THE LAW OF TORT

AUSTRALIA
The Law Book Company Ltd.
Sydney : Melbourne : Brisbane

CANADA AND U.S.A.
The Carswell Company Ltd.
Agincourt, Ontario

INDIA
N. M. Tripathi Private Ltd.
Bombay

ISRAEL
Steimatzky's Agency Ltd.
Jerusalem : Tel Aviv : Haifa

MALAYSIA : SINGAPORE : BRUNEI
Malaysian Law Journal (Pte.) Ltd.
Singapore

NEW ZEALAND
Sweet & Maxwell (N.Z.) Ltd.
Wellington

PAKISTAN
Pakistan Law House
Karachi

WINFIELD AND JOLOWICZ

ON

TORT

TENTH EDITION

BY

W. V. H. ROGERS, M.A.

Of Gray's Inn, Barrister;
Lecturer in Law in the University of Nottingham

LONDON
SWEET & MAXWELL
1975

First Edition	(1937)	The Author
Second Edition	(1943)	,, ,,
Third Edition	(1946)	,, ,,
Fourth Edition	(1948)	,, ,,
Fifth Edition	(1950)	,, ,,
Sixth Edition	(1954)	T. Ellis Lewis
Seventh Edition	(1963)	J. A. Jolowicz and T. Ellis Lewis
Eighth Edition	(1967)	J. A. Jolowicz and T. Ellis Lewis
Ninth Edition	(1971)	J. A. Jolowicz with T. Ellis Lewis and D. M. Harris
Tenth Edition	(1975)	W. V. H. Rogers
Second Impression	(1977)	,, ,,

SBN Hardback 421 17910 4
Paperback 421 17920 1

Published by
Sweet & Maxwell Limited of
11 New Fetter Lane, London
and printed in Great Britain
by Fletcher & Son Ltd,
Norwich

PREFACE TO NINTH EDITION

THE most obvious change in this edition is in its description. Sufficient time has now elapsed and sufficient alterations have been made to the text since Winfield himself last saw it that it has seemed to me inappropriate any longer to offer the book as if it were his alone, brought up to date. The order of presentation, though unchanged since the last edition, is quite different from that adopted by Winfield, much of his original material has been either omitted or completely rewritten, and there is a good deal in the book which never appeared in Winfield's work at all. The collaboration implied by the linking of my name with his did not, of course, ever actually take place, but the book as it stands still contains his *ipsissima verba* in several passages and cannot properly be attributed to either one of us alone. If it can be considered in its present version to be such a book as Winfield might have thought a satisfactory continuation of his work, had he lived to see it, I shall be content.

The chapter headings and their order in this edition are the same as in the last, but substantial alterations have been made to the text in a number of places, as much in the search for greater clarity as in the attempt to keep the book abreast of developments in the law itself. The length of the book has also been reduced by some pruning and rewriting, but not, unfortunately, to the extent that a comparison of the number of pages in the two editions might suggest; this edition has more lines to each page than did the last. A few introductory pages have been added to inform the reader of the crisis now facing the law of tort in so far as it deals with compensation for personal injuries, but I have conceived it still to be my task to describe the law as it is and as it may develop within the general framework of a system of civil liability. I have not attempted, therefore, either to describe fully or to assess the various proposals which have been made and which would substitute for the law of civil liability a different system altogether. Whatever the relation of tort to other branches of the law, it undoubtedly forms part of the law of civil responsibility as administered by the courts, and it is that with which this book is concerned.

As on previous occasions I have enjoyed the help of Dr. Ellis Lewis but, to my great regret, his health has prevented him from contributing more than the revised chapter on Animals, a task made especially troublesome for him by the fact that the Animals Act only became law at so late a stage in the preparation of the book. The chapters on Nuisance and the Rule in *Rylands* v. *Fletcher* have been taken over by my former pupil Dr. D. M. Harris who, after three years of research into these and allied subjects, is particularly well qualified and to whom I am most grateful. For the errors and omissions which may blemish the rest of the book, I am alone responsible.

I should like to thank Mr. R. Spicer for preparing the Index and the publishers for preparing the Tables. For reasons outside their control and outside mine, work on this edition could not be started until an uncomfortably recent date, but they remained unflustered and, as always, patient, courteous and kind in dealing with the manuscript and the alterations to proof under considerable pressure of time.

The law is in general stated in the light of materials available to me on June 1, 1971, but it has been possible occasionally to add references of a slightly later date.

J. A. J.

Trinity College,
  Cambridge.
July, 1971

PREFACE TO TENTH EDITION

IN 1971 *Winfield* became *Winfield and Jolowicz.* Let it be said immediately that although most of the work of preparing this edition fell to another editor, this is still Tony Jolowicz' book. The arrangement of material remains unchanged and except in a few isolated instances I have confined myself to seeking to bring the ninth edition up to date.

The shadow of Lord Pearson's Royal Commission lies heavily over large portions of this book and though that body has not yet published any recommendations, the almost universal assumption is that we shall follow New Zealand down the road of state insurance for personal injuries. No doubt the normal difficulties of framing and enacting legislation—not to speak of finding the money—will ensure that the courts will be dealing with substantial numbers of personal injury cases throughout the normal span of an edition of this book, but it would take an inveterate gambler to back the survival for a longer period of anything resembling the present system. For the academic lawyer the probable future shape of the law raises serious problems. There will remain substantial portions of the law dealt with in this book of which every student will require a knowledge, but will we be able to go on with a mutilated course in torts, or will we offload what is left on to other parts of the syllabus—intentional torts and defamation to constitutional law; nuisance and its relatives to land law; conversion, economic torts and *Hedley, Byrne* into some variant of commercial law? Not only shall we find some strange and ill-assorted bedfellows, but the principles of the law of civil responsibility for harms will be in danger of losing what general coherence they now possess. However, by that time some of our other conceptual classifications may well be ripe for revision.

The law is in general stated on the basis of materials available to me on November 1, 1974, though it has been possible to incorporate later developments at certain points. At one stage I planned to anticipate the enactment of the Trade Union and Labour Relations (Amendment) Bill, but this scheme was a victim of the House of Lords' onslaught on the " closed shop " clause. The reader should note the following changes or proposals for change.

(i) The Social Security Act 1975 has repealed and replaced most of the social welfare legislation referred to in Chapter 1. For our purposes, however, the basic structure of the system remains unchanged.

(ii) Faulks J.'s committee on defamation has reported (1975, Cmnd. 5909). Among its most important recommendations are:

restriction of the right to trial by jury; a drastic pruning of the jury's functions in assessing damages; the abolition of the distinction between libel and slander; the reduction of the limitation period to three years; and the introduction of a limited right of action in respect of defamation of the dead.

(iii) A Limitation Bill is now before Parliament based on the 20th Report of the Law Reform Committee (1974, Cmnd. 5630). Its main provisions seek to remedy the problems which have arisen over the interpretation of the Limitation Act 1963 (p. 655, *post*), but it also makes changes affecting persons under disability and confers on the courts in personal injury and fatal accident cases a power to set aside a defence of limitation if it would be fair to do so.

(iv) There is urgent need for guidance from the Court of Appeal on the question of whether failure to wear a seat belt is normally contributory negligence (p. 111, *post*). Though every case must be considered on its own facts, it would be fair to say that on a numerical basis the decisions are now evenly balanced with the present trend towards the answer " No." It is perhaps ironic that in a recent case the unfortunate plaintiff injured herself by tripping over a belt: *Donn* v. *Schacter* [1975] **R.T.R.** 238.

I should like to thank S. H. Bailey and W. I. Hooker for their helpful (and sometimes provocative) advice on many points. For the errors and omissions which remain, I alone am responsible. I should also like to thank the publishers for preparing the Tables and Index and for their patience and courtesy, despite the external factors which made the final stages of the work a rather desperate race against time.

W. V. H. R.

Nottingham.
June 29, 1975

CONTENTS

TABLE OF CASES

xiii

TABLE OF STATUTES

REFERENCES TO YEAR BOOKS

CHAPTER 1

MEANING OF LAW OF TORT

NUMEROUS attempts have been made in the past, with varying degrees
of lack of success, to define " a tort " or " tortious liability." Winfield's definition of tortious liability is discussed below, but no definition,
however good, can satisfy the primary need of the opening chapter of
a book of this kind which must be to tell the student what the book
is about. We should begin, therefore, with description rather than
definition and must be content to sacrifice accuracy and completeness
for the sake of simplicity.

With the warning, then, that what follows is not exact, the law
of tort may be said to be concerned with the allocation or redistri-
bution of those losses which are bound to occur in our society. It is
obvious that in any society of people living together numerous conflicts
of interest will arise and that the actions of one man or group of men
will from time to time cause damage to others. This damage may take
many forms—injury to the person, physical damage to property, damage
to financial interests, injury to reputation and so on—and whenever a
man suffers damage he is inclined to look to the law for redress. But
the granting of redress by the law means that some person or group of
persons will be required by the law to do or refrain from doing something—normally, but not invariably, to pay money to the sufferer by
way of compensation. It follows that the law cannot decree that whenever a man suffers loss or damage he should automatically be entitled
to redress. There must be some reason in any given case for calling on
another to provide it, or, in other words, for shifting the loss. In fact
the law cannot even go so far as to order every person whose action
may be regarded as morally culpable to make redress to those who
suffer by it: " Acts or omissions which any moral code would censure
cannot in a practical world be treated so as to give a right to every
person injured by them to demand relief. In this way rules of law arise
which limit the range of complainants and the extent of their remedy." [1]

It is the business of the law of tort to determine when the law will
and when it will not grant redress for damage suffered, and the rules
for liability whereby it does this are the subject of this book. We may
say, therefore, that if a plaintiff has suffered damage in circumstances
covered by the rules for liability stated in a book on the law of tort,
then, assuming the rules to be correctly stated, the plaintiff has been
the victim of a tort; by this we mean no more than that a tort is a wrong
whose victim is entitled to redress.[2] It does not follow, however, that

---

[1] *Donoghue* v. *Stevenson* [1932] A.C. 562, 580, *per* Lord Atkin.
[2] See *S.C.M. (United Kingdom) Ltd.* v. *Whittall & Son Ltd.* [1971] 1 Q.B. 337, 347–348,
per Winn L.J. But the law of tort is as much about *non*-liability as it is about liability:
Jolowicz, " The Law of Tort and Non-Physical Loss " (1972) 12 J.S.P.T.L. 91.

1

a person who has suffered damage without being the victim of a tort as thus defined is necessarily without redress. He may be entitled to it under the rules of some other branch of law such as the law of contract or quasi-contract or by the rules of equity, as for a breach of trust.

It was mainly in order to mark off the law of tort from these other branches of the law that Winfield formulated his well-known definition of tortious liability, and to this we shall return. First, however, it is necessary to emphasise that the law of tort, like those other branches of the law, is concerned with questions of *liability*. An action founded upon tort is an action between persons, either natural or artificial (*i.e.*, corporations), and the outcome can only be that one of them, the defendant, is or is not liable to do or refrain from doing something at the suit of the other. If there is no defendant whose liability can be established according to the principles of the law, then the plaintiff is left without redress.[3]

As will be seen, much of the law of tort is concerned with the problem of accidental injury to the person or damage to property, and the general approach of the law of tort to this problem rests on two broad principles. Both are subject to a number of exceptions and qualifications but by and large it is the case first that the victim of accidental injury or damage is entitled to redress through the law of tort if, and only if, his loss was caused by the fault of the defendant or of those for whose fault the defendant must answer, and secondly that the redress due from the defendant whose liability is established should, as nearly as possible, be equivalent in value to the plaintiff's loss. Until comparatively recently neither of these principles was subjected to serious challenge and it was regarded as almost axiomatic that, if no one was at fault, then the victim of accidental injury to the person must bear his loss himself.[4] The development of insurance, both national and private, has now led many commentators to take a different view. This book is concerned with the law of tort, not with an assessment of the views and proposals of those of its critics who would replace much of it by something else,[5] but no student of this branch of the law can any longer assume that the two broad principles just referred to will continue to be regarded as sacrosanct, particularly since the appointment in 1973 of a Royal Commission to consider the whole question of compensation for death and personal injury. Substantial reforms are possible in the not too distant future, and it is essential,

---

[3] *i.e.*, without redress so far as the law of tort is concerned. See *post*, pp. 6–11.

[4] " Nowadays, if somebody is unfortunate enough to meet with an accident from which some injury results, it is always thought that there ought to be somebody to pay. I think that idea is getting far too common. It is not for every injury that a person may sustain in the course of everyday life that he or she can recover compensation; it can only be recovered if that injury is due to the fault of somebody who owes a duty to that person ": *Bell* v. *Travco Hotels Ltd.* [1953] 1 Q.B. 473, 478, *per* Lord Goddard C.J.

[5] To change the basis of *liability* (*post*, p. 5) would be to reform the law of tort. To introduce a technique of insurance in place of liability (*post*, p. 8) would be to abolish it in favour of a totally different technique for dealing with a particular social problem.

therefore, that the reader of a book such as this should have the broad outline of contemporary criticism of the law in mind.

The principle that a person should be called upon to pay for damage caused by his fault may be thought to have an affinity with the criminal law (which the law of tort as a whole certainly did have much earlier in its history) in the sense that one of its purposes is to prevent conduct which is harmful. It is no doubt true that at least those parts of the law which deal with premeditated conduct do help to serve this purpose as well as that of deciding whether or not redress for damage already suffered should be ordered: newspaper editors, for example, take steps to avoid the publication of defamatory matter, and trade union officials have recognised the efficiency of the law of tort as an instrument for controlling conduct by demanding, and receiving, statutory exemption from some of its provisions so as to secure for themselves greater freedom of industrial action.[6] It is, however, extremely doubtful whether those parts of the law which relate to accidental injury, and especially the major topic of liability for negligence (which is expressed in the form of a directive to people to exercise care to avoid injuring others) has any worthwhile effect in assisting the purpose of accident prevention.[7] A generalised instruction to people to take care is of little practical use in guiding their behaviour in a given situation [8] and, as we shall see, in most cases the " sanction " for breach of the duty, liability to pay damages, rarely produces a more than trivial reduction in the negligent defendant's own resources.

Be this as it may, the sister principle that, in general, a person should not be called upon to pay for damage unless it was caused by his own fault, or that of others for whose fault he must answer, seems to depend upon the assumption that if a person is held liable to pay damages he will have to find the necessary money from his own resources. If the assumption is correct, then the principle probably accords with what most people would regard as fair, but in reality both the principle and the assumption no longer represent the truth. Recognition by the law that one person may have to answer for the fault of another, that is, the principle of " vicarious liability," [9] has its most important manifestation in the rule that an employer is liable for the torts of his employees done in the course of their employment,

---

[6] See *post*, pp. 467–471.

[7] See *e.g.*, Ison, *The Forensic Lottery*, pp. 80–89; Elliott and Street, *Road Accidents*, pp. 244–245: Atiyah, *Accidents, Compensation and the Law*, pp. 545–559; Lord Parker C.J., " Compensation for Accidents on the Road " (1965) 18 C.L.P. 1, 10. *Cf.* Lord MacDermott (C.J. of Northern Ireland), *Record of the Third Commonwealth and Empire Law Conference*, 1965, pp. 721–722. In any case, the amount of the damages is related to the extent of the plaintiff's damage and not to the gravity of the defendant's " offence," which makes the award of damages an unsatisfactory sanction. For a carefully-argued defence of the deterrence theory, see Stoljar, " Accidents, Costs and Legal Responsibility " (1973) 36 M.L.R. 233. Stoljar, however, assumes that a large proportion of the compensation already paid by the tort system would be transferred to a system of insurance.

[8] See *Brown* v. *National Coal Board* [1962] A.C. 574, 594–595, *per* Lord Radcliffe.

[9] See Chap. 25, *post*.

and this means that in the majority of accident cases it is not the person at fault who is the defendant but his employer,[10] and the employer's fault is unlikely to be in question at all. Even more importantly, the great spread of insurance against legal liability, now actually compulsory so far as road accidents affecting third parties [11] and most industrial accidents [12] are concerned, has had the result that, far more often than not, the damages for which a defendant in an accident case is held liable are actually paid not by him but by his insurer. It is true that he has had to pay in advance for his insurance cover and that he may have to pay more in the future if the insurer considers that he or his employees are more than ordinarily likely to cause further accidents, but the link between fault and the obligation to find the money to pay for its consequences in an individual case is extremely tenuous. And where the defendant is in the business of supplying goods or services to the public this link is more tenuous than ever for the cost of obtaining insurance cover will be reflected in the price charged to the public or in a reduced profit margin so that those who actually pay it are either the consumers or the shareholders or both.

These considerations do much to destroy the validity of fault as a criterion of liability in the law of tort; fault becomes irrelevant once it ceases to be the person whose fault caused the damage who has to pay for its consequences. It also becomes difficult to see what justification remains for the great disparity in the treatment accorded by the law to the victim of fault, who recovers substantial sums by way of damages, and the victim of an accident which cannot be proved to have been the fault of anyone, who recovers nothing.[13] Add to this that the fault principle is very expensive in operation because it requires that the facts of every case be carefully investigated to see who, if anyone, was at fault,[14] and no one should be surprised that

---

[10] The employee remains liable but even if he is sued along with his employer it is extremely unlikely that he will actually have to pay any part of the damage himself. See however, *Lister* v. *Romford Ice & Cold Storage Co. Ltd.* [1957] A.C. 555, *post*, pp. 532–534.

[11] Road Traffic Act 1972, s. 143.

[12] Employers' Liability (Compulsory Insurance) Act 1969, s. 1.

[13] *Dunne* v. *N.W. Gas Board* [1964] 2 Q.B. 806 is a striking example amongst reported cases but it must be borne in mind that an unknown number of claims are stifled at birth because the victim's solicitor advises him that he will be unable to prove the fault of anyone. A survey in Oxford of 90 serious road accident injury cases found that 55 per cent. of victims recovered no tort damages at all: see (1969) N.L.J. 492. Existing welfare benefits now account for a much greater proportion of the compensation paid to accident victims than do tort damages: Lees and Doherty, " Compensation for Personal Injury," *Lloyds Bank Review*, April 1973, No. 108, p. 18.

[14] This expense is not, of course, limited to the expense of trials in those actions which reach the court. Insurance companies, for example, must maintain claims investigation departments of a size which would not otherwise be necessary and so a larger proportion of premiums is absorbed in operating costs. See Atiyah, *op. cit.*, pp. 494–495 and Lees and Doherty, *loc. cit.* Note also that the result of an investigation into fault cannot always be relied on to produce the right answer in view of the great dependence of the investigatory process upon the powers of observation and recollection of eye witnesses. According to one estimate, the chances of a court making a finding of relevant facts concerning a road accident case which accurately corresponds with what happened may

modern literature is replete[14a] with proposals of one kind or another for its partial or complete abolition and replacement with different rules for enabling the victims of accidental damage to recover some compensation.

Despite its present insistence on fault as a prerequisite of liability, the law of tort does contain certain limited principles of strict liability, *i.e.*, liability imposed without proof of fault, and in the opinion of some writers the solution to the present difficulties lies in the wider and more sophisticated use of those principles. The basic structure of the law and the technique of legal liability should be retained, but the principles upon which liability is decided should be altered. What, in their opinion, is needed is to find a new principle whereby the law can decide that a defendant is, or is not, strictly liable to pay damages to the plaintiff and to do away, at least to a very substantial extent, with the present rules of liability for fault. One way of doing this would be to hold a defendant strictly liable if the plaintiff's injury was caused by his use of a legally recognised " dangerous thing " or his performance of a legally recognised " dangerous activity." [15] A different, and rather more complex, method is to develop a concept of risk against the background of insurance. An accident can be said to be the materialisation of a risk, and liability can be allocated by replacing the question " Whose fault was it that this accident occurred ? " by the question " Whose risk was it that this accident might occur? " The answer to this question is to be found in the economics and practicability of insurance. It should be recognised by the law that the normal sequel to the imposition of liability is that persons potentially subject to liability will protect themselves against its consequences by insurance. It should also be recognised by the law that where no one is liable for a given injury, then the victim must bear his loss himself unless he has insured against the risk that it might occur.[16] The question " Whose risk was it that this accident might occur? " can thus be translated into " Should the risk of this kind of accident be disposed of by liability insurance, or is it right, against the background of insurance, that the victim should bear his own loss or pay for his own insurance against it? " In short, the law should be reformed by the abolition or

---

be no more than 50 per cent.: Elliott and Street, *op. cit.*, p. 243. See also Ison, *op. cit.*, pp. 10–12, 74–77; Atiyah, *op. cit.*, pp. 470–473.

[14a] For the student, the most accessible bibliography and the best survey of the various alternatives is Hepple and Matthews, *Tort, Cases and Materials*, 1974, pp. 11–24, 667–729.

[15] See the Law Commission's Report on Civil Liability for Dangerous Things and Activities (Law Com. No. 32), 1970; Hamson [1973] C.L.J. 52, 244. *Cf.* Tunc, " Tort Law and the Moral Law " [1972 A] C.L.J. 247 and [1973] C.L.J. 241.

[16] This self-evident truth appears sometimes to be overlooked. See, *e.g.*, *S.C.M. (United Kingdom) Ltd.* v. *W. J. Whittall and Son Ltd.* [1971] 1 Q.B. 337, 344, where the Court of Appeal held that the defendants were not liable for the plaintiff's loss of profits caused by their negligence, and Lord Denning M.R. said that the risk should be borne by the whole community who suffer the losses rather than the defendant who may or may not be insured against the risk. The result of the decision was, however, that the plaintiff, not the whole community, had to carry the loss.

virtual abolition of liability for fault, and a thorough-going reappraisal
made of the scope and function of strict liability.[17]

It is believed that reform along these lines is possible and that if
achieved it would give to the law of tort a new and valuable lease of
life.[18] The suggestion does, however, leave open the relationship
between the remedy provided by the law of tort and the various other
possible sources of compensation to the victims of accidental injury.
Two of these sources, both of which are independent of any prior
arrangement made by the victim for his own protection and are thus
different from such sources of financial benefit as personal accident
insurance, must be briefly mentioned here.

By virtue of the Criminal Injuries Compensation Scheme, instituted
on a non-statutory basis in 1964,[19] victims of crimes of violence may be
entitled to recover compensation out of public funds. The Scheme is
administered by the Criminal Injuries Compensation Board and the
moneys are provided by Parliament. The claimant presents his case
directly to the Board and the compensation is calculated in a manner
approximately equivalent to the assessment of damages in an action
founded upon tort. It is obvious that the persons entitled to compensation under this Scheme are generally also entitled to damages at law for
it is almost inconceivable that the victim of a crime of violence is not
also the victim of a tort. It is, however, equally obvious that the legal
remedy in cases covered by the Scheme will almost invariably be valueless to the victim for the simple reason that even if the assailant is
identified and sued to judgment the chances of his being able to pay
substantial damages are negligible. Whatever its merits or demerits,[20]
therefore, the Scheme can be seen as supplementary to the law of tort,
not as overlapping it, and, in any case, a person compensated under it
must undertake that he will repay what he receives out of any damages
he may recover by a legal claim.

Of far greater importance in its implications for the law of tort is
the modern system of social security as it exists in this country. The
law governing social security is extremely complicated and can only
be touched on here,[21] but at least some of the financial benefits which

---

[17] See Jolowicz, " Liability for Accidents " [1968] C.L.J. 50. It will, of course, be a
difficult and possibly a continuing, but not an impossible, task to determine the appropriate
allocation of strict liability. It will also be necessary to decide whether the fault of the
plaintiff, if a contributory factor to his injury, should operate to negative or reduce
the liability of a defendant. Some may think it unjust that the carelessness of an accident
victim should not affect his legal remedy, but the admission of contributory negligence as
a defence would require the same kind of investigation into the facts as does the present
law, and so a major advantage of the reform would be lost. For contributory negligence
see *post*, pp. 106–118.

[18] See, however, Ison, *op. cit.*, pp. 37–41. *Nettleship* v. *Weston* [1971] 2 Q.B. 691.

[19] H.C. Deb., 5th Series, Vol. 657, w.a., cols. 89 *et seq.* See now, for the revised Scheme,
H.C. Deb., 5th Series, Vol. 784, w.a., cols. 99–104. Atiyah, *op. cit.*, Chap. 13.

[20] Atiyah, *ubi supra*, is severely critical of the Scheme and its theoretical foundation.

[21] The most convenient description of the relevant aspects of social security will be
found in Atiyah, *op. cit.*, Chaps. 14–16, brought up to date by Hepple and Matthews,
op. cit., pp. 693–698. See also Calvert, *Welfare Law* (1974). The Social Security Act 1975
consolidates earlier enactments and makes certain alterations in the system of benefits.

it provides must be borne in mind today by every student of the law of tort. In the first place, although no one is compelled to make use of it, the National Health Service will provide to every accident victim the medical attention he requires and he need incur no expense on that account. In addition the system provides for the payment of money to the victims of personal injury in one of two ways.[21a]

(i) Industrial Injuries. The National Insurance (Industrial Injuries) Act 1965 [22] covers industrial injuries [23] suffered by persons employed under contracts of service [24] and provides for a variety of benefits payable to injured workmen or, in the case of fatal accidents, their dependants. For a period of six months an injured person is entitled to receive " industrial injury benefit," which means the payment to him of a flat-rate weekly sum the amount of which depends upon the size of his family, plus an earnings related supplement equal to one third of the amount of his earnings between £10 and £30 per week and 15 per cent. of his earnings between £30 and £42, provided that the total amount he receives does not exceed 85 per cent. of his average weekly earnings.[25] If the injury has long-term consequences then the injured man receives a disablement pension [26] which is calculated by reference to the extent of his disability,[27] and in addition, if he is unable to work after the expiry of six months from his accident, he will normally be entitled to the " sickness benefit " and dependants' allowances of the general (non-industrial) insurance scheme.[28]

(ii) Non-industrial Injuries. Cases of injury falling outside the National Insurance (Industrial Injuries) Act 1965 are dealt with in the same way as is illness and the benefits are regulated principally by the National Insurance Act 1965. This Act, which deals with many other matters as well, such as unemployment, retirement and maternity benefits, provides for the payment of " sickness benefit " to a person who by reason of sickness (which includes non-industrial injury) is unable to work. This benefit is similar to but less generous than industrial injuries benefit and the earnings related supplement is payable for the first six months as in the case of an industrial injury. There is no time limit for the payment of sickness benefit but, on the other hand, there

---

[21a] Supplementary benefit may, of course, be payable in any case.

[22] This Act repeals and replaces the Act of 1946 which itself abolished the old system of " workmen's compensation " and introduced the present system.

[23] i.e., accidental injuries (including certain prescribed industrial diseases) " arising out of and in the course of his employment ": s. 5 (1).

[24] The self-employed are thus excluded: Sched. 1.

[25] National Insurance Act 1966, s. 2. The supplement is payable only after the first two weeks of incapacity. Since the benefits themselves are not taxable and since a period of absence from work is likely to reduce the amount of tax payable in the course of a year, the true value of the benefits will be greater than their actual monetary amounts: Atiyah, op. cit., pp. 362–368.

[26] Or, in the case of a minor disablement, a gratuity.

[27] A disablement pension or gratuity is not intended to replace lost earnings but is based wholly on an objective assessment of the disability.

[28] Other benefits such as " constant attendance allowance " (National Insurance (Industrial Injuries) Act 1965, s. 15) and increases of disablement pension on account of unemployability or in cases of special hardship are payable in appropriate cases.

is no equivalent to the disablement pension nor is there any possibility
that an injured person can receive the other special benefits available in
case of very severe injury under the scheme for industrial injuries.[29]

It has been shown recently that the level of the benefits available
under the National Insurance Acts is now such that they are at least
equivalent in value to, or even greater than, the net financial loss
suffered by a person whose injury prevents him from working for a
relatively short period of time.[30] This was not the case when the present
system of national insurance was introduced in 1946, and when the
Committee on Alternative Remedies reported in that year [31] no recommendation for the abolition of actions in tort for personal injuries in
any class of case was made. Even now the benefits of national insurance
are not equivalent to the " full compensation " of the law of tort for
they contain no element of compensation for " pain and suffering "
or " loss of amenity." [32] Nevertheless, the overlap between the law of
tort and social security has become undeniably more striking as the
extent of the latter has been enlarged, and this fact, added to general
dissatisfaction with the principle of liability for fault, has led to a
conviction on the part of many that the only satisfactory solution to the
problem of compensation for personal injury lies in a centralised
system of insurance. At the present time, therefore, it is almost certain
that the majority of writers, but not necessarily the majority of those
affected,[33] favour radical reform and the total or partial abolition of the
law of tort so far as it relates to compensation for personal injuries.

Many commentators, it is true, have concentrated their attention
on one or two classes of accident only, especially road accidents and
industrial accidents,[34] on the ground that these are numerically the
most important.[35] Others, however, would extend their proposals so
that all accidental injuries, and even disease as well, should receive
similar treatment from the law governing social security to the exclusion
of the law of tort.[36] It is not possible to examine the various proposals

---

[29] See note 28, *supra.*

[30] Atiyah, *op. cit.*, p. 365. The longer a man is unable to work the less the benefits
suffice to replace his financial loss.

[31] Final Report of the Committee on Alternative Remedies 1946 (Cmd. 6860).

[32] These heads of damage are described below, pp. 563–572.

[33] See, *e.g.*, the report of a conference held under the auspices of the Industrial Law
Society on " Personal Injuries—Social Insurance or Tort Liability ": (1969) 119 New
L.J. 957.

[34] See, *e.g.*, Elliott and Street, *op. cit.*; Payne, " Compensating the Accident Victim "
(1960) 13 C.L.P. 85. Lord Parker C.J., " Compensation for Accidents on the Road "
(1965) 18 C.L.P. 1; " Compensation for Victims of Road Traffic Accidents," Memorandum
of the Committee of Justice on No-Fault Insurance (1973). Of the extensive American
literature, see especially Keeton and O'Connell, *Basic Protection for the Traffic Victim—
A Blueprint for Reforming Automobile Insurance*, and for France, where there is already
substantial liability without fault, see Tunc, *La Sécurité Routière.* See Hepple and Matthews,
Tort, Cases and Materials, App. G, for a survey of the Canadian and American " no-
fault " insurance schemes for road accidents, which provide varying degrees of basic
cover, leaving negligence liability to operate above this level.

[35] But it is the fact that accidents in the home account for almost as many deaths and
serious injuries as do those on the road: Atiyah, *op. cit.*, p. 27, Table 1.

[36] Atiyah, *op. cit.*; Ison, *op. cit.*

here. What is common to almost all of them, however, is that in one way or another they seek to substitute the technique of insurance for that of liability at law: an insurance fund is to be brought into existence and administered by a central authority—in the opinion of many the only plausible authority is the state [37]—and an injured person is to be given a virtually automatic right to receive payment out of the fund. Various methods of financing the fund have been proposed, the general ideas of which seem to be twofold; first that abolition of tort liability would release large sums of money which are now inefficiently used for the compensation of a limited number of accident victims and secondly that the costs of the insurance could be equitably met by some form of selective taxation. Thus, for example, Professor Ison proposes that to the extent that the costs borne by the fund are attributable to identifiable activities they should be a charge on those activities and the rest should be raised by a system of contributions similar to that now used by the existing national insurance scheme.[38]

A scheme operating on principles broadly akin to those mentioned above is now in operation in New Zealand [39] providing for earnings-related compensation by periodical payments [40] of 80 per cent. of the injured person's loss (up to a limit of $200 per week) with no reduction on account of contributory negligence.[41] The scheme is administered by a State Accident Compensation Commission, though a supporting role is still left to insurance companies. Finance is provided by three self-contained funds, the Earners' Fund (supported by levies on employers and self-employed persons), the Motor Vehicle Fund (supported by levies on vehicles and vehicle licence holders) and the Supplementary Fund [42] (supported by ordinary taxation).

Reference has not yet been made to the second broad principle on which the present law is based, namely, that compensation should be " full " in those cases in which liability is imposed.[43] It is obvious, however, that retention of this principle in a system under which the victims of all accidents, or all accidents of a given kind, are automatically entitled to compensation would be prohibitively expensive,[43a]

---

[37] Ison, *op. cit.*, p. 56.   [38] *Op. cit.*, pp. 56–58.
[39] Accidents Compensation Act 1972; Accidents Compensation Amendment (No. 2) Act 1973. The Act is based, with some important changes, upon the Report of the Royal Commission of Inquiry into Compensation for Personal Injury in New Zealand (1967: the " Woodhouse Report "). For a review of the scheme, see Harris, " Accident Compensation in New Zealand: A Comprehensive Insurance System " (1974) 37 M.L.R. 361; Palmer, " Compensation For Personal Injury: A Requiem for the Common Law in New Zealand " (1973) 21 Amer. Jo. Comp. Law 1; Marks (1973) 46 A.L.J. 516.
[40] One of the major obstacles to accurate compensation under the present system is that damages have to be awarded on a lump-sum basis.
[41] But there is no compensation for wilful self-injury.
[42] The original scheme covered only earners and victims of motor accidents. The Supplementary Fund became necessary upon its extension to non-earners injured otherwise than on the road.
[43] The principle as applied at present is subject to the rule that damages may be reduced on account of the plaintiff's contributory negligence: *post*, pp. 106–118. Contributory negligence has no place in an insurance system.
[43a] With regard to loss of income alone, it is probable that under a social security scheme either a very large amount of money would have to be found out of additional

and none of the more radical schemes which have been mentioned does
in fact provide for it [44]; the emphasis in all of them is on compensation
for loss of income although some allowance is also made for payments
in respect of actual disability.[45] The major element of damages which
would be eliminated is, therefore, the non-pecuniary " loss, " *i.e.*,
" pain and suffering " and " loss of amenity " or " loss of enjoyment
of life. " It is, no doubt, true that " loss " of this description is very
different from the loss of something having an obvious monetary value
and damages are at present awarded more by way of " solace for
unpleasantness and misfortune " than by way of replacement of something of which a person has been deprived.[46] It is also true that it is
very difficult to find a basis for the assessment of damages for non-
pecuniary loss under the present law.[47] It can therefore be argued
that no great harm would be done to anyone if, in future, compensation for " pain and suffering " and the like were given to no one and it
has even been said that compensation for actual disability itself is hard
to justify so long as income losses are not adequately compensated in
so many cases.[48] On the other hand, a system under which those
injured persons who are too old or too young to suffer any income loss
can receive no monetary compensation, whatever the circumstances
of their injury,[49] is unlikely to prove an attractive one to many people
and there is no *a priori* reason for saying that those who suffer pain
or loss of amenity are undeserving of such solace as the payment of
money can bring them. The basic argument of the radical reformers
is that compensation of this kind should be given to none until such
time as the basic income losses of all can be restored through the
chosen compensation system. The New Zealand scheme which was
finally put into operation compromised on this issue by providing for
(by English Standards) fairly small lump sums for loss of function
(based on a schedule of degrees of disability) and for pain and suffering
and loss of amenities.[1]

The choice for the future lies between the basically individualistic

---

taxation or levels of compensation would have to be set substantially below full common
law damages. Not only do many victims of road and industrial accidents recover nothing
under the tort system, but one would be bringing in a class of victims who are almost
entirely outside the tort system, *viz.*, those injured in the home, a class of the same numerical order as road accident victims.

[44] The cost of replacing liability for fault by the selective imposition of strict liability
(*ante*, pp. 5–6) would depend on the extent to which strict liability was imposed.

[45] See, *e.g.*, Ison, *op. cit.*, pp. 55, 56; Woodhouse Report, para. 201 and Appendix
II. *Cf.* Elliott and Street, *op. cit.*, pp. 274–276. Atiyah, *op. cit.*, pp. 526, 611–615, would
place this kind of compensation in a low priority category and would probably not be
unhappy to see it disappear altogether.

[46] See Atiyah, *op. cit.*, pp. 523–527. So much is virtually admitted by the courts themselves: *e.g.*, Rushton v. *National Coal Board* [1953] 1 Q.B. 495, 502, *per* Romer L.J.

[47] *Post*, pp. 569–572.

[48] Atiyah, *op. cit.*, pp. 611–612.

[49] Consider, for example, the public reaction to the plight of the children who were
born deformed as a result of the use of the drug thalidomide by their mothers during
pregnancy and see S. v. *Distillers Co.* (*Biochemicals*) *Ltd.* [1970] 1 W.L.R. 114.

[1] See Harris, *loc. cit.*, pp. 372–373. The maximum aggregate award under both heads
is $12,500.

approach of the common law (whether reformed or not) and the collective approach of social security or some similar method for providing all injured persons with a right to compensation from some central fund. Looked at solely from the point of view of the most efficient distribution of the money available for compensation, the arguments are all in favour of the social security approach. But in the end the question is one of social policy and even of politics: of deciding what proportion of its wealth society can, and should, spend on the assistance of the victims of misfortune. If the social security approach prevails, we shall sooner or later have to consider why we give preferential treatment to the victims of accidents over the victims of disease or congenital disability.[2]

Definition of tortious liability [3]

Tortious liability arises from the breach of a duty primarily fixed by the law; this duty is towards persons generally and its breach is redressible by an action for unliquidated damages.

It will be noticed that this definition does not indicate what conduct is and what is not sufficient to·involve a person in tortious liability. It is not a material definition but a formal one intended to distinguish tortious liability from liability of other kinds. As such it contains much that is still instructive and will be considered here for that reason as much as for reasons of piety, but, as will appear, we can no longer agree that it does altogether achieve its purpose.

(i) *Primarily fixed by the law*

It was Winfield's view that tortious duties exist by virtue of the law itself and are not dependent upon the agreement or consent of the persons subjected to them. I am under a duty not to assault you, not to slander you, not to trespass on your land, because the law says I am under such a duty and not because I have agreed with you to undertake such a duty. Winfield therefore considered that tortious liability could for this reason be distinguished from contractual liability and from liability on bailment, neither of which can exist independently of the parties' or at least of the defendant's agreement or consent. There are, however, several instances of what is undoubtedly tortious liability for the existence of which some prior consent on the part of the defendant is essential. The liability of the occupier of

---

[2] *Cf.* the way in which enormous public sympathy was mobilised for the thalidomide children who are in fact a very small proportion of the children born with serious disabilities.

[3] For other definitions, see Winfield, *Province of the Law of Tort* (1931), Chap. XII. For a collection and discussion of English and American definitions, see Prosser, *Torts*, 4th ed., Chap. 1. Winfield's definition is preferred by Clerk & Lindsell, *Torts*, 13th ed., p. 1. See too Stone, " Touchstones of Tort Liability " (1950) 2 Stanford L.Rev. 259. On problems of classification, see Jolowicz (ed.) *The Division and Classification of the Law* (1970); Hadden, " Contract, Tort and Crime: The Forms of Legal Thought " (1971) 87 L.Q.R. 240.

premises to his visitor, for example, which is now governed by the
Occupiers' Liability Act 1957, is based upon breach of a duty of care
owed by the occupier to persons whom he has permitted to enter upon
his premises. The duty owed to trespassers, *i.e.*, persons who enter
without his consent, if any, is by no means the same.[4] Again, the duty
of care owed by the driver of a car to his gratuitous passenger is,
doubtless, a tortious one, but its existence is dependent upon the driver's
agreement to the presence of the passenger in his car.

If it is not true that all tortious duties arise independently of the
will of the defendant, it is equally not true that contractual duties are
always dependent upon that will. Not only is there the obvious point
that the duty not to break one's contracts is itself a duty imposed by
the law, but it is also the case that contractual liability may exist
even in the absence of any true consent between the parties. Whether
or not there is a contract normally depends upon the outward manifestations of agreement by the parties, not on their subjective states
of mind.[5]

A slightly better mode of differentiation between tortious and
contractual liability, it is suggested, is to be found in the proposition
that in tort the content of the duties is fixed by the law whereas the
content of contractual duties is fixed by the contract itself. If I consent to your entry upon my premises then the duty which I owe to
you is the duty fixed by the Occupiers' Liability Act, *i.e.*, by the
law itself, but whether, for example, my duty is to deliver to you
ten or twenty tons of coal can only be discovered from the contract
between us. Even this distinction, however, is by no means always
valid for today in many cases the content of contractual duties is also
fixed by the law. Statute provides, for example, that certain quite
specific obligations shall be contained in contracts for the sale or hire-
purchase of goods[6] and it is now no longer true as once, perhaps,
it was, that implied terms in a contract, in the absence of a statutory
rule, are always to be based upon the presumed intention of the
parties.[7] Conversely, there are tortious duties which are subject to
variation by agreement, whether or not that agreement amounts in
law to a contract between the parties.[8]

(ii) *The duty in tort is towards persons generally*

The reference here is, of course, to the primary duty, *i.e.*, the duty

---

[4] *Post*, Chap. 10.

[5] See, *e.g.*, *Smith* v. *Hughes* (1871) L.R. 6 Q.B. 597, 607, *per* Blackburn J.; *Frederick
E. Rose (London) Ltd.* v. *William H. Pim, Jnr. & Co. Ltd.* [1953] 2 Q.B. 450, 460, *per*
Denning L.J. Cheshire & Fifoot, *Law of Contract*, 8th ed., p. 24; Treitel, *The Law of
Contract*, 3rd ed., p. 1.

[6] Sale of Goods Act 1893; Supply of Goods (Implied Terms) Act 1973. See too Acts
such as the Terms and Conditions of Employment Act 1959, under which a term may be
compulsorily implied into a contract of employment.

[7] *Lister* v. *Romford Ice & Cold Storage Co. Ltd.* [1957] A.C. 555, especially at p. 594,
per Lord Tucker.

[8] Occupiers' Liability Act 1957, s. 2 (1); *Ashdown* v. *Williams (Samuel) & Sons Ltd.*
[1957] 1 Q.B. 409; *Wooldridge* v. *Sumner* [1963] 2 Q.B. 43. See *post*, pp. 183–185, 614–622.

not to trespass, not to slander and so on, for breach of which tortious liability is imposed. The breach of such a duty gives rise to a remedial duty, *i.e.*, a duty to make redress, and this is always owed to a specific person or persons whatever the source of the liability.[9] In Winfield's view, however, if the primary duty is towards a specific person or specific persons, it cannot arise from tort. He admitted that in some instances it is hard to say who exactly are " persons generally " [10] but claimed that the element of generality was an important factor in the definition and that it was sufficiently workable in the majority of cases.

It appears, however, that everything depends upon the level of abstraction at which the duty is expressed. It can, no doubt, be truly stated that by virtue of the law of tort I am under a duty not to convert to my own use the goods of anybody else, while my contractual duty to deliver goods which I have sold is owed only to the person to whom I have sold them. But this is to compare two statements at different levels. Just as I have a general duty not to commit the tort of conversion, so I have a general duty not to commit breaches of contract.[11] If, on the other hand, we descend to the particular, then just as my duty to deliver certain goods is owed only to their buyer, so also my duty not to convert certain goods to my own use is owed only to the person in possession, or having the immediate right to possession, of them.

Quasi-contractual liability. We may here conveniently make use of the idea of the primary duty to mark off from the law of tort one other branch of law, namely, quasi-contractual liability. This signifies liability imposed upon a particular person to pay money to another person on the ground of unjust enrichment.[12] A good example is the liability to repay money which has been paid under a mistake of fact. I owe you £10. I pay the £10 to your twin brother, whom I mistake for you, and he honestly believes that he is entitled to the money. Now he is, of course, legally bound to repay the money to me and so is under a remedial duty. But it cannot be said that this remedial duty is the result of the breach of some primary duty, as would be the case in tortious and, indeed, also in contractual liability. It would be meaningless to say that your twin brother was under a duty not to accept the money from me or that he was ever under a relevant duty of any kind save the remedial duty to return the money to me because otherwise he would be unjustly enriched at my expense. The remedial duty in tort always springs from the breach of a primary

---

[9] Friedmann, Book Review (1955) 33 Can. Bar Rev. 245; H. F. Jolowicz, *Lectures on Jurisprudence*, p. 359.

[10] Winfield, *op. cit.*, 230.

[11] *Cf. ibid.*, 229. See Poulton, " Tort or Contract " (1966) 82 L.Q.R. 346, 351–352.

[12] See Winfield, *op. cit.*, Chap. VII; Winfield, *Law of Quasi-Contracts;* Jackson. *History of Quasi-Contract;* Goff and Jones, *Restitution*, especially at pp. 3–5.

duty of some kind. But in quasi-contract there is no primary duty whatsoever.

(iii) *Breach of the duty is redressible by an action for unliquidated damages*

As a preliminary point, the distinction between liquidated and unliquidated damages must be made clear. Where the plaintiff in an action sues for a predetermined and inelastic sum of money, he is claiming liquidated damages. But where he seeks to recover such an amount as the court, in its discretion, is at liberty to award, he is claiming unliquidated damages, and this is so even where he has specified a particular sum of money in his pleadings.[13]

Other remedies

The *action for unliquidated damages* is one pretty sure test *of tortious liability* and it has some show of express judicial approval.[14] But we hasten to add that it is by no means the only remedy for a tort, and that, for some torts, it is not even the primary remedy.[15] Nevertheless, the possibility of bringing such an action is not fettered by any of the conditions which attach to other remedies and the courts must at least hear what the plaintiff in an action for damages has got to say, even if they come to the conclusion that the defendant has, in the circumstances of the case, nothing to which he need answer.[16]

Tort and crime distinguished

It would appear then that the possibility of an action for unliquidated damages is one of the factors in tortious liability. And this serves to distinguish it from *criminal liability*. A crime is a wrong the sanction of which involves punishment.[17] What then is punishment? Death, imprisonment (provided it is not merely imprisonment which is terminable by the act of the prisoner himself),

---

[13] The award cannot be of a sum greater than the amount claimed if an amount is specified in the pleadings, but leave to amend the statement of claim can be granted even after verdict: McGregor, *Damages*, 13th ed., p. 944.

[14] *Hulton* v. *Hulton* [1917] 1 K.B. 813, 820, 822–823, 824. *Cf. Re Great Orme Tramways Co.* (1934) 50 T.L.R. 450; *Att.-Gen.* v. *Canter* [1938] 2 K.B. 826; affirmed [1939] 1 K.B. 326 (action to recover penalty under Income Tax Acts not a cause of action in tort). Salmond, *Torts*, 16th ed., pp. 8–9. Prosser, *Torts*, 4th ed., p. 2.

[15] For the other remedies which may be available in a case of tort, see Chap. 27, *post.*

[16] Winfield, *op. cit.*, 231–233.

[17] Kenny, *Outlines of Criminal Law*, 16th ed. (1952), p. 539. The relevant chapter is omitted from later editions. Kenny added that the sanction must be remissible (*i.e.,* capable of forgiveness) by the Crown alone, if remissible at all. Winfield suggested that this leads to the vicious circle: " What is a crime? Something that the Crown alone can pardon. What, then, is it that the Crown alone can pardon? A crime." *Province of the Law of Tort*, pp. 196–197. See, generally, Kenny, *op. cit.*, pp. 538–547; Winfield, *op. cit.*, Chap. VIII; Allen, *Legal Duties*, pp. 221–252 (The Nature of a Crime). Glanville Williams, " The Definition of a Crime " (1955) 8 *Current Legal Problems* 107, argues that the whole of the law of procedure must be taken into account in a definition of a crime. See also Jolowicz, *op. cit.*, pp. 347–358.

and pecuniary fines.[17a] Now it will be instantly perceived that death and imprisonment have nothing in common with the unliquidated damages which are claimed in an action in tort. But the distinction is not so obvious in the case of a fine which, according to the Magistrates' Courts Act 1952 [18] is " any pecuniary penalty or pecuniary forfeiture or pecuniary compensation payable under a conviction." The powers of the criminal courts to award compensation have recently been rationalised and consolidated by the Powers of Criminal Courts Act 1973.[19] Broadly speaking, the court may order a convicted person to pay compensation for any " personal injury, loss or damage " resulting from the offence, though there are some important exclusions. Thus the compensation awardable by a magistrates' court is not to exceed £400, and road accidents and claims by dependants of a deceased person are totally excluded from the compensation provisions.[20] Clearly, in many cases an application to the criminal court may be a much more sensible proceeding than an action in tort. The compensatory sums awarded under these provisions are, until the court specifies their exact amount, quite uncertain. In other words, they are just as much " unliquidated " as are damages in tort. But there is one peculiar feature which marks them off from damages in tort. In every case they are obtainable only *in addition to some punishment*, or order in the nature of punishment, inflicted or made by the court. Thus, in crime, unliquidated damages which benefit the injured party are not claimable in the first instance; but in tort they may be.[21]

Tort and breach of trust distinguished

The test of an action for unliquidated damages might also be used to distinguish a tort from a *breach of trust*. If a trustee misappropriates property which he holds upon trust for a beneficiary, the beneficiary can claim compensation. But that compensation is measured by the loss which the trust property has suffered.[22] It is ascertainable before the beneficiary commences his action. It is, therefore, not an " unliquidated " sum of money. Indeed, it is not damages of any sort, liquidated or unliquidated. But a much better way of differentiating tort from breach of trust is to regard the whole law of trusts as a division of the law of property which is fairly detachable from other parts of our law. The administration of trusts

---

[17a] There are, of course, now several other methods of dealing with offenders: see generally the Powers of Criminal Courts Act 1973.

[18] 15 & 16 Geo. 6 & 1 Eliz. 2, c. 55, s. 126 (1).

[19] c. 62, ss. 35–38. The power to make compensation orders should only be used in straightforward cases: *R.* v. *Daly* [1974] 1 W.L.R. 133. See also the power to order restitution under s. 28 of the Theft Act 1968.

[20] But see the Criminal Injuries Compensation Scheme, *ante*, p. 6.

[21] Winfield, *op. cit.*, pp. 201–203. *Cf.* (1940) 4 *Journal of Criminal Law* 432–438.

[22] Lewin, *Law of Trusts*, 16th ed., p. 670; Hanbury, *Modern Equity*, 9th ed., pp. 396–400; Snell, *Equity*, 27th ed., pp. 276–277.

has for centuries been within the province of a special court which is
now represented by the Chancery Division of the High Court.
Although questions relating to trusts do incidentally arise in the
common law courts,[23] it is better to take advantage of the fact that
they belong more properly to the jurisdictional *enclave* of Chancery
and to leave them there. That course is more consistent with their
history and with the opinion of any legal practitioner at the present
day.[24]

Quasi-contractual liability

That tortious liability is remediable by an action for unliquidated
damages also serves as another ground for distinguishing it from
quasi-contractual liability. In quasi-contract the measure of the
defendant's liability is almost always the extent to which he has been
unjustly enriched, not the extent to which the plaintiff has suffered
loss.

Tort and liability on bailment

A bailment is a delivery of goods on a condition, express or
implied, that they shall be restored to the bailor, or according to his
directions, as soon as the purpose for which they are bailed has been
completed.[25] The person who delivers the goods is called a " bailor,"
the person to whom they are delivered is the " bailee." Common
examples of bailment are hire of goods, such as hire of a car from a
garage; gratuitous loan of goods, such as lending this book to a
friend; and pawn or pledge. Now, supposing that the bailee misuses
or damages the goods he is, of course, liable in a civil action to the
bailor. Is this liability to be distinguished from liability in tort?
Many bailments arise out of contract, but the better opinion is that it
is possible for bailment to exist without contract [26] and where this
is the case, as in the gratuitous loan of something for the use of the
borrower, the liability is a tortious one. Winfield's opinion, however,
was that the bailee's liability is not tortious because, he said, the duty
arises from a relation, that of bailor and bailee, which is created by
the parties. No one need be a bailee if he does not wish to be one
and no one can have liability for the safe custody of goods thrust
upon him against his will—a fact which is frequently ignored by
pushing tradesmen who send goods to persons who have never asked
for them.[27] It is certainly true that a man cannot be subjected to

---

[23] A striking example is *Hawkesley* v. *May* [1956] 1 Q.B. 304.
[24] Winfield, *op. cit.*, Chap. VI, for a fuller discussion of the relation of tort to breach
of trust.
[25] Sir William Jones, *Treatise on the Law of Bailment* (1781), p. 1; Paton, *Bailment
in the Common Law*, Chap. I.
[26] Winfield, *Province of the Law of Tort*, pp. 97–99; Paton, *op. cit.*, p. 40; Holdsworth,
H.E.L. iii, 450.
[27] See *post*, pp. 414–416. Winfield's view is set out in full in *Province of the Law of
Tort*, Chap. 5, where he makes the point that bailment is more fittingly regarded as a

the duties of a bailee without his consent, but as we have already seen, there are duties which are undoubtedly tortious and which can only exist if there has been some prior agreement between the parties. There seems to be no good reason for distinguishing the common law duties of a bailee from duties of this kind. If the bailor's claim is necessarily founded upon some specific provision in a contract, then, no doubt, the bailee's liability is not tortious but contractual, but if the bailor's claim rests upon a breach by the bailee of one of the bailee's common law duties, then his liability is as much attributable to the law of tort as is the claim of a visitor against the occupier of premises under the Occupiers' Liability Act.[28]

Law of obligations

At this stage we may, perhaps, claim to have given some reason why a book on the law of tort need not concern itself with quasi-contract, crime or breach of trust, and to have gone a little way towards distinguishing tortious from contractual liability.[29] A further point may now be mentioned to assist in making this last distinction, namely, that if the plaintiff in a given case can succeed only if he can prove a contract with the defendant, then the defendant's liability, if any, cannot be tortious. If, for example, I wish to claim damages from you on the ground that you did not call at my house to collect my television set for repair, I can only succeed if you have contracted to collect the set and any liability you may incur cannot be in tort. On this approach, however, it must be conceded that with changes in the law itself a topic may move from the law of contract into the law of tort. An important instance of this occurred in 1963.[30] Before that date it was a rule of English law that there could be no liability for a carelessly made misstatement leading to financial loss unless the defendant came under a duty of care created by a contract [31] (or unless there was a " fiduciary relationship " [32]). In 1963, however, the House of Lords held that there might be a duty of care in certain circumstances even in the absence of a contract—in other words, that there might be a tortious duty.[33]

---

distinct branch of the law of property under the title " Possession " than as appropriate to either the law of contract or the law of tort. We do not dissent from this view, but " Possession " is not a principle of liability and the possessor's rights of action are most conveniently regarded as arising out of contract or out of tort, or both. We therefore prefer the view now stated in the text. See, however, *Building and Civil Engineering Holidays Scheme Management Ltd.* v. *Post Office* [1966] 1 Q.B. 247, 261, *per* Lord Denning M.R.

[28] *Turner* v. *Stallibrass* [1898] 1 Q.B. 56, esp. *per* Collins L.J. at p. 59; *Morris* v. *C. W. Martin & Sons Ltd.* [1966] 1 Q.B. 716; *Lee Cooper Ltd.* v. *Jeakins & Sons Ltd.* [1967] 2 Q.B. 1; *Chesworth* v. *Farrar* [1967] 1 Q.B. 407; *Gilchrist Watt and Sanderson Pty. Ltd.* v. *York Products Pty. Ltd.* [1970] 1 W.L.R. 1262 (P.C.).

[29] For a recent discussion of this, see Poulton, " Tort or Contract " (1966) 82 L.Q.R. 346.

[30] *Hedley Byrne & Co. Ltd.* v. *Heller & Partners Ltd.* [1964] A.C. 465.

[31] *Candler* v. *Crane, Christmas & Co.* [1951] 2 K.B. 164.

[32] *Nocton* v. *Ashburton (Lord)* [1914] A.C. 932.

[33] *Hedley Byrne & Co. Ltd.* v. *Heller & Partners Ltd., supra.*

This example—and many others are to be found in the history of tort—may make it appear that there is no enduring reason for distinguishing tortious from contractual liability, and there is, moreover, plentiful opportunity for both forms of liability to co-exist on one and the same set of facts.[34] A dentist who contracts to pull out my tooth is, of course, liable to me for breach of contract if he injures me by an unskilled extraction. But he is also liable to me for the tort of negligence; for every one who professes skill in a calling is bound by the law, agreement or no agreement, to show a reasonable amount of such skill.[35] I cannot recover damages twice over, but I may well have alternative claims for damages under different heads of legal liability. Would it not, therefore, be advantageous to bring tortious and contractual liability together in one book under some such title as " The Law of Obligations "? There is a great deal to be said for this but, to be logical, a book on the law of obligations ought also to include both quasi-contract and trusts as well as the whole of contract and of tort, and would become unmanageably large. The book would also have to contain a great deal of material having only indirect connection with problems of the incidence of liability. Books on contract or on trusts are, no doubt, concerned with the incidence of liability for loss or damage suffered, as are those on tort, but there liability only forms a part, and sometimes a small part, of their subject-matter. Equally, if not more important, are such questions as the ways in which a contract may be concluded or a trust set up, the various modes of discharge or dissolution and the nature of the property rights these institutions may create. But the central question for the law of tort is always that of liability, and it is this which really forms the link between the various topics covered in this book. We are not here concerned with the creation of legal relationships or rights of property, though it may be necessary to mention them incidentally from time to time. Our concern is only with the rules of liability for damage done. " The study of the law of tort is . . . a study of the extent to which the law will shift the losses sustained in modern society from the person affected to the shoulders of him who caused the loss." [36]

---

[34] See Weir, *Casebook on Tort*, 3rd ed., p. 1.

[35] *Edwards* v. *Mallan* [1908] 1 K.B. 1002.

[36] Wright, " Introduction to the Law of Torts " (1944) 8 C.L.J. 238. " In these days the form of remedy is hardly an appropriate way to define substantive rights and liabilities. The province of tort is to allocate responsibility for injurious conduct ": Lord Denning (in a review) (1947) 63 L.Q.R. 517. Prosser, *op. cit.*, pp. 5–6; Seavey, " Principles of Torts " (1942) 56 Harv.L.R. 72. Compensation is, however, not the only purpose of the law of tort: there are four possible bases of the action for damages in tort—appeasement, justice (*i.e.*, the moral principle that one who by his fault has caused damage ought as a matter of justice to make compensation), deterrence and compensation—and each of these will be found to receive different emphasis according to the particular branch of the law under consideration. No one theory adequately explains the whole of the law. See Glanville Williams, " Aims of the Law of Tort " (1951) 4 *Current Legal Problems* 137 for a full analysis by this approach. Damage for which compensation is not recoverable is known as *damnum sine injuria*. " Injury (*injuria*) is limited to actionable wrong, while ' damage,' in contrast with injury, means loss or harm incurring in fact, whether actionable as an injury or not ": *Crofter Hand Woven Harris Tweed Co. Ltd.* v. *Veitch* [1942] A.C.

THE FOUNDATION OF TORTIOUS LIABILITY

Winfield's definition of tortious liability has been criticised on the ground that it is formal, not material, and does nothing to indicate the lawfulness or otherwise of a given act. This, it seems, Winfield admitted for he agreed that the layman must be told that no one but a professional lawyer can say whether or not the loss inflicted on him by the action or inaction of a neighbour will entitle him to a remedy by civil action against that neighbour [37] and added, " a layman is not remarkable for wisdom if he imagines that he can safely say that he is entitled to sue his neighbour for tort or for breach of contract, or for any conceivable claim without consulting a professional lawyer first."

A satisfactory material definition of tort is almost certainly an impossibility, but Winfield did devote several pages of earlier editions of this work to discussion of a familiar controversy concerning the foundation of tortious liability which has some bearing on the problem of a material definition. Salmond had asked, [38] " Does the law of torts consist of a fundamental general principle that it is wrongful to cause harm to other persons in the absence of some specific ground of justification or excuse, or does it consist of a number of specific rules prohibiting certain kinds of harmful activity, and leaving all the residue outside the sphere of legal responsibility? " and had chosen the second alternative. Winfield preferred the other view,[39] but latterly he modified it as follows: From a narrow practical point of view, the second theory will suffice, but from a broader outlook, the first is valid. If we concentrate attention on the law of tort at the moment (which is what most practitioners do), entirely excluding the development of the law, past and future, then it corresponds to the second theory. If we take the wider view that the law of tort has grown for centuries and is still growing, then the first theory seems to be at the back of it. It is the difference between treating a tree as inanimate for the practical purposes of the moment (e.g., for the purpose of avoiding collision with it, it is as lifeless as a block of marble) and realising that it is animate because we know that it has grown and is still growing. The caution and slowness which usually mark the creation of new rules by the judges tend to mask the fact that they have been created; for they have often come into existence only by a series of analogical extensions spread over a long period of time. To vary the metaphor, the process has resembled the sluggish movement of the glacier rather than the catastrophic charge of the avalanche. But when once a new tort has

---

435, 442, *per* Viscount Simon L.C. There may also be cases of *injuria sine damno, e.g.* *Ashby* v. *White* (1703) 2 Ld.Raym. 938.

[37] The question was put by Jenks, " The Province of Tort in English Law " (1932) 14 J.C.L. 207, 210.

[38] *Torts*, 2nd ed. (1910), pp. 8–9.

[39] " The Foundation of Liability in Tort " (1927) 22 Col.L.Rev. 1–11, reprinted in *Select Legal Essays*, pp. 3–14. *Province of Tort*, Chap. III. For other literature, see Glanville Williams, " The Foundation of Tortious Liability " (1939) 7 C.L.J. 111.

come into being, it might fairly seem to have done so, if the whole history of its development is taken into account, in virtue of the principle that unjustifiable harm is tortious.

Where the courts hold that the harm is justifiable, there is, of course, no tort. And they may hold that it is justifiable for any one or more of several reasons. The plaintiff may be asking them to do what they think Parliament is more fitted to do; or he may be alleging a particular tort, without giving proof of some essential requisite of it; or he may be taking an exaggerated view of what is necessary to his own comfort or prosperity; or he may be demanding the creation of a remedy which would throw out of gear other parts of the law. But, subject to these restrictions and looking at the law of torts in the whole of its development, Winfield still inclined to the first theory.

" Evidence," in the sense of judicial dicta, can be found to support either view,[40] but, so far as is known, neither forms the *ratio decidendi* of a single case. Furthermore, since the supporters of the second view do not deny that the law of tort is capable of development, or even that new heads of liability can come into existence, and since the supporters of the first view admit that no action will lie if the conduct which caused the harm was justifiable,[41] the difference between them is perhaps less than is sometimes supposed.

Summing up his investigation into the controversy, Professor Glanville Williams says this,[42] " The first school has shown that the rules of liability are very wide. The second school has shown that some rules of absence of liability are also very wide. Neither school has shown that there is any general rule, whether of liability or of non-liability, to cover novel cases that have not yet received the attention of the courts. In a case of first impression—that is, a case that falls under no established rule or that falls equally under two conflicting rules—there is no ultimate principle directing the court to find for one party or the other . . . . Why should we not settle the argument by saying simply that there are some general rules creating liability . . . and some equally general rules exempting from liability . . . . Between

---

[40] Such as Pratt C.J.'s famous " Torts are infinitely various, not limited or confined " in *Chapman* v. *Pickersgill* (1762) 2 Wils. 145, 146. To take two modern examples, in *Furniss* v. *Fitchett* [1958] N.Z.L.R. 396, 401 Barrowclough C.J. said, " The well known torts do not have their origin in any all embracing general principle of tortious liability." In *Bollinger* v. *Costa Brava Wine Co. Ltd.* [1960] Ch. 262, 283 Danckwerts J. said, " The substance of [the argument for the defendants] was that, before a person can recover for loss which he suffered from another person's act, it must be shown that his case falls within the class of actionable wrongs. But the law may be thought to have failed if it can offer no remedy for the deliberate act of one person which causes damage to the property of another."

[41] " What is justifiable conduct? This, of course, is the whole question of tortious liability. If it means justifiable in law, the statement merely means that you must compensate for harms (and it will be noticed that what *kind* of harms is not specified) unless the law says you are not obliged to. In other words we still have to decide what losses the law deems worthy of compensation, and what are the circumstances producing such harm which will be considered sufficient to entail liability ": Wright, " Introduction to the Law of Torts " (1944) 8 C.L.J. at p. 240.

[42] " The Foundation of Tortious Liability " (1939) 7 C.L.J. at p. 131; Salmond, *Torts*, 16th ed., pp. 15–17, Prosser, *Torts*, 4th ed., pp. 3–4; Wright, *loc. cit.* at p. 240.

the two is a stretch of disputed territory, with the courts as an unbiased boundary commission. If, in an unprovided case, the decision passes for the plaintiff, it will be not because of a general theory of liability but because the court feels that here is a case in which existing principles of liability may properly be extended." [43]

---

[43] " The truth is there is no single integrating principle of tort liability save one so broad that it answers nothing ": Fleming James, " Tort Law in Midstream " (1959) 8 *Buffalo Law Review* 315, 320. " The law of tort has fallen into great confusion, but, in the main, what acts and omissions result in responsibility and what do not are matters defined by long-established rules of law from which judges ought not wittingly to depart and no light is shed upon a given case by large generalisations about them ": *Victoria Park Recreation Grounds Co. Ltd.* v. *Taylor* (1937) 58 C.L.R. 479, 505, *per* Dixon C.J. Nevertheless, in the United States, there is now some development of a " prima facie tort " theory which is to the general effect that, " prima facie, the intentional infliction of temporal damages is a cause of action, which, as a matter of substantive law, whatever may be the form of the pleading, requires a justification if the defendant is to escape ": *Aikens* v. *Wisconsin*, 195 U.S. 194 (1904), *per* Holmes J. This theory has proved useful in enabling the courts to give a remedy where none of the traditional torts is available, and a similar idea has been canvassed in this country (see, *e.g.*, *Mogul Steamship Co.* v. *McGregor, Gow & Co.* (1884) 23 Q.B.D. 598, 613, *per* Bowen L.J.). But this theory still leaves unanswered the question, what is justifiable? And in so far as it suggests that the defendant has a burden of proof in matters of law, it can hardly be accepted. (See Glanville Williams, *loc. cit.*, p. 112.) For the " prima facie tort," see " The Prima Facie Tort Theory " (1952) 52 Col.L.Rev. 503; (1956) 41 *Cornell Law Quarterly* 507; Forkosch, " An Analysis of the ' Prima Facie Tort ' Cause of Action " (1957) 42 *Cornell Law Quarterly* 465; " Abstaining from Wilful Injury and the Prima Facie Tort Doctrine " (1958) 10 *Syracuse Law Review* 53.

CHAPTER 2

GENERAL CHARACTERISTICS OF TORTIOUS LIABILITY

1. Forms of action

The chief source of our law of tort is the common law as opposed to the statute law. This, of course, signifies that it is for the most part based on decided cases and owes its development to the activity of the judges more than to the activity of Parliament. It also means that the law of tort has grown up, like other branches of our law, behind a screen of legal procedure. Until the mid-nineteenth century, the question which arose when a plaintiff sued a defendant for some alleged injury was not " Has the defendant broken some duty which he owed to the plaintiff? " but " Has the plaintiff any form of action against the defendant, and, if so, what form? " If he could not fit his claim into one of the recognised forms of action, he had no legal grievance. An action was (and indeed still is) usually commenced by a royal writ issued from the Chancery, which in this sense signified not a court of law, but a government department, one of whose functions was the creation and issue of these writs. It was known also as the *officina brevium* which has been conveniently translated as " the writ-shop," for a plaintiff could not get a writ without paying for it. For a very considerable period of our legal history the shape of the law was no more than a classification of writs.

The writs that remedied the injuries which in modern time are called torts were principally the writ of trespass and the writ of trespass on the case or " case." [1] Trespass in common parlance now signifies unauthorised entry on another person's land, but in law it has a wider signification. The writ of trespass lay for injuries to land or to goods, or to the person. But it was limited to injuries which were direct and immediate such as those sustained by a person struck by a log which is thrown into the highway. It did not extend to indirect or consequential injuries, such as those sustained by a person who stumbled over the log while it lay in the highway. But these indirect injuries came to be remediable through the action on the case. These two classes of action, " trespass " and " case," existed side by side for centuries and to them we owe most of our law of tort. There were, however, definite distinctions between these two forms of action and until the nineteenth century it was vital for a plaintiff to choose correctly between them.[2] Only after the reforms of that century had broken up the cast-iron

---

[1] See Milsom, " Not doing is no Trespass " [1954] C.L.J. 105; " Trespass from Henry III to Edward III " (1958) 74 L.Q.R. 195, 407, 561.

[2] See Prichard, " Trespass, Case and the Rule in *Williams* v. *Holland* " [1964] C.L.J. 234.

moulds of procedure did it cease to be necessary " to canvass the niceties of the old forms of action. Remedies now depend upon the substance of the right, not on whether they can be fitted into a particular framework." [3] Nevertheless a knowledge of the forms of action is still necessary for the understanding of the old authorities and of the classification of much of the modern law. Moreover in some instances the existence and nature of tortious liability depend upon the form of action which would have been appropriate under the old procedure. Maitland's famous phrase, " The forms of action we have buried, but they still rule us from their graves," [4] has been repeated often enough to become a *cliché*. One does not venture to polish any aphorism of Maitland's but we shall see that in some respects it may be questioned whether the forms of action have not been buried alive.[5]

2. Forms of liability

There are different ways in which liability in tort may arise:

(a) Liability may be imposed as a legal consequence of a person's act, or of his omission if he is under a legal duty to act.[6] Liability may also be imposed upon one person as the legal consequence of the act or omission of another person with whom he stands in some special relationship such as that of master and servant. This is known as vicarious liability and is the subject of a separate chapter.[7]

(b) In some cases liability is based upon fault; sometimes an intention to injure is required but more often negligence is sufficient. In other cases, which are called cases of strict liability, liability is in varying degrees independent of fault.

(c) Whereas most torts require damage resulting to the plaintiff which is not too remote a consequence of the defendant's conduct, a few, such as trespass in some, or perhaps all, of its various forms and libel, do not require proof of actual damage.

INTENTION OR NEGLIGENCE OR THE BREACH OF A STRICT DUTY

Intention

This signifies full advertence in the mind of the defendant to his conduct, which is in question, and to its consequences, together with a desire for those consequences. But it is essential to add that the interpretation of this definition by the law is often technical.

---

[3] *Nelson* v. *Larholt* [1948] 1 K.B. 339, 343, *per* Denning J. See also *Dies* v. *British and International Mining and Finance Corporation* [1939] 1 K.B. 724, 738, *per* Stable J.; *Abbott* v. *Sullivan* [1952] 1 K.B. 189, 200, *per* Denning L.J.
[4] *Equity* (ed. 1916), p. 296.
[5] *e.g.*, the distinction between trespass to land and private nuisance still turns upon the old distinction between trespass and case. See, *e.g.*, *Esso Petroleum Co. Ltd.* v. *Southport Corporation* [1956] A.C. 218, where the judgment of Devlin J. at first instance is also reported. For proceedings in the Court of Appeal see [1954] 2 Q.B. 182.
[6] See Weir, *Casebook on Tort*, 3rd ed. pp. 5–7.
[7] Chap. 25, *post.*

To begin with, it is impossible for the law to do more than to infer a man's intention, or indeed any other mental state of his, from his conduct. The law may frequently attribute to him an intention which a metaphysician would at most consider very doubtful. Centuries ago, Brian C.J. said: " It is common knowledge that the thought of man shall not be tried, for the Devil himself knoweth not the thought of man." [9] On the other hand, Bowen L.J. in 1885, had no doubt that " the state of a man's mind is as much a fact as the state of his digestion." [10] There is no contradiction in these dicta. All that Brian C.J. meant was that no one can be perfectly certain of what passes in the mind of another person. But Brian would certainly not have dissented from the proposition that in law what a man thinks must be deduced from what he says and does; and that is all that Bowen L.J. meant.

Then, again, although intention always implies desire for the consequence of an act or omission, many a wrongdoer has found himself responsible in law for consequences which he not only did not " desire " in the layman's sense of the term but to which he did not even advert. This results from the rule that " a party must be considered, in point of law, to intend that which is the necessary or natural consequence of that which he does." [11] If I fire a gun at your dog, wishing merely to scare it, and in fact some of the pellets hit it, it does not lie in my mouth to say that I intended only to scare it and not to hit it. And it would be equally idle for me, at any rate in the law of tort, to say that I never wished to hit you, if in fact some of the shot glanced off the ground and wounded you who were standing near your dog. These are simple examples and, indeed, they are consonant with common sense.

Negligence

As a mental element in tortious liability, negligence usually signifies total or partial inadvertence of the defendant to his conduct and/or its consequences. In exceptional cases there may be full advertence to both the conduct and its consequences. But, in any event, there is no desire for the consequences, and this is the touchstone for distinguishing negligence from intention. A simple example of total inadvertence is that of a signalman who falls asleep and thus causes a railway collision. An illustration of full advertence to one's conduct and its consequences without any desire for the latter is *Vaughan v. Menlove*.[12] There the defendant had been warned that his haystack was likely to overheat and to take fire which might spread to the land of his neighbour. He said that he would chance it, and he was held

---

[9] Year Book Pasch. 17 Edw. 4, fol. 2, pl. 2.

[10] *Edgington* v. *Fitzmaurice* (1885) 29 Ch.D. at p. 483. See Glanville Williams, *Criminal Law—General Part*, s. 13, Intention.

[11] *R.* v. *Harvey* (1823) 2 B. & C. 257, 264; *D.P.P.* v. *Smith* [1961] A.C. 290. Though no longer completely true for the criminal law (Criminal Justice Act 1967, s. 8) there is no reason to doubt the validity of this rule in the law of tort.

[12] (1837) 3 Bing.N.C. 468.

liable for the damage which occurred when the stack actually took fire.

We are concerned at this point with negligence merely as a state of mind. But it also has the further meaning of an independent tort, with the specific name of " negligence." Its treatment as such must be postponed until we come to deal with specific torts.[13]

Breach of strict duty

In some torts, the defendant is liable even though the harm to the plaintiff occurred without intention or negligence on the defendant's part. Thus it was laid down in the celebrated case of *Rylands* v. *Fletcher* [14] that " if a person brings or accumulates on his land anything which, if it should escape, may cause damage to his neighbours, he does so at his peril. If it does escape and cause damage, he is responsible, however careful he may have been, and whatever precautions he may have taken to prevent damage." This is sometimes styled " absolute " liability, but the epithet is misplaced, as there are possible defences even to torts of this kind, *e.g.*, the act of God excludes liability under the rule in *Rylands* v. *Fletcher*.[15] Liability in nuisance *may* be strict where the defendant himself or someone for whom he is responsible has created the nuisance.[16] Liability for breach of a statutory duty is not, as a rule, dependent on proof of negligence,[17] and where an Act requires something to be done without qualification contravention of the statute automatically establishes liability.[18]

" Reasonable " and " reasonable man "

It is convenient to insert here an explanation of the terms " reasonable " and " reasonable man." They recur so frequently in the law of tort, and indeed in every branch of the law,[19] that their meaning must be grasped at the outset of this exposition. As to the law of tort, reasonableness is an essential ingredient in the law of negligence, whether that word be used to indicate an independent tort or a mental element in the commission of certain other torts; and more will be said of this in the chapter on Negligence.[20] But there are many other

---

[13] *Post*, Chap. 5.
[14] (1868) L.R. 3 H.L. 330, 340.
[15] *Post*, pp. 376–377; (1926) 42 L.Q.R. 37.
[16] *Rapier* v. *London Tramways Co.* [1893] 2 Ch. 588, 599, *per* Lindley L.J.; *Sedleigh-Denfield* v. *O'Callaghan* [1940] A.C. 880, 904. " Negligence is not a necessary condition of a claim in nuisance ": *per* Lord Wright. See *post*, pp. 320–324.
[17] *Galashiels Gas Co.* v. *O'Donnell* [1949] A.C. 275, 282, *per* Lord Morton, 286, *per* Lord MacDermott (absolute duty to maintain lift—Factories Act 1937, ss. 22 (1) and 152 (2)); *Carroll* v. *Barclay (Andrew) & Sons Ltd.* [1948] A.C. 477, 487, *per* Lord Normand (absolute obligation to fence dangerous machinery). But a statute may prescribe that reasonable care is all that is required, or that something shall be done so far as is reasonably practicable. See Munkman, *Employer's Liability*, 7th ed., pp. 193–202; *post*, pp. 135–136.
[18] *John Summers & Sons Ltd.* v. *Frost* [1955] A.C. 740. Liability under the Nuclear Installations Act 1965 will exist even if the damage is attributable to act of God, but not if it is attributable to hostile action in the course of armed conflict: *ibid.*, s. 13 (4).
[19] (1931) 45 Harv.L.R. 125–126. Eldredge, *Modern Tort Problems*, pp. 1–24.
[20] *Post*, Chap. 5.

torts in which, in one way or another, the idea appears. If any broad sense can be extracted from the various significations of " reasonable conduct " it might be described as the behaviour of the ordinary man in any particular event or transaction, including in such behaviour obedience to the special directions (if any) which the law gives him for his guidance in that connection. This is, of course, an abstraction. Lord Bowen visualised the reasonable man as " the man on the Clapham omnibus "; an American writer as " the man who takes the magazines at home, and in the evening pushes the lawn mower in his shirt sleeves." [23] He has not the courage of Achilles, the wisdom of Ulysses or the strength of Hercules, nor has he "the prophetic vision of a clairvoyant." [24] He will not anticipate folly in all its forms, but he never puts out of consideration the teachings of experience and so will guard against the negligence of others when experience shows such negligence to be common. [25] He is a reasonable man but he is neither a perfect citizen nor a " paragon of circumspection." [26] This is good so far as it goes, but it must be added that where a person exercises any calling, the law requires him, in dealing with other people in the course of that calling, to exhibit the degree of skill or competence which is usually associated with its efficient discharge. [27] Nobody expects the man on the Clapham omnibus to have any skill as a surgeon, a lawyer, a docker, or a chimney-sweep unless he is one; but if he professes to be one, then the law requires him to show such skill as any ordinary member of the profession or calling to which he belongs, or claims to belong, would display.

The description of " reasonable " just given is, and can only be, a rough approximation to exactness. As was indicated in it, if the law gives special directions for the guidance of the ordinary man, he must regulate his conduct by them if his conduct is to be regarded as reasonable. Now these directions are often so precise and technical that a man, if he is to ascertain and act upon them, strikes one as anything but a commonplace person, and seems to need the Clapham lawyer at his elbow on many occasions. Here the judicial method, being what it is, shows two rather conflicting tendencies. One is to get as near exactness as may be in the rules relating to what is regarded as reasonable. The

[23] Cited by Greer L.J. in *Hall* v. *Brooklands Auto Racing Club* [1933] 1 K.B. 205, 224. See the American *Restatement of the Law of Torts*, Vol. II, ss. 289, 290, p. 769, " What is customarily regarded as requisite for the protection of others, rather than that of the average man in the community." Eldredge, *Modern Tort Problems*, p. 3, " The reasonable man is a fiction—he is the personification of the court and jury's social judgment."

[24] *Hawkins* v. *Coulsdon & Purley U.D.C.* [1954] 1 Q.B. 319, 341, *per* Romer L.J. *Pace* Lord Bramwell, who occasionally attributed to the reasonable man the agility of an acrobat and the foresight of a Hebrew prophet.

[25] *L.P.T.B.* v. *Upson* [1949] A.C. 155, 173, *per* Lord Uthwatt; 176, *per* Lord du Parcq; *Lang* v. *London Transport Executive* [1959] 1 W.L.R. 1168, 1175, *per* Havers J.

[26] *A. C. Billings & Sons Ltd.* v. *Riden* [1958] A.C. 240, 255, *per* Lord Reid. For a brilliant caricature of " this excellent but odious creature " see Sir Alan Herbert, *Uncommon Law*, pp. 1–5.

[27] General and approved practice may, however, fall below the standard of the reasonable man, and if so, it is not a good defence. *Post*, p. 68.

other is to recognise that complete exactness is neither attainable nor desirable.[28] Nor is this all. The judge has to decide what " reasonable " means, and it is inevitable that different judges may take variant views on the same question with respect to such an elastic term.[29] An extreme example of this was a case in which " reasonable cause " was an element and the very same act was held by an appellate criminal court to be a felony punishable with penal servitude for life, and by an appellate civil court to be not even a tort.[30] But conflicts of this sort are very unusual, and although we shall find the reasonable man doing some things which a moralist would regard as quixotic and a good many other things which he would condemn as slovenly or even cowardly, yet the law upon the whole strikes a fair average between these extremes.

Several other phrases will be encountered in the law reports which have sometimes, but not always, a meaning equivalent to " reasonable." Such are " fair," " just," " natural justice." Like certain other phrases (e.g., " judicial discretion "), they show that although law and ethics are distinct topics, it is impossible to make or to administer a civilised system of law without taking account of current ethical ideas.[31]

MOTIVE AND MALICE

Motive may be conveniently treated here. It signifies the reason for conduct. Unfortunately it has become entangled with the word " malice " which is used quite differently in the law of tort. It may mean what the layman usually takes it to be—" evil motive "; or it may signify doing an act wilfully without just cause or excuse.[32] This latter meaning has really nothing to do with motive but refers to intention, a term which ought to be confined to advertence to conduct and its desired consequences, and which is quite colourless as to the motive which influences the actor; we are not concerned with it here.

Motive generally irrelevant

As to motive in its proper meaning, the general rule is that, if conduct

---

[28] The latter tendency is dominant at the present day, but with the diminishing use of juries in civil cases there is a danger that judges' decisions of fact may come to be treated as laying down detailed rules of law: *Qualcast (Wolverhampton) Ltd.* v. *Haynes* [1959] A.C. 743, esp. *per* Lord Somervell at pp. 757–758, *per* Lord Denning at pp. 759–761.

[29] *Glasgow Corporation* v. *Muir* [1943] A.C. 448, 457, *per* Lord Macmillan, who deals with some of the attributes of a reasonable man.

[30] *R.* v. *Denyer* [1926] 2 K.B. 258; *Hardie & Lane Ltd.* v. *Chilton* [1928] 2 K.B. 306; *post*, p. 454. This conflict was resolved in *Thorne* v. *Motor Trade Association* [1937] A.C. 797. *Cf.* the differing views expressed in the Court of Appeal and in the House of Lords in *Woods* v. *Duncan* [1946] A.C. 401.

[31] Winfield, " Ethics in English Case Law," (1931) 45 Harv.L.R. 112–135, reprinted in *Select Legal Essays* (1952), pp. 266–282.

[32] Bayley J. in *Bromage* v. *Prosser* (1825) 4 B. & C. 247, 255; Bowen L.J. in *Mogul Steamship Co. Ltd.* v. *McGregor, Gow & Co.* (1889) 23 Q.B.D. 598, 612; Lord Watson, in *Allen* v. *Flood* [1898] A.C. 1, 94. Fridman, " Malice in the Law of Torts " (1958) 21 M.L.R. 484. In earlier times one of the meanings of malice was " harmfulness " quite independently of any human mental element. *E.g.*, in Paynel, *Salerne's Regim.* (a book on health A.D. 1528), " such wyne doth alay the malice of ye meate."

is presumptively unlawful, a good motive will not exonerate the defendant, and that, if conduct is lawful apart from motive, a bad motive will not make him liable.

We shall see that there are several exceptions to the second part of this rule. To the first part of it defences like necessity and private defence are exceptions, for they depend to a certain extent on a good motive on the part of the defendant.

The general irrelevancy of evil motive was affirmed by the House of Lords in *Bradford Corporation* v. *Pickles*.[33] Pickles was annoyed at the refusal of the Corporation of Bradford to purchase his land in connection with the scheme of water supply for the inhabitants of the town. In revenge, he sank a shaft on his land. The water which percolated through his land in unknown and undefined channels from the land of the corporation on a higher level was consequently discoloured and diminished when it passed again to the lower land of the corporation. For this injury Pickles was held not liable. " It is the act," said Lord Macnaghten, " not the motive for the act that must be regarded. If the act, apart from motive, gives rise merely to damage without legal injury, the motive, however reprehensible it may be, will not supply that element." [34] Three years later this was again emphasised by the House of Lords in *Allen* v. *Flood* [35] and, for better or worse,[36] it remains the general rule today. As we shall see, however, there are certain exceptional cases in which the evil motive of the defendant, if proved, will tip the scales of liability against him.

---

[33] [1895] A.C. 587; *Crofter Hand Woven Harris Tweed Co.* v. *Veitch* [1942] A.C. 435, 442, *per* Viscount Simon L.C. See also *Perera* v. *Vandiyar* [1953] 1 W.L.R. 672.
[34] [1895] A.C. at p. 601. See further as to this case, *post*, pp. 331–332.
[35] [1898] A.C. 1.
[36] Gutteridge, " Abuse of Rights " (1933) 5 C.L.J. 22; Allen, *Legal Duties* (1931), pp. 95–118; Ames in *Selected Essays on the Law of Torts* (1924), pp. 150–161; Holmes, *ibid.* pp. 162–175; Roscoe Pound, *Spirit of the Common Law* (1921), pp. 202–203; Friedmann, *Legal Theory*, 5th ed., p. 554.

CHAPTER 3

NOMINATE TORTS

IN the course of English legal history certain forms of tortious liability have gained specific names, such as assault, battery, libel, slander, nuisance and negligence. The fact that they acquired such names was due to mere accidents of terminology traceable probably to their frequent occurrence. In the following chapters it is proposed to deal with these particular torts. But it is important to remember that they do not exhaust the content of tortious liability. Outside these nominate torts there are wrongs which are well known to exist but which have no compendious name; beyond these again are wrongs which may possibly be torts, but of which it is impossible to say whether they are such or not. Thus, as a family group, torts may be divided into those which received names soon after birth, those which seem to be awaiting baptism in their riper years and those whose paternity is uncertain enough to make it doubtful whether they ought to be included in the family at all.

It is also important to remember that these nominate torts are not exclusive of one another and that there is no reason why a given set of facts should not contain the elements of several of them. Since the plaintiff does not, today, have to specify the particular tort on which he wishes to rely,[1] all that is necessary for his success is that the facts of his case should include those essential to liability under one tort, without at the same time including any which are fatal to that liability. But the whole sequence of events leading up to the plaintiff's damage may include the essentials of more than one tort, and where this is so the position is simply that there is more than one reason why the plaintiff should succeed.[2]

On the other hand, though a case may sometimes be so clear that it is unnecessary for the plaintiff, through his counsel at the hearing, to identify which of the particular torts do, in his opinion, entitle him to a remedy, it is normally prudent for him to do so. Judges are presumed to know the law, but they are entitled to and should receive the assistance of counsel. Furthermore, though there is today considerable latitude to a party to amend his pleadings even at the trial, no one is allowed to lead evidence of facts which he has not pleaded. It is therefore necessary for counsel for the plaintiff, in settling the statement of claim, to plead all the facts which are essential to the particular tort

---

[1] R.S.C., Ord. 18, r. 7. *Lever Brothers Ltd.* v. *Bell* [1931] 1 K.B. 557, 583, *per* Scrutton L.J.

[2] *Letang* v. *Cooper* [1965] 1 Q.B. 232, 242–244, where Diplock L.J. states that a " cause of action " is simply a factual situation the existence of which entitles one person to obtain from the court a remedy against another person.

or torts on which he intends to rely. He cannot, however, simply plead all the facts which led up to the plaintiff's injury for this would be to go back to the creation of the world. He is bound to select from the whole complex of facts those which are relevant to his client's claim in point of law. And this, of course, he cannot do save by reference to particular torts. Suppose that the defendant has said of the plaintiff, a shopkeeper, that the plaintiff habitually sells goods which he knows to have been stolen. Here the defendant's words prima facie fall under the tort known as " slander of title"[3] and also within that form of the tort of defamation known as "slander actionable *per se*."[4] Now it is not normally an essential of the tort of defamation that the defendant should have used the words maliciously, but this is an essential of slander of title. If, therefore, the plaintiff wishes to make use in argument of that tort he must allege in his pleading that the defendant acted with malice. Otherwise, even though the defendant was in fact malicious, he will be precluded from proving this at the trial and so will fail to bring his case within slander of title. He will thus lose the advantage of an alternative line of argument which, on the facts as they actually occurred, should have been open to him.

We may say, therefore, that the law of tort is divided over the various nominate torts which we are now to consider, but life itself is not similarly divided. The law of tort may say, " If A, B and C, then liability in negligence " and also " If A, B and D then liability in nuisance." Life may produce A, B, C, D, E, F, G, H. If it does, and assuming E, F, G and H to be legally irrelevant, the plaintiff should plead and prove " A, B, C, D. " If he does he is entitled to succeed under the rules both of negligence and of nuisance. But this conclusion cannot, of course, be reached by one who is not familiar with the essentials of each particular tort.

The grouping of particular torts which have acquired names in any sort of classification is of no value except for purposes of exposition. And even for that it cannot possibly be scientifically complete. Following his definition of tortious liability, Winfield made the liability of the defendant and not the right of the plaintiff the root of his classification while the modern tendency is to adopt the other course. The order followed in the succeeding chapters adheres strictly to neither course but has as its principal aim no more than the avoidance so far as possible of repetition and of references forward to later chapters. The object is comprehensibility and the convenience of the reader who wants to begin at the beginning and go on to the end. The result is neither " historical " nor " scientific." If it is convenient, that is enough.

---

[3] *Post*, pp. 234–239.
[4] *Post*, pp. 245–249.

CHAPTER 4

TRESPASS TO THE PERSON [1]

IN its original legal meaning "trespass" signified no more than "wrong," [2] and in early times the great bulk of trespasses were dealt with in the local courts. A trespass which was also a breach of the king's peace, however, fell within the jurisdiction of the king's courts, and in course of time the allegation that the trespass was committed *vi et armis* came to be used as common form in order to preserve the jurisdictional propriety of an action brought in those courts, whether or not there was any truth in it.[3] In its developed form the writ of trespass covered injuries to land, to goods and to the person, but the first two are today more conveniently considered in separate chapters.

There is no doubt that as a matter of history trespass to the person might be committed negligently, *i.e.*, inadvertently as well as by intention,[7] and this is probably still true today.[8] In view of modern developments in this branch of the law, however,[9] the availability of trespass to the person in a case of inadvertent injury is of little more than academic interest and we shall confine our attention in this chapter to intentional trespass to the person, of which there are three main forms, namely, assault, battery and false imprisonment. Mention will also be made of intentional physical harm not falling within the tort of trespass.[10]

ASSAULT AND BATTERY [11]

Battery is the intentional application of force to another person.

Assault is an act of the defendant which causes to the plaintiff reasonable apprehension of the infliction of a battery on him by the defendant.

In popular language the word " assault " is used to describe either or both of these torts, but in this chapter it will be used in its strict sense. So, to throw water at a person is an assault but if any drops

---

[1] See Weir, *Casebook on Tort*, 3rd ed., Chap. 8. Introduction.

[2] Milsom, *Historical Foundations of the Common Law*, p. 244; Milsom, " Trespass from Henry III to Edward III " (1958) 74 L.Q.R. 195, 407, 561.

[3] See, *e.g.*, the case of 1317 cited by Milsom, *op. cit.*, p. 248.

[7] *Weaver* v. *Ward* (1616) Hob. 134; *Dickenson* v. *Watson* (1681) T. Jones 205; *Dodwell* v. *Burford* (1670) 1 Mod. 24; *Gibbon* v. *Pepper* (1695) 2 Salk. 637; 1 Ld.Raym. 38; 4 Mod. 404; *Scott* v. *Shepherd* (1773) 2 W.Bl. 892.

[8] *Covell* v. *Laming* (1808) 1 Camp. 497; *Eisener* v. *Maxwell* [1951] 1 D.L.R. 816; [1951] 3 D.L.R. 345, 348; *Fowler* v. *Lanning* [1959] 1 Q.B. 426; *Letang* v. *Cooper* [1965] 1 Q.B. 232, 243, *per* Diplock L.J. *Cf. ibid.* at pp. 239–240, *per* Lord Denning M.R.

[9] See *post*, pp. 81–83.

[10] Trespass to the person is also the parent of some of the torts described in Chap. 20, *post*, " Injuries Affecting Family and Service Relationships."

[11] Weir, *Casebook on Tort*, 3rd ed., pp. 282–284.

31

fall upon him it is battery [12]; riding a horse at a person is an assault but riding it against him is a battery. Pulling away a chair, as a practical joke, from one who is about to sit on it is probably an assault until he reaches the floor, for while he is falling he reasonably expects that the withdrawal of the chair will result in harm to him. When he comes in contact with the floor, it is a battery. Throwing over a chair on which another person is actually sitting is either a battery or one of the forms of residuary trespass to the person; either way the defendant is liable.[13]

Meaning of force

Any physical contact with the body of the plaintiff is sufficient to amount to " force ": there is a battery when the defendant shoots the plaintiff from a distance just as much as when he strikes him with his fist, and, probably, the infliction of such things as heat or light, if in such a degree as to cause injury or discomfort, will also suffice.[14] Nor is physical hurt necessary, at least if the act is done with hostile intent. " The least touching of another in anger is a battery," said Holt C.J. in 1704,[18] and in a later case in the same year he said laconically of spitting in a man's face, " it is a battery." [19] On the other hand, Holt C.J. also said, " if two or more meet in a narrow passage, and without any violence or design of harm, the one touches the other gently, it will be no battery " [20] and it has been held that touching another in the course of conversation or in order to draw his attention to something is again no battery.[21] Winfield seems to have thought that the everyday collisions of ordinary life such as occur in an underground station during the rush-hour do amount technically to batteries, for he said that " every day scores of trivial assaults and batteries are committed which never find their way into the law courts owing to the rough common sense and humour of mankind. It is not so much *de minimis non curat lex* as *de minimis non agit sapiens*." No doubt, if a person

---

[12] *Pursell* v. *Horne* (1838) 3 N. & P. 564; and, as Pollock noted (*Torts*, 15th ed., p. 159), there is much older authority in Reg.Brev. (ed. 1687), 108b (*de liquore calido super aliquo projecto*).

[13] *Per* Gibbs C.J. in *Hopper* v. *Reeve* (1817) 7 Taunt. 698, 700. *Nash* v. *Sheen* [1953] C.L.Y. 3726 (application of a " tone-rinse " to plaintiff's hair without her consent by defendant, a hairdresser to whom she went for a permanent wave, was a trespass). See Weir, *Casebook on Tort*, 3rd ed., p. 284.

[14] Russell, *Crimes*, 12th ed., pp. 652–653. But mere passive obstruction does not constitute force: *Innes* v. *Wylie* (1844) 1 C. & K. 257, 263, *per* Lord Denman L.J. *Cf. Bruce* v. *Dyer* (1966) 58 D.L.R. (2d) 211, 216–217, *per* Ferguson J. (H.Ct. of Ontario) and *Fagan* v. *Metropolitan Police Commissioner* [1969] 1 Q.B. 439. According to the American *Restatement of Torts*, § 18, it is battery if I daub with filth a towel which I hope that you will use, and you unwittingly use it and befoul your face. In English law this would appear to fall more naturally under intentional physical harm other than trespass to the person: *post*, pp. 43–44.

[18] *Cole* v. *Turner*, 6 Mod. 149. *Cf.* the *Restatement of Torts*, § 29, where mere touching without harm is not trespass to the person.

[19] *R.* v. *Cotesworth* 6 Mod. 172.

[20] *Cole* v. *Turner, supra.*

[21] *Turbervell* v. *Savadge* (1669) 1 Mod. 3; *Coward* v. *Baddeley* (1859) 4 H. & N. 478. *Cf. Ashton* v. *Jennings* (1674) 2 Lev. 133 and *Donnolly* v. *Jackman* [1970] 1 W.L.R. 562.

uses violence to force his way " in a rude and inordinate manner " or if there is a struggle of such violence that actual harm may be caused, then a battery will have been committed,[22] but it is submitted that mere accidental contacts between persons in a crowd are not even technically tortious.[23]

Meaning of act

For battery there must be a voluntary act by the defendant. I do not commit battery against you if X seizes my arm and uses it like a club. Here X, and X alone, is liable. The " act " which is essential in assault involves some bodily movement in the common sense of that term. Thus mere words are not an assault. *Meade's Case,*[24] though it was actually concerned with an indictment for murder, contains a dictum which may be taken to apply to the law generally: " no words or singing are equivalent to an assault." [25] Threats of personal violence which are purely oral and do not lead to injury in a man's business or freedom of action are not actionable at all. But if he has just cause to fear that the threatener will do him bodily harm, he can apply to the magistrates for the threatener to be bound over to keep the peace. Words accompanying a menacing gesture may negative its appearance of being an assault, as where the defendant laid his hand upon his sword, and said, " If it were not assize-time, I would not take such language from you "; as it was assize-time, he was held not to have committed an assault.[27]

Pointing a pistol

Pointing a loaded pistol at a person is, of course, an assault. But what if the pistol be unloaded? In the only civil case on the question, *Blake* v. *Barnard* (1840), Lord Abinger C.B. ruled that " If the pistol was not loaded it would be no assault." [28] In *R.* v. *St. George*, a criminal case of the same year, the actual question was whether the accused could be convicted of a particular form of statutory assault if the weapon were unloaded, but Parke B., *obiter,* had no doubt that it would be a common law assault to point an unloaded weapon at a person at such a short distance that, if loaded, it might do injury.[29] Principle and common sense favour this view. Assault involves reason-

---

[22] *Cole* v. *Turner, supra.*

[23] A plausible, if rather artificial, explanation of what is in truth a rule of common sense may be that a person consents to minor accidental contacts, but does not consent either to the deliberate use of force to any extent or to even accidental roughness to a degree that renders actual harm at all likely. See Street, *Law of Torts,* 5th ed., p. 19.

[24] (1823) 1 Lewin 184.

[25] But see Street, *Law of Torts,* 5th ed., p. 22.

[27] *Turbervell* v. *Savadge* (1669) 1 Mod. 3. *Cf. Barton* v. *Armstrong* [1969] 2 N.S.W.R. 451.

[28] 9 C. & P. 626, 628. It has been said that the case " turned entirely on a point of pleading " ((1939) 7 C.L.J. 67n.), but a study of the report shows that it was a point of pleading that was vital to the substance of the action.

[29] 9 C. & P. 483, 491–493. *R.* v. *James* (1844) 1 C. & K. 530, another criminal case on the same statute, is usually supposed to conflict with this, but Turner has shown that this is incorrect: (1939) 7 C.L.J. 63–67.

able apprehension of impact of something on one's body, and that is exactly what occurs when a firearm is pointed at one by an aggressor. It ought to be an assault whether it is loaded or unloaded, unless the person at whom it is levelled knows it to be unloaded, or unless his distance from the weapon was so great that any reasonable person would have believed that he was out of range.[30]

Interception of blow

An assault will still have been committed even if the actual blow consequent upon it is intercepted or prevented by some third person. In *Stephens* v. *Myers* [31] the plaintiff was in the chair at a parish meeting. The defendant, who sat at the same table some six or seven places away from the plaintiff, became vociferous and by a large majority it was resolved that he be expelled. He said he would rather pull the plaintiff out of the chair than be ejected and he advanced with clenched fist upon the plaintiff, but was stopped by the churchwarden who sat next but one to the plaintiff. He was held to be liable for assault. If, however, the plaintiff has no reasonable belief that the defendant has present ability to affect his purpose, it is presumably not an assault: *e.g.*, where A, who is in a train moving out of a station, shakes his fist at B who is on the platform.

Does battery include assault?

Some authorities make *fear* on the part of the plaintiff an ingredient in assault.[32] If " fear " merely means " reasonable apprehension of force or harm," this is correct, but if it means " alarm," the decided cases do not support the view that the plaintiff must experience fear of this kind.[33] No doubt in most circumstances there is alarm, but that is not essential. A courageous man might feel no alarm at an impending blow, but he is not to be penalised for being brave, and the defendant would still be liable. As to battery, there are examples of it in which the plaintiff has no opportunity of experiencing fear or any other sensation *before* the force is applied: *e.g.*, a blow from behind inflicted by an unseen assailant.[34] Hence, it would seem that battery does not always include assault.[35]

Offences against the Person Act

Assault and battery are crimes as well as torts, and the Offences

---

[30] Much the same view is expressed in Pollock, *Torts*, 15th ed., pp. 159–160; Salmond, *Torts*, 16th ed., p. 124, and Street, *Law of Torts*, 5th ed., pp. 21–22. See also Fleming, *Law of Torts*, 4th ed., p. 27; Weir, *Casebook on Tort*, 3rd ed., pp. 255–256. It is adopted in the American *Restatement of Torts*, § 29.

[31] (1830) 4 C. & P. 349.

[32] Pollock, *Torts*, 15th ed., p. 159; Addison, *Torts*, p. 158.

[33] For the like reason the ambiguous word " threat " has been omitted from the definitions. The American *Restatement*, Vol. 1, § 24, uses the word " apprehension."

[34] A biblical instance in point is the slaying of Sisera by Jael, the wife of Heber the Kenite. She drove a tent-peg through his head while he was asleep.

[35] *Contra*, Pollock, *Torts*, 15th ed., p. 160.

against the Person Act 1861 [36] makes criminal proceedings in certain circumstances a bar to any subsequent civil proceedings. By sections 42 to 45, where a person is prosecuted before a court of summary jurisdiction and, after a hearing on the merits,[37] either the summons is dismissed and a certificate of dismissal is granted by the magistrates or he is convicted and has served his imprisonment or paid the whole amount awarded against him,[38] no further proceedings, civil or criminal, for the same cause, shall lie at the instance of anyone against that person. The Act is only a defence (a) if the proceedings are instituted by or on behalf of the party aggrieved, and not by someone else; (b) if the summons is dismissed on the merits of the case and not for some technical defect; or (c) if the proceedings are summary and not by way of indictment. It relieves the party from all further proceedings whether at the suit of the party assaulted or of anyone else. If a servant is assaulted and thereby prevented from carrying out his duties to his master, the master may in certain circumstances sue for loss of service, but if the Act applies, it is a defence to an action by the master and by the servant.[39] The Act does not prevent proceedings against anyone other than the defendant, so that the conviction of a servant for an assault committed in the course of his employment is no bar to an action against his master.[40]

FALSE IMPRISONMENT [41]

This is the *infliction of bodily restraint which is not expressly or impliedly authorised by the law.*

Both " false " and " imprisonment " are somewhat misleading terms. " False " does not here necessarily signify " mendacious " or " fallacious," but is used in the less common sense of " erroneous " or " wrong." [42] And it is quite possible to commit the tort without " imprisonment " of a person in the common acceptation of that term. In fact neither physical contact nor anything resembling a prison is necessary. If a lecturer locks his class in the lecture-room after the usual time for dismissal has arrived, that is false imprisonment; so, too, if a man be restrained from leaving his own house or any part of

---

[36] 24 & 25 Vict. c. 100. See North, " Civil and Criminal Proceedings for Assault " (1966) 29 M.L.R. 16.

[37] *Reed* v. *Nutt* (1890) 24 Q.B.D. 669 (prosecutor obtained summons, did not attend to give evidence, magistrates dismissed summons, and granted defendant certificate of dismissal. Held, certificate invalid, not having been given after a hearing on the merits, and therefore, no bar to an action); *Ellis* v. *Burton* [1975] 1 All E.R. 395 (guilty plea).

[38] It has been held in the county court that these actions afford no defence to a person who has been convicted and bound over in his own recognisances: *Gibbons* v. *Harris* [1956] C.L.Y. 8611; *Toomey* v. *Condon* (1962) 112 L.J. 497.

[39] *Masper* v. *Brown* (1876) 1 C.P.D. 97.

[40] *Dyer* v. *Munday* [1895] 1 Q.B. 742.

[41] Weir, *Casebook on Tort*, 3rd ed., pp. 274–282.

[42] Salmond, *Torts*, 16th ed., p. 125, n. 38.

it,[43] or be forcibly detained in the public streets.[44] " Imprisonment," says the old *Termes de la Ley*,[45] " is the restraint of a man's liberty whether it be in the open field, or in the stocks or cage in the street, or in a man's own house, as well as in the common gaol. And in all these places the party so restrained is said to be a prisoner, so long as he hath not his liberty freely to go at all times to all places whither he will, without bail or mainprize." [46]

Knowledge of plaintiff

This definition (with due elimination of the archaisms in it) was accepted by the Court of Appeal in *Meering* v. *Grahame-White Aviation Co. Ltd.*[47] It had been held in *Grainger* v. *Hill* [48] that imprisonment is possible even if the plaintiff is too ill to move in the absence of any restraint. In *Meering's* case the court went much farther by holding that the tort is committed even if the plaintiff did not know that he was being detained.[49] The facts were that the plaintiff, being suspected of stealing a keg of varnish from the defendants, his employers, was asked by two of their police to go with them to the company's office. He assented and at his suggestion they took a short cut there. On arrival he was taken or invited to go to the waiting-room, the two policemen remaining in the neighbourhood. In an action for false imprisonment the defence was that the plaintiff was perfectly free to go where he liked, that he knew it and that he did not desire to go away. But it was held by a majority of the Court of Appeal that the defendants were liable because the plaintiff from the moment that he came under the influence of the police was no longer a free man. Atkin L.J. said: " It appears to me that a person could be imprisoned without his knowing it. I think a person can be imprisoned while he is asleep, while he is in a state of drunkenness, while he is unconscious, and while he is a lunatic. . . . Of course the damages might be diminished and would be affected by the question whether he was conscious of it or not." The learned Lord Justice's ground for this opinion was that, although a person might not know he was imprisoned, his captors might be boasting elsewhere that he was.[50] But this argument seems to

---

[43] *Warner* v. *Riddiford* (1858) 4 C.B.(N.S.) 180.

[44] Blackstone, Comm., iii, 127. *Cf.* the wedding guest detained by Coleridge's Ancient Mariner:

" He holds him with his glittering eye—
The wedding-guest stood still,
And listens like a three years' child,
The Mariner hath his will."

Would restraint by post-hypnotic suggestion suffice? There seems to be no reason why it should not be false imprisonment if the victim would not have assented to it.

[45] Its first edition was about 1520.

[46] A person bailed is theoretically in the custody of his sureties; a person mainprized (now wholly obsolete) is at large.

[47] (1920) 122 L.T. 44, 51, 53.

[48] (1838) 4 Bing.N.C. 212.

[49] *Contra* the American *Restatement of Torts*, §§ 35, 42.

[50] 122 L.T. at pp. 53–54.

be relevant rather to the tort of defamation, or injury to a man's reputation, than to false imprisonment, which is an injury to his person. Perhaps the actual decision in *Meering's* case is justifiable on the ground that restraint of personal liberty is a very serious matter, but it would have been more satisfactory if the court had been unanimous and if they had dealt with the earlier Court of Exchequer case, *Herring* v. *Boyle*,[51] which was a decision the other way and which does not appear to have been even cited in *Meering's* case.

Restraint must be complete

The tort is not committed unless motion be restrained in every direction. In *Bird* v. *Jones* [52] the defendants wrongfully enclosed part of the public footway on Hammersmith Bridge, put seats in it for the use of spectators of a regatta on the river, and charged for admission to the enclosure. The plaintiff insisted on passing along this part of the footpath, and climbed over the fence of the enclosure without paying the charge. The defendants refused to let him go forward, but he was told that he might go back into the carriage-way and cross to the other side of the bridge if he wished. He declined to do so and remained in the enclosure for half an hour. The defendants were held not to have committed false imprisonment.

Means of escape

If a person has the means of escape, but does not know it, it is submitted that his detention is nevertheless false imprisonment unless any reasonable man would have realised that he had an available outlet. Thus if I pretend to turn the key of the door of a room in which you are and take away the key, it would seem unreasonable if you made no attempt to see whether the door was in fact locked. A more difficult case is that in which you have a duplicate key in your pocket but have forgotten its existence.[53] A reasonable man may suffer from a lapse of memory.

Defences

Most of the defences depend upon conditions which in general negative liability in tort.[54] Some particular cases may be mentioned here.

---

[51] (1834) 1 Cr.M. & R. 377 (boy wrongfully kept at school during holidays, but he was not cognisant of the restraint: held, no action lay); Weir, *Casebook on Tort*, 3rd ed., p. 274.

[52] (1845) 7 Q.B. 742; Weir, *Casebook on Tort*, 3rd ed., p. 274.

[53] As was the case of Christian when he was imprisoned by Giant Despair in Doubting Castle.

[54] *Post*, pp. 614 *et seq.* See too *Liversidge* v. *Anderson* [1942] A.C. 206 (Reg. 18B of the Defence (General) Regulations 1939). *Cf. Kuchenmeister* v. *Home Office* [1958] 1 Q.B. 496 (Aliens Order 1953); *Buxton* v. *Jayne* [1960] 1 W.L.R. 783 (Lunacy Act 1890).

Reasonable condition

It is no tort to prevent a man from leaving your premises because he will not fulfil a reasonable condition subject to which he entered them. In *Robinson* v. *Balmain Ferry Co. Ltd.*[55] the plaintiff paid a penny for entry to the defendants' wharf from which he proposed to cross the river by one of the defendants' ferry-boats. A boat had just gone and, as there was not another one for twenty minutes, the plaintiff wished to leave the wharf and was directed to the turnstile which was its exit. There he refused to pay another penny which was chargeable for exit, as was stated on a notice-board, and the defendant declined to let him leave the wharf unless he did pay. The Judicial Committee held that this was not false imprisonment. "There is no law requiring the defendants to make the exit from their premises gratuitous to people who come there upon a definite contract which involves their leaving the wharf by another way. . . . The question whether the notice which was affixed to these premises was brought home to the knowledge of the plaintiff is immaterial, because the notice itself is immaterial." [56] And the court regarded the charge of a penny for exit as reasonable.

The House of Lords reached the same result in *Herd* v. *Weardale, etc., Co. Ltd.*,[57] where a miner, in breach of his contract of employment with the defendants, refused to do certain work allotted to him in the mine, and demanded to be taken to the surface by the lift five hours before his shift expired. He was not allowed to leave for twenty minutes. The defendants were held not liable.[58]

Arrest

A lawful arrest is, of course, no false imprisonment and it follows that a person who arrests another in pursuance of a valid warrant cannot be sued.[59] The common law concerning arrest without warrant is exceedingly complicated, and it is not made much easier by the enactment of certain rules by the Criminal Law Act 1967 [59a] for these do little more than make the necessary changes consequential upon the abolition by that Act of the old distinction between felonies and misdemeanours. They do not constitute a complete code of law upon the subject.[60]

---

[55] [1910] A.C. 295. Amos, "A Note on Contractual Restraint of Liberty" (1928) 44 L.Q.R. 464.

[56] [1910] A.C. at p. 299; *Cf.* Viscount Haldane L.C. in *Herd* v. *Weardale Steel Co. Ltd.* [1915] A.C. 67, 72.

[57] [1915] A.C. 67.

[58] Similar questions would arise with a person getting on the wrong omnibus, discovering his mistake and not being allowed by the conductor to get off unless he pays the minimum fare; or with a student who mistakenly enters the wrong lecture-room and is not allowed by the lecturer to leave until the end of the hour on the ground that this will interrupt the discourse. In each of these cases the decision must, having regard to all the facts, turn upon whether (a) the mistake was a reasonable one, and (b) the condition as to exit was a reasonable one. *Cf.* Street, *Torts*, 5th ed., p. 25, n. 8.

[59] See *post*, p. 599.   [59a] c. 58, s. 2.

[60] *Ibid.* s. 2 (7).

The Act replaces the distinction between felonies and misdemeanours with one between arrestable and non-arrestable offences: arrestable offences are those for which the sentence is fixed by law,[60a] those for which under any enactment [61] a person may on a first conviction be sentenced to imprisonment for five years or more, and attempts to commit such offences. (The Act) preserves the difference existing at common law between the powers of constables and of private citizens and may be summarised as follows: any person may arrest without warrant anyone who is, or whom he with reasonable cause suspects to be, in the act of committing an arrestable offence.[62] Where an arrestable offence has actually been committed, whether by the person arrested or not, any person may arrest anyone whom he with reasonable cause suspects to be guilty of the offence,[63] but an arrest by a constable on the ground of reasonable suspicion will be lawful even if in fact no arrestable offence has been committed.[64] Finally, a constable, but not a private person, may arrest anyone whom he, with reasonable cause, suspects to be about to commit an arrestable offence.[65]

In addition to the powers of arrest given in relation to arrestable offences, any person may use such force, including arrest, as is reasonable in the circumstances in the prevention of crime, or in effecting or assisting in the lawful arrest of offenders, suspected offenders or persons unlawfully at large,[66] and innumerable statutes create specific powers of arrest in connection with the offences which they create.[67] Where such special statutory powers exist the courts have in some cases taken the strong course of holding the constable exempt from liability for false imprisonment if, though the person arrested has not in fact committed the offence, the constable honestly and on reasonable grounds believes that he has committed it [68]; nor is it material that the statute apparently permits such arrest only if the person is actually committing the offence; examples are the arrest of a person who appears to be drunk while in charge of a motor-vehicle [69] or of a woman who appears to be importuning men for the purposes of

---

[60a] *e.g.* murder.

[61] Common law offences are thus excluded from the category of arrestable offences, but a power of arrest without warrant may exist independently of the Act, as where there is a breach of the peace. See Clerk & Lindsell, *Torts*, 13th ed., pp. 355–358.

[62] s. 2 (2).   [63] s. 2 (3).

[64] s. 2 (4). Note the retention of the anomalous rule in *Walters* v. *W. H. Smith & Son Ltd.* [1914] 1 K.B. 595 whereby the liability of a private person for false imprisonment may depend upon the outcome of a criminal trial (not necessarily of the person arrested) which takes place after the arrest was made. A private person arresting on suspicion of an arrestable offence must prove not only reasonable grounds for his suspicion but also that the arrestable offence in question has been committed by someone.

[65] s. 2 (5).

[66] s. 3 (1). See, *e.g.*, *R.* v. *Duffy* [1967] 1 Q.B. 63.

[67] See Clerk & Lindsell, *Torts*, 13th ed., pp. 360–366, 1131–1137. There was at common law no power of arrest without warrant in respect of misdemeanours or suspected misdemeanours and this, perhaps, explains the proliferation of special statutory powers. It would be of considerable assistance to both police and public if these powers could be consolidated.

[68] *Jones* v. *Cook* [1961] C.L.Y. 6679 is a modern example.

[69] *Trebeck* v. *Croudace* [1918] 1 K.B. 158; *Wiltshire* v. *Barrett* [1966] 1 Q.B. 312.

prostitution.[70] In such cases there is a conflict of interest between the private persons whose liberty ought to be respected and the public safety and good order sought to be preserved by immediate interference with the supposed offender.[71] However, the House of Lords in *Barnard* v. *Gorman* [72] declined to lay down any principle more exact than that each statute must be construed on its merits, and, on the facts before them, there was no need to go beyond that. But the law as it now stands certainly casts a heavy responsibility on a constable who may have to decide at a moment's notice a point that has puzzled the appellate courts several times.[73]

Where the lawfulness of an arrest depends upon reasonable cause for suspicion, it is for the defendant to prove the existence of such reasonable cause [74] and for the court to decide whether he has discharged this burden of proof. Reasonable suspicion is less than prima facie proof, but there must be reasonable suspicion that the offence in question has actually been committed; there is, for example, a wide gap between suspicion that a man was driving a lorry at a particular time and place and suspicion that he was driving it recklessly or dangerously.[75] The test, as expressed by Diplock L.J. against the background of the common law, is " whether a reasonable man, assumed to know the law and possessed of the information which was in fact possessed by the defendant, would believe that there was reasonable and probable cause " for the arrest [76] and these words can, *mutatis mutandis*, be applied to " reasonable cause " for suspicion under the Act of 1967. In *Dallison* v. *Caffery*,[77] where a theft had undoubtedly been committed, the defendant police officer had received trustworthy information that the plaintiff had been identified as the man responsible, and it was held that therefore the arrest was justified. In *Hogg* v. *Ward*,[78] on the other hand, a police constable was held liable for arresting the plaintiff on a mistaken charge of theft made by the owner of some harness because the constable ought to have known from the plaintiff's open use of the property and his immediate state-

---

[70] *Isaacs* v. *Keech* [1925] 2 K.B. 354. But see Lord Wright in *Barnard* v. *Gorman* [1941] A.C. 378, 394. *Cf. Ledwith* v. *Roberts* [1937] 1 K.B. 232.

[71] *Isaacs* v. *Keech, supra*, at p. 360, *per* Bankes L.J.

[72] [1941] A.C. 378. Emphasis may be placed on the need for immediate action by the police in order to remove a source of danger to the public, as where an officer finds a person in charge of a motor car who appears to be unfit through drink or drugs: *Wiltshire* v. *Barrett, supra*.

[73] See the observations of Davies and Salmon L.JJ. in *Wiltshire* v. *Barrett, supra*, at pp. 329 and 333.

[74] *Dumbell* v. *Roberts* [1944] 1 All E.R. 326; *Dallison* v. *Caffery* [1965] 1 Q.B. 348; *Stapeley* v. *Annetts* [1970] 1 W.L.R. 20.

[75] *Hussien* v. *Chong Fook Kam* [1970] A.C. 943, 947, *per* Lord Devlin. Note that prima facie proof must consist of admissible evidence, but suspicion can take into account other matters as well: *ibid.* at p. 949.

[76] *Dallison* v. *Caffery, supra*, at p. 371; *Broughton* v. *Jackson* (1852) 18 Q.B. 378, 385, *per* Lord Campbell C.J.

[77] *Supra*.

[78] (1858) 27 L.J.Ex. 443; *Hussien* v. *Chong Fook Kam, supra*.

ment of facts which raised a reasonable inference that he had acquired it honestly, that arrest was not justifiable in the circumstances.

Information of charge. Where a policeman (or a private person) arrests X, the general principles as to informing X of the ground on which he is arrested may be summarised as follows: X must, in ordinary circumstances, be informed of the true ground of his arrest. The policeman is not entitled to be silent as to the reason for the arrest or to give a reason which is not true. If he does either of these things he is guilty of false imprisonment, subject to certain exceptions the range of which is not entirely settled, but which include the following. X need not be informed of the reason for his arrest if the circumstances are such that he must be aware of the general nature of the alleged offence for which he is seized; nor can he legally complain if it was practically impossible to give him the information owing to his own fault; *e.g.*, if he made an immediate counter-attack on the policeman or if he ran away. In any event, the policeman need not state the reason for the arrest in technical or precise language, provided he conveys to X the substance of the charge against him. These principles were laid down by Viscount Simon in *Christie* v. *Leachinsky* [79] and were expressly or tacitly approved by the other noble and learned Lords. In that case, the police arrested X without a warrant for an alleged misdemeanour under the mistaken impression that a statute authorised them to do so, and when sued by X for false imprisonment they pleaded that they had reasonable grounds for suspecting that X had also committed the felony of larceny. The plea was held bad because they had not informed X of the charge of larceny.

Duty of arrester. A person arrested without a warrant may be released if there is no sufficient reason for detaining him,[80] but otherwise he must be taken either before a magistrate or a police officer, not necessarily forthwith, but as soon as is reasonably possible.[81] The vital question is " whether, in all the circumstances, the accused person has been brought before a justice of the peace within a reasonable time, it being always remembered that that time should be as short as is reasonably practicable." [82] In this respect a police officer has greater powers than a private person, for what is reasonable conduct on the part of a police officer may not be the same as what would

---

[79] [1947] A.C. 573, 587–588. " The decision in *Christie's* case does not mean that if an officer is arresting a deaf person he has to possess himself of an ear trumpet, or something of that sort or shout at the top of his voice. He must do what a reasonable person would do in the circumstances." *Tims* v. *John Lewis & Co. Ltd.* [1951] 2 K.B. 459, 467, *per* Lord Goddard C.J.; *ibid.* on appeal [1952] A.C. 676, 681, *per* Lord Porter; *Wheatley* v. *Lodge* [1971] 1 W.L.R. 29. See also *R.* v. *Kulynycz* [1971] 1 Q.B. 367.

[80] *Wiltshire* v. *Barrett* [1966] 1 Q.B. 312. In this case it was argued that the fact that the plaintiff was neither detained nor released on bail but was released unconditionally rendered an otherwise lawful arrest unlawful. As Salmon L.J. observed (at p. 334) the point was ingenious but not novel. See *Cokayne* v. *Manyngham* (1470) Year Book 10 Edw. IV & 9 Hen. VI; S.S. Vol. 47, p. 156. See also *McCloughan* v. *Clayton* (1816) Holt N.P. 478.

[81] See also Magistrates' Courts Act 1952 (15 & 16 Geo. 6 & 1 Eliz. 2, c. 55), s. 38.

[82] *John Lewis & Co. Ltd.* v. *Tims* [1952] A.C. 676, 691–692, *per* Lord Porter.

be reasonable conduct on the part of a private arrester.[83] In a case of suspected theft, for instance, a detective constable may take the suspected person to his own house to see whether any of the stolen property is there,[84] but it is unlikely that a private person would be entitled to act in this way. On the other hand even a private arrester is not always bound to take the arrested person directly before a magistrate or to a police station. For example, a person arrested in the street by a store detective on suspicion of having stolen goods from the store may be taken back there while the matter is reported to the store manager, and may be detained there while the police are sent for.[85]

Remedies

They are (a) self-help; (b) habeas corpus; (c) action for damages. No one who is unlawfully restrained need wait until he is released before seeking redress. He can use self-help in order to escape, and he, or anyone on his behalf, can apply for a writ of habeas corpus to secure his release.

Distinction from abuse of procedure

A defendant may be liable for false imprisonment even though he did not personally detain the plaintiff, so long as he acted through an intermediary who exercised no independent discretion of his own. In *Austin* v. *Dowling* [87] a police inspector refused to take the responsibility of arresting B on a charge made by A, but finally did arrest B when A signed the charge sheet. It was held that A could be liable for false imprisonment. There can, however, be no false imprisonment if a discretion is interposed between the defendant's act and the plaintiff's detention. If, for example, A makes a charge against B before a magistrate and the magistrate then decides to order the arrest of B, A has set in motion not a ministerial but a judicial officer exercising a discretion of his own and A cannot be liable for false imprisonment.[88] He may, however, be liable for abuse of legal procedure, an entirely different matter which is considered in detail in a later chapter. For the present it is sufficient to note that whereas in false imprisonment the plaintiff need prove no more than his detention, leaving it to the defendant to prove its lawfulness if he can,[89] in malicious prosecution, the best known form of abuse of procedure, the plaintiff must prove that the defendant (a) instituted a prosecution of him which (b) ended in his favour and (c) was instituted without reasonable and probable cause and (d) was malicious. It is true that the plaintiff may still succeed

---

[83] *Dallison* v. *Caffery* [1965] 1 Q.B. 348, 371, *per* Diplock L.J.
[84] *Ibid.* at p. 367, *per* Lord Denning M.R. *Cf. Wright* v. *Court* (1825) 4 B. & C. 596.
[85] *John Lewis & Co. Ltd.* v. *Tims, supra.*
[87] (1870) L.R. 5 C.P. 534. *Cf. Pike* v. *Waldrum* [1952] 1 Lloyd's Rep. 431. See also Weir, *Casebook on Tort*, 3rd ed., pp. 279–282.
[88] *Austin* v. *Dowling, supra*, at p. 540, *per* Willes J.; *Sewell* v. *National Telephone Co. Ltd.* [1907] 1 K.B. 557.
[89] *Ante*, p. 40.

in the absence of both (a) and (b) if he was actually arrested[90] but he must still prove as distinct matters both absence of reasonable and probable cause and also malice.

INTENTIONAL PHYSICAL HARM OTHER THAN TRESPASSES TO THE PERSON[91]

An act wilfully done which is calculated to cause, and actually does cause, physical harm to another person is a tort although it may not, according to current practice, be treated either as a trespass to the person or as any other specific tort.

This statement of principle is quite modern and its limits have not been explored in the law courts. It was laid down by Wright J. in *Wilkinson* v. *Downton*,[92] where A, by way of practical joke, falsely told the plaintiff, a married woman, that her husband had met with an accident whereby both his legs were broken. She believed this and was so violently upset by the consequent nervous shock that she had a serious illness. A was held liable. Some attempt was made by counsel to base the claim on deceit as a tort, but the learned judge indicated that this would have been an extension of that tort, presumably because it is necessary that there the injured party should be intended to *act* upon the false statement and should have acted upon it, and here the plaintiff could scarcely be said to have acted in any way. Wright J. preferred the following ground: " The defendant has . . . wilfully done an act calculated to cause harm to the plaintiff —that is to say, to infringe her legal right to personal safety, and has in fact thereby caused physical harm to her. That proposition without more appears to me to state a good cause of action there being no justification alleged for the act." [93]

Since *Wilkinson* v. *Downton* no other example of the principle in that case has appeared in the English reports, except *Janvier* v. *Sweeney*,[94] in which on similar facts *Wilkinson's* case was approved by the Court of Appeal. At any rate, there is no ground for thinking that the principle in *Wilkinson* v. *Downton* is inapplicable unless the harm *is* nervous shock. That is too narrow a view. If the plaintiff, when she heard the news, had broken her arm in falling in a faint, the defendant would have been equally liable; or, if I suddenly shout at a child who is crossing an unfenced plank over a stream and the child, as I intend, loses its balance and gets a ducking, surely I am just as

---

[90] *Melia* v. *Neate* (1863) 3 F. & F. 757; *Roy* v. *Prior* [1971] A.C. 470. See *post*, Chap. 22, and Fridman, " Compensation of the Innocent " (1963) 26 M.L.R. 481.

[91] Weir, *Casebook on Tort*, 3rd ed., pp. 267–268.

[92] [1897] 2 Q.B. 57.

[93] [1897] 2 Q.B. at pp. 58–59.

[94] [1919] 2 K.B. 316. *Cf. Bunyan* v. *Jordan* (1937) 57 C.L.R. 1 (High Court of Australia). See also Fleming, *Torts*, 4th ed., pp. 32–36, and Wright, *Cases on the Law of Torts*, 4th ed., pp. 22–29.

much liable as if it had sustained illness from a nervous shock.[94a] Nor need the principle be limited to harm arising from a *statement*, *e.g.*, if I scare a person into a nervous shock by dressing up as a ghost. Again, the administration of a noxious drug to an unwitting victim may be another illustration of this tort, although it would not be the tort of battery for there is no application of force (if accompanied by false representations, it might also be the tort of deceit). The principle would also extend to the intentional infection of another person with disease (inadvertent infection is probably the tort of negligence [95]). If the disease is a venereal one contracted from cohabitation, the position is doubtful, although it is hard to see why fraudulent concealment by the person suffering from the disease should not negative the victim's consent to cohabitation and thus make the infection a tortious battery.[96]

[94a] See *Slatter* v. *British Railways Board* (1966) 110 S.J. 688, a case of negligence.
[95] Clerk & Lindsell, *Torts*, 13th ed., pp. 513–515.
[96] *Post*, p. 619.

CHAPTER 5

NEGLIGENCE

As was stated earlier,[1] negligence may mean a mental element in tortious liability or it may mean an independent tort. In this chapter we are concerned with negligence as an independent tort.[2]

ESSENTIALS OF NEGLIGENCE

Negligence as a tort is the breach of a legal duty to take care which results in damage, undesired by the defendant, to the plaintiff. Thus its ingredients are: (a) A legal duty on the part of A towards B to exercise care in such conduct of A as falls within the scope of the duty. (b) Breach of that duty. (c) Consequential damage to B. As we shall see, however, these ingredients cannot always be kept apart, and it has been said that "they are simply three different ways of looking at one and the same problem." [3] In considering them separately, therefore, it must be borne in mind that their separation is, to some extent at least, artificial.[4]

1. Duty to take care [5]

✗ It is not for every careless act that a man may be held responsible in law, nor even for every careless act that causes damage. He will only be liable in negligence if he is under a legal duty to take care. It may be objected that " duty " is not confined to the law of negligence and that it is an element in every tort, because there is a legal duty not to commit assault or battery, not to commit defamation, not to commit nuisance and so forth. But all that " duty " signifies in these other torts is that you must not commit them. It throws no light on their essential ingredients. Thus it will not tell us what the plaintiff must prove in assault in order to be successful. Breach of it is not one of the internal factors which constitute these other torts.

---

[1] *Ante*, p. 24.

[2] For its history, see Winfield, " The History of Negligence in the Law of Torts " (1926) 42 L.Q.R. 184 (*Select Legal Essays* 30); Fifoot, *History and Sources of the Common Law*, Chap. 8.

[3] *Roe* v. *Minister of Health* [1954] 2 Q.B. 66, 85, *per* Denning L.J. For a more elaborate analysis, see Clerk & Lindsell, *Torts*, 13th ed., pp. 457–458.

[4] It is also to be borne in mind that the courts are almost invariably concerned with the problem of negligence *ex post facto*. Their decisions do not relate to what a man ought or ought not to do, but to what a man ought or ought not to have done and thus to the tort of negligence as a whole, not simply to one or other of its ingredients. Though a decision is said to turn on, say, absence of a duty of care, this is no more than one judge's analysis. Another might equally well have said that there was a duty but no breach. See *Woods* v. *Duncan* [1946] A.C. 401, and *post*, p. 60.

[5] See generally, Weir, *Casebook on Tort*, 3rd ed., Chap. 1.

But in the tort of negligence breach of " duty " is the chief ingredient of the tort; in fact there is no other except damage to the plaintiff.

Though there is nothing in the terminology used by the judges to indicate it, the concept of the duty of care performs two distinct functions.[6] If the plaintiff is to succeed it must be established first that the circumstances in which his damage was caused were capable of giving rise to a duty of care, and, secondly, that the defendant actually owed him a duty on the particular facts of the case. The first of these requirements raises questions of law, and the duty may be termed the " notional duty," [7] while the second raises questions of mixed law and fact. It is the latter which sometimes shades off into questions of breach of duty or remoteness of damage.

(i) *Notional duty*

Winfield thought that in theory the concept of duty might well be eliminated from the tort of negligence, for it got there by an historical accident and it seemed to him to be superfluous. Every case could be just as well decided on some ground not depending on duty at all—sufficiency of evidence for the jury, contributory negligence, remoteness of damage, inevitable accident, *volenti non fit injuria*.[8] On the other hand Professor Lawson [9] points out that there are limits to the action of negligence which have nothing to do with the factors referred to by Winfield. These are factors which are relevant in this field of negligence but they do not explain why, for example, the vendor of a defective house is not generally liable at common law [9a] or why a person who fails in a prosecution cannot be made liable without proving malice. These are matters of policy which English law expresses by saying that there is no duty of care and no satisfactory substitute for the concept has been devised whereby the scope of liability for negligence may be controlled.[12]

Criterion of duty. How is the judge to determine whether there is, or is not, a duty? His task is easy where earlier decisions have established one. Time out of mind it has been held that men must use care in driving vehicles on the highway, in handling deadly implements or sub-

---

[6] See Dias, " The Duty Problem in Negligence " [1955] C.L.J. 198 and " The Breach Problem and the Duty of Care " (1956) 30 Tulane L.Rev. 377; Lawson, *loc. cit., infra,* note 9; Clerk & Lindsell, *Torts,* 13th ed., pp. 458–488. See also Morison, " A Re-examination of the Duty of Care " (1948) 11 M.L.R. 9; Weir, *Casebook on Tort,* 3rd ed., pp. 8–10.

[7] The phrase is Dias's in [1955] C.L.J. at p. 205.

[8] " Duty in Tortious Negligence " in *Select Legal Essays.* See, too, Buckland, " The Duty to Take Care " (1935) 51 L.Q.R. 637; Buckland, *Some Reflections on Jurisprudence,* pp. 110–115.

[9] " Duty of Care in Negligence; a Comparative Study " (1947) 22 Tulane L.Rev. 111–130; Lawson, *Negligence in the Civil Law,* pp. 31–36.

[9a] But see now the Defective Premises Act 1972, *post,* pp. 199–201.

[12] Marsh, " The History and Comparative Law of Invitees, Licensees and Trespassers " (1953) 69 L.Q.R. 182, 183–184. The modern law of negligence is not concerned with the simple issue of fact: " Has the defendant behaved reasonably in all the circumstances of the case?" There are always exceptional cases in which other values have legal priority to the protection of the plaintiff from what a reasonable man would call " negligence of the defendant."

stances, in plying their trades where their neighbours are about; and for circumstances much more particular than these which may create a duty there is a wealth of decisions in the reports. But what is a judge to do if, as often happens, there is no precedent exactly in point? Is there simply a closed list of " notional " duties so that unless the plaintiff can rely upon an established duty he is bound to fail? Is there a general principle by means of which the existence of a particular notional duty can be logically determined? Or is there no principle of law at all, so that the decision in a novel type of case must be founded upon considerations of a non-legal character?

The first view, that liability for negligence can exist only if the case is covered by a duty which has already been recognised has few supporters today. It is put most forcibly by Landon: " Negligence is not actionable unless the duty to be careful exists. And the duty to be careful only exists where the wisdom of our ancestors has decreed that it shall exist." [13] Certainly it is true that in denying the existence of a duty in some cases the judges have done so on the ostensible ground that no authority for such a duty exists,[14] but they have not hesitated to produce a new duty when it has seemed right to them to do so. Lord Macmillan has said that " the categories of negligence are never closed," [15] and the argument to the contrary has been rejected in terms.[16]

Is there, then, any general principle? The first attempt to formulate a principle was made by Brett M.R. in *Heaven* v. *Pender*,[17] and the most famous and the most important generalisation is that of Lord Atkin in *Donoghue* v. *Stevenson*.[18]

" In English law there must be, and is, some general conception of relations giving rise to a duty of care, of which the particular cases found in the books are instances. The liability for negligence, whether you style it such or treat it as in other systems as a species of ' culpa,' is no doubt based upon a general public sentiment of moral wrongdoing for which the offender must pay. But acts or omissions which any moral code would censure cannot in a practical world be treated so as to give a right to every person injured by them to demand relief. In this way rules of law arise which limit the range of complainants and the extent of their remedy. The rule that you are to love your neighbour becomes, in law, you must not injure your neighbour; and the lawyer's question, Who is my neighbour? receives a restricted reply. *You must take*

---

[13] (1941) 57 L.Q.R. at 183; Pollock, *Torts*, 15th ed., p. 326. See also *Home Office* v. *Dorset Yacht Co. Ltd.* [1970] A.C. 1004, 1045, *per* Viscount Dilhorne, dissenting.

[14] " There has to be a breach of a duty which the law recognises, and to ascertain what the law recognises regard must be had to the decisions of the courts ": *Deyong* v. *Shenburn* [1946] K.B. 227, 233, *per* du Parcq L.J.

[15] *Donoghue* v. *Stevenson* [1932] A.C. 562, 619. Lord Devlin has said that he takes this dictum " quite literally ": *Hedley Byrne & Co. Ltd.* v. *Heller & Partners Ltd.* [1964] A.C. 465, 531.

[16] *Haseldine* v. *Daw* [1941] 2 K.B. 343, 358–359, *per* Scott L.J. See, too, *Jackson* v. *Mayfair Window Cleaning Co.* [1952] 1 All E.R. 215, 218, *per* Barry J.

[17] (1883) 11 Q.B.D. 503, 509. Bowen and Cotton L.JJ. dissociated themselves from his statement of the principle, *ibid.* at p. 599.

[18] [1932] A.C. 562, 580; Weir, *Casebook on Tort*, 3rd ed., p. 15.

reasonable care to avoid acts or omissions which you can reasonably foresee would be likely to injure your neighbour. Who, then, in law is my neighbour? The answer seems to be—persons who are so closely and directly affected by my act that I ought reasonably to have them in contemplation as being so affected when I am directing my mind to the acts or omissions which are called in question." [19]

In *Donoghue* v. *Stevenson*, a manufacturer of ginger-beer had sold to a retailer ginger-beer in an opaque bottle. The retailer resold it to A who treated a young woman of her acquaintance to its contents. These included the decomposed remains of a snail which had found its way into the bottle at the factory. The young woman alleged that she became seriously ill in consequence and sued the manufacturer for negligence. There was of course no contractual duty on the part of the manufacturer towards her, but a majority of the House of Lords held that he owed her a duty to take care that the bottle did not contain noxious matter and that he would be liable if that duty was broken. The House of Lords here had only to decide as a *matter of law* whether a duty of care existed,[20] and it was never actually decided whether a *breach* of that duty had taken place.[21] With great respect to the noble and learned lords who dissented, they appear to have been influenced in their judgment by the fallacy that *because* there was no contractual liability on the manufacturer's part to the plaintiff *therefore* there could be no liability in tort. This fallacy was injected into our law in 1842,[22] it was a *non sequitur* destined to have expensive consequences for the English litigant and it died a hard death in *Donoghue's* case. The Judicial Committee of the Privy Council, in following *Donoghue's* case in 1935 in *Grant* v. *Australian Knitting Mills Ltd.*,[23] gave it decent burial. The same facts may give rise to both contractual and tortious liability, but it is wrong to assume that, because A is bound by a contract to B, therefore harm resulting from A's breach of that contract to C, a third party, can never give rise to liability in tort on A's part to C.[24] On the contrary, the entering upon work, whether or not in pursuance of a contract with B, may place A under a duty of care to C.[25] In such a case the duty is cast upon A by law because he entered upon the work, not because he made a contract, but nevertheless the contract, if any, is not necessarily an

---

[19] Italics supplied. Lord Macmillan's speech is equally important and instructive ([1932] A.C. at pp. 605–623). *McArdle* v. *Andmac Roofing Co.* [1967] 1 W.L.R. 356, 363–364, *per* Sellers L.J.

[20] [1932] A.C. 562, 579.

[21] See Ashton-Cross's note (1955) 71 L.Q.R. 472, and Weir, *Casebook on Tort*, 3rd ed., p. 21.

[22] By some dicta in *Winterbottom* v. *Wright* (1842) 10 M. & W. 109. Historically, the fallacy is intelligible: Winfield, " Duty in Tortious Negligence " in *Select Legal Essays*, at p. 86.

[23] [1936] A.C. 85, 101–102.

[24] Winfield, *Province of Tort*, pp. 73–76. *Greene* v. *Chelsea B.C.* [1954] 2 Q.B. 127, 138, *per* Denning L.J.

[25] *A. C. Billings & Sons Ltd.* v. *Riden* [1958] A.C. 240.

irrelevant circumstance for it determines the task upon which A entered.[26]

Qualifications of Lord Atkin's test. *Donoghue* v. *Stevenson* thus rid the law of the contract fallacy and provided authority for the proposition that a notional duty is owed independently of contract by a manufacturer to the ultimate consumer of his product. In addition, it is certain that Lord Atkin's statement of principle has been largely responsible for the great development of the tort of negligence since 1932. However, that statement cannot and must not be treated as if it were a statutory provision laying down a universal rule for decision.[27] No one has ever suggested that the whole of the law of tort can be reduced to the question of what the defendant ought reasonably to have foreseen,[28] and even where the tort of negligence would appear to be the most apt in the circumstances Lord Atkin's test is subject to the following qualifications.

(i) *Omissions as opposed to acts.*[29] There is no general duty to act positively for the benefit of others. An adult who stands by and watches a child drown in four feet of water (provided he does not stand in some relationship to the child [29a]) may have to answer before some higher tribunal somewhere, sometime, but he is not accountable for negligence in the English courts,[30] yet he has omitted to do what the reasonable man would do to his neighbour. Most of the cases of apparent omission where there is a duty to act are really cases of commission where the defendant has created the dangerous situation,[30a] such as the liability of the occupier of dangerous premises towards his visitors.[31] In those cases there is some benefit accruing to the actor " and the price of that benefit which the law exacts is that he shall take affirmative steps to make a

---

[26] *Voli* v. *Inglewood Shire Council* [1963] Qd.R. 256, 268, *per* Windeyer J. (H.Ct. of Australia); *Clay* v. *A. J. Crump & Sons Ltd.* [1964] 1 Q.B. 533; *McArdle* v. *Andmac Roofing Co.* [1967] 1 W.L.R. 356; *Gilchrist Watt and Sanderson Pty. Ltd.* v. *York Products Pty. Ltd.* [1970] 1 W.L.R. 1262 (P.C.) *Cf. Bagot* v. *Stevens Scanlan & Co. Ltd.* [1966] 1 Q.B. 197; *Lee Cooper Ltd.* v. *C. H. Jeakins & Sons Ltd.* [1967] 2 Q.B. 1.

[27] *Hedley Byrne & Co. Ltd.* v. *Heller & Partners Ltd.* [1964] A.C. 465, 482, *per* Lord Reid; *ibid.* at pp. 524–525, *per* Lord Devlin; *Home Office* v. *Dorset Yacht Co. Ltd.* [1970] A.C. 1004, 1027, *per* Lord Reid; *ibid.* at p. 1034, *per* Lord Morris.

[28] Heuston, " *Donoghue v. Stevenson* in Retrospect " (1957) 20 M.L.R. 1, 14–15.

[29] Weir, *Casebook on Tort*, 3rd ed., pp. 59–73; Pollock, *Torts*, 15th ed., p. 333; Winfield· " Duty in Tortious Negligence " in *Select Legal Essays*, pp. 91–92, distinguishes between omission as the foundation of a duty to take care, which is extremely rare, and omission as the breach of an acknowledged duty, which is very common. See, too, Lawson, *Negligence in the Civil Law*, pp. 31–36; Lawson, " Duty of Care in Negligence " (1947) 22 Tulane L.Rev. 124–130. Wright, " Negligent ' Acts or Omissions,' " 19 Can. Bar Rev. 465–481.

[29a] *McCallion* v. *Dodd* [1966] N.Z.L.R. 710 (N.Z. C.A.).

[30] Eldredge, *Modern Tort Problems*, p. 12. See *Horsley* v. *Maclaren* [1971] 2 Lloyd's Rep. 410 (Sup.Ct. of Canada). Linden, " Rescuers and Good Samaritans " (1971) 34 M.L.R. 241, castigates the basic rule, examines its foundation in policy and suggests that the attitude of the courts is changing. See also Binchy, " The Good Samaritan at the Crossroads: A Canadian Signpost " (1974) 25 N.I.L.Q. 147.

[30a] It seems that there is a general principle that he who creates a danger, albeit innocently, must take steps to remedy it: *Johnson* v. *Rea Ltd.* [1962] 1 Q.B. 373; *McKinnon* v. *Burtatowski* [1969] V.R. 899.

[31] *Post*, pp. 165–201. *Cf. Jordan House Ltd.* v. *Menow* (1973) 38 D.L.R. (3d) 105 (Sup. Ct. of Canada).

situation reasonably safe."[32] However, while there is no general positive duty on the defendant to assist the plaintiff[33] or to protect him from a danger created by another,[34] a defendant who undertakes to carry out some service for the plaintiff's benefit may in certain circumstances be liable in tort for breach of his undertaking even though no act of his inflicts damage on the plaintiff. The limits of this principle are not easy to state, but it may be said with confidence that, in cases of personal injury, if the defendant undertakes to assist the injured or endangered plaintiff and the defendant breaks that undertaking, he will be liable for any loss caused by that breach if, by reason of the reliance of the plaintiff or some other person upon the undertaking, the plaintiff is deprived of other sources of assistance.[34a] It seems probable that the same principle extends to damage to property [34b] and even perhaps to pure economic loss [34c] if the case is one where the law is prepared to compensate that kind of damage at all.[34d]

(ii) *Occupiers' liability.* The duty owed by the occupier of premises to his lawful visitors is no longer dependent upon the common law at all, but is contained in the Occupiers' Liability Act 1957.[35]

(iii) *Real property.* As between vendor and purchaser, or lessor and lessee, of real property, the test has no application, because the law was clearly settled long before *Donoghue* v. *Stevenson.*[36] However, important alterations have now been made by statute in this branch of the

[32] Eldredge, *op. cit.*, p. 14. See *post,* for the distinction between sale and gift with regard to dangerous chattels. Payne, "Tort of Negligence" (1953) 6 *Current Legal Problems* 243–246.

[33] "The heart of the nonfeasance rule consists in the peremptory refusal to attach legal sanctions to gratuitous undertakings to confer a benefit on the promisee, as there is no more sacrosanct axiom in our jurisprudence than that a promise without consideration will not be enforced ": Fleming, *Torts,* 4th ed., p. 143.

[34] *The Majfrid* [1942] P. 43, 145 (C.A.); *Deyong* v. *Shenburn* [1946] K.B. 227, 233. See, however, *Goldman* v. *Hargrave* [1967] 1 A.C. 645, *post,* pp. 337–339 and *Home Office* v. *Dorset Yacht Co. Ltd.* [1970] A.C. 1004, *post,* pp. 56–58.

[34a] *Semble, Wood* v. *Thurston* (1951) *The Times,* May 25; *Barnett* v. *Chelsea and Kensington Hospital Management Committee* [1969] 1 Q.B. 428; and see *Horsley* v. *Maclaren* [1971] 2 Lloyd's Rep. 410 (Sup.Ct. of Canada). See also *Zelenko* v. *Gimbel Bros.* (1935) 287 N.Y.S. 134 (P taken ill in D's store. D put P in sick room and left her there for six hours without treatment, whereby she died. *Held,* D was liable for P's death).

[34b] In *East Suffolk Rivers Catchment Board* v. *Kent* [1941] A.C. 74 (see Weir, *Casebook on Tort,* 3rd ed., p. 59) the Board had statutory power to repair sea walls but were under no duty to do so. A high tide broke the sea wall and flooded the plaintiff's land. The Board sent an inexperienced man with poor equipment and the repair took 178 days. It was proved that with reasonable skill it could have been done in 14 days. A majority of the House of Lords held that the Board was not liable in negligence, but it is significant that the plaintiff put forward no evidence that if the Board had not intervened he would have done the work himself or got someone else to do it for him: [1940] 1 K.B. 319, 339–340 (C.A.), [1941] A.C. 74, 107. See also, however, *Dutton* v. *Bognor Regis U.D.C.* [1972] 1 Q.B. 373 (Weir, *Casebook,* 3rd ed., p. 64), which virtually imposes a liability for mere failure to confer a benefit on the plaintiff and which is very difficult to reconcile with the *Kent* case: see Miller (1973) 36 M.L.R. 199 and Rogers [1972A] C.L.J. 211; *cf.* Slutsky (1973) 36 M.L.R. 656.

[34c] *Wilkinson* v. *Coverdale* (1793) 1 Esp. 75; but *cf. Thorne* v. *Deas* (1809) 4 Johns 84 (U.S.).

[34d] See pp. 51–53, *post.*

[35] *Post,* pp. 173–187.

[36] *Cavalier* v. *Pope* [1906] A.C. 428; *Bottomley* v. *Bannister* [1932] 1 K.B. 458. All that is said on this subject in *Dutton* v. *Bognor Regis U.D.C.* [1972] 1 Q.B. 373 is pure dicta since the vendor-builder was not a party to the case.

law.[36a] Similarly, the settled principles of the law of nuisance are not to be subverted by an appeal to the duty of care concept.[36b]

(iv) *Negligent misstatements.* Prior to the decision of the House of Lords in *Hedley Byrne & Co. Ltd.* v. *Heller & Partners Ltd.*[37] in 1963 the Court of Appeal had held that there could be no liability in tort for negligent misstatement [38] and it was not until 1962 that it was held that this rule applied only where the misstatement led to pecuniary as distinct from physical injury or damage.[39] Even today, though the House of Lords has now held that a person may be under a duty to take care in making statements, it is clear that mere foreseeability of loss is not enough. For the duty to exist something in the nature of a " special relationship " between the parties is required.[40]

(v) *Economic loss.* Though primarily concerned with liability for misstatement, *Hedley Byrne & Co. Ltd.* v. *Heller & Partners Ltd.* also raised the problem of liability for economic loss since the plaintiffs suffered only that, not personal injury or physical damage to any property of theirs. In the course of his speech Lord Devlin castigated as nonsensical the distinction sought to be drawn between physical and economic loss and pointed out that where there has been physical injury or damage, economic loss is normally recoverable without difficulty. The injured workman, for example, who suffers loss of wages as a result of his injury is clearly entitled to damages on that account and, in Lord Devlin's view, it is absurd to say that the interposition of the physical injury makes a difference of principle.[41] Nevertheless, subject to certain exceptions the most important of which are statutory,[42] the courts have consistently declined to award damages for negligence causing economic loss except where that loss is immediately consequential upon injury to the plaintiff's person or his property.[42a] This was settled as long ago as 1875 in *Cattle* v. *Stockton Waterworks Co.*[43] and has been reaffirmed on several occasions since *Hedley Byrne & Co.* v. *Heller & Partners Ltd.* was

---

[36a] See *post,* pp. 198–201.
[36b] *Smith* v. *Scott* [1973] Ch. 314.
[37] [1964] A.C. 465.
[38] *Le Lievre* v. *Gould* [1893] 1 Q.B. 491; *Candler* v. *Crane Christmas & Co.* [1951] 2 K.B. 164. See also the *Hedley Byrne* case in the C.A.: [1962] 1 Q.B. 396.
[39] *Clayton* v. *Woodman & Son (Builders) Ltd.* [1962] 2 Q.B. 533.
[40] *Hedley Byrne & Co. Ltd.* v. *Heller & Partners Ltd., supra; Mutual Life and Citizens' Assurance Co. Ltd.* v. *Evatt* [1971] 2 W.L.R. 23 (P.C.). This question is considered fully *post,* pp. 221–233.
[41] [1964] A.C. at pp. 516–517; *Ministry of Housing* v. *Sharp* [1970] 2 Q.B. 223, 278, *per* Salmon L.J.
[42] The Fatal Accidents Acts 1846–1959. See *post,* pp. 502–511. Had the common law allowed damages to be awarded for loss suffered as the result of the death of another, those Acts would have been unnecessary.
[42a] See Atiyah, " Negligence and Economic Loss " (1967) 83 L.Q.R. 248. There is now, however, a body of support for the view that a plaintiff may recover where he suffers economic loss in averting the threat of physical injury: *Dutton* v. *Bognor Regis U.D.C.* [1972] 1 Q.B. 373, 396 *per* Lord Denning M.R.; *Rivtow Marine Ltd.* v. *Washington Iron Works* (1973) 40 D.L.R. (3d) 530, 549 *per* Laskin J. (Sup.Ct. of Canada). The principles of liability where economic loss is intentionally caused are considered *post,* Chap. 21.
[43] (1875) L.R. 10 Q.B. 453; *Simpson & Co.* v. *Thomson, Burrell* (1877) 3 App.Cas. 279.

decided.[43a] In *Spartan Steel & Alloys Ltd.* v. *Martin & Co. (Contractors) Ltd.*[44] the defendant's servants negligently damaged an electricity cable belonging to the electricity board and thereby cut off the supply of power to the plaintiff's factory for fourteen hours. As a result, the " melt " then in the furnace depreciated in value by £368 and the plaintiff suffered further losses of £400, the profit on that melt, and £1,767, the profit on four further melts which could have been carried out during the period when there was no electricity supply. The plaintiff recovered for the first two of these losses but not for the third, for that was not damage to the plaintiff's property nor was it consequential upon any such damage. The approach in such cases has traditionally been that of denial of duty,[44a] though remoteness of damage has also been called in aid.[44b] It has recently been said that there is no particular virtue in either approach in this context since it is all at bottom a matter of legal policy [44c]; but be this as it may, it is still perfectly clear that in general the mere fact that economic loss is the foreseeable consequence of a negligent act is still insufficient to entitle the plaintiff who suffers that loss to recover damages.[44d] The main policy factors lying behind denial of liability in this area are as follows: (1) While the physical damage ensuing from an act is normally [44e] limited fairly narrowly by the laws of nature, the effect on economic interests may be almost limitless. (2) Therefore liability insurance may be unobtainable at reasonable rates or at all.[44f] (3) In many cases, though the total loss resulting from an incident may be enormous it is spread among so many

---

[43a] The best known of the earlier cases are *Société Anonyme de Remorquage à Hélice* v. *Bennetts* [1911] 1 K.B. 243; *Chargeurs Réunis Compagnie Française de Navigation à Vapeur* v. *English and American Shipping Co.* (1921) 9 Ll.L.R. 464. The more recent cases include *Weller & Co. Ltd.* v. *Foot and Mouth Disease Research Institute* [1966] 1 Q.B. 569; *The World Harmony* [1967] P. 341; *Electrochrome Ltd.* v. *Welsh Plastics Ltd.* [1968] 2 All E.R. 205; *British Celanese Ltd.* v. *A. H. Hunt Capacitors Ltd.* [1969] 1 W.L.R. 959: *Margarine Union G.m.b.H.* v. *Cambay Prince Steamship Co. Ltd.* [1969] 1 Q.B. 219; *Dynamco Ltd.* v. *Holland and Hannen and Cubitts (Scotland) Ltd.* [1971] S.L.T. 150; *S.C.M. (United Kingdom) Ltd.* v. *Whittall & Son Ltd.* [1971] 1 Q.B. 337. The so-called principle of " parasitic " damages exemplified in *Seaway Hotels Ltd.* v. *Gragg (Canada) Ltd. and Consumer Gas Co.* (1960) 21 D.L.R. (2d) 264 will not assist a plaintiff in an action arising out of the negligent interruption of supplies or services: *Spartan Steel & Alloys Ltd.* v. *Martin & Co. (Contractors) Ltd.* [1973] Q.B. 27.

[44] [1973] Q.B. 27 (C.A.). Weir, *Casebook on Tort*, 3rd ed., p. 38; Jolowicz [1973] C.L.J. 20; Jacobs (1973) 36 M.L.R. 314.

[44a] See the cases cited in note 43a, *ante*.

[44b] *S.C.M. (United Kingdom) Ltd.* v. *Whittall & Son Ltd.* [1971] 1 Q.B. 337, 345 *per* Lord Denning M.R. *Cf.* Winn L.J. at 347.

[44c] *Spartan Steel & Alloys Ltd.* v. *Martin & Co. (Contractors) Ltd.* [1973] Q.B. 27, 37 *per* Lord Denning M.R.

[44d] *Cf. Rivtow Marine Ltd.* v. *Washington Iron Works* (1973) 40 D.L.R. (3d) 540 (Sup.Ct· of Canada). It is submitted that the statements in the *Spartan Steel* case, *supra*, do not mean that the traditional principle has gone, but merely that its policy basis should be recognised.

[44e] But not necessarily. Fleming James, " Limitations on Liability for Economic Loss Caused by Negligence: A Pragmatic Appraisal " (1972–73) 12 J.S.P.T.L. 105, instances damage from nuclear installations (for which, however, there are special statutory provisions: see pp. 386–389, *post*) and the London and Chicago fires.

[44f] See Alexander " The Law of Tort and Non-Physical Loss: Insurance Aspects " (1972–73) 12 J.S.P.T.L. 119 and the report of the discussion in *ibid*, pp. 173–176.

victims that it is not catastrophic for any of them.[44g] On the other hand, it may be that these fears of open-ended liability and multiplicity of claims are exaggerated [44h] and that the problems could be handled on a more specific plane by the proper application of the principles of duty and remoteness.[44i]

It will normally be fairly easy to distinguish between recoverable damage and pure economic loss, but the task can sometimes be difficult. Thus in one case where due to the negligence of A and B a house was built with defective foundations, sold to C and then resold by him to D, who suffered loss through cracking of the walls, a majority of the Court of Appeal held that D's loss was not mere economic loss and hence was recoverable in tort [44j]; the other member of the court, however, thought that a house with defective foundations leading to cracking was indistinguishable from a carelessly manufactured (but non-dangerous) product which quickly disintegrates and that in such a case the cause of action, if any, generally lay in contract not in tort.[44k]

Even if taken subject to the above qualifications, however, the principle stated by Lord Atkin in *Donoghue* v. *Stevenson* does not in truth provide an answer to the question whether or not a notional duty exists in a given case but rather to the different question whether, on the facts and assuming a notional duty, the particular defendant owes a duty to the particular plaintiff. According to Lord Atkin the duty of care is owed to " neighbours," and " neighbours " are then carefully defined. The test is not one of physical proximity [45] but of foresight. My neighbours are " persons who are so closely and directly affected by my act that I ought reasonably to have them in contemplation as being so affected *when I am directing my mind to the acts or omissions which are called in question.*" [46] It is not the existence of some relationship between

---

[44g] *Spartan Steel & Alloys Ltd.* v. *Martin & Co. (Contractors) Ltd.* [1973] Q.B. 27, 38–39 *per* Lord Denning M.R. It may be, however, that on the particular facts of the case the plaintiff is the only victim and does in fact suffer a very serious loss. In such a case the loss rests upon one pair of shoulders, but the victim's, not the wrongdoer's. If, on the other hand, the victim has taken out " interruption insurance " against interference with his production, then the burden is spread over many shoulders, perhaps the whole community's. Only by examining the insurance position, both actual and potential, can it be determined whether a decision for or against the plaintiff is likely to cause the loss to be borne by the community or some section of it, or by an individual.

[44h] Similar arguments were put forward against the extensions of liabilities made in *Donoghue* v. *Stevenson* (pp. 202–211, *post*) and *Hedley, Byrne & Co. Ltd.* v. *Heller & Partners Ltd.* (pp. 221–233, *post*).

[44i] See *Spartan Steel & Alloys Ltd.* v. *Martin & Co. (Contractors) Ltd.* at [1973] Q.B. 45 *per* Edmund Davies L.J.

[44j] *Dutton* v. *Bognor Regis U.D.C.* [1972] 1 Q.B. 373, Lord Denning M.R. and Sachs L.J.

[44k] Stamp L.J. who, however, thought that the inspecting council (but not the builder) were liable in tort for this sort of economic loss. See further Miller (1973) 36 M.L.R. 199 and Rogers [1972A] C.L.J. 211.

[45] See *per* Lord Atkin himself in *Donoghue* v. *Stevenson* [1932] A.C. at p. 581 and *Farr* v. *Butters Bros. & Co.* [1932] 2 K.B. 606, 613–614, *per* Scrutton L.J. Indeed, physical proximity is irrelevant, for it may exist and yet give rise to no legal duty, *e.g.* where I build so as to obstruct my neighbour's prospect (as distinct from his right of light); and conversely it may not exist and yet there may be a legal duty, *e.g.*, where a harmful thing is manufactured in Newcastle and causes injury to someone living in Southampton.

[46] [1932] A.C. at p. 580. Italics added.

the parties—such as that of manufacturer and consumer—which makes the plaintiff the defendant's neighbour, but the fact that the defendant ought reasonably to have the plaintiff in contemplation when directing his mind to the acts or omissions which are called in question, *i.e.*, the alleged acts of negligence themselves. It follows that the test can only be applied *ex post facto*. Assuming a notional duty of care and assuming careless conduct on the part of the defendant, Lord Atkin's test enables the court to decide whether the defendant was in breach of a duty which he owed to the plaintiff. But it does not enable the court to say whether a notional duty existed in the first place.

The point can be illustrated by the decision in *Bourhill* v. *Young*.[47] X, a fishwife, alighted from a tramcar. While the driver was helping her to put her fish basket on her back, Y, a motor-cyclist, passed the tram and immediately afterwards negligently collided with Z's motor-car. Y was killed. X did not see Y or the accident, which occurred about fifteen yards off, her view being obstructed by the tram, but she heard the collision and, after Y's body had been removed, she approached the spot and saw the blood left on the road. In consequence she sustained a nervous shock and gave birth to a stillborn child of which she was eight months pregnant. She sued the personal representatives of Y for Y's negligence but the House of Lords held that she could not recover on the ground that Y owed her no duty. It has already been stated that it has been settled time out of mind that men must use care in driving vehicles on the highway, and the decision in *Bourhill* v. *Young* does not, of course, controvert that proposition. But it was found as a fact that injury to X, in all the detailed circumstances of the case, was not foreseeable and this had the legal consequence that Y owed her no duty. As Lord Russell of Killowen put it, after citing Lord Atkin's speech in *Donoghue* v. *Stevenson*, a duty of care " only arises towards those individuals of whom it may be reasonably anticipated that they will be affected by the act which constitutes the alleged breach." [47a]

The element of policy.[47b] *Donoghue* v. *Stevenson* is undoubtedly one of the great " land-mark " cases of the law [47c] and Lord Atkin's state- ment of principle has certainly played a major part in the modern development of the tort of negligence. Nevertheless, until quite recently, the approach to that statement of principle by the courts has been

---

[47] [1943] A.C. 92; Weir, *Casebook on Tort*, 3rd ed., p. 34. See also *Palsgraf* v. *Long Island Railroad* (1928) 248 N.Y. 339; *Woods* v. *Duncan* [1946] A.C. 401; *Clay* v. *Ministry of Transport and Civil Aviation* [1960] 1 Lloyd's Rep. 517.

[47a] [1943] A.C. at p. 102. " The duty to take care is the duty to avoid doing or omitting to do anything the doing or omitting to do which may have as its reasonable and probable consequence injury to others, and the duty is owed to those to whom injury may reasonably and probably be anticipated if the duty is not observed ": *ibid.* at p. 104, *per* Lord Macmillan. *Cf.* Lord Macmillan's speech in *Donoghue* v. *Stevenson* itself [1932] A.C. at pp. 618–621.

[47b] Symmons, " The Duty of Care in Negligence: Recently Expressed Policy Elements " (1971) 34 M.L.R. 394, 528.

[47c] *Home Office* v. *Dorset Yacht Co. Ltd.* [1970] A.C. 1004, 1027, *per* Lord Reid; *ibid.* at p. 1059, *per* Lord Diplock.

ambivalent. In some cases, even, occasionally, when the facts fell within one of the generally recognised exceptions already mentioned,[48] liability has been imposed upon a careless defendant ostensibly upon the ground that the damage caused was foreseeable, that Lord Atkin's principle applied, and so that a duty of care was owed [48a]: in others the limitations of the principle and the absence of specific authority have been stressed and a duty of care accordingly denied, notwithstanding that the damage was foreseeable.[48b] Academic writers have, however, for some time insisted that the application of a legal rule is insufficient by itself to enable the existence or non-existence of a duty of care to be determined,[48c] and in recent years there has been an increasing willingness on the part of the judges to admit that considerations of policy must, from time to time, play a major part in the making of decisions.[49] For some, it is true, the word " policy " itself is still repugnant; Lord Morris, for example, has doubted whether the court is called upon to make a decision of policy " where reason and good sense will at once point the way " [49a] but, with respect, this is the same thing differently expressed. The use of the word " policy " indicates no more than that the court must decide not simply whether there is or is not a duty, but whether there should or should not be one, taking into account both the established framework of the law and also the implications that a decision one way or the other may have for the operation of the law in our society.[49b] So, for example, in *Rondel* v. *Worsley* [49c] the decision of the House of Lords that a barrister owes no legal duty of care to his client so far as his work in the conduct of litigation is concerned was avowedly based upon the judgment by the House that in order to fulfil his duty to the court and to the administration of justice the barrister must be relieved of the possibility that actions for negligence might be brought against him by disgruntled

---

[48] *e.g.*, *Clay* v. *Crump* [1964] 1 Q.B. 533, where the negligence complained of consisted in nothing more than an omission: Weir [1964] C.L.J. 23, 24; Weir, *Casebook on Tort*, p. 73; *Driver* v. *William Willett (Contractors) Ltd.* [1969] 1 All E.R. 665.

[48a] In addition to *Clay* v. *Crump, supra*, see *Cunard* v. *Antifyre Ltd.* [1933] 1 K.B. 551; *Barnes* v. *Irwell Valley Water Board* [1939] 2 K.B. 21; *Buckland* v. *Guildford Gas Light & Coke Co.* [1949] 1 K.B. 410; *Davis* v. *St. Mary's Demolition Co. Ltd.* [1954] 1 W.L.R. 592; *Clayton* v. *Woodman & Sons (Builders) Ltd.* [1962] 2 Q.B. 533, revd. on its facts [1962] 1 W.L.R. 585; *Commissioner for Railways* v. *McDermott* [1967] A.C. 169; *Goldman* v. *Hargrave* [1967] 1 A.C. 645; *McArdle* v. *Andmac Roofing Co.* [1967] 1 W.L.R. 356; *Barnett* v. *Chelsea and Kensington Hospital Management Committee* [1969] 1 Q.B. 428.

[48b] *e.g.*, *Deyong* v. *Shenborn* [1946] K.B. 227; *Commissioner for Railways* v. *Quinlan* [1964] A.C. 1054, and the cases on economic loss cited *supra*, p. 52, n. 43a.

[48c] Fleming, " Remoteness and Duty " (1953) 31 Can. Bar Rev. 471; Green, *Judge and Jury*, Chaps. 3 and 4—" The Duty Problem "; Prosser, *Torts*, 4th ed., pp. 325–326; Morison, " Re-examination of the Duty of Care " (1948) 11 M.L.R. 1; Prosser, " Palsgraf Revisited " (1953) 52 Michigan L.Rev. 1. See also Clerk & Lindsell, *Torts*, 13th ed., pp. 474–475.

[49] One of the clearest statements to this effect is that of MacDonald J. in the Canadian case of *Nova Mink Ltd.* v. *Trans-Canada Airlines Ltd.* [1951] 2 D.L.R. 241.

[49a] *Home Office* v. *Dorset Yacht Co. Ltd.* [1970] A.C. 1004, 1039.

[49b] On the other hand, the appeal to policy, like all new fashions, is liable to be somewhat overdone: see *Rootes* v. *Shelton* (1967) 116 C.L.R. 383, 386–387 (Aust.H.C.), *per* Kitto J.

[49c] [1969] 1 A.C. 191, discussed *post*, pp. 63–64.

clients. Similarly, the principles governing the recoverability of economic loss have now been stated to rest solely upon the policy of the law.[49d] Another example, one of the most striking, of the effect of policy is *Hanratty* v. *Lord Butler of Saffron Walden*, [49e] where the court denied the possibility of any cause of action against the Home Secretary for negligence in advising the Crown on the exercise of the prerogative of mercy. The reason for this immunity was to enable the Home Secretary to exercise his great responsibility independently, without fear of others or influence from any quarter.[50]

The most recent and the most important discussion of the matters now under consideration occurred in *Home Office* v. *Dorset Yacht Co. Ltd.*,[50a] where a preliminary point of law was brought before the House of Lords in the following circumstances: the Home Office were sued for the negligence of some Borstal officers who were in charge of a group of Borstal trainees. The boys had been working on an island in Poole harbour and during the night some of them escaped owing, it was alleged, to the negligence of the officers. The boys went aboard a yacht moored near by and caused the yacht to collide with the plaintiffs' yacht which suffered considerable damage in consequence. The Home Office denied that its officers owed any relevant duty of care to the plaintiffs.

It is to be observed that this case concerned physical damage to property and so fell more nearly within the class of case habitually thought of as coming within Lord Atkin's principle than did either *Rondel* v. *Worsley* or the economic loss cases, and also that the damage was the plainly foreseeable consequence of allowing Borstal boys to escape from control while on a small island. On the other hand, there is no general duty of care to prevent other persons from causing damage,[50b] and the power of the defendants to detain and control the boys was derived wholly from statute. The Home Office therefore argued that the officers' duty to control the boys was owed exclusively to the Crown, there being no private remedy for breach of this statutory duty.[50c] In addition it was strenuously argued that the imposition of a duty of care in the circumstances might lead to excessive caution in the administration of Borstal institutions and thus hamper the training of young delinquents as required by statute; experience had shown that the duty to train such people is better carried out by using activities outside rather than within the confines of an institution.[51] Public

---

[49d] See *ante*, pp. 51–53.
[49e] (1971) *The Times*, May 13. *Cf. Welbridge Holdings* v. *Metropolitan Corpn. of Greater Winnipeg* (1971) 22 D.L.R. (3d) 470 (Sup.Ct. of Canada).
[50] This is similar to the reason adopted in *Rondel* v. *Worsley*, *supra*, and rejected in *Home Office* v. *Dorset Yacht Co. Ltd.* (p. 57, *post*). See Symmons, *loc. cit.*, p. 528.
[50a] [1970] A.C. 1004. Weir, *Casebook on Tort*, 3rd ed., p. 27. See also the decision of the Court of Appeal [1969] 2 Q.B. 412 and Hamson, " Escaping Borstal Boys and the Immunity of Office " [1968] C.L.J. 273.
[50b] *Ante*, p. 50.
[50c] For claims based upon breach of statutory duty, see *post*, Chap. 8.
[51] [1970] A.C. at p. 1014.

policy demanded, therefore, that the Home Office and the officers be immune from liability.

In dealing with these arguments all of their Lordships agreed that *Donoghue* v. *Stevenson* did not provide a conclusive answer on the ground of foreseeability, although it is noteworthy that Lords Reid, Morris and Pearson [51a] all seem to adopt the view that foreseeability of damage does in general lead to the existence of a duty of care unless there is some reason to the contrary. In the words of Lord Reid, " *Donoghue* v. *Stevenson* . . . may be regarded as a milestone, and the well-known passage in Lord Atkin's speech should, I think, be regarded as a statement of principle. It is not to be treated as if it were a statutory definition. It will require qualification in new circumstances. But I think the time has come when we can and should say that it ought to apply unless there is some justification or valid explanation for its exclusion. For example, causing economic loss is a different matter."

Statements such as this, however, seem to attempt to create some kind of presumption of law; they cannot, it is submitted, mean more than that where there is foreseeability of damage the court will be disposed to decide in favour of the existence of the duty in the absence of convincing *argument* (not *evidence*) to the contrary; they cannot, therefore, actually relieve the court of the need to exercise that freedom of choice with which it is inescapably endowed.[51b] The clearest recognition of this is to be found in the speech of Lord Diplock and, indeed, his Lordship goes so far as to give an explanation of the methods employed when the court makes a policy decision.[51c]

So far as the actual decision in the case is concerned, the majority of the House of Lords, Viscount Dilhorne dissenting, agreed in holding that a duty of care existed. Their Lordships' reasons were not in all respects the same, but the objection that there is no general duty to prevent damage from being done by others was disposed of by drawing attention to certain analogous cases in which a duty of care existed [52]: though not conclusive, these cases were sufficient to enable the House to hold that the present case could be brought within the scope of the exceptions rather than the rule. The argument based expressly on public policy was met mainly by emphasising that the duty is one of care only

---

[51a] *Ibid.* at pp. 1027, 1034, 1054 respectively.

[51b] Unless, of course, the court adopts the view of Viscount Dilhorne, dissenting, to the effect that, in the absence of authority in favour of the existence of a duty, no duty exists at common law and that the power of creating new duties lies exclusively with the legislature: [1970] A.C. at pp. 1045, 1051. In *Smith* v. *Scott* [1973] Ch. 314 Pennycuick V.-C. refused to extend the duty of care principle so as to make a landlord liable for unauthorised nuisances by his tenants (see *post*, p. 340) but he does not seem to have denied absolutely the power of an appellate court to do so.

[51c] [1970] A.C. at pp. 1058–1064. See also the judgment of Lord Denning M.R. [1969] 2 Q.B. at p. 426: " It is, I think, at bottom a matter of public policy which we, as judges, must resolve. This talk of ' duty ' or ' no duty ' is simply a way of limiting the range of liability for negligence."

[52] *e.g. Ellis* v. *Home Office* [1953] 2 Q.B. 135; *Carmarthenshire County Council* v. *Lewis* [1955] A.C. 549; *Smith* v. *Leurs* (1945) 70 C.L.R. 256 (H.Ct. of Aus.). Special regard was had to the statement of Dixon J., *ibid.* at pp. 261–262.

and, as we shall see, the standard of care called for in any case must be judged in the light of all the circumstances of the case. A Borstal officer is not negligent merely because he does something which is foreseeably likely to lead to an escape and to damage being done by the escaper: " It is not negligence to keep an open Borstal, nor to let the boys have a great deal of freedom." [52a] The duty of care only requires Borstal officers to exercise the discretion conferred upon them in a reasonable manner [52b] and to take such care for the protection of the neighbours and their property as is consistent with the due carrying out of the Borstal system.[52c] Indeed, if Lord Diplock's view is accepted, before a court can even entertain the question whether some act or omission of an officer qualifies as negligence, it must first find that that act or omission was *ultra vires*, *i.e.*, either contrary to instructions from the Home Office or so unrelated to the purpose of reformation of trainees that no reasonable person could reach a bona fide conclusion that it was conducive to that purpose.[53] Only thus, in his Lordship's opinion, can the court reconcile the public interest in maintaining the freedom of the Home Office to decide upon the operation of the Borstal system (the importance of which was acknowledged by all) and the public interest that Borstal officers should not be allowed to be completely disregardful of the interests of persons likely to be injured by their carelessness without the law providing redress to those who in fact suffer injury.[53a]

Important though this case certainly is in relation to its particular facts,[53b] it is, perhaps, even more important for its recognition that the question whether or not a duty of care exists in a given case is not always one which the court can answer by simply applying an existing legal rule or formula to the facts before it. So far as the notional duty is concerned, therefore, the position seems to be this. Certain relations between the parties in a variety of situations have been recognised by the courts as giving rise to a legal duty to take care not to injure; other relations have been held by the courts not to do so. But where the precise situation is not already covered by authority, the judge has to make a creative choice whether or not to raise a duty of care on the facts before him. The factors which guide the judge in this creative process cannot be precisely identified. They obviously include the existing law and the way in which it has developed: the policy decision will undoubtedly be influenced by a general conception of what ought to give rise to a duty of care which will be revealed by an examination of existing authority, and it is here that

---

[52a] [1969] 2 Q.B. at p. 427, *per* Lord Denning M.R.; [1970] A.C. at p. 1035, *per* Lord Morris; *ibid.* at p. 1069, *per* Lord Diplock.

[52b] [1970] A.C. at p. 1031, *per* Lord Reid.

[52c] *Ibid.* at p. 1056, *per* Lord Pearson.

[53] [1970] A.C. at pp. 1068–1071. Lord Reid's approach seems to reach a similar conclusion though for different reasons; *ibid.* at p. 1032. *Cf. Welbridge Holdings* v. *Winnipeg* (1971) 22 D.L.R. (3d) 470.

[53a] See also *ibid.* at pp. 1056–1057, *per* Lord Pearson.

[53b] See, however, Hamson, *loc. cit.*, at p. 276, where it is suggested that the right question was not asked at all. Ganz, " Compensation for Negligent Administrative Action " [1973] P.L. 84 reviews the extra-judicial routes to compensation.

general statements of the characteristics of conduct and relationships giving rise to liability, such as that of Lord Atkin, are of the greatest value.[54] They also include a balancing of the relative values of the conflicting interests involved: as Lord Pearson observed in *Home Office* v. *Dorset Yacht Co. Ltd.*, " the needs of the Borstal system, important as they no doubt are, should not be treated as so paramount and all-important as to require or justify complete absence of care for the safety of the neighbours and their property and complete immunity from any liability for anything that the neighbours may suffer," [54a] In the end, however, it has to be acknowledged that " how wide the sphere of the duty of care in negligence is to be laid depends ultimately upon the courts' assessment of the demands of society for protection from the carelessness of others." [54b]

(ii) *Duty in fact*

It is not enough for the plaintiff to prove circumstances which give rise to a notional duty, for he must also establish that the defendant owed a duty of care to him; he cannot build on a wrong to someone else.[55] The motor-cyclist in *Bourhill* v. *Young* may have been negligent towards the owner of the car with whom he collided, but that did not avail the pursuer, for he was under no duty to her. The test for the existence of a duty owed to the plaintiff is, in substance, the " neighbour " principle stated by Lord Atkin in *Donoghue* v. *Stevenson*,[56] i.e., the foresight of the reasonable man. Was injury to the plaintiff the reasonably fore-seeable consequence of the defendant's acts or omissions? [57] In answering this question all the circumstances must be taken into account, including the whole sequence of events leading up to the accident. It is not enough to establish a duty of care that injury to the plaintiff would have been foreseeable if caused by an entirely different sequence of events from that which in fact occurred.[58]

On the other hand, it is not required that the plaintiff should necessarily be identifiable by the defendant. It is enough that he should be one of a class within the area of foreseeable injury. In *Haley* v. *London Electricity Board* [59] the defendants, with statutory authority, excavated a trench in the street. They took precautions for the protec-

---

[54] *Hedley Byrne & Co. Ltd.* v. *Heller & Partners Ltd.* [1964] A.C. at pp. 524–525, *per* Lord Devlin; *Home Office* v. *Dorset Yacht Co. Ltd.* [1970] A.C. at p. 1038, *per* Lord Morris; *ibid.* at p. 1059, *per* Lord Diplock.
[54a] [1970] A.C. at pp. 1056–1057; *ibid.* at pp. 1039–1040, *per* Lord Morris.
[54b] *Hedley Byrne & Co. Ltd.* v. *Heller & Partners Ltd.*, *supra*, at p. 536, *per* Lord Pearce.
[55] *Bourhill* v. *Young* [1943] A.C. 92, 108, *per* Lord Wright; *King* v. *Phillips* [1953] 1 Q.B. 429.
[56] *Ante*, p. 48.
[57] See *Woods* v. *Duncan* [1946] A.C. 401; *Roe* v. *Minister of Health* [1954] 2 Q.B. 66; *Booker* v. *Wenborn* [1962] 1 W.L.R. 162.
[58] *Woods* v. *Duncan*, *supra*: " To ask, who is the neighbour to whom I owe a duty in respect of my act, may be in part answered by saying that he at least is not my neighbour who cannot be affected by my act, unless there is some intervening event which I cannot reasonably foresee ": *ibid.* at p. 442, *per* Lord Simonds.
[59] [1965] A.C. 778; *Carmarthenshire County Council* v. *Lewis* [1955] A.C. 549.

tion of passers-by which were sufficient for normal sighted persons, but the plaintiff, who was blind, suffered injury because the precautions were inadequate for him. It was held that the number of blind persons who go about the streets alone was sufficient to require the defendants to have them in contemplation and to take precautions appropriate to their condition.

It has already been indicated that a test of this kind for the existence of a duty of care can only be applied *ex post facto*, for the subject-matter to which the test of reasonable foresight is to be applied is the very act or omission of the defendant which is alleged to constitute the negligence itself.[60] It is impossible, therefore, always to keep separate from one another questions of the existence of a duty in fact and questions of the breach of that duty. The foresight of the reasonable man is of critical importance to both questions and in practice it matters not at all whether the form of the decision is that there was a duty but no breach or that there was no duty.[61] Sometimes, as we shall see, additional factors enter into the question of breach of duty, but once it is appreciated that the duty under consideration is not the notional duty but the duty in fact, then, commonly, discussion of the existence of the duty and of breach of duty are but two ways of dealing with the same point.[62] We shall therefore consider " reasonable foresight " and " reasonable care " more fully in the next section.

The fact remains, however, that the existence of the duty of care and breach of that duty are regularly treated as separate ingredients of the tort of negligence and this has one obvious practical advantage. In some cases there is no doubt whatever that the defendant's conduct was negligent towards someone; what is seriously in issue is whether the defendant was negligent towards the plaintiff, and this is most conveniently considered in terms of duty. In other cases—and these form the majority—there is no doubt that if the defendant was negligent at all then he was negligent towards the plaintiff, and these cases are most conveniently discussed in terms of breach.

---

[60] *Ante*, p. 54.

[61] See the varying analyses of the House of Lords in *Woods* v. *Duncan* [1946] A.C. 401, and *Haley* v. *London Electricity Board* [1965] A.C. 778. Morison, " Re-examination of the Duty of Care " (1948) 11 M.L.R. 9.

[62] See Fleming, " Remoteness and Duty " 31 Can. Bar Rev. 486; Fleming James, " The Scope of Duty in Negligence Cases " 47 North Western Univ.L.Rev. 778. " It is, on final analysis, the need for care lest someone be injured that both creates the duty and determines what amounts to a breach of it ": *Voli* v. *Inglewood Shire Council* [1963] Qd.R. 256, 267, *per* Windeyer J. (H.Ct. of Australia). Compare *Grange Motors (Cwmbran) Ltd.* v. *Spenser* [1969] 1 W.L.R. 53 with *Clarke* v. *Winchurch* [1969] 1 W.L.R. 69, two cases on similar facts decided by the C.A. in the same month. In the first it was held that a postman who signalled to an approaching motorist to come on owed and on the facts was in breach of a duty of care to another motorist approaching from the opposite direction. In the second it was held that a bus driver who stopped and signalled to the driver of a parked car to move out from the side of the road and across the line of traffic owed no duty to the driver of a moped who, approaching from behind the bus overtook it and collided with the car. There is no conflict between these cases: the first is a decision that on the facts the postman was negligent; the second is a decision on the facts that the bus driver was not.

2. Breach of duty [63]

Criterion of " the reasonable man "

The test for deciding whether there has been a breach of duty is laid down in the oft-cited dictum of Alderson B., in *Blyth* v. *Birmingham Waterworks Co.*[64]: " Negligence is the omission to do something which a reasonable man, guided upon those considerations which ordinarily regulate the conduct of human affairs, would do, or doing something which a prudent and reasonable man would not do."

The general characteristics of the reasonable man have already been described.[65] Since he is an abstraction, the standard of reference he provides can be applied to particular cases only by the intuition of the court. The standard is objective and impersonal in the sense that it eliminates the personal equation and is independent of the idiosyncrasies of the particular person whose conduct is in question,[66] but it cannot eliminate the personality of the judge. " It is . . . left to the judge to decide what, in the circumstances of the particular case, the reasonable man would have in contemplation, and what, accordingly, the party sought to be made liable ought to have foreseen." [67] In the following pages we describe some of the factors taken into account by the judges in reaching their conclusions.

Imperitia culpae adnumeratur [68]

Where anyone is engaged in a transaction in which he holds himself out as having professional skill, the law expects him to show the average amount of competence associated with the proper discharge of the duties of that profession, trade or calling, and if he falls short of that and injures someone in consequence, he is not behaving reasonably. Thus, where a brewing company owned a ship which was regularly used for the carriage of their stout from Dublin to Liverpool and Manchester, it was held that the Board of Directors of the company must

---

[63] Weir, *Casebook on Tort*, 3rd ed., Chap. 2.

[64] (1856) 11 Ex. 781, 784.

[65] *Ante*, pp. 25–27.

[66] *Cf. Goldman* v. *Hargrave* [1967] 1 A.C. 645 where the Privy Council held that the standard ought to be to require of the defendant what it is reasonable to expect of him *in his individual circumstances*. " Less must be expected of the infirm than of the able-bodied . . . he should not be liable unless it is clearly proved that he could, and reasonably in his individual circumstance should, have done more ": *ibid.* at p. 524, *per* Lord Wilberforce. This approach must be carefully limited to its actual context, namely, the duty of an occupier of land to take active steps to put an end to a hazard on his land which has arisen through an act of God or of a third party for whom he is not responsible. A similar principle is now applicable to the comparable situation of occupier's liability to trespassers, but it is not appropriate in an ordinary action for negligence.

[67] *Glasgow Corporation* v. *Muir* [1943] A.C. 448, 457, *per* Lord Macmillan. Weir, *Casebook on Tort*, 3rd ed., p. 95. Bannerman, " Negligence—The Reasonable Man and the Application of the Objective Test in Anglo-American Jurisprudence " (1969) 6 U.G.L.J. 69.

[68] Weir, *Casebook on Tort*, 3rd ed., pp. 117–129. Compare the view of the majority of the Privy Council on the standard of care called for by this maxim in *Mutual Life and Citizens' Assurance Co. Ltd.* v. *Evatt* [1971] 2 W.L.R. 23, 29–32 with that of Lords Reid and Morris, *ibid.* at pp. 37–39.

exercise the same degree of care and skill in the management of the ship as would any other shipowner.[69] " The law must apply a standard which is not relaxed to cater for their factual ignorance of all activities outside brewing: having become owners of ships, they must behave as reasonable shipowners." [70] The rule *imperitia culpae adnumeratur* is just as true in English law as in Roman law.[70a] This rule must, however, be applied with some care to see that too high a degree of skill is not demanded. A passer-by who renders emergency first-aid after an accident is not required to show the skill of a qualified surgeon. Nor is a householder who does some small job of repair or replacement about his house required to show that degree of skill which might be required of a professional carpenter working for reward. He need only do his work with the skill of a reasonably competent carpenter doing the work in question.[70b] The position in the converse case, where the defendant possesses *more* than normal skill or experience, is not so clearly covered by authority. It has been suggested that he, too, is held only to the standard of normal competence, though the position may not be the same in contract.[70c]

It is notable that in most professions and trades each generation convicts its predecessor of ignorance and that there is a steady rise in the standard of competence incident to them. The surgeon must exercise such care as accords with the standards of reasonably competent medical men at the time [71] and, if he has in fact greater than average knowledge of any risks, he may be obliged to take more than average precautions,[71a] but he is not an insurer against every accidental slip.[72] He must keep himself reasonably up to date and cannot " obstinately and pig-headedly carry on with the same old technique if it has been proved to be contrary to what is really substantially the whole of informed medical opinion." [73] On the other hand he is not negligent if he acts in accordance with a practice accepted

---

[69] *The Lady Gwendolen* [1965] P. 294 (" actual fault " under the Merchant Shipping Act 1894, s. 503); *Griffiths* v. *Arch Engineering Co. Ltd.* [1968] 3 All E.R. 217.

[70] *Ibid.* p. 350, *per* Winn L.J.; *Freeman* v. *Marshall & Co.* (1966) 200 E.G. 777.

[70a] Buckland & McNair, *Roman Law and Common Law*, 2nd ed., pp. 259–260.

[70b] *Wells* v. *Cooper* [1958] 2 Q.B. 265. See also *Phillips* v. *William Whiteley Ltd.* [1938] 1 All E.R. 566 where it was held that a jeweller, piercing ears for earrings, is not bound to take the same precautions as a surgeon, but such as may reasonably be expected of a jeweller. This case is easily distinguishable (but see Clerk and Lindsell, *Torts*, 13th ed., pp. 516–517) from the normal run of cases because the plaintiff voluntarily entered into a relationship with a person who, she knew, did not profess surgical standards. *Quaere*, however, whether *Phillips* v. *Whiteley* can stand with *Nettleship* v. *Weston* [1971] 2 Q.B. 691 (Weir, *Casebook on Tort*, 3rd ed., p. 81) where a majority of the Court of Appeal held that a learner driver was required, *vis-à-vis* his instructor, to come up to the standard of an ordinary, competent driver. It is clear that the decision was strongly influenced by the insurance position in the case, but it would seem difficult to confine it to road traffic. See further Rogers [1972A] C.L.J. 24; (1971) 87 L.Q.R. 444.

[70c] *Duchess of Argyll* v. *Beuselinck* [1972] 2 Lloyd's Rep. 172, 183 *obiter per* Megarry J.

[71] *Bolam* v. *Friern Hospital Management Committee* [1957] 1 W.L.R. 582.

[71a] *Stokes* v. *Guest, Keen and Nettlefold (Bolts and Nuts) Ltd.* [1968] 1 W.L.R. 1776, 1783, 1786, *per* Swanwick J. *Cf.* n. 70c, *supra.*

[72] *Roe* v. *Ministry of Health* [1954] 2 Q.B. 66.

[73] *Hunter* v. *Hanley*, 1955 S.L.T. 213; cited in *Bolam* v. *Friern Hospital Management Committee* (*supra*). *Chin Keow* v. *Govt. of Malaysia* [1967] 1 W.L.R. 813.

at the time as proper by a responsible body of medical opinion skilled in the particular form of treatment even though there is a body of competent professional opinion which might adopt a different technique.[74] Again, a solicitor " is liable for the consequences of ignorance or non-observance of the rules of practice of this [*sc.* the High] Court; for the want of care in the preparation of the cause for trial; or of attendance thereon with his witnesses: and for the mismanagement of so much of the conduct of a cause as is usually and ordinarily allotted to his department of the profession," [75] Barristers, on the other hand, were for long thought to be immune from liability for professional negligence on the ground that no contractual relation exists between them and their clients,[76] but this reason is no longer sufficient [77] and the whole matter was reconsidered by the House of Lords in *Rondel* v. *Worsley*.[78] As has been mentioned, in the opinion of the House of Lords, the due administration of justice and the existence of the barrister's duty to the court require that he be immune from liability for negligence in connection with litigation; moreover, as several of their Lordships pointed out, if the rule were otherwise one undesirable consequence would be the need to retry, in the action against the barrister, the issues which originally arose between his client and the other party to the litigation out of which the action for negligence arose.[79] This reasoning applies as much to the solicitor advocate as to the barrister, and the House agreed that in principle he too is protected,[80] but it does not apply to the work done by a barrister which is unconnected with actual litigation. So far as such work is concerned, the majority of their Lordships, speaking with varying degrees of emphasis, held that the barrister is liable for negligence like any other professional man.[81]

---

[74] *Bolam* v. *Friern Hospital Management Committee (supra).* For the duty of a casualty officer in a hospital to see a person who presents himself to the casualty department, see *Barnett* v. *Chelsea and Kensington Hospital Management Committee* [1969] 1 Q.B. 428.

[75] *Fletcher & Son* v. *Jubb* [1920] 1 K.B. 275, 279. See also *Duchess of Argyll* v. *Beuselinck* [1972] 2 Lloyd's Rep. 172. The duty of care owed by a solicitor to his client arises by way of contract only, but it does not follow that in the absence of a contractual relation with the plaintiff he cannot be liable in tort. See the cases cited *post,* p. 239, n. 60. On the standard of care expected of an estate agent dealing with rented property, see *Button* v. *Alfred Savill, Curtis and Henson* (1970) 218 E.G. 1417.

[76] *Swinfen* v. *Lord Chelmsford* (1860) 5 H. & N. 890; *Kennedy* v. *Broun* (1863) 13 C.B. (N.S.) 677. See Roxburgh, " *Rondel* v. *Worsley*: The Historical Background " (1968) 84 L.Q.R. 178; Baker, " Counsellors and Barristers " [1969] C.L.J. 205.

[77] *Hedley Byrne & Co. Ltd.* v. *Heller & Partners Ltd.* [1964] A.C. 465.

[78] [1969] 1 A.C. 191. See also the judgments of Lawton J. and the Court of Appeal, [1967] 1 Q.B. 443 and Roxburgh, " *Rondel* v. *Worsley*; Immunity of the Bar " (1968) 84 L.Q.R. 513, Jolowicz. " Immunity from Suit and the Legal Profession " [1967] C.L.J. 10; [1968] C.L.J. 23.

[79] See [1969] 1 A.C. at p. 230, *per* Lord Reid; *ibid.* at pp. 248–253, *per* Lord Morris.

[80] According to Lord Reid, the solicitor is protected when he is carrying out work in litigation which would have been carried out by counsel if counsel had been engaged in the case: [1969] 1 A.C. at p. 232. This gives rise to obvious problems of demarcation which are probably best left open until it becomes necessary to resolve them; *ibid.* at p. 294, *per* Lord Pearson. See, however, *ibid.* at pp. 284–285, *per* Lord Upjohn.

[81] The duty of care is independent of contract and arises when the barrister undertakes the work he is instructed to do: [1969] 1 A.C. at pp. 231–232, *per* Lord Reid; *ibid.* at p. 244, *per* Lord Morris; *ibid.* at pp. 285–286, *per* Lord Upjohn; *ibid.* at pp. 293–294, *per* Lord Pearson. Lord Pearce, *ibid.* at pp. 276–277, dissented on this point. There remains the question of the dividing line between that part of the barrister's work to which the

" Reasonable " varies with circumstances

Whether the care that has been taken is or is not reasonable is a question the answer to which must vary with circumstances. No reasonable man handles a stick of dynamite and a walking-stick in the same way. But that is not an admission that there are different degrees of negligence in the law of tort in the sense that negligence may possibly be " gross " or " ordinary " or " slight." Either there is a breach of the duty of care or there is not, but it does not follow that every error of judgment or mistake amounts to negligence. There must be a falling below the standard of care called for by the circumstances of the case. This, it is submitted, is the reconciliation between apparently contradictory statements such as that of Lynskey J. that " gross negligence is not known to the English common law so far as civil proceedings are concerned " [82] and that of Lord Upjohn that a barrister will only be liable if guilty of " crassa negligentia or gross negligence by some really elementary blunder." [83] A barrister will not be guilty of a breach of the duty of care he owes to his client in respect of work unconnected with litigation merely because his opinion turns out to be wrong or he overlooks one of a number of relevant authorities, but there is no reason why the general duty of care owed by him should be different from that owed by any other professional man. [84]

Factors of the objective standard

The standard of care is that of the hypothetical reasonable man and in applying this standard it is necessary to ask what, in the circumstances, the reasonable man would have foreseen. [86] This question is not always susceptible of only one possible answer. " What to one judge may seem far-fetched may seem to another both natural and probable." [87] Nevertheless, in most cases the courts can apply the standard of care of the reasonable man with some confidence for it is to be assumed that the judges who staff them have the qualities of that hypothetical creature well in mind. In some cases, however, the question of the foreseeability of an event will depend upon whether or not a particular item of knowledge is to be imputed to the reasonable man and in these cases it is of particular importance to remember that what is in question is *foreseeability*, not *probability*. The *probability* of a

duty of care attaches and that part to which it does not. It is respectfully suggested that Lord Upjohn's proposal that immunity should operate from the time of the letter before action is too arbitrary.

[82] *Pentecost* v. *London District Auditor* [1951] 2 K.B. 759, 764; *ibid.* at p. 766, *per* Lord Goddard C.J. " Generally speaking in civil cases ' gross ' negligence has no more effect than negligence without an opprobrious epithet ": *Caswell* v. *Powell Duffryn Associated Collieries Ltd.* [1940] A.C. 152, 175, *per* Lord Wright.

[83] *Rondel* v. *Worsley* [1969] 1 A.C. 191, 287; *Purves* v. *Landell* (1845) 12 C. & F. 91.

[84] *Ante*, p. 62.

[86] As we have already seen, this question is also of importance to the existence of a duty in fact (*ante*, p. 59). According to one view it is again of critical importance to the problem of remoteness of damage: *Overseas Tankship (U.K.) Ltd.* v. *Morts Dock & Engineering Co. Ltd. (The Wagon Mound)* [1961] A.C. 388 (*post*, pp. 92–99).

[87] *Glasgow Corporation* v. *Muir* [1943] A.C. 448, 457, *per* Lord Macmillan.

consequence does not depend upon the knowledge or experience of anybody, but its reasonable *foreseeability* can only be discovered if it is first decided what knowledge and experience is to be attributed to the reasonable man in the circumstances.

In *Roe* v. *Minister of Health* [88] R. was, in 1947, a patient in a hospital and Dr. G., an anaesthetist, administered a spinal anaesthetic to him in preparation for a minor operation. The anaesthetic was contained in a glass ampoule which had been kept before use in a solution of phenol and unfortunately some of the phenol had made its way through an " invisible crack " into the ampoule. It thus contaminated the anaesthetic, with the result that R. became permanently paralysed from the waist down. Dr. G. was aware of the consequences of injecting phenol, and he therefore subjected the ampoule to a visual examination before administering the anaesthetic, but he was not aware of the possibility of " invisible cracks." Had he been aware of this possibility the danger to R. could have been eliminated by adding a powerful colouring agent to the phenol so that contamination of the anaesthetic could have been observed. It was held that he was not negligent in not causing the phenol to be coloured because the risk of invisible cracks had not been drawn to the attention of the profession until 1951 and " care has to be exercised to ensure that conduct in 1947 is only judged in the light of knowledge which then was or ought reasonably to have been possessed. In this connection the then-existing state of medical literature must be had in mind." [89] But the then-existing state of medical literature did not make R.'s injury any less *probable* than it would have been after 1951.

Whether the defendant has been guilty of a breach of his duty of care or not is a question of fact, and propositions of good sense which are applied by one judge in one case should not be regarded thereafter as propositions of law.[90] On the other hand situations do tend to repeat themselves and it is permissible to look at decisions of the courts to see how the standard of the reasonable man should be applied.[91] The result is that in each case a balance must be struck between the magnitude of the risk and the burden to the defendant in doing (or not doing) what it is alleged he should (or should not) have done. " The law in all cases exacts a degree of care commensurate with the

---

[88] [1954] 2 Q.B. 66. Weir, *Casebook on Tort*, 3rd ed., p. 124. See, too, Walsh J.'s careful analysis of the problem in *Miller Steamship Co. Pty. Ltd.* v. *Overseas Tankship (U.K.) The Wagon Mound (No. 2)* [1963] 1 Lloyd's Rep. 402, revd. on the facts [1967] 1 A.C. 617 (P.C.) *Cf. Overseas Tankship (U.K.) Ltd.* v. *Morts Dock & Engineering Co. Ltd. (The Wagon Mound)* [1961] A.C. 388.

[89] [1954] 2 Q.B. at p. 92, *per* Morris L.J.; *Graham* v. *Co-operative Wholesale Society Ltd.* [1957] 1 W.L.R. 511; *Jones* v. *Dennison* [1971] R.T.R. 174.

[90] See, *e.g.*, *Easson* v. *London & North Eastern Ry.* [1944] K.B. 421, 426, *per* du Parcq L.J.; *Woods* v. *Durable Suites Ltd.* [1953] 1 W.L.R. 857; *Qualcast (Wolverhampton) Ltd.* v. *Haynes* [1959] A.C. 743; *Cavanagh* v. *Ulster Weaving Co. Ltd.* [1960] A.C. 145; *Brown* v. *Rolls-Royce Ltd.* [1960] 1 W.L.R. 210.

[91] *Hazell* v. *British Transport Commission* [1958] 1 W.L.R. 169. See generally Charlesworth, *Negligence* 5th ed.; Bingham, *All the Modern Cases on Negligence*, 2nd ed.

risk." [92] In some cases, where there is only a remote possibility of injury no precautions need be taken for " one must guard against reasonable probabilities, not fantastic possibilities," [93] but this means no more than that if the risk is very slight the defendant may have behaved reasonably though he did nothing to prevent the harm.[94] If his act was one for which there was in any case no justification he may still be liable so long only as the risk of damage to the plaintiff is not such that a reasonable man would brush it aside as far-fetched.[95] Theoretically at least, in every case where a duty of care exists the courts must consider whether the risk was sufficiently great to require of the defendant more than he has actually done.

(a) **Magnitude of the risk.** Two elements go to make up the magnitude of the risk, the likelihood that injury will be incurred [96] and the seriousness of the injury that is risked. In *Bolton* v. *Stone* [97] the plaintiff was standing on the highway in a road adjoining a cricket ground when she was struck by a ball which a batsman had hit out of the ground. Such an event was foreseeable and, indeed, balls had to the defendant's knowledge occasionally been hit out of the ground before. Nevertheless, taking into account such factors as the distance from the pitch to the edge of the ground, the presence of a seven foot fence and the upward slope of the ground in the direction in which the ball was struck, the House of Lords considered that the likelihood of injury to a person in the plaintiff's position was so slight that the cricket club was not negligent in allowing cricket to be played without having taken additional precautions such as increasing the height of the fence. As Lord Reid said, " I think that reasonable men do in fact take into account the degree of risk and do not act upon a bare possibility as they would if the risk were more substantial." [98] On the other hand, in *Hilder* v. *Associated Portland Cement Manufacturers Ltd.*[99] the plaintiff's husband was riding his motor-cycle along a road outside a piece of open land, occupied by the defendants, where children were permitted to play football, when a ball was kicked into the road and caused him to have an accident. The conditions were such that the likelihood of injury to passers-by was much greater than in *Bolton* v. *Stone* and accordingly the defendants were held liable for having permitted football to be played on their land without having taken any additional precautions.

---

[92] *Read* v. *J. Lyons & Co. Ltd.* [1947] A.C. 156, 173, *per* Lord Macmillan, " As the danger increases, so must the precautions increase." *Lloyds Bank Ltd.* v. *Railway Executive* [1952] 1 All E.R. 1248, 1253, *per* Denning L.J.; *Cf. Goldman* v. *Hargrave* [1967] 1 A.C. 645, 663, *per* Lord Wilberforce, and see *ante*, p. 60, n. 66.

[93] *Fardon* v. *Harcourt-Rivington* (1932) 146 L.T. 391, 392, *per* Lord Dunedin.

[94] *Bolton* v. *Stone* [1951] A.C. 850, 886–889, *per* Lord Radcliffe.

[95] *The Wagon Mound* (*No.* 2) [1967] 1 A.C. 617, 643–644, *per* Lord Reid.

[96] *i.e.*, the *foreseeable*, not the objective, likelihood. See *ante*, p. 65.

[97] [1951] A.C. 850. Weir, *Casebook on Tort*, 3rd ed., p. 100.

[98] *Ibid.* at p. 865; *Brewer* v. *Delo* (1967) 117 New L.J. 575. *Cf. The Wagon Mound* (*No.* 2) [1967] 1 A.C. 617, 642, *per* Lord Reid.

[99] [1961] 1 W.L.R. 1434.

The relevance of the seriousness of the injury was recognised by the House of Lords in *Paris* v. *Stepney Borough Council*[1] after having been denied by the Court of Appeal in the same case.[2] In that case the plaintiff, a one-eyed man employed by the defendants, was working in conditions involving some risk of eye injury, but the likelihood of injury was not sufficient to call upon the defendants to provide goggles to a normal two-eyed workman. In the case of the plaintiff, however, goggles should have been provided for, whereas the risk to a two-eyed man was of the loss of one eye, the plaintiff risked the much greater injury of total blindness.

In assessing the magnitude of the risk it is important to notice that the duty of care is owed to the plaintiff himself and therefore that if he suffers from some disability which increases the magnitude of the risk to him that disability must be taken into account so long as it is or should be known to the defendant.[3] If it is unknown and could not reasonably have been known to the defendant then it is, of course, irrelevant.[4]

(b) The importance of the object to be attained. Asquith L.J. summed it up by saying that it is necessary to balance the risk against the consequences of not taking it. " As has often been pointed out, if all the trains in this country were restricted to a speed of five miles an hour, there would be fewer accidents, but our national life would be intolerably slowed down. The purpose to be served, if sufficiently important, justifies the assumption of abnormal risk." [6] In *Watt* v. *Hertfordshire County Council*[7] W., a fireman, was injured by the movement of a heavy jack when travelling with it in a lorry not specially equipped for carrying it. A woman had been trapped under a heavy vehicle and the jack was urgently required to save her life. It was held that the fire authorities had not been negligent for the risk involved to W. was not so great as to prohibit the attempt to save life. But if the same accident had occurred in a commercial enterprise W. could have recovered. " The commercial end to make profit is very different from the human end to save life or limb." [8] A fire authority has been held liable for damage

---

[1] [1951] A.C. 367.
[2] [1950] 1 K.B. 320.
[3] *Paris* v. *Stepney Borough Council* [1951] A.C. 367; *Haley* v. *London Electricity Board* [1965] A.C. 778; *Baxter* v. *Woolcombers* (1963) 107 S.J. 553 (plaintiff's low intelligence relevant to standard of care due to him but not to question of contributory negligence); *Thorne* v. *Northern Group Hospital Management Committee* (1964) 108 S.J. 484.
[4] *Bourhill* v. *Young* [1943] A.C. 92, 109–110, per Lord Wright. See also *Darvill* v. *C. & J. Hampton Ltd.* (1972) 13 K.I.R. 275, though the decision went on the pleadings.
[6] *Daborn* v. *Bath Tramways* [1946] 2 All E.R. 333, 336 (left-hand drive ambulance during emergency period of war not negligent in turning right without giving a signal). *Cf. Quinn* v. *Scott* [1965] 1 W.L.R. 1004 (National Trust negligent in not felling dangerous tree near highway. Safety of public must take precedence over preservation of the amenities). See also the discussion of the nature of the duty owed by Borstal officers in *Home Office* v. *Dorset Yacht Co. Ltd.* [1970] A.C. 1004, *ante*, pp. 56–57.
[7] [1954] 1 W.L.R. 835. Weir, *Casebook on Tort*, 3rd ed., p. 102.
[8] *Ibid.* p. 838, *per* Denning L.J. The purpose of catching a speeding motorist does not, apparently, justify a police motor-cyclist in driving any differently from an ordinary driver on his private occasions: *Gaynor* v. *Allen* [1959] 2 Q.B. 403. What if the motorist

caused by a fire engine which went through a red light on the way to a fire [8a]; but in proceedings of an entirely different type the Court of Appeal has refused to declare unlawful a fire authority order stating that drivers were allowed to go through red lights.[8b]

(c) **Practicability of precautions.** The risk must be balanced against the measures necessary to eliminate it, and the practical measures which the defendant could have taken must be considered.[9] In *Latimer* v. *A.E.C.*[10] a factory floor became slippery after a flood. The occupiers of the factory did everything possible to get rid of the effects of the flood, but nevertheless the plaintiff was injured and then sought to say that the occupiers should have closed down the factory. The House of Lords held that the risk of injury created by the slippery floor was not so great as to justify, much less require, so onerous a precaution. On the other hand, the greater the risk, the less weight will be given to the factor of cost, and in any case the courts will not view with favour a defence based simply upon the cost, in terms of money, of the required precaution.[11]

General and approved practice.[12] " A defendant charged with negligence can clear [himself] if he shows that he has acted in accord with general and approved practice." [13] This means that it must be approved

---

were wanted for murder? Neither a police constable (*Dyer* v. *Bannell* (1965) 109 S.J. 216) nor any other driver (*Barna* v. *Hudes Merchandising Corporation* (1962) 106 S.J. 194; Weir, *Casebook on Tort*, 3rd ed., p. 139), is guilty of negligence merely because he exceeds the speed limit. But a police constable, like other drivers, must remember that other road users will not expect his speed in a built-up area. See also *Hurlock* v. *Inglis* (1963) 107 S.J. 1023 (100 m.p.h. not automatically negligence but defendant liable in absence of explanation of enormous skid).
[8a] *Ward* v. *L.C.C.* [1938] 2 All E.R. 341.
[8b] *Bucocke* v. *G.L.C.* [1971] 1 Ch. 655.
[9] See *Haley* v. *London Electricity Board* [1965] A.C. 778; *Stokes* v. *Guest Keen and Nettlefold* (*Bolts and Nuts*) *Ltd.* [1968] 1 W.L.R. 1776.
[10] [1953] A.C. 643; *Jones* v. *Barclays Bank* [1949] W.N. 196; *Whiteford* v. *Hunter* [1950] W.N. 533; *McCarthy* v. *Coldair Ltd.* [1951] 2 T.L.R. 1226. *Cf. Bolton* v. *Stone* [1951] A.C. 850, 867, *per* Lord Reid: " I think that it would be right to take into account not only how remote is the chance that a person might be struck but also how serious the consequences are likely to be if a person is struck; but I do not think that it would be right to take into account the difficulty of remedial measures." The risk involved in taking a precaution may actually outweigh the advantages of taking it: *Morris* v. *West Hartlepools Steam Navigation Co. Ltd.* [1956] A.C. 552; *Bolam* v. *Friern Hospital Management Committee* [1957] 1 W.L.R. 582.
[11] *Morris* v. *Luton Corporation* [1946] 1 All E.R. 1, 4, *per* Lord Greene M.R. The report of the case at [1946] K.B. 116 is incomplete. *Cf. Hicks* v. *British Transport Commission* [1958] 1 W.L.R. 493, 505, *per* Parker L.J.; *Aiken* v. *Port of London Authority* [1962] 2 Lloyd's Rep. 30. See also *Henderson* v. *Carron* (1889) 16 R. (Ct. of Sess.) 633; *Christmas* v. *General Cleaning Contractors* [1952] 1 K.B. 141, 149, *per* Denning L.J. (affd. [1953] A.C. 180); *H. & A. Scott Ltd.* v. *J. Mackenzie Stewart & Co. Ltd.*, 1972 S.L.T.(Notes) 69. There may be situations in which an activity must be abandoned altogether if adequate safeguards cannot be provided. In *Goldman* v. *Hargrave* [1967] 1 A.C. 645, 663–664, the Privy Council treated the question of the actual monetary cost of the precautions as a material factor, but the case must be read in the light of its particular facts. *Ante*, p. 61, n. 66.
[12] Munkman, *Employer's Liability*, 7th ed., pp. 41–47; Fricke, " General Practice in Industry " (1960) 23 M.L.R. 653.
[13] *Vancouver General Hospital* v. *McDaniel* (1934) 152 L.T. 56, 57, *per* Lord Alness (methods of preventing infection in hospital); approved in *Whiteford* v. *Hunter* [1950] W.N. 553, with a caveat by Lord MacDermott that such expressions are meaningless unless used in relation to some particular condition or state of affairs. *Wright* v. *Cheshire*

by those qualified to judge, but also in the last resort by the court itself with the aid of expert evidence, and the courts have not hesitated to hold that a general practice is in fact negligent.[11] " Neglect of duty does not cease by repetition to be neglect of duty." [15] Speaking of an employer's duty of care to his workmen, Lord Dunedin said in an often cited passage: " Where the negligence of the employer consists of what I may call a fault of omission, I think it absolutely necessary that the proof of that fault of omission should be one of two kinds— either to show that the thing which he did not do was a thing which was commonly done by other persons in like circumstances, or to show that it was a thing which was so obviously wanted that it would be folly in anyone to neglect to provide it." [16] Despite occasional protests against a tendency to water down this test,[17] however, it seems that today the " Dunedin formula " means no more than that " when the court finds a clearly established practice ' in like circumstances ' the practice weighs heavily in the scale on the side of the defendant and the burden of establishing negligence, which the plaintiff has to discharge, is a heavy one." [18]

Evidence of negligence

The Civil Evidence Act 1968 [18a] reverses the common law rule that a conviction may not be used as evidence in civil proceedings [18b] and provides that if a person is proved to have committed an offence then he shall be taken to have committed that offence unless the contrary is proved. It follows that a plaintiff in an action for negligence may be entitled to succeed simply on proof that the defendant has been convicted

---

County Council [1952] 2 All E.R. 789 (C.A.) (general and approved practice in connection with gymnastics at a school); *Rich* v. *L.C.C.* [1953] 1 W.L.R. 895 (C.A.); *Simmons* v. *Pennington & Son* [1955] 1 W.L.R. 183 (C.A.) (solicitors following general conveyancing practice); *Graham* v. *Co-operative Wholesale Society Ltd.* [1957] 1 W.L.R. 511.

[14] *Lloyds Bank Ltd.* v. *Savory* [1933] A.C. 201; *Markland* v. *Manchester Corporation* [1934] 1 K.B. 566; *Barkway* v. *South Wales Transport Co. Ltd.* [1950] A.C. 185; *Paris* v. *Stepney B.C.* [1951] A.C. 367; *General Cleaning Contractors* v. *Christmas* [1953] A.C. 180; *Morris* v. *West Hartlepools Steam Navigation Co. Ltd.* [1956] A.C. 552; *Cavanagh* v. *Ulster Weaving Co. Ltd.* [1960] A.C. 145; *Macdonald* v. *Scottish Stamping and Engineering Co.*, 1972 S.L.T.(Notes) 73; *cf. Foufoulas* v. *F. G. Strong Pty. Ltd.* (1970) 44 A.L.J.R. 361 (Aust. H.C.).

[15] *Bank of Montreal* v. *Dominion Guarantee, etc., Co. Ltd.* [1930] A.C. 659, 666, *per* Lord Tomlin.

[16] *Morton* v. *Dixon (William) Ltd.*, 1909 S.C. 807.

[17] *e.g., per* Lord Morton, dissenting, in *Morris* v. *West Hartlepools Steam Navigation Co. Ltd.* [1956] A.C. at p. 558.

[18] *Morris* v. *West Hartlepools Steam Navigation Co. Ltd.* [1956] A.C. at p. 579, *per* Lord Cohen; *Paris* v. *Stepney B.C.* [1951] A.C. 367; *Cavanagh* v. *Ulster Weaving Co. Ltd.* [1960] A.C. 145; *Brown* v. *Rolls-Royce Ltd.* [1960] 1 W.L.R. 210 (H.L.); *Henderson* v. *Henry E. Jenkins & Sons* [1970] A.C. 282; *Foufoulas* v. *F. G. Strong Pty. Ltd.* (1970) 44 A.L.J.R. 361 (Aust. H.C.). S. 37 (5) of the Road Traffic Act 1972 provides that " a failure on the part of a person to observe a provision of the Highway Code shall not of itself render that person liable to criminal proceedings of any kind, but any such failure may in any proceedings (whether civil or criminal . . .) be relied upon by any party to the proceedings as tending to establish or to negative any liability which is in question in those proceedings." On this, see *Powell* v. *Phillips* [1972] 3 All E.R. 864.

[18a] c. 64, s. 11.

[18b] *Hollington* v. *F. Hewthorn & Co. Ltd.* [1943] K.B. 587.

of an offence in respect of conduct which is now complained of as negligent [19] unless the defendant can discharge the burden of proving that he was not negligent.[19a] The Act thus shifts the legal burden of proof on to the defendant once his conviction is proved.[19b] In the absence of proof of a relevant conviction, however, the legal burden of proof rests throughout with the plaintiff, and if at the conclusion of the evidence it has not been proved on a balance of probabilities [20] that the defendant was negligent, then the plaintiff fails.[21] In cases tried by jury, however, it is necessary to distinguish between the question whether there is evidence of negligence—which must be answered by the judge— and whether negligence is actually proved—which is for the jury.[22] If the judge considers that no evidence of negligence exists he must not allow the case to go to the jury. " A scintilla of evidence, or a mere surmise [23] that there may have been negligence on the part of the defendants, clearly would not justify the judge in leaving the case to the jury." [24] So too, if the plaintiff's evidence is equally consistent with the absence as with the presence of negligence on the part of the defendant, the case ought not to go to the jury.[25] On the other hand, if there is evidence from which negligence could be reasonably inferred, the judge must not withhold the case from the jury merely because in his view negligence has not been established.

This division of function came to be important, and at one time a large percentage of the appeals in negligence litigation was upon the question whether the judge had been right in allowing the case to go to the jury or in withholding it from them. So far as cases tried by jury are concerned there has been no change in the law, but today jury trials in negligence cases are very rare. Though the position is also theoretically the same in actions tried by judge alone—the position is simply that the judge must answer both questions—in practice the distinction between the two questions is obscured. At the conclusion of the evidence the judge answers the single question, Has the plaintiff proved that the

---

[19] *Wauchope* v. *Mordecai* [1970] 1 W.L.R. 317.

[19a] For differing views concerning the extent of this burden, see *Stupple* v. *Royal Insurance Co. Ltd.* [1971] 1 Q.B. 50, 71–73, *per* Lord Denning M.R. (with whom Winn L.J. substantially agreed, *ibid.* at pp. 74–75) and *ibid.* at pp. 75–76, *per* Buckley L.J. Care must be taken to distinguish between the effect of s. 11 and the effect of s. 13, by virtue of which proof of conviction of an offence is *conclusive* evidence that the convicted person did commit the offence if the question is relevant to an issue arising in an action for libel or slander. See *post*, p. 268.

[19b] *Stupple* v. *Royal Insurance Co. Ltd.*, *supra*.

[20] This is the normal standard of proof in civil cases. The more serious the allegation (*e.g.*, an allegation of fraud) the higher the degree of probability that is required: *Hornal* v. *Neuberger Products Ltd.* [1957] 1 Q.B. 247.

[21] *Brown* v. *Rolls-Royce Ltd.* [1960] 1 W.L.R. 210. Note the distinction drawn by Lord Denning between the legal and the provisional burdens of proof: *ibid.* pp. 215–216. *Henderson* v. *Henry E. Jenkins & Sons* [1970] A.C. 282, 301, *per* Lord Pearson.

[22] For a modern statement, see *Bolton* v. *Stone* [1951] A.C. 850, 858–859, *per* Lord Porter.

[23] For the distinction between conjecture and inference, see *Jones* v. *G.W.Ry.* (1931) 142 L.T. 194, 197, *per* Lord Buckmaster, 202, *per* Lord Macmillan and compare this case with *Wakelin* v. *L. & S.W. Ry.* (1886) 12 App.Cas. 41.

[24] *Toomey* v. *L.B. & S.C.Ry.* (1857) 3 C.B.(N.S.) 146, 150, *per* Williams J.

[25] *Cotton* v. *Wood* (1860) 8 C.B.(N.S.) 568.

defendant was negligent? The result is a difference in the approach taken by appellate courts to trials by jury and to trials by judge alone. In the former, unless the jury's verdict is perverse, an appellate court will interfere only on the ground of error on the part of the judge in allowing the case to go to the jury, in admitting or rejecting certain evidence, or in his direction to the jury. In an appeal from the decision of a judge alone, on the other hand, though the appellate court will accept the judge's findings of primary fact, it will decide for itself the conclusions or inferences to be drawn from them.[26]

The decline in the use of juries has thus led to a corresponding decline in importance of the question whether there is evidence of negligence, and this question is not really raised even when the defendant submits, at the conclusion of the plaintiff's evidence, that there is no case for him to answer. If the trial is by judge alone, then, because of the obvious inconvenience of asking the judge for an opinion before the evidence is complete, the defendant must elect to call no evidence at the same time that he makes his submission.[27] Since the defendant is bound by his election the case thus falls to be decided once and for all on the evidence presented.[28] In a trial by jury the judge probably has a discretion whether or not to put the defendant to his election,[29] but even if he does not the result is much the same. In *Payne* v. *Harrison* [30] the trial judge rejected the submission that there was no case to answer and the defendant proceeded to call his evidence, which, as it happened, proved the relevant negligence beyond doubt. His appeal on the ground that the judge had been wrong to reject his submission failed on the ground, *inter alia*, that the defendant, having chosen to call evidence, could not subsequently ask to have that evidence ignored.

It is not enough, of course, that there is evidence of negligence on the part of someone. There must be evidence of negligence on the part of the defendant, and this sometimes causes difficulty where the acts of more than one person are in question. In *Bray* v. *Palmer* [31] the plaintiffs' motor-cycle and the defendant's motor-car came into head-on collision in the middle of the road. The plaintiffs' evidence was in direct conflict with the defendant's, and the trial judge held that although the accident was due exclusively to the negligence of one side or the other, he was unable to decide between them. He therefore dismissed both the plaintiffs' claim

---

[26] *Watt* v. *Thomas* [1947] A.C. 484; *Benmax* v. *Austin Motor Co. Ltd.* [1955] A.C. 370; Goodhart, " Appeals on Questions of Fact " (1955) 71 L.Q.R. 402. A good many cases even in the House of Lords are today concerned almost exclusively with inferences and conclusions of fact, *i.e.*, whether or not the primary facts proved amount to negligence. For an example, see *Barnes* v. *Hampshire County Council* [1969] 1 W.L.R. 1563.

[27] *Alexander* v. *Rayson* [1936] 1 K.B. 169; *Parry* v. *Aluminium Corporation Ltd.* [1940] W.N. 44.

[28] If after a submission of no case the judge decides in favour of the defendant the Court of Appeal may, if it is so minded, reverse the decision and enter judgment for the plaintiff without affording the defendant an opportunity to call his evidence: *Goulding* v. *Ministry of Works* (1955), unreported, cited Salmond, *Torts*, 16th ed., p. 238.

[29] *Young* v. *Rank* [1950] 2 K.B. 510.

[30] [1961] 2 Q.B. 403.

[31] [1953] 1 W.L.R. 1455.

and the defendant's counterclaim. The Court of Appeal took the view
that a not unlikely inference was that both parties were equally to blame
and ordered a new trial. They indicated, however, that the judge's
decision as it stood was tantamount to a denial of justice,[32] and that he
should have formed some conclusion on the matter one way or the other.
In point of fact, in cases of this kind where there is really no evidence
to enable the court to distinguish between two drivers involved in an
accident, the correct inference will commonly be that both drivers were
equally to blame.[33] In the Canadian case of *Cook* v. *Lewis*,[34] however, no
similar inference was possible. A and B were out shooting and fired
simultaneously in the direction of C, who was injured, but it was impossible for C to prove which of them had injured him. The case had to be
sent for retrial, but on the issue of substance the Supreme Court of
Canada expressed the view that C could recover. They adopted the
principle that where two defendants have committed acts of negligence
in circumstances that deprive the plaintiff of the ability to prove which
of them caused his damage, the burden is cast upon each of the defendants to exculpate himself, and if both fail to discharge this burden, then
both are liable. It is doubtful, however, whether this principle forms
part of English law. The basic rule is that the plaintiff must prove his
case on a balance of probabilities, and if it is no more likely that one
defendant was negligent than that the other was negligent then no case
is proved against either.[35] The only qualification seems to be that if a
plaintiff sues two defendants and his difficulties in proving which of
them was negligent are due to their failure to call available evidence,
adverse inferences may be drawn. But if all available evidence is called
and the natural inference is that the accident was due to negligence on
the part of one or other of the defendants but not of both, then the
plaintiff will fail.[36] Where, however, the defendant is in law responsible
for the negligence of all the possible tortfeasors, the plaintiff " is not
required to lay his finger on the exact person in all the chain who was

---

[32] [1953] 1 W.L.R. at p. 1459, *per* Jenkins L.J.

[33] *Baker* v. *Market Harborough Industrial Co-operative Society*; *Wallace* v. *Richards
Ltd.* [1953] 1 W.L.R. 1472; *France* v. *Parkinson* [1954] 1 W.L.R. 581; *W. & M. Wood
(Haulage) Ltd.* v. *Redpath* [1967] 2 Q.B. 520. *Davison* v. *Leggett* (1969) 133 J.P. 552 takes
the matter very far. *Cf. Nesterczuk* v. *Mortimore* (1965) 39 A.L.J.R. 288 (H.Ct. of
Australia), and see *The Anneliese* [1970] 2 All E.R. 29 for the position under the Maritime
Conventions Act 1911, s. 1 (1) (a).

[34] [1951] S.C.R. 830; [1952] 1 D.L.R. 1; noted by Glanville Williams (1953) 31 Can. Bar
Rev. 315–317; (1953) 72 *Law Notes* 194. Hogan, " *Cook* v. *Lewis* Re-examined " (1961)
24 M.L.R. 331. See also *Summers* v. *Tice* (1948) 5 A.L.R. (2d) 91.

[35] It would be exceedingly difficult to apply the principle of *Cook* v. *Lewis* to a situation
involving numerous possible defendants.

[36] *Baker* v. *Market Harborough Industrial Co-operative Society* [1953] 1 W.L.R. 1472,
1475, *per* Somervell L.J.; *Salt* v. *Imperial Chemical Industries* [1958] C.L.Y. 2251 (C.A.);
Wotta v. *Haliburton Oil Well Cementing Co.* [1955] 2 D.L.R. 785; *Nesterczuk* v. *Mortimore*
(1965) 39 A.L.J.R. 288 (H.Ct. of Australia). *Cf. Roe* v. *Minister of Health* [1954] 2 Q.B.
66, 82, *per* Denning L.J. The learned Lord Justice's judgment in *Baker* v. *Market Harborough Industrial Co-operative Society*, *supra*, is equivocal on this point. If in an action
against two defendants the plaintiff makes out a prima facie case that one or both of them
was negligent, then he is entitled to have the case tried out between all the parties:
Hummerstone v. *Leary* [1921] 2 K.B. 664.

responsible." [37] It is enough if he has proved that someone for whom the defendant must answer has been negligent.

Res ipsa loquitur [38]

In order to discharge the burden of proof placed upon him it is usually necessary for the plaintiff to prove specific acts or omissions on the part of the defendant which will qualify as negligent conduct. Sometimes, however, the circumstances are such that the court will be prepared to draw an inference of negligence against the defendant without hearing detailed evidence of what he did or did not do. Thus, for example, the presence of an unlighted vehicle on the road at night will, if there is no other lighting, be regarded as prima facie evidence of negligence on the part of the driver.[38a] It is important to appreciate, however, that this means no more than that, in the absence of an explanation from the defendant, the plaintiff has discharged his burden of proof. The inference of negligence is by no means irrebuttable, [38b] and the nature of the evidence required from the defendant in rebuttal will depend in each case on the strength of the inference against him and the standard of care called for in the circumstances. In *Henderson v. Henry E. Jenkins & Sons*,[39] where the plaintiff's husband was killed by a heavy lorry whose brakes failed on a steep hill, the defendants pleaded that the brake failure was due to a latent defect in the main brake fluid pipe. They proved that they had cleaned and carried out visual inspections of the pipe at the proper intervals and that the cause of its failure was corrosion in a part of the pipe which could only be inspected by removing the pipe itself from the vehicle. Notwithstanding that neither the manufacturers of the vehicle nor the Ministry of Transport recommended removal of the pipe for inspection in normal circumstances, it was held by a majority of the House of Lords that the defendants had not done sufficient to rebut the inference that they had been negligent: they should have gone on to show that nothing had occurred in the life of the vehicle which would cause abnormal corrosion or call for special inspection or treatment.

---

[37] *Grant* v. *Australian Knitting Mills* [1936] A.C. 85, 101, *per* Lord Wright; *Cassidy* v. *Ministry of Health* [1951] 2 K.B. 343; *Roe* v. *Minister of Health* [1954] 2 Q.B. 66; *Walsh* v. *Holst & Co. Ltd.* [1958] 1 W.L.R. 800.

[38] Ellis Lewis, " A Ramble with *res ipsa loquitur* " (1951) 11 C.L.J. 74–92; O'Connell, " *Res ipsa loquitur*: The Australian Experience " [1954] C.L.J. 118–132; Underhay (1936) 14 Can. Bar Rev. 287–294; Baker (1950) 24 Australian L.J. 194–198; Prosser (1949) 37 California L.Rev. 183–234; Atiyah, " *Res ipsa loquitur* in England and Australia " (1972) 35 M.L.R. 337. The principle appears as early as *Christie* v. *Griggs* (1809) 2 Camp. 79; its Latin form is much later. It is untraceable in the civil law, although Prof. Buckland and Mr. Ashton-Cross state that phrases like " *res loquitur ipsa* " and " *res ipsa dixit* " occur in Cicero and other lay literature.

[38a] *Hill-Venning* v. *Beszant* [1950] 2 All E.R. 1151; *Parish* v. *Judd* [1960] 1 W.L.R. 867; *Moore* v. *Maxwells of Emsworth Ltd.* [1968] 1 W.L.R. 1077.

[38b] It was rebutted in the second and third of the cases cited in the last note.

[39] [1970] A.C. 282; *Barkway* v. *South Wales Transport Co. Ltd.* [1950] 1 All E.R. 392; *Pearce* v. *Round Oak Steel Works Ltd.* [1969] 1 W.L.R. 595. In the last named case, also involving a latent defect, the defendants called no evidence. *Cf. Pearson* v. *North Western Gas Board* [1968] 2 All E.R. 669.

The strength of the inference of negligence raised by the extensive corrosion of the pipe and the extremely high standard of inspection and maintenance required of a person who sends a heavy lorry on a journey involving the descent of a steep hill justify the heavy burden placed on the defendants in this case. In other circumstances the inference will be rebutted more easily, but in each case the question is the same: has the defendant rebutted the inference of negligence raised against him by the plaintiff's evidence? The position has, however, been complicated and obscured by the use in many cases of the maxim *res ipsa loquitur*. As Morris L.J. has said, the maxim " possesses no magic qualities: nor has it any added virtue, other than that of brevity, merely because it is expressed in Latin. When used on behalf of a plaintiff it is generally a short way of saying: ' I submit that the facts and circumstances which I have proved establish a prima facie case of negligence against the defendant.' . . . There are certain happenings that do not normally occur in the absence of negligence, and upon proof of these a court will probably hold that there is a case to answer." [40] In other words the maxim does no more than express in three words what has just been said. Nevertheless, it has given rise to a disproportionate amount of discussion and perhaps also to the development of detailed rules which do more than realise its simple underlying basis.

Conditions for application.[40a] The principal requirement is that the mere fact of the accident having happened should tell its own story and raise the inference of negligence so as to establish a prima facie case against the defendant. The story must be clear and unambiguous; if it may tell one of half a dozen stories the maxim is inapplicable.[41] This single requirement is, however, commonly divided into two on the basis of Erle C.J.'s famous statement in *Scott* v. *London and St. Katherine Docks Co.*[42] " There must be reasonable evidence of negligence. But where the thing is shown to be under the management of the defendant or his servants, and the accident is such as in the ordinary course of things does not happen if those who have the management use proper care, it affords reasonable evidence, in

---

[40] *Roe* v. *Minister of Health* [1954] 2 Q.B. 66, 87–88, *per* Morris L.J., *ibid.* at p. 80, *per* Somervell L.J.; *Ballard* v. *North British Ry.*, 1923 S.C. (H.L.) 43, 53, *per* Lord Dunedin, 56, *per* Lord Shaw; *Easson* v. *L.N.E. Ry.* [1944] K.B. 421, 425, *per* du Parcq L.J.; *Barkway* v. *South Wales Transport Co. Ltd.* [1950] 1 All E.R. 392, 403, *per* Lord Radcliffe; *Anchor Products Ltd.* v. *Hedges* (1966) 115 C.L.R. 493 (H.Ct. of Aus.); *Lloyde* v. *West Midlands Gas Board* [1971] 1 W.L.R. 749.

[40a] It is unnecessary specifically to plead the maxim: *Bennett* v. *Chemical Construction (G.B.) Ltd.* [1971] 1 W.L.R. 1571.

[41] *Carruthers* v. *MacGregor*, 1927 S.C. 816, 823, *per* Lord Murray; *Cole* v. *De Trafford* [1918] 2 K.B. 528; 11 C.L.J. 82–83.

[42] (1865) 3 H. & C. 596 (six bags of sugar fell on plaintiff whilst lawfully passing doorway of defendant's warehouse. Defendants called no evidence. Held, sufficient evidence of negligence). This passage has been said to be " the formulation of all subsequent authority ": *Moore* v. *R. Fox & Sons* [1956] 1 Q.B. 596, 611, *per* Evershed M.R. See also *Britannia Hygienic Laundry Co.* v. *Thornycroft & Co.* (1926) 95 L.J.K.B. 237; *Halliwell* v. *Venables* (1930) 143 L.T. 215; *Ellor* v. *Selfridge & Co. Ltd.* (1930) 46 T.L.R. 236; *Mahon* v. *Osborne* [1939] 2 K.B. 14; *Easson* v. *L.N.E. Ry.* [1944] K.B. 421; *Barkway* v. *South Wales Transport Co.*, 94 S.J. 95; [1950] 1 All E.R. 392; *Bolton* v. *Stone* [1951] A.C. 850, 859.

the absence of explanation by the defendants, that the accident arose from want of care." The two requirements are thus (i) that the " thing " causing the damage be under the control of the defendant or his servants,[43] and (ii) that the accident must be such as would not in the ordinary course of things have happened without negligence.

(i) *Control.* The point of this requirement is that the happening of the accident must be evidence of negligence on the part of the defendant or of someone for whose negligence he is responsible. A mere right to control, as opposed to actual control, is therefore sufficient [44] and it is not always necessary that all the circumstances be under the defendant's control.[45] But if the events leading up to the accident were, or might well have been, under the control of others besides the defendant, then the mere happening of the accident is insufficient evidence against the defendant.[45a] In *Gee* v. *Metropolitan Ry.*[46] the plaintiff leant lightly against the door of an underground train not long after it had left a station. The door flew open, causing the plaintiff to fall out, and it was held that there was evidence of negligence against the railway company. On the other hand, in *Easson* v. *L.N.E. Ry.*[47] where the plaintiff, a boy aged four, fell through a door of a corridor train about seven miles from its last stopping place it was held that the defendants did not have sufficient control over the door for *res ipsa loquitur* to apply. " It is impossible to say that the doors of an express corridor train travelling from Edinburgh to London are continuously under the sole control of the railway company. . . . Passengers are walking up and down the corridors during the journey and get in and out at stopping places." [48] The fact that the door came open could as well have been due to interference by a passenger as to the negligence of the defendants' servants.

(ii) *The accident must be such as could not in the ordinary course of things have happened without negligence.* The question here is whether the fact of the accident itself justifies the inference of negligence and this means not only that all the circumstances must be considered, but that they must be considered in the light of common experience and knowledge. In effect the judge takes judicial notice

---

[43] It is sufficient if an independent contractor employed by the defendant has control, provided that the circumstances are such that the defendant will be liable for the negligence of his independent contractor: *Walsh* v. *Holst & Co. Ltd.* [1958] 1 W.L.R. 800. *Post*, pp. 536–540. See also *ante*, p. 72.

[44] *Parker* v. *Miller* (1926) 42 T.L.R. 408.

[45] *McGowan* v. *Stott* (1930) 143 L.T. 217; *Chapronière* v. *Mason* (1905) 21 T.L.R. 633; *Grant* v. *Australian Knitting Mills* [1936] A.C. 85; *Moore* v. *R. Fox & Sons* [1956] 1 Q.B. 596.

[45a] The true principle therefore appears to be not that the plaintiff must show any positive control in the defendant but rather that outside interference is unlikely: *Lloyde* v. *West Midlands Gas Board* [1971] 1 W.L.R. 749.

[46] (1873) L.R. 8 Q.B. 161; *Burns* v. *N.B. Ry.*, 1914 S.C. 754; *Brookes* v. *L.P.T.B.* [1947] 1 All E.R. 506.

[47] [1944] 2 K.B. 421; *Lloyde* v. *West Midlands Gas Board* [1971] 1 W.L.R. 749.

[48] [1944] K.B. at p. 424, *per* Goddard L.J. See too *O'Connor* v. *British Transport Commission* [1958] 1 W.L.R. 346 and *McLeod* v. *Glasgow Corpn.*, 1971 S.L.T.(Notes) 64.

of the common experience of mankind.[49] It is common experience which shows that a barrel will not fall from an upstairs window onto a passer-by in the street if those in charge take proper care[50] or that two railway trains belonging to the same company will not collide without negligence on the part of the company or its servants.[51] So also, if a vehicle strikes a person on the pavement[52] or moves onto the wrong side of the road into the path of oncoming traffic,[53] there is a prima facie case of negligence against the driver: and this is not displaced merely by proof that the defendant's vehicle skidded.[54] Indeed, an unexplained and violent skid is itself evidence of negligence.[55] On the other hand, the mere fact that a fire spread from an ordinary domestic grate is not sufficient[56] for "everyone knows fires occur through accidents which happen without negligence on anybody's part."[57]

If it is the common experience of mankind which enables the inference of negligence to be drawn from the fact of the accident having happened then it might be thought that in cases outside the range of common experience, such as those involving surgical operations, *res ipsa loquitur* could not apply. This was the view of Scott L.J. in *Mahon* v. *Osborne*,[58] where a swab was left in the body of a patient after an abdominal operation, but the modern trend is to permit the maxim to be used. A plaintiff is entitled to say, " I went into hospital to be cured of two stiff fingers. I have come out with four stiff fingers, and my hand is useless. That should not have happened if due care had been used. Explain it, if you can."[59] And there seems no reason why the plaintiff should not call expert witnesses to show that the accident would not have occurred without negligence. Otherwise he may find himself put to an impossible burden of proof and in the result fail to establish what in truth is a valid claim simply because the judge lacks the experience to draw the appropriate inferences.[60]

---

[49] Ellis Lewis, *loc. cit.* at p. 80.   [50] *Byrne* v. *Boadle* (1863) 2 H. & C. 722.
[51] *Skinner* v. *L.B. & S.C. Ry.* (1850) 5 Ex. 787. Of the many other cases see, *e.g.* *Chaproniere* v. *Mason* (1905) 21 T.L.R. 633 (stone in bun); *Fosbroke-Hobbes* v. *Airwork Ltd.* [1937] 1 All E.R. 108 (aeroplane crashing immediately after take-off); *Grant* v. *Australian Knitting Mills* [1936] A.C. 85 (excess of sulphites in woollen pants); *Colvilles Ltd.* v. *Devine* [1969] 1 W.L.R. 475 (explosion in hose carrying oxygen).
[52] *Ellor* v. *Selfridge & Co. Ltd.* (1930) 46 T.L.R. 236; *Watson* v. *Thomas S. Witney & Co. Ltd.* [1966] 1 W.L.R. 57.
[53] *Richley (Henderson)* v. *Faull* [1965] 1 W.L.R. 1454.
[54] *Laurie* v. *Raglan Building Co. Ltd.* [1942] 1 K.B. 152. This, it is submitted, is all that is meant by Lord Greene M.R.'s statement (*ibid.* at p. 154) that " the skid itself is neutral." If the vehicle's presence in the wrong place is due to a skid and the skid is proved to have occurred without negligence then there is, of course, no negligence: *Hunter* v. *Wright* [1938] 2 All E.R. 621; *Browne* v. *De Luxe Car Services* [1941] 1 All E.R. 383.
[55] *Hurlock* v. *Inglis* (1963) 107 S.J. 1023; *Richley (Henderson)* v. *Faull, supra.*
[56] *Sochacki* v. *Sas* [1947] 1 All E.R. 344.
[57] *Ibid.* at p. 345, *per* Lord Goddard C.J.
[58] [1939] 2 K.B. 14. Goddard L.J., dissenting, thought that *res ipsa loquitur* could be used.
[59] *Cassidy* v. *Ministry of Health* [1951] 2 K.B. 343, 365, *per* Denning L.J.; *Roe* v. *Minister of Health* [1954] 2 Q.B. 66. *Cf. MacDonald* v. *Pottinger* [1953] N.Z.L.R. 196.
[60] See *Fish* v. *Kapur* [1948] 2 All E.R. 176 where, however, the plaintiff's expert witnesses helped to negative the inference of negligence.

(iii) *Absence of explanation.* It is sometimes said that there is a third requirement for the application of the maxim, namely, that there must be no evidence of the actual cause. of the accident. All this seems to mean, however, is that, if the facts are sufficiently known, the question ceases to be whether they speak for themselves, and the only question is whether on the facts as established, negligence is to be inferred or not.[61] The mere fact that the plaintiff attempts, and fails, to prove some specific act of negligence on the part of the defendant does not, of itself, deprive him of the benefit of the maxim [61a] and, of course, even its actual exclusion does not necessarily lead to the conclusion that the defendant was not negligent. In *Barkway* v. *South Wales Transport Co. Ltd.*[62] B. was travelling as a passenger in the defendants' omnibus and was killed when it veered across the road and fell over an embankment. A great deal of evidence was given by the defendants and it was established that the cause of the accident was a defect in one of the tyres which might have been discovered beforehand if the defendants had required their drivers to report occurrences which could result in " impact fractures." The House of Lords held that as the cause of the accident was known *res ipsa loquitur* did not apply, but that on the facts the negligence of the defendants was established.

Effect of the maxim. We have seen that in the case of trial by jury the judge must not leave the case to the jury if there is no evidence of negligence.[63] In such a case, if the plaintiff successfully raises a plea of *res ipsa loquitur* the judge must obviously reject a submission by the defendant that there is no evidence for the jury. It would not seem to follow, however, that if the defendant gives no evidence and yet the jury's verdict is in his favour, the verdict is necessarily perverse.[64] The inference of negligence raised by the mere fact of the accident may sometimes be irresistible, but it will not always be so. In theory the same should be true in cases tried by judge alone. The judge may hold that *res ipsa loquitur* applies, reject a submission of no evidence and yet, without hearing evidence for the defence, give judgment for the defendant. In practice, however, it is impossible for a judge sitting alone to distinguish so sharply between his functions as judge of law and as judge of fact. If he is not prepared to hold that, in the absence of some evidence from the defendant, the plaintiff has

---

[61] *Barkway* v. *South Wales Transport Co. Ltd.* [1950] 1 All E.R. 392; *Bolton* v. *Stone* [1951] A.C. 850, 859, *per* Lord Porter.

[61a] *Anchor Products Ltd.* v. *Hedges* (1966) 115 C.L.R. 493 (H.Ct. of Aus.).

[62] [1950] 1 All E.R. 392.

[63] *Ante*, pp. 70–71.

[64] See, *e.g.*, *Langham* v. *Governors of Wellingborough School* (1932) 101 L.J.K.B. 513; *Easson* v. *L.N.E. Ry.* [1944] K.B. 421, 423, *per* Goddard L.J., 425, *per* du Parcq L.J.; Street, *Torts*, 5th ed., p. 137; 11 C.L.J. at p. 84. In *Davis* v. *Bunn* (1936) 56 C.L.R. 246, 267–268 Evatt J. thought that where the doctrine applies, and the defendant gives no evidence, the jury are not bound to find for the plaintiff, because the maxim only raises a presumption of fact, and the cogency of the presumption varies with the circumstances.

sufficiently proved negligence by proving the fact of the accident alone, he will not hold that *res ipsa loquitur* applies.[65] At least in cases tried by judge alone, therefore, a decision that *res ipsa loquitur* applies is a decision that the plaintiff is entitled to judgment unless the defendant can exonerate himself. A burden of some kind is cast upon the defendant.

The burden on the defendant. What, then, must the defendant do to discharge this burden? In principle, if the maxim is no more than a convenient way of expressing the idea that the plaintiff can raise a prima facie case by circumstantial evidence, the answer can only be that he must do sufficient to rebut the inference of negligence raised by the plaintiff, and what that entails will, as we have seen, vary with the strength of the inference and the standard of care called for in the circumstances. Certainly the defendant will be exonerated if he shows how the accident actually occurred and if this true explanation is consistent with due care on his part[66]; and if he cannot do this he will still escape liability if he proves that there was no lack of care on his part or on the part of persons for whom he is responsible.[67] According to some authorities on *res ipsa loquitur,* however, if the defendant cannot do one of these two things, then the plaintiff is entitled to judgment without more. In *Moore* v. *R. Fox & Sons,*[68] where the Court of Appeal was doubtful whether or not the maxim applied, Evershed M.R. expressed his intention of dealing with the case on the assumption that it did not apply and also " on the alternative view that, although at the end of her case the plaintiff might have established a prima facie case of negligence, nevertheless the onus remained throughout on the plaintiff, so that the question for the determination of the court *in the latter alternative* is whether, upon the evidence as a whole, the right inference is one in favour of the plaintiffs or of the defendants." [69]

This, with respect, is difficult to understand for it appears to cast upon the defendant a different burden according to whether the case

---

[65] Even where he finds negligence proved a judge may still deny that the case is one of *res ipsa loquitur* though the meaning of this is unclear (see *post,* pp. 78–79). In *Moore* v. *R. Fox & Sons* [1956] 1 Q.B. 596, Evershed M.R. (with whom Birkett L.J. concurred) dealt with the case on the assumption that *res ipsa loquitur* applied and on the assumption that it did not. Romer L.J. preferred the view that it did not. But all three agreed that the plaintiff was entitled to succeed. See also *Barkway* v. *South Wales Transport Co.* [1950] 1 All E.R. 392, *ante; Pearson* v. *North Western Gas Board* [1968] 2 All E.R. 669.

[66] *Barkway* v. *South Wales Transport Co. Ltd.* [1948] 2 All E.R. 460, 471, *per* Asquith L.J.; *Colvilles Ltd.* v. *Devine* [1969] 1 W.L.R. 475.

[67] *Woods* v. *Duncan* [1946] A.C. 401; *Walsh* v. *Holst & Co. Ltd.* [1958] 1 W.L.R. 800; *Swan* v. *Salisbury Construction Co. Ltd.* [1966] 1 W.L.R. 204. Something more than a bare statement to this effect by the defendant himself is necessary: *Ludgate* v. *Lovett* [1969] 1 W.L.R. 1016.

[68] [1956] 1 Q.B. 596; *Walsh* v. *Holst & Co. Ltd., supra.* See Ellis Lewis [1956] C.L.J. 150.

[69] [1956] 1 Q.B. at p. 607. Italics added. Evershed M.R. also spoke of a case of *res ipsa loquitur* as " a case in which the onus has been cast upon the defendants." It is submitted that neither the dictum of Asquith L.J. in *Barkway* v. *South Wales Transport Co. Ltd.,* [1948] 2 All E.R. 460, 471, nor the observations of Lord Radcliffe in *Esso Petroleum Co.* v. *Southport Corporation* [1956] A.C. 218, 243, on which the Master of the Rolls relied, go so far as this.

is or is not one of *res ipsa loquitur*. But what is the hallmark of a case of *res ipsa loquitur*? What persuades a court to use the maxim instead of saying simply that the plaintiff's evidence is sufficient to raise an inference of negligence? In *Henderson* v. *Henry E. Jenkins & Sons*,[70] for example, although *res ipsa loquitur* was pleaded by the plaintiff, the phrase itself appears in none of the speeches in the House of Lords, and in *Barkway* v. *South Wales Transport Co. Ltd.*,[71] it was actually held that once the full facts were known, as a result of the evidence given by the defendants, *res ipsa loquitur* ceased to apply and the only question was whether negligence should be inferred. This decision cannot have meant that the legal burden of proof was affected. Moreover, *Moore* v. *R. Fox & Sons* seems even to deny to the defendant the opportunity of challenging the application of the maxim if, at the conclusion of the plaintiff's case, the judge has formed the view that it does apply, for it was held in that case that hypothetical explanations of the accident put forward by the defendant, even if consistent with the absence of negligence, cannot suffice to discharge the burden cast upon him by the maxim. In a well-known passage Lord Dunedin observed that " if the defenders can show a way in which the accident may have occurred without negligence, the cogency of the fact of the accident by itself disappears, and the pursuer is left as he began, namely, that he has to show negligence." [72] In *Moore* v. *R. Fox & Sons* Evershed M.R., while pointing out that this passage occurred in a dissenting speech, evidently accepted that it applied when the question was whether the facts justified the application of the maxim, but denied that it applied to " the consequences which properly follow when a case of *res ipsa loquitur* has once been established by the plaintiff." [73] This distinction is unconvincing.[74] If the defendants in *Moore* v. *R. Fox & Sons* had contended that the explanations they proffered tended to show that *res ipsa loquitur* did not apply, instead of contending that they had discharged the burden cast upon them by the maxim, might the result have been different?

The effect of *res ipsa loquitur* has been discussed in two recent decisions of the House of Lords but the result is unfortunately by no means clear. In *Henderson* v. *Henry E. Jenkins & Sons*[75] the victim was killed by the defendants' runaway lorry. The accident resulted from a brake failure caused by a hole in the brake pipe. The defendants had carried out all proper maintenance on the lorry but the hole had occurred in a part of the brake pipe which could not be inspected except

---

[70] [1970] A.C. 282, *ante*, p. 73. See also the cases concerning unlighted motor vehicles on the road at night, cited *ante*, p. 73, n. 38a.

[71] [1950] 1 All E.R 392, *ante*, p. 77.

[72] *Ballard* v. *North British Ry.*, 1923 S.C. (H.L.) 43, 54.

[73] [1956] 1 Q.B. at p. 614.

[74] Ellis Lewis [1956] C.L.J. at pp. 152–153. *National Trust Co. Ltd.* v. *Wong Aviation Ltd.* [1969] 2 Lloyd's Rep. 340 (Sup.Ct. of Can.).

[75] [1970] A.C. 282.

by removing the pipe altogether and in normal practice this was not done until a mileage well above that of the lorry had been attained. There was no further evidence as to the cause of the failure. A majority of the House of Lords held the defendants liable. Lord Pearson speaks in terms of *res ipsa loquitur* raising no special rule of law and effecting no change in the formal burden of proof,[76] but the speeches of the other members of the majority seem more consistent with the view that the effect of the maxim is to alter the legal burden of proof.[77] Certainly, the *result* of the case seems to support the latter view. The cause of the corrosion in the brake pipe remained in the realm of speculation, it being possible only to say that " something unusual " [78] had happened and " there was no evidence *at all* what this ' something unusual ' was, whether the defendants knew or ought to have known of it, and what precautions should have been adopted to deal with it. The truth was that the issue of negligence or no-negligence was simply not proved either way." [79] The speeches in the other case, *Colvilles Ltd.* v. *Devine* [79a] seem to support the view that the maxim has no effect on the legal burden of proof, [79b] but it has been suggested that as in *Henderson* v. *Jenkins* the *result* supports the other view.[79c]

The whole issue seems to require further elucidation by the House of Lords,[79d] though it must be admitted that in trial by judge alone the issue is comparatively rarely of practical importance.[79e] The tenor of the Commonwealth authorities is against giving the maxim the more rigorous effect of reversing the burden of proof, but this attitude may depend upon the greater prevalence of the civil jury outside England.[79f]

---

[76] [1970] A.C. 282, 301. His statement that " if in the course of the trial there is proved a set of facts which raises a prima facie inference that the accident was caused by negligence on the part of the defendants, the issue will be decided in the plaintiff's favour unless the defendants by their evidence provide some answer which is adequate to displace the prima facie inference " seems to conflict with the original basic principle that the maxim *justifies* rather than *compels* a conclusion, but this is no doubt a reflection of the virtual disappearance of the civil jury.

[77] [1970] A.C. 282 at p. 291, *per* Lord Reid; at p. 300, *per* Lord Donovan.

[78] [1970] A.C. 282, 291.

[79] Atiyah, *loc. cit.*, at 340.

[79a] [1969] 1 W.L.R. 475.

[79b] Thus Lord Donovan said at [1969] 1 W.L.R. 479, " that it was for the [defendants] to show that the accident was just as consistent with their having exercised due diligence as with their having been negligent. In that way the scales which had been tipped in the plaintiff's favour by the doctrine of *res ipsa loquitur* would be once more in the balance, and the plaintiff would have to begin again and prove negligence in the usual way." *Cf.* this passage with Asquith L.J.'s use of the same metaphor to produce the opposite conclusion in *Barkway* v. *South Wales Transport Co. Ltd.*, 94 S.J. 95; [1948] 2 All E.R. 460, 471. Whatever view be taken of the effect of the maxim, Lord Donovan's use of the metaphor is the more accurate because even in the case of a true presumption affecting the legal burden of proof the facts supporting the presumption are not evidence which can be compared in weight with the other party's rebutting evidence.

[79c] Atiyah, *loc. cit.*, at p. 344.

[79d] See Lord Upjohn in *Colvilles Ltd.* v. *Devine* at [1969] 1 W.L.R. 478.

[79e] *Cf.* the views of Lord Reid on the presumption of legitimacy in *S.* v. *McC.* [1972] A.C. 24, 41.

[79f] *Government Insurance Officer of New South Wales* v. *Fredrichberg* (1968) 118 C.L.R. 403 (Aust. H.C.); *Temple* v. *Terrace Transfer Ltd.* (1966) 57 D.L.R. (2d) 631. See also Fleming, *Torts*, 4th ed., pp. 266–270.

As to the so-called rule in *The Merchant Prince* [1892] P. 179 (C.A.) and its relationship with *res ipsa loquitur*, see Street, *Torts*, 5th ed., p. 138, n.2.

TRESPASS TO THE PERSON AND NEGLIGENCE [80]

The preceding pages have emphasised that for liability in negligence the plaintiff must discharge the burden of proving that the defendant was negligent. On the other hand, it was at one time widely thought that liability in trespass was such that " if the injury be done by the act of the party himself at the time, or he be the immediate cause of it, though it happens accidentally or by misfortune, yet he is answerable in trespass." [81] If this were correct, then a plaintiff would succeed in trespass in many cases in which an action for negligence would certainly fail. It is probable, however, that liability in trespass was never so strict as this,[82] and in *Stanley* v. *Powell* [83] it was clearly held that in the absence of negligence the defendant is not liable. That case, however, did not go so far as entirely to equate trespass to the person and negligence, and until 1959 the prevailing opinion was that the burden of proof in the two torts was different.[84] In negligence the burden of proving a failure to exercise due care rests with the plaintiff, but in trespass it was thought that the defendant must affirmatively prove that he was not negligent. In other words, once the plaintiff had shown a direct injury caused by the act of the defendant, the defendant was liable unless he proved inevitable accident.

To this rule about the burden of proof in trespass, cases concerning accidents on the highway were regarded as exceptions since it had for long been the rule that where a plaintiff has been injured by an accident on the highway he must sue in negligence or, if he sues in trespass to the person, he must prove that the trespass was done negligently.[85] The origin of this rule is obscure and Winfield, in common with most other writers, regarded it as both exceptional and historically unjustifiable.[86] Nevertheless in *National Coal Board* v. *Evans* [87] Cohen L.J. said that he could see no logical reason for restricting it to highway accidents, and in *Fowler* v. *Lanning* [88] Diplock J. held generally that the burden of proving negligence in actions for unintentional trespass

---

[80] See Milner " The Retreat of Trespass " (1965) 18 C.L.P. 20; Fridman, " Trespass or Negligence " (1971) 9 Alberta L.Rev. 250; Trinidade, " Some Curiosities of Negligent Trespass " (1971) 20 I.C.L.Q. 706; Weir, *Casebook on Tort*, 3rd ed., pp. 253–260.

[81] *Leame* v. *Bray* (1803) 3 East 593, 600, *per* East J.

[82] Winfield, " The Myth of Absolute Liability " (1926) 42 L.Q.R. 37; *cf.* Milsom, (1958) 74 L.Q.R. at pp. 582–583. See also Winfield and Goodhart, " Trespass and Negligence " (1933) 49 L.Q.R. 359; *Fowler* v. *Lanning* [1959] 1 Q.B. 426, 433, *per* Diplock J.

[83] [1891] 1 Q.B. 86, in effect following *Holmes* v. *Mather* (1875) L.R. 10 Ex. 261.

[84] Winfield and Goodhart, *loc. cit.* at pp. 376–377; Goodhart (1951) 67 L.Q.R. 434–435; Salmond, *Torts*, 12th ed., p. 311 (see now 16th ed., pp. 138–139); Clerk & Lindsell, *Torts*, 11th ed., p. 51 (see now 13th ed., p. 341); Street, *Torts*, pp. 14–15, left the point open (see now 5th ed., p. 17).

[85] *Holmes* v. *Mather* (1875) L.R. 10 Ex. 261; *Phillips* v. *Britannia Hygienic Laundry Co. Ltd.* [1923] 1 K.B. 539, 552–553, affd. on other grounds, [1923] 2 K.B. 832; *Gayler & Pope Ltd.* v. *Davies & Son Ltd.* [1924] 2 K.B. 75; *Southport Corporation* v. *Esso Petroleum Co. Ltd.* [1956] A.C. 218, 225–227, *per* Devlin J., affd. by the House of Lords, *ibid.*

[86] Winfield and Goodhart, *loc. cit.* at 376.

[87] [1951] 2 K.B. 861, 875.

[88] [1959] 1 Q.B. 426. Weir, *Casebook on Tort*, 3rd ed., p. 261. See (1959) 75 L.Q.R. 161; Glanville Williams [1959] C.L.J. 33; Dworkin (1959) 22 M.L.R. 538; *Beals* v. *Hayward* [1960] N.Z.L.R. 131; Davis (1960) 23 M.L.R. 674.

to the person lies upon the plaintiff. " This," he said, " has been unquestioned law in highway cases ever since *Holmes* v. *Mather*,[89] and there is no reason in principle, nor any suggestion in the decided authorities, why it should be any different in other cases." [90]

As Diplock J. admitted, his conclusion was contrary to a "formidable body of academic opinion," and in the High Court of Australia Windeyer J. has declined to follow it.[91] Nevertheless, in *Letang* v. *Cooper* [92] the Court of Appeal not only affirmed it but, perhaps, took it a step further. In that case the defendant drove his car over the legs of the plaintiff, who was sunbathing on a piece of grass outside a hotel where cars were parked. She did not issue the writ in her action until more than three years later, and this meant that a claim in negligence ¡was statute barred,[93] but she argued that she had an alternative claim n trespass which was not. This argument succeeded before Elwes J.[94] but was rejected by the Court of Appeal, one of the reasons being that actions for unintentional trespass to the person fall within the statutory words " actions for damages for negligence." Diplock L.J. considered that a cause of action is simply a factual situation the existence of which entitles a person to obtain a remedy from the court and that an action founded upon a failure to exercise reasonable care is an action for negligence notwithstanding that it can also be called an action for trespass to the person.[95] Lord Denning M.R. expressed his agreement with *Fowler* v. *Lanning* but added, " I would go this one step further: when the injury is not inflicted intentionally, but negligently, I would say that the only cause of action is negligence and not trespass." [96]

For all practical purposes, therefore, there is no significant difference between unintentional trespass to the person and the tort of negligence,[96a] and the differences that do remain, such as the rule that in trespass the injury must be direct, cannot affect the decision of actual cases.[97] If the plaintiff fails to prove that the defendant was negligent

---

[89] (1875) L.R. 10 Ex. 261.
[90] [1959] 1 Q.B. at 439. The same result had been reached in Massachusetts as long ago as 1850 (*Brown* v. *Kendall*, 6 Cush (60 Mass.) 292. *Cf. Kopka* v. *Bell Telephone Co. of Pennsylvania* (1952) 91 A. (2d) 232). For Canada see *Walmsley* v. *Humenick* [1954] 2 D.L.R. 232.
[91] *McHale* v. *Watson* (1964) 111 C.L.R. 384. For the proceedings on appeal, where Windeyer J.'s decision was affirmed without reference to this point, see (1966) 39 A.L.J.R. 458.
[92] [1965] 1 Q.B. 232; Weir, *Casebook on Tort*, 3rd ed., p. 264; Dworkin (1965) 28 M.L.R. 92.
[93] Limitation Act 1939, s. 2 (1), as amended by the Law Reform (Limitation of Actions etc.) Act 1954, s. 2 (1). See *post*, pp. 665–666.
[94] [1964] 2 Q.B. 53.
[95] [1965] 1 Q.B. at pp. 242–244. As to this reasoning see Jolowicz [1964] C.L.J. 200.
[96] [1965] 1 Q.B. at p. 240.
[96a] But Heuston in Salmond, *Torts*, 16th ed., p. 138, (where it is suggested that *Fowler* v. *Lanning* might be overruled by the House of Lords) points out that the burden of proof issue is of great practical importance.
[97] The other differences are (1) that trespass is actionable *per se*; (2) that a master is probably not liable in trespass for the tort of his servant; (3) that the maxim *res ipsa loquitur* does not, perhaps, apply in trespass; (4) that trespass has no " duty " element; (5) that the test for remoteness of damage in trespass is probably directness, not foreseeability; (6) that it is uncertain whether contributory negligence is a defence to an uninten-

then his claim will not succeed even if the injury was direct. If he proves negligence and the injury is consequential only, he will succeed in negligence, and this is all that matters. It is of no concern to anyone that a claim in trespass would fail.[98]

3. Consequent damage

The third ingredient of the tort of negligence is that the plaintiff's damage must have been caused by the defendant's breach of duty and must not be too remote a consequence of it. Discussion of this ingredient thus involves consideration of remoteness of damage, a topic relevant in all torts and not only in the tort of negligence. It is in cases of negligence, however, that problems of remoteness of damage most commonly arise, and some problems in negligence—especially that of liability for nervous shock—can only be dealt with against the background of the tort of negligence as a whole. Although a topic of general importance throughout the law, therefore, remoteness of damage will be dealt with in the next chapter.

---

tional trespass. The existence of some of these differences is doubtful, and none seems to have much practical consequence. (1) Unless the rule *de minimis non curat lex* applies, a trespass to the person is bound to cause some damage, however slight (Diplock L.J. considers that actual damage is necessary in unintentional as distinct from intentional trespass to the person: [1965] 1 Q.B. at pp. 244–245. Lord Denning M.R. supports the view that a negligently inflicted injury is not trespass on the ground that if it were it would be actionable without proof of damage, " and that is not the law today ": *ibid.* at p. 240. But this assumes what it seeks to prove. (2) A master is liable in " case " for the trespass of his servant committed in the course of the employment (*post*, pp. 516–532) and it matters not that he is not also liable in trespass. (3) If *res ipsa loquitur* applies, the defendant is liable in negligence and again it matters not that he is not also liable in trespass. It is not easy to see why *res ipsa loquitur* did not avail the plaintiff in *Fowler* v. *Lanning*: see Glanville Williams [1959] C.L.J. 34–35. (4) It is difficult to believe that where in negligence the law denies a notional duty for reasons of policy that this policy could be evaded by an action in trespass. As for duty in fact, it is not surprising that the cases on trespass are not concerned with the issue since (a) the injury must be direct and (b) inevitable accident provides a defence. (5) The distinction between directness and foreseeability has to a large extent been " smudged " in cases subsequent to *The Wagon Mound* (*No. 1*) (see pp. 92–98, *post*). (6) It is true that a Canadian statute on contributory negligence was held not to apply to an action for trespass in *Hollebone* v. *Barnard* [1954] 2 D.L.R. 278. Yet the definition of " fault " in the English Law Reform (Contributory Negligence) Act 1945, s. 4 is, it is submitted, amply wide enough to include trespass (*cf.* the somewhat narrower formulation in s. 2 (1) of the Law Reform (Limitation of Actions) Act 1954, which has been held applicable to trespass). *Lane* v. *Holloway* [1968] 1 Q.B. 379 (C.A.) and *Gray* v. *Barr* [1971] 2 Q.B. 554 (C.A.) do not carry the contrary argument since they were concerned with intentional violence.

[98] The case of *Sadler* v. *South Staffs, etc., Tramways Co.* (1889) 23 Q.B.D. 17, which was not cited in either *Fowler* v. *Lanning* or *Letang* v. *Cooper*, may present a difficulty to the complete assimilation of trespass to the person and negligence but is best regarded as *sui generis*: *Phillips* v. *Britannia Hygienic Laundry Co. Ltd.* [1923] 1 K.B. 539.

CHAPTER 6

REMOTENESS OF DAMAGE AND CONTRIBUTORY NEGLIGENCE [1]

Remoteness of damage and measure of damages

Even if the plaintiff proves every other element in tortious liability, he will lose his action or, in the case of torts actionable *per se*, fail to recover more than nominal damages, if the harm which he has suffered is too remote a consequence of the defendant's conduct, or, as it is somewhat loosely said, if the damage is too remote. Remoteness of damage is thus concerned with the question whether damages may be recovered for particular items of the plaintiff's loss. As such it is logically distinct from and anterior to the question of measure of damages which is concerned with the calculation of the amount of pecuniary compensation which the defendant must pay in respect of those items of the plaintiff's loss which are not too remote.[1a] Measure of damages will therefore be dealt with at a later stage.[2]

REMOTENESS OF DAMAGE [3]

Causation in fact

To ask whether a given item of damage is too remote a consequence of a given breach of duty for the person in breach of duty to be liable for it is, essentially, to ask whether the breach of duty was, *as a matter of law*, a cause of the damage. Before one reaches the question of remoteness, therefore, it must be decided that the breach of duty was, *as a matter of fact*, a cause of the damage, and the burden of proving this rests with the plaintiff.[4] If he fails to prove on a balance of

---

[1] Weir, *Casebook on Tort*, 3rd ed., Chap. 4 and Chap. 5, Sect. 1.

[1a] *Bourhill* v. *Young* [1943] A.C. 92; *The Argentino* (1888) 13 P.D. 191, 196, *per* Lord Esher M.R. Slade and Wilson, "A Re-examination of Remoteness" (1952) 15 M.L.R. 458–459; Pollock, *Torts*, 15th ed. (1951), p. 23. *Cf.* Chapman, Book Review [1964] C.L.J. 136, 138. "Measure of damages" is sometimes used where remoteness is meant, *e.g.*, *The Wagon Mound* (*No. 2*) [1967] 1 A.C. 617, 638, *per* Lord Reid, but it must be admitted that the two questions sometimes run into one another. Thus it is doubtful whether in *The Daressa* [1971] 1 Lloyd's Rep. 60 the court was correct to consider the recovery of the plaintiffs' lost "operating subsidy" as a question of remoteness governed by the principle of foreseeability, since the measure of damages for loss of use of a profit-earning chattel is probably assessed without reference to whether the amount of the profit was foreseeable (see p. 582, *post*). The line between remoteness and measure of damages is peculiarly difficult to draw in a case like *Liesbosch Dredger* v. *Edison SS.* [1933] A.C. 448 (see *post*, pp. 101–102).

[2] *Post*, Chap. 27.

[3] See generally Hart and Honoré, *Causation in the Law* (1959); Glanville Williams, "Causation in the Law" [1961] C.L.J. 62; McGregor, *Damages*, 13th ed., Chap. 6.

[4] *Metropolitan Ry.* v. *Jackson* (1877) 3 App.Cas. 193; *Wakelin* v. *L. & S.W. Ry.* (1886) 12 App.Cas. 41; *Bonnington Castings Ltd.* v. *Wardlaw* [1956] A.C. 613; *Clarke* v. *E. R. Wright & Son* [1957] 1 W.L.R. 1191; *Curran* v. *William Neill & Son* (*St. Helens*) *Ltd.* [1961] 1 W.L.R. 1069.

probabilities [5] that the breach of duty was in fact one of the causes of his damage then his claim must fail. In *Barnett* v. *Chelsea and Kensington Hospital Management Committee* [6] three night-watchmen, one of whom was the plaintiff's husband, called early in the morning at the defendants' hospital and complained of vomiting after drinking tea. The nurse on duty consulted a doctor by telephone and he said that the men should go home and consult their own doctors later in the morning. Later the same day the plaintiff's husband died of arsenical poisoning and the coroner's verdict was one of murder. In failing to examine the deceased the doctor was guilty of a breach of his duty of care, but this breach was not a cause of the death because, even if the deceased had been examined and treated with proper care, the probability was that it would have been impossible to save his life. The plaintiff's claim therefore failed.

Although more than one approach to the question of factual causation is possible,[7] for the practical purposes of the law that most generally adopted is the so-called " but-for " test of causation. If the result would not have happened but for a certain event then that event is a cause.[8] On this test every result has an infinite number of causes and it is subject to the objection that it becomes "Adam-and-Eve " causation. " What is the use of defining cause so widely that it goes back to the primeval slime ? " [9] The answer is that the " but-for " test enables us to eliminate the irrelevant. Generally speaking the law is concerned to know whether a particular event—the defendant's breach of duty— was a cause of the plaintiff's damage. If that damage would have occurred even if the breach of duty had not occurred then the breach of duty is not a cause of the damage. In *The Empire Jamaica*,[1] a maritime

---

[5] See *Gardiner* v. *Motherwell Machinery and Scrap Co. Ltd.* [1961] 1 W.L.R. 1424 (H.L.Sc.). A finding that the defendants' breach of duty materially increased the risk of injury to the plaintiff may amount, for practical purposes, to a finding that the breach of duty materially contributed to the injury in the absence of positive proof to the contrary: *McGhee* v. *N.C.B.* [1973] 1 W.L.R. 1 (dermatitis; medical evidence only able to show that risk increased by defendants' breach of duty).

[6] [1969] 1 Q.B. 428; *Lampert* v. *Eastern National Omnibus Co.* [1954] 1 W.L.R. 1047; *Quinn* v. *Burch Bros. (Builders) Ltd.* [1966] 2 Q.B. 370, 393–394, *per* Salmon L.J.; *British Road Services Ltd.* v. *Arthur V. Crutchley & Co. Ltd.* [1968] 1 All E.R. 811. *Cf. Kelly* v. *W:R.N. Contracting Ltd.* [1968] 1 W.L.R. 921. *Cf. Schneider* v. *Eisovitch* [1960] 2 Q.B. 430 and *Malcolm* v. *Broadhurst* [1970] 3 All E.R. 508, in both of which cases the learned judges seem to have overlooked the necessity that the defendant's breach of duty—not some other act or omission of his—must have caused the plaintiff's damage.

[7] Hart and Honoré, *op. cit.*, Part I; Glanville Williams, *loc. cit.*, pp. 62–79.

[8] " Subject to the question of remoteness, causation is a question of fact. If the damage would not have happened but for a particular fault, then that fault is the cause of the damage; if it would have happened just the same, fault or no fault, the fault is not the cause of the damage. It is to be decided by the ordinary plain common sense of the business ": *Cork* v. *Kirby Maclean Ltd.* [1952] 2 All E.R. 402, 406–407, *per* Denning L.J.; *Macrae* v. *Swindells* [1954] 1 W.L.R. 597.

[9] Glanville Williams, *loc. cit.* at p. 64.

[1] [1957] A.C. 386; *Corn* v. *Weir's (Glass) Ltd.* [1960] 1 W.L.R. 577; *Performance Cars Ltd.* v. *Abraham* [1962] 2 Q.B. 33; *Smith* v. *Auckland Hospital Board* [1965] N.Z.L.R. 191 (patient consents to exploratory operation on incorrect advice of doctor that no risk involved. Operation carefully carried out but patient suffers harm. Sufficient probability that patient would not have consented to operation if correct advice had been given). See also *Brown* v. *Rolls-Royce Ltd.* [1960] 1 W.L.R. 210.

collision was caused by the negligence of the officer of the watch on board the ship of that name. Contrary to the provisions of relevant legislation the officer did not hold the necessary certificate of competence, and the question was whether this fact was a cause of the collision.[2] The evidence showed that the officer was in fact fully competent and that if application had been made for exemption from the requirements of the legislation this would have been granted. It followed that even if there had been no breach of those requirements the officer would still have been on watch at the time and the collision would still have occurred. There was, therefore, no causal connection between the breach and the collision.[3]

The application of the " but-for " test of causation involves a hypothetical inquiry and the test cannot be regarded as an infallible rule of thumb. Not everyone will always agree that the hypothetical absence of some factor would or would not have affected the final result. This can be illustrated by reference to actions brought by workmen against their employers on the ground of the employers' failure to provide some item of safety equipment. Is it a defence to such an action that even if the equipment had been provided the workman would not have used it? In one case [4] the Court of Appeal answered this question with a clear negative: " If a person is under a duty to provide safety-belts or other appliances and fails to do so, he cannot be heard to say: ' Even if I had done so, they would not have been worn.' " [5] Subsequently, however, the House of Lords has reiterated the need for the plaintiff to prove causation [6] and this dictum is no longer correct. " The judge *may* infer the omission to be a cause, but he is not bound to do so. If, at the end of the day, he thinks that, whether the duty was omitted or fulfilled, the result would have been the same, he is at liberty to say so." [7]

In *Cutler* v. *Vauxhall Motors Ltd.*[8] the plaintiff grazed his right ankle in an accident for which the defendants were responsible. A few months later a condition of varicosity which had existed since before the accident was discovered in both the plaintiff's legs and, because of an ulcer set up by the graze, it was decided to operate at once to deal with this condition. The operation caused the plaintiff to suffer some pain and also to lose earnings amounting to £173. He was, of course, entitled to damages for the graze, but the trial judge

---

[2] The question arose because the shipowners sought to limit their liability under s. 503 of the Merchant Shipping Act 1894.

[3] See the discussion of this case by Glanville Williams, *loc. cit.*, pp. 73–75.

[4] *Roberts* v. *Dorman Long & Co. Ltd.* [1953] 1 W.L.R. 942.

[5] *Ibid.* at p. 946, *per* Lord Goddard C.J. See also *ibid.* at p. 951, *per* Hodson L.J.

[6] *Bonnington Castings Ltd.* v. *Wardlaw* [1956] A.C. 613.

[7] *Qualcast (Wolverhampton) Ltd.* v. *Haynes* [1959] A.C. 743, 762, *per* Lord Denning; *Nolan* v. *Dental Manufacturing Co.* [1958] 1 W.L.R. 936; *Wigley* v. *British Vinegars Ltd.* [1964] A.C. 307; *McWilliams* v. *Sir William Arrol & Co. Ltd.* [1962] 1 W.L.R. 295 (H.L.Sc.); *James* v. *Hepworth & Grandage Ltd.* [1968] 1 Q.B. 94. Weir, *Casebook on Tort*, 3rd ed., p. 160.

[8] [1971] 1 Q.B. 418; *Zumeris* v. *Testa* [1972] V.R. 839.

and the majority of the Court of Appeal held that he was entitled to nothing in respect of the losses due to the operation because the condition of varicosity was unconnected with the accident and was such that it would have required operative treatment within four or five years. Russell L.J. dissented on the ground that the losses due to the operation had *certainly* been suffered by the plaintiff whereas the future need to operate had there been no accident was a *probability*, not a certainty. He therefore thought it appropriate that the defendants should be held liable for a proportion of those losses. Russell L.J.'s view of the facts seems the more accurate, but, accepting the majority view, the decision is a correct, if somewhat hard, application of the " but-for " test. Even if the accident had not occurred the plaintiff would have sustained the losses due to the operation and so the defendants' breach of duty did not cause them; on the contrary, their sole cause was the plaintiff's pre-accident condition of varicosity. It may happen, however, that there are two breaches of duty, either one of which alone would have been sufficient to cause the plaintiff's damage, and then the " but-for " test is inadequate for it gives the result that neither is a cause. Where two such breaches of duty occur simultaneously, no particular problem is generally thought to arise and both tortfeasors are held fully liable for the loss.[9] But where one follows the other then the difficulties are greater for the question is no longer simply that of deciding whether one or the other breach of duty is a cause of the plaintiff's loss; the court has to decide the extent to which each tortfeasor is liable for the end result.

In *Baker* v. *Willoughby*,[10] as a result of the defendant's negligence, the plaintiff suffered an injury to his left leg and, taking both past and future losses into account the judge assessed his damages, on a basis of full liability,[11] at £1,600. Before the trial, however, and while the plaintiff was working at the new job he had taken up after his accident, he was the victim of an armed robbery in the course of which he suffered gunshot wounds to his left leg of such severity that the leg had to be amputated. The defendant therefore argued that his liability was limited to the loss suffered before the date of the robbery; all loss suffered thereafter was merged in and flowed from the robbery. On a strict application of the " but-for " test this argument was correct and it succeeded in the Court of Appeal. But, as Lord Pearson observed in the House of Lords, the argument, though formidable, must not be allowed to succeed because it produced manifest injustice.[12] The

---

[9] Glanville Williams, *loc. cit.*, at pp. 75–77. For contribution between tortfeasors, see *post*, pp. 548–551.

[10] [1970] A.C. 467. For the judgment of Donaldson J. which was restored by the House of Lords, see [1969] 1 Q.B. 38. McGregor, " Successive Causes of Personal Injury " (1970) 33 M.L.R. 378; Strachan, " The Scope and Application of the ' But For ' Causal Test," *ibid.* 386; Goodhart (1970) 86 L.Q.R. 291; Cohn, *ibid.* 449.

[11] The plaintiff was guilty of contributory negligence assessed at 25 per cent.

[12] [1970] A.C. at p. 495. Note that it is not wholly true that the plaintiff would have lost his leg even if he had not suffered the accident for which the defendant was responsible because he had had to change his employment as a result of his original injury. But it

extent of the plaintiff's disability was not reduced by the supervening event of the robbery [13] and, even if they could have been successfully sued to fruitful judgment, the robbers would have been liable only for depriving the plaintiff of an already damaged leg.[14] The only way to avoid the unacceptable result that even in theory the plaintiff would not be entitled to recover the whole of his loss in such a case is to hold that the first tortfeasor remains liable for so much of the plaintiff's loss as would have been suffered even if the second tort had never taken place, and to hold that the second tortfeasor is liable to the extent that he has increased the plaintiff's loss.[15] The subsequent loss by the plaintiff of his leg therefore had no effect on the defendant's liability to him.

The " but-for " test must not, therefore, be regarded as a rule of thumb for determining causation in fact in every case.[16] Indeed, causation in fact can hardly be dealt with as a matter of general legal principle for too much depends upon the circumstances and probabilities of each case. The only thing that can be said with confidence and generality is that the plaintiff must prove on a balance of probabilities that the defendant's breach of duty was a cause of his damage. It is on the assumption that this is so that the ensuing discussion of remoteness of damage proceeds.

Remoteness

Theoretically the consequences of any conduct may be endless, but no defendant is responsible _ad infinitum_ for all the consequences of his wrongful conduct, however remote in time and however indirect the process of causation, for otherwise human activity would be unreasonably hampered.[17] The law must draw a line somewhere, it

---

could not be contended that the defendant's negligence had caused him to be shot: _Carslogie Steamship Co. Ltd._ v. _Royal Norwegian Government_ [1952] A.C. 292, _post_, p. 103.

[13] Plaintiff's counsel conceded that if this had been the case the damages to which the plaintiff would otherwise have been entitled would have fallen to be reduced; _e.g._, if the first injury had resulted in shock and loss of sight, the second in shock and restoration of sight: [1970] A.C. at p. 484.

[14] _Performance Cars Ltd._ v. _Abraham_ [1962] 1 Q.B. 33; _Baker_ v. _Willoughby_ [1970] A.C. at p. 493, _per_ Lord Reid; _ibid._ at p. 495, _per_ Lord Pearson. An argument that the robbers would in theory be liable for the whole of the plaintiff's loss because they had deprived him of his right of action against the defendant was rejected ([1970] A.C. at p. 496, _per_ Lord Pearson). In any case, to have held that the plaintiff had a complete remedy against the robbers would have brought him little comfort.

[15] Cases in which the first tortfeasor's breach of duty would have caused no damage at all if the second breach of duty had not occurred raise different problems and are discussed below, pp. 103–105. In such cases both breaches of duty satisfy the " but-for " test of causation.

[16] For discussion of other complex situations, see McGregor and Strachan, _loc. cit._, and authorities there cited.

[17] A Frenchman, in celebrating the restoration of Alsace to France in 1919, fired a revolver which burst and injured him. His claim that his injuries were due to the outbreak of war in 1914 was rejected by the Metz Pensions Board as too remote: _The Times_, February 6, 1933. For Continental law see Hart & Honoré, _op. cit._, Part III. Social security law may be concerned with issues which are very similar to remoteness of damage: for example, where industrial injury benefit is payable in respect of an accident " arising out of and in the course of employment."

cannot take account of everything that follows a wrongful act, some consequences must be abstracted as relevant not on grounds of pure logic, but simply for practical reasons.[18] Bacon's rendering of the maxim *in jure non remota causa sed proxima spectatur* has often been cited. " It were infinite for the law to consider the causes of causes, and their impulsions one of another: therefore it contenteth itself with the immediate cause, and judgeth of acts by that without looking to any further degree." [19] Of course this does not tell us what is an " immediate " cause, and we shall see that the common law has probed the matter more deeply than the maxim does. But any student who expects a scientific analysis of causation will be grievously disappointed. Up to a certain point the common law does touch upon metaphysics. But no test of remoteness of causation put forward by Anglo-American courts would satisfy any metaphysician. On the other hand, no test suggested by metaphysicians would be of any practical use to lawyers. " Causation is to be understood as the man in the street, and not as either the scientist or the metaphysician would understand it." [20] " The choice of the real or efficient cause from out of the whole complex of the facts must be made by applying common sense standards." [21] The rather unscientific way in which lawyers are apt to approach the problem is shown in their use of metaphors about causation, such as chains, rivers, transmission gears, conduit pipes, nets, insulators,[22] or phrases expressive of it, such as " *causa causans* and *causa sine qua non*," " direct cause and intervening cause," " effective cause and ineffective cause," " *nova causa interveniens* "; but all these merely conceal the puzzle and do not solve it. In fact, neither metaphor nor catchword will release judges from the effort or agony of deciding each case on its merits with such help as they can get from some very general principles. This may not be systematic, but what is often forgotten by critics is that the judges would do no better if they tried to be more exact. For, as Lord Sumner said, " The object of a civil inquiry into cause and consequence is to fix liability on some responsible person and to give reparation for damage done. . . . The trial of an action for damage is not a scientific inquest into a mixed sequence of phenomena, or

---

[18] *Liesbosch Dredger* v. *Edison SS.* [1933] A.C. 449, 460, *per* Lord Wright.

[19] *Maxims of the Law* (1630), Reg. 1. For other views of Bacon's meaning, see Beale in *Selected Essays in the Law of Torts* (1924), pp. 730 *et seq.*, and McLaughlin in (1925–26) 39 Harv.L.R. 156, n. 30; and for some criticisms of Bacon, see Jeremiah Smith, *ibid.* 652–654.

[20] *Yorkshire Dale Steamship Co. Ltd.* v. *Minister of War Transport* [1942] A.C. 691, 706, *per* Lord Wright.

[21] *Ibid.* 706. In *S.C.M. (United Kingdom) Ltd.* v. *Whittall and Son Ltd.* [1971] 1 Q.B. 337 (*ante*, p. 52), where the plaintiffs' economic loss was held to be irrecoverable for policy reasons, Lord Denning M.R. based his decision on the legal ground that the plaintiffs' damage was too remote, not that the defendants owed no duty of care.

[22] Goodhart, *Essays in Jurisprudence*, p. 131, n. 8.

an historical investigation of the chapter of events. . . . It is a practical inquiry." [24]

Such principles as we have are no earlier than the nineteenth century.[25] Until then no one seems to have made use of Bacon's maxim,[26] and the courts either took refuge in scraps of scholastic logic about *causa causans* and *causa causata*,[27] or indulged in the mistiest generalities, such as, " he that does the first wrong shall answer for all consequential damages," [28] or " the damages must be the legal and natural consequence " [29] of the wrongful act. Then the phrase " natural and proximate consequence " creeps in.[30] " Proximate " was a misplaced adjective, for it suggested that the event which occurs immediately before the harm suffered by the plaintiff is always to be selected by the law as the determinant cause of that harm. But that is not necessarily so. If A throws a lighted squib into a crowd and it falls upon B who, in alarm, at once throws it away and it falls upon C, who does the like, and the squib ends its journey by falling upon D, exploding and putting out his eye, here A's act is held to be the proximate cause of the damage, though in fact it was the act farthest from the damage, not the one nearest to it.[31]

Since 1850 two competing views of the test of remoteness of consequence have been current in the law.[32] According to the first, *consequences are too remote if a reasonable man would not have foreseen them* [33]; according to the second, if a reasonable man would have foreseen any damage to the plaintiff as likely to result from his act, then *he is liable for all the direct consequences of it suffered by the plaintiff, whether a reasonable man would have foreseen them or not*. To put the second view another way, reasonable foresight is relevant to the question, " Was there any legal duty owed by the defendant to the plaintiff to take care ?" It is irrelevant to the question, " If the defendant broke a legal duty, was the consequence of this breach too remote ?" What ought to have been reasonably contemplated " goes to culpability, not to compensation." [34]

In 1921, in the case known as *Re Polemis*,[35] the Court of Appeal

[24] *Weld-Blundell* v. *Stephens* [1920] A.C. at p. 986. See, too, Goddard L.J. in *Duncan* v. *Cammell, Laird Ltd.* (1944) 171 L.T. 186, 199, quoting Lord Wright in *Liesbosch Dredger* v. *Edison SS.* [1933] A.C. 449, 460.

[25] Two important American studies on the topic are in *Selected Essays on the Law of Torts* (1924), pp. 649–730 (Jeremiah Smith), pp. 730–755 (Joseph H. Beale).

[26] Beale, *op. cit.*, p. 732.

[27] *Earl of Shrewsbury's Case* (1610) 9 Rep. 46, 50b.

[28] *Roswell* v. *Prior* (1700) 12 Mod. 636, 639; *Scott* v. *Shepherd* (1773) 2 W.Bl. 892, 898, 899.

[29] *Vicars* v. *Wilcocks* (1806) 8 East 1, 3.

[30] *e.g.*, *Ward* v. *Weeks* (1830) 7 Bing. 211, 212.

[31] *Scott* v. *Shepherd* (1773) 2 W.Bl. 892.

[32] Both have been described by a great variety of phrases and in *H.M.S. London* [1914] P. 72, 77–78, Evans P. collected eight specimens. See Lord Sumner's criticism of some of them in *Weld-Blundell* v. *Stephens* [1920] A.C. 956, 983–984.

[33] First propounded by Pollock C.B. in *Rigby* v. *Hewitt* (1850) 5 Ex. 240, 243; *Greenland* v. *Chaplin* (1850) 5 Ex. 243, 248.

[34] *Weld-Blundell* v. *Stephens, supra,* at p. 984, *per* Lord Sumner.

[35] *Re Polemis and Furness, Withy & Co. Ltd.* [1921] 3 K.B. 560. Weir, *Casebook on Tort*, 3rd ed., p. 163.

apparently settled English law in favour of the second rule. In 1961, however, in the case known as *The Wagon Mound* [36] on appeal from New South Wales, the Judicial Committee of the Privy Council roundly declared *Re Polemis* to be wrong and decided the case before it on the basis of the first rule. As a decision of the Privy Council, *The Wagon Mound* is not formally binding on any English court, but, as we shall see, the reception given to it here has been such that it would be idle to contend before an English court today that it does not represent the law. Nevertheless we must begin with some account of *Re Polemis* and of the second rule, if only because the developments since *The Wagon Mound* have to a great extent blunted its original impact and in some respects have produced results very similar to those which would have been achieved by the application of the *Re Polemis* principle.

Re Polemis. In *Re Polemis* [38] a ship was hired under a charter which excepted both the shipowner and the charterers from liability for fire. Among other cargo the charterers loaded a quantity of benzine in tins. During the voyage the tins leaked and thus there was a good deal of vapour in the hold. At a port of call stevedores, who were the servants of the charterers, negligently let a plank drop into the hold while they were shifting the cargo. A rush of flames at once followed and the ship was totally destroyed. The charterers were held liable for the loss— nearly £200,000. The fire exception clause did not help them, because there was no express statement that it covered negligence on the part of servants. And, as the fall of the plank was due to servants for whom they were responsible, the charterers were liable for all direct consequences of the negligence, even though they could not have been reasonably anticipated. None of the court except Scrutton L.J. defined " direct " consequence. He said that damage is indirect if it is " due to the operation of independent causes having no connection with the negligent act, except that they could not avoid its results." [39]

In *Re Polemis* itself, as well as in the earlier case of *Smith* v. *L. & S.W. Ry.*,[40] there are passages which seem to suggest that once an act has been found to be negligent in the sense that injury to someone is foreseeable, then any person directly injured by it can recover even though it is unforeseeable that *he* might suffer damage in any way. This, however, would clearly conflict with the basic principle that before liability in negligence can exist there must be a breach of a duty owed to the plaintiff.[41] The question of the defendant's initial liability, *i.e.*, has he committed a tort against the plaintiff, must be distinguished from the secondary question of remoteness of damage, *i.e.*, for what conse-

---

[36] *Overseas Tankship (U.K.) Ltd.* v. *Morts Dock & Engineering Co. Ltd.* (*The Wagon Mound*) [1961] A.C. 388. Weir, *Casebook on Tort*, 3rd ed., p. 165.
[38] [1921] 3 K.B. 560. For report in court below, see 26 Com.Cas. 281: for pleadings, see (1931) 4 C.L.J. 125–145.
[39] [1921] 3 K.B. at p. 577.
[40] (1870) L.R. 6 C.P. 14.
[41] *Ante*, pp. 59–60.

quences of the defendant's conduct is the plaintiff entitled to recover compensation.[42] If it was not reasonably foreseeable that the defendant's act or omission would lead to any damage to the plaintiff,[43] then there is no initial liability.[44] In *Re Polemis* it was foreseeable that the dropping of the plank would cause some damage to the ship and the initial breach of duty was thus established. The case is no authority for liability to the " unforeseeable plaintiff."

Re Polemis never attracted the detailed consideration of the House of Lords, though in *Liesbosch Dredger* v. *S.S. Edison*[45] that court restricted its operation to the immediate physical consequences of the negligent act.[46] In subsequent years some distinguished members of the Court of Appeal stated the rule of remoteness in phrases which, if consistent with *Re Polemis*, were not coincident with the rule laid down there,[47] but in *Thurogood* v. *Van den Berghs and Jurgens*[48] the Court of Appeal unanimously affirmed the binding character of the *Re Polemis* principle.[49]

The Wagon Mound. After *Thurogood's* case, *Re Polemis* was expressly applied on more than one occasion,[56] and it might have been thought that it had been restored to favour. In *The Wagon Mound*,[57] however, the Judicial Committee of the Privy Council, through Viscount Simonds, expressed its unqualified disapproval of *Re Polemis* and refused to follow it. Viscount Simonds also criticised Lord Sumner's dictum that foreseeability " goes to culpability not to compensation "[58] as having

---

[42] " A failure to observe the distinction between the cause of action and the measure of damages has led to confusion in the attacks of some lawyers who have criticised in general terms the authority of *Re Polemis* ": Lord Wright, " *Re Polemis* " (1951) 14 M.L.R. 393, 399. See also *Thurogood* v. *Van den Berghs & Jurgens Ltd.* [1951] 2 K.B. 537, 555, per Asquith L.J.

[43] Or, perhaps, to the particular interest of the plaintiff actually affected. It would not have assisted the pursuer in *Bourhill* v. *Young* [1943] A.C. 92 if she had, by chance, been the owner of the vehicle with which the motor-cyclist collided. See Street, *Torts*, 2nd ed., pp. 113 and 146 and authorities there cited.

[44] For criticism of the distinction between initial liability and remoteness of damage, see *The Wagon Mound* [1961] A.C. at p. 425. Goodhart, " Liability and Compensation " (1960) 76 L.Q.R. 567.

[45] [1933] A.C. 448. See the observations of Viscount Simonds on this case: *The Wagon Mound* [1961] A.C. 388, 423–424.

[46] See *post*, pp. 101–102.

[47] Greer L.J. even equated the rule as to remoteness in tort with what is known as the first rule in *Hadley* v. *Baxendale* (1854) 9 Ex. 341, 354, governing remoteness in contract: *The Edison* [1932] P. 52, 70–71 (see further the 9th ed. of this work, p. 93). The House of Lords has now categorically stated that the rules in contract and tort are different: *C. Czarnikow Ltd.* v. *Koufos* [1961] 1 A.C. 350. But see Hamson, " Contract and Tort: Measure of Damages " [1968] C.L.J. 14.

[48] [1951] 2 K.B. 537, 555.

[49] *Ibid.* at p. 552, per Asquith L.J.: " The actual damage may be wholly different in character, magnitude or in the detailed manner of its incidence, from anything which could reasonably have been anticipated." As to this case, see further Goodhart, " The Imaginary Necktie and the Rule in *Re Polemis* " (1952) 68 L.Q.R. 514; Glanville Williams, " Causation in the Law " [1961] C.L.J. 62, 71.

[56] *Pigney* v. *Pointer's Transport Services Ltd.* [1957] 1 W.L.R. 1121; *Schneider* v. *Eisovitch* [1960] 2 Q.B. 430.

[57] *Overseas Tankship (U.K.) Ltd.* v. *Morts Dock & Engineering Co. Ltd. (The Wagon Mound)* [1961] A.C. 388. Weir, *Casebook on Tort*, 3rd ed., p. 165.

[58] In *Weld-Blundell* v. *Stephens* [1920] A.C. at p. 984.

" perpetuated an error which has introduced much confusion into the law," [59] and said that this proposition is " fundamentally false." [60]

The facts of The Wagon Mound may be summarised as follows: O. T. Ltd. were charterers by demise of The Wagon Mound, an oil-burning vessel which was moored at the C. Oil Co.'s wharf in Sydney harbour for the purpose of taking on fuel oil. Owing to the carelessness of O. T. Ltd.'s servants a large quantity of fuel oil was spilt on to the water, and after a few hours this had spread to M. D. Ltd.'s wharf about 600 ft. away, where another ship, the Corrimal, was under repair. Welding operations were being carried out on the Corrimal, but when M. D. Ltd.'s manager became aware of the presence of the oil he stopped the welding operations and inquired of the C. Oil Co. whether they might safely be continued. The result of this inquiry, coupled with his own belief as to the non-inflammability of fuel oil in the open, led him to give instructions for the welding operations to continue, though with all precautions to prevent inflammable material from falling into the oil. Two days later the oil caught fire and extensive damage was done to M. D. Ltd.'s wharf.

Two findings of fact are important: (a) It was unforeseeable that fuel oil spread on water would catch fire [61]; (b) some foreseeable damage was caused to M.D. Ltd.'s wharf from the spillage of the oil in that the oil had got onto the slipways and interfered with their use. The case was dealt with, therefore, on the footing that there was a breach of duty and direct damage, but that the damage caused was unforeseeable. At the trial and on appeal to the Full Court of the Supreme Court of New South Wales it was held, following Re Polemis, that O.T. Ltd. were liable,[62] but the Privy Council reversed their decision [63] and held that Re Polemis should no longer be regarded as good law. " It is the foresight of the reasonable man which alone can determine responsibility. The Polemis rule by substituting ' direct ' for ' reasonably foreseeable ' consequence leads to a conclusion equally illogical and unjust." [63a]

Notwithstanding the fact that Re Polemis is a decision of the Court

---

[59] [1961] A.C. at p. 417.

[60] Ibid. at p. 425. Cf. Alston v. Marine & Trade Insurance Co. Ltd., 1964 (4) S.A. 112, 115, per Hiemstra J. (Witwatersrand Local Div. of S.C. of S.A.).

[61] This finding was reached after the learned judge had heard expert evidence on the matter, but this evidence, it is submitted, should not have influenced him. What was in issue was the foresight of the reasonable man in the position of O.T. Ltd., or rather of its servants. What " a distinguished scientist " could have foreseen was irrelevant. In Overseas Tankship (U.K.) Ltd. v. Miller Steamship Co. Pty. Ltd. (The Wagon Mound (No. 2)) [1967] A.C. 617, an action by the owners of the Corrimal for damage caused to their ship by the same fire, the Privy Council, on somewhat different evidence, held that the damage was foreseeable. See post, p. 98.

[62] For the proceedings before Kinsella J., see [1958] 1 Lloyd's Rep. 775 and for those before the Full Court, see [1959] 2 Lloyd's Rep. 692.

[63] So far as the cause of action in negligence was concerned; the action was remitted to the Full Court on the issue of nuisance, but was not proceeded with. In The Wagon Mound (No. 2), supra, the Privy Council held that the test of reasonable foreseeability applies also to a cause of action in nuisance. See post, pp. 98, 321.

[63a] [1961] A.C. at p. 424.

of Appeal and was clearly affirmed by the same court in 1951 in
Thurogood's case, most writers seem to have accepted *The Wagon
Mound* as decisive of English law.[64] More significantly, in every case
since *The Wagon Mound*, English judges seem to have side-stepped
the point of precedent and to have accepted the Privy Council's
decision as law even though in no case so far has it been strictly necessary for them to choose between the two decisions.[65] In *Hughes* v.
Lord Advocate,[66] though *The Wagon Mound* was barely mentioned
by their Lordships and *Re Polemis* not at all, the speeches in the House
of Lords are more consistent with the former than with the latter case,
and Lord Reid has stated more than once that *The Wagon Mound*
represents the law.[67] It is, therefore, extremely unlikely that the rule in
Re Polemis will ever be resurrected under its own name. It may be,
however, that when the disturbance created by the Privy Council's
decision has finally subsided, the end-result will be found to be little
different from what went before.

The essence of the decision is that in negligence foreseeability is
the criterion not only for the existence of a duty of care but also for
remoteness of damage, and the Privy Council clearly attached importance to the supposed illogicality of using different tests at different stages of the inquiry in any given case. " If some limitation must
be imposed upon the consequences for which the negligent actor is
to be held responsible—and all are agreed that some limitation there
must be—why should that test (reasonable foreseeability) be rejected
which, since he is judged by what the reasonable man ought to foresee,
corresponds with the common conscience of mankind, and a test (the
' direct ' consequence) be substituted which leads to nowhere but the
never-ending and insoluble problems of causation." [68] It might have been
thought from this that the effect of *The Wagon Mound* was restricted
to actions for negligence, or at least to cases in which foreseeability

---

[64] *e.g.* Goodhart, " Obituary: *Re Polemis* " (1961) 77 L.Q.R. 175; Glanville Williams,
" The Risk Principle " (1961) 77 L.Q.R. 179; Fridman, " Negligence and Remoteness "
(1961) 111 L.J. 609, 624 (where it is said to be justifiable to treat *The Wagon Mound* as if
it were a decision of the House of Lords); McGregor, *Damages*, 13th ed., p. 71, n. 28.
Cf. Street, *Torts*, 5th ed., p. 141; James, " Polemis: The Serpent in Eden " [1961] J.B.L.
252. For a full list of articles in which *The Wagon Mound* is discussed, see Dias, " Remoteness of Liability and Legal Policy " [1962] C.L.J. 178, n. 2: " Trouble on Oiled Waters:
Problems of *The Wagon Mound* (*No.* 2) " [1967] C.L.J. 62, 63, n. 4.
[65] *Smith* v. *Leech Brain & Co. Ltd.* [1962] 2 Q.B. 405, 415, *per* Lord Parker C.J.; *Stevens*
v. *Bermondsey & Southwark Group Hospital Management Committee* (1963) 107 S.J. 478,
per Paull J.; *Doughty* v. *Turner Manufacturing Co. Ltd.* [1964] 1 Q.B. 518, 525, *per* Lord
Pearce; 528, *per* Harman L.J. (whether or not *The Wagon Mound* is binding, " we ought
to treat it as the law "); 532, *per* Diplock L.J. (*Re Polemis* " is no longer law "); *Stewart*
v. *West African Terminals Ltd.* [1964] 2 Lloyd's Rep. 371; *Bradford* v. *Robinson Rentals
Ltd.* [1967] 1 W.L.R. 337; *Cook* v. *Swinfen* [1967] 1 W.L.R. 457, 461, *per* Lord Denning
M.R.; *Tremain* v. *Pike* [1969] 1 W.L.R. 1556; *Wieland* v. *Cyril Lord Carpets Ltd.* [1969]
3 All E.R. 1006; *Malcolm* v. *Broadhurst* [1970] 3 All E.R. 508; *Draper* v. *Hodder* [1972]
2 Q.B. 556; *Robinson* v. *The Post Office* [1974] 2 All E.R. 737.
[66] [1963] A.C. 837.
[67] *The Wagon Mound* (*No.* 2) [1967] A.C. 617, 636; *Home Office* v. *Dorset Yacht Co.
Ltd.* [1970] A.C. 1004, 1027. See also *C. Czarnikow Ltd.* v. *Koufos* [1969] A.C. 350, 385–386,
390, *per* Lord Reid; *ibid.* at p. 422, *per* Lord Upjohn.
[68] *The Wagon Mound* [1961] A.C. 388, 423, *per* Viscount Simonds.

of damage is relevant to liability.[69] In *The Wagon Mound (No.* 2),[70] however, the Privy Council held that foreseeability is the test for remoteness of damage in cases of nuisance also, and, though they pointed out that liability in many cases of nuisance depends on fault and thus on foreseeability, they stated that the same test must apply even where this is not so. There now seems every likelihood that foreseeability will be held to be the test of remoteness in other torts as well, whether or not it is the test of liability.[70a]

On this basis it follows that " the foresight of the reasonable man " may have acquired a new and different meaning. If a man may be liable notwithstanding that he neither could nor should have foreseen any harmful consequences of his act whatever, it is meaningless to say that the extent of his liability is limited to what he ought reasonably to have foreseen. In *Galashiels Gas Co. Ltd.* v. *O'Donnell,*[71] for example, the defendants had a lift at their gas works and the lift, so far as anyone could discover, was in perfect condition both before and after the accident. Nevertheless, on a single isolated occasion something went wrong for reasons no one could ascertain and as a result the plaintiff's husband was killed. The defendants were held liable for breach of an absolute statutory duty,[72] but how can it realistically be said that they could have foreseen the death of the deceased? What can be said—and this seems now to be the meaning of " reasonably foreseeable " when remoteness is in issue—is that a reasonable man, told of the way in which the lift went wrong, would not be surprised to learn that the deceased had been killed. The test for liability in a case of negligence is the foresight of the reasonable man in the position of the defendant when he is doing or is about to do the act alleged to constitute the breach of duty. If foresight is the test for remoteness, however, it can only be the foresight of the reasonable man in the position of the defendant when the act constituting the breach of duty has been done.[73]

" Reasonable foresight " as the test for remoteness of damage is thus not quite the same as " reasonable foresight " as the test for the

[69] Their Lordships expressly reserved the question of remoteness of damage under " the so-called rule of ' strict liability ' exemplified in *Rylands* v. *Fletcher* " ((1868) L.R. 3 H.L. 330, *post*, pp. 358–382).

[70] [1967] A.C. 617. See Dias, "Trouble on Oiled Waters: Problems of *The Wagon Mound (No.* 2) " [1967] C.L.J. 62.

[70a] But it has been said that a plaintiff in an action for deceit may recover even for unforeseeable damage: *Doyle* v. *Olby (Ironmongers)* [1969] 2 Q.B. 158, 167, *per* Lord Denning M.R.

[71] [1949] A.C. 275.

[72] Factories Act 1937, s. 22 (1), now Factories Act 1961, s. 22 (1).

[73] See Dias, *loc. cit.* at pp. 68, 77–82. *Cf. Millard* v. *Serck Tubes Ltd.* [1969] 1 W.L.R. 211, where the Court of Appeal held that once a part of machinery is found to be " dangerous " within s. 14 (1) of the Factories Act 1961, which means that it is a *foreseeable* cause of injury, and it is unfenced in breach of the section, it matters not that the plaintiff's injury occurred in an unforeseeable way, so long as the injury would not have occurred if the duty to fence had been fulfilled. The judgments, which refer to no decisions on remoteness of damage, provide admirable, if unintentional, examples of the operation of the rule in *Re Polemis* at its most straightforward.

existence of a duty of care, and it is still further qualified by the fact that neither the precise extent of the damage nor the precise manner of its infliction need be foreseeable. So much, indeed, has been expressly stated by Lord Denning M.R.: " It is not necessary that the precise concatenation of circumstances should be envisaged. If the consequence was one which was within the general range which any reasonable person might foresee (and was not of an entirely different kind which no one would anticipate) then it is within the rule that a person who has been guilty of negligence is liable for the consequences." [74] In *Hughes* v. *Lord Advocate* [75] employees of the Post Office opened a manhole in the street and in the evening left the open manhole covered by a canvas shelter, unattended and surrounded by warning paraffin lamps. The plaintiff, a boy aged eight, took one of the lamps into the shelter and was playing with it there when he stumbled over it and it fell into the manhole. A violent explosion followed and the plaintiff himself fell into the hole, sustaining terrible injuries from burns. It was quite unpredictable that a lamp might explode, but the Post Office men were in breach of duty in leaving the manhole unattended because they should have appreciated that boys might take a lamp into the shelter and that, if the lamp fell and broke, they might suffer serious injury from burning. So the lamp, a known source of danger, caused injury through an unforeseeable sequence of events, but the defendants were nevertheless held liable.

On facts such as these, therefore, the rejection of *Re Polemis* has made no difference so far as the actual result is concerned. *The Wagon Mound* does, however, introduce the requirement that the foreseeable damage must be of the same " kind " as the damage which actually occurred. In point of fact even under *Re Polemis* it was probably necessary to distinguish between three very broad " kinds " of damage, namely injury to the person, damage to property and pure financial loss,[76] but *The Wagon Mound* certainly demands a more elaborate classification of " kinds " of damage than that: in the case itself damage to the plaintiffs' wharf was foreseeable and damage to the plaintiffs' wharf occurred. It follows that, in the Privy Council's judgment, a distinction must be taken between damage by fouling, which was foreseeable, and damage by fire, which occurred. The difficulty is to know how narrowly the kind of damage in question in any given case must be defined. In *Tremain* v.

---

[74] *Stewart* v. *West African Terminals Ltd.* [1964] 2 Lloyd's Rep. 371, 375; *Bradford* v. *Robinson Rentals Ltd.* [1967] 1 W.L.R. 337, 344–345, *per* Rees J. See also *Donaghey* v. *Boulton & Paul Ltd.* [1968] A.C. 1, dealing with liability for breach of statutory duty.

[75] [1963] A.C. 837. Weir, *Casebook on Tort*, 3rd ed., p. 174. *Cf. Doughty* v. *Turner Manufacturing Co. Ltd.* [1964] 1 Q.B. 518 and see the discussion of this case in Clerk & Lindsell, *Torts*, 13th ed., pp. 214–215.

[76] This is based on the " interest theory " which, though not the subject of any judicial decision, has the support of Lord Wright: *Bourhill* v. *Young* [1943] A.C. 92, 110; " *Re Polemis* " (1951) 14 M.L.R. 393, 400; Payne, " Direct Consequences of a Negligent Act " (1952) 5 *Current Legal Problems* 188; " Negligence and Interest," a Comment (1955) 18 M.L.R. 43; Machin, " Negligence and Interest " (1954) 17 M.L.R. 405.

Pike [77] the rat population on the defendant's farm was allowed to become unduly large and the plaintiff, a herdsman on the farm, contracted leptospirosis, otherwise known as Weil's disease, in consequence. Even on the assumption that the defendants had been negligent in failing to control the rat population,[78] Payne J. held that the plaintiff could not succeed. Weil's disease is extremely rare and is caused by contact with rats' urine, and in the learned judge's opinion it was therefore both unforeseeable and " entirely different in kind " from such foreseeable consequences as the effects of a rat-bite or food poisoning from contaminated food: the plaintiff could not simply say that rat-induced disease was foreseeable and rat-induced disease occurred.[79]

If *Tremain* v. *Pike* is rightly decided then a fairly high degree of precision in classifying kinds of damage is required.[80] It is respectfully suggested, however, that the case is out of line with the general trend of decisions since *The Wagon Mound*. Apart from the tendency in some cases to give a broad definition of foreseeable consequences,[81] it is clear that two other principles have survived *The Wagon Mound*: the so-called " egg-shell skull " rule [82] and the principle that the defendant is not relieved of liability because the damage was more extensive than might have been foreseen.[83] Furthermore, the House of Lords, in emphasising the difference between the rules of remoteness in contract and in tort has given to the word " foreseeable " a meaning which is far removed from " probable " or " likely." The rule in tort, Lord Reid has said, imposes a much wider liability than that in contract; " the defendant will be liable for any type of damage which is reasonably foreseeable as liable to happen *even in the most unusual case*, unless the risk is so small that a reasonable man would in the whole circumstances feel justified in neglecting it." [84]

As this passage indicates, foreseeability is a relative, not an absolute, concept. In *The Wagon Mound* the Privy Council accepted and based its reasoning on the trial judge's finding that the defendant did not know and could not reasonably be expected to have known that furnace oil was capable of being set afire when spread on water.[85] In *The Wagon*

---

[77] [1969] 1 W.L.R. 1556; (1970) 86 L.Q.R. 151. *Cf. Bradford* v. *Robinson Rentals Ltd.* [1967] 1 W.L.R. 337; *Malcolm* v. *Broadhurst* [1970] 3 All E.R. 508.

[78] The defendant's negligence in this respect was not actually made out.

[79] His Lordship's suggested method of avoiding the question about what is meant by difference in kind by asking instead the direct question whether on the facts leptospirosis was reasonably foreseeable, succeeds only by assuming one particular answer to the question: [1969] 1 W.L.R. at p. 1561. *Cf.* the opinion of Edmund Davies L.J. in *Draper* v. *Hodder* [1972] 2 Q.B. 556 that the foreseeable risk of the infant plaintiff being injured by being bowled over by the dogs would justify the imposition of liability where the dogs *attacked* him.

[80] Fridman and Williams, " The Atomic Theory of Negligence " (1971) 45 A.L.J. 117.

[81] See *ante*, p. 96.

[82] See *post*, p. 100.

[83] See *post*, p. 100.

[84] *C. Czarnikow Ltd.* v. *Koufos* [1969] 1 A.C. 350, 385; *ibid.* at p. 411, *per* Lord Hodson; *ibid.* at p. 422, *per* Lord Upjohn. Italics added. James, " Foresight at Sea " [1968] J.B.L. 303.

[85] [1961] A.C. at p. 413.

Mound (*No.* 2), however, somewhat different evidence was presented [86] and in the Privy Council the trial judge's finding to similar effect, not being a primary finding of fact but an inference from other findings, was rejected. There was, it was held, a real risk of fire such as would have been appreciated by a properly qualified and alert chief engineer and this, given the fact that there was no justification for discharging oil into Sydney Harbour in any case, was sufficient to fix liability on the defendants. In other words, the mere fact that the damage suffered was unlikely to occur does not relieve the defendant of liability if his conduct was unreasonable—a proposition very little different from that contained in *Re Polemis* itself. On the facts of that case, notwithstanding the arbitrator's finding that the spark which caused the explosion was not reasonably foreseeable, there was, surely, a " real risk " that the vapour in the hold might be accidentally ignited and there was, of course, no justification for dropping the plank into the hold.

The competing rules compared

It seems, therefore, that *The Wagon Mound* has made little difference to the law in terms of practical result, and, indeed, Viscount Simonds indicated that this would probably be so in *The Wagon Mound* itself.[87] That case has, however, undoubtedly produced a change of principle and even now its full effect cannot be fully known. It is right, therefore, to conclude with some brief discussion of its merits as compared with those of *Re Polemis*. Much has been written on this subject [88] but two points only can be considered here:

(a) **Simplicity.** The Privy Council laid much stress upon the difficulties of the directness test. If foreseeability is treated as a question of fact to be decided once and for all at the trial, then, no doubt, the task of the appellate courts is made easier by the change, but the application of the law to the facts is made correspondingly more difficult.[89] If, on the other hand, questions of foreseeability are open in the appellate courts—and *The Wagon Mound* (*No.* 2) indicates that they are— then there seems no reason for supposing that the foreseeability test is any easier than directness. On the contrary, not only does the change from the one to the other raise the question of the meaning of " kind " of damage but it " gets rid of the difficulties of determining causal connection by substituting the difficulty of determining the range and extent of foresight of the hypothetical reasonable man." [90] The fact is that the issue of remoteness of damage is not susceptible to short cuts. " There is no substitute for dealing with the particular facts, and con-

---

[86] See Lord Reid's explanation of this, [1967] A.C. at pp. 640–641, and Dias, *loc. cit.* at pp. 63–65.
[87] [1961] A.C. at p. 422.
[88] See *ante*, p. 94, n. 64.
[89] This must be a matter for concern not only to trial judges but also to counsel and solicitors when consulted about the settlement of an action.
[90] Walker, " Remoteness of Damage and *Re Polemis* " 1961 S.L.T. 37.

sidering all the factors that bear on them, interlocked as they must be. Theories . . . have not improved at all on the old words ' proximate ' and ' remote ' with the idea they convey of some reasonable connection between the original negligence and its consequences, between the harm threatened and the harm done." [91]

(b) **Fairness.** According to the Privy Council the test of directness works unfairly: " It does not seem consonant with current ideas of justice or morality that for an act of negligence, however slight or venial, which results in some trivial foreseeable damage the actor should be liable for all consequences however unforeseeable and however grave, so long as they can be said to be ' direct.' " [92] It is no doubt hard on a negligent defendant that he should be held liable for unexpectedly large damages, but it is not clear that the final outcome is any fairer if the plaintiff is left without redress for damage which he has suffered through no fault of his own. Bearing in mind that negligence involves the creation of an *unreasonable* risk of causing some foreseeable damage to the plaintiff it might be thought that even though "justice" may be impossible of achievement where unforeseeable damage occurs,[93] greater injustice is produced by *The Wagon Mound* than by *Re Polemis*.[94]

Rules as to remoteness

We have tried to state the general principles and we can now consider some of the more detailed rules relating to remoteness. The reports are replete with illustrations of them, and there is a corresponding danger of mistaking examples for hard-and-fast rules.

1. *Intended consequences*

Intended consequences are never too remote.[95] " The intention to injure the plaintiff . . . disposes of any question of remoteness of damage." [96] Moreover, it must be recollected that the law presumes, or at least there is an inference of fact, that a man intends the necessary and natural consequences of his conduct, even though a psychologist might say that they formed no part of his original intention. *Scott* v. *Shepherd* [97] is the classical instance of this. The man who

---

[91] Prosser, " Palsgraf Revisited " (1953) 52 Michigan L.Rev. 1, 32.
[92] [1961] A.C. at p. 422.
[93] Prosser, " Palsgraf Revisited " (1953) 52 Michigan L.Rev. 1, 17.
[94] *Cf.* Glanville Williams, " The Risk Principle " (1961) 77 L.Q.R. 179–180. See, too, Weir (1961) 35 Tulane L.Rev. 619, 626, and the observations of Walsh J., the trial judge in *The Wagon Mound* (*No.* 2) [1963] 1 Lloyd's Rep. 402, 412.
[95] The American *Restatement of Torts*, §§ 870, 915, qualifies the rule by adding, " except where the harm results from an outside force the risk of which is not increased by the defendant's act." But this exception is unreal, for all the illustrations are explicable on some other ground (*e.g.*, *volenti non fit injuria*) or are merely cases in which all the consequences were not intended. See also Glanville Williams, " The Risk Principle " (1961) 77 L.Q.R. at pp. 200–202; Hart and Honoré, *Causation in the Law* (1959) pp. 150–160.
[96] *Quinn* v. *Leatham* [1901] A.C. 495, 537, *per* Lord Lindley.
[97] *Ante*, p. 90.

first threw the squib certainly intended to scare somebody or other. With equal certainty he did not, in common parlance, " intend " to hurt the plaintiff, much less to destroy his eye. But he was nevertheless held liable to the plaintiff, because the law insists, and insists quite rightly, that fools and mischievous persons must answer for consequences which common sense would unhesitatingly attribute to their wrongdoing.[98]

2. Unintended consequences

(a) **Existing states of affairs.** (i) Pecuniary amount of the damage. It is clear that this is a question of assessment of damages rather than of remoteness [98a] and foreseeability is here irrelevant. Thus if the defendant injures a high income earner or a valuable piece of property he cannot argue that he had no reason to expect the amount of loss to be so great.[98b]

(ii) Extent of the damage. If the accident occurs in a foreseeable way the defendant will be liable even though the damage is much greater in extent than would have been anticipated.[98c] It has sometimes been suggested that the " egg-shell skull " rule (see below) is an example of this principle, but this does not seem correct.[98d]

(iii) The " egg-shell skull " principle. *The Wagon Mound* has not displaced the principle that the defendant must take his victim as he finds him.[98e] It has for long been the law that " if a man is negligently run over or otherwise negligently injured in his body, it is no answer to the sufferer's claim for damages that he would have suffered less injury, or no injury at all, [98f] if he had not had an unusually thin skull or an unusually weak heart." [98g] The same (or a similar) [98h]

---

[98] See the admirable analysis in Pollock, *Torts*, 15th ed., pp. 25–27.

[98a] Fleming, *Torts*, 4th ed., p. 180, neatly says that it is concerned not with responsibility for unexpectable consequences, but for the unexpectable cost of expected consequences.

[98b] The point is perhaps so obvious that the only express authority for it appears to be the celebrated dictum of Scrutton L.J. in *The Arpad* [1934] P. 189, 202. The rule is probably the same where the high value is not " intrinsic " but comes from the existence of exceptionally profitable contracts: *Liesbosch Dredger* v. *Edison S.S.* [1933] A.C. 449, 461. See McGregor, *Damages*, 13th ed., pp. 106–109.

[98c] One of the few clear examples of this is *Vacwell Engineering* v. *B.D.H. Chemicals* [1971] 1 Q.B. 88 (minor explosion foreseeable; huge explosion took place because plaintiffs put number of ampoules in same sink). See also *Bradford* v. *Robinson Rentals Ltd.* [1967] 1 W.L.R. 337 (exposure causing frostbite) and *Richards* v. *State of Victoria* [1969] V.R. 136 (blow causing brain damage).

[98d] The suggestion seems to be made by Lord Wright in the *Liesbosch* case *supra* at p. 461 and by Lord Parker C.J. in *Smith* v. *Leech Brain & Co. Ltd.* [1962] 2 Q.B. 405, 415. But the law does not regard personal injury as indivisible (see *ante*, pp. 96–97) and damage in the form of cancer triggered off by a burn (as in *Smith* v. *Leech Brain*) seems different in kind from the burn.

[98e] But not his family: *McLaren* v. *Bradstreet* (1969) 113 S.J. 471.

[98f] This goes too far: there must be a breach of a duty owed to the plaintiff and if no damage at all could have been foreseen to a person of normal sensitivity and the plaintiff's abnormal sensitivity was unknown to the defendant, then he is not liable: *Bourhill* v. *Young* [1943] A.C. 92, 109–110, *per* Lord Wright; *Cook* v. *Swinfen* [1967] 1 W.L.R. 457; *cf. Collard* v. *Paul A. Sanders* [1971] C.L.Y. 1161.

[98g] *Dulieu* v. *White* [1901] 2 K.B. 669, 679, *per* Kennedy J. See this principle applied post-*Wagon Mound* in *Smith* v. *Leech Brain & Co. Ltd.* [1962] 2 Q.B. 405; *Warren* v. *Scruttons* [1962] 1 Lloyd's Rep. 497; *Lines* v. *Harland and Wolff* [1966] 2 Lloyd's Rep.

Footnote 98h on p. 101

principle operates when the plaintiff's injury is exacerbated by a combination of his abnormality and some external force which foreseeably and naturally intervenes after the accident, e.g., medical treatment to which he is allergic.[981]

(iv) Plaintiff's impecuniosity. In *Liesbosch Dredger* v. *Edison S.S.*[98j] the *Edison*, by negligent navigation, fouled and sank the dredger *Liesbosch*, whose owners were under contract with a third party to complete a piece of work within a given time. They were put to much greater expense in fulfilling this contract because they were too poor to buy a substitute for the dredger. The House of Lords held that they could recover as damages the market price of a dredger comparable to the *Liesbosch* and compensation for loss in carrying out the contract between the date of the sinking and the date on which the substituted dredger could reasonably have been available for work, for the measure of damages in such cases is the value of the ship to her owner as a going concern at the time and place of the loss, and, in assessing that value, regard must naturally be paid to her pending engagements [98k] but the claim for extra expenses due to poverty was rejected, because the plaintiff's want of means was an extraneous matter which made this special loss too remote. Lord Wright (with whose speech the rest of the House concurred) distinguished *Re Polemis* (then the leading case on remoteness) on the ground that the injuries there suffered were the " immediate physical consequences of the negligent act," and he added, " Nor is the appellants' financial disability to be compared with that physical delicacy or weakness which may aggravate the damage in the case of personal injuries, or with the possibility that the injured man in such a case may be either a poor labourer or a highly paid professional man. *The former class of circumstances goes to the extent of actual physical damage and the latter goes to interference with profit-earning capacity; whereas the appellants' want of means was, as already stated, extrinsic.*" [981]

It is not possible to give any logical reason why the law regards the plaintiff's impecuniosity as extrinsic but takes into account his physical

---

400; *Boon* v. *Thomas Hubback* [1967] 1 Lloyd's Rep. 281; *Wieland* v. *Cyril Lord Carpets Ltd.* [1969] 3 All E.R. 1006; *Malcolm* v. *Broadhurst* [1970] 3 All E.R. 508. Goodhart, " Liability and Compensation " (1960) 76 L.Q.R. 567, 577 suggests that though it is unusual to find a man with an egg-shell skull " it is not so extraordinary as to make the consequences unforeseeable." *Cf.* Williams, " The Risk Principle " (1961) 77 L.Q.R. 179; James, " *Polemis*: The Scotch'd Snake " [1962] J.B.L. 146.

[98h] It has been said that this is a logical corollary of the egg-shell skull principle: *Stephenson* v. *Waite Tileman Ltd.* [1973] N.Z.L.R. 152 (N.Z.C.A.).

[98i] *Robinson* v. *Post Office* [1974] 2 All E.R. 737 (C.A.). But negligent treatment might amount to a *novus actus interveniens: ibid.*, p. 748. See also *Bloor* v. *Liverpool Derricking and Carrying Co. Ltd.* [1936] 3 All E.R. 399; *Winteringham* v. *Rae* (1966) 55 D.L.R. (2d) 108.

[98j] [1933] A.C. 448. See the observations of Viscount Simonds on this case: *The Wagon Mound* [1961] A.C. 388.

[98k] [1933] A.C. 448, 463–464.

[981] *Ibid.* at p. 461. Italics supplied. The principle has even been applied to a case of fraud: *Clements* v. *Bawns Shipping Co.* (1948) 81 Ll.L.R. 232.

disability. The rule is one of policy,[98m] but it should be noted that a similar policy finds expression in two other areas of the law: the principles that (a) impecuniosity is not a frustrating event in the law of contract [98n] and (b) damages are not available for non-payment of a debt.[98o] The *Liesbosch* rule is not, however, beyond challenge in the House of Lords since there are contract cases which take account of impecuniosity [98p] and there is authority that even in cases of tort the plaintiff's impecuniosity may excuse his failure to mitigate his loss.[98q]

(b) Intervening acts or events. Everyone agrees that a consequence is too remote if it follows a " break in the chain of causation " or is due to a *nova causa interveniens*. This means that although the defendant's breach of duty is a cause of the plaintiff's damage in the sense that it satisfies the " but-for " test of causation in fact, nevertheless in the eyes of the law some other intervening event is regarded as the sole cause of that damage. Three classes of case fall to be considered, namely (a) where a natural event occurs independently of the act of any human being; (b) where the event consists of the act or omission of a third party; (c) where the event consists of the act or omission of the plaintiff himself. It should not be thought, however, that in any of these cases the law will be particularly astute to attribute the plaintiff's damage to a single cause. There is no objection to a finding that the separate torts of two independent actors were both causes of the damage, and where this is so the plaintiff may recover in full from either of them.[99] Nor is there any objection to a finding that the defendant's breach of duty and the plaintiff's own fault were both causes of the plaintiff's damage. On the contrary, such a finding is a condition precedent to the operation of the law of contributory negligence.[100]

(i) Intervening natural event. It is, of course, impossible for anything to happen in the physical world without the operation of natural forces, but sometimes the plaintiff suffers damage as the immediate result of a natural event which occurs independently of the defendant's breach of duty but which would have caused the plaintiff no damage if the breach of duty had not occurred. In such a case, if the breach of duty has neither increased the likelihood that the plaintiff will suffer damage nor rendered him more susceptible to damage, it will not be

---

[98m] See Lord Wright, " Legal Essays and Addresses," p. 113.
[98n] See *Davis Contractors Ltd.* v. *Fareham U.D.C.* [1956] A.C. 696; see also Treitel, *Law of Contract*, 3rd ed., p. 107.
[98o] This has been doubted: *Trans Trust S.P.R.L.* v. *Danubian Trading Co.* [1952] 2 Q.B. 297, 306, *per* Denning L.J.
[98p] The *Trans Trust* case, *supra*; *Muhammad* v. *Ali* [1947] A.C. 414.
[98q] *Clippens Oil Co.* v. *Edinburgh and District Water Trustees* [1907] A.C. 291, 303, *obiter per* Lord Collins. See also *Robbins of Putney* v. *Meek* [1971] R.T.R. 345 (contract). In *Martindale* v. *Duncan* [1973] 1 W.L.R. 574, however, Davies L.J. said that the *Liesbosch* was "authority for the proposition that impecuniosity is no excuse for not mitigating damage." On the problem of distinguishing between remoteness and mitigation see McGregor, *Damages*, 13th ed., pp. 58–59.
[99] *Grant* v. *Sun Shipping Co. Ltd.* [1948] A.C. 549. For contribution between tortfeasors, see *post*, pp. 548–551. [100] *Post*, pp. 106–117.

treated as a cause of the damage. Thus, in *Carslogie Steamship Co. Ltd.* v. *Royal Norwegian Government* [1] the plaintiffs' ship was damaged in a collision for which the defendant's ship was wholly responsible. After temporary repairs which restored the ship to a seaworthy condition she set out on a voyage to the United States, a voyage which she would not have made had the collision not occurred. During her crossing of the Atlantic she suffered extensive damage due to heavy weather, and on her arrival in the United States the collision damage was permanently repaired at the same time that the heavy weather damage was dealt with. It was held in the House of Lords that the plaintiffs were not even entitled to damages for the loss of the use of their ship while the collision damage was being repaired because that time was used also for the repair of the heavy weather damage. There was no question of the defendants being liable for the heavy weather damage itself: that damage " was not in any sense a consequence of the collision, and must be treated as a supervening event occurring in the course of a normal voyage." [2]

(ii) Intervening act of a third party. If the defendant's breach of duty has done no more than provide the occasion for an entirely independent act by a third party and that act is the immediate cause of the plaintiff's damage, then it will amount to a *nova causa interveniens* and the defendant will not be liable.[3] This, however, may not be the case if the act of the third party was not truly independent. In *The Oropesa* [4] a collision occurred between the ship of that name and another ship, the *Manchester Regiment*, for which both ships were to blame. The *Manchester Regiment* was severely damaged and her master decided to cross to the *Oropesa* in one of the ship's boats to discuss salvage arrangements with the master of the *Oropesa*. The boat overturned in heavy seas before reaching the *Oropesa* and nine of the men on board, one of whom was the plaintiff's son, were drowned. The question was whether his death was caused by the negligence of the *Oropesa*,[5] or whether the master's action in taking to the boat constituted a *nova causa interveniens*. It was held that that action could not be severed from the circumstances affecting the two ships, that the " hand of the casualty lay heavily " upon the *Manchester*

---

[1] [1952] A.C. 292; *Cutler* v. *United Dairies (London) Ltd.* [1933] 2 K.B. 297; *Vinnyey* v. *Star Paper Mills Ltd.* [1965] 1 All E.R. 175.
[2] [1952] 1 All E.R. at p. 22, *per* Viscount Jowitt. Not all of his Lordship's speech is reported in the Law Reports. It seems that if the supervening event had been detention caused by an outbreak of war, the defendants would have been liable: *Monarch S.S. Co.* v. *Karlshamns Oljifabriker* [1949] A.C. 196.
[3] *Weld-Blundell* v. *Stephens* [1920] A.C. 956; *Harnett* v. *Bond* [1925] A.C. 669; *S.S. Singleton Abbey* v. *S.S. Paludina* [1927] A.C. 16.
[4] [1943] P. 32; Weir, *Casebook on Tort*, 3rd ed., p. 177; *The City of Lincoln* (1890) 15 P.D. 15; *Summers* v. *Salford Corporation* [1943] A.C. 283, 296–297, *per* Lord Wright; *Cook* v. *S.* [1966] 1 W.L.R. 635.
[5] It is irrelevant to this question that the negligence of the *Manchester Regiment* leading to the collision may also have been a cause of the death.

Regiment, and so that it was caused by and flowed from the collision.[6] " To break the chain of causation it must be shown that there is something which I will call ultroneous, something unwarrantable, a new cause which disturbs the sequence of events, something which can be described as either unreasonable or extraneous or extrinsic." [7]

In *The Oropesa*, the action of the master was not itself tortious: he was not guilty of a breach of duty to the deceased in ordering him into the boat, but that fact is of itself unimportant. The intervening act will not necessarily amount to a *nova causa interveniens* even if it is negligent or otherwise tortious as against the plaintiff.[7a] In *Haynes* v. *Harwood* [8] the defendants' servant left a two-horse van unattended in a street where there were a good many children about. A mischievous boy threw a stone at the horses and caused them to bolt and the plaintiff was injured in consequence. It was held the boy's act did not sever the causal connection between the negligence of leaving the van unattended and the plaintiff's damage. Indeed, it was negligent to leave the van unattended in a place where there were children precisely because a mischievous child might do something to cause the horses to bolt.[9] Even theft, if to be anticipated as the likely outcome of the breach of duty, will not break the chain of causation. In *Stansbie* v. *Troman* [10] a decorator was at work at a house and left it for two hours to get some wallpaper. He was alone at the house and had been told by the householder to close the front door whenever he left the house. Instead of doing so he left the door unlocked and during his absence a thief entered the house and stole a diamond bracelet and some clothes. The Court of Appeal held that he was liable for their loss.

It should not be thought from these cases that no act of a third party which is foreseeable is capable of being a *nova causa interveniens*. The third party's action must have been something very likely to happen if it is not to be regarded as breaking the chain of causation.[11] Otherwise it remains true, as Lord Sumner has said, that " in general . . . even though A. is in fault, he is not responsible for injury to C. which B., a stranger to him, deliberately chooses to do. Though A. may have given the occasion for B.'s mischievous activity, B. then becomes a new and independent cause. . . . It is hard to steer clear of metaphors. Perhaps one may be forgiven for saying that B. snaps the chain of causation; that he is no mere conduit pipe through

---

[6] [1943] P. at p. 37, *per* Lord Wright.
[7] *Ibid.* at p. 39, *per* Lord Wright.
[7a] See *e.g.*, *West* v. *Hughes of Beaconsfield Ltd.* [1971] R.T.R. 298.
[8] [1935] 1 K.B. 146; *Lynch* v. *Nurdin* (1841) 1 Q.B. 29; *Hill* v. *New River Co.* (1868) 9 B. & S. 303; *Shiffman* v. *Grand Priory etc.* [1936] 1 All E.R. 557; *Davies* v. *Liverpool Corporation* [1949] 2 All E.R. 175; *Philco Radio, etc., Corporation Ltd.* v. *J. Spurling Ltd.* [1949] 2 K.B. 33; Weir, *Casebook on Tort*, 3rd ed., p. 181.
[9] [1935] 1 K.B. 147 at p. 153, *per* Greer, L.J.
[10] [1948] 2 K.B. 48; *Palmer & Harvey* v. *Cook* [1963] C.L.Y. 2678; *Petrovitch* v. *Callinghams* [1969] 2 Lloyd's Rep. 386. See too *Hinds* v. *Direct Supply Co.* [1966] C.L.Y. 5210.
[11] *Home Office* v. *Dorset Yacht Co. Ltd.* [1970] A.C. 1004, 1030, *per* Lord Reid.

which consequences flow from A. to C., no mere moving part in a transmission gear set in motion by A.; that, in a word, he insulates A. from C." [12]

(iii) Intervening act of the plaintiff. Where it is the plaintiff's own act or omission which, in combination with the defendant's breach of duty, has brought about his damage, then the problem is generally seen as one of contributory negligence./ Before there can be any question of contributory negligence, however, it is necessary that both the plaintiff's lack of care and the defendant's breach of duty shall be found to have been causes of the plaintiff's damage and in some cases, especially those in which the plaintiff seeks to recover for damage suffered in a second accident, the defendant has been exonerated on the ground that the plaintiff's conduct amounted to a *nova causa interveniens*. In *McKew* v. *Holland & Hannen & Cubitts (Scotland) Ltd.*[13] the pursuer had suffered an injury in an accident for which the defenders were liable and as a result he occasionally lost control of his left leg which gave way under him. Some days after this accident he went to inspect a flat which was approached by a steep stair between two walls and without a handrail. On leaving the flat he started to descend the stair holding his young daughter by the hand and going ahead of his wife and brother-in-law who had accompanied him. Suddenly he lost control of his left leg, threw his daughter back in order to save her, and tried to jump so as to land in an upright position instead of falling over down the stairs. As a result he sustained a severe fracture of his ankle. The House of Lords agreed that the pursuer's act of jumping in the emergency in which he found himself did not break the chain of causation, but that it had been broken by his conduct in placing himself unnecessarily in a position where he might be confronted by just such an emergency, when he could have descended the stair slowly and carefully by himself or sought the assistance of his wife or brother-in-law.

The basis of the decision of the House of Lords in this case was that the pursuer's conduct amounted to a *nova causa interveniens* because, even though it may have been foreseeable, it was unreasonable in the circumstances.[14] If he had had no reasonable alternative to acting as he did his conduct would not have broken the chain of causation. In *The Calliope*[15] a collision occurred between two ships in the River Seine as a result of the negligence of both. The *Calliope*

---

[12] *Weld-Blundell* v. *Stephens* [1920] A.C. 956, 986.
[13] [1969] 3 All E.R. 1621 (H.L.Sc.); *The San Onofre* [1922] P. 243. *Cf. Wieland* v. *Cyril Lord Carpets Ltd.* [1969] 3 All E.R. 1006. *Pigney* v. *Pointer's Transport Services Ltd.* [1957] 1 W.L.R. 1121, Weir, *Casebook on Tort*, 3rd ed., p. 184, is a remarkable case in which a man's suicide did not make his death too remote a consequence of an accident for which the defendants were responsible and which induced in him a condition of acute anxiety neurosis. This case was decided on the rule in *Re Polemis* and might, perhaps have been decided differently under *The Wagon Mound*.
[14] [1969] 3 All E.R. at p. 1623, *per* Lord Reid.
[15] [1970] P. 172.

was on her way down river but in view of the damage she had sustained it was decided to turn her round and proceed up river to an anchorage to await the ebb-tide. Then she was to be turned round again to resume her journey to the sea. The first part of this manoeuvre was carried out successfully, but the following morning, when the ship endeavoured to turn round for the second time, she grounded twice and suffered further damage. Brandon J. found that this would not have happened but for the negligence of the Chief Officer of the *Calliope* but held that this negligence did not amount to a *nova causa interveniens* and so that the owners of the other ship must bear partial responsibility for that further damage.[16] Although the manoeuvre of turning round was a difficult one and was made more difficult by the presence of thick fog, the learned judge evidently accepted that the decision of those in charge of the *Calliope* to attempt it was not unreasonable. It is this fact which distinguishes the case from *McKew* v. *Holland & Hannen & Cubitts (Scotland) Ltd.*[17] In both cases the injured party had placed himself in a position in which the consequences of the other party's breach of duty might lead to further damage; in *The Calliope* the decision to do so was reasonable, in *McKew* v. *Holland & Hannen & Cubitts (Scotland) Ltd.* it was not.

CONTRIBUTORY NEGLIGENCE [17a]

If the plaintiff's injuries have been caused partly by the negligence of the defendant and partly by his own negligence,[18] then, at common law, the plaintiff can recover nothing. This rule of " contributory negligence " [19] first appeared at the beginning of the nineteenth century, though the general idea is traceable much earlier.[20] In *Butterfield* v. *Forrester*,[21] A wrongfully obstructed a road by putting a pole across it. B, riding violently on the road in the dusk, was overthrown by the pole and injured. The pole was discernible at a distance of 100 yards. It was held that A was not liable to B. Bayley J. said: " If he had used ordinary care he must have seen the obstruction; so that the accident appeared to happen entirely from his own fault "; and Lord Ellenborough C.J. added: " One person being at fault will not dispense with another's using ordinary care of himself."

The common law rule produced hardship where one of the two negligent parties suffered the greater loss although his negligence was

---

[16] The judgment of Brandon J. is of particular importance for the law governing the apportionment of damages for it introduces the possibility of sub-apportionment in appropriate cases. See *post*, p. 115, n. 75.

[17] Compare *The Guildford* [1956] P. 364 with *The Fritz Thyssen* [1968] P. 255.

[17a] Weir, *Casebook on Tort*, 3rd ed., Chap. 5, s. 1.

[18] The burden of proving the plaintiff's negligence lies with the defendant: *Heranger (Owners)* v. *S.S. Diamond* [1939] A.C. 94, 104, *per* Lord Wright.

[19] There is a wealth of literature on the topic, the most useful work being Glanville Williams, *Joint Torts and Contributory Negligence*, Part II.

[20] Thus the strict liability of an innkeeper for the safe-keeping of his guest's goods was negatived if the goods were stolen by the guest's own fault: *Sanders* v. *Spencer* (1567) 3 Dyer 266b. See also Holdsworth, *H.E.L.*, iii, p. 378.

[21] (1809) 11 East 60.

not the major cause of the accident. Accordingly, the courts modified the defence of contributory negligence by the so-called rule of last opportunity. This enabled the plaintiff to recover notwithstanding his own negligence, if upon the occasion of the accident the defendant could have avoided the accident while the plaintiff could not.[22] The authorities were confused,[23] and confusion was made worse confounded by the extension of the rule, in *British Columbia Electric Ry.* v. *Loach*,[24] to cases of " constructive last opportunity." This meant that if the defendant would have had the last opportunity but for his own negligence, he was in the same position as if he had actually had it, and the plaintiff again recovered in full. There are cogent reasons for denying that either of these rules was derived from those concerning remoteness of damage [25] but they seem on the whole to have been regarded by the courts as if they were, and it is perhaps fair to say that in the result the ultimate question was, " Who caused the accident ? "

Whether it is based upon remoteness of damage or not, if it means that in every case the person whose negligence came last in time is solely responsible for the damage, the rule of last opportunity is clearly illogical. It is not surprising, therefore, that when apportionment of the damages between plaintiff and defendant became possible in cases of maritime collision under the Maritime Conventions Act 1911,[26] the rule began to receive adverse criticism. In *Admiralty Commissioners* v. *SS. Volute* [27] the House of Lords held that even where the defendant's negligence is subsequent to that of the plaintiff, nevertheless the plaintiff's negligence is still contributory to the collision if there is not " a sufficient separation of time, place, or circumstance " between the plaintiff's negligence and the defendant's negligence to make the defendant's negligence the sole cause of the collision. " Upon the whole I think that the question of contributory negligence must be dealt with somewhat broadly and upon common-sense principles as a jury would probably deal with it. And

---

[22] The authority usually regarded as supporting the rule of last opportunity is *Davies* v. *Mann* (1842) 10 M. & W. 546. Plaintiff fettered the fore feet of his donkey and negligently turned it loose on the highway. Defendant, driving his wagon and horses faster than he should have done, collided with and killed the donkey. Defendant liable because by the exercise of ordinary care he might have avoided the consequences of plaintiff's negligence. Neither in this case nor in *Butterfield* v. *Forrester* (*supra*) was the phrase " contributory negligence " used. *Davies* v. *Mann* was approved by the House of Lords in *Radley* v. *L. & N.W. Ry.* (1876) 1 App.Cas. 759.

[23] See Munkman, *Employer's Liability*, 7th ed., p. 539, n. 1 for a short summary of the controversy, and MacDermott J. in *Ross* v. *McQueen* [1947] N.I. 81–83, for reasons for the confusion. For a full discussion, see Glanville Williams, *op. cit.*, Chap. 9.

[24] [1916] 1 A.C. 719. This case has come in for much adverse criticism and " the truth is that no one knows precisely what it settled ": Glanville Williams, *op. cit.*, p. 234. But it was approved by the House of Lords in *McLean* v. *Bell* (1932) 147 L.T. 262.

[25] Glanville Williams, *op. cit.*, pp. 236–255.

[26] 1 & 2 Geo. 5, c. 57, s. 1.

[27] [1922] 1 A.C. 129, 144–145; *Anglo-Newfoundland and Development Co.* v. *Pacific Steam Navigation Co.* [1924] A.C. 406; *The Eurymedon* [1938] P. 41; applied in *Boy Andrew* v. *St. Rognvald* [1948] A.C. 140, 146, 154–155.

while no doubt, where a clear line can be drawn, the subsequent negligence is the only one to look to, there are cases in which the two acts come so closely together, and the second act of negligence is so much mixed up with the state of things brought about by the first act, that the party secondly negligent, while not held free from blame . . . might, on the other hand, invoke the prior negligence as being part of the cause of the collision so as to make it a case of contribution." [28] In this case the damages were apportionable under the Act of 1911, but in *Swadling* v. *Cooper*,[29] the House regarded the decision in *The Volute* as of general application, with the result that the plaintiff in similar circumstances on land could recover nothing.

The Law Reform (Contributory Negligence) Act 1945[30] applies the principle on which the Maritime Conventions Act 1911[31] was based to contributory negligence on land and today, therefore, the damages may be apportioned wherever both parties have been negligent and both have contributed to the damage.

Present law

Act of 1945

Section 1 (1) of the Act of 1945 provides as follows: " Where any person suffers damage as the result partly of his own fault and partly of the fault of any other person or persons, a claim in respect of that damage shall not be defeated by reason of the fault of the person suffering the damage, but the damages recoverable in respect thereof shall be reduced to such extent as the court thinks just and equitable having regard to the claimant's share ,in the responsibility for the damage." [32] By section 4, damage includes loss of life and personal injury.[33] There is no doubt that it also includes injury to property for that was so before the Act. By the same section " fault " means

---

[28] [1922] 1 A.C. at p. 144, *per* Viscount Birkenhead L.C. Viscount Finlay said of Lord Birkenhead's speech in this case that it was " a great and permanent contribution to our law on the subject of contributory negligence, and to the science of jurisprudence ": *ibid.* at p. 145. But there is a strong rumour that the speech was actually written by Lord Phillimore: Goodhart, " On Remembering some Lawyers " (1963) 7 J.S.P.T.L.(N.S.) 174, 181.

[29] [1931] A.C. 1.

[30] 8 & 9 Geo. 6, c. 28.

[31] The Act of 1911 is unaffected by the Act of 1945.

[32] The section does not operate to defeat any defence arising under a contract, nor can the amount of damages recoverable exceed the limit fixed by any contract or enactment applicable to the claim: s. 1 (2) and (6). The court must find and record the total damages which would have been recoverable had the claimant not been at fault; if the case is tried with a jury, they assess the total amount of the damages and also the extent to which they are to be reduced. S. 1 (3) makes the Law Reform (Married Women and Tortfeasors) Act 1935, s. 6 (*post*, pp. 558–661), apply where two or more persons are concerned. The Act binds the Crown: Crown Proceedings Act 1947, s. 4 (3).

[33] It probably includes physical and economic damage, all damages which might have been awarded at common law apart from the plaintiff's own fault, including physical injury resulting from shock: Glanville Williams, *op. cit.*, pp. 116–118, 317. It does not include damages which a person, who has himself suffered no damage to person or property, would have been entitled to recover as contribution but for the effect of s. 6 (1) of the Law Reform (Married Women and Tortfeasors) Act 1935. *Drinkwater* v. *Kimber* [1952] 2 Q.B. 281, 290, *per* Singleton L.J.; *ibid.* at pp. 293–297, *per* Morris L.J.

negligence, breach of statutory duty or other act or omission which gives rise to a liability in tort or would, apart from the Act, give rise to the defence of contributory negligence.[34]

Causation [34a]

Although the Act has done away with some of the artificiality of the old law,[35] its intention is to alter only the legal consequences of contributory negligence and not the general rules for determining whether or not a case of contributory negligence exists.[36] It is still perfectly possible that although plaintiff and defendant were both negligent one or other of them must bear the whole of the loss. In *Stapley* v. *Gypsum Mines Ltd.*[37] S. and D. were two miners of equal status employed in the defendants' mine. They were ordered by their foreman to bring down an unsafe part of the roof and not to return to their normal work until they had done so. They tried unsuccessfully to bring down the roof and then, by a joint decision, abandoned the effort and returned to their work. The roof fell and S. was killed. His widow sued the defendants on the ground that D.'s negligence, for which they were vicariously liable, had been a cause of her husband's death and in the House of Lords her claim succeeded. D's negligence in disobeying orders was a cause of S.'s death, though S. himself had been guilty of contributory negligence.[38] This decision was reached by a bare majority of the House of Lords, overruling a unanimous decision of the Court of Appeal, but this indicates no more than a difference of opinion concerning the app-

---

[34] See Glanville Williams, *op. cit.*, pp. 318–319, 328, 390. The application of the Act to actions for breach of contract is a vexed question. The problem has sometimes been evaded by finding a tortious duty in addition to a contractual one and purporting to apply the Act to the former: *Sole* v. *W. J. Hallt Ltd.* [1973] Q.B. 574, criticised by Jolowicz, [1973] C.L.J. 209. The best view seems to be that if the contract imposes a duty to take care, the Act is applicable to breach of that duty: see *Sayers* v. *Harlow U.D.C.* [1958] 1 W.L.R. 623; *Quinn* v. *Burch Bros. (Builders) Ltd.* [1966] 2 Q.B. 370 (affd. on other grounds, *ibid.*); *Artingstoll* v. *Hewen's Garages Ltd.* [1973] R.T.R. 197; *De Meza* v. *Apple* [1974] 1 Lloyd's Rep. 508. *Cf. Driver* v. *William Willett (Contractors) Ltd.* [1969] 1 All E.R. 665 (apportionment between *defendants* under Law Reform (Married Women and Tortfeasors) Act 1935: see *post*, pp. 548–551.

[34a] It is clear that what is relevant is causation of the damage, not causation of the accident: *O'Connell* v. *Jackson* [1972] 1 Q.B. 270 (C.A.) (crash helmet).

[35] There is no longer the same temptation to avoid finding a small element of contributory negligence on the part of the plaintiff and " each problem should be approached broadly avoiding the fine distinctions which were apt to be drawn when some slight act of negligence on the part of the plaintiff might defeat his claim altogether ": *Boy Andrew (Owners)* v. *St. Rognvald (Owners)* [1948] A.C. 140, 155, *per* Lord Porter; *Sayers* v. *Harlow U.D.C.* [1958] 1 W.L.R. 623, 630, *per* Lord Evershed M.R.; Glanville Williams, *op. cit.*, p. 354.

[36] *Davies* v. *Swan Motor Co.* [1949] 2 K.B. 291, 310, *per* Bucknill L.J.; 322, *per* Denning L.J. This was the view of Lord Simon himself, expressed extra-judicially: Salmond, *Torts*, 16th ed., p. 531, n. 35.

[37] [1953] A.C. 663, followed on the issue of causation in *Imperial Chemical Industries Ltd.* v. *Shatwell* [1965] A.C. 656 (Viscount Radcliffe dissenting). For cases in which the plaintiff's negligence was held to be the sole cause of his damage notwithstanding the defendant's breach of duty, see, *e.g.*, *Norris* v. *W. Moss & Sons Ltd.* [1964] 1 W.L.R. 346; *Rushton* v. *Turner Brothers Asbestos Co. Ltd.* [1960] 1 W.L.R. 96; *McWilliams* v. *Sir William Arrol & Co. Ltd.* [1962] 1 W.L.R. 295 (H.L.Sc.).

[38] S.'s share of the responsibility for his death was held to be 80 per cent.

lication of the law to the facts.[39] All of their lordships agreed that causation is as important now as it was before the Act of 1945, and Lord Porter said,[40] " I agree, indeed, with the opinion which has been commonly held since the decision of *Admiralty Commissioners* v. *SS. Volute (Owners)*,[41] viz., that the abolition of the rule that any contributory negligence, however small, on the part of a plaintiff defeated his claim, has no effect on causation. It enables the court (be it judge or jury) to seek less strenuously to find some ground for holding the plaintiff free from blame or for reaching the conclusion that his negligence played no part in the ensuing accident inasmuch as owing to the change in the law the blame can now be apportioned equitably between the two parties. What was the cause of an event, however, leads to an inquiry of the same nature as existed before the change." [42]

Duty of care

ᐧᑌ The existence of a duty of care is, of course, essential to a cause of action for negligence, but for contributory negligence it is quite unnecessary that the plaintiff should owe a duty to the defendant. All that is required is that the plaintiff should have failed to take reasonable care for his own safety.[43] It is essential, however, that the plaintiff's lack of care for his own safety should be a contributory factor to the accident which caused his damage. In *Jones* v. *Livox Quarries Ltd.*[44] the plaintiff was riding on the towbar at the back of a " traxcavator " vehicle in order to return from his place of work to the canteen when the driver of another vehicle negligently drove into the back of the traxcavator and caused him injury. The plaintiff was held partly to blame for the accident, and his damages were reduced accordingly, because the risk that the traxcavator might be run into from behind was one to which he had exposed himself. But the result would have been otherwise if, for example, he had been hit in the eye by a shot from a negligent sportsman. In that case his presence on the traxcavator would have been only part of the history.[45]

---

[39] *Imperial Chemical Industries Ltd.* v. *Shatwell* [1965] A.C. 656, 670, *per* Lord Reid; 679–680, *per* Lord Hodson.
[40] [1953] A.C. 663 at p. 677 (a dissenting speech). See also *ibid.* at p. 681, *per* Lord Reid; *ibid.* at p. 684, *per* Lord Tucker; *ibid.* at p. 687, *per* Lord Asquith (dissenting).
[41] *Supra*, pp. 107–108.
[42] See also *National Coal Board* v. *England* [1954] A.C. 403; *Sayers* v. *Harlow U.D.C.* [1958] 1 W.L.R. 623; Weir, *Casebook on Tort*, 3rd ed., p. 186. *Cf. Judson* v. *British Transport Commission* [1954] 1 W.L.R. 585.
[43] *Nance* v. *British Columbia Electric Ry.* [1951] A.C. 601, 611, *per* Viscount Simon. See *Davies* v. *Swan Motor Co. (Swansea) Ltd.* [1949] 2 K.B. 291 for a full discussion. *Cf. Dawrant* v. *Nutt* and see Dias [1961] C.L.J. 17. Nevertheless, it will often be the case, as where there is a collision between two vehicles, that the plaintiff does owe a duty of care to the defendant. A duty is essential if the defendant wishes to counterclaim against the plaintiff in respect of his own damage.
[44] [1952] 2 Q.B. 608; *Davies* v. *Swan Motor Co. (Swansea) Ltd.*, *supra*; *Cork* v. *Kirby Maclean Ltd.* [1952] 2 All E.R. 402.
[45] [1952] 2 Q.B. at p. 616, *per* Denning L.J. See also *ibid.* at p. 612 *per* Singleton L.J.; at p. 618, *per* Hodson L.J.

Standard of care

The standard of care in general is the same as that in negligence itself,[46] and is in the same sense objective and impersonal.[47] However careless a man may have been, therefore, he is not guilty of contributory negligence if his conduct was not foreseeably likely to result in his own injury: " A person is guilty of contributory negligence if he ought reasonably to have foreseen that, if he did not act as a reasonable, prudent man, he might be hurt himself; and in his reckonings he must take into account the possibility of others being careless." [48] The degree of want of care which will constitute contributory negligence varies with the circumstances and the line must be drawn " where mere thoughtlessness or inadvertence or forgetfulness ceases and where negligence begins." [49]

As with any other aspect of the law of negligence the standard of care demanded by the law may be adjusted to meet changing conditions: a good example of this is the recent move towards treating non-use of car safety-belts as contributory negligence.[49a]

Children

There is no age below which, as a matter of law, it can be said that a child cannot be guilty of contributory negligence,[50] but the age of the child is a circumstance which must be considered in deciding whether it has been guilty of contributory negligence.[51] In *Yachuk* v. *Oliver Blais Co. Ltd.*,[52] Y., a boy aged nine years, bought from O. B. Co. some gasoline (a highly inflammable liquid), falsely stating

---

[46] *Billings & Sons Ltd.* v. *Riden* [1958] A.C. 240. *Bittner* v. *Tait-Gibson Optometrists Ltd.* (1964) 44 D.L.R. (2d) 113, Ontario C.A. " Fault " in the Act of 1945 does not include some fault falling short of negligence: *Jones* v. *Price* [1963] C.L.Y. 2316. See also *Clayards* v. *Dethick* (1848) 12 Q.B. 439; *Sayers* v. *Harlow U.D.C.* [1958] 1 W.L.R. 623.

[47] See *ante*, p. 60. *Baxter* v. *Woolcombers* (1963) 107 S.J. 553 (plaintiff's low intelligence does not affect standard of care).

[48] *Jones* v. *Livox Quarries Ltd.* [1952] 2 Q.B. 608, 615, per Denning L.J. See also *Grant* v. *Sun Shipping Co.* [1948] A.C. 549, 567, per Lord du Parcq. *Cf. Hawkins* v. *Ian Ross (Castings) Ltd.* [1970] 1 All E.R. 180.

[49] *Caswell* v. *Powell Duffryn Collieries Ltd.* [1940] A.C. 152, 176, per Lord Wright. For a case in which the plaintiff, a police officer, deliberately placed himself in a position of danger in the course of his duty and was held not guilty of contributory negligence, see *Hambley* v. *Shepley* (1967) 63 D.L.R. (2d) 94 (Ont.C.A.).

[49a] See, *e.g.*, *Pasternack* v. *Poulton* [1973] 1 W.L.R. 476. A reduction of one-third was made in *McGee* v. *Francis Shaw & Co.* [1973] R.T.R. 409. See further Linden, " Seat Belts and Contributory Negligence, " 49 Can.B.R. 475. But it has been doubted whether a finding of contributory negligence is correct unless the passenger knows the driver to be drunk or incompetent: *Challoner* v. *Williams* [1974] R.T.R. 221 (distinguishing *O'Connell* v. *Jackson* [1972] 1 Q.B. 270). At the time when *O'Connell* v. *Jackson* held that failure to wear a crash-helmet was contributory negligence, the wearing of such head-gear was not compulsory, but it now is. The lapsed Road Traffic Bill 1974 proposed to make the wearing of seat-belts compulsory.

[50] *Cf. Gough* v. *Thorne* [1966] 1 W.L.R. 1387, 1390, per Lord Denning M.R. A child of five has been held guilty of contributory negligence: *McKinnel* v. *White*, 1971 S.L.T. (Notes) 61; and see *Speirs* v. *Gorman* [1966] N.Z.L.R. 897.

[51] Clerk & Lindsell, *Torts*, 13th ed., pp. 583-585. *Cf.* Glanville Williams, *op. cit.*, p. 355; *Whitehouse* v. *Fearnley* (1964) 47 D.L.R. (2d) 472, Br. Columbia S.C.; *Lynch* v. *Nurdin* (1841) 1 Q.B. 29; *Culkin* v. *McFie & Sons Ltd.* [1939] 3 All E.R. 613; *Jones* v. *Lawrence* [1969] 3 All E.R. 267.

[52] [1949] A.C. 386 (J.C.); *French* v. *Sunshine Holiday Camp (Hayling Island) Ltd.* (1963) 107 S.J. 595.

that his mother wanted it for her car. In fact, he used it to play with, and, in doing so, was badly burnt by it. It was held by the Judicial Committee that O. B. Co. were negligent in supplying gasoline to so young a boy and that Y. had not been guilty of contributory negligence for he neither knew nor could be expected to know the properties of gasoline. Although Lord Denning M.R. has said that a child should not be found guilty of contributory negligence " unless he or she is blameworthy," [53] it is not thought that the characteristics of the particular child other than its age are to be considered. The question is whether an " ordinary " child of the plaintiff's age—not a " paragon of prudence " nor a " scatter-brained " child—would have taken any more care than did the plaintiff.[54]

Even if the injury is due to the negligence of the child's parent or guardian in looking after it, the child may still recover unless this negligence was the sole cause of the accident. This has long been recognised as the correct view. At one time it was held that the child was " identified " with the negligence of his guardian and thus had no action,[55] but this singular method of visiting the sins of the father upon the children received its death blow in 1888,[56] and in 1933 *Oliver* v. *Birmingham, etc., Omnibus Co. Ltd.*[57] drove the last nail in its coffin. A, an infant of four years, was crossing the road in the care of B, his grandfather. In the middle of the road, the defendants' omnibus approached without any warning and consequently startled B, who let go of A's hand. It then struck and injured A. The defendants were held liable to A in spite of B's " contributory " negligence.[58]

Workmen

It has been suggested that in actions by workmen against their employers for injuries sustained at work the courts are justified in taking a more lenient view of careless conduct on the part of the plaintiff than would otherwise be justified, and that it is not for every risky thing which a workman in a factory may do that he is to be held to have been negligent.[59] Regard must be had to the dulling of the sense of danger through familiarity, repetition, noise, confusion, fatigue and preoccupation with work.[60] Where, however, the operation leading up to the

---

[53] *Gough* v. *Thorne, supra*, at p. 1390. *Jones* v. *Lawrence, supra*, refers to the need for *culpable* want of care by the child for his own safety.
[54] [1966] 1 W.L.R. at p. 1391, *per* Salmon L.J.
[55] *Thorogood* v. *Bryan* (1849) 8 C.B. 115; *Waite* v. *N.E. Ry.* (1858) E.B. & E. 719, 728.
[56] *The Bernina* (1888) 13 App.Cas. 1. *Cf.* Pollock, *Torts*, pp. 363–365, and an anonymous and undated brochure, " Negligence, Contributory Negligence and Damage sustained by a Third Party," Launceston, Tasmania. Glanville Williams, *op. cit.*, §§ 89, 117 (2).
[57] [1933] 1 K.B. 35.
[58] But the defendants would today have recovered contribution from B under the Law Reform (Married Women and Tortfeasors) Act 1935, *post*, pp. 548–551. See *McCallion* v. *Dodd* [1966] N.Z.L.R. 710 (C.A. of N.Z.); *cf.* *Hahn* v. *Conley* (1971) 45 A.L.J.R. 631 (Aust.H.C.).
[59] On the contributory negligence of workmen, see Munkman, *Employer's Liability*, 7th ed., Chap. 20.
[60] *Flower* v. *Ebbw Vale Steel, Iron and Coal Co. Ltd.* [1934] 2 K.B. 132, 139–140, *per* Lawrence J., cited with approval by Lord Wright, *ibid.* [1936] A.C. 206, 214; *Caswell* v.

accident is divorced from the bustle, noise and repetition that occurs in such places as factories these considerations cannot apply and, indeed, it may be that they are only relevant where the workman's cause of action is founded upon his employer's breach of statutory duty.[61]

Rule of last opportunity

Whether or not the so-called rule of last opportunity with its extension to constructive last opportunity was ever a true rule of law, it is not one today.[62] The fact that either the plaintiff or the defendant had the last opportunity of avoiding the accident may in a particular case and as a matter of common sense lead the court to hold that a "clear line" exists between the two negligences, but that is all. If A, with full knowledge of the dangerous situation created by B's negligence, nevertheless " presses on regardless," it may well be held that his negligence alone is to be taken into account. But it does not follow from this that the person who by his own negligence does not come to know of a dangerous situation which reasonable care on his part would have revealed is to be treated more leniently. No single " rule " can cover every factual situation, and each case must be considered on its facts.

Statutory duty

It was settled by the House of Lords in 1939 that contributory negligence is a defence to an action for breach of statutory duty,[63] and the general principles of contributory negligence are the same as where the cause of action is founded upon negligence. In practice, however, especially where the statute creates an absolute obligation to secure the existence of a certain state of affairs, e.g. that dangerous parts of machinery shall be securely fenced,[64] questions of contributory negligence may be treated rather differently. It has often been stated that statutes such as the Factories Act exist to protect

---

Powell Duffryn Collieries Ltd. [1940] A.C. 152, 166, *per* Lord Atkin; 176–179, *per* Lord Wright; *Grant* v. *Sun Shipping Co.* [1948] A.C. 549, 567, *per* Lord du Parcq; *Hawkins* v. *Ian Ross (Castings) Ltd.* [1970] 1 All E.R. 180.

[61] *Staveley Iron & Chemical Co.* v. *Jones* [1956] A.C. 627, 642, *per* Lord Reid; 647–648, *per* Lord Tucker; *Hicks* v. *British Transport Commission* [1958] 1 W.L.R. 493; *Quintas* v. *National Smelting Co.* [1961] 1 W.L.R. 401, 411, *per* Willmer L.J. *Cf. ibid.* 408–409, *per* Sellers L.J. Disobedience is not necessarily contributory negligence: *Westwood* v. *Post Office* [1974] A.C. 1.

[62] Today the rule seems on the whole to have been mercifully forgotten. Its existence is implicitly denied by Lord Pearce in *The Miraflores and The Abadesa* [1967] 1 A.C. 826, 847–848, and in *Chisman* v. *Electromation (Export) Ltd.* (1969) 6 K.I.R. 456 it was rejected by the Court of Appeal. Though it might have been in point in some recent cases, it has not been mentioned. See, *e.g.*, *Uddin* v. *Associated Portland Cement Manufacturers Ltd.* [1965] 2 Q.B. 582; *Wright* v. *Imperial Chemical Industries Ltd.* (1965) 109 S.J. 232; *Hawkins* v. *Ian Ross (Castings) Ltd.* [1970] 1 All E.R. 180. For a more cautious view, see Salmond, *Torts*, 16th ed., pp. 538–541. For the position in the early years after the 1945 Act, see the 9th ed. of this work, p. 113, n. 62.

[63] *Caswell* v. *Powell Duffryn Associated Collieries Ltd.* [1940] A.C. 152 (Factories Act); *Sparks* v. *Edward Ash Ltd.* [1943] K.B. 223 (Pedestrian Crossing Places Regulations). For the action for breach of statutory duty, see *post*, Chap. 8.

[64] Factories Act 1961, s. 14 (1).

workmen from the consequences of their own carelessness,[65] and the courts will therefore be slow to hold a workman guilty of contributory negligence where the defendant is in breach of his statutory duty.[66] Furthermore, even if the workman's negligence involves him in a breach of his own statutory duty his claim is not defeated by the maxim *ex turpi causa non oritur actio*.[67] On the other hand, given the nature of some statutory duties, it can happen that the defendant's breach is brought about wholly and exclusively by the plaintiff's own breach of his duty, and in such a case the plaintiff can recover nothing.[68]

Dilemma produced by negligence

Where the defendant's negligence has put the plaintiff in a dilemma, the defendant cannot escape liability if the plaintiff, in the agony of the moment, tries to save himself by choosing a course of conduct which proves to be the wrong one, provided the plaintiff acted in a reasonable apprehension of danger and the method by which he tried to avoid it was a reasonable one.[69] If those conditions are satisfied he committed no contributory negligence.[70]

A famous illustration of the principle is *Jones* v. *Boyce* (1816),[71] where the plaintiff was a passenger on the top of the defendant's coach and, owing to the breaking of a defective coupling rein, the coach was in imminent peril of being overturned. The plaintiff, seeing this, jumped from it and broke his leg. In fact the coach was not upset. Lord Ellenborough C.J. directed the jury that if the plaintiff acted as a reasonable and prudent man would have done, he was entitled to recover, although he had selected the more perilous of the two alternatives with which he was confronted by the defendant's negligence; and the jury gave a verdict for the plaintiff. But where all that the plaintiff is threatened with is mere personal inconvenience of

---

[65] *Staveley Iron & Chemical Co.* v. *Jones* [1956] A.C. 627, 648, *per* Lord Tucker; *Hutchinson* v. *L. & N.E. Ry.* [1942] 1 K.B. 481. *Cf. Reilly* v. *B.T.C.* [1956] 1 W.L.R. 76, 81.

[66] See, *e.g.*, *John Summers & Sons Ltd.* v. *Frost* [1955] A.C. 740. Nevertheless, cases in which workmen are held partly and even substantially to blame for their own injuries are exceedingly common. See, *e.g.*, *Cork* v. *Kirby Maclean Ltd.* [1952] 2 All E.R. 402; *Jones* v. *Richards* [1955] 1 W.L.R. 444; *Williams* v. *Sykes & Harrison Ltd.* [1955] 1 W.L.R. 1180; *Hodkinson* v. *H. Wallwork & Co. Ltd.* [1955] 1 W.L.R. 1195 (plaintiff 90 per cent. to blame); *Quinn* v. *Horsfall & Bickham Ltd.* [1956] 1 W.L.R. 652; *Uddin* v. *Associated Portland Cement Manufacturers Ltd.* [1965] 2 Q.B. 582.

[67] *National Coal Board* v. *England* [1954] A.C. 403. See *post*, pp. 626–628.

[68] *Ginty* v. *Belmont Building Supplies Ltd.* [1959] 1 All E.R. 414; Weir, *Casebook on Tort*, 3rd ed., p. 188; *Ross* v. *Portland Cement Manufacturers Ltd.* [1964] 1 W.L.R. 768; *Boyle* v. *Kodak Ltd.* [1969] 1 W.L.R. 661. See further, *post*, pp. 136–137.

[69] Glanville Williams, *op. cit.*, pp. 360–364.

[70] The rule is equally applicable in favour of the defendant where there is contributory negligence on the part of the plaintiff which has forced the dilemma upon him instead of upon the plaintiff: *Swadling* v. *Cooper* [1931] A.C. at p. 9; *McLean* v. *Bell* (1932) 147 L.T. 262, 263.

[71] 1 Stark. 493; *The Bywell Castle* (1879) 4 P.D. 219; *United States of America* v. *Laird Line Ltd.* [1924] A.C. 286; *Admiralty Commissioners* v. *SS. Volute* [1922] 1 A.C. 129, 136; *Sayers* v. *Harlow U.D.C.* [1958] 1 W.L.R. 623. See, too, Lord Blackburn in *Stoomvaart Maatschappij Nederland* v. *P. & O.S.N. Co.* (1880) 5 App.Cas. 876, 891; and Brett L.J. in *Woodley & Co.* v. *Michell & Co.* (1883) 11 Q.B.D. 47, 52–53.

a trifling kind, he is not entitled to run a considerable risk in order to get rid of it; *e.g.*, if the door of a railway-carriage in which he is travelling is so ill-secured that it keeps flying open, but he can avoid the draught by sitting elsewhere, it is his own fault if he falls out in trying to shut it (after several earlier unsuccessful attempts) while the train is in motion.[72]

Contributory negligence of the plaintiff's servants or agents [73]

As between the plaintiff and the defendant each is identified with any third person for whom he is vicariously responsible. The rule that the negligence of a servant in the course of his employment is imputed to his master applies whether the master is the plaintiff or the defendant. But the contributory negligence of an independent contractor for whom the plaintiff is not responsible does not affect the plaintiff's action. If X has charge of the person or property of A, A is not for that reason identified with X, hence if an accident happens owing to the negligence of X and a third person, Y, A may sue Y and recover in full, even though X could not.

Apportionment of damages

In a case of contributory negligence the damages recoverable by the plaintiff are to be reduced " to such extent as the court thinks just and equitable having regard to the claimant's share in the responsibility for the damage." [74] This may seem simple enough at first sight, though the problem may be complex when there are successive accidents which are causally connected with one another,[75] and in the majority of cases the judges give little by way of reason for their assessments of the extent to which the plaintiff's damages should be reduced. The matter is commonly treated as one of fact, and appellate courts will only vary an assessment in extreme cases unless

---

[72] *Adams* v. *L. & Y. Ry.* (1869) L.R. 4 C.P. 739.
[73] Glanville Williams, *Contributory Negligence*, pp. 428–456.
[74] Law Reform (Contributory Negligence) Act 1945, s. 1 (1); Glanville Williams, *op. cit.*, Chaps. 16–19; Payne, " Reduction of Damages for Contributory Negligence " (1955) 18 M.L.R. 344. The equivalent provision in the Maritime Conventions Act 1911, s. 1 (1), lays down that " the liability to make good the damage or loss shall be in proportion to the degree in which each vessel was in fault," but the principles of apportionment are the same under both Acts: *Davies* v. *Swan Motor Co.* (*Swansea*) *Ltd.* [1949] 2 K.B. 291, 319, *per* Evershed L.J.; *Rees* v. *The Admiralty* (1960) unreported, cited by Willmer L.J. in *Quintas* v. *National Smelting Co. Ltd.* [1961] 1 W.L.R. 401, 418; *The Miraflores and The Abadesa* [1966] P. 18, 33, *per* Willmer L.J. (dissenting, but not on this point. For the proceedings in the H.L., see [1967] 1 A.C. 826). The principles are also the same for the apportionment of responsibility between tortfeasors under the Law Reform (Married Women and Tortfeasors) Act 1935, s. 6 (*post*, pp. 548–551): *Ingram* v. *United Automobile Service Ltd.* [1943] K.B. 612. But see Payne, *loc. cit.* at pp. 345–346.
[75] *The Miraflores and The Abadesa* [1967] 1 A.C. 826; *The Calliope* [1970] P. 172. In the latter case Brandon J. held that where the first accident is caused partly by the negligence of the defendant and partly by the negligence of the plaintiff and then the plaintiff suffers further, consequential, damage which is caused partly by the first accident and partly by his own further negligence, there must be a sub-apportionment of responsibility for that consequential damage.

the trial judge can be said to have erred in principle or failed to take some relevant factor into account.[76]

Broadly speaking, two principal criteria of " responsibility " suggest themselves, causation and blameworthiness or culpability.[77] If the plaintiff's lack of care for his own safety is to be taken into account at all, it is, as we have seen, necessary that his own negligence should have been a cause of his damage, but as a basis for apportionment causation has been severely criticised. " To attempt to apportion damages by reference to degree of participation in the chain of causation is a hopeless enterprise, for it has no necessary connection with anything that would appeal to the ordinary person as being just and equitable." [78] Nevertheless there is high authority for the view that both causation and blameworthiness must be taken into account.[79] It would seem, however, that no hard-and-fast rule can be laid down. Degrees of causation may be impossible of rational assessment, but concentration exclusively upon comparative blameworthiness will tend in some cases to defeat the purpose of the Contributory Negligence Act. Where the defendant's liability is based upon breach of a strict common law or statutory duty he may have been guilty of no blameworthy behaviour at all, in which case if comparative blameworthiness were the sole criterion, even slight contributory negligence would prevent the plaintiff from recovering any damages.[80] Naturally the courts have been unwilling to reach such a conclusion; on the contrary, as has been recently stated, the protection intended to be given by strict statutory duties must not be emasculated by the " side-wind of apportionment." [81]

It has been persuasively argued, therefore, that once the liability of the defendant has been established, regard should be had only to the plaintiff's conduct in assessing the extent to which the damages

---

[76] Of the many authorities, see *The Macgregor* [1943] A.C. 197, 200–201, *per* Lord Wright; *Brown* v. *Thompson* [1968] 1 W.L.R. 1003, 1009–1011, *per* Winn L.J.; *The Jan Laurenz* [1973] 1 Lloyd's Rep. 329. Nevertheless appellate courts, and especially the House of Lords, have from time to time varied apportionments of damages quite freely: *Stapley* v. *Gypsum Mines Ltd.* [1953] A.C. 663; *National Coal Board* v. *England* [1954] A.C. 403; *Davison* v. *Apex Scaffolds Ltd.* [1956] 1 Q.B. 551; *Quintas* v. *National Smelting Co.* [1961] 1 W.L.R. 401; *Kerry* v. *Carter* [1969] 1 W.L.R. 1372; *Jennings* v. *Norman Collison Ltd.* [1970] 1 All E.R. 1121.

[77] Culpability should be measured by the degree of departure from the standard of the reasonable man rather than by *moral* blameworthiness. " A drunken motorist is to be disciplined not for his intoxication but for his negligence ": Fleming, *Law of Torts*, 4th ed., p. 220; *Pennington* v. *Norris* (1956) 96 C.L.R. 10.

[78] Glanville Williams, " The Two Negligent Servants " (1954) 17 M.L.R. 66, 69. " Causation itself is difficult enough; degrees of causation would really be a nightmare ": Chapman (1948) 64 L.Q.R. 28.

[79] *Davies* v. *Swan Motor Co.* [1949] 2 K.B. 291, 326, *per* Denning L.J.; *Stapley* v. *Gypsum Mines Ltd.* [1953] A.C. 663, 682, *per* Lord Reid; *The British Aviator* [1965] 1 Lloyd's Rep. 271; *The Miraflores and The Abadesa, supra,* especially *per* Lord Pearce [1967] 1 A.C. at p. 845; *Brown* v. *Thompson, supra,* at p. 1008, *per* Winn L.J.

[80] Denning J. seems to have accepted the logic of this in *Lavender* v. *Diamints Ltd.*; [1948] 2 All E.R. 249, 252, but the Court of Appeal held that the plaintiff was not guilty of contributory negligence at all: [1949] 1 K.B. 585.

[81] *Mullard* v. *Ben Line Steamers Ltd.* [1970] 1 W.L.R. 1414, 1418, *per* Sachs L.J. *McGuiness* v. *Key Markets Ltd.* (1973) 13 K.I.R. 249.

should be reduced.[82] Comparative blameworthiness cannot be assessed when the defendant's liability is not based upon moral fault, but "the legal effects of contributory negligence follow only from morally culpable conduct." [83] This may, in fact, very possibly explain the way in which judges often approach the problem of apportionment, but there seem to be two reasons why it cannot be accepted as universally valid. First, it is not invariably true that contributory negligence involves blameworthiness, e.g., where it consists itself in a breach of statutory duty,[84] and, secondly, it is not in truth always possible to ignore the nature of the defendant's liability. In *Quintas* v. *National Smelting Co.*[85] Devlin J. held that the defendants had not been guilty of negligence but had broken their statutory duty and assessed the plaintiff's contributory negligence at 75 per cent. The Court of Appeal, by a majority, held that the defendants were not guilty of breach of statutory duty but had been guilty of negligence and therefore reduced Devlin J.'s assessment to 50 per cent. " The respective responsibilities of the parties, and what is just and equitable having regard thereto, can only properly be assessed when it has been found what the plaintiff in fact did and what the defendants failed in their duty to do. The nature and extent of the defendants' duty is, in my view, highly important in assessing the effect of the breach or failure of duty on the happening of the accident giving rise to the plaintiff's claim and on the conduct of the plaintiff. There is an interaction of factors, acts and omissions to be considered." [1]

The result is, therefore, that there is no single principle for the apportionment of damages in cases of contributory negligence, and certainly no mathematical approach is possible.[2] No doubt the extent of the plaintiff's lack of care for his own safety must be a major factor in all cases, but the court is directed by the statute to do what is "just and equitable." The matter is thus one for the discretion of the court,[3] and, though the discretion must be exercised judicially, it is both unnecessary and undesirable that the exercise of the discretion be fettered by rigid rules requiring the court to take some aspects of the given case into account and to reject others.

---

[82] Payne, *loc. cit.*
[83] *Ibid.* at p. 347.
[84] *Laszczyk* v. *National Coal Board* [1954] 1 W.L.R. 1426.
[85] [1960] 1 W.L.R. 217; [1961] 1 W.L.R. 401. See also the example given by Lord Pearce in *The Miraflores and The Abadesa* [1967] 1 A.C. at p. 845.
[1] [1961] 1 W.L.R. at p. 408, *per* Sellers L.J. It may be relevant, also, whether the plaintiff's claim is founded upon negligence or nuisance: *Trevett* v. *Lee* [1956] 1 W.L.R. 113, 122, *per* Evershed M.R.
[2] *Connor* v. *Port of Liverpool Stevedoring Co.* [1953] 2 Lloyd's Rep. 604; *Williams* v. *Port of Liverpool Stevedoring Co.* [1956] 1 W.L.R. 551.
[3] Where there is a jury it is a question for the jury: s. 1 (6). However, subject to the *de minimis* principle, a court which has found *some* contributory negligence has no power to disregard it if it thinks it just and equitable so to do: *Boothman* v. *British Northrop Ltd.* (1972) 13 K.I.R. 112.

CHAPTER 7

NERVOUS SHOCK

WINFIELD thought it was not clear from the authorities whether nervous shock is a substantive tort or a particular instance of damage flowing from the commission of some particular tort.[1] On balance, he preferred the latter view, and this may account for his treatment of the topic under Remoteness. It should not be thought that its present treatment in a separate chapter indicates a different opinion. Nervous shock is a form of personal injury for which damages may or may not be recoverable according to the circumstances of the particular case. " The crude view that the law should take cognisance only of physical injury resulting from actual impact has been discarded, and it is now well recognised that an action will lie for injury by shock sustained through the medium of the eye or the ear without direct contact. The distinction between mental shock and bodily injury was never a scientific one, for mental shock is presumably in all cases the result of, or at least accompanied by, some physical disturbance in the sufferer's system." [2] A decision of the Judicial Committee in 1888 [3] proceeded on erroneous ideas about pathology and was never followed in the other courts.[4] The fallacy lay in supposing that " bodily " or " physical " injury must exclude " mental " injury as being too remote. Damages cannot be given for the mere sensation of fear or mental distress,[5] but when fear or any other sensation produces a definite illness, that consequence is no more remote than a broken bone or an open wound.[6]

Once it is realised that " true nervous shock is as much a physical injury as a broken bone or a torn flesh wound," [7] it might be thought that nothing further need be said on the subject save that the ordinary principles of liability for personal injury apply. As Lord Macmillan

[1] Cf. Wright J. in Wilkinson v. Downton [1897] 2 Q.B. 57, 58–59; Kennedy J. in Dulieu v. White [1901] 2 K.B. 669, 671, and Phillimore J., ibid. 682, 685; Bankes and Duke L.JJ. in Janvier v. Sweeney [1919] 2 K.B. 316, 321–322, 327; Bankes and Atkin L.JJ. in Hambrook v. Stokes [1925] 1 K.B. 141, 146, 154, 158; Lord Shaw in Coyle v. John Watson Ltd. [1915] A.C. 1, 13, approving Palles C.B. in the Irish case of Bell v. G.N. Ry. of Ireland (1890) 26 L.R.Ir. 428, 437; Owens v. Liverpool Corporation [1939] 1 K.B. 394. The American Restatement of Torts, Vol. 1, § 17, reckons nervous shock as an illustration of the tort of bodily harm rather than as a consequence of it. Cf. Professor C. Magruder in (1936) 49 Harv.L.R. 1033–1067; Bohlen, Studies in the Law of Torts (1926), pp. 252–290.
[2] Bourhill v. Young [1943] A.C. 92, 103, per Lord Macmillan.
[3] Victorian Railway Commissioners v. Coultas (1888) 13 App.Cas. 222.
[4] See cases cited in note 1.
[5] Dulieu v. White [1901] 2 K.B. 669, 673, per Kennedy J.; Behrens v. Bertram Mills Circus Ltd. [1957] 2 Q.B. 1, 27–28, per Devlin J.; Cook v. Swinfen [1967] 1 W.L.R. 457, 461, per Lord Denning M.R.; Hinz v. Berry [1970] 2 Q.B. 40.
[6] For the assessment of damages for nervous shock and the distinction between " sorrow and grief " for which damages are not recoverable and " nervous shock and psychiatric illness " for which damages are recoverable, see Hinz v. Berry [1970] 2 Q.B. 40.
[7] Eldredge, Modern Tort Problems, p. 76.

has said, however, " in the case of mental shock there are elements of greater subtlety than in the case of an ordinary physical injury and these elements may give rise to debate as to the precise scope of legal liability." [8] Where the shock is the result of an intentional wrongful act there is in fact no particular difficulty and, as we have seen, it was in a case of shock that Wright J. laid down his general principle concerning wilful acts calculated to cause harm.[9] In the case of negligence, however, the courts have not been prepared to apply the ordinary principles of liability without qualification.[9a] In part, no doubt, this has been due to their fear of fraudulent claims, [10] but a more significant point is that the literal application of the ordinary concept of foreseeability as used in negligence cases generally would produce a more extensive liability for shock than the courts have so far been prepared to accept. It is, for example, foreseeable that the relations of an accident victim will be informed of his death or injury and that they may suffer shock on hearing the news, but it is regarded as self-evident that " a wife or mother who suffers shock on being told of an accident to a loved one cannot recover damages from the negligent party on that account." [11] There is, therefore, general agreement to the effect that there must be some limitations to liability for nervous shock over and above those created by the ordinary principles of negligence, but there is little agreement as to their nature and scope. Some judges have attempted to make use of the concept of remoteness of damage,[12] but more commonly it has been the concept of duty which has been employed.[13] There is, however, no consistency in the way different judges, even in the same case, have dealt with the problem, and no clear principle emerges from the decisions.

In *Dulieu* v. *White* [14] the facts alleged [15] were that the plaintiff, a pregnant woman, was behind the bar of her husband's public-house when the defendant's servant so negligently drove a pair-horse

---

[8] *Bourhill* v. *Young* [1943] A.C. 92, 103.
[9] *Wilkinson* v. *Downton* [1897] 2 Q.B. 57. *Ante*, p. 43.
[9a] *Abramzik* v. *Brenner* (1967) 65 D.L.R. (2d) 651 (Sask. C.A.) at p. 654, *per* Culliton C.J.S.
[10] *Victorian Railway Commissioners* v. *Coultas* (1888) 13 App.Cas. 222, 225–226 *per* Sir Richard Couch. More than one judge has, however, declared his confidence " in the capacity of legal tribunals to get at the truth in this class of claim ": *Hambrook* v. *Stokes Bros.* [1925] 1 K.B. 141, 158, *per* Atkin L.J. See also Goodhart, " Shock Cases and the Area of Risk " (1953) 16 M.L.R. 14; Rendall, " Nervous Shock and Tortious Liability " (1962) 2 Osgoode Hall L.J. 291, 292.
[11] *King* v. *Phillips* [1953] 1 Q.B. 429, 441, *per* Denning L.J.; *Schneider* v. *Eisovitch* [1960] 2 Q.B. 430, 442, *per* Paull J.
[12] The formal ground for refusing a remedy in *Victorian Railway Commissioners* v. *Coultas* (1888) 13 App.Cas. 222 and in *Smith* v. *Johnson & Co.* (1897), unreported, referred to by Kennedy J. in *Dulieu* v. *White* [1901] 2 K.B. 669, 675, was that the damage was too remote, but in neither case would the ordinary rule of remoteness, whether that of directness or of foreseeability, have justified this conclusion. In *King* v. *Phillips* [1953] 1 Q.B. 429, Denning L.J. held that the plaintiff's damage was too remote.
[13] *Dulieu* v. *White* [1901] 2 K.B. 669; *Bourhill* v. *Young* [1943] A.C. 92; *King* v. *Phillips* [1953] 1 Q.B. 429.
[14] [1901] 2 K.B. 669.
[15] The decision was on a point of law raised by the pleadings.

van as to drive it into the public-house. The plaintiff was not physically injured, but she suffered shock which resulted in serious illness and the premature birth of her child. It was held that on these facts the plaintiff was entitled to recover, but Kennedy J. introduced the limitation that the shock must have been due to fear for her own personal safety. " A has, I conceive, no legal duty not to shock B's nerves by the exhibition of negligence towards C, or towards the property of B or C." [16] This would certainly have proved an effective limit on the scope of the liability, for it goes without saying that the plaintiff's fear must have been reasonable in the circumstances [17] but it is intellectually unsatisfying and was decisively rejected by a majority of the Court of Appeal in *Hambrook* v. *Stokes Bros.*[18] By S's negligence, his unattended lorry started to run violently down a steep and narrow street. H saw it coming and was terrified for the safety of her children from whom she had just parted [19] and who had turned a bend in the street out of her sight. Bystanders told her immediately afterwards that a child answering to the description of one of her own had been injured. She sustained a nervous shock and died in consequence. Bankes and Atkin L.JJ. held that S was liable for her death and rejected the limitation proposed by Kennedy J. " Assume two mothers crossing this street at the same time when this lorry comes thundering down, each holding a small child by the hand. One mother is courageous and devoted to her child. She is terrified, but thinks only of the damage to the child, and not at all about herself. The other woman is timid and lacking in the motherly instinct. She also is terrified, but thinks only of the damage to herself and not at all about her child. The health of both mothers is seriously affected by the mental shock occasioned by the fright. Can any real distinction be drawn between the two cases ? Will the law recognise a cause of action in the case of the less deserving mother and none in the case of the more deserving one ? Does the law say that the defendant ought reasonably to have anticipated the non-natural feeling of the timid mother, and not the natural feeling of the courageous mother ? I think not." [20]

Having thus rejected Kennedy J.'s proposed limitation, the Court of Appeal substituted a different one which, if accepted, will at least have the effect of restricting liability for shock to persons in the general

---

[16] [1901] 2 K.B. at p. 675. " The difficulty in these cases is to my mind not one as to the remoteness of the damage, but as to the uncertainty of there being any duty ": *ibid.* 685, *per* Phillimore J.

[17] *Cooper* v. *Caledonian Ry.* (1902) 4 F. 880; *Ross* v. *Glasgow Corpn.*, 1922 S.C. 527.

[18] [1925] 1 K.B. 141. But see Havard, " Reasonable Foresight of Nervous Shock " (1956) 19 M.L.R. 478, where it is observed that from the medical point of view the most likely cause of illness through shock is fear for one's own safety, " one reason for this being that the very excessive discharge (through the ' autonomic nervous system ') which it initiates is directed solely towards protecting him from immediate danger to his own personal safety " (at p. 482).

[19] *Cf.* Havard, *loc. cit.* at p. 486.

[20] [1925] 1 K.B. at p. 151, *per* Bankes L.J.; *ibid.* at p. 157, *per* Atkin L.J. See too *Chadwick* v. *British Railways Board* [1967] 1 W.L.R. 912, 918–920, *per* Waller J. *Cf.* [1925] 1 K.B. at pp. 162–164, *per* Sargant L.J., dissenting.

vicinity of the accident. More than one factor may have played its part in producing H's shock, for she did not only see the lorry careering down the street, she also learnt from bystanders that a child answering to the description of one of hers had been injured.[21] It was made clear, however, that S would be liable only if the shock resulted from what H either saw or realised by her own unaided senses, and not from something which someone told her.[22] This cannot be justified on the ground that shock following the report of an accident is always unforeseeable, but it does provide a reasonable means of drawing a line for the practical purposes of the law [23]; it is a derogation from the general principles of negligence which is called for by the " elements of greater subtlety " which exist in cases of nervous shock.[24]

In *Hambrook* v. *Stokes Bros.* there was an admission of negligence in the pleadings, and this meant that the breach of a duty owed to H was admitted by S.[25] It was not, therefore, necessary for the Court of Appeal to consider the circumstances in which a duty of care exists in cases of nervous shock.[26] Even if Kennedy J.'s limitation is rejected and that of *Hambrook* v. *Stokes Bros.* accepted, there remains the vital question whether a person who witnesses an accident and suffers shock in consequence, but is himself in no personal danger, can recover. In *Smith* v. *Johnson* [27] a man was killed by the defendant's negligence in the sight of the plaintiff, but the plaintiff failed to recover for the shock he suffered at the sight. In *Dooley* v. *Cammell Laird & Co.*,[28] on the other hand, the defendants' negligence led to the breaking of the rope of a crane so that its load fell into the hold of a ship where men were working. The plaintiff was the driver of the crane and was himself in no personal danger, but he suffered shock from witnessing the danger to the men in the hold, and Donovan J. held that he was entitled to succeed. The learned judge clearly denied the requirement of physical danger to the plaintiff. There was a breach of a duty owed to the plaintiff because the defendants should have had him in contemplation as likely to be affected

---

[21] Other factors also may have contributed to the shock. After the crash H went to her children's school, where she found her two boys, but her daughter was missing, and she then went to the hospital, where she found the girl, who had been knocked down and seriously injured by the lorry.

[22] At p. 152, *per* Bankes L.J.; at p. 159, *per* Atkin L.J.; at p. 165, *per* Sargant L.J.; *Abramzik* v. *Brenner* (1967) 65 D.L.R. (2d) 651 (Sask.C.A.).

[23] See also *Bourhill* v. *Young* [1943] A.C. 92; Goodhart, " *Bourhill* v. *Young* " (1944) 8 C.L.J. 265, 273. *Cf. Schneider* v. *Eisovitch* [1960] 2 Q.B. 430.

[24] In *The Wagon Mound* [1961] A.C. 388, 426, the Judicial Committee accepted as correct Denning L.J.'s statement in *King* v. *Phillips* [1953] 1 Q.B. 429, 441 that " the test of liability for nervous shock is foreseeability of injury by shock." It is respectfully submitted that this cannot always be true.

[25] At p. 156, *per* Atkin L.J.

[26] Atkin L.J. nevertheless considered that a duty was made out on the facts, apart from the admission in the pleadings [1925] 1 K.B. 156–158.

[27] (1897), unreported. See *Dulieu* v. *White* [1901] 2 K.B. 669; Pollard v. Makarchuk (1958) 16 D.L.R. (2d) 225; *Chadwick*
v. *British Railways Board* [1967] 1 W.L.R. 912. Liability was admitted on facts similar to *Dooley's* case in *Carlin* v. *Helical Bar Ltd.* (1970) 9 K.I.R. 154; *Mt. Isa Mines Ltd.* v. *Pusey* (1971) 46 A.L.J.R. 88 (Aust. High Ct.).

[28] [1951] 1 Lloyd's Rep. 271; *Pollard* v. *Makarchuk* (1958) 16 D.L.R. (2d) 225; *Chadwick* v. *British Railways Board* [1967] 1 W.L.R. 912. Liability was admitted on facts similar to *Dooley's* case in *Carlin* v. *Helical Bar Ltd.* (1970) 9 K.I.R. 154; *Mt. Isa Mines Ltd.* v. *Pusey* (1971) 46 A.L.J.R. 88 (Aust. High Ct.).

(*i.e.*, shocked) if the rope broke.[29] If these cases cannot be reconciled—and the task of reconciliation would seem extremely hard [30]—which of them should be regarded as correct?

The facts of *Bourhill* v. *Young* [31] have already been set out, and it will be recalled that the House of Lords held that there had been no breach of duty to the plaintiff because no injury to her could reasonably have been foreseen. The present point was not, therefore, directly raised, but nevertheless it was discussed. Unfortunately, however, the House of Lords did not speak with one voice on the matter. Dr. Goodhart suggests that it is reasonable to interpret the judgments in the case as being concerned only with foresight of emotional injury, but he agrees that there are also dicta indicating that a plaintiff can recover for nervous shock only if he was so placed that a physical injury to him could have been foreseen.[32] Even the decision in *Hambrook* v. *Stokes Bros.* provoked disagreement. Lord Wright expressed approval of it—" it now lays down the law "—and Lord Porter impliedly did so, but Lord Russell preferred the dissenting judgment of Sargant L.J. while Lords Thankerton and Macmillan reserved their opinions. Though the only case in which the House of Lords has so far considered liability for nervous shock, *Bourhill* v. *Young* does little to clarify the law.

In *King* v. *Phillips* [33] the defendant's taxicab, driven by his servant, was negligently backed into a small boy on a tricycle and slightly damaged both. The boy's mother heard him scream and, looking out of an upstairs window some seventy yards away, saw the tricycle under the taxicab but could not see the boy. She suffered shock

---

[29] It is worth noting that Donovan J. had no doubt that the plaintiff could recover against the first defendants for breach of a statutory duty which required " precautions to be taken to ensure the safety of all persons employed." It was against the second defendants only that the plaintiff had to prove the existence of a duty at common law. In *Boardman* v. *Sanderson* [1964] 1 W.L.R. 1317 (decided 1961) A, the driver of a car, B, his friend, and B's son were travelling together. They stopped for petrol and A asked B to go into the office to pay. B and his son got out of the car and, while B was in the office, A negligently backed the car into B's son. B heard the boy's screams and rushed to help him. The Court of Appeal held that B was entitled to recover damages for nervous shock. " I think I need say no more than that if the facts of this particular case are fitted to the concept of negligence, it is clear that a duty was owed by the defendant not only to the infant but to the near relatives of the infant who were, *as he knew*, on the premises, within earshot, and likely to come upon the scene if any injury or ill befell the infant ": *per* Ormerod L.J. at p. 1322. The ratio of this case is so narrow that it does not take the matter very far. What if A had not known, but should have known, of B's presence in the vicinity or if B had not been or was not known by A to be a near relative? See Dworkin, " An Unreported Nervous Shock Decision " (1962) 25 M.L.R. 353. *Cf. Lawrence* v. *C. J. Evans (Properties) Ltd.* [1965] C.L.Y. 2672.

[30] The explanation of *Smith* v. *Johnson* given by Kennedy J. in *Dulieu* v. *White* is that the defendant " neither intended to affect the plaintiff injuriously nor did anything which could reasonably or naturally be expected to affect him injuriously," but this seems to postulate an excessive degree of fortitude in the reasonable man.

[31] [1943] A.C. 92; *ante*, p. 54; Weir, *Casebook on Tort*, 3rd ed., p. 34.

[32] " The Shock Cases and Area of Risk " (1953) 16 M.L.R. 14, 20; *King* v. *Phillips* [1953] 1 Q.B. at p. 441, *per* Denning L.J.; *The Wagon Mound* [1961] A.C. at p. 426, *per* Viscount Simonds. See also Rendall, " Nervous Shock and Tortious Liability " 2 Osgoode Hall L.J. 290, where many of the cases are reviewed.

[33] [1953] 1 Q.B. 429; Goodhart, " Emotional Shock and the Unimaginative Taxicab Driver " (1953) 69 L.Q.R. 347. *Cf. Boardman* v. *Sanderson, supra.*

as a result, but the Court of Appeal, affirming McNair J.,[34] held
that although the taxicab driver was in breach of a duty of care he
owed to the boy, the mother could not recover. Singleton and Hodson
L.JJ. both reached their conclusions on the ground that the driver
owed no duty to the mother, but the similarity of their judgments
ends there. Hodson L.J. seems to have accepted Kennedy J.'s limitation,
for he suggests that had there been no admission of negligence in
Hambrook v. *Stokes Bros.* that case would have been overruled by the
House of Lords in *Bourhill* v. *Young*,[35] but Singleton L.J. would
have been prepared to hold that a duty existed if either physical ôr
emotional injury had been foreseeable. " I find it difficult to draw a
distinction between damage from physical injury and damage from
shock; prima facie, one would think that, if a driver should reasonably
have foreseen either, and damage resulted from the one or the other,
the plaintiff would be entitled to succeed." [36] He found it unnecessary
to consider " this somewhat academic point," however, for he accepted
and agreed with McNair J.'s finding that on the facts no reasonable
driver or hypothetical bystander would have anticipated damage of any
kind to the plaintiff. Denning L.J. also held that foreseeability of
emotional injury is sufficient and, indeed, went so far as to say that
the test adopted in *Bourhill* v. *Young* "was not foreseeability of
physical injury, but foreseeability of emotional shock." [37] Moreover, in his view, the driver owed a duty to the plaintiff in *King* v.
Phillips itself and on this point the case was indistinguishable from
Hambrook v. *Stokes Bros.* In *King* v. *Phillips*, however, the damage
suffered by the plaintiff was too remote, for " the slow backing of
the taxicab was very different from the terrifying descent of the runaway lorry. The taxicab driver cannot reasonably be expected to have
foreseen that his backing would terrify a mother seventy yards away,
whereas the lorry driver ought to have foreseen that a runaway lorry
might seriously shock the mother of children in the danger area." [38]
This reasoning is difficult to follow: first, as Dr. Goodhart observes,
" it is not immediately obvious why a mother should receive less of a
shock when she sees her child being slowly run over than when it is
done rapidly." [39] Secondly, if the fact was that no injury of any kind
was foreseeable to the plaintiff as a consequence of the actual negligence

---

[34] [1952] 2 All E.R. 459.
[35] [1953] 1 Q.B. at p. 444.
[36] [1953] 1 Q.B. at p. 437; *Boardman* v. *Sanderson* [1964] 1 W.L.R. 1317.
[37] *Ibid.* at p. 438. Approved in *The Wagon Mound* [1961] A.C. 388, 426. See too
Abramzik v. *Brenner* (1967) 65 D.L.R. (2d) 651, 658, *per* Culliton C.J.S. where, however,
the learned judge seems to have considered the ambit of foreseeability of nervous shock to
be narrower than that of physical injury. The finding of fact in this case that nervous
shock, suffered by the mother of three children on being told by her husband that two of
them had been killed and the third injured in an accident, was unforeseeable by the driver
of the car in which they were travelling who was responsible for the accident, is unexplained
and difficult to understand.
[38] At p. 442.
[39] *Loc. cit.* at p. 354.

alleged against the driver, then, whether the test of remoteness is directness or foreseeability, the decision should be that there was no breach of duty, not that a duty existed but that the damage was too remote.[40]

It is obvious, then, that the authorities are in a state of confusion, and the confusion is only slightly reduced by the preponderance of modern opinion in *Bourhill* v. *Young* and *King* v. *Phillips* that the problem in cases of nervous shock is one of duty and not of remoteness. Duty, it is agreed, depends upon foreseeability, but foreseeability, a vague concept at the best of times, is of quite exceptional vagueness when nervous shock is in issue. We have suggested earlier that it is foreseeable that the relatives of an accident victim may suffer shock on being told of the accident, at least if the victim suffers serious injury or is killed, but is it foreseeable that a witness of an accident, whether related to the victim or not, will suffer shock? This, it is said, must depend upon the standard of susceptibility of a normal person, unless the abnormality is known or ought to be known to the defendant,[41] but is a mother or a pregnant woman " normal " for the purposes of this rule? If I negligently run over a child I ought, perhaps, to foresee that his mother will probably be somewhere near, but what if, as is highly probable, I was not aware until after the accident that a child was there at all? [42] It will not always be true to say that I ought to have known of the presence of the child and so by implication of the presence also of his mother. My negligence against the child can be established by showing that I ought to have known that someone, adult or child, might be where the child in fact was. What, again, of the bystander who is unrelated to the victims or potential victims of the accident, such as the plaintiff in *Dooley* v. *Cammell Laird & Co.*[43] Does the liability of the negligent actor depend upon the extent and character of the physical damage he has caused or upon the extent and character of the physical damage he should have foreseen, which may not be the same, or upon neither of these things? [44]

---

[40] In *Schneider* v. *Eisovitch* [1960] 2 Q.B. 430, the plaintiff's husband was killed and the plaintiff herself injured in an accident caused by the negligence of the defendant. The plaintiff was rendered unconscious in the accident, and when she recovered consciousness in hospital she suffered additional shock on being told of her husband's death. Paull J. held that she could recover for this shock because the news of her husband's death was a consequence which flowed directly from the breach of duty to the plaintiff. But this, it is respectfully submitted, is an erroneous application of causation. It was not the breach of duty to the plaintiff, but the identical but distinct breach of duty to her husband, which caused the news of his death to reach her. See Jolowicz [1960] C.L.J. 156. A similar criticism, it is submitted, applies to *Malcolm* v. *Broadhurst* [1970] 3 All E.R. 508, 511.

[41] *Bourhill* v. *Young* [1943] A.C. at p. 110, *per* Lord Wright. But once the breach of duty is shown, then the plaintiff can recover in full even though his particular susceptibility leads him to suffer more than normal injury.

[42] See the important Australian case of *Chester* v. *Waverley Corporation* (1939) 62 C.L.R. 1. Lord Wright has said that Evatt J.'s dissenting judgment in this case " will demand the consideration of any judge who is called upon to consider these questions ": *Bourhill* v. *Young* [1943] A.C. at p. 110.

[43] [1951] 1 Lloyd's Rep. 271; *ante*, p. 121.

[44] Perhaps Denning L.J. had this sort of point in mind when he distinguished between the slow backing of a taxicab and the terrifying descent of a runaway lorry: *King* v. *Phillips* [1953] 1 Q.B. at p. 442.

There is an almost infinite number of questions of this kind which could be asked, but the courts have regularly treated questions of foreseeability as questions of fact. In view of the vagueness of foreseeability in the context of nervous shock, this means that the courts can base almost any conclusion on a finding that shock was or was not foreseeable in the circumstances, and this has to all intents and purposes been acknowledged by Lord Wright. In *Owens* v. *Liverpool Corporation* [45] a tramcar belonging to the defendants was negligently driven into a hearse, and the coffin was overturned and in danger of falling into the road. Four mourners in a following carriage suffered shock as a result and the Court of Appeal held that they were entitled to recover.[46] In *Bourhill* v. *Young* [47] Lord Wright said, " It is here, as elsewhere, a question of what the hypothetical reasonable man, viewing the position, I suppose, *ex post facto*, would say it was proper to foresee. What danger of particular infirmity that would include must depend on all the circumstances, but generally, I think, a reasonably normal condition, if medical evidence is capable of defining it, would be the standard. The test of the plaintiff's extraordinary susceptibility, if unknown to the defendant, would in effect make him an insurer. The lawyer likes to draw fixed and definite lines and is apt to ask where the thing is to stop. I should reply *it should stop where the good sense of the jury or of the judge decides*.[47a] I should myself be disposed, as at present advised, to say that it should have stopped short of judgment for the plaintiff in *Owens* v. *Liverpool Corporation*. The particular susceptibility there was to my mind beyond any range of normal expectancy or of reasonable foresight." Conversely, in *Chadwick* v. *British Railways Board*,[47b] the plaintiff's husband had acted as a volunteer rescue worker at the scene of a major rail disaster. As a result of the horror of his experiences he became ill with an anxiety neurosis. Although he had suffered psycho-

---

[45] [1939] 1 K.B. 394. The case was expressly disapproved by three members of the House of Lords in *Bourhill* v. *Young*: at p. 100, *per* Lord Thankerton; at p. 110, *per* Lord Wright; at p. 116, *per* Lord Porter.

[46] The court was inclined to doubt the trial judge's finding that the plaintiffs did in fact suffer shock at all, but MacKinnon L.J. said, " It may be that the plaintiffs are of that class which is peculiarly susceptible to the luxury of woe at a funeral, and may be disastrously disturbed by any untoward accident to the trappings of mourning. Nevertheless, one who is guilty of negligence to another must put up with idiosyncrasies of his victim that increase the likelihood or extent of damage to him." This, with respect, is a misapplication of the thin-skull rule. The peculiar susceptibility of the mourners could only have been relevant to the existence of a duty if it was known to the driver of the tramcar.

[47] [1943] A.C. at p. 110.

[47a] These words were adopted by Lord Denning M.R. in *Cook* v. *Swinfen* [1967] 1 W.L.R. 457, 462, where his Lordship seems to have interpreted them as referring to the good sense of the trial judge, not that of an appellate court.

[47b] [1967] 1 W.L.R. 912. Mr. Chadwick died of causes unconnected with the case and the action was brought on behalf of his estate. It is respectfully submitted that the judge's reasoning was unnecessarily complicated. Given the fact that the plaintiff's husband was not abnormally susceptible and given the " rescue principle " (*post*, pp. 623–626), would it not have been sufficient to hold that his illness was a foreseeable consequence of the defendants' admitted negligence in causing the accident? See n. 49a, *infra*.

neurotic symptoms a good many years before, he was not likely to relapse under the ordinary stresses of life, there was nothing in his personality to put him outside the ambit of contemplation and the defendants were therefore liable.

In the existing state of the authorities any propositions regarding liability in negligence for nervous shock must be put forward only with considerable diffidence. With this caveat it is submitted that the law may be summarised as follows:

1. If it was not reasonably foreseeable that the plaintiff would suffer injury of any kind as a result of the defendant's negligent act, then he cannot recover.[48]

2. If it was reasonably foreseeable that the plaintiff would suffer nervous shock as a result of the defendant's negligence, but only by being informed of it after the event, then again he cannot recover.[49]

3. If it was reasonably foreseeable that a normally susceptible person [49a] placed in the plaintiff's position would have suffered nervous shock from what he observed by his own unaided senses [49aa] as a result of the defendant's negligence, or if the particular susceptibility to shock of the plaintiff was known to the defendant, then probably the plaintiff can recover.[50]

4. If it was reasonably foreseeable that the plaintiff would suffer physical injury as a result of the defendant's negligence, i.e., if he was himself placed in danger of physical injury, then probably he can recover even though he suffers only nervous shock.

5. If the plaintiff suffers shock through reasonable fear for his own safety as a result of the defendant's negligence, then he can certainly recover.[51]

In all the above propositions it is presumed that the defendant failed to exercise due care and that the damage was not, on general

---

[48] *Bourhill* v. *Young* [1943] A.C. 92; *King* v. *Phillips* [1953] 1 Q.B. 429.
[49] *Hambrook* v. *Stokes Bros.* [1925] 1 K.B. 141.
[49a] Cf. the views of Windeyer J. in *Mt. Isa Mines Ltd.* v. *Pusey* (1971) 46 A.L.J.R. 88.
[49aa] It is probable now that the plaintiff may succeed if he has witnessed the aftermath rather than the accident: *Benson* v. *Lee* [1972] V.R. 879; *Marshall* v. *Lionel Enterprises Inc.* (1971) 25 D.L.R. (3d) 141. The apparently contrary decisions in *Chester* v. *Waverley Corpn.* (1939) 62 C.L.R. 1 and *Bourhill* v. *Young* [1943] A.C. 92 may be regarded as simply decisions on foreseeability.
[50] *Bourhill* v. *Young* [1943] A.C. at p. 109, *per* Lord Wright; at p. 119, *per* Lord Porter; *Dooley* v. *Cammell Laird & Co.* [1951] 1 Lloyd's Rep. 271; *King* v. *Phillips* [1953] 1 Q.B. 429; *Boardman* v. *Sanderson* [1964] 1 W.L.R. 1317. In *Furniss* v. *Fitchett* [1958] N.Z.L.R. 396 the defendant was the medical adviser to the plaintiff and her husband. The husband was anxious to obtain a separation from his wife and asked the defendant for a certificate regarding her health to show to his lawyer. The defendant gave a certificate stating that the plaintiff exhibited symptoms of paranoia. The contents of this certificate were made known to the plaintiff during proceedings for maintenance brought by her against her husband, and she suffered shock in consequence. The Supreme Court of New Zealand held that the defendant was liable as he knew that publication of the content of the certificate to the plaintiff was likely to be harmful to her and that such publication was likely. Cf. *Guay* v. *Sun Publishing Co.* [1952] 2 D.L.R. 479 (negligent misstatement in newspaper that plaintiff's husband and three children had been killed in an accident. No liability for nervous shock as publication was made in good faith); Macintyre (1953) 31 Can. Bar Rev. 773.
[51] *Dulieu* v. *White* [1901] 2 K.B. 669.

principles, too remote. In short, if the ordinary principles of liability in negligence indicate that the plaintiff has no cause of action, then he can no more recover for nervous shock than for any other injury. But even if the ordinary principles of liability in negligence suggest that the plaintiff is entitled to a remedy it does not necessarily follow that he can recover damages for shock.[52]

---

[52] See *King* v. *Phillips* [1953] 1 Q.B. at pp. 438–439, where Denning L.J. suggests that if the plaintiff in *Bourhill* v. *Young* had been physically injured she could have recovered. *Sed quaere.*

CHAPTER 8

BREACH OF STATUTORY DUTY [1]

THE EXISTENCE OF LIABILITY

The old rule

Where a statutory duty is imposed upon a person or body of persons and that duty is broken, liability to the penalty under the statute is of course incurred. It has, however, for long been the rule in the case of some statutes, that an action in tort may be brought by anyone who is injured by their breach.[2] Indeed, until the nineteenth century the view seems to have been taken that wherever a statutory duty is created, any person who can show that he has sustained harm from its non-performance can bring an action against the person on whom the duty is imposed.[3] During the first half of the nineteenth century, however, a different view began to be taken,[4] and in *Atkinson* v. *Newcastle Waterworks Co.*[5] the Court of Appeal's doubts about the old rule were so strong as to amount to disapproval of it. With the vast increase in legislative activity[6] of modern times, if the old rule were still law it might lead to unjust, not to say absurd, results in creating liabilities wider than the legislature can possibly have intended.

Extinguishment of common law rights

Where a common law right already in existence is extinguished by a statute, of course it disappears, but where the statute does not expressly or by necessary implication do this, there is no presumption that such is its effect.[7] Indeed, it is quite possible that it may leave the old right

---

[1] Thayer, " Public Wrong and Private Action " (1914) 27 Harv.L.R. 317; Morris, " The Role of Criminal Statutes in Negligence Actions " (1949) 49 Col.L.Rev. 21; Glanville Williams, " The Effect of Penal Legislation in the Law of Tort " (1960) 23 M.L.R. 233; Fricke, " The Juridical Nature of the Action upon the Statute " (1960) 76 L.Q.R. 240; Weir, *Casebook on Tort*, 3rd ed., Chap. 3.

[2] Statute of Westminster II (1285), c. 50; Fricke, *loc. cit.*, p. 240.

[3] " Where-ever a statute enacts anything, or prohibits anything, for the advantage of any person, that person shall have remedy to recover the advantage given him, or to have satisfaction for the injury done him contrary to the law by the same statute; for it would be a fine thing to make a law by which one has a right, but no remedy in equity ": *Anon.* (1704) 6 Mod. 26, *per* Holt C.J. Com.Dig. tit. " Action upon Statute," F; *Ashby* v. *White* (1703) 2 Ld.Raym. 938; *Couch* v. *Steel* (1854) 3 E. & B. 402.

[4] *Doe* v. *Bridges* (1831) 1 B. & Ad. 847.

[5] (1877) 2 Ex.D. 441, criticising *Couch* v. *Steel* (1854) 3 E. & B. 402.

[6] The law considered in this chapter applies to subordinate as well as to parliamentary legislation.

[7] Craies, *Statute Law*, 6th ed., Chap. 11, *National Coal Board* v. *England* [1954] A.C. 403; *Barnes* v. *Irwell Valley Water Board* [1939] 1 K.B. 21 (no breach of statutory duty to supply pure water in pipes, but breach of common law duty to supply pure water at point at which it was received); *Read* v. *Croydon Corporation* (1939) 108 L.J.K.B. 72 (breach of statutory and common law duty to supply pure and wholesome water); *Kilgollan* v. *William Cooke & Co. Ltd.* [1956] 1 W.L.R. 527 (no breach of statutory duty to fence dangerous parts of machinery but breach of employer's duty at common law). The point is made expressly by the Mines and Quarries Act 1954, s. 193.

128

existing side by side with the new one it creates, and it is, for example, extremely common for a claim for breach of statutory duty to be joined with one for negligence in actions by workmen against their employers.[8]

Creation of new rights

If an entirely new duty is imposed upon someone by statute and consequently a new right is conferred upon someone else, the question arises whether that right is enforceable by an action in tort. " The only rule which in all circumstances is valid is that the answer must depend on a consideration of the whole Act and the circumstances, including the pre-existing law, in which it was enacted." [9] The question is thus, at least in theory, one of ascertaining the intention of Parliament, and where Parliament has stated or clearly implied its intention in the wording of the Act, no difficulty exists.[10] Moreover, where a duty is imposed by statute but no sanction of any kind is provided, there is a presumption that a person injured by its breach has a right of action.[11] In the overwhelming majority of statutes, however, a sanction is provided for breach of the duty in the form either of a penalty or of administrative action [12] and yet the statute is silent on the question whether a civil remedy for breach is intended to exist.[13]

Ascertaining the intention of Parliament

Not the least of the difficulties in seeking to discover the intention, or rather presumed intention, of Parliament is that it is not altogether clear which of two diametrically opposed initial presumptions actually prevails. According to one view " prima facie a person who has been injured by the breach of a statute has a right to recover damages from the person committing it unless it can be established by considering the whole of the Act that no such right was intended to be given." [14]

---

[8] See Chap. 9, *post.*

[9] *Cutler* v. *Wandsworth Stadium Ltd.* [1949] A.C. 398, 407, *per* Lord Simonds; *ibid.* at p. 412, *per* Lord Normand; *Ministry of Housing* v. *Sharp* [1970] 2 Q.B. 223, 273, *per* Salmon L.J.

[10] *e.g.*, Mines and Quarries Act 1954, s. 159: " For the removal of doubts it is hereby declared that the owner of a mine or quarry is not absolved from liability to pay damages in respect of a contravention, in relation to the mine or quarry, by a person employed by him of—(a) a provision of this Act. . . ." See also Resale Prices Act 1964, s. 4 (2); Mineral Workings (Off-Shore Installations) Act 1971, s. 11; and p. 386 *et seq., post.*

[11] *Doe* v. *Bridges* (1831) 1 B. & Ad. 847, 859, *per* Lord Tenterden C.J.; *Square* v. *Model Farm Dairies (Bournemouth) Ltd.* [1939] 2 K.B. 365, 375, *per* Slesser L.J.; *Cutler* v. *Wandsworth Stadium Ltd.* [1949] A.C. 398, 407, *per* Lord Simonds; *Att.-Gen.* v. *St. Ives R.D.C.* [1960] 1 Q.B. 312; *Reffell* v. *Surrey C.C.* [1964] 1 W.L.R. 358; Weir, *Casebook on Tort*, 3rd ed., p. 144, *Ministry of Housing* v. *Sharp, supra*, at p. 267, *per* Lord Denning M.R.

[12] As under the Education Act 1944, s. 99; *Watt* v. *Kesteven C.C.* [1955] 1 Q.B. 408. *Cf. Reffell* v. *Surrey C.C., supra*, where Veale J. regarded the Education Act 1944 and the Standards for School Premises Regulations 1959 as providing no sanction for their breach and accordingly applied the presumption that an injured person has a right of action.

[13] In *Keating* v. *Elvan Reinforced Concrete Co. Ltd.* [1968] 1 W.L.R. 722, the fact that the Public Utilities Street Works Act 1950 contains provisions creating civil liabilities in favour of public authorities was regarded as a reason for holding that it gives no right of action to individuals.

[14] *Monk* v. *Warbey* [1935] 1 K.B. 75, 81, *per* Greer L.J. (but *cf.* the same Lord Justice's approval in the same case of a dictum of Atkin L.J. in *Phillips* v. *Britannia Hygienic*

According to the other view, however, "where an Act creates an obligation, and enforces the performance in a specified manner, we take it to be a general rule that performance cannot be enforced in any other manner." [15] The second of these views has the greater measure of acceptance today [16] but whichever is preferred, it must at once be qualified by the statement that it is subject to a large number of exceptions. It is probably unwise, therefore, when investigating the position under a given statute to start with a presumption of any kind. There are, however, certain indications which have been treated by the courts as pointing with more or less force one way or the other.

Statutes for the benefit of a class. It is sometimes said that an important criterion is whether the statute was passed for the benefit of an ascertainable class of persons [17] and, though Atkin L.J. denied the validity of this test,[18] it has since been said by Romer L.J. to be " of cardinal importance." [19] It may, indeed, be easier to hold that a civil remedy is intended where by its very nature the statute is capable of benefiting only a limited class of persons,[19a] but nevertheless, as a matter of principle the opinion of Atkin L.J. is to be preferred. " It would be strange if a less important duty, which is owed to a section of the public, may be enforced by action, while a more important duty owed to the public at large cannot." [20] The apparently similar distinction between a statutory duty which is a public duty only and one which is owed as well to the party aggrieved [21] seems to amount to no more than the distinction between a duty for the breach of which an action lies and one for which it does not and thus assumes what it seeks to establish.

The type of harm to be prevented. A more useful guide, perhaps, is to be found in an examination of the kind of mischief the statute was intended to prevent. If it is exactly the type of harm which the plaintiff has suffered, that is a strong argument in favour of his right

---

Laundry Co. [1923] 2 K.B. 832, 841, apparently to the opposite effect). See, too, *Groves* v. *Wimborne* (*Lord*) [1898] 2 Q.B. 402, 407, *per* A. L. Smith L.J.; *Solomons* v. *R. Gertzenstein Ltd.* [1954] 2 Q.B. 243, 260, *per* Birkett L.J.

[15] *Doe* v. *Bridges* (1831) 1 B. & Ad. at p. 859, *per* Lord Tenterden C.J.

[16] See, *e.g.*, *Pasmore* v. *Oswaldtwistle U.D.C.* [1898] A.C. 387; *Phillips* v. *Britannia Hygienic Laundry Co.* [1923] 2 K.B. 832; *Cutler* v. *Wandsworth Stadium Ltd.* [1949] A.C. 398; *J. Bollinger* v. *Costa Brava Wine Co.* [1960] Ch. 262; *Sephton* v. *Lancashire River Board* [1962] 1 W.L.R. 623.

[17] *Phillips* v. *Britannia Hygienic Laundry, supra,* at pp. 838, 840, *per* Bankes L.J.

[18] *Ibid.* at p. 841.

[19] *Solomons* v. *R. Gertzenstein Ltd.* [1954] 2 Q.B. 243, 265. See also *per* Birkett L.J., *ibid.* at p. 261; Fricke, *loc. cit.* at pp. 264–265.

[19a] As in *Warder* v. *Cooper* [1970] Ch. 495. (Breach of the Rent Act 1965, s. 32 (1), which in certain circumstances prohibits the owner of premises from enforcing his right to recover possession against the occupier of them otherwise than by proceedings in the court, is a tort against an evicted occupier.)

[20] *Phillips* v. *Britannia Hygienic Laundry Co.* [1923] 2 K.B. at p. 841. Romer L.J.'s opinion was *obiter,* but Atkin L.J.'s was approved in *Monk* v. *Warbey* [1952] 1 K.B. 75. *Cf. Rowley* v. *Chatham* [1970] R.T.R. 462.

[21] *e.g., Clarke* v. *Brims* [1947] K.B. 497, 505, *per* Morris J.

to sue. In *Monk* v. *Warbey* [22] the defendant had permitted his car to be driven by an uninsured driver and thereby committed an offence against the Road Traffic Act 1930, s. 35.[23] Owing to the negligence of that driver the plaintiff was injured but could recover no damages from him as he was destitute of means. It was held that the very purpose of the section was to provide protection against uninsured drivers and, accordingly, that the defendant was liable to the plaintiff.[24] On the other hand, it seems clear that a major purpose of the Motor Cars (Use and Construction) Order 1904 [25] was to prevent damage from unroadworthy vehicles to other property on the highway, but it was held in *Phillips* v. *Britannia Hygienic Laundry Co.*[26] that no action in tort lay for a breach of the Order.

The nature of the penalty. In *Groves* v. *Wimborne* [27] the statute made any occupier of a factory, who did not properly fence dangerous machinery, liable to a fine of £100; and it provided that the whole or any part of the fine might be applied, if the Secretary of State should so determine, for the benefit of the person injured by the occupier's neglect. A boy employed in the factory of the defendant was caught by an unfenced cogwheel and his arm had to be amputated. The Court of Appeal held that he was entitled to recover £150. It was true that the whole or part of the fine fixed by the Act might be applied for his benefit, and it was therefore arguable that he had no remedy outside the statute. But to this it was answered that there was no *certainty* that any part of the fine would be awarded to him, and, even if it were awarded, its upward limit of £100, it was said,[28] made it incredible that Parliament would have regarded that as a sufficient and exclusive compensation for mutilation or death.[29] That reasoning based upon the inadequacy of the statutory penalty is unreliable is shown, however, by a comparison of this case with *Atkinson* v. *Newcastle Waterworks Co.*[30] Parliament had required

[22] [1935] 1 K.B. 75; applied in *Corfield* v. *Groves* [1950] W.N. 116.
[23] See now Road Traffic Act 1972, s. 143.
[24] The court must look at the realities of the matter, and it is not necessary to show that the driver will *never* pay: *Martin* v. *Dean* [1971] 2 Q.B. 208. Where the lack of insurance has no connection with the injury suffered, *Monk* v. *Warbey* does not apply: *Daniels* v. *Vaux* [1938] 2 K.B. 203; nor where there is no liability under the Act of 1930: *Goodbarne* v. *Buck* [1940] 1 K.B. 771; *Gregory* v. *Ford* [1951] 1 All E.R. 121. Glanville Williams, *loc. cit.*, p. 259, regards *Monk* v. *Warbey* as an " improper type of judicial invention," but its general approach has been echoed in more recent cases, *e.g.*, *Ministry of Housing* v. *Sharp* [1970] 2 Q.B. 223; *Warder* v. *Cooper* [1970] Ch. 495, and see the comment in Weir, *Casebook on Tort*, 3rd ed., p. 150.
[25] See now the Road Traffic Act 1972, s. 40 and the Motor Vehicles (Construction and Use) Regulations 1969, as amended.
[26] [1923] 2 K.B. 832; Weir, *Casebook on Tort*, 3rd ed., p. 148, *Clarke* v. *Brims* [1947] K.B. 497. Contrast *L.P.T.B.* v. *Upson* [1949] A.C. 155 with *Coote* v. *Stone* [1971] 1 W.L.R. 279.
[27] [1898] 2 Q.B. 402.
[28] At p. 408, *per* A. L. Smith L.J.; p. 414, *per* Rigby L.J.; pp. 416–417, *per* Vaughan Williams L.J.
[29] Other examples are *Dormont* v. *Furness Ry.* (1883) 11 Q.B.D. 496; *Ross* v. *Rugge-Price* (1876) 1 Ex.D. 269.
[30] (1877) 2 Ex.D. 441. *Cf. Read* v. *Croydon Corpn.* [1938] 4 All E.R. 631.

the defendant company, which supplied Newcastle with water, to keep certain pipes, to which fire-plugs were fixed, charged with water at a certain pressure and had fixed a £10 penalty, no part of which could be awarded to any individual, for failure to do so. Fire broke out on the plaintiff's property and, in consequence of the defendants' breach of their obligation, could not be extinguished. It was held that the Act being in the nature of a bargain between the defendant company and Parliament for the supply of water to the city, it could not have been the intention that the company should become virtually insurers of the safety from fire, so far as water can produce that safety, of all the houses in the district. The fact that the Act itself provided no compensation to individuals was regarded more as an argument against civil liability than for it.[31]

Other criteria. Other criteria are also sometimes used and, for example, a civil remedy has been refused on the ground that the existing common law remedies were adequate,[32] but despite the existence of the employer's general duties at common law[33] this has never prevented the courts from holding that a remedy exists for breach of statutory safety provisions.[34] It seems, therefore, that there is no general rule except that the question whether a right of action exists in any given case must depend upon the construction of the statute in question. In practice, however, this means that in many cases the courts profess to seek the intention of Parliament on a question to which in all probability it gave no consideration. " This process of looking for what is not there, unaided by any compelling presumptions, naturally leads to the most surprising diversity of outcome." [35]

It can scarcely be maintained that this is a satisfactory situation. As Lord du Parcq has pointed out,[36] the draftsmen of Acts of Parliament are aware of the principles—and lack of principles—applied by the courts to fill the gaps left in legislation, and it can be argued, therefore, that the silence of a statute on the question of civil remedies for its breach is a deliberate invitation to the courts to decide the question for themselves. But if this is so, then the pretence of seeking

---

[31] In the case of breach of some other obligations, *e.g.*, the obligation to supply water to householders, a penalty was payable to the aggrieved individual. It was conceded by the plaintiff that in such cases no civil remedy could exist: 2 Ex.D. at p. 447, *per* Lord Cairns L.C.

[32] *Phillips* v. *Britannia Hygienic Laundry Co.* [1923] 2 K.B. 832, 842, *per* Atkin L.J.; *Square* v. *Model Farm Dairies Ltd.* [1939] 2 K.B. 365.

[33] Chap. 9, *post.*

[34] Conversely the fact that the common law affords no remedy to a highway user for injury caused by animals straying onto the highway did not lead the courts to grant a civil remedy for the statutory offence of allowing animals to stray onto the highway (Highways Act 1959, s. 135): Glanville Williams, *loc. cit.* at p. 246; *Heath's Garage Ltd.* v. *Hodges* [1916] 2 K.B. 370; *Searle* v. *Wallbank* [1947] A.C. 341. See too *Keating* v. *Elvan Reinforced Concrete Co. Ltd.* [1968] 1 W.L.R. 722, 728, *per* Widgery L.J. See now Animals Act 1971, s. 8 (1), *post*, p. 393.

[35] Glanville Williams, *loc. cit.* at p. 244.

[36] *Cutler* v. *Wandsworth Stadium Ltd.* [1949] A.C. 398, 411; *Solomons* v. *R. Gertzenstein Ltd.* [1954] 2 Q.B. 243, 267, *per* Romer L.J.

the non-existent intention of Parliament should be abandoned. Not only does it involve an unnecessary fiction, but it may lead to decisions being made on the basis of insignificant details of phraseology instead of matters of substance. If the question whether a person injured by breach of a statutory obligation is to have a right of action for damages is in truth a question to be decided by the courts, let it be acknowledged as such and some useful principles of law developed.[37]

In the prevailing state of the law, therefore, there is little if any principle beyond the vague invocation of the intention of Parliament, but there have been numerous decisions on particular statutes so that in many cases it is already settled that a right of action does or does not exist.[38] It is not enough, however, for a plaintiff simply to prove the breach of a statute for which, generally speaking, a right of action has been held to exist. There are other elements in the tort of breach of statutory duty which we must now consider.

ELEMENTS OF THE TORT

1. The duty must be owed to the plaintiff

Some statutory duties are so expressed as to limit the classes of person for whose benefit they exist, and where this is so it is a question of the construction of the statutory provision in question whether the plaintiff is a member of the protected class. If he is not, then his action for breach of statutory duty cannot succeed. In *Hartley* v. *Mayoh & Co.*,[40] for example, a fireman was electrocuted while fighting a fire at the defendants' factory. His widow relied, *inter alia*, upon a breach by the defendants of their obligations under certain statutory regulations, but these existed only for the protection of " persons employed," and firemen did not come within this description. The claim for breach of statutory duty therefore failed.

2. The injury must be of the kind which the statute is intended to prevent

If the object of the statute was to prevent mischief of a particular kind, one who suffers from its non-observance loss of a different

---

[37] For a case decided by reference to principle and policy rather than the supposed intention of Parliament see *Hargreaves* v. *Bretherton* [1959] 1 Q.B. 45 (no action in tort for perjury). See also *Badham* v. *Lambs Ltd.* [1946] K.B. 45; *Biddle* v. *Truvox Engineering Co.* [1952] 1 K.B. 101. See also Morris, *loc. cit.*

[38] Thus *Groves* v. *Wimborne* [1898] 2 Q.B. 402 virtually settled that an action for damages lies for breach of the safety provisions of successive Factories Acts (but *cf. Biddle* v. *Truvox Engineering Co.* [1952] 1 K.B. 101, no action against seller of unfenced machine for breach of s. 17 (2)). Professor Glanville Williams' statement that when legislation concerns industrial welfare it results in absolute liability while in all other cases it is ignored (*loc. cit.* p. 233), an admitted over-simplification, is perhaps less true than it was when written. See *e.g., Sephton* v. *Lancashire River Board* [1962] 1 W.L.R. 623; *Rippingale Farms Ltd.* v. *Black Sluice Internal Drainage Board* [1963] 1 W.L.R. 1347; *Ministry of Housing* v. *Sharp* [1970] 2 Q.B. 223; *Warder* v. *Cooper* [1970] Ch. 495, all of which are cases quite unrelated to industrial welfare. It is also the case that many statutory duties are less than absolute.

[40] [1954] 1 Q.B. 383; *Wingrove* v. *Prestige & Co.* [1954] 1 W.L.R. 524; *Herbert* v. *Harold Shaw Ltd.* [1959] 2 Q.B. 138. *Cf. Lavender* v. *Diamints Ltd.* [1949] 1 K.B. 585; *Canadian Pacific Steamships Ltd.* v. *Bryers* [1958] A.C. 485; *Smith* v. *Supreme Wood Pulp Co. Ltd.* [1968] 3 All E.R. 753.

kind cannot twist its remedy into an action for his own recoupment. In *Gorris* v. *Scott*[41] the defendant, a shipowner, was under a statutory duty to provide pens for cattle on his ship in order to lessen the risk of murrain among them. The plaintiff's sheep were swept overboard in consequence of lack of such pens. The defendant was held not liable, because it was no part of the purpose of the statute to protect cattle against the perils of the sea.[42] The modern tendency is, however, not to apply this decision too strictly,[43] and it has been said that if the plaintiff's damage is of the kind that the statute was designed to prevent, then it does not matter that it occurred in a way not contemplated by the statute.[44] On the other hand the House has affirmed that a workman who is injured by a dangerous part of machinery which flies out of a machine and hits him cannot base a claim on the statutory obligation that dangerous parts of machinery " shall be securely fenced."[45] The object of this provision, it has been said is " to keep the worker out, not to keep the machine or its product in."[46] It is only if he comes into contact with the dangerous part of the machine, therefore, that the workman can rely upon breach of the obligation to fence, and an injury caused in a different way is not covered.

3. The defendant must be guilty of a breach of his statutory obligation

Two points must be noted here. In the first place, many statutes and statutory regulations have strictly defined spheres of application, and outside their proper sphere they are irrelevant. To take a typical example, the Shipbuilding and Ship-repairing Regulations 1960, which lay down an elaborate code of safety precautions to be observed in the construction and repair of ships, do not in general apply to the construction and repair of ships not exceeding 100 feet in length, and many actions for injury caused by acts or omissions which would have amounted to breaches of the Factories Acts had they occurred in a factory have failed on the ground that the place where they in fact occurred was not a factory as defined.[47] In *Chipchase* v. *British Titan*

---

[41] (1874) L.R. 9 Exch. 125; *Bailey* v. *Ayr Engineering Co. Ltd.* [1959] 1 Q.B. 183.

[42] This decision may easily be misunderstood unless it is realised that the plaintiffs made no claim whatever apart from the statute. If, quite apart from this statutory duty, the defendant had been negligent so that the sheep would have been washed overboard, pens or no pens, then the plaintiffs could have recovered either for breach of contract or for the tort of negligence. As it was, they relied on the statutory obligation and on nothing else.

[43] *Grant* v. *National Coal Board* [1958] A.C. 649; *Gatehouse* v. *John Summers & Sons Ltd.* [1953] 1 W.L.R. 742; *Littler* v. *G. L. Moore (Contractors) Ltd.* [1967] 1 W.L.R. 1241; *Donaghey* v. *Boulton & Paul Ltd.* [1968] A.C. 1; *McInally* v. *Frank B. Price & Co. (Roofings) Ltd.*, 1971 S.L.T.(Notes) 43.

[44] *Donaghey* v. *Boulton & Paul Ltd.*, *supra*, at p. 26, *per* Lord Reid. Note the similarity to the development at common law subsequent to *The Wagon Mound*.

[45] Factories Act 1961, s. 14; *Close* v. *Steel Co. of Wales Ltd.* [1962] A.C. 367 (Lords Denning and Morris dissenting on this point); *Sparrow* v. *Fairey Aviation Co. Ltd.* [1964] A.C. 1019.

[46] *Nicholls* v. *F. Austin (Leyton) Ltd.* [1946] A.C. 493, 505, *per* Lord Simonds.

[47] A recent example is *Longhurst* v. *Guildford, etc., Water Board* [1963] A.C. 265.

Products Co.[48] a workman was injured when he fell from a platform nine inches wide and six feet above the ground. Statutory regulations required that " every working platform from which a person is liable to fall more than six feet and six inches shall be . . . at least 34 inches wide " [49] and it was argued that the case was so nearly within the regulations that the court ought to take them into account. The argument was rejected and the defendants were held not liable either for breach of statutory duty, for there was none, or for negligence at common law.

The second point which it is necessary to make is that the measure of the defendant's obligation in every case must be found in the statute itself and that no single standard of conduct exists. In some cases the statute imposes an unqualified obligation, *i.e.*, an absolute duty, that a certain state of affairs shall exist, and in such cases the non-existence of that state of affairs constitutes the breach.[50] In *John Summers & Sons Ltd.* v. *Frost*,[51] for example, a workman in a factory was injured when his thumb came into contact with a revolving grinding wheel. The Factories Act required [52] that " every dangerous part of any machinery . . . shall be securely fenced," and there was a hood over the grinding wheel which covered most of it. There was, however, a part of the wheel unguarded and if this had not been so the grinding wheel could not have been used. It was held that there had been a breach of the statutory obligation that dangerous parts be " securely fenced," and that it was no answer that secure fencing of a grinding wheel would render it unusable. In other cases,[53] however, the obligation may be qualified by some such words as " so far as is reasonably practicable," and where this is so, it has been said, the obligation adds little to that which exists at common law.[54] Again, the obligation may be " to take such steps as may be necessary " [55] and this, it appears, falls somewhere between the duty that a given state of affairs shall exist and a duty that it shall exist " so far as is reasonably prac-

---

[48] [1956] 1 Q.B. 545. *Cf. Blamires* v. *Lancashire & Yorkshire Ry.* (1873) L.R. 8 Ex. 283; *Thomas Stone Shipping Ltd.* v. *Admiralty* [1953] P. 117; *Butt* v. *Inner London Authority* (1968) 118 New L.J. 254.

[49] Building (Safety, Health and Welfare) Regulations 1948, reg. 22 (c).

[50] *Galashiels Gas Co.* v. *Millar* [1949] A.C. 275. " The fact that the rung gave way establishes . . . beyond question that the ladder was not in an efficient state and was not in good repair at that time "; *Cole* v. *Blackstone & Co.* [1943] K.B. 615, *per* Macnaghten J.; *Reffell* v. *Surrey C.C.* [1964] 1 W.L.R. 358.

[51] [1955] A.C. 740; *Davies* v. *Owen* [1919] 2 K.B. 39.

[52] Factories Act 1937, s. 14 (1). Now Factories Act 1961, s. 14 (1).

[53] Including other sections of the Factories Act itself.

[54] *Levesley* v. *Thomas Firth & John Brown Ltd.* [1953] 1 W.L.R. 1206, 1210, *per* Denning L.J. referring to the Factories Act 1937, s. 26 (1) (now Factories Act 1961, s. 29 (1)); *Jenkins* v. *Allied Ironfounders Ltd.* [1970] 1 W.L.R. 304. For cases where a duty of care which would not have existed at common law was created by statute, see *Sephton* v. *Lancashire River Board* [1962] 1 W.L.R. 623; *Ministry of Housing* v. *Sharp* [1970] 2 Q.B. 223. Where the duty is to the effect that something shall be done " so far as is reasonably practicable " it is for the defendant to prove the impracticability, not for the plaintiff to prove that it was reasonably practicable: *Nimmo* v. *Alexander Cowan & Sons Ltd.* [1968] A.C. 107.

[55] *e.g., Mines and Quarries Act* 1954, s. 48.

ticable." That the necessary steps were not reasonably practicable will be no answer to an allegation of breach of this duty, but there will be no breach if the necessity of the steps was not and could not have been known before the event.[56]

4. The breach of duty must have caused the damage

At one time the view was taken, at least where statutory duties aimed at promoting safety were concerned, that if a breach of the duty and damage of the kind that it was intended to prevent were shown, the onus shifted to the person in breach of his duty to prove that the breach of the duty was not the cause of the damage.[57] Now, however, it has been made clear that the injured person must prove the causal connection between the breach of duty and the damage as in any other case, and that no presumption exists in his favour.[58] In general, therefore, no distinction is to be drawn between actions for common law negligence and actions for breach of statutory duty so far as causation is concerned.[59] There is, however, one rather special kind of case, peculiar to actions for breach of statutory duty, which must be mentioned, namely that in which the act or omission of the plaintiff himself has the legal result that both plaintiff and defendant are in breach of the same duty.

In *Ginty* v. *Belmont Building Supplies Ltd.*[59a] the plaintiff was an experienced workman in the employment of the defendants who were roofing contractors. Statutory regulations binding upon both parties required that crawling boards should be used for work done on fragile roofs and, although boards had been provided by the defendants, the plaintiff neglected to use them and fell through a roof in consequence. In law both plaintiff and defendants were in breach of their statutory duties, but Pearson J. held that the plaintiff's claim failed altogether because the defendants' breach consisted of and was co-extensive with his own wrongful act.[59b] In other words, there was no wrongful act but the plaintiff's own, and " it would be absurd if, notwithstanding the employer having done all he could reasonably be expected to do

---

[56] *Brown* v. *National Coal Board* [1962] A.C. 574; [1961] 1 Q.B. 603 (C.A.); Hamson [1961] C.L.J. 20; [1962] C.L.J. 26; *Tomlinson* v. *Beckermet Mining Co. Ltd.* [1964] 1 W.L.R. 1043; *John G. Stein & Co. Ltd.* v. *O'Hanlon* [1965] A.C. 890.

[57] *Lee* v. *Nursery Furnishings Ltd.* [1945] 1 All E.R. 387; *Vyner* v. *Waldenberg Bros. Ltd.* [1946] K.B. 50.

[58] *Bonnington Castings Ltd.* v. *Wardlaw* [1956] A.C. 613; *McWilliams* v. *Sir William Arrol & Co.* [1962] 1 W.L.R. 295 (H.L.); *Wigley* v. *British Vinegars Ltd.* [1964] A.C. 307. It is enough if the plaintiff establishes on a balance of probabilities that the breach of duty contributed materially to the damage: *ibid.*; *Quinn* v. *Cameron & Robertson Ltd.* [1958] A.C. 9.

[59] *Bonnington Castings Ltd.* v. *Wardlaw* [1956] A.C. 613, 624, per Lord Tucker. Just as in cases at common law (*ante*, pp. 105–106) the plaintiff's own act may sometimes be such that it amounts in effect to a *nova causa interveniens*: *Rushton* v. *Turner Bros. Asbestos Co.* [1960] 1 W.L.R. 96; *Horne* v. *Lec Refrigeration Ltd.* [1965] 2 All E.R. 898, but this is rare. See, *e.g.*, *Denyer* v. *Charles Skipper and East Ltd.* [1970] 1 W.L.R. 1087; *Stocker* v. *Norprint Ltd.* (1971) 10 K.I.R. 10.

[59a] [1959] 1 All E.R. 414; *Manwaring* v. *Billington* [1952] 2 All E.R. 747.

[59b] [1959] 1 All E.R. at p. 424.

to ensure compliance, a workman, who deliberately disobeyed his employer's orders and thereby put the employer in breach of a regulation, could claim damages for injury caused to him solely by his own wrongdoing." [60]

Although the result reached in *Ginty* v. *Belmont Building Supplies Ltd.* has been judicially described as " obvious," [60a] the scope of the decision is restricted. If the plaintiff establishes the defendant's breach of duty and that he suffered injury as a result, he establishes a prima facie case against the defendant. The defendant will escape liability only if he can rebut that prima facie case by proof that the only act or default of anyone which caused the breach was that of the plaintiff himself.[60b] It follows that where some fault is to be attributed to the defendant, as where an employer calls upon a workman to do a job beyond his proper competence,[61] fails to provide adequate instructions or supervision,[61a] is responsible for some independent fault,[61b] or encourages him in his own breach of statutory duty,[61c] then the plaintiff is entitled to recover some damages, even though they may be substantially reduced on account of his contributory negligence.

DEFENCES

1. Volenti non fit injuria [62]

It was for long thought that this defence was not available in actions for breach of statutory duty.[63] In 1964, however, the House of Lords held that this is only so where a workman sues his employer for breach of the employer's statutory duty.[64] In all other cases the defence is available.[65]

2. Contributory negligence

Before the Law Reform (Contributory Negligence) Act 1945 the contributory negligence of the plaintiff was a complete defence to an

---

[60] *Boyle* v. *Kodak Ltd.* [1969] 1 W.L.R. 661, 665–666, *per* Lord Reid. " To say you are liable to me for my own wrongdoing is neither good morals nor good law ": *ibid.* at p. 673, *per* Lord Diplock.

[60a] *Donaghey* v. *Boulton & Paul Ltd.* [1968] A.C. 1, 24, *per* Lord Reid.

[60b] *Boyle* v. *Kodak Ltd.* [1969] 1 W.L.R. at pp. 672–673, *per* Lord Diplock.

[61] *Byers* v. *Head Wrightson & Co. Ltd.* [1961] 1 W.L.R. 961; *Ross* v. *Associated Portland Cement Manufacturers Ltd.* [1964] 1 W.L.R. 768 (H.L.).

[61a] *Jenner* v. *Allen West & Co. Ltd.* [1959] 1 W.L.R. 554; *Ross* v. *Associated Portland Cement Manufacturers Ltd.*, *supra*; *Boyle* v. *Kodak Ltd.* [1969] 1 W.L.R. 661.

[61b] *McMath* v. *Rimmer Bros. (Liverpool) Ltd.* [1962] 1 W.L.R. 1; *Leach* v. *Standard Telephones & Cables Ltd.* [1966] 1 W.L.R. 1392. *Donaghey* v. *Boulton & Paul Ltd.* [1968] A.C. 1; *Keaney* v. *British Railways Board* [1968] 1 W.L.R. 879. It appears that the fault for which the employer is responsible need not be such as to suffice as an independent ground of action.

[61c] *Barcock* v. *Brighton Corporation* [1949] 1 K.B. 339; *Laszczyk* v. *National Coal Board* [1954] 1 W.L.R. 1426.

[62] *Post*, pp. 614–626.

[63] *Baddeley* v. *Granville (Earl)* (1887) 19 Q.B.D. 423; *Wheeler* v. *New Merton Board Mills* [1933] 2 K.B. 669; *Alford* v. *N.C.B.* [1952] 1 All E.R. 754, 757, *per* Lord Normand.

[64] *Imperial Chemical Industries Ltd.* v. *Shatwell* [1965] A.C. 656.

[65] *Imperial Chemical Industries Ltd.* v. *Shatwell*, *supra*, concerned an action by a workman against his employer on the ground of a fellow employee's breach of statutory duty, but the generalisation is implicit in the reasoning of the House of Lords.

action for breach of statutory duty [66] and now, therefore, it is a reason for reducing the damages which he may recover. This matter has already been considered.[67]

3. Delegation

It is clear that in the ordinary way it is no defence for a person subjected to a statutory duty to claim that he has delegated the duty or its performance to another person.[68] In some cases, however, it seems to have been thought that delegation may be a defence where performance of the tasks necessary to secure compliance with the statutory obligation has been delegated to the plaintiff himself.[69] Nevertheless, although some specific requirements for the defence of delegation were laid down,[70] in no case did the plaintiff actually fail in his action on the express ground that the defendant's statutory duty had been delegated to him [71] and the doctrine has now fallen into disrepute. In *Ginty* v. *Belmont Building Supplies Ltd.*,[72] in a passage subsequently approved by the Court of Appeal,[73] Pearson J. doubted its soundness. " There has been a number of cases . . . in which it has been considered whether or not the employer delegated to the employee the performance of the statutory duty. In my view, the law which is applicable here is clear and comprehensible if one does not confuse it by seeking to investigate this very difficult and complicated question whether or not there was a delegation. In my view, the important and fundamental question in a case like this is not whether there was a delegation, but simply the usual question: Whose fault was it? . . . If the answer to that question is that in substance and reality the accident was solely due to the fault of the plaintiff, so that he was the sole author of his

---

[66] *Caswell* v. *Powell Duffryn Associated Collieries* [1940] A.C. 152.

[67] *Ante*, pp. 113–114. A possible technical explanation of the result in *Ginty* v. *Belmont Building Supplies Ltd.* [1959] 1 All E.R. 414, *ante*, p. 136 (if one be needed), is that in that case the odd situation prevailed that the accident was caused *wholly* by the fault of the plaintiff *and wholly* by the (identical) fault of the defendant while the Act of 1945 governs the case where " any person suffers damage as the result *partly* of his own fault *and partly* of the fault of any other person." So the Act did not apply and at common law a person whose own fault was a cause of his injury can recover nothing: [1959] 1 All E.R. at p. 424, *per* Pearson J.

[68] *Gray* v. *Pullen* (1864) 5 B. & S. 970; *Whitby* v. *Burt, Boulton & Hayward Ltd.* [1947] K.B. 918. See *post*, p. 539.

[69] See, *e.g.*, *Vincent* v. *Southern Ry.* [1927] A.C. 430; *Smith* v. *Baveystock & Co.* [1945] 1 All E.R. 531; *Vyner* v. *Waldenberg Bros.* [1946] K.B. 50; *Gallagher* v. *Dorman, Long & Co.* [1947] 2 All E.R. 38; *Barcock* v. *Brighton Corpn.* [1949] 1 K.B. 339.

[70] See, *e.g.*, *Beale* v. *Gomme Ltd.* (1949) 65 T.L.R. 543; *Manwaring* v. *Billington* [1952] 2 All E.R. 774.

[71] The judgment of Lord Goddard in *Smith* v. *Baveystock & Co.* [1945] 1 All E.R. 531, 533–534 may be an exception, but *cf.* the judgment of du Parcq L.J. at p. 535 and see Pearson J.'s explanation of the case in *Ginty* v. *Belmont Building Supplies Ltd.* [1959] 1 All E.R. 414, 425. In *Barcock* v. *Brighton Corpn.* [1949] 1 K.B. 339, Hilbery J. seems to have held that the defence of delegation defeated the claim for breach of statutory duty, but he held the defendants liable at common law.

[72] [1959] 1 All E.R. 414, 423–424.

[73] *McMath* v. *Rimmer Bros. Ltd.* [1962] 1 W.L.R. 1, 6. See also *Jenner* v. *Allen West & Co.* [1959] 1 W.L.R. 554.

own wrong, he is disentitled to recover." [74] It is submitted, therefore, that there is no special defence of delegation of a statutory duty and, indeed, that any other view would conflict with the general principle that no duty can be delegated.[75]

NATURE OF THE ACTION

As we have seen, in addition to showing that the statute upon which his claim is founded does give rise to a right of action in damages the plaintiff must also prove that the duty imposed by the statute was owed to him and that its breach caused his damage. The tort of breach of statutory duty thus has a resemblance to the tort of negligence in which the plaintiff must similarly prove the breach of a duty owed to him and consequent damage,[77] and breach of statutory duty is therefore sometimes called " statutory negligence." In *Lochgelly Iron & Coal Co.* v. *M'Mullan* [78] an action was brought under the Coal Mines Act 1911 [79] in respect of an accident caused by the collapse of a roof in a coal mine and it became necessary to decide whether breach of the statutory duty amounted to " personal negligence " for the purposes of the Workmen's Compensation Act 1925, which was then in force. The House of Lords held that it did and that the action was in substance one for negligence, the only important difference being that " whereas at the ordinary law the standard of duty must be fixed by the verdict of a jury, the statutory duty is conclusively fixed by the statute." [80] " I find the result to be that the employer is alleged to have committed a breach of a duty owed by him to his servant to take a particular precaution (namely, support of the roof) for his servant's safety whereby the servant was injured. In my opinion that state of facts constitutes negligence of the employer; and I am unable to conceive of any accurate definition of negligence which would exclude it. All that is necessary to show is a duty to take care to avoid injury; and if the particular care to be taken is prescribed by statute, and the duty to the injured person to take the care is likewise imposed by statute, and the breach is proved, all the essentials of negligence are present. I cannot think that the true position is, as appears to be suggested, that in such cases negligence only exists where the tribunal of fact agrees with the legislature that the precaution is one that ought to be taken. The very object of the legislation is to put that particular precaution beyond controversy." [81]

---

[74] " Fault is not necessarily equivalent in this context to blameworthiness. The question really is whose conduct caused the accident ": *Ross* v. *Associated Portland Cement Manufacturers Ltd.* [1964] 1 W.L.R. 768, 777, *per* Lord Reid.

[75] *Ross* v. *Associated Portland Cement Manufacturers Ltd.*, *supra*, at p. 776, *per* Lord Reid. [77] *Ante*, p. 45.

[78] [1934] A.C. 1; *David* v. *Britannic Merthyr Coal Co.* [1909] 2 K.B. 146.

[79] Now Mines and Quarries Act 1954.

[80] [1934] A.C. at p. 23, *per* Lord Wright.

[81] [1934] A.C. at p. 9, *per* Lord Atkin; *Lewis* v. *Denye* [1940] A.C. 921, 924–925, *per* Viscount Simon L.C.

This view approximates to that taken in the majority of jurisdictions in the United States that breach of a statute is " negligence *per se*," and is tantamount to saying that the statute " concretises " the common law duty of care by putting beyond controversy the question whether reasonable care in the circumstances required that a particular precaution be taken.[82] The concretisation theory, however, cannot explain the cases where no common law duty of care exists,[83] nor is it satisfactory or even sensible to describe as a failure to take care the breach of such duties as the unqualified obligation that dangerous parts of machinery " shall be securely fenced." [84] In fact there have been many decisions in which a defendant has been acquitted of negligence but held liable for breach of a statutory duty [85] and the modern tendency is certainly to treat the two causes of action as independent of one another. There may be resemblances between them, but, said Lord Wright,[86] " it is essential to keep in mind the fundamental differences of the two classes of claim."

It is submitted that the modern tendency to treat negligence and breach of statutory duty as separate causes of action is to be preferred to the earlier tendency to equate the two and that it better represents the true nature of the action for breach of statutory duty. In negligence the existence of the duty depends upon reasonable foresight, and the duty, if it exists, is always the same, namely, to exercise reasonable care in the circumstances. The existence of a statutory duty, on the other hand, depends upon the criteria laid down in the statute itself, and the strictness of the duty may vary not only from one statute to another, but from section to section within the same statute.

The view that breach of statutory duty is a tort distinct from negligence probably explains the existing case law better than the view that breach of statutory duty is equivalent to negligence, and there is little authority for a third possible view, namely, that breach of statutory duty is evidence of negligence.[87] Not only are there the cases already referred to in which a person is acquitted of negligence but held liable for breach of statutory duty; there are also cases in which a person has fulfilled his statutory obligation but is nevertheless held guilty of negligence.[88] It must be admitted, however,

---

[82] See Glanville Williams, *loc. cit.*, pp. 252 *et seq.*

[83] *e.g. Ashby* v. *White* (1703) 2 Ld.Raym. 938; *Monk* v. *Warbey* [1935] 1 K.B. 75; *Sephton* v. *Lancashire River Board* [1962] 1 W.L.R. 623; *Rippingale Farms Ltd.* v. *Black Sluice Internal Drainage Board* [1963] 1 W.L.R. 1347; *Ministry of Housing* v. *Sharp* [1970] 2 Q.B. 223; *Warder* v. *Cooper* [1970] Ch. 495.

[84] Factories Act 1961, s. 14 (1). See *John Summers Ltd.* v. *Frost* [1955] A.C. 740, *ante*, p. 135.

[85] For recent examples, see, *e.g., Kelly* v. *W.R.N. Contracting Ltd.* [1968] 1 W.L.R. 921; *Denyer* v. *Charles Skipper and East Ltd.* [1970] 1 W.L.R. 1087.

[86] *L.P.T.B.* v. *Upson* [1949] A.C. 155, 169.

[87] But see Glanville Williams, *loc. cit.*, pp. 249 *et seq.*

[88] *e.g. Kilgollan* v. *William Cooke & Co.* [1956] 1 W.L.R. 527; *Kimpton* v. *Steel Co. of Wales* [1960] 1 W.L.R. 527; *Bux* v. *Slough Metals Ltd.* [1973] 1 W.L.R. 1358. See also the different views expressed in the Court of Appeal in *Quintas* v. *National Smelting Co.*

that the view here expressed does nothing to assist in answering the question with which we began this chapter—how is it to be determined whether a particular statute gives rise to an action for damages? So far as the treatment accorded to this question in the judgments is concerned, this gives rise to no theoretical difficulty for in each case it is a question of construction of the statute in order to ascertain the intention of Parliament. As we have seen, however, Parliament rarely expresses an intention on the matter, and the view that breach of statutory duty is equivalent to negligence, or is evidence of negligence, at least solves the problem where a duty of care exists independently of the statute. Nevertheless, it is submitted, the latter view is not that of English law today. " A claim for damages for breach of a statutory duty intended to protect a person in the position of the particular plaintiff is a specific common law right which is not to be confused in essence with a claim for negligence. . . . I have desired before I deal specifically with the regulations to make it clear how in my judgment they should be approached, and also to make it clear that a claim for their breach may stand or fall independently of negligence. There is always a danger if the claim is not sufficiently specific that the due consideration of the claim for breach of statutory duty may be prejudiced if it is confused with the claim in negligence." [89]

[1961] 1 W.L.R. 401 (*per* Sellers and Danckwerts L.JJ., defendants liable for negligence but not liable for breach of Factories Act; *per* Willmer L.J., defendants not liable for negligence but liable for breach of Factories Act). *Cf. Wishart* v. *Bradley & Craven* (1963) 107 S.J. 554. In *Morris* v. *National Coal Board* [1963] 1 W.L.R. 1382 the plaintiff's claim for breach of statutory duty failed in the Court of Appeal. The court held that although on the facts the question whether there had been negligence arose, that question was not open as the case had been presented exclusively on the issue of breach of statutory duty.

[89] *L.P.T.B.* v. *Upson* [1949] A.C. 155, 168–169, *per* Lord Wright.

CHAPTER 9

EMPLOYERS' LIABILITY [1]

INTRODUCTORY

SINCE 1948, when the National Insurance (Industrial Injuries) Act 1946 [1a] came into force, there has been in operation a national insurance system under which benefits are payable to the victims of industrial accidents and to sufferers from certain prescribed industrial diseases. Both employer and workman contribute to the Industrial Injuries Fund [2] and, generally speaking, any person employed under a contract of service or apprenticeship is entitled to the benefits provided by the Act. Benefits [3] are payable in respect of personal injury by accident "arising out of and in the course of insurable employment." An accident arising in the course of the employment is deemed, in the absence of evidence to the contrary, to have arisen out of that employment. [4] If the employee was, at the time of the accident, disobeying any statutory or other regulations applicable to his employment, or disobeying his master's orders, the accident is nevertheless deemed to arise out of and in the course of the employment, provided (a) the accident would be deemed so to have arisen if there had been no disobedience, and (b) the act was done for the purpose of, and in connection with, the employer's trade or business. [5] The employee is insured against injuries sustained while travelling to and from work in transport provided by his employer [6] or while acting in an emergency (actual or supposed) on his employer's premises, for instance, averting damage by fire. The Act is administered by the Department of Health and Social Security and not by the ordinary courts. Claims under the Act are not a matter for the employer, they are made against the state, and their validity depends in no way upon proof of the fault or breach of duty of the employer.

The Act of 1946 replaced the Workmen's Compensation Acts, the first of which was enacted in 1897, and these Acts too, though in a different way, provided compensation to an injured workman without requiring him to prove the fault or breach of duty of his employer. It has thus been possible since 1897 for an injured workman to receive some compensation independently of the ordinary law governing the

---

[1] See Munkman, *Employer's Liability*, 7th ed. *passim*.
[1a] Since repealed and replaced by the National Insurance (Industrial Injuries) Act 1965 (c. 52).
[2] The Fund also receives a contribution from the Exchequer: Act of 1965, s. 2.
[3] See *ante*, pp. 6–8.
[4] s. 6.
[5] s. 7.
[6] s. 8.

civil liability of his employer, but it has never been the case that the compensation that he could receive in this way was equivalent in value to the damages he could recover in a successful action at law against his employer.[7] Moreover, under the law now in force the workman is entitled to retain his benefits under the Act of 1965 and also to bring an action for damages against his employer.[8] There has thus always been a strong incentive for a workman whose case offers reasonable prospects of success to bring an action against his employer, and today those prospects have been considerably enhanced by the abolition of the rule that contributory negligence is a complete defence [9] and of the doctrine of common employment.[10] Actions by workmen against their employers are, in fact, amongst the most numerous to be dealt with by the courts.[10a]

The recorded history of employers' liability does not start until 1837,[11] and then it began by denying the workman a remedy. *Priestley* v. *Fowler*,[12] decided in that year, is generally regarded as the *fons et origo* of the doctrine of common employment, which held that the employer was not liable to his employee for injury caused by the negligence of another employee, but the case really went further than that. It came close to denying that an employer might be liable to his workmen on any grounds,[13] and there can be no doubt that the judges of the first half of the nineteenth century viewed with alarm the possibility of widespread liability for industrial accidents.[14] Nevertheless, by 1858, if not earlier, common employment was recognised to be an exception to the ordinary principle that a master is liable for the tort of his servant done in the course of the servant's employment.[15] It was said to rest upon the theory that the contract of service contained an implied term to the effect that the servant agreed to run the risks naturally incident to the employment, including the risk of negligence on the part of his fellow employees,[16] but it did not follow that he

---

[7] See, however, *ante*, p. 8. Benefits can today frequently replace the earnings lost by the injured man but they give little or no compensation in respect of the non-pecuniary losses.

[8] The damages recoverable for loss of earnings are subject to a deduction of one-half of the value of the insurance benefits: Law Reform (Personal Injuries) Act 1948, s. 2. See *post*, p. 573.

[9] Law Reform (Contributory Negligence) Act 1945, *ante*, pp. 108–117.

[10] *Post*, p. 144.

[10a] Under the Employers' Liability (Compulsory Insurance) Act 1969 all employers other than the nationalised industries, local authorities and the police are compelled to maintain insurance against their liability to their workmen. Such insurance was, of course, extremely common before the Act. For criticism of the Act, see Hasson, I.L.J. 3 (1974) 79.

[11] Munkman, *Employer's Liability*, 7th ed., p. 3.

[12] (1837) 3 M. & W. 1; *Farwell* v. *Boston and Worcester Railroad Corpn.* (1842) 4 Metcalf 49; 149 R.R. 262.

[13] " The mere relation of the master and the servant can never imply an obligation on the part of the master to take more care of the servant than he may reasonably be expected to do of himself ": *per* Lord Abinger C.B. at p. 6; *Seymour* v. *Maddox* (1851) 16 Q.B. 327.

[14] Striking instances are the judgments of Pollock C.B. in *Vose* v. *Lancs. & Yorks. Ry.* (1858) 27 L.J.Ex. 249 and of Bramwell B. in *Dynen* v. *Leach* (1857) 26 L.J.(N.S.)Ex. 221.

[15] *Post*, pp. 516–536.

[16] *Bartonshill Coal Co.* v. *Reid* (1858) 3 Macq. 266 (H.L.).

agreed to take the risk of negligence on the part of the employer himself. If the employer had been negligent the workman's claim was still defeated if he had been guilty of contributory negligence,[17] or even if he merely knew of the danger,[18] but something of a general principle had emerged. If the workman was injured by the employer's own negligence he could recover,[19] but if he was injured by the negligence of a fellow employee he could not.[20]

During the second half of the nineteenth century judicial opinion veered in favour of the workman, and efforts began to be made to limit the scope of common employment. The doctrine was not finally abolished, however, until 1948 [21] and, though much restricted in scope before that date,[22] the harshness of the law was chiefly modified by the evasion of common employment through the development of the rule that an employer was liable for an injury to his workman caused by his own negligence or breach of statutory duty.[23] So far as the latter is concerned, no particular difficulty seems to us to exist: if a duty is placed directly upon the employer by statute, then he does not discharge that duty by entrusting its performance to another.[24] But how can an employer be personally negligent unless he actually takes a hand in the work himself, a physical impossibility where the employer is not a human individual but, as was increasingly the case during the nineteenth century and is now the general rule, a limited company with independent legal personality? Such an employer can only act through its servants, and if they are negligent the doctrine of common employment applies and relieves the employer of liability.[25]

The answer to this difficulty was found in the concept of duties personal to the employer, for the careful performance of which the employer remained responsible even though the tasks necessary to discharge the duties were entrusted to a servant. " It is quite clear," said Lord Herschell,[26] " that the contract between employer and employed involves on the part of the former the duty of taking

---

[17] *Senior* v. *Ward* (1859) 1 El. & El. 385.

[18] *Alsop* v. *Yates* (1858) 2 L.J.Ex. 156; *Williams* v. *Clough* (1858) 3 H. & N. 258. In *Smith* v. *Baker & Sons* [1891] A.C. 325, the House of Lords finally held that mere knowledge did not defeat the workman's claim: *post*, pp. 617–618.

[19] Early cases include *Brydon* v. *Stewart* (1855) 2 Macq. 30; *Tarrant* v. *Webb* (1856) 25 L.J.C.P. 261; *Roberts* v. *Smith* (1857) 26 L.J.Ex. 319. *Cf. Dynen* v. *Leach* (1857) 26 L.J.(N.S.)Ex. 221.

[20] The negligent employee was, of course, liable, but he was seldom worth suing.

[21] Law Reform (Personal Injuries) Act 1948, s. 1 (1). Contracting out of the Act is forbidden: *ibid.* s. 1 (3).

[22] See, *e.g.*, *Radcliffe* v. *Ribble Motor Services* [1939] A.C. 215; *Graham* v. *Glasgow Corporation* [1947] A.C. 368; *Lancaster* v. *L.P.T.B.* [1948] 2 All E.R. 796 (H.L.).

[23] It was settled in *Groves* v. *Wimborne* [1898] 2 Q.B. 402 that common employment afforded no defence in an action brought against the employer for breach of his statutory duty. The Employers' Liability Act 1880 (repealed by the Law Reform (Personal Injuries) Act 1948, s. 1 (2) also excluded the defence in a limited number of defined cases.

[24] *Ante*, p. 138.

[25] Subject to the Employers' Liability Act 1880 it was no answer to the defence of common employment that the negligent servant was the plaintiff's superior: *Wilson* v. *Merry* (1868) L.R. 1 H.L.(Sc.) 326.

[26] *Smith* v. *Baker* [1891] A.C. 325, 362.

reasonable care to provide proper appliances, and to maintain them in a proper condition, and so to carry on his operations as not to subject those employed by him to unnecessary risk. Whatever the dangers of the employment which the employed undertakes, amongst them is certainly not to be numbered the risk of the employer's negligence and the creation or enhancement of danger thereby engendered." [27] Later, in the famous case of *Wilsons and Clyde Coal Co.* v. *English*,[28] Lord Wright redefined the employer's duty as threefold: "the provision of a competent staff of men, adequate material, and a proper system and effective supervision." [29] The duty is not absolute, for it is fulfilled by the exercise of due care and skill. "But it is not fulfilled by entrusting its fulfilment to employees, even though selected with due care and skill." [30]

Before the abolition of common employment, therefore, it was important to maintain carefully the distinction between a breach of the employer's personal duty, for which he was liable, and the mere negligence of a fellow employee, for which he was not.[31] "There is a sphere in which the employer must exercise his discretion and there are other spheres in which foremen and workmen must exercise theirs. It is not easy to define these spheres, but where the system or mode of operation is complicated or highly dangerous or prolonged or involves a number of men performing different functions, it is naturally a matter for the employer to take the responsibility of deciding what system shall be adopted. On the other hand, where the operation is simple and the decision how it shall be done has to be taken frequently, it is natural and reasonable that it should be left to the foreman or workmen on the spot." [32]

With the abolition of the doctrine of common employment in 1948,[33] the employer became liable as much for the negligence of a fellow servant of the plaintiff acting in the course of his employment as for breach of his personal duty, and it thus became unnecessary always to distinguish between the two kinds of wrongdoing. Nevertheless the concept of the employer's personal duty was not destroyed, and the employer is today liable either vicariously or for breach of his personal duty.[34] Additionally, in many forms of employment there are numerous and detailed statutory duties which are imposed directly upon employers and these have the effect of increasing his overall liability for injury suffered by his workmen. Vicarious liability is the subject of a separate

---

[27] *Cf.* the views of Lord Bramwell, dissenting, at pp. 345–346.
[28] [1938] A.C. 57.
[29] *Ibid.* at p. 78, citing Lord MacLaren in *Bett* v. *Dalmeny Oil Co.* (1905) 7 F. 787, quoted with approval by Lord Shaw in *Butler* v. *Fife Coal Co.* [1912] A.C. 149, 173–174.
[30] *Ibid., per* Lord Wright.
[31] See, *e.g., Speed* v. *Thomas Swift* [1943] K.B. 557; *Winter* v. *Cardiff R.D.C.* [1950] 1 All E.R. 819 (H.L.).
[32] [1950] 1 All E.R. at pp. 822–823, *per* Lord Oaksey.
[33] Law Reform (Personal Injuries) Act 1948, s. 1 (1).
[34] See *Staveley Iron & Chemical Co.* v. *Jones* [1956] A.C. 627, discussed *post*, p. 542; Weir, *Casebook on Tort*, 3rd ed., p. 216.

chapter and here we shall consider the employer's personal duty to his employees, but in view of the mass of statutory duties in existence, to consider the common law alone would give a false picture of the present law of employer's liability. We shall also, therefore, consider some of the more significant of these duties and their effect upon employer's liability as a whole.

It is also necessary to make some mention of the Health and Safety at Work Act 1974,[34a] though the immediate impact of this upon the matters discussed in this chapter will be slight. The Report of the Committee on Safety and Health at Work [34b] made severe criticisms of the existing industrial safety legislation which, in their view, required a determined effort at revision, harmonisation and up-dating. This aim is pursued by the Act, which gives power to repeal existing statutes and replace them by provisions in regulations.[34c] The regulations will continue to give rise to civil liability,[34d] but until they are drafted and put into effect, the present statutory and regulatory provisions will remain in force. An important development is the introduction by the Act of a generalised duty upon employers to ensure, so far as is reasonably practicable, the health, safety and welfare at work of all his employees.[34e] This duty is in some respects reminiscent of the employer's common law duty of care towards his workers, though the duty under the Act is supported only by penal sanctions and does not give rise to any civil liability.[34f]

COMMON LAW

Since the employer is now liable to his employee for an injury caused by a fellow employee, it might be thought that there is no longer value in retaining the concept of the employer's personal duty.[35] The enormous majority of workmen are in the service of corporate employers who are in reality not capable of negligence, or anything else, so why not treat every case as one of vicarious liability? One answer to this may be that habits of thought acquired under the rule of common employment have survived its abolition, but in fact the concept of the personal duty continues to serve a useful purpose. In many cases it is obviously much more convenient to say that a given state of affairs

---

[34a] C. 37. See Carby-Hall, " Health and Safety at Work Act 1974 " (1974) 118 S.J. 635, 655. As to commencement, see *ibid.*, pp. 637–638.

[34b] Cmnd. 5034 (1972). The Committee also proposed a more far-reaching inquiry into the basis of compensation for work-accidents. This is now within the terms of reference of the Royal Commission on Compensation for Personal Injuries.

[34c] For the matters within the regulation-making power, see Scheds. 3 and 5. Note that the regulation-making power allows the Secretary of State wide powers of modification of existing provisions.

[34d] s. 47 (2).

[34e] See s. 2.

[34f] s. 47 (1). For " approved codes of practice " and their relevance in *criminal* proceedings, see ss. 16 and 17.

[35] See *Sullivan* v. *Gallagher & Craig*, 1960 S.L.T. 70, 76, *per* Lord Justice-Clerk Thomson; Weir, *Casebook on Tort*, 3rd ed., p. 238.

or a given event proves a breach by the employer of his personal duty than to say that some employee must somehow have been negligent for that state of affairs to exist or for that event to come about. If a workman is injured because no one has taken the trouble to provide him with an obviously necessary safety device, it is sufficient and in general satisfactory to say that the employer has not fulfilled his duty. It is unnecessarily complicated to say that someone whose duty it was to provide the device in question, or someone whose duty it was to see that there was someone else to consider what safety devices were required and to provide them, must have been negligent and therefore that the employer is liable. Again, in many cases the only person involved in the sequence of events leading up to the accident is the plaintiff himself and yet his employer is liable, e.g., because the plaintiff should not have been left alone to do the job. In terms of vicarious liability this would have to be explained by saying that some other employee had somehow failed in his duty of organising the work. It is simpler, and no less accurate, to say that the employer himself was in breach of his duty.

It is not only for its convenience, however, that the continued use of the employer's personal duty is justified. True vicarious liability exists only where a servant has committed a tort in the course of his employment,[36] but the employer's liability is not so restricted. Though the scope of the liability is now in some doubt,[37] there are cases in which the workman's injury is attributable to the negligence of an independent contractor and yet the employer is liable for breach of his personal duty to the workman. Moreover, though employer's liability is most commonly dealt with as a matter of tort, it is also a matter of contract,[38] and the workman's contract of service is made with his employer, not with his fellow employees. Duties which exist by virtue of express or implied terms in the contract of employment must, therefore, be duties owed by the employer himself. Theoretically at least, the employer's vicarious liability for his servants' negligence, which is a liability in tort, must be distinct.[39]

Nature of employer's duty

We have already noticed Lord Wright's threefold division of the employer's duty—" the provision of a competent staff of men, adequate material and a proper system and effective supervision " [40]—and it is convenient to adhere approximately to this in an exposition of the law. In truth, however, there is but one duty, a duty to take reasonable care

---

[36] *Post*, pp. 540–543.
[37] See *Davie* v. *New Merton Board Mills* [1959] A.C. 604; *Sumner* v. *William Henderson & Sons Ltd.* [1964] 1 Q.B. 450 (set aside on procedural grounds [1963] 1 W.L.R. 823); *post*, pp. 153–156.
[38] *Matthews* v. *Kuwait Bechtel Corporation* [1959] 2 Q.B. 57.
[39] See Jolowicz [1959] C.L.J. 163, 164–165.
[40] *Wilsons and Clyde Coal Co.* v. *English* [1938] A.C. 57, 78; *ante*, p. 145.

so to carry on operations as not to subject the persons employed to unnecessary risk.[41] " In case there is any doubt about the meaning of ' unnecessary ' I would . . . take the duty as being a duty not to subject the employee to any risk which the employer can reasonably foresee, or, to put it slightly lower, not to subject the employee to any risk which the employer can reasonably foresee and which he can guard against by any measure, the convenience and expense of which are not entirely disproportionate to the risk involved." [42]

In many respects, therefore, the duty is similar to the duty of care in the tort of negligence generally, but expressed in terms appropriate to the relationship of employer and employee.[42a] As we shall see, the duty of the employer cannot, as can an ordinary duty of care, always be discharged by the employment of an independent contractor,[43] but it is nevertheless a duty of care, not an absolute duty,[44] and it is for the plaintiff to prove its breach. If a workman cannot prove negligence, whether by direct evidence or with the aid of the maxim res ipsa loquitur, an action based upon breach of the employer's personal duty must fail. With this in mind we can consider the various branches of the employer's common law duty to his workmen.

(i) Competent staff of men

The duty to take reasonable care to provide a competent staff of men is still extant, but it is of comparatively little importance since the abolition of common employment. If, however, an employer engages a person with insufficient experience or training for a particular job and as a result a workman is injured, it may well be that there is a breach of this branch of the employer's duty.[45]

In one situation of a slightly different kind, however, this branch of the employer's liability retains its importance. If one employee is injured by the violent horseplay of another, or is actually assaulted by him, it is most unlikely that the employer will be liable vicariously, for the horseplay or the attack will not have been done in the course

---

[41] e.g., Smith v. Baker [1891] A.C. 325, 362, per Lord Herschell; Wilson v. Tyneside Window Cleaning Co. [1958] 2 Q.B. 110.

[42] Harris v. Brights Asphalt Contractors [1953] 1 Q.B. 617, 626, per Slade J.

[42a] The special relationship of employer and worker may impose positive duties of assistance or protection: thus an employer may be obliged to provide medical assistance in cases of illness or injury in no way attributable to him (Kasapis v. Laimos [1959] 2 Lloyd's Rep. 378) or to warn his workers to be medically examined if he learns that past working conditions, which were then regarded as proper, have caused a danger of disease (Wright v. Dunlop Rubber Co. (1971) 11 K.I.R. 311).

[43] Post, pp. 153–156.

[44] Winter v. Cardiff R.D.C. [1950] 1 All E.R. 819, 823, per Lord MacDermott; Davie v. New Merton Board Mills [1959] A.C. 604.

[45] See Butler v. Fife Coal Co. [1912] A.C. 149. So regarded, a case of this kind would not give rise to the question whether negligence is to be judged subjectively or objectively. If a man who has never previously operated a crane is put in charge of one and an accident results, despite the exercise by him of all the care of which he is, subjectively, capable, there might be difficulties in saying that the employer is vicariously liable for his negligence. In a question whether the employer is personally in breach of his duty no such difficulty exists.

of the employment.[45a] It may be, however, that the employer should have known of his employee's playful or vicious propensities and have taken steps to prevent them from resulting in injury to another. In that case he may be liable for breach of his personal duty.[46]

(ii) *Adequate plant and equipment*

The employer must take reasonable care to provide his workmen with the necessary plant and equipment, and is therefore liable if an accident is caused through the absence of some item of equipment which was obviously necessary or which a reasonable employer would recognise to be needed.[47] He must also take reasonable care to maintain the plant and equipment in proper condition, and in the case of complex or dangerous machinery this will probably mean instituting a regular system of inspection.[48] What is required in each case, however, is reasonable care according to the circumstances, and in some cases it may be legitimate to rely upon the workman himself to rectify simple defects in the plant he is using.[49] The duty extends to the installation of necessary safety devices on dangerous machinery [50] and the provision of protective equipment when required,[51] but the employer does not warrant the safety of plant and equipment. At common law, therefore, he is not liable if an accident is caused by some latent defect in equipment which could not have been discovered by the exercise of reasonable care on the part of persons for whose negligence he is answerable.[52] By the Employer's Liability (Defective Equipment) Act 1969,[52a] however, if an employee is injured in the course of his employment in consequence of a defect in equipment provided by his employer and the defect is due to the fault of a third party, whether identified or not, then the injury is deemed to be also attributable to the negligence of the employer. Today, therefore, if a workman can show, for example,

---

[45a] *O'Reilly* v. *National Rail and Tramway Appliances Ltd.* [1966] 1 All E.R. 499. *Cf. Chapman* v. *Oakleigh Animal Products Ltd.* (1970) 8 K.I.R. 1063.

[46] *Hudson* v. *Ridge Manufacturing Co.* [1957] 2 Q.B. 348; *Veness* v. *Dyson, Bell & Co.* [1965] C.L.Y. 2691. *Cf. Smith* v. *Crossley Bros.* (1951) 95 S.J. 655; *Coddington* v. *International Harvester Co. of Great Britain Ltd.* (1969) 6 K.I.R. 146.

[47] *Williams* v. *Birmingham Battery and Metal Co.* [1899] 2 Q.B. 338; *Lovell* v. *Blundells & Crompton & Co.* [1944] 1 K.B. 502; *Ross* v. *Associated Portland Cement Manufacturers Ltd.* [1964] 1 W.L.R. 768 (H.L.). It is not always necessary, however, for the employer to adopt the latest improvements: *Toronto Power Co.* v. *Paskwan* [1915] A.C. 734, per Sir Arthur Channell. See also *O'Connor* v. *B.T.C.* [1958] 1 W.L.R. 346.

[48] e.g., *Murphy* v. *Phillips* (1876) 35 L.T. 477. Even this may not always be sufficient: *Barkway* v. *S. Wales Transport Co.* [1950] A.C. 185; *Pearce* v. *Round Oak Steel Works Ltd.* [1969] 1 W.L.R. 595.

[49] *Munkman, op. cit.,* p. 112; *Bristol Aeroplane Co.* v. *Franklin* [1948] W.N. 341; *Richardson* v. *Stephenson Clarke Ltd.* [1969] 1 W.L.R. 1695.

[50] *Jones* v. *Richards* [1955] 1 W.L.R. 444; *Lovelidge* v. *Anselm Odling & Sons Ltd.* [1967] 2 Q.B. 351. See also *Naismith* v. *London Film Productions* [1939] 1 All E.R. 794.

[51] *Qualcast Ltd.* v. *Haynes* [1959] A.C. 743, per Lord Denning. But see *Brown* v. *Rolls-Royce* [1960] 1 W.L.R. 210.

[52] *Davie* v. *New Merton Board Mills* [1959] A.C. 604. *Cf. Taylor* v. *Rover Co. Ltd.* [1966] 1 W.L.R. 1491; *Pearce* v. *Round Oak Steel Works Ltd., supra.*

[52a] c. 37. The Act came into force on October 25, 1969, its main purpose being to reverse on its facts the result of *Davie* v. *New Merton Board Mills Ltd., supra.* Its bearing on the wider implications of that case is considered *post,* p. 155.

that a tool he was using was defective in such a way that there must, on a balance of probabilities, have been negligence or other fault in its manufacture, and that his injury was caused by that defect, then the employer as well as the manufacturer will be liable to him, whether or not the employer was in any way to blame.[52b] The principal advantage of this from the workman's point of view is that he is relieved of any need to identify and sue the manufacturer of defective equipment provided by his employer.

(iii) *Safe place of work*

Though not expressly mentioned by Lord Wright in *Wilsons and Clyde Coal Co.* v. *English*,[53] it is clear that the employer's duty of care extends to the place of work [54] and in some cases may even also apply to the means of access to the place of work.[55] No particular difficulty exists where the place of work is in the occupation or control of the employer, but it must be recalled that the duty is one of reasonable care only and thus that the employer is not obliged to take unreasonable precautions even against foreseeable risks.[56] At one time, however, it was thought that because an employer had no control over premises in the occupation of a third party he could owe no duty in respect of those premises,[57] but it is now clear that this is wrong.[58] The duty of care remains, but what is required for its performance may well be different where the place of work is not under the employer's control. " The master's own premises are under his control: if they are dangerously in need of repair he can and must rectify the fault at once if he is to escape the censure of negligence. But if a master sends his plumber to mend a leak in a private house, no one could hold him negligent for not visiting the house himself to see if the carpet in the hall creates a trap. Between these extremes are countless possible

---

[52b] The employer is entitled to raise the defence of contributory negligence against the workman and may seek to recover indemnity or contribution from the person to whose fault the defect is attributable. He cannot, however, contract out of the liability imposed by the Act.

[53] [1938] A.C. 57; *ante*, p. 145.

[54] *e.g.*, *Cole* v. *De Trafford (No. 2)* [1918] 2 K.B. 523, 535, *per* Scrutton L.J.; *Davidson* v. *Handley Page* [1945] 1 All E.R. 235, 236, *per* Lord Greene M.R. At the lowest, the employer's duty to his employee in respect of premises occupied by the employer must be the common duty of care under the Occupiers' Liability Act 1957, but probably it is stricter than that duty: *post*, pp. 153–156.

[55] *Ashdown* v. *Samuel Williams & Sons* [1957] 1 Q.B. 409, 430–432, *per* Parker L.J.; *Smith* v. *National Coal Board* [1967] 1 W.L.R. 871 (H.L.). The employer can be subject to no duty of care so far as the means of access consists of a public highway, but if the employee has to cross private property, whether the employer's own or that of a third party, the duty should exist.

[56] *Latimer* v. *A.E.C.* [1953] A.C. 643; *Thomas* v. *Bristol Aeroplane Co.* [1954] 1 W.L.R. 694. Nor is he liable for a defect which would not have been revealed by inspection: *Bevan* v. *Milford Haven Dry Dock Co.* [1962] 2 Lloyd's Rep. 281; *O'Reilly* v. *National Rail and Tramway Appliances Ltd.* [1966] 1 All E.R. 499.

[57] *Taylor* v. *Sims and Sims* [1942] 2 All E.R. 375; *Cilia* v. *H. M. James & Sons* [1954] 1 W.L.R. 721. *Cf. Hodgson* v. *British Arc Welding Co.* [1946] K.B. 302. In any case the duty in respect of a safe system of work (*post*, pp. 151–152) continues: *General Cleaning Contractors* v. *Christmas* [1953] A.C. 180.

[58] *Wilson* v. *Tyneside Window Cleaning Co.* [1958] 2 Q.B. 110; *Smith* v. *Austin Lifts* [1959] 1 W.L.R. 100 (H.L.); *Clay* v. *A. J. Crump & Sons Ltd.* [1964] 1 Q.B. 533.

examples in which the court may have to decide the question of fact:
Did the master take reasonable care so to carry out his operations as
not to subject those employed by him to unnecessary risk? . . . So
viewed, the question whether the master was in control of the premises
ceases to be a matter of technicality and becomes merely one of the
ingredients, albeit a very important one, in a consideration of the
question of fact whether, in all the circumstances, the master took
reasonable care." [59]

(iv) *Safe system of working*

This, the most frequently invoked branch of the employer's duty,
is also the most difficult to define, but it includes " the physical lay-out
of the job—the setting of the stage, so to speak—the sequence in which
the work is to be carried out, the provision in proper cases of warnings
and notices and the issue of special instructions. A system may be
adequate for the whole course of the job or it may have to be modified
or improved to meet the circumstances which arise; such modifications
or improvements . . . equally fall under the head of system." [60] The
employer's duty in respect of the system of working is most evident
where the work is of regular or routine nature, but its application is
not limited to such cases. Even where a single act of a particular kind
is to be performed, the employer may have an obligation to organise
the work if it is of a complicated or unusual kind or if a large number
of men are involved.[61] In each case it is a question of fact whether a
reasonable employer would have left it to his men to decide for themselves how the job should be done.[62]

In devising a system of working the employer must take into account
the fact that workmen are often heedless of their own safety,[63] and
this has two consequences. First, the system should so far as possible
minimise the danger of a workman's own foreseeable carelessness.
Secondly, the employer must also exercise reasonable care to see that

---

[59] *Wilson* v. *Tyneside Window Cleaning Co.* [1958] 2 Q.B. 110, 121–122, *per* Pearce L.J.
The employer's duty extends similarly to the plant and equipment of a third party:
Biddle v. *Hart* [1907] 1 K.B. 649; *Gledhill* v. *Liverpool Abattoir Utility Co.* [1957] 1 W.L.R.
1028.

[60] *Speed* v. *Thomas Swift & Co.* [1943] K.B. 557, 563–564, *per* Lord Greene M.R.
Although Lord Greene himself disclaimed exhaustiveness for his definition, Lord Simon
thought that it carried the analysis to the furthest point that could be reached: *Colfar* v.
Coggins & Griffith (Liverpool) [1945] A.C. 197, 202.

[61] *Winter* v. *Cardiff R.D.C.* [1950] W.N. 193, 200, *per* Lord Reid; *Byers* v. *Head
Wrightson & Co.* [1961] 1 W.L.R. 961; *Boyle* v. *Kodak Ltd.* [1969] 1 W.L.R. 661. The fact
that an untrained young man with indifferent English is a member of a team may call for
special precautions by the employer: *Hawkins* v. *Ian Ross (Castings) Ltd.* [1970] 1 All E.R.
180, 186, *per* Fisher J. *Cf. Brennan* v. *Techno Constructions* [1962] C.L.Y. 2069; *Vinnyey*
v. *Star Paper Mills Ltd.* [1965] 1 All E.R. 175.

[62] Since the abolition of common employment the employer is liable vicariously for
the negligence of the person in charge of the operation, but this cannot assist the plaintiff
if he was himself in charge or if no workman was guilty of negligence.

[63] *General Cleaning Contractors* v. *Christmas* [1953] A.C. 180, 189–190, *per* Lord
Oaksey; *Smith* v. *National Coal Board* [1967] 1 W.L.R. 871, 873, *per* Lord Reid; *Kerry*
v. *Carter* [1969] 1 W.L.R. 1372.

his system of working is complied with and that the necessary safety precautions are observed.[64] As Lord Denning has pointed out,[65] however, this is not a proposition of law but a proposition of good sense, so that proof that a workman was never actually instructed to wear necessary protective clothing is not itself proof of negligence.[66]

Scope of duty

The employer's duty of care concerns not only the actual work of his employees, but also all such acts as are normally and reasonably incidental to a man's day's work,[67] and the mere fact that an employee disobeys an order does not necessarily deprive him of the protection of his employer's duty, though he may, of course, be guilty of contributory negligence.[68] But the special duty of the employer exists only where the relationship of master and servant exists[69] and so an independent contractor employed to do work cannot rely upon that duty.[70] It is important to notice, however, that although the employer's duty springs from the relationship of master and servant generally, the duty is owed individually to each workman, so that circumstances concerning the particular workman which are known or which ought to be known to the employer will affect the precautions which the employer must take in order to fulfil his duty. Thus in *Paris* v. *Stepney Borough Council*[71] the plaintiff had only one eye and it was therefore held that he should have been provided with goggles even though the risk involved in his work was not so great as to require the provision of goggles to a normal two-eyed man doing a similar job. Conversely, " an experienced man dealing with a familiar and obvious risk may not reasonably need the same attention or the same precautions as an

---

[64] *General Cleaning Contractors* v. *Christmas* [1953] A.C. 180; *Clifford* v. *Charles H. Challen & Son* [1951] 1 K.B. 495; *Crookall* v. *Vickers-Armstrong Ltd.* [1955] 1 W.L.R. 659; *Nolan* v. *Dental Manufacturing Co.* [1958] 1 W.L.R. 936. *Cf. Woods* v. *Durable Suites* [1953] 1 W.L.R. 857; *Bux* v. *Slough Metals Ltd.* [1973] 1 W.L.R. 1358.

[65] *Qualcast (Wolverhampton) Ltd.* v. *Haynes* [1959] A.C. 743, 760.

[66] *Ibid.* " I deprecate any tendency to treat the relation of employer and skilled workman as equivalent to that of a nurse and imbecile child ": *Smith* v. *Austin Lifts* [1959] 1 W.L.R. 100, 105, *per* Viscount Simonds.

[67] *Davidson* v. *Handley Page Ltd.* [1945] 1 All E.R. 235.

[68] *Rands* v. *McNeil* [1955] 1 Q.B. 253 (but no breach of duty on the facts).

[69] *Savory* v. *Holland & Hannen & Cubitts (Southern) Ltd.* [1964] 1 W.L.R. 1158, which might be thought to deny this, should not, it is submitted, be so understood. See *Baxter* v. *Central Electricity Generating Board* [1965] 1 W.L.R. 200; *Field* v. *E. E. Jeavons & Co. Ltd.* [1965] 1 W.L.R. 996. In *Davies* v. *Prison Commissioners* [1963] C.L.Y. 2866 the Prison Commissioners denied that the relationship of master and servant existed between themselves and a prisoner but accepted a similar responsibility for the prisoner's safety. Of course the fact that the plaintiff is not the servant of the defendant does not of itself mean that the defendant owes the plaintiff no duty of care at all, but the duty is not owed " to such a high degree ": *Field* v. *E. E. Jeavons & Co. Ltd.*, *supra*, at p. 1002, *per* Lord Upjohn.

[70] *Herbert* v. *Harold Shaw Ltd.* [1959] 2 Q.B. 138; *Inglefield* v. *Macey* (1967) 117 New L.J. 101. The relationship of master and servant is most frequently in issue where the master's vicarious liability is in question, and the topic is considered more fully *post*, pp. 518–523. For the position with regard to volunteer workers see *Baxter* v. *Central Electricity Generating Board*, *supra*, and Munkman, *op. cit.*, pp. 565–568.

[71] [1951] A.C. 367. *Cf. James* v. *Hepworth & Grandage Ltd.* [1968] 1 Q.B. 94.

inexperienced man who is likely to be more receptive of advice or admonition." [72]

Strictness of the duty

As has been emphasised in the foregoing paragraphs and has been constantly reiterated by the courts, the employer's duty is a duty of care only and, though a high standard is required, there are limits to the protection which the employer must provide, even against foreseeable risks to his employee.[73] In *Withers* v. *Perry Chain Co.*[74] the plaintiff had previously contracted dermatitis from contact with grease in the course of her work and was therefore given by her employers the driest work they had available. This work she accepted without protest but nevertheless she again contracted dermatitis and sued her employers on the ground that, knowing that she was susceptible to dermatitis, they should not have permitted her to do work carrying a risk of causing that disease. Her action was dismissed by the Court of Appeal because the employers had done everything they reasonably could have done to protect the plaintiff short of refusing to employ her at all. " In my opinion there is no legal duty on an employer to prevent an adult employee from doing work which he or she is willing to do. If there is a slight risk . . . it is for the employee to weigh it against the desirability, or perhaps the necessity, of employment. The relationship of master and servant is not that of a schoolmaster and pupil. . . . It cannot be said that an employer is bound to dismiss an employee rather than allow her to run a small risk." [75]

Independent contractors

It might be supposed, therefore, that an employer who entrusts some task to a third party (not a servant), whose competence he has taken reasonable care to ascertain, has thereby discharged his own duty of reasonable care. To state the law in this way, however, would be to deny the *ratio decidendi* of *Wilsons and Clyde Coal Co.* v. *English* [76] that the employer's duty is personal and is not discharged simply by the appointment of a competent person to carry out the necessary tasks. In that case the defendant employers were held liable in respect of an injury sustained by a miner because the system of working was not reasonably safe. The system had been devised by the manager of the mine, a fellow servant of the plaintiff, to whom the employers

---

[72] *Qualcast (Wolverhampton) Ltd.* v. *Haynes* [1959] A.C. 743, 754, *per* Lord Radcliffe. Note that it is not the nature of the duty that changes, only the result of its application to the facts: *McPhee* v. *General Motors Ltd.* (1970) 8 K.I.R. 885.

[73] See, *e.g.*, *Latimer* v. *A.E.C.* [1953] A.C. 643. For the standard of care in negligence generally see *ante*, pp. 61–69. The criterion of general and approved practice (*ante*, p. 68) is of particular importance in actions against employers.

[74] [1961] 1 W.L.R. 1314.

[75] At p. 1320, *per* Devlin L.J. See also *Foufoulas* v. *F. G. Strang Pty. Ltd.* (1970) 44 A.L.J.R. 361 (Aust. H.C.).

[76] [1938] A.C. 57; *ante*, p. 145.

were obliged by statute [77] to leave the matter, but yet, despite the existence of common employment and despite the fact that the employers personally had done everything they possibly could, they were held to be in breach of their duty to the plaintiff. Their duty was "the employer's personal duty, whether he performs or can perform it himself, or whether he does not perform it or cannot perform it save by servants or agents. A failure to perform such a duty is the employer's personal negligence." [78] The employer's liability, therefore, not being a vicarious liability, was not defeated by the doctrine of common employment.

There can be little doubt that the concept of the employer's personal duty was developed in order to reduce the hardship created by the doctrine of common employment. In practical effect, however, it extends to cases which never were covered by that doctrine, for it involves the proposition that the employer's duty is not so much a duty to take reasonable care as a duty that care be taken. It thus carries the implication that the employer is liable in respect of matters covered by the personal duty for damage caused by the negligence of others, in particular independent contractors. A man can be liable vicariously only for the torts of his servants done in the course of their employment, but a duty that care be taken is not fulfilled if anyone concerned is guilty of a failure to take care.[79] It is, indeed, usually accepted that an employer is liable for the negligence of an independent contractor employed by him,[80] but it is necessary to consider whether this deduction from the *ratio decidendi* of *Wilsons and Clyde Coal Co.* v. *English* has been affected by the later decision of the House of Lords in *Davie* v. *New Merton Board Mills*.[81]

The facts in *Davie's* case were simple. The plaintiff was working with a hammer and a drift—a metal tool intended to be struck by the hammer—when a particle of metal chipped off the drift and entered his eye. He had been provided with the drift by his employers and they had bought it from reputable suppliers who had in turn bought it from the manufacturers. To all outward appearance the drift was in good condition, but in fact the metal of which it was made was excessively hard as a result of negligence in the course of manufacture. The position was thus that the manufacturers, but no one else,[81a] had been guilty of negligence, and the manufacturers were held liable on

---

[77] Coal Mines Act 1911, s. 2 (4).

[78] [1938] A.C. at pp. 83–84, *per* Lord Wright. See also *per* Lord Thankerton at pp. 64–65; *per* Lord Macmillan at p. 75; *per* Lord Maugham at pp. 87–88.

[79] See *post*, pp. 536–539.

[80] *e.g., Paine* v. *Colne Valley Electricity Supply Co.* [1938] 4 All E.R. 803; Charlesworth, *Negligence*, 5th ed., pp. 946–947.

[81] [1959] A.C. 604. See the important discussion of this case by Lord Justice-Clerk Thomson in *Sullivan* v. *Gallagher & Craig*, 1960 S.L.T. 70, 75–77; Weir, *Casebook on Tort*, 3rd ed., pp. 233 and 238.

[81a] *Cf. Taylor* v. *Rover Co. Ltd.* [1966] 1 W.L.R. 1491, where the employers had been negligent.

the principle of *Donoghue* v. *Stevenson*.[82] At first instance,[83] Ashworth J. also held that the employers were liable on the ground that their personal duty was broken by the negligence of the manufacturers,[84] but his decision was reversed by the Court of Appeal [85] and the House of Lords.[86] It was held that the employers had discharged their duty by buying from a reputable supplier a standard tool whose latent defect they had no means of discovering.[87]

So far as injury resulting from defective equipment is concerned, the result of *Davie's* case has now been reversed by the Employer's Liability (Defective Equipment) Act 1969,[88] and it is submitted that the employer's duty can still be regarded as in general a duty that care be taken. This is certainly true for cases covered by the Act, and there is nothing in *Davie's* case to prevent the employer from being liable for the negligence of an independent contractor in many other kinds of case.[89] The principal effect of the decision is to deny the liability of an employer where the negligence in question is not that of an independent contractor to whom the employer has delegated some task, but is that of a stranger to him, such as the manufacturer of a standard tool. No doubt, if a lorry driver delivering goods to a factory were negligently to run into and injure a workman, the workman's employer would not be liable, and *Davie's* case confirms that this is so. The lorry driver cannot, however, reasonably be described as the independent contractor of the employer, his negligence does not negative the exercise of care in the performance of the employer's personal duty for it is unrelated to any aspect of that duty, and the employer has delegated nothing to him; the authority of *Davie's* case is hardly necessary for the exoneration of the employer. But if, for example, a gas fitter negligently installs a gas appliance at the employer's premises with the result that a workman is injured by an explosion, then, it is submitted, the employer's personal duty with regard to the safety of the place of work has not been fulfilled and he is liable,

---

[82] [1932] A.C. 562; *ante*, p. 48.

[83] [1957] 2 Q.B. 368; *Donnelly* v. *Glasgow Corpn.*, 1953 S.C. 107.

[84] Jenkins L.J., dissenting in the Court of Appeal, described the employer's duty as " an absolute duty to take reasonable care which can be discharged only by showing that all reasonable care has in fact been taken to ensure the soundness of the tools provided, and not by showing that the employer entrusted to somebody else the taking of all reasonable care, or assumed that somebody else had taken all reasonable care, to ensure the soundness of those tools ": [1958] 1 Q.B. 210, 234.

[85] [1958] 1 Q.B. 210, Jenkins L.J. dissenting; Goodhart, " A Master's Liability for Defective Tools " (1958) 74 L.Q.R. 397.

[86] [1959] A.C. 604; Webber, " Safety of Tools and Employer's Liability " (1959) 12 *Current Legal Problems* 56.

[87] The House of Lords approved the decision of Finnemore J. in *Mason* v. *Williams & Williams Ltd.* [1955] 1 W.L.R. 549, where the judge had not been " embarrassed by the citation of authority ": [1959] A.C. at p. 617, *per* Viscount Simonds.

[88] *Ante*, p. 149.

[89] See [1959] A.C. at p. 621, *per* Viscount Simonds; *ibid.* at p. 629, *per* Lord Morton; *ibid.* pp. 645–646, *per* Lord Reid; *ibid.* at pp. 646–647, *per* Lord Tucker; *ibid.* at p. 652, *per* Lord Keith.

whether or not the workman is entitled to rely upon the Act of 1969.[90] The Act has, certainly, not reversed the principle of *Davie's* case, but it has deprived that principle of effect in the class of case in which it was, potentially, most important. For all practical purposes, therefore, it can be accepted that the implication contained in the *ratio decidendi* of *Wilsons and Clyde Coal Co.* v. *English*,[91] that an employer is liable for the negligence of his independent contractors, still represents the law.[92]

BREACH OF STATUTORY DUTY [93]

The employer's common law duty to his workman exists by virtue of the relationship of master and servant and therefore applies wherever that relationship exists, but no similar generalisation is possible in the case of duties imposed by statute. The application of those duties is governed purely and simply by the statute which creates them. Nevertheless the number of statutory duties which affect the employer's liability to his workman in one way or another is now so great that for the enormous majority of workmen it is no longer true to say simply that their employers' duty is the common law duty described above. That duty always exists, but in factories, in mines and quarries, on building sites, and in most other forms of employment,[1] a host of specific obligations are superimposed upon it by statute and statutory regulations. It would be out of the question in a book of this kind, however, to consider in detail even a limited number of these obligations,[2] and the purpose of the following paragraphs is to do no more than show how a few of the more important of them operate in relation to employer's liability. For the solution of any particular problem there is no alternative to an examination of the relevant legislation itself.

1. Factories

The earlier legislation [3] is now consolidated in the Factories Act 1961,[4] Part II of which deals with " Safety (General Provisions)." [5]

---

[90] *Sumner* v. *William Henderson & Sons Ltd.* [1964] 1 Q.B. 450. The judgment of Phillimore J. was later set aside ([1963] 1 W.L.R. 823) but for procedural reasons only.
[91] *Ante*, pp. 153–154.
[92] Under the Hague Rules, the carrier of goods by sea must " exercise due diligence to make the ship seaworthy," and there may be an analogy between this duty and the employer's. In a question concerning the carrier's liability a distinction apparently exists between the manufacturer of the ship, for whose negligence the carrier is not liable, and the repairer of the ship, for whose negligence the carrier is liable. See *Angliss (W.) & Co. (Australia) Proprietary* v. *P. & O. Steam Navigation Co.* [1927] 2 K.B. 456 and *Riverstone Meat Co. Pty.* v. *Lancashire Shipping Co.* [1961] A.C. 807. In the latter case it was regarded as almost self-evident that the carrier is in general liable for the negligence of independent contractors. See, *e.g., per* Viscount Simonds at p. 843.
[93] For the action for breach of statutory duty in general, see Chap. 8, *ante.* For the Health and Safety at Work Act 1974, see p. 146, *ante.*
[1] See, *e.g.*, Agriculture (Safety, Health and Welfare Provisions) Act 1956; Offices, Shops and Railway Premises Act 1963.
[2] Two substantial and important books are devoted almost exclusively to the Factories Act 1961 and the regulations made thereunder: *Redgrave's Factories Acts*, 21st ed. (1966); Samuels, *Factory Law*, 8th ed. (1969).
[3] Chiefly the Factories Acts of 1937, 1948 and 1959.

Footnotes 4 and 5 on p. 157

A great variety of matters are dealt with in this Part of the Act [6] but the majority of actions are based either upon the sections dealing with the fencing of machinery or upon those dealing with the condition of the factory premises.

Sections 12 to 16 cover the fencing of machinery, and the general rule is laid down that flywheels and moving parts of prime movers,[7] transmission machinery,[8] and "every dangerous part" of other machinery,[9] shall be securely fenced. In deciding whether a part of machinery is dangerous, a question around which a substantial body of case-law has developed, the basic question is whether it is foreseeably likely to cause injury, and in assessing this not only the careful but the careless and inattentive workman must be borne in mind.[10] This does not mean, however, that it must be foreseen that a workman will act with total disregard for his own safety.[11] The fencing provided must be of substantial construction and, subject to certain restricted exceptions,[12] must be kept in position while the parts required to be fenced are "in motion or use."[13] The duty to fence is absolute, in the sense that difficulty or even impossibility of complying and at the same time leaving the machine in a usable condition affords no defence,[14] but the requirement that the fencing be "secure" does not

---

[4] The duties created by the Act are for the most part imposed upon the occupier of the factory, not upon the employer as such, but in the vast majority of cases the occupier and the employer are one and the same.

[5] This is the most important Part of the Act for present purposes, but it does not follow that no action for damages can be brought for breach of a section in some other Part of the Act: *Nicholson* v. *Atlas Steel Foundry & Engineering Co.* [1957] 1 W.L.R. 613 (H.L.); *Thornton* v. *Fisher & Ludlow Ltd.* [1968] 1 W.L.R. 655, both concerning sections contained in Part I, "Health (General Provisions)"; *Reid* v. *Westfield Paper Co.*, 1957 S.C. 218, concerning a section contained in Part III, "Welfare (General Provisions)."

[6] *e.g.*, hoists and lifts, lifting tackle, cranes, dangerous fumes, steam boilers and means of escape in case of fire.

[7] s. 12 (1). For definition of "prime mover," see s. 176 (1).

[8] s. 13 (1). For definition of "transmission machinery," see s. 176 (1).

[9] s. 14 (1). There is no duty to fence the dangerous parts of machinery constructed in the factory and not part of the equipment used in the processes of the factory: *Parvin* v. *Morton Machine Co.* [1952] A.C. 515. *Aliter* where the machinery though not yet in use, has been installed in the factory where it is to be used: *Irwin* v. *White, Tomkins & Courage Ltd.* [1964] 1 W.L.R. 387 (H.L.).

[10] See, *e.g.*, *Hindle* v. *Birtwistle* [1897] 1 Q.B. 192; *Walker* v. *Bletchley Flettons Ltd.* [1937] 1 All E.R. 170; *Mitchell* v. *North British Rubber Co.*, 1945 S.C.(J.) 69; *John Summers & Sons* v. *Frost* [1955] A.C. 740; *Close* v. *Steel Co. of Wales* [1962] A.C. 367; *Cross* v. *Midland and Low Moor Iron and Steel Co. Ltd.* [1965] A.C. 343; *F. E. Callow (Engineers) Ltd.* v. *Johnson* [1971] A.C. 335.

[11] *Higgins* v. *Harrison* (1932) 25 B.W.C.C. 113; *Carr* v. *Mercantile Produce Co.* [1949] 2 K.B. 601; *Pearce* v. *Stanley-Bridges Ltd.* [1965] 1 W.L.R. 931.

[12] Parts which are in such a position or of such construction as to be as safe as if they were securely fenced need not be fenced: ss. 12 (3), 13 (1), 14 (1): *Atkinson* v. *L.N.E.R.* [1926] 1 K.B. 313; *Hodkinson* v. *Henry Wallwork* [1955] 1 W.L.R. 1195. Operations at unfenced machinery are permitted only in the exceptional cases allowed for by s. 16 of the Act and the Operations at Unfenced Machinery Regulations 1938 and 1946.

[13] s. 16. These words have given rise to considerable trouble. See *e.g.*, *Richard Thomas & Baldwins Ltd.* v. *Cummings* [1955] A.C. 321; *Knight* v. *Leamington Spa Courier Ltd.* [1961] 2 Q.B. 253; *Stanbrook* v. *Waterlow & Sons Ltd.* [1964] 1 W.L.R. 825; *Mitchell* v. *W. S. Westin Ltd.* [1965] 1 W.L.R. 297; *Horne* v. *Lec Refrigeration Ltd.* [1965] 2 All E.R. 898.

[14] *Davies* v. *Thomas Owen & Co.* [1919] 2 K.B. 39; *John Summers & Sons Ltd.* v. *Frost* [1955] A.C. 740.

mean that it must protect the workman against every possible kind of injury. In the first place there is no duty to guard against an unforeseeable danger such as might be caused by a machine going wrong in a way which could not be reasonably anticipated.[15] Secondly, the duty to fence applies only to parts of the machinery,[16] not to material or components upon which the machine is performing some operation.[17] Thirdly, there is no duty that the fencing shall protect the workman from being struck by something ejected from the machine, whether part of the material on which the machine is working [18] or part of the machine itself.[19] " Fencing, in my opinion, means the erection of a barricade to prevent any employee from making contact with the machine, not an enclosure to prevent broken machinery from flying out." [20] But if a workman is injured by coming into contact with a part of machinery which is required to be fenced, then, unless the accident was due entirely to his own fault,[21] he is automatically entitled to recover. The liability of the occupier of the factory for breach of his obligation to fence is independent of any fault on his part and exists even though the workman at the time of his accident was engaged " on a frolic of his own." [21a]

Safety of the factory premises is dealt with chiefly by sections 28 and 29, the former covering specific matters such as the construction and maintenance of floors and the provision of handrails for staircases, while the latter deals generally with the safety of workplaces and means of access thereto.[22] The sections impose duties of two main kinds; the

---

[15] *Eaves* v. *Morris Motors* [1961] 2 Q.B. 385; *cf. Rogers* v. *George Blair & Co.* (1971) 11 K.I.R. 391. But if a part of machinery is dangerous, in the sense that it is a foreseeable cause of injury, and is unfenced, then it is irrelevant that the plaintiff's accident occurred in an unforeseeable way: *Millard* v. *Serck Tubes Ltd.* [1969] 1 W.L.R. 211.

[16] See *Quintas* v. *National Smelting Co.* [1961] 1 W.L.R. 401; *Lovelidge* v. *Anselm Odling & Sons Ltd.* [1967] 2 Q.B. 351; *British Railways Board* v. *Liptrot* [1969] 1 A.C. 136 for the meaning of " machinery."

[17] *Bullock* v. *G. John Power (Agencies)* [1956] 1 W.L.R. 171; *Kilgollan* v. *William Cooke Ltd.* [1956] 1 W.L.R. 527; *Eaves* v. *Morris Motors* [1961] 2 Q.B. 385. There is no duty to prevent a tool which the workman is holding from coming into contact with the machine and thus causing an injury: *Sparrow* v. *Fairey Aviation Co. Ltd.* [1964] A.C. 1019. In considering whether a part is dangerous regard must be had to the operation of the machine in the course of normal working. So a part may be dangerous even though danger only arises through the juxtaposition of the part and material on which the machine is working: *Midland and Low Moor Iron and Steel Co. Ltd.* v. *Cross* [1965] A.C. 343; *F. E. Callow (Engineers) Ltd.* v. *Johnson* [1971] A.C. 335. *Cf. Pearce* v. *Stanley-Bridges Ltd.* [1965] 1 W.L.R. 931; *Hindle* v. *Joseph Porritt & Sons Ltd.* [1970] 1 All E.R. 1442.

[18] *Nicholls* v. *Austin (Leyton) Ltd.* [1946] A.C. 493.

[19] *Carroll* v. *Andrew Barclay & Sons* [1948] A.C. 477; *Close* v. *Steel Co. of Wales* [1962] A.C. 367. But see the powerful dissenting judgment of Lord Denning in the latter case.

[20] *Carroll* v. *Andrew Barclay & Sons, supra,* at p. 486, *per* Lord Porter.

[21] *Rushton* v. *Turner Bros.* [1960] 1 W.L.R. 96; *Horne* v. *Lec Refrigeration Ltd.* [1965] 2 All E.R. 898.

[21a] *Uddin* v. *Associated Portland Cement Manufacturers Ltd.* [1965] 2 Q.B. 582; *Allen* v. *Aeroplane and Motor Aluminium Castings Ltd.* [1965] 1 W.L.R. 1244; see also *Westwood* v. *Post Office* [1974] A.C. 1. *Cf. Napieralski* v. *Curtis (Contractors) Ltd.* [1959] 1 W.L.R. 835. Carelessness of his own safety will, of course, lead to a reduction of the workman's damages on the ground of contributory negligence.

[22] s. 29 (1). S. 29 (2) deals with the specific case of a man working at a place from which he is liable to fall more than six feet six inches.

unqualified obligation, for example, that " all ladders shall be soundly constructed and properly maintained," [23] and the qualified obligation, for example, that safe means of access [23a] shall, " so far as is reasonably practicable," be provided and maintained.[24] If a rung of a ladder breaks then, without more, a breach of duty is established,[25] but the absence of " safe means of access " does not always involve a breach, for it must have been " reasonably practicable " to provide and maintain it.[26] In other words, liability depends upon whether the risk in question is sufficiently great to call for the measures necessary to eliminate it.[27] On the other hand, the burden of proving that the measures necessary were not " reasonably practicable " rests with the defendant,[28] and therefore a workman who proves that he suffered injury because of the absence of a safe means of access establishes at least a prima facie case. It is true that the House of Lords has more than once observed that after all the evidence has been produced the initial burden of proof is rarely of importance,[28a] but the fact remains that in the absence of evidence that the measures necessary were not reasonably practicable, the plaintiff is entitled to succeed. He is thus in a stronger position when attempting to negotiate an agreed settlement of his claim and in the early stages of litigation, even if not in the appellate courts, if he can rely upon the section than if he has to shoulder the burden of proving negligence at common law.

As with the sections prescribing the duty to fence dangerous machinery, the application of these sections has inevitably developed a fair degree of technicality. Until 1959 there was no general duty with regard to the safety of a man's place of work, as opposed to the means of access to that place, and a good many cases therefore turned

---

[23] s. 28 (5). " Maintained " means " maintained in an efficient state, in efficient working order, and in good repair." See *Latimer* v. *A.E.C.* [1953] A.C. 643.

[23a] Including means of access passing over articles being repaired or manufactured in the factory, such as ships: *Gardiner* v. *Admiralty Commissioners* [1964] 1 W.L.R. 590 (H.L.Sc.).

[24] s. 29 (1). A third type of duty is contained in s. 28 (4): " All openings in floors shall be securely fenced, *except in so far as the nature of the work renders such fencing impracticable.*" A precaution may be " practicable " without being " reasonably practicable," and may be " impracticable " without being actually impossible: *Jayne* v. *National Coal Board* [1963] 2 All E.R. 220: and a precaution may be " practicable " even though the risks inherent in setting up the precaution exceed the probable benefit to be gained from it: *Boyton* v. *Willment Bros.* [1971] 1 W.L.R. 1625, *obiter.* See also, on the difference between such duties and the common law, *Wallhead* v. *Ruston and Hornsby Ltd.* (1973) 14 K.I.R. 285. For discussion of the correct approach to the problem of "obstructions," see *Marshall* v. *Ericsson Telephones Ltd.* [1964] 1 W.L.R. 1367.

[25] *Cole* v. *Blackstone & Co.* [1943] K.B. 615.

[26] See especially *Levesley* v. *Firth & Brown Ltd.* [1953] 1 W.L.R. 1206; *Braham* v. *J. Lyons & Co. Ltd.* [1962] 1 W.L.R. 1048; *Jenkins* v. *Allied Ironfounders Ltd.* [1970] 1 W.L.R. 304 (H.L.Sc.). The last-named is a case on s. 28 (1) which also contains the words " so far as is reasonably practicable."

[27] *McCarthy* v. *Coldair Ltd.* [1951] 2 T.L.R. 1226. Where there is a safe route and the workman unpredictably chooses another and unsafe route, there is no breach of the subsection: *Donovan* v. *Cammell Laird & Co.* [1949] 2 All E.R. 82.

[28] *Nimmo* v. *Alexander Cowan & Sons Ltd.* [1968] A.C. 107; Weir, *Casebook on Tort,* 3rd ed., p. 52.

[28a] *Dorman Long (Steel) Ltd.* v. *Bell* [1964] 1 W.L.R. 333, 335, *per* Lord Reid; *Jenkins* v. *Allied Ironfounders Ltd.* [1970] 1 W.L.R. 304, 312, *per* Lord Guest.

upon the distinction between the two.[29] Now, however, this defect
in the law has been remedied and the subsection reads: " There shall,
so far as is reasonably practicable, be provided and maintained safe
means of access to every place at which any person has at any time
to work, and every such place shall, so far as is reasonably practicable,
be made and kept safe for any person working there." [30] Nevertheless
cases such as *Davies* v. *De Havilland Aircraft Co.*,[31] in which it was
held that no duty under the section was owed to a workman walking
along a passage to the canteen for his mid-morning break, are not
decided differently today.[31a] Equally the duties in respect of the things
specified in section 28 apply only to those things and not to other
things, however similar they may be and however reasonable it may
appear that a similar duty should exist. A plankway between gantries
100 feet above the ground, for example, is not a " floor " and therefore
the widow of a workman who was killed when he fell through an
aperture in the plankway could not rely upon the requirement that
" all openings in floors shall be securely fenced." [32] In a case of this
kind the question is not one of what is reasonable, but whether the
words used in the section are " apt to cover or describe the circumstances in question in any particular case." [33]

2. Mines and quarries

The previous legislation is now collected together, in a modified
form, in the Mines and Quarries Act 1954 and in regulations made
under the Act,[34] Part III of the Act dealing with safety in mines and
Part V with safety in quarries. Almost every aspect of safety is dealt
with in the Act or regulations, and it is a feature of the legislation
that many duties are imposed directly upon individuals such as
managers, inspectors and shotfirers. It is, however, expressly provided
that the owner of the mine shall be liable for the breach of such a
duty by one of his servants.[35] It is also a feature of the legislation that
although it contains numerous unqualified obligations, there is a
general provision that in any case [36] it shall be a defence to prove
that it was " impracticable to avoid or prevent the contravention." [37]

---

[29] e.g., *Lovell* v. *Blundells & Crompton & Co.* [1944] K.B. 502; *Hopwood* v. *Rolls-Royce Ltd.* (1947) 176 L.T. 514; *Dorman Long & Co.* v. *Hillier* [1951] 1 All E.R. 357.
[30] s. 29 (1).
[31] [1951] 1 K.B. 50; *Rose* v. *Colvilles Ltd.*, 1950 S.L.T.(Notes) 72; *Dryland* v. *London Electrical Manufacturing Co.* (1949) 99 L.J. 665.
[31a] *Cockady* v. *Bristol Siddeley Engines Ltd.* (1965) 115 L.J. 661.
[32] s. 28 (4); *Tate* v. *Swan Hunter & Wigham Richardson Ltd.* [1958] 1 W.L.R. 39.
[33] *Bath* v. *B.T.C.* [1954] 1 W.L.R. 1013, 1015, *per* Somervell L.J. (dry-dock not an " opening " in a floor); *Kimpton* v. *Steel Co. of Wales* [1960] 1 W.L.R. 527 (three steps wedged into a platform not a " staircase ").
[34] Especially the Miscellaneous Mines Regulations 1956.
[35] s. 159.
[36] Both actions for damages and prosecutions.
[37] s. 157. The equivalent provision in the Coal Mines Act 1911, s. 102 (8), contained the words " not reasonably practicable " and the standard of liability has thus presumably been raised.

The burden of proving the impracticability rests squarely on the defendant and he must do more than prove that he took all reasonable care,[38] but at least it seems likely that no such decision as *John Summers & Sons* v. *Frost*[39] need be reached under the Act of 1954. In what follows, therefore, the existence of this general defence must be borne in mind.

One of the most important topics dealt with by the Act is the security from falls of the roads and working places in a mine, and numerous detailed rules concerning support are laid down. Under earlier legislation[40] there was also the general obligation that "the roof and sides of every travelling road and working place shall be made secure . . ." and it has been held that this created an absolute duty.[41] Now, however, in place of this impersonal obligation the manager of the mine is personally subjected to the duty to take such steps as may be necessary for keeping the road or working place secure,[42] and in order to determine what steps may be necessary to achieve this result, he must also take the necessary steps to secure that he is in possession of all relevant information.[43] This imposes a less than absolute duty, and there is no breach if the manager has merely failed to take steps the necessity for which could not have been discovered until after the accident.[44] On the other hand, the duty that all parts and working gear of machinery used in the mine "shall be of good construction, suitable material, adequate strength and free from patent defect, and shall be properly maintained"[45] does create an absolute duty[46] and therefore as soon as there is a patent, *i.e.*, observable, defect, there is a breach. It makes no difference that at the time of the accident the defect had not in fact and could not have been observed.[47] Similarly, the duty imposed upon the manager of a quarry " to secure that any quarrying operations . . . are so carried on as to avoid danger from falls "[48] means that he must achieve the

---

[38] *Sanderson* v. *N.C.B.* [1961] 2 Q.B. 244. Impracticability must be proved by evidence, " not deduced by casual inference ": *per* Holroyd Pearce L.J., *ibid.* at p. 252. The defence may succeed, however, if the precaution required by a regulation is impracticable even though the work could have been done in a different way altogether so as not to invoke the regulation in question at all: *Morris* v. *National Coal Board* [1963] 1 W.L.R. 1382.

[39] [1955] A.C. 740, *ante*, p. 135. S. 82 (1) of the Act of 1954 provides that " every fly-wheel and every other dangerous exposed part of any machinery . . . shall be securely fenced."

[40] Coal Mines Act 1911, s. 49.

[41] *Lochgelly Iron and Coal Co.* v. *M'Mullan* [1934] A.C. 1.

[42] s. 48 (1).

[43] s. 48 (2).

[44] *Brown* v. *N.C.B.* [1962] A.C. 574. See also *John G. Stein & Co. Ltd.* v. *O'Hanlon* [1965] A.C. 890; *Tomlinson* v. *Beckermet Mining Co. Ltd.* [1964] 1 W.L.R. 1043; *Soar* v. *National Coal Board* [1965] 1 W.L.R. 886; *Aitken* v. *N.C.B.*, 1973 S.L.T.(Notes) 48. If insecurity is shown it is for the defendant to prove performance of the requirements of the section: *Sinclair* v. *National Coal Board*, 1963 S.L.T. 296; *Beiscak* v. *National Coal Board* [1965] 1 W.L.R. 518.

[45] s. 81 (1).

[46] *Hamilton* v. *N.C.B.* [1960] A.C. 633.

[47] *Sanderson* v. *N.C.B.* [1961] 2 Q.B. 244.

[48] s. 108 (1).

result that no fall shall produce any danger.[49] The nature of the duty in each case depends purely and simply upon the way it is expressed in the appropriate section of the Act.

EMPLOYERS' LIABILITY

Despite the view sometimes expressed that an action for breach of statutory duty is identical with an action for negligence,[50] in the context of employers' liability the two are kept wholly distinct and some judges have even expressed concern lest the employer's common law duty be so enlarged that it becomes indistinguishable from a duty created by statute.[51] Nevertheless the subject-matter of both kinds of duty, so far as the law of tort is concerned, is the same, namely, the employer's liability to pay damages to his injured workman. It is the combined effect of the common law duty and such statutory duties as apply which governs the liability of the employer in any given case.[52]

At common law the employer's duty is a duty of care and it follows that the burden of proving negligence rests with the plaintiff workman throughout the case.[53] It has even been said that if he alleges a failure to provide a reasonably safe system of working the plaintiff must plead, and therefore prove, what the proper system was and in what relevant respects it was not observed.[54] It is true that the severity of this particular burden has been somewhat reduced,[55] but it remains clear that for a workman merely to prove the circumstances of his accident will normally be insufficient.[56] Where a statutory duty applies, on the other hand, the employer's duty is often absolute, so that no question of negligence arises at all, and even where it is qualified by such words as " so far as reasonably practicable " it is for the employer to prove that it was not reasonably practicable to avoid the breach.[57] It follows that the existence of a relevant statutory duty will almost invariably ease the task of the workman in establishing his employer's liability.

There is nothing intrinsically wrong in a system of law which sometimes imposes liability upon an employer without requiring the workman to prove negligence and sometimes does not. The common law generally requires proof of negligence as a precondition to liability, but the legislature, it may be said, has seen fit in specific cases to modify

---

[49] *Brazier* v. *Skipton Rock Co.* [1962] 1 W.L.R. 471; *Sanderson* v. *Millom Hematite Ore & Iron Co. Ltd.* [1967] 3 All E.R. 1050.

[50] *Ante*, pp. 139–141.

[51] *Latimer* v. *A.E.C. Ltd.* [1953] A.C. 644, 658, *per* Lord Tucker.

[52] This is, of course, a truism for any branch of the law of tort, but it is of particular significance here owing to the enormous number of statutory duties which exist.

[53] *Brown* v. *Rolls-Royce Ltd.* [1960] 1 W.L.R. 210 (H.L.) provides a striking example.

[54] *Colfar* v. *Coggins & Griffith (Liverpool)* [1945] A.C. 197, 203, *per* Viscount Simon L.C.

[55] *Dixon* v. *Cementation Co.* [1960] 1 W.L.R. 746.

[56] The workman may be entitled to rely upon the maxim *res ipsa loquitur* (*ante*, pp. 73–80) but cases in which it is of assistance are comparatively rare. See, *e.g.*, the doubts expressed in *Moore* v. *R. Fox & Sons* [1956] 1 Q.B. 596.

[57] *Ante*, p. 161.

the common law and relieve the workman of this burden. " The Factories Acts and the elaborate regulations made under them testify to the care with which the common law has been altered, adjusted and refined in order to give protection and compensation to the workman." [58] It is legitimate to inquire, however, whether the statutory modifications of the common law duty of care were really enacted with an eye to actions for damages by injured workmen and whether the combination of common law and statutory duties does in fact produce a coherent body of law.

A comprehensive answer to these questions would require an examination of the whole mass of statutes and statutory regulations which impose specific duties upon employers, but it is perhaps not unfair to express some doubts about the matter without undertaking this mammoth task. Although by now Parliament may be assumed to know the way in which the courts will treat breaches of the duties it creates, it can safely be said that the primary object of most of the legislation in question is not the modification of the law of employers' liability. It is to secure, so far as the enactment of specific duties can do so, the maximum protection for the workman against injury. This has, indeed, been expressly acknowledged in the House of Lords,[59-60] and the point emerges clearly from the change introduced by the Mines and Quarries Act 1954 in the obligation regarding the security of the roads and working places of a mine.[61] Formerly, the duty was expressed impersonally and was unqualified, but now the manager of the mine is directed to take such steps as may be necessary. " This was no doubt inserted as the result of the disaster in 1951 at the Knockshinnoch Colliery, when the duties were so distributed among the officials that ' what was everybody's business was nobody's business.' So in 1954 Parliament declared that it is the duty of the *manager* to see to the security of the road." [62] It can scarcely be argued that the purpose of the change was to modify the law governing the employer's liability for damages even though this was its incidental effect.[63]

The result of incorporating into the law of employer's liability the manifold duties enacted for the purpose of preventing accidents has inevitably been the creation of technical and often irrational distinctions, and it is the existence of these distinctions which gives rise to dissatisfaction with this branch of the law. We have already noticed,

---

[58] *Davie* v. *New Merton Board Mills* [1959] A.C. 604, 627, *per* Viscount Simonds.

[59-60] *Gill* v. *Donald Humberstone & Co. Ltd.* [1963] 1 W.L.R. 929, 933–934, *per* Lord Reid; 941–942, *per* Lord Devlin. See also *Alford* v. *N.C.B.* [1952] 1 All E.R. 754, 757 (H.L.), *per* Lord Normand; *Brown* v. *N.C.B.* [1962] A.C. 574, 594, *per* Lord Radcliffe.

[61] *Ante*, p. 161.

[62] *Brown* v. *N.C.B.*, *supra* at p. 597, *per* Lord Denning.

[63] It is not denied that a change may sometimes be made with this object. The purpose of adding the duty that places of work shall be safe, so far as reasonably practicable, to the section dealing with means of access to those places was presumably to avoid discussion of the distinction between the two. See *ante*, p. 160.

for example, that the duty created by the Factories Act that dangerous parts of machinery shall be securely fenced does not extend to protecting the workman from injury caused by material or even fragments of the machine itself which are ejected from it.[64] From the point of view of accident prevention it may be impracticable to legislate against this kind of thing,[65] but that is a poor reason for requiring a workman so injured to prove negligence while allowing his fellow workman, injured by direct contact with a dangerous part, an automatic right to damages.[66] Yet over and over again one will find in this branch of the law that the all-important question of the burden of proof turns upon a point of the purest technicality, for which no justification in terms of principle or expediency is to be found. It is, no doubt, too late now for the courts themselves to rid the law of these technicalities, but if the law of employers' liability were more generally realised to consist of both the common law and the statutory duties and their combined effect considered as a whole, the birth of still more technical distinctions might be avoided.[67] It is not likely that the problem will be substantially ameliorated by the implementation of the Health and Safety at Work Act 1974,[68] for the main effect of that will simply be to transfer the provisions creating liability from statutes to regulations, and the " conflict " between penal and compensation purposes will still remain.

---

[64] *Ante*, p. 158.

[65] In *Eaves* v. *Morris Motors Ltd.* [1961] 2 Q.B. 385, 400, Pearson L.J. suggested that the reason why no regulations have been made for the fencing of dangerous materials (Factories Act 1961, s. 14 (6)) lies in the difficulty of drafting general provisions for the fencing of such things.

[66] This is the effect of *Close* v. *Steel Co. of Wales* [1962] A.C. 367. See the criticism of Lord Hailsham L.C. in *F. E. Callow* (*Engineers*) *Ltd.* v. *Johnson* [1971] A.C. 335, 342–343.

[67] Perhaps Lord Hailsham's speech in *F. E. Callow* (*Engineers*) *Ltd.* v. *Johnson, supra,* marks the beginning of a somewhat less technical approach to this part of the law. *Cf.* however, the concurring speech of Lord Donovan, *ibid.* at p. 355 and the dissenting speech of Viscount Dilhorne, *ibid.* at pp. 354–355.

[68] See *ante*, p. 146.

CHAPTER 10

LIABILITY FOR LAND AND STRUCTURES [1]

INTRODUCTION

THE title of this chapter requires a brief explanation. It would be misleading to style the topic " liability for premises," although that would be natural antithesis to " liability for chattels " in the next chapter. But in fact it would be too narrow to be exact, for the rules now to be discussed are not limited to immovable property like open land, houses, railway stations and bridges, but have been extended to movables like taxicabs, omnibuses, railway carriages, gangways and scaffolding.[2] All these, except land, can be included in the elastic term " structures." As it therefore covers some things which are chattels, it may be asked what the distinction is between chattels in this connection and elsewhere. It seems to be this. The defendant, where dangerous structures of a movable kind are concerned, retains control of them, whereas under the " chattel " type of liability the control and very often the full ownership of the chattel has passed to someone else who is subsequently injured by it. A less solid distinction is that with movable structures the plaintiff is injured by entry upon them; that is not usually so with chattels, indeed the chattel is generally so small that " entry " upon it in the common sense of that term is not possible.

At common law the liability for dangerous structures (which for brevity's sake we shall generally use henceforth to include land) formed a special subhead of the general doctrine of negligence.[3] The duties of the occupier were, however, cast in a descending scale to four different kinds of persons. The highest degree of care was owed by the occupier to one who entered in pursuance of a contract with him; a less degree was due to the " invitee " who (without any contract) entered on business of interest both to himself and the occupier; still less was due

---

[1] North, *Occupiers' Liability* (1971) is the leading treatment. The American *Restatement of the Law of Torts* 2d, Chap. 13, should be studied for comparative purposes, and James, " Liability of Occupiers of Land " (1954) 63 Yale L.J. 148–182, 603–638; Marsh, " The History and Comparative Law of Invitees, Licensees and Trespassers " (1953) 69 L.Q.R. 182, 359; Law Reform Committee's Third Report, Occupier's Liability to Invitees, Licensees and Trespassers, Cmd. 9305 (1954); Odgers [1955] C.L.J. 1; *ibid.* " Occupiers' Liability: A Further Comment " [1957] C.L.J. 39; Bowett, " Law Reform and Occupier's Liability " (1956) 19 M.L.R. 172; Newark, " The Occupiers' Liability (Northern Ireland) Act " (1958) 12 N.I.L.Q. 203; Payne, " The Occupiers' Liability Act " (1958) 21 M.L.R. 359.
[2] *Francis* v. *Cockrell* (1870) L.R. 5 Q.B. 501; *Maclenan* v. *Segar* [1917] 2 K.B. 325; *Haseldine* v. *Daw* [1941] 2 K.B. 343 (lift); *Pratt* v. *Richards* [1951] 2 K.B. 208 (scaffolding).
[3] *Glasgow Corporation* v. *Muir* [1943] A.C. 448, 461, *per* Lord Wright, and in (1953) 2 Univ. of West Austr. Annual Law Rev. 543; *London Graving Dock* v. *Horton* [1951] A.C. 737. As the Occupiers' Liability Act 1957 imposes a duty of care upon the occupier, this remains true today: *Wheat* v. *E. Lacon & Co. Ltd.* [1966] A.C. 522, 578, *per* Lord Denning.

165

to the "licensee" who came, with the occupier's permission, on business of interest to himself but of none to the occupier; and scarcely any at all to a trespasser. The distinctions between these various classes of entrant were never finally settled, however, and in some cases at least they worked arbitrarily.[4] Though their significance was reduced by some of the later decisions,[5] this branch of the law as a whole remained the subject of criticism.[6] It was, therefore, referred to the Law Reform Committee in 1952 and as a result of the Committee's Report [7] the Occupiers' Liability Act 1957 was passed. This Act, speaking generally, reduces classes of entrant to two—lawful visitors and trespassers— and provides a single "common duty of care" which is now owed by an occupier to all his lawful visitors. The Act can, however, be understood only with the pre-existing common law in mind and before considering its provisions therefore it is necessary to describe briefly the rules of the common law.

THE COMMON LAW

1. Duty under contract

Where A enters B's structure under a contract entitling him to do so B's duty depends upon the terms of the contract, but it is rare for the contract to deal expressly with this matter. The duty depends, therefore, upon a term to be implied into the contract and this, at least in theory, will vary from one contract to another. In practice, however, it appears that the common law recognised only two types of implied term. The more stringent, appropriate where the main purpose of the contract was the use of the structure in question, amounted to a warranty by the occupier that the structure was as safe for the purposes contemplated by the contract as reasonable care and skill on the part of anyone could make it.[8] The less stringent, which probably differed little if at all from the duty owed to an invitee,[9] and which was appropriate where the use of the structure was merely ancillary to the main purpose of the contract, amounted to a warranty by the occupier that he, and perhaps his independent contractors,[10]

---

[4] e.g., Fairman v. Perpetual Investment Building Society [1923] A.C. 74; Jacobs v. L.C.C. [1950] A.C. 361.

[5] Esp. Pearson v. Lambeth Borough Council [1950] 2 K.B. 353; Hawkins v. Coulsdon & Purley U.D.C. [1953] 1 W.L.R. 882, affd. [1954] 1 Q.B. 319; Slater v. Clay Cross Co. Ltd. [1956] 2 Q.B. 264.

[6] See, e.g., Wallis-Jones, "Liability of Public Authorities as Occupiers of Dangerous Premises to Persons Entering as of Right" (1949) 65 L.Q.R. 367.

[7] Third Report (Occupiers' Liability to Invitees, Licensees and Trespassers) 1954, Cmd. 9305. Post, pp. 171–173.

[8] Francis v. Cockrell (1870) L.R. 5 Q.B. 501; Maclenan v. Segar [1917] 2 K.B. 325. Cf. Hall v. Brooklands Auto Racing Club [1933] 1 K.B. 205.

[9] Weigall v. Westminster Hospital (1936) 52 T.L.R. 301.

[10] Thomson v. Cremin [1953] 2 All E.R. 1185 appeared to hold that an invitee could recover for negligence on the part of an independent contractor employed by the occupier and the contractual duty could hardly be less onerous than that which existed independently of the contract. It was an open question whether the discovery of Thomson v. Cremin (the case was decided in 1941, but not brought to the general notice of the legal profession until the publication of the 11th ed. of Salmond on Torts in 1953) removed the

had taken reasonable care to see that the structure was reasonably safe.[11] It was often difficult to determine to which class a given contract belonged, and *Bell* v. *Travco Hotels Ltd*.[12] suggested that the duty might vary according to the part of the structure where the injury was sustained.

2. Liability in tort to an invitee: Rule in Indermaur v. Dames [13]

Between the invitor and the invitee there had to be a common or joint interest, perhaps not exclusively of a material or pecuniary character, but the exact scope of " common," " joint " and " material " had not been clearly defined, and it may have been sufficient only that the invitor had a material interest in the invitee's visit.[14] " The leading distinction between an invitee and a licensee is that, in the case of the former, invitor and invitee have a common interest, while the licensor and licensee have none." [15] A usual example of an invitee is the person who enters a shop or other place of business with a view to doing business with the shopkeeper or proprietor, whether or not he actually buys anything or otherwise does business.[16] A guest who is invited to dine by the occupier, on the other hand, is not an invitee, but a mere licensee.

The occupier's duty towards his invitee is expressed by the rule in *Indermaur* v. *Dames* laid down in 1866.[17] The plaintiff was a journeyman gas-fitter employed by X. Under a contract with the defendant, X had fixed a patent gas-regulator in the sugar-refinery of the defendant. X had directed the plaintiff to test some burners on the premises in connection with this regulator. While doing so, the plaintiff without any fault on his own part fell through an unfenced shaft and was injured. The defendant was held liable to him. There was no earlier decision exactly in point [18] and the judgment of the Court of Common

---

distinction between the two kinds of-implied term: Cmd. 9305, para. 4. But see *Green* v. *Fibreglass Ltd.* [1958] 2 Q.B. 245, questioning the effect of *Thomson* v. *Cremin*; Weir, *Casebook on Tort*, 3rd ed., p. 241.

[11] *Gillmore* v. *L.C.C.* (1938) 159 L.T. 615; *Bell* v. *Travco Hotels Ltd.* [1953] 1 Q.B. 473. See also *The Cawood III* [1951] P. 270.

[12] *Supra.*

[13] (1866) L.R. 1 C.P. 274. See Friedmann, 21 Can. Bar. Rev. 79–90.

[14] This was the view of Scott L.J. in *Haseldine* v. *Daw* [1941] 2 K.B. 343, 352, and preferred by the Law Reform Committee (Cmd. 9305, para. 7), though they admitted that the weight of authority might be against them.

[15] *Mersey Docks and Harbour Board* v. *Procter* [1923] A.C. 253, 272, *per* Lord Sumner; *Jacobs* v. *L.C.C.* [1950] A.C. 361, 372, *per* Lord Simonds.

[16] *Indermaur* v. *Dames* (1866) L.R. 1 C.P. 274, 287. The dividing line between an invitee and a licensee may be difficult to draw (*Fairman* v. *Perpetual Investment Building Society* [1923] A.C. 74) and on occasion the occupier's " interest " in the visit of his invitee has been very slight. See, *e.g.*, *Stowell* v. *Railway Executive* [1949] 2 K.B. 519 (father going to station to meet daughter arriving by train held an invitee because of the railway's interest that he should help her with her luggage); *Jennings* v. *Cole* [1949] 2 All E.R. 191.

[17] L.R. 1 C.P. 274; affirmed L.R. 2 C.P. 311.

[18] In *Southcote* v. *Stanley* (1864) 1 H. & N. 247, 250–251, Bramwell B. had emitted some dicta about the invitee which appeared to put him on a level with the licensee, but the problem was not really attacked until *Indermaur* v. *Dames*: see Pollock, *Torts*, p. 394.

Pleas, which was delivered by Willes J., was the starting-point of a new form of tortious liability. The essential part of it was as follows [19]:

" The class to which the customer belongs includes persons . . . who go upon business which concerns the occupier, and upon his invitation, express or implied. And with respect to such a visitor at least, we consider it settled law, that he, using reasonable care on his part for his own safety, is entitled to expect that the occupier shall on his part use reasonable care to prevent damage from unusual danger, which he knows or ought to know [20]; and that, where there is evidence of neglect, the question whether such reasonable care has been taken, by notice, lighting, guarding, or otherwise, and whether there was contributory negligence in the sufferer, must be determined by a jury as a matter of fact."

These words have been the subject of consideration in innumerable cases and were treated much as if contained in an Act of Parliament.[21] Fortunately the cases need no longer be considered in detail and it suffices to make the following two points:

(i) The occupier had no duty to the invitee unless there was an unusual danger of which he knew or ought to have known, and the duty was not to prevent unusual danger, but to use reasonable care to prevent damage from unusual danger.

(ii) It was laid down in *London Graving Dock Co. Ltd.* v. *Horton* [22] that if the invitee had full knowledge of the nature and extent of the danger then the occupier could not be in breach of his duty,[23] but probably this only applied if the invitee, as between himself and the occupier, was free to act upon his knowledge.[24]

3. Liability in tort to a licensee

A licensee (or " bare licensee ") was one who had express or implied permission to enter for his own purposes, but not for the occupier's business or material interest. Such was a guest whom the occupier had asked to dinner or to stay with him.[25] Whether the invitation were prompted by benevolence or social reasons was of no moment,

---

[19] L.R. 1 C.P. at p. 288.

[20] " Ought to know " necessarily involves a finding of negligence for liability: Tucker L.J. in *Jones* v. *Barclays Bank Ltd.* [1949] W.N. 266. The duty of the occupier is not " absolute ": see Lord Uthwatt in *Read* v. *Lyons & Co. Ltd.* [1947] A.C. 156, 186–187.

[21] The draftsman of the Occupiers' Liability Act 1957 is recorded as expressing the hope that " instead of having the judgment of Willes J. construed as if it were a statute, one is to have a statute which can be construed as if it were a judgment of Willes J." See *Roles* v. *Nathan* [1963] 1 W.L.R. 1117, 1122, *per* Lord Denning M.R.

[22] [1951] A.C. 737. See Lord Wright (1951) 67 L.Q.R. at pp. 532–534 (Book Review.)

[23] *Aliter* if the invitee's knowledge of the danger was incomplete: *Smith* v. *Austin Lifts Ltd., supra.*

[24] *Greene* v. *Chelsea Borough Council* [1954] 2 Q.B. 127, 139–140, *per* Denning L.J.; *Slater* v. *Clay Cross Co.* [1956] 2 Q.B. 264, 271, *per* Denning L.J. *Cf. A. C. Billings & Sons* v. *Riden* [1958] A.C. 240, 246, *per* Lord Somervell.

[25] But business might be so combined with hospitality as to make the visitor an invitee, *e.g.*, a parent asked to attend speech-day at a school where his child is a pupil: *Griffiths* v. *St. Clement's School, Liverpool* [1938] 3 All E.R. 537. For liability of requisitioning authority to licensee in occupation, see *Greene* v. *Chelsea B.C., supra.*

for the law did not take account of the worldly advantage which the host might remotely have in view.[26]

The licensee, in order to retain his rights as such, must keep within the bounds of the permission accorded to him.[27] The duty towards him may be thus stated:

The occupier must warn a licensee of any concealed danger (or trap) of which the occupier knows.

The principle behind this duty was that the licensee, who was allowed to enter for his own purposes exclusively, could not complain of the condition of the structure: he must take it as he finds it.[28] The licensor could not, however, allow his licensee to fall into a trap of which he actually knew,[29] and this leads to the idea that the chief difference between the duty owed to an invitee and that owed to a licensee lay in the fact that an invitee could recover for damage caused by an unusual danger of which the invitor *ought to have known*, while the licensee could recover only if the licensor *actually knew* of the concealed danger.[30] In the later cases, however, it was held that the test of the licensor's knowledge was objective, *i.e.*, if he knew of the physical facts which constituted the danger and a reasonable man having that knowledge would appreciate the risk involved, the licensor was not excused by his own failure to appreciate the risk.[31] According to Denning L.J. this development reduced the distinction between the two duties " to vanishing point." [32]

4. Liability in tort to a trespasser

The law governing the duty of an occupier towards a trespasser is not affected by the Occupiers' Liability Act 1957. It will, therefore, be considered after discussion of the provisions of that Act.

Activity duty

It seems to have been settled by 1954,[33] and perhaps by a very much earlier date,[34] that the distinctions between the various classes of lawful entrant were irrelevant where the injury was caused not by

---

[26] Hamilton L.J. in *Latham* v. *R. Johnson & Nephew Ltd.* [1913] 1 K.B. 398, 410.

[27] *Jenkins* v. *G.W. Ry.* [1912] 1 K.B. 525. *Cf. Braithwaite* v. *S. Durham Steel Co.* [1958] 1 W.L.R. 986.

[28] *Latham* v. *R. Johnson & Nephew Ltd.* [1913] 1 K.B. 398; *Perkowski* v. *Wellington Corporation* [1959] A.C. 53. The law was likened to that concerning gifts: *Gautret* v. *Egerton* (1866) L.R. 2 C.P. 371.

[29] An obvious danger cannot be a trap even if the licensee himself fails to observe it: *Perkowski* v. *Wellington Corporation, supra.*

[30] " The distinction between a concealed danger and an unusual danger was a narrow one. All concealed dangers are unusual dangers but an unusual danger is not necessarily concealed ": Cmd. 9305, para. 27.

[31] *Hawkins* v. *Coulsdon and Purley U.D.C.* [1954] 1 Q.B. 319.

[32] *Slater* v. *Clay Cross Co. Ltd.* [1956] 2 Q.B. at p. 269; *Wheat* v. *E. Lacon & Co. Ltd.* [1966] A.C. 552, 577, per Lord Denning.

[33] *Dunster* v. *Abbott* [1954] 1 W.L.R. 58, 62, per Denning L.J.; *Slade* v. *Battersea and Putney Hospital Management Committee* [1955] 1 W.L.R. 207; *Slater* v. *Clay Cross Co. Ltd.* [1956] 2 Q.B. 264; *Heard* v. *New Zealand Forest Products* [1960] N.Z.L.R. 329.

[34] *Tebbutt* v. *Bristol & Exeter Ry.* (1870) L.R. 6 Q.B. 73.

the static condition of the structure but by the current activities of the occupier. The class to which the entrant belonged governed the " occupancy duty " which was owed towards him, but not the " activity duty." [35] At common law there can in fact be two duties existing concurrently—the special duty arising out of the particular relationship between the occupier and the entrant and the general duty arising from other elements in the situation creating an additional relationship between them. " Occupation of premises is a ground of liability and is not a ground of exemption from liability." [35a] The inherently dangerous activity of running trains through a level crossing lawfully used by the public, for example, imposes upon the railway authority a duty to use all reasonable care which is independent of and additional to the duty owed by the authority as occupiers of the crossing to persons lawfully entering upon it.[35b] In *Slater* v. *Clay Cross Co. Ltd.*[36] the plaintiff, a licensee, was walking along a narrow tunnel on a railway track owned and occupied by the defendants when she was struck by a train driven by the defendants' servant. It was held that the driver was negligent and that therefore the plaintiff was entitled to recover. Her status, provided only that she was lawfully in the tunnel, was of no importance. " If a landowner is driving his car down his private drive and meets someone lawfully walking upon it, then he is under a duty to take reasonable care so as not to injure the walker; and his duty is the same no matter whether it is his gardener coming up with his plants, a tradesman delivering goods, a friend coming to tea, or a flag seller seeking a charitable gift." [37]

It is a matter of controversy whether the common duty of care now imposed on occupiers towards all lawful entrants replaces the " activity duty " as well as the " occupancy duty." On the one hand it is enacted that the rules provided by the Occupiers' Liability Act " shall have effect, in place of the rules of the common law, to regulate the duty which an occupier of premises owes to his visitors in respect of dangers due to the state of the premises *or to things done or omitted to be done on them.*" [38] On the other hand it is also en-

---

[35] Newark, " *Twine* v. *Bean's Express Ltd.*" (1954) 17 M.L.R. 102.

[35a] *Commissioner for Railways* v. *McDermott* [1967] A.C. 169, 186, *per* Lord Gardiner L.C. (P.C.)

[35b] *Commissioner for Railways* v. *McDermott, supra.*

[36] [1956] 2 Q.B. 264.

[37] *Ibid.* at p. 269, *per* Denning L.J.; *Perkowski* v. *Wellington Corporation* [1959] A.C. 53, 67, *per* Lord Somervell. The " activity duty " does not cover activities affecting the state of the structure before the entrant goes onto it: *Perkowski* v. *Wellington Corporation, supra. Cf. Slade* v. *Battersea and Putney Hospital Management Committee* [1955] 1 W.L.R. 207. On the other hand, it is not necessary that the defendant's negligence should itself be immediately connected with the activity in question: *Commissioner for Railways* v. *McDermott* [1967] A.C. 169, where the plaintiff was run over by a train because she had tripped and fallen at a level crossing which was in a defective condition and remained lying with her feet across the line, presumably dazed or unconscious, when the train approached. There was no negligence in the actual running of the train. See especially, *per* Lord Gardiner L.C. at p. 189.

[38] s. 1 (1).

acted that those rules " shall regulate the nature of the duty imposed
by law *in consequence of a person's occupation or control of premises
. . .,*" [39] and it can hardly be said that the " activity duty " is imposed
in consequence of a person's occupation or control of premises.
It arises, generally speaking, by the application of the ordinary principles
of negligence and applies equally to occupiers and non-occupiers.[40]
It is submitted that the better view is that the Act does not affect
the activity duty, for its principal purpose was to rid the law of the
distinction between invitees and licensees, and that distinction was
without importance in a case to which the " activity duty " applied.[41]
The question seems academic, however, for there can be little if any
practical difference between the duty of care in negligence and the
common duty of care as applied to current activities.[42]

The Law Reform Committee's Report [43]

Although there is much else besides, the principal criticisms of
the Committee are directed to the distinctions drawn between the
various classes of entrant and the various duties owed by the occupier.
The view of Atkin L.J. that, subtle and confusing though these distinctions may be, " they correspond to real differences in the nature of
the user of property and in the reasonable claims to protection of
those who are permitted such use," [44] is rejected and the common law
found to be defective in many respects. We cannot here examine all
the criticisms and recommendations of the Committee [45] but the most
significant may be summarised as follows:

1. Though in principle the duty owed by the occupier to a person
entering under contract should be governed by the contract, the distinction drawn in the cases between the two types of implied term
is unsatisfactory. There is no precise test for the application of one
of two or more standards of care of differing degrees of stringency. Save
where an express provision exists in the contract, a uniform standard
of care should be applied to all contractual entrants and in practice
this should be the same as for other lawful entrants.[46]

---

[39] s. 1 (2).

[40] *Riden* v. *Billings & Sons* [1957] 1 Q.B. 46, 56, *per* Denning L.J. Affd. [1958] A.C. 240.

[41] Clerk & Lindsell, *Torts*, 13th ed., pp. 595–596; Street, *Law of Torts*, 5th ed., p. 181;
North, *op. cit.*, p. 81; Payne, " The Occupiers' Liability Act " (1958) 21 M.L.R. 359,
367–368. *Contra* Salmond, *Torts*, 16th ed., pp. 263–264. If, however, the activity is that of
another visitor it is difficult to escape the logical conclusion that the occupier's liability,
if any, is based on the Act: see North, *op. cit.*, pp. 86–87.

[42] Clerk & Lindsell, *Torts*, 13th ed., p. 596. For the common duty of care, see *post*,
pp. 178–182. There are dicta in *British Railways Board* v. *Herrington* [1972] A.C. 877,
929, 942 rejecting any distinction between occupancy and activity duties, but this is in
the context of liability to trespassers which falls entirely outside the Act.

[43] Cmd. 9305, 1954; Odgers [1955] C.L.J. 1; Heuston (1955) 18 M.L.R. 271; Bowett,
" Law Reform and Occupier's Liability " (1956) 19 M.L.R. 172.

[44] *Coleshill* v. *Manchester Corporation* [1928] 1 K.B. 776, 791.

[45] See Odgers, *loc. cit.*, pp. 5–7.

[46] Para. 54.

2. There is " a certain air of reasonableness " [47] in the distinction between invitees and licensees when applied to the simple illustrations of a customer entering a shop and a person allowed purely for his own convenience to take a short cut across a field. Applied over " the whole range of almost infinitely variable circumstances in which one person may come upon the premises of another," however, the distinction is productive of capricious and unreasonable results. Various examples are given—*e.g.* a man who goes into a shop, not to buy something but to ask the way to some place (licensee), but seeing something he wants in the shop buys it or even merely inquires its price (invitee)—and the artificiality of the distinction is then demonstrated in this passage.[48] " A reasonable occupier of premises surely does not say to himself (for instance) ' These steps are dangerously slippery with frozen snow but they don't amount to a trap. I am expecting no visitors except Jones, who is coming to dinner. He is a mere licensee, and I need not do anything about the steps so far as he is concerned. There may of course also be a casual visitor or so. But they too will be mere licensees. So I need do nothing about the steps for their benefit either.' Nor, on the other hand, does he say to himself ' I must clear the snow off the steps because Brown is coming to see me on business. He will be an " invitee," and if he slips on the steps I may find myself liable to him in damages.' Surely the reasonable occupier's thought is more likely to be ' These steps are dangerous. I must clear the snow off them. Otherwise someone coming to the house may slip and get hurt.' " Though the distinction between invitees and licensees has not worked manifest injustice,[49] this relatively satisfactory result has not been achieved without some straining of the conception of " material interest " and of the differences between the two standards of care.[50]

3. Although the standard of duty laid down by Willes J. in *Indermaur* v. *Dames* [51] is prima facie adequate and fit for adoption as a general rule for all cases of lawful entry it is subject to two specific criticisms:

(a) The gloss on the rule contained in *London Graving Dock* v. *Horton* [52] that full knowledge and appreciation of the nature and extent of the risk is a bar to any action by the injured invitee is likely to work injustice.

(b) If the decision in *Thomson* v. *Cremin* [53] made an occupier invariably and in all circumstances liable to his invitee for the negligence of an independent contractor, the duty is unduly high.

---

[47] Para. 63.
[48] Para. 67. See, too, *Dunster* v. *Abbott* [1954] 1 W.L.R. 58, 61–62, *per* Denning L.J.
[49] Except in such cases as *Fairman* v. *Perpetual Investment Building Society* [1923] A.C. 74 and *Jacobs* v. *L.C.C.* [1950] A.C. 361.
[50] Para. 73.
[51] (1886) L.R. 1 C.P. 274, 288; *ante*, p. 167.
[52] [1951] A.C. 737; *ante*, p. 168.
[53] [1956] 1 W.L.R. 103; *ante*, p. 166, n. 10.

4. The principal recommendations therefore, are that the distinction between invitees and licensees should be abolished and that the occupier should owe a duty to every person coming upon the premises at his invitation or by his permission, express or implied, to take such care as in all the circumstances of the case is reasonable to see that the premises are reasonably safe for use by the visitor for the purpose to which the invitation or permission relates.[54]

THE OCCUPIERS' LIABILITY ACT 1957 [55]

Scope of the Act

As we have already seen, the Act probably does not affect the " activity duty " [56] but it substitutes for the various " occupancy duties " a single common duty of care owed by the occupier to all his " visitors." The definition of " occupier " remains the same as at common law and " visitors " are those persons who would at common law be treated as either invitees or licensees.[57] As it is provided that the duty owed to a person entering under contract shall also be the common duty of care in all cases where the nature of the duty depends upon a term to be implied in the contract,[58] it may be generally stated that the common duty of care is now owed by an occupier to all his lawful visitors. In accordance with the Law Reform Committee's recommendation [59] the law governing the occupier's liability to trespassers was not affected by the Act and it is thus necessary to distinguish between lawful and unlawful entrants on to the structure. As before, the occupier's duties apply not only to land and buildings but also to fixed and movable structures,[60] and they govern his liability in respect of damage to property as well as injury to the person, including the property of persons not themselves visitors.[61] The Act also made certain alterations in the liability of a landlord to the visitors of his tenants though these have now been replaced by further legislation.[62]

Occupier

The duty under the Act is imposed upon the " occupier," but the important question is not so much " Who occupies the structure?," using the word " occupy " in its normal sense, as " Who has control over it? " The word occupier is simply a convenient one to denote

[54] Para. 78 (i) and (ii).
[55] Odgers, " Occupiers' Liability: A Further Comment " [1957] C.L.J. 39; Payne, " The Occupiers' Liability Act " (1958) 21 M.L.R. 359.
[56] Ante, pp. 170–171.
[57] s. 1 (2).
[58] s. 5 (1). An entrant under contract may sue the occupier in both contract and tort: Sole v. W. J. Hallt [1973] 2 W.L.R. 171.
[59] Para. 80.
[60] s. 1 (3) (a). Bunker v. Charles Brand & Son Ltd. [1969] 2 Q.B. 480.
[61] s. 1 (3) (b). AMF International Ltd. v. Magnet Bowling Ltd. [1968] 1 W.L.R. 1028. For a full examination of this somewhat confused issue, see North, op. cit., pp. 94–112.
[62] Post, p. 201.

a person who has a sufficient degree of control over premises to put him under a duty of care towards those who come lawfully upon the premises.[63] An owner in possession is, no doubt, an " occupier "; an owner who has demised the premises to another and parted with possession is not.[64] But an absentee owner may " occupy " through his servant and remain subject to the duty [65] and he may also be subject to it though he has contracted to allow a third party to have the use of the premises.[66] On the other hand, it is not necessary that an " occupier " should have any estate in land [67] or even exclusive occupation.[68] There may thus be more than one " occupier " of the same structure or part of the structure.[69] " The foundation of occupier's liability is occupational control, i.e., control associated with and arising from presence in and use of or activity in the premises." [70] Such occupational control may perfectly well be shared between two or more people, but where this is so, though each is under the same common duty of care, it does not follow that what that duty requires of each of them is necessarily itself the same.[71]

Visitors

The common duty of care is owed by the occupier to all his " visitors," [72] and " visitors " are those persons who would at common law be treated as invitees or licensees.[73] For all practical purposes, therefore, the distinction between invitees and licensees is abolished [74] and the important matter is to distinguish a visitor from a trespasser. No difficulty exists where the occupier has given an express invitation or permission to the entrant, but the absence of such invitation or permission does not necessarily mean that the entrant is a trespasser. He may have the implied permission of the

---

[63] *Wheat* v. *Lacon & Co. Ltd.* [1966] A.C. 552, 577, *per* Lord Denning.
[64] A landlord may, nevertheless, be liable under the Act if he is in breach of a covenant to repair and the conditions of s. 4, as amended, are fulfilled. See *post*, p. 201.
[65] *Wheat* v. *Lacon & Co. Ltd.*, *supra*. A company can only occupy through its servants: *ibid.* at p. 571, *per* Viscount Dilhorne.
[66] *Wheat* v. *Lacon & Co. Ltd.*, *supra*; *Fisher* v. *C.H.T. Ltd.* (*No.* 2) [1966] 2 Q.B. 475. See also, *e.g.*, *Hawkins* v. *Coulsdon & Purley U.D.C.* [1954] 1 Q.B. 319; *Greene* v. *Chelsea Borough Council* [1954] 2 Q.B. 127, where requisitioning authorities were held to occupy requisitioned houses which were being lived in by persons they had placed in them. *Cf. Kearney* v. *Eric Waller Ltd.* [1967] 1 Q.B. 29.
[67] *Humphreys* v. *Dreamland (Margate) Ltd.* (1930) 144 L.T. 529.
[68] *Hartwell* v. *Grayson Rollo and Clover Docks Ltd.* [1947] K.B. 901; *Donovan* v. *Cammell Laird & Co.* [1949] 2 All E.R. 82.
[69] *Wheat* v. *Lacon & Co. Ltd.*; *Fisher* v. *C.H.T. Ltd.* (*No.* 2), *supra*; *AMF International Ltd.* v. *Magnet Bowling Ltd.* [1968] 1 W.L.R. 1028.
[70] *Wheat* v. *Lacon & Co. Ltd.*, *supra* at p. 589, *per* Lord Pearson.
[71] *Ibid.* at p. 581, *per* Lord Denning; 585–586, *per* Lord Morris; 587, *per* Lord Pearce.
[72] Except in so far as he is free to and does extend, restrict, modify or exclude the duty: s. 2 (1), *post*, pp. 183–185.
[73] s. 1 (2).
[74] Following the recommendation of the Law Reform Committee: Cmd. 9305, para. 78 (1). " It is true that this is not done in so many words, but no significance is to be attached to this omission. A legal distinction is abolished by depriving it of legal consequence ": Payne, " The Occupiers' Liability Act, 1957 " (1958) 21 M.L.R. 359, 360. *Cf.* Salmond, *Torts*, 16th ed., p. 265, n. 72.

occupier or he may enter by authority of the law. So far as the latter is concerned, there was at common law some doubt as to his status, for the balance of authority was against the existence of a special class of persons entering "as of right" [75] Some, such as firemen attending a fire [76] or police in execution of a search warrant, who have statutory rights of entry in the execution of their duties, were probably invitees.[77] Others, such as members of the public entering recreation grounds,[78] were probably only licensees. Now, however, it is expressly provided [79] that persons who enter premises for any purpose in the exercise of a right conferred by law are to be treated as permitted by the occupier to be there for that purpose, whether they in fact have his permission or not [80] and the occupier thus owes them the common duty of care. On the other hand, although the wording of the Act [81] seems wide enough to convert a person using a public or private right of way into a visitor, in fact the old law remains unchanged [82] and the owner of the highway or servient tenement has no obligation to maintain its safety. A highway may be full of ruts and holes at the date of dedication or become ruinous later, and it may be that, if there is a highway authority in charge of it, the authority is liable [83]; but for mere omission the occupier is not liable, although he may be if he digs a pit in it.[84]

Implied permission

It is a question to be decided on the facts of each case whether the occupier has impliedly given permission to a person to enter upon his structure, and the onus of proving an implied permission rests upon the person who claims that it existed.[86] The simplest example of implied permission is also the commonest in practice. Any person who enters the occupier's premises for the purpose of communicating with him will be treated as having the occupier's tacit permission unless he

---

[75] *Sutton* v. *Bootle Corporation* [1947] 1 K.B. 359, 366, *per* Asquith L.J.; *London Graving Dock Co.* v. *Horton* [1951] A.C. 737, 764, *per* Lord MacDermott.

[76] *Hartley* v. *Mayoh & Co.* [1954] 1 Q.B. 383.

[77] It appears that some 10,000 civil servants have the right to enter private premises without the permission of the occupier. See *Punch*, CCXLI, p. 129 (July 26, 1961).

[78] *Sutton* v. *Bootle Corporation* [1947] 1 K.B. 359; *Pearson* v. *Lambeth B.C.* [1950] 2 K.B. 353. For a full treatment of the problem, see the 6th ed. of this work, pp. 692–696. See also Cmd. 9305, paras. 37–38.

[79] s. 2 (6).

[80] But a person entering any premises in exercise of rights conferred by virtue of an access agreement or order under the National Parks and Access to the Countryside Act 1949 is not a visitor for the purposes of the Occupiers' Liability Act, s. 1 (4). It seems that, though he is not a trespasser and so is not subject to removal by the occupier, the occupier's duty with regard to the safety of such a person is no higher than if he were a trespasser: Act of 1949, ss. 60 (1) and 66 (2).

[81] s. 2 (6).

[82] *Greenhalgh* v. *British Railways Board* [1969] 2 Q.B. 286.

[83] Highways (Miscellaneous Provisions) Act 1961, *post*, pp. 355–357.

[84] *Gautret* v. *Egerton* (1867) L.R. 2 C.P. 371, 373, *per* Willes J. For proposals affecting entrants under the National Parks Act 1949 and users of rights of way, in the event that the position of trespassers is ameliorated by statute, see Law Commission Working Paper No. 52, paras. 37–40.

[86] *Edwards* v. *Railway Executive* [1952] A.C. 737. See *post*, p. 176.

knows or ought to know that he has been forbidden to enter [87]; *e.g.*, by a notice " no canvassers, hawkers or circulars." [88] The occupier may, of course, withdraw this licence by refusing to speak or deal with the entrant, but if he does so the entrant has a reasonable time in which to leave the premises before he becomes a trespasser.[89] Other cases depend very much upon their particular facts and it is difficult to state any general rule. This much, however, is clear in principle: the facts must support the implication from the occupier's conduct that he has permitted entry,[90] not merely tolerated it, for knowledge is not tantamount to consent and failure to turn one's premises into a fortress does not confer a licence on anyone who may seek to take advantage of one's inaction.[90a] This said, it must, however, be admitted that in some cases the courts have gone to surprising lengths in implying licences in the teeth of the facts. The classic example is *Lowery* v. *Walker.*[90b] For thirty-five years the public had used a short cut across a farmer's field to a railway station. He had often interfered with them in doing so, but had never taken legal proceedings against them to stop them trespassing, because most of them were customers for his milk. The House of Lords upheld a finding that they were licensees, not trespassers, and that one of them who was mauled by a savage horse, which the farmer had turned into the field without notice, could recover against him. A number of decisions in this category concern children, and it has been suggested that it might be rather easier to imply a licence in favour of a child; but there seems no good reason why this should be so and such a view seems inconsistent with *Edwards* v. *Railway Executive.*[90c] The plaintiff, a boy of nine, got through a fence dividing a recreation ground from a railway, climbed up the embankment to fetch a ball on the other side of the railway line and was injured by a passing train. For many years children had climbed through the

---

[87] *Robson* v. *Hallett* [1967] 2 Q.B. 393; *Christian* v. *Johanesson* [1956] N.Z.L.R. 664; Cmd. 9305, para. 67. *Cf. Dunster* v. *Abbott* [1954] 1 W.L.R. 58, 59–60, *per* Denning L.J.; and *Great Central Ry.* v. *Bates* [1921] 3 K.B. 578. The policeman in the last case, despite some unguarded dicta of Lord Sterndale M.R., was not acting in the execution of his duty: du Parcq J. in *Davis* v. *Lisle* [1936] 2 K.B. 434, 439–440. Nor would he now be assisted by the Occupiers' Liability Act 1957, s. 2 (6) (see *ante*, p. 175).

[88] *Quaere* as to the effect of " Private " or " Keep Out " in such cases: *cf. Christian* v. *Johanesson, supra*, at p. 666.

[89] *Robson* v. *Hallett, supra*.

[90] *Edwards* v. *Railway Executive* [1952] A.C. 737; *Phipps* v. *Rochester Corpn.* [1955] 1 Q.B. 450, 455. It is what may properly be inferred that counts, not the occupier's actual intention.

[90a] " Repeated trespass of itself confers no licence; the owner of a park in the neighbourhood of a town knows probably only too well that it will be raided by young and old to gather flowers, nuts or mushrooms whenever they get an opportunity. But because he does not cover his park wall with a *chevaux de frise* or post a number of keepers to chase away intruders how is it to be said that he has licensed that which he cannot prevent?": *Edwards* v. *Railway Executive, supra*, at p. 746, *per* Lord Goddard C.J.

[90b] [1911] A.C. 10; *Cooke* v. *Midland G.W. Ry. of Ireland* [1909] A.C. 229 (the facts must be supplemented from the report of the case in the lower courts: [1908] 2 Ir.R. 242). More easily supportable are the decisions in: *Oldham* v. *Sheffield Corporation* (1927) 136 L.T. 681; *Coleshill* v. *Manchester Corporation* [1928] 1 K.B. 776; *Purkis* v. *Walthamstow B.C.* (1934) 151 L.T. 30; *Phipps* v. *Rochester Corpn.* [1955] 1 Q.B. 450.

[90c] [1952] A.C. 737.

fence by breaking the wire to slide down the embankment. The Railway Executive knew this and had repaired the fence whenever damage had been observed. It was held that there was no evidence of any licence to enter the railway land.

In many cases the court has been astute to find an implied licence because of the severity of the law relating to liability to trespassers. The trespasser's position has now been improved [90d] and it is likely that implied permission will be rather less readily found,[90e] but the courts will still have to grapple with the problem of the implied licence, for there remains a considerable difference between the duty owed to a trespasser and to a visitor under the Occupiers' Liability Act.

The duty owed to a visitor does not extend to anyone who is injured by going where he is expressly or impliedly warned by the occupier not to go, as where a man falls over a cliff by getting on the wrong side of railings erected by the proprietor who has also put up a notice of the danger of going near the cliff [91]; or where a tradesman's boy deliberately chooses to go into a pitch dark part of the premises not included in the invitation and falls downstairs there.[92] Further, the duty does not protect a visitor who goes to a part of the premises where no one would reasonably expect him to go.[93] A person, who has two pieces of land and invites the public to come on one of them, can, if he chooses, limit the invitation to that one of the two pieces; but if the other piece is contiguous to the first piece, he may be held to have invited the public to come to both pieces.[94] Again, the plaintiff cannot succeed if, although rightly on the structure, he makes a use of it alien to the invitation. " When you invite a person into your house to use the staircase you do not invite him to slide down the banisters." [95] So, where a stevedore in loading a ship was injured by making use of the hatch covers for loading, although he knew that a statutory regulation forbade this practice in his own interests, it was held that he had no remedy.[96] In fact, in all these cases the plaintiff ceases to be a visitor and becomes a mere trespasser.[97] Where, however, the negligence of the occupier causes the visitor to take an involuntary

---

[90d] See post, pp. 187–190.

[90e] " The 'licence' treated as having been granted in such cases was a legal fiction employed to justify extending to meritorious trespassers, particularly if they were children, the benefit of the duty which at common law an occupier owed to his licensees . . .": British Railways Board v. Herrington [1972] A.C. 877, 933, per Lord Diplock.

[91] Anderson v. Coutts (1894) 58 J.P. 369.

[92] Lewis v. Ronald (1909) 101 L.T. 534; distinguished in Prole v. Allen [1950] 1 All E.R. 476.

[93] Mersey Docks and Harbour Board v. Procter [1923] A.C. 253, where there was a great difference of opinion as to the application of this principle to the facts; cf. Walker v. M. R. Co. (1886) 55 L.T. 489; Lee v. Luper [1936] 3 All E.R. 817; Gould v. McAuliffe [1941] 2 All E.R. 527; Periscinotti v. Brighton West Pier (1961) 105 S.J. 526.

[94] Pearson v. Coleman Bros. [1948] 2 K.B. 359, 375 (Lord Greene M.R.).

[95] Scrutton L.J. in The Carlgarth [1927] P. 93, 110. In any case, the common duty of care only applies where the visitor is using the premises for the purposes for which he is invited or permitted to be there: s. 2 (2), infra.

[96] Hillen v. I.C.I. (Alkali) Ltd. [1936] A.C. 65.

[97] Lord Atkin, ibid. 69–70.

step outside the area in which he is permitted to be, he does not thereby cease to be a visitor to whom a duty of care is owed.[98]

The common duty of care

The common duty of care, owed to all visitors and also where the duty of the occupier depends upon a term to be implied in a contract, is defined as " a duty to take such care as in all the circumstances of the case is reasonable to see that the visitor will be reasonably safe in using the premises for the purposes for which he is invited or permitted to be there." [99] The question whether the occupier has fulfilled his duty to the visitor is thus dependent upon the facts of the case,[1] and, though the purpose of the visit may be a relevant circumstance, it can no longer be conclusive as it so often was before when it governed the status of the entrant. All the circumstances must be taken into account. If, for example, the owner of an inn permits the resident manager to accept paying guests, both are " occupiers " in relation to such guests, but while the owner may be liable for injury caused to them by a structural defect such as the collapse of a staircase, the manager alone would be liable for injury caused by a defect in his own furnishings, such as a dangerous hole in the carpet of the living room.[2]

The Act itself gives some guidance in applying the common duty of care, and it is laid down [3] that the relevant circumstances include the degree of care and of want of care that may be looked for in the particular visitor, " so that (for example) in proper cases:

(a) an occupier must be prepared for children to be less careful than adults [4]; and

(b) an occupier may expect that a person, in the exercise of his calling, will appreciate and guard against any special risks ordinarily incident to it, so far as the occupier leaves him free to do so." [5]

Paragraph (b) echoes the common law concept of " unusual danger " in the duty owed to an invitee, for an unusual danger was defined as one not usually found in carrying out the task which the invitee had in hand,[6] and the paragraph clearly preserves such decisions as *Bates* v. *Parker*,[7] to the general effect that " where a householder

---

[98] *Braithwaite* v. *S. Durham Steel Co.* [1958] 1 W.L.R. 986.
[99] s. 2 (2).
[1] For a case in which the House of Lords gave full consideration to the application of the duty to the facts before them, see *Wheat* v. *Lacon & Co. Ltd.* [1966] A.C. 552. The similarity of the duty to the common law duty of care is demonstrated in *Simms* v. *Leigh Rugby Football Club Ltd.* [1969] 2 All E.R. 923.
[2] *Wheat* v. *Lacon & Co. Ltd.*, *supra*, at pp. 585–586, *per* Lord Morris; 587, *per* Lord Pearce.
[3] s. 2 (3).
[4] The occupier's liability to children is considered *post*, pp. 191–197.
[5] See *Woollins* v. *British Celanese Ltd.* (1966) 110 S.J. 686.
[6] *London Graving Dock Co.* v. *Horton* [1951] A.C. 737.
[7] [1953] 2 Q.B. 231; *Christmas* v. *General Cleaning Contractors* [1952] 1 K.B. 141; affd. [1953] A.C. 180; Cmd. 9305, para. 77 (iii); *Roles* v. *Nathan* [1963] 1 W.L.R. 1117, 1123, *per* Lord Denning M.R.

employs an independent contractor to do work, be it of cleaning or repairing, on his premises, the contractor must satisfy himself as to the safety or condition of that part of the premises on which he is to work." [8] In *Roles* v. *Nathan* [9] two chimney sweeps were killed by carbon monoxide gas while attempting to seal up a " sweep hole " in the chimney of a coke-fired boiler, the boiler being alight at the time, but the occupier was held not liable for their deaths, partly at least on the ground that paragraph (b) applied.[10] As Lord Denning M.R. said, " When a householder calls in a specialist to deal with a defective installation on his premises, he can reasonably expect the specialist to appreciate and guard against the dangers arising from the defect." [11] But the result might no doubt have been different if, for example, the stairs leading to the cellar where the boiler was had given way,[12] for that would not have been a special risk ordinarily incidental to the calling of a sweep.

Specific aspects

Two specific aspects of the common duty of care are also dealt with. Regard is to be had to all the circumstances of the case, so that (for example):

Warning

" (a) Where damage is caused to a visitor by a danger of which he had been warned by the occupier, the warning is not to be treated without more as absolving the occupier from liability, unless in all the circumstances it was enough to enable the visitor to be reasonably safe." [13] In most cases, probably, a warning of the danger will be sufficient to enable the visitor to be reasonably safe and so amount to a discharge by the occupier of his duty of care, but if, for some reason, the warning is not sufficient then the occupier remains liable.[14] There are, after all, some situations in which a reasonable man incurs a known risk and the question now, therefore, is whether such a situation existed on the particular facts of the case. It is clear too, since a warning of the danger is not necessarily sufficient to constitute performance of the occupier's duty, that the decision in *London Graving Dock Co.* v. *Horton* [15] is no longer good law.[16] In that case, it will be recalled, the

---

[8] *Ibid.* at p. 235, *per* Lord Goddard C.J.
[9] *Supra*; Weir, *Casebook on Tort*, 3rd ed., p. 115.
[10] [1963] 1 W.L.R. 1117, 1123–1125, *per* Lord Denning M.R. Pearson L.J. dissented on the interpretation of the evidence but not on the law. Harman L.J., while not differing from Lord Denning, preferred to base his judgment in favour of the defendant upon the fact that the sweeps had been actually warned of the danger.
[11] [1963] 1 W.L.R. at p. 1123.
[12] *Ibid.*; *Bird* v. *King Line* [1970] 2 Lloyd's Rep. 349.
[13] s. 2 (4) (*a*). The warning may be given by the occupier's agent: *Roles* v. *Nathan*, *supra*.
[14] See the different opinions expressed in the Court of Appeal about the warning given in *Roles* v. *Nathan*, *supra*.
[15] [1951] A.C. 737, *ante*, p. 168.
[16] *Roles* v. *Nathan*, *supra*, at p. 1124, *per* Lord Denning M.R.

House of Lords held that an invitee could not succeed if he had full knowledge of the nature and extent of the danger. Now, however, as in cases where he has actually received a warning, the question is whether a visitor with knowledge of the danger reasonably incurred it.[17]

Independent contractor

" (b) Where damage is caused to a visitor by a danger due to the faulty execution of any work of construction, maintenance or repair [18] by an independent contractor employed by the occupier, the occupier is not to be treated without more [18a] as answerable for the danger if in all the circumstances he had acted reasonably in entrusting the work to an [18b] independent contractor and had taken such steps (if any) as he reasonably ought in order to satisfy himself that the contractor was competent and that the work had been properly done." [19] It was the opinion of the Law Reform Committee that the decision of the House of Lords in *Thomson* v. *Cremin* [20] had settled that as a general rule an invitor was liable to his invitee for damage due to the shortcomings of an independent contractor employed by him,[21] and it is the purpose of this paragraph to restore the law to the state in which it was formerly believed to be.

In *Haseldine* v. *Daw* [22] H was going to visit a tenant in a block of flats belonging to D and was injured when the lift fell to the bottom of its shaft as a result of the negligence of a firm of engineers employed by D to repair the lift. It was held that D, having employed a competent firm of engineers to make periodical inspections of the lift, to adjust it and to report on it, had discharged the duty owed to H, whether H was an invitee or licensee. As Scott L.J. observed, " the landlord of a block of flats, as occupier of the lifts, does not profess as such to be either an electrical or, as in this case, a hydraulic engineer. Having no technical skill he cannot rely on his own judgment, and the duty of care towards his invitees requires him to obtain and follow good technical advice. If he did not do so, he would, indeed, be guilty of negligence. To hold him responsible for the misdeeds of his independent contractor would be to make him insure

---

[17] *Bunker* v. *Charles Brand & Son Ltd.* [1969] 2 Q.B. 480, 489, *per* O'Connor J. For contributory negligence in relation to the occupier's liability, see *post*, pp. 182–183.

[18] These words include failure to take adequate precautions to protect visitors or their property from risks arising in the course of the work: *AMF International Ltd.* v. *Magnet Bowling Ltd.* [1968] 1 W.L.R. 1028, 1043, *per* Mocatta J. (failure of builder in the course of constructing a building to take adequate precautions against flooding).

[18a] For possible meanings of this cryptic phrase see North, *op. cit*., p. 144.

[18b] How can it ever be unreasonable to employ *a* (as opposed to *the*) contractor?

[19] s. 2 (4) (*b*); s. 3 (2); *O'Connor* v. *Swan & Edgar* (1963) 107 S.J. 215; *Gibson* v. *Skibs A/S Marina, etc.* [1966] 2 All E.R. 476. The burden of proving that the danger was due to the fault of an independent contractor rests with the occupier: *Christmas* v. *Blue Star Line* [1961] 1 Lloyd's Rep. 94; *AMF International Ltd.* v. *Magnet Bowling Ltd.* [1968] 1 W.L.R. 1028, 1042–1043, *per* Mocatta J.

[20] [1956] 1 W.L.R. 103.

[21] Cmd. 9305, para. 26. See, however, *Green* v. *Fibreglass Ltd.* [1958] 2 Q.B. 245.

[22] [1941] 2 K.B. 343.

the safety of his lift. That duty can only arise out of contract. . . . " [23]
In *Woodward* v. *Mayor of Hastings*,[24] on the other hand, a pupil
at a school for which the defendants were responsible fell and was
injured on an icy step which had been negligently left in a dangerous condition by a cleaner. Even assuming that the cleaner was
an independent contractor, it was held that the defendants were liable
and *Haseldine* v. *Daw* was distinguished. Technical knowledge was
required in the maintenance and repair of a lift, but such considerations
were not relevant in *Woodward's* case. " The craft of the charwoman
may have its mysteries, but there is no esoteric quality in the nature
of the work which the cleaning of a snow-covered step demands." [25]

Where an independent contractor has been employed, therefore,
the question today is whether the occupier himself has done all that
reasonable care requires of him. He must take reasonable steps to
satisfy himself that the contractor he employs is competent, and, if
the character of the work permits, he must take similar steps to see
that the work has been properly done. In fact, where the work is
especially complex, as with the construction of a large building or a
ship, he may even have to cause the independent contractor's work to
be supervised by a properly instructed architect or other professional
man.[25a] As the dictum of Scott L.J. indicates, there are many cases
in which the technical nature of the work to be done will require the
occupier to employ an independent contractor and he will be negligent
if he attempts to do it himself. This does not mean, however, that a
householder must not himself undertake some ordinary domestic
repair such as the fixing of a new door handle. Provided that he does
the work with the care and skill of a reasonably competent carpenter
he has fulfilled his duty.[26]

Darkness

It was at one time held, at least of licensees, that " in darkness
where they cannot see whether there is danger or not, if they will walk
they walk at their peril." [27] It appears, however, that this statement
was too sweeping even for the common law. " There is no absolute
rule of law that in all cases a licensee moving in the dark takes the risk

---

[23] *Ibid.* at p. 356. See also *per* Goddard L.J. at p. 374.
[24] [1945] K.B. 174.
[25] *Ibid.* at p. 183, *per* du Parcq L.J.
[25a] *AMF International Ltd.* v. *Magnet Bowling Ltd.* [1968] 1 W.L.R. 1028, 1044, 1045–
1047, *per* Mocatta J. His Lordship also held that the negligence of the architect or other
supervisor would not itself involve the occupier in liability for otherwise, in technical cases,
the common duty of care would become equivalent to the obligation of an insurer.
Negligence in supervision would not fall under s. 2 (4) (*b*), but it must be remembered that
the purpose of s. 2 (4) is to insist that in determining whether the common duty of care
has been discharged, regard is to be had to all the circumstances. Paragraphs (*a*) and (*b*)
are introduced by the words " so that (for example) " and there is no reason for saying
that an occupier is necessarily liable for the negligence of his independent contractor
except when s. 2 (4) (*b*) applies.
[26] *Wells* v. *Cooper* [1958] 2 Q.B. 265; Weir, *Casebook on Tort*, 3rd ed., p. 117.
[27] *Latham* v. *R. Johnson & Nephew* [1913] 1 K.B. 398, 411, *per* Hamilton L.J.; *Mersey
Docks & Harbour Board* v. *Procter* [1923] A.C. 253, 274, *per* Lord Sumner.

of any danger which in daylight would be obvious." [28] Probably the question whether the occupier is liable for a danger which would have been obvious had the place been lighted depends, both at common law and under the Occupiers' Liability Act, upon whether the permission given to the visitor to go there is permission to go there whether it is lighted or not.[29] If it is, then the occupier must take reasonable care to make the place safe by lighting or otherwise eliminating the danger.

Volenti non fit injuria

Although knowledge of the danger does not of itself deprive the visitor of his remedy, the defence of *volenti non fit injuria* [30] remains available to the occupier. The occupier has no obligation to a visitor in respect of risks willingly accepted as his by the visitor.[31]

Contributory negligence

Even after the passage of the Law Reform (Contributory Negligence) Act 1945 there was some doubt whether an invitee who had failed to take reasonable care for his own safety could recover any damages at all.[32] This doubt derived from Willes J.'s formulation of the rule in *Indermaur* v. *Dames* [33] that the invitee, " *using reasonable care for his own safety*, is entitled to expect that the occupier shall on his part use reasonable care . . ." and it received some support from the House of Lords' decision in *London Graving Dock Co.* v. *Horton*.[34] It is to be borne in mind, however, that when Willes J. delivered his judgment the contributory negligence of the plaintiff was in any case a complete bar to his recovery, and the prevailing view when the Occupiers' Liability Act was passed was that contributory negligence on the part of an invitee merely operated to reduce the damages he might otherwise have recovered.[35] It was a specific recommendation of the Law Reform Committee that the Contributory Negligence Act should apply in cases of breach of the common duty of care [36] and, though this is not laid down in so many words in the Occupiers' Liability Act, it appears to be implicit in the wording of the Act.[37] It follows that where the

---

[28] *Hawkins* v. *Coulsdon and Purley U.D.C.* [1953] 1 W.L.R. 882; affd. [1954] 1 Q.B. 319.
[29] *Hogan* v. *P. & O. Steam Navigation Co.* [1959] 2 Lloyd's Rep. 305. See also *Campbell* v. *Shelbourne Hotel* [1939] 2 K.B. 534, and compare *Walker* v. *Midland Ry.* (1886) 55 L.T. 489; *Irving* v. *L.C.C.* (1965) 109 S.J. 157.   [30] *Post,* pp. 614–626.
[31] s. 2 (5). See *Bunker* v. *Charles Brand & Son Ltd.* [1969] 2 Q.B. 480, 488–489, *per* O'Connor J.
[32] See Payne, " The Occupiers' Liability Act " (1958) 21 M.L.R. 359, 366–367.
[33] (1866) L.R. 1 C.P. 274; *ante,* p. 167.
[34] [1951] A.C. 737.
[35] Glanville Williams, *Joint Torts and Contributory Negligence,* pp. 319–324; *Slater* v. *Clay Cross Co.* [1956] 2 Q.B. 264, 271, *per* Denning L.J.
[36] Cmd. 9305, para. 78 (ix).
[37] Esp. s. 2 (3). Clerk & Lindsell, *Torts,* 13th ed., p. 609; Street, *Law of Torts,* 5th ed., p. 184. It is submitted that the statement of Diplock L.J.: " My neighbour does not enlarge my duty of care for his safety by neglecting it himself " (*Wheat* v. *Lacon & Co. Ltd.* [1966] 1 Q.B. 335, 372), which was approved by Viscount Dilhorne in the House of Lords [1966] A.C. at p. 576, is not inconsistent with the statement in the text. The point is that a person cannot, by carelessness of his own safety, thereby put an occupier in breach of the common duty of care.

occupier is in breach of the common duty of care and the visitor is at the same time careless of his own safety, the damages will be apportioned in accordance with the Act of 1945.[38]

Exclusion of occupier's duty

We have seen that the occupier may be able to discharge his duty merely by warning the visitor of the danger and also that no duty is owed in respect of risks willingly accepted by the visitor. A further and distinct ground on which the occupier may escape liability is that he has excluded his duty altogether, for the Act provides that the occupier owes the same duty, the common duty of care, to all his visitors " except in so far as he is free to and does extend, restrict, modify or exclude his duty to any visitor or visitors by agreement or otherwise." [39] Obviously this allows modification or exclusion of the common duty of care by an express term in a contract between occupier and visitor, but the words " by agreement or otherwise " apply to other cases as well, and there is no doubt that the law as laid down in the Court of Appeal's decision in *Ashdown* v. *Samuel Williams & Sons* [40] is given statutory force. In that case, decided shortly before the Occupiers' Liability Act became law, the plaintiff was a licensee on land belonging to the defendants when she was knocked down and injured by railway trucks which were being negligently shunted along a railway line on their land. Various notices had been posted by the defendants to the effect that every person on the land was there at his own risk and should have no claim against the defendants for any injury whatsoever, and it was found as a fact that they had taken reasonable steps to bring the conditions contained in the notices to the plaintiff's attention. It was held, therefore, that the plaintiff could not recover.[40a]

The general principle that it is competent to an occupier of land to restrict or exclude any liability he might otherwise be under to any licensee of his, including liability for his own or his servant's negligence, by conditions aptly framed and made known to the licensee was not disputed in *Ashdown's* case.[41] Nevertheless it came under powerful

---

[38] *Ante*, pp. 115–117.

[39] s. 2 (1). *Cf.* the Law Reform Committee's recommendation: Cmd. 9305, para. 78 (iii). See Gower, " A Tortfeasor's Charter?" (1956) 19 M.L.R. 582; (1957) 20 M.L.R. 181; Odgers, " Occupiers' Liability: A Further Comment " (1957) C.L.J. 39, 42–54; Payne, " The Occupiers' Liability Act " (1958) 21 M.L.R. 359, 364–365; Clerk & Lindsell, *Torts*, 13th ed., pp. 610–614.

[40] [1957] 1 Q.B. 409; *Wilkie* v. *L.P.T.B.* [1947] 1 All E.R. 258. *Cf. Henson* v. *L.N.E. Ry.* [1947] 1 All E.R. 653, esp. at p. 656, *per* Scott L.J. *Ashdown's* case was followed by a majority of the Court of Appeal in *White* v. *Blackmore* [1972] 2 Q.B. 651. The decision in that case might have been different if there had been a contractual licence, but *cf.* Roskill L.J. at 675–676.

[40a] It seems now that one modification will have to made to the doctrine of *Ashdown's* case: since *British Railways Board* v. *Herrington* [1972] A.C. 877 an occupier owes a duty of common humanity to a trespasser, whereas when *Ashdown's* case was decided he owed only a duty not to harm deliberately or recklessly (see *post*, p. 187). It seems probable that this duty of common humanity cannot be excluded on the basis of a conditional licence, since a licensee can hardly be in a worse position than a trespasser. But *volenti non fit injuria* may still be available.

[41] [1957] 1 Q.B. at p. 421.

criticism from Professor Gower,[42] principally on the ground that the absence of a contract between the plaintiff and the defendant should have been fatal to the defence. While admitting that a licence can be granted subject to conditions, Professor Gower argues that the power to impose conditions otherwise than by contract is not unlimited: " Obviously I can make my permission subject to a condition that the licensee shall not take a dog. If he does, he ceases to be a licensee and becomes a trespasser. It by no means follows, however, that I can effectively make my permission subject to a term that although the licensee remains a licensee I shall not be subject to the liabilities of a licensor . . . it is submitted that I can only do so if the licensee has contracted to release me from these obligations." [43] The decision in *Ashdown's* case and its confirmation by the Occupiers' Liability Act do, however, seem to accord with general principle. If I can exclude you from my property altogether, why can I not permit you to enter upon any terms that I like to make? The result might, indeed, be construed as a contract whereby you give up what would otherwise be your legal rights in return for my allowing you to enter, but this construction is not essential to the validity of the conditions.[44] The occupier can say simply: " You have your choice: stay out of my premises or enter them on my terms. You will be a trespasser unless you have my permission. I give it subject to your agreeing that I owe you no duty. If later you claim to have entered without so agreeing you must admit you have entered without my permission and you will indeed be a trespasser." [45]

The occupier's power to exclude the common duty of care is, however, governed by the words "in so far as he is free to " do so. Clearly, therefore, the Occupiers' Liability Act does not enlarge the power which existed at common law, and does not override any specific statutory prohibitions against the exclusion of liability.[46] Moreover, it is submitted, since the power to exclude the duty depends upon the occupier's right to prevent the visitor from entering the premises altogether, it cannot exist in the case of a person entering in the exercise of a right conferred by law.[47] Whether there are other cases in which the occupier is not free to exclude his duty remains to be seen.[48]

It will be noticed that *Ashdown's* case [49] was concerned not with the static condition of the land on which the plaintiff was a licensee but with

---

[42] *Loc. cit.*
[43] 19 M.L.R. at p. 536.
[44] It was rejected by Lord Greene M.R. in *Wilkie* v. *L.P.T.B.* [1947] 1 All E.R. 258, 260. *Cf. Gore* v. *Van Der Lann* [1967] 2 Q.B. 31, and Odgers, " The Strange Case of Mrs. Gore " (1970) 86 L.Q.R. 69.
[45] Clerk & Lindsell, *Torts*, 13th ed., p. 611. On the other hand, as Lord Denning M.R. forcibly points out in *White* v. *Blackmore* [1972] 2 Q.B. 651, 665–666, this approach derogates severely from the purpose of s. 2 (4) (*a*) of the Act.
[46] *e.g.,* Road Traffic Act 1960, s. 151.
[47] *Ante,* p. 175.
[48] The effect of a contract between the occupier and a third party under which the occupier is bound to permit the visitor to enter is considered below.
[49] *Ashdown* v. *Samuel Williams & Sons* [1957] 1 Q.B. 409.

the current activities of the occupier. Clearly, therefore, the power to exclude liability is not restricted to the static condition of the structure, but it is less easy to justify the existence of that power with regard to current activities. " There is much to be said for an occupier who is prepared to grant a gratuitous licence provided he is not put to trouble or expense in inspecting or maintaining his property: there is less to be said for one who claims a right to shoot, drive, shunt or blast without taking reasonable care." [50] It is difficult, nevertheless, to see how the occupier's right to exclude his duty could have been restricted. To forbid exclusion of the duty altogether would be to penalise those occupiers who are willing to allow persons onto their land for purposes of interest exclusively to the visitors, while a distinction between classes of visitor would restore the common law distinction between licensees and invitees which it was the object of the Act to abolish.[51]

Effect of contract on occupier's liability to third parties

It was the opinion of the Law Reform Committee [52] that where a person contracts with the occupier for the use of premises on the footing that he is to be entitled to permit third persons to use them, the duty owed by the occupier to those third persons is the same as that owed to the other party to the contract.[53] This could lead to a person being deprived of his rights by a contract to which he was not a party and of whose provisions he was unaware. It is therefore provided by the Act that " where an occupier of premises is bound by contract to permit persons who are strangers to the contract [54] to enter or use the premises, the duty of care which he owes to them as his visitors cannot be restricted or excluded by that contract, but (subject to any provision of the contract to the contrary) shall include the duty to perform his obligations under the contract, whether undertaken for their protection or not, in so far as those obligations go beyond the obligations otherwise involved in that duty." [55] Furthermore, where a tenancy, including a statutory tenancy which does not in law amount to a tenancy, requires either the landlord or the tenant to permit persons to enter premises of which he is the occupier, the section applies as if the tenancy were a contract between the landlord and the tenant.[56]

This section has a twofold effect. The occupier cannot by contract reduce his obligations to visitors who are strangers to the contract to a level below that imposed by the common duty of care. If, however, the

---

[50] Odgers [1957] C.L.J. at p. 54.
[51] For a possible compromise, see Odgers [1957] C.L.J. at p. 48. The Law Commission (Working Paper No. 52) has proposed either (a) an absolute ban on exempting conditions in notices, tickets, etc. as to personal injury or (b) a test of reasonableness in all cases: para. 63.
[52] On the authority of *Fosbroke-Hobbes* v. *Airwork Ltd.* [1937] 1 All E.R. 108.
[53] Cmd. 9305, para. 55. See, too, para. 79.
[54] Defined in s. 3 (3).
[55] s. 3 (1).
[56] s. 3 (4).

contract requires him to take some precaution not required in the circumstances by that duty, the visitor shall have the benefit of that precaution. If, for example, A contracts with B to allow B and C to use his premises and the contract provides that the premises shall be lit during the hours of darkness, C has a right of action against A for injury due to A's failure to light the premises, whether or not such failure would amount to a breach of the common duty of care.[57] It is provided, however, that the section shall not have the effect, unless the contract so provides, of making an occupier who has taken all reasonable care liable for dangers due to the faulty execution of any work of construction, maintenance or repair or other like operation by persons other than himself, his servants or persons acting under his direction and control.[58]

It is an open question whether the occupier, though unable to restrict his duty to third parties by a provision in the contract itself, can do so by publishing a notice as in *Ashdown* v. *Samuel Williams & Sons*.[59] Though there are arguments to the contrary,[60] it is submitted that this is a case where the occupier is not " free to " restrict or exclude his duty of care and that the alternative view tends to defeat the object of the section.[61]

Damage to property

The Act provides [62] that the rules which it enacts shall apply " in like manner and to the like extent as the principles applicable at common law to an occupier of premises and his invitees or licensees would apply to regulate— . . . the obligations of a person occupying or having control over any premises or structure in respect of damage to property, including the property of persons who are not themselves his visitors."[62a] Clearly, therefore, where property lawfully on the premises is damaged by a structural defect of the premises,[63] whether it actually belongs to a visitor or not, the question in each case is whether the occupier has discharged the common duty of care. Where there has been a

---

[57] There is no general duty upon a landlord to light a common staircase at all times of darkness: *Irving* v. *L.C.C.* (1965) 109 S.J. 157.

[58] s. 3 (2). The wording of this subsection differs from that of s. 2 (4) (*b*), *ante*, p. 180 but the effect of the two subsections is probably the same: Clerk & Lindsell, *Torts*, 13th ed., p. 617. *Cf.* Street, *Law of Torts*, 5th ed., p. 190; North, *op. cit.*, pp. 145–147.

[59] [1957] 1 Q.B. 409; *ante*, p. 183.

[60] Payne, *loc. cit.* at pp. 369–370. The subsection itself only prohibits restriction or exclusion of the duty by the contract, and was enacted following the Law Reform Committee's view that it is undesirable for a person's rights to be capable of limitation by contractual provisions which may be entirely unknown to him: Cmd. 9305, para. 55.

[61] Clerk & Lindsell, *Torts*, 13th ed., p. 615; Street, *Law of Torts*, 5th ed., p. 190; North, *op. cit.*, pp. 151–152.

[62] s. 1 (3) (*b*). North, *op. cit.*, pp. 94–112 (based on the author's article, " Damage to Property and the Occupiers' Liability Act 1957 " (1966) 30 Conv.(N.S.) 264).

[62a] The last phrase would seem to allow an action by an owner who is not a visitor, as in *Drive Yourself Lessey's Pty. Ltd.* v. *Burnside* [1959] S.R.(N.S.W.) 390: but *cf.* North, *op. cit.*, pp. 101–105.

[63] *e.g.*, if, with your permission, I leave my car in the drive outside your house and a tile falls off the roof and damages it: *AMF International Ltd.* v. *Magnet Bowling Ltd.* [1968] 1 W.L.R. 1028. Damages may be recovered not only in respect of actual damage to the property but also in respect of consequential financial loss: *ibid.* at pp. 1049–1051, *per* Mocatta J.

bailment, however, as where goods are deposited in a warehouse, the liability of the warehouse-keeper will not depend upon the common duty of care but upon his duty under the bailment or special contract. The rules contained in the Occupiers' Liability Act replace only the principles of the common law formerly applicable between the occupier and his invitee or licensee. They do not affect the relationship of bailor and bailee. Furthermore, the Act does not effect a change in the common law rule that an occupier has no duty to protect the goods of his visitor from the risk of theft by third parties.[64]

LIABILITY TO TRESPASSERS

The duty of an occupier to a trespasser is unaffected by the Occupiers' Liability Act.[65] Once the decision has been reached that the plaintiff was indeed a trespasser the common law alone applies, but the common law on this matter has recently undergone very substantial alteration and development in *British Railways Board* v. *Herrington*.[66] Detailed consideration of the well-known earlier cases would now be out of place, but the progress of the law up to *Herrington's* case may be summarised as follows.[67] The basic principle was laid down by the House of Lords in the Scottish appeal of *Robert Addie & Sons (Collieries) Ltd.* v. *Dumbreck*,[68] to the effect that an occupier was only liable to a trespasser in respect of some wilful act " done with deliberate intention of doing harm . . . or at least some act done with reckless disregard of the presence of the trespasser." [69] Over thirty years later in *Videan* v. *British Transport Commission* [70] a majority of the Court of Appeal attempted to mitigate the severity of the law by imposing on the occupier in respect of " activities " (as opposed to the static condition of the premises) a duty of care based on foreseeability, but this was decisively rejected by the Privy Council in *Commissioner for Railways* v. *Quinlan*,[71] which reaffirmed the *Addie* doctrine.[72] Thus matters stood until 1972.

---

[64] *Tinsley* v. *Dudley* [1951] 2 K.B. 18. See also *Ashby* v. *Tolhurst* [1937] 2 K.B. 242; *Deyong* v. *Shenburn* [1946] K.B. 227; *Edwards* v. *West Herts Group Hospital Management Committee* [1957] 1 W.L.R. 418. *Cf.* Bowett, " Law Reform and Occupiers' Liability " (1956) 19 M.L.R. 172, 183.

[65] *Aliter* in Scotland: Occupier's Liability (Scotland) Act 1960. See *McGlone* v. *British Railways Board*, 1966 S.C.(H.L.) 1. The question of acts done by way of defence against trespassers is considered later, *post*, pp. 632–633.

[66] [1972] A.C. 877; (1972) 88 L.Q.R. 310; Matthews [1972A] C.L.J. 214; Miller (1972) 35 M.L.R. 410; Weir, *Casebook on Tort*, 3rd ed., p. 74. The Privy Council has restated the law for Australia in the same terms: *Southern Portland Cement Ltd.* v. *Cooper* [1974] 1 All E.R. 87.

[67] For more detail, see the 9th edition of this book, pp. 189 *et seq.*

[68] [1929] A.C. 358.

[69] *Ibid.*, at p. 365, *per* Lord Hailsham L.C. The difficult and factually very similar case of *Excelsior Wire Rope Co. Ltd.* v. *Callan* [1930] A.C. 404 was commonly regarded as an example of such " reckless disregard."

[70] [1963] 2 Q.B. 650. The third member of the court, Pearson L.J., rejected the activity/static condition distinction and put forward a duty of " common humanity " which is taken up and explained in *Herrington's* case.

[71] [1964] A.C. 1054.

[72] In fact, this decision was not so faithful to the *Addie* principle as it seemed: *Southern Portland Cement Ltd.* v. *Cooper*, *supra*, at pp. 93–96.

In *British Railways Board* v. *Herrington* the defendants were the occupiers of an electrified railway line which ran alongside a meadow where children played, and a path led across the meadow to the fence bounding the line. On both sides of the line the fence was in a dilapidated condition and people had been using the broken down fence to take a short cut across the line. In April 1965 the local station master, who was responsible for this part of the line, was informed that children had been seen on the line, but the only action he took was to inform the police. In June 1965 the plaintiff, then aged six, walked over the fence on to the line, where he came into contact with a live rail and suffered serious injuries. It was admitted that he was a trespasser on the line and the defendants, who called no evidence, therefore argued on the authority of *Addie's* case that they owed him no duty. The House of Lords upheld a decision for the plaintiff, though for reasons different from those which actuated the courts below.[73]

Because there are five separate speeches, analysing the law at length and by no means proceeding on identical reasoning, it is difficult to express precisely the *ratio decidendi* of *Herrington's* case and meticulous parsing of the words of individual speeches would be dangerous; but the following propositions may be made.

The fundamental principle is that there is still a distinction for the purposes of occupiers' liability between trespassers and lawful visitors. To assimilate the duties in respect of the two classes would not be a proper compromise between the requirement of civilised behaviour and the rights of landowners to enjoy their property. Not only does the fact that the plaintiff is a trespasser make his presence and actions less foreseeable than those of a lawful visitor, but also in many cases it would be impracticable for an occupier to prevent a trespasser getting into a position of danger. Accordingly, the correct level of duty towards a trespasser is to be sought not by asking whether the occupier has taken all reasonable care, but by asking whether the occupier has acted in accordance with common humanity or according to common standards of civilised behaviour.[74] The difference between this standard and the ordinary negligence formula is demonstrated at the levels both of deciding whether the duty is owed to the individual plaintiff and of determining the content of this duty. Thus the occupier is not to be expected to institute any checks or investigations either as to the presence of the trespasser or of dangers on his premises. With regard to the former matter the occupier will be under no duty unless " a reasonable man, knowing only the physical facts which the occupier actually knew, would appreciate that a trespasser's presence at the point and time of danger was so likely that in all the circumstances

---

[73] The Court of Appeal ([1971] 2 W.L.R. 477) had been able to bring the case within the *Addie* formula.

[74] [1972] A.C. 877 at 898–899, 909, 922, 936–937.

it would be inhumane not to give him effective warning of the danger." [75] Whether a reasonable man would regard inaction as inhumane will, of course, depend upon the gravity of the danger, so that a minefield or a live electric rail demand steps for the trespasser's protection even though the likelihood of trespass is far less than would cause a reasonable man to take steps to protect trespassers against more innocuous perils.[76] With regard to the occupier's knowledge of the danger, there is a similar combination of subjective and objective for his duty will arise if he has actual knowledge of " physical facts which a reasonable man would appreciate involved danger of serious injury to the trespasser." [77]

In relation to the content of the duty owed to a trespasser the fundamental principle is again conditioned by the fact that the trespasser has forced himself uninvited into a relationship of proximity with the occupier. The principle is that the trespasser must take the occupier as he finds him with regard to the latter's knowledge, ability and resources, so that an impecunious occupier with little assistance may be excused from doing something which a large organisation with ample staff would be expected to do.[78] This hybrid standard of what is reasonable for the individual defendant seems to be identical to that adopted in the law of nuisance in relation to an occupier's duty to remove dangers for whose creation he was not responsible [79] and represents a similar attempt to arrive at a fair allocation of liability for a risk which is forced upon the defendant. More generally, and whatever the capacities of the individual occupier, his duty will not usually extend to being required to take effective steps to keep intruders out—there is no duty to fence against trespassers [80]—and adequate warnings will therefore normally exculpate the occupier. However, there may be cases, for example involving young children, where some more effective steps may be necessary on the occupier's part.[81]

Liability of non-occupiers

This is a problem which remains unresolved by *Herrington's* case, though it contains dicta on the point. Suppose the defendant is not the occupier but the occupier's servant or a contractor or even a mere visitor to the premises, can he shelter behind the comparatively low level of duty which is owed to a trespasser even after *Herrington's* case ?[82]

---

[75] *Ibid.*, at p. 941, *per* Lord Diplock. Lord Reid said, at p. 899, that the occupier must know of a " substantial probability " of a trespass, a test adopted by Edmund Davies L.J. in *Pannett* v. *P. McGuinness & Co. Ltd.* [1972] 2 Q.B. 599 and by Lawton L.J. in *Westwood* v. *Post Office* [1973] Q.B. 591, reversed on other grounds [1974] A.C. 1.

[76] *Ibid.*, at pp. 920, 940.

[77] *Ibid.*, at p. 940, *per* Lord Diplock. *Cf.*, in a different context, *Hawkins* v. *Coulsdon and Purley U.D.C.* [1954] 1 Q.B. 319.

[78] [1972] A.C. at 899, 920–921, 942.

[79] See *post*, pp. 337–338.

[80] [1972] A.C. at 909, 920, 941.

[81] *Ibid.*, at pp. 923–924, 941.

[82] A non-occupier is, as a general rule, liable for dangers which he creates on the premises of another: see *post*, pp. 197–198.

What authority there is, is to the effect that as between the trespasser and the non-occupier, trespassory status as such [83] is irrelevant. In *Buckland* v. *Guildford Gas Light and Coke Co.*[84] the defendants had provided electric current for a farmer by high-voltage wires on poles over his fields, and the wires passed over and very close to the top of a tree which was easy to climb. A girl aged thirteen years came on to the farmer's land, climbed the tree and was killed by electrocution from the wires. Morris J. held that the defendants were liable for they ought to have foreseen the danger caused by their erection of the wires so close to the top of the tree. The girl was not a trespasser with respect to the defendants, and, even if they had proved that she was a trespasser to the farmer, their liability was on a different basis; they had not taken reasonable care to protect climbers from the danger of the wires and they ought to have foreseen the likelihood of the girl's climbing the tree. The balance of the dicta in *Herrington's* case point towards the removal of any sharp distinction between occupiers and non-occupiers in this respect, so that the plaintiff's being a trespasser would be relevant in a claim against either.[85]

Present status of Herrington's case

The Lord Chancellor referred the issue of occupiers' liability to trespassers to the Law Commission for examination in the light of *Herrington's* case and the Commission has made provisional proposals.[86] The Commission thinks that *Herrington's* case is unsatisfactory in that there is not sufficient consistency among the five speeches to provide a reasonable degree of certainty in the law and the distinction made between the concepts of " humanity " and " reasonableness " is likely to be unworkable.[87] The Commission has provisionally proposed the imposition of a duty of reasonable care, the trespassory status of the entrant being a matter to be considered in the light of all the circumstances of the case. Though opinions may differ as to whether this sets the right standard, as a matter of principle it seems unlikely that it would in practice impose an excessive burden upon occupiers.[88]

---

[83] On the facts, a trespasser might of course be unforeseeable when a lawful visitor would not.

[84] [1949] 1 K.B. 410; *Davis* v. *St. Mary's Demolition and Excavation Co. Ltd.* [1954] 1 W.L.R. 592; *Creed* v. *McGeogh & Sons Ltd.* [1955] 1 W.L.R. 1005. However, Fleming (1966) 82 L.Q.R. 25 points out that none of the decisions deals with the position of a servant as opposed to an independent contractor. Even if the servant does not share his master's " immunity," it seems clear that one cannot evade that immunity by the device of vicarious liability.

[85] Lord Wilberforce at [1972] A.C. 914 and Lord Pearson at 929. *Cf.* Lord Diplock at p. 943.

[86] Working Paper No. 52 (1973).

[87] Though the Court of Appeal found little difficulty in applying the *Herrington* case in *Pannett* v. *P. McGuinness & Co. Ltd.* [1972] 2 Q.B. 599, that case perhaps demonstrates how uncertain is the line between reasonableness and humanity and suggests that appellate courts may have great difficulty in preventing trial courts imposing a fairly stringent duty upon occupiers. However, the idea of humanity is in itself no more uncertain than that of reasonableness.

[88] Something very like the Law Commission's proposal has been the law in Scotland since the Occupiers' Liability (Scotland) Act 1960; but see Lord Reid's comment upon the

LIABILITY TO CHILDREN

The disposition of children of tender years to mischief has given their elders nearly as much trouble in the law courts as outside them, but English law has traditionally refused as a matter of legal theory to make any distinction between the child entrant on the premises and the adult. Children do not form any special class in the law and must be treated as lawful visitors or as trespassers, for " infancy as such is no more a status conferring rights, or a root of title imposing obligations on others to respect it, than infirmity or imbecility." [89] On the other hand in its application the law cannot fail to take account of the fact that children are more vulnerable than adults and do not always behave as adults would, and we must examine the results of this recognition in two contexts.

1. Child trespassers

In principle, the question whether a child is a trespasser is to be decided according to exactly the same criteria as apply in the case of an adult. In the past, however, the courts went to great lengths to imply licences on behalf of child plaintiffs even though the conceptions of licence or permission were virtually without meaning as applied to children [90]; but this tendency has probably received a check as a result of *British Railways Board v. Herrington*.[91]

If the child was held to be a trespasser, the position formerly was that exactly the same principles of liability applied as if he had been an adult,[92] but *Herrington's* case now draws a distinction between these two classes of trespasser for, though the duty owed to both is that of " common humanity," the case recognises that precautions which would be sufficient to protect an adult trespasser are not necessarily effective in relation to children. Thus if there is a substantial probability of intrusion by children too young to appreciate the danger or understand a warning notice, the occupier's duty " may require the provision of an obstacle to their approach to the danger sufficiently difficult to surmount as to make it clear to the youngest unaccompanied child likely to approach the danger, that beyond the obstacle is for-

---

Scottish situation in [1972] A.C. at 898. The Commission questions whether the standard of care should vary according to the occupier's individual resources because liability insurance is " a device for distributing loss which can lessen the burden which might otherwise fall upon the impecunious individual defendant ": but this ignores the fact that a defendant with a serious risk on his premises and without the means to remedy it might find it impossible to obtain insurance or might find his policy invalidated if he failed to declare that risk.

[89] *Glasgow Corporation* v. *Taylor* [1922] 1 A.C. 44, 67, *per* Lord Sumner; *Latham* v. *R. Johnson & Nephew Ltd.* [1913] 1 K.B. 398, 407, *per* Farwell L.J.

[90] *Commissioner of Railways* (*N.S.W.*) v. *Cardy* (1961) 104 C.L.R. 274; *Commissioner for Railways* v. *Quinlan* [1964] A.C. 1054.

[91] See *ante*, p. 177.

[92] Several of the leading cases, including *Addie* v. *Dumbreck*, concerned children; see *ante*, p. 187.

bidden territory." [93] Every case must depend upon its particular facts but *Pannett* v. *P. McGuinness & Co. Ltd.*[94] provides an illustration of the application of these principles. The defendants were engaged in the demolition of a warehouse which was close to a public park. At one stage the defendants found it necessary to remove the hoardings around the site and light fires. They knew that these fires would be attractive to children so they posted three men to watch the fires and warn off children. The plaintiff, aged five, had been warned off by these men but on the afternoon in question, soon after school hours, the men were absent from the site. The plaintiff entered the building, fell into a fire and was seriously burned. The Court of Appeal upheld a decision for the plaintiff. In view of the situation of the warehouse, the attractiveness of fires to children and the time of the accident, there was a serious risk of which the defendants were in fact aware and they were responsible for the negligence of their servants in failing to exercise proper supervision. The plaintiff was aware that he ought not to go into the warehouse, but this was not, in view of his age, sufficient protection, for he could not fully appreciate the danger of the fires.

2. Licensees

If the child is lawfully on the land, then the occupier owes to him the common duty of care under the Occupiers' Liability Act, but since the distinction between invitees and licensees was rarely of importance in cases involving children, the cases decided before the Act are probably, for the most part, still good law. Certainly the common duty of care, like the common law duty before it, requires that the characteristics of children be taken into account [95-17] and in particular the occupier must appreciate that " in the case of an infant, there are moral as well as physical traps. There may accordingly be a duty towards infants not merely not to dig pitfalls for them, but not to lead them into temptation." [18] In *Glasgow Corporation* v. *Taylor* [19] it was alleged that a child aged seven had died from eating poisonous berries which he had picked from a shrub in some public gardens under the control of the corporation. The berries looked like cherries or large blackcurrants and were of a very tempting appearance to children. They thus constituted an " allurement " to the child. The corporation was aware of their poisonous nature, but nevertheless

---

[93] *British Railways Board* v. *Herrington* [1972] A.C. 877, 940, *per* Lord Diplock. In the case of very young children, it seems better to say that the obstacle must be effective to stop them rather than to warn them that further progress is unlawful. In any case, as Dixon J. pointed out in *Cardy's* case, *supra*, at p. 322, " the warning required is not that trespassing is not tolerated but that entry may be dangerous."

[94] [1972] 2 Q.B. 599; *cf. Penny* v. *Northampton B.C.* (1974) The Times, July 20.

[95-17] Occupiers' Liability Act 1957, s. 2 (3) (*a*). *Moloney* v. *Lambeth B.C.* (1968) 64 L.G.R. 440.

[18] *Latham* v. *R. Johnson & Nephew Ltd.* [1913] 1 K.B. 398, 415, *per* Hamilton L.J.

[19] [1922] 1 A.C. 44.

the shrub was not properly fenced from the public nor was any warning given of its deadly character. It was held that these facts disclosed a good cause of action.

On the facts of *Glasgow Corporation* v. *Taylor* it could, no doubt, be said that the child had no right to take the berries and, indeed, that in relation to the bush he was a trespasser. However, even if the child's permission to be on the land does not extend to the actual object on which he injured himself, nevertheless, so long as that object is an " allurement," the very fact of its being left there unguarded as a temptation to the child may itself constitute a breach of the occupier's duty. A rule of this sort was first recognised in *Lynch* v. *Nurdin*,[20] where the defendant's servant had left a horse and cart unattended in the street and the plaintiff, aged under seven, had been injured while playing with it. The servant's " most blameable carelessness " had tempted the child, who had merely indulged his natural instincts in playing with the cart, and the defendant was held liable. Since then the principle has been applied in several cases involving the occupier of land. In *Holdman* v. *Hamlyn*,[21] where a boy of ten was injured on a threshing machine, it was argued that he was a trespasser on the machine. To this du Parcq L.J. answered [22]: " The truth is, however, that he was an invitee, at any rate down to the moment when the threshing machine proved an irresistible temptation. If the boy strayed beyond the strict limit imposed by the terms of the invitation, it was because of the failure of the defendant's agent to guard him against a dangerous allurement, and, if he can properly be called a trespasser at all, the trespass was a natural and probable result of the negligence of the defendant's agent. A defendant who has lured an invitee into a forbidden area cannot thereafter treat him as a trespasser."

No liability where no allurement

If there be no allurement, trap, invitation or dangerous object placed upon the land, the occupier is not liable. Such was the law laid down in *Latham* v. *R. Johnson & Nephew Ltd.*,[23] where the child was injured by playing on a heap of stones and was held to have no remedy, because it is a normal use of land to deposit stones on it, and they are no more of a danger than cows or donkeys, if indeed

---

[20] (1841) 1 Q.B. 29; *Harrold* v. *Watney* [1898] 2 Q.B. 320; *Creed* v. *McGeoch & Sons Ltd.* [1955] 1 W.L.R. 1005. *Cf. Donovan* v. *Union Cartage Co. Ltd.* [1933] 2 K.B. 71; *Liddle* v. *Yorkshire (North Riding) C.C.* [1934] 2 K.B. 101. In *Mangan* v. *Atterton* (1866) L.R. 1 Ex. 239 Bramwell B. not only held that a child aged four who had crushed his fingers in the cogs of a machine exposed for sale in a public street was unable to recover damages but was inclined to think that if the machine had been of specially delicate construction and had been injured by the child's fingers the child would have been liable to the owner. This is certainly not the law today: see *Clark* v. *Chambers* (1878) 3 Q.B.D. 327, where it was already impliedly rejected.
[21] [1943] K.B. 664; *Williams* v. *Cardiff Corporation* [1950] 1 K.B. 514; *Gough* v. *N.C.B.* [1954] 1 Q.B. 191.
[22] [1943] K.B. at p. 668.
[23] [1913] 1 K.B. 398, 407.

as much. What is an allurement or trap must be inferred from the facts of each case. As Hamilton L.J. said in this case [24]: " a trap is a figure of speech, not a formula. It involves the idea of concealment and surprise,[25] of an appearance of safety under circumstances cloaking a reality of danger " [26]; and he added: " In some cases the answer may rest with the jury, but it must be a matter of law to say whether a given object can be a trap in the double sense of being fascinating and fatal." Hence, the thing which caused the harm may be so innocuous in itself as not to be a trap, or, although it may be a trap to begin with, it may cease to be one because it is reasonably well protected, or because the danger is obvious even to the child injured by it, or because adequate warning has been given to children to keep away from it. Thus there is no inherent danger in a sound, stationary and immobile vehicle, like an unhorsed van, left unattended in the street.[27] And unguarded water, natural or artificial, is in the same category according to an *obiter dictum* of Scrutton L.J. in *Liddle* v. *Yorks* (*North Riding*) *C.C.*[28] In that case there was adequate warning and the risk was obvious. The defendants' workmen, in carrying out a road improvement, had to leave a large quantity of soil temporarily against a new retaining wall. The heap and the wall were near the highway but on land not yet dedicated to the public. The heap formed a slope giving easy access to the top of the wall. Children had always been warned off when the workmen were there. On a Saturday afternoon, after the workmen had left, a boy aged seven years, who had previously been warned off, climbed up the heap, sat on the wall and, in trying to show his companions how bees flew, fell backwards and was injured. The defendants were held not liable, for the danger of falling off the wall was obvious to the child, quite apart from the fact that he was a trespasser because he had been forbidden to go there.

Very young children

In the case of very young children, however, there is scarcely anything which may not prove a danger to them, and there exists a dilemma to which Hamilton L.J. drew attention in *Latham* v. *R. Johnson & Nephew Ltd.*[29]: " The child must take the place as he finds it and take care of himself; but how can he take care of himself? If his injury is not to go without legal remedy altogether by reason of his failure

---

[24] *Ibid.* at pp. 415, 416.
[25] The context requires the insertion of this comma; see the collateral report in 82 L.J.K.B. 258.
[26] Evidently the occupier must himself be aware of the danger or else his failure to appreciate it must be unreasonable: *Sutton* v. *Bootle Corporation* [1947] K.B. 359, 369, *per* Asquith L.J. See also *Ellis* v. *Fulham B.C.* [1938] 1 K.B. 212.
[27] *Donovan* v. *Union Cartage Co. Ltd.* [1933] 2 K.B. 71, distinguishing *Lynch* v. *Nurdin* (1841) 1 Q.B. 29, where there was a horse harnessed to the vehicle.
[28] [1934] 2 K.B. 101, 112. There is nothing insidious about a hole in the ground which is, therefore, not an allurement: *Perry* v. *Thomas Wrigley Ltd.* [1955] 1 W.L.R. 1164.
[29] [1913] 1 K.B. 398, 414.

to use a diligence which he could not possibly have possessed, the owner of the close might be practically bound to see that the wandering child is as safe as in a nursery." The means of escape from this dilemma which was favoured by Hamilton L.J. himself was the concept of the conditional licence, first proposed by Lindley J. in 1880.[30] According to this view the circumstances may evidence the attachment of a condition to the licence or permission to enter, namely, that the child shall only enter if accompanied by a person in charge capable of seeing and avoiding obvious perils and thus of placing both himself and his charge in the position of an ordinary licensee both able and bound to look after himself.[31]

This approach was favourably received in several cases [32] and was apparently accepted as correct by the Court of Appeal in *Bates* v. *Stone Parish Council*,[33] where, however, it was held that the circumstances did not evidence the attachment of a condition to the plaintiff's permission to enter. There are, however, difficulties involved in the concept of the conditional licence, for, where the condition is held to exist, the unaccompanied child must be a trespasser and so would be unable to recover even in respect of a danger which by any standard constituted a trap. This and other problems [34] led Devlin J. to the view that if it were followed up the conditional licensor would soon become a legal fiction and the terms of the supposed licence would be mainly lawyers' inventions. In *Phipps* v. *Rochester Corporation*,[35] therefore, he preferred to adopt a more flexible approach.

In *Phipps* v. *Rochester Corporation* the plaintiff, a boy aged five, was out blackberrying with his sister, aged seven, and they walked across a large open space which formed part of a housing estate being developed by the defendants. In the course of laying a sewer the defendants had dug a long deep trench about two-and-a-half feet wide in the middle of the open space and the soil from the trench had been heaped along one side of it to a height of about four feet. To an adult, therefore, the danger was quite obvious, and the plaintiff's sister managed to avoid it by walking round the end of the trench. The plaintiff, however, fell in and broke his leg. There was evidence that children frequently went onto the open space and that the defendants had done nothing to keep them off, and Devlin J. held, therefore,

---

[30] *Burchell* v. *Hickisson* (1880) 50 L.J.C.P. 101, 102.
[31] *Latham* v. *R. Johnson & Nephew Ltd.* [1913] 1 K.B. 398, 414, *per* Hamilton L.J. *Cf.* the view of the same learned judge (then Lord Sumner) in *Glasgow Corporation* v. *Taylor* [1922] 1 A.C. 44, 67.
[32] Most of them are reviewed by Devlin J. in *Phipps* v. *Rochester Corporation* [1955] 1 Q.B. 450.
[33] [1954] 1 W.L.R. 1249. *Cf. Dyer* v. *Ilfracombe Urban District Council* [1956] 1 W.L.R. 218.
[34] *e.g.* what degree of incapacity calls for the attachment of the condition and what must be the qualifications of the companion?
[35] [1955] 1 Q.B. 450; Hall Williams (1955) 18 M.L.R. 393; (1955) 71 L.Q.R. 170; *Gwynne* v. *Dominion Stores* (1963) 43 D.L.R. (2d) 290 (Manitoba Q.B.); Weir, *Casebook on Tort*, 3rd ed., p. 110.

that the plaintiff was a licensee. Nevertheless he refused to hold that
the plaintiff's licence was subject to the condition that he must be
accompanied by some responsible person, and preferred the view that
in measuring the duty of the licensor, the habits of prudent parents in
relation to little children should be taken into account.[36] On the facts,
it was not prudent for a parent to have allowed two small children to go
alone on the open space in question or, at least, a prudent parent
would have satisfied himself that the place held no dangers for the
children, and if he had done so he would have seen the trench and
taken steps to prevent his children going there while it was still open.
The defendants were entitled to assume that parents would behave
in this prudent way and therefore, although the plaintiff was a licensee,
the defendants were not in breach of their duty to him.

Before the Occupiers' Liability Act 1957 came into force, there
might have been some difficulty in saying that the judgment of Devlin
J. in *Phipps* v. *Rochester Corporation*[37] contained the true rule of law,
for *Bates* v. *Stone Parish Council*,[38] in which the Court of Appeal
appears to have accepted the doctrine of the conditional licence, was
not cited.[39] Now, however, the question in each case is whether the
occupier has fulfilled his common duty of care, and in deciding this
" regard is to be had to all the circumstances."[40] Where young children
are concerned, it is submitted, one of the circumstances which should
clearly be taken into account in measuring the occupier's obligation
is the degree of care for their children's safety which the occupier may
assume will be exercised by the parents.[41]

Devlin J.'s judgment concedes that there may be places to which
parents of small children may reasonably allow them to go unaccompanied, *e.g.*, recognised playing-grounds for such children, but it
squarely places the primary responsibility for the safety of small children
upon the parents. " It is their duty to see that such children are not
allowed to wander about by themselves, or at the least to satisfy
themselves that the places to which they do allow their children to go
unaccompanied are safe for them to go to. It would not be socially
desirable if parents were, as a matter of course, able to shift the burden
of looking after their children from their own shoulders to those of
persons who happen to have accessible bits of land."[42]

In deciding whether an occupier has discharged the common duty

---

[36] Authority for this approach is to be found in the speech of Lord Shaw in *Glasgow
Corporation* v. *Taylor* [1922] 1 A.C. 44, 61.
[37] [1955] 1 Q.B. 450.
[38] [1954] 1 W.L.R. 1249.
[39] Devlin J. actually said that the doctrine of the conditional licence had not been
mentioned in any of the cases in the preceding 30 years in which one might have expected
it to be discussed: [1955] 1 Q.B. at p. 472.
[40] s. 2 (4). The specific instances contained in the subsection are examples only and do
not restrict its generality.
[41] See *O'Connor* v. *British Transport Commission* [1958] 1 W.L.R. 346; *McCullie* v.
Butler [1959] C.L.Y. 2207; *Nicholson* v. *Zoological Society* [1960] C.L.Y. 2127.
[42] [1955] 1 Q.B. at p. 472.

of care in respect of a young child, therefore, the kind of conduct
to be expected from the child's parents is to be taken into account.
If, in the circumstances, the occupier should anticipate that young
children will come onto his structure unaccompanied, then, indeed,
he must make it as safe as a nursery, but in general, and allowing
for the social habits of the neighbourhood,[43] he will have discharged
his duty if the place is reasonably safe for a child who is accompanied by the sort of guardian whom the occupier is in the circumstances entitled to expect him to have.[44] If the child is in fact accompanied by a guardian, then the question will be whether the occupier
ought to have foreseen that the source of the child's injury would be
a danger to the child, bearing in mind the guardian's responsibility
for the child's safety.[45] There seems no reason, at least in theory,
why the child's injury should not in an appropriate case be attributed
both to the occupier's breach of the common duty of care and to
the negligence of the guardian. In such a case the occupier will be liable
in full to the child, but presumably could recover contribution from
the guardian.[46]

LIABILITY OF NON-OCCUPIERS

Contractors

The liability of a contractor towards trespassers has already been
considered.[47] In relation to injuries caused by a contractor to a lawful
visitor it is clear that the ordinary principles of negligence, not the
special rules of occupiers' liability, apply,[48] though the distinction will
rarely be of importance since the Occupiers' Liability Act. In *A. C.
Billings & Sons Ltd.* v. *Riden* [49] contractors had been employed to
reconstruct the front approach to a house, and in the course of the
work they had left the access to the house in a dangerous condition.
As a result, the plaintiff, a lady of 71 who had been visiting
the house, was injured when she tried to leave. She knew of the danger
and could not, therefore, have recovered if the contractors had owed
her only the duty of licensors,[50] but it was held by the House of Lords

[43] *Phipps* v. *Rochester Corporation* [1955] 1 Q.B. at p. 472.
[44] Whether the occupier is entitled to assume that young children will be accompanied
by an adult guardian will depend upon the facts. In *Coates* v. *Rawtenstall B.C.* [1937]
3 All E.R. 602 an intelligent boy of 14 was held to be a competent guardian for a boy of
three and a quarter while in a recreation ground maintained by the defendants.
[45] *O'Connor* v. *British Transport Commission* [1958] 1 W.L.R. 346.
[46] Law Reform (Married Women and Tortfeasors) Act 1935, s. 6, *post*, p. 548. See
McCallion v. *Dodd* [1966] N.Z.L.R. 710 (C.A. of N.Z.). For contributory negligence of
children, see *ante*, pp. 111–112.
[47] See *ante*, p. 189.
[48] *Miller* v. *South of Scotland Electricity Board*, 1958 S.C.(H.L.) 20, 37, *per* Lord
Denning. It is, of course, possible for a contractor to be an occupier within the meaning
of this Act: *A.M.F. International Ltd.* v. *Magnet Bowling Ltd.* [1968] 1 W.L.R. 1028.
[49] [1958] A.C. 240; *Clayards* v. *Dethick* (1848) 12 Q.B. 439; *Dominion Natural Gas Co.
Ltd.* v. *Collins* [1909] A.C. 640; *Kimber* v. *Gas Light & Coke Co.* [1918] 1 K.B. 439;
Haseldine v. *Daw & Son Ltd.* [1941] 2 K.B. 343; *Whitby* v. *Burt, Boulton & Hayward Ltd.*
[1947] K.B. 918. See too *Hartley* v. *Mayoh & Co.* [1954] 1 Q.B. 383.
[50] The case arose before the Occupiers' Liability Act.

that the position of the contractors was not the same as the occupier's. In the words of Lord Reid, they were " under a duty to all persons who might be expected lawfully to visit the house, and that duty was the ordinary duty to take such care as, in all the circumstances of the case, was reasonable to ensure that visitors were not exposed to danger by their actions." [51]

Vendors and lessors

The law governing the liability of vendors and lessors of defective premises is, if anything, even more complex after the Defective Premises Act 1972 than it was before, for an exposition of the common law remains necessary not only to cover the significant number of cases which fall outside that Act but also for an understanding of the Act itself.

1. The common law

In accordance with the general principles of negligence, there is no reason why the builder, vendor or lessor of a house should not have been liable for an injury resulting from a dangerous condition created by his negligence even though the injury was suffered after the house was sold or let,[53] and, provided the builder is not himself the vendor or lessor, there is, today, no doubt that at common law he is so liable, unless, of course, the damage is too remote.[54] Once he has ceased to be in occupation, however, the vendor or lessor, even if he is also the builder, is probably not liable, apart from express or implied contractual terms,[55] unless he has acted fraudulently.[56] So far as leases are

---

[51] [1958] A.C. at p. 250; *ibid.* at pp. 259–260, *per* Lord Cohen; *ibid.* at pp. 263–264, *per* Lord Somervell. *Johnson* v. *Rea Ltd.* [1961] 1 W.L.R. 1400 provides an interesting example, and perhaps an extension, of the liability of a non-occupier for the condition of premises.

[53] In Winfield's note on *Otto* v. *Bolton, infra* (1936) 52 L.Q.R. 313, he suggests that if no one had ever sued in tort for injury arising from a ruinous house until after *Donoghue* v. *Stevenson*, the jerry-builder would then have been held to be the " neighbour " of the injured person.

[54] *Sharpe* v. *E. T. Sweeting & Son Ltd.* [1963] 1 W.L.R. 665, following *Gallagher* v. *McDowell Ltd.* [1961] N.I. 26 (C.A. of N.I.). Ellis Lewis [1963] C.L.J. 23.

[55] In relation to sales, there is at common law no implied term as to fitness in a contract for sale of land; but in a contract for the sale of a house to be built or completed there is an implied term that the house will be reasonably fit for habitation: *Miller* v. *Cannon Hill Estates Ltd.* [1931] 2 K.B. 113. In relation to leases, there is at common law an implied warranty in the letting of furnished premises that they are fit for occupation at the commencement of the tenancy: *Collins* v. *Hopkins* [1923] 2 K.B. 617. In addition, there are certain non-excludable, statutory implied terms. By the Housing Act 1957, s. 6, there is implied into contracts for the letting of houses at very low rents an undertaking by the landlord that they are, and will be kept, fit for human habitation. By the Housing Act 1961, ss. 32 and 33, there is imposed upon the landlord an obligation to carry out certain repairs where a house is let for a term of less than seven years (see *O'Brien* v. *Robinson* [1973] A.C. 912). Though sounding in contract and therefore actionable only at the suit of the tenant, the above implied terms in leases would indirectly avail third parties because they would create an obligation under what is now s. 4 of the Defective Premises Act 1972, *infra.*

[56] *Bottomley* v. *Bannister* [1932] 1 K.B. 458; *Otto* v. *Bolton* [1936] 2 K.B. 46. " The fact that the owner is also the builder does not remove the owner's immunity, but when the builder is not the owner he enjoys no such immunity ": *Sharpe* v. *E. T. Sweeting & Son Ltd., supra*, at p. 675, *per* Nield J. It is probable, however, that the vendor or lessor is liable at common law for negligence in work which he does on premises after the sale

concerned, the reason given by Erle C.J. in 1863 [57] and repeated constantly in later cases [58] is that " fraud apart, there is no law against letting a tumbledown house," and the general rule is *caveat* lessee or *emptor* as the case may be.[59] The family and guests of the lessee or purchaser are in even worse case, for they have no possibility of any contractual action against the lessor or vendor.[60]

The above statement of the law is supported by the authorities in point, but grave doubt has been cast upon it by powerful dicta in the Court of Appeal in *Dutton* v. *Bognor Regis U.D.C.*[61] In that case the builder of the defective house (who had sold it to an intermediate purchaser) was a party to the original proceedings but settled for a comparatively small sum. Nevertheless, in an appeal by another party Lord Denning M.R. and Sachs L.J. stated categorically that the doctrine of *Donoghue* v. *Stevenson* applied to realty as well as to personalty and that the builder/vendor's immunity was no longer law. The logic of this position would seem to extend beyond the builder/ vendor to the " mere " vendor and to the lessor [62]; but any plaintiff relying on the dicta might face grave problems, for they are difficult to support according to the commonly understood doctrine of precedent in the Court of Appeal.[63]

2. The Defective Premises Act 1972

The foregoing principles were widely regarded as unsatisfactory, and the Law Commission recommended the intervention of Parliament.[64] Their proposals were brought to fruition in the Defective Premises Act 1972,[65] which came into force on January 1, 1974. The provisions of the Act cannot be excluded or restricted by any agreement.[66]

Duty to build dwellings properly. Section 1 of the Act imposes upon persons who undertake work for, or in connection with, the provision

---

or the commencement of the lease; *Malone* v. *Laskey* [1907] 2 K.B. 141, to the contrary, was overruled in *A. C. Billings & Son Ltd.* v. *Riden* [1958] A.C. 240. See too *Ball* v. *L.C.C.* [1949] 2 K.B. 159, 167, *per* Tucker L.J.

[57] *Robbins* v. *Jones* (1863) 15 C.B.(N.S.) 221, 240.

[58] *e.g., Cavalier* v. *Pope* [1906] A.C. 428, 430, *per* Lord Macnaghten; *Bottomley* v. *Bannister, supra*, at p. 469, *per* Scrutton L.J. In the case of sales the almost universal practice of having a survey was no doubt some justification for the rule.

[59] *Cheater* v. *Cater* [1918] 1 K.B. 247. The rule is not limited to the physical condition of the land but extends to the existence of legal restrictions on its user: *Edler* v. *Auerbach* [1950] 1 K.B. 329; *Hill* v. *Harris* [1965] 2 Q.B. 601.

[60] *Robbins* v. *Jones, supra; Cavalier* v. *Pope, supra; Otto* v. *Bolton, supra.*

[61] [1972] 1 Q.B. 373. See further on this case, *ante*, p. 50.

[62] See Lord Denning M.R. at p. 393.

[63] The leading case on builder-vendors, *Bottomley* v. *Bannister*, is itself a Court of Appeal decision, and was not overruled in *Donoghue* v. *Stevenson. Cavalier* v. *Pope*, the leading authority on leases, was overruled on its facts by the Occupiers' Liability Act 1957, s. 4, but the general principle upon which the case was based has not before been departed from.

[64] *Civil Liability of Vendors and Lessors for Defective Premises*, Law Com. No. 40, 1970.

[65] North (1973) 36 M.L.R. 628; Samuels (1973) 37 Conv.(N.S.) 314.

[66] s. 6 (3).

of a dwelling [67] a statutory duty to see that the work taken on is done in a workmanlike or professional manner, with proper materials and so that as regards that work the dwelling will be fit for habitation when completed.[68] The range of persons on whom the duty is imposed is therefore much wider than the building firm itself and would include the architect and surveyor and any subcontractors involved,[69] though the manufacturer of standard components is outside the scope of the duty. The duty is owed not only to the person ordering the work but also to every person who then or later acquires an interest (whether legal or equitable) in the dwelling [70]; this open-ended liability is, however, mitigated by the fact that for limitation purposes any cause of action is deemed to accrue at the time when the dwelling is completed.[71]

The operation of section 1 will be greatly limited in practice by section 2, which excludes dwellings covered by an " approved scheme " of purchaser protection, i.e., that operated by the National House Building Council.[72] In practice, therefore, since nearly all new houses are covered by the N.H.B.C. scheme, the operation of section 1 will tend to be confined to conversions and alterations, to which that scheme does not apply.[72a]

Duty of care not abated by disposal of premises. Section 3 provides that where work of construction, repair, maintenance or demolition or any other work is done on or in relation to premises,[73] any duty of care owed, because of the doing of the work, to persons who might reasonably be expected to be affected by the defects in the state of the premises created by the doing of the work shall not be abated by the subsequent disposal [74] of the premises by the person who owed the

---

[67] Industrial and commercial premises are therefore outside the Act. As to dwellings excluded from the Act see *infra*, note 72.

[68] This is in some ways stricter than a duty of care. It corresponds closely with the implied warranty at common law in a contract for the construction of a house (see *ante*, note 55). and in that context it has been held that the warranty in relation to materials is strict: *Hancock* v. *B. W. Brazier (Anerley) Ltd.* [1966] 1 W.L.R. 1317. The wording suggests that the position is the same under the Act.

[69] But note the important provisions in s. 1 (2), (3) which will generally relieve a person of liability if he does the work properly in accordance with instructions given by another. This would appear to cover not only the builder upon whom the client imposes detailed specifications, but also the sub-contractor who receives instructions from the builder.

[70] " The analogy is not with the common law of tort but rather with the rule contained in the Bills of Lading Act 1855 that a subsequent purchaser of goods carried by sea succeeds to the rights of the person who contracted with the carrier thereof ": Weir, *Casebook on Tort*, 3rd ed., p. 24.

[71] s. 1 (5). The limitation period will generally be six years, but three years for personal injuries. In view of the existence of s. 3 it is perhaps odd that s. 1 covers personal injuries at all.

[72] Under the National House-Building Council scheme the purchaser is protected for up to 10 years, but from the third to the tenth years there is cover only against major structural defects.

[72a] However, s. 71 of the Health and Safety at Work Act 1974 (which is not yet in force) creates civil liability for contravention of building regulations. It is unclear (see s. 71 (4)) whether this covers the type of loss primarily contemplated by s. 1 of the Defective Premises Act.

[73] This, unlike s. 1, is not confined to " dwellings." Omissions apparently give rise to no liability.

[74] " Disposal " includes a letting: s. 6 (1).

duty. The effect of this is to abolish the *caveat emptor* or lessee rule as far as the law of tort is concerned and, of course, to allow a cause of action to members of the family or guests of the purchaser.[75]

Landlord's duty of care. If a landlord retains part of his premises in his own occupation and demises the rest (*e.g.*, the staircase and lifts in a block of flats) he, of course, remains responsible for defects in the part so retained.[76] However, under section 4 of the Defective Premises Act (which replaces a similar but narrower provision in section 4 of the Occupiers' Liability Act 1957)[77] a landlord with a duty or right to repair is under a duty in tort with respect to demised premises. Where premises are let under a tenancy which puts on the landlord an obligation to the tenant for the maintenance or repair of the premises, the landlord owes to all persons [78] who might reasonably be expected to be affected by defects in the state of the premises a duty to take such care as is reasonable in all the circumstances to see that they are reasonably safe from personal injury or damage to their property caused by a defect within the repairing obligation. The duty is owed if the landlord knows or ought to have known of the defect. Where the landlord has only a right to enter and repair, he is treated for the purposes of this section (but for no other purpose) as if he were under an obligation to the tenant to repair, but will be under no liability to the tenant by virtue of the section in respect of any defect in the state of the premises arising from, or continuing because of, a failure to carry out an obligation expressly imposed on the tenant by the tenancy.[79]

---

[75] There is some degree of overlap with s. 1, though the position is not entirely clear: (1) A plaintiff suffering personal injuries may also sue under s. 1 if the premises are a dwelling and he has an interest therein and the duty under that section may be somewhat stricter than a duty to take care: see *ante*, note 68. (2) It is uncertain whether a claim may be made under s. 3 by a person with an interest in the premises in respect of a defect which does not cause any personal injury or damage to other property (s. 1 clearly covers such a defect), *e.g.*, the defect in *Dutton* v. *Bognor Regis U.D.C.* [1972] 1 Q.B. 373. S. 3 seems merely to remove an obstacle to the existence of a common law duty and a non-dangerous defect in the premises *might* be considered mere economic loss (*contra, Dutton's* case): see further *ante*, p. 53. The matter is not merely academic, since the provisions of s. 1 are confined to dwellings unprotected by an approved scheme; s. 3 applies to all premises, whether or not protected by such a scheme.

[76] *Cunard* v. *Antifyre* [1933] 1 K.B. 551; *Taylor* v. *Liverpool Corpn.* [1939] 3 All E.R. 329. *Cf. Shirvell* v. *Hackwood Estates Ltd.* [1938] 2 K.B. 577 and Hamson (1938) 2 M.L.R. 215; (1938) 54 L.Q.R. 459.

[77] For detailed consideration of this, see the 9th ed. of this work and North, *Occupiers' Liability*, Chap. 12.

[78] Including the tenant. Subject to contributory negligence, the tenant appears to be able to sue even where the lease requires him to give notice to the landlord of the want of repair and he fails to do so. A trespasser may also be a person who might reasonably be expected to be affected. The landlord's duty does not appear to be confined to persons on the premises. S. 4 therefore also creates a liability in nuisance, see p. 341, note 69a, *post*.

[79] If, therefore, the lease required the tenant to repair but reserved to the landlord a right to enter and do so, the tenant could not sue, but a visitor of his could. S. 4 of the Occupiers' Liability Act " imported " into the landlord's duty the considerations and defences in relation to the common duty of care expressed in s. 2. S. 4 of the Defective Premises Act does not do so.

CHAPTER 11

LIABILITY FOR CHATTELS

NATURE OF THE LIABILITY

Classification of dangerous chattels

There is no doubt that in the past the law recognised the existence of a special category of " dangerous chattels," liability for which was treated in legal literature and practice as a separate compartment of the law of tort. Before the decision in *Donoghue* v. *Stevenson*,[1] while the " contract fallacy " remained in full vigour, it was broadly true to say that apart from contract there was no general duty of care with regard to chattels.[2] The duty only existed if either the chattel causing the damage was of the class of dangerous chattels or if it was dangerous for some reason actually known to the defendant.[3] In *Dominion Natural Gas Co.* v. *Collins & Perkins*[4] the defendants installed a natural gas supply at the premises of the plaintiffs' employers and allowed the safety valve to discharge into part of the building instead of leading the gas out to the open air. As a result an explosion occurred for which the defendants were held liable, and Lord Dunedin said: " There being no relation of contract between the [defendants] and the plaintiffs, the plaintiffs cannot appeal to any defect in the machine supplied by the defendants which might constitute breach of contract. There may be, however, in the case of any one performing an operation, or setting up and installing a machine, a relationship of duty. What that duty is will vary according to the subject-matter of the things involved. It has, however, again and again been held that in the case of articles dangerous in themselves, such as loaded firearms, poisons, explosives, and other things ejusdem generis, there is a peculiar duty to take precaution imposed upon those who send forth or instal such articles when it is necessarily the case that other parties will come within their proximity."[5]

Criticism of the classification

The classification of chattels into those which are dangerous and those which are not is, however, an unsatisfactory one. Lord Dunedin

---

[1] [1932] A.C. 562.

[2] *Winterbottom* v. *Wright* (1842) 10 M. & W. 109.

[3] *Dixon* v. *Bell* (1816) 5 M. & S. 198; *Longmeid* v. *Holliday* (1851) 6 Ex. 761; *Earl* v. *Lubbock* [1905] 1 K.B. 253; *Blacker* v. *Lake & Elliot Ltd.* (1912) 106 L.T. 533. *Cf. George* v. *Skivington* (1869) L.R. 5 Ex. 1.

[4] [1909] A.C. 640.

[5] [1909] A.C. at p. 646. In addition to the cases already cited, see *Thomas* v. *Winchester* (1852) 6 N.Y.R. 397; *Parry* v. *Smith* (1879) 4 C.P.D. 325.

himself agreed that there is an element of danger in every chattel [6] and Scrutton L.J. confessed that he did not understand the difference " between a thing dangerous in itself, as poison, and a thing not dangerous as a class, but by negligent construction dangerous as a particular thing. The latter, if anything, seems to me the more dangerous of the two; it is a wolf in sheep's clothing instead of an obvious wolf." [7] Nevertheless, even after *Donoghue* v. *Stevenson* [8] had demonstrated that a duty of care could exist in respect of something not belonging to the class of dangerous chattels, the terminology persisted [9] and some cases were actually decided against the plaintiff on the express ground that the chattel which caused his injury was not a dangerous chattel. [10] On the other hand, it is thought that with one exception [11] the result in those cases would have been the same if the classification had been ignored and the ordinary rules of negligence applied, always bearing in mind, of course, that in accordance with those rules, what is a reasonable amount of care in one set of circumstances may not be so in another. It is true that the law expects of a man a great deal more care in carrying a pound of dynamite than a pound of butter, or in keeping a bottle of poison than a bottle of lemonade, but that is the result of the general law of negligence, not of the application of a special rule of law concerning dangerous things. [12]

It is suggested that sufficient time has now elapsed since the decision in *Donoghue* v. *Stevenson* for the category of dangerous things to be abandoned, and the signs are that the judges have come to this conclusion. In *Beckett* v. *Newalls Insulation Co. Ltd.*, [13] which concerned an explosion of gas from a portable gas cylinder, Singleton L.J. agreed that " there really is no category of dangerous things; there are only some things which require more and some which require less care " [14]; in at least three cases concerning guns, which, like gas cylinders, are

---

[6] *Oliver* v. *Saddler & Co.* [1929] A.C. 584, 599.

[7] *Hodge* v. *Anglo-American Oil Co.* (1922) 12 Ll.L.Rep. 183, 187. See Stallybrass, " Dangerous Things and the Non-Natural User of Land " (1929) 3 C.L.J. 376.

[8] [1932] A.C. 562.

[9] It received the approval of Lord Wright in *Glasgow Corporation* v. *Muir* [1943] A.C. 448, 463–464. Neither Lord Atkin nor Lord Macmillan condemned the classification in *Donoghue* v. *Stevenson* ([1932] A.C. at pp. 596, 611–612 respectively) but it seems that neither regarded dangerous chattels as a special category to which a distinct principle of law should be applied.

[10] *Wray* v. *Essex C.C.* [1936] 2 All E.R. 97; *Ricketts* v. *Erith B.C.* [1943] 2 All E.R. 629; *Ball* v. *L.C.C.* [1949] 2 K.B. 159. In some others the plaintiff succeeded on the ground that the chattel was a dangerous chattel: *Burfitt* v. *Kille* [1939] 2 K.B. 743; *Watson* v. *Buckley* [1940] 1 All E.R. 174.

[11] *Ball* v. *L.C.C.*, *supra.* This case is almost certainly overruled by *A. C. Billings & Sons* v. *Riden* [1958] A.C. 240.

[12] *Cf.* Clerk & Lindsell, *Torts*, 13th ed., pp. 532–536, which adheres to the classification but emphasises that the law relating to both categories forms part of the law of negligence. The classification is probably still necessary for the purposes of the rule in *Rylands* v. *Fletcher* (1868) L.R. 3 H.L. 330, *post*, pp. 358–382.

[13] [1953] 1 W.L.R. 8.

[14] His Lordship was quoting with approval the argument of Sir Hartley Shawcross Att.-Gen. in *Read* v. *J. Lyons & Co.* [1947] A.C. 156, 161. For this case, see *post*, pp. 362–363.

obvious " dangerous chattels," no mention of any special rule of law was made but the ordinary law of negligence applied [15]; and now Chapman J. has stated positively that " things dangerous in themselves have gone into limbo as a category since *Read* v. *J. Lyons & Co. Ltd.*" [16] There is no liability in tort for damage caused by a chattel unless there is negligence, and there is no class of chattel in respect of which there is no liability for negligence. There is simply the ordinary rule that the greater the risk the greater the precautions that must be taken to obviate it.[17]

INCIDENCE OF THE LIABILITY

Liability to immediate transferee

Where the plaintiff is injured by a chattel which was transferred to him under a contract with the defendant, then the plaintiff will often be able to claim damages for the breach of some term, express or implied, in the contract. So, for example, in *Godley* v. *Perry* [18] the plaintiff, a boy of six, was injured when a catapult which he had bought from the defendant broke, and it was held that he was entitled to damages for breach of the terms implied into the contract by the Sale of Goods Act 1893. Where the transfer is gratuitous, on the other hand, then, according to the older authorities, unless the chattel belongs to the class of dangerous chattels, the transferor is liable only for wilful or reckless conduct, and this means that he cannot be liable if he did not actually know of the defect or danger which caused the plaintiff's injury.[19] The force of these authorities is, however, greatly weakened if not altogether destroyed by the decision in *Donoghue* v. *Stevenson* [20] and there is no reason today for holding that the defendant's ignorance of the danger is in itself sufficient to protect him from liability if in the circumstances he ought to have known of it. The fact that the transfer is gratuitous is, certainly, an important matter to be taken into

---

[15] *Donaldson* v. *McNiven* [1952] 2 All E.R. 691; *Newton* v. *Edgerley* [1959] 1 W.L.R. 1031; *Gorely* v. *Codd* [1967] 1 W.L.R. 19. See also *Bebee* v. *Sales* (1916) 32 T.L.R. 413; *Hatfield* v. *Pearson* (1956) 6 D.L.R. (2d) 593; *Hinds* v. *Direct Supply Co. (Clapham Junction) Ltd.* [1966] C.L.Y. 5210.

[16] *Griffiths* v. *Arch Engineering Co. (Newport) Ltd.* [1968] 3 All E.R. 217, 220.

[17] *Read* v. *J. Lyons & Co.*, *supra*, at pp. 172–173, *per* Lord Macmillan; *ibid.* 180–181, *per* Lord Simonds. There has, however, been a suggestion that the category of dangerous things should be reconstituted and a rule of strict liability imposed. See the Law Commission's Report on Civil Liability for Dangerous Things and Activities (Law Com. No. 32), 1970, *ante*, p. 5.

[18] [1960] 1 W.L.R. 9. Of the many other examples see, *e.g.*, *Hyman* v. *Nye* (1880) 6 Q.B.D. 685; *Bamfield* v. *Goole and Sheffield Transport Co.* [1910] 2 K.B. 94; *Grant* v. *Australian Knitting Mills Ltd.* [1936] A.C. 85; *Andrews* v. *Hopkinson* [1957] 1 Q.B. 229; *Vacwell Engineering Co. Ltd.* v. *B.D.H. Chemicals Ltd.* [1971] 1 Q.B. 88.

[19] " The principle of law as to gifts is, that the giver is not responsible for damage resulting from the insecurity of the thing, unless he knew its evil character at the time, and omitted to caution the donee ": *Gautret* v. *Egerton* (1867) L.R. 2 C.P. 371, 375, *per* Willes J.; *Coughlin* v. *Gillison* [1899] 1 Q.B. 145.

[20] " The decision in *Donoghue* v. *Stevenson* makes the earlier cases on gifts quite out of date ": *Hawkins* v. *Coulsdon U.D.C.* [1954] 1 Q.B. 319, 333, *per* Denning L.J.; *Griffiths* v. *Arch Engineering Co. Ltd.* [1968] 3 All E.R. 217, 220, *per* Chapman J.; Marsh, " Liability of the Gratuitous Transferor " (1950) 66 L.Q.R. 39.

account in assessing the standard of care required of the transferor, but it does not have the result that the gratuitous transferor owes no duty of care to the transferee.[21] It is submitted that the transferor's liability in tort to the immediate transferee is today governed by the same general principles of negligence as govern his liability to anybody else.[22]

Liability to ultimate transferee

Before *Donoghue* v. *Stevenson* [23] was decided in 1932 it was doubtful whether the transferor of a chattel owed any duty to the ultimate transferee (in the absence of a contractual relationship between them) unless the chattel belonged to the class of dangerous chattels or was actually known to the transferor to be dangerous.[24] Winfield has traced the doubt, vacillation and conflict of authorities elsewhere,[25] and it is unnecessary to go back beyond *Donoghue* v. *Stevenson* itself. The real issue in that case may be stated as follows: if A is under a contract with B and breaks the contract, C, who is injured by the breach, cannot sue A in contract for there is none between A and C; can he, however, sue A in tort, or is the whole of A's duty limited to his contract with B?

Donoghue v. *Stevenson* finally established by a majority of three to two that apart from contract, apart from any special rule about dangerous chattels, there are circumstances in which A owes a duty of care to C for the breach of which he is liable in negligence. Lord Atkin laid down the following principle for both Scots and English law: " *A manufacturer of products, which he sells in such a form as to show that he intends them to reach the ultimate consumer in the form in which they left him with no reasonable possibility of intermediate examination and with the knowledge that the absence of reasonable care in the preparation or putting up of the products will result in an injury to the consumer's life or property,*[25a] *owes a duty to the consumer to take that reasonable care.*" [26]

---

[21] In *Philco Radio etc. Corporation Ltd.* v. *J. Spurling Ltd.* [1949] 2 K.B. 33, negligence was admitted where the defendants mistakenly delivered to the plaintiffs a quantity of film scrap without any warning of its inflammable nature. It may be that the law was as stated in the text even before *Donoghue* v. *Stevenson*: *Oliver* v. *Saddler & Co.* [1929] A.C. 584. In *Clarke* v. *Army & Navy Co-operative Society Ltd.* [1903] 1 K.B. 155 the defendants were held liable for a failure to warn on the ground that they actually knew of the danger, but the evidence really established only that they ought to have known of it.

[22] *Andrews* v. *Hopkinson, supra*; *Griffiths* v. *Arch Engineering Co. Ltd., supra*; *Vacwell Engineering Co. Ltd.* v. *B.D.H. Chemicals Ltd.* [1971] 1 Q.B. 88, 109–110, *per* Rees J.

[23] [1932] A.C. 562, *ante*, pp. 47–48.

[24] If the fraud of the transferor could be proved he would be liable for that: *Langridge* v. *Levy* (1837) 2 M. & W. 519; (1838) 4 M. & W. 337 The liability in respect of dangerous chattels has been said not to rest upon knowledge (*Burfitt* v. *Kille* [1939] 2 K.B. 743, 747, *per* Atkinson J.) but if the classification of a chattel as dangerous means anything, it must mean that everyone is presumed to know that it is dangerous.

[25] " Duty in Tortious Negligence " in *Select Legal Essays*, p. 70; Bohlen, " Liability of Manufacturers to Persons other than their Immediate Vendees " (1929) 45 L.Q.R. 343.

[25a] *Cf.* the views expressed in *Dutton* v. *Bognor Regis U.D.C.* [1972] 1 Q.B. 373.

[26] [1932] A.C. 562, 599.

Developments of Donoghue v. Stevenson. The importance of *Donoghue* v. *Stevenson* for the general law of negligence has already been indicated,[27] but the decision is also the foundation of the modern law concerning the narrower topic of liability for chattels, and the developments since 1932 may be conveniently collected in the following form.[28]

(i) *Extension of persons liable.* The principle has been extended from manufacturers to include repairers,[29] fitters, erectors,[30] assemblers,[31] in other words to persons who have done something active to create the danger. If the essential basis of *Donoghue's* case is that someone has negligently manufactured a defective chattel and that neither the transferee nor the ultimate consumer could have been expected to examine it, then it would seem that the principle of the case should not generally apply to suppliers, that is, vendors, bailors and donors of chattels who are unaware of the defect and have done nothing active to create or contribute to the defect or danger, for such persons cannot reasonably have foreseen that there was risk of injury to the ultimate user. Affirmative duties to inspect are not generally imposed except as the price of a benefit.[32] Today, however, the courts are more willing to take the view that a supplier should in certain circumstances make inquiries or carry out an inspection of the chattel, and if it is dangerous for some reason of which the supplier should have known, his failure to warn of it will amount to negligence. In *Andrews* v. *Hopkinson*,[33] by arrangement with the plaintiff the defendant sold a second-hand car to a finance company and the company hired the car to the plaintiff under a hire-purchase agreement. The car was some eighteen years old, and the defendant, who was a dealer in second-hand cars, had taken no steps to see that it was in a roadworthy condition although the car had been in his possession for a week. In fact the car had a defective steering mechanism which caused the plaintiff to have an accident a week after he took delivery of the car. Evidence showed that in an old car the danger spot is the steering mechanism and that the defect in question could have been discovered by a competent mechanic if the car had been

---

[27] *Ante*, pp. 54–57.
[28] See Glanville Williams, " Negligent Contractors and Third Parties " (1942) 92 L.J.Newsp. 115, 124, 132, and Underhay, " Manufacturer's Liability: recent developments of *Donoghue* v. *Stevenson* " (1936) 14 Can. Bar Rev. 283–310. Heuston, in Salmond's *Torts*, 16th ed., pp. 310–317; Heuston, " *Donoghue* v. *Stevenson* in Retrospect " (1957) 20 M.L.R. 1.
[29] *Malfroot* v. *Noxal* (1935) 51 T.L.R. 551; *Stennett* v. *Hancock* [1939] 2 All E.R. 578; *Herschtal* v. *Stewart & Ardern* [1940] 1 K.B. 155; *Haseldine* v. *Daw* [1941] 2 K.B. 343.
[30] *Brown* v. *Cotterill* (1934) 51 T.L.R. 21.
[31] *Howard* v. *Furness Houlder Ltd.* [1936] 2 All E.R. 296.
[32] Eldredge, *Modern Tort Problems*, p. 265; *Bottomley* v. *Bannister* [1932] 1 K.B. 458, 480, *per* Greer L.J.
[33] [1957] 1 Q.B. 229. Heuston considers that the decision is justified by the social importance of preventing defective vehicles being allowed on the highways: Salmond's *Torts*, 16th ed., p. 312. See, too, *White* v. *John Warwick & Co.* [1953] 1 W.L.R. 1285; *Griffiths* v. *Arch Engineering Co. Ltd.* [1968] 3 All E.R. 217.

jacked up. McNair J. held that the defendant was liable and said [34]: " Having regard to the extreme peril involved in allowing an old car with a defective steering mechanism to be used on the road, I have no hesitation in holding that the defendant was guilty of negligence in failing to make the necessary examination, or at least in failing to warn the plaintiff that no such examination had been carried out." Similarly suppliers may be liable if they carelessly represent the goods to be harmless without having made any adequate tests,[35] but it should not be thought that these cases impose a general duty on suppliers to subject all their goods to an exhaustive examination. The duty to examine will only arise if in all the circumstances they could reasonably be expected to carry out an examination. A second-hand car dealer may be expected to discover a patent defect in the steering mechanism of one of his cars, and a manufacturer and supplier of chemicals must take reasonable care to discover and give warning of industrial hazards arising out of the chemicals he supplies,[36] but a retail grocer, for example, cannot be expected to discover that tinned food is contaminated. Unless the contamination was caused by his negligence or he actually knew of it, his only liability is to the actual purchaser under the contract of sale. If a third party becomes ill on eating the contaminated food, his remedy, if any, is against the manufacturer.

(ii) *Extension of subject-matter.* The principle has been extended from articles of food and drink and includes, *inter alia,* kiosks,[37] tombstones,[38] hair dye,[39] industrial chemicals,[40] lifts,[41] motor-cars [42] and pants.[43] Likewise the term " consumer " includes the ultimate user of the article [44] or anyone who is within physical proximity to it.[45]

---

[34] [1957] 1 Q.B. 229, 237.

[35] *Watson* v. *Buckley, Osborne, Garrett & Co.* [1940] 1 All E.R. 174 (distributors of a dangerous hair dye held liable because they advertised it as positively harmless and requiring no tests); *Devilez* v. *Boots Pure Drug Co.* [1962] C.L.Y. 2015; *Goodchild* v. *Vaclight* [1965] C.L.Y. 2669; *Fisher* v. *Harrods* [1966] C.L.Y. 8148. Street, *Torts,* 5th ed., p. 171, suggests that retailers have a duty to carry out those checks which a retailer who sells those goods would reasonably be expected to make. See also Fleming, *Torts,* 4th ed., p. 451.

[36] *Vacwell Engineering Co. Ltd.* v. *B.D.H. Chemicals Ltd.* [1971] 1 Q.B. 88. In this case Rees J. regarded the argument, kept open by counsel for the defendant, that where parties are in a contractual relationship the terms of the contract govern and it is not open to one of them to sue the other for a tort as a " novel proposition." It is respectfully submitted that it is not novel (see, *e.g., Bagot* v. *Stevens Scanlan & Co. Ltd.* [1966] 1 Q.B. 197) but it is wrong. An appeal from the judgment of Rees J. was settled: [1971] 1 Q.B. 111n.

[37] *Paine* v. *Colne Valley Electricity Supply Co.* [1938] 4 All E.R. 803.

[38] *Brown* v. *Cotterill* [1934] 51 T.L.R. 21.

[39] *Watson* v. *Buckley* [1940] 1 All E.R. 174.

[40] *Vacwell Engineering Co. Ltd.* v. *B.D.H. Chemicals Ltd.* [1971] 1 Q.B. 88.

[41] *Haseldine* v. *Daw* [1941] 2 K.B. 343.

[42] *Herschtal* v. *Stewart & Ardern* [1940] 1 K.B. 155; *Andrews* v. *Hopkinson* [1957] 1 Q.B. 229.

[43] *Grant* v. *Australian Knitting Mills* [1936] A.C. 85.

[44] *Grant* v. *Australian Knitting Mills, supra*; *Griffiths* v. *Arch Engineering Co. Ltd.* [1968] 3 All E.R. 217; *Cassidy* v. *Imperial Chemical Industries Ltd.* (1972) *The Times,* November 2.

[45] *Brown* v. *Cotterill, supra* (child injured by falling tombstone); *Sternett* v. *Hancock* [1939] 2 All E.R. 578 (pedestrian hit by flange of lorry wheel).

(iii) *Possibility of alternative cause.* In *Grant* v. *Australian Knitting Mills Ltd.,*[46] the Judicial Committee held that the defendants were liable to the ultimate purchaser of some pants which they had manufactured and which contained a chemical that gave the defendant a skin disease when he wore them. It was argued for the defendants that as they despatched the pants in paper packets of six sets there was greater possibility of intermediate tampering with the goods before they reached the user than there was with the sealed bottle in *Donoghue's* case, but the court held that " the decision in that case did not depend on the bottle being stoppered and sealed; the essential point in this regard was that the article should reach the consumer or user subject to the same defect as it had when it left the manufacturer." [47] Mere possibility of interference did not affect their liability. There must, however, be sufficient evidence that the defect existed when the article left the manufacturer's hands and that it was not caused later. In *Evans* v. *Triplex Safety Glass Co. Ltd.,*[48] the plaintiff bought a motorcar fitted with a " Triplex Toughened Safety Glass " windscreen of the defendants' manufacture. A year later, when the car was being used, the windscreen suddenly and for no apparent reason broke into many fragments and injured the occupants of the car. The defendants were held not liable for the following reasons: (a) the lapse of time between the purchase and the accident; (b) the possibility that the glass may have been strained when screwed into its frame; (c) the opportunity of intermediate examination by the intermediate seller and (d) the breaking of the glass may have been caused by something other than a defect in manufacture. User of the article by the plaintiff for a purpose materially different from that for which the maker designed it or which he might reasonably be taken to have contemplated will also defeat a claim, but use for a different but similar purpose does not *ipso facto* absolve him from liability. The question here is one of fact and degree,[49] and it is suggested that the right thing to ask is whether the cause of the plaintiff's injury was the defect in the article or the plaintiff's own misuse of it.[50]

(iv) *Intermediate examination.* As originally formulated by Lord Atkin the principle applies where there is " no reasonable possibility of intermediate examination." If, then, the plaintiff himself actually knows of the danger and disregards it the defendant is not liable [51]

---

[46] [1936] A.C. 85.
[47] *Ibid.* at pp. 106–107.
[48] [1936] 1 All E.R. 283. *Cf.* Mason v. *Williams & Williams Ltd.* [1955] 1 W.L.R. 549.
[49] *Davie* v. *New Merton Board Mills Ltd.* [1957] 2 Q.B. 368, 378–379, *per* Ashworth J. The manufacturers' liability was not in issue on appeal: [1959] A.C. 604.
[50] If both are causes, then damages should be apportioned under the Law Reform (Contributory Negligence) Act 1945, as in *Griffiths* v. *Arch Engineering Co. Ltd.* [1968] 3 All E.R. 217.
[51] *Farr* v. *Butters Bros. & Co.* [1932] 2 K.B. 606. Perhaps in cases of this kind the damages should now be apportioned under the Law Reform (Contributory Negligence) Act 1945. See Glanville Williams, *Joint Torts and Contributory Negligence,* p. 325.

unless, indeed, he should have foreseen that the plaintiff was bound to disregard it.[52] Nor is he liable if the danger was known to a third person whose duty it was to withdraw the chattel from circulation [53] or if he has given a sufficient warning to an intermediary who disregards it. In *Kubach* v. *Hollands* [54] a manufacturer sold the article (a chemical) to an intermediary with an express warning that it had to be tested before use. The intermediary resold the article without making the test and without passing on the warning. The manufacturer was not liable for the resulting injury, but the intermediary was. Decisions since *Donoghue* v. *Stevenson* have, however, made it clear that the mere existence of an opportunity for inspecting the goods after the defendant has parted with them is not enough to exonerate him. In *Griffiths* v. *Arch Engineering Co. Ltd.*[55] the plaintiff borrowed from the first defendants a portable grinding tool which had been lent to them by its owners, the second defendants. The tool was in a dangerous condition because an incorrect part had been fitted to it at some time by a servant of the owners, and the plaintiff was injured in consequence. Although the first defendants had an opportunity of examining the tool, the owners of it had no reason to suppose that an examination would actually be carried out and they were liable to the plaintiff.

There must, therefore, be at least a reasonable probability that an examination sufficient to reveal the danger will be carried out if the defendant is to escape liability. Even so, however, " it is difficult to see why a person who has created a dangerous situation should be held not liable on the ground that it has not been abated by another whose duty it was to do so." [56] With the modern reaction against theories of last opportunity and attributions of responsibility to one only of multiple causes,[57] it is submitted that the time has come to acknowledge that the question of intermediate examination is simply an aspect of breach of duty or of causation, as the case may be.[57a] In *Kubach* v. *Hollands* [58] there was no breach of duty on the part of the manufacturer because there was nothing wrong in his putting his product into circulation with a warning. In *Taylor* v. *Rover Co. Ltd.*,[59] on the other hand, where the chattel had been negligently manufactured but its defect was known to the plaintiff's employers before his

---

[52] *Denny* v. *Supplies and Transport Co. Ltd.* [1950] 2 K.B. 374.
[53] *Taylor* v. *Rover Co. Ltd.* [1966] 1 W.L.R. 1491.
[54] [1937] 3 All E.R. 907; *Holmes* v. *Ashford* [1950] 2 All E.R. 76; *Gledhill* v. *Liverpool Abattoir Utility Co. Ltd.* [1957] 1 W.L.R. 1028.
[55] [1968] 3 All E.R. 217; *Herschtal* v. *Stewart & Ardern Ltd.* [1940] 1 K.B. 155; *Andrews* v. *Hopkinson* [1957] 1 Q.B. 229. These cases are preferable to *Dransfield* v. *British, etc., Cables Ltd.* (1937) 54 T.L.R. 155, which Goddard L.J. has said was wrongly decided: *Haseldine* v. *Daw & Son Ltd.* [1941] 2 K.B. 343, 376. See also *Paine* v. *Colne Valley Electricity Co. Ltd.* [1938] 4 All E.R. 803; *Mason* v. *Williams & Williams Ltd.* [1955] 1 W.L.R. 549.
[56] Goodhart (1941) 57 L.Q.R. 163.
[57] Fleming, *Torts*, 4th ed., p. 446.
[57a] *The Diamantis Pateras* [1966] 1 Lloyd's Rep. 179, 188.
[58] *Supra.*
[59] [1966] 1 W.L.R. 1491.

accident and yet nothing was done about it, it was held that there had been a break in the chain of causation between the manufacturer's negligence and the plaintiff's damage. If there is both a breach of duty and a causal connection between the negligence and the damage, then it is submitted, the fact that there was even a probability of intermediate examination should not be treated as automatically exonerating the defendant altogether; and this seems to be the result of the most recent cases.[60]

(v) *Extension to containers, etc.* The duty of reasonable care extends not only to the manufacture, erection or repair of the product itself but also to any container,[61] package or pipe,[62] in which it is distributed, and to the labels, directions or instructions for use that accompany it.[63]

(vi) *Burden of proof.* The duty owed is that of reasonable care[64] and the burden of proving negligence is on the plaintiff. In *Donoghue* v. *Stevenson*[65] itself Lord Macmillan said that in a case such as that there was no justification for applying the maxim *res ipsa loquitur*, but whether the maxim may be invoked or not, the question in each case is whether the plaintiff has given sufficient evidence to justify the inference of negligence against the defendant. He is not required to specify what the defendant did wrong[66] and, indeed, any other rule would stultify the principle of *Donoghue* v. *Stevenson*, for normally it will be impossible for a plaintiff to bring evidence of particular negligent acts or omissions occurring in the defendant's manufacturing processes. In *Mason* v. *Williams & Williams Ltd.*[67] the plaintiff was injured while using a cold chisel manufactured by the defendants and which was too hard for its purpose. Finnemore J. accepted that *res ipsa loquitur* could

---

[60] *Power* v. *Bedford Motor Co.* [1959] I.R. 391; *Voli* v. *Inglewood Shire Council* [1963] Qd.R. 256 (H.Ct. of Australia); *Clay* v. *A. J. Crump & Sons Ltd.* [1964] 1 Q.B. 533. If the plaintiff himself neglects to use an opportunity of examination which he could reasonably be expected to use, the case is one of contributory negligence. If an intermediary is guilty of similar neglect, the case is one for the apportionment of responsibility between several defendants under the Law Reform (Married Women and Tortfeasors) Act 1935. See also Salmond, *Torts*, 16th ed., pp. 313–315; Fleming, *Torts*, 4th ed., pp. 446–447.

[61] *Donoghue* v. *Stevenson* [1932] A.C. 585, *per* Lord Atkin, who, at p. 595, disapproved of Horridge J.'s decision in *Bates* v. *Batey & Co.* [1913] 3 K.B. 351; *ibid.* at p. 604, *per* Lord Thankerton; *ibid.* at pp. 616–617, *per* Lord Macmillan.

[62] *Barnes* v. *Irwell Valley Water Board* [1938] 2 All E.R. 650.

[63] *Watson* v. *Buckley* [1940] 1 All E.R. 174; *Holmes* v. *Ashford* [1950] 2 All E.R. 76; *Vacwell Engineering Co. Ltd.* v. *B.D.H. Chemicals Ltd.* [1971] 1 Q.B. 88.

[64] A manufacturer is not liable on the ground only that an independent contractor employed by him had been negligent: *Taylor* v. *Rover Co. Ltd.* [1966] 1 W.L.R. 1491.

[65] [1932] A.C. at p. 622. The dictum was clearly *obiter*. Cf. *Chapronière* v. *Mason* (1905) 21 T.L.R. 633; Fleming, *Torts*, 4th ed., pp. 447–449.

[66] *Grant* v. *Australian Knitting Mills Ltd.* [1936] A.C. 85, *ante*, p. 208. " If excess sulphites were left in the garment, that could only be because someone was at fault. The appellant is not required to lay his finger on the exact person in all the chain who was responsible, or to specify what he did wrong. Negligence is found as a matter of inference from the existence of the defects taken in conjunction with all the known circumstances ": *ibid.* at p. 101, *per* Lord Wright. It may be observed that the phrase *res ipsa loquitur* appears nowhere in the opinion.

[67] [1955] 1 W.L.R. 549; *Davie* v. *New Merton Board Mills Ltd.* [1957] 2 Q.B. 368. Cf. *Evans* v. *Triplex Safety Glass Ltd.* [1936] 1 All E.R. 283; *Moorhead* v. *Thomas Smith & Sons Ltd.* [1963] 1 Lloyd's Rep. 164.

not be invoked but held that since the plaintiff had established that nothing had happened to the chisel after it left the defendants' factory which could have caused the excessive hardness, the defendants' negligence was established. It is suggested that the plaintiff will generally discharge his burden of proof by showing that the article was defective and that, on a balance of probabilities, the defect arose in the course of manufacture [68] by the defendant.[69] It may be, however, that the defendant can rebut the inference of negligence by proving that he did exercise reasonable care, even though he cannot affirmatively prove that the defect arose after the article left his hands.[70] The duty is not to ensure that the goods are perfect but to take reasonable care to see that there exists no defect which is likely to cause injury.[71]

---

[68] Or repair, etc, according to the business of the defendant.

[69] Whether this is described as the application of *res ipsa loquitur* or not seems to be a mere matter of terminology. See *ante*, pp. 78–79.

[70] *Daniels* v. *White & Sons* [1938] 4 All E.R. 258. Defendants manufactured lemonade and a consumer was injured by some carbolic acid which, for some unknown reason, had got into the bottle. Held not liable, for they had established " a foolproof method " of filling and cleaning the bottles and adequate supervision. Reconciliation of this case with *Grant* v. *Australian Knitting Mills Ltd., supra,* is difficult. For criticism, see Goodhart (1939) 55 L.Q.R. 6; Anon., *ibid.* 352.

[71] *Daniels* v. *White & Sons, supra,* at p. 261, *per* Lewis J. Although the law has advanced quite rapidly since *Donoghue* v. *Stevenson,* that liability for damage caused by defective chattels should continue to be governed by the law of negligence does not command universal approval. See *e.g.,* Weir, *Casebook on Tort,* 3rd ed., at pp. 21–22; Jolowicz, " The Protection of the Consumer and Purchaser of Goods under English Law " (1969) 32 M.L.R. 1. *Cf.* the Final Report of the Committee on Consumer Protection (Cmnd. 1781) 1962, § 417. In the United States there has been a considerable development in the field of " products liability " leading to the imposition of strict liability and liability for " breach of warranty " independently of contract. See Prosser, " The Fall of the Citadel (Strict Liability to the Consumer) " (1966) 50 Minn.L.Rev. 791. For a lucid account of the American position, see Pasley, " The Protection of the Purchaser and Consumer under the Law of the U.S.A." (1969) 32 M.L.R. 241.

CHAPTER 12

LIABILITY FOR STATEMENTS

WORDS, especially if untrue, are capable of causing loss in several different ways. They may injure a man's reputation, if they are defamatory and published to a third party; they may cause direct injury by shock to the person to whom they are addressed; they may cause him to act in reliance upon them and suffer loss or damage as a result; or they may cause him to act in reliance upon them and so cause loss or damage to someone else. The first of these cases is covered by the tort of defamation which is the subject of a separate chapter [1] while the second is exemplified by *Wilkinson* v. *Downton*,[2] to which we have already referred.[3] In this chapter we are concerned mainly with the other types of case.

Since the famous case of *Pasley* v. *Freeman* [4] in 1789, it has been the rule that A is liable in tort to B if he knowingly or recklessly (*i.e.*, not caring whether it is true or false) makes a false statement to B with intent that it shall be acted upon by B, who does act upon it and thereby suffers damage. This is the tort of deceit, and for liability in deceit the defendant must make the statement with knowledge of its falsity or at least reckless whether it is true or false.[5] It was for long thought that this meant that there could be no liability in tort for a false statement honestly made, however negligent its maker may have been and however disastrous its consequences: a careless man is not a dishonest one. Now, however, the House of Lords has held that there may in certain circumstances be a duty of care upon the maker of a statement,[6] and thus that a person may be liable for a false statement honestly but negligently made. Such liability cannot be brought under the tort of deceit—it is liability for negligence and not for fraud—but its existence has a profound bearing on liability for statements as a whole. As we have seen,[7] the plaintiff in an action for damages does not have to specify the particular tort on which he wishes to rely and all that is necessary is that he should prove the facts required for liability under

---

[1] Chap. 13, *post.*

[2] [1897] 2 Q.B. 57.

[3] *Ante*, p. 43. There seems no reason in principle why negligence by words leading directly to nervous shock should not be actionable, but cases will be rare. For an example, see *Furniss* v. *Fitchett* [1958] N.Z.L.R. 396 (Sup.Ct. of N.Z.), and *cf. Guay* v. *Sun Publishing Co.* [1952] 2 D.L.R. 479 (Sup.Ct. of Canada).

[4] (1789) 3 T.R. 51; Weir, *Casebook on Tort*, 3rd ed., p. 459.

[5] *Derry* v. *Peek* (1889) 14 App.Cas. 337; Weir, *Casebook on Tort*, 3rd ed., p. 461. In one instance, the law allows (but does not compel) the making of a false statement: Rehabilitation of Offenders Act 1974, s. 4 (2).

[6] *Hedley Byrne & Co. Ltd.* v. *Heller & Partners Ltd.* [1964] A.C. 465. See, too, the Misrepresentation Act 1967 (c. 7), s. 2.

[7] *Ante*, pp. 29–30.

at least one tort. If, therefore, there may be liability in negligence it is of little more than academic interest that absence of fraudulent intent is fatal to a claim founded on deceit. Nevertheless, because the scope of liability for negligent misstatement is still uncertain it is convenient first to set out briefly the requirements of deceit.

ESSENTIALS OF DECEIT

The five things that the plaintiff has to establish in a common law action of deceit may be summarised as follows [8]:

1. There must be a representation of fact made by words or conduct.
2. The representation must be made with the intention that it should be acted upon by the plaintiff, or by a class of persons which includes the plaintiff, in the manner which resulted in damage to him.
3. It must be proved that the plaintiff has acted upon the false statement.
4. It must be proved that the plaintiff suffered damage by so doing.[9]
5. The representation must be made with knowledge that it is false. It must be wilfully false, or at least made in the absence of any genuine belief that it is true.

1. A false statement of fact

Representations

The statement may, of course, be oral or written. It may also be implied from conduct. If the defendant deliberately acts in a manner calculated to deceive the plaintiff and the other elements of the tort are present, the defendant is as much liable for deceit as if he had expressly made a false statement of fact.[10] Subject to what is said below,[11] however, mere silence, however morally wrong, will not support an action for deceit.[12]

Promises and other statements of intention

It is commonly said that mere promises are not statements of fact, but this is misleading, for every promise involves a statement of present intention as to future conduct. " There must be a misstatement of an existing fact: but the state of a man's mind is as much a fact as the state of his digestion." [13] If, then, I make a promise believing that I

---

[8] *Bradford Building Society* v. *Borders* [1941] 2 All E.R. 205, 211, *per* Lord Maugham.
[9] The damage is the gist of the action: *Smith* v. *Chadwick* (1884) 9 App.Cas. 187, 196, *per* Lord Blackburn; *Briess* v. *Woolley* [1954] A.C. 332.
[10] *Ward* v. *Hobbs* (1878) 4 App.Cas. 13, 26, *per* Lord O'Hagan; *Bradford Building Society* v. *Borders* [1942] 1 All E.R. 205, 211, *per* Lord Maugham; Clerk & Lindsell, *Torts*, 13th ed., p. 908; Salmond, *Torts*, 16th ed., p. 394. For a criminal case, see *R.* v. *Barnard* (1837) 7 C. & P. 784 and Smith, *The Law of Theft*, 2nd ed., pp. 74 *et seq.*
[11] *Post*, pp. 215–217.
[12] *Bradford Building Society* v. *Borders, supra*, at p. 211, *per* Lord Maugham, citing *Peek* v. *Gurney* (1873) L.R. 6 H.L. 377, 390, *per* Lord Chelmsford; *ibid.* at p. 403, *per* Lord Cairns.
[13] *Edgington* v. *Fitzmaurice* (1885) 29 Ch.D. 459, 483, *per* Bowen L.J.; *Clydesdale Bank Ltd.* v. *Paton* [1896] A.C. 381, 394; *per* Lord Herschell. *Cf. ibid.* at p. 397, *per* Lord Davey.

shall fulfil it, the reason that I am not liable for deceit if I do not fulfil it is not that my promise was not a statement of fact, but that the statement of fact involved in the promise was true. If at the time I made it I had no intention of fulfilling my promise, I may be liable for deceit. So in *Edgington* v. *Fitzmaurice* [14] directors of a company were held liable for deceit in procuring the public to subscribe for debentures by falsely stating in a prospectus that the loan secured by the debentures was for the purpose of completing buildings of the company, purchasing horses and vans and developing the trade of the company; in fact the directors intended to use it for paying off pressing liabilities. [15]

Opinion

A statement of opinion frequently carries within itself a statement of fact. A man who says " I believe X to be honest " is making a statement of fact as to his state of mind, and if it is untrue there is no reason why, if the other requirements of the tort are met, he should not be held liable for deceit. Often also an expression of opinion carries the implication that the person expressing it has reasonable grounds for it, and where this is not the case he may be guilty of a misstatement of fact. [16]

Statements of law

As a matter of general principle a misstatement of law ought to be a sufficient misstatement of fact for the purposes of deceit provided at least that the parties are not on an equal footing with respect to knowledge of the law or to general intelligence. [17] A great many statements which we should not hesitate to describe as statements of fact involve inferences from legal rules [18] and the distinction between law and fact is by no means as precise as might at first appear. So, in *West London Commercial Bank Ltd.* v. *Kitson*, [19] where directors of a company, knowing that the private Act of Parliament which incorpor-

---

[14] *Supra*; Weir, *Casebook on Tort*, 3rd ed., p. 463.

[15] There is said to be an exception to this, namely, that a purchaser may freely state his intention to pay no more than a certain sum or a vendor his intention to accept no less than a certain sum: Rolle Abr.101, pl. 16 (1598); *Vernon* v. *Keys* (1810) 12 East 632; affd. *sub. nom. Vernon* v. *Keyes* (1812) 4 Taunt. 488. The exception must not, however, be carried too far: Pollock in 11 R.R.Pref. vi–vii, and *Torts*, 15th ed., p. 213, n. 6; *Haygarth* v. *Wearing* (1871) L.R. 12 Eq. 320.

[16] *Brown* v. *Raphael* [1958] Ch. 636, a case of innocent misrepresentation in contract. *Cf. Haycraft* v. *Creasy* (1801) 2 East 92, and see Pollock, *Torts*, 15th ed., p. 212, n. 12.

[17] Direct authority for this proposition is lacking but the view stated in the text is shared by Clerk & Lindsell, *Torts*, 13th ed., p. 906; Salmond, *Torts*, 16th ed., p. 396; Fleming, *Torts*, 4th ed., p. 557; Street, *Torts*, 5th ed., p. 378. A deliberate false statement of law is sufficient for the offence of obtaining property by deception: Theft Act 1968 (c. 60), s. 15 (4).

[18] " There is not a single fact connected with personal *status* that does not, more or less, involve a question of law. If you state that a man is the eldest son of a marriage, you state a question of law, because you must know that there has been a valid marriage, and that that man was the first-born son after the marriage. . . . Therefore, to state it is not a representation of fact seems to arise from a confusion of ideas. It is not the less a fact because that fact involves some knowledge or relation of law ": *Eaglesfield* v. *Marquis of Londonderry* (1876) 4 Ch.D. 693, 703, *per* Jessel M.R.

[19] (1884) 13 Q.B.D. 360.

ated the company gave them no legal power to accept bills of exchange, nevertheless represented to the plaintiff that they had such authority there was held to have been deceit. " Suppose I were to say I have a private Act of Parliament which gives me power to do so and so. Is not that an assertion that I have such an Act of Parliament? It appears to me to be as much a representation of a matter of fact as if I had said I have a particular bound copy of ' Johnson's Dictionary.' " [20] If the representation is of a pure proposition of law and not a deduction from a rule of law there may be greater difficulty in treating it as a statement of fact, but there is no reason for holding that a solicitor, for example, can never be liable in deceit for a misstatement of law to his client.[21] It is not easy to see what argument can be produced the other way. To urge that everyone is presumed to know the law is to carry into the law of deceit a distinction between law and fact which, artificial enough in any event,[22] was never invented for the purpose of shielding swindlers. On the other hand, professional lawyers dealing with each other at arm's length would doubtless be deemed equal and if one falsely alleged to the other something purporting to be a pure proposition of law, this could scarcely ground an action for deceit.[23]

Silence

Some sort of statement or representation there must be, but a probable qualification of this is that, where a man is under a legal duty to speak and deliberately holds his tongue with the intention of inducing the other party to act upon the belief that he did not speak because he had nothing to say, that is fraud.[24] What constitutes such a duty is a matter of law. It often arises under a contract and most of the decisions on innocent misrepresentation by reason of such silence, and most of the dicta on fraudulent misrepresentation from the same cause, are on contract.[25] But the duty may arise in other ways and, whatever its origin may be, there is no reason to think that breach of it cannot be deceit if the other essentials of that tort are present. Moreover, *suppressio veri* may amount to *suggestio falsi* if it is " such a partial and fragmentary statement of fact, as that the withholding of that which is not stated makes that which is stated absolutely false " [26]; *e.g.*, where a husband

---

[20] *Ibid.* at p. 363, *per* Bowen L.J.

[21] There is, of course, a contract between solicitor and client, and a solicitor may be liable for a negligent misstatement: *Otter* v. *Church, Adams, Tatham & Co.* [1953] Ch. 280.

[22] For an extreme statement of the fiction, see *Rashdall* v. *Ford* (1866) L.R. 2 Eq. 750, 754–755, *per* Page-Wood V.-C.

[23] One professional lawyer would not normally act in a professional capacity in reliance upon another's statement of law, and an action between such persons founded upon a false statement of law would therefore fail on the ground that the plaintiff did not rely upon the statement: *post*, pp. 218–219.

[24] Lord Blackburn in *Brownlie* v. *Campbell* (1880) 5 App.Cas. 925, 950.

[25] Kerr, *Fraud and Mistake*, 7th ed., pp. 50 *et seq.*

[26] *Peek* v. *Gurney* (1873) L.R. 6 H.L. 377, 403, *per* Lord Cairns: " Half the truth will sometimes amount to a real falsehood ": *ibid.* at p. 392, *per* Lord Chelmsford; *Arkwright* v. *Newbold* (1881) 17 Ch.D. 301, 317–318, *per* James L.J.; *Briess* v. *Woolley* [1955] A.C. 333.

whose income is £800 a year is under agreement to pay half to his wife, writes to her saying: " I send £300, half my income "—that would be a lie. It makes no difference if he sends her £300 and says nothing, for it would be an implied statement that it is half his income, and he is guilty of deceit.[27]

Statements which prove to be false. What is the position of A, who makes a true statement to B and then discovers, before B acts upon it, that it has become false? Does the law permit A to remain silent or does it compel him to correct B's false impression under pain of an action of deceit? It is submitted that the latter answer is in general correct. The tort of deceit is not complete when the representation is made. It only becomes complete when the misrepresentation—not having been corrected in the meantime—is acted upon by the representee.[28] The proper question in any case, therefore, is whether the statement was false when it was acted upon, not when it was made,[29] and so a person whose true statement becomes false to his knowledge before it is acted upon should be liable in deceit if he does not correct it.[30]

Closely akin to this is another problem. Suppose that A's statement was false from the very beginning, but that when he made it he honestly believed it to be true and then discovers later and before B has acted upon it that it is false. Must he acquaint B with this? Here, again, equity has a decided answer, whereas the common law is short of any direct decision. In *Reynell* v. *Sprye* [31] a deed was cancelled by the Court of Chancery because A had not communicated the falsity of his belief.[32] As to the wider liability to an action of deceit, it might be inferred from a dictum of Lord Blackburn that it exists.[33]

However we treat the question, there is no substantial difference between the two problems just put,[34] and the weight of the leading textbooks is decidedly in favour of the view that A is guilty of deceit in both of them if he withholds from B the further information.[35] This certainly ought to be the law where there is plenty of time to retract the statement and where the result of not doing so is certain to result in widespread loss or damage (as in the case of a company prospectus) or in

---

[27] *Legh* v. *Legh* (1930) 143 L.T. 151, 152, *per* MacKinnon L.J.
[28] *Briess* v. *Woolley* [1954] A.C. 333, 353, *per* Lord Tucker; *ibid.* at p. 349, *per* Lord Reid; Weir, *Casebook on Tort*, 3rd ed., p. 465.
[29] Spencer Bower, *Actionable Misrepresentations*, 3rd ed., p. 84.
[30] See *Incledon* v. *Watson* (1862) 2 F. & F. 841; *With* v. *O'Flanagan* [1936] Ch. 575, 584, *per* Lord Wright; *Bradford Building Society* v. *Borders* [1941] 2 All E.R. 205, 220. *Cf. Arkwright* v. *Newbold* (1881) 17 Ch.D. 301, 325, *per* Cotton L.J.; 329, *per* James L.J.
[31] (1852) 1·De G.M. & G. 660, 708–709.
[32] See, too, Jessel M.R. in *Redgrave* v. *Hurd* (1881) 20 Ch.D. 1, 12–13.
[33] *Brownlie* v. *Campbell* (1880) 5 App.Cas. 925, 950.
[34] Except that in the latter case the statement was false from the moment it was made, while in the former it was not. Since it is impossible for a man to make a false statement of his intention while believing it to be true, it would appear that the qualification stated below has no application to the solution of the second problem put.
[35] Pollock, *Torts*, 15th ed., pp. 216–217; Salmond, *Torts*, 16th ed., p. 395; Clerk & Lindsell, *Torts*, 13th ed., pp. 915–916; Fleming, *Torts*, 4th ed., p. 555.

physical danger or serious business loss to even one person.[36] But it must not be taken too far. As we have seen, a false statement of intention is a sufficient misrepresentation of fact to support an action of deceit, and the difference between a false statement of intention and a breach of a promise is that in the latter case the promisor believes what he says about his intention. The subsequent breach of promise shows, however, that at some time his intention must have changed, but it does not follow that his failure to inform the promisee of his change of intention is fraudulent. Suppose that B has booked (but not paid for) an unreserved seat on A's motor coach at 9 a.m., and that A tells him correctly that he intends to start the journey at 11 a.m. Suppose that A, finding that the vehicle is full by 10.30, starts then without informing B of his change of plans, because it would take nearly half an hour to find B. Here, A has certainly committed a breach of contract, but it is wrong to style his silence as to the changed circumstances deceit, even though it is admittedly intentional. It is really no more than a churlish indifference to a breach of contract.[37]

One more possible case of silence raises no difficulty. If A knowingly makes a false statement to B, but before B acts upon it subsequent events have turned the statement into a true one, this is not deceit. Thus in *Ship* v. *Crosskill*,[38] a false allegation in a prospectus, that applications for more than half the capital of the company had been subscribed, had become true before the plaintiff made his application for shares, and it was held that there was no misrepresentation for which relief could be given to him. " If false when made but true when acted upon there is no misrepresentation." [39]

2. The intent

The statement must be made with intent that the plaintiff shall act upon it. So long as that is satisfied, it need not be made to him either literally or in particular. In *Langridge* v. *Levy*,[40] the seller of a defective gun which he had falsely and knowingly warranted to be sound, was held liable to the plaintiff who was injured by its bursting, although it was the plaintiff's father to whom the gun had been sold, but who had acquainted the seller with the fact that he intended his sons to use it. If, however, the statement is made to a limited class of persons, no one outside that class can sue upon it. Thus a company prospectus is ordinarily confined in its scope to the original shareholders. For false statements in it they can sue, but purchasers

---

[36] It is submitted that the tort is not committed if there is no time for the statement to be retracted or corrected before it is acted upon.

[37] See Clerk & Lindsell, *Torts*, 13th ed., p. 904.

[38] (1870) L.R. 10 Eq. 73.

[39] *Briess* v. *Woolley* [1954] A.C. 333, 353, *per* Lord Tucker.

[40] (1837) 2 M. & W. 519; 4 M. & W. 337. See Clerk & Lindsell, *Torts*, 13th ed., pp. 921–922. *Cf. Gross* v. *Lewis Hillman Ltd.* [1970] Ch. 445.

of the shares from them cannot do so [41]; but circumstances may quite possibly make the prospectus fraudulent with respect even to them, as where it is supplemented by further lying statements intended to make persons who are not original allottees of the shares buy them in the market.[42] The intent need not be to cause damage to the plaintiff; it is enough that the plaintiff was intended to act on it and did act on it in the manner contemplated. The defendant is liable whether he actually intended damage to ensue or not.[43]

3. The plaintiff must rely on the statement

There is no such reliance and therefore no actionable deceit if the fraud consists in some defect in an article sold which is so obvious that the purchaser must have discovered it if he had inspected the article. In other words, if the defect is a patent one, and one of which the purchaser is as good a judge as the vendor, the vendor is not bound to point it out.[44] On the other hand, in *Central Ry. of Venezuela* v. *Kisch*,[45] directors of a company made deceitful statements in a prospectus and were held liable to a shareholder defrauded thereby, although the prospectus stated that certain documents could be inspected at the company's office and, if the shareholder had taken the trouble to do so, he would have discovered the fraud.[46] Indeed, if the fraud is not obvious, it will not help the defendant that he inserted an express clause in a contract with the plaintiff that the plaintiff must verify all representations for himself and not rely on their accuracy, for " such a clause might in some cases be part of a fraud, and might advance and disguise a fraud." [47]

It is to be noted, too, in this connection that knowledge of the plaintiff's agent is not to be imputed to the plaintiff; *e.g.*, where a house-agent acting for the plaintiff knew that a prospective tenant of the plaintiff's house was a woman of immoral character, but the plaintiff was unaware of this.[48]

---

[41] *Peek* v. *Gurney* (1873) L.R. 6 H.L. 377. But see Gower, *Modern Company Law*, 3rd ed., pp. 320–322, where it is suggested that the rule in *Peek* v. *Gurney* may no longer be generally applicable. The question of to whom it was contemplated the false statement would be communicated is one of fact and if A makes a false statement to B with the intention that C will hear of it and act upon it, he cannot escape liability by telling B that it is for B's private use only: *Commercial Banking Co. of Sydney Ltd.* v. *R. H. Brown &. Co.* [1972] 2 Lloyd's Rep. 360 (H.Ct. of Aust.).
[42] *Andrews* v. *Mockford* [1896] 1 Q.B. 372.
[43] *Polhill* v. *Walter* (1832) 3 B. & Ad. 114; *Edgington* v. *Fitzmaurice* (1885) 29 Ch.D. 459, 482; *Brown Jenkinson & Co. Ltd.* v. *Percy Dalton (London) Ltd.* [1957] 2 Q.B. 621.
[44] *Horsfall* v. *Thomas* (1862) 1 H. & C. 90. The application of this proposition to the facts has provoked a good deal of criticism, and Cockburn C.J. dissented altogether from *Horsfall* v. *Thomas* in an *obiter dictum* in *Smith* v. *Hughes* (1871) L.R. 6 Q.B. 597, 605, but in Pollock's opinion this dictum did not appear to have been followed, at any rate down to 1911, or to have commanded the assent of the profession: *Shepherd* v. *Croft* [1911] 1 Ch. 521, 530, n. 1.
[45] (1867) L.R. 2 H.L. 99.
[46] So, too, *Dobell* v. *Stevens* (1825) 3 B. & C. 623.
[47] *S. Pearson & Son Ltd.* v. *Dublin Corporation* [1907] A.C. 351, 360, *per* Lord Ashbourne.
[48] *Wells* v. *Smith* [1914] 3 K.B. 722.

Ambiguity

In the case of an ambiguous statement the plaintiff must prove (a) the sense in which he understood the statement; (b) that in that sense it was false; and (c) that the defendant intended him to understand it in that sense or deliberately made use of the ambiguity with the express purpose of deceiving him.[49] It does not follow because the defendant uses ambiguous language that he is conscious of the way in which the plaintiff will understand it. Unless the defendant " is conscious that it will be understood in a different manner from that in which he is honestly though blunderingly using it, he is not fraudulent. An honest blunder in the use of language is not dishonest." [50] An ambiguous statement must therefore be taken in the sense in which the defendant intended it to be understood, and however reasonable a plaintiff may be in attaching the untrue meaning to the statement, there is no deceit unless the defendant intended his words to be taken in that sense. " The question is not whether the defendant in any given case honestly believed the representation to be true in the sense assigned to it by the court on an objective consideration of its truth or falsity, but whether he honestly believed the representation to be true in the sense in which he understood it albeit erroneously when it was made." [51] In *Smith* v. *Chadwick*,[52] the prospectus of a company alleged that " the present value of the turnover or output of the entire works is over £1,000,000 sterling *per annum*." Did this mean that the works had *actually* turned out in one year produce worth more than a million, or at that rate *per* year? If so, it was untrue. Or did it mean only that the works were *capable* of turning out that amount of produce? If so, it was true. The plaintiff failed to prove that he had interpreted the words in the sense in which they were false, so he lost his action. On the question of the actual meaning of the statement, the noble and learned Lords were evenly divided,[53] but there is no doubt that if an allegation is deliberately put forth in an ambiguous form with the design of catching the plaintiff on that meaning of it which makes it false, it is fraudulent and indeed is aggravated by a shabby attempt to get the benefit of a fraud without incurring the responsibility.[54]

---

[49] *Smith* v. *Chadwick* (1884) 9 App.Cas. 187, 201, *per* Lord Blackburn; *Arkwright* v. *Newbold* (1881) 17 Ch.D. 301, 324, *per* Cotton L.J.

[50] *Angus* v. *Clifford* [1891] 2 Ch. 449, 472, *per* Bowen L.J.; *Smith* v. *Chadwick* (1882) 20 Ch.D. 27, 79, *per* Lindley L.J.; *Gross* v. *Lewis Hillman Ltd.* [1970] Ch. 445.

[51] *Akerhielm* v. *De Mare* [1959] A.C. 789, 805 (P.C.), *per* Lord Jenkins. This proposition is subject to the limitation that the meaning placed by the defendant on the representation may be so far removed from the sense in which it would be understood by any reasonable person as to make it impossible to hold that the defendant honestly understood the representation to bear the meaning claimed by him and honestly believed it in that sense to be true: *ibid.* Note that where liability for a negligent, as distinct from a fraudulent, misstatement is in issue, the important question concerns the sense in which the plaintiff, not the defendant, understood it: *W. B. Anderson & Sons Ltd.* v. *Rhodes (Liverpool) Ltd.* [1967] 2 All E.R. 850, 855–856, *per* Cairns J.

[52] (1884) 9 App.Cas. 187.

[53] Lord Selborne and Lord Bramwell thought that it had the first meaning, Lord Blackburn and Lord Watson that it had the second.

[54] *Ibid.* at p. 201, *per* Lord Blackburn.

4. Damage

The plaintiff must prove that he has suffered damage in consequence of acting upon the statement. Such damage will usually be financial but it may consist of personal injury or damage to property [55] and it has also been held that loss of possession of a regulated tenancy under the Rent Acts, even without actual financial loss, will suffice.[55a] In principle the plaintiff is entitled, so far as money can do it, to be put into the position in which he would have been if the fraudulent statement had not been made, not that in which he would have been if it had been true,[56] and the defendant must make reparation for all the actual losses which flow from his deceit. Where the plaintiff has been induced to buy property by a fraudulent representation, therefore, he may recover not only the difference between the price he paid and the actual value of the property at the time of the sale [57] but also any consequential loss which he may have suffered so long as this is not too remote.[58] Moreover, it seems, such damage will only be too remote if it was the result of the plaintiff's own unreasonable behaviour, for example in trying for too long to revive a moribund business or, presumably, if it was the result of a *nova causa interveniens*: it is not too remote merely because it was not reasonably foreseeable by the defendant.[59] On the other hand the plaintiff must, of course, give credit for any benefit he may have received from the transaction into which he entered as a result of the deceit.

5. The statement must be made with knowledge of its falsity or recklessly

This rule is the result of the decision in *Derry* v. *Peek*,[60] where the House of Lords made it clear that blundering but honest belief in an allegation cannot be deceit. For liability in deceit the defendant must either know his statement to be false or else must be reckless, *i.e.*,

---

[55] *Langridge* v. *Levy* (1837) 2 M. & W. 519; (1838) 4 M. & W. 337; *Burrows* v. *Rhodes* [1899] 1 Q.B. 816.

[55a] *Mafo* v. *Adams* [1970] 1 Q.B. 548.

[56] The rule thus differs from that governing the damages recoverable for a breach of contract and a plaintiff in deceit cannot normally recover in respect of prospective gains which he was expecting: *McConnel* v. *Wright* [1903] 1 Ch. 546, 554–555, *per* Collins M.R.; *Bango* v. *Holt* (1971) 21 D.L.R. (3d) 66.

[57] In *Hornal* v. *Neuberger Products Ltd.* [1957] 1 Q.B. 247, the plaintiff was induced to buy a lathe by the fraudulent representation that it was fit for immediate use. Although it was worth in its actual condition what the plaintiff had paid for it, he was put to seven weeks' delay in preparing it for use and was awarded damages for this delay.

[58] *Doyle* v. *Olby (Ironmongers) Ltd.* [1969] 2 Q.B. 158, following a dictum of Lord Atkin in *Clark* v. *Urquhart* [1930] A.C. 28, 67–68 and McGregor, *Damages*, 13th ed., pp. 909–916. See also *N.Z. Refrigerating Co.* v. *Scott* [1969] N.Z.L.R. 30 (N.Z. Sup.Ct.); *Parna* v. *G. & S. Properties* (1969) 5 D.L.R. (3d) 315 (Ont.C.A.).

[59] *Doyle* v. *Olby (Ironmongers) Ltd.*, *supra*, at p. 167, *per* Lord Denning M.R.; *ibid.* at p. 168, *per* Winn L.J. Apparently the decision in *The Wagon Mound* [1961] A.C. 388 (*ante*, pp. 94–95) does not apply in cases of deceit. This seems correct, but *The Wagon Mound* was not cited in *Doyle* v. *Olby (Ironmongers) Ltd.* In an appropriate case damages may also be recovered for such matters as worry, strain, anxiety, unhappiness and physical inconvenience; *Doyle* v. *Olby (Ironmongers) Ltd.*, *supra*, at p. 170, *per* Winn L.J.; *Mafo* v. *Adams* [1970] 1 Q.B. 548. As to exemplary damages, see *post*, p. 556, n. 30.

[60] (1889) 14 App.Cas. 337; Weir, *Casebook on Tort*, 3rd ed., p. 461.

without knowing whether his statement is true or false he must be consciously indifferent whether it is the one or the other.[61] The facts of *Derry* v. *Peek* were that the directors of a tramway company issued a prospectus in which they stated that they had parliamentary powers to use steam in propelling their trams. In fact the grant of such powers was subject to the consent of the Board of Trade. The directors honestly but mistakenly believed the giving of this consent to be a merely formal matter; it was, however, refused. The company was wound up in consequence and the plaintiff, who had bought shares in it on the faith of the prospectus, instituted an action for deceit against the directors. The House of Lords, reversing the decision of the Court of Appeal, gave judgment for the defendants, holding that a false statement made carelessly and without reasonable ground for believing it to be true could not be fraud, though it might furnish evidence of it. A careless man is not a dishonest man and no amount of argument will prove he is one.

LIABILITY FOR NEGLIGENT MISSTATEMENT

Derry v. *Peek* settled that liability for deceit is liability for dishonest and not for careless statements, but for many years the case was treated as authority for more than that, for the House of Lords was taken to have held that there could be no tortious liability of any kind for a misstatement so long only as it was not dishonest. Earlier there had been at least one case in which damages for a negligent misstatement had been awarded,[62] but this was later held by the Court of Appeal to be inconsistent with and overruled by *Derry* v. *Peek*.[63] As late as 1950 Devlin J. was prepared to state categorically that " negligent misstatement can never give rise to a cause of action." [64] After *Donoghue* v. *Stevenson* [65] had been decided, more than one attempt was made to argue that the position had been changed,[66] but apart from evoking a notable dissenting judgment from Denning L.J.,[67]

---

[61] " A man may be said to know a fact when once he has been told it and pigeonholed it somewhere in his brain where it is more or less accessible in case of need. In another sense of the word a man knows a fact only when he is fully conscious of it. For an action of deceit there must be knowledge in the narrower sense; and conscious knowledge of falsity must always amount to wickedness and dishonesty ": *Armstrong* v. *Strain* [1951] 1 T.L.R. 856, 871, *per* Devlin J. For recklessness, see *Angus* v. *Clifford* [1891] 2 Ch. 449, 471, *per* Bowen L.J.; *Derry* v. *Peek* (1889) 14 App.Cas. 337, 371, *per* Lord Herschell.

[62] *Cann* v. *Willson* (1888) 39 Ch.D. 39.

[63] *Le Lievre* v. *Gould* [1893] 1 Q.B. 491. See also *Angus* v. *Clifford* [1891] 2 Ch. 449; *Low* v. *Bouverie* [1891] 3 Ch. 82.

[64] *Heskell* v. *Continental Express Ltd.* [1950] 1 All E.R. 1033, 1042. The statement was approved by Cohen L.J., subject to the qualification that there could be liability where there is a contractual or a fiduciary relationship: *Candler* v. *Crane, Christmas & Co.* [1951] 2 K.B. 164, 198. See now *Hedley Byrne & Co. Ltd.* v. *Heller & Partners Ltd.* [1964] A.C. 465, 532, *per* Lord Devlin.

[65] [1932] A.C. 562.

[66] *Old Gate Estates Ltd.* v. *Toplis* [1939] 3 All E.R. 209; *Candler* v. *Crane, Christmas & Co.* [1951] 2 K.B. 164.

[67] *Candler* v. *Crane, Christmas & Co., supra.*

these attempts met with no success. Only Parliament it was thought, could introduce a duty to take care in making statements, as it did in the case of company directors by the Directors Liability Act 1890,[68] passed a year after the decision in *Derry* v. *Peek*. Other statutory duties of care in making statements also exist, the most important of which is contained in the Misrepresentation Act 1967.[69] Section 2 (1) provides that where a person has entered into a contract after a misrepresentation has been made to him by another party to the contract, then, if the representor would have been liable in damages if the representation had been made fraudulently, he shall be so liable unless he proves that he had reasonable grounds to believe and did believe up to the time the contract was made that the representation was true.[70] On the other hand, as long ago as 1914, in *Nocton* v. *Lord Ashburton*,[71] the House of Lords itself pointed out that *Derry* v. *Peek* had not ruled out every form of liability independent of statute but that for fraud. Not only could there be liability in contract,[72] but it could exist in equity as well. A fiduciary relationship, such as that between solicitor and client, is capable of giving rise to a duty of care in making statements for breach of which the plaintiff may recover compensation.

It is certain that *Nocton* v. *Lord Ashburton* was decided in equity and not at common law,[73] but fortunately for the subsequent development of the law the distinction between law and equity was blurred throughout the speeches of their Lordships and even an admittedly wrong order for an inquiry into damages—a common law remedy— was allowed to stand on the ground that its replacement by the correct order for equitable redress would not in the circumstances make any difference.[74] Strictly speaking, *Nocton* v. *Lord Ashburton* decides only that where a relationship recognised by equity as fiduciary [75] exists, an equitable remedy may be given for misstatement, and it is probable that the House of Lords in that case did not consider that a common law duty of care could exist without a contract. Fifty years later,

---

[68] 53 & 54 Vict. c. 64. Its provisions are now contained in the Companies Act 1948 (11 & 12 Geo. 6, c. 38), s. 43.

[69] c. 7. Another example is contained in the Land Charges Act 1925, s. 17. See *Ministry of Housing* v. *Sharp* [1970] 2 Q.B. 223. (See now L.C.A. 1972, s. 10 (3).)

[70] Discussion of this provision must be sought in works on the law of contract. See, *e.g.*, Cheshire and Fifoot, *The Law of Contract*, 8th ed., p. 256; Treitel, *The Law of Contract*, 3rd ed., pp. 289–292; Atiyah and Treitel, "Misrepresentation Act 1967" (1967) 30 M.L.R. 369. Whether or not the situation envisaged by the subsection is covered also by the common law since the decision in *Hedley Byrne & Co. Ltd.* v. *Heller & Partners Ltd.* [1964] A.C. 465, the liability which it creates is not identical with that created by the common law: Treitel, *ibid.* The Act was passed to give effect (subject to certain modifications) to the Tenth Report of the Law Reform Committee (Cmnd. 1782) which was presented in July 1962, *i.e.*, before the House of Lords' decision in *Hedley Byrne*.

[71] [1914] A.C. 932.

[72] This was always admitted.

[73] The clearest speech from this point of view is that of Lord Dunedin, but see also, *e.g.*, *per* Viscount Haldane L.C. at pp. 946, 954, 957.

[74] *Per* Viscount Haldane L.C. at p. 958; *per* Lord Dunedin at p. 965. In *Woods* v. *Martins Bank Ltd.* [1959] 1 Q.B. 55, Salmon J. held that a fiduciary relationship existed and awarded the plaintiff damages for misstatement.

[75] See Sealy, "Some Principles of Fiduciary Obligation" [1963] C.L.J. 119, 137–140.

however, in *Hedley Byrne & Co. Ltd.* v. *Heller & Partners Ltd.*,[76] the House was able to rely on *Nocton* v. *Lord Ashburton* as showing that *Derry* v. *Peek* governed only liability in deceit and so that they were not precluded from holding that a tortious duty of care in making statements might exist. In the words of Lord Devlin,[77] "There was in *Derry* v. *Peek*, as the report of the case shows, no plea of innocent or negligent representation and so their Lordships did not make any pronouncement on that. I am bound to say that had there been such a plea I am sure that the House would have rejected it. As Lord Haldane said, their Lordships must ' be taken to have thought ' that there was no liability in negligence.[78] But what your Lordships may be taken to have thought, though it may exercise great influence upon those who thereafter have to form their own opinion on the subject, is not the law of England. It is impossible to say how their Lordships would have formulated the principle if they had laid one down. They might have made it general or they might have confined it to the facts of the case. They might have made an exception of the sort indicated by Lord Herschell [79] or they might not. This is speculation. All that is certain is that on this point the House laid down no law at all."

The facts of *Hedley Byrne & Co. Ltd.* v. *Heller & Partners Ltd.*[80] were that the plaintiffs, who were advertising agents, were anxious to know whether they could safely give credit to a company, Easipower, on whose behalf they had entered into various advertising contracts, and they therefore sought bankers' references about Easipower. For this purpose the plaintiffs' bankers approached the defendants, who were Easipower's bankers, and on two occasions the defendants gave favourable references. These were passed on to the plaintiffs by their bankers and, although the defendants did not know who the plaintiffs were and had in fact marked their communications to the plaintiffs' bankers " Confidential. For your private use. . .," they did know that the inquiry was made in connection with an advertising contract. They must also have known that the references were to be passed on to a customer.[81] In reliance on these references the plaintiffs incurred expenditure on Easipower's behalf and, when Easipower went into liquidation, they suffered substantial loss. This loss they sought to recover from the defendants in an action based upon the defendants' alleged negligence in giving favourable references concerning Easipower.

---

[76] [1964] A.C. 465; Weir, *Casebook on Tort*, 3rd ed., p. 46.
[77] *Ibid.* pp. 518–519.
[78] *Nocton* v. *Lord Ashburton* [1914] A.C. 932, 947.
[79] 14 App.Cas. 337, 360.
[80] [1964] A.C. 465. See Stevens, " *Hedley Byrne* v. *Heller*: Judicial Creativity and Doctrinal Possibility " (1964) 27 M.L.R. 121; Goodhart, " Liability for Innocent but Negligent Misrepresentations " (1964) 74 Yale L.J. 286; Honoré, " Hedley Byrne & Co. Ltd. *v.* Heller & Partners Ltd." (1965) 8 J.S.P.T.L.(N.S.) 284; Weir, " Liability for Syntax " [1963] C.L.J. 216; Gordon, " Hedley Byrne *v.* Heller in the House of Lords " (1964) 38 A.L.J. 39, 79.
[81] [1964] A.C. at p. 482, *per* Lord Reid; *ibid.* at p. 503, *per* Lord Morris.

At first instance McNair J. held that the defendants owed no duty to the plaintiffs, and this decision was affirmed in the Court of Appeal [82] both on the ground that the case was covered by authority [83] and also on the ground that it would not be reasonable to impose upon a banker an obligation to exercise care when informing a third party of the credit-worthiness of his client.[84] In the House of Lords the decision in favour of the defendants was affirmed, but none of their Lordships based his decision on a general rule of non-liability for negligent misstatement. On the contrary, Lords Reid, Devlin and Pearce held that, assuming the defendants to have been negligent, the only reason for exonerating them was that the references had been given " without responsibility." [85] Lord Hodson and, perhaps, Lord Morris considered that even without this denial of responsibility there was no duty of care on the facts, but nevertheless agreed that a duty of care in making statements was a legal possibility.

Before *Hedley Byrne* the position with regard to negligent misstatement was, in short, that there could be no liability apart from contract or fiduciary relation or, perhaps, in a case of physical damage to person or property. Now, at the least, it is clear that a duty of care may exist in other circumstances,[86] but the scope and extent of the duty remains obscure. As with *Donoghue* v. *Stevenson*, the implications of *Hedley Byrne* are very great, but its actual effect upon the law can only emerge with time.

The factual situation in *Hedley Byrne* differed from the ordinary case of negligence in two main aspects. The damage resulted from reliance on a misstatement, not from an act, and was pecuniary or economic, not physical. Despite Lord Devlin's strongly worded rejection of a distinction between physical and economic damage,[87] it remains the law, as we have already mentioned,[88] that damages for economic loss cannot be recovered simply because such loss was the foreseeable consequence of the defendant's negligence. Before turning to the effect of *Hedley Byrne* itself we must now consider the significance of the fact that the defendant's alleged negligence consisted not of an act but of a misstatement.

---

[82] [1962] 1 Q.B. 396.

[83] Especially *Le Lievre* v. *Gould* [1893] 1 Q.B. 491; *Candler* v. *Crane, Christmas & Co.* [1951] 2 K.B. 164.

[84] [1962] 1 Q.B. 396, 414, *per* Pearson L.J.

[85] See *post*, pp. 231–232.

[86] It has been said that their Lordships' observations on the duty of care were *obiter* since their actual decision was against liability: *Rondel* v. *Worsley* [1967] 1 Q.B. 443, 514, *per* Danckwerts L.J.; speech of Sir Milner Holland, Q.C., to the Annual General Meeting of the Bar, 1963, cited Stevens, *loc. cit.* p. 125, n. 14; Gordon, *loc. cit.* Such a view seems not only pedantic but wrong (Dias [1963] C.L.J. 221; Salmond, *Torts*, 16th ed., p. 208); *W. B. Anderson & Sons Ltd.* v. *Rhodes (Liverpool) Ltd.* [1967] 2 All E.R. 850, 857, *per* Cairns J.; *Smith* v. *Auckland Hospital Board* [1965] N.Z.L.R. 191 (N.Z.C.A.). See too *Mutual Life and Citizens' Assurance Co. Ltd.* v. *Evatt* [1971] A.C. 793.

[87] [1964] A.C. at pp. 516–517.

[88] *Ante*, pp. 51–53.

Misstatement

In *Hedley Byrne* itself, Lord Morris said that he could see no essential reason in logic for distinguishing injury which is caused by reliance upon words from injury which is caused by, for example, reliance upon the safety for use of the contents of a bottle of hair wash or a bottle of some consumable liquid.[89] It is, of course, true that if a duty of care is assumed to exist then there is no logical reason for the distinction and it is also true that many cases of negligence which have never been regarded as raising the problem of misrepresentation nevertheless contain as an essential element in the sequence of events a misrepresentation, express or, more commonly, implied. No harm would have come to the pursuer in *Donoghue* v. *Stevenson* [90] if there had been no implied representation that the ginger beer was fit for human consumption.[91] Furthermore, there are cases in which the distinction between word and deed is for all practical purposes non-existent. Quite apart from contract, a doctor is as much liable for negligently advising his patient to take a certain drug as he is for negligently injecting the drug himself.[92] The fact remains, however, that if negligence in word were to be treated in precisely the same way as negligence in deed the result would be a liability far more extensive than the courts are prepared to accept.[93] Whereas, speaking generally, foreseeability of harm, or at least of physical harm, is sufficient to establish a duty to act with reasonable care, it is clear from *Hedley Byrne* itself that for a duty of care in speech or writing something more is needed. Their Lordships were in general agreement that *Donoghue* v. *Stevenson* had little, if any, direct bearing on the problem of negligent misstatement and that a duty of care will exist in relation to statements only if there is a " special relationship " between the parties.[94] Without such a limitation there would be liability " in an

---

[89] [1964] A.C. at p. 496. *Cf.* the speeches of Lord Reid at pp. 482–483 and Lord Pearce at p. 534, which recognise the necessity for distinguishing between word and deed. The explanation of the apparent disagreement seems to be that whereas Lord Morris is assuming a duty to exist, Lords Reid and Pearce are concerned with that very question. See also *Mutual Life and Citizens' Assurance Co. Ltd.* v. *Evatt* [1969] A.L.R. 3, 9, *per* Barwick C.J. (revd. [1971] A.C. 793).

[90] [1932] A.C. 562.

[91] See also *Watson* v. *Buckley, Osborne Garrett & Co. Ltd.* [1940] 1 All E.R. 174; *Sharp* v. *Avery* [1938] 4 All E.R. 85; *Holmes* v. *Ashford* [1950] 2 All E.R. 76; *Devilez* v. *Boots Pure Drug Co.* (1962) 106 S.J. 552. An interesting American example is *Pease* v. *Sinclair Refining Co.*, 104 F. (2d) 183 (2nd Cir. 1939). Fleming, *Torts*, 4th ed., pp. 161–163.

[92] This, it is submitted, is equivalent to the position as it was seen by Salmon J. in *Clayton* v. *Woodman & Sons (Builders) Ltd.* [1962] 2 Q.B. 533. The Court of Appeal took a different view of the facts and held that the point decided by the learned judge did not arise: [1962] 1 W.L.R. 585. See also *The Appollo* [1891] A.C. 499 and the examples given by Denning L.J. in *Candler* v. *Crane, Christmas & Co.* [1951] 2 K.B. 164, 173, 179.

[93] Consider the familiar example of the marine hydrographer whose careless omission of a reef from his published chart leads to the loss of a ship: *Candler* v. *Crane, Christmas & Co.* [1951] 2 K.B. 164, 183, *per* Denning L.J.

[94] See too *W. B. Anderson & Sons Ltd.* v. *Rhodes (Liverpool) Ltd.* [1967] 2 All E.R. 850, 853, *per* Cairns J.

indeterminate amount for an indefinite time and to an indeterminate class." [95]

Effect of Hedley Byrne [96]

The most significant consequence of the decision in *Hedley Byrne* is that it is now possible for the courts to hold in certain circumstances that a special relationship exists and therefore that one person owes another a duty of care in the giving of information or advice. The decision does not, however, specify exactly what those circumstances are, and it remains to be seen to what extent the courts will think it right to avail themselves of the opportunity created by the House of Lords for the expansion of liability for negligent misstatement.

The core of the reasoning in *Hedley Byrne* is that the duty of care arises from an undertaking, express or implied, by the defendant that he will exercise care in giving information or advice, and that this undertaking need not be supported by consideration.[97] On this basis it can be accepted that if there is an express undertaking of care the duty will certainly exist, but the important and difficult question is to know when an undertaking will be implied. Certainly this will not be the case where the advice or information is given on a purely social occasion, but it has been held that a dealer who also acted as a commission agent owed a duty of care to sellers of goods when he told them that a company on whose behalf he was purchasing those goods could safely be given credit.[98] Bankers advising third parties as to the credit of their customers are within *Hedley Byrne* itself [99] and a duty of care is also owed by accountants who provide information to persons contemplating transactions with their employers.[1] It has been

---

[95] *Ultramares Corporation* v. *Touche* (1931) 255 N.Y.Rep. 170, *per* Cardozo C.J. The clearest explanation of the reasons for a distinction between negligence in word and negligence in deed is in the speech of Lord Reid [1964] A.C. at pp. 482–483. That a person's potential liability is very extensive may seem on the face of it a poor reason for relieving him of a duty of care, but it is, nevertheless, one which has for long appealed to the judges.

[96] The clearest discussion is Honoré, " Hedley Byrne & Co. Ltd. *v*. Heller & Partners Ltd." (1965) 8 J.S.P.T.L.(N.S.) 284.

[97] But see *Mutual Life and Citizens' Assurance Co. Ltd.* v. *Evatt* [1969] A.L.R. 3, 11–12, *per* Barwick C.J. Notwithstanding that a different view commended itself to a majority of the Privy Council ([1971] A.C. 793, *post*, pp. 228–230) the judgment of the learned Chief Justice contains the most important judicial discussion of this branch of the law since *Hedley Byrne* itself. Stevens, *loc. cit.* at p. 129, considers that the House of Lords has to some extent undermined the doctrine of privity of contract.

[98] *W. B. Anderson & Sons Ltd.* v. *Rhodes (Liverpool) Ltd.* [1967] 2 All E.R. 850. See on this case *Mutual Life and Citizens' Assurance Co. Ltd.* v. *Evatt* [1971] A.C. 793, 809, *per* Lord Diplock. It has been held in the county court that a fuel merchant may be liable to a nurseryman for making negligent assurances about deliveries of fuel: *Charrington Gardner Lockett (London) Ltd.* v. *B. K. Tarry* [1964] C.L.Y. 2565.

[99] See also *Woods* v. *Martins Bank Ltd.* [1959] 1 Q.B. 55, approved in *Hedley Byrne*. But a bank which advises its client that a third person contracting with the client " ought to be satisfied " with the financial arrangements is not undertaking any duty of care with respect to the third person: *McInerny* v. *Lloyds Bank Ltd.* [1974] 1 Lloyd's Rep. 246.

[1] *Candler* v. *Crane, Christmas & Co.* [1951] 2 K.B. 164 was overruled and the dissenting judgment of Denning L.J. approved in *Hedley Byrne*. The House also considered that *Cann* v. *Willson* (1888) 39 Ch.D. 39 should not have been overruled by *Le Lievre* v. *Gould* [1893] 1 Q.B. 491, but that the latter case, though its reasoning was wrong, was probably

held in New Zealand that, independently of contract, a doctor owes his patient a duty to reply with reasonable care to the patient's questions,[2] and in both Canada and New Zealand that an estate agent acting for a vendor of property owes a duty to a potential purchaser of it to take reasonable care in providing information about it.[3] A Canadian court has held that a seller of products may be liable under *Hedley Byrne* for negligent misrepresentations made before the contract is concluded [3a]; but a New Zealand court has declined to hold that a contractor responding to an invitation to tender for the supply of goods owes any duty to act with care in fixing his price.[3b] On balance, the applicability of *Hedley Byrne* to pre-contract negotiations seems established,[3c] though its limits in this context remain to be worked out.

In all of these cases it was both foreseeable by the defendant that the plaintiff would rely upon his statement and reasonable for the plaintiff to do so; if in a given case either of these elements is lacking, as they would be if the statement were made on a social occasion, it can confidently be predicted that no duty of care will be held to exist.[4] In *Hedley Byrne* itself none of their Lordships was willing to lay down precise criteria for the existence of the special relationship and thus of the duty and, indeed for the most part they preferred to rely upon broad statements of general principle capable of being applied to a wide range of factual situations. Thus, for example, Lord Morris,[5] with the agreement of Lord Hodson,[6] said that " it should now be regarded as settled that if someone possessed of a special skill undertakes, quite irrespective of contract, to apply that skill for the assistance of another person who relies upon such a skill, a duty of care will arise. The fact that the service is to be given by means of or by the instrumentality of words can make no difference. Furthermore, if in

---

correctly decided on its facts. See further *Dimond Manufacturing Co. Ltd.* v. *Hamilton* [1969] N.Z.L.R. 609 (N.Z.C.A.); Whincup, " Further Adventures of Hedley Byrne " (1969) 119 New L.J. 1073.

[2] *Smith* v. *Auckland Hospital Board* [1965] N.Z.L.R. 191. In this case reliance upon the statement led to personal injury, not to pure financial loss.

[3] *Dodds* v. *Millman* (1964) 45 D.L.R. (2d) 472; *Barrett* v. *J. R. West Ltd.* [1970] N.Z.L.R. 789. *Bango* v. *Holt* (1971) 21 D.L.R. (3d) 66. See also *Hodgson* v. *Hydro-Electric Commission of the Township of Nepean* (1972) 28 D.L.R. (3d) 174 (electricity authority giving estimate of heating costs); and *cf. Sulzinger* v. *C. K. Alexander Ltd.* (1971) 24 D.L.R. (3d) 137 (insurance adjuster retained by insurers in dispute with plaintiff under no duty of care to plaintiff).

[3a] *Sealand of the Pacific Ltd.* v. *Ocean Cement Ltd.* (1973) 33 D.L.R. (3d) 625; *cf. J. Nunes Diamonds Ltd.* v. *Dominion Electric Co.* (1972) 26 D.L.R. (3d) 699 (Can.Sup.Ct.) and the Misrepresentation Act 1967.

[3b] *Holman Construction Ltd.* v. *Delta Timber Co. Ltd.* [1972] N.Z.L.R. 1081 (defendant mistakenly quoted too low a price; plaintiff relied on this in entering into head contract; defendant discovered mistake and withdrew tender before plaintiff accepted it.) *Cf. Hodgson* v. *Hydro-Electric Commission etc.*, *supra.*

[3c] *Esso Petroleum Co. Ltd.* v. *Mardon* (1974) *The Times*, August 2 (pre-contract representations by lessor); *Dillingham Constructions* v. *Downs* [1972] 2 S.R.(N.S.W.) 49; *Morrison-Knudson International Co. Inc.* v. *The Commonwealth* (1972) 46 A.L.J.R. 265.

[4] See *Mutual Life and Citizens' Assurance Co. Ltd.* v. *Evatt*, *supra*, at p. 36, *per* Lords Reid and Morris.

[5] [1964] A.C. at pp. 502–503.

[6] *Ibid.* at p. 514.

a sphere in which a person is so placed that others could reasonably rely upon his judgment or his skill or upon his ability to make careful inquiry, a person takes it upon himself to give information or advice to, or allows his information or advice to be passed on to, another person who, as he knows or should know, will place reliance upon it, then a duty of care will arise." Though the formulations in the other speeches are not quite the same,[7] they are not inconsistent with this statement of the law and perhaps it may be said, therefore, that in general the foreseeability and reasonableness of the plaintiff's reliance upon the defendant's words are not only necessary but are also sufficient for the duty of care to arise.[8] In *Mutual Life and Citizens' Assurance Co. Ltd.* v. *Evatt*,[9] however, the majority of the Privy Council took a more restricted view.

The facts of *Evatt's* case were that the plaintiff, who was a policy holder in the defendant company, sought advice from the company as to the financial soundness of another company, " Palmer," with which it was closely associated. In reliance upon the information he was given the plaintiff refrained from realising his investment in Palmer and invested further sums in that company. The information he was given was incorrect and he lost his money. The case came before the Privy Council on a procedural question as to the sufficiency of the plaintiff's declaration,[1] the objection to it being that it alleged neither that the defendant company was in the business of supplying information or advice nor that it had let it be known that it claimed to possess the necessary skill to do so and was prepared to exercise due diligence to give reliable advice. It was held by the majority that the omission was fatal.

If the reasoning of the majority of the Privy Council is adopted in the future there can be no doubt that the decision will act as a powerful brake on the development of liability for negligent misstatement.

---

[7] *Ibid.* at p. 486, *per* Lord Reid; *ibid.* at p. 539, *per* Lord Pearce. Lord Devlin, *ibid.* at p. 530, was prepared to adopt any of the statements of the rule given by his brethren but preferred to say that the duty of care exists wherever there is a relationship " equivalent to contract," *i.e.*, where there is an assumption of responsibility in circumstances in which but for the absence of consideration, there would be a contract. Lord Devlin's view does not, however, mean that to incur liability for negligent misstatement, the defendant must have intended to make a contract: *McInerny* v. *Lloyds Bank Ltd.* [1973] 2 Lloyd's Rep. 389, 400 (on appeal [1974] 1 Lloyd's Rep. 246). See too the judgment of Barwick C.J. in *Mutual Life and Citizens' Assurance Co. Ltd.* v. *Evatt* (1968) 122 C.L.R. 556.

[8] See Weir, " Liability for Syntax " [1963] C.L.J. 216, 217. The statement in the text is, it is submitted, consistent with the minority opinion in *Evatt's* case ([1971] A.C. at 811) even though their Lordships considered the appropriate question to be whether the advice was given on a business occasion (*ibid.* at p. 811). On the facts this comes to the same thing.

[9] [1971] A.C. 793; (1971) 87 L.Q.R. 147; Farmer [1971] C.L.J. 189; Rickford (1971) 34 M.L.R. 328; Hodgin, " Fortunes of Hedley Byrne " [1972] J.B.L. 27; Lindgren, " Professional Negligence in Words and the Privy Council " (1972) 46 A.L.J. 176; Stevens, " Two Steps Forward and Three Back! Liability for Negligent Words " (1972) 5 N.Z.U.L.R. 39; Harvey, " Negligent Statements—The Wilderness Revisited " (1970) 120 New L.J. 1155.

[1] The appeal was on the defendants' demurrer to the plaintiff's declaration in accordance with the old form of procedure still current in New South Wales.

Instead of a broad general principle of great flexibility, liability will be confined to those who are actually in the business of supplying advice or information and to those, surely very few, others, who let it be known that they claim to possess skill and competence in the matter of an inquiry comparable to that possessed by those who are in the business of advising on the subject-matter of the inquiry.[2] The decision is, however, no more than a majority decision of the Privy Council and should not be regarded as conclusive of the problem so far as English law is concerned.[3]

An important premise from which the conclusion of the majority depends was that the imposition of a duty of care presupposes an ascertainable standard of skill, competence and diligence with which the adviser is, or has represented himself to be, acquainted: if he is not in the business of supplying information or advice he cannot reasonably be expected to know the standard to which he is required to conform and so he cannot be held to have accepted the responsibility of conforming to it.[4] As was pointed out in the minority opinion, however, a duty to take care is not the same as a duty to conform to a particular standard of skill, and there is no ground for saying that a specially skilled man must exercise care while a less skilled man need not do so. " One must assume a reasonable man who has that degree of knowledge and skill which facts known to the inquirer (including statements made by the adviser) entitled him to expect of the adviser, and then inquire whether a reasonable man could have given the advice which was in fact given if he had exercised reasonable care." [5] The view of the majority seems contrary to the very nature of a duty of care, while that of the minority shows how such a duty is to be applied in the special case of one person advising another. It is suggested, therefore, that *Evatt's* case should not be regarded as imposing a rigid limit on the scope of *Hedley Byrne* at least so far as English law is concerned,[6] and that it is preferable to adhere to a general statement such as that

---

[2] [1971] A.C. at pp. 805–806, *per* Lord Diplock. His Lordship conceded that the absence of the missing characteristic of the relationship considered to be essential in the case under consideration would not in all circumstances be fatal, as, perhaps, where the adviser has a financial interest in the transaction, upon which he gives his advice. This would avoid a conflict with *W. B. Anderson & Sons Ltd.* v. *Rhodes (Liverpool) Ltd.* [1967] 2 All E.R. 850.

[3] The majority decision reversed a majority decision of the High Court of Australia which in its turn upheld a majority decision of the Court of Appeal of the Supreme Court of New South Wales. Of the appellate judges who heard the case, seven decided in favour of the plaintiff and six against. Moreover the majority in the Privy Council " explained " certain passages in the speeches of Lords Reid and Morris in *Hedley Byrne* in a manner which those two learned Lords, who formed the minority in the Privy Council, were at pains to deny: [1971] A.C. at p. 813. It is of interest to note that the passage from the speech of Lord Morris, cited in the text, is one of those " explained " by the majority and that Lord Hodson, notwithstanding his agreement with and repetition of it in *Hedley Byrne* ([1964] A.C. at p. 514), shared in the majority opinion.

[4] [1971] A.C. at pp. 802–808. Considerable reliance was placed on *Low* v. *Bouverie* [1891] 3 Ch. 82 which was not overruled by *Hedley Byrne.*

[5] *Ibid.* at p. 812, *per* Lords Reid and Morris.

[6] So much is admitted in the opinion itself: [1971] A.C. at p. 809. See also *Esso Petroleum Co. Ltd.* v. *Mardon* (1974), *The Times*, August 2.

of Lord Morris which is capable of application to a wide range of circumstances.[7] It may be, however, that no duty should be imposed unless the defendant has held himself out in some way as possessing skill or knowledge relevant to the subject matter of the plaintiff's inquiry.[8]

A further difficult problem thrown up by *Hedley Byrne* concerns the range of the duty, for, as is evident from the well-known example of the marine hydrographer,[9] the number of persons who may rely on a statement is potentially enormous and would not be sufficiently limited by the test of foreseeability.[10] Accordingly, it has been said that the information or advice must be " sought or accepted by a person on his own behalf or on behalf of an identified or identifiable class of persons "[11] and it is also probably necessary that the defendant should be able to foresee not merely reliance of some kind by the plaintiff but the particular transaction which he has in mind.[11a]

Hedley Byrne has not affected the immunity of an arbitrator acting honestly, for that is founded on public policy in view of the nature of his office.[11b]

The standard of duty

In *Hedley Byrne* and also in *Evatt's* case there are references to a " duty of honesty " which, it is said, a person may incur even if he is not subjected to the duty which exists where there is a special relationship.[12] The meaning of this is not clear; it may be that the duty of

---

[7] In *Evatt's* case Lords Reid and Morris observe that it is quite common practice for businesses to perform gratuitous services for their customers with the object of retaining or acquiring their goodwill and that all concerned would be surprised to learn that in doing so the businesses come under no duty to exercise care: [1971] A.C. at p. 811. Whether or not such businesses could be held to be in the business of giving advice is unclear, but in view of the actual decision in *Evatt's* case it may be surmised that the majority of the Privy Council would consider that they were not, unless it was part of their business to give advice.

[8] This seems to be the view of Lords Morris, Hodson and Pearce in *Hedley Byrne*, and all cite with approval the statement of Lord Loughborough in *Shiells* v. *Blackburne* (1789) 1 H.Bl. 158 that " if a man gratuitously undertakes to do a thing to the best of his skill, where his situation or profession is such as to imply skill, an omission of that skill is imputable to him as gross negligence." The limitation was applied by Wilson J. in the Supreme Court of New Zealand in *Jones* v. *Still* [1965] N.Z.L.R. 1071. *Cf.*, however, the decision of the same court in *Barrett* v. *J. R. West Ltd.* [1970] N.Z.L.R. 789, the opinion of Lords Reid and Morris in *Evatt's* case ([1971] A.C. at p. 812) and that of Barwick C.J. in the High Court of Australia (1968) 122 C.L.R. at p. 574.

[9] See *Candler* v. *Crane, Christmas & Co.* [1951] 2 K.B. 164, 182–183.

[10] But see *McInerny* v. *Lloyds Bank Ltd.* [1974] 1 Lloyd's Rep. 246, 253, *per* Lord Denning M.R. dissenting.

[11] *Evatt's* case, *supra*, at (1968) 122 C.L.R., p. 570, *per* Barwick C.J. Note that the actual identity of the inquirer need not be known: see *Hedley Byrne* itself. For examples of " third party reliance " see *Dimond Manufacturing Co. Ltd.* v. *Hamilton* [1969] N.Z.L.R. 609 and *Gordon* v. *Moen* [1971] N.Z.L.R. 526.

[11a] Or a transaction substantially identical therewith: *Restatement* 552. See *Ultramares Corp.* v. *Touche* (1931) 255 N.Y. 170 and *Glanzer* v. *Shepherd* (1922) 233 N.Y. 170. Honoré, *loc. cit.* at pp. 288, 289. *Cf. Sutcliffe* v. *Thackrah* [1974] 2 W.L.R. 295, 319.

[11b] But this immunity by no means necessarily extends to an expert appointed as valuer by two parties to a transaction: *Sutcliffe* v. *Thackrah* [1974] 2 W.L.R. 295. *Quaere* whether *Arenson* v. *Arenson* [1973] Ch. 346 was correctly decided on its facts.

[12] *Hedley Byrne* [1962] 1 Q.B. 396, 414–415, *per* Pearson L.J. approved by Lords Reid, Morris and Hodson in the House of Lords: [1964] A.C. at pp. 489, 503–504, 512; *Evatt's* case [1971] A.C. at p. 801, *per* Lord Diplock.

honesty is the same as the duty to refrain from the tort of deceit [13] or it may mean something more so that, for example, a person subject to it must not give the impression that his advice is based on research into records when it is not, and must disclose any financial interest he may have in the advice he is giving.[14] The recognition of a duty of honesty in the first sense serves no useful purpose; in the second sense it may have some advantages [15] but it is suggested that it is unnecessary. The concept of reasonable care, correctly used, is adequate to enable the courts to impose more precisely the appropriate level of obligation by its use than by distinguishing the duty of care from the duty of honesty. The duty of care is not a duty to take every possible care; still less is it a duty to be right.[16] It is the familiar duty to take such care as, in all the circumstances, is reasonable. If it is unreasonable to expect a banker answering a query about a customer to spend time and trouble in searching records and so on, then a duty of reasonable care would not require him to do so. There is no need to say that the banker has no duty of care, only a duty not to tell lies.[17]

Disclaimer of responsibility

It must not be overlooked that, in the result, judgment in *Hedley Byrne* went to the defendants and this, at least in the opinion of the majority, was because they had supplied the information " without responsibility." [18] On the basis that the duty arises from an undertaking to exercise care, it is probably inevitable that a defendant should incur no liability if he makes it clear from the outset that he accepts no responsibility for his statement. " A man cannot be said voluntarily to be undertaking a responsibility if at the very moment that he is said to be accepting it he declares that he is not." [19] It seems likely, therefore, that the duty under *Hedley Byrne* can exist only where the defendant has been too careless of his own interests or too proud to protect himself by such a declaration. Otherwise the recipient of the statement has the choice of acting upon it or not at his peril, which was the position before *Hedley Byrne*.[20]

---

[13] In which case " we have travelled to the village church via the moon, because no one doubts that a person giving information to another owes a duty to abstain from deceit; at least where he intends his information to be acted on ": Honoré, *loc. cit.* at p. 291. *Cf.* Stevens, *loc. cit.* at p. 146.   [14] Honoré, *ibid.*
[15] It is possible to exclude the duty of care by appropriate words, but only an express disclaimer of an intention to make the statement honestly could exclude a duty of honesty. See *infra.*
[16] *Evatt's* case [1971] A.C. at p. 812, *per* Lords Reid and Morris.
[17] See *Hedley Byrne* [1962] 1 Q.B. at pp. 414–415, *per* Pearson L.J. It is respectfully submitted that the view adopted by the minority in *Evatt's* case of the nature of a duty of care is more accurate than that of the majority. See *ante*, p. 229.
[18] Lord Hodson and, perhaps, Lord Morris would have reached the same conclusion even in the absence of the disclaimer: *ante*, p. 224.
[19] [1964] A.C. at p. 533, *per* Lord Devlin.
[20] Clerk & Lindsell, *Torts*, 13th ed., p. 468. *Cf.* the approach of Barwick C.J. in *Evatt's* case (1968) 122 C.L.R. at p. 570; *Ministry of Housing* v. *Sharp* [1970] 2 Q.B. 223, 268, *per* Lord Denning M.R.; *ibid.* at p. 279, *per* Salmon L.J. Stevens, *loc. cit.* at pp. 150–155, is critical but admits that the undermining of the power of disclaimer will require " judicial valour."

There would seem to be the following qualifications to the power to disclaim responsibility:

(i) A person guilty of the tort of deceit will remain liable whatever he may have said by way of disclaimer.[21]

(ii) The duty of honesty, if different from the duty to abstain from deceit, will not be excluded by a disclaimer save in the unlikely event that the defendant has expressly stated that he does not propose to give an honest answer.

(iii) Words of exclusion should, following the normal practice, be interpreted *contra proferentem*, but in this connection it must be borne in mind that there is no duty stricter than the duty of care to be excluded.[22] Thus, it is submitted, the letters " E. & O.E." (Errors and Omissions Excepted) which are printed at the bottom of many documents should not be treated as sufficient in themselves to exclude the duty of care.

(iv) The disclaimer must have been made before or at the time that the defendant supplies the information or advice. Once a responsibility has been accepted it cannot be avoided save by agreement between the parties.[23]

Lord Tenterden's Act

By the Statute of Frauds 1677 promises that are guarantees must be in writing and signed by the party to be charged or his agent in order to make them actionable. After *Pasley* v. *Freeman*[24] it appeared that the action of deceit provided a way for plaintiffs to evade the statute by alleging not that the defendant had given a guarantee but that he had fraudulently represented that a third party might safely be given credit. To block this evasion of the statute the Statute of Frauds Amendment Act 1828 (commonly called Lord Tenterden's Act), s. 6, was passed providing, in effect, that a false representation as to credit cannot be sued upon unless it is made in writing and signed by the party to be charged.[25]

The section clearly covers fraudulent representations as to a person's credit, but it does not apply to an action between contracting parties in respect of advice negligently given.[26] " Section 6 appears to me, upon its plain meaning to be confined to actions brought upon misrepresentations as such, and not to bar redress for failure to perform any

---

[21] [1964] A.C. at p. 540, *per* Lord Pearce.
[22] [1964] A.C. at pp. 492–493, *per* Lord Reid; at p. 540, *per* Lord Pearce.
[23] This seems to be suggested by Lord Devlin [1964] A.C. at p. 533, and would accord with general principle.
[24] (1789) 3 T.R. 51, *ante*, p. 212.
[25] The requirement is more stringent than that contained in the Statute of Frauds itself, for signature by an agent is not sufficient: *Swift* v. *Jewsbury* (1874) L.R. 9 Q.B. 301. This applies when the defendant is a company, and there is no mode in which a company can sign other than by an agent. Thus an incorporated bank is not responsible for a fraudulent representation as to credit signed by a manager of one of its branches: *Hirst* v. *West Riding Union Banking Co. Ltd.* [1901] 2 K.B. 560.
[26] *Banbury* v. *Bank of Montreal* [1918] A.C. 626.

contractual or other duty." [27] The section was not considered in *Hedley Byrne*, and rightly so, for it has no more place in actions for tortious negligence than it has in actions founded upon contract.[27a] Nevertheless it is strange that what would be a defence in an action for fraud should not be one in an action for negligence. It would be even stranger if a defendant against whom negligence is alleged could affirmatively set up his own fraudulent intent and plead the statute. Presumably, however, such a plea could be struck out on the general ground that no one should be allowed to take advantage of his own wrongful act.

Injury to third parties

It is not only the person who relies upon a statement who may suffer if the statement turns out to be untrue. Reliance on a statement made by A to B may sometimes lead B to act in a manner detrimental to C, and the question then arises, if A's statement is false, whether C can sue A. A doctor employed by an insurance company may incorrectly inform the company that an applicant for a life insurance policy is a bad risk, with the result that the company demands a higher premium than normal or refuses the applicant altogether; a solicitor may give to his client incorrect advice about the way to effect a gift of certain of his assets, with the result that the intended donee never receives his gift; a newspaper may publish incorrectly that a trader has gone out of business with the result that the trader loses custom. Since the decision in *Hedley Byrne*, can it be said that in any of these or similar cases the maker of the statement owes any duty to the person who is affected?

If the basis of the decision in *Hedley Byrne* is, as has been suggested, that a duty of care is owed to the plaintiff where he reasonably and foreseeably relies on the defendant's words, then that decision has no direct application here, for the would-be plaintiff does not rely upon the defendant's words at all. On the other hand, in the tort most commonly known as " slander of title " [28] it has for long been recognised that A may be liable to C if he makes a false *and malicious* statement to B about C, his property or his business which causes C to suffer damage.[29] It is suggested that there is an analogy between this tort, which touches on our present problem, and the tort of deceit. Both are concerned with false statements and damage resulting from

---

[27] *Ibid.* at p. 640, *per* Lord Finlay L.C.

[27a] *W. B. Anderson & Sons Ltd.* v. *Rhodes (Liverpool) Ltd.* [1967] 2 All E.R. 850; *Evatt's* case (1968) 122 C.L.R. at p. 580, *per* Barwick C.J.

[28] The tort is known by various names, of which " slander of title " is still the most usual, though the tort has little, if anything, in common with defamation. (See *Hatchard* v. *Mège* (1887) 18 Q.B.D. 771, 775, *per* Day J.) Salmond calls it " injurious falsehood " but he uses this also for the tort of " passing off " (*post*, pp. 471–476), to which, perhaps, it does not apply so exactly. Winfield considered it to be more closely allied to unlawful trade competition than to any other heading.

[29] For its origins, see Holdsworth, H.E.L., viii, 351–353.

them, but in the case of deceit the plaintiff must have suffered damage as a result of his own reliance upon the statement, while in slander of title the plaintiff must have suffered damage as a result of another's reliance upon it. There is, it is true, an apparent difference between the principles of liability in the two torts: for liability in deceit the defendant must have known his statement to be false, while in slander of title the defendant must have been malicious. But this difference is more apparent than real. Though proof that the defendant knew his statement to be false may not in itself be proof of malice, it is certainly evidence of it [30] and, conversely, a man who honestly believes his statement to be true cannot be guilty of slander of title.[31]

There is thus a fairly close, though not exact, parallel between the law governing liability for statements made to and relied on by the plaintiff as it was before *Hedley Byrne* and the law governing liability for statements made by A to B, reliance upon which by B causes damage to C. The House of Lords was able in *Hedley Byrne* to hold that there might sometimes be a duty of care despite the rule in *Derry v. Peek* [32] that the defendant must know his statement to be false. So, it is submitted, despite the rule of slander of title that the defendant must be malicious, the House of Lords could at some future date hold that there may be a duty of care in situations apparently covered by that rule.

It must be emphasised that *Hedley Byrne* itself has no direct bearing on our present problem and any argument founded upon it could rely only on analogy and on the general tenor of their Lordships' speeches. It must also be emphasised that so far there is extremely little English authority suggesting that a duty of care might exist. Before turning to what can be no more than speculation about possible future development, therefore, it is desirable to set out the elements of the tort of slander of title, for these will remain the essential ingredients of liability unless and until the House of Lords makes the appropriate extensions to *Hedley Byrne*.

Slander of title

Most of the modern cases are concerned with rival traders and nearly all the cases, old and new, are instances of interference with business, if not unlawful competition. A common form of the tort is impugning the plaintiff's title to goods; *e.g.*, a false assertion that the defendant has a lien on goods which the plaintiff had bought from X and which X consequently refuses to deliver to the plaintiff.[33] But this

---

[30] *Greers Ltd.* v. *Pearman & Corder Ltd.* (1922) 39 R.P.C. 406. In *Cellactite and British Uralite* v. *H. H. Robertson* [1957] C.L.Y. 1989, C.A. 1957 No. 227, the Court of Appeal accepted recklessness as sufficient to justify the inference of malice.
[31] *Balden* v. *Shorter* [1933] Ch. 427; *Loudon* v. *Ryder* (*No.* 2) [1953] Ch. 423.
[32] (1889) 14 App.Cas. 337, *ante*, pp. 221–224.
[33] *Green* v. *Button* (1835) 5 L.J.Ex. 81. *Cf. Gutsole* v. *Mathers* (1836) 1 M. & W. 495; *Malachy* v. *Soper* (1836) 3 Bing.N.C. 371; *Riding* v. *Smith* (1876) 1 Ex.D. 91; *Loudon* v. *Ryder* (*No.* 2) [1953] Ch. 423.

is not essential, and in one of the best-known cases the words used by the defendant, a newspaper proprietor, imported that the plaintiff had ceased to carry on business.[34] There seems no reason, however, why liability should be restricted to trade, and in *Barrett* v. *Associated Newspapers Ltd.*[35] the plaintiff's claim was based on a false assertion by the defendants that his house was haunted.

Essentials of the tort [36]

(i) *A false statement to some person other than the plaintiff*

The statement may be oral or written and even conduct conveying a false representation may be sufficient.[37] It is for the plaintiff to prove that the statement is false and there is no presumption in his favour.[38] If the statement is due to the plaintiff's own fault, he has no claim.[39]

(ii) *Malice*

Knowledge of the falsehood of the statement or even recklessness whether it be true or false may be sufficient,[40] but probably malice here generally means some indirect, dishonest or improper motive.[41] Certainly mere carelessness is not enough.[42] In *Greers Ltd.* v. *Pearman & Corder Ltd.*[43] the defendants were held to have acted maliciously in alleging falsely that the plaintiffs had infringed their trade mark for chocolates, which included the words " Bouquet Brand," for the defendants had repeatedly disclaimed any right to the exclusive use of these words years before the plaintiffs had employed them. In such circumstances, the mere fact that the defendants had made such an allegation constituted malice. " Honest belief," said Scrutton L.J.,[44] " in an unfounded claim is not malice; but the nature of the unfounded claim may be evidence that there is not an honest belief in it. It may be so unfounded that the particular fact that it is put forward may be evidence that it is not honestly believed." A bona fide assertion of

---

[34] *Ratcliffe* v. *Evans* [1892] 2 Q.B. 524; *Joyce* v. *Motor Surveys Ltd.* [1948] Ch. 252; Weir, *Casebook on Tort*, 3rd ed., p. 484.

[35] (1907) 23 T.L.R. 666; *Sheperd* v. *Wakeman* (1662) 1 Sid. 79.

[36] *Royal Baking Powder Co.* v. *Wright, Crossley & Co.* (1900) 18 R.P.C. 95, 99, *per* Lord Davey; *Reuter* (*R. J.*) *Co. Ltd.* v. *Muhlens* [1954] Ch. 50, 74, *per* Evershed M.R.; *Mayer* v. *Pluck* (1971) 223 E.G. 33, 219.

[37] *Wilts United Dairies* v. *Robinson & Sons* [1958] R.P.C. 94.

[38] Clerk & Lindsell, *Torts*, 13th ed., pp. 1051–1052. Note that in defamation the falsity of the defamatory words is presumed in the plaintiff's favour until the defendant proves their truth. *Post*, p. 266.

[39] *Vacha* v. *Gillett* (1934) 50 Ll.L.R. 67, 74–75.

[40] *Cellactite and British Uralite* v. *H. H. Robertson* [1957] C.L.Y. 1989, *ante*, p. 234, n. 30.

[41] *London Ferro-Concrete Co.* v. *Justicz* (1951) 68 R.P.C. 261, 265, *per* Birkett L.J. (C.A.); *cf. Joyce* v. *Motor Surveys Ltd.* [1948] Ch. 252, 254. An intent to injure is not necessary: *Wilts United Dairies* v. *Robinson* [1957] R.P.C. 220, affd. without considering this point [1958] R.P.C. 94.

[42] *Balden* v. *Shorter* [1933] Ch. 427; *Loudon* v. *Ryder* (*No. 2*) [1953] Ch. 423. (Where no malice is proved an action for damages for slander of title will not lie, but if the defendant's claim is nevertheless wrongful, the plaintiff is entitled to a declaration as to the plaintiff's title.)

[43] (1922) 39 R.P.C. 406.

[44] *Ibid.* 417.

title, though mistaken, if made in protection of one's own interest is not malicious.

(iii) Damage

Save in cases falling within the provisions of section 3 (1) of the Defamation Act 1952, proof of special damage is required,[45] but this requirement is satisfied by proof of a general loss of business where the falsehood in its very nature is intended, or is reasonably likely, to produce and actually does produce in the ordinary course of things, such loss; for there are businesses, like those of an auctioneer or a publican, where the customers are often so fleeting in their patronage that it would be almost impossible for the plaintiff to name in particular such of them as have ceased to deal with him in consequence of the defendant's tort.[46] By section 3 (1) of the Defamation Act 1952 it is no longer necessary to allege or prove special (*i.e.*, actual) damage (a) if the words complained of are published in writing or other permanent form [47] and are calculated to cause pecuniary damage to the plaintiff; or (b) if the words complained of are calculated to cause pecuniary damage to the plaintiff in respect of any office, profession, calling, trade or business held or carried on by him at the time of the publication.

A statement by one trader that his own goods are superior to those of another (mere " puffing "), even if it is false, malicious and causes damage to that other, is not actionable; for courts of law cannot be converted into advertising agencies for trying the relative merits of rival productions.[49]

Liability for negligence

It has already been suggested that there is nothing in the authorities to prevent the House of Lords from holding that in certain circumstances A may owe a duty of care to C not to make false statements about him to B. In one class of case, moreover, this result has in effect already been achieved. A doctor called in to certify that a person should be admitted to a mental hospital owes a duty of care to that person even though he is called in by and acts on behalf of another,[50] and Denning L.J. has said that this is because " the doctor knows that his certificate is required for the very purpose of deciding whether the man should be

---

[45] *White* v. *Mellin* [1895] A.C. 154; *Royal Baking Powder Co.* v. *Wright & Co.* (1900) 18 R.P.C. 95, 99.

[46] *Ratcliffe* v. *Evans* [1892] 2 Q.B. 524, 533; *Leetham* v. *Rank* (1912) 57 S.J. 111; *Hargrave* v. *Le Breton* (1769) 4 Burr. 2422; *Evans* v. *Harries* (1856) 1 H. & N. 251; *Worsley & Co. Ltd.* v. *Cooper* [1939] 1 All E.R. 290; Kerly, *Trade Marks*, 9th ed., p. 495.

[47] *Fielding* v. *Variety Incorporated* [1967] 2 Q.B. 841. Broadcasting is publication in permanent form (s. 3 (2)). If a plaintiff takes advantage of the section he cannot lead evidence of special damage: *Calvet* v. *Tomkies* [1963] 1 W.L.R. 1397.

[49] *White* v. *Mellin* [1895] A.C. 154, 164–165; *Hubbuck & Sons Ltd.* v. *Wilkinson* [1899] 1 Q.B. 86.

[50] *Hall* v. *Semple* (1862) 3 F. & R. 33; *Everett* v. *Griffiths* [1921] A.C. 631; *Harnett* v. *Fisher* [1927] A.C. 573; *De Freville* v. *Dill* (1927) 96 L.J.K.B. 1056 (all decided under earlier statutes. See now Mental Health Act 1959, ss. 25–29). No proceedings may be brought without the leave of the court: *ibid.* s. 141 (1) and (2).

detained or not." [51] We must now inquire whether there is any reason to anticipate that a duty of care will be held to exist in any other class of case.

In *Ministry of Housing* v. *Sharp*,[52] a land-owner had been refused permission to develop certain land and had been paid compensation by the Ministry under the Town and Country Planning Act 1954. This payment was subject to the condition that if permission to develop was granted at a later date the compensation would be repayable by the developer, and the Ministry's right to obtain such repayment was registered in accordance with that Act and the Land Charges Act 1925.[52a] Some time later the owner re-applied for and was granted permission to develop, and he then sold the land with planning permission. The purchaser (B) caused a search to be made in the register and the clerk who prepared the certificate (A) carelessly omitted the Ministry's (C's) charge. The certificate was conclusive in favour of the purchaser [53] who thus took the land free of the obligation to repay the Ministry, the Ministry lost its right to be repaid, and sued, *inter alios*, the local council as the clerk's employer. It was held in the Court of Appeal that the clerk owed a duty of care to the Ministry for the breach of which the council was liable.

It is tempting to regard this case as one in which it was held that A owed a duty of care to C not to make careless misstatements to B which led B to act to the detriment of C, but it is submitted that on a true analysis the case is of little assistance on the point and is unique.[54] Much turns on the effect of the certificate, a matter on which the law is obscure,[55] and the vital question is whether it was the actual purchase of the land (*i.e.*, the act of B in reliance on the statement of A) or the issue of the certificate itself (*i.e.*, the act of A) which destroyed the Ministry's right to recover its money. This cannot be investigated here, but it is submitted that, whether or not the certificate was conclusive in favour of anyone other than the purchaser (or intending purchaser) to whom it was issued, in the events which occurred it was the actual issue of the certificate rather than the purchase of the land, which caused the Ministry's loss. This means that it was the act of A, not the act of B in reliance upon the statement of A, which caused C's damage. *Ministry of Housing* v. *Sharp* is thus only of indirect assistance on the

---

[51] *Candler* v. *Crane, Christmas & Co.* [1951] 2 K.B. 164, 183. Denning L.J. agrees that an insurance company's doctor owes no duty to the insured person: *ibid.*

[52] [1970] 2 Q.B. 223; *Dutton* v. *Bognor Regis U.D.C.* [1972] 1 Q.B. 373.

[52a] The Land Charges legislation has now been consolidated in the Land Charges Act 1972.

[53] Land Charges Act 1925, s. 17 (3).

[54] [1970] 2 Q.B. at p. 278, *per* Salmon L.J.

[55] s. 17 (3) (now s. 10 (4), Land Charges Act 1972) read, " In favour of a purchaser or an intending purchaser, as against persons interested under or in respect of matters or documents whereof entries are required or allowed . . . the certificate, according to the tenor thereof, shall be conclusive, affirmatively or negatively, as the case may be."

point under discussion, but it does at least demonstrate that a duty of care in making statements can arise out of a general relationship of " proximity." The clerk must and should have foreseen that unless the search was conducted and the certificate prepared with reasonable care, any chargee whose charge was carelessly omitted from the certificate would be likely to suffer damage, and that was enough. Indeed, in the view of Salmon L.J.,[55a] there was as close a degree of proximity between the clerk and the Ministry as there was between the parties in *Donoghue* v. *Stevenson* itself.

It is obvious that any extension of the duty of care to the kind of situation under consideration is something to be undertaken only with great caution; certainly it cannot be the law that A owes a duty to C whenever he can reasonably foresee loss to C resulting from his false statement to B. On the other hand, there are circumstances in which the proximity between A and C is very much closer than this. A may, for example, know not only C's actual identity but also the precise loss that his negligence will inevitably cause. At least where A is a professional man advising or giving information to B in the course of his professional duties, as where A is a solicitor, B a testator and C an intended beneficiary of B's will, is there any reason why A should not be liable to C if his negligence leads to B's will being declared invalid so that C loses his inheritance?

The question here is essentially one of policy, as was frankly admitted by the Californian court in a case decided in favour of a disappointed beneficiary,[56] and it is submitted that the question should not be answered by a flat denial of the possibility of a duty in all cases. It should be answered in each case by the balancing of a variety of factors such as the extent to which the transaction was intended to affect the plaintiff, the foreseeability of harm to him, the closeness of the connection between the defendant's conduct and the injury suffered and the policy of preventing future harm.[57] The general principle of negligence and the concept of proximity are sufficiently adaptable to take account of factors such as these, and it is to be recalled that Lord Devlin has said [58] that he takes quite literally Lord Macmillan's dictum that " the categories of negligence are never closed." [59] There is no reason why the courts should feel themselves incapable of distinguishing between cases in which there should and cases in which

---

[55a] [1970] 2 Q.B. at p. 278. See also *ibid.* at pp. 268–269, *per* Lord Denning M.R. Cross L.J. doubted the existence of a duty on the facts of the case, but was not willing to dissent: *ibid.* at p. 291.

[56] *Biakanja* v. *Irving* (1958) 49 Cal. (2d) 647; *Lucas* v. *Hamm,* 56 Cal. (2d) 583. In the latter case it was found that there was no negligence.

[57] *Biakanja* v. *Irving, supra, per* Gibson C.J.

[58] [1964] A.C. at p. 531; *Mutual Life and Citizens' Assurance Co. Ltd.* v. *Evatt* [1971] A.C. 793, *per* Lord Diplock.

[59] *Donoghue* v. *Stevenson* [1932] A.C. 562, 619.

there should not be liability and it is to be hoped that they will not reject out of hand the opportunity created by *Hedley Byrne* of making cautious progress towards a principle of liability for negligence in this class of case.[60]

---

[60] There is a difficulty in the case of solicitors in that it has been held in several cases that a client's only cause of action against his solicitor lies in contract (*Groom* v. *Crocker* [1939] 1 K.B. 194; *Bailey* v. *Bullock* [1950] 2 All E.R. 1167) and this has survived *Hedley Byrne: Clark* v. *Kirby Smith* [1964] Ch. 506. See also *Bagot* v. *Stevens Scanlan & Co.* [1966] 1 Q.B. 197 (architect) and *Cook* v. *Swinfen* [1967] 1 W.L.R. 457, 461, *per* Lord Denning M.R. It is submitted that these cases should not be construed as meaning that a solicitor can never be liable for professional negligence in the absence of contract. See the Scottish case of *Donaldson* v. *Haldane* (1840) 7 Cl. & F. 762 (H.L.) and Poulton, " Tort or Contract " (1966) 82 L.Q.R. 346, 360–363. *Hall* v. *Meyrick* [1957] 2 Q.B. 455, in which there are dicta which could be read as implying the contrary, was pleaded solely as a claim in contract.

CHAPTER 13

DEFAMATION [1]

DEFINITION

Defamation is the publication of a statement which tends to lower a person in the estimation of right-thinking members of society generally; or which tends to make them shun or avoid that person.

Many writers define defamation simply as the publication of a statement which tends to bring a person " into hatred, contempt or ridicule." But this is not quite exact, for a statement may possibly be defamatory even if it does not excite in reasonable people feelings quite so strong as hatred, contempt or ridicule [2]; and the definition is defective in omitting any reference to the alternative of " tending to shun or avoid." This addition is necessary, for falsely imputing insolvency or insanity to a man is unquestionably defamation, although, far from tending to excite hatred, contempt or ridicule, it would rouse only pity and sympathy in the minds of reasonable people,[3] who would nevertheless be inclined to shun his society. And Slesser L.J. took this view in *Youssoupoff* v. *Metro-Goldwyn-Mayer Pictures Ltd.*, where a cinematograph film falsely imputed that the plaintiff, a Russian princess, had been raped or seduced by the notorious monk, Rasputin, for this tended " to make the plaintiff be shunned and avoided and that without any moral discredit on her part." [4] A statement which disparages a man in his reputation in relation to his office, profession, calling, trade or business may be defamatory, *e.g.* the imputation of some quality which would be detrimental or the absence of some quality which is essential to the successful carrying on of his office, trade or profession, such as want of ability, incompetence and, of course, dishonest or fraudulent conduct.[5]

---

[1] The leading monograph is Gatley, *Libel and Slander*, 7th ed. (1974). Other works are Odgers, *Libel and Slander*, 6th ed. (1929); Fraser, *Libel and Slander*, 7th ed. (1936); Bower, *Actionable Defamation*, 2nd ed. (1923); Carter-Ruck, *Libel and Slander* (1972); Weir, *Casebook on Tort*, 3rd ed., Chap. 14.

[2] *e.g. Tournier* v. *National, etc. Bank of England* [1924] 1 K.B. 461; *Drummond-Jackson* v. *B.M.A.* [1970] 1 W.L.R. 691, 700, *per* Sir Gordon Willmer.

[3] *Pace* Juvenal: Nil habet infelix paupertas durius in se Quam quod ridiculos homines facit. (Sat. iii, 152–153.)

[4] (1934) 50 T.L.R. 581, 587. But would reasonable people shun the society of a woman who had the misfortune to be raped? (1935) 51 L.Q.R. 281–282. Slesser L.J. saw the difficulty but dismissed it with the remark: " It is to shut one's eye to realities to make these nice distinctions."

[5] *Turner* v. *Metro-Goldwyn-Mayer Pictures Ltd.* [1950] 2 All E.R. 449; *Angel* v. *H. H. Bushell & Co. Ltd.* [1968] 1 Q.B. 813; *Drummond-Jackson* v. *B.M.A.* [1970] 1 W.L.R. 688. The statement must disparage the reputation of the plaintiff personally; it is not enough that it disparages only the goods which he sells: *South Hetton Coal Co. Ltd.* v. *North Eastern News Association Ltd.* [1894] 1 Q.B. 133, 139, *per* Lord Esher M.R. But to disparage a professional man's technique is to disparage him as a professional man; to say of a dentist that he uses a bad technique is to say that he is a bad dentist: *Drummond-Jackson* v. *B.M.A., supra,* at p. 699, *per* Lord Pearson. *Cf. ibid.* at p. 694, *per* Lord Denning M.R. (dissenting).

The words must tend to give rise to the feelings mentioned in the definition.[6] But on the part of whom? The answer is the reasonable man. This rules out on the one hand persons who are so lax or so cynical that they would think none the worse of a man whatever was imputed to him, and on the other hand those who are so censorious as to regard even trivial accusations (if they were true) as lowering another's reputation, or who are so hasty as to infer the worst meaning from any ambiguous statement. It is not these, but the ordinary citizen, whose judgment must be taken as the standard. He is neither unusually suspicious nor unusually naive and he does not always interpret the meaning of words as would a lawyer for he " is not inhibited by a knowledge of the rules of construction." [7] He may thus more freely read an implication into a given form of words, " and, unfortunately, as the law of defamation has to take into account, is especially prone to do so when it is derogatory." [8] The question, as Lord Atkin suggested, is " Would the words tend to lower the plaintiff in the estimation of right-thinking members of society generally? " [9] So, if the plaintiff can prove only that the statement tends to discredit him with one special class of persons, it is. not defamatory unless reasonable people in general would take the same view.[10] Suppose that A is a member of a club which bans the wearing of coloured shirts and that B falsely accuses him of openly wearing one. That may tend to make A unpopular with members of the club, but B has committed no defamation; had A been accused of misappropriating the club funds, the case would have been otherwise; for while right-minded persons in general are indifferent to the hue of other people's underwear, they dislike dishonesty in any quarter; but there is nothing dishonest or dishonourable in openly breaking a club rule of this sort.[11] Similarly, to say of a man that he has put in motion the proper machinery for suppressing crime, in that he has reported certain acts, wrongful in law, to the police, cannot be defamatory.[12]

The law of defamation is in many respects irrational and hair-splitting. Its historical development is responsible for an excess of judicial subtlety and an elaboration of technical rules and distinc-

---

[6] Proof that they actually did give rise to it is unnecessary: *Hough* v. *London Express Newspaper* [1940] 2 K.B. 507, 515, *per* Goddard L.J.: " If words are used which impute discreditable conduct to my friend, he has been defamed to me, although I do not believe the imputation, and may even know that it is untrue."

[7] *Lewis* v. *Daily Telegraph Ltd.* [1964] A.C. 234, 258, *per* Lord Reid.

[8] *Ibid.* at p. 277, *per* Lord Devlin. This is in marked contrast with the old approach to slander typified by *Holt* v. *Astgrigg* (1608) Cro.Jac. 184, *post*, p. 249.

[9] *Sim* v. *Stretch* [1936] 2 All E.R. 1237, 1240.

[10] *Cf.* Lord Hailsham in *Tolley* v. *Fry & Sons Ltd.* [1931] A.C. 333, 339; McCardie J. n *Myroft* v. *Sleight* (1921) 90 L.J.K.B. 883, 886, citing Farwell L.J. in *Leetham* v. *Rank* (1912) 57 S.J. 111; *Miller* v. *David* (1874) L.R. 9 C.P. 118.

[11] This seems to be the reconciliation of apparently inconsistent statements in some of the textbooks; *e.g.* Gatley, *op. cit.*, pp. 21–22; Fraser, *op. cit.*, pp. 8–9.

[12] *Byrne* v. *Deane* [1937] 1 K.B. 818, Greer L.J. dissenting. See also Donovan J.'s summing-up in *Grech* v. *Odhams Press Ltd.*, cited in [1958] 2 All E.R. at p. 464. *Cf. Mawe* v. *Piggott* (1869) I.R. 4 C.L. 54.

tions. Not everyone would agree with Diplock L.J. that it has passed beyond redemption by the courts, but his Lordship's recommendation of it as a fit topic for the attention of the Law Commission should not be neglected.[13] Many of the difficulties facing the law of defamation stem from the fact that it seeks to serve a number of different and not wholly reconcilable purposes.[14]

Distinction between libel and slander

A libel consists of a defamatory statement or representation in permanent form; if a defamatory meaning is conveyed by spoken words or gestures it is slander. Examples of libel, as distinguished from slander, are a picture, statue, waxwork effigy, or any writing, print, mark or sign exposed to view. On the other hand, defamation in the manual language of the deaf and dumb, and mimicry and gesticulation generally (e.g. holding up an empty purse to indicate that the plaintiff has robbed the defendant[15]) would probably be slander, because the movements are more transient. These examples show that it is only broadly true to say that libel is addressed to the eye, slander to the ear.[16] Moreover, broadcasting, both radio and television,[17] and theatrical performances[18] are, by statute, treated as publication in permanent form, i.e. as libel.

It needs no demonstration that if an oral utterance is communicated orally it is a slander that is published, or that if a written statement is shown to a third person, it is a libel that is published. But further, if an oral statement by A is written down by B and shown by B to C, it is a libel, not a slander, that B has published. No doubt A's original uttering of the words to B may have been slander, but then the communication was oral; whereas disclosure of the writing by B to C is not oral. Conversely, if A writes to B a letter defamatory of X and B reads it aloud to C, it ought to be a slander that is published by B, not a libel; but the balance of authority is the other way, although it has very little reasoning in support of it.[19] If I dictate a defamatory letter to my typist the cause of action is

---

[13] Slim v. Daily Telegraph Ltd. [1968] 2 Q.B. 157, 179; Broadway Approvals Ltd. v. Odhams Press Ltd. (No. 2) [1965] 1 W.L.R. 805, 825, per Russell L.J.; Boston v. W. S. Bagshaw & Sons [1966] 1 W.L.R. 1126, 1135, per Diplock L.J.; Pollock, Torts, 15th ed., p. 177. On trial by jury, see Rothermere v. Times Newspapers Ltd. [1973] 1 W.L.R. 448.

[14] See Veitch, " Defamation Awards in Context " (1973) 2 Anglo-American L.R. 473.

[15] Lord Ellenborough C.J. in Cook v. Cox (1814) 3 M. & S. 110, 114.

[16] Fraser, op. cit., pp. 4–5.

[17] Defamation Act 1952, ss. 1, 16.

[18] Theatres Act 1968, s. 4. Performances given on domestic occasions in private dwellings are excepted from this provision: ibid. s. 7.

[19] In Forrester v. Tyrrell (1893) 9 T.L.R. 257, the C.A., following dicta in the Case de Libellis Famosis (1605) 5 Rep. 125a, and in Lamb's Case (1611) 9 Rep. 59b, held it to be libel. See too Robinson v. Chambers [1946] N.I. 148. In Osborn v. Boulter [1930] 2 K.B. 226, 231, 237 Scrutton and Slesser L.JJ. were of opinion obiter that the reading back by a typist of a dictated statement, in the presence of a third party, was a slander; contra, Greer L.J. at p. 236. Forrester v. Tyrrell was not cited.

slander as regards the publication to her.[20] If she reads it back to me or hands it back as a typed letter it would seem that *she* has not by that act published defamatory matter,[21] nor have I published it as a libel, since although I can be liable for a publication of a libel through my agent, I can hardly publish it to *myself*. If the letter is sent out by me or by my typist on my behalf to a third party, I shall be liable for the libel published to the third party. In this connection it has been questioned whether defamatory matter on a gramophone is, as such, libel or only potential slander.[22] If the test be, as we have suggested, " What is the mode of publication? " it seems to be potential slander.[23] Of course the record as such is in permanent form, but that does not settle the point, for matter on the record is not communicated to anyone until a needle is applied to the record, and then it takes the form of speech. No doubt the defamation may have been communicated to anyone who happened to be present while the speaker was consigning it to the record, but *then* the words were spoken and therefore slanderous; that, however, throws no light on what their reproduction by the needle would be.[24] The Court of Appeal in *Youssoupoff* v. *Metro-Goldwyn-Mayer Pictures Ltd.* [25] had no doubt that defamatory matter embodied in a " talking " cinematograph film was a libel. " There can be no doubt that, so far as the photographic part of the exhibition is concerned, that is a permanent matter to be seen by the eye, and is the proper subject of an action for libel, if defamatory. I regard the speech which is synchronised with the photographic reproduction and forms part of one complex, common exhibition as an ancillary circumstance, part of the surroundings explaining that which is to be seen." [26] This reasoning neatly solves any difficulty which might be felt where the gramophone and the picture film are combined to make a " talking " film, but it still leaves open the question whether a gramophone record unaccompanied by any pictorial representation is libel or slander.

Differences between slander and libel

The distinction between libel and slander is purely historical and is obviously antiquated in relation to modern inventions.[27] Nevertheless,

---

[20] It may be a publication on a privileged occasion and so protected on that ground; see *post*, pp. 293–294.

[21] *Eglantine Inn Ltd.* v. *Smith* [1948] N.I. 29, 33. It is submitted that the dicta in *Osborn* v. *Thomas Boulter & Son* [1930] 2 K.B. 226 are concerned with the situation where defamatory matter is dictated and read back then and there from the notes in the presence of a third party, and not with the question of reading out a defamatory document.

[22] Pollock, *Torts*, 15th ed., p. 176, n. 1. See further *Chicken* v. *Ham, Uncommon Law* (A. P. H.), 71.

[23] (1935) 51 L.Q.R. 281–283; 573–574. *Contra*, Landon, in Pollock, *Torts*, 15th ed., p. 176.

[24] *Semble*, matter confided to a parrot is slander when repeated by the bird to another person. *Cf. Chicken* v. *Ham, supra*, at p. 75, *per* Lord Lick.

[25] (1934) 50 T.L.R. 581.

[26] *Ibid., per* Slesser L.J. at p. 587.

[27] A strong committee in 1843 recommended the abolition of the distinction: Spencer Bower, *op. cit.*, pp. 289–290; *cf.* Holdsworth, H.E.L., viii, 378; but the Defamation Committee, 1948 (Cmd. 7536), by a majority (Wade and O'Sullivan dissenting) refused

there are two important differences in their legal consequences. First, libel, if it tends to provoke a breach of the peace, is a crime as well as a tort. Slander, as such, is never criminal, although spoken words may be punishable as being treasonable, seditious, blasphemous or the like.

Secondly, libel is actionable *per se*, *i.e.* without proof of special damage. In slander, special damage must be proved except in the cases stated in the next section.

The rules as to libel are thus more severe for the defendant, and this is said to be justifiable on the ground that libel is much more permanent in character and, so, more likely to do harm to the person defamed; moreover, there is an irresistible tendency on the part of most people to believe almost anything they see in print and if a lie appears in a newspaper, even if it is nailed to the counter, it is not likely that everyone who read and believed the lie will also read a possible apology in a succeeding issue of the same newspaper.

Special damage

" Special " damage is a phrase which has been rightly criticised as either meaningless or misleading and " actual " damage has been suggested as a more accurate expression.[28] But whatever be the adjective used, it signifies that no damages are recoverable merely for loss of reputation by reason of the slander, and that the plaintiff must prove loss of money or of some temporal or material advantage estimable in money. If there is only loss of the society of one's friends, that is not enough. Hence, while loss of your friend's hospitality is special damage, exclusion from the religious congregation to which you belong is not; for a dinner has temporal and material value, while spiritual communion has none in this connection.[29]

Where there is no need to prove special damage in defamation, the plaintiff can recover general damages for the injury to his reputation without adducing any evidence that it has in fact been harmed, for the law presumes that *some* damage will arise in the ordinary course of things. It is enough that the immediate tendency of the words is to impair his reputation. If the plaintiff contends that special damage has been suffered in addition to general damages, he must allege it in his pleadings and prove it at the trial, but even if he breaks down on this point, he can still recover general damages.[30]

Damage must of course not be too remote. The general principles as to this have already been discussed,[31] and the only peculiarity in

---

to recommend the abolition of the distinction. See Wade, 66 L.Q.R. 348, 357. In Scotland, no differentiation is made between libel and slander. (Cmd. 7536, para. 40.)

[28] Bower, *op. cit.*, Art. 13. See, too, Bowen L.J. in *Ratcliffe* v. *Evans* [1892] 2 Q.B. 524. " Special damage " has other meanings with which the present meaning should not be confused: Jolowicz, " The Changing Use of ' Special Damage ' and its Effect on the Law " [1960] C.L.J. 214.

[29] *Roberts* v. *Roberts* (1864) 5 B. & S. 384; *Davies* v. *Solomon* (1871) L.R. 7 Q.B. 112.

[30] Odgers, *op. cit.*, p. 305; Gatley, *op. cit.*, pp. 415–416.

[31] *Ante*, pp. 84–106.

defamation is that illness arising from mental worry induced by slander not actionable *per se* is damage which is too remote,[32] although in slander actionable *per se*, libel, and other torts, that is not now the law provided the damage amounts to nervous shock.[33] The exception has been defended on the ground that otherwise the courts might be pestered with an infinity of trumpery or groundless actions.[34]

It was held in an old case [35] that if A slanders B so that B is wrongfully dismissed by C from C's employment, A is not liable to B, because the " special damage must be the legal and natural consequences of the words spoken," and that A is no more responsible for C's unlawful act than he would be if B's neighbours, believing A's lie to be true, were to duck B in a horse-pond. But this reasoning cannot now be regarded as law, for although the case has not been actually overruled (indeed, on the facts the decision may have been correct), yet the *ratio decidendi* encountered strong adverse criticism in later cases in the House of Lords and in other courts. In *Lynch* v. *Knight*,[36] Lord Wensleydale said: " To make the words actionable by reason of special damage, the consequence must be such as, taking human nature as it is, with its infirmities, and having regard to the relationship of the parties concerned, might fairly and reasonably have been anticipated and feared would follow from the speaking the words." [37] In other words, if A does an unlawful act to B, the chain of causation may possibly be severed by the unlawful act of C, but it does not follow that it must necessarily be severed thereby.[38]

" Unauthorised " repetition of the words by other persons will make the damage too remote,[39] unless there is a legal or moral duty to repeat them,[40] or the defendant intends them to be repeated or, probably, the repetition is the natural and probable consequence of the original publication.[41]

SLANDER ACTIONABLE PER SE

The exceptional cases in which slander is actionable without proof of special damage are:

---

[32] *Allsop* v. *Allsop* (1860) 5 H. & N. 534.

[33] *Ante*, p. 118; Gatley, *op. cit.*, pp. 105 and 605.

[34] Wright J. in *Wilkinson* v. *Downton* [1897] 2 Q.B. 57, 60.

[35] *Vicars* v. *Wilcox* (1806) 8 East 1.

[36] (1861) 9 H.L.C. 577, 600.

[37] See, too, *Bowen* v. *Hall* (1881) 6 Q.B.D. 333, 339 and *cf. Longdon-Griffiths* v. *Smith* [1950] 2 All E.R. 662, 678 (not reported on this point in other reports).

[38] *Ante*, pp. 104–105. See, too, Gatley, *op. cit.*, pp. 100–102.

[39] *Ward* v. *Weeks* (1830) 7 Bing. 211; *Parkins* v. *Scott* (1862) 1 H. & C. 153.

[40] *Derry* v. *Handley* (1867) 16 L.T. 263; Clerk and Lindsell, *Torts*, 13th ed., pp. 1032–1035.

[41] *Speight* v. *Gosnay* (1891) 60 L.J.Q.B. 231; *Ward* v. *Lewis* [1955] 1 W.L.R. 9; *Cellactite and British Uralite* v. *H. H. Robertson Co.* [1957] C.L.Y. 1989. For the application of a similar rule to libel, see *Weld-Blundell* v. *Stephens* [1920] A.C. 956, 987, 999; *Cutler* v. *McPhail* [1962] 2 Q.B. 292.

1. Imputation of a criminal offence

Imputation of a criminal offence punishable with imprisonment.
There must be direct imputation of the offence, not merely of suspicion
of it,[42] and the offence must be punishable by imprisonment in the first
instance.[43] If the slander goes into details of the offence charged, it is
not actionable *per se* if the details are inconsistent with one another,
as in *Jackson* v. *Adams*,[44] where the defendant said to the plaintiff, a
churchwarden, " Who stole the parish bellropes, you scamping rascal ? "
As the possession of the ropes was vested in the churchwarden, theft
of them by the plaintiff was impossible.[45] But there is authority for the
proposition that the basis of the rule, that imputation of a criminal
offence is actionable *per se*, is the probability of social ostracism of the
plaintiff and not his jeopardy of imprisonment [46]; this seems inconsistent with *Jackson* v. *Adams*.

2. Imputation of disease

*Imputation of a contagious or infectious disease likely to prevent other
persons from associating with the plaintiff.* There is some uncertainty
about this exception, nonetheless so because there is no reported
decision on it later than 1844,[47] nor are the modern monographs on
defamation entirely in agreement on the topic.[48] It has always included
venereal disease and, in olden times, plague and leprosy. Perhaps at the
present day it covers any disease which is infectious or contagious
whether it be " owing to the visitation of God, to accident, or to the
indiscretion of the party therewith afflicted " [49]; for, although an
accusation of smallpox was held in 1599 not to be actionable at all,
the decision turned upon a rule of interpretation now extinct.[50]

---

[42] *Simmons* v. *Mitchell* (1880) 6 App.Cas. 156, P.C.
[43] *Hellwig* v. *Mitchell* [1910] 1 K.B. 609. It is not enough that imprisonment may be
inflicted for non-payment of a fine which has been imposed: *Ormiston* v. *G.W. Ry.*
[1917] 1 K.B. 598.
[44] (1835) 2 Bing.N.C. 402.
[45] Perhaps this case would have been decided differently if the Theft Act 1968 had
been law.
[46] *Gray* v. *Jones* (1939) 160 L.T. 361. In *D. & L. Caterers Ltd.* v. *D'Ajou* [1945] K.B.
364, the C.A. left open the question whether a slander which imputes to a corporation
an offence which, in the case of an individual, is punishable with imprisonment is actionable *per se*. It is submitted that, as the law stands at present, the answer ought to be in
the negative, for if the basis of this species of slander actionable *per se* is jeopardy of
imprisonment, a corporation, being an artificial person, cannot be imprisoned; and if
its basis is the probability of social ostracism, a corporation cannot as such be subjected
to *social* ostracism, though ostracism of it as a trading body is possible. See Gatley, *op.
cit.*, pp. 78–79, 376.
[47] *Bloodworth* v. *Gray*, 7 Man. & G. 334.
[48] Gatley, *op. cit.*, pp. 84–85; Odgers, *op. cit.*, pp. 44–45; Fraser, *op. cit.*, pp. 32–33;
Bower, *op. cit.*, pp. 25–26.
[49] Bacon, Abr., 7th ed. (1832), vii, 266–267 (slander). The Defamation Committee
(Cmd. 7536), para. 45, suggested it covered " such contagious skin complaints as are
often caused by personal uncleanliness."
[50] *James* v. *Rutlech*, 4 Rep. 17a; ambiguous words were there interpreted *mitiori sensu*,
i.e. in the sense more favourable to the defendant. Hence at that time to charge a person
with " pox " (which might mean venereal disease or smallpox) was regarded as an accusation of the less repulsive ailment—smallpox. In *Villers* v. *Monsley* (1769) 2 Wils. 403, there
were *obiter dicta* that oral imputation of the itch was not actionable, but the case itself
was one of libel, not slander.

3. Imputation of unchastity

Imputation of unchastity [51] *or adultery to any woman or girl.* This is a statutory exception created by the Slander of Women Act 1891,[52] which also provides that in this exception, " the plaintiff shall not recover more costs than damages, unless the judge shall certify that there was reasonable ground for bringing the action." [53]

4. Imputation of unfitness or incompetence

Imputation of unfitness, dishonesty or incompetence in any office, profession, calling, trade or business held or carried on by the plaintiff at the time when the slander was published. This is by far the most important because the most frequently invoked exception. At common law its scope was severely restricted by the rule that the slander must be spoken of the plaintiff in the way of his office so that it was not, for example, slander actionable *per se* to say of a schoolmaster that he had committed adultery with one of the school cleaners.[54] Now, however, it is provided by section 2 of the Defamation Act 1952, " In an action for slander in respect of words calculated to disparage the plaintiff in any office, profession, calling, trade or business held or carried on by him at the time of publication, it shall not be necessary to allege or prove special damage whether or not the words are spoken of the plaintiff in the way of his office, profession, calling, trade or business." It is thought, therefore, that any words spoken of a man which are reasonably likely to injure him in his office, profession, calling, trade or business will be actionable *per se*.[55]

At common law a distinction was taken between profitable and purely honorary offices, and in the case of the latter slander was not actionable *per se* unless, if true, it would have been a ground for removing the plaintiff from his office.[56] The wording of section 2 of the Defamation Act 1952, however, appears to be wide enough to be interpreted so as to put an end to this distinction.[57]

Reason for exceptions

Two questions may well be asked by the student. One is, " Why

---

[51] Held in *Kerr* v. *Kennedy* [1942] 1 K.B. 409 to include an imputation of lesbianism.
[52] 54 & 55 Vict. c. 51, s. 1. See Odgers, *op. cit.*, pp. 61–63.
[53] See *Russo* v. *Cole* [1966] 1 W.L.R. 248.
[54] *Jones* v. *Jones* [1916] 2 A.C. 481; *De Stempel* v. *Dunkels* (1937) 54 T.L.R. 289; 55 T.L.R. 655; *Hopwood* v. *Muirson* [1945] K.B. 313 (" The slander was upon the solicitor as a man; not upon the man as a solicitor ").
[55] It matters not how humble the office may be, so long as it is lawful (Gatley, p. 90, Clerk and Lindsell, *Torts*, 13th ed., p. 942) and a man may hold more than one office at the same time: *Bull* v. *Vazquez* [1947] 1 All E.R. 334. The exception does not include slander calculated to disparage the plaintiff in the performance of a duty compulsorily imposed upon citizens: *Cleghorn* v. *Sadler* [1945] K.B. 325 (firewatching in wartime).
[56] *e.g. Alexander* v. *Jenkinson* [1892] 1 Q.B. 797. To say of a justice of the peace, " He is an ass and a beetle-headed justice," was not actionable *per se*, for it imputes ignorance of the law and he need know none (cited in *How* v. *Prinn* (1702) 2 Salk. 695; Holt 652).
[57] Clerk and Lindsell, *Torts*, 13th ed., p. 944. *Cf.* Gatley, p. 88; *Robinson* v. *Ward* (1958) 108 L.J. 491. A false charge of dishonesty even though not a ground for removal is in any case actionable *per se*: *Booth* v. *Arnold* [1895] 1 Q.B. 571.

should some, but not all, slanders be actionable *per se*? " The other is, " Why has not the distinction been applied to libels? " The answers to both questions are historical.[58]

As to the first, in early times, apart from some inadequate statutes, defamation was not actionable at common law, but was redressible only in the ecclesiastical or the local courts. Then the common law courts, fearing that their ecclesiastical brethren might monopolise jurisdiction here, gradually allowed an action upon the case for written or spoken words. But just because it was an action upon the case, damage had to be proved. Here, then, the law made a false start. What it ought to have remedied was insult; what it did remedy was insult *plus* pecuniary loss. Damage, not insult, became the gist of the action, subject to the exceptions just discussed.

Probably the oldest of these is the imputation of a criminal offence punishable with imprisonment. No satisfactory explanation of this has ever been given.[59] At any rate, the qualification that the offence must be punishable with imprisonment is untraceable in the Year Books, inconsistent with principle, contrary to practice in the sixteenth and early seventeenth centuries and was not recognised until 1642. It was adopted in order to put a check upon the increase of actions for words.[60]

The other exceptions developed later. One would be tempted to say that the common origin of all the exceptions (apart from the statutory one due to the Slander of Women Act 1891) was that accusations of crime, of contagious disease, of incompetence or dishonesty in one's business are so obviously likely to lead to damage that it would have been foolish to insist upon evidence of it, and to some extent this does seem to have influenced the courts; but it is not a complete explanation.

When these exceptions were established, distinctions of the most ridiculous artificiality were taken by the courts, although there was a praiseworthy motive at the back of them. The Star Chamber was trying to suppress duelling, and persons who had been insulted consequently resorted to the law courts which became flooded with slander actions. The judges were probably right in trying to stem a spate of litigation on disputes often of a trumpery nature, but they were certainly wrong in the mode which they adopted. They dissected the meaning of oppro-

---

[58] Holdsworth, " Defamation in the Sixteenth and Seventeenth Centuries " (1924) 40 L.Q.R. 302, 397; (1925) 41 L.Q.R. 13, esp. at 40 L.Q.R. 388–400; 41 L.Q.R. 14–17.

[59] Holdsworth suggests that it originated in the days when the common law courts were trying to distinguish between words which they would hold to be actionable, and words which were actionable only in an ecclesiastical court. Thus, if A called B a " traitor " or a " thief," as treason and theft were punishable in the common law courts, they held that lying imputations of these offences were also triable there. But if A called B a " heretic" or an " adulterer," as heresy and fornication were cognisable only in an ecclesiastical court, false accusations of them were not reckoned as actionable in a common law court. This is clear enough, but how does it explain the fact that the common law courts, where they *did* entertain such actions, departed from their own rule about proof of special damage?

[60] 40 L.Q.R. 399, n. 7.

brious epithets with as much care as if they had been technical terms in a conveyance of property.[61] Probably the most absurd example was *Holt* v. *Astgrigg*,[62] where the defendant said: " Sir Thomas Holt struck his cook on the head with a cleaver, and cleaved his head; the one part lay on the one shoulder and another part on the other." Was this an accusation of homicide? No, because it was not averred that the cook was killed. Decisions like this made an action for slander in the seventeenth century more like a lottery than a legal proceeding, and their evil effects are felt at the present day.

As to the second question, " Why is it unnecessary ever to prove special damage in libel? " the answer in brief is this: The old common law action on the case for words applied to both spoken and written words, but actions for written words must, in view of the backward state of printing and the check upon publication which resulted from the necessity of procuring a government licence for it, have been considerably rarer than actions for spoken words. Then, when printing became commoner, defamatory words were dealt with in the Court of Star Chamber principally as a crime. Next, the Star Chamber fell and the common law courts invented an action for libel quite distinct from the action on the case for spoken words. This they did in 1670 in *King* v. *Lake*.[63] And they decided that no damage need be proved, perhaps because the Star Chamber had occasionally given damages, perhaps also because duelling had to be suppressed; and if the plaintiff were driven to proving damage, he might have found the burden so heavy that he would have preferred to vindicate his character with his sword in Leicester Fields rather than by an action in Westminster Hall.[64]

ESSENTIALS OF DEFAMATION GENERALLY

Whether defamation consists of libel or slander the following requisites are common to both, and must be proved by the plaintiff:

1. The words must be defamatory.
2. They must refer to the plaintiff.
3. They must be " maliciously " published.

1. The words must be defamatory

As we have seen, to be defamatory the words must tend to lower the plaintiff's reputation in the estimation of right-minded persons, or must tend to cause him to be shunned or avoided. For the issue to be decided, therefore, it is essential to know the very words on which the

---

[61] Matters may not be so very different today. See *Slim* v. *Daily Telegraph Ltd.* [1968] 2 Q.B. 157, 171–177, *per* Diplock L.J. (a case of libel).
[62] (1608) Cro.Jac. 184. *Barrons* v. *Ball* (1613), *ibid.* 331, and *Cooper* v. *Smith* (1617), *ibid.* 423, are similar curiosities.
[63] Hardres 470.
[64] Holdsworth, *loc. cit.* at 40 L.Q.R. 397–398; 41 L.Q.R. 14–17.

plaintiff founds his claim. A plaintiff is not entitled to bring a libel action on a letter which he has never seen and of the contents of which he is unaware but which he merely suspects to have been written and to contain words defamatory of him.[65]

Abuse

It is commonly said that mere vulgar spoken abuse is neither defamation nor indeed any other tort [66] but this needs some explanation. Spoken words which are prima facie slanderous are not actionable if it is clear that they were uttered merely as general vituperation *and* were so understood by those who heard them.[67] This makes the manner in which the words were spoken very important in determining whether they were mere vituperation or slander. It is possible that the same word may or may not be slanderous according as it is said deliberately in cold blood, or is bawled out at the height of a violent quarrel.[68] " The manner in which the words were pronounced, and various other circumstances might explain the meaning of the word." So Sir James Mansfield C.J. in *Penfold* v. *Westcote* [69] where the defendant called out, " Why don't you come out you blackguard, rascal, scoundral [*sic*], Penfold, you are a thief," and it was left to the jury to say whether the general abusive terms accompanying " thief " reduced " thief " itself to mere abuse; and the jury gave a verdict for the plaintiff.

The speaker of the words must take the risk of his hearers construing them as defamatory and not simply abusive, and the burden of proof is upon him to show that a reasonable man would not have understood them in the former sense.[70]

If the words be written, not spoken, they cannot be protected as mere abuse,[71] for the defendant had time for reflection before he wrote and his readers may know nothing of any heated dispute or other circumstances which may have led him to write what he did; but it is quite possible for them to be not defamatory for some other reason.

Although there is no civil remedy for mere vituperation, a person may be bound over by justices of the peace to be of good behaviour if he utters rash, quarrelsome or unmannerly words which tend to a breach of the peace or which deter an officer from doing his duty.[72]

---

[65] *Collins* v. *Jones* [1955] 1 Q.B. 564.

[66] " For mere general abuse spoken, no action lies ": Mansfield C.J. in *Thorley* v. *Kerry* (1812) 4 Taunt. 355, 365; Pollock C.B. and Wilde B. in *Parkins* v. *Scott* (1862) 1 H. & C. 153, 158, 159.

[67] Gatley, *op. cit.*, pp. 45–46, 59, 82–83; Odgers, *op. cit.*, pp. 41–43; Fraser, *op. cit.*, p. 31; Salmond, *Torts*, 16th ed., p. 143. See, too, Pound in *Selected Essays on the Law of Torts* (1924), pp. 110–118.

[68] *Field* v. *Davis* [1955] C.L.Y. 1543 (defendant called plaintiff, who was a married woman, " a tramp." Held, this expression was capable of a defamatory meaning but considering the obvious temper of the defendant, it was understood by those who heard it as mere abuse). See also *Australian Newspaper Co. Ltd.* v. *Bennett* [1894] A.C. 284; *Gwynne* v. *Wairarapa Times-Age Ltd.* [1972] N.Z.L.R. 586.

[69] (1806) 2 B. & P.(N.R.) 335.

[70] Gatley, *op. cit.*, p. 45.

[71] Gatley, *op. cit.*, p. 82. But see Salmond, *Torts*, 16th ed., p. 143.

[72] Stone's *Justices' Manual*, title " Surety for good behaviour."

Function of jury

In determining whether the words are defamatory, the functions of judge and jury must be carefully distinguished.[73] After fierce controversy, Fox's Libel Act 1792,[74] which professed to be a declaratory Act, allotted to the jury in a criminal trial for libel the task of deciding whether the words are defamatory or not; the Act was necessary because judges had been usurping this function and had thereby warped criminal trials for seditious libels into modes for securing the conviction of political offenders. The provision of Fox's Act with respect to criminal libel has long been regarded as also applicable to civil actions for defamation.

Function of judge

The power given to the jury by Fox's Act is not unlimited and the judge can exercise control in three ways.

First, if he decides to leave the case to the jury, he must tell them what defamation means in law.

Secondly, if he thinks that no reasonable man could regard the words as defamatory, he must withdraw the case from the jury.[75] "To put it from the point of view of an appellate court, the question of libel or no libel should have been left to the jury if it cannot be said that twelve men could not reasonably have come to the conclusion that the words were defamatory." [76] *Capital and Counties Bank Ltd.* v. *Henty* [77] is a leading case on this. Henty & Sons, a firm of brewers, were in the habit of receiving, in payment from their customers, cheques on various branches of the Capital and Counties Bank, which the bank cashed for the convenience of Hentys at a particular branch of which X was manager. In consequence of a squabble with X, Hentys sent a printed circular to a large number of their customers (who knew nothing of the squabble), "Henty & Sons hereby give notice that they will not receive in payment cheques drawn on any of the branches of the Capital and Counties Bank." The circular became known to other persons and there was a run on the bank, which sued Hentys for libel on the ground that the circular imputed insolvency. There was much difference of opinion in the courts below, and it was only after hearing

---

[73] Despite the general decline of jury trial in civil cases, the majority of actions for defamation are still tried by jury: see *Rothermere* v. *Times Newspapers Ltd.* [1973] 1 W.L.R. 448.　　　　　　　　　　　　　　　　　　　　　　　　[74] 32 Geo. 3, c. 60.
[75] *Turner* v. *Bowley* (1896) 12 T.L.R. 402; *Nevill* v. *Fine Art Insurance Co. Ltd.* [1897] A.C. 68; *Sim* v. *Stretch* [1936] 2 All E.R. 1237, H.L.; *Jones* v. *Skelton* [1963] 1 W.L.R. 1362, P.C. Only in a very clear case will the court dispose of the matter on an application to strike out the action: *Drummond-Jackson* v. *B.M.A.* [1970] 1 W.L.R. 688. The dissenting judgment of Lord Denning M.R. carries an important criticism of present-day practice. It seems that an interlocutory ruling refusing to hold that words are incapable of a defamatory meaning does not bind the trial judge to hold that they are so capable: *Morgan* v. *Odhams Press Ltd.* [1970] 1 W.L.R. 820.
[76] *Turner* v. *Metro-Goldwyn-Mayer Pictures Ltd.* [1950] 1 All E. R. 449, 454, *per* Lord Porter; *Morris* v. *Sanders Universal Products* [1954] 1 W.L.R. 67. Words may still be capable of a defamatory meaning even though they make it clear that the law was on the plaintiff's side: *Clarke* v. *Associated Newspapers* [1955] C.L.Y. 1542.
[77] (1882) 7 App.Cas. 741.

the case twice argued that the House of Lords, by a majority of four to one, held that the circular, taken in conjunction with the circumstances of its publication, did not constitute evidence from which any reasonable person would infer such an imputation; that there was no case to go to the jury; and that the defendants were not liable. Lord Selborne L.C. said that the fact that some customers showed the circular to strangers was not the fault of Hentys, who had not authorised the communication,[78] and that where words in their natural meaning were not libellous, evidence must be brought to show that reasonable men might be led to understand them in a libellous sense. Both these propositions are unexceptionable and there are no doubt many reasons why a creditor may refuse to accept a cheque on a particular bank. Yet it might be thought that the first reason that would occur to any reasonable person would be that the bank was financially unsound. The decision has been subjected to considerable criticism [79] and recently Salmon L.J. has said that the principles, never better formulated than in *Henty's* case, were perhaps never worse applied.[80]

Generally the controversy is whether the words are capable of bearing a defamatory meaning at all, but in *Lewis* v. *Daily Telegraph Ltd.*[81] the defendants admitted that the words were defamatory. What they denied was that the words were defamatory in the particular sense alleged by the plaintiffs. The defendants had published a paragraph in their newspaper stating that officers of the City of London Fraud Squad were investigating the affairs of the plaintiff company and the plaintiffs alleged that these words carried the meaning that the company's affairs were conducted fraudulently or dishonestly. By a majority the House of Lords decided that the words were not capable of bearing that meaning. As Lord Devlin pointed out, one cannot make a rule about the fundamental question—what is the meaning which the words convey to the ordinary man—but the ordinary sensible man is not capable of thinking that whenever there is a police inquiry there is guilt. Otherwise " it would be almost impossible to give accurate information about anything." [82]

Thirdly, if the words are obviously defamatory, the judge, although he cannot directly tell the jury that they are so, may nevertheless indicate to them that the evidence cannot bear any other interpretation. If, in spite of this, they find a verdict for the defendant, a new trial will be ordered on appeal.[83] But this is so stark an interference

---

[78] 7 App.Cas. 746–747.
[79] Scrutton L.J. in *Youssoupoff* v. *Metro-Goldwyn-Mayer Pictures Ltd.* (1934) 50 T.L.R. 581, 594, thought that the law and the facts got pretty far apart from each other in *Henty's* case; and see *per* Goddard L.J. in *Hopwood* v. *Muirson* [1945] K.B. 313, 318.
[80] *Slim* v. *Daily Telegraph Ltd.* [1968] 2 Q.B. 157, 187.
[81] [1964] A.C. 234; Weir, *Casebook on Tort*, 3rd ed., p. 426.
[82] *Ibid.* at pp. 285—286.
[83] *Levi* v. *Milne* (1827) 4 Bing. 195; Sankey L.J. in *Broome* v. *Agar* (1928) 138 L.T. 698, 701–702; Scrutton L.J. *ibid.* 699, and in *Youssoupoff* v. *Metro-Goldwyn-Mayer Pictures Ltd.* (1934) 50 T.L.R. 581, 584; Lord Buckmaster in *Lockhart* v. *Harrison* (1928) 139 L.T. 521, 523.

with the normal functions of a jury that the courts are very loth to make such an order, and examples of it in the reports are rare indeed.[84]

Innuendo

The words of which the plaintiff complains may be either (a) defamatory in their natural and ordinary meaning or (b) defamatory only, or additionally to (a), in the light of facts and circumstances known to persons to whom the words were published.

As to (a) words can, of course, convey different meanings to different people [85] and the plaintiff is not obliged to give an interpretation of the words either in his statement of claim or in his evidence.[86] It is as defamatory of A to say that justice miscarried when he was acquitted of murdering X, as it is to say outright that he did murder X.[87] But it must be remembered that, as Lord Blackburn said, " there are no words so plain that they may not be published with reference to such circumstances, and to such persons knowing these circumstances, as to convey a meaning very different from that which would be understood from the same words used under different circumstances." [88] Or, we might add, at different periods of history, and this makes it hazardous to say dogmatically of any epithet that it is or is not, for all time and in all places and circumstances, defamatory. To call a man a " cony-catcher " would convey little to most people today but at one time it was a well-known word for a swindler. Conversely, most people nowadays know what the Mafia is and so words alleging that a company is controlled by the Mafia are defamatory in their natural and ordinary meaning.[89] If the words are fairly capable of several meanings, some defamatory and some innocent, the case should be left to the jury.[90] But where the statement has only one reasonable meaning which is harmless, the court will not torture into it a defamatory meaning which

---

[84] *Broome* v. *Agar* (1928) 138 L.T. 698.
[85] See *Slim* v. *Daily Telegraph Ltd.* [1968] 2 Q.B. 157, 171–177, *per* Diplock L.J. It is respectfully submitted that his Lordship overstates the difficulties when he insists that the legal process requires that a single " right " meaning be given to the words for the purposes of the action. Cannot a jury or a judge alone recognise and award damages upon the basis that the words may convey different meanings to different reasonable people? *Cf. ibid.,* *per* Lord Denning M.R. at pp. 168–169.
[86] *Cadam* v. *Beaverbrook Newspapers Ltd.* [1959] 1 Q.B. 413, 525, *per* Morris L.J.; *Lewis* v. *Daily Telegraph Ltd.* [1964] A.C. 234, 265, *per* Lord Morris; *Jones* v. *Skelton* [1963] 1 W.L.R. 1362, P.C.
[87] See *Loughans* v. *Odhams Press Ltd.* [1963] 1 Q.B. 299, as explained by Upjohn L.J. in *Grubb* v. *Bristol United Press Ltd.* [1963] 1 Q.B. 309, 331–333. *Hoare* v. *Silverlock* (1848) 12 Q.B. 624 is, perhaps, an extreme example.
[88] *Capital and Counties Bank* v. *Henty* (1882) 7 App.Cas. 741, 771.
[89] *Associated Leisure Ltd.* v. *Associated Newspapers Ltd.* [1970] 3 W.L.R. 101.
[90] *Cassidy* v. *Daily Mirror Newspapers Ltd.* [1929] 2 K.B. 331, 339–340, *per* Scrutton L.J.; *Newstead* v. *London Express Newspapers Ltd.* [1940] 1 K.B. 377, 396, *per* du Parcq L.J.; *English, etc. Society Ltd.* v. *Odhams Press Ltd.* [1940] 1 K.B. 440; *Sim* v. *Stretch* [1936] 2 All E.R. 1237, 1241 where Lord Atkin cited Brett L.J. in *Capital and Counties Bank* v. *Henty* (1880) 5 C.P.D. 514, 541: " It seems to me unreasonable that when there are a number of good interpretations, the only bad one should be seized upon to give a defamatory sense to the document." *Turner* v. *Metro-Goldwyn-Mayer Pictures Ltd.* [1950] 2 All E. R. 449, 454; *Pyke* v. *Hibernian Bank* [1950] I.R. 195; *Jones* v. *Skelton* [1963] 1 W.L.R. 1362, 1370, *per* Lord Morris.

no doubt is possible, but which can be reached only by inventing facts which are not disclosed and are in fact non-existent.

Where, however, the words are not defamatory in their natural and ordinary meaning, or where the plaintiff wishes to rely upon an additional defamatory meaning in which they were understood by persons having knowledge of particular facts, then an innuendo is required. This is a statement by the plaintiff of the meaning which he attributes to the words,[91] and he must prove the existence of facts to support that meaning.[92] If such facts do not exist, the innuendo fails and may be struck out of the statement of claim,[93] though the plaintiff may still fall back on the natural and ordinary meaning of the words.[94] Separate causes of action exist in respect of that meaning and of each innuendo that is proved.[95]

One of the best-known cases of the successful use of the innuendo is *Tolley* v. *Fry & Sons Ltd.*[96] The plaintiff, a famous amateur golfer, was caricatured by the defendants, without his knowledge or consent, in an advertisement of their chocolate which depicted him with a packet of it protruding from his pocket. A caddy was represented with him, who also had a packet of chocolate the excellence of which he likened, in some doggerel verse, to the excellence of the plaintiff's drive. The plaintiff alleged in his innuendo that the defendants thereby meant that the plaintiff had agreed to let his portrait be exhibited for advertisement, that he had done this for gain, and that he had thus prostituted his reputation as an amateur golfer. The House of Lords held that the caricature, as explained by the evidence, was capable of being thus construed; for golfers testified that any amateur golfer who assented to such advertisement might be called upon to resign his membership of any reputable club, and it also appeared from correspondence between the defendants and their advertising agents that they were quite alive to the possible effect of the advertisement on the plaintiff's amateur status.

This type of innuendo, the " true " innuendo, should be distinguished from the " false " innuendo in which the plaintiff does not rely upon extrinsic facts to support the defamatory meaning of the words, but merely states a particular inference which, he says, is to be

---

[91] The plaintiff is bound by the meaning he attributes to the words in the innuendo as pleaded: " *Truth* " (*N.Z.*) *Ltd.* v. *Holloway* [1960] 1 W.L.R. 997, P.C.

[92] Since 1949 these facts must be pleaded with proper particularity: R.S.C., Ord. 82, r. 3 (1).

[93] *Grubb* v. *Bristol United Press Ltd.* [1963] 1 Q.B. 309, applying *Capital and Counties Bank* v. *Henty* (1882) L.R. 7 App.Cas. 741. *Cf. Loughans* v. *Odhams Press Ltd.* [1963] 1 Q.B. 299.

[94] *Lewis* v. *Daily Telegraph Ltd.* [1963] 1 Q.B. 340, affd. [1964] A.C. 234.

[95] Common Law Procedure Act 1852; *Watkin* v. *Hall* (1868) L.R. 3 Q.B. 896; *Sim* v. *Stretch* [1936] 2 All E.R. 1237; *Grubb* v. *Bristol United Press Ltd.*, *supra*; *Lewis* v. *Daily Telegraph Ltd.*, *supra*. It is important to distinguish carefully between these separate causes of action. There may be a defence to some but not to others. Nevertheless, Lord Devlin has doubted the value of the rule: [1964] A.C. at p. 279.

[96] [1931] A.C. 333.

drawn from the words themselves.[97] Here the plaintiff is not alleging a separate cause of action, but is relying upon the natural and ordinary meaning of the words.[98] For example, " if the defendant published of John Smith: ' His name is certainly not George Washington,' then, however much the defendant may argue that the words were a harmless truism concerned merely with nomenclature, the natural and ordinary implication of the words is that John Smith is untruthful; and presumably the jury would find that to be the ordinary meaning of the words." [99] The basic rule in such a case is that it is unnecessary to plead an innuendo explaining George Washington's reputation for truthfulness, but such a restrictive approach has led to difficulties: not only is the line between the true and false innuendo difficult to draw, but the defendant may be put in serious difficulty where, although the words clearly do not demand a true innuendo, their meaning is obscure or they are open to a number of interpretations.[1] The courts sought to meet this difficulty by stressing the desirability of pleading any meaning alleged by the plaintiff which was not immediately obvious on reading the words,[2] but this has proved insufficient and the Court of Appeal in a series of recent decisions has stated that unless the defamatory statement has only one meaning which is clear and explicit it is *necessary* for the fair trial of the action for the plaintiff to plead the meaning he ascribes to the words.[3] For pleading purposes, therefore, the distinction between true and false innuendoes has become blurred.

Juxtaposition. Mere juxtaposition to noxious matter may make an otherwise innocent representation defamatory. The most famous instance of this is *Monson* v. *Tussauds Ltd.*[4] where the defendants,

---

[97] Lord Devlin regrets the use of " true " and " false," but he agrees that there is a difference between the " legal " innuendo, which requires supporting facts, and the " popular " innuendo, which may not: *Lewis* v. *Daily Telegraph Ltd., supra*, at pp. 279–280.

[98] *Jones* v. *Skelton* [1963] 1 W.L.R. 1362, 1370–1371, *per* Lord Morris.

[99] *Grubb* v. *Bristol United Press Ltd.* [1963] 1 Q.B. 309, 327, *per* Holroyd Pearce L.J. See also the examples given by Davies L.J., *ibid.*, at pp. 336–337.

[1] " The time has surely come when specialist practitioners in the field of defamation must do some re-thinking about the desirability of pleading innuendoes far more freely than appears to have been done during the last 15 or 20 years.": *S. & K. Holdings Ltd.* v. *Throgmorton Publications Ltd.* [1972] 1 W.L.R. 1036, 1041, *per* Edmund Davies L.J.

[2] *Lewis* v. *Daily Telegraph, supra*; see also *Longhams* v. *Odhams Press Ltd.* [1963] 1 Q.B. 299; *Grubb* v. *Bristol United Press Ltd., supra*; *Drummond-Jackson* v. *B.M.A.* [1970] 1 W.L.R. 688, 694, *per* Lord Denning M.R.

[3] *Allsop* v. *Church of England Newspaper Ltd.* [1972] 2 Q.B. 161; *S. & K. Holdings Ltd.* v. *Throgmorton Publications Ltd., supra*; *D.D.S.A. Pharmaceuticals Ltd.* v. *Times Newspapers Ltd.* [1973] 1 Q.B. 21. In *Slim* v. *Daily Telegraph Ltd.* [1968] 2 Q.B. 157, 175, Diplock L.J. said that if a plaintiff sets out in his statement of claim particular defamatory meanings, then he is in effect estopped from contending at the trial that the words bear a more injurious meaning, but he may contend that they bear some other, less injurious but still defamatory, meaning. But if plaintiffs are to be encouraged, in the interests of clarity, to plead their interpretations of the natural and ordinary meanings of words, they should not be penalised by too severe an application of this rule. Otherwise the result will be that they will keep their options open by reverting to the old practice of pleading every possible defamatory meaning, however far-fetched, which the ingenuity of their counsel can devise. See also *ibid.* at pp. 184–186, *per* Salmon L.J.

[4] [1894] 1 Q.B. 671; *Garbett* v. *Hazell, Watson and Viney Ltd.* [1943] 2 All E.R. 359.

who kept a waxworks exhibition, had exhibited a wax model of the plaintiff, with a gun, in a room adjoining the " Chamber of Horrors." The plaintiff had been tried for murder in Scotland and released on a verdict of " Not Proven " and a representation of the scene of the alleged murder was displayed in the Chamber of Horrors. The Court of Appeal considered that though in all the circumstances the case was not clear enough for the issue of an interlocutory injunction, the exhibition was capable of being found by a jury to be defamatory. On the other hand, the mere fact that an article about the plaintiff appeared in a newspaper where numerous articles attacking dishonest business men had appeared on other occasions was held incapable of carrying a defamatory inference.[5] If reliance is placed upon juxtaposition it must be shown that a reasonable man, seeing the two objects together, would draw from their relative positions an inference defamatory of the plaintiff.

Knowledge of defendant immaterial. It is immaterial whether the defendant knew, or did not know, of external facts which turn a presumptively innocent statement into a defamatory one. He must take the risk of that, and he is liable either way, provided the defamatory meaning which is alleged could reasonably have been put upon the words. In *Cassidy* v. *Daily Mirror Newspapers Ltd.*[6] the defendants published in their newspaper a photograph of one C. and Miss X together with the words, " Mr. C., the race-horse owner, and Miss X, whose engagement has been announced." Mrs. C. was, and was known among her acquaintances, as the lawful wife of C., although she and C. were not living together. The information on which the defendants based their statement was derived from C. alone, and they had made no effort to verify it from any other source. Mrs. C. sued them for libel, the innuendo being that C. was not her husband but lived with her in immoral cohabitation. A majority of the Court of Appeal held that the innuendo was established and, the jury having found that the publication conveyed to reasonable persons an aspersion on the plaintiff's moral character, that she was entitled to damages.[7]

2. The words must refer to the plaintiff

If the plaintiff is mentioned by name, there is usually no difficulty about this, and it is to be observed that there is no requirement that

---

[5] *Wheeler* v. *Somerfield* [1966] 2 Q.B. 94. In *Astaire* v. *Campling* [1966] 1 W.L.R. 34 it was held that a newspaper article identifying by name a " Mr. X " about whom derogatory articles had appeared in other newspapers was not capable of a defamatory meaning.

[6] [1929] 2 K.B. 331.

[7] Followed in *Hough* v. *London Express Newspaper Ltd.* [1940] 2 K.B. 507, where it was pointed out that it need not be proved that reasonable persons actually did so understand the words; it is enough to prove that the words were published to persons having knowledge of the special facts, and so might understand the words in the secondary and defamatory sense: see Gatley, *op. cit.*, p. 47. Both cases were, however, criticised by Lord Denning M.R. in *Morgan* v. *Odhams Press Ltd.* [1970] 1 W.L.R. 820, 929–829, but, *semble*, only on the ground that the libel did not adequately refer to the plaintiff. See *post*, p. 257.

the defendant should have intended to refer to the plaintiff. In *Hulton & Co.* v. *Jones*,[8] H. & Co. were newspaper proprietors and published in their paper a humorous account of a motor festival at Dieppe in which imputations were cast on the morals of one Artemus Jones, a churchwarden at Peckham. This person was intended to be, and was believed by the writer of the article and the editor of the paper to be, purely fictitious. In fact there was a barrister named Artemus Jones, who was not a churchwarden, did not live at Peckham and had taken no part in the Dieppe festival. He sued H. & Co. for libel, and friends of his swore that they believed that the article referred to him. The jury returned a verdict for the plaintiff and the House of Lords refused to disturb this. They held that if reasonable people would think the language to be defamatory of the plaintiff it was immaterial that the defendants did not intend to defame him. In *Newstead* v. *London Express Newspaper Ltd.*,[9] the Court of Appeal carried *Hulton* v. *Jones* farther in two directions. They held that (a) the principle applies where the statement truly relates to a *real* person, A, and is mistakenly but reasonably thought to refer to another real person, B; and (b) absence of negligence on the defendant's part is relevant only in the sense that it may be considered by the jury in determining whether reasonable people would regard the statement as referring to the plaintiff; otherwise it is no defence. In *Newstead's* case, the statement was that " Harold Newstead, thirty-year-old Camberwell man," had been convicted of bigamy. This was true of a Camberwell barman of that name, but it was untrue of the plaintiff, Harold Newstead, aged about thirty, who assisted his father in a hairdressing business in Camberwell. The defendants were held liable.[10]

Material may be defamatory of the plaintiff even though it does not mention him by name and even if it contains no " key or pointer " indicating that it refers to him. Thus in *Morgan* v. *Odhams Press Ltd.*,[11] a newspaper article alleged that a girl had been kidnapped by a dog-doping gang. At the relevant time the girl had been staying at the plaintiff's flat and the plaintiff produced six witnesses who swore that they understood from the article that he was connected with the gang. A majority of the House of Lords held that these facts constituted sufficient material to leave to the jury. The test of whether the words " refer to the plaintiff " in the special sense here used is whether a hypothetical, sensible reader, having knowledge of the special circum-

---

[8] [1910] A.C. 20. Applied by Scrutton and Slesser L.JJ. in *Youssoupoff* v. *Metro-Goldwyn-Mayer Pictures Ltd.* (1934) 50 T.L.R. 581, 582–583, 587. Weir, *Casebook on Tort*, 3rd ed., p. 431.

[9] [1940] 1 K.B. 377. *Cf. Shaw* v. *London Express Newspaper Ltd.* (1925) 41 T.L.R. 475, and see *Boston* v. *W. S. Bagshaw & Sons* [1966] 1 W.L.R. 1126, 1131, *per* Lord Denning M.R.; 1134, *per* Harman L.J.

[10] But the damages were assessed at ½d.

[11] [1971] 1 W.L.R. 1239; (1971) 87 L.Q.R. 452. *Astaire* v. *Campling* (p. 256 (note 5, *supra*)) was distinguished because in that case, although the article referred by name to the plaintiff, it did not itself defame him.

stances, would believe that the plaintiff was referred to, and due allowance must be made for the fact that such a reader will not give a sensational article in a popular newspaper the attention which a lawyer would bestow on a perusal of evidence.[12] Nor is it relevant that no person who actually read the defamatory words believed them true.[13]

Defamation of a class

The question whether an individual can sue in respect of words which are directed against a group, or body, or class of persons generally was considered by the House of Lords in *Knuppfer* v. *London Express Newspaper Ltd.*,[14] and the law may be summarised as follows: (a) The crucial question is whether the words were published " of the plaintiff " in the sense that he can be said to be personally pointed at [15] rather than the application of any arbitrary general rule subject to exceptions that liability cannot arise from words published of a class. (b) Normally where the defamatory statement is directed to a class of persons no individual belonging to the class is entitled to say that the words were written or spoken of himself. " No doubt it is true to say that a class cannot be defamed as a class, nor can an individual be defamed by a general reference to the class to which he belongs." [16] As Willes J. said in *Eastwood* v. *Holmes*, " If a man wrote that all lawyers were thieves, no particular lawyer could sue him unless there was something to point to the particular individual." [17] What the psalmist said in haste of all men was not defamatory even if it had been untrue. (c) Words which appear to apply to a class may be actionable if there is something in the words, or the circumstances under which they were published which indicates a particular plaintiff or plaintiffs.[18] (d) Again if the reference is to a limited class or group, *e.g.* trustees, members of a firm, tenants of a particular building, so that the words can be said to refer to each member, all will be able to sue.[19] (e) Whether there is any evidence on which the words can be regarded as capable of referring to the plaintiff

---

[12] The minority in *Morgan* dissented because they thought there was no material in the article which a reasonable man could sensibly infer to apply to the plaintiff: they did not accede to the " key or pointer " argument which had found favour in the court below.

[13] At p. 1246, *per* Lord Reid, who refers to it as a proposition so obvious that no one has had the hardihood to dispute it.

[14] [1944] A.C. 116; Weir, *Casebook on Tort*, 3rd ed., p. 435; *Schloimovitz* v. *Clarendon Press* (1973) *The Times*, July 6. The Report on Defamation, Cmd. 7536, paras. 30–32, did not recommend any general change in the existing law to deal with group defamation.

[15] *Cf. Braddock* v. *Bevins* [1948] 1 K.B. 586, 588–589. The law as to qualified privilege at elections as stated in this case has been altered by s. 10, Defamation Act 1952. *Plummer* v. *Charman* [1962] 1 W.L.R. 1469. As to evidence to identify the plaintiff as the person libelled, see *Jozwiak* v. *Sadek* [1954] 1 W.L.R. 275; *Bottomley* v. *Bolton* (1970) 115 S.J. 61.

[16] *Per* Lord Porter in *Knuppfer* v. *London Express Newspaper Ltd.*, *supra*, at p. 124.

[17] (1858) 1 F. & F. 347, 349.

[18] *Cf. Le Fanu* v. *Malcolmson* (1848) 1 H.L.C. 637.

[19] *Browne* v. *D. C. Thomson*, 1912 S.C. 359; *Foxcroft* v. *Lacey* (1613) Hob. 89. Seventeen men indicted for conspiracy, and A said, " These defendants are those that helped to murder Henry Farrer." *Held*, each of the seventeen could bring a separate action against A. See also *MacKay* v. *Southern Co.* (1956) 1 D.L.R. (2d) 1.

is a matter of law for the judge.[20] If there is such evidence then it is a question of fact whether the words lead reasonable people who know the plaintiff to the conclusion that they do refer to him.

Just as an innuendo may mark out the plaintiff as one member of a class, so it may show that the description of a single person, real or fictitious, refers to him. Thus in *J'Anson* v. *Stuart*,[21] a newspaper paragraph stated, " This diabolical character, like Polyphemus the man-eater, has but one eye, and is well known to all persons acquainted with the name of a certain noble circumnavigator." It was clear that the plaintiff was the person indicated on his giving proof that he had one eye and bore a name similar to that of Anson, the famous admiral.

" Unintentional Defamation " within the Defamation Act 1952, s. 4

It has been seen above that liability for an imputation defamatory of the plaintiff does not depend on the intention of the person responsible for the main publication [22] of the statement either with regard to reference to the plaintiff,[23] or with regard to knowledge of facts which make a statement innocent on the face of it defamatory of the plaintiff.[24] Defamation may thus be " unintentional," and in its result produce hardship, especially, perhaps, for the writers of fiction and their publishers. Either or both may find themselves at the mercy of any unscrupulous person whose name happens to be the same as that of a fictitious character. Accordingly a change in the law has been introduced by section 4 of the Defamation Act 1952. This provides a procedure whereby, in the case of words *published innocently* as defined by the section, a defendant may avoid liability to pay damages if he is willing to publish a reasonable correction and apology, and pay the plaintiff's costs and expenses reasonably incurred as a consequence of the publication in question. The section may be summarised as follows:

1. It applies only to words published innocently as defined by the section,[25] *i.e.* if and only if the following conditions are satisfied:

   (a) " that the publisher did not intend to publish them of and concerning that other person, and did not know of

---

[20] " In deciding this question the size of the class, the generality of the charge and the extravagance of the accusation may all be elements to be taken into consideration, but none of them is conclusive. . . . Each member of a body, however large [would be] defamed when the libel consisted in the assertion that no one of the members of a community was elected unless he had committed a murder ": *Knuppfer's Case* [1944] A.C. 116, 124, *per* Lord Porter.

[21] (1787) 1 T.R. 748; *Jozwiak* v. *Sadek* [1954] 1 W.L.R. 275.

[22] See *post*, p. 263, for innocent dissemination by persons who take a subordinate part in the distribution of a libel.

[23] *Hulton* v. *Jones* [1910] A.C. 20; *Newstead* v. *London Express* [1940] 1 K.B. 377; *ante*, p. 257.

[24] *Cassidy* v. *Daily Mirror* [1929] 2 K.B. 331; *Hough* v. *London Express* [1940] 2 K.B. 507; *ante*, p. 256.

[25] s. 4 (5).

circumstances by virtue of which they might be understood to refer to him [26]; or

(b) that the words were not defamatory on the face of them, and the publisher did not know of circumstances by virtue of which they might be understood to be defamatory of that person,[27]

and in either case that the publisher exercised all reasonable care in relation to the publication [28]; and any reference in this subsection to the publisher shall be construed as including a reference to any servant or agent of his who was concerned with the contents of the publication."

2. A person who has published words alleged to be defamatory of another person may, if he claims that the words were published innocently in relation to that other person, make an offer of amends, which must be expressed to be made for the purposes of the section and must be accompanied by an affidavit specifying the facts relied upon by the person making it to show that the words in question were published innocently in relation to the aggrieved party.[29]

3. *An offer of amends* under the section is an offer—

(a) in any case to publish or join in the publication of a suitable correction and apology; and

(b) where copies of a document or record containing the words have been distributed by or with the knowledge of the person making the offer, to take such steps as are reasonably practicable on his part for notifying persons to whom copies have been so distributed that the words are alleged to be defamatory of the party aggrieved.[30]

4. *If the offer of amends is accepted by the party aggrieved, and duly performed,* no proceedings for libel or slander may be taken or continued by that party against the party making the offer in respect of the publication in question.[31]

5. *If the offer of amends is not accepted by the party aggrieved then it is a defence* in any proceedings by him for libel or slander to prove:

(a) that the words were *published innocently* in relation to the plaintiff [32];

---

[26] *Cf. Hulton* v. *Jones* [1910] A.C. 20; *Newstead* v. *London Express* [1940] 1 K.B. 377.
[27] *Cf. Cassidy* v. *Daily Mirror* [1929] 2 K.B. 331; *Hough* v. *London Express* [1940] 2 K.B. 507.
[28] *Ross* v. *Hopkinson* [1956] C.L.Y. 5011 (plaintiff an actress using stage name of J. S. Defendant wrote book with minor character an actress called J. S. *Held*, that the defendant could have checked whether there was in fact an actress called J. S. and therefore he had not exercised all reasonable care). *Cf. Solomon* v. *Simmons, The Times,* April 10, 1954, cited Clerk and Lindsell, *Torts,* 13th ed., p. 958, n. 48.
[29] s. 4 (1) (2).
[30] s. 4 (3).
[31] s. 4 (1) (a). The liability of any other person jointly responsible for the publication is unaffected.   [32] s. 4 (1) (b); *ante,* p. 264.

(b) that the offer was made as soon as practicable after the defendant received notice that they were or might be defamatory of the plaintiff [33]; and

(c) that if the publication was of words of which the defendant was not the author that the words were written by the author without malice.[34] Moreover for the purposes of this defence no evidence, other than evidence of facts specified in the affidavit which accompanied the offer of amends, is admissible to prove that the words were published innocently.[35]

3. The words must be " maliciously " published

Publication is the communication of the words to at least one person other than the person defamed.[36] Communication to the plaintiff himself is not enough, for defamation is an injury to one's reputation, and reputation is what other people think of a man, and not his own opinion of himself.[37] It is normally said that the words must be published " maliciously," but this is purely formal. Though the word is usually inserted in the plaintiff's statement of claim, no one takes any notice of it at the trial except for the purpose of inflating damages where there has been spite or deliberateness. As we shall see, however, malice in the sense of spite or evil motive— " express malice " as it is commonly called to distinguish it from merely formal malice—will defeat the defences of fair comment and qualified privilege.

The handing back by a printer to the author of a defamatory document printed in the ordinary course of business is not of *itself* a publication by the printer so as to make him liable [38]; nor is the handing back to the employer by a clerk or typist of a document copied or made to the employer's order a publication by the clerk or typist.[39] But there is, of course, publication *to* the printer by the author when he hands the document over, and if the author intends further publication, as where a person writes a letter to the editor of a newspaper for publication in the paper, the author is liable in respect of that publication also.[40]

---

[33] *Ibid.* An offer made six weeks after complaint of the libel was received from the plaintiff was held to be too late in *Ross* v. *Hopkinson* [1956] C.L.Y. 5011.
[34] s. 4 (5).
[35] s. 4 (2).
[36] *Bata* v. *Bata* [1948] W.N. 366.
[37] In criminal libel publication to the prosecutor alone suffices, but then the reason why libel is a crime is not merely because it assails the reputation, but also because it tends to a breach of the peace. In Scots law, publication to persons other than the pursuer is unnecessary even in civil proceedings, but that is because defamation is regarded by the system as an injury to a man's feelings as well as to his reputation: *Mackay* v. *M'Cankie* (1883) 10 Rettie 537.
[38] *Eglantine Inn Ltd.* v. *Smith* [1948] N.I. 29.
[39] *Ibid.* at p. 33, *per* Andrews L.C.J.
[40] *Cutler* v. *McPhail* [1962] 2 Q.B. 292. The damage which flows from the original publication to the editor includes the damage caused by the republication in the paper, for that is what the author intended. Even if there has been a release of the separate cause of action arising from publication in the paper, therefore, the author remains liable. " It matters not whether the damages caused by the repetition of the libel are sued for as part of the damage flowing from the original publication to the editor, or separately as the damages flowing from the publication in the newspaper ": *ibid.* at p. 299, *per* Salmon J.; *Gardiner* v. *Moore* [1969] 1 Q.B. 55.

The statement must be intelligible to the recipient of it. There is no publication of it if it is in a foreign language which he does not understand, or if he is too deaf to hear it, or too blind to read it, or if he did not realise that it referred to the plaintiff.[41] Nor is there any publication if a person gets to know of the statement through his own wrongful act which is destitute of any authority on the part of the defendant and which is not decisively caused by the defendant's negligence. In *Huth* v. *Huth*,[42] the defamatory matter was in an unsealed letter sent through the post and the letter was opened and read by an inquisitive butler. As it was no part of his duty to do this, there was no publication for which the defendant was responsible. No doubt the defendant did an unwise thing in not sealing the envelope, but the behaviour of the butler was not a direct consequence of his sending the letter. But there would have been a publication by the defendant if the letter, whether sealed or unsealed, had not been marked " private " and had been opened and read by the plaintiff's correspondence clerk in the course of his duty.[43] The court was much pressed with the argument that this letter was in exactly the same position as a postcard or a telegram. The legal presumption is that these are published on being sent through the Post Office without any proof that any one did in fact read them. It might be urged that a third person is no more entitled to read a postcard than an unsealed letter, and that the publication is due to the wrongful act of the third person just as much in the one case as in the other. But that is not the real basis of the distinction. What it really turns upon is practical necessity in the law of evidence. As the Court of Appeal pointed out in *Huth* v. *Huth*, the presumption as to postcards is based on the fact that it is practically impossible to *prove* that any third person did read it, although it is highly probable that someone did. Moreover, the presumption is a rebuttable one, although it is very difficult to conceive that such rebutting evidence could be given.[44]

Husband and wife

Communication of defamatory matter by a husband to his wife, or vice versa, is not a publication, for what passes between them is protected on the ground that any other rule " might lead to disastrous results to social life." [45] But communication by a third party to one spouse of matter defamatory of the other spouse is publication; husband and wife are still, for some purpose of the law, one person,

---

[41] *Sadgrove* v. *Hole* [1901] 2 K.B. 1.
[42] [1915] 3 K.B. 32. *Cf. Theaker* v. *Richardson* [1962] 1 W.L.R. 151 (husband opened sealed letter addressed to wife. Jury found publication). There, however, the facts were unusual and the Court of Appeal's decision, by a majority, was no more than that the jury's verdict was not perverse.
[43] [1915] 3 K.B. at pp. 40, 43–44, *per* Lord Reading C.J., Swinfen Eady L.J.
[44] *Ibid.*, at pp. 39–40, *per* Lord Reading C.J. The court will not take judicial notice of the fact that husbands read their wives' letters, but this may nevertheless be something which the defendant should anticipate in some cases: *Theaker* v. *Richardson* [1962] 1 W.L.R. 151, 157, *per* Holroyd Pearce L.J.
[45] *Wennhak* v. *Morgan* (1888) 20 Q.B.D. 635, 639, *per* Manisty J.

but not " for the purpose of having the honour and feelings of the husband assailed and injured by acts done or communications made to the wife." [46]

Repetition

Every repetition of defamatory words is a fresh publication and creates a fresh cause of action.[47] This is strikingly illustrated by a libel in a newspaper. Not only is the writer of the article liable, but so is the editor, the printer, the publisher, the proprietor of the paper,[48] and (subject to what is said below) even the newsagent or the boy who sells it in the street. But there are qualifications of this. It is true that absence of knowledge that the matter is defamatory or of intention to injure the plaintiff is, by itself, no excuse for the defendant, and it is equally true that it is a very lame defence to plead, " I tell the tale as 'twas told to me," for it is usually by idle repetition that lies are propagated. But, on the other hand, a person is not responsible for the publication of a statement which is put in circulation by one who is not his agent, express or implied.

(a) By mere distributor. So much is clear, but beyond this lies the question, " Is a person liable who had not been negligent with respect to publication?" The answer to this is neither easy to ascertain nor entirely self-consistent. The modern law is to be found chiefly in cases connected with newspapers and printed books. Those who are concerned with the mere mechanical distribution of such matter—newsagents, circulating libraries, booksellers (and presumably bookbinders) —are in a safer position than those who are primarily concerned with its production—authors, newspaper proprietors, publishers, printers, editors. Any one of the former is presumptively liable, but he has a good defence if he can prove (a) that he was innocent of any knowledge of the libel contained in the work disseminated by him; and (b) that there was nothing in the work or in the circumstances in which it came to him or was disseminated by him which ought to have led him to suppose that it contained a libel; and (c) that when the work was disseminated by him, it was not by any negligence on his part that he did not know that it contained the libel.[49] These requisites, which were laid down by Romer L.J. in *Vizetelly* v. *Mudie's Select Library Ltd.*,[50] were adopted

---

[46] *Wenman* v. *Ash* (1853) 13 C.B. 836, 844–845, *per* Maule J.; *Theaker* v. *Richardson, supra.*

[47] " *Truth* " (*N.Z.*) *Ltd.* v. *Holloway* [1960] 1 W.L.R. 997; *Cutler* v. *McPhail* [1962] 2 Q.B. 292. As to joinder of actions, see Odgers, *op. cit.*, pp. 484–489. Law of Libel Amendment Act 1888, s. 5; Defamation Act 1952, s. 13.

[48] *Cutler* v. *McPhail* [1962] 2 Q.B. 292; *Gardiner* v. *Moore* [1969] 1 Q.B. 55. See Report on Defamation, Cmd. 7536, paras. 116–137, as to joint liability for defamation and *cf. Gardiner* v. *Moore, supra,* at p. 817, *per* Thesiger J., referring to the effect of *Egger* v. *Viscount Chelmsford* [1965] 1 Q.B. 248 (*post,* p. 296).

[49] See Report on Defamation, Cmd. 7536, paras. 112–115. " The defence, commonly referred to as ' innocent dissemination,' is strictly a defence of ' never published.' "

[50] [1900] 2 Q.B. 170, 180.

by Scrutton L.J. in *Bottomley* v. *Woolworth & Co.* [51]; but in the later case of *Sun Life Assurance Co. of Canada* v. *W. H. Smith & Son Ltd.*, the learned Lord Justice thought that (b) and (c) might be simplified by combining them in the single question, " Ought the defendant to have known that the matter was defamatory; *i.e.* was it due to his negligence in conducting his business that he did not know? " [52]

In *Vizetelly's* case, the proprietors of a circulating library were held liable because they took no steps to ascertain whether their books contained libels and had overlooked a publisher's circular requesting the return of copies of this particular book. Contrast with this *Martin* v. *Trustees of British Museum*,[53] where the defendants were held not liable for allowing readers in the British Museum to see books containing libellous matter, there being no negligence on the part of the defendants,[54] and later cases in which judgments were given in favour of newsagents and booksellers who satisfied the three conditions stated above.[55] The law could scarcely be otherwise for if it were we should be a short step from holding that a railway company ought to be liable for transporting bundles of newspapers in its vans. "A newspaper is not like a fire; a man may carry it about without being bound to suppose that it is likely to do an injury." [56]

(b) By producer of print. A sterner view is taken of the responsibilities of those who actually produce printed matter. The proprietor of a newspaper (with whom must be included its editor, printer and publisher) is liable even if he was not negligent [57] in embodying the libel in his journal. He can, of course, set up any other defence appropriate to defamation—truth, fair comment, privilege. He can establish a general negation of liability, like *volenti non fit injuria*; but he cannot successfully contend that he was not negligent except for the purpose of mitigating damages or, in appropriate cases, for the purpose of availing himself of the procedure and defence under section 4 of the Act.[58] The law may seem to be severe, but it must be borne in mind that much greater currency is given to the matter which is multiplied by journals than to spoken (except broadcast) or written statements.

As to propagation of defamatory matter by the ordinary person, he is not liable if he can disprove negligence. He will be liable if he leaves his correspondence about, if he inadvertently puts letters in the wrong envelopes, or if he speaks too loudly; but not if a thief or other

---

[51] (1932) 48 T.L.R. 521.
[52] (1934) 150 L.T. 211.
[53] (1894) 10 T.L.R. 338.
[54] What is the position of the owner of a private library who lends a book to a friend, or who permits a guest to use the library; or of a railway passenger who lends a fellow-traveller a magazine? Presumably, the same as that of a newsagent or bookseller.
[55] *Emmens* v. *Pottle* (1885) 16 Q.B.D. 354; *Weldon* v. *Times Book Club Co. Ltd.* (1911) 28 T.L.R. 143; *Bottomley* v. *Woolworth & Co. Ltd.* (1932) 48 T.L.R. 521.
[56] *Emmens* v. *Pottle* (1885) 16 Q.B.D. at p. 358, *per* Bowen L.J.
[57] *Cassidy's* case and *Newstead's* case, *ante*, pp. 256–257.
[58] *Ante*, pp. 259–261.

unauthorised person puts a letter of his in circulation or reads it himself. What constitutes negligence must be a question of fact in each case.[59]

If defamatory matter is imposed upon the defendant's property by the unauthorised act of a third person, is the defendant bound to remove the matter when he becomes aware of it and knows, or has reasonable grounds for suspecting, that it is defamatory? Certainly he must remove it where he can do so without any difficulty or expense: e.g. if it be a typed document affixed to a wall of his house, for otherwise he is a party to publication.[60] And, probably, the same is true even if the removal of the defamatory matter is more difficult, save, perhaps, in the unlikely event that it is so difficult that it can be achieved only by the virtual destruction and rebuilding of the wall.[61]

Assent to publication

If the plaintiff expressly or impliedly assents to the publication of matter which is true on the face of it, the defendant is not liable [62]; and this is so even if it appears that some persons may interpret the statement in a sense much more prejudicial to the plaintiff than is warranted by the plain meaning of the words. After all, that is a possibility which the plaintiff ought to have considered before he assented to publication, and he cannot be heard to complain that words which, in their ordinary meaning, are true have been construed by third parties in a sense contemplated neither by him nor by the defendant. In *Cookson* v. *Harewood*,[63] the plaintiff sued the defendants for libel because they had published a true statement that the plaintiff had been warned off all pony racing courses under their control. The plaintiff had submitted to the rules of the Pony Turf Club which the defendants controlled, and one of these rules was that the stewards of the club might, in their absolute discretion, warn off any person. Warning off might be occasioned by mere negligence of the delinquent as well as by less reputable causes. The plaintiff contended that if, by innuendo, the jury interpreted the statement as meaning that he had been guilty of corrupt and fraudulent practices, then the defendants were liable. But the Court of Appeal held that this argument was unsound. Scrutton L.J. said,[64] " It has seemed to me all through this case that these questions about innuendoes are quite beside the mark. If you get a true statement and an authority to publish the true statement, it does not matter in the least what people will understand it to mean. The plaintiff had submitted to the jurisdiction [of the Pony Turf

---

[59] Gatley, *op. cit.*, pp. 108–109. See also *Theaker* v. *Richardson* [1962] 1 W.L.R. 151.
[60] *Byrne* v. *Dean* [1937] 1 K.B. 818.
[61] *Cf. Byrne* v. *Dean, supra*, at p. 838, *per* Greene L.J.
[62] The Supreme Court of New Zealand has held that there is no assent to publication where the defamatory matter is first sent to the plaintiff himself and he, being under a duty to do so, sends it on to other persons: *Collerton* v. *MacLean* [1962] N.Z.L.R. 1045.
[63] [1932] 2 K.B. 478n.
[64] [1932] 2 K.B. at p. 482.

Club]. The stewards have authority to publish the decision in the Racing Calendar, and if it is defamatory, it does not matter in the slightest what exact shade of meaning you are to put upon the obviously defamatory statement." [65] Judgment for the defendants was affirmed.

It should be observed that this defence, which has also been regarded as an instance of *volenti non fit injuria*,[66] has nothing whatever to do with the defence of qualified privilege. Emphasis of this is necessary because some expressions in *Chapman* v. *Ellesmere* might give the contrary impression.[67] As will be seen, when we come to deal with it, privilege, if it is established, negatives liability for any statement whether it is prima facie untrue or is untrue only by innuendo, and whether consent has been given to the publication or not; or, to put it in another way, privilege, truth and consent are three entirely separate defences. Another distinction between privilege and consent to publication is this: It is for the law to say whether privilege in any form exists. Parties cannot by mere agreement create it.[68] But they can, as they did in *Cookson* v. *Harewood*, agree that one of them shall be entitled to publish the truth about the other, and such an agreement will exclude liability for defamatory innuendoes which may be put upon a correct but bald statement of facts.

DEFENCES

In addition to the defence of assent to publication and the provisions of section 4 of the Defamation Act 1952, there are three specialised defences to an action for defamation. These are:

1. Justification (or truth).
2. Fair comment.
3. Privilege which may be (a) absolute or (b) qualified.

1. Justification (or truth)

The plaintiff need not prove that the statement is false, for the law presumes that in his favour. But the defendant can plead "justification" (the technical name for truth here), and if he can establish it by evidence he has a good defence even though he may have been actuated by ill-will or spite.[69] It is not that the law has any special relish

---

[65] Approved by Lord Hanworth M.R. and Slesser L.J. in *Chapman* v. *Ellesmere* [1932] 2 K.B. 431, 451, 464, and *semble* by the Court of Appeal in *Pritchard* v. *Greyhound Racing Association Ltd.* (1933) 176 L.T.J. 393; (1934) 177 L.T.J. 90.

[66] Slesser L.J. in *Chapman* v. *Ellesmere* [1932] 2 K.B. at p. 463; *contra*, Romer L.J. at p. 474.

[67] [1932] 2 K.B. at pp. 450–451, 468, *per* Lord Hanworth M.R., Slesser L.J.

[68] *Cf.* Denning L.J. in *Russell* v. *Norfolk* (*Duke*) [1949] 65 T.L.R. 225, 232: " If the publication in the Racing Calendar is no wider than the occasion warrants, it is privileged. This might be the case even if the rules did not contain any provision on the matter, but any doubt is removed by the fact that the rules, to which the plaintiff has assented, empower the stewards to publish the decision in the Racing Calendar. That is, in effect, a consent by the plaintiff to this mode of publication, though consent cannot create a privilege where none would otherwise exist."

[69] But see the important exception in relation to " spent convictions " under the Rehabilitation of Offenders Act 1974: p. 297, *post*.

for the indiscriminate infliction of truth on other people, but defamation is an injury to a man's reputation, and if people think the worse of him when they hear the truth about him that merely shows that his reputation has been reduced to its proper level. At the same time justification may be a dangerous plea if it is the only one which the defendant decides to adopt, for if he fails in it the jury are likely to regard his conduct as wanton and to return a verdict for heavier damages.[70]

Must be true in substance

Subject to the fact that the question whether a minor inaccuracy is sufficient to defeat the defence of justification is one for the jury,[71] it is a general principle that " the justification must be as broad as the charge, and must justify the precise charge." [72] To justify the repetition of a defamatory statement already made, therefore, the defendant must prove that the content of the statement was true, not merely that it was made. If I say to you, " Smith told me that Brown swindled his creditors," I can justify this only by proof that Brown did swindle his creditors; it is idle to show merely that Smith gave me the information.[73] It follows that although the defence of justification is distinct from the question whether words are defamatory, the two are interlocked to some extent.[74] In *Lewis* v. *Daily Telegraph Ltd.*,[75] for example, the defendants were clearly able to justify the literal meaning, admittedly itself defamatory, of their statement that the Fraud Squad was investigating the plaintiff company's affairs, and so once the House of Lords had held that the words were incapable of meaning that the plaintiffs had been guilty of fraud the case was at an end. In *Cadam* v. *Beaverbrook Newspapers Ltd.*,[76] on the other hand, the defendants published a statement that a writ had been issued against the plaintiff for conspiracy to defraud and they sought to justify this by proving that such a writ had indeed been issued. On an interlocutory appeal the Court of Appeal held that it could not be said that proof of the issue of the writ could not justify some conceivable defamatory meaning that somebody

---

[70] *Simpson* v. *Robinson* (1848) 12 Q.B. 511; *Associated Leisure Ltd.* v. *Associated Newspapers Ltd.* [1970] 3 W.L.R. 101. Cf. *Broadway Approvals Ltd.* v. *Odhams Press Ltd.* (*No. 2*) [1965] 1 W.L.R. 805, 814, *per* Sellers L.J.; 825, *per* Davies L.J. *Loughans* v. *Odhams Press Ltd.* [1963] C.L.Y. 2007 is a remarkable case. The defendants published a statement which bore the meaning that the plaintiff had murdered a certain person. Although he had been acquitted by a criminal jury the defendants pleaded justification. The civil jury in the action for libel found that this defence succeeded.
[71] *Alexander* v. *North-Eastern Ry.* (1865) 6 B. & S. 340.
[72] Odgers, *op. cit.*, p. 149; *Bishop* v. *Latimer* (1861) 4 L.T. 775.
[73] " *Truth* " (*N.Z.*) *Ltd.* v. *Holloway* [1960] 1 W.L.R. 997. If the action were brought by Smith on the innuendo that, Brown being notoriously honest, the words meant that Smith was an unreliable and dishonest person, proof that Smith did use the words could amount to justification. Note the distinction between the statement " It is rumoured that X is guilty of fraud " and the statement " It is rumoured that X is suspected of fraud ": *Lewis* v. *Daily Telegraph Ltd.* [1964] A.C. 234, 283–284, *per* Lord Devlin.
[74] *Cadam* v. *Beaverbrook Newspapers Ltd.* [1959] 1 Q.B. 413, 423, *per* Hodson L.J.
[75] *Supra.* For facts see *ante*, p. 252.
[76] *Supra*; *Hennessy* v. *Wright* (1888) 57 L.J.Q.B. 594.

might say was the ordinary meaning of the words, and the issue of justification must therefore be allowed to go to the jury. It must be for the jury to decide whether proof that the writ had been issued justified the natural and ordinary meaning of the words, whatever the jury itself might decide the natural and ordinary meaning to be.[77] Moreover, at common law, if a defamatory statement contains more than one charge, then each must be justified,[78] but this has been altered by section 5 of the Defamation Act 1952 to the extent that the defence of justification does not fail " if the words not proved to be true do not materially injure the plaintiff's reputation having regard to the truth of the remaining charges." [79]

In the past the application of the principles concerning the defence of justification gave rise to particular difficulty where the defamatory statement was to the effect that the plaintiff had been convicted of a criminal offence. At common law a conviction was not even prima facie evidence of guilt for the purposes of other proceedings, and this meant that the defendant had to prove the guilt of the plaintiff over again if the defence of justification was to succeed.[80] Now, however, it is provided by section 13 of the Civil Evidence Act 1968 [81] that in an action for libel or slander in which the question whether a person committed a criminal offence is relevant, proof that he stands convicted of the offence is conclusive evidence that he did commit it.

Innuendo

If words are held to be capable of an innuendo put upon them by the plaintiff, then the defendant must, if he wishes to justify, prove the truth of the meaning raised by the innuendo just as much as if the words were plain in their signification. But the defendant may justify part of the statement if it is severable from the rest without embarrassing the plaintiff in his pleading, or he may justify the natural and ordinary meaning of the words and not the innuendo. As to the rest, he may plead privilege if that plea is applicable, or he may leave it unjustified with, or without, an apology.[82]

2. Fair comment

It is a defence to an action for defamation that the statement is a fair comment on a matter of public interest.

---

[77] The jury need not disentangle its verdict. Fox's Libel Act, *ante,* p. 251, gives the jury the right to give a general verdict for the plaintiff or the defendant as the case may be. See also *Barnes* v. *Hill* [1967] 1 Q.B. 579.

[78] *e.g. Helsham* v. *Blackwood* (1851) 11 C.B. 111.

[79] Report of the Committee on the Law of Defamation, Cmd. 7536, paras. 79–82; Gatley, *op. cit.,* p. 158. " *Truth* " (*N.Z.*) *Ltd.* v. *Avery* [1959] N.Z.L.R. 274; *Anders* v. *Gas* (1960) 104 S.J. 211, cited Clerk and Lindsell, *Torts,* 13th ed., p. 970.

[80] This he did not always succeed in doing: *Hinds* v. *Sparks* [1964] Crim.L.R. 717; *Goody* v. *Odhams Press Ltd.* [1967] 1 Q.B. 333. *Cf.* the observations of Greer L.J. in *Cookson* v. *Harewood* [1932] 2 K.B. 478n., 485.

[81] 1968, c. 64. See *Levene* v. *Roxhan* [1970] 1 W.L.R. 1322.

[82] *Fleming* v. *Dollar* (1889) 23 Q.B.D. 388; *Davis* v. *Billing* (1891) 8 T.L.R. 58.

Honest criticism ought to be, and is, recognised in any civilised system of law as indispensable to the efficient working of any public institution or office, and as salutary for private persons who make themselves or their work the object of public interest. " Others abide our question, thou art free " may be true of Shakespeare in literature. In law it is not true of him or of anybody else. The defence has been recognised for a long time in English law,[83] and, although criticism of government and of public functionaries was not always so freely allowed as today,[84] it is now fully recognised as one of the essential elements of freedom of speech which is not to be whittled down by legal refinement.[85]

The requisites of fair comment

(a) **The matter commented on must be of public interest.** It is a question for the judge, not the jury, whether the matter is of public interest.[86] No principle for decision is laid down, the books contenting themselves with examples,[87] but the public interest is not confined within narrow limits and covers matters in which the public is legitimately *interested* as well as matters in which it is legitimately *concerned*.[88] It ranges from the behaviour of a Prime Minister or of a sanitary authority to the conduct of a flower show and includes the conduct of every public man and every public institution [89] but it is not limited to what is sometimes called " public life." [90] The presentation of a new play or the sudden closure of one enjoying a successful run,[91] the publication of a book, the exhibition of a picture, the conduct of a newspaper,[92] the claim of a company to use a pedestrian way for vehicular traffic,[93] and even criticism publicly made [94] may all be the subject of fair comment.

(b) **It must be an expression of opinion and not an assertion of fact.** It is not always easy to draw this distinction. To describe the line,

" A Mr. Wilkinson, a clergyman," [95]

as the worst in English poetry is obviously comment, for verification

---

[83] e.g. *Dibdin* v. *Swan* (1793) 1 Esp. 28.
[84] *Wason* v. *Walter* (1868) L.R. 4 Q.B. 73, 93–94, *per* Cockburn C.J.
[85] *Slim* v. *Daily Telegraph Ltd.* [1968] 2 Q.B. 157, 170, *per* Lord Denning M.R.; *Silkin* v. *Beaverbrook Newspapers Ltd.* [1958] 1 W.L.R. 743, 747, *per* Diplock J.
[86] *South Hetton Coal Co. Ltd.* v. *N.E. News Association* [1894] 1 Q.B. 133, 141, *per* Lopes L.J.
[87] e.g. Odgers, *op. cit.*, pp. 169–180; Gatley, *op. cit.*, pp. 311–320; Clerk and Lindsell, *Torts*, 13th ed., pp. 1009–1011.
[88] *London Artists Ltd.* v. *Littler* [1969] 2 Q.B. 375, 391, *per* Lord Denning M.R.
[89] See *Kelly* v. *Sherlock* (1866) L.R. 1 Q.B. 686, 689, *per* Bramwell B.
[90] The former exclusion from fair comment of the affairs of private institutions as exemplified by *Gathercole* v. *Miall* (1846) 15 M. & W. 319 is, it is submitted, no longer law. This seems implicit in the decision of the Court of Appeal in *London Artists Ltd.* v. *Littler*, *supra*.
[91] *London Artists Ltd.* v. *Littler*, *supra*.
[92] *Kemsley* v. *Foot* [1952] A.C. 345.
[93] *Slim* v. *Daily Telegraph Ltd.* [1968] 2 Q.B. 157.
[94] *Turner* v. *M.G.M. Pictures Ltd.* [1950] 1 All E.R. 449, 463, *per* Lord Greene M.R.
[95] A parody of Wordsworth in Benson's *Life of Fitzgerald*.

of it as a fact is impossible. But some cases are much nearer than that
to the border-line between comment and fact. In *Dakhyl* v. *Labouchere* [96] the plaintiff described himself as " a specialist for the treatment
of deafness, ear, nose, and throat diseases." The defendant described
him as " a quack of the rankest species." Was this comment or an
allegation of fact? It was held by the House of Lords that it might be
comment.[97] Again, calling a man a fornicator or a swindler looks like
a statement of fact, but what is calling him " immoral " or " a sinner "?
Are immorality and sin facts or matters of opinion? To this there is no
dogmatic answer. Every statement must be taken on its merits. The
very same words may be one or the other according to the context.
To say that " A is a disgrace to human nature," is an allegation of
fact. But if the words were, " A murdered his father and is therefore a
disgrace to human nature," the latter words are plainly a comment on
the former.[98] Hence a critic should take pains to keep his facts and the
comment upon them severable from one another, for if it is not
reasonably clear that the matter purports to be comment, he cannot
plead fair comment as a defence.[99]

(c) The comment must be fair. For comment to be fair it must first
of all be based upon true facts in existence when the comment was
made.[1] You cannot invent untrue facts about a man and then comment
upon them.[2] To this, however, there is one necessary exception, namely,
that fair comment may be based upon an untrue statement which is
made by some person upon a privileged occasion, *e.g.* a statement
made by a witness in the course of judicial proceedings, and properly
attributed to him.[3] Moreover if the comment is upon the statement of
another person, even if the statement was not made on a privileged
occasion, the statement need not always be proved to be true, for in
some cases such proof is impossible. If A publishes a statement that
" There are men on the planet Mars " and B criticises this allegation as
unfounded, B's criticism may well be fair comment, for it is based on
fact in the sense that it refers to an assertion actually made by A.
B is not bound to prove that there are men on Mars—in fact it is the
very thing that he denies. Suppose, however, that A's statement were

---

[96] [1908] 2 K.B. 325n.
[97] See, too, their decision in *Turner* v. *Metro-Goldwyn-Mayer Pictures Ltd.* [1950]
W.N. 33 and *cf. London Artists Ltd.*v. *Littler* [1969] 2 Q.B. 375.
[98] Gatley, *op. cit.*, pp. 295–296.
[99] *Hunt* v. *Star Newspaper Co. Ltd.* [1908] 2 K.B. 309, 320, *per* Fletcher-Moulton L.J.;
London Artists Ltd. v. *Littler* [1969] 2 Q.B. 375, 395, *per* Edmund Davies L.J. It is for the
judge to rule whether words are capable of being regarded as comment and for the jury
to decide whether they are: *Jones* v. *Skelton* [1963] 1 W.L.R. 1362, 1379, 1380, *per* Lord
Morris.
[1] *Cohen* v. *Daily Telegraph Ltd.* [1968] 1 W.L.R. 916.
[2] See the dictum of Kennedy J. in *Joynt* v. *Cycle Trade Publishing Co.* [1904] 2 K.B.
292, 294; approved in *Hunt* v. *Star Newspaper Co. Ltd.* [1908] 2 K.B. 309, 317, 320; *Silkin*
v. *Beaverbrook Newspapers Ltd.* [1958] 1 W.L.R. 743, 746; *London Artists Ltd.* v. *Littler*
[1969] 2 Q.B. 375. *Cf. Lyon* v. *Daily Telegraph Ltd.* [1943] K.B. 746.
[3] *Mangena* v. *Wright* [1909] 2 K.B. 958; *Grech* v. *Odhams Press Ltd.* [1958] 1 Q.B. 310;
[1958] 2 Q.B. 275, 285, *per* Jenkins L.J.

false and defamatory of C, then if B repeats it with some comment of his own, and C sues B for defamation, B cannot successfully plead fair comment unless his comment is a repudiation of the lie; for any other kind of comment of his would be an acceptance of a lie put in circulation by A; *i.e.* comment based upon what is untrue.

It is not necessary, however, that all the facts upon which the comment is based should themselves be stated in the alleged libel. The question is whether there is a sufficient substratum of fact stated *or indicated* in the words which are the subject-matter of the action and whether the facts or subject-matter on which comment is made are indicated with sufficient clarity to justify comment being made. The substratum of fact, facts, or subject-matter may be indicated impliedly in the circumstances of the publication.[4] In *Kemsley* v. *Foot*[5] the defendant had published a newspaper article under the heading "Lower than Kemsley." The article was violently critical of the conduct of a newspaper not owned by the plaintiff and contained no reference to the plaintiff other than the heading. The House of Lords held that the defence of fair comment was open to the defendant as in the circumstances the conduct of the Kemsley Press in its publications was sufficiently indicated as the fact on which the comment was made, and if the jury found that the comment was such as an honest, though possibly prejudiced, man might make the defence of fair comment would be established.

Comment and justification. The relation of justification (or truth) to fair comment must be carefully noted. We start with two propositions. First, justification and fair comment are totally independent defences; the defendant can, and often does, plead them alternatively, and it is quite possible for fair comment to succeed while justification fails. " It may be said in the appropriate circumstances that a man's conduct is discreditable and it may be a fair comment to make, although a jury is not prepared to find that the substance of the comment was true." [6] Secondly, it is impossible for the defendant to succeed in a plea of fair comment unless he is commenting on facts, *i.e.* on what is " true " in the qualified sense of that word stated above. No comment can be fair if it is upon something which the defendant has invented or distorted, and if the alleged facts relied upon as the basis for comment turn out to be untrue, a plea of fair comment avails the defendant nothing, even though they expressed his honest view.[7] Where the facts on which the comment is made are fully set out in the alleged libel, then, subject to section 6 of the Defamation Act 1952, each fact must be shown to be true to enable the defence of fair comment to succeed in relation to

---

[4] *Kemsley* v. *Foot* [1952] A.C. 345, 356–357, *per* Lord Porter.
[5] [1952] A.C. 345; Weir, *Casebook on Tort*, 3rd ed., p. 445.
[6] *Broadway Approvals Ltd.* v. *Odhams Press Ltd. (No.* 2) [1965] 1 W.L.R. 805, 817–818, *per* Sellers L.J. See also *ibid.* at p. 823, *per* Davies L.J.
[7] *London Artists Ltd.* v. *Littler* [1969] 2 Q.B. 375, 395, *per* Edmund Davies L.J.

the comment.[8] And to that extent the defendant must prove the truth of facts, unless that much is conceded in his favour by the plaintiff; but his defence is still fair comment and not justification. Since 1952, however, the defence of fair comment does not fail by reason only that the truth of every allegation of fact contained in the alleged libel is not proved. It is enough " if the expression of opinion is fair comment having regard to such of the facts alleged or referred to in the words complained of as are proved." [9]

The " rolled-up " plea. In this connection the so-called " rolled-up " plea has caused much perplexity. By it the defendant alleges that " in so far as the words complained of consist of allegations of fact, they are true in substance and in fact, and in so far as they consist of expressions of opinion they are fair comments made in good faith and without malice upon the said facts, which are matters of public interest." The original object of this plea (which was sanctioned in 1890 [10]) was to make it clear that the defendant proposed to prove the truth of the facts on which he had commented. As has just been said, no comment can be fair unless it is comment upon facts. The plea was therefore one of fair comment and not of justification, and the sole reason for its use was that it was difficult to frame the plea in any other way if facts and comment were so mixed up in the defendant's imputation as to be inextricable. But then it often occurred that the defamatory statement did not happen to include all the facts upon which the defendant had made his comment; of course it would be much tidier from the lawyer's point of view if critics always took care to include all the facts, but when a man is uttering or writing criticism he generally knows little about the law of defamation and even less about the niceties of pleading in it. At any rate if he had not included all the facts, and were sued for defamation, he would be compelled to go outside his defamatory statement to collect the rest of the facts upon which his comment was based. Therefore the concluding words of the above plea, " they are fair comments made . . . upon the said facts which are matters of public interest," could not, with respect to the italicised words, be accurate.

---

[8] Kemsley v. Foot [1952] A.C. 345, 358, 361–362. Where the facts are not published to the world at large, but are contained in the particulars delivered, they are not the subject-matter of the comment, but facts alleged to justify that comment. Since they are not published otherwise than in the particulars, which are privileged, it is unnecessary that the truth of all of them be proved and it is enough if the defendant establishes sufficient of the facts to support the comment in the eyes of the jury. " Twenty facts might be given in the particulars and only one justified, yet if that one fact were sufficient to support the comment so as to make it fair, a failure to prove the other nineteen would not of necessity defeat the defendant's claim ": ibid. at p. 358, per Lord Porter.

[9] Defamation Act 1952, s. 6. See Truth (N.Z.) Ltd. v. Avery [1959] N.Z.L.R. 274, where it was held: (a) that fair comment is a defence to comment only and not to defamatory statements of fact, and that s. 6 has not altered the law in this respect; (b) that where there is any defamatory sting in any of the facts on which the comment is based these defamatory statements of fact can only be defended by a successful plea of justification with, now, the benefit of s. 5 of the Defamation Act 1952; Clerk and Lindsell, Torts, 13th ed., pp. 1004–1005; Broadway Approvals Ltd. v. Odhams Press Ltd. [1964] 2 Q.B. 683, 685–686, per Lawton J.; ibid. (No. 2) supra, at p. 818, per Sellers L.J.

[10] Penrhyn v. Licensed Victuallers' Mirror, 7 T.L.R. 1; Gatley, op. cit., pp. 437–438.

So the practice sprang up of omitting them and the plea simply wound up, " they are fair comments made in good faith and without malice on a matter of public interest." [11] This was most unfortunate, for it gave rise to the idea that the plea was one of justification and fair comment, " rolled-up " together; and it took a decision of the House of Lords in *Sutherland* v. *Stopes* [12] to remind the profession that it was still a plea of fair comment and of nothing else. The result now is that the plea ought not to be used at all in the mutilated form described above. A better plan, if all the facts are not included in the defamatory statement, is not to make use of the rolled-up plea, but to plead fair comment and then to set out particulars of the facts upon which the defendant commented.[13] Where the rolled-up plea is used it no longer has the advantage it had prior to 1949 that the defendant could not be compelled to say what parts of the statement are allegations of fact and what parts are comment.[14]

Fairness. Finally we must consider the " fairness " of the comment itself. The principles upon which this is determined are not easy to state with precision, but it is at least clear that for comment to be fair it is not necessary that the jury should accept it as correct and therefore that the test is not what the ordinary reasonable man would think about the subject-matter of the comment. If the defendant was " an honest man expressing his genuine opinion on a subject of public interest, then no matter that his words conveyed derogatory imputations: no matter that his opinion was wrong or exaggerated or prejudiced; and no matter that it was badly expressed so that other people read all sorts of innuendoes into it; nevertheless, he has a good defence of fair comment. His honesty is the cardinal test. He must honestly express his real view. So long as he does this, he has nothing to fear, even though other people may read more into it." [15] On the other hand, criticism cannot be used as a cloak for mere invective, nor for personal imputations not arising out of the subject-matter or not based on fact.[16] " The

---

[11] Odgers, *op. cit.,* pp. 514–516.

[12] [1925] A.C. 47.

[13] Odgers, *op. cit.,* pp. 515–516. But see *London Artists Ltd.* v. *Littler* [1969] 2 Q.B. 375.

[14] See R.S.C., Ord. 82, r. 3 (2), added in 1949, requiring the defendant where the rolled-up plea is used to furnish particulars stating which of the words complained of he alleges are statements of fact and of the facts and matters he relies on in support of the allegation that the words are true. This follows the recommendation of the Report on Defamation, Cmd. 7536, paras. 173–177. Particulars of the facts relied on may also be ordered where the rolled-up plea is not used, but only an ordinary plea of fair comment: *Cunningham-Howie* v. *Dimbleby Ltd.* [1951] 1 K.B. 360; *London Artists Ltd.* v. *Littler* [1969] 2 Q.B. 375, 391, *per* Lord Denning M.R.; *Lord* v. *Sunday Telegraph Ltd.* [1971] 1 Q.B. 235. As to the former practice, see *Aga Khan* v. *Times Publishing Co.* [1924] 1 K.B. 675; *Tudor-Hart* v. *British Union* [1938] 2 K.B. 329.

[15] *Slim* v. *Daily Telegraph Ltd.* [1968] 2 Q.B. 157, 170, *per* Lord Denning M.R.; *Silkin* v. *Beaverbrook Newspapers Ltd.* [1958] 1 W.L.R. 743, 747, *per* Diplock J.; *McQuire* v. *Western Morning News Co. Ltd.* [1903] 2 K.B. 100.

[16] *London Artists Ltd.* v. *Littler, supra,* at p. 399, *per* Widgery L.J. The rule that juries must not substitute their own views for those of the critic is a salutary one, but probably the more competent a jury is to judge the matter criticised, the harder it will be to observe the rule. A jury of law teachers, in considering the fairness of criticisms on this book,

question is not whether the comment is justified in the eyes of the judge or jury, but whether it is the honest expression of the commentator's real view and not mere abuse or invective under the guise of criticism." [17]

Mere violence in criticism does not make it unfair. Moderation here " is only used to express the idea that invective is not criticism. It certainly cannot mean moderate in the sense that that which is deemed by a jury, in the case of a literary criticism, extravagant and the outcome of prejudice on the part of an honest writer is necessarily beyond the limit of the fair comment." So Collins M.R., in *McQuire* v. *Western Morning News Co. Ltd.*,[18] where a critique of a play imputed that it was dull, vulgar and degrading, and the Court of Appeal, in giving judgment for the defendants, held that the case ought not even to have been left to the jury.[19] Nor need comment on a literary production be confined to criticism of it as literature. " It can be criticised for its treatment of life and morals as freely as it can for bad writing, *e.g.* it can be criticised as having an immoral tendency." [20]

Whether comment can be fair if bad motives are imputed to the plaintiff depends upon circumstances, and certainly the law is now more lenient to critics on this point than it was a century ago.[21] Where a man's conduct may be rightly open to ridicule and disapprobation, it would nevertheless be wrong to charge him with base, sordid or wicked motives unless there were so much ground for the charge as to make it clear not only that the defendant honestly believed it to be true but also that he had foundation for his belief.[22] " Where the public conduct of a public man is open to animadversion, and the writer who is commenting upon it makes imputations on his motives, which arise fairly and legitimately out of his conduct, so that a jury shall say that the criticism was not only honest but also well founded, an action is not maintainable." This was the rule laid down by Cockburn L.C.J. in the

---

would have to make a considerable effort to restrain themselves from assessing it by their own opinions of the book.

[17] *Turner* v. *Metro-Goldwyn-Mayer Pictures Ltd.* [1950] 1 All E.R. 449, 461, *per* Lord Porter.

[18] [1903] 2 K.B. at p. 110. *Cf.* a reviewer's opinion that Keats' " Endymion " was a poem of " calm, settled, imperturbable idiocy." This is violent enough, but is not on that account unfair.

[19] A test given by Lord Esher M.R. in *Merivale* v. *Carson* (1887) 20 Q.B.D. 275, 281 was, " Would any fair man, however prejudiced he may be, however exaggerated or obstinate his views, have said that which this criticism said of the work which is criticised?" In *Turner* v. *Metro-Goldwyn-Mayer Pictures Ltd.* [1950] W.N. 83, 97, Lord Porter said he should adopt the words of Lord Esher except that he would substitute " honest " for " fair," lest some suggestion of reasonableness instead of honesty should be read in.

[20] *Kemsley* v. *Foot* [1952] A.C. 345, 356, *per* Lord Porter.

[21] Odgers, *op. cit.*, pp. 182–184.

[22] Gatley, *op. cit.*, p. 728 cites as the true test the words of Buckley L.J. in *Peter Walker Ltd.* v. *Hodgson* [1909] 1 K.B. 239, 253 (relied upon in *Harris* v. *Lubbock* (1971), *The Times*, October 21, but only partially reported): " if [the defendant] shows that the imputation . . . although defamatory, and although not proved to have been founded in truth, yet was an imputation in a matter of public interest, made fairly and bona fide as the honest expression of the opinion which the defendant held on the facts truly stated, and was in the opinion of the jury warranted by the facts, *in the sense that a fair-minded man might upon those facts bona fide hold that opinion* " (emphasis added).

oft-cited case of *Campbell* v. *Spottiswoode*.[23] Dr. Campbell, a dissenting minister, published in his newspaper (the *British Ensign*) a scheme for inserting in it a series of letters on converting the Chinese and for promoting the circulation of copies of the paper in which these letters appeared in order to call attention to the importance of this evangelising work. The defendant imputed in another newspaper that Dr. Campbell's alleged aim of propagating the gospel in China was "a mere pretext for puffing an obscure newspaper" (the *Ensign*). It was held that, though the defendant believed this to be true, he had no defence; for what he believed had no foundation at all.

For the rest, a sound canon of criticism in both law and literature is that it should attack a man's work and not the man himself. "Show me an attack," said Lord Ellenborough C.J.,[24] " on the moral character of this plaintiff, or any attack upon his character unconnected with his authorship, and I should be as ready as any judge who ever sate here to protect him."

__(d) The comment must not be malicious.__ Malice here means evil motive.[25] Until 1906 there was considerable doubt whether private spite on the critic's part could make his comment unfair.[26] In theory it is possible to judge a man's work fairly even if you hate him, though it is not easy in practice. However, in that year the Court of Appeal held, in the only successful libel action ever brought against the proprietors of *Punch*, that malice may negative fairness: *Thomas* v. *Bradbury, Agnew & Co. Ltd.* [27] In that case, the book reviewer of *Punch* showed both by his review of the plaintiff's book and by his demeanour in the witness-box and elsewhere personal hostility to the plaintiff, and judgment for £300 damages was affirmed.

In *Lyon* v. *Daily Telegraph Ltd.*[28] the defendants published in their newspaper a letter criticising a public entertainment given by the plaintiffs. The letter was signed " A. Winslow " and gave as an address " The Vicarage, Wallington Road, Winchester." In fact there was no

---

[23] (1863) 3 B. & S. 769, 777; Weir, *Casebook on Tort*, 3rd ed., p. 441; *Dakhyl* v. *Labouchere* [1908] 2 K.B. 325n., 329; *Hunt* v. *Star Newspaper Co.* [1908] 2 K.B. 309, 319–320; and see *Kemsley* v. *Foot* [1952] A.C. 345, 358–360. *Cf.* Report on Defamation, Cmd. 7536, para. 85.

[24] *Carr* v. *Hood* (1808) 1 Camp. 355, 358. Carlyle's opinion of Charles Lamb that he was a " pitiful rickety, gasping, staggering, stammering, tom-fool " seems to have erred on the side of a personal attack.

[25] It is discussed more fully in relation to qualified privilege, *post*, pp. 294–296.

[26] Even now the point has not been settled by the House of Lords, but in *Broadway Approvals Ltd.* v. *Odhams Press Ltd.* (*No.* 2) [1965] 1 W.L.R. 805, 822, Davies L.J. considered a submission that the defence of fair comment might not be defeasible by express malice to be " a very remarkable one."

[27] [1906] 2 K.B. 627 (distinguished in *Longdon-Griffiths* v. *Smith* [1951] 1 K.B. 295); Weir, *Casebook on Tort*, 3rd ed., p. 448. By R.S.C., Ord. 82, r. 6, first made in 1949 on the recommendation of the Report on Defamation, Cmd. 7536, paras. 182–187, where the defendant pleads fair comment or privilege " no interrogatories as to the defendant's sources of information or grounds of belief shall be allowed." In *Adams* v. *Sunday Pictorial Newspapers Ltd.* [1951] 1 K.B. 354, the C.A. held this also prohibits interrogatories as to the actual information and knowledge of the defendant.

[28] [1943] K.B. 746.

such place in Winchester, nor was any " Winslow " traceable in a clerical directory. But the comment itself was fair and the Court of Appeal held that the fictitious name and address did not constitute malice so as to make it unfair. A newspaper is under no duty to verify the name and address of a correspondent, or to prove that the writer honestly held the opinion expressed in the comment; if the rule were otherwise it would lay far too heavy a burden on the Press in relation to free discussion of matters of public interest.[29]

Judge and jury. If an allegation of malice is raised in answer to a plea of fair comment, the burden of proving malice rests with the plaintiff. The judge must not allow the case to go to the jury, therefore, unless he is satisfied that there is evidence to support a finding that the defendant was malicious.[30] It is probable that a similar rule also applies where the question is simply whether the words of the comment itself reveal its unfairness. If the judge has ruled that the matter is of public interest and if the words are comment, not statements of fact, the judge should not allow the case to go to the jury unless there is some evidence of unfairness.[31] Proof of malice is no more than one special way of proving that the comment is unfair.[32] But questions of the unfairness of the comment are essentially questions of opinion to be formed on reading the passage complained of and they should, therefore, normally be left to the jury.[33]

Fair comment and privilege

It is disputed whether fair comment is properly regarded (a) as a right which everyone has, or (b) as a species of qualified privilege.[34] Judicial dicta are in conflict upon the question. Collins M.R. in *Thomas's* case (*supra*) regarded fair comment and qualified privilege as " governed by precisely the same rules," [35] but this was inconsistent with an earlier opinion of Lord Esher M.R. in *Merivale* v. *Carson* [36] and with other dicta. And more recently Diplock J. has described fair comment as " the right of the public, which means you and me, and the

---

[29] If it had been proved that the writer did not honestly hold the opinion which he expressed, that would have negatived fairness of the comment in an action against him; but would it have deprived the newspaper of the defence of fair comment? This point was left open by the C.A. See *Gros* v. *Cook* (1969) 113 S.J. 408 and Gatley, *op. cit.*, pp. 340–341.

[30] See *Broadway Approvals Ltd.* v. *Odhams Press Ltd.* (*No. 2*) [1965] 1 W.L.R. 805.

[31] *McQuire* v. *Western Morning News Co. Ltd.* [1903] 2 K.B. 100; *Turner* v. *Metro-Goldwyn-Mayer Pictures Ltd.* [1950] 1 All E.R. 449, 461–462, *per* Lord Porter; *Jones* v. *Skelton* [1963] 1 W.L.R. 1362, 1378, *per* Lord Morris, where, however, it is pointed out that considerations as to where the onus of proof lies are not often of great consequence when both parties have had every opportunity to adduce all the evidence they wish to call. *Cf. Burton* v. *Board* [1929] 1 K.B. 301, 306, *per* Sankey L.J. Clerk and Lindsell, *Torts*, 13th ed., pp. 1001–1002; Salmond, *Torts*, 16th ed., p. 190.

[32] See the observations of Collins M.R. in *Thomas* v. *Bradbury, Agnew & Co. Ltd.* [1906 2 K.B. 627, 638–641.

[33] This seems to have been the view of Diplock J. in *Silkin* v. *Beaverbrook Newspapers Ltd.* [1958] 1 W.L.R. 743, 749.

[34] Explained *post*, pp. 282–296.

[35] [1906] 2 K.B. at p. 641.

[36] (1887) 30 Q.B.D. 275, 280.

newspaper editor, and the man . . . on the Clapham omnibus, to express their views honestly and fearlessly on matters of public interest " [37] while a privilege attaches only to particular people on particular occasions. The monographs on defamation and the textbooks on tort are, on balance, against the view of Collins M.R.[38] Probably they are correct; fair comment and qualified privilege are separate in their nature, but it is only the House of Lords who can now finally settle the conflict. The chief objections to the second view are two. First, so far as the contents of the statement go, mere honest belief in them on the part of the defendant is enough to preserve qualified privilege if the case is one that falls under qualified privilege at all; but the fact that a comment is based upon honest belief does not necessarily make it fair.[39] Secondly, malice, and nothing but malice, will rebut qualified privilege, whereas comment may be unfair in other ways than by being malicious: e.g. if it is upon matter which the law regards as not open to comment at all.

3. Privilege

In addition to the cases covered by the defence of fair comment the law recognises that there are other occasions on which freedom of communication without fear of an action for defamation is more important than the protection of a person's reputation. Such occasions are said to be " privileged," [40] and the privilege may be either absolute or qualified. Absolute privilege covers cases in which complete freedom of communication is regarded as of such paramount importance that actions for defamation cannot be entertained at all: a person defamed on an occasion of absolute privilege has no legal redress, however outrageous the untrue statement which has been made about him and however malicious the motive of the maker of it. Qualified privilege, on the other hand, though it also protects the maker of an untrue defamatory statement, does so only if the maker of the statement acted honestly and without malice. If the plaintiff can prove " express malice " [41] the privilege is displaced and he may recover damages, but it is for him to prove malice, once the privilege has been made out, not for the defendant to disprove it. It is for the jury to decide whether malice has been proved, but it is for the judge to rule whether or not the occasion is a privileged one.[42]

---

[37] *Silkin* v. *Beaverbrook Newspapers Ltd.*, *supra* at p. 746. In *London Artists Ltd.* v. *Littler* [1968] 1 W.L.R. 607, Cantley J. dealt as separate issues with the two defences of privilege and fair comment. The unsuccessful defendant appealed only on the latter issue, a course which caused no difficulty in the Court of Appeal although it would have done if the court had regarded fair comment as a species of privilege.

[38] Fraser, *op. cit.*, p. 105; Odgers, *op. cit.*, p. 158; Gatley, *op. cit.*, p. 293; Pollock, *Torts*, 15th ed., pp. 190–191; Salmond, *Torts*, 16th ed., pp. 182–183; Clerk and Lindsell, *Torts*, 13th ed., pp. 1001–1002. *Contra*, Bower, *op. cit.*, p. 322; and Radcliffe in (1907) 23 L.Q.R. 97–99.

[39] Blackburn J. in *Campbell* v. *Spottiswoode* (1863) 3 B. & S. 769, 781.

[40] The term " privilege " has been severely criticised by Bower, *op. cit.*, Appendix VIII, but its use is inveterate.

[41] See *ante*, p. 261.   [42] *Adam* v. *Ward* [1917] A.C. 309.

Absolute privilege

This includes:

(i) *Statements in Parliament.* The Bill of Rights 1688 provides that " the freedom of speech and debates or proceedings in Parliament ought not to be impeached or questioned in any court or place out of Parliament." [43] This has the effect not only of conferring absolute privilege upon statements in Parliament, but also of preventing a plaintiff from using statements in Parliament as evidence of malice in respect of statements made outside it.[44]

(ii) *Reports, papers, votes and proceedings ordered to be published by either House of Parliament.* The Parliamentary Papers Act 1840,[45] by establishing this, put an end to a bitter and unedifying dispute between the House of Commons and the Law Courts.

(iii) *Judicial proceedings.* Whatever is stated, whether orally or in documentary form, in a judicial proceeding is absolutely privileged. It does not matter how false or malicious the statement may be, and it does not matter who makes it—the judge,[46] the jury, the parties, the advocates,[47] or the witnesses.[48] Protection does not, however, extend to an entirely irrelevant answer of a witness unprovoked by any question as if, for example, to counsel's question, " Were you at York on a certain day? " the witness replied, " Yes, and A B picked my pocket there." [49] But the privilege is given a wide application and extends to anything a witness might naturally and reasonably say when giving evidence with reference to the subject-matter of the proceedings; it is not limited by any technical considerations of relevance.[50] Similarly, although a judge is not protected if he makes a defamatory statement in a matter over which he has no jurisdiction,[51] this is so only if he

---

[43] 1 W. & M., sess, 2, c. 2. The Bill was declared to be law by 2 W. & M., c. 1 (1689). See *Dingle* v. *Associated Newspapers Ltd.* [1960] 2 Q.B. 405 (the case proceeded to the H.L. on another point [1964] A.C. 371). As to a letter by an M.P. to a Minister as a proceeding in Parliament, see *Re Parliamentary Privilege Act, 1770* [1958] A.C. 331, P.C. As to colonial legislatures, see *Chenard & Co.* v. *Joachim Arissol* [1949] A.C. 127, P.C.

[44] *Church of Scientology* v. *Johnson-Smith* [1972] 1 Q.B. 522. *Quaere* as to the position if the *defendant* sought to rely on statements in Parliament to rebut an inference of malice.

[45] 3 & 4 Vict. c. 9. Extracts or abstracts of such reports have, however, only qualified privilege under s. 3, *post*, p. 282.

[46] *Glick* v. *Hinchcliffe* (1967) 111 S.J. 927 is a modern example. See further *post*, p. 595 and *Royal Aquarium Society Ltd.* v. *Parkinson* [1892] 1 Q.B. 431, 451, *per* Lopes L.J.

[47] *Munster* v. *Lamb* (1883) 11 Q.B.D. 588, 603–604, *per* Brett M.R. See also *Rondel* v. *Worsley* [1969] 1 A.C. 191, *ante*, pp. 63–64. A barrister is, of course, subject to the discipline of his Inn of Court and a solicitor to that of the Law Society, and any advocate may incur the penalties of contempt of court for insolence to the judge or the use of violent or abusive language to the jury: Oswald, *Contempt of Court*, 3rd ed. (1910), pp. 50–52; Borrie and Lowe, *The Law of Contempt* (1973).

[48] *Seaman* v. *Netherclift* (1876) 2 C.P.D. 53. For a full historical review of the authorities, see Pigot C.B. in *Kennedy* v. *Hilliard* (1859) 10 Irish Common Law Reports 195. Where a solicitor is briefing the evidence of a witness to be given on an occasion of absolute privilege, the occasion of the briefing is covered by the same privilege: *Thompson* v. *Turbott* [1962] N.Z.L.R. 298; *Lincoln* v. *Daniels* [1962] 1 Q.B. 237, 257–262, *per* Devlin L.J.

[49] *Seaman* v. *Netherclift, supra*, at pp. 56–57, *per* Cockburn C.J.

[50] *Ibid.*, at p. 60, *per* Bramwell J.A.

[51] *Case of the Marshalsea* (1612) 10 Rep. 68b, 76a.

knew, or had the means of knowing, of the defect which deprived him of jurisdiction.[52]

Judicial privilege, in the wide sense explained above, applies not only to any ordinary law court but also whenever there is an authorised inquiry which, though not before a court of justice, is before a tribunal which has similar attributes,[53] *e.g.* a military court of inquiry, or the Disciplinary Committee of the Law Society.[54]

Communication between solicitor and client. Any professional communication between solicitor and client is privileged, but apart from communications made in connection with litigation, which are absolutely privileged, it is uncertain whether the privilege is absolute or qualified.[55] The Court of Appeal in *More* v. *Weaver* [56] held that it was absolute, but the House of Lords in *Minter* v. *Priest* [57] found it unnecessary to decide the question and preferred to leave it open. On principle, no strong reason seems to have been advanced for regarding the privilege as absolute. It ought to be only in the most exceptional cases that, in the interests of the public, privilege should be ranked as absolute, and surely a solicitor and his client are sufficiently protected if they are conceded qualified privilege for their transactions with each other.

The privilege has been regarded as *ejusdem generis* with " judicial privilege," [58] but the affiliation is a loose one, for it is not confined to the walls of a law court and extends to communications which have nothing to do with litigation, *e.g.* the drawing of a client's will. One restriction on it is that the communication must be a professional one. First, the relationship of solicitor and client must be proved, and it is regarded as sufficiently established for this purpose if, though the solicitor does not ultimately accept a retainer, the statement were made in communications passing between him and a prospective client with a view to retainer.[59] Secondly, what passes between them when the

---

[52] *Calder* v. *Hackett* (1839) 3 Moo.P.C. 28; *Mayor of London* v. *Cox* (1867) L.R. 2 H.L. 239, 263, *per* Willes J. See also p. 598, *post.*

[53] Lord Esher M.R. in *Royal Aquarium Society Ltd.* v. *Parkinson* [1892] 1 Q.B. 431, 442. Approved in *O'Connor* v. *Waldron* [1935] A.C. 76, 81. Applied in *Smith* v. *National Meter Co. Ltd.* [1945] 2 All E.R. 35. See also *Thompson* v. *Turbott, supra,* and *Constable* v. *Jagger* (1972), *The Times,* March 16.

[54] *Addis* v. *Crocker* [1961] 1 Q.B. 11. That the Committee sits in private makes no difference provided that its functions are otherwise similar to those of a court of justice. *Cf. Lincoln* v. *Daniels* [1962] 1 Q.B. 237. No absolute privilege covers complaints to the Bar Council concerning a barrister's conduct as such complaints are not steps in an inquiry before the Senate of the Inns of Court which alone has disciplinary powers over barristers. *Quaere* whether a complaint made to the barrister's Inn of Court would be absolutely privileged. Proceedings before the Inns of Court themselves are absolutely privileged: *Marrinan* v. *Vibart* [1963] 1 Q.B. 234, affd. [1963] 1 Q.B. 528. See also, *post,* p. 597.

[55] Distinguish this.privilege in the law of defamation from the privilege in the law of evidence which enables a client to prevent his legal adviser from disclosing any professional communication. The point is clearly taken by Lord Atkin in *Minter* v. *Priest* [1930] A.C. 558, 578 *et seq.*

[56] [1930] A.C. 558.

[57] *More* v. *Weaver, supra,* at pp. 521–523, *per* Scrutton L.J.

[58] [1928] 2 K.B. 520.

[59] *Minter* v. *Priest* [1930] A.C. 558.

relationship has been established is privileged if, within a very wide and generous ambit of interpretation, it is fairly referable to the relationship,[60] or (to put it in another way) if it consists of " professional communications passing for the purpose of getting or giving professional advice." [61] This would exclude a piece of gossip interjected by the client in a conversation on, say, land registration: *e.g.* " Have you heard that Jones has run off with Mrs. Brown" [62] Another illustration is *Minter* v. *Priest*,[63] where the House of Lords held that conversations relating to the business of obtaining a loan for the deposit sum to be paid on the purchase of land fall under the professional work of a solicitor, but that conversations about speculation in land to enable the solicitor to share in the profits do not and that slanders of third persons uttered by the solicitor in the course thereof are not privileged.

(iv) *Communications made by one officer of state to another in the course of his official duty*. In *Chatterton* v. *Secretary of State for India*,[64] the plaintiff was an officer in the Indian Staff Corps. The defendant, in the course of his duty, wrote to the Under-Secretary of State that the Commander-in-Chief in India and the Government of India recommended the removal of the plaintiff to the half-pay list as an officer, and the letter stated the reasons for the recommendation. The Court of Appeal held that an order dismissing the plaintiff's action for libel as vexatious had been rightly made, on the ground that it would be injurious to the public interest to allow such an inquiry, for it would tend to deprive officers of state of their freedom of action in matters concerning the public weal. If an action for defamation were permitted, it would place their official conduct at the mercy of a jury who might to that extent substitute themselves for the officials in governing the country. The more recent decision in *Isaacs & Sons Ltd.* v. *Cook* [65] shows that the fact that a report relates to commercial matters does not in itself preclude it from being one relating to state matters.

The extent of this head of absolute privilege is, however, somewhat uncertain.[66] One High Court judge has suggested that it does not extend to officials below the rank of Minister, though they may, of course, have qualified privilege,[67] and in *Merricks* v. *Nott-Bower* [68] the Court of Appeal refused to strike out a claim for libel based on a report on two police officers written by a Deputy Commissioner of the Metropolitan Police to the Commissioner. In the words of Lord

---

[60] *Ibid.* at pp. 568, 586, *per* Lords Buckmaster and Thankerton.
[61] *Ibid.* at p. 581, *per* Lord Atkin.
[62] *More* v. *Weaver* [1928] 2 K.B. at p. 525, *per* Scrutton L.J.
[63] [1930] A.C. 558.
[64] [1895] 2 Q.B. 189.
[65] [1925] 2 K.B. 391.
[66] For a particular case covered by statute, see Parliamentary Commissioner Act 1967 (c. 13), s. 10 (5).
[67] Henn-Collins J. in *Szalatnay-Stacho* v. *Fink* [1946] 1 All E.R. 303. The Court of Appeal ([1947] K.B. 1) made no reference to this point.
[68] [1965] 1 Q.B. 57.

Denning M.R.,[69] " it is not so clearly the subject of absolute privilege that the courts ought to strike out the claim on that ground today." The position of reports made pursuant to military duty is also doubtful. In *Dawkins* v. *Lord Paulet* [70] a majority of the Court of Queen's Bench held that a report on a lieutenant-colonel made by a major-general to the adjutant-general of the Army was covered by absolute privilege, but Cockburn C.J. delivered a strong dissenting judgment and in *Dawkins* v. *Lord Rokeby* [71] the Exchequer Chamber congratulated themselves on the fact that the question was still open for consideration by the House of Lords.

The argument generally advanced for absolute rather than qualified privilege is to the effect that a man will perform his duties better by being released from the fear of being sued than by being given an easily substantiated defence if he is sued, but this is as true of the nationalised industries and private concerns as it is of the state.[72] Absolute privilege should be reserved for those cases alone in which complete freedom of communication is so important that it is right to deprive the citizen of his remedy for all defamatory statements made about him including even those made maliciously. No one could claim that this is true of all communications between all servants of the Crown. It is respectfully submitted, therefore, that the caution of the Court of Appeal in *Merricks* v. *Nott-Bower* [73] was fully justified and that care should be taken not to extend absolute privilege further than can be shown to be really necessary. It is no less in the interest of the state that justice should be done to the citizen than that the machinery of government should be able to work without fear of legal action.

(v) *Fair and accurate newspaper and broadcast reports of judicial proceedings in the United Kingdom.* Section 3 of the Law of Libel Amendment Act 1888 [74] provides that a fair and accurate report in any newspaper [75] of proceedings publicly heard before any court exercising judicial authority within the United Kingdom shall, if published contemporaneously [76] with such proceedings, be privileged; but that this shall not authorise the publication of any blas-

---

[69] *Ibid.* at p. 68; *Richards* v. *Naum* [1967] 1 Q.B. 620.

[70] (1869) L.R. 5 Q.B. 94.

[71] (1873) L.R. 8 Q.B. 255, 272. On appeal the decision of the House of Lords was based on the ground that the defendant was a witness before a tribunal which must be regarded as a judicial body: (1875) L.R. 7 H.L. 744.

[72] No question of official secrets is involved, for writers of official communications may be protected by an evidentiary privilege which has nothing to do with the law of defamation. See Clerk and Lindsell, *Torts,* 13th ed., pp. 978–979; *Duncan* v. *Cammell, Laird & Co. Ltd.* [1942] A.C. 624; *Conway* v. *Rimmer* [1968] A.C. 910.

[73] [1965] 1 Q.B. 57.

[74] 51 & 52 Vict. c. 64. Cited as amended by the Defamation Act 1952, s. 8.

[75] By s. 1 of this Act, the word " newspaper " shall have the same meaning as in the Newspaper Libel and Registration Act 1881 and covers publications at intervals not exceeding 26 days. *Cf.* the definition of " newspaper " for the purpose of s. 7 of the Defamation Act 1952—at intervals not exceeding 36 days.

[76] See the Criminal Justice Act 1967, s. 5.

phemous or indecent matter.[77] The protection of the section is extended to broadcast reports from a broadcasting station within the United Kingdom.[78] After a long period of uncertainty it was at last decided in 1964 that the privilege created by the statute is absolute.[79] Qualified privilege would in any case exist at common law.[80]

Qualified privilege

This includes—

(i) *Fair and accurate reports of parliamentary proceedings*

The long battle between reporters and Parliament on this matter belongs to Constitutional Law rather than to the Law of Tort. However, in 1868, *Wason* v. *Walter* [81] settled the privilege of faithful reports. The court regarded the privilege as on the same footing as reports of judicial proceedings: *i.e.* the advantage of publicity outweighed any private injury resulting from publication. This qualified privilege at common law is not limited to reports in newspapers and will cover other reports, *e.g.* broadcast reports. The publication by means of printing or broadcasting of extracts from or abstracts of reports, papers, votes or proceedings published by order of either House of Parliament is given the protection of qualified privilege by statute.[82]

In order to qualify as fair and accurate the report does not have to be a full précis of the debate: a " parliamentary sketch " may properly select those portions of the debate which will be of interest to the public.[83] What matters is whether the report is fair and accurate in so far as the debate concerned the plaintiff's reputation.[84]

---

[77] The report is still privileged even if it includes defamatory interruptions by A in proceedings between B and C, provided that they are connected in some way with the proceedings: *Farmer* v. *Hyde* [1937] 1 K.B. 728. See also *Burnett and Hallamshire Fuel Ltd.* v. *Sheffield Telegraph and Star Ltd.* [1960] 1 W.L.R. 502. (Report of opening speech by counsel or solicitor.)

[78] Defamation Act 1952, s. 9.

[79] *McCarey* v. *Associated Newspapers Ltd.* [1964] 1 W.L.R. 855 (the Court of Appeal subsequently ordered a new trial on the issue of damages only: [1965] 2 Q.B. 112). Though the ruling was given only at first instance, it is unlikely to be challenged and is in conformity with the opinion of most writers and of the Committee on the Law of Defamation: Cmd. 7536, para. 92.

[80] *Post,* pp. 283–284.

[81] L.R. 4 Q.B. 73. The decision was a strong piece of judicial legislation, for two earlier, but abortive, attempts had been made to get Parliament to sanction this privilege. It would have been hard indeed if the plaintiff had succeeded in his action, for he had procured a peer to present to the House of Lords a scandalously false attack on Sir Fitzroy Kelly, then newly appointed Chief Baron of the Court of Exchequer, and the Lord Chancellor had described the petition as a perpetual record of the plaintiff's falsehood and malignity. *The Times* newspaper accurately reported this proceeding and thereupon the plaintiff sued the publishers for libel. The action was dismissed.

[82] Parliamentary Papers Act 1840, s. 3, as extended by s. 9 (1) of the Defamation Act 1952: *Mangena* v. *Lloyd* (1908) 98 L.T. 640; *Mangena* v. *Wright* [1909] 2 K.B. 958; *Associated Newspapers Ltd.* v. *Dingle* [1964] A.C. 371. The privilege extends to fair comment upon the extracts or abstracts, but if a newspaper " adds its own spice and prints a story to the same effect as the parliamentary paper, and garnishes and embellishes it with circumstantial detail, it goes beyond the privilege and becomes subject to the general law ": *ibid.* at p. 411, *per* Lord Denning. The Defamation Act 1952, s. 7 and Sched., give qualified privilege as regards publications in newspapers or by broadcasting to reports of proceedings in public of the legislatures of any part of Her Majesty's dominions outside Great Britain; *post,* p. 285.

[83] *Cook* v. *Alexander* [1974] Q.B. 279.   [84] At p. 291.

(ii) *Fair and accurate* [85] *reports of judicial proceedings which the public may attend* [86]

This applies to the proceedings of any court of justice, high or low. " For this purpose," said Lord Campbell C.J.,[87] " no distinction can be made between a court of pie poudre and the House of Lords sitting as a court of justice." Nor, according to the better opinion, does it matter whether the court had jurisdiction or not, for it would be harsh to expect the reporter to be an infallible judge of a matter upon which the court itself is often in doubt.[88] Again, it is immaterial whether the proceedings are *ex parte* or interlocutory or are adjourned from time to time. " The privilege applies to a fair and correct account of proceedings published before the final decision is arrived at, if in the end there must be a final decision. . . If it were not so, the ridiculous result would follow that, where the trial of a case of the greatest public interest lasted fifty days, no report could be published until the case was ended." [89] Reporters, therefore, need not wait until the final decision is rendered, but they must recollect that any comment, as distinct from fair and accurate reproduction, must be postponed until the decision is given; otherwise they may make themselves liable to the penalties for contempt of court or to an injunction,[90] for intermediate comment is likely to prejudice the minds of a jury in a jury action and might conceivably influence the judge. This common law privilege is not limited to newspapers, but covers reports in pamphlets or in a broadcast or any other form of publication.

Qualifications. The following points with respect to this species of privilege are noteworthy. First, if the proceedings are not public, it does not apply, for the ground of the privilege is that, if the public are entitled to be present in a court, they are also entitled to be informed of what goes on in their absence.[91] Secondly, the privilege presumably does not apply if publication is forbidden, either by law [92] or by an order of the court.[93] Thirdly, even at common law it is a criminal offence to publish obscene matter, so qualified privilege will not cover a report of that,[94] and this common law restriction was drawn

---

[85] *Mitchell* v. *Hirst, etc. Ltd.* [1936] 3 All E.R. 872; *Burnett and Hallamshire Fuel Ltd.* v. *Sheffield Telegraph and Star Ltd.* [1960] 1 W.L.R. 502.

[86] *Usill* v. *Hales* (1878) 3 C.P.D. 319. For an analysis of the reasons for the existence of this privilege, see *Webb* v. *Times Publishing Co.* [1960] 2 Q.B. 535, 557–562, *per* Pearson J. See also *Burnett and Hallamshire Fuel Ltd.* v. *Sheffield Telegraph and Star Ltd., supra.*

[87] *Lewis* v. *Levy* (1858) E.B. & E. 537, 554.

[88] The dictum of Lopes J. in *Usill* v. *Hales* (1878) 3 C.P.D. 319, 329 is preferable to that of Lord Coleridge C.J. at p. 324. See Odgers, *op. cit.*, pp. 254–255; Gatley, *op. cit.*, pp. 260–261.

[89] *Kimber* v. *Press Association Ltd.* [1893] 1 Q.B. 65, 71, *per* Lord Esher M.R.

[90] *Brook* v. *Evans* (1860) 29 L.J.Ch. 616.

[91] *Per* Romer L.J. in *Chapman* v. *Ellesmere* [1932] 2 K.B. 431, 475. The remarks of Greer L.J. in *Cookson* v. *Harewood, ibid.* 485, are not really in conflict with this. Reports of the findings or decision of a domestic tribunal if published in a newspaper may be privileged under the Defamation Act 1952, s. 7. *Post*, p. 285.

[92] Criminal Justice Act 1967 (c. 80), s. 3.

[93] *Brook* v. *Evans* (1860) 29 L.J.Ch. 616.

[94] *Re The Evening News* (1887) 3 T.L.R. 255.

tighter by the Judicial Proceedings (Regulation of Reports) Act 1926,[95] the object of which was to call a halt to the practice of some newspapers of reporting the more salacious details of a certain type of legal proceedings, for the mere purpose of inflating their circulation. Fourthly, qualified privilege does not attach automatically to all fair and accurate reports of proceedings in the courts of foreign countries. Such reports are only privileged if the public interest in this country requires their publication, as would be the case, for example, with a report of a decision of the United States Supreme Court on an important question of commercial law or where the proceedings in the foreign court throw light upon or are connected with the administration of justice in England. But a report of a judicial proceeding wholly concerned with an alleged scandalous affair between Mrs. X and Mr. Y is unlikely to have a legitimate interest for the English public and is likely to appeal only to idle curiosity or a desire for gossip. It will not, therefore, be privileged.[96]

(iii) *Certain fair and accurate reports published in newspapers or broadcast from a station in the United Kingdom*

Section 7 of the Defamation Act 1952 [97] affords qualified privilege to the publication in a newspaper or in a broadcast for general reception of the reports or other matters specified in the Act. The reports or matters so privileged are divided into two categories, the first [98] comprising statements which are privileged " without explanation or contradiction," and the second [99] statements which are privileged " subject to explanation or contradiction." As regards statements in the second category, the defence of qualified privilege is lost if it is proved that the defendant has been requested by the plaintiff to publish in the newspaper in which (or, if by broadcast, in the manner in which) the original publication was made, a reasonable letter or statement by way of explanation or contradiction, and has refused or neglected to do so, or has done so in a manner not adequate or reasonable having regard to all the circumstances.[1] In neither case is protection

---

[95] 16 & 17 Geo. 5, c. 61. Children and Young Persons Act 1933 (23 Geo. 5, c. 12), ss. 39, 49; Magistrates' Courts Act 1952 (15 & 16 Geo. 6 & 1 Eliz. 2, c. 55), ss. 58, 59 (newspaper reports of domestic proceedings in magistrates' courts); Domestic and Appellate Proceedings (Restriction of Publicity) Act 1968, s. 2; Children and Young Persons Act 1969, s. 10.

[96] *Webb* v. *Times Publishing Co.* [1960] 2 Q.B. 535; Payne, " Qualified Privilege " (1961) 24 M.L.R. 178. For the special case of international courts and courts exercising jurisdiction in the Commonwealth, see *post*, p. 285. Note that a newspaper is not privileged merely because its article is of great public interest: *Truth (N.Z.) Ltd.* v. *Holloway* [1960] N.Z.L.R. 69; *London Artists Ltd.* v. *Littler* [1968] 1 W.L.R. 607. In neither case was the point raised on appeal: [1960] 1 W.L.R. 997; [1969] 2 Q.B. 375.

[97] ss. 7, 9 (2) (3), and the Schedule to the Act. This replaces the more restricted protection formerly given by the Law of Libel Amendment Act 1888, s. 4.

[98] See Part I, Schedule to the Defamation Act 1952.

[99] See Part II, Schedule to the Defamation Act 1952.

[1] s. 7 (2), Defamation Act 1952. *Khan* v. *Ahmed* [1957] 2 Q.B. 149' (a general letter demanding a full apology and withdrawal is not a request within the subsection. What is required is a special request that there should be published either a contradiction or an explanation in the words of the letter or in terms put forward by the person alleging that he has been libelled).

given to the publication of any matter which is prohibited by law or of
any matter which is not of public concern and the publication of which
is not for the public benefit.[2]

The reports and other matters the publication of which is to have
qualified privilege are listed in the Schedule to the Act and cover:

I. Statements privileged without explanation or contradiction.[3]
(1) Fair and accurate reports of proceedings in public of legislatures
of any part of Her Majesty's dominions outside Great Britain, of
international organisations and international conferences of which
the United Kingdom is a member, of international courts, of public
inquiries appointed by the Government or legislature of any part
of Her Majesty's dominions outside the United Kingdom.

(2) Fair and accurate reports of judicial proceedings of courts
exercising jurisdiction throughout any part of Her Majesty's dominions
outside the United Kingdom or of any proceeding before a British
court-martial held outside the United Kingdom.[4]

(3) A fair and accurate copy of or extract from any register kept
in pursuance of any Act of Parliament which is open to inspection
by the public, or of any document which is required by the law of
any part of the United Kingdom to be open to inspection by the public.

(4) A notice or advertisement published by or on the authority
of any court within the United Kingdom or any judge or officer of
such a court.

II. Statements privileged subject to explanation or contradiction.[5]
(1) Fair and accurate reports of the findings or decisions (in relation
to members or persons subject by contract to the control of the association) of certain associations or the committees or governing bodies
thereof, *i.e.*

(a) an association formed in the United Kingdom for the purpose
of promoting or encouraging the exercise of or interest in
any art, science, religion or learning, and empowered by its
constitution to exercise control over or adjudicate upon matters
of interest or concern to the association, or the actions or
conduct of any persons subject to such control or adjudication;

(b) an association formed in the United Kingdom for the purpose
of promoting or safeguarding the interests of any trade, business,

---

[2] s. 7 (3), *e.g.* reports of a torrent of abusive interruptions which have nothing to do
with the purpose for which the meeting was summoned are not privileged (*Kelly* v.
O'Malley (1889) 6 T.L.R. 62) nor remarks made at a company shareholders' meeting as
to the guilt of a servant of the company and not relating to its financial affairs: *Ponsford*
v. *Financial Times* (1900) 16 T.L.R. 249. See *Boston* v. *W. S. Bagshaw & Sons* [1966]
1 W.L.R. 1126, 1132, *per* Lord Denning M.R.
[3] Schedule to the Act, Part I, paras. 1–7.
[4] Such reports may also be privileged independently of s. 7: *Webb* v. *Times Publishing
Co.* [1960] 2 Q.B. 535, *ante*, p. 284.
[5] Sched., Part II, paras. 8–12.

industry or profession, or of the persons carrying on or engaged in any trade, business, industry or profession, and empowered by its constitution to exercise control over or adjudicate upon matters connected with the trade, business, industry or profession, or the actions or conduct of those persons;

(c) an association formed in the United Kingdom for the purpose of promoting or safeguarding the interests of any game, sport or pastime to the playing or exercise of which members of the public are invited or admitted and empowered by its constitution to exercise control over or adjudicate upon persons connected with or taking part in the game, sport or pastime.[6]

(2) Fair and accurate reports of the proceedings of any public meeting held in the United Kingdom.

A public meeting is defined as " a meeting bona fide and lawfully held for a lawful purpose and for the furtherance or discussion of any matter of public concern, whether the admission to the meeting is general or restricted." [7]

(3) Fair and accurate reports of the proceedings at any meeting or sitting in any part of the United Kingdom of:

(a) any local authority or committee thereof;

(b) any justice or justices of the peace acting otherwise than as a court exercising judicial authority;

(c) any commission, tribunal, committee or person appointed for the purposes of any inquiry by Act of Parliament, by Her Majesty or by a Minister of the Crown;

(d) any person appointed by a local authority to hold a local inquiry in pursuance of any Act of Parliament;

not being a meeting or sitting admission to which is denied to representatives of newspapers and other members of the public.[8]

(4) Fair and accurate reports of proceedings at a general meeting of a public company.

(5) A copy or a fair and accurate report or summary of any notice or other matter issued for the information of the public by or on

---

[6] The publication in *The Times* of the decision of the domestic tribunal in *Chapman* v. *Ellesmere* [1932] 2 K.B. 431 would now be covered.

[7] The meaning of " public meeting " may now be wider than before the Act, and a meeting may be " public " even though it is open only to members of the association holding the meeting and their guests: *Khan* v. *Ahmed* [1957] 2 Q.B. 149. Whether a meeting is a " public meeting " is a question of law for the judge to decide: *ibid.*

[8] See the Public Bodies (Admission to Meetings) Act 1960 (8 & 9 Eliz. 2, c. 67). Subject to certain exceptions, *e.g.* where publicity would be prejudicial to the public interest by reason of the confidential nature of the business to be transacted, any meeting of a local authority or other body exercising public functions (listed in a Schedule to the Act) must now be open to the public: s. 1 (1), (2), (3). Where meetings are required to be open a newspaper may receive on request a copy of the agenda and other documents (s. 1 (4) (*b*)) and these may also be supplied to members of the public attending the meeting. If the supply of such documents involves the publication of defamatory matter, it is protected by qualified privilege: s. 1 (5).

behalf of any government department, officer of state, local authority, or chief officer of police.[9]

(iv) *Statements made by A to B about C (a) which A is under a legal, moral or social duty to communicate to B and which B has a corresponding interest in receiving; or (b) where A has an interest to be protected and B is under a corresponding legal, moral or social duty to protect that interest* [10]

" If fairly warranted by any reasonable occasion or exigency, and honestly made, such communications are protected for the common convenience and welfare of society." [11] A very common example is that of a former employer giving the character of a servant to a prospective employer.

It was thought at one time that, so long as the recipient (who must be some person other than the plaintiff [12]) had an interest in hearing the statement, it was immaterial that the communicator had no interest in making it. But in *Watt* v. *Longsdon*,[13] the Court of Appeal dispelled this view and emphatically adopted the rule that reciprocity of interest is essential.[14] B was a foreign manager of the X Co. He wrote to the defendant, a director of the company, a letter containing gross charges of immorality, drunkenness and dishonesty on the part of the plaintiff, who was managing director of the company abroad. The defendant wrote a reply to B in which he stated his own suspicions of the plaintiff's immorality and asked B to get confirmation of B's own allegations in order that the defendant might communicate them to the plaintiff's wife whom the defendant stated to be an old friend of his. Then, without waiting for any corrobation of B's statement, the defendant showed B's letter to S, the chairman of the board of directors and largest shareholder in the company, and also to the plaintiff's wife. All the allegations against the plaintiff were false. He sued the defendant for libel (a) in writing what he did to B; (b) in communicating B's letter to S; (c) in communicating B's letter to the plaintiff's wife. The defendant pleaded qualified privilege. The Court of Appeal had little difficulty in holding that (a) the defendant's letter to B was privileged, because both B and the defendant had a common interest in the affairs of the company, and that entitled them to discuss the behaviour of the plaintiff as another employee of the company and to collect further information for the chairman of the company; (b)

---

[9] *Boston* v. *W. S. Bagshaw & Sons* [1966] 1 W.L.R. 1126.
[10] See Lord Greene M.R. in *De Buse* v. *McCarthy* [1942] 1 K.B. 156, 164; and in *Braddock* v. *Bevins* [1948] 1 K.B. 580, 589–593. The law relating to qualified privilege at elections as stated in *Braddock's* case has been altered by the Defamation Act 1952, s. 10. *Plummer* v. *Charman* [1962] 1 W.L.R. 1469.
[11] Parke B. in *Toogood* v. *Spyring* (1834) 1 C.M. & R. 181, 193; cited by Scrutton L.J. in *Watt* v. *Longsdon* [1930] 1 K.B. 130, 143.
[12] *White* v. *Stone Ltd.* [1939] 2 K.B. 827.
[13] [1930] 1 K.B. 130; Weir, *Casebook on Tort*, 3rd ed., p. 344.
[14] *Phelps* v. *Kemsley* (1942) 168 L.T. 18, 21. This does not mean that both parties must have a duty or both an interest: one may have an interest and the other a duty, as in the common case of a servant's character. See *Beach* v. *Freeson* [1971] 2 W.L.R. 805.

the defendant's communication of B's letter to S was privileged, because a duty to make it arose both from the fact of employment in the same company and from the possibility that S might be asked by the plaintiff for a testimonial if the plaintiff were to seek another situation. But the court held that (c) the communication of the letter to the plaintiff's wife was not privileged. No doubt she had the strongest possible interest in hearing a statement about her husband's moral conduct; no doubt also there may be occasions on which a friend of the wife is under a duty, or has a corresponding interest, in informing her of statements about her husband—indeed each case must depend on its own circumstances, the nature of the information and the relation of the speaker to the wife.[15] But here the defendant had no sufficient interest or duty, for the information came from a very doubtful source and he had neither consulted the plaintiff nor obtained any confirmation of outrageous accusations before passing them to the wife.

Test of duty. The determination of whether a duty to communicate the matter does or does not exist is a question for the judge. It is easy enough for him to decide where the duty is a legal one, but where it is alleged to be moral or social, what test is he to adopt? Naturally, no criterion of any affair of ethics or of social relations can be more than an approximate one, but unfortunately the authorities do not show complete agreement on even an approximate test. Lindley L.J. said in *Stuart* v. *Bell*[16]: " The question of moral or social duty being for the judge, each judge must decide it as best he can for himself. I take moral or social duty to mean a duty recognised by English people of ordinary intelligence and moral principle, but at the same time not a duty enforceable by legal proceedings, whether civil or criminal." If " all or, at all events, the great mass of right-minded men in the position of the defendant would have considered it their duty under the circumstances " to give the information, then the learned Lord Justice thought that the privilege arose. But Scrutton L.J. in *Watt* v. *Longsdon*[17] asked, " Is the judge merely to give his own view of moral and social duty, though he thinks that a considerable portion of the community hold a different opinion? Or is he to endeavour to ascertain what view the great mass of right-minded men would take? " It is suggested that the answer to this is that the judge's view if, as is probable, it takes account of the arguments of counsel on each side, as well as of his own personal predilections, is the nearest approach that is possible to the ascertainment of public opinion. You cannot subpoena

---

[15] Scrutton L.J. [1930] 1 K.B. at pp. 149–150.

[16] [1891] 2 Q.B. 341, 350. Cited by Scrutton and Greer L.JJ. in *Watt* v. *Longsdon* [1930] 1 K.B. at pp. 144, 153. *Cf. Phelps* v. *Kemsley* (1942) 168 L.T. 18. *Bridgman* v. *Stockdale* [1953] 1 W.L.R. 704 (statement by invigilator to the class at an examination on a trade course that a trainee had " cribbed " privileged on ground of common interest).

[17] [1930] 1 K.B. at p. 144; *Beach* v. *Freeson, supra,* at pp. 812–813, *per* Geoffrey Lane J.

as witnesses a portion of the community in order to discover what they regard as a moral duty. At any rate, it is a fallacy to suppose that the mere existence of any relationship (*e.g.* host and guest) will suffice to raise the duty without weighing all the circumstances of the particular case before the court; and this seems to be the explanation of some decisions in which it looks as if facts which really constituted malice (*i.e.* abuse of the privilege) were regarded as showing that the privilege had never existed at all.[18]

In this privilege a distinction has been drawn between a statement which is made in answer to an inquiry and one which is merely volunteered. Certainly, where there has been a request for the information, that is useful evidence towards showing that the privilege exists, particularly if the case is on the border-line,[19] but it does not follow that because the information is given unasked there can be no privilege. A man is but a poor citizen, to say nothing worse of him, if he is deliberately silent when he sees the lives of the public likely to be imperilled or the property of another person in obvious danger of being stolen or destroyed by one whom he honestly believes to be a drunkard or a thief.[20] And decided cases show that something less than such urgency as this may be enough to establish privilege for a volunteered statement.[21]

Trade protection societies. Two decisions on reports as to the financial stability of tradesmen must be distinguished. Trade protection societies are often formed for the purpose of supplying such information to inquirers, and the law has to steer some middle course between allowing third persons to help a tradesman to protect himself against dealing with insolvent persons and " safeguarding commercial credit against the most dangerous and insidious of all enemies—the dissemination of prejudicial rumour, the author of which cannot be easily identified, nor its medium readily disclosed." [22] In *Macintosh* v. *Dun*,[23] the defendants carried on business as a trade protection society under the title " The Mercantile Agency." X, one of the subscribers to the agency, asked for information about the credit of the plaintiffs who were ironmongers. The agency replied unfavourably and, as it turned out, untruly. In an action for libel, the Judicial Committee of the Privy Council held that there was no privilege, for the defendants were only collectors of information which they were ready to sell to their customers, and it was immaterial whether the customer bought the information across the counter or whether he enjoyed the privilege of being enrolled as a subscriber and paid his fee in advance. In *London*

---

[18] See *Angel* v. *H. H. Bushell & Co. Ltd.* [1968] 1 Q.B. 813, 830, *per* Milmo J.

[19] *Macintosh* v. *Dun* [1908] A.C. 390, 399, *per* Lord Macnaghten.

[20] *Coxhead* v. *Richards* (1846) 2 C.B. 569, 609–610; *Boston* v. *W. S. Bagshaw & Sons* [1966] 1 W.L.R. 1126.

[21] Gatley, *op. cit.*, pp. 200 *et seq.*; *Beach* v. *Freeson*, *supra*.

[22] Lord Buckmaster L.C. in *London Association, etc.* v. *Greenlands Ltd.* [1916] 2 A.C. 15, 26.

[23] [1908] A.C. 390.

Association for Protection of Trade v. *Greenlands Ltd.*,[24] the facts were much the same except that the appellants there did not trade for profit and that the secretary to their association collected and supplied the information about Messrs. Greenlands to X. The House of Lords held that the communication was privileged on the ground that the secretary, in supplying it, was acting, not as agent of the association as a whole but as the confidential agent of X; for if X had the right to make inquiries on his own account, he equally had the right to make them through an agent and the agent was under a duty to report to him. But had the association itself any such privilege? The question could not be directly decided by the House of Lords owing to procedural blunders in the court of first instance but it may be deduced from the speech of Lord Buckmaster [25] that the privilege exists if (a) the association consists of persons who are themselves interested in trade, and (b) it exercises control over the person who on their behalf procures the information and over the manner in which he procures it, and (c) it does not conduct its business purely for purposes of gain.[26] In *Macintosh* v. *Dun* not one of these conditions was satisfied; in the *Greenlands* case all were.

This kind of qualified privilege may quite well exist where the people interested in the receipt of the information are very numerous.[27] Thus it would appear from *Chapman* v. *Ellesmere* [28] that the stewards of the Jockey Club had qualified privilege for statements published by them relating to the conduct of trainers and other persons connected with the running of horse-races under the rules of the club, for the stewards owe all persons interested in racing conducted under those rules a duty to give them such information [29]; but the medium of communication must be a proper one, and it was held in this case that, while publication in the Racing Calendar satisfied this condition because both the plaintiff and the defendants had agreed upon this, publication in *The Times* did not, because the racing community could be adequately informed of the decisions of the Jockey Club without broadcasting them to the public in general.[30] One occasion where a

---

[24] [1916] 2 A.C. 15.

[25] At pp. 26–27.

[26] It may be that (c) is not always necessary. See *ibid.* at p. 42, *per* Lord Parker; *Watt* v. *Longsdon* [1930] 1 K.B. 130, 148, *per* Scrutton L.J.

[27] Even, very occasionally, the whole of the newspaper-reading public: *Adam* v. *Ward* [1917] A.C. 309. But see *infra*, note 30.

[28] [1932] 2 K.B. 431; applied in *Russell* v. *Duke of Norfolk* [1949] 65 T.L.R. 225.

[29] The clearest statement on this point is that of Romer L.J. at pp. 473–474. Lord Hanworth M.R. at pp. 449–450 seems to have held the same view. *Contra* Slesser L.J. at pp. 465–467.

[30] Note that the parties' assent here was to the *mode* of exercising qualified privilege. Any expressions in the judgments which might indicate that the parties could *create* qualified privilege by agreement cannot be supported for it is the court alone which settles whether qualified privilege exists or not. As regards the publication in a newspaper of the findings or decisions of such a tribunal, qualified privilege now arises under s. 2, Defamation Act 1952, and Sched., para. 8 (c). " So far as I know, there is no authority in which a letter published in the press has been held to be privileged, except when it was published as a matter of duty, as in the case of *Adam* v. *Ward* ([1917] A.C. 309), or where

qualified privilege may have arisen at common law by virtue of interest is now limited by section 10 of the Defamation Act 1952, which provides that a defamatory statement published by or on behalf of a candidate in any election to a local government authority or to Parliament shall not be deemed to be published on a privileged occasion on the ground that it is material to a question in issue in the election, whether the person by whom it is published is qualified to vote at the election or not.[31]

(v) *Where A and B have a common interest in the statement made by A to B about the plaintiff* [32]

It is impossible to classify the cases in which such a common interest arises. Whether it exists or not is a question of law for the judge and probably the principle upon which he ought to resolve it cannot be put more exactly than to say that " the law never sanctions mere vulgar curiosity or officious meddling in the concerns of others." [33] Nor will an honest belief that there is a common interest suffice to create it, if in law there is none.[34]

The common interest may be a pecuniary one, such as a communication made by an insurance company to its policy-holders about an agent of the company [35]; or it may be professional, such as a letter written by an auctioneer to other auctioneers in the area about a person who had " purchased " goods at an auction and removed them without paying,[36] or the " screening " of a barrister by the Benchers of his Inn of Court after he has been disbarred.[37] But a general interest in church architecture confers no privilege on the imputations of a clergyman on an architect employed to restore a church of which the clergyman was neither an incumbent, nor a

---

it is published by a defendant in answer to a public attack which had been made upon him ": *Cutler* v. *McPhail* [1962] 2 Q.B. 292, 296, *per* Salmon J. But if the subject-matter of the letter is comment on a matter of public interest then the defence of fair comment may be available.

[31] The section reverses the decision in *Braddock* v. *Bevins* [1948] 1 K.B. 580, 589–593 on this point; *Plummer* v. *Charman* [1962] 1 W.L.R. 1469.

[32] Lord Greene M.R. in *De Buse* v. *McCarthy* [1942] 1 K.B. 156, 164, 166–167 referred to the fact that this privilege has been stated as requiring a common interest " in the subject-matter " of the communication. He thought these words were too vague to be worth inclusion. He distinguished *Hunt* v. *Great Northern Ry.* [1891] 2 Q.B. 189 as a decision which brings out very clearly " the distinction between a case where there was an obvious interest to receive it ": *Bridgman* v. *Stockdale* [1953] 1 W.L.R. 704.

[33] Odgers, *op. cit.*, p. 232.

[34] *Ley* v. *Hamilton* (1935) 153 L.T. 384, 385; *Davidson* v. *Barclays Bank Ltd.* [1940] 1 All E.R. 316, 322, *per* Hilbery J.: " You cannot by making a mistake create the occasion for making a defamatory communication." For criticism of this case, see *Pyke* v. *Hibernian Bank* [1950] I.R. 195, 220–223, *per* Black J.

[35] *Nevill* v. *Fine Art and General Insurance Co.* [1897] A.C. 68; *Smythson Ltd.* v. *Cramp & Sons Ltd.* [1943] 1 All E.R. 322; the appeal to the H.L., [1944] A.C. 329, was upon a different point.

[36] *Boston* v. *W. S. Bagshaw & Sons* [1966] 1 W.L.R. 1126.

[37] Odgers, *op. cit.*, pp. 236–237. For other examples see *Laughton* v. *Bishop of Sodor and Man* (1872) L.R. 4 P.C. 495; *Winstanley* v. *Bampton* [1943] K.B. 319; *Angel* v. *H. H. Bushell & Co. Ltd.* [1968] 1 Q.B. 813. It is doubtful how far professional communications about his client made by a solicitor to the opposing solicitor are privileged: *Groom* v. *Crocker* [1939] 1 K.B. 194.

patron, nor a parishioner.[38] Fair comment may of course be a defence in such a case provided its requisites are satisfied.

It would seem, although the English authorities are somewhat discordant, that a clergyman who prays for, or preaches at, another person for some sin which the clergyman expressly or impliedly alleges against him, has no privilege.[39] No doubt all men are sinners, but an admission of general iniquity is one thing, an accusation of personal sin is quite another, and the proper way for a pastor to rebuke it is in private and not in the pulpit, unless indeed public admonition of sin is one of the tenets of the particular form of worship which he professes and the plaintiff has become a member of his congregation on that understanding. If the imputation is true, of course, the plea of justification will be available. Whether fair comment can be pleaded presumably depends on the circumstances of the case; if the allegation of sin is based on a matter of fact which is fairly open to public comment (*e.g.* the behaviour of a public librarian in admitting books of a provocatively erotic character into the library) one does not see why this form of comment on it should be in any worse plight than, say, newspaper criticism; but purely private peccadilloes do not appear to be a fit matter for public comment at all.

(vi) *Statements in protection of oneself or of one's property* [40]

An example of defence of one's property would be a master's warning to servants not to associate with a former fellow-servant whom he had dismissed for dishonesty.[41] Another illustration is *Osborn* v. *Boulter*,[42] where a publican complained to the brewers who supplied him with beer that it was of poor quality. They retorted that they had heard rumours that the poorness of the beer was due to the watering of it by the publican, and they published this statement to a third party. It was held to be privileged. The case was regarded by the Court of Appeal as illustrative of the type of privilege which is based on the fact that A's statement to B is in protection of an interest of his own and

---

[38] *Botterill* v. *Whytehead* (1879) 41 L.T. 588.

[39] *Greenwood* v. *Prist* (*or Prick*) (1584), cited in Cro.Jac. 91, 1 Camp. 270, and 13 St.Tr. 1387 (best report), is the other way, but it was declared not to be law in *Hearne* v. *Stowell* (1841) 11 A. & E. 726. Both Irish and Scots law support the statement in the text: *Magrath* v. *Finn* (1877) I.R. 11 C.L. 152; *Dudgeon* v. *Forbes* (1833) 11 S. 1014.

[40] *Turner* v. *M.G.M. Pictures Ltd.* [1950] 1 All E.R. 449, 470–471, *per* Lord Oaksey. " There is . . . an analogy between the criminal law of self-defence and a man's right to defend himself against written or verbal attacks. In both cases he is entitled to defend himself effectively, and he only loses the protection of the law if he goes beyond defence and proceeds to offence. That is to say, the circumstances on which he defends himself, either by acts or by words, negative the malice which the law draws from violent acts or defamatory words." See Gatley, *op. cit.*, pp. 240–245.

[41] *Somerville* v. *Hawkins* (1851) 10 C.B. 583.

[42] [1930] 2 K.B. 226, 233, *per* Scrutton L.J. " Brewers supplying beer and a licensee who receives it are quarrelling about its character. That is clearly a privileged occasion within the principle laid down in *Toogood* v. *Spyring* (1834) 1 Cr.M. & R. 181, because it is in the interest of one party to defend himself and the interest of the other to receive and consider the defence. The privilege is not lost where a man defending himself and making charges against another reads a letter to his servant on whose information he is making the charges and says, ' Is that correct?' Nor was it lost by dictating it to his clerk." *Meekings* v. *Henson* [1964] 1 Q.B. 472.

B is under a corresponding duty to protect it.[43] But it falls just as well under this head, and indeed the reports and textbooks draw no very sharp lines of division between these and some other species of qualified privilege.

(vii) *Statements made to the proper authorities in order to procure the redress of public grievances*

Such would be a complaint to the Post Office concerning the alleged delinquencies of a local postmaster,[44] or to the Home Secretary that a local magistrate had incited people to break the peace,[45] or to a bishop that a clergyman in his diocese was reputed to have had a fight with the local schoolmaster.[46] Probably a complaint to the Bar Council concerning the professional conduct of a barrister is also protected by qualified privilege despite the fact that the Council can do no more than pass on the complaint to the barrister's Inn of Court.[47] The grievance need not be one which especially affects the complainant. If it does, he will probably have an additional kind of qualified privilege —statements made in self-protection.[48]

The complaint, in order to be privileged, must be addressed to the right person, *i.e.* to someone who has some power of redressing the grievance. Meticulous selection of the proper official is not necessary. A petition for an inquiry into the conduct of a magistrate and for his removal from office was held to be correctly addressed to the Home Secretary; for, although power of removing a magistrate is with the Lord Chancellor, yet the memorial to the Home Secretary was in effect a petition to the Crown, who might direct the inquiry to be made by the Home Secretary, and the Lord Chancellor would then, if necessary, act upon the results of it.[49] On the other hand, the Home Secretary has no sort of control over a clerk to the justices of the peace, and a petition to him alleging corruption on the part of that official is not privileged.[50]

(viii) *Third persons*

Where a communication is made on a privileged occasion, the privilege is not lost merely because there is publication to a third person

---

[43] *Ante*, pp. 287–291.
[44] *Woodward* v. *Lander* (1834) 6 C. & P. 548.
[45] *Harrison* v. *Bush* (1855) 5 E. & B. 344; *R.* v. *Rule* [1937] 2 K.B. 375. (R wrote to the Member of Parliament for his constituency a letter containing defamatory statements about a constable and a justice of the peace for his district, in relation to their offices. Held R and the Member of Parliament had sufficient common interest to make it a publication on a privileged occasion.) *Cf. Rivlin* v. *Bilainkin* [1953] 1 Q.B. 485.
[46] *James* v. *Boston* (1845) 2 C. & K. 4.
[47] *Lincoln* v. *Daniels* [1962] 1 Q.B. 237, 269, per Danckwerts L.J.; Devlin L.J., *ibid.* at p. 264, expressly left the point open. Disciplinary jurisdiction is in fact now exercised by the Senate of the Inns of Court.   [48] *Ante*, p. 292.
[49] *Harrison* v. *Bush* (1855) 5 E. & B. 344, 350–351. See also *Lincoln* v. *Daniels, supra.* If the recipient of the petition has an interest in the subject-matter of the complaint, qualified privilege may arise by virtue of common interest: *R.* v. *Rule* [1937] 2 K.B. 375; *De Buse* v. *McCarthy* [1942] 1 K.B. 156, 170.
[50] *Blagg* v. *Sturt* (1846) 10 Q.B. 899. *Hebditch* v. *MacIlwaine* [1894] 2 Q.B. 54 is to the same effect, although, like so many cases on qualified privilege, it may be, and indeed was, treated under another head of qualified privilege.

in the usual course of business, as where a letter sent by A to B is first dictated by A to his secretary and typed by her. " The person exercising the privilege is entitled to take all reasonable means of so doing, and those reasonable means may include the introduction of third persons, where that is reasonable and in the ordinary course of business." [51] As a matter of common sense it must also be the law that if A sends to B a letter which is defamatory of B himself and, in the usual course of business, first dictates that letter to his secretary, B should not be able to sue in respect of the publication to the secretary.[52] There is, however, the difficulty that where the defamatory matter is contained in a communication between the defamer and the defamed no question of privilege properly so called arises, for there is no publication.[53] If, then, a privilege cannot be set up between the defamer *and his secretary*, it would appear that an actionable publication has occurred. In *Boxsius* v. *Goblet Freres* [54] and in *Osborn* v. *Thomas Boulter & Son* [55] it seems to have been assumed that a privilege exists between defamer and defamed on the ground of common interest, but the assumption, though convenient, is illogical.[56] The solution proposed by Stallybrass,[57] that there is a " new head of privileged occasion for statements not otherwise actionable published to third persons in the reasonable and usual course of business," is to be preferred.[58]

Express malice

As has been said above, a plea of qualified privilege can be rebutted by proof of express malice, and malice in this connection [59] may mean either (a) lack of belief in the truth of the statement or (b) use of the privileged occasion for an improper purpose. Lack of belief in the truth of the statement is generally conclusive as to malice, except in a case where a person is under a duty to pass on defamatory reports made by some other person.[60] Mere carelessness, however, or even honest

---

[51] *Edmonson* v. *Birch & Co. Ltd.* [1907] 1 K.B. 371, 380, *per* Collins M.R.; *Boxsius* v. *Goblet Freres* [1894] 1 Q.B. 842; *Roff* v. *British and French Chemical Manufacturing Co.* [1918] 2 K.B. 677; *Osborn* v. *Thomas Boulter & Son* [1930] 2 K.B. 226. *Pullman* v. *Walter Hill & Co. Ltd.* [1891] 1 Q.B. 524, to the contrary, has been distinguished out of existence. For other cases see *Taylor* v. *Hawkins* (1851) 16 Q.B. 308 (witness present when servant dismissed for dishonesty); *Crisp* v. *Gill* (1857) 29 L.T.(o.s.) 82.

[52] *Aliter* if the communication is not made in the usual course of business, *e.g.* if the defamatory matter is purely personal.

[53] *White* v. *J. & F. Stone Ltd.* [1939] 2 K.B. 827.

[54] *Supra.*

[55] *Supra.*

[56] *Cf.* Goodhart, " Defamatory Statements and Privileged Occasions " (1940) 56 L.Q.R. 262; Salmond, *Torts*, 16th ed., pp. 180–181.

[57] (1943) 59 L.Q.R. 276, 278 (a review of the 2nd edition of this work).

[58] Winfield's own view (see 5th ed., p. 298) was to the effect that communication to the secretary was no publication if the communication to the addressee, being the person defamed, was itself no publication. See also *Restatement of Torts*, §§ 577, comment (h); 604, comment (c).

[59] " Malice " is almost as unfortunate here as in the formal allegation of malicious publication (see p. 261, *ante*): a mere love of gossip will defeat the privilege, but this is not malice in the popular sense.

[60] *Horrocks* v. *Lowe* [1974] 2 W.L.R. 282, 291, *per* Lord Diplock. *Stuart* v. *Bell* [1891] 2 Q.B. 341 is a good example of this type of case.

belief produced by irrational prejudice, does not amount to malice [61]: " despite the imperfection of the mental process by which the belief is arrived at it may still be ' honest.' The law demands no more." [62] Even an honest belief will not, however, protect the defendant if he uses the privileged occasion for some purpose other than that for which the privilege is accorded by law: if his dominant motive is spite or if he acts for some private advantage he will be liable. [63]

Evidence of malice

The question of malice is one for the jury and may be left to them at large, provided, of course, that there is some evidence of it. It is not necessary for the judge to draw the attention of the jury to every possible item of evidence of malice; nor is it required that the jury be told that they may act on any single such item, even though there is also evidence to negative malice. [64]

Evidence of malice may be found in the publication itself. If the language used is utterly beyond or disproportionate to the facts, that may lead to an inference of malice, [65] but the law does not weigh words in a hair balance and it does not follow that merely because the words are excessive there is therefore malice. [66]

Malice may also be inferred from the relations between the parties before or after publication or from the conduct of the defendant in the course of the proceedings themselves, as, for example, where the defendant persisted in a plea of justification while nevertheless making no attempt to prove it. [67] But the mere pleading of justification is not itself evidence of malice even though the plea ultimately fails; on the contrary, it may point more to honesty than to malice. [68]

There may also be evidence of malice in the mode of publication and this is commonly illustrated by wider dissemination of the statement

---

[61] *Horrocks* v. *Lowe, supra.* As in the tort of deceit, recklessness is here equivalent to intention, for it equally involves lack of honest belief. It is not clear whether in *Smith* v. *Hodgeskins* (1633) Cro.Car. 276 the defendant's state of mind was reckless or intentional.

[62] *Horrocks* v. *Lowe, supra*, at p. 291, *per* Lord Diplock.

[63] *Horrocks* v. *Lowe, supra.*

[64] *Boston* v. *W. S. Bagshaw & Sons* [1966] 1 W.L.R. 1126, not following a dictum of Lord Porter in *Turner* v. *M.G.M. Pictures Ltd.* [1950] 1 All E.R. 449, 455.

[65] *Spill* v. *Maule* (1869) L.R. 4 Ex. 232, 236; *Adam* v. *Ward* [1917] A.C. 309, 327, 330, 335; *Sun Life Assurance Co. of Canada* v. *Dalrymple* (1965) 50 D.L.R. (2d) 217, Sup.Ct.

[66] *Nevill* v. *Fine Art, etc. Co. Ltd.* [1895] 2 Q.B. 156, 170, *per* Lord Esher M.R. If in the course of the editing of a newspaper article certain vital matters were omitted or inserted so as to make the article more exciting or scandalous that might be evidence of malice, but " a newspaper would too readily be deprived of the privilege of fair comment if the editing of news by omissions or additions were of itself to be held more consistent with malice than with its absence ": *Broadway Approvals Ltd.* v. *Odhams Press Ltd.* (*No. 2*) [1965] 1 W.L.R. 805, 815, *per* Sellers L.J. (" Malice is not established by forensic imagination, however eloquently and subtly expressed ": *ibid.*).

[67] *Simpson* v. *Robinson* (1848) 12 Q.B. 511.

[68] *Broadway Approvals Ltd.* v. *Odhams Press Ltd.* (*No. 2*), *supra*, at p. 825, *per* Davies L.J. A plea of justification should not, of course, be made unless the defendant has evidence of the truth of the statement, and if that evidence only comes to light at a later stage, leave to amend the defence by adding the plea may be given so long as the defendant has not been guilty of delay or failure to make proper inquiries at an earlier stage: *Associated Leisure Ltd.* v. *Associated Newspapers Ltd.* [1970] 2 Q.B. 450.

than is necessary, such as circulating it on a postcard instead of in an enclosed letter, or saying it at the top of one's voice so that bystanders who have no proper interest in it overhear.[69] An alternative way of reaching the same result is to say that the privilege which covers publication by A to B does not in general cover the distinct, if contemporaneous, publication to C.[70]

Privilege, agents and malice

When a defamatory communication is made by several persons on an occasion of qualified privilege, only those against whom express malice is actually proved are liable.[71] This may seem self-evident, but until recently it was thought that where a defamatory communication was published by an agent, the agent's only protection was by way of an ancillary privilege derived from his principal, so that the malice of the principal destroyed the protection of the agent.[72] Now, however, in *Egger* v. *Viscount Chelmsford*,[73] the Court of Appeal has declared this to be wrong. The malice of an agent may make the innocent principal liable in some cases on the ordinary principles of vicarious liability,[74] but the malice of the principal, cannot do the same for the innocent agent.

The decision in *Egger* v. *Viscount Chelmsford* accords well with common sense—it would be absurd to hold a typist liable because her employer was malicious.[75] But there remains the difficulty that except where the agent has for some reason a privilege of his own (which Davies LJ. thought to be the case in *Egger* v. *Viscount Chelmsford* itself [76]) his protection can only be derived from the privilege of his principal. If, then, the malice of the principal does not destroy the protection of the agent, it follows that the derivative privilege survives the destruction of the privilege from which it is derived and has an independent existence of its own. In effect, therefore, the Court of Appeal has created a new head of privilege, namely, publication by an agent in circumstances in which his principal has a prima facie privilege to make the defamatory communication.[77]

---

[69] *Sadgrove* v. *Hole* [1901] 2 K.B. 1; *Oddy* v. *Paulet* (1865) 4 F. & F. 1009; *Chapman* v. *Ellesmere* [1932] 2 K.B. 421, 474–475, *per* Romer L.J.

[70] But on this approach, it may be that the privilege is destroyed even though there is no malice: *Cutler* v. *McPhail* [1962] 2 Q.B. 292; but *cf. Angel* v. *H. H. Bushell & Co. Ltd.* [1968] 1 Q.B. 813.

[71] *Longdon-Griffiths* v. *Smith* [1951] 1 K.B. 295; *Meekins* v. *Henson* [1964] 1 Q.B. 472.

[72] *Smith* v. *Streatfeild* [1913] 3 K.B. 764; *Adam* v. *Ward* [1917] A.C. 309, 320, *per* Lord Finlay L.C.; 340–341, *per* Lord Atkinson.

[73] [1965] 1 Q.B. 248; Weir, *Casebook on Tort*, 3rd ed., p. 451.

[74] *Fitzsimons* v. *Duncan and Kemp & Co. Ltd.* [1908] 2 I.R. 483; *Angel* v. *H. H. Bushell & Co. Ltd., supra; Gros* v. *Cook* (1969) 113 S.J. 408. For vicarious liability generally, see Chap. 25, *post*.

[75] Even though she could recover a full indemnity under the Law Reform (Married Women and Tortfeasors) Act 1935: *post*, pp. 548–551.

[76] [1965] 1 Q.B. at p. 272.

[77] This goes further than the recommendations of the Committee on the Law of Defamation, which, in any event, were not accepted by Parliament, and, indeed, section 4 (6) of the Defamation Act 1952 recognises and proceeds upon the principle of *Smith* v. *Streatfeild*. See further on *Egger* v. *Viscount Chelmsford*, Armitage [1965] C.L.J. 30.

Apology

An apology for the defamatory statement by the defendant may mitigate damages and its absence may aggravate them,[78] but it cannot affect his liability.[79] He is quite entitled, apart from any statute, to make such an apology, and an Act of 1843, commonly styled Lord Campbell's Act,[80] enables the defendant to employ what may be called a statutory apology. Section 1 provides that in any action for defamation the defendant, after duly notifying the plaintiff in writing of his intention to do so, may give evidence in mitigation of damages that he made or offered an apology to the plaintiff before the action began, or as soon afterwards as he had an opportunity of doing so if the action had commenced before he had such opportunity. Section 2 provides that in an action for libel contained in a newspaper or other periodical publication, the defendant may plead that he inserted the libel without actual malice and without gross negligence,[81] and that he inserted in the publication a full apology.[82] An Act of 1845[83] amended section 2 by requiring that the defendant must pay money into court by way of amends at the time of delivering the plea. It was held in *Hawkesley* v. *Bradshaw*[84] that the defence of justification could be pleaded as an alternative to the plea under section 2. Under the present rules of procedure, a defendant in any action for debt or damages may pay money into court, with or without an admission of liability,[85] and in an action for defamation it may be advantageous to the defendant to combine an apology with payment under this rule of procedure.[86]

A full apology need not be an abject one, but it does at least require a complete withdrawal of the imputation and an expression of regret for having made it.[87] To say that a man has manners not fit for a pig and then to retract that by saying that his manners are fit for a pig would merely aggravate damages.

THE REHABILITATION OF OFFENDERS ACT 1974[88]

Some mention must be made here of this important legislation, though it has many provisions unconnected with the law of defamation and a

---

[78] *Fielding* v. *Variety Incorporated* [1967] 2 Q.B. 841.

[79] Apart from cases when the defence is open for unintentional defamation under Defamation Act 1952, s. 4. *Ante*, pp. 265–267.

[80] 6 & 7 Vict. c. 96.

[81] *Bell* v. *Northern Constitution* [1943] N.I. 108 (failure of a newspaper company to make any inquiry as to the authentication of a telephone notice for publication was gross negligence).

[82] If the periodical is published at intervals exceeding one week, it is enough if he offered to insert the apology in any periodical publication selected by the plaintiff.

[83] 8 & 9 Vict. c. 75.   [84] (1880) 5 Q.B.D. 302.

[85] R.S.C., Ord. 22, r. 1; Gatley, *op. cit.*, p. 348. See also *ibid.* 346–347; and see *Bell* v. *Northern Constitution* [1943] N.I. 108, where the money was paid into court by way of amends under the Libel Acts 1843, 1845, and under Ord. 22, r. 1.

[86] Gatley, *op. cit.*, p. 348.

[87] See Odgers, *op. cit.*, pp. 330–333.

[88] The Act comes into force on July 1, 1975, or on such earlier date as the Secretary of State may by order appoint.

full account of it must be sought elsewhere. The Act seeks to rehabilitate offenders by restricting or forbidding the disclosure of " spent convictions," which, broadly speaking, means convictions for offences in respect of which the offender has received a sentence not exceeding 30 months' imprisonment and where a specified time (the " rehabilitation period "—varying from five to 10 years, depending on the sentence) has elapsed since the conviction. A rehabilitated person is then to " be treated for all purposes in law as a person who has not committed or been charged with or prosecuted for or convicted of or sentenced for the offence . . . the subject of that conviction." [89] However, this is severely limited with respect to proceedings for defamation by section 8 (3) which provides that nothing shall prevent a defendant in such an action from " relying on any defence of justification or fair comment or of absolute or qualified privilege which is available to him or restrict the matters he may establish in support of any such defence." At this point, however, the Act introduces a novel concept into English law, for it goes on to provide that a defendant shall not be entitled to rely upon the defence of justification if the publication is proved to have been made with malice.[90] " Malice " is nowhere defined, but its normal meaning is that the statement is either made without belief in its truth or for an improper purpose.[91] In this context, however, it can mean only the latter, since section 13 of the Civil Evidence Act 1968, which is unaffected by this Act, provides that for the purposes of defamation, conviction of an offence is conclusive evidence of guilt.[92]

---

[89] s. 4 (1).
[90] s. 8 (5).
[91] See p. 294, *ante*.
[92] See p. 268, *ante*.

The position of the writer of a reference after this Act is curious. He is not obliged to disclose a spent conviction of which he knows and is under no liability to the addressee for failing to do so (s. 4 (2)). But if he chooses to disclose such a conviction he may plead non-malicious privilege.

The Act also restricts the defence of privilege based upon a fair and accurate report of judicial proceedings if the report contains a reference to inadmissible evidence of a spent conviction: s. 8 (6), (7).

CHAPTER 14

TRESPASS TO LAND [1]

TRESPASS DEFINED

TRESPASS to land is the name given to that form of trespass which is constituted by unjustifiable interference with the possession of land. Contrary to popular belief trespass is not criminal in the absence of some special statute which makes it so,[1a] but an entry upon another's land is tortious whether or not the entrant knows that he is trespassing.[2] It is no defence that the only reason for his entry was that he had lost his way or even that he genuinely but erroneously believed that the land was his.[3]

Since the decision in *Fowler* v. *Lanning*,[4] it may be asked whether liability for trespass to land, like that for trespass to the person, requires proof of intention or negligence on the part of the defendant, but the question is of little practical interest, for the majority of trespasses to land are, in the nature of things, self-evidently intentional. I intend to enter upon your land if I consciously place myself upon what proves to be your land, even though I neither knew nor could reasonably have known that it was not mine. It is true that land adjoining a highway may be unintentionally entered as the result, for example, of a motor accident, but in such cases it was clear long before *Fowler* v. *Lanning* that the plaintiff must prove negligence.[5] Other cases of unintentional entry are more likely to occur in the imagination than in real life—I may, perhaps, fall or be thrown from my window into your garden. In the latter case there has been no act on my part and so I cannot be liable in any event.[6] Otherwise it is today probably correct in principle that you must prove negligence on my part,[7] but the principle is unlikely to be of much practical importance.

---

[1] Weir, *Casebook on Tort*, 3rd ed., Chap. 8, section 5.

[1a] The familiar notice, " Trespassers will be prosecuted " is thus, normally, no more than a " wooden falsehood." The punitive element which originally attached to trespass finally disappeared in 1694 but it had fallen into obsolescence long before that date: Winfield, *Province of the Law of Tort*, p. 11. However, a conspiracy to trespass is in certain cases an offence: *R.* v. *Kamara* [1973] 3 W.L.R. 198, H.L. See also the proposals in Law Commission Working Paper No. 54 (1974).

[2] *Conway* v. *George Wimpey & Co. Ltd.* [1951] 2 K.B. 266, 273-274; *Jolliffe* v. *Willmett & Co.* (1970) 120 New L.J. 707. By the Limitation Act 1623, s. 5, if the defendant disclaims any title to the land and proves that his trespass was involuntary or negligent and that he had tendered sufficient amends before the action was brought, he has a defence to an action of trespass. *Cf. Basely* v. *Clarkson* (1682) 3 Lev. 37. If this case is still good law the scope of the defence is extremely restricted. See Williams, *Liability for Animals*, p. 196.

[3] Hence the possibility, long appreciated, of using trespass as a means of testing title.

[4] [1959] 1 Q.B. 426. See *ante*, pp. 81-82.

[5] See, *e.g.*, *River Wear Commissioners* v. *Adamson* (1877) 2 App.Cas. 743 and *ante*, p. 81.

[6] Though I could, no doubt, be required to leave.

[7] *Mann* v. *Saulnier* (1959) 19 D.L.R. (2d) 130; Salmond, *Torts*, 16th ed., p. 39; Fleming, *Torts*, 4th ed., p. 39.

On the face of it the law looks harsh, and the appearance of harshness is enhanced by the fact that trespass is actionable *per se, i.e.* whether or not the plaintiff has actually suffered any damage.[8] In earlier times, however, trespass was so likely to lead to a breach of the peace that even unwitting and trivial deviations on to another person's land were reckoned unlawful. At the present day there is, of course, much greater respect for the law in general and appreciation of the security which it affords, and the theoretical severity of the rules as to land trespass is hardly ever exploited in practice. It is true that " legal theory has nothing to do with the fact that a great deal of trespassing is tolerated by reasonable owners and occupiers as being substantially harmless," [9] but nobody except a churl would drag into court a person who takes a short cut across his meadow without doing any visible injury to it. Moreover, there are cases where a trespass is justified by the common law and many modern statutes confer a right of entry upon private property.[10]

POSSESSION

Trespass to land, like the tort of trespass to goods which is considered in a later chapter, consists of interference with possession,[11] and it is necessary to say something here of this concept.[12] Our law has, however, not worked out a consistent theory of possession, and its meaning may turn upon the context in which it is used.[13] Broadly speaking the law recognises two kinds of possession—possession in fact and possession in law.

1. Possession in fact

Sometimes known also as " custody," " detention " or " *de facto* possession," this may be defined as " any power to use the thing and exclude others . . . if accompanied by the *animus possidendi*, provided that no one else has the *animus possidendi* and an equal or greater power." [14] Possession in fact, whether of goods or land, obviously extends to things which are beyond a person's immediate physical control. I do not lose the possession of my house and its contents

---

[8] *Entick v. Carrington* (1765) 2 Wils.K.B. 275, 291, *per curiam*; Blackstone, Comm., iii, 209–210.

[9] Pollock and Wright, *Possession* (1888), p. 45.

[10] *Post*, pp. 309–310.

[11] " The distinction between the actions of trespass and trover is well settled: the former is founded on possession: the latter on property ": *Ward* v. *Macauley* (1791) 4 T.R. 489, 490, *per* Lord Kenyon C.J.; *Smith* v. *Milles* (1786) 1 T.R. 475, 480, *per* Lord Ashhurst J.; *Thompson* v. *Ward* [1953] 2 Q.B. 153, 158–159, *per* Lord Evershed M.R.

[12] A more elaborate discussion of possession will be found in earlier editions of this work. See further Pollock and Wright, *Essay on Possession in the Common Law*; Lightwood, *Possession of Land*; Paton, *Bailment*, pp. 6–25; Paton, *Jurisprudence*, 3rd ed., Chap. 22; Dias, *Jurisprudence*, 3rd ed., Chap. 12; Harris, " The Concept of Possession in English Law," *Oxford Essays in Jurisprudence*, p. 69.

[13] *Towers & Co. Ltd.* v. *Gray* [1961] 2 Q.B. 351, 361, *per* Lord Parker C.J.

[14] Terry, *Principles of Anglo-American Law*, p. 268, cited with approval in Pollock and Wright, *op. cit.*, p. 13.

when I leave it to go to my office, but some sort of power to use the property and to exclude others there must be. If, for example, two persons both lay claim to the same article at a bargain sale, and neither has yet contracted to buy it, possession remains with the owner; neither can sue the other even if one of them has the thing in his hands and the other snatches it from him.[15] But each case depends upon its own facts, and generalisation is not made easier when it is appreciated that what is sufficient possession to support an action of trespass against one person may not be sufficient against another. In *Fowley Marine (Emsworth) Ltd.* v. *Gafford*[16] both the plaintiffs and the defendants had laid permanent moorings in a tidal creek, the plaintiffs in reliance upon a " paper title " to the creek, the defendants in reliance upon permission they had obtained from a person then claiming to be the owner of it. It was held that whether or not the plaintiff's paper title was a good one, the acts of the plaintiffs and their predecessors amounted to assertions of ownership or the right to possession because they considered themselves entitled to do them by virtue of their paper title. Their possession was therefore sufficient to support an action against the defendants, whose claim to be entitled to lay moorings did not depend on any claim to possession of the creek. It would not, however, have been sufficient if the defendants had shown a better paper title to the creek than their own.[17]

Protection of possession in fact

Possession in fact confers no actual right of property, but a possessor may nevertheless maintain trespass against anyone who interferes who cannot himself show that he has the right to recover possession immediately.[18] A stranger cannot rely in his defence upon another person's right to possess (the " *jus tertii* ") unless he can prove that he acted with that person's authority.[19] Even wrongful possession, such as that acquired by a thief, will, in principle, be protected except against the owner of the thing stolen or someone acting lawfully on his behalf.[20] On the other hand it seems that a guest in an hotel or a

---

[15] *Young* v. *Hichens* (1844) 6 Q.B. 606. *Cf. Wilson* v. *Lombank Ltd.* [1963] 1 W.L.R. 1294, *post*, p. 404, where neither party had title but the plaintiff did have possession and so could sue in trespass.

[16] [1968] 2 Q.B. 618; *Williams Brothers Direct Supply Ltd.* v. *Raftery* [1958] 1 Q.B. 159; *Wuta-Ofei* v. *Danquah* [1961] 1 W.L.R. 1238, P.C.; *Ocean Estates Ltd.* v. *Pinder* [1969] 2 A.C. 19, P.C.

[17] " If there are two persons in a field, each asserting that the field is his, and each doing some act in assertion of the right of possession, and if the question is, which of those two is in actual possession, I answer the person who has the title is in actual possession and the other is a trespasser ": *Jones* v. *Chapman* (1849) 2 Exch. 803, 821, *per* Maule J.

[18] *Wuta-Ofei* v. *Danquah* [1961] 1 W.L.R. 1238; *Wilson* v. *Lombank Ltd.* [1963] 1 W.L.R. 1294.

[19] *Chambers* v. *Donaldson* (1809) 11 East 65; *Nicholls* v. *Ely Beet Sugar Factory* [1931] 2 Ch. 84. The position as regards Crown land may be different: *Harper* v. *Charlesworth* (1825) 4 B. & C. 574; *Georgian Cottagers' Association Inc.* v. *Corporation of Township of Flos and Kerr* (1962) 32 D.L.R. (2d) 547 (Ontario).

[20] The most obvious reason for this is to avoid encouraging breaches of the peace. See further Pollock and Maitland, *History of English Law*, 2nd ed., ii, pp. 40 *et seq. Cf. Browne* v. *Dawson* (1840) 12 Ad. & E. 624.

lodger probably does not have possession, and if this is so he cannot maintain trespass against an intruder,[21] although a tenant (who has possession in law) can certainly maintain trespass against a stranger, and even against his landlord, unless, of course, the landlord's entry was effected in accordance with the provisions of the lease.[22]

2. Possession in law

Possession in law differs from possession in fact in that it exists only if the possessor has the intention " not merely to exclude the world at large from interfering with the thing in question, but to do so on [his] own account and in [his] own name." [23] Normally possession in law exists in conjunction with possession in fact, but its practical significance is that in certain cases a person may part with possession in fact but retain possession in law and so remain entitled to maintain trespass.[24] Neither a servant who is given custody of his master's goods nor a bailee at will acquires possession in law; this remains with the master or the bailor who can thus sue for trespass even though the goods were in the hands of the servant or the bailee at the material time.[25] Conversely the lessor of land gives up possession in law as well as in fact to his tenant and can only bring trespass during the continuance of the lease if the wrongful act has caused permanent damage to the land, leading to a reduction in the value of his reversion, such as would result from the cutting of trees or the pulling down of buildings.[26] In other cases it is generally a question of fact whether a person had the necessary intention for him to acquire possession in law. For example, in *Williams Brothers Direct Supply Ltd.* v. *Raftery* [27]

---

[21] *Allan* v. *Liverpool Overseers* (1874) L.R. 9 Q.B. 180, 191–192, *per* Blackburn J., adopted by Davies L.J. in *Appah* v. *Parncliffe Investments Ltd.* [1964] 1 W.L.R. 1064, 1069–1070. It would be strange, however, if a lodger to whom exclusive occupation of a room had been given could not sue an intruder in trespass. Winfield was of the opinion, following *Hurst* v. *Picture Theatres Ltd.* [1915] 1 K.B. 1, that once a railway passenger has occupied his seat he has possession of it even if he temporarily vacates it; the lodger would seem to be in a stronger position. See too Weir's questions following *White* v. *Bayley* (1861) 10 C.B.(N.S.) 227, *Casebook on Tort*, 3rd ed., p. 286, and *cf.* Salmond, *Torts*, 16th ed., pp. 45–46; Clerk and Lindsell, *Torts*, 13th ed., pp. 741–742.

[22] *Lane* v. *Dixon* (1847) 3 C.B. 776. *Aliter* if there was only an oral contract for a lease, unenforceable by virtue of the Law of Property Act 1925, s. 40: *Delaney* v. *T. P. Smith Ltd.* [1946] K.B. 393; Weir, *Casebook on Tort*, 3rd ed., p. 285. A tenant in occupation under an unenforceable contract can certainly maintain trespass against a stranger: *ibid.* at p. 397, *per* Tucker L.J.

[23] Pollock and Wright, *op. cit.*, p. 17.

[24] Possession in law, when separated from possession in fact, is thus a legal fiction the purpose of which is to enable one who does not have possession in fact to make use of the legal remedies for interference with possession.

[25] *Lotan* v. *Cross* (1810) 2 Camp. 464; *Ancona* v. *Rogers* (1876) 1 Ex.D. 285, 292, *per* Mellish L.J.; *U.S.A.* v. *Dollfus Mieg et Cie S.A.* [1952] A.C. 582, 605, *per* Earl Jowitt. See too *Meux* v. *Great Eastern Ry.* [1895] 2 Q.B. 387. The bailee at will and, perhaps, the servant has sufficient possession in fact to maintain trespass against a stranger: *Nicolls* v. *Bastard* (1835) 2 C.M. & R. 659, 660, *per* Parke B., *arguendo*.

[26] *Ward* v. *Macauley* (1791) 4 T.R. 489; *Mayfair Property Co.* v. *Johnston* [1894] 1 Ch. 508; *Jones* v. *Llanrwst U.D.C.* [1911] 1 Ch. 393; Salmond, *Torts*, 16th ed., pp. 119–120.

[27] [1958] 1 Q.B. 159; *Leigh* v. *Jack* (1879) 5 Ex.D. 264; *Wuta-Ofei* v. *Danquah* [1961] 1 W.L.R. 1238; *Ocean Estates Ltd.* v. *Pinder* [1969] 2 A.C. 19, P.C. See also the cases on finding, *post*, pp. 426–428.

the defendant had erected fencing and sheds on land belonging to the plaintiffs and claimed to have been in possession of the land for more than 12 years so as to have acquired a squatter's title under the Limitation Act 1939. The plaintiffs had bought the land for development and, though prevented from developing it, had never abandoned their intention of doing so when the opportunity arose. The defendant had done nothing to keep them off the land and nothing that he had done was inconsistent with their contemplated use of it. They had therefore never lost possession to the defendant, his claim to a squatter's title failed, and he was liable in trespass.

Immediate right to possess: trespass by relation

The immediate right to possess, sometimes also known as constructive possession,[28] signifies the lawful right to retain possession when one has it or to acquire it when one has not. Without possession it is not sufficient to support an action of trespass[29] but, owing to the willingness of the courts to extend the superior protection afforded by the older law to possession as distinct from ownership, it has for long been the law that once a person entitled to immediate possession actually enters upon the land and so acquires possession, he is deemed to have been in possession from the moment that his right to it accrued.[30] This fiction, known as trespass by relation, has the result that he can sue for acts of trespass committed while he was actually out of possession and it also provides the foundation for the claim in respect of " mesne profits," that is, the claim for the damage suffered by a person as a result of having been kept out of the possession of his land.[31]

INTERFERENCE

Interference with the possession of land sufficient to amount to trespass may occur in many ways. The most obvious example is unauthorised walking upon it or going into the buildings upon it, but it is equally trespass if I throw things on to your land or allow my cattle to stray on to it from my land, and even if I do no more than place my ladder against your wall.[32] And if you have given me permission to enter your land and I act in excess of the permission or remain on your land after it has expired, then, again, I am a trespasser.[33] The one restriction is

---

[28] For an explanation of this term, see *Alicia Hosiery Ltd.* v. *Brown Shipley & Co. Ltd.* [1970] 1 Q.B. 195, 207, *per* Donaldson J.

[29] It is, however, sufficient for an action of conversion and is explained more fully in connection with that tort, *post*, pp. 421–423.

[30] See *Dunlop* v. *Macedo* (1891) 8 T.L.R. 43 and Clerk and Lindsell, *Torts*, 13th ed., pp. 743–744.

[31] The action for mesne profits is explained *post*, p. 315.

[32] *Westripp* v. *Baldock* [1938] 2 All E.R. 779; affd. [1939] 1 All E.R. 279; *Gregory* v. *Piper* (1829) 9 B. & C. 591.

[33] *Hillen* v. *I.C.I. (Alkali) Ltd.* [1936] A.C. 65; *Canadian Pacific Ry.* v. *Gaud* [1949] 2 K.B. 239, 249, *per* Cohen L.J.; *ibid.* at pp. 254–255, *per* Singleton L.J. But a lessoc holding over after the termination of his lease is no trespasser, for trespass can only be committed against the person in present possession of the land: *Hey* v. *Moorhouse* (1839)

that for trespass the injury must be direct and immediate. If it is indirect or consequential, there may well be a remedy (usually for nuisance or for negligence), but whatever it is it will not be trespass. If I plant a tree on your land, that is trespass. But if the roots or branches of a tree on my land project into or over your land, that is a nuisance.[34]

Trespass on highway

It is obvious that a person who uses a highway for the purpose of travelling from one place to another commits no trespass against anyone, but it is not the case that a member of the public may do upon the highway whatever he pleases; apart from the criminal law and the law of public nuisance, if he does something going beyond the reasonable use of the highway for the purpose of passing along it and matters incidental thereto,[35] he commits trespass against the person in possession of the soil on which the highway rests.[36] In *Hickman* v. *Maisey* [37] the plaintiff, as the owner of land crossed by a highway, had possession of the soil underlying the highway. The defendant, a " racing tout," had for a considerable period of time walked to and fro on a 15-yard stretch of the highway for the purpose of observing and taking notes of trials of racehorses which were being conducted on the plaintiff's land. It was held that he was a trespasser. As in all cases of trespass, however, only the person having possession can complain of it and, accordingly, the fact that a person on the highway is a trespasser upon it does not relieve lawful users of the highway of any duty of care they may owe to him in accordance with the ordinary law of negligence.[38]

Trespass to subsoil

Any intrusion upon the subsoil is just as much a trespass as entry upon the surface, and subsoil and surface may be possessed by different persons. If A is in possession of the surface and B of the subsoil, and I walk upon the land, that is a trespass against A, but not against B. If I dig holes vertically in the land, that is a trespass against both A and B. If I bore a tunnel from my land into B's subsoil, that is a trespass against B only.[39]

---

6 Bing.N.C. 52. *Cf. Minister of Health* v. *Bellotti* [1944] K.B. 298 (licensee holding over after termination of licence and after lapse of reasonable time, becomes a trespasser).
[34] *Smith* v. *Giddy* [1904] 2 K.B. 448, 451; *Davey* v. *Harrow Corporation* [1958] 1 Q.B. 60. As to removal of the intruding growth, see *post*, pp. 585–586.
[35] See *e.g. Harrison* v. *Duke of Rutland* [1893] 1 Q.B. 142, 145–147, *per* Lord Esher M.R.; *ibid.* pp. 152–154, *per* Lopes L.J.; *ibid.* at pp. 155–160, *per* Kay L.J.; *Iveagh* v. *Martin* [1961] 1 Q.B. 232, 273, *per* Paull J. In *Randall* v. *Tarrant* [1955] 1 W.L.R. 255 a car was parked in a narrow lane while some of its occupants trespassed in the adjoining field. It was held that the parked car did not constitute a trespass to the highway.
[36] At common law this is the person whose land abuts upon the highway. *Cf. Tithe Redemption Commission* v. *Runcorn U.D.C.* [1954] Ch. 383, and Highways Act 1959, ss. 226–228.
[37] [1900] 1 Q.B. 752; *Harrison* v. *Duke of Rutland, supra*: *Liddle* v. *Yorkshire (North Riding) C.C.* [1934] 2 K.B. 101, 125–127, *per* Slesser L.J.
[38] *Farrugia* v. *G.W. Ry.* [1947] 2 All E.R. 565.
[39] *Cox* v. *Glue* (1848) 5 C.B. 533.

Interference with airspace [40]

Lord Ellenborough once expressed the view that the invasion of the air space above a man's land could not be trespass unless there was some actual contact with the land itself.[41] Now, however, it is clear that this is incorrect, and in *Kelsen* v. *Imperial Tobacco Co.*[42] McNair J., after a full review of the authorities, held that an advertising sign erected by the defendants on their own property, which projected into the airspace above the plaintiff's shop, created a trespass. Even if the plaintiff has suffered no damage at all, he is entitled to an injunction, but the court has the power to suspend its operation, and this means, in practice, that, if the invasion is intended to last only for a limited period of time an unmeritorious plaintiff can be deprived of an advantage he seeks to obtain from a purely technical trespass.[43]

Although it must now be taken as settled that an intrusion into the air space at a relatively low height constitutes trespass, it is doubtful to what height a person can possess the air space above his land, and certainly the maxim *cujus est solum ejus est usque ad coelum* [44] is not to be taken literally. It is submitted that possession does not extend to a height beyond that which can reasonably be held to be within the control of the occupier. If a man has a high building, then an intrusion into the air space immediately above it is as much a trespass as an intrusion immediately above a single storey house. The passage of an aircraft several thousands of feet above, on the other hand, will not amount to a trespass because it cannot be said that the possessor of the land has any power to use and exclude others from the air space through which the aircraft flies.[45] But if an aircraft, or anything from it, falls upon the land or comes into contact with a structure on it, that is trespass, no matter what the height from which it fell.

Whether or not an aircraft flying at a reasonable height above the ground constitutes a trespass at common law, it is certain that privately owned aircraft, including those belonging to national and commercial airlines, which fly at such a height do not commit trespass for it is

---

[40] The best treatment of the topic is McNair, *The Law of the Air*, 3rd ed., pp. 31–64, 99–128, 281–288. See also Moller, *Law of Civil Aviation*, Chaps. V, VI; Shawcross and Beaumont, *Air Law*, 3rd ed., Chap. 25.

[41] *Pickering* v. *Rudd* (1815) 4 Camp. 219, 220–221; *Clifton* v. *Viscount Bury* (1887) 4 T.L.R. 8. *Cf. Kenyon* v. *Hart* (1865) 6 B. & S. 249, 252, per Blackburn J., *arguendo.* Lord Ellenborough considered that if the plaintiff suffered any damage from such an invasion, his remedy lay in an action on the case.

[42] [1957] 2 Q.B. 334; Weir, *Casebook on Tort*, 3rd ed., p. 289.

[43] *Woollerton and Wilson Ltd.* v. *Richard Costain Ltd.* [1970] 1 W.L.R. 411, where the plaintiffs had refused an offer of £250 per week to allow the jib of a crane used in building operations to swing over their premises. The plaintiffs did not allege any inconvenience or danger to themselves and were seeking to exploit the artificial value which the air space had acquired as a result of the defendants' needs. The case was doubted in *Charrington* v. *Simons & Co. Ltd.* [1971] 1 W.L.R. 598, but it is submitted that the judge's exercise of discretion was justified.

[44] For this maxim, see McNair, *op. cit.*, App. I, pp. 393–397, and for its application in International Law with regard to national sovereignty in outer space, see Schick, " Space Law and Space Politics " (1961) 10 I.C.L.Q. 681.

[45] See the general definition of possession given *ante*, p. 300.

specifically so provided by the Civil Aviation Act 1949.[46] The Act also provides, however, that if material loss or damage is caused to any person or property by, or by a person in, or an article or person falling from an aircraft while in flight, taking off [47] or landing, then, unless the loss or damage was caused or contributed to by the negligence of the person by whom it was suffered, damages are recoverable without proof of negligence or intention or other cause of action as if the loss or damage had been caused by the wilful act, neglect, or default of the owner of the aircraft.[48]

Continuing trespass

Trespass, whether by way of personal entry or by placing things on the plaintiff's land, may be " continuing " and give rise to actions *de die in diem* so long as it lasts. In *Holmes* v. *Wilson*,[49] highway authorities supported a road by wrongfully building buttresses on the plaintiff's land, and they paid full compensation in an action for trespass. They were nevertheless held liable in a further action for trespass, because they had not removed the buttresses. Nor does a transfer of the land by the injured party prevent the transferee from suing the defendant for continuing trespass.[1]

Mere omission to remove something from the land which was lawfully there to begin with is not continuing trespass, although if the thing does damage to the land after it ought to have been removed, an action for negligence or nuisance will lie.[2] Nor is it continuing trespass if a man merely omits to restore land to the same condition (apart from removing anything which he has put on it) in which he found it: *e.g.* if he fails to fill up a pit which he has dug upon his neighbour's land. He is, of course, liable in trespass for the original digging and perhaps for negligence if anyone falls into the pit, but for the mere omission to fill up the pit he is liable neither for trespass nor for any other tort.[3]

---

[46] 12 & 13 Geo. 6, c. 67, s. 40 (1). Compliance with the provisions of Part II of the Act and of Orders in Council made thereunder is a condition of this statutory exemption from liability. The section does not apply to military aircraft belonging to or exclusively employed in the service of Her Majesty. Civil aircraft belonging to or exclusively employed by the Crown were brought within s. 40 by the Civil Aviation (Crown Aircraft) Order 1970 (S.I. No. 289).

[47] This expression appears to be confined to the period after the pilot has come to the take-off position: *Blankley* v. *Godley* [1952] 1 All E.R. 436n.

[48] There is a proviso to the effect that if the owner's liability arises only by virtue of the section and if a legal liability to pay damages for the loss in question exists in some other person, then the owner is entitled to be indemnified by that other person.

[49] (1839) 10 A. & E. 503.

[1] *Hudson* v. *Nicholson* (1839) 5 M. & W. 437; followed in *Konskier* v. *Goodman Ltd.* [1928] 1 K.B. 421.

[2] *Shapcott* v. *Mugford* (1696) 1 Ld.Raym. 187, 188; trespass *vi et armis* does not apply to non-feasance. It is difficult to reconcile *Konskier's* case *supra*, with this principle, for on the facts of that case there was no trespass to begin with and therefore none that could be regarded as continuing: nevertheless, the C.A. held that there was a continuing trespass; a sufficient ground for the decision would have been that the limited licence given to the defendants had ended.

[3] *Clegg* v. *Dearden* (1848) 12 Q.B. 576, 601.

DEFENCES

1. Licence

For the purposes of trespass, the best definition of licence is that given by Sir Frederick Pollock. A licence is "that consent which, without passing any interest in the property to which it relates, merely prevents the acts for which consent is given from being wrongful." [4] In the law of real property it is important to distinguish a licence from interests in land like leases, easements or *profits à prendre*, existing at law. These confer rights *in rem*, *i.e.* rights which avail against persons generally, including, of course, the lessor or grantor himself, whereas a licence normally gives only a right *in personam* against the licensor. But the distinction seems to have little importance so far as defences to trespass are concerned. A man is not a trespasser if he is on land with the permission, express or implied,[5] of the possessor, and that is all that matters for present purposes.[6]

Revocation

A bare licence, *i.e.* one granted otherwise than for valuable consideration, may be revoked at any time, and so may many contractual licences, even though revocation may involve the licensor in liability for breach of contract.[7] After revocation the licensee becomes a trespasser, but he must be allowed a reasonable time in which to leave and to remove his goods.[8] Some contractual licences are, however, irrevocable because revocation in breach of contract would be prevented by the grant of an equitable remedy to the licensee. A licence coupled with an interest is irrevocable because, although the licence itself—the bare permission to enter—is only a right *in personam*, it confers a right *in rem* to something when you have entered. "A licence to hunt in a man's park and carry away the deer killed to his own use; to cut down a tree in a man's ground, and to carry it away the next day to his own use, are licences as to the acts of hunting and cutting down the tree, but as to the carrying away of the deer killed

---

[4] *Torts*, 15th ed., p. 284.

[5] See *Robson* v. *Hallett* [1967] 2 Q.B. 939, 950–951, *per* Lord Parker C.J.; *ibid.* at pp. 953–954, *per* Diplock L.J. For the purposes of the crime of burglary (of which trespassory entry is an ingredient) the question is whether the defendant honestly (not reasonably) believed in his right to enter: see the extraordinary case of *R.* v. *Collins* [1973] Q.B. 100.

[6] *Armstrong* v. *Sheppard and Short Ltd.* [1959] 2 Q.B. 384, 399, *per* Lord Evershed M.R.; Weir, *Casebook on Tort*, 3rd ed., p. 303. Earlier editions of this work contained a full discussion of the difficult topic of licences (see 6th ed., pp. 383–393) but the subject is today better left to books on real property. See Cheshire, *Modern Law of Real Property*, 11th ed., pp. 566–573; Megarry and Wade, *Law of Real Property*, 3rd ed., pp. 775–783.

[7] *Thompson* v. *Park* [1944] K.B. 408. *Cf. Kerrison* v. *Smith* [1897] 2 Q.B. 445; *King* v. *David Allen & Sons Ltd.* [1916] 2 A.C. 54.

[8] *Cornish* v. *Stubbs* (1870) L.R. 5 C.P. 334; *Canadian Pacific Ry.* v. *R.* [1931] A.C. 414; *Minister of Health* v. *Bellotti* [1944] K.B. 289; *Robson* v. *Hallett*, *supra*.

and the tree cut down, they are grants." [9] Until the tree or deer is carried away the licence is irrevocable.[10]

A contractual licence may also be irrevocable even if it is not coupled with an interest, but the circumstances in which this will be so are not finally settled. It seems, however, that the following conclusion is warranted by the cases.[11] Whether a contractual licence is revocable is a question of construction of the contract in the light of relevant and admissible circumstances.[12] It will be irrevocable if such is the intention of the parties, and this may be inferred from the terms of the contract, the character of the transaction, and the attendant circumstances that the licence is intended to endure for a definite or ascertainable period.[13] Where it is granted for a limited period and for a definite purpose, it will be irrevocable until the accomplishment of the purpose.[14] If the licensee has begun performance of the act or purpose licensed, and observes the terms of the contract, the licensor will be restrained by injunction from revoking the licence in breach of contract or from acting upon the purported revocation.[15] Thus the licensee acquires a right which destroys the defence of " trespasser " which the licensor could otherwise plead to an action for assault.[16]

If a licence has been executed, it cannot be revoked in the sense that the licensee can be compelled to undo what he has lawfully done. If I allow you to post bills on my hoarding, I can cancel my permission, but I cannot force you to remove bills that you have already stuck there. So in *Liggins* v. *Inge* [17] where an oral licence had been given to lower a river bank and make a weir above the licensor's mill, it was held that the licensor could not sue the licensee for continuing the weir which the latter had erected. But the rule that an executed licence is irrevocable applies only where the

---

[9] *Thomas* v. *Sorrell* (1672) Vaughan 330, 351, *per* Vaughan C.J.

[10] The court in *Wood* v. *Leadbitter* (1845) 13 M. & W. 838, 844–845; *Wood* v. *Manley* (1839) 11 A. & E. 34; *Jones & Sons Ltd.* v. *Tankerville* [1909] 2 Ch. 440, 442, *per* Parker J. *Cf. Frank Warr & Co. Ltd.* v. *L.C.C.* [1904] 1 K.B. 713; *Clore* v. *Theatrical Properties Ltd.* [1936] 3 All E.R. 483.

[11] See especially *Hurst* v. *Picture Theatres Ltd.* [1915] 1 K.B. 1; Weir, *Casebook on Tort*, 3rd ed., p. 297; *Winter Garden Theatre (London) Ltd.* v. *Millennium Productions Ltd.* [1948] A.C. 173; *Bendall* v. *McWhirter* [1952] 2 Q.B. 466; *Hounslow* v. *Twickenham Garden Developments Ltd.* [1971] Ch. 233. *Cf. Wood* v. *Leadbitter* (1845) 13 M. & W. 838; *Cowell* v. *Rosehill Racecourse Co. Ltd.* (1937) 56 C.L.R. 605.

[12] *Winter Garden* case [1946] 1 All E.R. 678, 680, *per* Lord Greene M.R.; *Re Spenborough U.D.C.'s Agreement* [1968] Ch. 139. *Cf. Winter Garden* case [1948] A.C. 173, 193, *per* Lord Porter; Wade, " What is a Licence " (1948) 64 L.Q.R. 57, 69.

[13] Walford (1947) 12 Conv.(N.S.) 126; Glanville Williams, 30 Can. Bar Rev. 1006; Mitchell, " Learner's Licence " (1954) 17 M.L.R. 211–219.

[14] *Winter Garden* case [1948] A.C. 173, *per* Lord Porter; *ibid.* at p. 189, *per* Lord Simon. See *Munro* v. *Balnagown Estates Co.*, 1949 S.L.T. 85.

[15] [1946] 1 All E.R. 678, 685, *per* Lord Greene M.R.; *Bendall* v. *McWhirter* [1952] 2 Q.B. 466, 478–483, *per* Denning L.J.

[16] Wade, *loc. cit.* at p. 76. *Errington* v. *Errington* [1952] 1 K.B. 290, 297–299 and *Bendall* v. *McWhirter* [1952] 2 Q.B. 466, 479–483, *per* Denning L.J. *Bendall* v. *McWhirter* has been overruled by *National Provincial Bank Ltd.* v. *Ainsworth* [1965] A.C. 1175 but, it is submitted, without affecting the statements in the text.

[17] (1831) 3 Bing. 682; *Davies* v. *Marshall* (1861) 10 C.B.(N.S.) 697. See Wade, *loc. cit.* at pp. 68–69.

licence can be construed as authorising the doing of exactly what has been done. It does not apply where there has been mere acquiescence in something which was never authorised before it was done.[18] Nor does it apply if its application would amount to the creation of an easement in favour of the licensee. An easement cannot be granted by parol and therefore, after the licence has been revoked, the plaintiff is prima facie entitled to an injunction restraining the continuation of the trespass.[19]

2. Justification by law

Acts which would otherwise be trespasses, whether to land, goods or the person, are frequently prevented from being so by the existence of some justification provided by the law. A person entering land in pursuance of arrangements made by a local authority for the public to have access to open country is not a trespasser so long as he complies with the specified conditions [20]; a person having parental authority commits no trespass by applying reasonable chastisement to a child [21]; a landlord commits no trespass if he distrains for rent.[22] Most importantly there are innumerable instances in which officers of the law are authorised to enter land, to take goods or to arrest or restrain a person, but these belong more to public than to private law and only one or two illustrations can be given here.[23] A policeman commits no trespass if he enters a public-house through an open door late at night in order to investigate a disturbance,[24] nor does a bailiff who enters private premises on civil process (e.g. to arrest a debtor on a warrant from the court), provided that he does not gain entry by breaking in.[25] Indeed a bailiff may even enter the house of a stranger to the debtor to execute process, but this he does at his peril. If the property of the debtor that he is to take or if the person whom he is

---

[18] *Canadian Pacific Ry.* v. *R.* [1931] A.C. 414, 428–429, *per* Lord Russell.

[19] *Armstrong* v. *Sheppard and Short Ltd.* [1959] 2 Q.B. 384. The right to an injunction is not unqualified and an injunction may be refused on the ground that the injury is trivial: *ibid.*

[20] National Parks and Access to the Countryside Act 1949 (12, 13 & 14 Geo. 6, c. 97), s. 60.

[21] *Post*, pp. 611–612.

[22] The leading work on distress is Daniels, *Law of Distress*, 7th ed. For distress damage feasant (the seizure of an animal or chattel by the possessor of land when it is wrongfully on the land and causing damage to it) see Williams, *Animals*, Chaps. I–VIII and the 7th ed. of this work, pp. 381–383. In respect of animals, there is now a statutory right of detention and sale: see pp. 399–400, *post*.

[23] The statutory rights of entry of gas and electricity boards were held in *Groves* v. *Eastern Gas Board* [1952] 1 K.B. 77 to authorise forcible entry where necessary and to constitute a defence of justification in an action of trespass. By the Rights of Entry (Gas and Electricity Boards) Act 1954 (2 & 3 Eliz. 2, c. 21) these rights are (except in a case of emergency) to be exercised only by consent of the occupier or under a warrant.

[24] *R.* v. *Smith* (1833) 6 C. & P. 216; *Thomas* v. *Sawkins* [1935] 2 K.B. 249; *Robson* v. *Hallett* [1967] 2 Q.B. 939. *Aliter* if he enters merely in order to put property there in a safer place: *Great Central Ry.* v. *Bates* [1921] 3 K.B. 578, 581; *Davis* v. *Lisle* [1936] 2 K.B. 434.

[25] The bailiff may enter by opening an unlocked door, but may not break open a locked one: *Semayne's Case* (1604) 5 Co.Rep. 91a; *Southam* v. *Smout* [1964] 1 Q.B. 308; *Vaughan* v. *McKenzie* [1969] 1 Q.B. 557.

to arrest is actually there, then he is justified, but otherwise he is a trespasser.[26] Nor is it only officers of the law who may be thus empowered. A private person may in certain circumstances arrest a criminal, and it is no trespass if he breaks into the house of another person in order to prevent him from murdering his wife,[27] or probably from committing other serious offences.[28]

Trespass ab initio

Where an entry upon land or other prima facie trespass is justified by the authority of the law itself, then, according to an ancient doctrine of the common law, if the actor abuses his authority he becomes a trespasser *ab initio*; his act is reckoned as unlawful from the very beginning, however innocent his conduct may have been up to the moment of the abuse.[29] The doctrine applies only if the authority is that of the law, not that of the other party concerned, and the abuse must be by a positive act, not a mere omission.[30] The explanations of these restrictions on the doctrine are historical,[31] but they show that its purpose, derived from its origin in the law of distress, was to provide protection against abuses of authority.

Seen in this light it would seem to be unduly optimistic to suppose that the doctrine has outlived its usefulness,[32] even given the modern limitation that partial abuse of an authority does not render everything done under it unlawful. For example, in *Elias* v. *Pasmore*[33] police had lawfully entered the plaintiff's premises in order to arrest a man, and while there they seized a number of documents, some of them unlawfully. It was held that this did not render their original entry a trespass. Now, however, the Court of Appeal has indicated that the doctrine as a whole is out of date, and, at least in Lord Denning's view, no longer law.[34] In *Chic Fashions (West Wales) Ltd.* v. *Jones*[35] police officers had obtained a warrant to search the plaintiff's shop for certain stolen goods. They found none of these goods but they did find and seize certain other goods which they reasonably but erroneously believed to have been stolen. It was held that the seizure of these goods was in fact lawful,[36] and no issue involving the doctrine

---

[26] *Southam* v. *Smout, supra.* " It is a case of justification not by faith but by works ": *ibid.* at p. 327, *per* Harman L.J. *Cf. Chic Fashions (West Wales) Ltd.* v. *Jones* [1968] 2 Q.B. 299.

[27] *Handcock* v. *Baker* (1800) 2 Bos. & P. 260.

[28] *Ibid.* 265, *per* Chambre J.

[29] *The Six Carpenters' Case* (1610) 8 Co.Rep. 146a. The older cases are epitomised in Viner's *Abridgement,* Vol. XX, 2nd ed. (1793), pp. 499–504.

[30] *Ibid.*

[31] Holdsworth, H.E.L., vii, pp. 499–501.

[32] *Pace* the Court of Appeal in *Chic Fashions (West Wales) Ltd.* v. *Jones* [1968] 2 Q.B. 299.

[33] [1934] 2 K.B. 164; *Harvey* v. *Pocock* (1843) 11 M. & W. 740; *Canadian Pacific Wine Co. Ltd.* v. *Tuley* [1921] 2 A.C. 417.

[34] *Chic Fashions (West Wales) Ltd.* v. *Jones* [1968] 2 Q.B. 299, 313, *per* Lord Denning M.R.; *ibid.* at p. 317, *per* Diplock L.J.; *ibid.* at p. 320, *per* Salmon L.J.

[35] *Supra.*

[36] This is now confirmed by the Theft Act 1968, s. 26 (3). *Cf.* Weir [1968] C.L.J. 193.

of trespass *ab initio* was raised. In connection with the somewhat different point that the later discovery that the goods had not been stolen did not render their original seizure unlawful, however, their Lordships criticised the doctrine as offending against the principle that subsequent events cannot render unlawful an act which was lawful when it was done. This principle is, in general, a sound one, but it should not be over-stressed. Not only may subsequent events illuminate the intent with which an act was originally done and thus assist in determining its lawfulness or unlawfulness,[37] but there are, and should continue to be, cases in which, in effect, the law withholds judgment on the lawfulness of an act for a time and allows it to depend upon subsequent events.[38] The doctrine of trespass *ab initio* enables this to be done in the important area of the protection of a man's person, goods and land against abuse of official power.

Remedies

The action for trespass, besides being used to remedy trespass as a pure tort, has also some varieties which are employed for the recovery of land and the profits thereof, and of these we shall speak in the next sections on ejectment and mesne profits.

Re-entry

The remedies for trespass as a pure tort need no special mention except the *right of re-entry*. The person entitled to possession can enter or re-enter the premises, but the Statutes of Forcible Entry, beginning with one of A.D. 1381,[39] require him to do so in a peaceable manner; otherwise he commits a crime punishable by imprisonment. But whatever his criminal liability may be, he is not civilly liable if he uses no more force than is necessary. After some conflicting opinions this was finally settled by the Court of Appeal in *Hemmings* v. *Stoke Poges Golf Club*.[40] The plaintiff, tenant of a cottage owned by the defendants, refused to quit it after notice had been duly given to him. The defendants thereupon entered the cottage and removed the plaintiff and his furniture with no more force than was necessary.

---

[37] This was one of the explanations of the doctrine of trespass *ab initio* itself given by Coke: 8 Co.Rep. 146b. Winfield ridiculed it (see 8th ed., p. 346) but even though it contains an element of fiction, it is submitted that it does have some merit.

[38] *Southam* v. *Smout* [1964] 1 Q.B. 308, *ante*, p. 310 and n. 26 provides one example, and there are others also. The power of a private person to arrest on reasonable suspicion of an arrestable offence exists only if the offence suspected has actually been committed (Criminal Law Act 1967, s. 2 (3), *ante*, p. 39), and this cannot be known until further investigations have been carried out. If a person enters upon land under authority of the National Parks and Access to the Countryside Act 1949, s. 60 (1) (*ante*, p. 309) and then commits a breach of the restrictions contained in the Second Schedule, it seems that he becomes a trespasser *ab initio*: the subsection has effect subject to the provisions of the Schedule (s. 60 (4)) and the Schedule itself provides that s. 60 (1) " shall not apply to a person who " does any of the forbidden acts on the land.

[39] 5 Ric. 2, st. 1, c. 7. See also 15 Ric. 2, c. 2, and 8 Hen. 6, c. 9.

[40] [1920] 1 K.B. 720, where the earlier authorities are considered.

He sued them for assault, battery and trespass, and they were held
not liable.

Action for the recovery of land (Ejectment)

By the action of ejectment, or, as it should now be called, the action
for the recovery of land, a person dispossessed of land can recover
it specifically. The story of this remedy is an old one and neatly exempli-
fies the use of fictions in the development of a legal system. It was
originally a species of the action for trespass to land, and was invented
for the benefit of the leaseholder, to whom the remedies of the freeholder were denied because he had mere " possession " of the land and
not that blessed and superior " seisin " which gave the freeholder very
adequate, if excessively dilatory, protection in the shape of the real
actions. Then, by a notable paradox, the action of ejectment was seen to
be so quick and efficient compared to the ponderous progress of the real
actions that the freeholder adopted it by a series of fictions. If, for
example, Smith, a freeholder, were seeking to recover the land from
Brown, he was allowed to pretend that he had leased the land to
John Doe, an imaginary person, and that John Doe had been ejected
by another non-existent person, Richard Roe (the " casual ejector ").
Then Smith began his action with Doe as the nominal plaintiff against
Roe as the nominal defendant, but he first served on Brown a notice
signed by " your loving friend, Roe," in which Roe informed Brown
that Roe claimed no interest in the land and advised Brown to defend
the action. The fictitious parties then disappeared and the stage was
cleared for the proceedings between Smith and Brown. The title of the
action was " John Doe on the demise [*i.e.* lease] of Smith *v.* Brown,"
or, more briefly, " Doe *d.* Smith *v.* Brown." It was useless for Brown
to protest against these fictions; he was not allowed to defend the action
unless he acquiesced in them.[41] The remarkable result was that the
question of ownership of land was fought under the guise of an action
of trespass.

These fictions have been long abolished,[42] and an action for the
recovery of land differs in no formal respect from any other action.
A special summary procedure has, however, been devised to enable
a plaintiff to obtain an order for possession, and a writ for its enforcement, against persons in occupation of his land if they entered or
remained there without his licence or consent, whether or not he is
able to identify all, or even any, of those persons.[43]

---

[41] Sometimes the fictitious names were more descriptive: *e.g. Fairclaim* v. *Shamtitle*
(1762) 3 Burr. 1290.
[42] By the Common Law Procedure Act 1852. For the history of the matter, see Holdsworth, H.E.L., iii, pp. 213–217; vii, pp. 4–23. The best account is in Maitland, *Equity*
(ed. 1916), pp. 352–355; reprinted separately as *Forms of Action* (1936), pp. 56–59. For an
unsuccessful attempt to resurrect Messrs. Doe and Roe, see *Re Wykeham Terrace* [1971]
1 Ch. 204, the effect of which is now reversed by R.S.C., Ord. 113, *post*, n. 43.
[43] R.S.C., Ord., 113. The procedure is also available in the County Court: C.C.R.,
Ord. 26. An occupier not named as a defendant can apply at any stage to be joined as a

A rule that has been repeatedly asserted is that in an action of ejectment the plaintiff must recover by the strength of his own title and not by the weakness of the defendant's,[44] and since the action for the recovery of land has taken the place of ejectment the rule has been recognised by both the House of Lords [45] and the Judicial Committee of the Privy Council.[46] The defendant need only allege that he is in possession, and the plaintiff must, if he can do so, positively prove that his own title is better. But when we ask what exactly he must prove in order to establish his title, the law does not appear to require much. It has been said, indeed, that he must do more than set up mere *de facto* possession which, as we have seen, will usually enable him to sue for trespass as a tort,[47] but this distinction between the action of ejectment and the action for pure trespass is a tenuous one in view of other authorities, the most important of which is *Asher* v. *Whitlock*,[48] where it was held that, if A takes possession of waste land without any other title than such seizure, he can maintain ejectment against B who subsequently enters on the land and who cannot show title or possession in anyone prior to A.[49] When, therefore, it is said that A's former possession raises only a presumption of title it must be confessed that this presumption is not easily upset.[50]

Jus tertii

It has already been noted that the defendant to an ordinary action of trespass cannot as a general rule set up the defence of *jus tertii*.[51] Is this rule applicable to the defendant to an action of ejectment? As the plaintiff there must prove his title, it would seem to be a corollary that if the evidence, whether it appear from the plaintiff's own case or be produced by the defendant, shows that some third person is entitled to the land, the plaintiff ought not to succeed; in other words, the defendant ought to be allowed to plead *jus tertii*. But whether this is the law has been greatly debated by various writers.[52] If, however, we limit ourselves

---

defendant and any order made may be set aside on such terms as the judge considers just. See *G.L.C.* v. *Lewis, The Times,* August 6, 1970; *Southwark London Borough Council* v. *Williams* [1971] 2 W.L.R. 467 (where the Court of Appeal excluded the defence of necessity) and editorial comment in (1970) 120 New L.J. 745 and 1173. The special procedure must be strictly complied with: *Re 9 Orpen Road, Stoke Newington* [1971] 1 W.L.R. 166.

[44] Lee C.J. in *Martin* d. *Tregonwell* v. *Strachan* (1742) 5 T.R. 107n. is said to have first formulated the rule: Wiren, "The Plea of *Ius Tertii* in Ejectment" (1925) 41 L.Q.R. 139, 145.

[45] *Danford* v. *McAnulty* (1883) 8 App.Cas. 456, 460, *per* Lord O'Hagan; *ibid.* at p. 462, *per* Lord Blackburn.

[46] *Emmerson* v. *Maddison* [1906] A.C. 569, 575, *per* Sir Alfred Wills.

[47] *Harper* v. *Charlesworth* (1825) 4 B. & C. 574, 589, *per* Bayley J.; *ibid.* at pp. 592–594, *per* Holroyd J.; Weir, *Casebook on Tort,* 3rd ed., p. 285.

[48] (1865) L.R. 1 Q.B. 1. See, too, *Doe* d. *Hughes* v. *Dyeball* (1829) Moo. & M. 346.

[49] Approved by the Judicial Committee in *Perry* v. *Clissold* [1907] A.C. 73, 79.

[50] *Whale* v. *Hitchcock* (1876) 34 L.T. 136.

[51] *Ante,* p. 301.

[52] For full discussion of the question, see Wiren, *loc. cit.*; Hargreaves, "Terminology and Title in Ejectment" (1940) 56 L.Q.R. 376; Holdsworth, "Terminology and Title in Ejectment—A Reply," *ibid.* 479.

to what has been actually decided by the courts, it appears that *jus tertii* is a defence. *Doe* d. *Carter* v. *Barnard* [53] is the leading authority to that effect. True, this decision received a glancing blow from Cockburn L.C.J. in *Asher* v. *Whitlock* [54] and a much harder knock from Lord Macnaghten in *Perry* v. *Clissold* [55] but the dicta of these learned judges were obiter, for in neither of these cases was *jus tertii* raised, nor indeed could it have been raised on the facts. Both cases decide no more than that if the plaintiff in ejectment once had *de facto* possession of land, that raises a presumption of title in his favour which mere subsequent possession of the defendant will not defeat. Neither of them decides that the plaintiff's claim cannot be upset by proof of *jus tertii;* indeed, *Asher* v. *Whitlock* implies that it can be.

Moreover, the principle which is supported by *jus tertii*—that the plaintiff must win by his own strength and not by his opponent's weakness—is a sound one. What he is seeking to establish is ownership of the land and, if it appears to be in anyone else, why should the defendant be compelled to give up possession to *him*? Against this it has been urged that if the plaintiff can win (as undoubtedly he can) if he once had *de facto* possession and the defendant can show nothing but a later *de facto* possession on his own part, then the plaintiff ought to win in any event because the law greatly respects possession. But that is a two-edged argument, for if the law respects possession which the plaintiff once had, why should it not equally respect possession which the defendant now has? And it sounds odd to insist that, because C is the real owner of land, B, who is in wrongful (but legally protected) possession of it, ought to give it up to A who once had wrongful possession of it.[56]

Whether or not *jus tertii* is in general a defence in an action of ejectment, it cannot be relied upon where the defendant has acquired possession from the plaintiff himself or from one through whom the plaintiff claims. The rule that a tenant is estopped from denying his landlord's title is well known, but a licensee is similarly estopped from

---

[53] (1849) 13 Q.B. 945.
[54] (1865) L.R. 1 Q.B. 1, 6.
[55] [1906] A.C. 73, 79–80.
[56] Winfield's account of this controversial topic has been left unchanged and it is not thought that either the dictum of Lord Diplock in *Ocean Estates Ltd.* v. *Pinder* [1969] 2 A.C. 19, 25 or the decision of the High Court of Australia in *Allen* v. *Roughley* (1955) 94 C.L.R. 98 (see Wade [1956] C.L.J. 177) would have led him to alter it. In that case Holdsworth's view that the plaintiff in ejectment must prove an absolutely good title and that therefore the *jus tertii* was a defence (H.E.L., vii, pp. 57–81) was rejected. But Winfield emphasises the strength of a case founded upon prior possession. Against a defendant in possession, however, the plaintiff must recover by the strength of his own title, and this he cannot do if the right to possession is proved to be in a third party. A plea of *jus tertii* is not made out merely by showing defects in the plaintiff's title. It must be proved that title is vested in some third party: Jolly, " The Jus Tertii and the Third Man " (1955) 18 M.L.R. 371. See further Salmond, *Torts*, 16th ed., p. 46; Fleming, *Law of Torts*, 4th ed., pp. 46–47. *Cf.* Clerk and Lindsell, *Torts*, 13th ed., pp. 765–766. *Georgian Cottagers' Association inc.* v. *Corporation of Township of Flos and Kerr* (1962) 32 D.L.R. (2d) 547 (Ontario). (Though *jus tertii* is not normally a defence against a plaintiff in possession, the defence is available where the plaintiff is in occupation of Crown land without the consent of the Crown. *Cf. Harper* v. *Charlesworth* (1825) 4 B. & C. 574.)

denying the title of his licensor,[57] and, indeed this rule of estoppel extends to anyone who is sued in ejectment by one from whom he derived his interest. " If a person obtains possession of land, claiming under a will or deed, he cannot afterwards set up another title to the land against the will or deed, though the deed or will did not operate to pass the land in question." [58]

Mesne Profits

The action for mesne profits is another species of the action for trespass and lies for the damage which the plaintiff has suffered through having been out of possession of his land. By Blackstone's time nothing but a shilling or some trivial sum was usually recoverable in the action of ejectment because it had been " licked into the form of a real action " [59] and its chief purpose had become the trial of the title to land.[60] If the claimant was successful, he got possession of the land but no compensation for having been kept out of it. The action for mesne profits enables the plaintiff to claim not only profits taken by the defendant during his occupancy, but also damages for deterioration and the reasonable costs of getting possession.[61] The Rules of the Supreme Court [62] enable a plaintiff in an action for the recovery of land to join with it a claim for mesne profits, and if he does so it is unnecessary for him to have entered the land before he sues. If he prefers he can still bring the action for mesne profits separately but in that event he must first enter, for the action is one of trespass; trespass is a wrong to possession, and until he enters he has not got it. Once he has entered, however, then, by the fiction of trespass by relation,[63] the plaintiff is deemed to have been in possession during the whole period for which he claims the mesne profits.

---

[57] *Doe* d. *Johnson* v. *Baytup* (1835) 3 Ad. & E. 188. A general denial in a pleading by a tenant does not amount to a sufficient denial of the landlord's title to cause a forfeiture of the lease: *Warner* v. *Sampson* [1959] 1 Q.B. 297.

[58] Lopes L.J. in *Dalton* v. *Fitzgerald* [1897] 2 Ch. 86, 93. Another exception to the permissibility of pleading *jus tertii* is suggested with some doubt in Salmond, *Torts*, 16th ed., p. 60. " If the defendant's possession is wrongful as against the plaintiff, the plaintiff may succeed though he cannot himself show a good title." But assuming that this is the law, has it any necessary connection with *jus tertii*?

[59] *Goodtitle* v. *Tombs* (1770) 3 Wils.K.B. 118, 120, *per* Wilmot C.J.

[60] Blackstone, Comm. iii, p. 205.

[61] " I have known four times the value of the mesne profits given by a jury in this sort of action of trespass ": *Goodtitle* v. *Tombs* (1770) 3 Wils.K.B. 118, 121, *per* Gould J. And see *Doe* v. *Filliter* (1844) 13 M. & W. 47; *Hall & Co. Ltd.* v. *Pearlberg* [1956] 1 W.L.R. 244.

[62] Ord. 15, r. 1.

[63] *Ante*, p. 303.

CHAPTER 15

NUISANCE [1]

PUBLIC AND PRIVATE NUISANCES

Public nuisance

Nuisances are divided into public and private, although it is quite possible for the same conduct to amount to both. A public nuisance is a crime, while a private nuisance is only a tort. A public or common nuisance is one which materially affects the reasonable comfort and convenience of life of a class of Her Majesty's subjects who come within the sphere or neighbourhood of its operation; the question whether the number of persons affected is sufficient to constitute a class is one of fact in every case, and it is sufficient to show that a representative cross-section of that class has been so affected for an injunction to issue.[1a] It is one which is so widespread in its range or so indiscriminate in its effect that it would not be reasonable to expect one person as distinct from the community at large [2] to take proceedings to put a stop to it. This definition is vague and it has been rightly said that nuisance " covers a multitude of sins, great and small." [3]

\ Public nuisances at common law include such diverse activities as carrying on an offensive trade, keeping a disorderly house, selling food unfit for human consumption, obstructing public highways and throwing fireworks about in the street. A variety of matters have been made nuisances by statute, particularly the Public Health Act 1936, Part III,[4] and the Clean Air Act 1956.[5] The Noise Abatement Act 1960 [6] makes noise or vibration which is a nuisance a statutory nuisance for the purpose of Part III of the Public Health Act 1936. The element which such public nuisances have in common with private nuisances like blocking up the ancient lights of a building or excessive playing on the piano is that of annoyance or inconvenience.

Special damage necessary for action for damages in public nuisance

So long as the public only or some section of it is injured no civil action can be brought for nuisance.[7] Where a public highway is

---

[1] Weir, *Casebook on Tort*, 3rd ed., Chap. 10.
[1a] *Att.-Gen.* v. *P.Y.A. Quarries Ltd.* [1957] 2 Q.B. 169, 184, *per* Romer L.J. (quarrying, blasting, stones and splinters projected from quarry, dust, noise and vibration).
[2] *Ibid.* at pp. 190–191, *per* Denning L.J.
[3] *Southport Corporation* v. *Esso Petroleum Co. Ltd.* [1954] 2 Q.B. 182, 196, *per* Denning L.J. For a peculiarly modern form of public nuisance see *Att.-Gen. for Ontario* v. *Orange Productions Ltd.* (1971) 21 D.L.R. (3d) 257.
[4] 26 Geo. 5 & 1 Edw. 8, c. 49.
[5] 4 & 5 Eliz. 2, c. 52. See also the Clean Air Act 1968 (c. 62).
[6] 8 & 9 Eliz. 2, c. 68, s. 1.
[7] The Attorney-General may, on the information of a private individual, maintain an action for nuisance: Robertson, *Civil Proceedings by and against the Crown*, p. 472. For the principle and history of this, see Blackstone, Comm. iv., pp. 303–308; Holdsworth, H.E.L., ix, pp. 236 *et seq.*

obstructed I cannot sue the obstructor for nuisance if I can prove no damage beyond being delayed on several occasions in passing along it and being obliged either to pursue my journey by a devious route or to remove the obstruction, for these are inconveniences common to everyone else.[8] The reason normally given for the rule is that it prevents multiplicity of actions, for if one were allowed to sue, a thousand might do so and this would lead to harsh results. If, for instance, a public body obstructed a highway temporarily for the purpose of draining, paving or lighting it and it was then discovered that owing to some technical error they had no authority to do so, they would be sufficiently punished by a criminal prosecution.[9] But where any person is injured in some way peculiar to himself, that is, if he can show that he has suffered some particular or special loss over and above the ordinary inconvenience suffered by the public at large, then he can sue in tort, e.g. if he falls into a trench unlawfully opened in a street and breaks his leg. Particular damage [10] is not limited to special damage in the sense of pecuniary loss actually incurred, e.g. in an action for negligence.[11] It may consist of proved general damage, such as inconvenience and delay, provided it is substantial, direct and not consequential and is appreciably different in nature or extent to that in fact suffered by the general public, although in another sense it is " general " and not " special " to him.[12] " Direct " here means damage other or different from the damage caused to the rest of the public. It is narrower than when " direct " is used in determining whether damage is too remote.[13] The case of *Rose* v. *Miles* [14] affords an illustration of such special damage. The defendant wrongfully moored his barge across a public navigable creek and thereby obstructed it so that the plaintiff, who had begun a journey on the creek with his barges before the obstruction was made, was obliged to unload them and to incur considerable expense in

---

[8] *Winterbottom* v. *Lord Derby* (1867) L.R. 2 Ex. 316, 321–322. " Even if he chose to incur expense to remove it. There must be some damage to himself, his trade or calling ": *per* Kelly C.B.

[9] *Winterbottom* v. *Lord Derby* (1867) L.R. 2 Ex. 316.

[10] *Rose* v. *Groves* (1843) 5 Man. & G. 613, 616. " It is not necessary to prove special damage in this action. It is sufficient to prove particular damage ": *per* Cresswell J.

[11] See *post* at pp. 560–561.

[12] *Walsh* v. *Ervin* [1952] V.L.R. 361, 368–369, *per* Sholl J. reviewing the English authorities. Fleming, *Torts*, 4th ed., pp. 347–342. Particular damage includes injury to plaintiff's person, wife, servant, loss of custom, depreciation in the actual value of the property by reducing or cutting off the approach to it. See Fridman, " The Definition of Particular Damage in Nuisance " (1953) 2 Annual L.Rev. (Univ. Western Australia) 490–503, who suggests that the test of difference in degree is neither justified by authority nor preferable as a matter of principle and common sense to the test of difference in kind. *Boyd* v. *G.N. Ry.* (1895) 2 I.R. 555 (doctor held up at level crossing for 20 minutes, recovered). For an example of the narrower approach, requiring difference in kind, see *Hickey* v. *Electric Reduction Co. of Canada Ltd.* (1970) 21 D.L.R. (3d) 368.

[13] *Overseas Tankship (U.K.) Ltd.* v. *The Miller Steamship Co. Pty.* [1967] 1 A.C. 617, 636, P.C.

[14] (1815) 4 M. & S. 101. See. too, *Harper* v. *Haden & Sons* [1933] Ch. 298, 303; *Metcalf* v. *Strawbridge Ltd.* [1937] 2 K.B. 102.

transporting their cargoes by land; and it was held that this was sufficient damage to support an action for nuisance.[15]

Private nuisance

Private nuisance may be described as *unlawful interference with a person's use or enjoyment of land, or some right over, or in connection with it.*[16] Generally, the essence of a nuisance is a state of affairs that is either continuous or recurrent, a condition or activity which unduly interferes with the use or enjoyment of land. Not every slight annoyance, therefore, is actionable. Stenches, smoke, the escape of effluent and a multitude of different things may amount to a nuisance *in fact* but whether they constitute an *actionable* nuisance will depend on a variety of considerations, especially the character of the defendant's conduct, and a balancing of conflicting interests.[17] In fact the whole of the law of private nuisance represents an attempt to preserve a balance between two conflicting interests, that of one occupier in using his land as he thinks fit, and that of his neighbour in the quiet enjoyment of his land.[18] Everyone must endure some degree of noise, smell, etc. from his neighbour, otherwise modern life would be impossible and such a privilege of interfering with the comfort of a neighbour is reciprocal. It is repeatedly said in nuisance cases that the rule is *sic utere tuo ut alienum non laedas*, but the maxim is unhelpful and misleading. If it means that no man is ever allowed to use his property so as to injure another, it is palpably false.[19] If it means that a man in using his property may injure his neighbour, but not if he does so unlawfully, it is not worth stating, as it leaves unanswered the critical question of when the interference becomes unlawful.[20] In fact, the law repeatedly recognises that a man may

---

[15] It was substantially more injurious to the plaintiff than to the general public, who might only have it in contemplation to use the creek: *per* Lord Ellenborough C.J., 4 M. & S. at p. 103. The leading case is *Iveson* v. *Moore* (1699) 1 Ld.Raym. 486 (colliery owner recovered in nuisance for loss of profit caused by highway obstruction which prevented workmen from coming to colliery and coal being carted away). In *Ricket* v. *Metropolitan Ry.* (1865) 5 B. & S. 156, 159–160, the Exch. Chamber summarised the law.

[16] Adopted by Scott L.J. in *Read* v. *Lyons & Co. Ltd.* [1945] K.B. 216 at p. 236; by Lord Goddard C.J. in *Howard* v. *Walker* [1947] 2 All E.R. 197 at p. 199; by Evershed J. in *Newcastle-under-Lyme Corporation* v. *Wolstanton Ltd.* [1947] Ch. 92 at p. 107 (his dictum on this point was unaffected by the appeal [1947] Ch. 427, at pp. 467–468); and by Windeyer J. in *Hargrave* v. *Goldman* (1963) 37 A.L.J.R. 277 at p. 283, affirmed [1967] 1 A.C. 645. For other definitions, see Pollock, *Torts*, 15th ed., p. 302; Salmond, *Torts*, 16th ed., pp. 51–55; Street, *Torts*, 5th ed., pp. 212–213.

[17] See *post*, pp. 325–332.

[18] " A balance has to be maintained between the right of the occupier to do what he likes with his own, and the right of his neighbour not to be interfered with ": *Sedleigh-Denfield* v. *O'Callaghan* [1940] A.C. 880 at p. 903, *per* Lord Wright.

[19] *Bamford* v. *Turnley* (1862) 3 B. & S. 66, at pp. 79, 83–84. " Liability is imposed only in those cases where the harm or risk to one is greater than he ought to be required to bear under the circumstances ": *per* Bramwell B. Weir, *Casebook on Torts*, 3rd ed., p. 339.

[20] The maxim has been described by Erle J. as an " ancient and solemn imposter ": *Bonomi* v. *Backhouse* (1858) E.B. & E. 622 at p. 643. See also the comments of the same judge in *Brand* v. *Hammersmith Ry.* (1867) L.R. 2 Q.B. 223, at p. 247. Holmes, *Harvard Essays*, 162 at p. 164 remarked that the " maxim teaches nothing but a benevolent yearning."

use his own land so as to injure another without committing a nuisance. It is only if such use is unreasonable that it becomes unlawful.

Nuisance to servitudes

We have so far been considering private nuisance as the interference with a person's use or enjoyment of land, and we have seen that in determining liability, the nature and quality of the defendant's conduct is a factor of great importance. In addition to this situation, however, the tort of nuisance provides a remedy for the infringement of a servitude,[21] such as the obstruction of a right of way or the blocking of a right to light.[22] In this type of nuisance, once the plaintiff has proved that he has suffered a substantial degree of interference,[23] the conduct of the defendant is in general irrelevant and the convenience of the locality, or the benefit of the activity in question to the community, or the care used by the defendant to avoid damage,[24] will not suffice to absolve him from liability. The plaintiff's right is paramount, and if the occupier of the servient tenement cannot prosecute his activities without infringing it, he must not perform them at all. This distinction led Lord Macnaghten in *Colls* v. *Home and Colonial Stores, Ltd.*[25] to regard the action for the interference with an easement as *sui generis*. The function of the action is to remedy the infringement of a right, not to compensate for the commission of a wrong.[26]

THE BASIC DIFFERENCES BETWEEN PUBLIC AND PRIVATE NUISANCE

Although claims (a) for a private nuisance, and (b) for particular damage resulting from a public nuisance have many features in common,[27] the rules relating to them are not identical. To succeed in private nuisance, the plaintiff must have an interest in land and consequently a non-occupier cannot recover damages for personal injuries,[28] whereas in public nuisance the plaintiff need have no interest in land and may recover for injury to the person or to property.

---

[21] *i.e.* easements, *profits à prendre* and natural rights.

[22] See the excellent account of this kind of nuisance in Salmond, *Torts*, 16th ed., pp. 72–74.

[23] *Jackson* v. *Duke of Newcastle* (1864) 3 De G.J. & Sm. 275 at p. 285, *per* Lord Hardwicke; *Colls* v. *Home and Colonial Stores Ltd.* [1904] A.C. 179 at p. 182, *per* Lord Halsbury L.C.; *Warren* v. *Brown* [1900] 2 Q.B. 722; *Petley* v. *Parsons* [1914] 2 Ch. 653.

[24] The natural right of the riparian owner to the continued flow of a stream in its natural condition is an exception. " It is only for unreasonable and unauthorised use of this common benefit that an action would lie ": *Embrey* v. *Owen* (1851) 6 Ex. 353 at p. 369, *per* Parke B. See generally *Swindon Waterworks Co.* v. *Wilts and Berks Canal Navigation Co.* (1875) L.R. 7 H.L. 697; *McCartney* v. *Londonderry and Lough Swilly Ry.* [1904] A.C. 301; Brett, " The Right to Take Flowing Water " (1950) 14 Conv.(N.S.) 154.

[25] [1904] A.C. 179.

[26] *Ibid.* at p. 186. Also *Price* v. *Hilditch* [1930] 1 Ch. 500 at p. 507, *per* Maugham J.

[27] *Sedleigh-Denfield* v. *O'Callaghan* [1940] A.C. 880 at pp. 905, 907, 918; *Halsey* v. *Esso Petroleum Co. Ltd.* [1961] 1 W.L.R. 683 at p. 699, *per* Veale J.

[28] *Post*, pp. 333–335.

The Standard of Liability in Nuisance [29]

One of the most difficult questions in the law of nuisance is the extent
to which proof of fault on the part of the defendant is essential to
liability.[29a] Looking at the problem another way, can a plaintiff succeed
in a claim in nuisance in circumstances in which a claim in negligence
would be unsuccessful? If a plaintiff can prove his case in negligence,
it may well be immaterial whether in addition the action of the defendant constitutes an actionable nuisance. On the other hand, if he cannot
discharge the burden of proving negligence, his claim may fail unless
(i) the facts bring him within the area of nuisance and (ii) the burden
of proof in nuisance is less or at least different.

In attempting to determine the standard of liability in nuisance,
it must always be borne in mind that the plaintiff has available two
remedies which require different considerations. These are: (i) an
injunction to restrain the defendant from commencing or continuing
an activity causing or threatening an interference [30]; (ii) an action for
damages to compensate the plaintiff for the injury he has suffered. In
the former the primary purpose of the remedy is to protect the plaintiff from further damage and the court is not principally concerned
with the defendant's culpability.[31] As the Law Commission has remarked, " consideration of the strictness of the duty is then out of
place—all that the court is concerned with is the question, " Should
the defendant be told to stop this interference with the plaintiff's
rights? " Whether or not the defendant knew of the smell or noise
or the like when it first began to annoy the plaintiff does not matter;
he becomes aware of it at the latest when the plaintiff brings his claim
before the court.[32] Because the court is not directly concerned with
the knowledge or culpability of the defendant liability appears to be
strict. In an action for damages, on the other hand, the courts have
traditionally been loth to penalise a defendant in the absence of fault,
and so the nature and quality of the defendant's activities are of far
greater importance. This distinction has not always been made by the
courts and one must beware of accepting as law generalisations in
injunction cases indicating that liability is strict.[33] The following
discussion is concerned principally with liability for damages.

The standard of liability in nuisance was recently discussed by the

---

[29] See generally: Friedmann, " Modern Trends in the Law of Torts " (1937) 1 M.L.R.,
pp. 39–48; Friedmann, " Negligence and the Overlapping of Torts " (1940) 3 M.L.R.,
pp. 305–309; Buxton, " The Negligent Nuisance " (1966) 8 U.Malaya L.R. 1 at pp. 2–6;
Buxton, " Nuisance and Negligence Again " (1966) 29 M.L.R. 676; Newark, " The
Boundaries of Nuisance " (1949) 65 L.Q.R. 480; Newark, " Trespass or Nuisance or
Negligence " (1954) 17 M.L.R. 579.

[29a] See, e.g. the differing views expressed in relation to nuisance by obstruction of the
highway in Dymond v. Pearce [1972] 1 Q.B. 496.

[30] Snell, Principles of Equity, 27th ed., Part VII, Chap. 6.

[31] Though this may, of course, affect the terms of the injunction.

[32] Report No. 32, " Civil Liability for Dangerous Things and Activities " at p. 25.

[33] e.g. Rapier v. London Tramways Co. [1893] 2 Ch. 588 at p. 560, per Lindley L.J.

Judicial Committee in *The Wagon Mound (No. 2)*.[34] This was an action in negligence and nuisance against the same defendants as in *The Wagon Mound (No. 1)* [35] by the owners of the *Corrimal*, which was being repaired in MD Ltd.'s wharf and was badly damaged in the fire. In the Australian court,[36] Walsh J. held that the plaintiffs' claim in negligence failed because fire damage was not reasonably foreseeable, but that they succeeded in their claim in nuisance because in his view liability in nuisance was not dependent on foreseeability. Both parties appealed to the Privy Council, who upheld the defendants' contention that foreseeability is a prerequisite to liability in nuisance and also accepted the plaintiffs' contention that fire damage was reasonably foreseeable,[37] so that the plaintiffs succeeded.

Lord Reid referred to the argument of counsel for the plaintiffs that negligence is not an essential element in determining liability for nuisance and continued [38]: " It is quite true that negligence is not an essential element in nuisance. Nuisance is a term used to cover a wide variety of tortious acts or omissions and in many negligence in the narrow sense is not essential. . . . And although negligence may not be necessary fault of some kind is almost always necessary and fault generally involves foreseeability." It is unfortunate that such an important statement of principle is expressed in difficult and ambiguous terms which are not defined [39] and the following discussion of the principles involved is put forward therefore with some diffidence.

It would seem that Lord Reid is drawing a distinction between negligence " in the narrow sense " and fault. The precise meaning of the

---

[34] [1967] 1 A.C. 617 *sub nom. Overseas Tankship (U.K.) Ltd.* v. *The Miller Steamship Co. Pty.*

[35] [1961] A.C. 388. See *ante* at pp. 92–99. This case was remitted to the Australian court for trial on the issue of nuisance, but the action was dropped.

[36] [1963] S.R.(N.S.W.) 948; [1963] 1 Lloyd's Rep. 402.

[37] In *The Wagon Mound (No. 1)* it had been found that fire damage was not reasonably foreseeable. In *The Wagon Mound (No. 2)*, Walsh J. found that it was foreseeable, though only as a remote possibility. The Privy Council stressed that in these circumstances it was not justifiable to neglect the risk, however small it was. It does not follow that whatever the circumstances may be, it is justifiable to neglect a risk of small magnitude. A reasonable man would only neglect such a risk if he had some valid reason for doing so: *e.g.* that it would involve considerable expense to eliminate the risk. There was no justification whatever for discharging the oil into the harbour. Not only was it an offence to do so, but it involved considerable financial loss. There could have been no question of balancing the advantages and disadvantages, it was their duty to stop the discharge immediately. [1967] 1 A.C. 617 at p. 643.

[38] *Ibid.* at p. 639; *cf. Leong Bee* v. *Ling Nam Rubber* [1970] 2 M.L.J. 45 (P.C.).

[39] See the article of R. W. M. Dias, " Trouble on oiled Waters; Problems of *The Wagon Mound (No. 2)* " [1967] C.L.J., pp. 62–82. He suggests that Lord Reid's statement quoted in the text means that " foreseeability is relevant as a test of remoteness in all cases of nuisance to determine whether the kind of interference is actionable, even though unreasonable conduct, such as negligence, which is based on foreseeability in another sense, may not be required " (at p. 82). In other words, if the defendant can foresee a limited interference of the kind that occurred, it is irrelevant if the extent of the interference that actually occurred is unforeseeable. Whilst this is correct and is in fact the *ratio* of the case, it may be doubted whether it is what Lord Reid had in mind at this point in his judgment. His discussion at this point is in response to the submission of counsel that in nuisance " negligence is not an essential element in determining *liability* " (at p. 639, italics added). He is therefore concerned with the relevance of fault and foreseeability to liability, not remoteness.

former is not made clear, but it is suggested that it is used by Lord Reid in the sense of a breach of a duty of care. Such conduct must always constitute fault but the two concepts are not identical because fault is wider than the breach of a duty of care. A person may still be legally at fault, even though a claim in negligence against him may fail. In certain circumstances he may, for instance, have taken reasonable care in conducting his activity, but he may still have *knowingly* fallen short of the standard set by law.[40] Provided that he could foresee that such was a possible consequence of engaging in his activity he may be deemed to be " at fault." As Lord Reid explained in *The Wagon Mound* (*No. 2*), " an occupier may incur liability for the emission of noxious fumes or noise although he has used the utmost care in building and using his premises." [41] The basis of liability is the *intentional* prosecution of an activity by the defendant.

In stating that in many cases of nuisance negligence " in the narrow sense " is not essential, Lord Reid seems to admit of the existence of two different types of liability in nuisance.

(i) *Cases in which negligence " in the narrow sense " is essential, i.e.* the plaintiff must prove the breach of duty of care. In general, the existence of a duty of care in this factual situation can be taken for granted; it must arise from the control the occupier exercises over his land and its proximity to adjacent land or the highway. The plaintiff will normally succeed if he can prove that the defendant has neglected to take reasonable precautions to prevent foreseeable damage and it is immaterial whether the cause of action is termed " nuisance " or " negligence." In *Bolton* v. *Stone*,[42] for instance, it was conceded by the plaintiff that the claim in nuisance would fail unless negligence were established. This proposition seems to have been accepted by Lord Wilberforce in *Goldman* v. *Hargrave*.[43] In holding the defendant liable for permitting the escape of a spontaneous fire, his Lordship said: " The tort of nuisance, uncertain in its boundary, may comprise a wide variety of situations, in some of which negligence plays no part, in others of which it is decisive. The present case is one where liability, if it exists, rests upon negligence and nothing else." [44]

(ii) *Cases in which negligence in the narrow sense is not essential, i.e.* those cases where the defendant has acted wrongfully (though not necessarily carelessly) in prosecuting his activity when it is reasonably

---

[40] Dias, *loc. cit.* at p. 68, who also gives other examples (at p. 67) of fault without negligence, *e.g.* where there is a " no duty " situation as in *Weller & Co.* v. *Foot and Mouth Disease Research Institute* [1966] 2 Q.B. 569.

[41] [1967] 1 A.C. 617 at p. 639. This sentence must be read in conjunction with the later proposition that in nuisance " fault of some kind is almost always necessary."

[42] [1951] A.C. 850. This was apparently accepted by the House, but Lord Reid reserved his opinion as to what constituted a public nuisance in such a case.

[43] [1967] 1 A.C. 645.

[44] *Ibid.* at p. 657. Lord Wilberforce continued: " whether it falls within or overlaps the boundaries of nuisance is a question of classification which need not be resolved." For the standard of care required, see *ante*, at p. 61, note 66 and *post*, at pp. 338–339.

foreseeable that damage to the plaintiff will result from it. It is not, for example, a defence to a factory owner whose factory has caused substantial inconvenience to an adjacent occupier that he took all reasonable care in siting, erecting and using the factory. " The amount of fumes or noise which he can lawfully emit is a question of degree and he or his advisers may have miscalculated what can be justified." [45] He may not have desired the consequences of his activity but he *deliberately* continued with it in the knowledge that, despite the care taken, damage might be caused to his neighbour. In this situation a claim in negligence may well fail, but prima facie a claim in nuisance will succeed. Once the plaintiff has established that his interest in land has been infringed to a substantial extent by an emanation from the defendant's land, the burden is on the defendant to show that, in all the circumstances, his use of his premises was *reasonable*. As Lord Denning has said in talking of public nuisance, " once the nuisance is proved and the defendant is shown to have caused it, then the legal burden is shifted onto the defendant to plead and prove a sufficient justification or excuse. If he fails to do so, he is held liable, whereas in an action for negligence, the legal burden in most cases remains throughout on the plaintiff." [46] The concept of reasonableness in nuisance will be analysed subsequently, and it need only be said at this stage that it differs materially from reasonableness in negligence.[47]

Of course, it may well be that the defendant *has* prosecuted his activity in a careless manner, but in this category, any such negligent conduct on the part of the defendant is an accidental factor which is irrelevant to a claim in nuisance. Whenever the factor of careless conduct is present, " precisely the same facts will establish liability in both nuisance and negligence," [48] but the bases of the two torts are distinct.

The fundamental problem, therefore, is to determine the criterion by which it is possible to distinguish the respective areas of application of these two different forms of liability in nuisance. There is a traditional distinction between the *creation* or *adoption* of a nuisance by the defendant and the *negligent continuance* of the nuisance. [49] An occupier " continues " a nuisance for the creation of which he is not responsible, if, once he knows or ought to know of its existence, he fails to take

---

[45] *The Wagon Mound* (*No. 2*) [1967] 1 A.C. at p. 639, *per* Lord Reid, who continues: " Or he may deliberately obstruct the highway adjoining his premises to a greater degree than is permissible, hoping that no-one will object."

[46] *Southport Corporation* v. *Esso Petroleum Company Ltd.* [1954] 2 Q.B. 182 at p. 197.

[47] *Post*, at pp. 325–332.

[48] *The Wagon Mound* (*No. 2*) [1967] 1 A.C. 617 at p. 639. In *Sedleigh-Denfield* v. *O'Callaghan* [1940] A.C. 880 at p. 904, Lord Wright stated that " Negligence is not an independent cause of action but is ancillary to the actual cause of action, which is nuisance." See also *Jacobs* v. *L.C.C.* [1950] A.C. 361 at p. 374, *per* Lord Simonds. Lord Wright intended his statement to apply to all types of nuisance.

[49] *e.g. Noble* v. *Harrison* [1926] 2 K.B. 332 at p. 338, *per* Rowlatt J.; *Barker* v. *Herbert* [1911] 2 K.B. 633 at pp. 636–637, *per* Vaughan Williams L.J. and at pp. 642–643, *per* Fletcher Moulton L.J.; *Sedleigh-Denfield* v. *O'Callaghan* [1940] A.C. 880 at pp. 904–908, *per* Lord Wright, and at p. 913, *per* Lord Romer.

reasonable precautions to abate it.[50] It may be argued that the second form of liability discussed above applies to the creation or adoption of a nuisance and the first form of liability to the negligent continuance of it.

Normally, a person who creates a nuisance situation will appreciate that some damage is an inevitable or likely consequence of his activities and accept the risk that such damage may be actionable.[51] In such circumstances there is no reason why he should not be prima facie liable for any damage and subject to the burden of proving that his conduct was reasonable according to the special meaning of that term in the law of nuisance.[52] In other circumstances, however, there may have been no reason to suppose that the type of activity carried on by the defendant would cause any damage at all to the plaintiff, provided that it was carried on with due care. In such a situation it is arguable that the defendant should not be under any prima facie liability and the burden of proving negligence should fall on the plaintiff.

It is suggested that the best criterion to distinguish the two forms of liability in nuisance is to be found in the nature of the defendant's conduct. If he was or ought to have been aware that it was an inevitable or likely consequence of his activity that damage would be caused to the plaintiff's interest then, providing the injury or interference is sufficiently substantial,[53] there is a prima facie case in nuisance and it is for the defendant to exculpate himself.[53a] Otherwise the plaintiff must himself prove that the defendant was negligent in the manner in which he prosecuted his activity or in failing to abate the nuisance. In essence the distinction is between the deliberate or reckless (if undesired) infliction of and the negligent infliction of harm. It must be admitted that the boundary between the two categories may at times be difficult to draw, but it is a difficulty that the courts have to face in other branches of the law of torts.[54]

---

[50] " With knowledge that a state of things existed which might at any time give rise to a nuisance they took no steps to remedy that state of affairs ": *Sedleigh-Denfield* v. *O'Callaghan, supra*, at p. 920, *per* Lord Porter.

[51] " The amount of fumes or noise which [an occupier] can lawfully emit is a question of degree and he or his advisers may have miscalculated what can be justified ": *Wagon Mound (No. 2), supra*, at p. 639.

[52] *Ante* at p. 323.

[53] *i.e.* is the interference a material one, " not merely according to elegant or dainty modes and habits of living, but according to plain and sober and simple notions among the English people." *Walter* v. *Selfe* (1851) 4 De G. & Sm. 315 at p. 322, *per* Knight-Bruce V.-C.; *Thompson-Schwab* v. *Costaki* [1956] 1 W.L.R. 335 (use of residential premises for prostitution a nuisance to adjoining owners, having regard to the usages of civilised society and to the character of the neighbourhood).

[53a] *Cf. Radstock Co-operation and Industrial Society Ltd.* v. *Norton Radstock U.D.C.* [1968] Ch. 605, 633–634, *per* Sachs L.J.

[54] The problem of direct injury to the person provides a good analogy. If the injury is intentional, the defendant is liable unless he can bring himself within a number of limited defences. If it is negligent, the plaintiff must now prove fault whether the cause of action is called trespass or negligence: *Fowler* v. *Lanning* [1959] 1 Q.B. 426; *Letang* v. *Cooper* [1965] 1 Q.B. 232. See also the occupier's liability for injury to a trespasser on his land: *ante*, at pp. 187–190. In *The Wagon Mound (No. 2)*, Lord Reid draws a distinction between nuisance cases such as *Sedleigh-Denfield* v. *O'Callaghan* and negligence. It is submitted that as the burden of proof in each case is the same, the difference is one of terminology only: see Friedmann, " Incidence of Liability for Nuisance " (1940) 4 M.L.R. 139; Lloyd

INTENTIONAL HARM—REASONABLENESS

In the case of intentional or reckless harm, then, the onus is on the defendant to excuse himself by showing that in all the circumstances he has acted reasonably " according to the ordinary usages of mankind living in . . . a particular society." [55] It is important to distinguish the meaning of this term in the law of nuisance from its use elsewhere in the law of tort, especially in negligence. In negligence, assuming that a duty of care has been established, the vital question is, " Did the defendant take reasonable care? " If he did, there can be no liability. In nuisance, however, the defendant does not necessarily escape liability even if he has taken reasonable care. " Reasonable " means something more than taking proper care. It signifies what is legally right between the parties, taking into account all the circumstances of the case, and some of these circumstances are often such as a man on the Clapham omnibus could not fully appreciate.[56] It is putting a comparatively simple proposition before him to tell him that he is liable for negligence if he carelessly drives his car against another person; but it is not so simple to tell him that, while he can make some noise on his premises, he must not make too much, or he will be liable for nuisance. Knocking a man down carelessly is a tort *simpliciter*; making a noise that irritates him is a tort only *sub modo*.

Thus it must often be a pure gamble whether I act lawfully in opening a particular business in a street. If I make an error of judgment in deciding whether the business is offensive or not, I shall not escape liability by proving that I took all reasonable care to prevent the business from being a nuisance.[57] This is far short of saying that taking care is irrelevant to liability for nuisance. If the defendant *has* conducted his trade or business in a proper manner, *i.e.* as a reasonable man would have done, he has gone some of the way towards making out a defence, but only some of the way[58]; and, conversely, he will be in danger of being held liable if he has taken no such reasonable care.[59] No precise or universal formula is possible. Whether an act constitutes a nuisance cannot be determined merely by an abstract

---

(1951) 14 M.L.R. 499; Millner, *Negligence in the Modern Law* at pp. 18, 184 *et seq.* Prosser, *Torts*, 4th ed., pp. 573–577, regards nuisance as a field of tortious liability, based on the particular interest invaded, and considers that a private nuisance may be caused maliciously, intentionally or negligently.

[55] *Sedleigh-Denfield* v. *O'Callaghan* [1940] A.C. 880 at p. 903, *per* Lord Wright.

[56] This paragraph was cited with approval in *Russell Transport Ltd.* v. *Ontario Malleable Iron Co. Ltd.* [1952] 4 D.L.R. 719, 731 by McRuer C.J. (Ont.H.C.). For summary of conflicting views on " unreasonable " see Robert E. Keeton, " Conditional Fault in the Law of Torts " (1959) 72 Harv.L.R. 432–433, n. 62; Fridman, " Nuisance and the Reasonable Milkman " (1955) Austr.L.J. 435–436, based on *Munro* v. *Southern Dairies* [1955] V.L.R. 332.

[57] Lindley L.J. in *Rapier* v. *London Tramways Co.* [1893] 2 Ch. 588, 600.

[58] *Stockport Waterworks Co.* v. *Potter* (1861) 7 H. & N. 160.

[59] *May* v. *Stoop* (1909) 25 T.L.R. 262 (crying children in a day nursery, no failure of care, no nuisance); *Leeman* v. *Montagu* [1936] 2 All E.R. 1677 (750 cockerels crowing between 2 and 7 a.m., no attempt to re-arrange the farm, held a nuisance); *Manchester Corporation* v. *Farnworth* [1930] A.C. 171; *Manners* v. *Chester* [1963] C.L.Y. 2561 (nuisance by noise, go-kart racing, injunction and damages granted).

consideration of the act itself, but by reference to all the circumstances of the particular case; the time and place of its commission, the seriousness of the harm, the manner of committing it, whether it is done maliciously or in the reasonable exercise of rights; and the effect of its commission, that is whether it is transitory or permanent, occasional or continuous; so that it is a question of fact whether or not a nuisance has been committed.[60] Certain of these factors will now be discussed in greater detail.

(1) *The extent of the harm and the nature of the locality* [61]

In the leading case of *St. Helen's Smelting Co. v. Tipping*,[62] the plaintiff acquired an estate in a manufacturing area. Among the works situated nearby were those of a copper smelting company. The vapours emanating from these works proved injurious to the trees on the plaintiff's estate. In the House of Lords Lord Westbury L.C. drew a distinction between nuisances producing material injury to property and nuisances causing sensible personal discomfort. In assessing whether the latter can constitute an actionable nuisance, it is necessary to take into account the nature of the locality. " If a man lives in a town, it is necessary that he should subject himself to the consequences of those operations of trade which may be carried on in his immediate locality, which are actually necessary for trade and commerce, and also for the enjoyment of property, and for the benefit of the inhabitants of the town and of the public at large." [63] Inevitably, therefore, interference which may be permissible in one area may not be permissible in another.[64] On the other hand, in the case of " sensible injury to the value of the property," [65] these considerations do not apply and the convenience of the locality for the particular trade in question cannot absolve a defendant from liability. The plaintiff therefore recovered damages.

It is easier to establish a nuisance causing material damage to property than one causing personal discomfort, for in the former case the damage is tangible and more easily observed and measured. In the case of non-tangible injuries, there must be something over and above the everyday inconveniences which are inevitable in the locality.

---

[60] *Bamford* v. *Turnley* (1862) 3 B. & S. 66 at p. 79, *per* Pollock C.B.; *Stone* v. *Bolton* [1949] 1 All E.R. 237 at pp. 238–239, *per* Oliver J. (approved as to nuisance [1950] 1 K.B. 201 (C.A.), and on other grounds [1951] A.C. 850). *Stone* v. *Bolton* is explained in *Overseas Tankship (U.K.) Ltd.* v. *Miller Steamship Co. Pty.* [1966] 3 W.L.R. 498 at pp. 510–511.

[61] Planning decisions as such are not conclusive one way or the other, though they may be relevant. In *Halsey* v. *Esso Petroleum Co. Ltd.* [1961] 1 W.L.R. 683, the plaintiff's house was in an area " zoned " as residential while the defendant's depot was in an area " zoned " as industrial.

[62] (1865) 11 H.L.C. 642. Weir, *Casebook*, 3rd ed., p. 342.

[63] *Ibid.* at p. 650; *Shoreham-by-Sea U.D.C.* v. *Dolphin Canadian Proteins Ltd.* (1972) 71 L.G.R. 261.

[64] " What would be a nuisance in Belgrave Square would not necessarily be so in Bermondsey ": *Sturges* v. *Bridgman* (1879) 11 Ch.D. 852 at p. 865, *per* Thesiger L.J.; *Polsue and Alfieri* v. *Rushmer* [1907] A.C. 121; *Andreae* v. *Selfridge & Co.* [1938] Ch. 1

[65] (1865) 11 H.L.C. 642 at p. 651.

" The law does not regard trifling inconveniences; everything is to be looked at from a reasonable point of view." [66] This distinction is not free from difficulties and its consequences do not seem to have been fully investigated by the courts,[67] but it was recently reiterated by Veale J. in *Halsey* v. *Esso Petroleum Co.*[68] The magnitude of the harm, therefore, and in some cases the nature of the locality are circumstances to be considered in determining whether the defendant has acted unreasonably.

(2) *Utility of the defendant's conduct*

Since nuisance is the law of give and take the court is inevitably concerned to some extent with the utility or general benefit to the community of the defendant's activity. Thus we must all put up with the rattle of early morning milk deliveries, though probably not with the same amount of noise made by drunken neighbours.[69] This approach, however, will only justify an injurious activity up to a certain point, and that point is reached when serious damage is being done to the plaintiff's property or livelihood. In such a case the court will not accept the argument that the plaintiff should put up with the harm because it is beneficial to the community as a whole, for that would amount to requiring him to carry the burden alone of an activity from which many others benefit.[70] Nor will the court in such a case adopt the device of awarding damages in lieu of an injunction, for that would amount to expropriation without the sanction of Parliament.[71] Indeed, in one case an Irish court enjoined a nuisance even though the order would have the effect of closing for three months the only cement factory in Ireland at a time when building was an urgent public necessity.[72]

(3) *Abnormal sensitivity*

In considering what is reasonable the law does not take account of abnormal sensitivity in either persons or property. If the only reason why a man complains of fumes is that he has an unusually sensitive nose or that he owns an exotic flower, he cannot expect any sympathy from the courts.

---

[66] *Ibid.* at p. 653.

[67] The *St. Helen's* case gave no test for determining exactly whether a nuisance is one to property or is one causing personal discomfort, and the test which it did give for the latter is rather vague. Noises or smells primarily cause only personal discomfort, but they may make a hotel uninhabitable. It is uninjured as a building, but there is material injury to the business carried on in it. Is this an injury to property? Where vibration, noise and smoke depreciate the selling value of land, this is an injury to property: *Hammersmith Ry.* v. *Brand* (1867) L.R. 1 Q.B. 130; 2 Q.B. 223; (1869) L.R. 4 H.L. 171. The same may apply to loss of custom: *Harper* v. *Haden & Sons Ltd.* [1933] Ch. 298, *post*, at p. 351. See Weir, *Casebook*, 3rd ed., at p. 344.

[68] [1966] 1 W.L.R. 683.

[69] This is demonstrated most clearly where the activity is actuated by malice, for malicious conduct can have no utility: see pp. 331–332, *post*.

[70] See Bohlen, *Studies in the Law of Torts*, p. 429.

[71] *Shelfer* v. *City of London Electric Co.* [1895] 1 Ch. 287; *Munro* v. *Southern Dairies* [1955] V.L.R. 332; *cf. Bottom* v. *Ontario Leaf Tobacco Co.* [1935] 2 D.L.R. 699.

[72] *Bellew* v. *Cement Co.* [1948] Ir.R. 61.

In *Heath* v. *Brighton (Mayor of)*[73] for example, the incumbent and trustees of a Brighton church sought an injunction to restrain noise from the defendants' electrical power station. There was no proof of diminution of the congregation or of any personal annoyance to anyone except the incumbent and he was not prevented from preaching or conducting his services; nor was the noise such as to distract the attention of ordinary healthy persons attending the church. An injunction was not granted. It seems that no regard should be had to the special needs of invalids, or to special occupational needs, for there is no redress for damage due solely to the exceptionally delicate nature of the operations carried on by an injured party.[74]

Robinson v. *Kilvert*[75] illustrates the point with regard to sensitive property. The defendant began to manufacture paper-boxes in the cellar of a house the upper part of which was in the occupation of the plaintiff. The defendant's business required hot and dry air and he heated the cellar accordingly. This raised the temperature on the plaintiff's floor and dried and diminished the value of brown paper which the plaintiff warehoused there; but it did not inconvenience the plaintiff's workmen nor would it have injured paper generally. It was held that the defendant was not liable for nuisance. " A man who carries on an exceptionally delicate trade cannot complain because it is injured by his neighbour doing something lawful on his property, if it is something which would not injure anything but an exceptionally delicate trade." [76] A man cannot increase the liabilities of his neighbour by applying his own property to special uses, whether for business or pleasure.[77] But once the nuisance is established, the remedies by way of damages or an injunction will extend to delicate and sensitive operations such as the growing of orchids.[78]

(4) *Temporary injury*

Where the plaintiff is claiming an injunction to restrain a nuisance, it will not be issued, except in extreme cases, if the nuisance is temporary and occasional only. The reason for this is that an

---

[73] (1908) 98 L.T. 718.

[74] *Bloodworth* v. *Cormack* [1949] N.Z.L.R. 1058 at p. 1064; *Murray* v. *Laus* [1960] N.Z.L.R. 126 (noise); *cf. Stretch* v. *Romford Football Club* (1971) 115 S.J. 741.

[75] (1889) 41 Ch.D. 88; *Whycer* v. *Urry* [1955] C.L.Y. 1939 (C.A. held practice of ophthalmic optician in a business area too specially delicate for protection); *Bridlington Relay* v. *Yorkshire Electricity Board* [1965] Ch. 436; Weir, *Casebook on Tort*, 3rd ed., p. 345. Plaintiffs carried on business of relaying television, sued defendants to prevent them from electrifying a cable so as to interfere with reception. Defendants offered plaintiffs an assurance that every effort would be made to suppress interference. Injunction not granted: [1965] C.L.J. 204–206; (1965) 115 L.J. 174–175.

[76] Lopes L.J., *ibid.* 97.

[77] *Eastern and S.A. Telegraph Co.* v. *Cape Town Tramways* [1902] A.C. 381 at p. 383. But there may be liability if defendant fails to adopt such reasonable and practicable precautions as could have avoided the damage without appreciable prejudice to his own interests. *Gandel* v. *Mason* [1953] 3 D.L.R. 65 (road contractors liable in nuisance and negligence, they knew of peculiar sensitivity of mink in whelping season); *Nova Mink* v. *T.C.A.* [1951] 2 D.L.R. 241 distinguished. *Cf. Rattray* v. *Daniels* [1959] 17 D.L.R. (2d) 134, 135–136 (another mink case, but no liability—no nuisance, and no negligence).

[78] *McKinnon Industries Ltd.* v. *Walker* [1951] 3 D.L.R. 577 at p. 581, *per* Lord Simonds.

injunction is a remedy depending on the discretion of the court and it will not be issued where damages would be an adequate remedy. In *Swaine* v. *G.N. Ry.*,[79] for example, manure heaps which were ordinarily inoffensive were occasionally rendered offensive by a delay in their removal and also by the presence of dead cats and dogs. The Court of Chancery declined to grant an injunction, leaving the plaintiff to his common law action for damages. An instance of the exceptional circumstances in which the court did grant an injunction was pile-driving carried on by night for building purposes; for to do it at that time was unreasonable.[80]

Where the claim is for damages, as distinct from an injunction, the duration of the alleged nuisance is one of the relevant factors in determining whether the defendant has acted unreasonably and is liable.[81] All other circumstances must be taken into account and they may on the one hand make a temporary annoyance a nuisance or, on the other, render it lawful. A man who pulls down his house for the purpose of building another no doubt causes considerable inconvenience to his neighbours and it may well be that he will take some months in the process; but if he uses all reasonable skill and care to avoid annoyance, that is not a nuisance, for life could scarcely be carried on if it were.[82] On the other hand, blocking up a highway for no more than a month may well be a nuisance because circumstances will usually make the resulting damage so much more serious.[83] Indeed, when the damage is of a serious character the fact that the event which caused it was momentary is not material. In *Midwood & Co. Ltd.* v. *Manchester (Mayor of)* [84] an electric main installed by the defendants fused. This caused an accumulation and explosion of gas from which a fire broke out which damaged the plaintiffs' goods. The defendants were held liable and the argument that a sudden accident could not properly be regarded as a nuisance was rejected.

---

[79] (1864) 4 De G.J. & S. 211, 215–216, where Turner L.J. stated the rule. He and Lord Cranworth had anticipated it in *Att.-Gen.* v. *Sheffield Gas Co.* (1852) 3 De G.M. & G. 304, and it was applied in *Att.-Gen.* v. *Cambridge Gas Co.* (1868) L.R. 4 Ch. 71; *Gosnell* v. *Aerated Bread Co. Ltd.* (1894) 10 T.L.R. 661, and *Att.-Gen.* v. *Preston (Mayor of)* (1896) 13 T.L.R. 14.

[80] *De Keyser's Royal Hotel Ltd.* v. *Spicer Bros. Ltd.* (1914) 30 T.L.R. 257.

[81] *Per* Pollock C.B. in *Bamford* v. *Turnley* (1862) 3 B. & S. 66, 79; 31 L.J.Q.B. 286, 292 (a dissenting judgment, but certainly not on this point); Bramwell B.'s expression at p. 294 is too wide. As to nuisance by noise and vibration and the appropriate remedy, see *Lebor* v. *Trans-World Airline Incorporated* (1953) 215 L.T. 116–117.

[82] Vaughan Williams J. in *Harrison* v. *Southwark and Vauxhall Water Co.* [1891] 2 Ch. 409, 413–414. *Cf. Andreae* v. *Selfridge & Co. Ltd.* [1938] Ch. 1, 6, *per* Sir Wilfrid Greene M.R.: " Common or ordinary use of land . . . does not mean that the methods of using land and building on it are in some way to be stabilised for ever. . . . New methods enable land to be more profitably used, either by digging down into the earth or mounting it up into the skies."

[83] *Iveson* v. *Moore* (1699) 1 Ld.Raym. 486.

[84] [1905] 2 K.B. 597, 605, *per* Collins M.R.; 609, *per* Romer L.J. The order provided that nothing therein contained should exonerate from any indictment action or proceeding for nuisance. The jury found defendants were negligent, but they were liable apart from this finding. The case could equally well have been decided on the principle of *Rylands* v. *Fletcher*, pp. 358–382, *post*—an isolated escape is actionable. *Charing Cross Electricity Supply Co.* v. *Hydraulic Power Co.* [1914] 3 K.B. 772, 778–779, 784.

When it is said therefore that the injury must be " of a substantial character, not fleeting or evanescent," [85] what is signified is that the temporary nature of the injury may be evidence, but certainly not conclusive evidence, that it is too trivial to be considered as a nuisance.[86]

A related problem is whether a defendant can be held liable in nuisance for an isolated escape. In the vast majority of cases, of course, private nuisances involve an interference for a substantial length of time with the enjoyment of neighbouring property,[87] and there is some authority to suggest that a continuing state of affairs is essential to liability in nuisance. In *Stone* v. *Bolton*, for instance, the plaintiff, whilst standing on the highway, was injured by a cricket ball which had been hit from the defendant's adjacent cricket ground. At first instance Oliver J. held that a nuisance connotes some degree of continuity; it must " be a state of affairs, however temporary, and not merely an isolated happening." [88] In the Court of Appeal, Somervell L.J. regarded the gist of the alleged nuisance, not as the isolated act of hitting a ball into the highway, but the organising and carrying on of a game on property adjacent to the highway thereby endangering the public in the exercise of its right of passage.[89] The frequency of the escape,[90] and presumably the gravity of the harm caused, are important factors in determining whether a dangerous state of affairs existed on the defendant's land. Even if the escape is isolated, if the harm caused by it is sufficiently grave that is evidence of a pre-existent dangerous state of affairs. In *Spicer* v. *Smee* [91] a fire which destroyed the plaintiff's bungalow was caused by defective electrical wiring installed in the defendant's adjacent bungalow. Atkinson J. held that there was a dangerous state of affairs on the defendant's property and held him liable in nuisance.[92] Presumably *Midwood's* case can be explained in the same way. As Thesiger J. remarked in *S.C.M. (United Kingdom) Ltd.* v. *W. J. Whittall & Son*

---

[85] Brett J. in *Benjamin* v. *Storr* (1874) L.R. 9 C.P. 400, 407; Weir, *Casebook on Tort*, 3rd ed., p. 155.

[86] *Cf. Fritz* v. *Hobson* (1880) 14 Ch.D. 542, 556.

[87] *Cunard* v. *Antifyre* [1933] 1 K.B. 551 at p. 557, *per* Talbot J.; *British Celanese Ltd.* v. *A. H. Hunt Ltd.* [1969] 1 W.L.R. 959 at p. 969, *per* Lawton J.

[88] [1949] 1 All E.R. 237 at p. 238.

[89] [1950] 1 K.B. 201 at p. 213: " Nuisance is the causing or permitting of a state of affairs from which damage is likely to result," *per* Jenkins L.J. at pp. 208-209. The element of nuisance was not discussed in the House of Lords, but Lord Reid reserved his opinion as to what constituted nuisance in cases of this character: [1951] A.C. 850 at p. 868. See also *Cunard* v. *Antifyre* [1933] 1 K.B. 551 at p. 557, *per* Talbot J.; *Att.-Gen.* v. *P.Y.A. Quarries Ltd.* [1957] 2 Q.B. 169 at p. 192, *per* Denning L.J.; *Hilder* v. *Associated Portland Cement Manufacturers Ltd.* [1961] 1 W.L.R. 1434 (football escaping onto road, liability in negligence, nuisance considered).

[90] Thus, *Castle* v. *St. Augustine's Links* (1922) 38 T.L.R. 615, where golf balls were repeatedly sliced onto the highway, is distinguishable, for there was substantial interference with the use of the road and a state of affairs which foreseeably threatened damage.

[91] [1946] 1 All E.R. 489.

[92] In *Sedleigh-Denfield* v. *O'Callaghan* [1940] A.C. 880 at pp. 895-896, Lord Atkin said that the defendants " created a state of things . . . from which . . . flooding on the plaintiff's ground might reasonably be expected to result," and were therefore liable in nuisance.

Ltd., " while there is no doubt that a single isolated escape may cause the damage that entitles a plaintiff to sue for nuisance, yet it must be proved that the nuisance arose from the condition of the defendant's land or premises or property or activities thereon that constituted a nuisance." [93]

(5) *Malice*

Is malice material in nuisance? If A's use of his own property causes to B annoyance which does not amount to a nuisance, will the fact that A's acts are done solely for the purpose of annoying B convert them into a nuisance?

In *Christie* v. *Davey,*[94] the defendant, exasperated by a considerable number of music lessons given by the plaintiff, a teacher of music whose residence was separated from that of the defendant only by a party-wall, interrupted the plaintiff's lessons by knocking on the party-wall, beating on trays, whistling and shrieking. North J. issued an injunction because the defendant had acted deliberately and maliciously for the purpose of annoying the plaintiff. The learned judge added: " If what has taken place had occurred between two sets of persons both perfectly innocent, I should have taken an entirely different view of the case." [95] Two years later, however, the House of Lords in *Bradford (Mayor of)* v. *Pickles* [96] asserted that a bad motive cannot make wrongful an act otherwise legal, and they reaffirmed this principle in *Allen* v. *Flood* [97]; but in neither decision was any reference made to *Christie* v. *Davey.*

In *Hollywood Silver Fox Farm Ltd.* v. *Emmett,*[98] Macnaghten J. followed *Christie* v. *Davey.* The defendant deliberately caused guns to be fired on his own land near the boundary of the plaintiff's land in order to scare the plaintiff's silver foxes during breeding-time. The vixens of these animals are extremely nervous during breeding-time and much damage was done in consequence of the defendant's act, which was motivated by pure spite.

Macnaghten J. considered that the intention of the defendant is

---

[93] [1970] 1 W.L.R. 1017 at p. 1031. The learned judge continued: " I am satisfied that one negligent act that causes physical damage to an electric cable does not thereby constitute a nuisance." Nuisance was not considered on appeal by the Court of Appeal: [1971] 1 Q.B. 337. In *British Celanese Ltd.* v. *Hunt,* Lawton J. considered that an isolated escape is actionable as a nuisance but did not discuss the need for a pre-existing state of affairs, although on the facts set out there was such a state: [1969] 1 W.L.R. 959, 969. On this, see the comments of Thesiger J. in *S.C.M.* v. *Whittall* at p. 1031.

[94] [1893] 1 Ch. 316; *Palmar* v. *Loder* [1962] C.L.Y. 2233 (perpetual injunction granted to restrain defendant from interfering with plaintiff's enjoyment of her flat by shouting, banging, laughing, ringing door-bells or otherwise behaving so as to cause a nuisance by noise to her).

[95] [1893] 1 Ch. at pp. 326–327.

[96] [1895] A.C. 587 (*ante*, p. 28).

[97] [1898] A.C. 1.

[98] [1936] 2 K.B. 468, 475; Weir, *Casebook on Tort,* 3rd ed., p. 348: distinguished in *Rattray* v. *Daniels* [1959] 17 D.L.R. (2d) 134 (Alberta S.C.) (noise of bulldozer damaging mink in whelping season): for discussion on *Emmett's* case see (1936) 52 L.Q.R. 460–461; (1957) 53 L.Q.R. 1–4.

relevant in determining liability in nuisance and granted an injunction and awarded damages to the plaintiff. It is submitted that this is the better view. The courts, in judging what constitutes a nuisance, take into consideration the purpose of the defendant's activity,[99] and acts otherwise justified on the ground of reciprocity if done wantonly and maliciously with the object of injuring a neighbour are devoid of any social utility and cannot be regarded as " reasonable." The element of unreasonableness in nuisance as a tort had been recognised long before *Bradford* v. *Pickles* and that decision did not affect the principle of nuisances of this type,[1] *i.e.* those in which the law recognises that a certain amount of discomfort is inevitable in life owing to the activities of one's neighbours, but also expects that neighbours by their mutual forbearance will lessen this discomfort as much as they are reasonably able. The law of private nuisance gives to each party a qualified privilege of causing harm to the other. When the activity of one party is motivated principally by malice, his privilege is at an end and he is liable for the damage he has caused.

In both *Christie* v. *Davey*[2] and *Hollywood Silver Fox Farm Ltd.* v. *Emmett*[3] the defendant interfered with a legally protected interest of the plaintiff and the issue was whether, in doing so, he had acted unreasonably. If, however, the defendant's activity has not infringed any such right or interest, the plaintiff has no cause of action and the defendant's motive is irrelevant. This was in fact the position in *Bradford (Mayor of)* v. *Pickles*[4] itself, where the defendant deliberately drained his land so as to diminish the water supply reaching the land of the plaintiffs. His purpose was to coerce the plaintiffs into purchasing his land. It had previously been established that no interest in percolating waters exists until appropriation,[5] and as no interest or right could therefore have been infringed, the motive of the defendant was not material.[6]

SOURCE OF THE INTERFERENCE

The interference need not emanate from the defendant's land, although commonly it does, for a trespasser or a contractor executing works there may be liable in nuisance.[7] A public nuisance may emanate from a high-

---

[99] *Harrison* v. *Southwark and Vauxhall Water Co.* [1891] 2 Ch. 409 at p. 414, *per* Vaughan Williams L.J.; *Bamford* v. *Turnley* (1862) 31 L.J.Q.B. 286, 294, *per* Bramwell B.; *Grant* v. *Fynney* (1872) L.R. 8 Ch.App. 8 at p. 12, *per* Lord Selborne L.C.

[1] But in nuisances which are injuries to servitudes, malice is irrelevant to liability.

[2] [1893] 1 Ch. 316.

[3] [1936] 2 K.B. 468.

[4] [1895] A.C. 587.

[5] *Acton* v. *Blundell* (1843) 12 M. & W. 324; *Broadbent* v. *Ramsbotham* (1856) 11 Exch. 602; *Chasemore* v. *Richards* (1859) 7 H.L.C. 349. See Clayberg, " The Law of Percolating Waters " (1915) 14 Mich.L.R. 119.

[6] This principle was recently reiterated in *Langbrook Properties Ltd.* v. *Surrey C.C.* [1969] 3 All E.R. 1424. See Fridman, " Motive in the English Law of Nuisance " (1954) 40 Va.L.R. 583-595.

[7] *Post*, p. 335.

way or a waterway, and there is some authority that an action for a private nuisance may be maintained for an interference which is unconnected with the user of land by the defendant.[8] It is generally of the essence of nuisance that the interference emanates from *outside* the plaintiff's land, but in one case it seems that this is not so: where plaintiff and defendant are co-occupiers of the land on which the nuisance originates, the plaintiff can sue if he is in sole occupation of the land *affected* by the nuisance.[9]

WHO CAN SUE

1. Private nuisance

Private nuisance has traditionally been a remedy available only to a person who has suffered an interference with an interest in land. " It is clear that to give a cause of action for private nuisance, the matter complained of must affect the property of the plaintiffs." [10] " He alone has a lawful claim who has suffered an invasion of some proprietary or other interest in land." [11] The occupier of land can always maintain an action in respect of an interference to it, as can a tenant in possession,[12] even if there is only a weekly tenancy [13] or a tenancy at will.[14] The duration of the tenancy and the gravity of the interference are factors to be considered in determining whether to grant an injunction, but where there is real injury to health and comfort it is possible that even a weekly tenant will be granted an injunction as well as damages.[13]

A person who has merely the use of land without either the possession of it or any other proprietary interest in it, *e.g.* a licensee without possession, such as a lodger or a guest, cannot sue in nuisance. For the same reason even members of the occupier's family cannot maintain an action in nuisance although of course if they suffer personal injuries [15] it is always open to them to sue in negligence. It may be,

---

[8] *Southport Corporation* v. *Esso Petroleum Co. Ltd.* [1956] A.C. 218, 225. Devlin J., *obiter*, " I can see no reason why, if the defendant as a licensee or trespasser misuses someone else's land, he should not be liable for a nuisance in the same way as an adjoining occupier would be ": [1954] 2 Q.B. at p. 204, Morris L.J. agreed; at p. 196, Denning L.J. took the contrary view; [1956] A.C. at p. 242, Lord Radcliffe agreed with Denning L.J. In *Hall* v. *Beckenham Corporation* [1949] 1 K.B. 716, 728, in entering judgment for the defendant, it was conceded that an action would lie against the persons creating the nuisance: *Halsey* v. *Esso Petroleum Co. Ltd.* [1961] 1 W.L.R. 683, 699–700; *Hargrave* v. *Goldman* (1963–64) 37 A.L.J.R. 277 at p. 283, *per* Windeyer J.; *Miller Steamship Co. Pty.* v. *Overseas Tankship (U.K.) Ltd.* [1963] 1 Lloyd's Rep. 402 at p. 427, *per* Walsh J.
[9] *Hooper* v. *Rogers* [1974] 3 W.L.R. 329, though the point was not in fact open to the defendant in the Court of Appeal.
[10] *Southport Corpn.* v. *Esso Petroleum Co.* [1953] 3 W.L.R. 773, at p. 776, *per* Devlin J.
[11] *Read* v. *J. Lyons & Co. Ltd.* [1947] A.C. 156 at p. 183, *per* Lord Simonds; *Cunard* v. *Antifyre Ltd.* [1933] 1 K.B. 551 at p. 557, *per* Talbot J.; *Southport Corpn.* v. *Esso Petroleum Co. Ltd.* [1954] 2 Q.B. 182, 193, *per* Denning L.J.; *Halsey* v. *Esso Petroleum Co. Ltd.* [1961] 1 W.L.R. 683 at p. 692, *per* Veale J. See West, " Nuisance or *Rylands* v. *Fletcher* " (1966) 30 Conv.(N.S.) 95 at p. 101.
[12] *Inchbald* v. *Robinson* (1869) L.R. 4 Ch. 388.
[13] *Jones* v. *Chappell* (1869) L.R. 20 Eq. 539 at p. 544.
[14] *Burgess* v. *City of Woodstock* [1955] 4 D.L.R. 615 (Ont.H.C.).
[15] *Malone* v. *Laskey* [1907] 2 K.B. 144 at pp. 153–154, *per* Fletcher Moulton L.J.; *Cunard* v. *Antifyre Ltd.* [1933] 1 K.B. 551.

however, that a licensee with exclusive possession has a sufficient interest in the land to be permitted to claim in nuisance.

The owner of an incorporeal hereditament such as an easement or profit can sue for disturbance of his right.[16]

A reversioner can bring an action in nuisance if he can show that there is a likelihood that permanent injury will be caused to the property and his right is then co-existent with that of the occupier. A permanent injury is one which will continue indefinitely unless something is done to remove it,[17] for example a building which infringes the right to ancient lights,[18] vibrations causing structural damage,[19] or the keeping locked a gate across a path over which the reversioner has a right of way [20]; but the emission of noise or fumes or other invasions of a temporary nature, even if they cause the tenants to leave, or reduce the letting value, will not suffice.[21]

It is doubtful whether there are any other persons who can maintain an action in private nuisance. Pollock was of the opinion that in some instances there may be a private nuisance where the plaintiff has no control, use or enjoyment of immovable property; e.g. the owner or master of a ship lying in a harbour might sue for a nuisance created by an occupier of the wharf or shore which made the ship uninhabitable,[22] but it would seem that this would be properly classified as a public nuisance.[23]

The need for an interest in land in private nuisance is an anomaly in the modern law. If A and his wife are injured [24] and their house damaged by an emission from B's adjoining property, it is unjust that A can recover for his personal injuries without proof of negligence as a consequence of his right to sue in nuisance for the damage to his property, whilst his wife will only be compensated if she can prove that B has acted in breach of his duty of care. The rule, however, is firmly entrenched in the law. " With possibly certain anomalous exceptions . . . possession or occupation is still the test " for a cause of action in nuisance.[25]

---

[16] Nicholls v. Ely Beet Sugar Factory Ltd. [1936] 1 Ch. 343 (destruction of fish by pollution); Weston v. Lawrence Weaver Ltd. [1961] 1 Q.B. 402 (physical damage to an easement of way without interference with right of passage not actionable).

[17] Jones v. Llanrwst U.D.C. [1911] 1 Ch. 393 at p. 404, per Parker J.

[18] Jesser v. Gifford (1767) 4 Burr. 2141.

[19] Colwell v. St. Pancras B.C. [1904] Ch. 707.

[20] Kidgill v. Moor (1850) 9 C.B. 364.

[21] Simpson v. Savage (1856) 1 C.B.(N.S.) 347; Cooper v. Crabtree (1882) 20 Ch.D. 589.

[22] Torts, 15th ed., p. 302.

[23] Wagon Mound (No. 2) [1967] 1 A.C. 617.

[24] It has been doubted whether nuisance lies at all for personal injuries (Halsey v. Esso Petroleum Co. Ltd. [1961] 1 W.L.R. 683, 692), but it seems to have been so assumed in Cunard v. Antifyre [1933] 1 K.B. 551 and Malone v. Laskey [1907] 2 K.B. 141.

[25] Sedleigh-Denfield v. O'Callaghan [1940] A.C. 880 at pp. 902–903, per Lord Wright; Vaughn v. Halifax Dartmouth Bridge Commission [1961] 29 D.L.R. (2d) 523 (Nova Sc. S.C.) (owner of car in car park cannot sue in nuisance).

2. Public nuisance

As we have seen,[26] if a public nuisance has been committed, any person who has suffered special damage can sue in respect of it. It may, for instance, be the occupier of adjacent property [26] and it may be a user of the highway.[27]

WHO CAN BE SUED [28]

1. The creator of the nuisance

In general the person who creates the nuisance by some act of misfeasance as opposed to a mere non-feasance may always be sued in respect of it, whether or not he is in occupation of the land on which it originates,[29] and it is no defence that the land is now occupied by someone else and that he has no power to abate the nuisance without committing a trespass.[30] That may seem unfair, but he did the first wrong and he must answer for the damage resulting from it.[31]

2. The occupier

The occupier of the premises where the nuisance exists is in general liable during the period of his occupancy.[32] This is simple enough where he himself created the nuisance, but further questions arise where it originated (i) with someone else lawfully on the premises; or (ii) with a trespasser or as a result of an act of God; or (iii) with someone from whom the occupier acquired the property.

(i) *Persons lawfully on premises.* If a nuisance is caused by the servant or agent of the occupier the latter is liable according to the ordinary rules of vicarious liability. Moreover, the occupier is liable for the acts of anyone under his control, such as members of his family or his guests.[33] For the same reason, a landowner is liable if he allows a gipsy

---

[26] *Ante,* pp. 316–318 and *post,* pp. 351–352.

[27] *e.g. Holling* v. *Yorkshire Traction Co. Ltd.* [1948] 2 All E.R. 662; *Dollman* v. *Hillman Ltd.* [1941] 1 All E.R. 355; *Hilder* v. *Associated Portland Cement Manufacturers* [1961] 1 W.L.R. 1434.

[28] Friedmann (1943) 59 L.Q.R. 63–71 for an admirable analysis of the authorities.

[29] *Southport Corporation* v. *Esso Petroleum Co. Ltd.* [1956] A.C. 218, 225. Devlin J., *obiter,* " I can see no reason why if the defendant as a licensee or trespasser misuses someone else's land, he should not be liable for a nuisance in the same way as an adjoining occupier would be "; *Newman* v. *Conair Aviation Ltd.* (1972) 33 D.L.R. (3d) 474; *Gertson* v. *Municipality of Metropolitan Toronto* (1973) 41 D.L.R. (3d) 646. In *Hall* v. *Beckenham Corporation* [1949] 1 K.B. 716, 728, in entering judgment for the defendant, Finnemore J. conceded that an action would lie against the persons creating the nuisance.

[30] *Thompson* v. *Gibson* (1841) 7 M. & W. 456. Public authorities creating a nuisance in the exercise of their functions are liable in nuisance as a private person unless they can rely on some statutory defence, and a nuisance cannot be defended unless it is the necessary and inevitable consequence of the acts authorised by the statute: *Metropolitan A.D.* v. *Hill* (1881) 6 App.Cas. 193. Difficulties connected with the liability of local authorities for pollution by sewage are reviewed in *Pride of Derby, etc. Association Ltd.* v. *British Celanese Ltd.* [1953] Ch. 149, C.A., and *Smeaton* v. *Ilford Corporation* [1954] Ch. 450.

[31] Holt C.J., *Rosewell* v. *Prior* (1701) 12 Mod. 635, 639.

[32] Friedmann, " Incidence of Liability in Nuisance " (1943) L.Q.R. 63–71; *Sedleigh-Denfield* v. *O'Callaghan* [1940] A.C. 880, " Deliberate act or negligence is not an essential ingredient, but some degree of personal responsibility is required," at p. 897, *per* Lord Atkin.

[33] See *post,* p. 373.

encampment to be made upon his land which by reason of its noise and insanitary condition is a nuisance to adjoining inhabitants.[34]

INDEPENDENT CONTRACTOR. As a general rule, a principal cannot be held liable for the acts or defaults of an independent contractor employed by him, but there are certain exceptions to this rule.[35] In some cases, for instance, the principal is said to be under a " non-delegable " duty to see that care is taken and if, in fact, damage is caused to a third party by the activity of the contractor, the principal will be liable, because he himself is thereby in breach of his duty of care.[35]

A person who engages in any activity which involves particular danger is under such a non-delegable duty of care [36] and this rule of course will cover some nuisance situations. In addition, an occupier will generally be liable for a nuisance created by his independent contractor. In *Bower* v. *Peate* [37] the defendant employed a contractor to do construction work on his land in the course of which the contractor undermined the support for the plaintiff's adjoining house. The defendant was held liable. In *Matania* v. *National Provincial Bank* [38] the occupier of the first floor of a building was liable to the occupier of the higher floors for a nuisance by dust and noise created by his independent contractor.

A principal whose contractor interferes with or creates a danger on the highway may be liable to anyone who in consequence suffers special damage. In *Hole* v. *Sittingbourne Ry.*,[39] for instance, a railway company had authority to build a bridge across a navigable river provided that they did not impede navigation. The contractors whom they employed constructed it so imperfectly that it would not open to let boats through. The company were held liable to a user of the highway. In *Holliday* v. *National Telephone Co.*[40] the defendants were empowered by statute to lay telephone wires in the highway. One of their contractors in the course of the work negligently immersed a defective blowlamp in a pot of solder and the plaintiff was injured in the resultant explosion. The defendants were held liable. A person who has statutory authority to interfere with the highway owes a duty to the public to exercise his authority carefully, and he cannot delegate the performance of this duty to an independent contractor.[41]

In the above cases, however, the source of the danger was actually on the highway. It was clearly established by the Court of Appeal in *Salsbury* v. *Woodland* [41] that an occupier of land adjacent to the highway who commissions a contractor to do work *on* his land is not liable

---

[34] *Att.-Gen.* v. *Stone* (1895) 12 T.L.R. 76.
[35] *Post* at pp. 536–540.
[36] *Ibid.*; *Honeywill and Stein Ltd.* v. *Larkin Bros.* [1934] 1 K.B. 191; *Rylands* v. *Fletcher* (1868) L.R. 3 H.L. 330; *Salsbury* v. *Woodland* [1970] 1 Q.B. 324.
[37] (1876) 1 Q.B.D. 321; *Dalton* v. *Angus* (1881) 6 App.Cas. 740.
[38] [1936] 2 All E.R. 633; *Duncan's Hotel (Glasgow) Ltd.* v. *J. & A. Ferguson Ltd.*, 1972 S.L.T.(Notes) 84.
[39] (1861) 6 H. & N. 488; *Gray* v. *Pullen* (1864) 5 B. & S. 970.
[40] [1899] 2 Q.B. 392.
[41] *Salsbury* v. *Woodland* [1970] 1 Q.B. 324 at p. 345, *per* Harman L.J.

merely because as a result of the negligence of the contractor injury is caused to a user of the highway. It would be different if the work involved especial risk to the users of the highway, or if the work was done in response to a " positive and continuing duty " [42] to keep the premises in repair as in *Tarry* v. *Ashton*.[43] In that case the occupier of a public house adjoining the highway was liable when a heavy lamp attached to the building fell on a passer-by. Although the defendant had employed an independent contractor to maintain the lamp in good repair, it was held that because of the contractor's negligence the occupier had failed to discharge his duty. " That duty was imposed on him before the contractor came and after the contractor had gone." [42] There was no such continuing duty in *Salsbury* v. *Woodland* and the defendant was not liable for the negligence of a tree feller he had engaged to cut down a tree on his land adjacent to the highway.

An employer is never liable for " collateral " negligence on the part of an independent contractor.[44]

(ii) *Nuisances created by a trespasser or resulting from an act of God.* An occupier is not liable for a state of affairs either created by a trespasser [45] or resulting from an act of God [46] unless either he adopts the nuisance by using the state of affairs for his own purposes or he " continues " the nuisance. An occupier continues a nuisance if once he has actual or constructive knowledge of its existence he fails to take reasonably prompt and efficient steps to abate it. He cannot of course be liable unless he is in a position to take effective steps to abate the nuisance.[47] This principle was enunciated by the House of Lords in relation to a nuisance created by a trespasser in the leading case of *Sedleigh-Denfield* v. *O'Callaghan*.[48] The defendant occupied land on which there was a ditch. A trespasser laid a pipe in it with a grating designed to keep out leaves, but placed in such an ill-chosen position that it caused a blockage of the pipe when a heavy rainstorm occurred, and in consequence the plaintiff's adjacent land was flooded. The storm occurred nearly three years after the erection of the grating and during that period, the defendant's servant who was responsible for cleansing the ditch, ought to have realised the risk of flooding presented by the obstruction. The defendant was held liable in nuisance. The House of Lords refused to draw any distinction in this connection

---

[42] *Ibid.* at p. 339, *per* Widgery L.J.

[43] (1876) 1 Q.B.D. 314.

[44] *Post*, p. 539.

[45] For more detailed discussion on this point see pp. 372–374, *post*.

[46] For more detailed discussion on this point see pp. 376–377, *post*.

[47] *Smeaton* v. *Ilford Corporation* [1954] Ch. 450 at p. 462; *Goldman* v. *Hargrave* [1967] 1 A.C. 645.

[48] [1940] A.C. 880. " An absentee owner or occupier oblivious of what is happening under his own eyes is in no better position than a man who looks after his property ": at p. 887, *per* Lord Maugham; Weir, *Casebook on Tort*, 3rd ed., p. 350; *Leanse* v. *Egerton* [1943] K.B. 323.

between public and private nuisance.[49] A trespasser who creates a nuisance is of course also liable.[50]

Although it had been clear even before *Sedleigh-Denfield* v. *O'Callaghan* that an occupier can be liable for continuing a nuisance created by a third party,[51] until recent times it was considered that he was never under a duty to abate a natural nuisance.[52] This rule of immunity was however decisively rejected by the Judicial Committee in the important case of *Goldman* v. *Hargrave*.[53] A tall redgum tree growing in the centre of the defendant's land was struck by lightning and began to burn. The defendant properly requested a tree feller to come and cut down the tree. Until the time the tree was felled, the defendant's conduct in relation to the fire was not open to criticism. However, instead of extinguishing the fire immediately the tree was felled by inundating it with water, the defendant left the tree to burn itself out and took inadequate steps to prevent the fire from spreading. In fact, in consequence of a strengthening of the wind and an increase in temperature, the fire spread onto the plaintiff's property. It was found that the method adopted by the defendant involved a foreseeable risk of the revival and spread of the fire and the defendant was held liable. In an admirable judgment Lord Wilberforce rejected the traditional policy of regarding occupation of land as a source of privilege and immunity. " It is only in comparatively recent times that the law has recognised an occupier's duty as one of a more positive character than merely to abstain from creating, or adding to, a source of danger or annoyance." [54] As regards such nuisances of omission, therefore, it is no longer relevant whether the state of affairs was originally created by a third party or by nature. Once the occupier becomes aware of the nuisance and fails to remedy it within a reasonable time, he may be liable for any damage it may cause, either to his neighbour or the user of the highway. " The basis of the occupier's liability lies not in the use of his land; in the absence of.' adoption ' there is no such use; but in the neglect of action in the face of something which may damage his neighbour." [55]

We have seen that in this nuisance situation, it is immaterial whether the cause of action is termed " nuisance " or " negligence "; the burden

---

[49] As suggested by Bankes L.J. in *Job Edwards* v. *Birmingham Navigation* [1924] 1 K.B. 341. The actual decision in the case may be valid on other grounds, though dicta in *Sedleigh-Denfield's* case leave even that uncertain: [1940] A.C. 880 at pp. 893, 918–919.
[50] *Ante* at p. 335.
[51] *e.g. Barker* v. *Herbert* [1911] 2 K.B. 633.
[52] *Giles* v. *Walker* (1890) 24 Q.B.D. 656; *Sparke* v. *Osborne* (1909) 7 C.L.R. 51; *Pontardawe U.D.C.* v. *Moore-Gwyn* [1929] 1 Ch. 656; *Neath R.D.C.* v. *Williams* [1951] 1 K.B. 115 (natural silting up of a watercourse—an interesting comparison with *Sedleigh-Denfield* v. *O'Callaghan, supra*). The rule of immunity did not extend to public nuisance: *Noble* v. *Harrison* [1926] 2 K.B. 332.
[53] [1967] 1 A.C. 645, Weir, *Casebook on Tort*, 3rd ed., p. 354; Harris [1967] C.L.J. 24–27.
[54] *Ibid.* at p. 657. In the High Court of Australia, Windeyer J. said: " The tendency of the law in recent times has been to lessen the immunities and privileges of landowners and occupiers and to increase their responsibility to others for what happens on their and ": [1964] A.L.R. 377 at p. 392.
[55] [1967] 1 A.C. 645 at p. 661.

of proof on the plaintiff is the same.[56] In determining the standard of care required the court cannot disregard the fact that the occupier is confronted with a nuisance not of his own creation, and because of this the court is entitled to consider the occupier's individual circumstances. As Lord Wilberforce said in a passage of great clarity: " The law must take account of the fact that the occupier on whom the duty is cast has, *ex hypothesi*, had this hazard thrust upon him through no seeking or fault of his own. His interest, and his resources, whether physical or material, may be of a very modest character either in relation to the magnitude of the hazard, or as compared with those of his threatened neighbour. A rule which required of him in such unsought circumstances in his neighbour's interest a physical effort of which he is not capable, or an excessive expenditure of money, would be unenforceable or unjust. One may say in general terms that the existence of a duty must be based upon knowledge of the hazard, ability to foresee the consequences of not checking or removing it, and the ability to abate it. . . . The standard ought to be to require of the occupier what is reasonable to expect of him in his individual circumstances." [57] This subjective test is an exception to the general rule in negligence [58] and is carefully limited by Lord Wilberforce to cases where the defendant was not himself responsible for the creation of the source of danger.

(iii) *Predecessor in title.* Where the nuisance existed before the occupier acquired the property he will be liable if it can be proved that he knew, or ought reasonably to have known, of its existence; but not otherwise. In *St. Anne's Well Brewery Co.* v. *Roberts*,[59] X owned an ancient inn, one side of which was bounded by the old city wall of Exeter. Y owned part of the wall. On either side of X's kitchen fireplace, recesses had at some time unknown been formed by excavations in the wall. Part of the wall belonging to Y collapsed and demolished the inn. X sued Y who was held not liable because he neither knew of the defect nor could have discovered it by reasonable diligence.[60] It is

---

[56] *Ante* at pp. 322–324.

[57] At p. 663. Lord Wilberforce proceeded to interpret some of the previous cases in this light. Thus in the *Job Edwards* case, to remove the hazard would have cost £1,000, therefore no liability. In *Pontardawe U.D.C.* v. *Moore-Gwyn*, the cost would have been between £300–£450: no liability.

[58] *Ante* at pp. 61–69.

[59] (1929) 140 L.T. 1. Followed in *Wilkins* v. *Leighton* [1932] 2 Ch. 106. *Cf. Hall* v. *Duke of Norfolk* [1900] 2 Ch. 165 (present occupier held not liable for " continuing " an excavation made by his predecessor which eventually caused a subsidence).

[60] In *Broder* v. *Saillard* (1876) 2 Ch.D. 692, defendant was a tenant of premises the stables of which were erected upon an artificial mound of earth which adjoined the plaintiff's house, and into which rain and drainage from the stables penetrated and so caused the plaintiff's wall to be damp. Defendant was held liable although he had no knowledge of the nuisance, but one must assume that there had not been such reasonable diligence on the defendant's part with respect to leakage from a soil-pipe. In *Humphries* v. *Cousins* (1877) 2 C.P.D. 239, a drain which began on defendant's premises passed under other houses and received their drainage and then returned under defendant's premises and passed under plaintiff's house. The return drain beneath defendant's premises was decayed and allowed the drainage to escape which passed into plaintiff's premises. Defendant was ignorant even of the existence of the return drain. " It is probable, however,

arguable that the standard of care discussed in *Goldman* v. *Hargrave* should apply also to this situation.

3. The landlord

In general, a landlord is not liable for a nuisance on the premises, as he is not in occupation; the proper person to sue is the tenant.[61] But the landlord is liable in the following circumstances.

(i) IF HE HAS AUTHORISED NUISANCE. The landlord is liable if he has expressly or impliedly authorised his tenant to create the nuisance. Where A let a field to B for working it as a lime quarry and B's acts in blasting the limestone and letting kiln smoke escape constituted a nuisance to C, A was held liable, for B's method of working the quarry was the usual way of getting lime and A was taken to have authorised it.[62] Here the liability of the landlord is not different from that of any principal who authorises his agent to commit a tort. The tenant, of course, is also liable. By way of contrast, a local authority who let a house to a " problem " family were not liable to be enjoined in respect of nuisance created by the family even though the authority could have terminated the lease for breaches of covenant.[63]

(ii) IF HE KNEW OF NUISANCE BEFORE LETTING. If the landlord knowingly lets premises on which there is a nuisance for which the landlord was in some way himself responsible, he will remain liable for it. A person who creates a nuisance is of course always responsible even though he is no longer in occupation of the land on which the nuisance exists.[64] Moreover the tenant may be liable for adopting or continuing the nuisance.

(iii) IF HE OUGHT TO HAVE KNOWN OF NUISANCE BEFORE LETTING. If he ought to have known of the nuisance at the date of the lease, the landlord is liable, but not if he had no reasonable grounds for suspecting its existence. This result has been attained gradually and by steps of doubtful consistency. In *Gandy* v. *Jubber*,[65] the plaintiff was lamed by slipping through a defective iron grating over the area of a house in the occupation of X. She sued the defendant, who had originally let the premises to X. The court[66] was of the opinion that there was no tenancy between the defendant and X and held that, even if there were one, the

---

that the principle of *Rylands* v. *Fletcher*, though not referred to in the case, would justify the decision, as suggested in *Winfield on Torts* ": *per* Lord Atkin in the *Sedleigh-Denfield* case [1940] A.C. at p. 898.

[61] *Cheetham* v. *Hampson* (1791) 4 T.R. 318.

[62] *Harris* v. *James* (1876) 45 L.J.Q.B. 545; *Rich* v. *Basterfield* (1847) 4 C.B. 783 was regarded by Blackburn J. as a decision on the facts, and by Lush J. as hair-splitting: *Pwllbach Colliery Co.* v. *Woodman* [1915] A.C. 634 at p. 639, " But permission to carry on a business is quite a different thing from permission to carry it on in such a manner as to create a nuisance, unless it is impossible in a practical sense to carry it on without committing a nuisance ": *per* Lord Loreburn.

[63] *Smith* v. *Scott* [1973] Ch. 314; criticised by Merritt [1973] J.P.L. 154.

[64] *Rosewell* v. *Prior* (1701) 12 Mod. 635; *Todd* v. *Flight* (1860) 9 C.B.(N.S.) 377.

[65] (1865) 5 B. & S. 78, 485; 9 B. & S. 15.

[66] 9 B. & S. 15; an undelivered judgment of the Exch. Chamber.

defendant was not liable because it was not alleged that the grating was defective at the time of the letting. But the court also considered that, if there had been a tenancy, the defendant would have been liable for the nuisance provided (a) it had existed at the date of the creation of the tenancy, and (b) the defendant had had notice of it, and (c) it was such as to be in its very essence and nature a nuisance at the date of letting and was not merely some defect capable of being rendered a nuisance by the tenant after the tenancy had begun; e.g. a cellar with a flap is not an obvious nuisance; it may or may not be one according to whether the flap was improperly left open or carefully closed.[67] The court considered that if the above three conditions were fulfilled, the lessor ought to be liable because it is only just that the owner of property receiving rent should be thus answerable. A sweeping dictum in the later case of *Nelson* v. *Liverpool Brewery Co.*[68] might imply that unless the landlord actually knew of the nuisance he could not be liable for it; but still later dicta have narrowed it and probably the rule now is that the landlord is liable not only if he knew of the defect but also if he could have ascertained it with reasonable care, whether it were obvious or not.[69]

(iv) WHERE LANDLORD RESERVES RIGHT TO ENTER AND REPAIR OR HAS IMPLIED RIGHT TO DO SO.[69a] In *Wilchick* v. *Marks* [70] the plaintiff was walking along the highway when she was injured by the fall of a defective shutter from X's house. X had let the house to Y and both X and Y knew of the defect. There was no covenant on either side to repair. Both were held liable. Y was liable because he was the occupier and also because, if the rule were otherwise and the landlord happened to be abroad, the damage might be done before he could be notified of the risk and called upon to repair it. X was liable because he had reserved to himself the right to enter and do repairs (though he was under no obligation to do them) and to that extent he exercised a measure of control over the premises. In *Heap* v. *Ind, Coope and Allsopp Ltd.*[71] the landlord was held liable by the Court of Appeal to a passer-by where he had not covenanted to do repairs but had expressly reserved the right to enter for the purpose of viewing the condition and making the necessary repairs at the tenant's expense, although he did not know of the want of repair. The tenant was not sued but was clearly liable.[72]

---

[67] *Ibid.*, and Blackburn J. in 5 B. & S. at p. 90. *Cf.* Lindley L.J. in *Gwinnell* v. *Eamer* (1875) L.R. 10 C.P. 658, 662.

[68] (1877) 2 C.P.D. 311. In any event the decision related to visitors *coming on* the premises and therefore belonged to a different branch of the law (" Liability for Land and Structures") *ante*, Chap. 10.

[69] *St. Anne's Well Brewery Co.* v. *Roberts* (1929) 140 L.T. 1; Goddard J. in *Wilchick* v. *Marks* [1934] 2 K.B. 56, 67–68.

[69a] In this and Case (v) below, the landlord also appears to be liable under s. 4 of the Defective Premises Act 1972 (p. 201, *ante*) though this seems to add little to the common law.

[70] [1934] 2 K.B. 56.

[71] [1940] 2 K.B. 476.

[72] *Ibid.*, 482. MacKinnon L.J. refers to it as " an irrefragable claim."

In *Mint* v. *Good* [73] the plaintiff was injured by the collapse of a wall on the highway, the wall being on premises which the defendant landlord had let to a weekly tenant, who was not sued in the action. The wall was found to be a nuisance due to its defective state of repair. The defendant had not contracted with the tenant to do repairs and had not reserved a right to enter on the property to do so. The Court of Appeal held that in a weekly tenancy such a right must be implied and the defendant was liable in nuisance. The Housing Act 1961 now provides that in any lease of a dwelling-house granted after October 24, 1961, for a term of *less* than seven years or any lease which is determinable by the lessor in less than seven years, there is an implied covenant by the lessor to keep in repair the structure and exterior (including drains, gutters and external pipes), and certain installations within the dwelling-house. It renders ineffective any provision in a tenancy which seeks to place these burdens on the tenant.[74] The landlord's liability does not exempt the tenant; he is also liable even if he does not know of the defect provided he could have ascertained it if he had used reasonable care.[75]

(v) WHERE COVENANT TO REPAIR. Hitherto we have assumed that neither landlord nor tenant is under an express covenant to repair. Suppose that there is such a covenant, that it is not observed and that a nuisance consequently arises which causes an injury to a third person, how does that affect the position?

If it is the tenant who has undertaken the repair, of course he is liable, but his liability is based on the fact that he is the occupier of the premises; any additional obligation which he may have undertaken by contract with the landlord cannot affect his liability in tort to third parties. Does such an undertaking exempt the landlord from liability for the nuisance? Clearly the landlord cannot be liable if he did not have actual or constructive knowledge of the defect, but in *Pretty* v. *Bickmore* [76] it was held that even if the landlord was aware of the nuisance he could not be liable where he had taken from his tenant a covenant to repair as he had done nothing to authorise the nuisance or its continuance. In the light of subsequent *obiter dicta*,[77] however, this

---

[73] [1951] 1 K.B. 517; Weir, *Casebook on Tort*, 3rd ed., p. 157. In the absence of evidence to the contrary, both parties must be taken to have contemplated that the landlord will do the necessary repairs: 521–522, 527. Somervell L.J. was not prepared to hold the landlord liable because he had previously done the repairs: 523. See *Sleafer* v. *Lambeth B.C.* [1959] 1 Q.B. 43 at pp. 56–57.

[74] 9 & 10 Eliz. 2, c. 65, ss. 32 and 33. These sections do not apply to any lease where the lessee has an option for a renewal which will bring the total term to seven years or more. Contracting out is forbidden, but the county court may, with the consent of the parties, allow s. 32 to be excluded or modified.

[75] Goddard L.J. in *Wilchick* v. *Marks* [1934] 2 K.B. 56. The dicta of Heath J. to the contrary in *Payne* v. *Rogers* (1794) 2 H.Bl. 350 are unsatisfactory.

[76] (1873) L.R. 8 C.P. 401. The fact of the landlord's knowledge appears more clearly in the reports in 28 L.T. 704 (Honeyman J.) and 21 W.R. 783. See however the comments of Sachs L.J. in *Brew Bros. Ltd.* v. *Snax (Ross) Ltd.* [1970] 1 Q.B. 612 at p. 637.

[77] Brett J. in *Gwinnell* v. *Eamer* (1875) L.R. 10 C.P. 658 at p. 661; Goddard J. in *Wilchick* v. *Marks* [1934] 2 K.B. 56 at p. 67; the C.A. in *Wringe* v. *Cohen* [1940] 1 K.B. 229 at pp. 235–236, 246.

view was of doubtful authority and was finally rejected by a majority of the Court of Appeal in the recent case of *Brew Bros. Ltd.* v. *Snax (Ross) Ltd.*[78] The liability of the landlord now depends in part on whether the nuisance existed on the premises at the commencement of the tenancy. If it did and was such that the landlord knew or ought to have known of its existence at the commencement of the tenancy he is liable and the covenant to repair is irrelevant.[79] " If the nuisance arises after the lease is granted, the test of an owner's duty to his neighbour depends on the degree of control exercised by the owner in law or in fact for the purpose of repairs." [80] He cannot therefore be liable if he has no right to enter the premises to inspect and effect repairs,[81] but such a right is readily inferred by the courts, particularly in a weekly tenancy.[82] Indeed in *Mint* v. *Good*,[83] Denning L.J. doubted whether a landlord can now exempt himself from liability to passers-by by taking a covenant from a tenant to repair premises adjoining a highway.[84] If the landlord does have a sufficient degree of control, it is no defence that the tenant is under a duty to repair. As Sachs L.J. remarked in *Brew Brothers Ltd.* v. *Snax (Ross) Ltd.*,[85] there is no reason why liability to a third party should be " shuffled off merely by signing a document which as between owner and tenant casts on the latter the burden of executing remedial work. The duty of the owner is to ensure that the nuisance causes no injury—not merely to get somebody else's promise to take the requisite steps to abate it." [86]

If it is the landlord who has undertaken to repair, he is liable. Such was the decision in *Payne* v. *Rogers*,[87] where Heath J. said that if the tenant, and not the landlord, were held liable this would encourage circuity of action because the tenant would then be able to obtain an indemnity from the landlord. A more satisfactory explanation is that in such circumstances the landlord has control of the premises. He may not be in occupation but his covenant to repair gives him a right of access to the premises for the very purpose of preventing the injury which has occurred.[88] Moreover, in *Wringe* v. *Cohen* the Court of Appeal held that where premises on a highway become dangerous and constitute a nuisance, so that they collapse and injure a passer-by or an adjoining owner, the occupier or owner of the premises, if he has under-

[78] [1970] 1 Q.B. 612.
[79] *Ibid.* at p. 638, *per* Sachs L.J., and at p. 644, *per* Phillimore L.J. Harman L.J. (at p. 643) appears to insist on actual knowledge.
[80] *Ibid.* at p. 638, following the judgment of Lord Denning and Birkett L.J. in *Mint* v. *Good* [1951] 1 K.B. 517 at pp. 528 and 529.
[81] See *post*, pp. 635–636.
[82] *Mint* v. *Good* [1951] 1 K.B. 517 at p. 523, *per* Somervell L.J.; at p. 527, *per* Denning L.J.; at p. 528, *per* Birkett L.J.
[83] [1951] 1 K.B. 517.
[84] *Ibid.* at p. 528.
[85] [1970] 1 Q.B. 612.
[86] *Ibid.* at pp. 638–639, following *Mint* v. *Good, supra,* at p. 527, *per* Denning L.J.
[87] (1794) 2 H.Bl. 350. So, too, dictum in *Nelson* v. *Liverpool Brewery Co.* (1877) 2 C.P.D. 311, 313.
[88] *Cf.* Collins M.R. in *Cavalier* v. *Pope* [1905] 2 K.B. 757, 762.

taken the duty to repair, is answerable, whether he knew or ought to have known of the danger or not.[89] A had let a house to B and the duty to keep it in repair was on A. A decayed gable-end fell from the house onto C's adjoining shop and destroyed its roof. It was held that A was liable to C in nuisance, whether A knew or ought to have known of the danger or not. It was conceded, however, that if the defect were due to either (a) a secret and unobservable operation of nature (e.g. subsidence under or near the foundations of the premises), or (b) the act of a trespasser, then neither landlord nor tenant would be liable, unless, with knowledge or means of knowledge, he were to allow the danger to continue.[90]

Where the landlord is under a duty to repair and injury to a third party has resulted from a breach of the duty, the tenant is also liable. In *Payne* v. *Rogers*,[91] Heath J. seemed to imply that in such circumstances the tenant cannot be liable, but in *St. Anne's Well Brewery Co.* v. *Roberts*, this view was correctly rejected by Lawrence L.J. " Any bargain," said the learned judge, " made by the person responsible to his neighbour or to the public that another person should perform that obligation may give rise to rights as between the two contracting parties, but does not, in my judgment, in any way affect any right of third parties, who are not parties or privy to such contract." [92] If this were not so, it would result in the continuation of the fallacy finally exposed in *Donoghue* v. *Stevenson* that if A is injured by B and the cause of the injury is the breach of a contractual obligation owed by C to B, A cannot sue B in tort. The tenant of course will be able to obtain an indemnity from his landlord.[93]

DAMAGE

If the nuisance is a public one, it has long been settled that the plaintiff must prove damage.[94] In the case of a private nuisance, however, although it is said that damage must be proved, the law will often presume it. In *Fay* v. *Prentice*[95] a cornice of the defendant's house

---

[89] [1940] 1 K.B. 229.

[90] [1940] 1 K.B. at p. 233. See (1940) 56 L.Q.R. 1; Friedmann (1940) 3 M.L.R. 305–309; (1943) 56 L.Q.R. 63, 68. See Salmond, *Torts*, 16th ed., p. 68, n. 62. *Wringe's* case and the *Sedleigh-Denfield* case are concerned with different types of nuisance, the former with nuisance arising from a failure to repair and the liability of landlord and tenant; the latter with nuisance created by a trespasser and the subsequent liability of the occupier: *per* Somervell L.J. in *Mint* v. *Good, supra*, at p. 387—they may raise different principles. *Hagen* v. *Goldfarb* [1961] 28 D.L.R. (2d) 746 (Nova Scotia S.C.) reviews the English decisions on the liability of landlord and tenant for negligence and nuisance.

[91] (1794) 2 H.Bl. 350.

[92] (1929) 140 L.T. 1, 8. The case was not one of landlord and tenant, but the C.A. in *Wringe* v. *Cohen* [1940] 1 K.B. 229, 245–246 apparently regarded the absence of knowledge on the part of the occupier as irrelevant in the *St. Anne's* case. But this was one more of the *obiter dicta* with which *Wringe's* case is replete, and it is contrary to the decision in the *St. Anne's* case.

[93] See Stallybrass in (1929) 45 L.Q.R. 118–121.

[94] Comyns, *Digest*, 5th ed. (1822), Action upon the Case for Nuisance (C.), and authorities there cited.

[95] (1845) 1 C.B. 828.

projected over the plaintiff's garden so that rain-water dripped from it on the garden, and it was held that the law would infer injury to the plaintiff without proof of it. This inference appears to apply to any nuisance where the damage is so likely to occur that it would be superfluous to demand evidence that it has occurred. The inference cannot be made if the discomfort is purely personal, for personal sensitivity to smells, smoke and the like varies considerably and it is only fair that evidence of substantial annoyance should be required.

Again, no present damage need be proved where the nuisance is to an easement or *profit à prendre*, at any rate where the claim is for damages as distinct from a mandatory injunction.[96] As a series of such acts or the continuation of one particular act is evidence of acquiescence by the plaintiff in the annoyance, if no remedy were available in these circumstances for merely presumed damage the plaintiff would be barred by prescription after 20 years from suing at all.[97] If damage were not presumed, it might be difficult to establish that any one act had caused it. In these cases, however, although no present damage need be proved, probability that substantial damage will ensue must be shown; otherwise the law would be redressing merely fanciful claims.[98] In *Nicholls* v. *Ely Beet Sugar Factory Ltd.*,[99] large quantities of refuse and effluent were alleged to have been discharged from the defendants' beet sugar factory into the river in which the plaintiff owned two several and exclusive fisheries. The Court of Appeal held that there was no need for him to prove pecuniary loss, the injury being one actionable *per se*, although he lost his action on the ground that he had failed to show that the defendant had caused the injury.[1]

DEFENCES

1. Coming to nuisance no defence

It is usually said that it is no defence to prove that the plaintiff came to the nuisance or that the place is a convenient one for committing it.

---

[96] There substantial damage must be proved, at any rate in infringement of light: *Colls* v. *Home and Colonial Stores* [1904] A.C. 179. The decision might, however, be interpreted rather as defining the limits of the right of light than as laying down any rule with respect to the necessity of proving damage. It is arguable that what the H.L. actually decided was that the right exists only with respect to a particular amount of light.

[97] *Cf.* Kelly C.B. in *Harrop* v. *Hirst* (1868) L.R. 4 Ex. 43, 45, 46–47; Lord Wright M.R. in *Nicholls* v. *Ely Beet Sugar Factory Ltd.* [1936] Ch. 343, 349–350. Both these cases were applied in *Marriage* v. *East Norfolk Rivers Catchment Board* [1949] 2 K.B. 456, with respect to the date upon which the cause of action arose, but no opinion was expressed on this point on appeal: [1950] 1 K.B. 284.

[98] *Kensit* v. *G.E. Ry.* (1884) 27 Ch.D. 122.

[99] [1936] Ch. 343. *Cf.* (1936) 52 L.Q.R. 463–465. In *Pride of Derby and Derby Angling Association Ltd.* v. *British Celanese Ltd.* [1953] Ch. 149, the C.A. reviews the authorities on nuisance to fisheries by discharge of sewage, statutory defences, the alleged distinction between nonfeasance and misfeasance of the local authority, and the remedy of injunction.

[1] Lord Wright M.R., at p. 349, adopted Sir Frederick Pollock's view (*Torts*, 15th ed., p. 283): " Disturbance of easements and the like, as completely existing rights of use and enjoyment, is a wrong in the nature of trespass, and remediable by action without any allegation or proof of specific damage; the action was on the case under the old forms of

What this means is that if the annoyance is unreasonable in that particular district, then the plaintiff can recover even if it has been going on long before he came there. In *Bliss* v. *Hall*[2] the defendant had set up a tallow-chandlery which emitted " divers noisome, noxious, and offensive vapours, fumes, smells and stenches " to the discomfort of the plaintiff, who had taken a house near it. It was held to be no defence that the business had been in existence for three years before the plaintiff's arrival, for he " came to the house . . . with all the rights which the common law affords, and one of them is a right to wholesome air." [3]

If, however, a man chooses to make his home in the heart of a coal-field or in a manufacturing district, he can expect no more freedom from the discomfort usually associated with such a place than any other resident. The oft-cited dictum that " What would be a nuisance in Belgrave Square would not necessarily be so in Bermondsey " [4] puts the matter concisely and needs only the addition that Belgrave Square may in course of time fall to the level of Bermondsey.[5] This test of the local standard does not apply to nuisance causing material damage to property.[6] It is confined to nuisance causing personal discomfort and even within this limit, it has much less to do with nuisances caused by the obstruction of ancient lights than those caused by noises and smells.[7]

2. Usefulness not in itself a defence

The mere fact that a process or business is useful to persons generally, in spite of its annoyance to the plaintiff, is no defence. One who keeps a pigsty, a tannery, a limekiln or an iron-foundry is pursuing a laudable occupation and possibly one of great benefit to the public, yet that by itself will not excuse him. In *Adams* v. *Ursell*[8] a fried-fish shop was held to be a nuisance in the residential part of a street where it was carried on. It was urged unsuccessfully that an injunction would cause great hardship to the defendant and to the poor people who were his customers. The defendant could engage in his business in an area where it would not constitute a nuisance and indeed the injunction granted did not extend to the whole street.

3. No defence that it is due to many

It is no defence that the nuisance was created by independent acts of different persons, although the act of any one of them was not *per se*

---

pleading, since trespass was technically impossible, though the act of disturbance might include a distinct trespass of some kind, for which trespass would lie at the plaintiff's option." [2] (1838) 4 Bing.N.C. 183.
   [3] Tindal C.J., *ibid.*, 186. So, too, *Elliotson* v. *Feetham* (1835) 2 Bing.N.C. 134.
   [4] *Sturges* v. *Bridgman* (1879) 11 Ch.D. 852, 865.
   [5] As to the effect of a contract not to sue for annoyance see *Andreae* v. *Selfridge &* *Co. Ltd.* [1936] 2 All E.R. 1413 (this point was not raised on appeal: [1938] Ch. 1).
   [6] *St. Helens Smelting Co.* v. *Tipping* (1865) 11 H.L.C. 642: see p. 326, *ante.*
   [7] *Fishenden* v. *Higgs and Hill* (1935) 153 L.T. 128, 140, *per* Romer L.J.
   [8] [1913] 1 Ch. 269: see also p. 327, *ante.*

unlawful; *e.g.* where 100 people independently leave 100 wheelbarrows in a place and the obstruction consists in the accumulation of these vehicles and not in the presence of any one of them.[9] To hold otherwise would be to compel the plaintiff to prove the precise degree of annoyance caused by each wrongdoer—a task which would often be impossible.

4. Twenty years' prescription a defence

Twenty years' continuance will, by prescription, legalise a private nuisance but not a public one.[10] The period will not commence to run until the nuisance is known by the plaintiff to exist. The secret discharge of pollution upon his premises cannot be a root of prejudice to his rights until he knows of, or suspects, it.[11] This qualification is of especial importance where the nuisance has been in existence before the plaintiff came to it. In *Sturges* v. *Bridgman*[12] a confectioner had for more than 20 years used large pestles and mortars in the back of his premises which abutted on the garden of a physician, and the noise and vibration were not felt to be a nuisance during that period. In other words there had been no actionable interference with the physician's enjoyment of his own property. Then, however, the physician built a consulting room at the end of his garden and, for the first time, found that the noise and vibration materially interfered with the pursuit of his practice. He was granted an injunction against the confectioner, whose claim to a prescriptive right failed because the interference had not been an actionable nuisance during the whole preceding period of 20 years.

5. Jus tertii

As we shall see in an action in conversion,[13] it is no defence for a person who has interfered with goods in the possession of the plaintiff to plead *jus tertii, i.e.* that some third party has a better title to the goods than the plaintiff. This rule has been extended to an action for a nuisance created by the pollution of a privately owned fishery. In

---

[9] *Thorpe* v. *Brumfitt* (1873) L.R. 8 Ch. 650, 656; *Lambton* v. *Mellish* [1894] 3 Ch. 163.
[10] For difficulties with respect to this rule, see Clerk and Lindsell, *Torts*, 13th ed., pp. 833–834. The right to commit a private nuisance may be acquired by prescription as an easement in cases where such right is capable of being an easement, *e.g.* a right to discharge rain-water from your eaves onto your neighbour's land. To acquire a right by prescription there must be certainty and uniformity " for the measurement and determination of the user by which the extent of the prescriptive right is acquired ": *per* Eve J. in *Hulley* v. *Silversprings Bleaching Co.* [1922] 2 Ch. 268, 281. There are dicta that a right may be acquired by prescription to annoy your neighbour by smoke, smells and noise, although the quantity of the inconvenience is constantly changing. There is no reported case when such a right has arisen by prescription: *Waterfield* v. *Goodwin* (1957) 105 L.J. 332; *Khyatt* v. *Morgan* [1961] N.Z.L.R. 1020, 1024.
[11] *Liverpool Corporation* v. *Coghill & Son Ltd.* [1918] 1 Ch. 307.
[12] (1879) 11 Ch.D. 852, 863: " Acts which are neither preventable nor actionable cannot be relied on to found an easement "; *Whycer* v. *Urry* [1955] C.L.Y. 1939, C.A. (ophthalmic optician's work of too delicate a character in a business area to be protected by the law of nuisance).
[13] *Post* at p. 424.

Nicholls v. *Ely Beet Sugar Factory*,[14] Farwell J. held that the defendant to such an action cannot plead *jus tertii*, but the learned judge left it open whether this applied to nuisance in general.

It is not obvious why the principle should have been stretched to nuisance of any kind, whether to a fishery or otherwise. To commit a nuisance to another person's property does not necessarily constitute a reflection on his title to it, which is the essence of conversion. In any case a person who wishes to bring an action in nuisance need have no more than possession of the property; in fact, he cannot sue unless he has possession. If that be the law, it would seem that *jus tertii* cannot afford a defence to an action in nuisance.[15]

6. Conduct permitted by statute

Conduct that otherwise would be a nuisance may be permitted by a statute [16]; but, in exercising the power conferred by the statute, reasonable care must be taken to prevent the occurrence of something so inconsistent with the extent of the power given by the statute that it is a nuisance.

7. Other defences

Other valid defences are: consent of the plaintiff, provided there is no negligence on the part of the defendant [17]; the act of a stranger, provided the occupier has no knowledge of it and is not negligent in not knowing of it [18]; the secret unobservable process of nature or an act of God [18]; contributory negligence subject to the provisions of the Law Reform (Contributory Negligence) Act 1945,[19] and in those cases

---

[14] [1931] 2 Ch. 84.

[15] In *Newcastle-under-Lyme Corporation* v. *Wolstanton Ltd.* [1947] Ch. 92, 109–110, Evershed J. expressed agreement with the above paragraph, and the Court of Appeal's reversal of part of his decision was on grounds not affecting this dictum; [1947] Ch. 427, 467–468. In *Nicholls'* case (*supra*) Farwell J. agreed with, and considered himself bound by, *Fitzgerald* v. *Firbank* [1897] 2 Ch. 96, a decision of Kekewich J. affirmed by the C.A. Farwell J., however, admitted that the point about *jus tertii* was not raised in the C.A., but he assumed that it must have been present to that court. It is respectfully urged that Kekewich J.'s judgment (at p. 97) proceeded on the correct ground that *jus tertii* is irrelevant in an action for nuisance because the very nature of the tort makes it so; that in the C.A. counsel did not raise the point again; and that this was why no reference was made to it in the judgment of the C.A. *Cf.* Scott L.J. in *Paine & Co. Ltd.* v. *St. Neots Gas Co.* [1939] 3 All E.R. 812, 816–817.

[16] *e.g.* Land Drainage Act 1930 (20 & 21 Geo. 5, c. 44). See *Marriage* v. *East Norfolk Rivers Catchment Board* [1950] 1 K.B. 284, C.A. For legalisation of nuisance by aircraft, see S.I. 1954 Nos. 751–753, 777. Pipe-lines Act 1962 (10 & 11 Eliz. 2, c. 58), s. 69 (no exoneration from liability for nuisance). *Dunne* v. *North Western Gas Board* [1964] 2 Q.B. 806, C.A. (reviews the authorities). See Clerk and Lindsell, *Torts*, 13th ed., pp. 834 *et seq.*, and *post* at pp. 374–376. For an excellent analysis of legislative authority in these cases, see Fleming, *Torts*, 4th ed., pp. 365–367.

[17] *Kiddle* v. *City Business Properties Ltd.* [1942] 1 K.B. 269. *Post* at p. 370.

[18] *Sedleigh-Denfield* v. *O'Callaghan* [1940] A.C. 880, 897; *Cushing* v. *Peter Walker & Son Ltd.* [1941] 2 All E.R. 693 (enemy bombing loosened slate on defendants' premises; reasonable inspection did not disclose this. Slate fell and injured plaintiff—held enemy action equivalent to act of a trespasser). *Cf. Wringe* v. *Cohen* [1940] 1 K.B. 229. Where, owing to want of repair, premises constitute a nuisance the owner or occupier is answerable whether he knew or ought to have known of the danger or not, but he is not responsible for some secret unobservable process of nature. See *post* at pp. 354–355.

[19] *Trevett* v. *Lee* [1955] 1 W.L.R. 113, 122.

where liability turns on negligence, inevitable accident would appear to be a defence.[20]

HIGHWAYS [21]

" Nuisance may be defined, with reference to highways, as any wrongful act or omission upon or near a highway, whereby the public are prevented from freely, safely, and conveniently passing along the highway." [22] In considering the general law of nuisance we have to some extent considered its application to highways. We must now discuss some of the applicable rules in greater detail and also certain other matters which have not yet been mentioned.

1. Which obstructions are actionable

Every obstacle on the highway does not constitute an actionable nuisance, for the highway would be scarcely usable if it were. The law requires of users of the highway a certain amount of " give and take " and each person is deemed to assume the normal risks of passage along the highway by way of inconvenience and even danger.[23] It is only when the defendant creates a risk which in the circumstances is unreasonable does it become actionable. For this reason, the repair of the water, gas and electric mains which run under the street, of the surface of the street itself, and the building and alteration of the houses bordering on it, all constitute lawful occasions, either under statutory powers or by the common law, for temporary interference with its free passage and its amenities.[24] And if shops and houses are to get any supplies, vehicles and persons must pause on the highway to deliver them. A temporary obstruction, provided it is reasonable in amount and duration, is permissible.[25] Whether it is so is a question of fact varying with the circumstances of each particular case. Nor is every

---

[20] See *Southport Corporation* v. *Esso Petroleum Co. Ltd.* [1956] A.C. 218, 226, *per* Devlin J., citing Blackburn J. in *Fletcher* v. *Rylands* (1866) L.R. 1 Ex. 265, 286 and Lord Blackburn in *River Wear Commissioners* v. *Adamson* (1877) 2 App.Cas. 743, 767.

[21] For a detailed account of the law, see Pratt and Mackenzie's *Law of Highway*, 21st ed., Chaps. 4–7; also Pearce and Meston, *op. cit.*, Chap. 6.

[22] *Jacobs* v. *L.C.C.* [1950] A.C. 361 at p. 375, *per* Lord Simonds: quoting Pratt and Mackenzie, *op. cit.*, 20th ed. at p. 106.

[23] " Traffic on the highways, whether by land or sea, cannot be conducted without exposing those whose persons or property are near to it to some inevitable risk, and . . . those who go on the highway or have their property adjacent to it, may well be held to do so subject to their taking on themselves the risk of injury from that inevitable danger." *Fletcher* v. *Rylands* (1866) L.R. 1 Ex. 265 at p. 286, *per* Blackburn J. See also the comments of the same judge in *River Wear Commissioners* v. *Adamson* (1877) 2 App.Cas. 743 at p. 767.

[24] Pratt and Mackenzie, *op. cit.*, Part I, Chaps. 7 and 8.

[25] *Harper* v. *Haden & Sons Ltd.* [1933] Ch. 298, 304; *Amalgamated Theatres* v. *Charles S. Luney* [1962] N.Z.L.R. 226, S.C. (permit granted under a by-law by a local authority to a contractor to execute works on a highway which obstruct public right of passage may exempt him from criminal liability but not from civil liability to persons aggrieved by the nuisance); *Almeroth* v. *W. E. Chivers & Sons Ltd.* [1984] 1 All E. R. 53 (pedestrian on highway is not obliged to keep his eyes on the ground to see whether there is any obstruction there). See Goodhart in (1937) 6 C.L.J. 161–174 (Public Meetings and Processions). As to " pickets " see *Hubbard* v. *Pitt* [1975] 2 W.L.R. 254 (on appeal, *The Times*, May 14, 1975).

permanent obstruction a nuisance.[26] These propositions are elementary but they need stating because it has been argued on the one hand that the highway can never be obstructed and on the other hand that obstruction can never give rise to an action for nuisance.[27]

In a number of cases the courts have been faced with problems arising from the parking or stopping of vehicles on the highway. If the vehicle is left [28] in such a position that it is a foreseeable source of danger to other road users then there is clearly liability in nuisance and the defendant's conduct would anyway amount to negligence.[29] It has been said, however, that, quite apart from foreseeability of danger, the defendant will be liable in nuisance if he so leaves his vehicle as to constitute an obstruction of the highway even though it does not constitute a risk to other road users.[30] Whether or not this view represents the law, it may be doubted whether the distinction drawn between nuisance and negligence in relation to a stationary vehicle on the highway has any justification in the modern law. As Professor Newark has pointed out,[31] such cases are more conveniently dealt with in negligence.[32] It is only because the factual situation became common before the development of the law of negligence that it was incorporated into public nuisance. With the emergence of negligence, it became for the most part irrelevant which cause of action was adopted by the plaintiff, as the burden of proof on him is the same. This duplication of action has given rise to confusion [33] and was justifiably criticised by Adams J. in the New Zealand case of *Everitt* v. *Martin*.[34] " It is well established," explained the learned judge, " that a duty rests on all users of the highway to exercise due care for the safety of other users; and, in regard to

---

[26] *Att.-Gen.* v. *Wilcox* [1938] Ch. 934.

[27] *Fritz* v. *Hobson* (1880) 14 Ch.D. 542, 552.

[28] It is important to distinguish between the man who deliberately parks his vehicle and the man who stops temporarily, *e.g.* to deal with an emergency: *Dymond* v. *Pearce* [1972] 1 Q.B. 496, 504, *per* Edmund Davies L.J. Thus if the driver, on finding his lights are out, stops the vehicle, this is not of itself a nuisance, though it may be so if he leaves it on the highway for an unreasonable time or without giving warning of its presence there or if the vehicle became unlit because of some fault on his part: *Maitland* v. *Raisbeck* [1944] K.B. 689, explaining and distinguishing *Ware* v. *Garston Haulage Co. Ltd.* [1944] K.B. 30 (for criticism, see Laskin (1944) 22 Can. Bar Rev. 468–471; (1945) 23 Can. Bar Rev. 265); *Parish* v. *Judd* [1960] 1 W.L.R. 867.

[29] This is not to say that it makes no difference that the liability is founded on nuisance, for, a " nuisance situation " being shown, it is up to the defendant to prove a sufficient justification or excuse: see p. 323, *ante*. It has been held that the statutory obligations in relation to the lighting of vehicles do not give rise to civil liability: *Clarke* v. *Brims* [1947] K.B. 497.

[30] *Dymond* v. *Pearce* [1972] 1 Q.B. 496. But see the contrary view of Edmund Davies L.J. at pp. 503 *et seq.*; *cf. Wickstead* v. *Murphy* [1975] 1 C.L. 257.

[31] " The Boundaries of Nuisance " (1949) 65 L.Q.R. 480 at p. 485. See also Pritchard, " Trespass, Case, and the Rule in *Williams* v. *Holland* " [1964] C.L.J. 234 at p. 237, note 24.

[32] In fact, many cases involving a dangerous obstruction of the highway are not pleaded in nuisance at all: *e.g. Tart* v. *G. W. Chitty & Co. Ltd.* [1933] 2 K.B. 453; *Baker* v. *E. Longhurst & Sons Ltd.* [1933] 2 K.B. 461 (though horse and cart were moving); *Tidy* v. *Battman* [1934] 1 K.B. 319; *Henley* v. *Cameron* (1949) 118 L.J.K.B. 989; *Hill-Venning* v. *Beszant* [1950] 2 All E.R. 1151; *Moore* v. *Maxwells of Emsworth Ltd.* [1968] 1 W.L.R. 1077.

[33] See materials in note 28.

[34] [1952] N.Z.L.R. 298.

highway accidents arising out of the user of the highway and giving rise to claims for injury to persons or to chattels, the law of negligence is sufficient, and any liability, which can be legitimately founded on nuisance, can be equally well, and I think more conveniently, based on negligence. The breach, by act or omission, of the duty to exercise due care is indeed the foundation of the liability." [35]

2. Special damage

We have seen that a person can only sue in public nuisance if he has suffered damage over and above that suffered by the rest of the public.[36] On occasions the application of this principle has proved complicated.

Loss of custom

In particular there is some conflict of judicial opinion as to whether a tradesman who has lost custom as a result of an unlawful obstruction can sue in respect of it. In *Wilkes* v. *Hungerford Market Co.*[37] it was held that he could but this was regarded as incorrect in *Ricket* v. *Metropolitan Ry.*[38] on the ground that loss of custom was too remote as it did not involve any interference with the use of the highway by the plaintiff. In other cases, however, it was held an obstruction which interfered with an easement of light was actionable and such damage appears just as direct or indirect as loss of custom. It is submitted that there is no reason in principle why a plaintiff who can prove loss of actual or even potential custom should not be allowed to recover damages in respect of it and this is supported by the balance of judicial opinion in more recent times.[39] In *Fritz* v. *Hobson*,[40] an unreasonable obstruction of a private way leading from the highway to the house and shop of an antique dealer was held to be actionable because it resulted in loss of custom to him.[41]

Somewhat akin to obstruction of this kind is the monopoly of a pavement by a theatre queue. A queue as such is perhaps not unlawful even if its occupation of the pavement makes foot-passengers deviate or access to shops difficult. It is only when it is unreasonable that the proprietors of the theatre which causes it are liable for nuisance;

---

[35] *Ibid.* at p. 300. Similarly C. A. Wright, "The Law of Torts: 1923–47" (1948) 26 Can. Bar Rev. 46 at p. 78.

[36] *Ante*, at pp. 316–318.

[37] (1835) 2 Bing.N.C. 281.

[38] (1865) 5 B. & S. 156 at pp. 160–162, *per* Erle C.J.; L.R. 2 H.L. 175 at p. 188, *per* Lord Chelmsford L.C., and at p. 199, *per* Lord Cranworth. This case was considered as having overruled the *Wilkes* case by Willes J. in *Beckett* v. *Metropolitan Ry.* (1867) L.R. 3 C.P. 82 at p. 100 and by Montague Smith J. in *Eagle* v. *Charing Cross Ry.* (1867) L.R. 2 C.P. 638 at p. 650.

[39] *Blundy, Clark & Co.* v. *L. & N.E. Ry.* [1931] 2 K.B. 334 at p. 352, *per* Greer L.J., and at p. 362, *per* Scrutton L.J.; *contra* Slesser L.J. at p. 372; *Harper* v. *Haden & Sons Ltd.* [1933] Ch. 298 at pp. 306–307, *per* Lord Hanworth M.R.; Lawrence L.J. preferred (at p. 315) to express no opinion; *Hubbard* v. *Pitt* [1975] 2 W.L.R. 254 (on appeal *The Times*, May 14, 1975).

[40] (1880) 14 Ch.D. 542.

[41] *Cf. Vanderpant* v. *Mayfair Hotel Co. Ltd.* [1930] 1 Ch. 138.

e.g. where the queue was at times five deep, extended far beyond the theatre itself and remained there for very considerable portions of time, it was held to be a nuisance to the plaintiffs, whose premises were adjacent to the theatre.[42] The defendant is not liable if, although the queue was one of prospective customers at his shop, he was not responsible for it because other circumstances (*e.g.* shortage of supplies in consequence of war) were the primary cause of it; nor will he be liable unless the plaintiff can prove damage.[43] But the defendant is liable if the obstruction by means of the queue is due to an unusual method of conducting business; *e.g.* by the sale of ice-cream from a window of the shop instead of inside the shop.[44]

Access to highway

The right of the owner of property adjoining a highway to have access to the highway is totally different from the right of passage along the highway.[45] The former is a private right of property and any obstruction of it is actionable,[46] whereas the latter is a public right, and no action will lie for an obstruction unless special or particular damage can be proved.[47] The private right of access is subject to the public right of passage, which is the higher right,[48] but the right of passage of the public is also subject to the private right of access to the highway and is liable to be temporarily interrupted by the adjoining owner.[49] The conflict of these two rights is resolved on the ordinary principle that a reasonable exercise of both must be allowed.[49] Interference with a private right of access may also be an interference with the public right of passage.[50]

3. Projections

These deserve special mention because the law is to some extent unsettled. It is clear that the mere fact that something (*e.g.* a tree, a

---

[42] *Lyons, Sons & Co.* v. *Gulliver* [1914] 1 Ch. 631; *diss.* Phillimore L.J. The C.A. approved *Barber* v. *Penley* [1893] 2 Ch. 447, where North J. examined the authorities in detail.

[43] *Dwyer* v. *Mansfield* [1946] K.B. 437.

[44] *Fabri* v. *Morris* [1947] 1 All E.R. 315.

[45] *Rose* v. *Groves* (1843) 5 Man. & G. 613; *Att.-Gen.* v. *Thames Conservators* (1862) 1 H. & M. 1, 31–33, *per* Page-Wood V.-C. (access to navigable river).

[46] *Walsh* v. *Ervin* [1952] V.L.R. 361 (anything sufficiently substantial to constitute an interference with his right of access enables the recovery, at least, of nominal damages); *Chaplin* v. *Mayor of Westminster* [1901] 2 Ch. 329 (transference of goods from highway across pavement to his premises is a right enjoyed by him as one of the public entitled to use the highway).

[47] *Boyce* v. *Paddington B.C.* [1903] 1 Ch. 109, 114, *per* Buckley J.

[48] *Vanderpant* v. *Mayfair Hotel Co.* [1930] 1 Ch. 138, 152–154, *per* Luxmoore J.

[49] *Marshall* v. *Blackpool Corporation* [1935] A.C. 16, 22, *per* Lord Atkin; *Farrell* v. *John Mowlem & Co. Ltd.* [1954] 1 Lloyd's Rep. 437, 439, 440, *per* Devlin J.; *Trevett* v. *Lee* [1955] 1 W.L.R. 113. For statutory encroachments on the right of access, see Cork [1952] J.P.L. 553–556.

[50] *Rose* v. *Groves* (1843) 5 Man. & G. 613, 620 (obstruction of access to public-house). " A private right of way is set up on the part of the plaintiff, he is not complaining of any public injury, but even if he were he discloses a sufficient cause of action ": *per* Tindal C.J.; *Fritz* v. *Hobson* (1880) 14 Ch.D. 542 (damages for interference with private right in respect of loss of custom, and also on the ground of particular injury from public nuisance).

clock, a sign, an awning or a corbel) projects over the highway from land or a building adjacent to it does not *per se* constitute an actionable nuisance. This must be so, for no conceivable damage is done to anyone and there is scarcely a garden or a building on the edge of the highway which would not have to be altered if the law were otherwise.[51] The rule is different where the projection is over private property because the rights of the proprietor of it are much wider than the limited right of the user of a highway.[52] If damage is done owing to the collapse of the projection on the highway or by some other mischief traceable to it, the occupier of the premises on which it stood is liable if he knew of the defect or ought, on investigation, to have known of it. At any rate that is the rule with respect to a thing that is naturally on the premises, *e.g.* a tree. In *Noble* v. *Harrison* [53] a branch of a beech tree growing on X's land overhung the highway and in fine weather suddenly broke and fell upon Y's vehicle passing along the highway. Neither X nor his servants knew that the branch was dangerous and the fracture was due to a latent defect undiscoverable by any reasonably careful inspection, and for this reason Y's action against X in nuisance failed.[54] In *Caminer* v. *Northern and London Investment Trust Ltd.*[55] the defendants in an action for (a) negligence or (b) nuisance were held not liable for either. They were lessees of land from which a tree fell onto a car driven by C, the plaintiff, on the highway. The fall of the tree was due to a disease of its roots of which there was no indication above ground. Evidence was also given that, if the tree had been trimmed or topped, it was unlikely that it would have fallen, but it did not appear to be dangerous to any of the witnesses called. On these facts, it was held by the House of Lords that the plaintiff had failed to prove that the defendants, as ordinary careful laymen (*i.e.* not experts), knew, or ought to have known, that the tree was dangerous, and therefore they were not liable.

With respect to artificial things (*e.g.* a lamp) which project and do damage there is a conflict of judicial opinion as to the precise nature of the liability for it. According to one view the duty is no greater than that with respect to natural projections,[56] whilst according to another

---

[51] *Noble* v. *Harrison* [1926] 2 K.B. 332, 337.

[52] *Ibid.* 340; and *Lemmon* v. *Webb* [1895] A.C. 1.

[53] [1926] 2 K.B. 332: applied in *Cunliffe* v. *Bankes* [1945] 1 All E.R. 459. See *Shirvell* v. *Hackwood Estates Co. Ltd.* [1938] 2 K.B. 577 and *Cunliffe* v. *Bankes* for remarks on care in looking after trees; *Brown* v. *Harrison* (1947) 177 L.T. 281 (owner of tree in obvious state of decay held liable); *Quinn* v. *Scott* [1965] 1 W.L.R. 1004 (National Trust held liable in negligence in failing to fell a dangerous tree near a highway as they had means of knowing it was diseased); *British Road Services* v. *Slater* [1964] 1 W.L.R. 498 (liability of occupier of land for failing to remedy a nuisance which he inherited—projecting branch of tree in the verge of a highway—does not arise, although source of the nuisance is plain to be seen, until occupier becomes aware of its being a nuisance, or with ordinary care should have become aware of it).

[54] A claim under the rule in *Rylands* v. *Fletcher* also failed: *post*, pp. 368–369.

[55] [1951] A.C. 88. Note Lord Radcliffe's *caveat* at 110–112.

[56] Blackburn J. in *Tarry* v. *Ashton* (1876) 1 Q.B.D. 314, 319; Wright J. in *Noble* v. *Harrison* [1926] 2 K.B. 332, 343–344. Both opinions were *obiter*.

view it is a strict one analogous to that formulated in *Rylands* v. *Fletcher* which would make the occupier of the premises liable even in the absence of negligence.[57] Until *Wringe* v. *Cohen*,[58] however, the balance of authorities supported the view that an occupier could only be liable for damage caused by non-repair if, with actual or constructive knowledge of the condition, he failed to remedy it.[59] As Vaughan Williams L.J. explained in *Barker* v. *Herbert*, " there can be no liability on the part of the possessor of land in such a case, unless it is shown either that he himself, or some person for whose action he is responsible, created that danger which constitutes a nuisance to the highway, or that he neglected for an undue time after he became, or, if he had used reasonable care, ought to have become, aware of it, to abate or prevent the danger or nuisance." [60] The occupier therefore could not be liable if he was justifiably unaware of the condition. In *Wringe* v. *Cohen*,[58] however, the Court of Appeal chose to rationalise the previous authorities and to formulate a rule of strict liability which was not warranted by them. " If, owing to want of repair, premises on a highway become dangerous and, therefore, a nuisance and a passer-by or an adjoining owner suffers damage by their collapse, the occupier, or owner if he has undertaken the duty of repair, is answerable whether he knew or ought to have known of the danger or not." [61] The unforeseeable act of a trespasser is a good defence and the Court of Appeal also held that the defendant would escape liability should the damage result from " a secret and unobservable operation of nature, such as subsidence under or near the foundations of the premises." [61]

As Professor Friedmann has pointed out, these exceptions seem to deprive the rule itself of much of its significance. " It can hardly be imagined that any damage caused neither by the act of a third person nor by a latent defect could be due to anything but knowledge or negligence of the occupier." [62] In subsequent cases the rule in *Wringe* v. *Cohen* has been interpreted restrictively. It might have been thought that an occupier whose tree projects over the highway would be in the same position as a defendant whose lamp overhangs the highway, although in the former case it would be easier for the defend-

---

[57] Lush and Quain JJ. in *Tarry's* case (*supra*) at p. 320; Rowlatt J., *obiter*, in *Noble's* case (*supra*) at p. 338.

[58] [1940] 1 K.B. 229; *ante* at p. 343.

[59] *Barker* v. *Herbert* [1911] 2 K.B. 633 at p. 636, *per* Vaughan Williams L.J., at p. 643, *per* Fletcher Moulton L.J. See the comments of Branson J. in *Ilford U.D.C.* v. *Beal and Judd* [1925] 1 K.B. 671 at p. 675 and contrast *Silverton* v. *Marriott* (1888) 59 L.T. 61 (defendant liable because failed to guard against danger of which aware); *St. Anne's Well Brewery Co.* v. *Roberts* (1929) 140 L.T. 1 (no difference between public and private nuisance); *Wilchick* v. *Marks* [1934] 2 K.B. 56 at pp. 67–68, *per* Goddard J.; *Palmer* v. *Bateman* [1908] 2 Ir.Rep. 393.

[60] [1911] 2 K.B. 633 at pp. 636–637.

[61] [1940] 1 K.B. 229 at p. 233.

[62] " Nuisance, Negligence and the Overlapping of Torts " (1940) 3 M.L.R. 305 at p. 309. See also *Sedleigh-Denfield* v. *O'Callaghan* [1940] A.C. 880 and Friedmann, " Incidence of Liability in Nuisance " (1943) 59 L.Q.R. 63.

ant to argue that the injury was caused by a latent defect.[63] In *British Road Services* v. *Slater*,[64] however, Lord Parker C.J. refused to hold a non-negligent occupier liable for damage caused by an overhanging branch. In other cases attempts have been made to distinguish between inactivity *causing* the nuisance and the mere continuance of an inherited nuisance.[65]

In effect, there is now little substantive difference between the rule in *Wringe* v. *Cohen* and ordinary fault liability. It may be, however, that under the rule an occupier may be liable for his non-negligent failure to appreciate the implications of a patent nuisance. The defendant is liable under the rule in *Wringe* v. *Cohen* because he or someone for whom he is responsible has been at fault. As Denning L.J. remarked in *Mint* v. *Good*,[66] " he is liable when structures fall into dangerous disrepair, because there must be some fault on the part of someone or other for that to happen." [67] It would seem, however, that the burden of proof on the plaintiff has been lessened. He need only show that the defendant had control over the defective premises, and that the injury resulted from their dangerous condition. This gives rise to a presumption that the defendant has failed in his duty to inspect and repair which can only be rebutted by proof that the accident was inevitable, *i.e.* it was not, nor could have been, avoided by reasonable inspection.[68]

4. The condition of the highway [69]

At common law a highway authority could not be liable for injury suffered by a user of the highway and resulting from the authority's failure to discharge its duty to keep the highway in repair. This immunity did not extend to misfeasance on the highway nor to acts of repair improperly performed. The distinction between misfeasance and non-feasance and the rule of immunity were criticised and eventu-

---

[63] This argument was accepted in the Irish case of *Lynch* v. *Dawson* [1946] Ir.Rep. 504 (plaintiff's lorry with high load ran in unusual circumstances into bough projecting from defendant's land. Defendant was liable even though he was justifiably unaware of the risk of an accident).

[64] [1964] 1 W.L.R. 498. Lord Parker refused to follow *Lynch* v. *Dawson, supra*, on the ground that *Sedleigh-Denfield* v. *O'Callaghan, supra*, had not been cited to the Irish Court, and said: " the present tendency of the law is not only to move further and further away from absolute liability but also more and more to assimilate nuisance and negligence " (at p. 504).

[65] *Cushing* v. *Peter Walker & Son Ltd.* [1941] 2 All E.R. 693 at p. 699, *per* Hallett J.; *Mint* v. *Good* [1951] 1 K.B. 517 at p. 524, *per* Somervell L.J. It is suggested that this is not a valid distinction. The failure of the occupier to discover and remedy an inherited nuisance is equally the cause of the damage. It results just as much from the occupier's breach of his duty to inspect and repair as does, *e.g.* the negligent failure to discover a defective gable-end.

[66] [1951] 1 K.B. 517.

[67] *Ibid.* at p. 526, *per* Denning L.J.

[68] *Mint* v. *Good* at p. 525, *per* Denning L.J.; *Spicer* v. *Smee* [1946] 1 All E.R. 489 at p. 494, *per* Atkinson J. The occupier is of course liable for the default of his independent contractor: *ante*, at pp. 336–337.

[69] See Pratt and Mackenzie, *op. cit.*, Chap. 4; Clerk and Lindsell, *Torts*, 13th ed., pp. 830–832.

ally the latter was abrogated by section 1 of the Highways (Miscellaneous Provisions) Act 1961 [70] which came into force on August 3, 1964. In any action against a highway authority for damage resulting from its failure to maintain a highway maintainable at the public expense, it shall be a defence (without prejudice to any other defence such as voluntary acceptance of risk and contributory negligence) to prove that the authority had taken such care as in all the circumstances was reasonably required [71] to secure that part of the highway to which the action relates was not dangerous for traffic. For the purpose of such a defence the court shall in particular have regard to:

1. the character of the highway, and the traffic which was reasonably to be expected to use it;

2. the standard of maintenance appropriate for a highway of that character and used by such traffic;

3. the state of repair in which a reasonable person would have expected to find the highway;

4. whether the highway authority knew, or could reasonably have been expected to know, that the condition of the part of the highway to which the action relates was likely to cause danger to users of the highway;

5. where the highway authority could not reasonably have been expected to repair that part of the highway before the cause of action arose, what warning notice of its condition had been displayed.[72]

The Act applies whether the plaintiff is suing in nuisance, negligence or for breach of a statutory duty.

In *Griffiths* v. *Liverpool Corporation*,[73] the Court of Appeal considered the nature of the liability under the statute. The plaintiff fell over a ridge of a flagstone which projected half an inch above the adjoining flagstone. It was found as a fact that the flagstone was a potential danger, and the majority of the Court of Appeal held the defendant liable. Diplock and Salmon L.JJ. considered that, irrespective of negligence, the highway authority is under an absolute statutory duty of repair subject to a defence that it has taken reasonable care, the onus of which falls on the authority. Sellers L.J., however, took the view that the provisions of section 1 " make negligence the essential and ultimate basis of a claim against a highway authority." [74]

Before the onus falls on the highway authority, however, the plaintiff " must make out a case that the highway was not reasonably safe, that

---

[70] 9 & 10 Eliz. 2, c. 63.

[71] *Pridham* v. *Hemel Hempstead Corpn.* (1970) 69 L.G.R. 523.

[72] s. 1. For the purpose of such a defence it shall not be relevant to prove that the highway authority had arranged for a competent person to carry out or supervise the maintenance of the part of the highway to which the action relates unless it is also proved that the authority had given him proper instructions with regard to the maintenance of the highway and that he carried out the instructions. This confirms *Hardaker* v. *Idle District Council* [1896] 1 Q.B. 335 (statutory duty non-delegable). *Cf.* collateral negligence of independent contractor, *post*, pp. 540–541.

[73] [1967] 1 Q.B. 374. See [1967] C.L.J. 21; (1967) 83 L.Q.R. 4.

[74] [1967] 1 Q.B. 374 at p. 386.

is, was dangerous to traffic." [75] There is an inevitable risk in travelling along the highway of unevenness in the pavement, and a highway is not to be criticised by the standards of a bowling green.[76] In *Littler* v. *Liverpool Corporation*,[77] Cumming-Bruce J. stated that the criterion to be applied in assessing whether any particular length of pavement is dangerous is that of reasonable foreseeability of danger. " A length of pavement is only dangerous if, in the ordinary course of human affairs, danger may reasonably be anticipated from its common use by the public. . . . It is a mistake to isolate and emphasise a particular difference in levels between flagstones unless that difference is such that a reasonable person who noticed and considered it would regard it as presenting a real source of danger." [78] In relation to danger to vehicular traffic, it has been held that the highway authority must provide not merely for model drivers, but for the normal run of drivers to be found on the roads and that includes those who make the mistakes which experience and common sense teach are likely to occur.[79]

In *Scott* v. *Green & Sons*,[80] it was held that section 154 (5) of the Highways Act 1959,[81] which imposes on an owner or occupier the duty to keep every vault arch and cellar under a street in good repair, does not give rise *per se* to a cause of action for breach of statutory duty. The statute does however give to the occupier sufficient control of any grating or flagstone over his cellar to enable him to effect repairs. Because of this, " he must use reasonable care to see that it is safe; and if he fails in his duty, he is liable in nuisance or negligence as the case may be." [82]

---

[75] *Littler* v. *Liverpool Corporation* [1968] 2 All E.R. 343 at p. 344, *per* Cumming-Bruce J., following *Meggs* v. *Liverpool Corporation* [1968] 1 W.L.R. 689.
[76] *Littler* v. *Liverpool Corporation, supra*, at p. 345; *Ford* v. *Liverpool Corporation* (1972) 117 S.J. 167.
[77] [1968] 2 All E.R. 343.
[78] *Ibid.* at p. 345.
[79] *Rider* v. *Rider* [1973] 1 Q.B. 505.
[80] [1969] 1 W.L.R. 301.
[81] 7 & 8 Eliz. 2, c. 25.
[82] [1969] 1 W.L.R. 301 at p. 302, *per* Lord Denning M.R.

CHAPTER 16

STRICT LIABILITY: THE RULE IN RYLANDS v. FLETCHER

HAVING considered the tort of nuisance, we now turn to a further tort which had its origins in nuisance but which has developed in such a way that it is now quite distinct from it. This is the rule in *Rylands* v. *Fletcher*.

THE RULE IN RYLANDS v. FLETCHER [1]

The facts of this case were as follows. B, a millowner, employed independent contractors, who were apparently competent, to construct a reservoir on his land to provide water·for his mill. In the course of the work the contractors came upon some old shafts and passages on B's land. They communicated with the mines of A, a neighbour of B, although no one suspected this, for the shafts appeared to be filled with earth. The contractors did not block them up, and when the reservoir was filled the water from it burst through the old shafts and flooded A's mines. It was found as a fact that B had not been negligent, although the contractors had been. A sued B and the House of Lords held B liable.

The litigation originated in an unusual way. It began as an action upon the case (apparently for negligence) at Liverpool Assizes, and A secured a verdict, subject to the award of an arbitrator, who was afterwards empowered by a judge's order to state a special case instead of making an award. This he did, and so the case came before the Court of Exchequer which, by a majority, decided in favour of the defendant. The Court of Exchequer Chamber unanimously reversed this decision and held the defendant liable, and the House of Lords affirmed their decision. The judgment of the Exchequer Chamber was delivered by Blackburn J. and it has become a classical exposition of doctrine.[2] " *We think that the true rule of law is, that the person who for his own purposes brings on his lands and collects and keeps there anything likely to do mischief if it escapes, must keep it in at his peril, and, if he does not do so, is* prima facie *answerable for all the damage which is the natural consequence of its escape.*"

This may be regarded as the " rule in *Rylands* v. *Fletcher*," but what follows is equally important. " He can excuse himself by showing that

---

[1] (1865) 3 H. & C. 774 (Court of Exchequer); (1866) L.R. 1 Ex. 265 (Court of Exchequer Chamber); (1868) L.R. 3 H.L. 330 (House of Lords) (Weir, *Casebook on Tort*, 3rd ed., p. 362). See generally: Bohlen, *Studies in the Law of Torts* (1926), Chap. 7; Fridman, " The Rise and Fall of *Rylands* v. *Fletcher* " (1956) 34 Can.Bar Rev. 810–823; Erskine Blackburn, " The Rule in *Rylands* v. *Fletcher* " (1961) 4 Can.Bar J. 39–50. Law Commission Report No. 32, *Civil Liability for Dangerous Things and Activities* (1970).
[2] (1866) L.R. 1 Ex. 265, 279–280.

the escape was owing to the plaintiff's default; or perhaps that the escape was the consequence of *vis major*, or the act of God; but as nothing of this sort exists here, it is unnecessary to inquire what excuse would be sufficient. The general rule, as above stated, seems on principle just. The person whose grass or corn is eaten down by the escaping cattle of his neighbour, or whose mine is flooded by the water from his neighbour's reservoir, or whose cellar is invaded by the filth of his neighbour's privy, or whose habitation is made unhealthy by the fumes and noisome vapours of his neighbour's alkali works, is damnified without any fault of his own; and it seems but reasonable and just that the neighbour, who has brought something on his own property which was not naturally there, harmless to others so long as it is confined to his own property, but which he knows to be mischievous if it gets on his neighbour's, should be obliged to make good the damage which ensues if he does not succeed in confining it to his own property. But for his act in bringing it there no mischief could have accrued, and it seems but just that he should at his peril keep it there so that no mischief may accrue, or answer for the natural and anticipated consequences. And upon authority, this we think is established to be the law whether the things so brought be beasts, or water, or filth, or stenches."

In the House of Lords, Lord Cairns L.C. held the defendant liable because he had made " a non-natural use " of his land, and the noble and learned Lord regarded the judgment of Blackburn J. as reaching the same result and he entirely concurred in it,[3] although the learned judge merely stated that there would be liability if something was brought onto the land " which was not naturally there."

Genesis of the principle

Such were the facts and decision in the case. Although Lord Cairns regarded the principles applicable as extremely simple,[4] it seems clear that the common law was faced by a new and important problem which could not be solved by merely applying the existing authorities.

This was not the first time that water had been collected in bulk, but hitherto those who indulged in the practice had generally been powerful bodies, like water or railway companies, who had acted under powers given them by legislation which at the same time made them liable for harm done by its escape. But here there was no statutory authority, and although there were several paths that seemed to lead to a solution, none of them went the whole way. Trespass did not really fit the case

---

[3] L.R. 3 H.L. 330, 338–340; *Porter (J. P.) Co. Ltd.* v. *Bell* [1955] 1 D.L.R. 62, 66: " The true situation seems to be that there is not one rule of *Rylands* v. *Fletcher* but two; and that Lord Blackburn's version or Lord Cairns' more flexible one is invoked according to the circumstances of the case in hand," *per* MacDonald J. " The complexity between a natural and non-natural user of land that has resulted from the words Lord Cairns used, and between dangerous and non-dangerous things, makes the application of the rule uncertain in some cases of fire and explosion ": *Hargrave* v. *Goldman* [1963–64] 37 A.L.J.R. 277, 283, *per* Windeyer J.

[4] (1868) L.R. 3 H.L. 330, 338.

because the harm was consequential, not direct.[5] Negligence was out of the question, even though the contractors were found to have been at fault, because it could not be said on the particular facts of the case that the defendant ought to have foreseen that the plaintiff's property could be affected by his operations.[6] As a result it was not thought necessary by the courts to discuss whether in these circumstances a principal could be held liable for the default of his independent contractor. For the same reasons nuisance was not appropriate.

A strenuous effort was made by Bramwell B. in the court below [7] to stretch another principle to meet this case—the principle that, if X by excavation withdraws lateral support from the land of Y his neighbour and thereby damages it, he is liable whether he has been negligent or not.[8] But here again there was nothing to show that X would be responsible for the misdoings of an independent contractor; and this objection could equally be raised against Blackburn J.'s examples of liability for cattle-trespass, damage done by savage animals and the escape of filth.

Look at the decision of the Exchequer Chamber how we may, it laid down a new principle. True, in the judgment itself it might appear that the court was making a pontifical statement of existing principle rather than laying down a new rule, for they regarded their own proposition as having been anticipated by Holt C.J. some 160 years earlier in *Tenant* v. *Goldwin* (1703),[9] and they cited as instances of it the rules relating to cattle-trespass, the escape of mischievous animals and nuisance by the escape of fumes. But in fact Holt C.J.'s decision related to the escape of filth and his formulation of principle was limited to that and to cattle-trespass; it was not nearly so sweeping as the rule expressed in *Rylands* v. *Fletcher*, which was reached by methods extremely characteristic of judicial development of the law—the creation of new law behind a screen of analogies drawn from existing law. And whatever views the Exchequer Chamber may have had about their decision, succeeding generations have regarded it as the starting-point of a liability wider than any that preceded it.[10]

Scope of extension

It seems unsound, then, to dismiss the rule as a convenient summary of the thoery underlying several specific torts which had existed long before 1868, or even as the old cattle-trespass rule raised to a high

---

[5] (1865) 3 H. & C. 773, 792–793, *per* Martin B. But see the judgment of Bramwell B. at p. 790.

[6] See the facts set out in (1865) 3 H. & C. p. 737, 777–778.

[7] 3 H. & C. 774, 789–790.

[8] *Backhouse* v. *Bonomi* (1861) 9 H.L.C. 503.

[9] 2 Ld.Raym. 1089.

[10] *Cf.* Newark, "The Boundaries of Nuisance" (1949) 65 L.Q.R. 480, 488. "What was novel in *Rylands* v. *Fletcher*, or at least clearly decided for the first time, was that as between adjacent occupiers an isolated escape is actionable."

power.[11] The substantial advances which it made on the earlier law were two:

1. In the direction of *things* for the escape of which an occupier of land is subjected to strict liability.

2. In the direction of the *persons* for whose defaults in connection with such escape the occupier is vicariously responsible.

As to 1, the court took a rule of liability which had been more or less clearly perceived in connection with the escape of fire, cattle or unruly beasts, and extended it to the escape of mischievous things generally. As to 2, they held in effect that the occupier from whose land these things escaped and did damage is liable not only for the default of his servant, but also for that of an independent contractor [12] and (as later decisions show) for that of anyone except a stranger.[13]

"Absolute" liability a misnomer

It was unfortunate that Blackburn J. chose to describe liability under the rule as resting upon " an absolute duty to keep it [*sc.* the water] in at his peril." [14] Though stated as a rule of absolute liability, there " are so many exceptions to it that it is doubtful whether there is much of the rule left." [15] The liability may be strict, but it is not absolute as the exceptions to the rule indicated by Blackburn J. himself show. Recently, moreover, as we shall see, the courts have tended to erode and rationalise the rule so as to reduce the ambit of strict liability and to bring the rule more into line with the predominant modern philosophy of no liability without fault. As a result of this development the rule in *Rylands* v. *Fletcher* is sometimes unavailable at times when it is most needed, *i.e.* when the plaintiff cannot prove that the defendant was at fault.

SCOPE OF THE RULE

Like all broad formulations of principle, the rule in *Rylands* v. *Fletcher* had to be worked out in detail by later decisions, and it has been

---

[11] See Salmond, *Torts*, 16th ed., pp. 320–321. But it is difficult to agree with the statement as to the four historical grounds of the rule in *Rylands* v. *Fletcher*. In three of them (liability for trespass, fire and nuisance) it is too strong to say that absence of fault on the defendant's part was no defence. As to trespass and fire, see (1926) 42 L.Q.R. 44–51; as to nuisance, see Viner, Abr. Nusance (H), Vol. xvi, pp. 27 *et seq.*, where several cases are cited which show that defendant was not liable, because in effect he was " without fault." See, too, Rolle, Abr. Nusans, B 2 (p. 137). As to instances of liability without proof of negligence, Lord Simon said it was " logically unnecessary and historically incorrect to refer to all these instances as deduced from one common principle ": *Read* v. *Lyons* [1947] A.C. 156, 167.

[12] It is true that the Exch.Ch. said it was not necessary to decide whether defendants were liable for the default of independent contractors (L.R. 1 Ex. at p. 287), but it is certain that if the action had been for negligence or (at that date) for nuisance, they would not have been liable for the wrongdoing of such contractors. In other words, the Exch.Ch. were extending the law in this respect.

[13] (1931) 4 Camb.L.J. 192–193.

[14] L.R. 1 Ex. at p. 279.

[15] *St. Anne's Well Brewery* v. *Roberts* (1928) 140 L.T. 1, p. 6 (C.A.), *per* Scrutton L.J.

applied to a remarkable variety of things.[16] Fire,[17] gas,[18] explosions,[19] electricity,[20] oil,[21] noxious fumes,[22] colliery spoil,[23] rusty wire from a decayed fence,[24] vibrations,[25] poisonous vegetation,[26] a flag-pole,[27] a " chair-o-plane "[28] and even noxious persons.[29]

Escape necessary

But unless there is an " escape " of the substance from the occupier's land, there is no liability under the rule [30]; this was the ground of the House of Lords' decision in Read v. Lyons & Co. Ltd.,[31] where the plaintiff was employed by the Ministry of Supply as an inspector of munitions in the defendants' munitions factory and, in the course of her employment there, was injured by the explosion of a shell that was being manufactured. It was admitted that high explosive shells were dangerous. The defendants were held not liable. There was no allegation of negligence on their part and Rylands v. Fletcher was inapplicable because there had been no " escape " of the thing that inflicted the injury. " Escape " was defined as " escape from a place where the defendant has occupation or control over land to a place which is outside his occupation or control." [32] Viscount Simon stated that Rylands v. Fletcher is conditioned by two elements which he called (a) " the condition of ' escape ' from the land of something likely to do mischief if it escapes," and (b) " the condition of ' non-natural ' user

---

[16] Neatly catalogued by Stallybrass in " Dangerous Things and the Non-Natural User of Land " (1929) 3 Camb.L.J. 382–385.

[17] Post, pp. 382–385.

[18] Batcheller v. Tunbridge Wells Gas Co. (1901) 84 L.T. 765.

[19] Miles v. Forest Rock, etc. Co. (1918) 34 T.L.R. 500; Rainham Chemical Works Ltd. v. Belvedere Fish Guano Co. Ltd. [1921] 2 A.C. 465.

[20] National Telephone Co. v. Baker (1893) 2 Ch. 186; Eastern and S. African Telegraph Co. Ltd. v. Cape Town Tramways Companies Ltd. [1902] A.C. 381; Hillier v. Air Ministry [1962] C.L.Y. 2084 (cows electrocuted by an escape of electricity from high-voltage cable laid under plaintiff's field, liability under Rylands v. Fletcher).

[21] Smith v. G.W. Ry. (1926) 135 L.T. 112.

[22] West v. Bristol Tramways Co. [1908] 2 K.B. 14.

[23] Att.-Gen. v. Cory Bros. Ltd. [1921] 1 A.C. 521.

[24] Firth v. Bowling Iron Co. (1878) 3 C.P.D. 254.

[25] Hoare & Co. v. McAlpine [1923] 1 Ch. 167.

[26] Crowhurst v. Amersham Burial Board (1878) 4 Ex.D. 5; Ponting v. Noakes [1894] 2 Q.B. 281.

[27] Shiffman v. Grand Priory, etc. [1936] 1 All E.R. 557 (obiter, it was decided on the ground of negligence).

[28] A species of centrifugal roundabout: Hale v. Jennings Bros. [1938] 1 All E.R. 579.

[29] Att.-Gen. v. Corke [1933] Ch. 89; but cf. Smith v. Scott [1973] Ch. 314, where it is suggested that this case could at least equally well have been decided on the basis that the landowner was in possession of the property and was himself liable for nuisances created by his licensees.

[30] Read v. Lyons & Co. Ltd. [1947] A.C. 156; Weir, Casebook on Tort, 3rd ed., p. 373; Howard v. Furness, etc. Lines Ltd. [1936] 2 All E.R. 781.

[31] [1947] A.C. 156; (1947) 63 L.Q.R. 159–163.

[32] Viscount Simon [1947] A.C. at p. 168; 177, per Lord Porter: " Escape from the place in which the dangerous object has been maintained by the defendant to some place not subject to his control "; 184–185, Lord Uthwatt shows that history supports the distinction between what happens within and what happens without a landowner's boundaries. But see comments of Law Commission, Report No. 32, p. 16. The authorities clearly establish that it is not necessary for the defendant to have any property interest in the land: Benning v. Wong (1969) 122 C.L.R. 249, 294, per Windeyer J.

of the land." [33] But the House of Lords emphasised that the absence of an " escape " was the basis of their decision.

Personal injuries

The House of Lords in *Read* v. *Lyons* [34] also considered whether under the rule in *Rylands* v. *Fletcher* a plaintiff can recover damages for personal injuries. According to Lord Macmillan, the rule " derives from a conception of mutual duties of neighbouring landowners " [35] and is therefore inapplicable to personal injuries. " An allegation of negligence," he continued, " is in general essential to the relevancy of an action of reparation for personal injuries." [36] Viscount Simon and Lord Simonds reserved their opinions on this question,[37] and Lord Porter considered that opinions expressed supporting the application of the rule to personal injuries are an undoubted extension of it, " and may some day require examination." [38]

Lord Macmillan's view must however be considered in context. It is clear that in the related tort of nuisance, an *occupier* can sue in respect of his personal injuries [39] and the same was established in the tort of cattle trespass.[40] Even after *Read* v. *Lyons*, therefore, there is no reason to doubt the correctness of decisions such as *Hale* v. *Jennings Bros.*[41] in which the Court of Appeal held that an occupier of land was entitled to damages for personal injuries under the rule in *Rylands* v. *Fletcher*. But before *Read* v. *Lyons*, the courts had gone further, holding that even a non-occupier may sue for personal injuries under the rule, and it is probably this development that their lordships had in mind. In *Shiffman* v. *Order of St. John*,[42] for instance, the plaintiff was injured in Hyde Park when he was struck by a falling flag-pole belonging to the defendants. Although it was found that the defendants had been at fault, Atkinson J. considered that, irrespective of this, the defendants would have been liable under the rule in *Rylands* v. *Fletcher*.[43]

Judged from a strictly historical point of view, Lord Macmillan's

---

[33] *Ibid.* 167; 173, Lord Macmillan, " Escape . . . and not-natural use of the land, whatever precisely that may mean." It seems that it must be an escape from land of the defendant and not an escape from a ship; *Miller Steamship Co. Ltd.* v. *Overseas Tankship (U.K.)* [1963] 1 Lloyd's Rep. 402, 426.
[34] *Supra.*
[35] At p. 173.
[36] At pp. 170–171.
[37] At pp. 168–169 and 180, respectively.
[38] At p. 178. In the Court of Appeal, Scott L.J. considered that the rule in *Rylands* v. *Fletcher* is restricted to damage to land: [1945] K.B. 216, 236. Compare his earlier inconsistent judgment in *Hale* v. *Jennings Bros.* [1938] 1 All E.R. 579.
[39] *Ante*, p. 334.
[40] *Wormald* v. *Cole* [1954] 1 Q.B. 614; as to the present position see p. 398, *post.*
[41] *Supra* (tenant of stall at a fairground injured by escape of defendant's chair-o-plane).
[42] [1936] 1 All E.R. 557. See also *Miles* v. *Forest Rock Granite Co. Ltd.* (1918) 34 T.L.R. 500 (C.A.). In *Wing* v. *L.G.O.* [1909] 2 K.B. 652, 665, Fletcher Moulton L.J. stated that the rule applies where " by excessive use of . . . [a] private right a person has exposed his neighbour's property or person to danger." It is clear from the context that this is not restricted to injury to an occupier. The previous authorities were not fully discussed by the House of Lords in *Read* v. *Lyons.*
[43] At p. 561.

approach is doubtless correct. It is, however, open to the criticism that it helps to preserve the anachronistic situation in which proprietary interests receive more protection than the interest in physical security. Perhaps because of this the courts have in subsequent cases generally declined to follow Lord Macmillan's view. In *Perry* v. *Kendricks Transport Ltd.*,[44] for instance, Parker L.J. did not " think it is open to this court to hold that the rule applies only to damage to adjoining land or to a proprietary interest in land and not to personal injury." [45] In *Weller* v. *Foot and Mouth Disease Research Institute*,[46] however, Widgery J. briefly held that the defendants could not be liable to the plaintiffs under the rule in *Rylands* v. *Fletcher*, because the plaintiffs, who were cattle auctioneers, had no interest in any land to which the virus could have escaped.[47] The plaintiffs' loss of business was pecuniary or economic damage.

Widgery J.'s conclusion that the plaintiffs could not recover under the rule for economic injury alone seems perfectly correct. But this is not due, it is suggested, to the absence of any proprietary interest on their part, but because in general a person cannot recover damages for such injury unless he has also suffered tangible physical injury.[48] This does not in the least mean that in all cases a plaintiff cannot recover under the rule unless he proves interference to his proprietary interest. It is submitted with respect that Widgery J.'s view is inconsistent with the trend of modern authorities and should not be followed.

Land

The rule as originally formulated refers to a person who for his own purposes brings on to his lands and collects and keeps there anything likely to do mischief if it escapes. The words *for his own purposes* will be discussed later.[49] The rule is not confined to the case of adjacent freeholders. It applies, for instance, to a local authority which is required by statute to receive sewage into its sewers.[50] It applies where the defendant has a franchise, such as a right to use land founded on a statute or upon private permission, e.g. for laying pipes to carry gas,[51] or cables for electricity.[52] One who uses land by permission of the

---

[44] [1956] 1 W.L.R. 85: *Benning* v. *Wong* (1969) 122 C.L.R. 249 (Aust.H.C.).

[45] At p. 92. Singleton L.J. at p. 87 assumed that an action for personal injuries was possible. See also *Dunne* v. *North Western Gas Board* [1964] 2 Q.B. 806, 836, *per* Sellers L.J.; *British Celanese Ltd.* v. *A. H. Hunt Ltd.* [1969] 2 All E.R. 1252, 1257, *per* Lawton J.; *Aldridge* v. *Van Patter* (1952) 4 D.L.R. 93, 105, *per* Spence J. *Contra* Salmond, *Torts*, 16th ed., at pp. 324–325.

[46] [1966] 1 Q.B. 569.

[47] At p. 588.

[48] *Ante*, pp. 51–54. See Goodhart, " Liability for Remote Consequences " (1966) 82 L.Q.R. 34; West, " Nuisance or *Rylands* v. *Fletcher* " (1966) 30 Conv.(N.S.) 95–105.

[49] At p. 373.

[50] *Smeaton* v. *Ilford Corporation* [1954] 1 Ch. 450, 469, 472.

[51] *Northwestern Utilities Ltd.* v. *London Guarantee Ltd.* [1936] A.C. 108, 118; *Read* v. *Lyons & Co. Ltd.* [1947] A.C. 156, 183. Lord Simonds did not consider it necessary to pronounce finally on these cases, but thought it possible that the rule extended to them.

[52] *Charing Cross Electricity Supply Co.* v. *Hydraulic Power Co.* [1914] 3 K.B. 772.

tenant or occupier (*i.e.* a licensee) and brings on to it a dangerous thing is liable for its escape.[53] Although there are conflicting dicta it seems that an owner who is not in occupation of the land at the time when the thing escapes is liable if he has authorised the accumulation,[54] and that anyone who collects the dangerous thing and has control of it at the time of the escape would be liable.[55]

Non-natural user

For some time before *Rylands* v. *Fletcher* the courts had been concerned with the extent of a person's liability for the escape of an accumulation of water from his land during the normal course of mining operations.[56] Their conclusions may be formulated as follows: if A conducts mining operations on his own land in such a way as to cause water to flood his neighbour's mine and the inundation is due to mere gravitation, A is not liable, but if the flooding is due to A's accumulation of the water (*e.g.* by pumping), A is liable. This distinction was developed in *Rylands* v. *Fletcher* into the rule that as a prerequisite to liability the defendant must have brought onto the land something " which was not naturally there." As one author has put it, non-natural use was originally " an expression of the fact that the defendant has artificially introduced onto the land a new and dangerous substance." [57]

This term " natural " is inherently confusing for it has two distinct meanings. In its primary sense it signifies " that which exists in or by nature and is not artificial." [58] The term was used in this sense by Lord Cairns in *Rylands* v. *Fletcher*. It also means, however, " that which is ordinary and usual, even though it may be artificial." [59] As Professor Newark has pointed out,[57] the courts now understand non-natural user in the latter sense. The most frequently quoted definition of non-natural user is that given by the Judicial Committee in *Rickards* v. *Lothian*,[60] " It must be some special use bringing with it increased danger to others and must not merely be the ordinary use of the land or such a use as is proper for the general benefit of the community." [61]

It is suggested that the concept of non-natural user is now understood by the courts as being similar to the idea of unreasonable risk in

---

[53] *Rainham Chemical Works* v. *Belvedere Fish Guano Co.* [1921] 2 A.C. 465.
[54] *Rainham Case* [1921] 2 A.C. 465, 476, 489. Contra, *St. Anne's Well Brewery Co.* v. *Roberts* (1928) 140 L.T. 1, 5; Charlesworth, *Negligence*, 5th ed., p. 273.
[55] *Rainham Case* [1921] 2 A.C. 465, 479. Cf. *Westhoughton Coal Co. Ltd.* v. *Wigan Coal Co. Ltd.* [1939] Ch. 800; *Powell* v. *Fall* (1880) 5 Q.B. 597, 599 (sparks escaping from traction engine on highway, owner liable).
[56] *e.g. Smith* v. *Kenrick* (1849) 7 C.B. 515; *Baird* v. *Williamson* (1863) 15 C.B.(N.S.) 376. Cf. *Rouse* v. *Gravelworks Ltd.* [1940] 1 K.B. 489.
[57] Newark in his important article " Non-natural User and *Rylands* v. *Fletcher* " (1961) 24 M.L.R. 557, 561.
[58] *Ibid.*, at p. 558.
[59] *Ibid.*
[60] [1913] A.C. 263.
[61] At pp. 279–280, *per* Lord Moulton, approved in *Read* v. *Lyons* [1947] A.C. 156, 169, *per* Viscount Simon.

negligence.[62] In *Read* v. *Lyons*, Lord Porter commented that " non-natural user seems to be a question of fact . . . and in deciding this question I think that all the circumstances of time and practice of mankind must be taken into consideration so that what may be regarded as dangerous or non-natural may vary according to the circumstances." [63] The courts balance the magnitude of the risk (*i.e.* the extent of the accumulation and the injury potential of the thing accumulated) with the desirability or necessity of the activity from the point of view of the defendant and the public. This equating of non-natural user with unreasonable risk in negligence seems to have been recognised by MacKenna J. in *Mason* v. *Levy Auto Parts of England Ltd.*[64] The defendants stored on their land large quantities of combustible materials which ignited in mysterious circumstances. In determining whether the defendants ought to be held liable under the rule in *Rylands* v. *Fletcher*, the learned judge considered that he ought to pay regard to (i) the quantities of combustible materials which the defendants brought onto the land; (ii) the way in which they stored them; and (iii) the character of the neighbourhood. " It may be," he concluded, " that these considerations would also justify a finding of negligence. If that is so, the end would be the same as I have reached by a more laborious, and perhaps more questionable route." [65]

As Lord Porter recognised,[66] it is inevitable that the courts' view of what is non-natural should change in response to changing social conditions and needs. A striking illustration of such a change is afforded by a comparison of some of the dicta in *Read* v. *Lyons* and the case of *Rainham Chemical Works Ltd.* v. *Belvedere Fish Guano Co.*[67] In the former, Lord Macmillan hesitated " to hold that in these days and in an industrial community it was a non-natural use of land to build a factory on it and conduct there the manufacture of explosives." [68] The House declined to consider itself bound by the *Rainham Chemicals* case [67] where it seems to have been taken for granted that such an activity constituted a non-natural use of land.

The identification of non-natural user with conduct creating an

---

[62] See Stallybrass, " Dangerous Things and the Non-Natural User of Land " (1929) 3 C.L.J. 376; Goodhart, " The Rule in *Rylands* v. *Fletcher* " (1947) 63 L.Q.R. 160, 163; Morris, " Absolute Liability for Dangerous Things " (1948) 61 Harv.L.R. 515, 520–523; Fridman, " The Rise and Fall of *Rylands* v. *Fletcher* " (1956) 34 Can.Bar Rev. 810.

[63] [1947] A.C. 176. *Cf. J. P. Porter Co. Ltd.* v. *Bell* [1955] 1 D.L.R. 62 which reviews the authorities.

[64] [1967] 2 Q.B. 530.

[65] At pp. 542–543.

[66] *Ante*, note 63.

[67] [1921] 2 A.C. 465.

[68] At p. 174. See generally pp. 174–175. It was a time of war. Viscount Simon expressed a similar view though more hesitantly: pp. 169–170. Lord Uthwatt at p. 187 declined to express an opinion. See also the comments of Scott L.J. in the Court of Appeal [1945] K.B. 216, 240. Lord Macmillan's view was adopted by Lawton J. in *British Celanese Ltd.* v. *A. H. Hunt Ltd.* [1969] 1 W.L.R. 959, 963–964: " The manufacturing of electrical and electronic components in the year 1964 . . . cannot be adjudged to be a special use. . . . The metal foil was there for use in the manufacture of goods of a common type which at all material times were needed for the general benefit of the community."

abnormal risk that ought not to be borne by the public has given to the courts a device for determining liability in accordance with what they consider to be public policy. There is no objective universal test of what is non-natural. The court must make its own value judgment on the defendant's conduct, taking into account its social utility and the care with which it is carried out. Because of this some of the early cases may require consideration.[69] It may well be, for example, that courts in the future will be reluctant to hold that the use of land as a reservoir to supply water to a great city is non-natural.[70]

The following have in the past been regarded as a natural user of land: water installations in a house or flat,[71] a fire in a domestic grate,[72] electric wiring[73] and gas pipes in a house or shop,[74] the ordinary working of mines and minerals on land,[75] erecting or pulling down houses or walls,[76] trees whether planted or self-sown (if not poisonous).[77] Generating steam on a steamship is not " non-natural." [78] But the storing of water as in *Rylands* v. *Fletcher*, or industrial water under pressure,[79] gas and electricity in bulk in mains is a non-natural use of land. It seems that keeping a motor-car in a garage with petrol in the tank,[80] and a motor-coach in a parking ground after the tank has been emptied is a non-natural use of land,[81] but the decisions have been criticised.[82]

---

[69] *Read* v. *Lyons* [1947] A.C. 156, 169–170, 173–174, 176.

[70] In *Dunne* v. *North Western Gas Board* [1964] 2 Q.B. 806, the Court of Appeal was reluctant to hold a nationalised industry liable in the absence of fault, but the contrary argument of Windeyer J. in *Benning* v. *Wong* (1969) 122 C.L.R. 249, 301 is compelling.

[71] *Rickards* v. *Lothian* [1913] A.C. 263.

[72] *Sochacki* v. *Sas* [1947] 1 All E.R. 344; *cf.* Williams [1973] C.L.J. 310, 311, 314.

[73] *Collingwood* v. *Home and Colonial Stores Ltd.* [1936] 3 All E.R. 200.

[74] *Miller* v. *Addie & Sons (Collieries) Ltd.*, 1934 S.C. 150.

[75] *Rouse* v. *Gravelworks Ltd.* [1940] 1 K.B. 489.

[76] *Thomas and Evans Ltd.* v. *Mid-Rhondda Co-operative Society* [1941] 1 K.B. 381.

[77] *Noble* v. *Harrison* [1926] 2 K.B. 332.

[78] *Howard* v. *Furness, etc. Ltd.* [1936] 2 All E.R. 781; *Eastern Asia Navigation Co. Ltd.* v. *Freemantle* (1951) 83 C.L.R. 353 (dealing with oil fuel in harbour berth for oil-burning vessels, a natural user); *Smeaton* v. *Ilford Corporation* [1954] Ch. 450, 472 (collection in sewer of large volume of noxious and inherently dangerous sewage by local authority, not a natural user); *Miller Steamship Co. Pty. Ltd.* v. *Overseas Tankship (U.K.) Ltd.* [1963] 1 Lloyd's Rep. 402, 426 (ship in harbour bunkering with furnace oil, a natural user); *Gertsen* v. *Municipality of Metropolitan Toronto* (1973) 41 D.L.R. (3d) 646 (landfill project using household waste which generated methane gas, not a natural user).

[79] *Charing Cross Electricity Supply Co.* v. *Hydraulic Power Co.* [1914] 3 K.B. 772; *Peters* v. *Prince of Wales Theatre Ltd.* [1943] K.B. 73, 76 (sprinkler system in theatre " ordinary and usual ").

[80] *Musgrove* v. *Pandelis* [1919] 2 K.B. 43; the criticism of this case by Romer L.J. in *Collingwood* v. *Home and Colonial Stores Ltd.* (1936) 155 L.T. 550, 553 was approved by Lord Porter in *Read* v. *Lyons* [1947] A.C. 156, 176; but followed in *Sturge* v. *Hackett* [1962] 1 W.L.R. 1257 (C.A.).

[81] *Perry* v. *Kendricks Transport Ltd.* [1956] 1 W.L.R. 85, 92. Parker L.J. considered *Musgrove* v. *Pandelis* was binding on the C.A.

[82] Goodhart (1956) 72 L.Q.R. 184–186, pointing out that insurance companies distinguish between petrol in the tank of a car, and petrol stored in bulk which is both more dangerous and unusual. *Cf. Mulholland and Tedd Ltd.* v. *Baker* [1939] 3 All E.R. 253, rule correctly applied.

Things naturally on the land [83]

The distinction between natural and non-natural user has at times been confused with the distinction between things naturally on the land and things artificially there.[84] The former defines the nature of the user of the land; the latter the cause of accumulation thereon. Only when it has been determined that the accumulation on the land is a deliberate one, need the court consider whether the defendant's user is non-natural. The rule in *Rylands* v. *Fletcher* applies only to things which the occupier brings onto his land and collects and keeps there. It was quickly established that the occupier could not be liable under the rule merely for permitting a spontaneous accumulation (*e.g.* of water, vegetation, birds) on his land,[85] or even for inducing a spontaneous accumulation as an undesired by-product of the normal working of the land.[86] In *Pontardawe R.D.C.* v. *Moore-Gwyn*,[87] for instance, there was no liability for the fall of rocks from an outcrop, when the fall was due to the natural process of weathering.

An occupier, therefore, is not liable to his neighbour under the rule in *Rylands* v. *Fletcher* for damage caused by ordinary trees which are self-sown because they are naturally on the land. Nor in general is he liable even if he has planted the trees because he has not used his land in an extraordinary or non-natural manner.[88] " To grow a tree is one of the natural users of the soil." [89] In contrast, in *Crowhurst* v. *Amersham Burial Board*,[90] the defendants planted on their land a yew tree which grew so as to project over onto the land of the plaintiff on which cattle were pastured. The leaves of yew trees are poisonous to cattle. The plaintiff's horse ate some leaves and died and the defendants were held liable under the rule in *Rylands* v. *Fletcher*. It was not in the circumstances a natural use of the land to plant on it a poisonous tree.

---

[83] See Goodhart in *Essays in Jurisprudence* (1931), Chap. 8, for an illuminating discussion of this topic. It is not confined to the rule in *Rylands* v. *Fletcher* but includes nuisance. Also Noel, " Nuisances from Land in its Natural Condition " (1934) 56 Harv. L.R. 772.

[84] Stallybrass, *loc. cit.*

[85] *e.g. Giles* v. *Walker* (1890) 24 Q.B.D. 656; *Sparke* v. *Osborne* (1909) 7 C.L.R. 51; *Seligman* v. *Docker* [1949] Ch. 53.

[86] *e.g. Wilson* v. *Waddell* (1876) 2 App.Cas. 95, following *Smith* v. *Kenrick, ante.* Contrast *Fletcher* v. *Smith* (1877) 2 App.Cas. 781; *Hurdman* v. *Great North Eastern Ry.* (1878) 3 C.P.D. 168.

[87] [1929] 1 Ch. 656.

[88] *Noble* v. *Harrison* [1926] 2 K.B. 332, 336, *per* Rowlatt J. and at p. 342, *per* Wright J.; *Davey* v. *Harrow Corpn.* [1958] 1 Q.B. 60, 71–73, *per* Lord Goddard C.J. The courts seem to impose a form of strict liability for damage by the encroachment of roots: *McCombe* v. *Read* [1955] 2 Q.B. 429; *Davey* v. *Harrow Corpn.*; Yale [1957] C.L.J. 137; Wedderburn [1958] C.L.J. 32; *Morgan* v. *Kyatt* [1964] 1 W.L.R. 475. Despite dicta to the effect that no distinction should be drawn between damage by roots and branches (*e.g. Lemmon* v. *Webb* [1894] 3 Ch. 1, 24, *per* Kay L.J.; *Davey* v. *Harrow Corpn.* at p. 70, *per* Lord Goddard C.J.) this seems to be the effect of these cases. It is, however, possible to argue that they are all based on presumed fault. It is common knowledge that the roots of certain trees spread. If the defendant plants or maintains such trees too near to the property of his neighbour, he cannot be heard to say that he could not have known of the extent of the roots.

[89] *Noble* v. *Harrison* [1926] 2 K.B. 332, 336, *per* Rowlatt J.

[90] (1878) 4 Ex.D. 5.

A further illustration of the application of these principles is afforded by the interesting case of *Giles* v. *Walker*.[91] Thistle-seed was blown in large quantities by the wind from the defendant's land to that of the plaintiff; it was held that " there can be no duty as between adjoining occupiers to cut the thistles, which are the natural growth of the soil," [92] and that the defendant was not liable. Upon the facts the decision seems to have been correct so far as the rule in *Rylands* v. *Fletcher* goes, for all that the defendant had done was to plough up some forest land on which there had previously been no thistles but from which, for some unexplained reason, an immense crop of them sprang up in two successive years. But even in relation to the rule in *Rylands* v. *Fletcher*, the principle seems to have been stated too widely. If, for example, an occupier deliberately plants weeds in large quantities, he would surely be liable under the rule for damage caused by their escape, for it is not a natural use of one's land to cultivate weeds in bulk.

Although a natural condition cannot give rise to liability under the rule in *Rylands* v. *Fletcher* it may still constitute a nuisance for which an occupier may be liable.[93] Moreover, an occupier will be liable if he deliberately causes the escape of things naturally on his land.[94]

Dangerous things

The phrase " essentially dangerous " has been much criticised both by judges (who nevertheless continue to use it—some of them with approval) and by writers.[95] It has been truly said that almost anything is potentially dangerous [96] and that the line between " essentially dangerous " and " not usually dangerous " is often evanescent. A gun would generally be reckoned as dangerous in itself, a chair as perfectly safe. Yet the chair, if it has a rotten leg, may be much more perilous than an old musket in the Tower armoury.[97]

But in spite of the uncertainty of the phrase we are only following English law if we adopt it. Under the rule in *Rylands* v. *Fletcher* it is relevant not only under the head which we are discussing, but in later cases it has been used as equivalent to " likely to do mischief," which is the phrase used by Blackburn J. in laying down the rule.[98] Subsequent

---

[91] (1890) 24 Q.B.D. 656; Harris [1967] C.L.J. at pp. 24–27.

[92] At p. 657, *per* Lord Coleridge C.J. Goodhart, *op. cit.* at p. 154, points out that the soil was not in its natural condition as it was ploughed up forest land. This point does not seem to have been taken in the case, presumably because the accumulation was a spontaneous result of the normal working of land. See *ante*.

[93] *Goldman* v. *Hargrave* [1967] 1 A.C. 645. See *ante*, pp. 337–339.

[94] *Whalley* v. *Lancashire and Yorkshire Ry.* (1884) 13 Q.B.D. 131.

[95] See Stallybrass's excellent analysis in (1929) 3 C.L.J. 376–397. (In some judgments, there is a confusion between dangerous and non-dangerous things, and natural and non-natural user, p. 395.) *Miller Steamship Co. Ltd.* v. *Overseas Tankship (U.K.) Ltd.* [1963] 1 Lloyd's Rep. 402, 426. It may be that furnace oil was not a " dangerous thing " within the rule in *Rylands* v. *Fletcher*; Walsh J. preferred to express no opinion on that.

[96] Lord Macmillan in *Read* v. *Lyons & Co. Ltd.* [1947] A.C. at p. 172; Lord Porter, *ibid.* 176.

[97] See *ante*, pp. 202–204.

[98] The source of this identification is the head-note in *Rylands* v. *Fletcher* (1868) L.R. 3 H.L. 330.

interpretation limits the rule to things which are likely to escape and in doing so bring increased danger to others.[99] It is difficult to find a test for " things " which come within the rule and equally difficult to find a test for " things dangerous in themselves." The two classes of things may overlap but should not be equated. Water is not " dangerous *per se*," yet it was the " thing " in *Rylands* v. *Fletcher* itself. Too much stress must not be laid upon Blackburn J.'s illustration in support of the rule,[1] for as pointed out by du Parcq L.J.,[2] he was not purporting to compile a representative list of " extra-hazardous " activities—it is not extra-hazardous to keep cows or maintain a privy. Blackburn J. was dealing with things which are harmless to others, so long as they are confined to a man's own property and was not considering at all the rights of those who are injured by dangerous chattels or premises which they have entered.

In its Report on Civil Liability for Dangerous Things and Activities,[3] the Law Commission has suggested that if there is a general basis on which strict liability is imposed, it is to be found in the notion of " special danger," *i.e.* activities involving " a more than ordinary risk of accidents or a risk of more than ordinary damage if accidents in fact result." Despite the great difficulties involved in formulating criteria, the Law Commission commends the concept of " special danger " as a basis for future development of the law.

DEFENCES TO THE RULE

In *Rylands* v. *Fletcher* possible defences to the rule were no more than outlined and we must look to later decisions for their development.

1. Consent of the plaintiff

Where the plaintiff has expressly or impliedly consented to the presence of the source of danger and there has been no negligence on the part of the defendant, the defendant is not liable.[4] The exception merely illustrates the general defence, *volenti non fit injuria*, and would not have needed special mention here but for the fact that the Court of Appeal and the House of Lords have considered it expedient to take particular notice of it. The main application of the principle of implied consent is found in cases where different floors in the same building are occupied by different persons and the tenant of a lower floor suffers damage as the result of water escaping from an upper floor.[5] In a block

---

[99] *Read* v. *Lyons* [1947] A.C. 156, 186; 176, " Dangerous in the sense that if it escapes, it will do damage."

[1] *Ibid.* 178, *per* Lord Porter.

[2] *Read* v. *Lyons* [1945] K.B. 216, 247–248.

[3] Report No. 32 (1970).

[4] *Gill* v. *Edouin* (1894) 71 L.T. 762; 72 L.T. 579; *Att.-Gen.* v. *Cory Bros. Ltd.* [1921] 1 A.C. 521, 538, 543, 545, 550. *Ross* v. *Fedden* (1872) L.R. 7 Q.B. 661 and *Kiddle* v. *City Business Properties Ltd.* [1942] 1 K.B. 269 are cases of this type.

[5] The doctrine has no application where the parties are *adjoining* occupants but there is no relationship of landlord and tenant between them (*Humphries* v. *Cousins* (1877)

of premises each tenant can normally be regarded as consenting to the presence of water on the premises if the supply is of the usual character, but not if it is of quite an unusual kind, or defective or dangerous, unless he actually knows of that. The defendant is liable if the escape was due to his negligence.[6]

2. Common benefit

Where the source of the danger is maintained for the common benefit .of the plaintiff and the defendant, the defendant is not liable for its escape. This is akin to the defence of consent of the plaintiff, and Bramwell B. in *Carstairs* v. *Taylor*[7] treated it as the same thing. There A had hired from B the ground floor of a warehouse, the upper part of which was occupied by B. Water from the roof was collected by gutters into a box, from which it was discharged by a pipe into drains. A rat gnawed a hole in the box and water leaked through it and injured A's goods. There was no negligence on B's part. B was held not liable. In *Peters* v. *Prince of Wales Theatre* (*Birmingham*) *Ltd.*,[8] the Court of Appeal regarded " common benefit " as no more than an element (although an important element) in showing consent in cases of the type of *Carstairs* v. *Taylor*. In other judicial dicta the exception has been regarded as an independent one.[9] The precise ambit of " common benefit " has never been properly determined. Until recently, for example, it was not considered to apply between consumers of gas or water and the public industries which supply them.[10] If an explosion occurs owing to the escape of gas, it does not seem to have been suggested that the defences of common benefit or consent of the plaintiff would be available to the defendants, possibly because the plaintiff has no choice as to the source of his supply of gas, whereas in other cases he can decide for himself whether he will accept the arrangement offered to him by his landlord. It is submitted that this is the correct approach, but in *Dunne* v. *North Western Gas Board*[11] Sellers L.J., delivering the judgment of the Court of Appeal, considered that common benefit was an important factor. " It would seem odd that

---

2 C.P.D. 239); but the position is not so clear when the parties are not landlord and tenant but are occupiers of the same building: *Kiddle* v. *City Business Properties Ltd.* [1942] 1 K.B. 269, 274; *Peters* v. *Prince of Wales Theatre* (*Birmingham*) *Ltd.* [1943] 1 K.B. 73.

   [6] *Prosser* v. *Levy* [1955] 1 W.L.R. 1224, 1233, C.A. (reviewing previous cases); [1956] C.L.J. 13–15. Kadirgamar, " The Escape of Water from Domestic Premises " (1973) 37 Conv.(N.S.) 179, points out that most of the difficulties arising from this and the next defence have been faced unnecessarily because in nearly all the cases (*cf. Western Engraving Co.* v. *Film Laboratories Ltd.* [1936] 1 All E.R. 106) the defendant's activity was a natural use of land. See also Salmond, *Torts*, 16th ed., p. 331 and Law Com. No. 32, p. 19.

   [7] (1871) L.R. 6 Ex. 217. So, too, *Northwestern Utilities Ltd.* v. *London Guarantee, etc. Co. Ltd.* [1936] A.C. 108, 120.

   [8] [1943] 1 K.B. 73, 78.

   [9] *Gill* v. *Edouin* (1894) 72 L.T. 579; *Anderson* v. *Oppenheimer* (1880) 5 Q.B.D. 602.

   [10] e.g. *Northwestern Utilities Ltd.* v. *London Guarantee, etc. Co. Ltd.* [1936] A.C. 108.

   [11] [1964] 2 Q.B. 806.

facilities so much sought after by the community and approved by
their legislators should be actionable at common law because they have
been brought to the places where they are required and have escaped
without negligence by an unforeseen series of mishaps." [12] In addition
the learned judge did not think that a nationalised industry can be
said to accumulate a substance for its own purposes.

3. Act of stranger

If the escape was caused by the unforeseeable act of a stranger, the
rule does not apply. In *Box* v. *Jubb* [13] the defendant's reservoir overflowed partly because of the acts of a neighbouring reservoir-owner
and the defendant escaped liability. The plaintiff also failed in his
claim in *Rickards* v. *Lothian* [14] where some third person deliberately
blocked up the waste-pipe of a lavatory basin in the defendant's
premises, thereby flooding the plaintiff's premises.[15] It has been suggested that the defence is limited to the " mischievous, deliberate and
conscious act of a stranger," [16] and therefore excludes his negligent
acts. However, as Jenkins L.J. pointed out in *Perry* v. *Kendricks
Transport Ltd.*,[17] the basis of the defence is the absence of any control
by the defendant over the acts of a stranger on his land and therefore
the nature of the stranger's conduct is irrelevant. The onus is on the
defendant to show that the escape was due to the unforeseeable act of
a stranger without any negligence on his own part.

If, on the other hand, the plaintiff can show that the act of the
stranger could reasonably have been anticipated or its consequences
prevented, the defendant will still be liable. In *Northwestern Utilities
Ltd.* v. *London Guarantee and Accident Co. Ltd.*,[18] an hotel belonging
to and insured by the plaintiffs was destroyed in a fire caused by the
escape and ignition of natural gas. The gas had percolated into the
hotel basement from a fractured welded joint in an intermediate
pressure main situated below street level and belonging to the defendants, a public utility company. The fracture was caused during the
construction of a storm sewer, involving underground work beneath
the defendants' mains, by a third party. The Privy Council accepted

---

[12] At p. 832.
[13] (1879) 4 Ex.D. 76. *Wilson* v. *Newberry* (1871) L.R. 7 Q.B. 31, 33 is perhaps another
instance of the rule but illustrates bad pleadings still better.
[14] [1913] A.C. 263; Weir, *Casebook on Tort*, 3rd ed., p. 366.
[15] Also *Perry* v. *Kendricks Transport Ltd.* [1956] 1 W.L.R. 85 (child threw a match into
an empty petrol tank which exploded and injured the plaintiff—defendants not liable).
[16] *Perry* v. *Kendricks Transport Ltd.* at p. 87, *per* Singleton L.J. Similarly in *Prosser* v.
Levy [1955] 1 W.L.R. 1224 by the same judge. The learned judge relies on *Philco, etc. Ltd.*
v. *J. Spurling Ltd.* [1949] 2 All E.R. 882 and *Dominion Natural Gas Co.* v. *Collins and
Perkins* [1909] A.C. 640, but these are authorities on *novus actus interveniens* and irrelevant
to the different question of breach of duty.
[17] At p. 90. Similarly *per* Parker L.J. In *Smith* v. *Great Western Ry.* (1926) 42 T.L.R.
391 the negligent act of a third party (failing to ascertain a defect in an oil tank) was held
to be a good defence, but this case was not brought to the attention of the court in *Prosser*
v. *Levy*.
[18] [1936] A.C. 108. See Lord Wright, *Legal Essays*, p. 124; Goodhart (1951) 4 C.L.P.
177.

that the defences of act of God and act of a third party prevent a plaintiff from succeeding in a claim based on the rule in *Rylands* v. *Fletcher* but held the defendants liable for negligence. The risk involved in the defendants' operations was so great that a high degree of care was expected of them. They knew of the construction of the sewer, and they ought to have appreciated the possibility of damage to their mains and taken appropriate action to prevent or rectify it.

While it is clear that a trespasser is a " stranger " for this purpose,[19] we can only conjecture who else is included in the term. For the defaults of his servants [20] in the course of their employment, the occupier is of course liable; he is also liable for the negligence of an independent contractor [21] unless it is entirely collateral [22]; for the folly of a lawful visitor [23] in tampering with a potentially dangerous machine provided for his amusement [24]; and it may well be for the misconduct of any member of his family on the premises, for he has control over them. Moreover, it has been argued that he ought to be responsible for guests or licensees on his land. But perhaps a distinction ought to be taken here. It would be harsh to hold a person liable for the act of every casual visitor who has bare permission to enter his land and of whose propensities to evil he may know nothing; *e.g.* an afternoon caller who leaves the garden gate open or a tramp who asks for a can of water and leaves the tap on. Possibly the test is, " Can it be inferred from the facts of the particular case that the occupier had such control over the licensee or over the circumstances which made his act possible that he ought to have prevented it? If so, the occupier is liable, otherwise not." [25]

In connection with this exception to the rule in *Rylands* v. *Fletcher*,[26] we must consider whether the rule applies to a danger created on the premises by the occupier's predecessor in title. It may be inferred from the decision in the *Northwestern Utilities* case that if the occupier knew, or might with reasonable care have ascertained, that the danger existed, he is liable for its escape. If, however, this condition is not satisfied, it is submitted that he ought not to be liable. There is no direct decision

---

[19] *Mandraj* v. *Texaco Trinidad Inc.* (1969) 15 W.I.R. 251.
[20] But a servant may be a stranger as in *Stevens* v. *Woodward* (1881) 6 Q.B.D. 318 (when he used a private lavatory to which he had been prohibited access and omitted to turn off the tap; employer not liable for flooding).
[21] *Balfour* v. *Barty-King* [1957] 1 Q.B. 496, 505–506, C.A., *per* Lord Goddard C.J. (the defendant has control of his independent contractor in that he chooses him, invites him to his premises to do work, can order him to leave at any moment, although it is left to the contractor how the work is to be done); [1957] C.L.J. 132–133.
[22] *Post*, pp. 539–540.
[23] *Ante*, pp. 174–178.
[24] *Hale* v. *Jennings* [1938] 1 All E.R. 579.
[25] In Salmond, *Torts*, 16th ed., pp. 333–334, the same criterion is adopted. Charlesworth, *Negligence*, 4th ed., pp. 258–263.
[26] " Unless one can visualise the accumulation in circumstances which do not constitute an ordinary user of the land of something likely to do mischief if it escapes, and which does escape from the defendant's land neither by act of God nor of third party, everything that is within *Rylands* v. *Fletcher* could also be negligence ": Street (1965) I.C.L.Q. 862, 870.

on the point, but the rule itself seems to make it essential that the defendant should " bring on his lands " the danger. It is true that this is qualified by the *Northwestern Utilities* case, but that decision does not apply to an occupier who neither knows nor could reasonably have discovered the existence of a danger created by his predecessor. Moreover, Eve J. in an obiter dictum in *Whitmores Ltd. v. Stanford* [27] said that the rule in *Rylands* v. *Fletcher* does not extend to making the owner of land liable for the consequences of the escape of a dangerous element brought on the owner's land by another person, not for the purposes of the owner but for the purposes of that other person.

It is evident from the *Northwestern Utilities* case that once the defendant proves the act of a stranger, the point is reached when a claim based on the rule in *Rylands* v. *Fletcher* merges into a claim in negligence, so that a plaintiff who cannot prove fault will not succeed. [26] The original basis of liability under the rule was responsibility for the creation of an exceptional risk which happened to ripen into injury. By means of the defence of act of a stranger the basis of the liability is shifted to responsibility for culpable failure to control the risk. The rule in *Rylands* v. *Fletcher* thus ceases to be available at the very moment when the plaintiff needs it. One can compare liability under the rule with the liability at common law for dangerous animals which was stricter. [28] It seems that the non-malicious act of a stranger is not a valid defence to the *scienter* action, because it is within the risk that must be accepted by anyone who knowingly chooses to keep a dangerous animal.

4. Statutory authority

The rule in *Rylands* v. *Fletcher* may be excluded by statute. Whether it is so or not is a question of construction of the particular statute concerned. In *Green* v. *Chelsea Waterworks Co.*,[29] for instance, a main belonging to a waterworks company, which was authorised by Parliament to lay the main, burst without any negligence on the part of the company and the plaintiff's premises were flooded; the company were held not liable. On the other hand, in *Charing Cross Electricity Co.* v. *Hydraulic Power Co.*,[30] where the facts were similar, the defendants were held to have no exemption upon the interpretation of their statute. The distinction between the cases is that the Hydraulic Power Co. were empowered by statute to supply water for industrial purposes, that is, they had permissive power but not a mandatory authority, and they were *under no obligation to keep their mains charged* with water

---

[27] [1909] 1 Ch. 427, 438.

[28] *Post*, pp. 392–402. The new, statutory liability is similarly strict.

[29] (1894) 70 L.T. 547; applied by the House of Lords in *Longhurst* v. *Metropolitan Water Board* [1948] 2 All E.R. 834.

[30] [1914] 3 K.B. 772. Where there is negligence of the sort occurring in *Northwestern Utilities Ltd.* v. *London Guarantee, etc. Co. Ltd.* [1936] A.C. 108, statutory authority will be no defence.

at high pressure, or at all. The Chelsea Waterworks Co. were authorised by statute to lay mains and *were under a statutory duty to maintain a continuous supply of water*; it was an inevitable consequence that damage would be caused by occasional bursts and so by necessary implication the statute exempted them from liability where there was no " negligence." [31] Where a statutory authority is under a mandatory obligation to supply a service, whether with a saving or nuisance clause (that nothing shall exonerate it from proceedings for nuisance) or whether without such a clause, the authority is under no liability for anything expressly required by statute to be done, or reasonably incidental to that requirement, if it was done without negligence. Where the statutory authority is merely permissive, with no clause imposing liability for nuisance, the authority is not liable for doing what the statute authorises, provided it is not negligent; but it is liable when there is a clause imposing liability for nuisance, even if it is not negligent.[32] As to the escape of water from reservoirs, even express statutory authority for their construction will not by itself exonerate their under-takers since the Reservoirs (Safety Provisions) Act 1930.[33] The Dol-garrog Dam disaster of 1925 led to the passing of this Act. A reservoir 1,400 feet above sea level and holding 200 million gallons of water burst and caused great devastation and loss of life.

One important question in this area awaits a final answer: if, on its proper instruction, the statutory authority exempts the undertaker from *Rylands* v. *Fletcher* liability and imposes only an obligation to use due care, upon whom does the burden of proof lie? A bare majority of the High Court of Australia [34] has held that the burden lies upon the plaintiff to prove lack of such care; but the contrary arguments of the minority seem more convincing in principle and allow for the grave difficulties facing a plaintiff with the task of proving negligence against the supplier of a public utility such as gas or electricity.[35]

The question whether the rule in *Rylands* v. *Fletcher* applies in all its strictness to local authorities has been considered but not decided.[36]

---

[31] *Smeaton* v. *Ilford Corporation* [1954] Ch. 450, 475–477. In the statute relating to the Hydraulic Power Co. there was a clause that nothing should exempt them from liability for any nuisance caused by them, there was no clause *in pari materia* in the statute relating to the Chelsea Waterworks Co. " Negligence " in this connection is not a very appropriate word for it means " adopting a method which in fact results in damage to a third person, except in a case where there is no other way of performing the statutory duty ": *per* Farwell J. in *Provender Millers (Winchester) Ltd.* v. *Southampton C.C.* [1940] Ch. 131, 140.

[32] *Dunne* v. *North Western Gas Board* [1964] 2 Q.B. 806, 833–837, C.A.; [1964] C.L.J. 25–27 (no negligence or breach of statutory duty, defendants not liable under *Rylands* v. *Fletcher* or in nuisance); Allen M. Linden, " Strict Liability, Nuisance and Legislative Authorization " (1966) Osgoode Hall L.J. 196–221, a useful discussion of the rule of statutory authority: Law Commission Report No. 32, pp. 20–21.

[33] 20 & 21 Geo. 5, c. 51, s. 7.

[34] *Benning* v. *Wong* (1969) 122 C.L.R. 249 (McTiernan, Menzies and Owen JJ.).

[35] Barwick C.J. and Windeyer J.; Sawer (1970) 33 M.L.R. 557; *cf. Manchester Corporation* v. *Farnworth* [1930] A.C. 171.

[36] *Pride of Derby, etc. Association Ltd.* v. *British Celanese Ltd.* [1953] Ch. 149, 172–177, *per* Evershed M.R.; 189–190, *per* Denning L.J.; *Benning* v. *Wong* (1969) 122 C.L.R. 249, 301, *per* Windeyer J.

In *Smeaton* v. *Ilford Corporation* [37] Upjohn J. found it unnecessary to express a concluded view on the question whether a local authority exercising statutory duties is altogether outside the rule as suggested by Denning L.J., or prima facie within the rule subject only to express or implied statutory modification as tentatively suggested by Evershed M.R. in the *Pride of Derby* case.[38]

5. Act of God

Where the escape is caused directly by natural causes without human intervention in " circumstances which no human foresight can provide against and of which human prudence is not bound to recognise the possibility," [39] the defence of act of God applies. This was recognised by Blackburn J. in *Rylands* v. *Fletcher* [40] itself and was first applied in *Nichols* v. *Marsland*.[41] In this case the defendant for many years had been in possession of some artificial ornamental lakes formed by damming up a natural stream. An extraordinary rainfall, " greater and more violent than any within the memory of witnesses " broke down the artificial embankments and the rush of escaping water carried away four bridges in respect of which damage the plaintiff sued. Judgment was given for the defendant; the jury had found that she was not negligent and the court held that she ought not to be liable for an extraordinary act of nature which she could not reasonably anticipate.

Whether a particular occurrence amounts to an act of God is a question of fact, but the tendency of the courts nowadays is to restrict the ambit of the defence, not because strict liability is thought to be desirable but because increased knowledge limits the unpredictable. In *Greenock Corporation* v. *Caledonian Ry.*,[42] the House of Lords criticised the application of the defence in *Nichols* v. *Marsland*, and four of their lordships cast doubt on the finding of facts by the jury in that case.[43] The Corporation constructed a concrete paddling pool for children in the bed of the stream and to do so they had to alter the course of the stream and obstruct the natural flow of the water. Owing to a rainfall of extraordinary violence, the stream overflowed at the pond, and a great volume of water, which would normally have been carried off by the stream, poured down a public street into the town and caused damage to the plaintiffs' property. The House of Lords held that the rainfall was not an act of God [44] and that the Corporation were

---

[37] [1954] Ch. 450, 478. See *ibid.* 462 as to the distinction between " discharge "— something caused or permitted—and " escape "—involuntary.

[38] See note 36.

[39] *Tennent* v. *Earl of Glasgow* (1864) 2 M.(H.L.) 22, 26–27, *per* Lord Westbury, approved by the House of Lords in *Greenock Corpn.* v. *Caledonian Ry.* [1917] A.C. 556. Also *AMF International Ltd.* v. *Magnet Bowling Ltd.* [1968] 1 W.L.R. 1028, 1039, *per* Mocatta J.

[40] (1866) L.R. 1 Ex. 265, 280.

[41] (1876) 2 Ex.D. 1.

[42] [1917] A.C. 556.

[43] *Ibid.* at pp. 573–574, 575, 580–581.

[44] Or *damnum fatale*, the equivalent in Scottish law.

liable. It was their duty " so to work as to make proprietors or occupiers on a lower level as secure against injury as they would have been had nature not been interfered with." [45] Similar considerations apply to an extraordinary high wind [46] and an extraordinary high tide. [47] Lightning, [48] earthquakes, cloudburst and tornadoes may be acts of God but there seems to be no English decision in which they have been involved.

In law, then, the essence of an act of God is not so much a phenomenon which is sometimes attributed to a positive intervention of the forces of nature, but a process of nature not due to the act of man [49] and it is this negative side which deserves emphasis. The criterion is not whether or not the event could *reasonably* be anticipated, but whether or not human foresight and prudence could reasonably recognise the *possibility* of such an event. [50] Even in such limited form, however, this defence, like the defence of act of a stranger, [51] shifts the basis of the tort from responsibility for the creation of an exceptional risk to culpable failure to control that risk. This has been criticised on the ground that an accidental escape caused by the forces of nature is within the risk that must be accepted by the defendant when he accumulates the substance on his land. [52] As Scrutton L.J. put it in his strong dissenting judgment in *Att.-Gen.* v. *Cory Bros.*, " the fact that an artificial danger escaped through natural causes was no excuse to the person who brought an artificial danger there." [53] Nevertheless, the defence is now firmly part of the law and brings the rule in *Rylands* v. *Fletcher* closer to the tort of negligence. As Lord Greene M.R. accepted in *J. & J. Makin Ltd.* v. *L.N.E.R.*, a proprietor can avoid the ordinary liability based on the rule in *Rylands* v. *Fletcher* if he can show that the water had escaped without his negligence. [54]

6. Default of the plaintiff

If the damage is caused solely by the act or default of the plaintiff himself, he has no remedy. In *Rylands* v. *Fletcher* itself, this was noticed as a

[45] At p. 579, *per* Lord Shaw. Similarly *per* Lord Finlay L.C. at p. 527; *per* Lord Dunedin at p. 577; *per* Lord Wrenbury at p. 583.
[46] *Cushing* v. *Walker & Son* [1941] 2 All E.R. 693, 695. " Before wind can amount to an act of God . . . the wind must not merely be exceptionally strong, but must be of such exceptional strength that no one could be reasonably expected to anticipate or provide against it," *per* Hallett J.
[47] *Greenwood Tileries Ltd.* v. *Clapson* [1937] 1 All E.R. 765, 772, *per* Branson J.
[48] *Nichols* v. *Marsland* (1875) L.R. 10 Ex. 255, 260, dictum of Bramwell B.
[49] " Something in opposition to the act of man ": Lord Mansfield in *Forward* v. *Pittard* (1785) 1 T.R. 27, 33.
[50] The former view was taken in *Nichols* v. *Marsland*, the latter in *Greenock Corporation* v. *Caledonian Ry.* [1917] A.C. 556.
[51] *Ante*, at pp. 372–374.
[52] Particularly, Goodhart, " The Third Man " (1951) 4 C.L.P. 177; " *Rylands* v. *Fletcher* Today " (1956) 72 L.Q.R. 184.
[53] (1919) 35 T.L.R. 570, 574 (fall of refuse in Rhondda Valley probably caused by the saturation of its inferior strata by an extraordinary rainfall). Also *Dixon* v. *Metropolitan Board of Works* (1881) 7 Q.B.D. 418, *per* Lord Coleridge C.J.
[54] [1943] 1 K.B. 467, 470 citing counsel, seemingly with approval. See Buxton, " The Negligent Nuisance " (1966) 8 U.Malaya L.R. at p. 7: the decision in *Nichols* v. *Marsland* " leaves very few cases where a defendant could be held liable who had not in fact been negligent."

defence.[55] If a person knows that there is a danger of his mine being flooded by his neighbour's operations on adjacent land, and courts the danger by doing some act which renders the flooding probable, he cannot complain.[56] So, too, in *Ponting* v. *Noakes*,[57] the plaintiff's horse reached over the defendant's boundary, nibbled some poisonous tree there and died accordingly, and it was held that the plaintiff could recover nothing, for the damage was due to the horse's own intrusion and, alternatively, there had been no escape of the vegetation. Had it been grown there expressly for the purpose of alluring cattle to their destruction, the defendant would have been liable, not on the grounds of *Rylands* v. *Fletcher*, but because he would have been in the position of one who deliberately sets traps baited with flesh in order to attract and catch dogs which are otherwise not trespassing at all.[58] Where the plaintiff is contributorily negligent, the apportionment provisions of the Law Reform (Contributory Negligence) Act 1945 will apply.

If the injury due to the escape of the noxious thing would not have occurred but for the unusual sensitiveness of the plaintiff's property, there is some conflict of authority whether this can be regarded as default of the plaintiff. In *Eastern & S. A. Telegraph Co. Ltd.* v. *Cape Town Tramways Companies Ltd.*,[59] an escape of electricity stored and used by the defendants in working their tramcars, interfered with the sending of messages by the plaintiffs through their submarine cable. The plaintiffs failed to recover as no tangible injury had been done to their property—no apparatus had been damaged. The defendants' operations were not destructive of telegraphic communication generally, but only affected instruments unnecessarily so constructed as to be affected by minute currents of the escaping electricity. With regard to such instruments it was said, " A man cannot increase the liabilities of his neighbour by applying his own property to special uses, whether for business or pleasure." [59] However, in *Hoare & Co.* v. *McAlpine*,[60] where vibrations from pile-driving caused structural damage to a large hotel on adjoining land, Astbury J. held it to be a bad plea that the vibrations had this effect only because the hotel was so old as to be abnormally unstable; but he found also that the evidence did not establish that it was in such a condition. Thus the question remains an open one, and it can hardly be said that the hotel proprietor had put his property to any special or unusually sensitive use.

---

[55] (1868) L.R. 3 H.L. 330, 340.

[56] *Lomax* v. *Stott* (1870) 39 L.J.Ch. 834; *Dunn* v. *Birmingham Canal Co.* (1872) L.R. 7 Q.B. 244. *Miles* v. *Forest Rock Granite Co. Ltd.* (1918) 34 T.L.R. 500 would be more helpful if the report had stated more exactly the finding of the jury. *Postmaster-General* v. *Liverpool Corporation* [1923] A.C. 587.

[57] [1894] 2 Q.B. 281; *cf. Cheater* v. *Cater* [1918] 1 K.B. 247.

[58] *Townsend* v. *Wathen* (1808) 9 East 277.

[59] [1902] A.C. 381, 393, P.C.; *Western Silver Fox Ranch Ltd.* v. *Ross and Cromarty C.C.*, 1940 S.C. 601, 604–606 (breeding silver foxes not a non-natural use of land).

[60] [1923] 1 Ch. 167. See Pollock's criticism of this decision in *Torts*, p. 377, n. (16), and (1923) 39 L.Q.R. 145–146; Charlesworth, *Negligence*, 5th ed., p. 278.

REMOTENESS OF DAMAGE

The Privy Council in 1961 stated that their Lordships had not found it necessary to consider the so-called rule of " strict liability " exemplified in *Rylands* v. *Fletcher* in relation to remoteness of damage.[61] In many cases the results of the escape of objects within the rule are likely to be unpredictable, and the inference is that foreseeability is not the test of remoteness.[62] The defendant cannot be liable *ad infinitum* and in Blackburn J.'s formulation of the rule, he " is prima facie answerable for all the damage which is the natural consequence of its escape." In *British Celanese Ltd.* v. *A. H. Hunt Ltd.* Lawton J. stated that the burden is on the plaintiff to prove " that the damage they suffered was the natural consequence of the escape and was of a kind recognised by the law." [63] The natural consequences of a water dam bursting are, *inter alia*, the inundation of the adjoining land, damage to buildings, roads and, maybe, personal injuries. If the water flows into the shaft of an adjoining coal mine with the result that the mine cannot be worked for six months the mine owner may recover damages, but the miners who lose their wages during that period have no remedy because such injury is not a type recognised by the law in these circumstances.[64] But if the escaping water flows into a carbide factory and thereby generates gas which causes a tremendous explosion, is the owner of the dam liable for this more extensive and perhaps unforeseeable damage by the explosion than would have been caused by the water alone? It has been suggested that the extent of the liability would have to be sought in policy.[65]

THE MODERN POSITION OF THE RULE IN RYLANDS v. FLETCHER [66]

The rule in *Rylands* v. *Fletcher*, then, had its origins in the law of private nuisance and has often been treated as a particular species of nuisance. In *Read* v. *Lyons*, for instance, Lord Simonds remarked that " the judgment of Blackburn J. in the case itself shows that the law of nuisance and the rule in *Rylands* v. *Fletcher* might in most cases be invoked indifferently." [67] The rule of course has in many senses a more restricted application than nuisance; there must be an

---

[61] *Overseas Tankship (U.K.) Ltd.* v. *Morts Dock and Engineering Co. Ltd. (The Wagon Mound)* [1961] A.C. 388, 427, " Nothing that they have said is intended to reflect on that rule."

[62] *McGregor on Damages*, 13th ed., p. 100. Causation must remain the test of the extent to which the defendant is liable under *Rylands* v. *Fletcher*. The defence based on the act of a stranger may be said to stem from the fact that the damage is causally too remote.

[63] [1969] 1 W.L.R. 959, 964.

[64] *Weller & Co.* v. *Foot and Mouth Disease Research Institute* [1966] 1 Q.B. 569, following *Cattle* v. *Stockton Waterworks Co.* (1875) L.R. 10 Q.B. 453, 457.

[65] Dias, " Remoteness of Damage and Legal Policy " [1962] C.L.J. 178, 194–195.

[66] See Winfield (1931) 4 C.L.J. 194–197; Friedmann, " Modern Trends in the Law of Torts " (1937) 1 M.L.R. 49–63; " Nuisance, Negligence and the Overlapping of Torts " (1940) 3 M.L.R. 305–309; *Law and Social Change*, pp. 75–82, 93–98; Wright, " The Law of Torts, 1923–1947 " (1948) 26 Can.Bar Rev. 47, 76–81.

[67] [1947] A.C. 156, 183.

accumulation, and it must be of a substance likely to cause injury if it escapes,[68] neither of which is essential to liability in nuisance. Moreover, the condition of non-natural user, though similar to unreasonable user in nuisance, normally involves some degree of exceptional risk which unreasonable user does not. Nevertheless in many factual situations, a plaintiff will succeed equally well either under the rule or in nuisance.[69]

Despite the original relationship of the rule to nuisance, however, the former has been developed in such a way that it provides a remedy which is basically quite different from nuisance. Private nuisance remains fundamentally a remedy for the infringement of a proprietary interest in land. There are, as we have seen,[70] different types of nuisance and because of this the burden of proof placed on the plaintiff varies. But the basic characteristic common to all types of private nuisance is that of interference with the plaintiff's proprietary interest in land. For this reason a non-occupier cannot maintain a claim in nuisance and an occupier's right to damages for his personal injuries is ancillary to his claim for compensation for damage to his property.[71] In contrast, it now seems good law that the rule in *Rylands* v. *Fletcher* protects all interests including the interest of a non-occupier, *e.g.* a user of the highway, in his personal security.[72] As one writer has put it, the rule provides a remedy for what is " essentially a wrong arising from occupation of land (and it is irrelevant whether the person suffering the injury occupies land or not)." [73] This serves to distinguish it quite fundamentally from nuisance.

At the same time as the area covered by the rule in *Rylands* v. *Fletcher* has been enlarged, the usefulness of the rule has been reduced by the unwillingness of the courts to apply it in circumstances where the defendant could not be said to have been at fault. In *Dunne* v. *North Western Gas Board*,[74] Sellers L.J. asserted that in the present time the defendant's liability in *Rylands* v. *Fletcher* itself " could simply have been placed on the defendant's failure of duty to take reasonable care," [75] and it seems a logical inference from this and from the judgment as a whole that the Court of Appeal considered the rule to have no useful function in modern times. Because of this policy, " the rule in *Rylands* v. *Fletcher*, by reason of its many limitations

---

[68] Law Commission No. 32 at p. 24.

[69] Compare *Midwood & Co. Ltd.* v. *Manchester Corporation* [1905] 2 K.B. 597 (nuisance) with *Charing Cross Electricity Co.* v. *Hydraulic Power Co.* [1914] 3 K.B. 772 (the rule in *Rylands* v. *Fletcher*).

[70] *Ante*, at pp. 320–324.

[71] *Ante*, at pp. 333–334.

[72] *Ante*, at pp. 363–364.

[73] West, *op. cit.* at p. 101. He defines nuisance as " essentially a wrong to occupation of land (whether the person causing the injury does so *qua* occupier of land or not)." See *British Celanese Ltd.* v. *A. H. Hunt Ltd.* [1969] 1 W.L.R. 959, 964, *per* Lawton J.

[74] [1964] 2 Q.B. 806.

[75] *Ibid.* at p. 831.

and exceptions, today seldom forms the basis of a successful claim in the courts." [76]

The most important restriction on any extended application of the rule is the requirement of non-natural user. As it is now interpreted,[77] this excludes from the ambit of the rule those accumulations which in the judgment of the court (there being no objective test) do not involve an unreasonable risk or an extraordinary use of land. Such an interpretation allows the courts to hold that a common activity such as the collection and storage of gas or water does not constitute a non-natural use of land, even though the injury potential of the activity is high. Moreover, in determining what is extraordinary or unreasonable the courts can have regard not only to the interests of the defendant but to the public interest as well.[77] The benefit to the public accruing from the activity in question was an important element in both *Read* v. *Lyons* [78] and *Dunne* v. *North Western Gas Board* [79] and was again emphasised in the recent case of *British Celanese Ltd.* v. *A. H. Hunt Ltd.*[80] In this case the defendants, who were manufacturers of electronic components, collected on their land a large number of strips of metal foil, light enough to be blown about in the wind. Lawton J. refused to regard this as a non-natural use of land. " The manufacturing of electrical and electronic components in the year 1964 . . . cannot be adjudged to be a special use nor can the bringing and storing on the premises of metal foil be a special use in itself. . . . The metal foil was there for use in the manufacture of goods of a common type which at all material times were needed for the general benefit of the community." [81] It would seem therefore that normal industrial activities properly carried out may no longer involve a non-natural use of land and many of the older authorities on this point will need reconsidering.

Moreover, as a result of the defences of act of God, act of a third party and statutory authority, the courts must investigate not only the reasonableness of the accumulation, but also the defendant's responsibility for its actual escape. The nature and quality of the defendant's conduct are therefore factors of great importance, and although the decisional process is different from that in negligence, the result is almost always the same. We have virtually reached the position where a defendant will not be considered liable when he would not be liable according to the ordinary principles of negligence.

Unfortunately, it is precisely at the point when the plaintiff cannot succeed in a claim in negligence that he needs to have recourse to the rule in *Rylands* v. *Fletcher*. It may well be contrary to modern judicial philosophy that a defendant should be liable in the absence of fault

---

[76] Law Commission, Report No. 32 at p. 7.
[77] *Ante*, at pp. 365–367.
[78] [1947] A.C. 156.
[79] [1964] 2 Q.B. 806.
[80] [1969] 1 W.L.R. 959.
[81] *Ibid.* at p. 963.

but this involves as its consequence that an innocent plaintiff should bear the loss. The injustice that may be caused by this was clearly illustrated by the case of *Pearson* v. *North Western Gas Board*.[82] The plaintiff was seriously and her husband fatally injured by an explosion of gas which also destroyed their home. On the facts of the case, even assuming the doctrine of *res ipsa loquitur* to operate in favour of the plaintiff, Rees J. was compelled to hold that the expert evidence adduced by the defendants rebutted any prima facie case in negligence. As the plaintiff was precluded from relying on the rule in *Rylands* v. *Fletcher* by the decision in *Dunne* v. *North Western Gas Board*,[83] the action failed. It is suggested that the decline of the rule in *Rylands* v. *Fletcher* in recent times has left the individual injured by the activities of our industrial society without adequate protection. It has been said on high authority that " to regard negligence as the normal requirement of responsibility in tort, and to look upon strict liability as anomalous and unjust seems to . . . mistake present values as well as past history. In an age when insurance against all forms of liability is commonplace, it is surely not surprising or unjust if law makes persons who carry on some kinds of hazardous undertakings liable for the harm they do, unless they can excuse or justify it on some recognisable ground." [84]

FIRE

Common law

Winfield has traced the history of the earlier forms of action available as remedies for damage caused by the spread of fire.[85] The usual remedy was the special action of trespass on the case for negligently allowing one's fire to escape in contravention of the general custom of the realm which we first hear of in *Beaulieu* v. *Finglam* (1401).[86] The allegation in the action for fire that the defendant *tam negligenter ac improvide* kept his fire that it escaped, referred to negligence in its older sense—one mode of committing a tort. Centuries later remedies became available under the rule in *Rylands* v. *Fletcher*,[87] in nuisance [88]

---

[82] [1968] 2 All E.R. 669.

[83] [1964] 2 Q.B. 806.

[84] *Benning* v. *Wong* (1969) 122 C.L.R. 249, 304, *per* Windeyer J. This judgment contains the most comprehensive judicial consideration of the present status of *Rylands* v. *Fletcher*.

[85] Winfield (1926) 42 L.Q.R. 46–50, or *Select Essays*, pp. 25–28; and (1931) 4 C.L.J. 203–206; Newark (1945) 6 N.I.L.Q. 134–141; Ogus, " Vagaries in Liability for the Escape of Fire " [1969] C.L.J. 104.

[86] Y.B.Pasch. 2 Hen. 4, f. 18, pl. 6, translated in Fifoot, *History and Sources of the Common Law* (1949) p. 166.

[87] *Jones* v. *Festiniog Ry.* (1866) L.R. 1 Ex. 265, fire included in " things likely to do mischief if they escape " and thus within *Rylands* v. *Fletcher*; *Powell* v. *Fall* (1880) 5 Q.B.D. 597; *Musgrove* v. *Pandelis* [1919] 2 K.B. 43; *Job Edwards Ltd.* v. *Birmingham Navigations* [1924] 1 K.B. 341, 351–352; *Collingwood* v. *Home and Colonial Stores Ltd.* [1936] 3 All E.R. 200, 205; *Balfour* v. *Barty-King* [1957] 1 Q.B. 496, 505, C.A. (Lord Goddard C.J. deals with the history of the action on the case from its origin to the present day).

[88] *Spicer* v. *Smee* [1946] 1 All E.R. 489.

and in negligence.[89] Although it is repeatedly said that at common law a man must keep his fire " at his peril," research shows that we cannot be sure that at any period in the history of the common law a man was absolutely liable for the escape of his fire.[90] He is liable for damage done by his fire if it has been caused wilfully,[91] or by his negligence, or by the escape without negligence of a fire which has been brought into existence by some non-natural user of the land. As has recently been emphasised, the last type of liability is not quite the same as liability under the rule in *Rylands* v. *Fletcher* in that the thing accumulated on the land does not itself escape. The criterion of liability is: " Did the defendants . . . bring to their land things likely to catch fire, and keep them there in such conditions that if they did ignite the fire would be likely to spread to the plaintiff's land? "[92] With this qualification liability is the same as under the rule in *Rylands* v. *Fletcher*.

Exactly what " *negligenter* " meant can only be conjectured, for the old authorities are confused, but it certainly excluded liability where the fire spread or occurred (a) by the act of a stranger[93] over whom he had no control, such as a trespasser,[94] and (b) by the act of God. He is responsible for the default of his servant,[95] his wife, his guest[96] or one entering his house with his leave[97] and for his independent contractor.[98] The second exception was established in *Tuberville* v. *Stamp*[99] where it was held that liability extended to a fire originating

---

[89] Bankes L.J. in *Musgrove* v. *Pandelis* [1919] 2 K.B. 43, 46, *per* Scrutton L.J.; *Job Edwards Ltd.* v. *Birmingham Navigations* [1924] 1 K.B. 341, 361.

[90] Winfield (1926) 42 L.Q.R. 46–50 or *Select Essays*, pp. 26–29; Jordan C.J. in *Commissioner for Railways* v. *Wise Bros. Pty.* (1946) 47 S.R.(N.S.W.) 233, on appeal Latham C.J. (1947) 75 C.L.R. 59, as to liability in general; *Edwards* v. *Blue Mountains C.C.* (1961) 78 W.N.(N.S.W.) 864 and (1962) 35 A.L.J. 392.

[91] If the damage is intentional it is a trespass or assault, *e.g.* deliberately throwing a lighted match on a haystack or a lighted firework in a man's face.

[92] *Mason* v. *Levy Auto Parts of England Ltd.* [1967] 2 Q.B. 530, 542, *per* MacKenna J.

[93] *Balfour* v. *Barty-King* [1957] 1 Q.B. 496, 504; *Tuberville* v. *Stamp* (1697) 1 Ld.Raym. 264; *H. N. Emanuel Ltd.* v. *G.L.C.* [1971] 2 All E.R. 835.

[94] Unless he has knowledge of the fire and fails to take steps to extinguish it within a reasonable time.

[95] But a servant acting outside the course of his employment is a stranger: *McKenzie* v. *McLeod* (1834) 10 Bing. 385.

[96] *Crogate* v. *Morris* (1617) 1 Brownl. 197; *Boulcott Golf Club Inc.* v. *Engelbrecht* [1945] N.Z.L.R. 556 (Finlay J. reviews the authorities).

[97] (1926) 42 L.Q.R. 46–50, where the authorities are examined. In the *Emanuel* case, *supra*, Lord Denning M.R. suggested that a person on the occupier's premises with leave and licence was a stranger for this purpose if in lighting the fire he acts contrary to anything the occupier could expect him to do. However, the New Zealand case of *Eriksen* v. *Clifton* [1963] N.Z.L.R. 605, cited in support of this proposition, seems in fact to be a case of liability for personal negligence, not vicarious liability.

[98] *Balfour* v. *Barty-King* [1957] 1 Q.B. 496 (defendant was held liable for a fire caused by an independent contractor whom he employed to thaw frozen pipes in an attic which contained large quantities of combustible material. Contractor used blow-lamp and caused a fire which spread and destroyed plaintiff's adjoining house. Havers J. held defendant liable for negligence of his independent contractor and also under *Rylands* v. *Fletcher*. C.A. affirmed decision but did not think it necessary to consider *Rylands* v. *Fletcher* as a separate head of liability, but had no doubt that it applied); [1957] C.L.J. 132–133; *Black* v. *Christchurch Finance Co.* [1894] A.C. 48.

[99] (1697) 1 Ld.Raym. 264. Lord Raymond gives the best report of the argument; but the record is set out in full by Salkeld (2 Salk. 726). *Balfour* v. *Barty-King, supra.* n. 98. *Eriksen* v. *Clifton* [1963] N.Z.L.R. 705, 707.

in a field as much as to one beginning in a house, but if the defendant kindles it at a proper time and place and the violence of the wind carry it to his neighbour's land, that is fit to be given in evidence. The common law liability still remains in all cases which are not covered by statutory provision.

Statutes

Fires beginning accidentally on the defendant's land

The common law liability has been modified in respect of fires spreading from the defendant's land by the Fires Prevention (Metropolis) Act 1774,[1] which provides that no action shall be maintainable against anyone in whose building or on whose estate a fire shall accidentally begin. This section of the Act is of general application and is not limited to London.[2] In *Filliter* v. *Phippard* [3] the word " accidentally " was interpreted restrictively so as to cover only " a fire produced by mere chance or incapable of being traced to any cause." [4] In other words a fire caused by negligence [5] or due to a nuisance [6] will give rise to a cause of action.

The immunity of a defendant under the statute is illustrated by *Collingwood* v. *Home and Colonial Stores Ltd.*[7] A fire broke out on the defendants' premises and spread to those of the plaintiff. It originated in the defective condition of the electrical wiring on the defendants' premises, but as there was no negligence on their part they were held not liable. Nor was the rule in *Rylands* v. *Fletcher* applicable for the installation of electric wiring, whether for domestic or trade purposes, was a reasonable and ordinary use of premises. Even if the fire is lit intentionally, providing it is lit properly, there is no liability if it spreads without negligence and causes damage, *e.g.* a spark jumps out of an ordinary household fire and causes it to spread.[8] It would be different, of course, if the fire were made too large for the grate.

However, the statute does not confer protection on one who was not at fault so far as the origin of the fire is concerned but who was negligent in letting it spread. In *Musgrove* v. *Pandelis*,[9] the plaintiff occupied rooms over a garage and let part of the garage to the defendant who kept a car there. The defendant's servant, who had little

---

[1] 14 Geo. 3, c. 78, s. 86.
[2] *Filliter* v. *Phippard* (1847) 11 Q.B. 347, 355. Estate applies to land not built upon.
[3] (1847) 11 Q.B. 347.
[4] *Ibid.* at p. 357, *per* Lord Denman C.J.
[5] *e.g. Mulholland and Tedd* v. *Baker Ltd.* [1939] 3 All E.R. 253, 255, *per* Asquith J. (paper lit and inserted in drainpipe to smoke out a rat, fire spread to packing case and exploded drum of paraffin. Liable in negligence and under the rule in *Rylands* v. *Fletcher*).
[6] *e.g. Spicer* v. *Smee* [1946] 1 All E.R. 489, 495, *per* Atkinson J. (defective electric wiring negligently installed by contractor caused fire, owner liable in nuisance or negligence).
[7] (1936) 155 L.T. 550.
[8] *Sochacki* v. *Sas* [1947] 1 All E.R. 344.
[9] [1919] 2 K.B. 43.

skill as a chauffeur, started the engine of the car and without any fault on his part the petrol in the carburettor caught fire. If he had acted like any chauffeur of reasonable competence he could have stopped the fire by turning off the tap connecting the petrol tank with the carburettor. He did not do so and the fire spread and damaged the plaintiff's property. The defendant was held liable, for the fire which did the damage was not that which broke out in the carburettor but that which spread to the car and this second or continuing fire did not " accidentally " begin.[10] The same principle applies where the fire originated as a consequence of an act of God. In *Goldman* v. *Hargrave*,[11] a redgum tree on the defendant's land was struck by lightning and caught fire in a fork eighty feet above ground. The defendant had the tree felled the following morning, but then, instead of extinguishing the fire with water as he could have done, he left it to burn itself out. Three days later a wind came up and revived the fire which spread to and damaged the plaintiff's land. It was held in the circumstances that the defendant was negligent in not completely extinguishing the fire and that the Act of 1774 provided no defence. The burden of proving such negligence is on the plaintiff; it is not for the defendant to prove that the fire was accidental.[12] Even though a plaintiff cannot prove negligence, if the fire originated from a non-natural user of the defendant's land, the Act of 1774 does not provide a defence and the defendant will be liable.[13]

Railway engines. Other statutes deal with the escape of sparks from railway engines. Where, as is commonly the case, a railway is constructed and worked under statutory powers, and there is no negligence in the construction or use of locomotives, there is no liability for fires caused by the escape of sparks from locomotives; such was the decision in *Vaughan* v. *Taff Vale Ry.*,[14] where the defendants had taken every precaution that science could suggest to prevent injury of this sort, and it was held that as Parliament had authorised the use of locomotives it was consistent with policy and justice that

---

[10] Also *Sturge* v. *Hackett* [1962] 1 W.L.R. 1257 (defendant was tenant of a ground-floor flat. To destroy some birds' nests attached to the walls of the flat, he lit a paraffin rag, applied it to the nest, which caught fire; the fire spread and destroyed the entire building. Held, the fire which caused the damage was the fire that got out of control, *viz.* the fire in the birds' nests and not that started by lighting the rag).

[11] [1967] 1 A.C. 645.

[12] *Mason* v. *Levy Auto Parts of England Ltd.* [1967] 2 Q.B. 530, 538–539, *per* MacKenna J. (discussing previous authorities).

[13] *Ibid.* at pp. 540–541. MacKenna J. after reviewing the authorities felt bound to follow them but did so reluctantly: " In holding that an exemption given to accidental fires, ' any law, usage or custom to the contrary notwithstanding,' does not include fires for which liability might be imposed upon the principle of *Rylands* v. *Fletcher*, the Court of Appeal (in *Musgrove* v. *Pandelis*) went very far."

[14] (1860) 5 H. & N. 679; *Jones* v. *Festiniog Ry.* (1868) L.R. 3 Q.B. 733 (sparks from railway engine caused fire, railway not worked under statutory powers, liable under *Rylands* v. *Fletcher*); *Powell* v. *Fall* (1890) 5 Q.B.D. 997; *Mansel* v. *Webb* (1918) 88 L.J.K.B. 323 (sparks from traction engine on highway causing fire, liability under *Rylands* v. *Fletcher*).

the defendants, in the absence of any negligence, should not be liable. But this view was rather hard upon farmers with crops adjacent to a railway line and a compromise was effected by the Railway Fires Acts 1905 and 1923,[15] which cast upon railways a liability not exceeding £200, even if the total damage claimed and done is much in excess,[16] for damage caused to agricultural land or agricultural crops for fire arising from the emission of sparks or cinders from their locomotives, although the locomotive was used under statutory powers. Presumably this puts the liability of the railway company up to £200 on the same level as that fixed by the common law and, on the other hand, does not deprive it of any of the defences pleadable at common law which are discussed above, e.g. default of the plaintiff.[17]

Strict liability under modern legislation

The dangers created by some modern industrial activities involving the use of toxic or polluting materials have created problems which the common law of negligence, nuisance and *Rylands* v. *Fletcher* might not be able to handle.[18] Accordingly, recent years have seen the enactment of a number of important statutory forms of liability for "environmental hazards." Full accounts of these Acts must be sought elsewhere, but the following is a summary of their provisions on civil liability.

Nuclear incidents [19]

The major factors requiring the enactment of legislation on liability for nuclear incidents were the risk of widespread damage, possibly involving losses of millions of pounds, from a single emission of ionising radiations and the possible injustice in the Limitation Acts owing to the long periods which might elapse between the impact of ionising radiations on the plaintiff and his suffering ascertainable damage.[20]

By the Nuclear Installations Act 1965 [21] no person other than the

---

[15] 5 Edw. 7, c. 11, s. 1; 13 & 14 Geo. 5, c. 27, s. 1.

[16] *Att.-Gen.* v. *G.W. Ry.* [1924] 2 K.B. 1; *Langlands (Swanley)* v. *British Transport Commission* [1956] 1 W.L.R. 890 (purpose of the Acts within the limit of £200 is to put the plaintiff in the position he would have been if the defendants had not been acting under statutory powers).

[17] *Groom* v. *G.W. Ry.* (1892) 8 T.L.R. 253, 256. In *Parker* v. *L.N.E. Ry.* (1945) 175 L.T. 137, defendants were held liable, as they had not adopted a modern invention used by other railways.

[18] It is not that the common law *could not* cope with disasters like the Torrey Canyon or Flixborough, but rather that the rules of liability are not sufficiently certain to avoid the possibility of protracted litigation.

[19] Street and Frame's *Law Relating to Nuclear Energy* (1966) is the leading work on this subject, and the editors of this work are indebted to them for clarifying such a complex series of statutes, statutory orders and international conventions.

[20] Street and Frame, *op. cit.*, p. 38. However, after the first Nuclear Installations Act in 1959, the Limitation Act 1963 to some extent mitigated this problem in all personal injury cases: see pp. 654–656, *post*.

[21] c. 57. This Act consolidates the law relating to nuclear installations, namely, the Nuclear Installations (Licensing and Insurance) Act 1959 (7 & 8 Eliz. 2, c. 46) and the Nuclear Installations (Amendment) Act 1965 (1965, c. 6). The Act came into force on December 1, 1965, except for s. 17 (5) (which bars enforcement in the United Kingdom of

United Kingdom Atomic Energy Authority shall use any site for the operation of nuclear plant unless a licence to do so has been granted in respect of that site by the Minister of Power.

Liability arises only when there is a nuclear incident which occurs at or in connection with certain nuclear installations, or in the course of transport of nuclear substances, and it can arise only in connection with licensed nuclear sites.[22] Section 7 (1) enacts:

" It shall be the duty of the licensee to secure that—

(a) no such occurrence involving nuclear matter as is mentioned in subsection (2) of this section causes injury to any person or damage to any property of any person other than the licensee, being injury or damage arising out of or resulting from the radio-active properties, or a combination of those and any toxic, explosive or other hazardous properties, of that nuclear matter; and

(b) no ionising radiations emitted during the period of the licensee's responsibility—

(i) from anything caused or suffered by the licensee to be on the site which is not nuclear matter; or

(ii) from any waste discharged (in whatever form) on or from the site, cause injury to any person or damage to any property of any person other than the licensee." [23]

The liability of the licensee under section 7 (1) (a), once damage within the Act is proved to have resulted, is a strict one, there is no need to prove negligence on the part of anyone.[24] Any person, other than the licensee, may sue provided he can prove " injury " (which means " personal injury " and includes loss of life) or " damage to any property." [25] There is no need that the dangerous matter should " escape " from the site on which it was kept onto other land. The Act creates a statutory right of action for damages, where injury or damage has been caused in breach of a duty.[26] Where liability in respect of the same injury is incurred by two or more persons, both or all of those persons shall be treated as jointly and severally liable in respect of that injury or damage.[27] It is a defence that the breach of duty under the Act is attributable to hostile action in the course of any armed conflict, but it is not a defence that it is attributable to a natural disaster, notwithstanding that the disaster is of such an exceptional character

---

certain foreign judgments), Nuclear Installations Act 1965 (Commencement No. 1) Order 1965 (No. 1880). Nuclear site licences are granted only to corporate bodies and are not transferable, s. 3 (1).

[22] s. 12.

[23] For other occurrences liability is confined to nuclear matter which is not excepted matter. " Nuclear matter " and " excepted matter " are defined in s. 26 (1).

[24] Street and Frame, op. cit., p. 52.

[25] Ibid. p. 53.

[26] ss. 12, 16.

[27] s. 17 (3).

that it could not reasonably have been foreseen.[28] The amount of compensation payable may be reduced by reason of the fault of the plaintiff, " but only if, and to the extent that, the causing of that injury or damage is attributable to the act of [' the plaintiff '] committed with the intention of causing harm to his person or property or with reckless disregard for the consequences of his act." [29] Under the Law Reform (Contributory Negligence) Act 1945 both the degree of blameworthiness and the causative potency of the act have to be considered in reducing damages.[30] But under the 1965 Act once the plaintiff is found to be intentional or reckless within the meaning of the subsection, the amount of the reduction rests solely on the extent to which the harm is caused by the plaintiff's act.[31] If after the plaintiff has been harmed his damages are increased by his failure to have proper medical attention, this failure by him to mitigate his damage would have prevented him from recovering that portion of his loss which is attributable to his omission, and it is doubtful whether section 13 (6) of the 1965 Act has a different effect.[32] It may well be that in an extreme case the plaintiff's claim will fail completely by a plea of ex turpi causa non oritur actio.[33] Section 12 (1) provides that " where any injury or damage has been caused in breach of a duty imposed " by the Act, then subject to certain exceptions " no other liability shall be incurred by any person in respect of that injury or damage." [34] Section 15 (1) enacts that " notwithstanding anything in any other enactment, a claim under the Act shall not be entertained after the expiration of 30 years from the date of the occurrence which gives rise to the claim, or, where that occurrence was a continuing one, or was one of a succession of occurrences all attributable to a particular happening " on a particular site, the date of the last event in the course of that occurrence or succession of occurrences is the relevant one. The period runs from the defendant's act, not from the infliction of damage.

The licensee must make such provision (either by insurance or some other means) as the Minister may, with the consent of the Treasury, approve for sufficient funds to be available up to a total of five million pounds in respect of each period as defined by section 19 of the Act. Section 16 (3) makes arrangements where the claim does not fall to be

---

[28] s. 13 (4) (a) and (b). Act of God, e.g. earthquake, is not a defence.
[29] s. 13 (6).
[30] Ante, pp. 115–117.
[31] Street and Frame, op. cit., p. 60.
[32] Ibid. p. 60.
[33] Ibid. p. 61.
[34] Ibid. pp. 61–66. The effect of the subsection may be summarised as follows: " Where ionising radiations are emitted as a result of defective equipment provided under contract with the licensee by a supplier, the section, it seems, prevents a person who suffers personal injury in consequence from suing the manufacturer or supplier, however negligent they might have been. It seems to prevent the supplier from being contractually liable to indemnify the licensee against damages payable to the victim by the licensee. It may prevent licensees from invoking Lister v. Romford Ice and Cold Storage Co. Ltd. (post, pp. 532–534) as a means of claiming an indemnity from the employee whose negligence actually caused the emission."

met by the licensee, because (a) it is in excess of the five million limit, or (b) it is made after the relevant 10-year period, or (c) it is a claim in respect of damage to the means of transport, the full satisfaction of which out of available funds is prevented by section 21 (1). Claims against the Atomic Energy Authority must be made to the Minister of Technology, those against government departments to the Minister in charge of the government department concerned, and in any other case to the Minister of Power.

The Act applies to occurrences outside the United Kingdom.[35]

Oil Pollution

The Merchant Shipping (Oil Pollution) Act 1971 [36] imposes civil liability upon the owner of a ship carrying a cargo of persistent oil in bulk for escape or discharge of persistent oil [37] from the ship. Liability extends to damage [38] caused in the United Kingdom, the cost of any measures reasonably taken for the purpose of preventing or reducing such damage, or damage caused by any measures so taken.[39] The Act provides three defences,[40] namely, that the discharge or escape—

(i)   resulted from an act of war, hostilities, civil war, insurrection or an exceptional, inevitable and irresistible natural phenomenon [41] or

(ii) was due wholly to anything done or left undone by another person, not being a servant or agent of the owner, with intent to do damage [42]; or

(iii) was due wholly to the negligence or wrongful act of a government or other authority in exercising its function of maintaining lights or other navigational aids.

The Act provides a complete code of liability of shipowners for such occurrences and any common law liability is abolished.[43] There are also provisions for compulsory insurance [44] and for limitation of liability where the occurrence was without the " actual fault or privity " of the shipowner.[45]

---

[35] s. 12 (1); Street and Frame's *Law Relating to Nuclear Energy*, pp. 74–85.

[36] C. 59. Forster, " Civil Liability of Shipowners for Oil Pollution," [1973] J.B.L. 23.

[37] Not necessarily the persistent oil in the cargo.

[38] " Damage " includes " loss " (s. 20 (1)). *Quaere* whether it extends to (i) personal injuries (*cf.* the Animals Act 1971, s. 11) (ii) mere loss of trade such as that suffered by hoteliers in the South West as a result of the *Torrey Canyon* incident.

[39] s. 1 (1).

[40] s. 2.

[41] *Cf.* " act of God," p. 376, *ante*; and see Forster, *loc. cit.*, p. 25.

[42] Thus the negligent act of a third party provides no defence.

[43] s. 3. This abolition extends to the liability of servants or agents of the owner and of salvors. Forster, *loc. cit.*, p. 30 n. 33 ignores on this point the general provisions of s. 1 (1), which makes the Act apply to bunkering oil as well as oil cargo. Any existing common law liability would, of course, continue to apply to the owner or master of another ship colliding with the oil carrier. The purpose of the obscurely worded s. 15 is apparently to allow recovery of the cost of preventive measures in respect of spillages of oil in situations to which the other provisions of the Act do not apply *e.g.* the discharge of bunkering oil from a dry cargo ship: see Hansard, H.L., Vol. 314, col. 1085.

[44] s. 10.

[45] s. 4. *Cf.* the Merchant Shipping Act 1894, s. 503.

The Law Reform (Contributory Negligence) Act 1945 applies to proceedings under the Act.[46]

Poisonous Waste

The Control of Pollution Act 1974 [47] provides that where any damage is caused by poisonous, noxious or polluting waste which has been deposited on land, any person who deposited it or caused or knowingly permitted it to be deposited is civilly liable for the damage,[48] provided that his act constituted an offence under section 3 (3) or section 18 (2) of the Act.[49] To constitute an offence under those sections the waste must have been deposited on an unlicensed site or in breach of the conditions in the licence,[50] must amount to an " environmental hazard " [51] and must have been deposited in such circumstances or for such a period that whoever deposited it there may reasonably be assumed to have abandoned it there or to have brought it there for the purpose of its being disposed as waste.[52] The Act provides the following defences to a civil action [53]:

(i)   that the defendant took care to inform himself, from others who were in a position to provide the information, as to whether the deposit would constitute an offence and had no reason to suppose that the information given to him was false or misleading [54];

(ii) that the defendant acted under instructions from his employer and neither knew nor had reason to suppose that the deposit was unlawful [55];

(iii) in the case of an action arising from making a deposit otherwise than in accordance with conditions specified in a disposal licence, that the defendant took all such steps as were reason-

---

[46] s. 1 (5). See Chap. 6, ante.

[47] C. 40. The Act comes into force on a day or days to be appointed, and with respect to liability for poisonous waste replaces the Deposit of Poisonous Wastes Act 1972. Unlike the Merchant Shipping (Oil Pollution) Act, supra, this Act does not abolish other forms of liability: s. 88 (5).

[48] Which here clearly includes personal injuries. Cf. n. 38, supra.

[49] s. 3 deals with " controlled waste," s. 18 with other waste.

[50] s. 3 (1).

[51] Defined in s. 4 (5) as a situation where " the waste has been deposited in such a manner or in such a quantity (whether that quantity by itself or cumulatively with other deposits of the same or different substances) as to subject persons or animals to a material risk of death, injury or impairment of health or as to threaten the pollution (whether on the surface or underground) of any water supply." The fact that waste is deposited in containers is not of itself to be taken to exclude any risk which might be expected to arise if the waste were not in containers (s. 4 (5) (b)); and the degree of risk of the hazards mentioned is to be assessed with particular regard " (a) to the measures, if any, taken by the person depositing the waste, or by the owner or occupier of the land, or others, for minimising the risk; and (b) to the likelihood of the waste, or any container in which it is deposited, being tampered with by children or others " (s. 4 (6)).

[52] s. 3 (3).

[53] The first three defences here mentioned are also defences to a criminal charge under the Act. However, one defence provided to a criminal charge is not available in civil proceedings: ss. 3 (4) (d), 88 (2).

[54] s. 3 (3) (a).

[55] s. 3 (3) (b).

ably open to him to ensure that the conditions were complied with [56];

(iv) the damage was wholly due to the fault of the person who suffered it [57];

(v) the damage was suffered by a person who voluntarily accepted the risk thereof.[58]

The Law Reform (Contributory Negligence) Act 1945 applies to liability arising under the Act.[59]

---

[56] s. 3 (3) (c).
[57] s. 88 (1) (a).
[58] s. 88 (1) (b).
[59] s. 88 (4) (b).

CHAPTER 17

ANIMALS [1]

AT common law a person might be liable for damage caused by an animal on one or more of three distinct grounds, namely, ordinary liability in tort, liability under the *scienter* rule [2] and liability for cattle trespass. The law has now been substantially modified with regard to two of these matters by the Animals Act 1971 [3]; but its structure is still in large measure the same and it is convenient to retain the common law headings for the purposes of exposition. [4]

ORDINARY LIABILITY IN TORT

There are many possible ways in which one may incur tortious liability through the instrumentality of an animal under one's control, but the fact that the agent happens to be animate rather than inanimate is immaterial, for while the common law, like other legal systems, [5] developed special or additional rules of liability for animals, it did not deny the applicability to them of the general law. A good example of this is nuisance, for you can be liable for nuisance through the agency of your animals, just as you can be for nuisance through the agency of anything else you own. A man who keeps pigs too near his neighbour's house commits a nuisance, but that is not solely because they are pigs. He would commit a nuisance just as much if what he owned were a manure heap. There is no independent tort called " nuisance by pigs " or " nuisance by animals." [6] Indeed, nuisance may be the only appropriate remedy where there is no " escape " and where the animal is not dangerous, *e.g.* obstruction of the highway by large numbers of animals, [7] or stench from pigs [8] or the crowing of cockerels. [9] Generally there is no liability for the escape of noxious animals on the defendant's land in the ordinary course of nature, such as rabbits, rats or birds. [10]

---

[1] The common law on this topic is covered by the exhaustive monograph of Glanville Williams, *Liability for Animals* (1939).

[2] This expression is properly confined to liability for animals which do not belong to a dangerous species, but is commonly used in the wider sense used here.

[3] 1971 c. 22. The Act came into force on October 1, 1971. The leading study of the modern law is North, *The Modern Law of Animals* (1972). See too Law Commission, Civil Liability for Animals, Law Com. No. 13, 1967.

[4] For the previous law, see the 8th ed. of this work, Chap. 17, and Law Com. No. 13.

[5] See Law Com. No. 13, n. 35.

[6] *Pitcher* v. *Martin* [1937] 3 All E.R. 918 illustrates negligence and nuisance committed through the agency of a dog; *Farrer* v. *Nelson* (1885) 15 Q.B.D. 258 nuisance through the agency of pheasants (distinguished in *Seligman* v. *Docker* [1949] 1 Ch. 53).

[7] *Cunningham* v. *Whelan* (1917) 52 Ir.L.T. 67.

[8] *Aldred's Case* (1610) 9 Co. 57b.

[9] *Leeman* v. *Montagu* [1936] 2 All E.R. 1677.

[10] *Brady* v. *Warren* [1900] 2 Ir. 632 (rabbits); *Seligman* v. *Docker* [1949] 1 Ch. 53 (wild pheasant increasing in numbers owing to favourable weather conditions). In an extreme case, however, there might be liability under the principle of *Goldman* v. *Hargrave* (p. 338 ante).

392

But if a landowner deliberately collects rabbits or game on his land for any purpose, he is liable for damage by them to neighbouring owners if it is caused by his "extraordinary, non-natural or unreasonable action." [11]

Again, if a dog-owner deliberately sets his dog on a peaceable citizen he is guilty of assault and battery in the ordinary way just as if he had flung a stone or hit him with a cudgel. So, too, if a man teaches his parrot to slander anyone, that is neither more nor less the ordinary tort of defamation than if he prefers to say it with his own tongue rather than with the parrot's. Similarly, ordinary trespass can be committed by means of animals. Trespass by beasts so often takes the form of cattle trespass (with which we deal separately) that one does not meet with many ordinary actions for trespass in the reports. However an indirect example is *Paul* v. *Summerhayes* [12] where fox hunters persisted in riding over the land of a farmer in spite of his protests and were held to have committed trespass.

Liability for animals may also be based on negligence. " Quite apart from the liability imposed upon the owner of animals or the person having control of them by reason of knowledge of their propensities, there is the ordinary duty of a person to take care either that his animal or his chattel is not put to such a use as is likely to injure his neighbour—the ordinary duty to take care in the cases put upon negligence." [13] In an action based upon the breach of such a duty to take care, the ordinary rules in an action of negligence apply. There is abundant authority to show that the action for negligence for harm done through animals is quite distinct from both the cattle trespass rule and the *scienter* rule. [14] In one respect, however, the common law failed to extend the principles of negligence to cases involving animals. It was the rule for centuries that if animals (or at least, ordinary tame animals) strayed from adjacent land on to the highway neither the owner of the animals nor the occupier of the land was liable for any ensuing damage even though it could have been prevented by controlling the animal or by fencing. [15] This immunity has now been abolished by the Animals Act 1971, [16] so that where damage is caused by animals straying on the

---

[11] *Farrer* v. *Nelson* (1885) 15 Q.B.D. 258, 260 (nuisance by unreasonable number of pheasants *brought* on the land); *Peech* v. *Best* [1931] 1 K.B. 1, 14; *Seligman* v. *Docker* [1949] 1 Ch. 53, 61–63. See Williams, *op. cit.*, pp. 235–262, for nuisance by wild animals, and (1956) 73 S.A.L.J. 335 for liability for escape of wild geese).

[12] (1878) 4 Q.B.D. 9.

[13] *Fardon* v. *Harcourt-Rivington* (1932) 146 L.T. 391, 392, *per* Lord Atkin; *Searle* v. *Wallbank* [1947] A.C. 341, 359–360.

[14] See *Draper* v. *Hodder* [1972] 2 Q.B. 556 (where a claim based upon *scienter* failed at the trial). Similarly, a claim might in some cases be founded upon the statutory variant of negligence created by the Occupiers' Liability Act 1957. See North, *op. cit.*, pp. 176, *et seq.*

[15] *Searle* v. *Wallbank* [1947] A.C. 341. For other cases see the 8th ed. of this work. The immunity had no application where the animal was brought on to the highway and then got out of control: *Gomberg* v. *Smith* [1963] 1 Q.B. 25.

[16] s. 8, which Lord Hailsham L.C. referred to as " the only [section] which it is really worth enacting ": Hansard, H.L., Vol. 312, cols. 887–888.

highway the question of liability is to be decided in accordance with the ordinary principles of negligence. It is provided, however, that if a person has a right to place animals on unfenced land, he is not to be regarded as in breach of a duty of care by reason only of his placing them there, so long as the land is in an area where fencing is not customary or is common land or a town or village green.[17] It is important to note that the Act will *not* require all landowners to fence against the highway: in moorland areas of Wales and the north of England this would be an intolerable burden and in such areas a motorist must be expected to be on the look out for straying livestock.[18]

LIABILITY FOR DANGEROUS ANIMALS

At common law the keeper of an animal was strictly liable, independently of negligence, for damage done by the animal if (a) the animal was *ferae naturae* (*i.e.* belonged to a dangerous species) or (b) the animal was *mansuetae naturae* (*i.e.* did not belong to a dangerous species) and he knew of its vicious characteristics.[19] These forms of strict liability have been retained by the Animals Act 1971 and, though they have been subjected to considerable modification, much of the old learning will continue to be relevant. It is, however, important to remember that the only source of the law is now the words of the Act and these must always prevail.

Animals belonging to a dangerous species

Where any damage is caused by an animal which belongs to a dangerous species, any person who is a keeper of the animal is liable for the damage.[20] A dangerous species is defined as " a species [21] (a) which is not commonly domesticated in the British Islands and (b) whose fully grown animals normally have such characteristics that they are likely, unless restrained, to cause severe damage or that any damage they may cause is likely to be severe." [22] A number of points arise on this definition. First, it seems that as was the case at common law in classifying animals as "*ferae naturae*," the question of whether an animal belongs to a dangerous species is one of law for the court. It is therefore to be expected that where an animal had been classified as *ferae naturae* at common law it will be regarded as belonging to a dangerous species

---

[17] s. 8 (2). Like many " by reason only " exceptions, this subsection is a fertile source of difficulties. Even without it, the owner would not be liable by reason *only* of placing his animals there, for there would have to be sufficient traffic to create a serious danger. For various problems of interpretation, see North, *op. cit.*, pp. 157–160. The subsection was applied in *Davies* v. *Davies* (1974) *The Times*, July 16: see (1974) 124 N.L.J. 683, 774.

[18] For statistics on road accidents involving animals see Law Com. No. 13, paras. 49–52. Dogs are in fact the major culprits.

[19] See Law Com. No. 13, paras. 4–9.

[20] s. 2 (1). For the definition of " keeper " see below.

[21] By s. 11, " species " includes sub-species and variety: see further note 28 below.

[22] s. 6 (2).

under the Act (*e.g.* a lion,[23] an elephant [24] and at least certain types of monkeys [25]). In two respects, however, the definition is wider than at common law in that the Act (a) renders a species dangerous if it poses a threat to property [26] and (b) allows for a species to be considered dangerous if it is not commonly domesticated in Britain, *even though it may be so domesticated overseas.*[27] Secondly, it will remain the case that once a species has been judicially classified as dangerous, then, subject to the doctrine of precedent, there is no room for distinctions based upon the fact that some variants or individual animals within the species may not in fact be at all dangerous: in other words, the law continues to ignore " the world of difference between the wild elephant in the jungle and the trained elephant in the circus . . . [which] is in fact no more dangerous than a cow." [28] Thirdly, the Act clearly adopts as the test of danger *either* " the greater risk of harm " *or* " the risk of greater harm ": an elephant may not in fact be very likely to get out of control and do damage, but *if* it does so, its bulk gives it a great capacity for harm.

For the purposes of this form of liability a person is a " keeper " of the animal if " (a) he owns the animal or has it in his possession; or (b) he is the head of a household of which a member under the age of 16 owns the animal or has it in his possession; and if at any time an animal ceases to be owned by or to be in the possession of a person, any person who immediately before that time was a keeper thereof . . . continues to be a keeper of the animal until another person becomes a keeper thereof . . . ." [29]

Other animals

Section 2 (2) provides:

" Where damage is caused by an animal which does not belong to a dangerous species, a keeper of the animal is liable for the damage . . . if:

(a) the damage is of a kind which the animal, unless restrained, was likely to cause or which, if caused by the animal, was likely to be severe; and

---

[23] *Murphy* v. *Zoological Society of London* [1962] C.L.Y. 68.

[24] *Behrens* v. *Bertram Mills Circus Ltd.* [1957] 2 Q.B. 1.

[25] Hale 1 P.C. 101; *cf. Brook* v. *Cook* (1961) 105 S.J. 684. As to other animals see Williams, *op. cit.*, pp. 292–294.

[26] The definition of " damage " in s. 11 is not exhaustive but does, it is submitted, include damage to property: see Law Com. No. 13, para. 15 (iii).

[27] Thus a camel is probably dangerous under the Act, though not *ferae naturae* at common law: *McQuaker* v. *Goddard* [1940] 1 K.B. 687 (which probably applied the wrong test at common law, anyway).

[28] *Behrens* v. *Bertram Mills Circus Ltd.*, *supra*, at p. 14. However, it is not clear to what extent the common law was prepared to distinguish among sub-species and the same problem will arise under the Act: see North, *op. cit.*, pp. 36–38.

[29] s. 6 (3). It is provided, however, by s. 6 (4) that where an animal is taken into and kept in possession for the purpose of preventing it from causing damage or of restoring it to its owner, a person is not a keeper of it by virtue only of that possession.

(b) the likelihood of the damage or of its being severe was due to characteristics of the animal which are not normally found in animals of the same species or are not normally so found except at particular times or in particular circumstances; and

(c) those characteristics were known to that keeper or were at any time known to a person who at that time had charge of the animal as that keeper's servant or, where that keeper is the head of a household, were known to another keeper of the animal who is a member of that household and under the age of sixteen."

The purpose of this somewhat complex provision is to preserve, with some modifications, the old rule of *scienter* liability for tame animals. Paragraph (a) follows the pattern of section 2 (1) in adopting likelihood of injury or likelihood that any injury that may be caused will be severe. Paragraph (b), however, is likely to give rise to difficulty with its concept of " abnormal " characteristics, if only because it may be so difficult to determine the " normal " characteristics of a species.[30] An example of the sort of case where a plaintiff might fail because of the first part of paragraph (b) is *Fitzgerald* v. *A. D. and E. D. Cooke Bourne Farms Ltd.*[31] where the injuries were inflicted by the frolics of a young filly; but in a case like *Barnes* v. *Lucille Ltd.*,[32] where the plaintiff was bitten by a bitch with pups, he would still presumably succeed, since the " normal " bitch is aggressive only at such times.

The requirement of knowledge in paragraph (c) is clearly of " actual " rather than of constructive knowledge, though a person who ought to know of his animal's vicious characteristics may, of course, still be liable for negligence. In some cases the knowledge is imputed to the keeper by process of law under paragraph (c), but this does not mean that knowledge of a person not mentioned in that paragraph will be irrelevant: if, for example, the wife of the keeper has knowledge of the animal's propensities it may be proper for the court to infer as a matter of fact that the keeper also knew of them.[33]

It should be noted with regard to both types of dangerous animals, that the Act, unlike the common law,[34] contains no requirement that the animal must escape from control, nor that there must be any sort of attack. If, therefore, an elephant slips or stumbles or a sheep transmits a virulent disease to another's flock, strict liability will apply.

The definition of " keeper " for this head of liability is the same as that for animals belonging to a dangerous species.

---

[30] See North, *op. cit.*, pp. 49–54.
[31] [1964] 1 Q.B. 249. With respect, there is room for the view that the Court of Appeal was too tender to fillies and too hard on " timorous persons, unused to horses."
[32] (1907) 96 L.T. 680.
[33] As in *Gladman* v. *Johnson* (1867) 36 L.J.C.P. 153.
[34] *Behrens* v. *Bertram Mills Circus Ltd., supra*, at p. 19; *Fitzgerald* v. *A. D. and E. D. Cooke Bourne Farms Ltd., supra*, at p. 270; Williams, *op. cit.*, p. 341.

Defences

The Act provides that it is a defence to an action brought under section 2 that the damage was wholly due to the fault of the person suffering it [35] or that he voluntarily assumed the risk thereof [36] (though a person employed as a servant by a keeper of the animal is not to be treated as accepting voluntarily risks incidental to his employment [37]). Contributory negligence, is, of course, a partial defence.[38]

There is special provision for injury to trespassers by dangerous animals. Section 5 (3) provides that a person is not liable under section 2 for any damage by an animal " kept on any premises or structure [39] to a person trespassing there, if it is proved either (a) that the animal was not kept there for the protection [40] of persons or property; or (b) (if the animal was kept there for the protection of persons or property) that keeping it there for that purpose was not unreasonable." It would seem unreasonable to protect your premises with a lion or a cobra, but not, it is submitted, with a fierce dog. This subsection does not, of course, affect any liability for negligence which the defendant may incur *qua* occupier of the premises or keeper of the animal, but there is little doubt that the keeping of guard dogs is consistent with the duty of common humanity to trespassers laid down in *British Railways Board* v. *Herrington*,[41] provided at least some warning of their presence is given.

LIABILITY FOR STRAYING LIVESTOCK

At common law the possessor of " cattle " [42] was strictly liable, independently of *scienter*, for damage done by them when they trespassed on the land of his neighbour.[43] Whatever may have been the original *rationale* of this form of liability, it was certainly not the same as that of *scienter*, for agricultural animals present no peculiar risk. However, the Law Commission recommend the retention of strict liability for this type of harm on the ground that it provided a simple method of allocating liability for what were usually comparatively small damages.[44] The law was, however, in need of considerable modification and the modern form of " cattle trespass " is found in section 4 of the Act, which provides:

---

[35] s. 5 (1).

[36] s. 5 (2).

[37] s. 6 (5). See North, *op. cit.*, pp. 73–76.

[38] s. 10.

[39] Not necessarily animals owned or kept by the occupier.

[40] This probably does not have to be a dominant purpose. Thus the old lady who keeps a dog partly for companionship and partly for protection would fail on (a), though her conduct would certainly be reasonable under (b).

[41] See p. 188, *ante.*

[42] " Cattle " or *avers* was a class virtually identical with livestock under the Act: see n. 45 *infra.*

[43] See Williams, *op. cit.*, Parts 2 and 3.

[44] Law Com. No. 13, paras. 62–63.

" (1) Where livestock [45] belonging [46] to any person strays [47] on to land in the ownership or occupation of another and—

    (a) damage is done by the livestock to the land or to any property on it [48] which is in the ownership or possession of the other person; [49] or

    (b) any expenses are reasonably incurred by that other person in keeping the livestock while it cannot be restored to the person to whom it belongs or while it is detained in pursuance of section 7 of [the] Act,[50] or in ascertaining to whom it belongs;

the person to whom the livestock belongs is liable for the damage or expenses, except as otherwise provided by [the] Act."

Defences to strict liability for straying livestock

The Act provides that there is no liability under this head for damage which is due wholly to the fault of the person suffering it [51] and that contributory negligence is a partial defence.[52] In this context default of the plaintiff is often closely bound up with fencing obligations and the Act therefore provides that damage " shall not be treated as due to the fault of the person suffering it by reason only that he could have prevented it by fencing; but [the defendant] is not liable . . . where it is proved that the straying of the livestock on to the land would not have occurred but for a breach by any other person, being a person having an interest in the land, of a duty to fence." [53] One other common law defence is preserved by the Act: the defendant is not liable under this form of liability if his livestock strayed on to the plaintiff's property from the highway and its presence there was a lawful use of the highway.[54] An example of this principle is the decision in *Tillet* v. *Ward*.[55]

---

[45] Defined in s. 11 as " cattle, horses, asses, mules, hinnies, sheep, pigs, goats and poultry [which is further defined as the domestic varieties of fowls, turkeys, geese, ducks, guinea-fowls, pigeons, peacocks and quails] and also deer not in the wild state."

[46] By s. 4 (2) livestock belongs to the person in whose possession it is. Finance companies owning herds under hire-purchase agreements may therefore rest easy in their corporate beds.

[47] The marginal note to s. 4 refers to " trespassing," but the enacting words do not. " Stray " is probably wide enough to cover the facts of *Ellis* v. *Loftus Iron Co.* (1874) L.R. 10 C.P. 10: *Wiseman* v. *Booker* (1878) 3 C.P.D. 184.

[48] Notwithstanding the general definition of " damage " in s. 11, it is submitted that the words of this paragraph make it clear beyond argument that damages are not recoverable for personal injuries under this section and *Wormald* v. *Cole* [1954] 1 Q.B. 614 is no longer law.

[49] The range of potential plaintiffs and their claimable losses is, with regard to property, rather wider than at common law: see North, *op. cit.*, pp. 94–96.

[50] See p. 399, *post.*

[51] s. 5 (1).

[52] s. 10.

[53] s. 5 (6). The law relating to the obligation to fence is notoriously complex and the Law Commission thought it inappropriate to deal with it other than by providing a relatively simple rule: Law Com. No. 13, n. 98. It should be noted that there is no requirement under s. 5 (6) that the duty in question be owed to the defendant. For a detailed comparison of s. 5 (6) with the common law position see North, *op. cit.*, Chap. 4.

[54] s. 5 (5). This does not, of course, remove any liability for negligence in such a case: *Gayler and Pope Ltd.* v. *Davies & Son Ltd.* [1924] 2 K.B. 75.

[55] (1882) 10 Q.B.D. 17.

X owned an ox which, while his servants were driving it with due care through a town, entered the shop of Y, an ironmonger, through an open door. It took three quarters of an hour to get it out and meanwhile it did some damage. X was held not liable to Y, for this was one of the inevitable risks of driving cattle on the streets. It would have made no difference if the ironmonger's door had been shut instead of open, and the ox had pushed its way through, or had gone through a plateglass window.[56]

Detention and sale of straying livestock

The common law provided a form of self-help remedy to a person harmed by straying livestock by way of distress damage feasant.[57] The Law Commission concluded that some remedy of this type should be retained but considered that the old remedy was so hedged about with limitations (in particular, it provided no power of sale) and obscurities that it would be better to create a new, statutory right. This is found in section 7 of the Act, which may be summarised as follows:

(i) The right of distress damage feasant is abolished in relation to animals.[58]

(ii) The occupier of land may detain any livestock which has strayed [59] on to his land and which was not then under the control of any person.[60]

(iii) He has, within 48 hours of exercising the right of detention, to give notice to the police and, if he knows the person to whom the livestock belongs, to that person.[61]

(iv) The right to detain the livestock ceases [62] if:

(a) the detainer has not complied with the provisions regarding notice; or

(b) the detainer is tendered sufficient money to satisfy any claim he may have for damage and expenses in respect of the straying livestock [63]; or

(c) he has no such claim and the person to whom the livestock belongs claims it.

---

[56] *Gayler and Pope Ltd.* v. *Davies & Son Ltd.* [1924] 2 K.B. 75. The driver of beasts which stray without his fault into property adjoining the highway is entitled to enter the property in order to get them out, and for that purpose he must be allowed such time as is reasonable in the circumstances: *Goodwin* v. *Cheveley* (1895) 28 L.J.Ex. 298.

[57] See Williams, *op. cit.*, Part I.

[58] The right is therefore abolished for *all* animals and the new remedy applies only to *livestock*, for the definition of which see n. 45, *supra*. The right of distress damage feasant remains in respect of other property, but it is practically moribund.

[59] The word " strayed " *may* not be wide enough to encompass livestock which have been driven on to the land, though the condition that the animals must not be under the control of any person (see n. 60, *infra*) suggests that the draftsman meant to include such a case.

[60] This was also a condition of the exercise of the common law right and is designed to prevent breaches of the peace.

[61] As to the person to whom livestock belongs, see note 46, *supra*.

[62] In the absence of a request for the return of the livestock, however, the detainer will not necessarily be liable for conversion or detinue.

[63] *i.e.* under s. 4.

(v) The detainer is liable for any damage caused to the livestock by failure to treat it with reasonable care and supply it with adequate food and water.

(vi) Where the livestock has been rightfully detained for not less than 14 days, the person detaining it may sell it at a market or by public auction, unless proceedings are then pending for the return of the livestock or for any claim for damages done by it or expenses incurred in detaining it.[63]

(vii) Where the net proceeds of sale exceed the amount of any claim the detainer may have for damages and expenses, the excess is recoverable from him by the person who would be entitled to the livestock but for the sale.[64]

REMOTENESS OF DAMAGE AND STRICT LIABILITY UNDER THE ACT

The Animals Act contains no provisions relating to remoteness of damage. The common law position was probably as follows. With regard to both forms of *scienter* liability and to cattle trespass the remoteness rule was probably that of directness of consequence rather than foreseeability since these heads of liability had affinities with *Rylands* v. *Fletcher*, which was expressly excluded from the ambit of the foreseeability test in *The Wagon Mound* (*No. 1*).[65] There were, however, at least two exceptions to the generality of this principle. First, in the case of *scienter* liability for animals *mansuetae naturae*, the keeper was only liable if the animal caused some harm of the kind to be expected from its known vicious characteristics [66]; secondly, in the case of cattle trespass, there was a rule that the damage had to be in accordance with the natural characteristics of the animal.[67] As to the position under the Act, one may guess that the basic principle will remain unchanged with directness of consequence as the test [68] and that the form of section 2 (2) means that with regard to liability for animals not belonging to a dangerous species the position will be fundamentally the same as at common law, since the damage must be of a kind made likely by the characteristics known to the keeper.[69] With regard to liability for straying livestock, however, there is nothing in the Act to support a principle comparable to that of the common law, so that the

---

[64] Presumably, if the net proceeds are *not* sufficient to meet the claim the detainer may sue for the excess. Further, the section makes no provision for the case where a detainer with no claim for damages or expenses exercises the power of sale which the section undoubtedly confers on him: the only sensible solution is to make him hold the proceeds on trust for the owner. These solutions, however, involve a fairly robust interpretation of the Act: North, *op. cit.*, pp. 119–120.

[65] See p. 379, *ante*.

[66] See Williams, *op. cit.*, p. 301. If, however, the animal committed a " direct " wrong of the type to be expected, the keeper was probably liable for other losses stemming from that injury, *e.g.* a disease caught from the bite of a vicious dog: Williams, p. 320.

[67] North, *op. cit.*, p. 103.

[68] North, *op. cit.*, pp. 47, 58, 107–108.

[69] See p. 396, *ante*.

keeper would be liable even for damage which it was abnormal or unnatural for the livestock to commit.[70]

PROTECTION OF LIVESTOCK AGAINST DOGS

Liability for attacks on livestock

Section 3 of the Animals Act re-enacts, with some modification, the form of strict liability formerly found in the Dogs Acts 1906–1928 and provides that where a dog causes damage by killing or injuring livestock,[71] any person who is a keeper [72] of the dog is liable for the damage.[73] The Act provides the following defences: that the damage was wholly due to the fault of the person suffering it [74]; that that person voluntarily accepted the risk of the damage [75]; and that the livestock was killed or injured on land on which it had strayed and either the dog belonged to the occupier or its presence on the land was authorised by the occupier.[76] Contributory negligence is a partial defence.[77]

Killing or injuring dogs to protect livestock

It may, in certain circumstances, be lawful for a person to kill or injure an animal belonging to another if this is necessary for the protection of his livestock or crops. The common law rule on this was laid down by the Court of Appeal in *Cresswell* v. *Sirl* [78] but this rule has been replaced, so far as the protection of livestock against dogs is concerned,[79] by section 9 of the Animals Act.

It is a defence [80] to an action for killing or injuring a dog to prove that:

(i) the defendant acted for the protection of livestock [81] and was a person entitled so to act; and

(ii) within 48 hours thereafter notice was given to the officer in charge of a police station.

A person is entitled to act for the protection of livestock if either the livestock or the land on which it is belongs [82] to him or to any person

---

[70] However, this is not likely to be of much practical importance now that liability for personal injuries is excluded from the ambit of s. 4.

[71] " Livestock " for this purpose is slightly wider than under s. 4, including pheasants, partridges and grouse in captivity: s. 11.

[72] " Keeper " has the same meaning as in s. 2: see note 29, *supra*.

[73] s. 3. See North, *op. cit.*, Chap. 7.

[74] s. 5 (1).

[75] s. 5 (2).

[76] s. 5 (4).

[77] s. 10.

[78] [1948] 1 K.B. 241.

[79] The rule in *Cresswell* v. *Sirl* continues to govern in the case of animals other than dogs, *e.g.* pigeons damaging crops, as in *Hamps* v. *Darby* [1948] 2 K.B. 311. See Clerk and Lindsell, *Torts*, 13th ed., pp. 292–293, 885; and the 8th ed. of this work, pp. 761–762.

[80] But not the only defence. A defendant who fails to make out the statutory defence (*e.g.* because he has not informed the police) may presumably fall back on the common law.

[81] For the definition in this context see note 71, *supra*.

[82] For this purpose an animal belongs to a person if he owns it or has it in his possession and land belongs to the occupier thereof: s. 9 (5).

under whose express or implied authority he is acting [83]; and he is deemed to be acting for their protection if and only if,[84] either:

(a) the dog is worrying or is about to worry the livestock and there are no other reasonable means of ending or preventing the worrying; or

(b) the dog has been worrying livestock, has not left the vicinity and is not under the control of any person and there are no practicable means of ascertaining to whom it belongs.[85]

---

[83] But if the livestock have strayed on to the land of another, there is no right under this section to shoot a dog which is lawfully on that land: s. 9 (2) (b).

[84] But the two following conditions are satisfied by reasonable belief on the defendant's part: s. 9 (4).

[85] This right to take punitive action in respect of an attack which is over is the major differance between s. 9 and *Cresswell* v. *Sirl*.

CHAPTER 18

TRESPASS TO GOODS [1]

Definition

Trespass to goods is a wrongful interference with the possession of them. It may take innumerable forms, such as scratching the panel of a coach,[2] removing a tyre from a car [3] or the car itself from a garage,[4] injuring or destroying goods, or, in the case of animals, beating [5] or killing [6] them, or infecting them with disease.[7] All that is necessary is that the harm done should be direct and not consequential (at any rate, as the law understands those terms) for otherwise the action, if any, must be case, not trespass. But physical contact is probably unnecessary; for chasing cattle has been a trespass time out of mind [8] and there is no reason to think that such chasing signifies actual beating or that a man is any the less liable for trespass to his neighbour's horse by scaring it off his neighbour's land than by putting a halter on it and leading it off; or for trespass to his neighbour's dog by putting poison where it can and does take it than by thrusting the substance down its throat.[9]

Whether the damage done must be substantial (*i.e.* whether the tort is actionable *per se*) is a matter of some doubt. According to an old case special damage must be proved where an animal is beaten,[10] but no reason was given for the decision,[11] and there must be many instances where, if mere touching of objects like wet paint, waxworks or exhibits in a picture gallery or museum, be not trespass, then their possessor would be without remedy. If the touching is intentional then there is no reason why it should not be trespass,[12] but the law may be otherwise if the touching is merely negligent. Diplock L.J. has said that actual damage is an essential ingredient in unintentional trespass to the

---

[1] In relation to this and the next chapter see Weir, *Casebook on Tort*, 3rd ed., Chap. 13 and Introduction.

[2] Alderson B. in *Fouldes* v. *Willoughby* (1841) 8 M. & W. 538, 549.

[3] *G. W. K. Ltd.* v. *Dunlop Rubber Co. Ltd.* (1926) 42 T.L.R. 376, 593.

[4] *Wilson* v. *Lombank Ltd.* [1963] 1 W.L.R. 1294.

[5] *Slater* v. *Swann* (1730) 2 Stra. 872.

[6] *Sheldrick* v. *Abery* (1793) 1 Esp. 55.

[7] *Anderson* v. *Buckton* (1719) 1 Stra. 192 carries the point, although Lord Tenterden C.J. disapproved of the case on another ground in *Daubney* v. *Cooper* (1830) 10 B. & C. 830. *Cf. Theyer* v. *Purnell* [1918] 2 K.B. 333, 341.

[8] *e.g. Farmer* v. *Hunt* (1610) 1 Brownl. 220; *Durant* v. *Childe* (1611) *ibid.* 221.

[9] Salmond, *Torts*, 16th ed., p. 92, and Addison, *Torts*, 8th ed. (1906) pp. 579–580, are to the like effect. The American *Corpus Juris*, Vol. 63 (1933), p. 892, seems to cite at least one authority in favour of this view; and the American *Restatement of Torts*, Vol. 1, § 217, Comment (b), regards scaring of animals to their injury as sufficient.

[10] *Slater* v. *Swann* (1730) 2 Stra. 872. *Cf. Everitt* v. *Martin* [1953] N.Z.L.R. 298: Davis (1953) 16 M.L.R. 525–526.

[11] It appears to be the only authority for Street's view in *Foundations of Liability* (1906), i. p. 16.

[12] This was Pollock's view: *Torts*, 15th ed., pp. 264–265. See also *Leitch & Co. Ltd.* v. *Leydon* [1931] A.C. 90, 106, *per* Lord Blanesburgh; Salmond, *Torts*, 16th ed., p. 93, Street, *Torts*, 5th ed., p. 31.

person,[13] and if this is so there is no reason for distinguishing the case of trespass to goods.

Since the decision in *Fowler* v. *Lanning*,[14] which held that in an action for unintentional trespass to the person the plaintiff must prove negligence on the part of the defendant, it is likely that the same is true in cases of trespass to goods, though the matter cannot be regarded as finally settled.[15] It is clear, however, that either an intentional or a negligent act was formerly sufficient and one who negligently killed another's pigeons,[16] or caused his ship to collide with another vessel,[17] was just as liable in trespass as if he had done these acts intentionally. In the later reports there is hardly any direct authority as to inadvertent trespass to goods, probably because the injured party preferred the action for the nascent tort of negligence for reasons which have been already detailed, and it may be that today only negligence is available.[18] But trespass obviously remains appropriate where one takes another's goods in the mistaken belief that he is entitled to do so.[19] In *Wilson* v. *Lombank Ltd.*[20] the plaintiff had " purchased " a car from a person who had no title to it and had sent it to a garage for repair. The defendant, believing, wrongly, that the car was his, removed it from the garage. It was held that the plaintiff had possession and that the defendant was liable in trespass.[21]

Possession essential

As trespass is an interference with possession, it follows that if the plaintiff were not in possession at the date of the alleged meddling, he cannot sue for trespass. He may be able to sue for conversion, but that is a different matter. " The distinction between the actions of trespass and trover is well settled: the former is founded on possession; the latter on property." [22]

Alleged exceptions

It is said that there are exceptions to this rule and that the following

---

[13] *Letang* v. *Cooper* [1965] 1 Q.B. 232, 244–245. Lord Denning M.R. went so far as to say that negligence is the only cause of action for unintended injury to the person (*ibid.* at p. 240) and presumably his Lordship would have said the same for unintended damage to goods. See *ante*, p. 82.

[14] [1959] 1 Q.B. 426; *ante*, pp. 80–83.

[15] *National Coal Board* v. *Evans* [1951] 2 K.B. 861 establishes that inevitable accident is a defence, but does not carry the point in the text, since the absence of negligence on the part of the defendants was established as in *Stanley* v. *Powell* [1891] 1 Q.B. 86. See *ante*, pp. 80–81.

[16] Br.Abr. *Trespass*, 63 (A.D. 1373). See, too, 74, 99.

[17] *Covell* v. *Laming* (1808) 1 Camp. 497.

[18] See note 13, *supra*, and *ante*, pp. 80–83.

[19] As in the case of excessive execution. Proof of malice is unnecessary: *Moore* v. *Lambeth County Court Registrar* (*No. 2*) [1970] 1 Q.B. 560.

[20] [1963] 1 W.L.R. 1294; *Colwill* v. *Reeves* (1811) 2 Camp. 575; Weir, *Casebook on Tort*, 3rd ed., p. 402.

[21] Notwithstanding the fact that the plaintiff had no title to the car and that the defendant had returned it to its true owner, the plaintiff recovered the full value of the car by way of damages. See *post*, p. 425, note 28.

[22] Lord Kenyon C.J. in *Ward* v. *Macauley* (1791) 4 T.R. 489, 490.

persons can sue for trespass although they had not possession: (a) A trustee against any third person who commits a trespass to trust chattels in the hands of the beneficiary. (b) An executor or administrator for trespasses committed to goods of the deceased after his death but before probate is granted to the executor or before the administrator takes out letters of administration. (c) The owner of a franchise (*e.g.* a right to take wreck or treasure trove) against anyone who seizes the goods before he himself can take them.[23] But it is questionable whether any of these exceptions is genuine. The language used in the authorities relating to the trustee is none too clear, but it indicates that the trustee has possession of chattels in the hands of the beneficiary, and not merely the right to possess them.[24] It does not follow from this that the beneficiary himself cannot sue, for if he holds the chattels he seems to have joint possession with the trustee.[25] Again, the executor and administrator have long been regarded as having the deceased's possession continued in them; when they assume office their title relates back to his death. They have not merely the right to possess: they are in possession.[26] Similarly, in the case of the franchise, possession is deemed to be with the owner of the franchise. In *Bailiffs of Dunwich* v. *Sterry*,[27] the plaintiffs had the right to wrecks at Dunwich and the defendant took a cask of whisky from a wreck before the plaintiffs could get it. The defendant was held liable for trespass, for " the right to the possession draws after it a constructive possession, which is sufficient to support the action." [28]

In a simple bailment determinable at will the bailor does not lose possession and may sue any wrongdoer other than his bailee in trespass.[29]

---

[23] Salmond, *Torts*, 16th ed., p. 95.
[24] *White* v. *Morris* (1852) 11 C.B. 1015; *Barker* v. *Furlong* [1891] 2 Ch. 172, a case of conversion, but Romer J. approved *White* v. *Morris*.
[25] Lewin, *Trusts*, 16th ed., p. 618.
[26] *Tharpe* v. *Stallwood* (1843) 5 M. & G. 760, 770; Pollock & Wright, *Possession*, pp. 146–147.
[27] (1831) 1 B. & Ad. 831.
[28] *Ibid.* 842; Pollock & Wright, *op. cit.*, p. 147.
[29] *Lotan* v. *Cross* (1810) 2 Camp. 464. The authorities are discussed in *Penfolds Wines Pty. Ltd.* v. *Elliott* (1946) 74 C.L.R. 204, 214–220, 226–236, 239–244; Paton, *Bailment*, Preface, ss. 3, 82; *U.S.A.* v. *Dollfus Mieg et Cie* [1952] A.C. 582, 605, 611–613; *Wilson* v. *Lombank Ltd.* [1963] 1 W.L.R. 1294.

CHAPTER 19

CONVERSION AND OTHER INJURIES TO GOODS

HISTORICAL

IT is impossible to give an intelligible account of conversion without an historical sketch of the action of trover which was the remedy for it; nor is trover completely understandable without some knowledge of the other actions for injuries to, or interference with, chattels. These remedies were, and indeed still are: (1) Detinue. (2) Replevin. (3) Trespass, besides (4) Trover. We proceed to consider them separately.

1. Detinue

If A unjustly detains B's goods, B's remedy is detinue. The action is one of the oldest in our law, for it is traceable to the twelfth century.[1] At common law the defendant had the option of giving up the goods or paying damages. He was allowed this alternative partly because medieval movables were often so perishable that the court could not undertake the responsibility of enforcing their restoration, partly because the law then regarded all things as having a legal price, and if the plaintiff got that, he got all that he ought to have.[2] As we shall see, it is now possible for the court to order specific restitution of the goods. The great drawback to detinue was that the defendant could defeat the plaintiff's claim by waging his law, i.e. by getting a number of compurgators to swear that they believed him to be oath-worthy although they knew nothing of the facts of the case. Nor was detinue of any use if the goods had been damaged by a bailee who nevertheless restored them to the bailor (or to his nominee); for the bailee was no longer detaining anything, and the bailor's only remedy was an action of trespass upon the case.[3] These disadvantages led to the almost complete supersession of detinue by trover by devices which are discussed below.[4]

2. Replevin

If A unlawfully takes B's goods by way of distress or otherwise, B's remedy is replevin. This action is also one of venerable origin

---

[1] Maitland, *Forms of Action* (1936), p. 48.

[2] *Ibid.* pp. 61–63.

[3] This may be inferred from Coke's argument in Y.B.Hil. 39 Hen. VI, f. 44, pl. 7. Later authorities are cited in Ames (" 33 Hen. VI " is a slip for " 39 Hen. VI ") in *Select Essays in Anglo-American Legal History*, iii, p. 441, and Holdsworth, *History of English Law*, iii, pp. 350–351. Fifoot, *History and Sources of the Common Law*, pp. 24–43.

[4] For the circumvention of detinue by case, see Milsom, " Not Doing is no Trespass " [1954] C.L.J. 105, 113–117.

and was very important in the Middle Ages, but by its very nature it was incapable of much expansion, and by 1770 the wider scope of trover had led to its use as an alternative—and something more —to replevin.[5]

3. Trespass

The action of trespass to goods was considered in Chapter 18. The point to emphasise is that it has always been a wrong to possession, and does not necessarily involve any assertion of a right to deal with the goods or any appropriation of them. If there were a taking of them, then the remedy was trespass *de bonis asportatis* and possibly trover might lie; if there were injury, but no taking, trespass would still lie, but not trover unless the possessor's title were called in question.[6]

4. Trover and Conversion [7]

The essence of conversion, the wrong for which trover was the remedy, is calling in question the title of another person to goods. It is dealing with them in such a way as to deprive the person entitled to them of their use and benefit, or it may consist in an absolute denial of his right to deal with them even though there be no physical interference with the possession of them.

Trover came into our law later than the other remedies just mentioned. Some such remedy was urgently needed. Detinue did not apply at all to *taking* goods but was limited to *keeping* them and, moreover, it could be stultified by the licensed perjury known as wager of law. Replevin was almost confined to wrongful distress. Trespass was a wrong to possession, not to the right to possess.

The history of trover has been well told and at length by several experts and we need do no more than give a bare outline of it here. It began as an action of trespass upon the case in which it was alleged that the defendant had converted the plaintiff's goods to his use. The first instance of such an allegation was in 1479.[8] Then by 1547 a series of fictions had considerably expanded the action. It was alleged (a) that the plaintiff was possessed of the goods; (b) that he accidentally lost them; (c) that the defendant found them; (d) that the defendant converted them to his own use.[9] The losing and finding might be pure fictions, but the defendant was not allowed to deny them. And so this action of trover became the remedy for a new tort—conversion.

---

[5] Maitland, *op. cit.*, p. 61; Holdsworth, *op. cit.*, iii, pp. 285–287.

[6] Many modern cases show this. Br.Abr. *Trespass*, 63 (A.D. 1373) will serve as an early illustration.

[7] Holdsworth, *op. cit.*, iii, pp. 285–287, 350–351, 450, 581–584; vii, pp. 403–513; viii, pp. 466–468; ix, p. 42; " Not Doing is no Trespass " Milsom [1954] C.L.J., 105, 114; Simpson, " The Introduction of the Action on the Case for Conversion " (1959) 75 L.Q.R. 364.

[8] Y.B.Hil. 18 Edw. 4, f. 23, pl. 5.

[9] Rastall, *Entries* (1596), 4b–5a.

Nineteenth-century legislation swept away these fictions and the action of trover has become the action for conversion. One of its remarkable developments historically was that conversion included not only appropriation to one's own use, but also disposition of the goods to another person and indeed any dealing with them in a manner adverse to the plaintiff and inconsistent with his right of dominion.[10] Still more notable was the way in which it encroached upon the spheres of detinue, trespass and replevin. The difficulty in extending it to cases covered by detinue was this: Conversion could be committed only by a positive act—misfeasance. Now detinue lay where a man was in possession of goods and refused to give them up. Could it be said that such a mere refusal was a positive act? The line between misfeasance and non-feasance is apt to be a fine one, and the courts after some hesitation took advantage of this and held mere refusal to redeliver to be conversion unless, of course, it were justified.[11] Detinue wilted considerably under this treatment and it was not until the abolition of the unpopular wager of law in 1833 and other procedural reforms in the early nineteenth century that it revived.

As to the action of trespass, there was a certain amount of give and take between it and trover, and at one time it looked as if any " asportation " (or moving) of property might be regarded not only as trespass to it but also as conversion of it. But this mischievously wide doctrine which would have made a scratch upon the panel of a coach a conversion of the whole vehicle [12] is certainly not law now, if it ever was.[13] As to replevin, it has long been settled that trover is an alternative to it. This was undoubtedly stretching a point, for wrongful distraint of goods is not a denial of the owner's title to them, since the goods are reckoned to be in the custody of the law.[14]

We can now state the present law as to these various remedies.

DETINUE

As has long been stated, this is the wrongful retention of the possession of a chattel. A good deal of litigation with respect to it has been concerned with the recovery of title deeds to land,[15] but it is by no means confined to that. It does not matter how possession of the chattel was acquired; it may have been by a bailment and then the bailee is liable in detinue if he holds over after the bailment is determined, or it may be by finding and then the finder is liable if he wrongfully refuses to give up the chattel to the owner, or it may be any other mode of

---

[10] Pollock, *Torts*, 15th ed., p. 270.
[11] Holdsworth, *op. cit.*, vii, pp. 405–415.
[12] Alderson B. in *Fouldes* v. *Willoughby* (1841) 8 M. & W. 540, 549.
[13] Holdsworth, *op. cit.*, vii, pp. 414–421.
[14] *Ibid.* iii, p. 286, n. 8; vii, pp. 415–416.
[15] See the cases in Roscoe, *Evidence in Civil Actions*, 20th ed. (1934), ii, pp. 1007–1008.

acquisition.[16] In *Singh* v. *Ali* [17] the plaintiff purported to buy a lorry from the defendant, but the contract of sale was void for illegality. Nevertheless, when the defendant removed the lorry from the plaintiff's possession and refused to return it, it was held that the plaintiff could maintain detinue.

What must be proved

The plaintiff must prove, first, that he is entitled to immediate possession of the chattel, and if there is any defect in his right to immediate possession he must fail.[18] Usually the defect arises from a right of adverse possession in a third party, but a defect arising from other causes may be equally fatal, *e.g.* that it would be unlawful to transfer the goods to him even although he is the true owner.[19] Secondly, that the defendant detained it after a proper demand had been made for its restoration.[20] A bailee is not obliged to return the chattel to the bailor; he must merely allow the bailor to collect it. Failure on the part of the bailee to comply with a demand that the chattel be returned to a particular address will not, therefore, sustain a claim in detinue.[21] On the other hand, it is no defence that the defendant has not got possession if he once had it and improperly parted with it: *e.g.* where an auctioneer mistakenly delivers an article to X which he has in fact sold to Y [22]; so, too, if the defendant carelessly lost it; but accidental loss excuses him provided he can prove the loss was not due to any fault of his own.[23]

A good defence is that the refusal to deliver was not an unqualified one but was subject to a reasonable condition that the plaintiff's claim should be verified. Where there is a bona fide doubt as to the plaintiff's title, the defendant is entitled to a reasonable time for investigation.

---

[16] Where the defendant acquires possession by virtue of an order of a magistrates' court made under the Police (Property) Act 1897, s. 1, the plaintiff must prove his title to the goods and cannot rely upon his former possession: *Irving* v. *National Provincial Bank Ltd.* [1962] 2 Q.B. 73.

[17] [1960] A.C. 167; *Belvoir Finance Co. Ltd.* v. *Stapleton* [1971] 1 Q.B. 210. See also *Stoneleigh Finance Ltd.* v. *Phillips* [1965] 2 Q.B. 537, an example of the not uncommon case where an owner in possession sells the goods but retains possession under a hire-purchase contract. If the new owner acquires an immediate right to possess he can claim in detinue. For the converse case of a bailee succeeding against his bailor in detinue see *City Motors (1933) Pty. Ltd.* v. *Southern Aerial Super Service Pty. Ltd.* (1961) 106 C.L.R. 477.

[18] See, *e.g.* *Jarvis* v. *Williams* [1955] 1 W.L.R. 71; *Tappenden* v. *Artus* [1964] 2 Q.B. 185.

[19] *Kahler* v. *Midland Bank Ltd.* [1950] A.C. 24, 33–34, *per* Lord Normand; *Garrett* v. *Arthur Churchill Ltd.* [1970] 1 Q.B. 92, *per* Lord Parker C.J. *Cf. Ghani* v. *Jones* [1970] 1 Q.B. 693. In a bailment terminable at the will of the bailor, the bailor as well as the bailee may sue, for the bailor has a right to immediate possession.

[20] *Gledstane* v. *Hewitt* (1831) 1 Cr. & J. 565, 570.

[21] *Capital Finance Co. Ltd.* v. *Bray* [1964] 1 W.L.R. 323; Weir, *Casebook on Tort*, 3rd ed., p. 409.

[22] *Jones* v. *Dowle* (1841) 9 M. & W. 19.

[23] *Reeve* v. *Palmer* (1858) 5 C.B.(N.S.) 84; *Roux* v. *Wiseman* (1857) 1 F. & F. 45; *Coldman* v. *Hill* [1919] 1 K.B. 443, 450; *Houghland* v. *R. R. Low (Luxury Coaches) Ltd.* [1962] 1 Q.B. 694; Weir, *Casebook on Tort*, 3rd ed., p. 411; *Alicia Hosiery Ltd.* v. *Brown Shipley & Co. Ltd.* [1970] 1 Q.B. 195. (Defendant whose possession was constructive only not liable for his bailee's refusal to deliver to the plaintiff.)

This is especially so with respect to property that has been lost or stolen and has come into the hands of an innocent defendant. He is not liable in detinue, or indeed on any ground, merely because he meets the plaintiff's demand by saying that he must make inquiries which any reasonable man would make; indeed, he would be taking foolish risks if he did otherwise.[24]

Jus tertii in detinue

Jus tertii is generally no defence to a bailee who is sued in detinue by his bailor, for a bailee is estopped from disputing his bailor's title. To this there are two exceptions: first, if he has been evicted by title paramount, *i.e.* if the article bailed to him has been taken from him by the true owner [25]; secondly, if he is defending the action on behalf and by the authority of the true owner.[26] There is no direct decision that *jus tertii* is a good defence where the defendant is in possession of goods otherwise than by bailment, *e.g.* by finding, but as the burden of proving his title is on the plaintiff, it is conceived that it would be a good defence; that is the rule in conversion, and the argument is equally strong where the defendant merely detains the goods.

Judgment and damages

At common law a defendant held liable in detinue was ordered to deliver up the chattel to the plaintiff or to pay its value as assessed and in either event to pay damages for its detention. The defendant thus in effect had the option either to return the chattel or pay its value.[27] By the Common Law Procedure Act 1854,[28] however, the court was given a discretionary power to deprive the defendant of this option and to order him to deliver up the chattel to the plaintiff. This power continues to exist and today a judgment in detinue may take one of three forms: (i) for the value of the chattel as assessed and damages; (ii) for the return of the chattel or recovery of its value as assessed and damages; or (iii) for the return of the chattel and damages.[29] Under the first form, which is appropriate where the chattel claimed is an ordinary article in commerce and damages are an adequate remedy,[30] the defendant loses his option of returning the chattel, but he can, of course, do so at any time before judgment and then his only liability will be for damages. If he does not return it before judgment, the

---

[24] *Clayton* v. *Le Roy* [1911] 2 K.B. 1031.
[25] This is the result of *Shelbury* v. *Scotsford* (1603) Yelv. 22; *Biddle* v. *Bond* (1865) 6 B. & S. 225, 233; *Rogers, Sons & Co.* v. *Lambert & Co.* [1891] 1 Q.B. 318, 328.
[26] *Rogers, Sons & Co.* v. *Lambert & Co.*, *supra*; *Blaustein* v. *Maltz & Co.* [1937] 2 K.B. 142 marks the limits of this exception and of the doctrine of *jus tertii* itself.
[27] A plaintiff seeking specific relief might try his luck in the Court of Chancery: *Re Scarth* (1874) L.R. 10 Ch.App. 234, 235, *per* Mellish L.J.
[28] 17 & 18 Vict. c. 125, s. 78.
[29] See the full discussion by Diplock L.J. in *General and Finance Facilities Ltd.* v. *Cooks Cars (Romford) Ltd.* [1963] 1 W.L.R. 644, 650–651; Weir, *Casebook on Tort*, 3rd ed., p. 415.
[30] *Whiteley Ltd.* v. *Hilt* [1918] 2 K.B. 808, 819.

plaintiff is entitled to judgment in this form.[31] Under the second form the defendant retains his option of returning the chattel but the plaintiff has the right, once its value has been assessed, of applying to the court for the enforcement of specific restitution by a writ of specific delivery which the court has a discretion to grant or refuse.[32] Under the third form, which is unusual but possible,[33] the only pecuniary sum recoverable is damages for detention and therefore valuation of the chattel is unnecessary.

When it is necessary for the value of the chattel to be assessed, the relevant date to be taken is the date of the verdict or judgment in the plaintiff's favour and not the date of the defendant's refusal to return it.[34] This is so because the plaintiff in detinue does not abandon his property in the goods when his cause of action arises by the defendant's refusal to return on demand, for the essence of detinue is that the plaintiff maintains and asserts his property in the goods up to the date of judgment.[35] The significance of the date of the refusal of the plaintiff's demand is that the defendant's failure to return the goods after that date becomes, and continues to be, wrongful, and damages are recoverable for wrongful " detention " after that date until the goods are returned or payment made of their value.[36] The date of the defendant's refusal cannot convert a claim for the return of the goods into a claim for payment of their value at that date.[37]

---

[31] R.S.C., Ord. 13, r. 3. This rule is, in its terms, applicable only to a judgment given in default of appearance, but Diplock L.J. treats its predecessor (R.S.C., Ord. 13, r. 6 of 1883) as of general application: *General and Finance Facilities* case, *supra*, at p. 650.
[32] R.S.C., Ord. 45, r. 4 (2). It is essential that the value of the chattel be separately assessed from the damages if this form of judgment is used: *General and Finance Facilities* case, *supra*. Where the chattel is on the premises of a third party, a defendant does not satisfy a judgment in this form by doing nothing. If he does not pay the value he must at least inform the plaintiff that he recognises his title to the chattel and that it is at his disposal: *Metals and Ropes Co. Ltd.* v. *Tattersall* [1966] 1 W.L.R. 1500. Cf. *Alicia Hosiery Ltd.* v. *Brown Shipley & Co. Ltd.* [1970] 1 Q.B. 195.
[33] *Hyams* v. *Ogden* [1905] 1 K.B. 246. R.S.C., Ord. 45, r. 4 (1).
[34] *Rosenthal* v. *Alderton & Sons Ltd.* [1946] 1 K.B. 374. If the defendant has acquired an interest in the goods the plaintiff can then only recover the value of his interest: *Belsize Motor Supply Co.* v. *Cox* [1914] 1 K.B. 244; *Whiteley Ltd.* v. *Hilt* [1918] 2 K.B. 808. " In a hire-purchase transaction there are two proprietary interests: the finance company's interest and the hirer's interest. If the hirer wrongfully sells the goods or the benefit of the agreement, in breach of the agreement, then the finance company are entitled to recover what they have lost by reason of his wrongful act. That is normally the balance outstanding on the hire-purchase price. But they are not entitled to more than they have lost ": *Wickham Holdings Ltd.* v. *Brooke House Motors Ltd.* [1967] 1 W.L.R. 295, 300–301, *per* Lord Denning M.R.; *Belvoir Finance Co. Ltd.* v. *Stapleton* [1971] 1 Q.B. 210.
[35] *Rosenthal* v. *Alderton & Sons Ltd.*, *supra*, at pp. 377–378, *per* Evershed J. At p. 379 he adds that where a bailor sues in detinue the value of goods that have been already converted is assessed as at the time of judgment " at any rate where he was not aware of the conversion at the time." See *Sachs* v. *Miklos* [1948] 2 K.B. 23. Paton, *Bailment*, p. 405, states that on a strict historical basis this qualification is unnecessary, but is added to prevent a plaintiff delaying his action to take advantage of a rising market.
[36] *Ibid.* 378.
[37] *Ibid.* 378. In *Beaman* v. *A.R.T.S.* [1948] 2 All E.R. 89, 93 (reversed on other grounds [1949] 1 K.B. 550), Denning J. thought there might be practical difficulties in reconciling *Rosenthal's* case with the general rule that damages in tort should be assessed at the time of the accrual of the cause of action, but detinue is " a continuing cause of action which accrues at the date of the wrongful refusal to deliver up the goods and continues until delivery up of the goods or judgment in the action for detinue ": *General and Finance*

As the gist of the grievance is mere unlawful detention, the damages will be nominal unless the plaintiff proves that he has suffered special damage.[38] In an action for detinue of railway scrip it was held that the jury was entitled in awarding damages to take into consideration the fall in value between the date of the defendant's refusal and the date of its return to the plaintiff under the order of the court.[39] As the scrip had been returned, the question of value or fall in value was relevant only under the head of damages, so the plaintiff in detinue is protected whether there is a rise or fall.[40] Where the defendant detains goods which the plaintiff normally lets on hire, the measure of damages will include a reasonable sum for hiring charges during the period of detention.[41]

REPLEVIN

By far the commonest use of replevin is where goods have been wrongfully seized by way of distress. Indeed, Coke [42] and Blackstone [43] thought that it had no other use, but there is enough show of common law authority to make it applicable to the recovery of property taken otherwise than by distress,[44] although it is very rarely so employed.

The procedure in the action is for the plaintiff to apply to the registrar of the county court, who will see that the goods alleged to have been wrongfully taken are restored to the plaintiff on his giving security to prosecute an action of replevin in the county court or in the High Court.[45] The plaintiff thus recovers his goods without having to await the outcome of an action while the defendant is protected by the security given by the plaintiff.

Replevin is available only if the taking of the goods was a trespass, for the allegation in the old pleadings was that the defendant " took and detained " the goods; hence it will not lie against a carrier who detains them, for he did not obtain possession by trespass though he may be liable in detinue or conversion.[46]

CONVERSION

Conversion may be defined as *any act in relation to the goods of a person which constitutes an unjustifiable denial of his title to them.*

Facilities Ltd. v. Cooks Cars (Romford) Ltd. [1963] 1 W.L.R. 644, 648, per Diplock L.J. See further Kiralfy, " The Problem of a Law of Property in Goods " (1949) 12 M.L.R. 424; Elliott, " Damages in Detinue and Conversion " (1951) 9 N.I.L.Q. 157.

[38] Anderson v. Passman (1835) 7 C. & P. 193.

[39] Williams v. Archer (1871) L.R. 6 C.P. 584, approved in Rosenthal's case [1946] 1 K.B. 374, 378.

[40] Paton, Bailment, p. 407.

[41] Strand Electric and Engineering Co. Ltd. v. Brisford Entertainments Ltd. [1952] 2 Q.B. 246, 252 (C.A.); Capital Finance Co. Ltd. v. Bray [1964] 1 W.L.R. 323, 329, per Lord Denning M.R.

[42] Co.Litt. 145b.

[43] Comm., iii, 146.

[44] Coleridge J.'s judgment in Mennie v. Blake (1856) 6 E. & B. 842, 846–850; Lord Ellenborough C.J. in Dore v. Wilkinson (1817) 2 Stark. 287, 288.

[45] County Courts Act 1959 (7 & 8 Eliz. 2, c. 22), ss. 104–106.

[46] Galloway v. Bird (1827) 4 Bing. 299; Mennie v. Blake (1856) 6 E. & B. 842.

What constitutes conversion

Conversion involves two concurrent elements: (a) a dealing with goods in a manner inconsistent with the right of the person entitled to them, and (b) an intention in so doing to deny that person's right or to assert a right which is inconsistent with such right. Where the act done is necessarily a denial of the other's right, however, or is an assertion of a right inconsistent therewith, as where he deals with the goods as his own, intention does not matter. Intention becomes material in those cases where goods are in the possession of somebody who acts as agent or bailee and the dealing with the goods is a transfer of custody from himself to somebody else, for there it may well be that the intention is not to exercise any right inconsistent with the right of the person entitled to them.[47]

It is possible for you to commit conversion of my goods by wrongfully (a) taking possession of them, or (b) abusing possession of them when you have already got it, or even (c) denying my title to them, although you have never had possession at all, provided your denial is absolute.

(a) Taking possession. As to taking possession of them, that by itself will not always be conversion. If I snatch your hat from your head with intent to steal it, that is conversion as well as trespass, but if I throw it at another person, that is trespass only, for I am not questioning your title to it.[48] So, too, if you shift my bicycle from a public stand for cycles in order to get at your own, and forget to replace mine so that it is stolen by someone, that may be trespass, but it is not conversion.[49]

Mere reception of goods

Where A, without lawful authority, transfers B's goods to C, the mere voluntary reception of them by C is in general conversion, however innocent C may be. This is abundantly supported by decisions with respect to receipt of goods by a buyer [50] and receipt of a cheque by a banker,[51] and there are judicial dicta that appear to regard the rule

---

[47] *Lancashire and Yorkshire Ry.* v. *MacNicoll* (1919) 88 L.J.K.B. 601, 605, *per* Atkin J.; adopted by Scrutton L.J. in *Oakley* v. *Lyster* [1931] 1 K.B. 148, 153 and by Lord Porter in *Caxton Publishing Co.* v. *Sutherland Publishing Co.* [1939] A.C. 178, 201–202.

[48] *Fouldes* v. *Willoughby* (1841) 8 M. & W. 540; *Price* v. *Helyar* (1828) 4 Bing. 597, 604, *per* Best C.J.

[49] *Cf. Bushel* v. *Miller* (1718) 1 Stra. 128.

[50] *Wilkinson* v. *King* (1809) 2 Camp. 335; *Farrant* v. —— (1822) 3 Stark. 130 (further reported as *Farrant* v. *Thompson*, 5 B. & Ald. 826); *Dyer* v. *Pearson* (1824) 3 B. & C. 38; *Hilbery* v. *Hatton* (1864) 2 H. & C. 822. *Ingram* v. *Little* [1961] 1 Q.B. 31 is a recent example. *Cf. Milford Mutual Facilities* v. *H. W. Hidson* [1962] C.L.Y. 3092.

[51] *Fine Art Society* v. *Union Bank of London* (1886) 17 Q.B.D. 705; *Gordon* v. *London City and Midland Bank* [1902] 1 K.B. 242, 265; *Morison* v. *London County and Westminster Bank* [1914] 3 K.B. 356, 364; *Reckitt* v. *Barnett* [1928] 2 K.B. 244, 263; [1929] A.C. 726; *Lloyds Bank* v. *Chartered Bank* [1929] 1 K.B. 40, 69; *Orbit Mining and Trading Co. Ltd.* v. *Westminster Bank Ltd.* [1963] 1 Q.B. 794. Under the Cheques Act 1957, s. 4, re-enacting and extending the Bills of Exchange Act 1882, s. 82, the banker has a defence if he has acted in good faith and without negligence.

as of general application.[52] Some qualifications of it for which there is good foundation are discussed below.[53] A more questionable exception appeared in *Spackman* v. *Foster*.[54] In 1859, A, without B's knowledge, obtained possession of the title deeds to B's lands and wrongfully deposited them with C to secure repayment of money lent to A by C. C took the deeds in good faith. In 1882, B discovered the loss of the deeds and demanded their return from C. C refused. B sued C for conversion. C pleaded that the action was barred by lapse of time under the Statute of Limitation. It was held that C's mere receipt of the deeds in 1859 was not conversion, that there was no conversion until the demand and refusal in 1882, that the Statute of Limitation was therefore not applicable and that C was liable. This decision was inconsistent with earlier authority [55] and, although it was followed by the Court of Appeal in *Miller* v. *Dell*,[56] neither case exhibited any reason for distinguishing innocent receipt of goods by way of pledge from similar receipt by way of sale,[57] and both cases were regarded by Denning J. in *Beaman* v. *A.R.T.S. Ltd.*[58] as reversed by the Limitation Act 1939, s. 3.[59]

The "involuntary bailee." Involuntary reception of goods is not conversion.[60] Such is the case of an innocent person into whose pocket a thief, in order to escape detection, inserts a purse which he has stolen from a third person. Even where the receiver knows that the thing

---

[52] " Certainly a man is guilty of a conversion who takes my property by assignment from another who has no authority to dispose of it; for what is that but assisting that other in carrying his wrongful act into effect ": Lord Ellenborough C.J. in *McCombie* v. *Davies* (1805) 6 East 538; cited with approval in the first five cases in last note; distinguished in *Spackman* v. *Foster, infra*, on the ground that in *McCombie's* case there was a demand that the innocent pledgee should restore the goods and a refusal by him to do so; *sed qu.*, for demand and refusal are not the only mode in which conversion can be committed.

[53] *Post*, pp. 414–416.

[54] (1883) 11 Q.B.D. 99.

[55] *Packer* v. *Gillies* (1806) 2 Camp. 336n.; *Boyson* v. *Cole* (1817) 6 M. & S. 14; *cf. Cole* v. *North Western Bank* (1875) L.R. 10 C.P. 354. None of these cases was cited in *Spackman* v. *Foster*.

[56] [1891] 1 Q.B. 468. The *obiter dicta* in *Union Credit Bank* v. *Mersey Docks, etc., Board* [1899] 2 Q.B. 205, 214–216 might also support *Spackman* v. *Foster*. Salmond, 16th ed., p. 103, supports the case, but Clerk and Lindsell, 13th ed., pp. 670–671, regard it as inconsistent with *McCombie* v. *Davies, supra*, the latter case being more in accordance with the general course of authorities. Street, *Torts*, 5th ed., p. 46, n. 10, is doubtful. The Law Reform Committee has recommended the reversal of the rule in *Spackman* v. *Foster*: 18th Report (Cmnd. 4774), para. 43.

[57] In *Miller* v. *Dell, supra*, at pp. 471–472, Lord Esher M.R. was emphatic that title deeds of land are not like ordinary chattels, but he certainly gave no hint that they were incapable of conversion. The American *Restatement of Torts*, § 223, draws no distinction between the pledgee and other recipients.

[58] [1948] 2 All E.R. 89, 93. Today *Spackman's* case would be decided the other way; the action would be barred six years from the date of the wrongful conversion by A, unless there was a fraudulent concealment of the cause of action, so that the running of time would be postponed under s. 26 (*b*) of the Limitation Act 1939: *Beaman* v. *A.R.T.S.* [1949] 1 K.B. 550, C.A. If the theft by A had been overt, there would be nothing to postpone the running of time under s. 2 or to prevent the operation of s. 3 six years after the theft. See *R. B. Policies at Lloyd's* v. *Butler* [1950] 1 K.B. 76.

[59] See *post*, p. 653.

[60] See Burnett, " Conversion by an Involuntary Bailee " (1960) 76 L.Q.R. 364.

belongs to someone else, he incurs no liability by having it thrust upon him.

It is no new thing for pushing tradesmen occasionally to send unsolicited goods to persons in the hope of making a sale, but recently this practice has developed to the extent that it has come to be regarded in some quarters as a serious social problem.[61] By virtue of the Unsolicited Goods and Services Act 1971 [62] the recipient of unsolicited goods is entitled in certain circumstances [63] to treat them as unconditional gifts after six months from receipt, or 30 days from notice to the sender, so long as the sender does not in the meantime take possession of them and the recipient does not unreasonably refuse to permit him to do so. Subject to this, the law relating to an involuntary bailee may be stated as follows:

1. He cannot, without his knowledge or consent, be made a bailee in the strict sense of that term. In *Lethbridge* v. *Phillips*,[64] L, a celebrated miniature painter, lent a miniature to B who wished to show it to the defendant. B sent it to the defendant without any previous knowledge or consent on the defendant's part. The miniature was much damaged by being placed near a large stove in the house of the defendant who was nevertheless held not liable to L.

2. Mere negligence on the part of the recipient with respect to the safe custody of the thing will not make him liable. So, in *Howard* v. *Harris*,[65] where a playwright sent the manuscript of a play to a theatrical producer who had never asked for it and who lost it, the producer was held not liable.

3. But he must not wilfully damage or destroy the thing.[66] The law has not, however, been fully explored here. It is simple enough with a small and imperishable article like a book or a fountain pen, but what of a parcel of fish or a piano which is delivered at my house in my absence? I can distrain them damage feasant, but what I want to do is to get rid of them and I am certainly not bound to incur the expense of packing and returning them. If the sender is traceable, probably the most sensible thing to do is to notify him that the goods are at his risk and to request him to fetch them; and if (as is likely with perishables) the goods become a nuisance, the recipient would surely be justified in abating the nuisance by destroying them, even without notice to the sender, if the emergency were so pressing as to leave him no time to give it.

---

[61] See *Which*, June 1969, 173.

[62] C. 30. The Act came into force on August 12, 1971.

[63] The goods must have been sent to the recipient with a view to his acquiring them; the recipient must not have had reasonable cause to believe that they were sent with a view to their being acquired for the purposes of a trade or business, and he must not have agreed either to acquire or to return them.

[64] (1819) 2 Starkie 544.

[65] (1884) Cababé & Ellis 253.

[66] " I am not bound to warehouse it, nor am I entitled to turn it into the street ": Bramwell B., *obiter*, in *Hiort* v. *Bott* (1874) L.R. 9 Ex. 86, 90.

4. The recipient does no wrong if he acts reasonably in trying to return the goods. In *Elvin and Powell Ltd.* v. *Plummer Roddis Ltd.*,[67] X, a swindler, directed the plaintiffs to supply the defendants at Brighton with £350 worth of coats. X then forged a telegram to the defendants: " Goods dispatched to your branch in error.—Sending van to collect. Elvin and Powell." Then a confederate of X called on the defendants, who delivered the coats to him under the impression that he was the plaintiffs' agent. The confederate disappeared. The plaintiffs sued the defendants for (a) negligence as bailees and (b) conversion. The jury negatived negligence and found that there was contributory negligence on the plaintiffs' part, and Hawke J. held that there was no conversion, for the defendants had acted reasonably.[68] Contrast with this case *Hiort* v. *Bott*,[69] where A mistakenly sent an invoice for barley to B (who had ordered none), which stated that B had bought the barley of A through G as broker; and A also sent B a delivery order which made the barley deliverable to the order of A or of B. G then told B there had been a mistake and got B to indorse the delivery order to himself. G thereby got hold of the barley, disposed of it and absconded. Here B was held liable to A for conversion. Had he merely handed the delivery order to G for return to A, the decision might have been otherwise, but by indorsing it to G he had gone far beyond what was necessary to secure the return of it to A.

(b) **Abusing possession.** Abuse of possession which the defendant already has may take many forms, such as sale accompanied by delivery of the plaintiff's goods or their documents of title to another,[70] pawning them,[71] or otherwise disposing of them. Even the use of a borrowed car for the transporting of uncustomed watches is a conversion of the car, for such conduct if discovered leads to the forfeiture of the car under the Customs and Excise Act 1952 and its consequent loss to the owner.[72] On the other hand, an omission on the part of the defendant is not enough to make him guilty of conversion even though it leads to the loss by the plaintiff of his goods. So, where the owner of a car leaves it in a car park, the attendant commits no conversion if he negligently allows a stranger to drive it away.[73] If, however, he wrong-

---

[67] (1933) 50 T.L.R. 158.   [68] So, too, *Batistoni* v. *Dance* (1908) 52 S.J. 202.
[69] (1874) L.R. 9 Ex. 86; Weir, *Casebook on Tort*, 3rd ed., p. 404. Criticised by Burnett, *loc. cit.* Note that the defendant was not, strictly, a bailee since he never had actual possession of the barley.
[70] *Hollins* v. *Fowler* (1875) L.R. 7 H.L. 757.
[71] *Parker* v. *Godin* (1728) 2 Stra. 813.
[72] *Moorgate Mercantile Co. Ltd.* v. *Finch* [1962] 1 Q.B. 701; Weir, *Casebook on Tort*, 3rd ed. p. 400. The Court of Appeal held that it was at least the probable result of such use of the car that the car would be forfeited and therefore that the defendant must be taken to have intended this result even though, no doubt, he hoped that it would not happen.
[73] *Ashby* v. *Tolhurst* [1937] 2 K.B. 242; *Tinsley* v. *Dudley* [1951] 2 K.B. 18. If a carrier negligently allows goods entrusted to him to be stolen he does not commit conversion, but he may be liable for negligence: *Lee Cooper Ltd.* v. *C. H. Jeakins & Sons Ltd.* [1967] 2 Q.B. 1. Cf. *Garnham, Harris and Elton Ltd.* v. *Alfred W. Ellis (Transport) Ltd.* [1967] 1 W.L.R. 940. See Weir [1965] C.L.J. 186.

fully and mistakenly delivers the car to the wrong person, he will, normally at least,[74] be liable for conversion.[75]

A mere bargain and sale or other attempted disposition of goods by a person without a transfer of possession, *i.e.* delivery, on the other hand, is not a conversion; the act is void and does not change the property or the possession.[76] But in those cases where a person in possession of goods to which he has no title may confer a good title on someone else by selling, pledging, or otherwise disposing of the goods,[77] then, since the true owner is deprived of his title to the goods, such a disposition constitutes conversion whether or not the goods are actually delivered.

The destruction of goods amounts to conversion and so does the alteration of their nature. If I make an omelette of your eggs or a statue out of your block of marble, that is conversion.[78] The question to whom the omelette and the statue belong is another matter, and Salmond points out that the attempts of the older lawyers to transplant the Roman law of *specificatio, confusio* and the like to our system are of small practical use at the present day. The better method of solving the question is to split it into, " Who owns the newly created thing? " and " Who is entitled to possession of it? " [79] The probable answer to the first inquiry is that ownership of material is unchanged by alteration of it; to the second, that the court will use its discretion in making an order for specific restitution and will award the thing to him whose interest is the more substantial, on condition that he pays the value of the other's interest. But if the thing is perishable, recovery of the value of the goods converted is the only remedy possible.

Demand and refusal

Proof of a demand by the plaintiff for the return of the goods met by a refusal of the defendant is one of the common ways of producing evidence of conversion for it tends to show that the defendant's detention of them is wrongful.[80] The refusal must, however, be unconditional or, if it is conditional, the condition must be an unreasonable one. It is certainly not unreasonable to refuse to give up a bank note which you pick up in the street to the first stranger who alleges it to be his, if you tell him that you must make further inquiries or that he must produce evidence which will authenticate his claim.[81] Whether the length of time

---

[74] See *Hollins* v. *J. Davy Ltd.* [1963] 1 Q.B. 844, where a contractual clause protected the defendant against liability for a misdelivery.

[75] *Sydney C.C.* v. *West* (1965) 39 A.L.J.R. 323 (H.Ct. of Australia).

[76] *Lancashire Waggon Co.* v. *Fitzhugh* (1861) 6 H. & N. 502.

[77] *e.g.* by sale in market overt: Sales of Goods Act 1893, s. 22. *Post*, p. 420.

[78] The bottling of wine entrusted to a person in cask may be evidence of conversion even if none of the wine is drunk, but much will depend on the circumstances of the bottling. If done to preserve the wine from deterioration it is not conversion. See *Philpott* v. *Kelley* (1835) 3 A. & E. 106.

[79] *Torts*, 16th ed., pp. 115–116. See Owen, " A Case of Specificatio " (1945) 104 L.J. 296.

[80] A wrongful detention can sometimes be shown without proof of demand and refusal: *London Jewellers Ltd.* v. *Sutton* (1934) 50 T.L.R. 193, 194.

[81] *Green* v. *Dunn* (1811) 3 Camp. 215n.; *Alexander* v. *Southey* (1821) 5 B. & Ald. 247; *Clayton* v. *Le Roy* [1911] 2 K.B. 1031.

spent in making these inquiries and the mode in which they are made are reasonable or not may be nice questions.[82]

(c) **Denying title.** There may be a conversion of goods even though the defendant has never been in physical or constructive possession provided that he has dealt with them in such a way as to amount to an absolute denial of the plaintiff's title, such as signing an order for the delivery of goods which are delivered under that order.[83] The denial must, however, be *absolute*. In *England* v. *Cowley*,[84] a landlord was held not to have committed conversion by merely telling the plaintiff, who held a bill of sale over the tenant's goods, that they were not to be removed until the tenant's arrears of rent had been paid. " It is not enough that a man should say that *something* shall not be done by the plaintiff; he must say that *nothing* shall " [85]; otherwise it would be conversion if one were to say to a man about to take his pistol out of a drawer in order to fight a duel, " You shall not take it."

In the much-discussed case of *Oakley* v. *Lyster* [86] the plaintiff had leased land from the tenant of a farm in order to dump there a large quantity of hard core and tar macadam he had obtained. Subsequently the defendant acquired the freehold of the land and claimed that this material belonged to him. He used a small quantity of it for his own purposes and his solicitors wrote to the plaintiff stating that it belonged to the defendant. They added, " You must not, therefore, attempt to remove any of the hard core, otherwise you will become a trespasser on our client's land." This claim, as was admitted at the trial, was quite unfounded, but as a result of the dispute the plaintiff lost a favourable opportunity to sell the material and in the meantime its value in the open market dropped substantially. On these facts the Court of Appeal held the defendant liable. The case has been criticised,[87] but less, it would appear, for its actual decision than for what it may be thought to imply. The defendant had, after all, not only used some of the material himself but had interfered with the plaintiff's right to deal with his property by denying, or purporting to deny, him access to it. The case should not be read as holding that a denial of the plaintiff's title, unaccompanied by any " dealing " with the goods, is a conversion.[88]

• [82] *e.g. Burroughes* v. *Bayne* (1860) 5 H. & N. 296, where the court was not unanimous.
[83] *Hiort* v. *Bott* (1874) L.R. 9 Ex. 86; *Van Oppen* v. *Tredegars* (1921) 37 T.L.R. 504; *Douglas Valley Finance Co. Ltd.* v. *S. Hughes (Hirers) Ltd.* [1969] 1 Q.B. 738; see also *Ernest Scragg & Sons Ltd.* v. *Perseverance Banking and Trust Co. Ltd.* [1973] 2 Lloyd's Rep. 101.
[84] (1873) L.R. 8 Ex. 126; Weir, *Casebook on Tort*, p. 407.
[85] Bramwell B., *ibid.* at p. 130.
[86] [1931] 1 K.B. 148.
[87] See Goodhart (1931) 46 L.Q.R. 168. It was applied by McNair J. in *Douglas Valley Finance Co. Ltd.* v. *S. Hughes (Hirers) Ltd., supra.*
[88] Salmond, *Torts*, 16th ed., p. 102; Clerk and Lindsell, *Torts*, 13th ed., pp. 650–652; Fleming, *Torts*, 4th ed., p. 61. Street, *Torts*, 5th ed., pp. 52–53, has the fullest discussion. The view that a mere denial of title should not be conversion is supported by the Law Reform Committee, 18th Report (Cmnd. 4774), para. 45. Note that a denial of title, if accompanied by malice, may amount to slander of title: Goodhart, *loc. cit.* at p. 171.

Bona fides of defendant. Honest but mistaken belief of the defendant that he had the right to deal with the goods is generally no defence.[89] In *Hollins* v. *Fowler*,[90] the House of Lords put this rule, which had been recognised long before, on a highly authoritative basis, for the puisne judges were summoned to advise them. B fraudulently obtained possession of cotton from Fowler. Hollins, a cotton broker who was ignorant of the fraud, bought it from B and resold it to another person, receiving only broker's commission. Hollins was held liable to Fowler for conversion of the cotton. Lord Ellenborough C.J. had said some 60 years earlier that " a person is guilty of conversion who intermeddles with my property and disposes of it, and it is no answer that he acted under authority from another, who had himself no authority to dispose of it. And the court is governed by the principle of law and not by the hardship of any particular case." [91] Thus judges have recognised the hardship of the rule, but they have also on the whole considered it to be inevitable in the not uncommon situation where one or two morally innocent persons has to suffer. The validity of this may be doubted, at least since the Law Reform (Contributory Negligence) Act 1945, and a more just result might be achieved in some cases by apportionment.[92] But even if it is inevitable that the whole loss should be borne by one of the innocent parties, why should it be the original owner who, as a general principle, receives the protection of the law? Often enough he will have given up possession to a rogue with the flimsiest of credentials while the defendant has acquired the goods not only in good faith but from a wholly reputable dealer who was himself deceived.[93]

There are, however, many exceptions to the rule that innocent mistake is no defence. It is necessary to emphasise this, for it has been somewhat hastily inferred that, because an auctioneer has been held liable for innocently selling goods of another person [94] and a sheriff for mistaken execution of a writ,[95] innocence is never a defence. That is not so. In this branch of the law, there are occasions on which

---

[89] Modern examples include *Jerome* v. *Bentley & Co.* [1952] 2 All E.R. 114; *Central Newbury Car Auctions Ltd.* v. *Unity Finance Ltd.* [1957] 1 Q.B. 371.

[90] (1875) L.R. 7 H.L. 757.

[91] *Stephens* v. *Elwall* (1815) 4 M. & S. 259, 261: followed in *Hollins* v. *Fowler* (*supra*); Blackburn J. at pp. 764–765, 769–770; Lord O'Hagan at p. 798. See Hardy Ivamy, " Conversion by Innocent Agents " (1951) 18 *Solicitor* 125–128.

[92] See *post*, pp. 432–433.

[93] *Central Newbury Car Auctions Ltd.* v. *Unity Finance Ltd.*, *supra*, seems a particularly hard decision. *Hollins* v. *Fowler*, *supra*, concerned an innocent handler rather than an innocent acquirer. The Law Reform Committee in its 12th Report, Cmnd. 2958 (1966) rejected a general scheme of apportionment in relation to the innocent acquirer. In its 18th Report, Cmnd. 4774 (1971) it says that the reasoning behind the 12th Report must equally apply to the position of the innocent handler. *A fortiori*, therefore, the innocence of the handler could not be made a complete defence for " such an extreme solution was not even considered by the committee in the case of the innocent acquirer."

[94] *Consolidated Co.* v. *Curtis* [1892] 1 Q.B. 495, where *National Mercantile Bank Ltd.* v. *Rymill* (1881) 44 L.T. 767 was distinguished (no conversion at all, quite apart from auctioneer's innocence). *Cf.* Scrutton L.J. in *Underwood Ltd.* v. *Bank of Liverpool* [1924] 1 K.B. 775, 790–791; Clerk and Lindsell, *Torts*, 13th ed., pp. 666–671.

[95] *Glasspole* v. *Young* (1829) 9 B. & C. 696.

a balance must be struck between two competing principles. One is that ownership of property must be protected. The other is that speedy commerce in goods should be facilitated. Business could scarcely be carried on if every time I bought goods I were to ask the seller to prove his right to sell them. The law therefore admits of a number of cases in which a bona fide purchaser of goods from A commits no conversion but actually obtains a good title to them even though the goods really belonged to B and B never intended to allow A to sell them.[96] B's remedy is against A alone.[97]

In addition to cases of this description there are others in which one who handles property in good faith commits no conversion. What is the position of X, who innocently interferes with B's goods either upon his own initiative or upon the instructions of A, when X's acts amount to nothing more than transport or custody of the goods? e.g. where a finder of goods removes them to a place of safety [98]; or where a railway company, acting upon A's directions, carries B's goods, honestly believing that A has B's authority to give such directions [99]; or where a wharfinger takes care of B's goods; or where a packer puts them up in parcels. Blackburn J., in Hollins v. Fowler, thought that, in accordance with earlier authorities, these acts would not be conversion and he suggested that the principle is that " one who deals with goods at the request of the person who has the actual custody of them, in the bona fide belief that the custodier is the true owner, should be excused for what he does if the act is of such a nature as would be excused if done by the authority of the person in possession, if he was a finder of the goods or intrusted with their custody. . . . A warehouseman with whom goods have been deposited is guilty of no conversion by keeping them, or restoring them to the person who deposited them with him, though that person turns out to have had no authority from the true owner." [1] It must be confessed that this test is a rather artificial one. We have first to pretend that, in the event of A wrongfully directing an innocent person X to do something to B's goods, A is in the position of a finder or custodian of the goods; and then we must ask ourselves, " Would X's acts have been excused if these were the facts? " If aye, then X committed no conversion. But allowing for this criticism, the test seems to be workable. It would protect all those persons in Hollins v. Fowler who merely handled the cotton ministerially, such as a carrier

---

[96] e.g. Sale of Goods Act 1893 (56 & 57 Vict. c. 71); Factors Act 1889 (52 & 53 Vict. c. 45); Bills of Exchange Act 1882 (45 & 46 Vict. c. 61). See e.g. Pacific Motor Auctions Pty. Ltd. v. Motor Credits (Hire Finance) Ltd. [1965] A.C. 867, P.C. and cf. Mercantile Credit Ltd. v. Hamblin [1965] 2 Q.B. 242. The Law Reform Committee has proposed a considerable extension of these cases: 12th Report, Cmnd. 2958 (1966).

[97] Ante, p. 417.

[98] Sorrell v. Paget [1950] 1 K.B. 252; Weir, Casebook on Tort, 3rd ed., p. 413.

[99] Misdelivery of the goods by either a carrier or a warehouseman will render him liable for conversion: Lancashire and Yorkshire Ry. v. MacNicoll (1919) 88 L.J.K.B. 601; Devereux v. Barclay (1819) 3 B. & Ald. 702.

[1] L.R. 7 H.L. at pp. 766–767. Aliter if the warehouseman has notice of the claim of the true owner: Winter v. Bancks (1901) 84 L.T. 504.

who merely received and delivered the goods in the ordinary way and it would not save the man who had sold the cotton to another. A solicitor of an undischarged bankrupt who receives after-acquired property on behalf of his client and transfers it to another agent, even with knowledge that that agent has been instructed to sell, is not liable for conversion at the suit of the trustee in bankruptcy, for the solicitor's act can be described as ministerial within the test laid down by Blackburn J.[2] Unfortunately, as Blackburn J. himself admitted, it is doubtful how far it goes. Does it protect X if A wrongfully gives him B's wheat to grind into flour and he innocently does so? The learned judge thought not (and indeed a mere finder of lost wheat could not authorise the grinding of it), and yet he felt that it would be hard to hold X liable. No doubt a finder of perishable commodities would be justified in taking any reasonable steps to preserve them pending the ascertainment of their owner; e.g. he would not commit conversion by making jam of strawberries if that were the only mode of preserving them. But cases like these might well be based on the general defence of necessity.[3]

Title of plaintiff

What kind of right to the goods must the plaintiff have in order that interference with it may amount to conversion? The answer is that he can maintain the action if at the time of the defendant's act he had (a) ownership and possession of the goods; or (b) possession of them; or (c) an immediate right to possess them, but without either ownership or actual possession [4]: but in this third case he will lose his action if the defendant proves that the title to the goods is in some third party. This seems to be the law, but it can be elicited only from a great confusion of terminology in the reports. Thus it is said in several cases that the plaintiff must have " a right of property in the thing and a right of possession " and that unless both these rights concur the action will not lie.[5] If " right of property " means " ownership," this might lead one to infer that no one can sue for conversion except an owner in possession at the date of the alleged conversion. But that is not so, for

---

[2] *Re Samuel (No. 2)* [1945] Ch. 408, C.A. " To involve conversion the act, looked at in isolation, must have the effect of depriving the true owner of his property "; 411, *per* Lord Greene M.R. If A lends B's plough to C without authority and C uses it thinking it is A's, such a use is not a conversion by C: Warren, *Trover and Conversion*, p. 101. See further *Penfolds Wines Ltd.* v. *Elliott* (1946) 74 C.L.R. 204, discussed in Paton, *Bailment*, pp. 65–66 and 387.

[3] *Post*, pp. 635–638.

[4] The definition of Atkin J. in *Lancashire and Yorks Ry.* v. *MacNicoll* (1919) 88 L.J.K.B. 601, 605 (adopted by Scrutton L.J. in *Oakley* v. *Lyster* [1931] 1 K.B. 148, 153, and by Lord Porter in *Caxton Publishing Co. Ltd.* v. *Sutherland Publishing Co. Ltd.* [1939] A.C. 178, 201–202) needs extension to include (c), *supra*. *Rogers* v. *Kennay* (1846) 9 Q.B. 594, 596: " Any person having a right to the possession of goods may bring trover in respect of the conversion of them, and allege them to be his property: and lien, as an immediate right of possession, was held to constitute such a property ": *per* Patteson J. *Bute (Marquess)* v. *Barclays Bank Ltd.* [1955] 1 Q.B. 202.

[5] *Gordon* v. *Harper* (1796) 7 T.R. 9, 12; *Bloxam* v. *Sanders* (1825) 9 B. & C. 941, 950; *Owen* v. *Knight* (1837) 4 Bing.N.C. 54, 57; *Bradley* v. *Copley* (1845) 1 C.B. 685.

a bailee has only possession and not ownership (which remains in the bailor), and yet the bailee can sue a third party for conversion.[6] And, as we shall see,[7] one who has mere possession at the date of the conversion can generally sue, and so can one who has no more than a right to possess, provided that no *jus tertii* is proved by the defendant.

Examples of right to possess

There is no need to enlarge upon (a) ownership and possession, or (b) possession, for possession was analysed in Chapter 14. But (c), the immediate right to possess, must be briefly examined. A reversionary owner out of possession certainly has not got it, *e.g.* a landlord of premises let together with furniture to a tenant whose term is still unexpired; if the furniture is wrongfully seized by the sheriff, it is the tenant and not the landlord who can sue for conversion.[8] Again, a servant in custody of his master's goods has not possession of them, for it is constructively in the master.[9] But if the master has made him a bailee of them so as to vest him with exclusive possession, then, like any other bailee of this sort, he has it; so, too, if goods are delivered to him to hand to his master, he has possession of them until he has done some act which transfers it to his master: *e.g.* a shop-assistant has possession of money paid to him by a customer until he puts it in the till. Up to that moment the master has only the right to possess. These examples are tolerably plain, but it must depend to a large extent on the facts of each case whether the law will attribute to a person the immediate right to possess. A bailor has it against a mere bailee at pleasure even if he never himself had actual possession of the goods and only acquired title by virtue of an illegal but completely executed contract of sale.[10] In *Manders* v. *Williams*,[11] brewers supplied porter in casks to a publican on condition that he returned the empty casks; held, they could maintain trover against a sheriff who took the casks in execution for the publican's debts, for directly they were emptied the right to immediate possession was in the brewers, the publican becoming a mere bailee at will.[12] So, too, if furniture dealers transfer furniture on hire-purchase to X with an express proviso that the hiring is to terminate without any notice if the goods are taken in execution for debt, they can sue the sheriff in trover if he levies execution on them.[13] Not that every dis-

---

[6] *Burton* v. *Hughes* (1824) 2 Bing. 173, 175.
[7] *Post*, pp. 424–428.
[8] *Gordon* v. *Harper* (1796) 7 T.R. 9.
[9] See Holmes, *The Common Law*, pp. 227–228; Pollock and Wright, *Possession in the Common Law*, pp. 58–60.
[10] *Belvoir Finance Co. Ltd.* v. *Stapleton* [1971] 1 Q.B. 210 (plaintiff finance company buys car from dealer and lets it on H.P. to defendant's employer. Contracts of sale and H.P. both illegal. Defendant " sells " car on behalf of employer. Liable for conversion).
[11] (1849) 4 Ex. 339.
[12] Distinguish *Bradley* v. *Copley* (1845) 1 C.B. 685, where, upon the construction of a bill of sale, demand was held to be necessary to confer the immediate right to possess.
[13] *Jelks* v. *Hayward* [1905] 2 K.B. 460; applied in *North General Wagon and Finance Co. Ltd.* v. *Graham* [1950] 2 K.B. 7, C.A.; applied in *Alexander* v. *Railway Executive* [1951] 2 K.B. 882; distinguished in *Reliance Car Facilities Ltd.* v. *Roding Motors* [1952] 2 Q.B. 844, C.A. (hiring terminable on notice, but no notice given).

position of goods let on hire-purchase constitutes conversion; the terms of the agreement must be scrutinised [14] and dealers and finance companies, in order to protect themselves, must draw their contracts with some minuteness as to forfeiture of the hirer's interest.

In a simple bailment, *i.e.* one which does not exclude the bailor from possession, an action for conversion against a third person is maintainable by either bailor or bailee [15]; by the bailee because he is in possession, by the bailor because it is said that his title to the goods draws with it the right to possession, that the bailee is something like his servant and that the possession of the one is equivalent to that of the other.[16] Nor is it material to the bailee's right of action that he is not liable over to the bailor for the third party's injury to the goods [17]; but the latter cannot be made liable twice over and if he has been cast in damages to the one, he cannot be sued by the other.[18]

A buyer of goods can sue the seller or a third party for conversion if he has ownership of the goods even though he has not yet got possession of them; but he cannot sue the third party if ownership has passed to such third person by reason of exceptions to the rule *nemo dat quod non habet,* *e.g.* by bona fide purchase for value in market overt [19]; the seller, however, is liable for conversion to the original buyer.

A person who is entitled to the temporary possession of a chattel and who delivers it back to the owner for a special purpose may, after that purpose is satisfied and during the existence of his temporary right, sue the owner for conversion of it [20]; *a fortiori* he can sue anyone else.

Co-owners

As between co-owners there is unity of possession, each is entitled to possession and use of the chattel, and the mere enjoyment in one way or another by one co-owner cannot amount to a wrong against the possession of another so as to constitute a conversion.

---

[14] *Whiteley Ltd.* v. *Hilt* [1918] 2 K.B. 808.

[15] *Nicolls* v. *Bastard* (1835) 2 C.M. & R. 659; 5 L.J.Ex. 7.

[16] Williams, *Personal Property,* 18th ed. (1926), p. 59; *Manders* v. *Williams* (1849) 4 Ex. 339, 344, *per* Parke B. The extension of remedies to the bailor was a gradual process (Holdsworth, H.E.L., iii, pp. 348–349), nor has any adequate explanation been offered why he should retain the " special property " in the goods which gives him a right to sue a third party for conversion; but, however that may be, it was recognised that he could sue trover as early as 1471: Y.B.Mich. 12 Edw. IV, f. 12a, *per* Brian C.J., C.P.

[17] *The Winkfield* [1902] P. 42. But the bailee must account to the bailor for the amount by which the damages recovered exceed the value of his own interest, and probably he holds this balance as trustee for the owner: *Eastern Construction Co. Ltd.* v. *National Trust Co. Ltd.* [1914] A.C. 197, 210, *per* Lord Atkinson; *Hepburn* v. *A. Tomlinson (Hauliers) Ltd.* [1966] A.C. 451, 467–468, *per* Lord Reid; 480, *per* Lord Pearce.

[18] Bacon, Abr., 7th ed. (1832), vii, p. 805. *Nicolls* v. *Bastard* (1835) 2 C.M. & R. 659, 660, *per* Parke B.

[19] *Ante,* p. 420. Note that if the goods remain in the seller's possession subject to his lien for their unpaid price, the buyer cannot sue a wrongdoer for conversion: *Lord* v. *Price* (1874) L.R. 9 Ex. 54; Weir, *Casebook on Tort,* 3rd ed., p. 399.

[20] *Roberts* v. *Wyatt* (1810) 2 Taunt. 268.

But one co-owner can sue the other for conversion if the wrongful act amounts to destruction of the property (*e.g.* a sale in market overt effectively destroys the property of the wronged owner) [21] or to complete exclusion of the plaintiff from it.[22] In *Nyberg* v. *Handelaar*,[23] there was held to be such complete exclusion when A and B were co-owners of a gold enamel box under an agreement that A was to have possession until it was sold. A entrusted B with its possession to take to an auctioneer for sale and B, instead of doing so, pledged the box with C as security for a debt of his own.

Jus tertii

As said above, it is quite possible for one who had only a right to possess at the date of the conversion to bring an action for it, subject to his being met by a plea of *jus tertii*, *i.e.* that some third party has a title superior to his own. It is necessary to examine more fully the extent of this plea.

(a) **Not available against possessor.** Where the plaintiff was *in possession* at the time of the conversion, the defendant cannot set up *jus tertii*. In *Armory* v. *Delamirie*,[24] a chimney-sweep's boy found a jewel and handed it to a goldsmith's apprentice to value. Under pretence of weighing it, he extracted the jewel from its setting and offered the boy the setting and 1½d. for the jewel. The boy took the first and refused the second and sued the goldsmith in trover. The defence that the boy was not the owner of the jewel was held to be bad; for the boy had possession of the jewel when he handed it to the apprentice and his parting with it for this particular and temporary purpose did not amount to parting with the possession which he had acquired by finding.[25] Later authorities are to the same effect, and the rule that " against a wrongdoer possession is title " and that possession raises a presumption of ownership has been said to be a very sensible one in the interests of the peace and quiet of the community.[26] An exception to the rule that *jus tertii* is not pleadable against a possessor occurs where the defendant " claims under it," [27] an expression which seems

---

[21] *Fenning* v. *Lord Grenville* (1808) 1 Taunt. 241, 249; see Derham, " Conversion by Wrongful Disposal as between Co-owners " (1952) 68 L.Q.R. 507–513.

[22] *Baker* v. *Barclays Bank Ltd.* [1955] 1 W.L.R. 822. *Cf. Union Bank of Australia Ltd.* v. *McClintock* [1922] 1 A.C. 240; *Commercial Banking Co. of Sydney* v. *Mann* [1961] A.C. 1.

[23] [1892] 2 Q.B. 202.

[24] (1721) 1 Stra. 505.

[25] The case itself does not show this, but it is to be inferred from the facts, and was assumed to be so by the C.A. in *The Winkfield* [1902] P. 42, 55. See, too, 1 Smith L.C., 13th ed. (1929), 393–394.

[26] Lord Campbell C.J. in *Jeffries* v. *G.W. Ry.* (1856) 5 E. & B. 802, 805; *Northam* v. *Bowden* (1855) 11 Ex. 70; *Glenwood Lumber Co. Ltd.* v. *Phillips* [1904] A.C. 405, 410. But the rule also gives rise to serious practical difficulties: see the Law Reform Committee's 18th Report, Cmnd. 4774 (1971), paras. 51–78. The Committee's proposals would allow the pleading of the *jus tertii* even against the possessor. The proposals also seek to mitigate the problem of double liability by various proceedings for joinder.

[27] Collins M.R. in *The Winkfield* [1902] P. 42, 54.

to mean that the defendant can set up the right of a third person if he has the authority of that person to do so.[28]

(b) Available against non-possessor. Where the plaintiff was *not in possession* at the time of the conversion, *i.e.* where he had only the right to possess, *jus tertii* can be pleaded by the defendant.[29] In *Leake* v. *Loveday*,[30] A bought goods of B and allowed B to remain in possession. B became bankrupt. B's assignees in bankruptcy made no claim to the goods and B still remained in possession of them. Later, the sheriff seized and sold them under a writ of *fieri facias* against B and handed the proceeds to B's assignees. A sued the sheriff in trover. Held, the sheriff might set up the assignees' title.

Why is *jus tertii* pleadable here and not where the plaintiff was in possession? The explanation is historical. If the act constituting conversion of the chattel also amounted to dispossession of the plaintiff, he had the same advantages in suing trover as if he were suing in trespass, and one of these advantages was (and still is) that the possession which the plaintiff had at the moment that the thing was taken from him is a good title against a wrongdoer.[31] But if the plaintiff were out of possession, then no act of conversion could also be an act of trespass, for trespass is a wrong to possession; the plaintiff must rely upon conversion alone, and as conversion is a tort against the plaintiff's title to the chattel, it is only fair that the defendant should be allowed to prove that the title is in someone else.[32]

Except against bailor. In one case, however, *jus tertii* is not pleadable even where the plaintiff has only a right to possess. A bailee, if sued by his bailor, is estopped from denying the plaintiff's title, although, of course, he may have some other defence. For the bailor, when he delivers the goods to the bailee, is regarded as representing to him that he may safely accept them and, on that representation, the bailee is deemed to promise to redeliver them. Having thus acknowledged that he holds the goods on the bailor's account, he cannot blow hot and blow cold by denying the bailor's title[33]; but he can do so if he has been evicted from the goods by someone having a title paramount to that of

---

[28] A neat decision on the point in conversion is untraceable, but dicta indicate that it is the law; *e.g. The Jupiter (No.* 3), [1927] P. 122, 137, *per* Hill J.; *ibid.* [1927] P. 250, 254, *per* Bankes L.J. The cases usually cited are on estoppel as between bailor and bailee. Two other exceptions to the rule about *jus tertii* are given in Salmond, *Torts*, 16th ed., pp. 110–111, namely, (a) where the defendant committed the act complained of by the authority of the true owner and (b) where he has already made satisfaction to the true owner by returning the property to him, but authority for either of these exceptions is lacking. The second seems to be negatived by *Wilson* v. *Lombank Ltd.* [1963] 1 W.L.R. 1294.

[29] This is denied by Atiyah, " A Re-examination of the *Jus Tertii* in Conversion " (1955) 18 M.L.R. 97. But see Jolly's reply, " The *Jus Tertii* and the Third Man," *ibid.* 371.

[30] (1842) 4 M. & G. 972.

[31] See *Wilson* v. *Lombank Ltd., supra.*

[32] Pollock and Wright, *Possession*, pp. 91–92. *Cf.* Holdsworth, H.E.L., vii, pp. 424–430.

[33] *Ross* v. *Edwards* (1895) 73 L.T. 100, 101. The rule is old enough: *e.g.* Martyn J. refers to it in Y.B.Pasch. 7 Hen. 6, f. 22, pl. 3. See also *Re Savoy Estate Ltd.* [1949] Ch. 622.

the bailor,[34] or if he is defending the action on behalf, and by the authority, of some third person. If he is subjected to competing claims by the bailor and some third party, he can escape the quandary by interpleader proceedings which enable him to drop out of the litigation and leave the other two to fight it out between themselves.[35]

It may be noted here that, quite apart from bailee and bailor, it is possible for a defendant in conversion to be estopped from denying that he has committed it, *e.g.* where he has made some negligent misrepresentation with respect to his title to the goods and the plaintiff has acted upon it and has thereby suffered damage [36]; but cases of this sort belong to the rules peculiar to estoppel, which cannot be detailed here.[37]

Finding

The popular saying that " Finding is keeping" is a dangerous half-truth, which needs a good deal of expansion and qualification to make it square with the law.

A finder of a chattel has such a title as will enable him to keep it against everyone, with two exceptions:

1. The rightful owner. Far from getting any title against him, the finder, if he appropriates the chattel, not only commits the tort of conversion,[38] but is also guilty of the crime of theft unless he appropriates the chattel in the belief that the owner cannot be discovered by taking reasonable steps.[39]

2. The possessor of the land on which the chattel is found. Subject to what is said below, the possessor of the land on which the chattel is found has a title superior to that of the finder.

It will be recollected that, in *Armory* v. *Delamirie*,[40] the chimney-sweep's boy was held to have a sufficient title to the jewel, which he had found, to enable him to maintain trover against the goldsmith to whose servant he had handed it for purposes of valuation. Now, no claim was made by the owner of the house in the chimney of which the jewel was presumably found.[41] But if he had made such a claim (assuming, of course, that he was not the owner of the jewel), would it have been successful? Certainly not against the true owner,[42] but he would probably have succeeded as against the finder. According to

---

[34] *Ross* v. *Edwards, supra*; *Biddle* v. *Bond* (1865) 6 B. & S. 225, distinguished in *Blaustein* v. *Maltz & Co.* [1937] 2 K.B. 142; *Re Banque des Marchands de Moscou* [1952] 1 All E.R. 1269.

[35] R.S.C., Ord. 17.

[36] *Seton* v. *Lafone* (1887) 19 Q.B.D. 68.

[37] They have been put under a rubric " Conversion by estoppel " in Salmond, *Torts*, 16th ed., p. 105, but the phrase is rather dangerous, for it tends to obscure the fact that estoppel is only a rule of evidence, not a cause of action: Everest and Strode, *Estoppel*, 3rd ed. (1923), pp. 1–2; the learned editor of Salmond admits this: *ibid.*, p. 105, n. 37.

[38] *Moffatt* v. *Kazana* [1969] 2 Q.B. 152.

[39] Theft Act 1968 (c. 60), ss. 1, 2 (1) (c).

[40] (1721) 1 Stra. 505. *Ante*, p. 424.

[41] The report does not state where it was found.

[42] *Moffatt* v. *Kazana* [1969] 2 Q.B. 152.

Pollock and Wright [43]: " The possession of land carries with it in general, by our law, possession of everything which is attached to or under that land, and in the absence of a better title elsewhere, the right to possess it also. And it makes no difference that the possessor is not aware of the thing's existence. . . . It is free to any one who requires a specific intention as part of a *de facto* possession to treat this as a positive rule of law. But it seems preferable to say that the legal possession rests on a real *de facto* possession constituted by the occupier's general power and intent to exclude unauthorised interference." This passage was made the *ratio decidendi* in *South Staffs Water Co.* v. *Sharman*,[44] where the plaintiffs employed the defendant to clean out a pool on their land and in doing so he found two gold rings in the mud. Their owner was untraceable, and it was held that the plaintiffs were entitled to them. Lord Russell C.J. said: " The general principle seems to me to be that where a person has possession of house or land, with a manifest intention to exercise control over it and the things which may be upon or in it, then if something is found on that land, whether by an employee of the owner or by a stranger, the presumption is that the possession of that thing is in the owner of the *locus in quo.*" [45] This general principle must, however, admit of the exception, as Lord Russell C.J. implies, that if there is evidence that the possessor of the land had no intention to exercise control over things found upon it, then he is not their possessor. In *City of London Corporation* v. *Appleyard* [46] two workmen on a building site in London found a large sum of money in a safe built into an old wall on the site. The site belonged to the Corporation but had been let by them on a building lease and the lease contained a clause providing that " every . . . article of value . . . found . . . upon any remains of former buildings . . . shall belong to the Corporation." McNair J. held that although the lessee, being in possession of the land, had a better title than the finders, by virtue of the lease itself it was the Corporation which was entitled to the money.[47]

The old case of *Bridges* v. *Hawkesworth* [48] is by no means easy to reconcile with the principle just stated. There the plaintiff entered the defendant's shop on business and picked up from the shop floor some bank notes dropped by an unknown person. Until then, the defendant did not know the notes were on his premises. The plaintiff handed them to the defendant to see if the owner could be traced. He could not, and

---

[43] *Possession*, p. 41.
[44] [1896] 2 Q.B. 44; *Elwes* v. *Brigg Gas Co.* (1886) 33 Ch.D. 562; *N. P. Bank Ltd.* v. *Katz* [1953] Ch. 88 (money hidden in matrimonial home); see [1954] C.L.J. 73; *City of London Corpn.* v. *Appleyard* [1963] 1 W.L.R. 982.
[45] [1896] 2 Q.B. at p. 47.
[46] [1963] 1 W.L.R. 982.
[47] Another example, suggested by Winfield, is that if A, while lawfully picnicking on X's land, throws away a half-empty sardine tin which is found and appropriated by B, B ought to get a good title to the tin. It would be absurd to hold that X is in possession of an article which, if he were aware of its existence, he would probably repudiate as noxious rubbish.
[48] (1851) 15 Jur. 1079 (the best report); 21 L.J.Q.B. 75.

it was held that the plaintiff was entitled to maintain trover for the notes against the defendant because "the notes never were in the custody of the defendant, nor within the protection of his house, before they were found" and it was a mistake to think "that the place in which the notes were found makes any legal difference" to the rule about the finder's title. But it seems possible for a man to have possession of a chattel even if he does not know that he has got it [49] so that the first of these reasons is questionable. And it might be thought that the second is inconsistent with the decisions in the later cases. It is true that in *Sharman's* case,[50] Lord Russell C.J. tried to distinguish *Bridges'* case, but the attempt was unfortunate. He said that there the notes were dropped and found in a public shop. This was not the *ratio decidendi* of *Bridges'* case,[51] and many difficulties may arise in determining whether a place is "public" or not. "Is the public," asks Dr. Goodhart, "invited to a doctor's consulting room, a solicitor's office, a tailor's shop, a theatre, a restaurant, or a store? For some purposes a theatre is a public place in law, while for others it is private; which is it for the purpose of possession?"[52] It can scarcely be urged that, in the light of the later cases, the facts in *Bridges'* case rebutted the presumption that the possessor of the land was the possessor of the bank notes, for the presumption ought to be a strong one, otherwise trespass and disorder on his premises would be encouraged, especially where the articles found there are valuable. It is submitted that *Bridges'* case ought to be overruled.[53]

DEFENCES TO CONVERSION AND OTHER TORTS TO GOODS

Some of the defences to conversion and other torts to goods call for special mention owing to their peculiar applicability to these wrongs. Such as licence, distress and retaking of goods. Contributory negligence must also be considered. The first two of these were considered in the

---

[49] *Ante*, p. 427.
[50] [1896] 2 Q.B. at p. 47.
[51] See Goodhart's pungent criticism in *Essays in Jurisprudence*, pp. 75–90.
[52] *Ibid.* p. 80.
[53] It was followed in *Hannah* v. *Peel* [1945] K.B. 509, but it is respectfully submitted that, if the analysis of the law in the text above is correct, Birkett J. might have based his decision on the ground that the defendant, though he owned the premises on which the plaintiff (who was lawfully on the premises) had found a brooch, had not occupied them until after the plaintiff had found the brooch. It seems to be implied in the *ratio decidendi* of *South Staffs Water Co.* v. *Sharman* (*ante*, p. 427) that unless the owner or possessor of land is (either personally or by his agent) also occupier of it, the presumption that he is possessor of any chattel on it does not arise. See Winfield (1945) 61 L.Q.R. 333–334. In *Hibbert* v. *McKiernan* [1948] 2 K.B. 142, where the King's Bench Division affirmed the conviction of a man for larceny of golf balls lost on some golf links on which he was trespassing, Lord Goddard C.J. (at p. 149) referred to Winfield's criticism of *Bridges* v. *Hawkesworth*, and considered that it is still open to the House of Lords to consider whether *Bridges* v. *Hawkesworth* ought to be overruled. The learned Chief Justice considered that the point did not arise in *Hibbert* v. *McKiernan*. In *Grafstein* v. *Holme* (1958) 12 D.L.R. (2d) 727, where the finder was the servant of the possessor of the land, the Ontario Court of Appeal distinguished *Bridges'* case. Marshall, "The Problem of Finding" (1950) 2 *Current Legal Problems* 68–85; Paton, *Bailment*, pp. 118–129; Tay, "Possession and the Modern Law of Finding" (1964) 4 Sydney L.R. 381.

chapter on Trespass to Land, to which they are also relevant.[54] It remains to examine the following:

Retaking of goods

This is a species of self-help. If A's goods are wrongfully in B's possession or control, there is no need for A to go to the expense of litigation to recover them. He can retake them, peaceably if he can, and in any event with no more force than is commensurate with the violence of B's resistance. Indeed, retaking may be his only opportunity of doing himself justice, for delay may mean destruction or conveying away of the goods by B, who may be quite incapable of paying their value.[55] It should be noted that, while maiming or wounding are not justifiable for simple recaption of property,[56] yet they may well become justifiable for another reason—self-defence. This may occur where B, in endeavouring wrongfully to resist A's attempt to recapture the goods, commits an assault upon A and so justifies A in using violence to protect himself. And if B's violence takes the form of assault with a deadly weapon, A may even inflict death if his own life is in peril. But as the test is that A must use no more force than is necessary, and as this necessity varies with the facts of each case, self-help is likely to be just as dangerous a remedy here as elsewhere.[57] Moreover, there are other qualifications of A's right to retake goods.[58]

Qualifications

(a) **With respect to persons.** He can retake the goods not only from B, the original tortfeasor, but even from a third person [59] subject to the apparent exceptions which arise where that third person has acquired a good title even against A.[60] Such exceptions are only apparent because A, having lost his right to the property, has got nothing which he can retake.

(b) **With respect to place.** There is no doubt that the person entitled to goods may enter and take them from the land of the first taker if the taker himself wrongfully put them there.[61] But it is by no means certain what the law is when the goods are on the premises of one who was not responsible for bringing them there and who has committed no tort with respect to them. The only case of any real assistance is *Anthony* v.

---

[54] See *ante*, pp. 307–311.

[55] Blackstone, Comm., iii, 4.

[56] Cf. *Whatford* v. *Carty* [1960] C.L.Y. 3258 (a criminal case); Weir, *Casebook on Tort*, 3rd ed., p. 326.

[57] See Branston (1912) 28 L.Q.R. 262–275, and Pollock, *Torts*, 15th ed., p. 293, n. 81, on *Blades* v. *Higgs* (1861) 10 C.B.(N.S.) 713; (1865) 11 H.L.C. 621.

[58] There are also certain important statutory restrictions upon the retaking of goods, the best-known of which are in the Consumer Credit Act 1974.

[59] *Quaere* as to the use of force in these circumstances: Clerk and Lindsell, *Torts* 13th ed., p. 556.

[60] *Ante*, p. 420.

[61] *Patrick* v. *Colerick* (1838) 3 M. & W. 483.

Haney,[62] and even there the dicta are *obiter* and, although of considerable weight, do not probe the question of recaption very deeply.[63] Tindal C.J. in that case [64] gave as examples of permissible retaking by A from the land of an innocent person, C, (a) where the goods have come there by accident; (b) where they have been feloniously taken by B and A follows them to C's land; (c) where C refuses to deliver up the goods or to make any answer to A's demand for them.

As to (a) accident, the Chief Justice's examples were A's fruit falling upon C's land, or A's tree falling upon it by decay or being blown upon it by the wind. By " accident " it seems clear that " inevitable accident " was meant. Negligent or intentional placing of goods on the land of another is a tort, *e.g.* where a cricket ball is hit by any ordinary stroke out of the ground into another person's premises or onto the highway. The occupier of the premises, far from being put under any obligation to allow the owner of the goods to enter and retake them, is entitled to distrain them damage feasant until the owner of the goods pays for such damage as they have done. Where, however, the entry of the goods was inevitable, not only is there no liability for trespass on the part of their owner, but the view that he can retake them seems to be right, even if there is no direct decision to that effect. It may be hard that the occupier of land should have no right to compensation for harm done by the fall of a large thing, like a tree, on his premises, but his plight is no worse than in any other instance of inevitable accident.

As to (b), the rule that if A's goods are feloniously taken by B, A may follow them onto C's land rests upon a passage in Blackstone [65] which commended itself to two of the judges in *Anthony* v. *Haney.*[66] The distinction between felonies and misdemeanours no longer exists [67] but there seems no reason why the rule, if it is a rule at all, should not apply wherever B's taking is criminal.[68]

As to (c), Tindal C.J. thought that where C refused to deliver up the goods or to answer A's demand, " a jury might be induced to presume a conversion from such silence, or at any rate the owner might in such case enter and take his property subject to the payment

---

[62] (1832) 8 Bing. 186.

[63] The scraps which are selected from old authorities and cited in this connection seem to be either irrelevant or to be contradicted in the very context in which they occur. *E.g.* in Y.B. 6 Edw. 4, f. 7, pl. 17 (1466: " Case of Thorns "), Brian C.J. and other judges opposed Catesby's argument as to the right of recaption. *Millen* v. *Hawery* (1624) Latch 13 is also inconclusive. Blackstone, Comm., iii, 45, says almost in the same breath that the owner can retake his goods " wherever he happens to find them " and then that " entering on the grounds of a third person is not allowable except where the goods have been feloniously stolen."

[64] 8 Bing. at pp. 192–193.

[65] Comm., iii, 4–5. His citations of 2 Rolle Rep. 55, 56, 208 and Rolle Abr. 565, 566 are unconvincing. In *Webb* v. *Beavan* (1844) 6 M. & G. 1055, Tindal C.J. was of opinion that this was at least arguable as a defence to trespass.

[66] 8 Bing. at pp. 192, 193.

[67] Criminal Law Act 1967 (c. 58), s. 1 (1).

[68] But there are practical difficulties here, too, for B's criminality might depend upon B's state of mind, of which A was ignorant: for example, B might have taken the property under a claim of right.

of any damage he might commit." [69] The learned Chief Justice had already dealt with inevitable accident, so that he was presumably contemplating a case in which the presence of A's goods on C's land was due, not to that, but to the tort of A or of someone else for whose act A was in some way or other responsible. If so, it is doubtful whether his dictum about A's right to retake the goods is law. Later dicta leave it quite uncertain whether A can do so where C's refusal to deliver up the goods amounts to detinue or conversion,[70] and they are decidedly against such a view where C's conduct in obstructing A's entry is neither; and this, too, even where the goods come on C's premises without any tort on A's part. Thus in *British Economical Lamp Co. Ltd.* v. *Empire Mile End Ltd.*,[71] C let his theatre to B. B did not pay his rent, so C re-entered and thus terminated the lease. B left in the theatre some detachable electric lamps which he had hired from A. A sued C for detinue of the lamps. It was held that the facts did not show any detinue and it was also said that C had done no wrong by not allowing A to enter and remove them. Note that neither A nor B had committed any tort to C in leaving the lamps there.[72] Thus it is not easy to predict what the law is either where the occupier of the land commits detinue or conversion by his refusal or where he is blameless. It may be argued on the one hand that where the owner of goods was under no tortious liability for their appearance on the occupier's land, he ought to be able to retake them in any event, provided he does no injury to the premises or gives adequate security for making good any unavoidable injury. On the other hand, it may be urged that self-help ought to be strictly limited even against a wrongdoer and forbidden altogether against one who is not a wrongdoer, except that retaking might be permitted in circumstances of inevitable accident or of necessity (*e.g.* where the goods are perishable or are doing considerable damage to the land and it is impossible to communicate speedily enough with the occupier or his agent). It has been held that the owner of a swarm of bees has no right to follow it onto another man's land,[73] but this is of no general assistance for, once the bees get onto that land they become again *ferae naturae* and the property of no one.

---

[69] 8 Bing. 192–193. The report in 1 L.J.C.P. 81, 84 omits the passage about the right to enter, subject to payment of damages; the report in 1 Moo. & Sc. 300, 308 omits any reference to the obligation to pay for the damage done.

[70] If C distrains the goods damage feasant and refuses to return them when A pays for the damage done by them, A can sue replevin, but that throws no light on the question whether he can retake them.

[71] (1913) 29 T.L.R. 386.

[72] *Ante*, p. 306. Maule J. in *Wilde* v. *Waters* (1855) 24 L.J.C.P. 193, 195 thought that if a former tenant of a house left a picture on the wall and the new tenant merely said " I don't want your chattel, but I shall not give myself any trouble about it," that would not be conversion; but this dictum is colourless with respect to the old tenant's right to retake the picture, and the same may be said of dicta in *Mills* v. *Brooker* [1919] 1 K.B. 555, 558, *per* Avory J. and *Ellis* v. *Noakes* [1932] 2 Ch. 98n., 104, *per* Lawrence J. In *Moffatt* v. *Kazana* [1969] 2 Q.B. 152, 156–157, Wrangham J. recognised the difficulty but found it unnecessary to deal with it.   [73] *Kearry* v. *Pattinson* [1939] 1 K.B. 471.

Tindal C.J. did not profess to make an exhaustive list of the cases in which recaption is permissible, but be the extent of this justification of trespass and conversion what it may, one thing is clear. The retaker, before he attempts to retake, must, if required to do so, explain to the occupier of the land or the person in possession of the goods the facts upon which his proposed action is based. A mere allegation that the goods are his, without any attempt to show how they came on the premises, will not do, for " to allow such a statement to be a justification for entering the soil of another, would be opening too wide a door to parties to attempt righting themselves without resorting to law, and would necessarily tend to breach of the peace." [74]

Contributory negligence

There is now in existence a body of academic opinion to the effect that in some cases of conversion at least, if the plaintiff's own negligence has contributed to his loss the damages should be apportioned under the Law Reform (Contributory Negligence) Act 1945,[75] and the moral case for this seems strong. Why, for example, should a plaintiff whose lack of ordinary care has enabled a thief to make off with his property recover its full value from an innocent third party who bought the property from the thief in good faith? It is true that it is the plaintiff's property and that the thief can pass no title, but as Devlin L.J. has suggested,[76] " the loss should be divided between them in such proportion as is just in all the circumstances. If it be pure misfortune, the loss should be borne equally; if the fault or imprudence of either party has caused or contributed to the loss, it should be borne by that party in the whole or in the greater part." The question is, however, whether this is at all possible as the law now stands.

It is submitted that the question is probably to be answered in the negative. In *Bank of Ireland* v. *Evans' Trustees* [77] the trial judge had directed the jury that if the plaintiffs' loss had been caused by their own negligence then the defendant was absolved, but of this the Lord Chancellor said, " I apprehend that there is no such principle of law. I think that there must be something that amounts to an estoppel, or something that amounts to a ratification, in order to make the negligence a good answer." [78] That case, it is true, was decided at a time when contributory negligence, if a defence at all, was a complete defence, and its use in cases of conversion would therefore have had the result of depriving a plaintiff of his property altogether on account of some initial carelessness. This consequence the courts were not prepared

---

[74] Tindal C.J. in *Anthony* v. *Haney* (1832) 8 Bing. 186, 191–192.
[75] Glanville Williams, *Joint Torts and Contributory Negligence*, pp. 210–212, 328; Salmond, *Torts*, 16th ed., p. 106; Burnett, " Conversion by an Involuntary Bailee," 76 L.Q.R. 364, 373–378. For contributory negligence generally, see *ante*, pp. 106–117.
[76] *Ingram* v. *Little* [1961] 1 Q.B. 31, 73–74.
[77] (1855) 5 H.L.C. 389.
[78] At p. 413. *Cf.* Burnett, *loc. cit.* at pp. 376, 377.

to accept. As Lord Macnaghten said, in a famous passage, " If I lose a dog and find it afterwards in the possession of a gentleman who bought it from somebody whom he believed to be the owner, it is no answer to me to say that he never would have been cheated into buying the dog if I had chained it up or put a collar on it or kept it under proper control. . . . If that be so, how can carelessness, however extreme, in the conduct of a man's own business preclude him from recovering his own property which has been stolen from him? " [79]

Now, however, contributory negligence is no longer a complete defence and an apportionment of the damages under the Act of 1945 might achieve more substantial justice between the parties. There is, however, no decisive English authority to suggest that the Act may apply in cases of conversion.[80] In *Central Newbury Car Auctions Ltd.* v. *Unity Finance Ltd.*,[81] the trial judge had found that the plaintiffs had been guilty of culpable negligence in parting with their property to the thief, but contributory negligence was not even considered. The case was argued on estoppel and the Court of Appeal held by a majority [82] that, on the facts, there was no estoppel and that the innocent defendants were liable in full.

There is, perhaps, no decisive authority against the defence of contributory negligence in those cases of conversion in which the defendant no longer has the plaintiff's property and did not benefit by his handling of it,[83] but it is submitted that the tenor of the authorities is against it.[84]

MEASURE OF DAMAGES [85]

Unlike detinue, conversion is a purely personal action and results in a judgment for pecuniary damages only.[86] Correctly understood, therefore, there is no reason to suppose that the damages for conversion are the same as those for detinue. In detinue the value of the chattel

---

[79] *Farquharson Bros. & Co.* v. *King & Co.* [1902] A.C. 325, 335–336.
[80] *Cf.* n. 84, *infra.*
[81] [1957] 1 Q.B. 371; *Jerome* v. *Bentley & Co.* [1952] 2 All E.R. 114.
[82] Denning L.J., dissenting, would have given judgment for the defendants. The possibility of apportionment was not discussed.
[83] Glanville Williams, *op. cit.*, p. 211, admits that contributory negligence can be no defence where the defendant has personally benefited from his tort.
[84] A proposal that the courts should be given the power to apportion the loss has been reluctantly rejected by the Law Reform Committee, principally on the ground that it would introduce a wide judicial discretion just where predictability is particularly important. But if their Report is implemented the innocent " purchaser " will acquire title to the goods in a much greater proportion of cases: Twelfth Report (1966) Cmnd. 2958. See Thornely, " Transfer of Title to Chattels by Non-Owners " [1966] C.L.J. 186. In *Lumsden* v. *London Trustee Savings Bank* [1971] 1 Lloyd's Rep. 114, Donaldson J. applied the Act to a case of conversion of a cheque. It would be unsafe to rely on this case in the more typical event of conversion of chattels. The Law Reform Committee has again rejected apportionment for contributory negligence in its 18th Report, Cmnd. 4774 (1971).
[85] The topic is fully discussed in McGregor, *Damages,* 13th ed., Ch. 31. See also Gordon, " Anomalies in the Law of Conversion " (1955) 71 L.Q.R. 346.
[86] *General and Finance Facilities Ltd.* v. *Cooks Cars (Romford) Ltd.* [1963] 1 W.L.R. 644, 649, *per* Diplock L.J.; Weir, *Casebook on Tort,* 3rd ed., p. 415.

is paid, if at all, as an alternative to its return and damages are awarded only for its detention. On the other hand, the value of the chattel is generally a most important element in the assessment of damages for conversion. It is to be expected, therefore, that in the ordinary course of events the damages awarded on a claim in conversion will be equal to the sum of the value of the chattel and damages for its detention on a claim in detinue where the facts give rise to claims in both forms.[87] It is submitted that no more than this should be read into Goddard L.J.'s statement that " the measure of damages is the same in conversion as it is in detinue where the facts are only that the defendant has the goods in his possession and could hand them over but would not." [88]

In general the measure of damages in conversion is the value of the chattel,[89] credit being given to the defendant for the return of the chattel or its equivalent.[90] After some initial hesitation [91] it now seems to be generally accepted that the value should be assessed at the date of the conversion,[92] and this is in accord with the principle that damages should be assessed at the date of the wrong.[93]

The value of the chattel at the date of the conversion may not, however, be the only element of the plaintiff's loss. In addition he may recover any special damage he pleads which the law does not regard as being too remote. So where a carpenter's tools were converted and he was thereby prevented from working, £10 above the value of the tools was awarded as special damage.[94] Damages may also extend to loss suffered while the article is being repaired,[95] and extra loss suffered by

---

[87] *Ibid.*

[88] *Sachs* v. *Miklos* [1948] 2 K.B. 23, 38–39.

[89] *Finch* v. *Blount* (1836) 7 C. & P. 478. Value is prima facie the market price; if there is no market price then it is the cost of replacement: *Hall* v. *Barclay* [1937] 3 All E.R. 620; *Martin* v. *L.C.C.* [1947] K.B. 628 (purchase tax must be included in assessing replacement cost). See generally Street, *Principles of the Law of Damages* (1962), Chap. 8.

[90] *Solloway* v. *McLaughlin* [1938] A.C. 247, 257–258; *Douglas Valley Finance Co. Ltd.* v. *S. Hughes (Hirers) Ltd.* [1969] 1 Q.B. 738.

[91] See, *e.g. Mercer* v. *Jones* (1813) 3 Camp. 477; *Greening* v. *Wilkinson* (1825) 1 C. & P. 625.

[92] *Caxton Publishing Co. Ltd.* v. *Sutherland Publishing Co. Ltd.* [1939] A.C. 178, 192, *per* Lord Roche; 203, *per* Lord Porter; *Douglas Valley Finance Co. Ltd.* v. *S. Hughes (Hirers) Ltd., supra; Belvoir Finance Co. Ltd.* v. *Stapleton* [1971] 1 Q.B. 210; *Elliott*, " Damages in Detinue and Conversion " (1951) 9 N.I.L.Q. 157; McGregor, *Damages*, 13th ed., pp. 668–678. One might infer from the Civil Procedure Act 1833 (3 & 4 Will. 4, c. 42), s. 29 of which allowed a jury to give damages in the nature of interest *over and above the value of the goods at the time of the conversion*, that the statute favoured this view of the common law, for it looks as if express legislation was necessary to make an exception to it; McGregor, *op. cit.*, p. 99, n. 15. S. 29 was repealed by the Law Reform (Miscellaneous Provisions) Act 1934 (24 & 25 Geo. 5, c. 41), s. 3. Moreover, Maule J., in *Reid* v. *Fairbanks* (1853) 13 C.B. 692, 728, regarded *Greening* v. *Wilkinson (supra)* as inconsistent with modern doctrine.

[93] On this view no particular difficulty is raised by the case where a plaintiff learns of the conversion of his chattel but delays taking action in the hope that its value will rise and his damages accordingly be increased. If any loss he may suffer over and above the value of the chattel at the date of the conversion is due to his own default, then he cannot recover in respect of it. See *Sachs* v. *Miklos* [1948] 2 K.B. 23.

[94] *Bodley* v. *Reynolds* (1846) 8 Q.B. 779.

[95] *Liesbosch Dredger* v. *Edison* [1933] A.C. 449.

the inability of the plaintiff to deliver goods to a third party to whom he had sold the goods before the defendant made away with them.[96]

An increment in the value of the chattel, which is due to the act of the defendant, is not claimable by the plaintiff; *e.g.* where the defendant, after committing conversion of the plaintiff's half-built ship, completed her, the plaintiff was not allowed to claim this addition to her value, for the defendant did not, by converting the vessel, take upon himself any liability to complete her.[97] On the other hand, when the increase in value is not due to the act of the defendant it is probable that the plaintiff is entitled to recover the extra value which has accrued before he knew or ought to have known of the conversion.[98] If the value falls the defendant is liable for the value at the date of the conversion.[99] If several acts of conversion have been committed at different dates by the defendant in respect of the same thing, he is responsible for any of them done at any time, and if the value of the thing was greater at one date than at another, he will have to pay the higher value.[1]

When conversion of a thing bailed is committed by a third person (*i.e.* one who is neither the bailor nor the bailee), the bailee can recover the full value of the thing from the third party, although he (the bailee) would have a good answer to the bailor if he were sued for the loss of the chattel. Thus, in *The Winkfield*,[2] mails were lost in a collision between ships one of which was carrying the mails. Now, the Postmaster-General was not liable to the senders of the letters and parcels for their loss. Yet he was held entitled to recover their value from the owners of the ship responsible for the accident. But he was also bound to pay to the bailors any excess above his own interest and this " serves to soothe a mind disconcerted by the notion that a person who is not himself the complete owner should be entitled to receive back the full value of the chattel converted or destroyed." [3] *The Winkfield* was actually a decision on negligence, but the same point had been settled with respect to conversion in *Swire* v. *Leach*.[4] The principle is not confined to the bailee, but extends to the finder of goods and apparently to anyone with a limited interest in them, if he was in possession at the time of conver-

---

[96] *France* v. *Gaudet* (1871) L.R. 6 Q.B. 199. *Cf. The Arpad* [1934] P. 189.
[97] *Reid* v. *Fairbanks* (1853) 13 C.B. 692, 727, *per* Jervis C.J.; *Munro* v. *Willmott* [1949] 1 K.B. 295. For the complications which arise where the defendant has incurred expense in making the goods saleable, as in cases of unauthorised mining, see McGregor, *op. cit.*, pp. 672–678; Gordon, " Anomalies in the Law of Conversion " (1955) 71 L.Q.R. 346. See also *Greenwood* v. *Bennett* [1973] Q.B. 195.
[98] McGregor, *op. cit.*, p. 671, relying on *Sachs* v. *Miklos* [1948] 2 K.B. 23. *Cf.* Elliott, *loc. cit.* at p. 164. *Aliter* if he knows or ought to have known of the conversion and unduly delays the action: *Sachs* v. *Miklos, supra.*
[99] *Solloway* v. *McLaughlin* [1938] A.C. 247 (conversion of shares).
[1] *Johnson* v. *Hook* (1883) 31 W.R. 812.
[2] [1902] P. 42, overruling *Claridge* v. *South Staffs Tramway Co.* [1892] 1 Q.B. 422. See Holdsworth, *History of English Law*, vii, pp. 448 *et seq.*, for the history of the matter; Weir, *Casebook on Tort*, 3rd ed., p. 550.
[3] Collins M.R. in *The Winkfield* [1902] P. 42, 60; *Hepburn* v. *A. Tomlinson* (*Hauliers*) *Ltd.* [1966] A.C. 451.
[4] (1865) 18 C.B.(N.S.) 479.

sion and probably, it is submitted, even if he has to rely upon a mere right to possess.[5] On the other hand, where the action is between persons each having an interest in the chattel, such as bailor and bailee, the measure of damage is the injury suffered and is limited, therefore, to the plaintiff's interest.[6]

Where a bailor has an immediate right to resume possession (e.g. where the bailment is gratuitous), he can recover the full value of the thing. Thus, either bailor or bailee can sue a third party for conversion, though judgment in favour of the one will bar an action by the other.[7] But if the bailment is one which excludes the bailor from possession, he cannot sue a third party for conversion during the currency of the bailment, for he has neither possession nor the immediate right to possess[8]; he can, however, sue for negligence, if the goods are destroyed or permanently injured by a negligent act which thus damages his reversionary interest.[9]

Some difficulty has arisen over chattels which are intrinsically valueless but have a value in that their possession confers rights on the holder. It is clear that the measure of damages for conversion of a negotiable instrument is prima facie the face value, not the value as paper,[10] but it has been held that this principle is inapplicable to non-negotiable documents such as holiday credit stamps.[11] With respect, this approach seems curiously narrow and may be inconsistent with other authorities.[12]

Judgment

The effect of a satisfied judgment in conversion is to vest in the defendant such title as was vested in the plaintiff whose judgment has

---

[5] Winfield held that the principle of The Winkfield did not apply to one who had merely a right to possess at the time of the conversion, for that would be inconsistent with the rule that jus tertii may be pleaded against him if he sued for conversion (semble from The Winkfield at pp. 55–56, per Collins M.R.; Clerk and Lindsell, Torts, 13th ed., p. 682; Salmond, Torts, 16th ed., p. 576). It was held in Bloxam v. Hubbard (1804) 5 East 407 that a co-owner of a ship who had not possession of it at the moment of its conversion could recover only the amount of his own interest. McGregor, Damages, 13th ed., p. 684, however, denies the authority of Bloxam v. Hubbard on this point and considers that such a plaintiff should recover the full value of the converted goods under The Winkfield. It is submitted that the latter view is to be preferred.

[6] Belsize Motor Supply Co. v. Cox [1914] 1 K.B. 244; Wickham Holdings Ltd. v. Brooke House Motors Ltd. [1967] 1 W.L.R. 295; Belvoir Finance Co. Ltd. v. Stapleton [1970] 3 W.L.R. 530.

[7] Manders v. Williams (1849) 4 Ex. 339; Nicolls v. Bastard (1835) 2 Cr.M. & R. 659; 5 L.J.Ex. 7.

[8] Gordon v. Harper (1796) 7 T.R. 9.

[9] Mears v. L. & S.W. Ry. (1862) 11 C.B.(N.S.) 850.

[10] Morison v. London County and Westminster Bank [1914] 3 K.B. 356.

[11] Building and Civil Engineering Holidays Scheme Management Ltd. v. Post Office [1964] 2 Q.B. 430. This decision was reversed in the Court of Appeal ([1966] 1 Q.B. 247), but the cause of action there was under the Crown Proceedings Act, not in conversion.

[12] The 18th Report of the Law Reform Committee, Cmnd. 4774 (1971), para. 90, points out that many valuable tokens in common use in modern life could be the subject of conversion. Cf. the conversion of title deeds, where the court may award as damages the full value of the estate if the defendant does not redeliver the deeds: Coombe v. Sanson (1822) 1 Dow. & Ry. 201.

been satisfied.[13] Conversion itself, however, does not divest the plaintiff of his property in the chattel converted [14] and until the judgment has been satisfied he may exercise all his rights as owner even after judgment has been given in his favour. In *Ellis* v. *John Stenning & Son* [15] A sold land to B, reserving to himself the right to cut and sell the uncut timber on the land. He then sold the timber to Ellis. B wrongfully removed some of the timber and Ellis obtained judgment against him for conversion but took no steps to enforce his judgment because B was insolvent. B sold the timber to Stenning and Ellis then sued Stenning for conversion of the timber. It was held that Stenning was liable because, the judgment against B not having been satisfied, title to the timber remained with Ellis. On the other hand, a judgment in conversion does not entitle the plaintiff to the assistance of the court or the executive, *i.e.* the sheriff, in recovering possession of the chattel.[16]

The Law Reform Committee's Report

The Law Reform Committee has published proposals for the fundamental alteration of the law governing trespass, conversion, detinue and the recaption of chattels.[17] Detailed consideration of these would be beyond the scope of this chapter, but the major proposals are as follows:

(i) Trespass to chattels, conversion and detinue should all be superseded by a new right to sue in tort in respect of any unlawful interference with the plaintiff's chattels. For practical reasons any legislation should retain the existing tort of conversion (modified as necessary), rather than attempt to codify the whole law relating to interference with chattels.

(ii) As well as possession or the immediate right to possession, any interest in the property (other than an equitable interest) should confer title to sue on the plaintiff.

(iii) An interference with the plaintiff's chattel should be treated as mere " innocent handling," and therefore not wrongful, if it was done on the instructions of the person in possession and in circumstances which gave the defendant no reason to suppose that that person was not entitled to give those instructions, and if the instructions were such as are normally within the implied authority of a hirer or custodian for reward to give.

(iv) The law governing the right to use the *jus tertii* as a defence should be amended so as to secure, as far as practicable, that

---

[13] *U.S.A.* v. *Dollfus Mieg et Cie S.A.* [1952] A.C. 582, 622, *per* Lord Tucker.
[14] *General and Finance Facilities Ltd.* v. *Cooks Cars (Romford) Ltd.* [1963] 1 W.L.R. 644, 649, *per* Diplock L.J.
[15] [1932] 2 Ch. 81.
[16] *General and Finance Facilities Ltd.* v. *Cooks Cars (Romford) Ltd.*, *supra*, at pp. 649–650, *per* Diplock L.J.
[17] 18th Report, Cmnd. 4774 (1971). The Report also contains a detailed account of the existing law. See also Bentley (1972) 35 M.L.R. 171.

third parties have an opportunity to join the action, that the defendant is not exposed to the risk of double liability and that the plaintiff's damages are measured in general by his real loss.

(v) The plaintiff in the action for wrongful interference should be free to claim—

    (a) specific restitution of the chattel and consequential damages; or

    (b) judgment in an alternative form for the return of the chattel or payment of an appropriate sum of money in lieu; or

    (c) a purely monetary judgment.

The court should have discretion as to which form of relief to grant.

CHAPTER 20

FAMILY AND SERVICE RELATIONSHIPS

THE archaic idea that those who interfere with a man's wife or child thereby interfere also with his proprietary rights, led to the development at common law of a number of tortious remedies available to him. As husband, he could obtain damages from one who enticed his wife away from him [1] or even harboured her if she left him voluntarily [2] and he could also obtain damages from an adulterer, originally by way of a distinct action for " criminal conversation " and, after the Divorce Court was established in 1857, by way of a claim in a petition for divorce or judicial separation. Independently of these remedies he could also claim damages from anyone who, by a tortious act against his wife, deprived him of her consortium (*i.e.* her society and service). As father, he had the benefit of the action usually known as the action for seduction but which was actually based not upon any outrage to him as head of the family but upon his loss of the services of his child. It was thus both wider and narrower in scope than its popular name suggests for it extended, for example, to loss of services resulting from an assault on a son,[3] but gave no redress to a father whose daughter was seduced if he lost no services as a result.[4]

For many years this part of the law was subjected to severe adverse criticism,[5] and now, finally, all the remedies mentioned have been abolished except that for loss of consortium.[6] This remedy too has been regarded as anomalous in modern conditions [7] and in 1952 the House of Lords refused for this reason to extend it so as to give a wife a remedy for loss of the consortium of her husband.[8] Recommendations

---

[1] *Winsmore* v. *Greenbank* (1745) Willes 577. After some hesitation it was ultimately held that a wife as well as a husband could sue for enticement: *Gray* v. *Gee* (1923) 39 T.L.R. 429.

[2] The action for harbouring was not available to a wife: *Winchester* v. *Fleming* [1958] 1 Q.B. 259, reversed without affecting this point: [1958] 3 All E.R. 51n.

[3] *Jones* v. *Brown* (1794) 1 Esp. 217.

[4] *e.g.* if the daughter was in the full-time service of another: *Hedges* v. *Tagg* (1872) L.R. 7 Ex. 283.

[5] For references, and for the law as it was prior to 1971, see 8th ed., pp. 521–532.

[6] Law Reform (Miscellaneous Provisions) Act 1970 (c. 33), ss. 4, 5. The Act came into force on January 1, 1971, and these sections follow the recommendations of the Law Commission: Family Law, Report on Financial Provisions in Matrimonial Proceedings, July 1969. Law Com. No. 25, paras, 101, 102. If a person deprives a parent of the services of his child otherwise than by " raping, seducing or enticing " the child the parent may still have a remedy but, it is submitted, only in accordance with the principles described below under the title Master and Servant, *post*, pp. 441–443.

[7] " So entirely has the concept of husband and wife changed since the time of Blackstone, that if the matter was *res integra* the law would refuse to give an action to the husband for loss of consortium due to negligence, but it is now too late to deny an action which has existed for hundreds of years ": *Best* v. *Samuel Fox & Co. Ltd.* [1952] A.C. 716, 732–733, *per* Lord Goddard. *Cf. Curran* v. *Young* (1965) 112 C.L.R. 99 (H.Ct. of Australia).

[8] *Best* v. *Samuel Fox & Co. Ltd., supra.*

for its abolition have, however, necessarily been coupled with proposals for the introduction of an alternative [9] for, anachronistic though it may be, the right to damages for loss of consortium continues to play a useful part in some classes of case. It is true that the husband's right to recover the expenses he has incurred for medical treatment needed by his wife might be based upon quasi-contract rather than upon loss of consortium, on the ground that a husband has a legal duty to maintain and comfort his wife,[10] but it may happen that the husband, perfectly properly, gives up his employment in order to be near his wife while she is in hospital. An action in quasi-contract for the consequent loss of earnings would, it is thought, be doomed to failure, but as the law now stands the husband can sometimes recover his loss on the basis that it was incurred as an alternative to loss of consortium.[11] It would, it is submitted, be wrong to deprive him altogether of this remedy. And how, if the action for loss of consortium is abolished, is the husband to recover the expenses he may incur in obtaining domestic help to replace his injured wife? [12] It has, however, been suggested that it is out of keeping with modern views that the remedy should be in the hands of the husband: accordingly, the latest plan for reform proposes that the remedy for loss to the family of an injured wife's services be given to the wife herself.[13]

According to the present law all that a husband need prove is that the defendant, by a tort committed against his wife, has caused him to suffer a loss of consortium. The husband's claim is quite distinct from that of the wife in respect of her own injuries. There are two separate claims for two separate torts [14] and the husband's damages are therefore unaffected by any contributory negligence of which his wife may have been guilty.[15] There is, however, a conflict of judicial opinion as to whether an action will lie for partial loss or impairment as dis-

---

[9] See Law Reform Committee's Eleventh Report (Loss of Services, etc.) (1963) Cmnd. 2017, para. 19; Law Commission's Published Working Paper No. 19: The Actions for Loss of Services, Loss of Consortium, Seduction and Enticement, 1968, paras. 46–87; Law Commission, Report on Personal Injury Litigation—Assessment of Damages, Law Com. No. 56 (1973), paras. 115–159. The proposals are discussed below, p. 579.

[10] Best v. Samuel Fox & Co. Ltd. [1952] A.C. 716, 733, per Lord Goddard; Kirkham v. Boughey [1958] 2 Q.B. 338, 342, per Diplock J.; Gage v. King [1961] 1 Q.B. 188. The husband's expenses in visiting his wife may also be recoverable on this basis as his visits may well be a factor in her recovery: Kirkham v. Boughey, supra, at p. 343.

[11] Behrens v. Bertram Mills Circus Ltd. [1957] 2 Q.B. 1; McNeill v. Johnstone [1958] 1 W.L.R. 888. Cf. Kirkham v. Boughey, supra; McDonnell v. Stevens, The Times, April 8, 1967. In the latter case it was conceded that if the wife had promised to recompense her husband if he stayed away from work to look after her, she could have recovered a reasonable sum with which to do so. See further, post, pp. 577–579.

[12] Toohey v. Hollier (1955) 92 C.L.R. 618 (H.Ct. of Australia); Ross Parsons, " Loss of Consortium " (1955) 18 M.L.R. 514; Hare v. B.T.C. [1956] 1 W.L.R. 250, 252, per Lord Goddard C.J. In Cutts v. Chumley [1967] 1 W.L.R. 742 Willis J. awarded a husband £5,200 for loss of consortium—£200 for the loss of her society and £5,000 for the loss of her services.

[13] Law Com. No. 56, paras. 156–159.

[14] Brockbank v. Whitehaven Ry. (1862) 7 H. & N. 834.

[15] Mallett v. Dunn [1949] 2 K.B. 180; Curran v. Young (1965) 112 C.L.R. 99 (H.Ct. of Australia). Cf. Enridge v. Copp (1966) 57 D.L.R. (2d) 239 (Sup.Ct. of B.C.). The position is unaffected by the Law Reform (Husband and Wife) Act 1962, post, p. 604.

tinct from total loss of consortium.[16] It is not easy to see why a husband should not have a remedy for a partial loss, for it may be necessary for him to pay others to perform those of the household duties which his wife's injuries prevent her from performing, and in the most recent cases [17] it has been held that the action for partial loss of consortium is well founded. It is to be hoped that these first instance decisions will be taken to have settled the matter until a thoroughgoing reform of this branch of the law has been achieved.

MASTER AND SERVANT

If a master is wrongfully deprived of his servant's services, he may be able to recover damages from the wrongdoer through one or more of three different actions, the actions of enticement and harbouring, and the action *per quod servitium amisit* for injury inflicted upon his servant.

1. Enticement

It is a tort to entice a servant away from his master if the servant thereby breaks his contract of service. This tort has now developed into the wider tort of inducement of breach of contract and is considered below.[18]

2. Harbouring

Harbouring without enticement must in the nature of things be rare, but it is certain that the common law still recognises this tort.[19] On the other hand, the plaintiff in an action for harbouring must prove that he has suffered damage, and this means that he must prove that had it not been for the harbouring the servant would have returned.[20] In modern conditions such proof will nearly always be impossible, and the action for harbouring is virtually obsolete.[21]

3. Per quod servitium amisit

Theoretically this action is not wholly distinct from those already mentioned, for like them it is originally based upon the idea that a master has a proprietary right to his servant's services. Now, however, the phrase " action *per quod servitium amisit* " is generally reserved for

---

[16] There are dicta both ways in *Best* v. *Samuel Fox & Co. Ltd.*, *supra*. See also the same case in the C.A. ([1951] 2 K.B. 639) and *Toohey* v. *Hollier* (1955) 92 C.L.R. 618 (H.Ct. of Australia); *Spaight* v. *Dundon* [1961] I.R. 201 (Eire Sup.Ct.); *Honsey* v. *Sykes & Leger* (1963) 37 D.L.R. (2d) 225 (Saskatchewan C.A.).

[17] *Lawrence* v. *Biddle* [1966] 2 Q.B. 504, followed in *Cutts* v. *Chumley* [1967] 1 W.L.R. 742.

[18] *Post*, pp. 445–453.

[19] *D. C. Thomson Ltd.* v. *Deakin* [1952] Ch. 646, 694, *per* Jenkins L.J.; *Jones Bros. (Hunstanton) Ltd.* v. *Stevens* [1955] 1 Q.B. 275. No action for harbouring will lie if the service has terminated: *Forbes* v. *Cochrane* (1824) 2 B. & C. 448.

[20] *Jones Bros. (Hunstanton) Ltd.* v. *Stevens* [1955] 1 Q.B. 275.

[21] Its abolition has been recommended by both the Law Reform Committee (Eleventh Report (Loss of Services, etc.) (1963) Cmnd. 2017, para. 23) and the Law Commission (Published Working Paper No. 19: The Actions for Loss of Services, Loss of Consortium, Seduction and Enticement, 1968, para. 89).

the case where the loss of services results from an injury suffered by the servant.[22]

The action *per quod servitium amisit* is ancient [23] and formerly had a considerable scope. The tortious act causing the servant's injury may be negligence as well as trespass [24] and it is unnecessary that the defendant should know of the master and servant relationship. The fact of the service is a sufficient foundation for the action.[25] Actions have succeeded in respect of servants of such diverse characters as travellers,[26] apprentices,[27] and even a music-hall performer.[28] In *Admiralty Commissioners* v. *SS. Amerika*,[29] however, the House of Lords refused to allow the action to be extended to the case where the servant was killed and stated that the law here was anomalous as being in conflict with the general rule that " the loss of A arising out of an injury whereby B is unable to perform his contract is not actionable." [30] Since then the scope of the action has been curtailed, and it has been held that the action is not available in the case of injury to a police officer [31] or a civil servant.[32] Indeed the Court of Appeal has held that the action is restricted to " menial " servants,[33] meaning by that term servants living as part of their master's households,[34] and if this is accepted, it follows that most modern employers, and certainly the Crown and all corporate employers, are excluded from bringing the action.

It can scarcely be denied that an action whose foundation is the master's proprietary right to his servant's services is anachronistic in the twentieth century, and once that foundation of the action is rejected

---

[22] " It is the better course, . . . ignoring the way in which the law has developed where the wrongdoer has procured the breach of the contract of service, to examine solely the case where the master has lost the services of a servant by reason of injury to the servant " : *Att.-Gen. for New South Wales* v. *Perpetual Trustee Co.* [1955] A.C. 457, 484, *per* Viscount Simonds.

[23] For its history see Gareth H. Jones, " Per Quod Servitium Amisit " (1958) 74 L.Q.R. 39.

[24] *Martinez* v. *Gerber* (1841) 3 M. & G. 88.

[25] *Att.-Gen. for New South Wales* v. *Perpetual Trustee Co.*, *supra* at p. 483, *per* Viscount Simonds; *Inland Revenue Commissioners* v. *Hambrook* [1956] 2 Q.B. 641, 671, *per* Parker L.J.

[26] *Martinez* v. *Gerber* (1841) 3 M. & G. 88.

[27] *Hodsoll* v. *Stallebrass* (1840) 11 Ad. & E. 301.

[28] *Mankin* v. *Scala Theodrome Co.* [1947] K.B. 257. See also *Bradford Corpn.* v. *Webster* [1920] 2 K.B. 135 (police officer) and *Att.-Gen.* v. *Valle Jones* [1935] 2 K.B. 209 (airman), but these cases are no longer good law: *Att.-Gen. for New South Wales* v. *Perpetual Trustee Co.* [1955] A.C. 641; *Commonwealth* v. *Quince* (1944) 68 C.L.R. 227.

[29] [1917] A.C. 38.

[30] *Admiralty Commissioners* v. *SS. Amerika* [1917] A.C. at p. 45, *per* Lord Parker; *Best* v. *Samuel Fox & Co.* [1952] A.C. 716, 731, *per* Lord Goddard; *Inland Revenue Commissioners* v. *Hambrook* [1956] 2 Q.B. 641, 660, *per* Denning L.J.

[31] *Att.-Gen. for New South Wales* v. *Perpetual Trustee Co.* [1955] A.C. 457.

[32] *Inland Revenue Commissioners* v. *Hambrook, supra.*

[33] *Ibid.* relying on *Taylor* v. *Neri* (1795) 1 Esp. 386. The correctness of this has been challenged on historical grounds (Gareth H. Jones, *loc. cit.*, 53–58) and the decision has not been followed in Australia: *Commissioner for Railways (N.S.W.)* v. *Scott* [1959] Argus L.R. 896.

[34] This is the meaning given to the term by Blackstone (i Comm. 425), but it is probably not the original meaning: see *Commissioner for Railways (N.S.W.)* v. *Scott, supra, per* Dixon C.J. at p. 899; *per* Windeyer J. at p. 931.

the interest that a master has in the performance by the servant of his *contractual* obligation is no different from that of any other contracting party in the performance of his contract. The restriction of the action *per quod servitium amisit* is, therefore, a step in the right direction, for the law generally affords no remedy for negligent interference with contractual rights.[35] There remains, however, the problem of the master who continues to pay wages to his servant during the servant's incapacity. If he is excluded from the action *per quod servitium amisit* he has no remedy against the wrongdoer at all.[36] Nor, at least where the payments by the master are really wages and not some other sort of benefit, can the servant recover damages for loss of wages from the wrongdoer and then reimburse his master, for the servant having been paid has lost no wages.[37] The wrongdoer's total liability is thus less than it otherwise would have been by the amount of the wages paid. It is, however, improbable that this factor has any significant effect upon the circumstances in which wages are paid by employers in those cases [38] and the Law Commission has recommended the abolition of the action *per quod servitium amisit* without the introduction of any new right of recovery by the master against the wrongdoer.[39]

---

[35] The tort of inducement of breach of contract (*post*, pp. 445–453) is a tort of intention.
[36] He cannot claim in quasi-contract: *Receiver for the Metropolitan Police District* v. *Croydon Corporation* [1957] 2 Q.B. 154.
[37] *Parry* v. *Cleaver* [1970] A.C. 1. See further pp. 573–574, *post*.
[38] Law Commission, Report on Personal Injury Litigation—Assessment of Damages, Law Com. No. 56 (1973), para. 148.
[39] Law Com. No. 56, para. 150. If the employer makes payments as a loan then this will not reduce the tortfeasor's liability and the loan would, of course, be repayable by the plaintiff.

CHAPTER 21

INTERFERENCE WITH CONTRACT OR BUSINESS [1]

IN this chapter we are concerned with a group of torts whose function
it is to protect some of a person's intangible interests—those which
may loosely be called his business interests—from unlawful interference.
As we have already seen, the law is slow to protect such interests from
negligently inflicted harm and we are here concerned only with liability
for intended harm. It is not possible, however, to say simply that whenever one man intentionally causes harm to another that is a tort for, as
we have also seen, motive is generally irrelevant in the law of tort. If my
act is lawful, the mere fact that my motive in performing it is to cause
damage to another will not make it tortious. On the other hand, it may
now be that the law has moved some way towards the principle that " it
is tortious intentionally to damage another by means of an act which
the actor was not at liberty to commit " [2] and certainly we do not wish to
suggest that an exhaustive list of nominate torts can be drawn up. If the
categories of negligence are not closed, still less should those of intentionally inflicted damage be circumscribed. But the law has developed
by way of distinct torts,[3] and it is convenient to retain that division here
for purposes of exposition.

Two further prefatory remarks are necessary. First, a great many of
the cases in this area of the law are concerned with industrial strife of
one kind or another and where this is so the common law is often
excluded or modified by the provisions of the Trade Union and Labour
Relations Act 1974. With certain exceptions not connected with trade
disputes, a trade union or employers' association cannot be sued in tort
at all and protection against liability is given in various ways to individuals who act in contemplation or furtherance of a trade dispute. We
must endeavour, therefore, first to ascertain the general law and then to
see shortly how it is affected when there is a trade dispute.[4]

Secondly, the torts considered in this chapter, though in the past
primarily of importance in industrial disputes, may come into question

---

[1] Heydon, *Economic Torts* (1973); Weir, *Casebook on Tort*, 3rd ed., Chap. 16.
[2] Weir, " Chaos or Cosmos? *Rookes, Stratford* and the Economic Torts " [1964] C.L.J.
225, 226. The High Court of Australia has said that the authorities already justify " a
proposition that, independently of trespass, negligence or nuisance but by an action for
damages upon the case, a person who suffers harm or loss as the inevitable consequence
of the unlawful, intentional and positive acts of another is entitled to recover damages
from that other ": *Beaudesert Shire Council* v. *Smith* (1966) 40 A.L.J.R. 211, 215, *per
curiam.* This principle, unlike that stated in the text, does not require that the acts of the
defendant should have been intended to harm the plaintiff, and for this reason it is respectfully submitted that it goes too far. See Dworkin and Harari, " The Beaudesert
Decision—Raising the Ghost of the Action upon the Case " (1967) 40 A.L.J. 296.
[3] These torts have different ingredients and it is still important to distinguish between
them for practical purposes: *Pete's Towing Services Ltd.* v. *N.I.U.W.* [1970] N.Z.L.R. 32,
41, *per* Speight J. (N.Z. Sup.Ct.).
[4] See *post*, pp. 467–471.

in cases of alleged unlawful competition between traders. However, a full consideration of " unfair competition " would involve the legislation dealing with trade marks, patents, copyrights and restrictive practices and these cannot be described in a general textbook on the law of tort.[5]

1. Interference with a subsisting contract

A commits a tort if, *without lawful justification, he intentionally interferes with a contract between B and C, (a) by persuading B to break his contract with C; or (b) by some other act, perhaps only if tortious in itself, which prevents B from performing his contract.*[6]

The existence of the tort of enticement of a servant has already been noticed. In course of time it became obvious that the remedies it furnished were too narrow to satisfy modern requirements. By the mid-nineteenth century the old idea that a servant had a status had weakened to the extent of giving him legal, if not economic, freedom to contract with whom he pleased and the idea of contract itself as a compartment of the law had become familiar. In 1853 a considerable extension of the law was made in *Lumley* v. *Gye*.[7] It was held on demurrer that the action for enticement was not confined to contracts between master and servant but that it applied also to those for rendering professional services; and that the defendant could be liable for inducing Johanna Wagner, a famous operatic singer, not to perform her contract with the plaintiff. The good sense of this extension was clear. It was argued that the plaintiff ought to be satisfied with his action for breach of contract against Miss Wagner, but the answer to that was that in many cases the defaulting party to the contract might be quite incapable of paying all the damages.[8] Moreover, it was law in 1853, and still may be at the present day, that the measure of damages in tort may in certain circumstances exceed that in contract.[9] *Bowen* v. *Hall*[10] and later decisions made it clear that intentionally and without lawful justification to induce or procure anyone to break a contract, whether of personal services or not, made by him with another is a tort actionable at the suit of that other[11] if damage results to him. This has been said to be based on the principle

---

[5] Reference should be made to specialist works, such as Kerly, *Trade Marks and Trade Names*, 10th ed.; Terrell, *Patents*, 12th ed.; Copinger and Skone James, *Copyright*, 11th ed.; Cunningham, *The Fair Trading Act* 1973. For the European law of competition see Cunningham, *Competition Law of the E.E.C.* With respect, it is difficult to support the view of Lord Denning M.R. in *Application des Gaz S.A.* v. *Falks Veritas Ltd.* [1974] 3 All E.R. 51, 58, that Arts. 85 and 86 of the Treaty of Rome give rise to new torts in English law: they do not appear to give rise to any direct liability in *damages*.

[6] *Quinn* v. *Leathem* [1901] A.C. 495; *D. C. Thomson Ltd.* v. *Deakin* [1952] Ch. 646; *J. T. Stratford & Son Ltd.* v. *Lindley* [1965] A.C. 269. See Payne, " The Tort of Interference with Contract " (1954) 7 *Current Legal Problems* 94; Grunfeld, " Inducing or Procuring Breach of Contract " (1953) 16 M.L.R. 86.

[7] 2 E. & B. 216; Guest and Hoffmann, " When is a Boycott Unlawful " (1968) 84 L.Q.R. 310; Hughes, " Liability for Loss caused by Industrial Action " (1970) 86 L.Q.R. 181; Weir, *Casebook on Tort*, 3rd ed., p. 474.

[8] Crompton J., 2 E. & B. 230-231.

[9] Erle C.J., *ibid.* 234.   [10] (1881) 6 Q.B.D. 333.

[11] But not at the suit of the contract breaker himself: *Boulting* v. *Association of Cinematograph, Television and Allied Technicians* [1963] 2 Q.B. 606, 639-640, *per* Upjohn L.J.

" that any violation of legal rights, including rights under contract, committed knowingly and without justification, is a tortious act." [12]

The essentials of the tort have been considered in a number of modèrn cases and may be stated as follows:

1. It must be established that A has brought about a breach of the contract between B and C, the causal connection between A's conduct and the breach requiring strict proof.[13] It is, therefore, not tortious to persuade a person lawfully to terminate a contract,[14] and there is no tort if the contract allegedly broken proves to be void.[15] On the other hand, if the contract is valid but unenforceable [16] it is submitted that it is actionable to procure its breach. The action would not be an indirect method of enforcing the contract against the other contracting party because it is against a third party and in tort.[17]

Reference has been, and for convenience will continue to be, made to " breach " of contract, but it is not certain that there must be an actual breach. In *Torquay Hotel Co. Ltd.* v. *Cousins* [18] an interlocutory injunction was issued to restrain the defendants from preventing oil companies from carrying out their contracts to deliver oil to the plaintiff's hotel notwithstanding that the contract with the principal supplier of oil contained a clause absolving it from liability if delivery was prevented by circumstances outside its control including, as in the event, labour disputes. In the opinion of Russell and Winn L.JJ.[19] the clause did not mean that non-delivery would not amount to a breach of contract by the supplier, but only that there would be no liability in damages for the breach. Lord Denning M.R., on the other hand, assumed that there had been no breach and held that the law should be extended to cover deliberate and direct interference with the execution of a contract even though no breach was brought about.[20] If this goes to the length of imposing liability in a case where A has done no more than persuade B to exercise an option open to him under the contract [21] then, it is

---

[12] *Temperton* v. *Russell* [1893] 1 Q.B. 715; *Southern Foundries Ltd.* v. *Shirlaw* [1940] A.C. 701; *cf. D. C. Thomson & Co. Ltd.* v. *Deakin* [1952] Ch. 646, 674, 676, *per* Evershed M.R., referring to Lord Macnaghten in *Quinn* v. *Leathem* [1901] A.C. 495, 510.

[13] *D. C. Thomson & Co. Ltd.* v. *Deakin* [1952] Ch. 646, 697–699, *per* Jenkins L.J.

[14] *Allen* v. *Flood* [1898] A.C. 1. But if A's efforts to bring the contract to an end within a certain time regardless of whether this will involve its breach do themselves bring about a situation in which B can lawfully terminate the contract, A remains liable to C, for he cannot rely upon his own wrongful act: *Emerald Construction Co. Ltd.* v. *Lowthian* [1966] 1 W.L.R. 691, 701, *per* Lord Denning M.R.

[15] *De Francesco* v. *Barnum* (1890) 45 Ch.D. 430; *Joe Lee Ltd.* v. *Dalmeny* [1927] 1 Ch. 300; *Said* v. *Butt* [1920] 3 K.B. 497.

[16] *e.g.* by virtue of the Law of Property Act 1925, s. 40.

[17] *Cf.* Heydon, *op. cit.,* p. 30.

[18] [1969] 2 Ch. 106. Weir, *Casebook on Tort,* 3rd ed., p. 522.

[19] *Ibid.* at pp. 143, 147.

[20] *Ibid.* at pp. 137–138. Winn L.J. found it unnecessary to decide the point but the view expressed *obiter* by the learned Lord Justice (at p. 147) implies at the least agreement with Lord Denning. See Hughes, *loc. cit.* at p. 192, n. 74.

[21] As seems to be contemplated by Winn L.J., *supra*; and see *Brekkes Ltd.* v. *Cattel* [1972] Ch. 105, 114. *Cf.* the formulation adopted in *Acrow (Automation) Ltd.* v. *Rex Chainbolt Inc.* [1971] 1 W.L.R. 1676, a decision which relied on the use of unlawful means; Wedderburn (1972) 35 M.L.R. 184.

respectfully submitted, it goes too far.[22] But it is clearly wrong that A should find a defence in the fact that the very conduct in respect of which he is sued happens to furnish B with a defence to an action for breach of contract which might be brought against him by C.[23] It is suggested, therefore, that for the purposes of this tort there is a " breach " of contract if there is non-performance of his contract by B and either B is liable to C in respect of that non-performance or, if he is not so liable, the sole reason for this is to be found in the conduct of A.[24]

2. The plaintiff must prove that he has suffered damage as a result of the breach of contract which has been procured.[25] Where, as will normally be the case, the breach is such as must in the ordinary course of business inflict damage on the plaintiff, he may suceed without proof of any particular damage [26]; but damage is the gist of the action and without it the plaintiff must fail.[27]

3. It is often stated that A must have acted with knowledge of the existence of the contractual relations between B and C,[28] and thus a question is raised as to the exact nature or degree of knowledge of the actual contract and its terms that is required.[29] It is submitted that this question need not give rise to difficulty, for the true principle is that A must have intended to bring about a breach of the contract between B and C or must have been recklessly indifferent whether a breach occurred or not. It is obvious that for this A must have some knowledge of the contract between B and C, but the extent of that knowledge does not need precise definition, as it will vary from case to case according to the nature of A's conduct.[30] In *Emerald Construction Co. Ltd.* v. *Lowthian* [31] the defendants knew of the existence of the contract between the plaintiffs

---

[22] In *Midland Cold Storage Ltd.* v. *Steer* [1972] Ch. 630, Megarry J. said: " I am certainly not prepared to hold on motion that, conspiracy or unlawful means apart, there is a tort of wrongfully inducing a person not to enter into a contract."
[23] [1969] 2 Ch. at pp. 137–138, *per* Lord Denning M.R. See also n. 14, *ante.*
[24] A similar but slightly more restricted view is propounded by Clerk and Lindsell, *Torts*, 13th ed., p. 386. See also Heydon, *op, cit.*, p. 30. In *G.W.K. Ltd.* v. *Dunlop Rubber Co. Ltd.* (1926) 42 T.L.R. 376, 593, *post*, p. 449, it is most unlikely that B would have been liable to C for breach of contract but this did not prevent A from being liable to him.
[25] *Goldsoll* v. *Goldman* [1914] 2 Ch. 603; *B.M.T.A.* v. *Salvadori* [1949] Ch. 556; *Sefton* v. *Tophams Ltd.* [1965] Ch. 1140.
[26] *Exchange Telegraph Co.* v. *Gregory* [1896] 1 Q.B. 147; *B.M.T.A.* v. *Salvadori, supra.*
[27] *Sefton* v. *Tophams Ltd., supra.* Cf. the view of the facts taken by Sellers L.J. at p. 1187 with that of Harman and Russell L.JJ. at pp. 1196 and 1206. For proceedings in the House of Lords, where this point did not arise, see [1967] A.C. 50.
[28] *D. C. Thomson & Co. Ltd.* v. *Deakin* [1952] Ch. 646; *British Homophone Ltd.* v. *Kunz* (1935) 152 L.T. 589; *British Industrial Plastics Ltd.* v. *Ferguson* (1940) 162 L.T. 313. But it may be that the tort can be committed where A innocently enters into a contract with B which is incompatible with B's prior contract with C and A subsequently discovers that prior contract: *Jones Bros. (Hunstanton) Ltd.* v. *Stevens* [1955] 1 Q.B. 275; *cf. H. C. Sleigh Ltd.* v. *Blight* [1969] V.R. 931. If it exists at all, this principle seems to be confined to contracts of service and to have some connection with the ancient action of harbouring.
[29] *Cf., e.g.* the statements of Evershed M.R. and Morris L.J. in *D. C. Thomson & Co. Ltd.* v. *Deakin, supra*, at pp. 687 and 702.
[30] In *J. T. Stratford & Son Ltd.* v. *Lindley* [1965] A.C. 269 the evidence was such that " the defendants must . . . be treated as possessing a sufficient knowledge of the existence and nature of these hiring contracts and as having intended to bring it about that they should be broken ": *per* Viscount Radcliffe at p. 328.
[31] [1966] 1 W.L.R. 691; *Daily Mirror Newspapers Ltd.* v. *Gardner* [1968] 2 Q.B. 762.

and their co-contractors but they did not know its precise terms and said that they assumed from their experience in other cases that it could be terminated by short notice. Nevertheless, the evidence showed that the defendants were determined to bring the contractual relationship to an end if they could, regardless of whether it was done in breach or not. The Court of Appeal held that this was sufficient to entitle the plaintiffs to an interlocutory injunction. On the other hand, it is not sufficient merely that A must have known that the persons reached by his exhortations must have contracts of some kind or other with other persons and that his exhortations might result in some breaches of them [32] nor is there any general duty actively to inquire about the existence of contracts between others.[33] If the intention to procure the breach of contract is established, no other mental element is required, and in particular " malice " in the ordinary sense of spite or ill will is not necessary.[34]

4. The means adopted to bring about the breach of contract may either consist of direct personal persuasion by A of B to break his contract with C or of indirect procurement of the breach. It is uncertain whether in the latter class of case the use of unlawful means is always a requirement of the tort.

(a) Direct persuasion. This is the primary form of the tort [35] exemplified by the facts alleged in Lumley v. Gye [36] itself. It is sometimes argued that direct persuasion applied by A to B not to perform his contract is itself the procurement of breach by unlawful means,[37] but the argument is circular and it seems better to recognise that at least in this form of the tort the use of unlawful means is not required.[38] So if A enters into a contract with B knowing that the contract is inconsistent with a prior contract of B's with C, A is liable to C.[39]

In this context a distinction may be taken between persuasion and mere advice,[40] and certainly if advice means " a mere statement of, or drawing of the attention of the party addressed to, the state of facts as they were," [41] the distinction is important, for the latter is not actionable. If, on the other hand, the advice is of a character obviously intended to

---

[32] D. C. Thomson & Co. Ltd. v. Deakin [1952] Ch. 646, 698, per Jenkins L.J.
[33] Leitch & Co. v. Leydon [1931] A.C. 90. See, too, the observations of Jenkins L.J. in D. C. Thomson & Co. Ltd. v. Deakin, supra. at p. 698.
[34] Quinn v. Leathem [1901] A.C. 495, 510, per Lord Macnaghten; S. Wales Miners' Federation v. Glamorgan Coal Co. Ltd. [1905] A.C. 239; D. C. Thomson & Co. Ltd. v. Deakin, supra, at p. 676, per Evershed M.R.
[35] D. C. Thomson & Co. Ltd. v. Deakin [1952] Ch. 646, 694, per Jenkins L.J.
[36] (1853) 2 E. & B. 216: S. Wales Miners' Federation v. Glamorgan Coal Co. Ltd. [1905] A.C. 239.
[37] e.g. per Jenkins L.J., ubi supra.
[38] So much is implicit in the judgment of Lord Denning M.R. in Torquay Hotel Co. Ltd. v. Cousins [1969] 2 Ch. 106, 138–139, and is affirmed by Speight J. in Pete's Towing Services Ltd. v. N.I.U.W. [1970] N.Z.L.R. 32, 45.
[39] B.M.T.A. v. Salvadori [1949] Ch. 556. It is no answer that B needed little, if any, persuasion: per Jenkins L.J., ubi supra. Cf. Batts Combe Quarry Ltd. v. Ford [1943] Ch. 51.
[40] e.g. D. C. Thomson & Co. Ltd. v. Deakin [1952] Ch. 646, 686, per Evershed M.R. See Report of the Royal Commission on Trade Unions and Employers' Associations, 1968, Cmnd. 3623, para. 891.
[41] Ibid. Cf. J. T. Stratford & Son Ltd. v. Lindley [1965] A.C. 269, 333, per Lord Pearce.

be acted upon, then it amounts to persuasion.[42] It is submitted that the issue is really one of intention and causation. If A's words were intended to cause and did cause B to break his contract with C, then they are actionable by C whatever their form.[43] So also " the fact that an inducement to break a contract is couched as an irresistible embargo rather than in terms of seduction does not make it any the less an inducement." [44]

(b) **Direct intervention.** This take the form of direct action by A on the person or property of B whereby B is disabled from performing his contract with C, as where A physically detains B [45] or steals B's specialised tools without which B cannot carry out his obligations.[46] A similar case exists where A interferes with the subject-matter of the contract in a way which if done by B would amount to a breach of the contract. In *G.W.K. Ltd.* v. *Dunlop Rubber Co. Ltd.*[47] B manufactured cars and contracted with C that all cars exhibited by B should be fitted with tyres of C's manufacture. At an exhibition A, who also manufactured tyres, secretly removed from B's cars tyres made by C and substituted tyres of his own manufacture. A was held liable to B for trespass to his goods and to C for unlawful interference with his contract with B.

(c) **Indirect intervention.** If, instead of persuading B to break his contract or causing him to do so by direct action against his person or property, A brings about the breach of the contract between B and C by operating through a third party, A may still be liable to C. In *J. T. Stratford & Son Ltd.* v. *Lindley* [48] C carried on business under two types of contract. Under the first he carried out repairs to barges belonging to B1 and under the second he let out barges on hire to various hirers (B2). He did not, however, employ any watermen himself: B1's barges were brought to his premises by their watermen, and under the contracts with B2 their watermen collected the barges and returned them to C when their jobs were completed. The defendants (A) were officials of a union to which all but a very few of the watermen in London belonged. In

---

[42] *Camden Nominees Ltd.* v. *Forcey* [1940] Ch. 352; *Torquay Hotel Co. Ltd.* v. *Cousins, supra,* at p. 147, *per* Winn L.J.
[43] The relative positions of the persons involved and the degree of anxiety to achieve his ends shown by the alleged inducer are both factors to be taken into account: *Square Grip Reinforcement Co. Ltd.* v. *Macdonald,* 1968, S.L.T. 65.
[44] *J. T. Stratford & Co. Ltd.* v. *Lindley* [1965] A.C. 269, 333, *per* Lord Pearce. *Cf.* Hughes, *loc. cit.* p. 185, n. 29.
[45] *D. C. Thomson & Co. Ltd.* v. *Deakin* [1952] Ch. 646, 678, *per* Evershed M.R.; 694–695, *per* Jenkins L.J.
[46] *Ibid.* at p. 702, *per* Morris L.J.
[47] (1926) 42 T.L.R. 376, 593.
[48] [1965] A.C. 269; Weir, *Casebook on Tort,* 3rd ed., p. 520; *D.C. Thomson & Co. Ltd.* v. *Deakin* [1952] Ch. 646, 678, 682, *per* Evershed M.R.; 696, *per* Jenkins L.J.; *Emerald Construction Co. Ltd.* v. *Lowthian* [1966] 1 W.L.R. 691; *Progressive Deliveries Ltd.* v. *Birmingham, The Times,* June 29, 1966. *Daily Mirror Newspapers Ltd.* v. *Gardner* [1968] 2 Q.B. 762 was originally treated by Lord Denning as a case of indirect intervention (*ibid.* at p. 781) but he subsequently revised his opinion: *Torquay Hotel Co. Ltd.* v. *Cousins* [1969] 2 Ch. 106, 109. See too Clerk and Lindsell, *Torts,* 13th ed., p. 387. The distinction, which may sometimes be difficult to draw, is of critical importance if, but only if, unlawful means are essential to liability for indirect intervention. See *post,* pp. 450–452.

order to strike at Mr. Stratford, the chairman of C, who was also the chairman of another company against which the union had a grievance, A issued instructions to members of the union not to man, service or tow barges belonging to C. Barges under load were to complete their jobs and when empty were to be " blacked " and tied up at the nearest mooring. The result of this embargo was, and was intended to be, to bring C's business to a standstill. The repair business stopped because the watermen would not deliver or redeliver barges which were to be or had been repaired and the hire business stopped because barges out on hire were not returned to C when empty. In proceedings by C against A for an interlocutory injunction, the House of Lords held that no tort was made out against A in respect of the contract with B1 because there was insufficient evidence that A knew of its existence, but he was liable for procuring breaches by B2 of the hiring contracts. A must have known that B2 was under a contractual obligation to return the empty barges to C and conduct aimed at preventing their return was therefore tortious.[49]

Unlawful means

We have already noticed that where direct persuasion is concerned the use of unlawful means is not required. Until recently, however, it was thought to be clear that in the other forms of the tort A was not liable even though he brought about a breach of the contract between B and C unless he had also made use of unlawful means. In *D. C. Thomson & Co. Ltd.* v. *Deakin* [50] the defendants escaped liability on this very ground and the Court of Appeal emphasised that, except in the case of direct persuasion, A cannot be liable unless the means employed were intrinsically unlawful. Any other rule, they thought, would be inconsistent with the basic principle that motive does not make unlawful an act which is otherwise lawful. In some of the more recent cases, however, the requirement of unlawful means was far less clearly insisted upon if, indeed, it was not abandoned altogether. In *J. T. Stratford & Son Ltd.* v. *Lindley* [51] the means used for procuring the breaches of the hiring contracts was the persuasion of the watermen not to return the barges to the plaintiffs and would thus have been " unlawful " only if the men's refusal to return barges to the plaintiffs were a breach of their contracts of employment. Nevertheless, the majority of their Lordships do not seem to have regarded the point as of any particular importance and Lord Pearce went so far as to say, " It is unnecessary for present

---

[49] Note the criticism voiced by Viscount Radcliffe of a principle in which liability depends upon the almost fortuitous circumstance that breaches of contract are involved: [1965] A.C. at pp. 329–330.

[50] [1952] Ch. 646. See *per* Evershed M.R. at p. 679; *per* Jenkins L.J. at pp. 693, 695–698; *per* Morris L.J. at p. 702.

[51] [1965] A.C. 269. Both Lord Upjohn (at p. 338) and Lord Donovan (at p. 342) relied on the fact that the men were in breach of their contracts. Lord Reid and Viscount Radcliffe also were of the opinion that the men were in breach, but they evidently thought that this fact gave the plaintiffs an additional ground of action. See *per* Lord Reid at p. 324 and *per* Viscount Radcliffe at p. 329.

purposes to decide whether the men's refusal to take barges to the plaintiffs was a breach of their contracts of employment with the hirers."[52] Similarly in *Emerald Construction Co. Ltd.* v. *Lowthian* [53] the important point was, as we have seen, that the defendants were determined to bring the plaintiff's contract to an end whether this meant a breach of it or not, and it was for this reason that the injunction was granted. The court seems to have attached no importance to the question whether or not the means adopted by the defendants were themselves lawful or unlawful.

The full implications of these decisions cannot yet be known. In *Daily Mirror Newspapers Ltd.* v. *Gardner* [54] Lord Denning M.R. took the view that unlawful means were no more required in a case of indirect intervention than in a case of direct persuasion but he later retracted this on, as he said, reading once again *D. C. Thomson & Co. Ltd.* v. *Deakin* with more time.[55] His Lordship did not, however, refer in this context to *J. T. Stratford & Son Ltd.* v. *Lindley*. There is, it is true, no suggestion in the speeches in that case that the House of Lords intended to overrule *D. C. Thomson & Co. Ltd.* v. *Deakin*, and care must be taken not to read too much into the decision for, being concerned with an interlocutory injunction only, the plaintiffs had to do no more than establish a prima facie case. That, however, is true also of *D. C. Thomson & Co. Ltd.* v. *Deakin* and there can be no doubt that if there is a conflict between that case and the *Stratford* case it is the *Stratford* case which must prevail.

The present state of the law on this matter in thus uncertain. Certainly it cannot safely be said that whenever and however A engineers a breach of a contract between B and C he commits a tort subject only to the defence of justification,[56] but at the same time it is doubtful whether the emphatic rejection of liability in *D. C. Thomson & Co. Ltd.* v. *Deakin* on the ground that the means for procuring the breach were not themselves unlawful can any longer be sustained. Perhaps, to adapt a statement of Viscount Radcliffe [57] to a slightly different context, the matter may in future be treated according to its substance without regard to the comparatively accidental issue whether intermediate procurement of breaches of contract or other unlawful means happen to have been employed.

The foregoing paragraphs must not be understood as casting any doubt upon a somewhat different proposition also emphasised in *D. C.*

---

[52] [1965] A.C. at p. 335.
[53] [1966] 1 W.L.R. 691.
[54] [1968] 2 Q.B. 762, 782.
[55] *Torquay Hotel Co. Ltd.* v. *Cousins* [1969] 2 Ch. 106, 138; *Pete's Towing Services Ltd.* v. *N.I.U.W.* [1970] N.Z.L.R. 32, 46.
[56] *Post*, pp. 452–453.
[57] *J. T. Stratford & Son Ltd.* v. *Lindley* [1965] A.C. 269, 330. Note also that several of their Lordships in the *Stratford* case seem to have thought that if unlawful means are used the plaintiff may have a cause of action even though no actual breach of any contract of his own is brought about: *e.g. per* Lord Reid at p. 324. As to this, see *post*, pp. 458–461.

Thomson & Co. Ltd. v. *Deakin*,[58] namely, that in a case of direct intervention the means advocated by A as distinct from those used by A himself must be unlawful. Subject to what has been said above about recklessness, if A advocates objects which can be achieved by lawful means, he is not liable merely because they can also be and are achieved by unlawful means. So the plaintiffs in the *Stratford* case would have failed if the non-return of the barges to them had not involved a breach of the hiring contracts, at least unless unlawful means had been used to prevent their return.[59]

Inducement by servant

If my servant, acting bona fide within the scope of his authority, procures or causes me to break a contract which I have made with you, you cannot sue the servant for interference with the contract; for he is my *alter ego* here, and I cannot be sued for *inducing* myself to break a contract, although I may be liable for *breaking* the contract. Such is the inference from *Said* v. *Butt*.[60] The plaintiff wished to get a ticket for X's theatre. He knew that X would not sell him one because they had quarrelled. He therefore persuaded a friend to procure him a ticket without disclosing his identity. When the plaintiff presented himself at the theatre, the defendant who was X's servant and managing director of the theatre, detected the plaintiff and refused to admit him. He sued the defendant for procuring a breach of his contract with X. The action was dismissed because there was no contract, since the identity of the plaintiff was, in the circumstances, material to the formation of the alleged contract; and alternatively, even if there had been a valid contract, the principle stated above would prevent the action from lying.[61] If the servant does not act bona fide, presumably he is liable on the ground that he has ceased to be his employer's *alter ego* [62] it is true; that even then he might still be acting in the course of his employment, but we must take it that this curious piece of metaphysics exempts the employer from vicarious responsibility for this particular tort.

Defence of Justification [63]

It is certain that justification is capable of being a defence to this tort, but what constitutes justification is incapable of exact definition.

---

[58] [1952] Ch. 646, 697–698, *per* Jenkins L.J.

[59] The point really goes to the question whether the defendant *intended* to procure a breach of contract. So also, it is submitted, does Jenkins L.J.'s other point (*ibid.* p. 697) that the breach must be a " necessary " consequence of the conduct advocated by A. This point was taken for the defendants in the *Stratford* case but, as Lord Pearce observed ([1965] A.C. at p. 333), " if the defendants intended to procure the breach, and successfully procured it as a reasonable consequence of their acts . . . it is not, in my opinion, a defence to say that the hirers could have somehow avoided the breaches."

[60] [1920] 3 K.B. 497, 506.

[61] Approved by Greer L.J. in *Scammell Ltd.* v. *Hurley* [1929] 1 K.B. 419, 443; *cf.* Scrutton and Sankey L.JJ. at pp. 436, 449.

[62] This paragraph was adopted by Evershed M.R. in the *Thomson* case ([1952] Ch. 646, 681), who added, " The difficulty is avoided if the act which the servant is procured to do is not an act in accordance with or under his contract, but is in breach or violation of it."

[63] See Heydon, " The Defence of Justification in Cases of Intentionally Caused Economic Loss " (1970) 20 Univ. of Toronto L.J. 139, 161–171 and Heydon, " Economic Torts," 33–39.

It has been said that regard must be had to the nature of the contract broken, the position of the parties to the contract, the grounds for the breach, the means employed to procure it, the relation of the person procuring it to the person who breaks the contract, and the object of the person procuring the breach. The advancement of one's own interests will not suffice, nor will that of the interests of one's own group,[64] but it has been held in New Zealand that action by a trade union to avoid involvement in industrial discord provoked by the plaintiff was covered by the defence of justification, especially bearing in mind the reasonable offer made by the defendant union, acceptance of which by the plaintiff would have enabled the contract in question to be completed.[65] In *Brimelow* v. *Casson* [66] persuasion of theatre proprietors by a theatrical performers' protection society to break their contracts with a theatrical manager was justified on the grounds that the wage paid by the manager to chorus girls was so low that they were induced to supplement it by resort to prostitution.[67] Justification may also exist where the person inducing the breach acts in pursuance of an existing legal right as where the contract, breach of which is procured by A, is one between B and C which B could not perform without breaking a contract existing between himself and A.[68] But the breach by C of his contract with A will not justify A in procuring B to break an independent contract with C.[69]

It has been suggested that pressure of moral obligation may amount to justification. *Brimelow* v. *Casson* lends some support to this, and there would surely be justification if a medical man advised a patient to give up his employment in the interests of his health. On the other hand, *Brimelow* v. *Casson* has been said to stand alone,[70] no decision has been based upon the existence of a moral obligation, and the dicta are conflicting.[71] It has also been suggested that the defence of justification can never succeed if unlawful means are used,[72] but this too is not certain.[73] All in all it seems that each case turns on its particular circumstances and that no general rule can be stated.[74]

---

[64] *South Wales Miners' Federation* v. *Glamorgan Coal Co.* [1905] A.C. 239; *Camden Nominees Ltd.* v. *Forcey* [1940] Ch. 352.
[65] *Pete's Towing Services Ltd.* v. *N.I.U.W.* [1970] N.Z.L.R. 32. See also *Posluns* v. *Toronto Stock Exchange* (1964) 46 D.L.R. (2d) 210, affd. (1968) 67 D.L.R. (2d) 165.
[66] [1924] 1 Ch. 302.
[67] See also *Stott* v. *Gamble* [1916] 2 K.B. 504; *Slade and Stewart Ltd.* v. *Haynes* (1969) 5 D.L.R. (3d) 736.
[68] *Smithies* v. *National Association of Operative Plasterers* [1909] 1 K.B. 310, 337, per Buckley L.J. *Aliter*, of course, where A contracted with B, knowing of B's contract with C.
[69] *Ibid*, at p. 341, per Kennedy L.J.
[70] *Camden Nominees Ltd.* v. *Forcey*, supra, at p. 366, per Simonds J.
[71] e.g. *South Wales Miners' Federation* v. *Glamorgan Coal Co.*, supra, at p. 255, per Lord Lindley (against); ibid. at pp. 245, 246, 249, per Lords Halsbury, Macnaghten and James (non-committal): *Crofter Hand-Woven Harris Tweed Co.* v. *Veitch* [1942] A.C. 435, 443, per Viscount Simon (for).
[72] 8th and earlier editions of this work (8th ed., p. 545); Street, *Torts*, 5th ed., p. 340.
[73] Clerk and Lindsell, *Torts*, 13th ed., p. 395; Heydon (1970) 20 University of Toronto L.J., pp. 178–182.
[74] *Pete's Towing Services Ltd.* v. *N.I.U.W.* [1970] N.Z.L.R. 32, 49, per Speight J.

2. Intimidation

The word " intimidation " when used in the present context signifies a threat delivered by A to B whereby A intentionally causes B to act (or refrain from acting) either to his own detriment or to the detriment of C. There are thus two forms of the tort, which will be considered separately but first two general points must be mentioned.

(a) " Threat " when used in this connection means " an intimation by one to another that unless the latter does or does not do something the former will do something which the latter will not like." [75] It is coercive and demands either action or abstention from action on the part of the recipient,[76] so a mere announcement by A that he proposes to strike B is not, for the purposes of the law, a " threat " and cannot of itself give rise to a claim for damages.[77] On the other hand, the fact that a threat is couched in polite and regretful language does not make it any the less a threat, and there is little value in the distinction which has been suggested between a warning and a threat.[78]

(b) For a threat as thus defined to be capable of giving rise to an action for damages on the part of anyone it must be a threat of an unlawful act. Anything that I may lawfully do I may also lawfully threaten to do, whatever the motive or purpose of my threat. This is an inescapable result of *Allen* v. *Flood*,[79] however unfortunate some of its consequences may be. Accordingly in *Hardie and Lane Ltd,* v. *Chilton*,[80] the Court of Appeal held that a threat by A, a trading association, to put B, one of its members, on a " stop list " (which would prevent B from getting goods from its members of the association) unless B paid a sum of money for having broken a rule of the association was not a tort.

(i) **Three-party intimidation.** Despite some earlier hesitations, it is now certain that A commits the tort of intimidation against C if he threatens B with conduct which is unlawful in relation to B and thereby causes B to act (or refrain from acting) in a way which causes damage to C. [81] It is not a requirement of this tort that B's conduct be in any way unlawful in relation to C.[82] An old illustration is *Garret* v. *Taylor*,[83] where the plaintiff was the lessee of a quarry and alleged that the defendant had " disturbed " his customers and his workmen by " threatening to

---

[75] *Hodges* v. *Webb* [1920] 2 Ch. 70, 89, *per* Peterson J.

[76] *J. T. Stratford & Son Ltd.* v. *Lindley* [1965] A.C. 269, 292, *per* Pearson L.J.

[77] *Ibid.* at pp. 283–284, *per* Lord Denning M.R.

[78] *Hodges* v. *Webb, supra,* at p. 87.

[79] [1898] A.C. 1; *Rookes* v. *Barnard* [1964] A.C. 1129, 1169, *per* Lord Reid.

[80] [1928] 2 K.B. 306. See also *Ware and De Freville Ltd.* v. *Motor Trade Association* [1921] 3 K.B. 40. *Hardie and Lane Ltd.* v. *Chilton* was approved by the House of Lords in *Thorne* v. *Motor Trade Association* [1937] A.C. 797. For the crime generally known as " blackmail " see Theft Act 1968 (c. 60), s. 21.

[81] There seems no doubt that it would also be the tort of intimidation against C if A threatened an unlawful act to B unless C acted to his detriment.

[82] *Rookes* v. *Barnard* [1964] A.C. 1129; Weir, *Casebook on Tort*, 3rd ed., p. 515. Note the difference between this tort and that of interference with a subsisting contract.

[83] (1620) Cro.Jac. 567; *Tarleton* v. *M'Gawley* (1793) Peake N.P. 270.

mayhem and vex them with suits if they bought any stones." It was held that on these facts the plaintiff had a good cause of action.

In *Rookes* v. *Barnard*,[84] decided by the House of Lords in 1964 and the leading authority on this tort, the plaintiff (C) was employed by B.O.A.C. (B) in their design office and the three defendants (A) were officials of the A.E.S.D. Union, two of them also being employees of B.O.A.C.[85] C had been but was no longer a member of the Union. In order to preserve 100 per cent. union membership in the design office and notwithstanding the fact that a strike would have involved the men in breaches of their contracts of employment,[86] A notified B of a resolution passed by members of the union that if C was not dismissed, " a withdrawal of labour of all A.E.S.D. Membership will take place." B yielded to this threat and lawfully terminated C's contract of employment. Owing to the provisions of the Trade Disputes Act 1906 [87] C could not rely upon a simple conspiracy to injure but in the House of Lords it was held that he was entitled to succeed on the ground of intimidation. The House held, agreeing with the Court of Appeal,[88] that there is a tort of intimidation, but they also held, reversing the Court of Appeal, that the tort extends to threats by A to break his contract with B and is not confined to threats of criminal or tortious conduct.

The essence of the tort lies in the coercion of B, through whom A intentionally inflicts damage upon C, but obviously the law cannot hold every form of coercion to be wrongful. If A tells his grown-up son, B, that he will stop B's allowance if B marries C, A may succeed, as is no doubt his intention, in depriving C of a profitable marriage, but he commits no tort against her, for he is perfectly entitled to stop B's allowance for any reason. The law has therefore adopted the natural dividing line between what is lawful and what is unlawful as against B, the person threatened.[89] In *Rookes* v. *Barnard* the threat of strike action involved a threat of breach of contract, and for this reason the defendants were liable: in the similar case of *Morgan* v. *Fry*,[90] on the other hand, the threat was to strike only after the expiry of a sufficient period of notice and so was a threat of lawful action in respect of which the defendants were not liable in tort.[91]

The decision in *Rookes* v. *Barnard* has given rise to a substantial

---

[84] *Supra.*

[85] Silverthorne, who was not employed by B.O.A.C., was a party to an unlawful conspiracy to threaten breaches of contract: *Rookes* v. *Barnard* at pp. 1210–1211.

[86] An unusual feature of the case is that, as the defendants admitted, the men's contracts of employment contained an express undertaking that no strike would take place.

[87] s. 1. See *post*, p. 467.

[88] [1963] 1 Q.B. 623.

[89] *Rookes* v. *Barnard* [1964] A.C. 1129, 1207, *per* Lord Devlin.

[90] [1968] 2 Q.B. 710; *Pete's Towing Services Ltd.* v. *N.I.U.W.* [1970] N.Z.L.R. 32.

[91] The decision in *Morgan* v. *Fry* in this respect was of doubtful validity, but in view of s. 13 of the Trade Union and Labour Relations Act 1974, where the action taken is in contemplation or furtherance of a trade dispute, no action will lie in any such case.

literature,[92] some of it critical, and much of the criticism has been directed to its operation in the sphere of industrial disputes. So far as that area is concerned the critics have had their way, and in cases where there is a trade dispute the effect of the decision was largely destroyed by the Trade Disputes Act 1965 and its successor, the Trade Unions and Labour Relations Act 1974.[93] From the legal point of view the criticism has been in the main to the effect that, as was indeed the opinion of the Court of Appeal,[94] if intimidation is extended to cover threats to break contracts " it would overturn or outflank some elementary principles of contract law," [95] notably the so-called rule of privity of contract, which holds that one who is not a party to a contract cannot found a claim upon it or sue for breach of it.

For the purposes of the tort of intimidation itself at least two answers are available to the privity of contract objection.[96] First it can be said not merely that C does not sue for breach of the contract between A and B, but that his cause of action actually depends upon the contract not having been broken. It is only because B yields to A's threat that it might be broken that C suffers damage at all. If B does not yield and the contract is broken, then A's threat has not caused C to suffer loss.[97] And if it be objected that A may act first (against B) and explain why afterwards, whereupon B acts to C's detriment, the answer is that it is not A's act which has caused C's loss but the implied threat that it will be repeated.[98] Alternatively it may be said bluntly that in all cases of intimidation, whatever the nature of the threatened act, C's cause of action is wholly independent of B's. C founds not upon the wrong, if any, done to B but on the fact that A has set out to injure him by the use of an unlawful weapon. " I can see no difference in principle between a threat to break a contract and a threat to commit a tort. If a third party could not sue for damage caused to him by the former I can see no reason why he should be entitled to sue for damage caused to him by the latter. A person is no more entitled to sue in respect of loss which he suffers

---

[92] Amongst the most important articles are: Hamson, " A Note on *Rookes* v. *Barnard* " [1961] C.L.J. 189; " A Further Note on *Rookes* v. *Barnard* " [1964] C.L.J. 159; Weir; " Chaos or Cosmos? *Rookes, Stratford* and the Economic Torts " [1964] C.L.J. 225; Hoffmann, " *Rookes* v. *Barnard* " (1965) 81 L.Q.R. 116; Wedderburn, " The Right to Threaten Strikes " (1961) 24 M.L.R. 572; " The Right to Threaten Strikes II " (1962) 25 M.L.R. 513; " Intimidation and the Right to Strike " (1964) 27 M.L.R. 257.

[93] See *post*, p. 470.

[94] [1963] 1 Q.B. 623.

[95] *Ibid.*, per Pearson L.J, at p. 695.

[96] See, however, Wedderburn, " Intimidation and the Right to Strike " (1964) 27 M.L.R. 257, 263–267.

[97] This is the line of reasoning that seems to be preferred by Lords Evershed, Hodson and Devlin: [1964] A.C. at pp. 1187–1188; 1200–1201; 1207–1208. Note that even though the contract between A and B is broken C may still suffer damage (Wedderburn, " Intimidation and the Right to Strike " (1964) 27 M.L.R. 257, 265, gives a good example) but his damage will not be caused by A's threat and so is not actionable under the head of intimidation. Whether it may be actionable at all is considered *post*, pp. 458–461.

[98] See, *e.g. Rookes* v. *Barnard* [1964] A.C. at pp. 1187–1188, *per* Lord Evershed; 1208–1209, *per* Lord Devlin.

by reason of a tort committed against someone else than he is entitled
to sue in respect of loss which he suffers by reason of breach of a
contract to which he is not a party. What he sues for in each case is
loss caused to him by the use of an unlawful weapon against him—
intimidation of another person by unlawful means." [99]

It is to be observed that this approach does more than answer the
privity of contract objection: it refutes its basic premise. The point
is " that the ' weapon,' *i.e.* the means, which the defendant uses to
inflict loss on the plaintiff, may be unlawful because it involves conduct wrongful towards a third party. There is no reason in principle
why such wrongful conduct should include torts and not breaches of
contract. One might argue about whether it is expedient for the law
to forbid the use of such acts as a means of causing loss, but the
privity doctrine is a red herring." [1] Indeed one might also ask why
the law should draw the line at threats of breach of contract and not
include within the tort of intimidation some threats against B even
though the acts threatened are not strictly unlawful. The answer lies
only in the structure of the law. There is a legal " chasm " [2] between,
for example, not entering into a contract and breach of an existing
contract, which will not easily be bridged.[3] Even subject to this limitation, however, the second approach to the privity objection opens the
way to a wider form of liability based on the use of unlawful means
and for this reason is to be preferred. The possibilities of this are
considered in a later section.

(ii) **Two-party intimidation.** There is little direct authority on the
position where A threatens B with an unlawful act and thereby causes
B to act (or refrain from acting) in a way which causes loss to B himself.[4] Nevertheless the general opinion seems to be that A commits
a tort, certainly where his threat is of violence,[5] and also, since *Rookes*
v. *Barnard*, where the threat is of any unlawful act within the meaning
of that case.[6] On the other hand, in *J. T. Stratford & Son Ltd.* v.

---

[99] *Rookes* v. *Barnard* [1964] A.C. at p. 1168, *per* Lord Reid. Lord Pearce's short discussion of the point, *ibid.* at pp. 1234–1235, is in accord with Lord Reid's approach.
Hoffmann and Weir, *loc. cit.*, prefer this approach. Hamson's view, *loc. cit.*, seems to
come between the two.
[1] Hoffmann, *loc. cit.* at p. 125.
[2] The word is Lord Herschell's: *Allen* v. *Flood* [1898] A.C. 1, 121.
[3] Hamson ([1961] C.L.J. at p. 193) says that what he suggests is that a threat of legal
injury is sufficient to constitute an intimidation. He adds, " I must not be taken as contending that intimidation should be limited to the threat of legal injury only, or that it is."
[4] There is no reason why the two-party and the three-party situations should not
co-exist on the same facts. In *Rookes* v. *Barnard* itself, for example, B.O.A.C. might have
wished to sue in respect of their loss of the services of Mr. Rookes.
[5] Old textbook authority cited by Pearson L.J. in *Rookes* v. *Barnard* [1963] 1 Q.B. at
p. 689 regards it as a form of trespass. See, *e.g.* Finch's *Law*, ed. of 1678, pp. 201–202.
Salmond, 16th ed., p. 370, considers that the tortious character of A's conduct " cannot
be doubted."
[6] The various dicta include: *Allen* v. *Flood* [1898] A.C. 1, 17, *per* Hawkins J.; *Rookes*
v. *Barnard* [1964] A.C. 1187, *per* Lord Evershed; [1963] 1 Q.B. 663, *per* Sellers L.J.;
J. T. Stratford & Son Ltd. v. *Lindley* [1965] A.C. 269, 285, *per* Lord Denning M.R.; 302,
305–306, *per* Salmon L.J.; 336, *per* Lord Pearce; *D. & C. Builders Ltd.* v. *Rees* [1966]

Lindley [7] Lord Reid said, " A case where a defendant presents to the plaintiff the alternative of doing what the defendant wants him to do or suffering loss which the defendant can cause him to incur is not necessarily *in pari casu* and may involve questions which cannot arise where there is intimidation of a third person." It is respectfully suggested that Lord Reid's caution is justified, principally on the ground that in the two-party situation there is normally a remedy already available to B, while in the three-party situation, if C cannot sue for intimidation he cannot sue at all.[8] If B is threatened with a breach of contract he may be able to treat the contract as repudiated and sue for anticipatory breach or, of course, he may await the breach and sue for damages; if he is threatened with a tort he may equally bring an action for damages if the tort is committed or bring an action for a *quia timet* injunction first.

It is submitted, therefore, that the two-party situation is properly distinguishable from the three-party situation and that it does not necessarily follow from *Rookes* v. *Barnard* that whenever A threatens B with an unlawful act, including a breach of his contract with B, he thereby commits the tort of intimidation. In fact the balance of advantage seems to lie in holding that where A threatens B with a breach of his contract with B, B should be restricted to his contractual remedies. The law should not encourage B to yield to the threat but should seek to persuade him to resist it.[9] If he suffers damage in consequence he will be adequately compensated by his remedy in damages for breach of contract, as his damage can scarcely be other than financial. Where, however, what is threatened is a tort, and especially if the threat is of violence, it is both unrealistic to insist that proceedings for a *quia timet* injunction afford him adequate protection against the consequences of resistance and unreasonable to insist that if violence is actually inflicted upon him he is adequately compensated by an award of damages thereafter. The view is preferred, therefore, that although A commits the tort of intimidation against B where he threatens B with violence or perhaps with any other tort, no independent tort is committed when all that is threatened is a breach of contract.

3. Interference by unlawful means [10]

In the ordinary simple situation in which A's act operates directly to cause injury to B, then, even if the injury was intended, B may

---

2 Q.B. 617, 625, *per* Lord Denning M.R. None of these dicta is, however, very strong, and those in the *Stratford* case are more concerned with the effect of the Trade Disputes Act 1906.

    [7] [1965] A.C. at p. 325.   [8] Hoffmann, *loc. cit.* at pp. 127–128.

    [9] See the example given by Hoffmann, *ibid.*

    [10] The idea that a primary lawful act, if intended or known to be likely to interfere with a person's trade or employment, was unlawful unless it could be justified was at one time current, but was described by Lord Dunedin in *Sorrell* v. *Smith* [1925] A.C. 700, 719 as " the leading heresy." See *Crofter Hand-Woven Harris Tweed Co. Ltd.* v. *Veitch* [1942] A.C. 435, 442, *per* Viscount Simon L.C.; *Rookes* v. *Barnard* [1964] A.C. 1129.

recover damages from A only if A's conduct amounts to a tort or breach of contract as against him [11] and it makes no difference that A's conduct is in some extrinsic sense unlawful. In *Chapman* v. *Honig* [12] A, a landlord, gave notice to quit the premises to his tenant, B, the notice being in accordance with the terms of the lease. A's purpose, however, was to punish B for having given evidence (under subpoena) in an action brought against A by another of his tenants and it followed that A was guilty of a criminal contempt of court.[13] Nevertheless the Court of Appeal held, by a majority, that B had no cause of action against A.[14] Similarly where the act done by A is an offence against a penal statute B has no claim against A unless the case falls within the scope of the ordinary action for breach of statutory duty.[15]

The position is otherwise, however, in the complex situation in which A uses B as a vehicle for the infliction of harm upon C.[16] In the case of three-party intimidation it is the unlawfulness in relation to B of the act threatened by A which renders A liable to C, and there is no reason why A should not equally be liable where the act, unlawful in relation to B, is not merely threatened but is actually carried out. In other words, A commits a tort against C if, with the intention and

---

[11] It is not unlawful to cause injury to a member of a trading or professional association by expelling him from that association in accordance with its rules, even if that causes him to lose his livelihood, at least if the expulsion is made in good faith: *Abbott* v. *Sullivan* [1952] 1 K.B. 189; *Lee* v. *Showmen's Guild of Great Britain* [1952] 2 Q.B. 329; *Byrne* v. *Kinematograph Renters Society Ltd.* [1958] 1 W.L.R. 762. *Cf. Lawlor* v. *Union of Post Office Workers* [1965] Ch. 712. If, however, the expulsion is in breach of the rules, then damages for breach of contract may be awarded even against a trade union: *Bonsor* v. *Musicians' Union* [1956] A.C. 104; *Edwards* v. *S.O.G.A.T.* [1971] Ch. 354. Nevertheless, if a trading or professional association has a monopoly control over a certain trade or profession such that no one can earn his living in it without the sanction of the association, a declaration or injunction may perhaps be obtained against it even in the absence of tort or breach of contract, as the law can act to protect a person against capricious or unreasonable denial of his right to work: *Nagle* v. *Feilden* [1966] 2 Q.B. 633. See also *Faramus* v. *Film Artistes' Association* [1964] A.C. 925, where, however, a trade union rule in unreasonable restraint of trade was held to be validated by the Trade Union Act 1871, s. 3. *Cf. Edwards* v. *S.O.G.A.T.*, *supra.*

[12] [1963] 2 Q.B. 502; Weir, *Casebook on Tort*, 3rd ed., p. 137. *Cf. Beaudesert Shire Council* v. *Smith* (1966) 40 A.L.J.R. 211 (H.Ct. of Aust.), p. 453, n. 2.

[13] *Att.-Gen.* v. *Butterworth* [1963] 1 Q.B. 696.

[14] It is not easy to reconcile *Acrow (Automation) Ltd.* v. *Rex Chainbelt Inc.* [1971] 1 W.L.R. 1676 with *Chapman* v. *Honig.* B had obtained an injunction to restrain C from breaking a contract. C purported to ignore the injunction and instructed A, suppliers of components for machines manufactured by B under licence from C, to cease supply. There was no contractual relationship between B and A. The Court of Appeal granted an injunction restraining A from carrying out C's instructions. A's stopping of the supply constituted interference in business by unlawful means, the unlawful means being A's aiding and abetting of C's contempt of court. *Chapman* v. *Honig* was not referred to by the court. See Wedderburn (1972) 35 M.L.R. 184.

[15] *Ante*, Chap. 8. Of course, as Davies L.J. observed in *Chapman* v. *Honig, supra*, at p. 523, most crimes are also torts, but where they are not the fact that they are committed with the intention of causing harm will not, it seems, make them so. *Cf. Weir, loc, cit.* at pp. 231–232.

[16] Weir, *ibid.* at p. 227, suggests that the difference between the two classes of case is merely one of fact, not of principle. " One can bloody one's neighbour's nose unaided, but to ruin him usually requires assistance; the defendant in the economic torts is commonly Iago, not Jehu." But a large corporation can often easily ruin its " neighbour " unaided. If it does so its liability depends not on the extrinsic unlawfulness of its conduct but on whether or not it has broken any duty owed to its " neighbour."

result of causing loss to C, he does an act which is primarily unlawful in relation to B. In *J. T. Stratford & Son Ltd.* v. *Lindley*,[17] the facts of which have been summarised above, two at least of their Lordships considered that if the defendants had used unlawful means—*i.e.* had committed against the barge hirers the tort of procuring breaches of their contracts with their men [18] the plaintiffs would have had a cause of action not only in respect of the breaches of the hiring contracts but also in respect of new business they were unable to undertake. " In addition to interfering with existing contracts," said Lord Reid,[19] " the defendant's action made it practically impossible for the appellants to do any new business with the barge hirers. It was not disputed that such interference with business is tortious if any unlawful means are used."

It is tolerably clear that actual violence, the procurement of breaches of contract, fraud [20] and probably any other tort constitute unlawful means for the purpose of this form of liability.[21] It is, however, uncertain whether the fact that the conduct is such as to constitute a crime or breach of statute is alone sufficient. In *Hargreaves* v. *Bretherton* [22] it was held that perjury leading to the conviction of the plaintiff was not capable of giving rise to a cause of action, and one reason, in addition to that of policy, may be that perjury, though criminal, is not unlawful in relation to the jury, which is the vehicle (B) used by the defendant (A) for inflicting harm on the plaintiff (C). On the other hand, in *Daily Mirror Newspapers Ltd.* v. *Gardner* [23] Lord Denning M.R. and Russell L.J. considered that a claim was entitled to succeed where the means used by A were not unlawful in relation to B,[24] but were unlawful in the sense that they offended against the Restrictive Trade Practices Act 1956.[25] It is respectfully submitted that the latter case should not be regarded as a binding authority on the point for it was decided principally on another ground [26] and no argument was addressed to the Court concerning the difference between means which are unlawful only in the sense that they are contrary to statute, and

---

[17] [1965] A.C. 269, *ante*, pp. 449–450; *Tarleton* v. *M'Gawley* (1793) Peake N.P. 270. See Hoffmann, *loc. cit.*, p. 121.
[18] This might have been affected by the Trade Disputes Act 1906, s. 3. *Post*, p. 467.
[19] [1965] A.C. at p. 324; *per* Viscount Radcliffe at p. 329.
[20] *National Phonograph Co. Ltd.* v. *Edison Bell Consolidated Phonograph Co. Ltd.* [1908] 1 Ch. 335.
[21] See Clerk and Lindsell, *Torts*, 13th ed., p. 410.
[22] [1959] 1 Q.B. 45. *Cf. National Phonograph Co. Ltd.* v. *Edison Bell Consolidated Phonograph Co. Ltd.* [1908] 1 Ch. 335, where the tort of deceit was made out.
[23] [1968] 2 Q.B. 762. *Cf. Davies* v. *Thomas* [1920] 2 Ch. 189, 202, *per* Warrington L.J. and see Clerk and Lindsell, *Torts*, 13th ed., pp. 410–411.
[24] See also *Acrow (Automation) Ltd.* v. *Rex Chainbelt Inc.*, *supra*.
[25] 4 & 5 Eliz. 2, c. 68, ss. 6 (7), 21. See also *Brokkes Ltd.* v. *Cattel* [1972] Ch. 305 and Kloss (1971) 34 M.L.R. 690, who points out that a contract in restraint of trade at common law does not constitute " unlawful means " in tort.
[26] Lord Denning M.R. and Davies L.J. held that the plaintiff was entitled to succeed on the ground of interference with contract. Davies L.J. expressed no opinion on the point here at issue, but Russell L.J. considered that the plaintiff's case on the basis of unlawful means was the stronger: [1968] 2 Q.B. at p. 785.

means which are primarily unlawful in relation to B.[27] The rationale of liability in this tort is that what A does in relation to B with the intention of injuring C is something which B is legally entitled to resist, not that it is something which, in more general terms, A is not permitted to do.[28] If the distinction drawn here is not maintained it will be difficult to avoid the conclusion that every crime is also a tort, and that, however desirable a rule it might be, is not the law in England.[29]

An even more important question is whether the actual breach by A of his contract with B is actionable on the part of C if the breach is committed with the intention and result of causing harm to C. The solution depends upon which of the two answers to the privity of contract objection given in *Rookes* v. *Barnard*[30] is preferred. It is submitted that the better view, in terms of logic as well as convenience, is that the rules of privity of contract are wholly irrelevant in this context and therefore, so long as A acts with the requisite intent and C suffers actual loss, A is as much liable to C for an act done in breach of his contract with B as he is for a threat of such an act. In both cases the nature of C's complaint is the same—that A has deliberately injured him by an act unlawful in relation to B, the vehicle used by A for causing harm.[31] It remains to be seen, however, whether this view will commend itself to the courts.

4. Conspiracy

In the forms of liability discussed in the preceding sections of this chapter the defendant is not liable unless he has either brought about an unlawful end (as where A persuades B to break his contract with C) or has employed unlawful means to bring about an end which may or may not itself be unlawful (as where A, by the threat of an unlawful act, forces B lawfully to terminate his contract with C). The tort of conspiracy takes two forms, one of which overlaps considerably with forms of liability already discussed. The tort is undoubtedly committed where two or more persons combine to injure a third party by unlawful means (that is, by acts which on the facts known to them, are unlawful[32]) and damage actually results.[33] Unlawful means for this purpose

---

[27] The defendant's argument was only to the effect that the means used were lawful within the Restrictive Trade Practices Act.

[28] *Pace* Lord Denning M.R.: [1968] 2 Q.B. at p. 139.

[29] *Cf.* Street, *Torts*, 5th ed., pp. 349–351. There is a much closer correspondence between crime and tort in the law of some other countries and the Italian penal code specifically enacts that every crime which has caused pecuniary or non-pecuniary damage obliges the guilty person to make compensation: art. 185.

[30] [1964] A.C. 1129. See *ante*, pp. 456–457.

[31] In the case of an actual breach of contract, C may find it more difficult to prove the necessary intent to injure him on the part of A than in the case of a threat, but that goes not to principle but to proof: Weir, *loc. cit.* at p. 229. It may be inappropriate in terms of policy to draw the line even at breach of contract, but that seems inevitable now without legislative intervention.

[32] *Churchill* v. *Walton* [1967] 2 A.C. 224, a case concerning criminal conspiracy. Knowledge that the means are unlawful is not required, but if the facts rendering them unlawful are not known, there is no liability.

[33] Damage is the gist of the *tort* of conspiracy.

include a tort, a crime and, probably, a breach of contract.[34] In this form, the tort of conspiracy is of little importance for two reasons: (a) if, as is commonly the case, the unlawful means are tortious in themselves towards the plaintiff he can in any case recover damages in respect of them and there is nothing to be gained by the addition of an allegation of conspiracy [35]; (b) in many other cases, the development of the tort of interference in trade by unlawful means [36] has made conduct actionable without combination. It is now, however, clear that the tort of conspiracy may be committed even though no illegal means are used and no independently unlawful ends are brought about. In fact, unlike the case where one person acts alone, if there is a combination of persons whose purpose is to cause damage to the plaintiff, that purpose may render unlawful acts which would otherwise be lawful.[37]

Though our early law knew a writ of conspiracy, this was restricted to the abuse of legal procedure, and the action on the case in the nature of conspiracy which came into fashion in the reign of Elizabeth I developed into the modern tort of malicious prosecution. Conspiracy as a crime approached the wide meaning it now has in the latter half of the seventeenth century, but as a tort its development only began in the latter half of the nineteenth century and the law remained obscure until the decision of the House of Lords in *Crofter Hand-Woven Harris Tweed Co. Ltd.* v. *Veitch* [38] in 1942. Even now it cannot be regarded as completely settled. Nor is there any really satisfactory explanation why the " magic of plurality " [39] should make something unlawful if it is not unlawful when done by one person alone. " The view that the explanation is to be found in the increasing power of numbers to do damage beyond what one individual can do is open to the obvious answer that this depends on the personality and influence of the individual. In the play, Cyrano de Bergerac's single voice was more effective to drive the bad actor Montfleury off the stage than the protests of all the rest of the audience to restrain him. The action of a single tyrant may be more potent to inflict suffering on the continent of Europe than a combination of less powerful persons." [40] The most

---

[34] See Heydon, *Economic Torts*, pp. 56–57. The inclusion of breach of contract seems a logical deduction from *Rookes* v. *Barnard* [1964] A.C. 1129.
[35] *Ward* v. *Lewis* [1955] 1 W.L.R. 9, 11, *per* Denning L.J.; *Bird* v. *O'Neal* [1960] A.C. 907, 922, *per* Lord Tucker; *Torquay Hotel Co. Ltd.* v. *Cousins* [1969] 2 Ch. 106, 120, *per* Stamp J. See Hughes, " The Tort of Conspiracy " (1952) 15 M.L.R. 209. If the allegation of conspiracy is brought in to gain some added advantage, *e.g.* in order to get in evidence which would not be admissible in a straight action in tort, it may be struck out: *Ward* v. *Lewis, supra,* at p. 11, *per* Denning L.J.
[36] See pp. 458–461, *ante*; Fleming, *Torts*, 4th ed., p. 616.
[37] Note, however, that where there is a trade dispute this form of conspiracy is not actionable. Furthermore, the scope of " unlawful means " conspiracy is also severely restricted. See pp. 468–469, *post*.
[38] [1942] A.C. 435; Weir, *Casebook on Tort*, 3rd ed., p. 509.
[39] *Pete's Towing Services Ltd.* v. *N.I.U.W.* [1970] N.Z.L.R. 32, 55, *per* Speight J.
[40] *Crofters' Case* [1942] A.C. at p. 443, *per* Viscount Simon L.C. In the same case Viscount Maugham (at p. 448) said that he had never felt any difficulty in seeing " the great difference between the acts of one person and the acts in combination of two or of of a multitude." *Cf. D.P.P.* v. *Withers* [1974] 3 All E.R. 984.

plausible explanation is the historical one that conspiracy as a crime, like libel, was developed by the Star Chamber and when taken over by the common law courts came to be regarded by them as not only a crime but also as capable of giving rise to civil liability.[41] Whatever the explanation, however, it must now be taken as clear " that there are cases in which a combination of individuals to act in a certain way, resulting in deliberate damage to others, is actionable, even though the same thing, if done by a single individual without any element of combination, would not expose him to liability." [42]

The crime of conspiracy has recently received the attention of the House of Lords [43] and it seems clear that a conspiracy of the type found in the *Crofter's* case is not now indictable.[44] It should not, however be deduced from this that such conduct is not tortious: the tort and the crime seem largely to have cut loose from their common origin.[45]

The Crofters' case

In the *Crofters'* case the House of Lords gave elaborate consideration to the main essentials of conspiracy and it is no longer necessary to make more than passing references to the " famous trilogy " [46] of *Mogul SS. Co. Ltd.* v. *McGregor Gow & Co.*,[47] *Allen* v. *Flood* [48] and *Quinn* v. *Leathem*,[49] which, together with *Sorrell* v. *Smith* [50] provided the main material with which the House had to work. The facts of the *Crofters'* case were as follows. The production of Harris tweed is an industry of the Isle of Lewis. Originally the yarn of the cloth was hand-spun from wool by the crofters of Lewis and was wholly produced in the Isle. By 1930, hand-spinning of wool had become commercially impracticable and thenceforth many of the weavers in Lewis imported yarn from the mainland. Five mill-owners in Lewis nevertheless spun yarn woven by the crofters. These mill-owners alleged that cloth woven on Lewis from mainland yarn could be sold much more cheaply than cloth made from yarn spun in Lewis. It was therefore to their interest to get a minimum price fixed for the cloth. Of the workpeople in their mills 90 per cent. were members of

---

[41] Holdsworth, *H.E.L.*, viii, 392, cited by Viscount Simon L.C., *ubi supra.*
[42] *Crofters' Case* [1942] A.C. 435, 444, *per* Viscount Simon L.C.
[43] *Kamara* v. *D.P.P.* [1974] A.C. 104; *D.P.P.* v. *Withers* [1974] 3 All E.R. 984.
[44] *Semble, D.P.P.* v. *Withers, supra.* A conspiracy is indictable if it is (a) a conspiracy to commit a crime, (b) a conspiracy to commit a tort involving " invasion of the public domain " or intended to inflict substantial harm on the victim, or (c) it falls within a residual class such as conspiracy to corrupt public morals, conspiracy to pervert the course of justice and conspiracy to defraud.
[45] In *Kamara, supra*, Lord Hailsham L.C. at p. 125, leaves open the question whether a conspiracy may be tortious, but not criminal. But unless the *Crofters'* case be overruled, this seems to be the inevitable conclusion under the modern law. Lord Porter in the *Crofters'* case at [1942] A.C. 488 thought that certain tortious conspiracies were not indictable.
[46] The phrase is Viscount Cave L.C.'s in *Sorrell* v. *Smith* [1925] A.C. 700, 711.
[47] [1892] A.C. 25; Weir, *Casebook on Tort*, 3rd ed., p. 477.
[48] [1898] A.C. 1; Weir, *Casebook on Tort*, 3rd ed., p. 488.
[49] [1901] A.C. 495; Weir, *Casebook on Tort*, 3rd ed., p. 495.
[50] *Supra*; Weir, *Casebook on Tort*, 3rd ed., p. 503.

the Transport and General Workers Union, and the Lewis dockers were also members of it. The union, with the object of getting all workpeople in the mills to be members of the union and of increasing their wages, approached the mill-owners who replied that they could not raise wages because of the competition of the crofters who wove yarn imported from the mainland. The union officials then put an embargo on the importation of yarn by ordering the Lewis dockers not to handle such yarn. They obeyed (without breaking any contract) and thus injured the trade of seven small producers of tweed who used imported yarn and who sued the union officials for conspiracy.

On these facts the House of Lords held that the defendants were not liable because the predominant purpose of the embargo was to promote the interests of members of the union rather than to injure the plaintiffs, and the actual outcome of the case thus does little more than follow the decision in *Sorrell* v. *Smith*.[51] Their Lordships made it clear, however, that if the predominant purpose of a combination is to injure another in his trade or business [52] or in his other legitimate interests [53] then, if damage results, the tort of conspiracy exists. We must now consider this in detail.

(a) **Purpose.** The most important feature of a tortious conspiracy where unlawful means are not used is that the object or purpose of the combination must be to cause damage to the plaintiff. It is not a matter of " intention " as that word is normally used in the law, for intention signifies not what a person is aiming at but what may reasonably be expected to flow from what he does, while for conspiracy the test is " what is in truth the object in the minds of the combiners when they acted as they did." [54] Malice in the sense of malevolence, spite or ill will is not an essential for liability [55]; what is required is that the combiners should have acted *in order that* (not *so that*) the plaintiff should suffer damage. If they did not act in order that the plaintiff should suffer damage they are not liable, however

---

[51] [1925] A.C. 700. In *Mogul S.S. Co. Ltd.* v. *McGregor Gow* [1892] A.C. 25 the defendant shipping companies had combined to offer reduced freight charges in order to gain a monopoly of the China tea trade. The plaintiff company, which was excluded from the combination, was driven out of the trade as a result, but had no cause of action as the object of the defendants was merely to extend their own trade and increase their profits, and they had used no unlawful means to achieve this legitimate, if selfish, purpose.

[52] This, so their Lordships held, had really been settled in *Quinn* v, *Leathem* [1901] A.C. 495, notwithstanding earlier doubts about the meaning of that case.

[53] [1942] A.C. at pp. 446–447, *per* Viscount Simon L.C.; at p. 451, *per* Viscount Maugham; at pp. 462, 478, *per* Lord Wright; *Thompson* v. *New South Wales Branch of the British Medical Association* [1924] A.C. 764.

[54] [1942] A.C. at p. 445, *per* Viscount Simon L.C. Nevertheless, though " purpose " is not the same as " intention," " in many cases the one is the parent of the other " (*ibid.* at p. 452, *per* Viscount Maugham) and a man's " intention " may furnish useful evidence of his " pupose."

[55] *Ibid.* at p. 450, *per* Viscount Maugham; 463, 469–471, *per* Lord Wright. Proof of malevolence coupled with proof of a lack of tangible benefit to the combiners would show a combination to be wrongful, but mere malevolence does not damage anyone. " I cannot see how the pursuit of a legitimate practical object can be vitiated by glee at the adversary's expected discomfiture ": *ibid.*, *per* Lord Wright.

selfish their attitude and however inevitable the plaintiff's damage may have been.[56]

Cases of mixed motive are common enough in individuals, and it is obvious that a combination of persons may have more than one purpose. Where this is so the question must be asked, what was the real or predominant purpose of the combination, and it is to be answered broadly as by a jury or judge of fact.[57] Difficulty may arise where the purposes of the various parties to the combination are different, but though each party may have his own private end to gain, if the joint aim is no more than a desire for prosperity or peace in industry, there is no tort.[58] On the other hand, if one of the parties is actuated merely by hate or vindictive spite he may be liable and if the others are aware of this and lend him their assistance then they too may be participants in the wrong.[59]

Precise definition of what is and what is not a legitimate purpose is probably not possible,[60] but the fact that we live in a competitive or acquisitive society has led English law, for better or for worse, to adopt the test of self-interest or selfishness as being capable of justifying the deliberate doing of lawful acts which inflict harm.[61] Acts done to forward or protect the defendants' trade or business interests are clearly justified, but it is not essential that the interest promoted be a material one.[62] In *Scala Ballroom (Wolverhampton) Ltd.* v. *Ratcliffe* [63] the plaintiffs refused to admit coloured persons to their ballroom but they did allow coloured musicians to play in the orchestra. The defendants were officials of the Musicians' Union, a union with many coloured members, and they gave notice to the plaintiffs that members of the union would not be permitted to play at the ballroom so long as the colour bar remained in operation. An injunction to restrain them from persuading their members not to play there was refused. On the other hand, in *Huntley* v. *Thornton* [64] damages were awarded against union officials whose object in keeping the plaintiff out of work was, as Harman J. found, to uphold " their own ruffled dignity. . . . It had become a question of the district committee's prestige; they were determined to use any weapon ready to their hand to vindicate their authority, and grossly abused the quite frightening powers at their command." [65]

---

[56] As may be expected from this, successful actions for conspiracy are rare.

[57] [1942] A.C. at p. 445, *per* Viscount Simon L.C.; at p. 478, *per* Lord Wright.

[58] *Ibid.* at p. 453, *per* Viscount Maugham; at p. 495, *per* Lord Porter.

[59] *Ibid.* at p. 495, *per* Lord Porter. Fleming, *Torts*, 4th ed., p. 621, takes a different view, holding that it is impossible for one person only to be liable for conspiracy.

[60] *Crofters' Case* [1942] A.C. at p. 446, *per* Viscount Simon L.C. For the change in judicial attitudes see Wedderburn, *The Worker and the Law*, pp. 21–25, 247–251.

[61] *Ibid.* at p. 472, *per* Lord Wright.

[62] Lord Wright (*ibid.* at p. 478) implies that a combination of parishioners to withhold subscriptions from the incumbent is not unlawful if the object is the promotion of the religious interests of the parish.   [63] [1958] 1 W.L.R. 1057.

[64] [1957] 1 W.L.R. 321; *Hutchison* v. *Aitchison* (1970) 9 K.I.R. 69.

[65] *Ibid.* at p. 341, *per* Harman J. Such a case was foreshadowed by Lord Wright in the *Crofters' Case* [1942] A.C. at p. 445.

Other examples of unlawful objects are given by their Lordships in the *Crofters'* case. " Mere busybodies " are probably not protected,[66] nor are those who are induced to join a combination by the payment of money and have no other interest to protect.[67] A combination to compel the plaintiff to pay a debt is apparently unlawful,[68] but where the object is to punish him it is necessary to distinguish between mere vindictive vengeance, which is unlawful, and the purpose of deterring others from similarly offending, which apparently is not.[69] If the object is to increase the effective strength of a trade union, it is lawful.[70]

The legitimate purpose of a combination is sometimes spoken of as its justification,[71] but this does not mean that a combination to do an act harmful to the plaintiff is necessarily actionable unless the defendants prove that it was justified. The burden of proof lies with the plaintiff throughout.[72] On the other hand, there may obviously be cases in which a plaintiff established a prima facie case by proving that he suffered damage from acts done in combination by the defendants, the natural and probable outcome of which was damage to him. This will cast a " provisional burden " on the defendants to set up their legitimate purpose, but does not affect the " legal burden " which remains with the plaintiff.[73] On the other hand, if the combination is one to use unlawful means, then the burden of justification, if justification is possible, lies with the defendant.[74]

(b) Combination.[75] There must, of course, be concerted action between two or more persons,[76] but it seems that there can be no conspiracy between an employer and his employees, at least where they merely go about their employer's business.[77] On the other hand, there seems no reason why an employer should not be vicariously

---

[66] *Ibid.* at p. 491, *per* Lord Porter.

[67] *Ibid.* at p. 451, *per* Viscount Maugham; at p. 460, *per* Lord Thankerton; at p. 480, *per* Lord Wright.

[68] *Giblan* v. *National Amalgamated Labourers' Union* [1903] 2 K.B. 600. What of the case where the defendants combine to compel the plaintiff to subscribe to an extraneous charity? *Per* Lord Porter [1942] A.C. at p. 493.

[69] *Crofters' Case* [1942] A.C. at p. 475; *Eastham* v. *Newcastle United Football Club Ltd.* [1964] Ch. 413, 453–454, *per* Wilberforce J.

[70] *Crofters' Case* [1942] A.C. at p. 493, *per* Lord Porter, citing *Hodges* v. *Webb* [1920] 2 Ch. 70; *White* v. *Riley* [1921] 1 Ch. 1. Note that the fact that the damage is disproportionate to the purpose sought to be achieved does not itself render the conspiracy actionable but it may cast doubt on the bona fides of the alleged purpose: nor is the court concerned with the expediency or otherwise of the policy adopted by the combiners: *Crofters' Case* [1942] A.C. at p. 447, *per* Viscount Simon L.C.

[71] *e.g. Sorrell* v. *Smith* [1925] A.C. 700, 712, *per* Viscount Cave L.C. See Heydon, [1970] 20 Univ. of Toronto L.J., pp. 150–151.

[72] *Crofters' Case* [1942] A.C. at p. 471, *per* Lord Thankerton; at p. 471, *per* Lord Wright; at p. 495, *per* Lord Porter. *Cf. ibid.* at p. 449, *per* Viscount Maugham.

[73] See *Brown* v. *Rolls-Royce Ltd.* [1960] 1 W.L.R. 210, 215, *per* Lord Denning.

[74] Clerk and Lindsell, *Torts*, 13th ed., pp. 421–422.

[75] See Fridman, " *Mens Rea* in Conspiracy " (1956) 19 M.L.R. 276.

[76] There can be no conspiracy between husband and wife, but they can, of course, conspire with others.

[77] Clerk and Lindsell, *Torts*, 13th ed., p. 414.

liable for a conspiracy involving his servants, and it is submitted, therefore, that a company may be liable in some cases for lawful action agreed upon by the directors if the purpose of that action was to cause damage to the plaintiff and if the agreement between the directors was reached in the course of their employment.

(c) **Overt act causing damage.** In contrast with the crime of conspiracy, an overt act causing damage is an essential of liability in tort. If, therefore, the acts relied on are incapable of being made part of any cause of action—e.g. evidence given by witnesses in a court of law—then the tort cannot be made out.[78] A sufficient element of damage is shown where expenses are necessarily incurred by the plaintiff in investigating and counteracting the machinations of the defendants.[79]

TRADE DISPUTES

A general textbook on the law of tort is not the place for an extended discussion of the specialised law relating to industrial disputes,[80] but the general law, and particularly the forms of liability considered in the preceding sections of this chapter, is so substantially modified by the Trade Union and Labour Relations Act 1974 that some account of the legislative intervention is necessary.

1. Trade Disputes Acts 1906 and 1965 [81]

The Trade Disputes Act 1906 was of enormous importance but only the briefest summary of its provisions can be attempted here. The Act:

(i) made trade unions completely immune from actions in tort, though it did not affect the liability of individuals;

(ii) rendered " conspiracy to injure " (i.e. without unlawful means [82]) not actionable in the context of trade disputes;

(iii) rendered inducement of breaches of contracts of employment not actionable in the context of trade disputes.

The Trade Disputes Act 1965 reversed *Rookes* v. *Barnard* [83] in trade dispute cases by rendering not actionable a threat to break or induce the breach of a contract of employment.

2. The Industrial Relations Act 1971

This Act set out to enlarge the range of civil remedies for wrongful acts done in contemplation or furtherance of " industrial disputes,"

---

[78] *Marrinan* v. *Vibart* [1963] 1 Q.B. 234, affd. *ibid.* 528.
[79] *B.M.T.A.* v. *Salvadori* [1949] Ch. 556.
[80] See Citrine, *Trade Union Law*, 3rd ed., pp. 551–629; Wedderburn, *The Worker and the Law*, 2nd ed., pp. 327–410; Grunfeld, *Modern Trade Union Law*, pp. 317–519. Unfortunately, all these works have been overtaken by legislative developments.
[81] See the 9th ed. of this work.
[82] See pp. 463–466, *ante.*
[83] See p. 455, *ante.*

but through the new statutory concept of unfair industrial practices, not through the law of tort.[84] Some of these unfair industrial practices were similar to certain varieties of torts and the common law was not wholly abolished. However, the Act was a disastrous failure for political reasons and was repealed by the Trade Union and Labour Relations Act 1974.

3. The Trade Union and Labour Relations Act 1974 [85]

When presented as a Bill, this Act was intended not merely to repeal the Industrial Relations Act but to grant a more extensive immunity against actions in tort than had been afforded by the Trade Disputes Acts of 1906 and 1965. However, amendments in Parliament produced an Act which is in this respect similar, though not identical, to the Acts of 1906 and 1965. At the time of writing there is before Parliament a further Bill which would amend the 1974 Act in such a way as to make it accord with the Labour Government's original intentions. This Bill is discussed later.

(a) **Trade unions.** No action in tort lies against a trade union or employers' association [86] in respect of any action alleged to have been done by or on behalf of that body and the immunity is not limited to trade disputes.[87] However, a measure of tort liability is imposed by section 14 (2), which provides that the union or association may be sued in its own name in respect of negligence, nuisance or breach of duty resulting in personal injury or breach of any duty connected with the ownership, occupation, possession, control or use of any property, real or personal,[88] if not arising from an act done in contemplation or furtherance of a trade dispute.

(b) **Conspiracy.** By section 13 (4) of the Act an agreement or combination of two or more persons to do or procure the doing of any act in contemplation or furtherance of a trade dispute [89] shall not be actionable in tort if the act is one which, if done without any such agreement, would not be actionable in tort. This provision has two main effects. First, it carries on the principle of section 1 of the Trade Disputes Act 1906 by rendering not actionable conspiracies which do not involve unlawful means.[90] Secondly, it restricts the scope of " unlawful means "

---

[84] There was a voluminous literature on this ill-fated Act. For a summary of its provisions concerning industrial disputes, see Salmond, *Torts*, 16th ed., Chap. 17.
[85] Wedderburn (1974) 37 M.L.R. 525; Perrins, *Labour Relations Law Now* (1975).
[86] " Special register " trade unions and corporate employers' associations are subject to somewhat different provisions.
[87] Trade Union and Labour Relations Act 1974 s. 14 (1). The immunity extends to actions against trustees and representative actions. S. 14 (1) (c) makes it clear that the immunity extends to an action for an injunction: cf. *Torquay Hotel Co. Ltd.* v. *Cousins* [1969] 2 Ch. 106.
[88] This is extraordinarily vague. Cf. Wedderburn, *loc. cit.*, p. 538.
[89] For definition, see p. 470, *post.*
[90] See p. 467, *ante.* See, however, Perrins, *op. cit.*, p. 64, who argues that s. 13 (4) is redundant in this context. If the defendants are genuinely acting in contemplation or furtherance of a trade dispute they have a legitimate purpose at common law and need no statutory protection: see p. 465, *ante.*

conspiracy by, in effect, providing that only a conspiracy to commit a *tort* is actionable in tort.[91]

(c) **Interference with subsisting contract.** Section 13 (2) of the Act may be shortly disposed of. " For the avoidance of doubt it is hereby declared that an act done in contemplation or furtherance of a trade dispute is not actionable in tort on the ground only that it is an interference with the trade, business or employment of another person, or with the right of another person to dispose of his capital or his labour as he wills." This merely repeats the so-called " second limb " of section 3 of the Trade Disputes Act which was passed at a time when it was thought that there might be a general tort of unjustifiable interference in trade without unlawful means—a " *Quinn* v. *Leathem* without the conspiracy " [92] Subsequent case law confirmed that there was no such tort and section 13 (2) is merely declaratory.[93]

Section 13 (1) (*a*) is considerably more important for, like earlier legislation, it provides that an act done in contemplation or furtherance of a trade dispute is not actionable in tort on the ground only that it induces another person to break a contract of employment.[94] The word " only " should be noted, for the protection is thereby confined to cases in which the defendant makes no use of unlawful means to procure the breach of contract and so commits no other, incidental tort. If the means are unlawful—*e.g.*, if he uses words amounting to defamation—he is not protected.

Section 13 (3) (*a*) lays to rest what might have become a substantial problem under the pre-1971 law. The Trade Disputes Act 1906 simply provided that direct inducement of breaches of contracts of employment was not actionable. But the effect of such inducement might well be the indirect procurement of breaches of commercial contracts and in that event it was at least arguable that the inducement, though not *actionable*, was still *unlawful* for the purpose of the tort of interference with contract by unlawful means.[95] Now, section 13 (3) (*a*) declares " for the avoidance of doubt " that an act which is not actionable by reason of section 13 (1) (*a*) shall not be regarded as an unlawful act or unlawful means for the purpose of establishing liability in tort.[96]

---

[91] This is achieved by the words " in tort " at the end of the subsection. S. 13 (3) is also theoretically applicable to conspiracy, but seems to add nothing to the protection given by s. 13 (4). The increasingly common tactic of a "sit-in " or "work-in " receives no protection from s. 13, since it involves a conspiracy to trespass.

[92] The phrase is Lord Devlin's: *Rookes* v. *Barnard*, *supra*, at p. 1216.

[93] *Quaere*, however, whether s. 13 (2) might not cover development of the direct interference with contract, short of breach, suggested in *Torquay Hotel Co. Ltd.* v. *Cousins*, p. 446, *ante*. See Wedderburn, *loc. cit.*, p. 539, n. 86.

[94] By s. 30 (1) " contract of employment " means a contract of service or of apprenticeship. If, therefore, an official of a union of university teachers persuaded members to withhold marks of internal examinations he would be protected by s. 13 (1); but if he persuaded them to withhold marks from other institutions at which they were external examiners he might not be so protected.

[95] For the conflicting judicial *dicta*, see the 9th edition of this book, p. 478, n. 64a.

[96] The original Bill also gave protection against *interference* with contract short of breach, no doubt with the decision in *Torquay Hotel Co. Ltd.* v. *Cousins* (p. 446, *ante*) in mind. As to whether s. 13 (2) could cover this case, see n. 93, *supra*.

(d) Intimidation. By section 13 (1) (b) of the Act an act done by a person in contemplation or furtherance of a trade dispute shall not be actionable in tort on the ground only that it consists in his threatening that a contract of employment (whether one to which he is a party or not) will be broken or that he will induce another person to break a contract of employment to which that other person is a party. This repeats section 1 (1) of the Act of 1965, passed as a Parliamentary response to the decision in *Rookes* v. *Barnard*.[97] If a threat consists of or includes a threat of an unlawful act other than the breach or procurement of the breach of a contract of employment [98] the threat remains actionable so long as the other conditions for the tort of intimidation are satisfied. The problem dealt with by section 13 (3) (a) in relation to inducing breaches of contracts of employment [99] is met in a similar way by section 13 (3) (b) in relation to threats of breach or inducement of breach: such acts are not unlawful for the purpose of interference with contract by unlawful means.[1]

(e) Trade disputes. In order to gain the protection of section 13 of the Act, the act done by the defendant must be " in contemplation or furtherance of a trade dispute." A trade dispute is comprehensively defined in section 29 (1) as a dispute [2] between employers and workers or between workers and workers [3] which is connected with one or more of the following: terms and conditions (including physical conditions) of employment; engagement, non-engagement, termination or suspension of employment or of duties of employment; allocation of work or duties of employment; matters of discipline; membership or non-membership of a trade union; facilities for union officials; machinery for negotiation or consultation and other procedures, including recognition of unions.

Finally, it should be noted that the scope of *ex parte* injunctions [4] is restricted by section 17, which provides that where an *ex parte* application for an injunction is made and the defendant claims, or in the opinion of the court would be likely to claim, that he acted in contemplation or furtherance of a trade dispute, the court shall not

---

[97] See p. 455, *ante*.

[98] *e.g.*, a commercial contract.

[99] See *supra*.

[1] The problem of interference with a contract which does not cause a breach (see notes 93 and 96, *supra*) arises equally where such interference is threatened.

[2] But by s. 29 (5) an act, threat or demand done or made by one person or organisation against another which, if resisted, would have led to a trade dispute with that other shall, notwithstanding that because that other submits to the act or threat or accedes to the demand no dispute arises, be treated for the purposes of the Act as being done or made in contemplation of a trade dispute with that other.

[3] It therefore remains the case that a dispute between employers and employers cannot be a trade dispute: *Larkin* v. *Long* [1915] A.C. 814. But a dispute between unions can be: *White* v. *Riley* [1921] 1 Ch. 1.
On the distinction between a " trade dispute " and a " political dispute " see *Sherard* v. *A.U.E.W.* [1973] I.C.R. 421.

[4] See p. 587, n. 83, *post*.

grant the injunction unless satisfied that all steps which in the circumstances were reasonable have been taken with a view to securing that notice of the application and an opportunity of being heard with respect to the application have been given to him. It thus becomes more difficult to rob the union side of the initiative in industrial disputes.[5]

4. The Trade Union and Labour Relations (Amendment) Bill. The Act of 1974 is undoubtedly open to two technical objections and may be open to a third objection of a policy or political nature. The first two objecttions are that it fails to take account of, and deal adequately with, the effect of the case law of the 1960's on the immunities conferred by the Acts of 1906 and 1965; and that it bears the marks of its somewhat bizarre legislative history.[6] The third objection (with the validity of which we are not concerned) is that the immunities conferred are simply too narrow for the proper exercise of trade union power. All three objections would be met by the enactment of clause 2 (2) of the Trade Union and Labour Relations (Amendment) Bill now before Parliament, which would substitute for the present section 13 (1) the following provision:

" (1) An act done by a person in contemplation or furtherance of a trade dispute shall not be actionable in tort on the ground only—

(a) that it induces another person to break a contract or interferes or induces any other person to interfere with its performance; or

(b) that it consists in his threatening that a contract (whether one to which he is a party or not) will be broken or its performance interfered with, or that he will induce another person to break a contract or to interfere with its performance."

This would have two major effects. First, it would stifle any possible outflanking of existing protection by development of the statements in *Torquay Hotel Co. Ltd.* v. *Cousins.*[7] Secondly, and more important, it would extend the existing protection to inducing breaches of, or interference with *commercial* contracts.[8] " Blacking " or the " secondary boycott " would no longer give rise to liability and the common law would, for practical purposes, have bowed out of the field of industrial disputes.[9]

5. Passing off

We have already seen that a full consideration of " unfair competition " would be beyond the scope of this book, so that such matters

---

[5] See Wedderburn, *loc. cit.*, pp. 538–539.
[6] On both these points, see Wedderburn, *loc. cit.*
[7] See notes 93 and 96, *supra.*
[8] S. 13 (3) (b) of the present Act is not confined to contracts of employment. This appears to be an error: Wedderburn, *loc. cit.*, p. 542.
[9] Another significant proposal is that in cl. 1 (d) of the Bill to extend protection to a trade dispute relating to matters occurring outside Great Britain. This gives liberty to take industrial action against multi-national companies.

as copyrights and patents must be sought elsewhere.[1] There remains the tort commonly known as " passing off." [2]

The essence of passing off is that one trader represents his goods (or his services) as those of another [3] and he commits the tort even if he does so innocently, that is, with no intention to deceive.[4] All that is necessary is that the get-up [5] or description of the plaintiff's goods should have become distinctive of them and that there is a probability of confusion between them and those of the defendant. Actual confusion on the part of a member of the purchasing public need not be proved,[6] but proof that it has occurred will obviously assist the plaintiff's case, especially if substantial damages are claimed and not only an injunction. Indeed it may be that if he knows nothing of the plaintiff's right the defendant cannot be liable for more than nominal damages.[7] The uncertainty on this point is probably due to the uncertainty which still exists about the theoretical basis of the action, namely, whether or not the plaintiff's right which is infringed is a right of property. It is submitted that the better view today is that, for most purposes, trade names and the like are the subject of property rights.[8]

Varieties of tort. The commonest forms of the tort are imitating the get-up or appearance of the plaintiff's goods, or selling them under the same or a similar name. In *White Hudson & Co. Ltd.* v. *Asian Organisation Ltd.*[9] the plaintiffs' medicated cough sweets had been sold

---

[1] See p. 445 n. 5, *ante*. Competition between traders is as such, of course, perfectly lawful, however ruinous it may be to those who are losers: *Gloucester Grammar School Case* (1410) Y.B.Hil. 11 Hen. 4, f. 47, pl. 21; *Mogul Steamship Co. Ltd.* v. *McGregor Gow & Co.* [1892] A.C. 25. *Ajello* v. *Worsley* [1898] 1 Ch. 274, carries the principle very far. Modern legislation regarding restrictive practices and monopolies attempts positively to encourage competition.

[2] See Kerly, *Trade Marks and Trade Names*, 10th ed., Chap. 17. Trade marks, patents and copyrights depend almost entirely upon statute. Other " common law " torts which may be relevant in this area include deceit (pp. 213–221, *ante*), slander of title (pp. 234–239, *ante*) and breach of confidence (pp. 493–494, *post*).

[3] *Spalding & Bros.* v. *A. W. Gamage Ltd.* (1915) 84 L.J.Ch. 449, 450, *per* Lord Parker. The basis of the action is a proprietary right in the goodwill of a business. Accordingly, an action may in some cases be maintained even though the plaintiff has ceased to carry on the business: *Ad-Lib Club Ltd.* v. *Granville* [1972] R.P.C. 673.

[4] *Singer Machine Manufacturers* v. *Wilson* (1877) 3 App.Cas. 376; *Cellular Clothing Co. Ltd.* v. *Maxton and Murray* [1899] A.C. 326, 334–335, *per* Lord Halsbury L.C. Originally fraud was a necessary element at common law but not in equity: *Millington* v. *Fox* (1838) 3 My. & Cr. 339. Note that the plaintiff does not in any case complain that he was himself deceived: *J. Bollinger* v. *Costa Brava Wine Co.* [1960] Ch. 262, 275, *per* Danckwerts J. See also *Sim* v. *H. J. Heinz Co. Ltd.* [1959] 1 W.L.R. 313, 319, *per* Hodson L.J.

[5] Thus it is not necessary that the public know the plaintiff's identity: *Hoffman-La Roche & Co. A.G.* v. *D.D.S.A. Pharmaceuticals Ltd.* [1972] R.P.C. 1.

[6] *Lee Kar Choo* v. *Lee Lian Choon* [1967] 1 A.C. 602.

[7] *Draper* v. *Trist* [1939] 3 All E.R. 513, 525, *per* Clauson L.J.; *ibid.* at p. 528, *per* Goddard L.J. *Cf. ibid.* at p. 519, *per* Greene M.R. The question was left open by the House of Lords in *Marengo* v. *Daily Sketch and Sunday Graphic Ltd.* (1948) 65 R.P.C. 242.

[8] *J. Bollinger* v. *Costa Brava Wine Co.*, *supra*; *ibid.* (*No.* 2) [1961] 1 W.L.R. 277.

[9] [1964] 1 W.L.R. 1466; *Lee Kar Choo* v. *Lee Lian Choon* [1967] 1 A.C. 602 (P.C.), where it is also pointed out that there may be passing off where the get-up of the defendant's goods is similar to that of the plaintiff, even though there is no infringement of the plaintiff's registered trade mark. See also *Hoffman-La Roche & Co. A.G.* v. *D.D.S.A. Pharmaceuticals Ltd.* [1972] R.P.C. 1.

in Singapore since 1953 in red cellophane wrappers bearing the word " Hacks." In 1958 the defendants began selling their cough sweets in Singapore in similar wrappers bearing the word " Pecto." It was proved that the majority of purchasers in Singapore were unable to read English and that many of them had, by 1958, acquired the habit of asking for " red paper cough sweets." Prior to 1953 no cough sweets had been sold in red cellophane wrappers and between 1953 and 1958 only the plaintiffs' had been so sold. On these facts the Privy Council held that the plaintiffs were entitled to an injunction restraining the defendants from offering cough sweets for sale in the " Pecto " wrapper without clearly distinguishing them from the plaintiffs'.

If the plaintiff's case is based on similarity or identity of name, then he must show that the name used actually connotes goods manufactured by him and is not merely descriptive of those goods.[10] This is a question of fact in each case, for descriptive words may by usage have become distinctively attached to the plaintiff's goods.[11] The leading case is *Reddaway* v. *Banham*,[12] where it was held that " camel hair belting," which originally signified nothing more than belting made of camel hair, had come to signify belting made by the plaintiffs.[13] A plaintiff undertakes no light burden of proof in trying to convince the court that a word in common use has become associated with his goods [14]—far heavier than in proving imitation of a device used as a trade mark. So a mere six months' use of the name " shampoomatic " for a carpet cleaner was insufficient to entitle the manufacturers to an injunction against its use by another company.[15] It is not always necessary, however, for the plaintiff to show that a word used by the defendant has become associated exclusively with the plaintiff's own goods. Thus the word " champagne " is not associated with any particular producer, but it is associated with a wine produced in the Champagne district of France, and producers of champagne were therefore entitled to an injunction restraining the defendants from describing their wine, produced in Spain, as " Spanish

---

[10] Thus " vacuum cleaner " was held to mean simply a cleaner working by suction and not necessarily one manufactured by the British Vacuum Cleaner Co.: *British Vacuum Cleaner Co. Ltd.* v. *New Vacuum Cleaner Co. Ltd.* [1907] 2 Ch. 312; *Fels* v. *Hedley & Co. Ltd.* (1903) 21 R.P.C. 91. *Cf. Wellcome* v. *Thompson* [1904] 1 Ch. 736.

[11] Equally, though once so attached, they may become so public and in such universal use as to be again *publici juris*: *Lazenby* v. *White* (1871) 41 L.J.Ch. 354; *Ford* v. *Foster* (1872) L.R. 7 Ch. 611, 628, *per* Mellish L.J. See also *J. Bollinger* v. *Costa Brava Wine Co. (No. 2)* [1961] 1 W.L.R. 277, 283; *Norman Kark Publications Ltd.* v. *Odhams Press Ltd.* [1962] 1 W.L.R. 380. *Cf.* Street, *Law of Torts*, 5th ed., p. 363.

[12] [1896] A.C. 199.

[13] And in 1931 it was held, upon the facts, that a Belgian manufacturer did not sufficiently distinguish his goods from the plaintiff's by describing them as " Lechat's camel hair belting ": *Reddaway & Co. Ltd.* v. *Hartley*, 48 R.P.C. 283.

[14] *Norman Kark Publications Ltd.* v. *Odhams Press Ltd.* [1962] 1 W.L.R. 380 (" Today "). The burden is lighter if the plaintiff can show that the defendant intended to produce confusion of his wares with those of the plaintiff: *Office Cleaning Services Ltd.* v. *Westminster Office Cleaning Association* [1944] 2 All E.R. 269, 271, *per* Luxmoore L.J. For proceedings in the H.L. see (1946) 63 R.P.C. 39.

[15] *Countess Housewares Ltd.* v. *Addis* [1964] R.P.C. 251. It was pointed out that the word was in part, though not wholly, descriptive.

champagne." [16] The law of passing off arose to prevent unfair trading and protects the property right of a trader in his goodwill, of which a word such as " champagne " may form a part.[17] A trader properly entitled to the use of such a word may therefore prevent its use by one not so entitled, even though persons other than the plaintiff may also lawfully use the word to describe their products.

Use of own name

As a general rule a person can freely use his own name, or one which he has acquired by reputation, although the use of it inflicts damage on someone else who has the same name.[18] This is, however, qualified to some extent by the law of passing off. In the leading case of *Parker-Knoll Ltd.* v. *Knoll International Ltd.*,[19] both parties were manufacturers of furniture, the plaintiff being a company well known in the United Kingdom and the defendant an American company which had only recently begun to trade in England. Notwithstanding that the defendant company did no more than use its own name on its furniture, the House of Lords, by a majority, granted an injunction to restrain it from continuing to do so without distinguishing its goods from those of the plaintiff.[20] The plaintiff has established that its name had come to denote goods made by it alone and not goods made by anyone else possessing or adopting [21] that name, and the use by the defendant of a similar name did, in the opinion of the majority, amount to the false representation that its goods were the plaintiff's goods. The central question in each case is, therefore, whether the name or description given by the defendant to his goods is such as to create a likelihood that a substantial section of the purchasing public will be misled into believing that his goods are the goods of the plaintiff.[22] That the defendant used his own name with no intention to deceive anybody does not mean that such a likelihood has not been created,

---

[16] *J. Bollinger* v. *Costa Brava Wine Co.* [1960] Ch. 262; *ibid.* (*No.* 2) [1961] 1 W.L.R. 277; *Vine Products Ltd.* v. *Mackenzie & Co. Ltd.* [1969] R.P.C. 1; *John Walker & Sons Ltd.* v. *Henry Ost & Co. Ltd.* [1970] 1 W.L.R. 917. On this case, see Cornish, " Unfair Competition? A Progress Report " (1972) 12 J.S.P.T.L. 126; *Shaw Bros.* (*Hong Kong*) v. *Golden Harvest* [1972] R.P.C. 559.

[17] [1961] 1 W.L.R. at p. 281, *per* Danckwerts J.

[18] *Brinsmead & Son Ltd.* v. *Brinsmead* (1913) 30 R.P.C. 493; *Jay's Ltd.* v. *Jacobi* [1933] Ch. 411; Kerly, *op. cit.*, pp. 320, 426–429. As to the use of a title of honour, see *Cowley* v. *Cowley* [1901] A.C. 450.

[19] [1962] R.P.C. 265; *Brinsmead & Son Ltd.* v. *Brinsmead* (1913) 30 R.P.C. 493; *Baume & Co.* v. *A. H. Moore Ltd.* [1958] Ch. 907.

[20] See *Parker-Knoll Ltd.* v. *Knoll International Ltd.* [1962] R.P.C. 243, 257–258, *per* Harman L.J. (proceedings subsequent to those in the House of Lords). Note the distinction, which may sometimes be difficult to draw in practice, between carrying on business in such a way as to represent that it is the business of another and describing one's goods in such a way as to represent that they are the goods of another. The rule against the former admits of the exception of the honest use of one's own name; the rule against the latter does not: *Rodgers* v. *Rodgers* (1924) 41 R.P.C. 277, 291, *per* Romer J.

[21] See *Massam* v. *Thorley's Cattle Food Co.* (1880) 14 Ch.D. 748, 760–761, *per* Bramwell L.J.

[22] *Parker-Knoll Ltd.* v. *Knoll International Ltd.*, *supra*, at pp. 278–279, *per* Lord Morris; *ibid.* at p. 285, *per* Lord Hodson; *ibid.* at pp. 289–290, *per* Lord Devlin. *Granada Group* v. *Ford Motor Co.* [1972] F.S.R. 103.

but proof that the defendant did intend to deceive, where it can be made, will, no doubt, materially assist the plaintiff's case. As has often been pointed out, if it was the defendant's object to deceive people into believing that his goods were the goods of the plaintiff, the court will not be reluctant to infer that he achieved his object.[23]

" *Garnishing* " *one's name.* So far we have spoken of use of one's name without any variation of it. If there is an alteration of it which is likely to mislead—" garnishing " of it, as the expression is—that is unlawful; thus a firm of wine-merchants, " Short's Ltd.," obtained an injunction against one, Short, who set up a similar business and styled it " Short's." [24]

Use of another's name. Unauthorised use of another's name (which is not also the user's name) is, of course, unlawful in so far as it falls within the law of passing off, *i.e.* representing B's goods or business to be the user's goods or business; and this also applies to cases where the defendant uses a fancy name adopted by the plaintiff.[25] But, apart from this, there is a rather wider rule that an injunction can be obtained to prevent A from using B's name in a way calculated to injure B in his property, business or profession.[26] Provided the tendency to injure is proved, this will enable a medical man to prevent unauthorised use of his name to puff a quack medicine.[27] In nearly all the cases, the defendant's use of the name was fraudulent or at least intentional, but there is some ground for thinking that mere accidental user would also be restrained.[28]

Damnum absque injuria. There can be no action for passing off where (a) there is no interference with another person's trade, *and* (b) there is no intent to injure or to deceive. If harm is suffered in such circumstances, it is *damnum absque injuria*, however much trouble and inconvenience it may cause. In *Day* v. *Brownrigg*,[29] X's house had for 60 years been called " Ashford Lodge." The house of Y, his neighbour, had been called " Ashford Villa " for 40 years. Y changed its name to " Ashford Lodge " and this caused much inconvenience and annoyance to X, who claimed an injunction to restrain Y from such alteration

---

[23] *Brinsmead & Son Ltd.* v. *Brinsmead, supra,* at p. 507, *per* Buckley L.J.; *Parker-Knoll Ltd.* v. *Knoll International Ltd., supra,* at p. 290, *per* Lord Devlin.
[24] *Short's Ltd.* v. *Short* (1914) 31 R.P.C. 294; *Parker & Son (Reading)* v. *Parker* [1965] R.P.C. 323. Perhaps *Heppells Ltd.* v. *Eppels Ltd.* (1928) 46 R.P.C. 96 is explicable on this ground.
[25] *Hines* v. *Winnick* [1947] Ch. 708. *Cf. McCulloch* v. *Lewis A. May Ltd.* [1947] 2 All E.R. 845; *Serville* v. *Constance* [1954] 1 W.L.R. 487.
[26] Smith and Williams L.JJ. in *Dockrell* v. *Dougall* (1899) 80 L.T. 556, 557, 558; *Byrne* J. in *Walter* v. *Ashton* [1902] 2 Ch. 282, 293; *Clark* v. *Freeman* (1848) 11 Beav. 112, which is the other way, has been repeatedly disapproved. *Henderson* v. *Radio Corporation Pty. Ltd.* [1969] R.P.C. 218 constitutes an extension of the principle of *Dockrell* v. *Dougall.*
[27] *Cf. Sim* v. *H. J. Heinz Co. Ltd.* [1959] 1 W.L.R. 313.
[28] *Ransom* v. *Old Chem Co.* (1896) 40 S.J. 846. See also 176 L.T. 343–344.
[29] (1878) 10 Ch.D. 294; *Street* v. *Union Bank of Spain and England* (1885) 30 Ch.D. 156.

of the name. It was held on demurrer that he had no cause of action. He made no allegation of malice, nor of intent to injure on Y's part, nor of slander of title, and the law does not recognise that a man can have a legal right to the exclusive use of any name that he chooses to affix to his property.

CHAPTER 22

ABUSE OF LEGAL PROCEDURE [1]

MALICIOUS PROSECUTION [2]
History

The history of this tort takes us back to the old writ of conspiracy which was in existence as early as Edward I's reign and was probably of statutory origin. It was aimed against combinations to abuse legal procedure and it fell into decay in the sixteenth century partly because of its narrow limitation to abuse by two or more persons and partly because the writ of maintenance supplanted it. Even then there was room for another remedy, for maintenance, although it applied to officious meddling in civil litigation, probably did not extend to malicious institution of criminal proceedings.[3] This gap was filled by an action upon the case in the nature of conspiracy. It was not very accurately named, for it lay against a single person as well as against those who acted in combination. Its beginnings are somewhat obscure, but it was coming into use in Elizabeth I's reign [4] and eventually became known as the action for malicious prosecution. Its progress was gradual, for it had to make its way between two competing principles—the freedom of action that every man should have in bringing criminals to justice and the necessity for checking lying accusations of innocent people.[5] For some time the judges oscillated between apprehension of scaring off a just accuser and fear of encouraging a false one; but *Saville* v. *Roberts* (1698) [6] put the action on a firm basis and indeed it is so much hedged about with restrictions and the burden of proof upon the plaintiff is so heavy that no honest prosecutor is ever likely to be deterred by it from doing his duty. On the contrary, now that in fact the enormous majority of prosecutions are brought by the police and reliance need no longer be placed upon the private citizen for this purpose, the law is open to the criticism that it is too difficult for the innocent to obtain redress.[7] It is notable how rarely an action is brought at all, much less a successful one, for this tort.[8]

---

[1] The law and its history are detailed in Winfield, *History of Conspiracy and Abuse of Legal Procedure* (1921), and *Present Law of Abuse of Legal Procedure* (1921). See, too, H. Stephen, *Malicious Prosecution* (1888).
[2] Winfield, *Present Law*, etc. Chap. 6; Weir, *Casebook on Tort*, 3rd ed., Chap. 17.
[3] Winfield, *History*, etc. p. 136; *Present Law*, etc. pp. 4–6. Maintenance as a tort survived until 1967 but has now been abolished: Criminal Law Act 1967 (c. 58), s. 14.
[4] Coke thought *Jerom* v. *Knight* (1587) 1 Leon. 107 was the first instance of it, but *Fuller* v. *Cook* (1584) 3 Leon. 100 is earlier: Winfield, *History*, pp. 118 *et seq.*
[5] See *Glinski* v. *McIver* [1962] A.C. 726, 741, *per* Viscount Simonds; *ibid.* at pp. 753–754, *per* Lord Radcliffe.
[6] 1 Ld.Raym. 374; 5 Mod. 394.
[7] See Fridman, " Compensation of the Innocent " (1963) 26 M.L.R. 481.
[8] But see *Tempest* v. *Snowden* [1952] 1 K.B. 130; *Leibo* v. *Buckman Ltd.* [1952] W.N. 547.

The action for malicious prosecution being an action on the case [9] it is essential for the plaintiff to prove damage, and in *Saville* v. *Roberts* [10] Holt C.J. classified damage for the purpose of this tort as of three kinds, any one of which might ground the action; malicious prosecution might damage a man's fame, or the safety of his person, or the security of his property by reason of his expense in repelling an unjust charge. A moral stigma will inevitably attach where the law visits an offence with imprisonment, [11] but there are today innumerable offences which are punishable only by fine. In such cases the plaintiff can only rely upon damage to his fame if the offence with which he is charged is necessarily and naturally defamatory of him, [12] and in effect the question is the converse of the question of law which is involved in actions for defamation. " Is the statement that the plaintiff was charged with the offence capable of a *non*-defamatory meaning? " [13] Thus a charge of wrongly pulling the communication cord in a railway train does not necessarily affect the fair fame of the accused and will not ground an action for malicious prosecution under Holt C.J.'s first head, [14] but it is otherwise where, *e.g.* the plaintiff is charged with deliberately travelling on a train without having paid his fare. [15] On the other hand, unless the plaintiff was awarded the equivalent of the taxed costs which he incurred in defending himself, the difference between the costs awarded in the criminal proceedings, if any, and the costs actually incurred is sufficient to ground the action under Holt C.J.'s third head. [16]

Assuming there is damage as explained above, the plaintiff must prove (a) that the defendant prosecuted him; and (b) that the prosecution ended in the plaintiff's favour; and (c) that the prosecution lacked reasonable and probable cause; and (d) that the defendant acted maliciously. We can take these point by point.

Essentials of the tort

(i) *Prosecution*

A prosecutor has been described as " a man actively instrumental

---

[9] In *Berry* v. *British Transport Commission* [1962] 1 Q.B. 306, 339, Ormerod L.J. suggested that the time may have come to consider the abolition of the distinction between actions on the case and other actions in tort.

[10] (1698) 1 Ld.Raym. 374; 5 Mod. 394.

[11] Clerk and Lindsell, *Torts*, 13th ed., p. 1060.

[12] *Berry* v. *British Transport Commission* [1961] 1 Q.B. 149, 166, following *Wiffen* v. *Bailey and Romford U.D.C.* [1915] 1 K.B. 600. This was not the original meaning intended by Holt C.J. (*Berry* v. *British Transport Commission, supra*, 160–163, *per* Diplock J.) and it has been criticised by the Court of Appeal; *Berry* v. *British Transport Commission* [1962] 1 Q.B. at p. 333, *per* Devlin L.J.; at pp. 335–336, *per* Danckwerts L.J. See also Prichard [1960] C.L.J. 171.

[13] *Berry* v. *British Transport Commission* [1961] 1 Q.B. 149, 166, *per* Diplock J.

[14] *Ibid.*; *Wiffen* v. *Bailey and Romford U.D.C.* [1915] 1 K.B. 600.

[15] *Rayson* v. *South London Tramways Co.* [1893] 2 Q.B. 304.

[16] *Berry* v. *British Transport Commission* [1962] 1 Q.B. 306, where *Wiffen* v. *Bailey and Romford U.D.C.* [1915] 1 K.B. 600 was held not binding on this point. It is otherwise where costs incurred in a civil action are concerned: *Quartz Hill Consolidated Gold Mining Co.* v. *Eyre* (1883) 11 Q.B.D. 674.

in putting the law in force," [17] but this is too vague to be of much assistance. Certainly it is not necessary that the defendant should himself conduct the prosecution; it is sufficient that he should have signed the charge and expressed to the police his willingness to attend court and give evidence against the accused.[18] Similarly, if A goes before a magistrate and positively asserts that he suspects B of having committed a crime and the magistrate thereupon issues a warrant for B's arrest, A has commenced a prosecution.[19] But if A does no more than tell the story of his loss to the magistrate, leaving it to him to determine whether the facts amount to an offence, he is not on that ground alone a prosecutor.[20] Nor is he necessarily a prosecutor because he was bound over by magistrates who committed a person for trial to prosecute at the trial.[21] It depends upon whether his conduct prior to being bound over was such as to make the binding over the natural and foreseeable consequence.[22]

(ii) *Favourable termination of the prosecution*

The plaintiff must show that the prosecution ended in his favour,[23] but so long as it did so it is of no moment how this came about, whether by a verdict of acquittal, or by discontinuance of the prosecution by leave of the court,[24] or by quashing of the indictment for a defect in it,[25] or because the proceedings were *coram non judice*,[26] or by nonsuit.[27] The effect of a *nolle prosequi* (staying by the Attorney-General of proceedings on an indictment) is open to question. An old case indicates that it is not a sufficient ending of the prosecution because it still leaves

[17] Lopes J. in *Danby* v. *Beardsley* (1880) 43 L.T. 603. In *Mohammed Amin* v. *Jagendra Kumar Bannerjee* [1947] A.C. 322, the Judicial Committee held that in malicious prosecution the test is not whether criminal proceedings have reached a stage at which they may be correctly described as a " prosecution," but whether they have reached a stage at which damage to the plaintiff results. No English authority was cited for this meaning of " prosecution," and, in the case itself, where an Indian magistrate had taken cognisance of the complaint by the defendant that an offence had been committed by the plaintiff, the Judicial Committee held that an action for malicious prosecution would lie. It is difficult to see why the proceedings could not " correctly be described as a prosecution."
[18] *Malz* v. *Rosen* [1966] 1 W.L.R. 1008. See also *Romegialli* v. *Marceau* (1963) 42 D.L.R. (2d) 481 (Ontario C.A.); *Casey* v. *Automobiles Renault Canada Ltd.* (1965) 54 D.L.R. (2d) 600 (Sup.Ct. of Canada).
[19] *Elsee* v. *Smith* (1822) 1 D. & R. 97; *Davis* v. *Noak* (1816) 1 Stark. 377; (1817) 6 M. & S. 29 (*sub tit. Davis* v. *Noake*); *Clarke* v. *Postan* (1834) 6 C. & P. 423; *Dawson* v. *Vasandu* (1863) 11 W.R. 516.
[20] *Cohen* v. *Morgan* (1825) 6 D. & R. 9; *Leigh* v. *Webb* (1800) 3 Esp. 164. The position may be otherwise if A knows his story to be false: *Pandit Gaya Parshad Tewari* v. *Sardar Bhagat Singh* (1908) 24 T.L.R. 884. See too *Roy* v. *Prior* [1971] A.C. 470, *post*, pp. 496–497.
[21] See Magistrates' Courts Act 1952 (15 & 16 Geo. 6 & 1 Eliz. 2, c. 55), s. 5.
[22] *Fitzjohn* v. *Mackinder* (1861) 9 C.B.(N.S.) 505. *Cf. Browne* v. *Stradling* (1836) 5 L.J.C.P. 295. Winfield, *Present Law*, pp. 176–179.
[23] *Parker* v. *Langly* (1713) 10 Mod. 145 and 209. This was not always the law: Winfield, *Present Law*, pp. 182–183.
[24] *Watkins* v *Lee* (1839) 5 M. & W. 270. Withdrawal of the charge, even if without prejudice to the right to recommence, has been held in Canada to be sufficient: *Romegialli* v. *Marceau* (1963) 42 D.L.R. (2d) 481 (Ontario C.A.); *Casey* v. *Automobiles Renault Canada Ltd.* (1965) 54 D.L.R. (2d) 600 (Sup.Ct. of Canada).
[25] *Jones* v. *Gwynn* (1712) 10 Mod. 148, 214.
[26] *Atwood* v. *Monger* (1653) Style 378.
[27] *Goddard* v. *Smith* (1704) 1 Salk. 21; 3 Salk. 245; 6 Mod. 261; 11 Mod. 56.

the accused liable to be indicted afresh on the same charge.[28] But this seems inconsistent with the broad interpretation put upon " favourable termination of the prosecution " which signifies, not that the accused has been acquitted, but that he has not been convicted.[29]

It was held in *Reynolds* v. *Kennedy* [30] that no action could lie if the plaintiff had been convicted, even if his conviction was later reversed on appeal, the reason apparently being that the original conviction showed conclusively that there was foundation for the prosecution. In a number of modern cases, however, it was the fact that the proceedings had terminated in the plaintiff's favour only as the result of an appeal, but nothing was made of this.[31] The question of reasonable and probable cause for the prosecution is an independent question and should not be regarded as finally answered in the defendant's favour on the ground only that a conviction was secured in a court of first instance. *Reynolds* v. *Kennedy* should no longer be regarded as good law.

Conviction procured by fraud. On the other hand, if a conviction stands, then the plaintiff cannot succeed in an action for malicious prosecution, and this is so even if the conviction is one against which there is no right of appeal and which has been obtained by the fraud of the prosecutor. In *Basébé* v. *Matthews*,[32] Byles J. thought that if the rule were otherwise every case would have to be retried on its merits, and Montague Smith J. feared that they would be turning themselves into a Court of Appeal where the legislature allowed none. Neither of these reasons is convincing, for the burden of proof in malicious prosecution is heavy enough to prevent convicted persons from using it as an indirect method of appeal,[33] but nevertheless *Basébé* v. *Matthews* still represents the law. It was followed in *Everett* v. *Ribbands* [34] where the plaintiff had been bound over to find sureties to be of good behaviour. He failed in an action for malicious prosecution, for the proceedings complained of had actually been determined against him.

(iii) *Lack of reasonable and probable cause*

There does not appear to be any distinction between " reasonable " and " probable " The conjunction of these adjectives is a heritage from

---

[28] *Goddard* v. *Smith, supra.*

[29] The question has been much litigated in America, where the *Restatement of Torts*, § 659, and the balance of the decisions are to the effect that *nolle prosequi* is a sufficient ending of the prosecution: 38 *Corpus Juris*, 444–445; so, too, decisions of the Supreme Courts of N.S.W. (*Gilchrist* v. *Gardner* (1891) 12 N.S.W. Law Rep. 184) and of British Guiana (*Khan* v. *Singh* (1960) 2 W.I.R. 441). See also *Romegialli* v. *Marceau, supra.*

[30] (1784) 1 Wils. 232.

[31] *Herniman* v. *Smith* [1938] A.C. 305; *Berry* v. *B.T.C.* [1962] 1 Q.B. 306; *Abbott* v. *Refuge Assurance Co. Ltd.* [1962] 1 Q.B. 432; *Blaker* v. *Weller* [1964] Crim.L.R. 311.

[32] (1867) L.R. 2 C.P. 684.

[33] Some support for this criticism may be found in *Churchill* v. *Siggers* (1854) 3 E. & B. 929, 937, *per* Lord Campbell C.J.; *Fitzjohn* v. *Mackinder* (1860) 8 C.B.(N.S.) 78, 92–93, *per* Willes J.

[34] [1952] 2 Q.B. 198; *Bynoe* v. *Bank of England* [1902] 1 K.B. 467.

the redundancies in which the old pleaders delighted,[35] and although it has been said that reasonable cause is such as would operate on the mind of a discreet man, while probable cause is such as would operate on the mind of a reasonable man,[36] this does not help us much, for it is difficult to picture a reasonable man who is not discreet.

The principal difficulty, and it is no minor one, in stating the law as to reasonable and probable cause arises from the division of function between judge and jury.[37] It has been recognised for centuries [38] that once a man has been acquitted by a criminal court, juries are too ready to award him damages against his prosecutor,[39] and therefore it is for the judge to decide whether the defendant had reasonable and probable cause for launching the prosecution,[40] but is is for the jury to decide any incidental questions of fact necessary for the judge's determination.[41] Moreover, this branch of the law is unusual in requiring the plaintiff to undertake the difficult task of proving a negative. It is for him to prove that the prosecutor did not have reasonable and probable cause, and not for the prosecutor to prove that he had.[42]

In *Herniman* v. *Smith* [43] the House of Lords approved and adopted the definition of reasonable and probable cause given by Hawkins J. in *Hicks* v. *Faulkner* [44] as " an honest belief in the guilt of the accused based upon a full conviction, founded upon reasonable grounds, of the existence of a state of circumstances, which, assuming them to be true, would reasonably lead any ordinarily prudent and cautious man placed in the position of the accuser, to the conclusion that the person charged was probably guilty of the crime imputed." This definition may, however, be over-elaborate for some cases,[45] and has even been said not to fit the ordinary run of cases.[46] It cannot serve as a substitute

---

[35] Winfield, *Present Law*, p. 192.

[36] *Broad* v. *Ham* (1839) 5 Bing.N.C. 722, 725, *per* Tindal C.J.

[37] *Glinski* v. *McIver* [1962] A.C. 726, 742, *per* Viscount Simonds.

[38] See *Pain* v. *Rochester and Whitfield* (1599) Cro.Eliz. 871, cited by Denning L.J. in *Leibo* v. *Buckman Ltd.* [1952] 2 All E.R. 1057, 1062.

[39] *e.g. Abrath* v. *North Eastern Ry.* (1886) 11 App.Cas. 247, 252, *per* Lord Bramwell; *Leibo* v. *Buckman Ltd., supra* at p. 1063, *per* Denning L.J.; *Glinski* v. *McIver, supra* at pp. 741–742, *per* Viscount Simonds; *ibid.* at pp. 777–778, *per* Lord Devlin. *Cf. ibid. per* Lord Radcliffe at p. 754.

[40] *Johnstone* v. *Sutton* (1786) 1 T.R. 510; *Herniman* v. *Smith* [1938] A.C. 305. It is doubtful whether the question is one of fact or law. Probably it is best regarded as a question of fact, but one which is to be treated in the same way as if it were a question of law: *Glinski* v. *McIver, supra* at p. 768, *per* Lord Devlin.

[41] The judge need put to the jury only questions on the salient issues of fact, for otherwise the questions would have no end: *Dallison* v. *Caffery* [1965] 1 Q.B. 348, 368, *per* Lord Denning M.R.

[42] *Abrath* v. *N.E. Ry.* (1883) 11 Q.B.D. 440; *Stapeley* v. *Annetts* [1970] 1 W.L.R. 20. *Green* v. *De Havilland* (1968) 112 S.J. 766, to the contrary, cannot be relied on. *Cf.* the rule in false imprisonment, *ante*, p. 40. If, when the principles of malicious prosecution were being laid down, the courts had been acquainted with the idea, now familiar, of a judge himself determining a disputed question of fact, the whole question of reasonable and probable cause would have been left to the judge, but it is now too late to achieve this result without legislation: *Glinski* v. *McIver, supra* at p. 778, *per* Lord Devlin.

[43] [1938] A.C. 305, 316, *per* Lord Atkin.

[44] (1878) 8 Q.B.D. 167, 171; affd. (1882) 46 L.T. 130.

[45] *Abbott* v. *Refuge Assurance Co.* [1962] 1 Q.B. 432, 452, *per* Upjohn L.J.

[46] *Glinski* v. *McIver* [1962] A.C. 726, 758, *per* Lord Denning.

for the rule of law which says that, in order to succeed in an action for malicious prosecution, the plaintiff must prove to the satisfaction of the judge that, at the time when the charge was made, there was an absence of reasonable and probable cause for the prosecution.[47] Various other definitions have been attempted, but perhaps the most helpful is that given by Lord Devlin in *Glinski* v. *McIver*.[48] Reasonable and probable cause " means that there must be cause (that is, sufficient grounds . . .) for thinking that the plaintiff was probably guilty of the crime imputed: *Hicks* v. *Faulkner*.[49] This does not mean that the prosecutor has to believe in the probability of conviction: *Dawson* v. *Vasandau*.[50] The prosecutor has not got to test the full strength of the defence; he is concerned only with the question of whether there is a case fit to be tried.[51] As Dixon J. (as he then was) put it, the prosecutor must believe that ' the probability of the accused's guilt is such that upon general grounds of justice a charge against him is warranted ': *Commonwealth Life Assurance Society Ltd.* v. *Brain.*" [52]

In many cases the issue of reasonable and probable cause raises only one question, namely, whether the facts admittedly known to and believed by the prosecutor when he launched the prosecution furnished him with reasonable and probable cause for so doing, and in such cases there is no question to be left to the jury. This question is for the judge alone.[53] Moveover, if the prosecutor knew, or, rather, thought he knew, certain facts, it matters not that those facts turn out to be false. " The defendant can claim to be judged not on the real facts but on those which he honestly, and however erroneously, believes; if he acts honestly upon fiction, he can claim to be judged on that." [54]

The judge's concern is essentially with the objective aspect of the question—whether there was reasonable and probable cause in fact—but the overall question is a double one, both objective and subjective: did the prosecutor actually believe and did he reasonably believe that he had cause for prosecution? [55] Not only must there be reasonable and probable cause in fact, but " it would be quite outrageous if, where a party is proved to believe that a charge is unfounded, it were to be

---

[47] *Ibid.*

[48] [1962] A.C. at pp. 766–767; *Dallison* v. *Caffery* [1965] 1 Q.B. 348, 371, *per* Diplock L.J.; Weir, *Casebook on Tort*, 3rd ed., p. 531; *ibid.* p. 315.

[49] (1878) 8 Q.B.D. 167.

[50] (1863) 11 W.R. 516, 518.

[51] On this point see also *Tempest* v. *Snowden* [1952] 1 K.B. 130, 139, *per* Denning L.J.; *Glinski* v. *McIver* [1962] A.C. 726, 759, *per* Lord Denning; *Dallison* v. *Caffery, supra,* at p. 376, *per* Diplock L.J. *Cf. Glinski* v. *McIver, supra,* at p. 756, *per* Lord Radcliffe; *Abbott* v. *Refuge Assurance Co.* [1962] 1 Q.B. 432, 463, *per* Davies L.J. (in a dissenting judgment). For the case where the prosecution acts on advice, see *post,* pp. 483–484.

[52] (1935) 53 C.L.R. 343, 382.

[53] *Leibo* v. *Buckman Ltd.* [1952] 2 All E.R. 1057, 1064, *per* Denning L.J.; *Glinsky* v. *McIver, supra,* at pp. 743–744, *per* Viscount Simonds; *ibid.* at p. 753, *per* Lord Radcliffe; *ibid.* at p. 760, *per* Lord Denning; *ibid.* at pp. 771–772, *per* Lord Devlin.

[54] *Glinski* v. *McIver* [1962] A.C. at p. 776, *per* Lord Devlin.

[55] *Ibid.* 768, *per* Lord Devlin; *Abbott* v. *Refuge Assurance Co.* [1962] 1 Q.B. 432, 453, *per* Upjohn L.J.

held that he could have reasonable and probable cause," [56] and the prosecutor himself must also honestly believe that he has reasonable and probable cause. His belief is a matter for the jury, not the judge, to determine, but the burden of proving lack of honest belief is on the defendant, and the question should only be put to the jury " in the highly unlikely event that there is cogent positive evidence that, despite the actual existence of reasonable and probable cause, the defendant himself did not believe that it existed." [57] If there is such evidence, then it is permissible to ask the jury whether the defendant honestly believed that the plaintiff was guilty of the offence with which he was charged, [58] but questions of guilt are not really for the prosecutor, [59] and it may be better, therefore, to ask the jury whether the prosecutor honestly believed in the case he put forward. [60]

In this connection a problem may arise where the prosecutor acts upon advice, as is commonly the case, for example, where the prosecution is undertaken by the police. The prosecutor, and thus the potential defendant in an action for malicious prosecution, is the individual police officer concerned, but as a matter of police organisation he will act upon the advice or instruction of his superior officers or of the legal department. [61] In principle the fact that the prosecutor has received advice should be regarded as no more than one of the facts to be taken into account, for if the prosecutor did not himself have an honest belief in the case he put forward it is irrelevant that he received advice before doing so. [62] In practice, however, if the prosecutor believes in the facts of the case and is advised by competent counsel before whom the facts are fairly laid that a prosecution is justified, it will be exceedingly difficult to establish lack of reasonable and probable cause. [63] An opinion of counsel favourable to the prosecutor is not

---

[56] *Haddrick* v. *Heslop* (1848) 12 Q.B. 268, 274, *per* Lord Denman C.J.; *Broad* v. *Ham* (1839) 8 Scott 40, 50, *per* Erskine J.

[57] *Dallison* v. *Caffery* [1965] 1 Q.B. 348, 372, *per* Diplock L.J.; *ibid.* at p. 368, *per* Lord Denning M.R.; *Glinski* v. *McIver* [1962] A.C. 726, 743–744, *per* Viscount Simonds; *ibid.* at p. 745, *per* Lord Radcliffe; *ibid.* at p. 768, *per* Lord Devlin. The mere argument that the facts known to the prosecutor were so slender or unconvincing that the prosecutor could not have believed in the plaintiff's guilt is not evidence; *ibid.* at p. 754, *per* Lord Radcliffe. See also *Watters* v. *Pacific Delivery Service* (1964) 45 D.L.R. (2d) 638 (Br.Columbia C.A.).

[58] *Glinski* v. *McIver, supra,* at p. 744, *per* Viscount Simonds; *ibid.* at pp. 755–756, *per* Lord Radcliffe.

[59] *Dallison* v. *Caffery* [1965] 1 Q.B. 348, 375–376, *per* Diplock L.J.

[60] *Tempest* v. *Snowden* [1952] 1 K.B. 130, 137, *per* Evershed M.R.; *ibid.* at p. 140, *per* Denning L.J.; *Glinski* v. *McIver, supra,* 760–761, *per* Lord Denning; *ibid.* at pp. 767–768, *per* Lord Devlin, but *cf. ibid.* at pp. 770–778.

[61] *Glinski* v. *McIver* [1962] A.C. 726, 744–745, *per* Viscount Simonds.

[62] *Ibid.* at pp. 756–757, *per* Lord Radcliffe; *ibid.* at p. 777, *per* Lord Devlin.

[63] *Abbott* v. *Refuge Assurance Co. Ltd.* [1962] 1 Q.B. 432, where Davies L.J. dissented on the facts. See also *Ravenga* v. *Macintosh* (1824) 2 B. & C. 693, 697, *per* Bayley J.; *Glinski* v. *McIver, supra* at pp. 744–745, *per* Viscount Simonds. A similar result will follow where a private citizen is advised by the police that the facts which he has reported constitute a particular offence: *Malz* v. *Rosen* [1966] 1 W.L.R. 1008. It is respectfully submitted, however, that Diplock L.J. overstates the strength of the defendant's position in such a case: *ibid.* at p. 1013.

conclusive, but it is a potent factor to be taken into account when deciding whether to prosecute.[64]

If there are several charges in the indictment, the rule as to reasonable and probable cause applies to all of them,[65] but where there is reasonable and probable cause for a prosecution on a lesser charge than that actually preferred, a question of degree may arise. " Where there is a charge of theft of 20s. and reasonable and probable cause is shown as regards 19s. of it, it may well be that the prosecutor, when sued for malicious prosecution, is entitled to succeed, because he was in substance justified in making the charge, even though he did so maliciously. But the contrary must surely be the case if the figures are reversed and reasonable and probable cause is shown as to 1s. only out of the 20s." [66]

(iv) *Malice*

Judicial attempts to define malice have not been completely successful. " Some other motive than a desire to bring to justice a person whom he [the accuser] honestly believes to be guilty " [67] seems to overlook the fact that motives are often mixed. Moreover, anger is not malice; indeed, it is one of the motives on which the law relies in order to secure the prosecution of criminals,[68] and yet anger is much more akin to revenge than to any desire to uphold the law. Perhaps we are nearer the mark if we suggest that malice exists unless the predominant wish of the accuser is to vindicate the law.[69] The question of its existence is one for the jury [70] and the burden of proving it is on the plaintiff.[71]

At one time malice was not always kept distinct from lack of reasonable and probable cause,[72] but a cogent reason for separating them is that, however spiteful an accusation may be, the personal feelings of the accuser are really irrelevant to its probable truth. The probability or improbability of X having stolen my purse remains the same however much I dislike X. And it has long been law that malice and lack of reasonable and probable cause must be separately proved. Want of reasonable and probable cause may be evidence of malice in cases where it is such that the jury may come to the conclusion that there was no

---

[64] *Abbott* v. *Refuge Assurance Co. Ltd.*, *supra* at p. 450, *per* Ormerod L.J.

[65] *Reed* v. *Taylor* (1812) 4 Taunt. 616. *Cf. Johnstone* v. *Sutton* (1786) 1 T.R. 510.

[66] *Leibo* v. *Buckman Ltd.* [1952] 2 All E.R. 1057, 1071, *per* Jenkins L.J.; *ibid.* at p. 1073, *per* Hodson L.J. *Cf.* the dissenting judgment of Denning L.J. *ibid.* at pp. 1066–1067.

[67] Cave J. in *Brown* v. *Hawkes* [1891] 2 Q.B. 718, 723; *Glinski* v. *McIver* [1962] A.C. 726, 766, *per* Lord Devlin.

[68] [1891] 2 Q.B. 722. But if the prosecutor's anger is aroused, not by his belief in the plaintiff's guilt but by some extraneous conduct of the plaintiff, then there may be evidence of malice: *Glinski* v. *McIver* [1962] A.C. 726 (plaintiff gave evidence for X on a criminal charge which the defendant, a police officer, believed to be perjured, and X was acquitted. If this was the reason for the plaintiff's prosecution on a charge of fraud, the prosecutor would have been malicious). See too *Heath* v. *Heape* (1856) 1 H. & N. 478.

[69] *Stevens* v. *Midland Counties Ry.* (1854) 10 Ex. 352, 356, *per* Alderson B. *Cf.* H. Stephen, *Malicious Prosecution* (1888), p. 37.

[70] *Mitchell* v. *Jenkins* (1833) 5 B. & Ad. 588; *Hicks* v. *Faulkner* (1878) 8 Q.B.D. 167, 175, *per* Hawkins J.

[71] *Abrath* v. *N.E. Ry.* (1886) 11 App.Cas. 247.

[72] Winfield, *Present Law*, p. 189.

honest belief in the accusation made.[73] If there was such an honest belief, the plaintiff must establish malice by some independent evidence, for malicious motives may co-exist with a genuine belief in the guilt of the accused.[74] If want of reasonable and probable cause is not proved by the plaintiff, the defect is not supplied by evidence of malice.[75] " From the most express malice, the want of probable cause cannot be implied." [76]

MALICIOUS PROCESS

For malicious prosecution the defendant must have " prosecuted," but there may also be liability if the defendant has maliciously and without reasonable and probable cause instituted some process short of actual prosecution, of which the most important example is the procuring of a warrant for the plaintiff's arrest. In *Roy* v. *Prior* [77] the defendant, a solicitor, was acting for the the defence of a man charged with a criminal offence. The plaintiff was a doctor who had attended the accused and the defendant issued a witness summons requiring him to be present to give evidence at the trial. According to the plaintiff, this summons was never served on him, but in any case he was not present at the trial and, on the defendant's instructions, the accused's counsel applied for a warrant for his arrest. In support of the application the defendant himself gave evidence to the effect that the plaintiff had been evading service of the summons. As a result the warrant was issued and the plaintiff was arrested at 1 a.m. and kept in custody until 10.30 a.m. on the same day, when he was brought before the court. The House of Lords held that if the plaintiff could prove that the defendant had acted maliciously and without reasonable and probable cause, as he alleged, then he was entitled to succeed.[78] On similar principles a person may also be liable for procuring the issue of a search warrant.[79]

MALICIOUS CIVIL PROCEEDINGS

Historically, there was no reason why the old action upon the case for conspiracy should not be extended to malicious civil proceedings as well

---

[73] *Brown* v. *Hawkes* [1891] 2 Q.B. 718, 722, *per* Cave J.; *Hicks* v. *Faulkner* (1878) 8 Q.B.D. 167, 175, *per* Hawkins J.

[74] *Brown* v. *Hawkes*, 726, *per* Lord Esher.

[75] *Turner* v. *Ambler* (1847) 10 Q.B.D. 252; *Glinski* v. *McIver, supra.*

[76] *Johnstone* v. *Sutton* (1786) 1 T.R. 510, 545; *Glinski* v. *McIver, supra,* at p. 744, *per* Viscount Simonds.

[77] [1971] A.C. 470.

[78] It matters not that the arrest was procured in the course of civil rather than criminal proceedings, though arrest on civil process is now exceptional. See *e.g. Daniels* v. *Fielding* (1846) 16 M. & W. 200; *Melia* v. *Neate* (1863) 3 F. & F. 757. The point decided by the House of Lords in *Roy* v. *Prior, supra,* was that the immunity from suit of a witness in respect of this evidence does not protect him from an action for maliciously procuring the issue of a warrant of arrest. The plaintiff is not suing on or in respect of the evidence. He is suing because he alleges that the defendant procured his arrest by means of judicial process which the defendant instituted both maliciously and without reasonable and probable cause: [1971] A.C. at p. 477, *per* Lord Morris.

[79] Winfield, *Present Law,* p. 203.

as to malicious criminal proceedings,[80] and it was in fact held to apply
(*inter alia*) to malicious procurement of excommunication by an
ecclesiastical court,[81] to bringing a second writ of *fi. fa.* against a man
when one had already been obtained [82] and perhaps to malicious arrest
of a ship.[83] In more modern times it has been laid down that it is available whenever the civil proceedings attack a man's credit in scandalous
fashion; *e.g.* malicious bankruptcy proceedings against him, or malicious
winding-up proceedings against a company.[84] The same requisites must
be satisfied as for malicious prosecution.

But does the law go still farther and make the malicious institution
of *any* civil proceeding actionable? There is no historical reason why it
should not, and it would seem curious to say that a man shall have an
action for maliciously taking bankruptcy proceedings against him, but
not for maliciously suing him for some scandalous tort like deceit.
However, there is no reported decision in favour of any such general
proposition. In *Corbett* v. *Burge* [85] a debtor who had been sued for a
debt which he had already paid was unsuccessful in an action against
the creditor for maliciously causing judgment to be entered against him,
because he could not prove any malice on the part of the creditor;
but it is impossible to make out from the report of the case whether he
would have been successful if he had proved malice. Apart from this
case, it has been urged against the general proposition, first, that the
person maliciously sued is adequately compensated by successfully
defending the action—which is patently false [86]—and, secondly, that
litigation must end somewhere—which is true as a fact but unconvincing
as an argument, for litigation should end only where common justice
has been done or at least attempted.[87] However, the legislature has
interfered in outrageous cases of this sort, for litigious monomaniacs
can be muzzled under the Supreme Court of Judicature (Consolidation)
Act 1925.[88]

---

[80] Winfield, *Present Law*, pp. 199, 202.
[81] *Hocking* v. *Matthews* (1670) 1 Vent. 86; *Gray* v. *Dight* (1677) 2 Show. 144. *Cf. Fisher*
v. *Bristow* (1779) 1 Doug. 215.
[82] *Waterer* v. *Freeman* (1617) Hob. 205, 266.
[83] *The Walter D. Wallet* [1893] P. 202.
[84] *Quartz Hill Gold Mining Co.* v. *Eyre* (1883) 11 Q.B.D. 674, 683, 689; *Brown* v.
Chapman (1762) 1 W.Bl. 427. For a modern example, where, however, the plaintiff failed,
see *Beechey* v. *William Hill* [1956] C.L.Y. 5442.
[85] (1932) 48 T.L.R. 626.
[86] Though awarded the costs of the action, the person sued will still be out of pocket,
for the costs to be paid by his opponent will be taxed and the taxed costs will not amount
to the total cost of the defence. But it is clearly settled that an award of taxed costs in a
civil case must be treated as if it amounted to a complete indemnity: *Quartz Hill Gold
Mining Co.* v. *Eyre* (1883) 11 Q.B.D. 674. The rule is otherwise as regards costs incurred
in defending a criminal charge: *Berry* v. *B.T.C.* [1962] 1 Q.B. 306. See the judgments of
Devlin and Danckwerts L.JJ. for full discussion.
[87] The rules in the American *Restatement of Torts*, §§ 674–675, are more satisfactory
than our law. *Cf.* Fridman, " Abuse of Legal Process " (1964) 114 L.J. 335.
[88] 15 & 16 Geo. 5, c. 49, s. 51, as amended by the Supreme Court of Judicature (Amendment) Act 1959 (7 & 8 Eliz. 2, c. 39), repealing and virtually re-enacting the Vexatious
Actions Act 1896 (59 & 60 Vict. c. 51). The legislation was needed, for in *Re Chaffers*
(1897) 45 W.R. 365 a person had within five years brought 48 civil actions against the

MAINTENANCE AND CHAMPERTY [89]

Maintenance means the improper stirring up of litigation by giving aid to one party to bring or defend a claim without just cause or excuse [90] while champerty is the particular form of maintenance which exists when the person maintaining the litigation is to be rewarded out of its proceeds. At common law a person guilty of either committed both a crime and a tort, but in modern times the defences became so numerous and the reasons for imposing liability so outdated that the law ceased to serve any useful purpose. As crimes and as torts, maintenance and champerty have now been abolished.[91]

Speaker of the House of Commons, the Archbishop of Canterbury, the Lord Chancellor and others. 47 of them were unsuccessful. See also *Att.-Gen.* v. *Vernazza* [1960] A.C. 965; *Re Langton* [1966] 1 W.L.R. 1575.

[89] For the history and former law see Winfield, *History of Conspiracy and Abuse of Legal Procedure*, pp. 131–160; *Present Law*, pp. 1–116; Bodkin, *Maintenance and Champerty*, and the 8th ed. of this work, pp. 585–592.

[90] *Re Trepca Mines Ltd.* (*No.* 2) [1963] Ch. 199, 219, *per* Lord Denning M.R.

[91] Criminal Law Act 1967 (c. 58), ss. 13 (1) (*a*), 14 (1). Note that a champertous agreement is still void for illegality so far as the law of contracts is concerned: *ibid.* s. 14 (2).

CHAPTER 23

MISCELLANEOUS AND DOUBTFUL TORTS

THIS chapter is concerned with three different types of injuries. First, there are some wrongs which are certainly torts, but the details of which are rather outside the scope of an elementary book on that topic; these may be styled " miscellaneous torts." Secondly, there are other injuries which are no doubt unlawful wrongs of some sort, but of which we cannot say with certainty that they are torts; these may be called " doubtful torts." Thirdly, there are some injuries which may not be unlawful at all; these we can call " doubtful wrongs."

MISCELLANEOUS TORTS

The most conspicuous of these is unlawful interference with a franchise. A franchise is a royal privilege, or branch of the Queen's prerogative, subsisting in the hands of a subject.[1] The forms of it are innumerable, but common examples are the franchise of a number of persons to be incorporated and subsist as a body politic, and franchises to have waifs, wrecks, estrays, treasure trove, royal fish, to hold markets or fairs, to take tolls for bridges and ferries.[2]

In another sense, " franchise " signifies the right to vote at a parliamentary or municipal election. In the famous case of *Ashby* v. *White*,[3] a returning officer was held liable in damages for wrongfully refusing to take the plaintiff's vote at a parliamentary election.[4]

Usurpation of the public office or interference with the discharge of it is a tort against the person rightly entitled to it. The remedy in tort seems to have been almost forgotten in modern legal literature [5] and the last reported English decision on it goes back to 1808.[6] The chief reason for its decline was the greater popularity of the quasi-contractual action for money had and received.[7] The chief characteristics of a " public

---

[1] Blackstone, Comm., ii, 37.

[2] Details are given in Clerk and Lindsell, *Torts*, 13th ed., Chap. 26. For recent examples, see *Iveagh* v. *Martin* [1961] 1 Q.B. 232; *Wyld* v. *Silver* [1963] 1 Q.B. 169.

[3] (1703) 2 Ld.Raym. 938; 1 Bro.Parl.Cas. 62. The best account of the case for students' purposes is in 1 Smith's L.C., 13th ed. (1929), 253. *Tozer* v. *Child* (1857) 7 E. & B. 377, carries the same point as to municipal elections.

[4] s. 50 of the Representation of the People Act 1949 provides that no action for damages shall lie in respect of the breach by a returning officer of his official duty. This negatives the decisions in *Ashby* v. *White* and *Tozer* v. *Child*. The remedy is now criminal, not civil; s. 50 (1) (2), *ibid.*

[5] Its history and the current law are developed by Winfield, " Interference with Public Office " (1940) 56 L.Q.R. 463.

[6] *Carrett* v. *Smallpage*, 9 East 330. A later Irish decision is *Lawlor* v. *Alton* (1873) 9 Ir.R.C.L. 160.

[7] First applied for this purpose in *Woodward* v. *Aston* (1676) 2 Mod. 95, and not much used (if at all) since 1872. Other remedies are mandamus, injunction, action for a declaration. They, too, are not now of common occurrence, perhaps because usurpation of public office has become less easy and profitable than in time past.

office " (apart from any statutory definition) are that it is a post the occupation of which involves the discharge of duties towards the community or some section of it, whether the occupier of the post is or is not remunerated.[8] It is not clear from the authorities whether the defendant can successfully plead an honest but mistaken belief as to his rights, in usurping or interfering with the office.[9] Damages are probably not limited to the amount of the fees that would have been received but for the usurpation.[10]

DOUBTFUL TORTS AND DOUBTFUL WRONGS

Four of these need mention—

1. Abuse of quasi-judicial powers

In many societies authority is given to certain of the members to exercise over the members at large a jurisdiction resembling that of an inferior court of justice: *e.g.* the General Medical Council over practitioners, the Stock Exchange Committee over stockbrokers, the Inns of Court over barristers, the Law Society over solicitors, a Watch Committee over its Chief Constable,[11] a University over its students [12] or any committee of a club over its members. Persons entrusted with these quasi-judicial powers act unlawfully if, in expelling or otherwise penalising a member, they fail to observe the terms of any particular statute, contract or agreement affecting the relationship with him; or, supposing that the instrument creating the society is silent upon the point, if they fail to observe the rules of natural justice. " Natural justice," as Lord Wright observed in his analysis of the term in *General Medical Council* v. *Spackman*,[13] " seems to be used in contrast with any formal or technical rule of law or procedure." The most important application of it to quasi-judicial functions is that a man must not be removed from office or membership, or otherwise dealt with to his disadvantage, without having fair and sufficient notice of the charge against him and being given an opportunity of defending himself.[14]

If these conditions are fulfilled, the law courts will not interfere, even if they think that the decision of the quasi-judicial body was wrong; even if they are not fulfilled, the proceedings will be declared void and the member will be reinstated and maintained in his rights until the matter

---

[8] Winfield, *loc. cit.*, at pp. 464–465.

[9] *Ibid.* at pp. 468–469. It is a defence according to the American *Restatement of Torts*, § 865.

[10] Winfield, *loc. cit.*, at pp. 469–470.

[11] *Ridge* v. *Baldwin* [1964] A.C. 40; Bradley, " A Failure of Justice and Defect of Police " [1964] C.L.J. 83.

[12] *R.* v. *Aston University Senate* [1969] 2 Q.B. 538; *John* v. *Rees* [1970] Ch. 345 (political party).

[13] [1943] A.C. 627, 640–645. Another good analysis is that of Maugham J. in *Maclean* v. *Workers' Union* [1929] Ch. 602.

[14] " Even God himself," said Fortescue J. in *Dr. Bentley's Case*, " did not pass sentence upon Adam before he was called upon to make his defence ": Campbell, *Lives of the Chief Justices* (1849), ii, p. 185; *Ridge* v. *Baldwin* [1964] A.C. 40; *R.* v. *Aston University Senate* [1969] 2 Q.B. 538, 552, *per* Donaldson J.

has been treated in regular fashion.[15] He may also in some cases recover damages.[16]

Winfield, who dealt with the matter at some length, concluded that the action lay in contract only, not in tort,[17] and subject to a possible line of development mentioned below,[18] it seems that later authorities confirm this view.[19]

2. Infringement of privacy [20]

This may be described as interference with another person's seclusion of himself, his family or his property from the public. The subject can be divided between privacy of property and personal privacy.

(i) *Privacy of property*

This is fairly well protected by the law, but the infringement of it is not an independent tort but a species of one or another of various torts, well known under other names. Thus, infringement of copyright, patents, designs, trade-marks and trade-names is adequately dealt with by the law relating to those topics. And there is some evidence that the courts are prepared to make use of this law to protect a man's privacy in the sense used above. In *Williams* v. *Settle* [21] the plaintiff's father-in-law had been murdered in circumstances which attracted publicity. The defendant, who had taken photographs at the plaintiff's wedding two years previously, sold one for publication in the national press. The copyright in the photographs was the plaintiff's and therefore the court was able to award him very heavy damages for the defendant's " scandalous conduct " which was " in total disregard not only of the legal rights of the plaintiff regarding copyright but of his feelings and his sense of

---

[15] *Fisher* v. *Keane* (1878) 11 Ch.D. 353; *John* v. *Rees* [1970] Ch. 345.

[16] *Bonsor* v. *Musicians' Union* [1956] A.C. 104.

[17] 6th ed., pp. 768–771.

[18] *Post*, pp. 495–496.

[19] *e.g. Bonsor* v. *Musicians' Union, supra; Abbott* v. *Sullivan* [1952] 1 K.B. 189. *Cf. Weinberger* v. *Inglis* [1919] A.C. 606, though this case, too, was probably not founded upon tort. The action may, of course, depend on particular statutory provisions, as in *Ridge* v. *Baldwin, supra*.

[20] The law on this topic is much more developed in the United States than in England and stems from a famous article, Warren and Brandeis, " The Right of Privacy " (1890) 4 Harv.L.R. 193. For the present position see Prosser, " Privacy " (1960) 48 Cal.L.Rev. 385, and a brief account by Mr. Justice Brennan, " Privacy in the United States " (1962) Vol. 5, No. 2, *The Lawyer* 7; *Restatement of Torts*, § 867. See further Winfield, " Privacy " (1931) 47 L.Q.R. 23; Neill, " The Protection of Privacy " (1962) 25 M.L.R. 393; Brittan, " The Right of Privacy in England and the United States " (1963) 37 Tulane L.R. 235; Justice Report, *Privacy and the Law*; Taylor, " Privacy and the Public " (1971) 34 M.L.R. 288. For continental law see Gutteridge and Walton, " Comparative Law of Privacy " (1931) 47 L.Q.R. 203, 219; Lipstein, " Protected Interests in the Law of Torts " [1963] C.L.J. 85, 96–98.

The Report of the Committee on Privacy, 1972 (Cmnd. 5012), contains much factual information on current threats to privacy and an appendix giving a detailed account of the various legal rules which may apply in this area.

[21] [1960] 1 W.L.R. 1072. See the observations on this case in *Rookes* v. *Barnard* [1964] A.C. 1129, 1225, *per* Lord Devlin.

family dignity and pride." [22] As to privacy of land, where there is actual entry upon it, the law of trespass almost, but not entirely, covers the ground. Where there is no entry on the land, the law of nuisance to some extent secures privacy. An unreasonable amount of noise is an actionable nuisance, but cheaper and more expeditious remedies are usually provided by borough by-laws to repress the itinerant organ-grinder or the raucous newsboy. [23] Where there is anything like watching or besetting a house, it is submitted that this also constitutes a nuisance. [24] For one form of infringement, however, there is no redress. Neither at law nor in equity will a court prevent a landowner from opening new windows which command a view of his neighbour's premises. [25] At one time there were traces of a different doctrine, [26] but the modern rule was clinched by the House of Lords in *Tapling* v. *Jones* in 1865. [27] It may create hardship in some cases, but in a densely populated country like England, the privacy of a man's landed property must give way to the building activities of his neighbours. [28]

(ii) *Personal privacy*

There is no English decision which recognises any unqualified right of personal privacy. Such authority as exists is against allowing any action for the publication of an accurate photograph or waxwork or other effigy of a person without his permission. [29] Thus, a defeated pugilist has no remedy against one who publishes an accurate photographic film of the fight in which he was beaten, for the law cannot take account of his annoyance at the result of a public competition in which he has been worsted. [30] This, however, will not exempt the exhibitor of the photograph or waxwork from an action for defamation if he places it, without any justification for doing so, in the company of likenesses of criminals, rogues, or other persons and thereby creates a tendency to injure the victim's reputation. [31]

A case of some importance and difficulty in this context is *Corelli*

---

[22] *Ibid.* at p. 1082, *per* Sellers L.J.
[23] *Kruse* v. *Johnson* [1898] 2 Q.B. 91; *Innes* v. *Newman* [1894] 2 Q.B. 292. See, too, Stone's *Justices' Manual, sub tit.* " Bye-Laws."
[24] *Lyons & Sons* v. *Wilkins* [1899] 1 Ch. 255; the principle of the decision stands, although subsequent legislation may have modified it with respect to trade unions: *Hubbard* v. *Pitt* [1975] 2 W.L.R. 254 (on appeal, *The Times*, May 14, 1975). *Cf.* the unreported case, referred to by the Committee on Privacy, *op. cit.*, p. 291, n. 19, of the dentist in Balham who failed to obtain any remedy against his neighbours who erected large mirrors in order to observe what was going on on his premises.
[25] *Turner* v. *Spooner* (1861) 30 L.J.Ch. 801.
[26] *Cherrington* v. *Abney* (1709) 2 Vern. 646 (an ill-reported case); Le Blanc J. in *Chandler* v. *Thompson* (1811) 3 Camp. 80.
[27] 11 H.L.C. 290.
[28] Nevertheless, in determining planning appeals the Minister may take a man's privacy into account. See the case cited by Neill, *loc. cit.* at p. 394, n. 7.
[29] The right of publication may, of course, be restrained by contract between the photographer and his subject: *Pollard* v. *Photographic Co.* (1888) 40 Ch.D. 345, or by copyright: *Williams* v. *Settle, supra.*
[30] *Palmer* v. *National Sporting Club Ltd.* (1906) Macgillivray, *Copyright Cases* (1905–10), p. 55; *Sports, etc. Agency* v. " *Our Dogs* " *Publishing Co. Ltd.* [1916] 2 K.B. 880; [1917] 2 K.B. 125.
[31] *Monson* v. *Tussauds Ltd.* [1894] 1 Q.B. 671.

v. *Wall.*[32] The defendants published and sold, without the consent of the plaintiff, a novelist, coloured postcards depicting bad portraits of her in imaginary incidents of her life. She sued for an injunction on two grounds—libel, and the publication of her portrait without her consent. Swinfen Eady J. refused to issue it on either ground. First, the evidence of the alleged libel was not clear enough to justify the issue of an interlocutory injunction (it must be recollected that in libel such an injunction is granted only in the clearest cases and that it does not follow that, because it is refused, an action for damages will not lie). Secondly, there was no authority for the proposition that " a private person was entitled to restrain the publication of a portrait of herself which had been made without her authority and which, although professing to be her portrait, *was totally unlike her.*" If the words italicised mean that a bad portrait of a person can never be defamatory, they cannot be supported in view of the later decision of the House of Lords in *Dunlop Rubber Co. Ltd.* v. *Dunlop,*[33] where portraits of Mr. Dunlop, falsely representing him as a foppish old gentleman, were published for advertising purposes by the company without his consent and it was held that an injunction against them for libel had been rightly issued by the court below. Suppose, however, that A has made some offensive invasion of B's personal privacy which is not defamatory, has B any remedy in tort? The civil law of defamation can give no remedy for (a) a statement which is true, or (b) a statement which does not affect a person's reputation, or (c) conduct which is not a " statement " at all. An example of each of these may be given. (a) If a newspaper, in describing a cricket match, states truly that " Jones slouched to the wicket, unshaven, unwashed and with a patch in his trousers," this is offensive enough, but it is not a civil libel. (b) A writes a letter to B prophesying ill luck to him unless he writes out and sends copies of the letter to ten other people. That is not defamatory, nor, probably, is it any other tort.[34] (c) A thrusts his conversation or company on a total stranger in a public place. There is no " representation " or " statement " here and it is difficult to see that it is actionable on any ground. Certainly it is not defamation.[35]

The balance of such authority as there is appears to be clearly against the existence of any independent tort of invasion of privacy,[36]

---

[32] (1906) 22 T.L.R. 532. *Cf. Prince Albert* v. *Strange* (1848) 2 De G. & Sm. 652; (1849) 1 H. & Tw. 1.

[33] [1921] 1 A.C. 367; *Tolley* v. *Fry & Sons Ltd.* [1931] A.C. 333.

[34] Winfield considered that it might conceivably be a private nuisance but we respectfully share a reviewer's doubts: Bromley (1964) 80 L.Q.R. at p. 583.

[35] The Committee on the Law of Defamation (1948 Cmd. 7536, pp. 10, 49) considered that no appropriate remedy for invasion of privacy falls within the general scope of the law of defamation, and that the law of defamation should not be extended to it.

[36] Against such an action: Swinfen Eady J. in *Corelli* v. *Wall* (1906) 22 T.L.R. 532; Greer L.J. in *Tolley* v. *Fry & Sons Ltd.* [1930] 1 K.B. 467, 478, in the C.A. (the point was not discussed in the H.L. [1931] A.C. 333). For such an action: perhaps Lord Halsbury in *Monson* v. *Tussauds Ltd.* [1894] 1 Q.B. 671, 687. Neutral: Collins J., *ibid.,* 769; and perhaps Horridge J. in *Sports, etc. Ltd.* v. " *Our Dogs* " *Publishing Co. Ltd.* [1916] 2 K.B. 880. *Cf.* Neill, *loc. cit.,* pp. 402–405.

though there is no direct decision on the point and it might be open to the House of Lords to hold otherwise. There have, however, been several attempts to get legislation on the subject. A Home Office Committee [37] has recently come out by a majority against the introduction of any general right of privacy, though proposing alteration or clarification of some existing legal rules. The majority came to this conclusion because in their view a general right would be too vague and uncertain and might interfere with freedom of speech. However, no one would suggest that there should be any unqualified right of privacy or that a person should in all circumstances be able to claim a right to be " let alone." Everyone must tolerate some publicity and nobody wishes daily newspapers to be like blue-books. It is only *offensive* invasions of privacy that are really objectionable. [38] There is no need to stop the propagation of news—even silly news—about people, or to stifle curiosity—even vulgar curiosity—about a neighbour's affairs; but there is a difference between " saltness and bitterness " and between ordinary inquisitiveness and unscrupulous abuse of a person's privacy for advertising or to boost circulation. [39]

3. Breach of confidence

The modern law gives considerable protection against disclosure or misuse of confidential information, though any detailed review would be out of place here, if only because the law rests upon an amalgam of doctrines drawn from contract, tort and equity. [40] The law of tort may be relevant in the area of confidence in two ways. First, misuse of confidential information may lead to liability for one of the nominate torts. Thus in *Ansell Rubber Co.* v. *Allied Rubber Industries* [41] the defendants were held liable in damages for inducing breach of contract [42] when they persuaded one of the plaintiffs' employees, in breach of his contractual

---

[37] Report of the Committee on Privacy, 1972 (Cmnd. 5012).

[38] Such as *Melvin* v. *Reid* (1931) 297 P. 91, and the case given by Mr. A. W. Lyon in his minority report to the Report of the Committee on Privacy.

[39] If such a limited right to privacy were established, truth would not, of course, be a defence and the right should clearly be capable of express or implied waiver. Some of the defamation heads of privilege could also be applied by analogy (see Mr. Brian Walden's Bill of November 26, 1969, printed in Appendix F to the Report of the Committee on Privacy). It would probably also be necessary to follow the lead of the American courts and treat the private sphere of a plaintiff's life as diminishing in area as he comes to occupy an increasingly public position.

[40] Thus the original (and probably still the primary) remedy in this field was the injunction.
For general surveys of this area of law see Turner, *The Law of Trade Secrets*; Jones, " Restitution of Benefits Obtained in Breach of Another's Confidence " (1970) 86 L.Q.R. 463; Dworkin, " Confidence in the Law," Inaugural Lecture, University of Southampton, 191; North, " Breach of Confidence: Is There a New Tort? " (1972) 12 J.S.P.T.L. 149; Law Commission Working Paper No. 58 (1974).

[41] [1967] V.R. 37. *Cf. British Industrial Plastics* v. *Ferguson* [1940] 1 All E.R. 479, where the defendants were unaware that any contract was being broken. It seems that a breach of confidence might be unlawful means for the tort of conspiracy: see *Spermolin* v. *Winter* [1962] C.L.Y. 2441.

[42] See pp. 445–453, *ante*.

duty of fidelity, to disclose his employer's trade secrets. Secondly, there is some support for the view that breach of confidence or unauthorised use of information given in confidence to another is an independent head of tortious liability. This view rests upon decisions where damages have been awarded in respect of such conduct even though there was no contractual nexus between the parties,[43] and in one of the cases the view has been expressed that the law has affinities with conversion.[44]

It is probably too early to say to what extent, if any, the law of confidence depends upon tort, but one fundamental issue remains obscure, namely the mental element required for liability. It is clear that an injunction may lie even against a person who comes into possession of information without knowledge of its confidentiality,[45] but there is some doubt as to the position where the plaintiff seeks damages or other form of monetary compensation. In *Seager* v. *Copydex Ltd.*[46] the Court of Appeal awarded damages against a defendant who was unaware that he was making use of confidential information, but if this is the general rule it is difficult to reconcile with the view that the law rests upon the equitable principle that the defendant should not be allowed to take an unfair advantage of the plaintiff.[47]

The Committee on Privacy proposed that the Law Commission be given the task of clarifying and stating in legislative form the law relating to breach of confidence.[48] The Commission has published provisional proposals which would base the law upon a new tort of breach of a statutory duty of confidence. Consideration of these proposals would be outside the scope of this work and reference should be made to the Commission's Working Paper.[49]

---

[43] *Seager* v. *Copydex Ltd.* [1967] 1 W.L.R. 923; *Seager* v. *Copydex Ltd.* (*No.* 2) [1969] 1 W.L.R. 809; *Nicrotherm Electrical Co. Ltd.* v. *Percy* [1956] R.P.C. 252 (upheld on other grounds [1957] R.P.C. 207). It is true that damages may be awarded in lieu of an injunction under Lord Cairns' Act 1858 but these cases did not purport to exercise that power. See generally North, *loc. cit. Cf.* Jones, *loc. cit.*, p. 491, who considers that rights in confidential information are based on a broad equitable principle and that the decision in the *Nicrotherm* case is " mildly revolutionary in that, by implying that a damages claim can succeed independently of any prayer for equitable relief, it presupposes a fusion of law and equity."

[44] *Seager* v. *Copydex Ltd.* (*No.* 2), *supra*, at pp. 813, 815, *per* Lord Denning M.R. and Winn L.J.

[45] *Stevenson, Jordan and Harrison Ltd.* v. *Macdonald and Evans* (1951) 68 R.P.C. 190 (affirmed on other grounds, (1952) 69 R.P.C. 10); *Fraser* v. *Evans* [1969] 1 Q.B. 349 at 361, *per* Lord Denning M.R. Since an injunction is a discretionary remedy, it does not, of course, follow that one will be granted: see Jones, *loc. cit.*, pp. 484–486. An injunction was refused in *Seager* v. *Copydex*, *supra*.

[46] *Supra.*

[47] The view that liability is " strict " might follow from regarding information as property and applying the analogy of conversion. However, it is submitted that *Seager* v. *Copydex* does not necessarily support the strict liability view, for although the defendants acted honestly, they clearly *ought* to have known that they were using confidential information and this should be enough to make them liable. For consideration of the position of the *bona fide* purchaser see Jones, *loc. cit.*, pp. 478–481.
North, *loc. cit.*, p. 170, suggests a third possible basis for an award of damages for breach of confidence, namely a form of common law protection analogous to the statutory protection provided for copyrights, patents and designs.

[48] Report of the Committee on Privacy, *op. cit.*

[49] Law Commission Working Paper No. 58 (1974).

4. Abuse of statutory or monopoly power over a person's means of livelihood

Whether or not this is a wrong at all must be regarded as very doubtful, unless, of course, it is associated with the commission of some established tort such as conspiracy or can be shown to amount to a breach of contract; and even if it is a wrong it may still be insufficient to support a claim for damages in tort. Nevertheless there are now beginning to appear some signs that if the defendant does as a matter of fact enjoy a discretionary power which puts him in a position to prevent the plaintiff from exercising his means of livelihood, then some duty is owed by him to the plaintiff as regards the employment of that power.[50] In *David* v. *Abdul Cader*[51] the Privy Council, in an appeal from Ceylon, thought that a person having a statutory discretion to grant or refuse licences for cinemas might perhaps be liable for maliciously refusing to grant a licence; in *Nagle* v. *Feilden*[52] the Court of Appeal refused to strike out an action against the Stewards of the Jockey Club in which it was alleged that the plaintiff had been refused a trainer's licence on the ground only that she was a woman. In the latter case Lord Denning M.R. said,[53] " When an association, who have the governance of a trade, take it upon themselves to license persons to take part in it, then it is at least arguable that they are not at liberty to withdraw a man's licence— and thus put him out of business—without hearing him. Nor can they refuse a man a licence—and thus prevent him from carrying on his business—in their uncontrolled discretion. If they reject him arbitrarily or capriciously, there is ground for thinking that the courts can intervene."

In neither of these cases could an action have been founded upon contract[54] and they are thus distinct from the cases concerned with, for example, wrongful expulsion from a trade union.[55] There is some reason for thinking, therefore, that a new head of liability in tort or a

---

[50] See Lloyd, " The Right to Work " (1957) 10 C.L.P. 36; *ibid.* " The Disciplinary Powers of Professional Bodies " (1950) 13 M.L.R. 281; *ibid.* (case note) (1958) 21 M.L.R. 661; *ibid.* " Natural Justice and the ' Warned off ' Bookmaker " (1963) 26 M.L.R. 412.

[51] [1963] 1 W.L.R. 834. The decision, which amounted to no more than a refusal to strike out the action, really turns on the Roman Dutch law, but their Lordships addressed some of their observations also to the English law. See also *Farrington* v. *Thomson* [1959] V.R. 286; Gould (1972) 5 N.Z.U.L.R. 105; Ganz [1973] P.L. 84.

[52] [1966] 2 Q.B. 633; Goodhart, " The Right to Work " (1966) 82 L.Q.R. 319; Weir, " Discrimination in Private Law " [1966] C.L.J. 165.

[53] [1966] 2 Q.B. at pp. 646–647. In *Faramus* v. *Film Artistes' Association* [1964] A.C. 925, where a trade union rule in restraint of trade was validated by the Trade Union Act 1871, s. 3, Lord Pearce said, " Since this union has a monopoly, exclusion from its membership prevents a man from earning his living in this particular profession. An absolute rule that so prevents any person who may have suffered a trivial conviction many years before is in restraint of trade and unreasonable. It is therefore void. . . .": *ibid.* at p. 946.

[54] See also *Abbott* v. *Sullivan* [1952] 1 K.B. 189, 216, *per* Morris L.J.; *Davis* v. *Carew-Pole* [1956] 1 W.L.R. 833.

[55] See, *e.g. Bonsor* v. *Musicians' Union* [1956] A.C. 104.

new right, the " right to work," is beginning to develop. There are, however, formidable difficulties in the way of such a development and in any case the nature of the " right to work " would have to be most carefully defined if the undoubted right of a person or group of persons to exclude strangers from their property or their association is not to be unduly circumscribed.[56] It must also be noticed that in *Nagle* v. *Feilden* Lord Denning M.R. seems to have thought that the plaintiff's remedies would be limited to a declaration and injunction, and if this is adhered to and damages refused, then whatever remedy there may be cannot be one in tort.

It is true that by declining to create a new head of liability in tort and limiting the remedies which may be available to those which are in the discretion of the court in every case, the courts would avoid the necessity of definition of the " right to work " and that this may be very desirable in the present uncertain state of things. On the other hand, if the courts do take the step of declaring unlawful an unreasonable denial to a person of the opportunity to pursue his chosen means of earning his living, then it would seem extremely hard that they should not also take the further step of awarding damages to him for any loss he may have suffered as a result of the unlawful act before the declaration or injunction can take effect.

It is necessary to end this section with the warning that any suggestion for tort liability here must be recognised as highly speculative. Only a few years ago an action such as that in *Nagle* v. *Feilden* would certainly have failed *in limine*. The Court of Appeal's refusal to strike out the statement of claim amounts to no more than a refusal to hold at the outset that the plaintiff had no possible cause of action, and so should be regarded as not much more than a straw in the wind.[57] Nevertheless, it is submitted, it would be unfortunate if the courts were to tie themselves to the " thoroughly artificial nexus of contract " [58] and it is to be hoped that the possibilities of an action in tort will at least be explored.[59]

---

[56] This right is described by Lloyd as " the inalienable right of Englishmen to decide whom they desire to consort with in the club-room ": " The Right to Work " (1957) 10 C.L.P. at p. 40. See also Wedderburn, *The Worker and the Law*, pp. 328–331

[57] After the Court of Appeal's decision the action was compromised and the plaintiff was granted her trainer's licence.

[58] The description is Lloyd's: (1958) 21 M.L.R. at p. 668.

[59] In relation to membership of, and exclusion from, trade unions the law seems to be describing a full circle. The Industrial Relations Act 1971 declared " unapproved " pre-entry closed shop agreements void and forbade exclusion from trade union membership by way of arbitrary or unreasonable discrimination. The Trade Union and Labour Relations Act 1974 now contains somewhat different provisions on arbitrary or unreasonable discrimination. The Trade Union and Labour Relations (Amendment) Bill will repeal those provisions and leave the common law (whatever that may be) to govern exclusion and expulsion from trade unions. However, if the views of Lord Denning in *Edwards* v. *S.O.G.A.T.* [1971] Ch. 354 be correct, there is perhaps not so much difference between the common law and the repealed provisions of the Industrial Relations Act 1971. For more detailed consideration of these matters see notes on employment law and administrative law.

Finally, it should be noted that by the Race Relations Act 1968 damages may be awarded for losses suffered as a result of unlawful racial discrimination in a number of fields of activity.[60] There are proposals for the enactment of similar provisions covering discrimination on grounds of sex.[61]

---

[60] See Lester and Bindman, *Race and Law* (1972).
[61] " Equality for Women," Cmnd. 5724 (1974). A Sex Discrimination Bill completed its passage through the House of Commons on May 18, 1975.

CHAPTER 24

DEATH IN RELATION TO TORT

CONSIDERED merely as a final catastrophe, death does not require a separate chapter in the law of tort, but it does have an important bearing on liability in tort and its legal effects are most conveniently considered in a separate chapter. The death of a person may affect tortious liability in two ways:

1. *It may possibly extinguish liability for a tcrt.* Here the question for discussion is: " If I have committed a tort against you (not involving your death), and either of us dies, does your right of action survive? "

2. *It may possibly create liability in tort.* Here the question is: " If I cause your death, is that a tort either (a) against you, so that your personal representatives can sue me for it; or (b) against persons who have an interest in the continuance of your life: *e.g.* your wife or children? "

DEATH AS EXTINGUISHING LIABILITY

At common law the general rule was that death of either party extinguished any existing cause of action in tort by one against the other. This was due in part to the historical connection of the action of trespass, from which much of our law of tort is derived, with the criminal law [1] and in part to the reference often made to the maxim " *actio personalis moritur cum persona* " which, though traceable to the fifteenth century,[2] probably did no more originally than state in Latin a long-established principle concerning torts such as assault and battery of which it was neither the historical cause nor the rational explanation.[3] Actions in contract generally escaped the rule,[4] and so too did those in which property had been appropriated by a deceased person and added to his own estate,[5] but it was not until 1934 that the defects of the law were forced on the attention of the legislature by the growth of motor traffic and its accompanying toll of accidents. If a negligent driver was killed in the accident which he himself had caused, nothing was recoverable from his estate or his insurer [6] by those whom he had injured. Accordingly,

---

[1] Pollock and Maitland, *History of English Law*, ii, p. 526. *Cf.* Milsom, " Trespass from Henry III to Edward III " (1960) 74 L.Q.R. at p. 584. Obviously a man's liability to be punished by the criminal law for some offence is extinguished by his death.

[2] Y.B. Mich. 18 Edw. 4, f. 15, pl. 17.

[3] Winfield, " Death as Affecting Liability in Tort " (1929) 29 Col.L.Rev. 239.

[4] *Pinchon's Case* (1611) 9 Rep. 86b, 88b.

[5] *Sherrington's Case* (1582) Sav. 40. See *Phillips* v. *Homfray* (1883) 24 Ch.D. 439 and Goff and Jones, *Restitution*, pp. 431–433.

[6] Insurance against third party risks was first made compulsory in 1930 (now Road Traffic Act 1972, s. 143) but the compulsory insurance is insurance against *liability*, so that in the absence of a tort the insurance company incurs no liability under a policy such as that required by the Act. However, " comprehensive " policies commonly provide for payment of limited compensation to the policyholder and certain passengers independently of fault.

the Law Reform (Miscellaneous Provisions) Act 1934 was passed to provide generally for the survival of causes of action in tort.[7] Its main provisions may be summarised as follows:

(a) **Survival of causes of action.** By section 1 (1) of the Act, all causes of action subsisting against or vested in any person on his death, except causes of action for defamation,[8] now survive against, or, as the case may be, for the benefit of his estate. The Act does not create a cause of action for death itself and has no bearing on the common law rule that no such cause of action exists. What it does is to provide for the survival of causes of action subsisting when the tortfeasor or the injured person dies. Thus, it having been held in *Flint* v. *Lovell* [9] that the damages in an action for personal injuries may include a sum in respect of the plaintiff's diminished expectation of life,[10] it follows that even when a person is killed " instantaneously " he dies possessed of a cause of action which survives [11] and his estate may recover damages not for his death, but for his loss of expectation of life.[12]

(b) **" Subsisting " action.** It may happen that a cause of action is not complete against a wrongdoer until after he has in fact died, as, for example, where damage is the gist of the action and no damage is suffered until after the death of the wrongdoer. In such a case no cause of action subsists against the wrongdoer at the date of his death and there is nothing to survive against his estate, so that, were there no provision in the Act to deal with the point, the person suffering the damage would be deprived of his remedy. Section 1 (4) provides, however, that where damage has been suffered as the result of a wrongful act in respect of which a cause of action would have subsisted had the wrongdoer not died before or at the same time as the damage was suffered, there shall be deemed to have subsisted against him before his death such cause of action as would have subsisted if he had died after the damage had been suffered. Thus if on facts similar to those of *Donoghue* v. *Stevenson.*[13] A, the negligent manufacturer of noxious ginger-beer, dies before the ultimate consumer, B, suffers damage from drinking it, B's cause of action against A's estate is preserved as it is regarded as arising before

---

[7] 24 & 25 Geo. 5, c. 41. The generality of the main provisions of the Act renders superfluous earlier statutory provisions concerning torts against property.

[8] Other causes of action were also excluded from the operation of the Act, but these have now been abolished by the Law Reform (Miscellaneous Provisions) Act 1970 (c. 33), ss. 4 and 5. If judgment has been obtained in an action for defamation, the judgment can be enforced even after the death of the defendant: *Rysak* v. *Rysak and Bugajaski* [1967] P. 179, a case concerning the now defunct claim for damages for adultery.

[9] [1935] 1 K.B. 354.

[10] For the assessment of damages for personal injury, including those for " loss of expectation of life," see *post*, pp. 562–580. It commonly occurs that a claim on behalf of a deceased person's estate is joined with one on behalf of his dependants under the Fatal Accidents Acts (*post*, pp. 512–514) and where this is done it normally matters little what sum is awarded to the estate. See, however, *Farmer* v. *Rash* [1969] 1 W.L.R. 160.

[11] *Morgan* v. *Scoulding* [1938] 1 K.B. 786.

[12] *Rose* v. *Ford* [1937] A.C. 826.

[13] [1932] A.C. 562, *ante*, p. 48.

A's death. Similarly if A is killed and B injured in an accident for which A and C are jointly responsible, C will be liable to B in full, but will have no cause of action for contribution under the Law Reform (Married Women and Tortfeasors) Act 1935 against A until he has met B's claim,[14] and this is bound to be after A's death. But by section 1 (4) the claim for contribution is deemed to have subsisted against A before his death and so survives against his estate.[15]

(c) **Damages recoverable.** (i) *Where the injured party dies,* the damages recoverable for the benefit of the estate (i) may not include exemplary damages, and (ii) shall, where the death has been caused by the act or omission which gives rise to the cause of action, be calculated without reference to any loss or gain to the deceased's estate consequent on his death, except that funeral expenses may be included.[16] Where, however, the death is unconnected with the act or omission which gives rise to the cause of action, it appears that substantial damages can be recovered even though the deceased himself, had he been alive when the action was brought, could only have recovered nominal damages.[17]

The commonest applications of the rule in (ii) are that it makes irrelevant any gain to the deceased's estate from a policy of insurance, and that, if the deceased had been entitled to an annuity or a life interest, the loss of the annuity or the life interest must be disregarded in calculating the damages. Subject to this, the damages recoverable are the same as would have been recoverable by the deceased himself had he not been killed, save that any award for loss of earnings or profits must be limited to the period during which the deceased survived his injury [18] and that funeral expenses may be recovered if they have been paid out of the estate of the deceased. The damages recovered form part of the estate of the deceased, they bear estate duty,[19] are available for the payment of his debts and pass under his will or upon his intestacy. If the deceased's death was caused partly by his own contributory negligence, the damages recoverable by his estate will be reduced under the Law Reform (Contributory Negligence) Act 1945.[20]

---

[14] *George Wimpey & Co.* v. *B.O.A.C.* [1955] A.C. 169; *Harvey* v. *R. G. O'Dell Ltd., Galway (Third Party)* [1958] 2 Q.B. 78, 108. *Post,* pp. 550–551.

[15] *Harvey* v. *R. G. O'Dell Ltd., Galway (Third Party), supra.* See, too, *Post Office* v. *Official Solicitor* [1951] 1 All E.R. 522.

[16] s. 1 (2). See *Hart* v. *Griffiths-Jones* [1948] 2 All E.R. 729; *Stanton* v. *Ewart F. Youlden Ltd.* [1960] 1 W.L.R. 543.

[17] *Otter* v. *Church, Adams, Tatham & Co.* [1953] Ch. 280. This was an action in contract for the negligence of a solicitor, which survived at common law. It is submitted, however, that the result would have been the same even if the plaintiff had had to rely upon the Act of 1934. *Cf.* Gray and Thompson, " The Measure and Remoteness of Damages " (1953) 16 M.L.R. 518.

[18] *Rose* v. *Ford* [1937] A.C. 826, 861; *Benham* v. *Gambling* [1941] A.C. 157, 167.

[19] *Hall* v. *Wilson* [1939] 4 All E.R. 85, 86. The same will apply to capital transfer tax: Finance Act 1975, ss. 22, 23.

[20] For contributory negligence generally, see *ante,* pp. 106–118.

(ii) *When the tortfeasor dies*, the ordinary measure of damage applies in an action brought against his estate.[21]

(d) **Time limitation.** Until recently special rules governed the time within which proceedings in tort had to be started against a deceased person's estate.[22] Now, however, those rules have been abolished [23] and the ordinary law for the limitation of actions applies, whether the action is brought against or for the benefit of the estate.[24]

(e) **Right of action is cumulative.** The rights conferred by the Act are in addition to, and not in derogation of, any rights conferred on the dependants of deceased persons by the Fatal Accidents Acts 1846 to 1959.[25]

DEATH AS CREATING LIABILITY

At common law the death of a person cannot be complained of as legal damage in an action in tort brought either by the deceased person's estate or by dependants of his who suffer loss by reason of his death. So far as the first part of the rule is concerned, the explanation is historical,[26] but it remains law today so that, as we have seen, the damages recoverable by a deceased person's estate for loss of earnings is limited to the period during which the deceased survived his injuries [27]: the Act of 1934 provides for the survival of the claim possessed by the deceased at his death, not for the creation of a head of claim in respect of the death itself.[28] The second part of the rule, which may not always have been the law,[29] is derived from the ruling of Lord Ellenborough in *Baker* v. *Bolton* [30] that, " in a civil court the death of a human being could not be complained of as an injury." [31] The plaintiff and his wife were passengers on the top of the defendants' stagecoach which was upset by the negligence of the defendants, " whereby the plaintiff himself was much bruised, and his wife was

---

[21] Where the tortfeasor's estate is insolvent any liability can be proved in the administration notwithstanding that the liability is for unliquidated damages in tort: s. 1 (6).

[22] For the old law, see the 8th ed. of this work, pp. 609–610.

[23] Proceedings Against Estates Act 1970 (c. 17).

[24] *Post*, p. 647. Provision is made by rules of court to enable proceedings to be started against an estate where no grant of probate or administration has been made: R.S.C., Ord. 15, r. 6A.

[25] s. 1 (5). This does not mean that if the dependants are the same persons as those entitled to the deceased person's estate they can recover twice over. See *post*, pp. 512–514.

[26] See Pollock and Maitland, *History of English Law*, ii, pp. 482–485; Holdsworth, H.E.L., ii, 362–364.

[27] *Ante*, p. 499. See further, *post*, p. 573, n. 61.

[28] Given the availability of the statutory remedy of the dependants of a deceased person under the Fatal Accidents Acts, *post*, pp. 502–511, there is no reason for altering this rule so as to enable damages to be awarded to a deceased person's estate in respect of the death itself. Difficulties do arise, however, where a person's expectation of life is substantially reduced by his injuries and yet he survives for a number of years so that no action under the Fatal Accidents Acts is available to his dependants. See *post*, pp. 572–573.

[29] Y.B. Mich. 43 Edw. 3, f. 23, pl. 16.

[30] (1808) 1 Camp. 493.

[31] The rule in *Baker* v. *Bolton* does not apply where the plaintiff's cause of action is founded upon contract: *Jackson* v. *Watson* [1909] 2 K.B. 193.

so severely hurt that she died about a month after." The plaintiff recovered £100 for his own bruises and for the loss of his wife's society up to the moment of her death, but nothing for such loss after that event.

Baker v. *Bolton* was only a ruling at Nisi Prius, not a single authority was cited and the report is extremely brief, but it was nevertheless upheld in later cases [32] and the seal of approval placed upon it by the House of Lords in *Admiralty Commissioners* v. *SS. Amerika*.[33] In that case a submarine of the Royal Navy was run into and sunk by the negligence of the steamship *Amerika*. The Admiralty Commissioners granted pensions to the relatives of those who were drowned in the submarine and then claimed the capitalised amount of the pensions from the owners of the *Amerika*. The claim failed, first, because of the rule in *Baker* v. *Bolton*; secondly, because the damages were too remote, since the pensions were not paid under any legal obligation upon the Admiralty, but were voluntary disbursements in the nature of compassionate allowances. With this second ground we are not here concerned, but why the rule in *Baker* v. *Bolton* should have been followed except on the ground of *vis inertiae* it is difficult to see.[34]

The Fatal Accidents Acts 1846–1959

The development of railways in England led to a great upsurge in the number of accidents, fatal and non-fatal, and this made a change in the law imperative for, while those who survived an accident could recover substantial damages, the dependants of those who were killed could recover nothing. Accordingly, in 1846, the Fatal Accidents Act,[35] otherwise known as Lord Campbell's Act, was passed and virtually overturned the common law so far as those dependants who are specified in the Act and in later legislation are concerned. The Act provides that whenever the death of a person [36] is caused by the wrongful act, neglect or default [37] of another, such as would (if death had not ensued) have entitled the injured person to sue and recover damages in respect thereof, then the person who would have been liable if death had not ensued shall be liable to an action for damages

---

[32] *Osborn* v. *Gillett* (1873) L.R. 8 Ex. 88; *Clark* v. *London General Omnibus Co. Ltd.* [1906] 2 K.B. 648.

[33] [1917] A.C. 38.

[34] The historical arguments of Lord Parker ([1917] A.C. at pp. 43–48) and Lord Sumner (*ibid.* at pp. 56–60) are unconvincing. See Holdsworth, H.E.L., iii, 676–677, and in (1916) 32 L.Q.R. 431–437.

[35] 9 & 10 Vict. c. 93.

[36] It is immaterial that the deceased was an alien, provided he was otherwise qualified to sue: *Davidson* v. *Hill* [1901] 2 K.B. 606. See Webb, " The Conflict of Laws and the English Fatal Accidents Acts " (1961) 24 M.L.R. 467.

[37] s. 1. This now includes any "occurrence " which gives rise to liability under Article 17 of the Warsaw Convention as amended at The Hague, 1955: Carriage by Air Act 1961, **s. 3,** *post,* p. 512. It also includes a breach of contract as well as a tort: *Grein* v. *Imperial Airways Ltd.* [1937] 1 K.B. 50.

on behalf of the dependants, notwithstanding the death of the person injured.

DEPENDANTS. The action lies for the benefit of the deceased's dependants,[38] a class of persons which has been considerably enlarged since it was first defined in 1846. Today it includes not only the deceased's wife, husband, parent, child,[39] grandparent and grandchild, but also any person who is or is the issue of a brother, sister, uncle or aunt of the deceased.[40] Moreover, in deducing any relationship an adopted person is to be treated as the child of the persons by whom he was adopted, a relationship by affinity as one by consanguinity and a relationship of the half blood as one of the whole blood. The stepchild of any person is to be treated as his child and an illegitimate person as the child of his mother and reputed father.[41] The action must normally be brought on behalf of the dependants by the executor or administrator of the deceased [42] but where there is no personal representative, or no action is brought by him within six months, any dependant who is entitled to benefit under the Act may sue in his own name on behalf of himself and the others.[43] The action must in any case be brought within three years of the death.[44]

NATURE OF ACTION. The right of action created by the Fatal Accidents Act is " new in its species, new in its quality, new in its principles, in every way new " [45]; it is not the deceased's own cause of action which is caused to survive, it is a new action for the benefit of his dependants. For this new cause of action to exist, however, it is necessary that the circumstances of his death should have been such that the deceased himself, had he been injured and not killed, could have sued for his injury. One must consider the hypothetical ability of the deceased to sue as at the

---

[38] The defendant must be supplied with particulars of the persons for whose benefit the action is brought, and if a person is left out, he can apply before verdict to be named as a party to benefit. But the court cannot consider a dependant not named in the proceedings and such a person can have no claim against the defendant. He may, however, have some legal or equitable remedy against the representative plaintiff: *Avery* v. *London & N.E. Ry.* [1938] A.C. 606, 613, *per* Lord Atkin. For a dependant's ability to intervene before judgment in proceedings in which she was not named, see *Cooper* v. *Williams* [1963] 2 Q.B. 567. *Cf. Voller* v. *Dairy Produce Packers Ltd.* [1962] 1 W.L.R. 960, where there appear to have been two distinct claims under the Fatal Accidents Acts in respect of the same death.

[39] Including a posthumous child: *The George and Richard* (1871) L.R. Ad. & E. 466.

[40] Fatal Accidents Act 1959, s. 1 (1). The Law Commission has recommended that the list be extended to include divorced spouses and " children of the family " within the meaning of s. 52 (1) of the Matrimonial Causes Act 1973: Law Com. No. 56, para. 262.

[41] *Ibid.* s. 1 (2).

[42] *Ibid.* s. 2. An executor's title to sue dates from the death, but an administrator must first obtain a grant of letters of administration: *Hilton* v. *Sutton Steam Laundry* [1946] K.B. 65; *Finnegan* v. *Cementation Co. Ltd.* [1953] 1 Q.B. 688. *Cf. Stebbings* v. *Holst & Co. Ltd.* [1953] 1 W.L.R. 603; *Bowler* v. *John Mowlem & Co.* [1954] 1 W.L.R. 1445.

[43] Fatal Accidents Act 1864, s. 1. If there is no executor or administrator, the dependants need not wait six months before suing: *Holleran* v. *Bagnell* (1879) 4 L.R.Ir. 740.

[44] s. 3, as amended by the Fatal Accidents Act 1864, s. 1 (27 & 28 Vict. c. 95), and the Law Reform (Limitation of Actions, etc.) Act 1954, s. 3. For the limitation period in cases of death on board ship, see *post*, p. 656.

[45] *Seward* v. *Vera Cruz* (1884) 10 App.Cas. 59, 70–71, *per* Lord Blackburn.

moment of his death, with the idea fictionally that death has not taken place.[46] If, therefore, the deceased had been run over in the street through nobody's fault but his own, there will be no claim on behalf of his dependants; nor will there be such a claim if by contract with the defendant the deceased had excluded any possibility of liability to himself,[47] but if the contract merely limited the amount of the defendant's liability, then the deceased could have sued for some damages, the way is open for the dependants' claim, and that claim, being independent of the deceased's, will not be affected by the limitation of liability.[48] Similarly the dependants have no claim if the deceased before his death had accepted compensation in satisfaction of his claim,[49] or had actually obtained judgment against the defendant, or if by the date of his death his claim had become statute barred.[50] But so long as the deceased's claim has not become statute barred when he dies, then the dependants have the full three years from the death in which to sue,[51] for their claim, which arises on the death, has no connection with the deceased's.[52] It is thus somewhat illogical, though doubtless good practical sense, that, since the Law Reform (Contributory Negligence) Act 1945,[53] if the deceased was himself partly to blame for the accident which caused his death, the damages recoverable by his dependants are reduced in proportion to his share of responsibility for the accident.[54] Before the Act of 1945, of course, the dependants could have recovered nothing for the deceased could not himself have sued. At the present time, were it not for express statutory provision to the contrary, they would be able to recover the full amount of their loss without reduction.

WHAT IS RECOVERABLE. The only guidance given by the Act is that the jury (today, the judge) may give damages as they think proportioned to the injury resulting from the death to the dependants [55]; it does not say on what principle they are to be assessed, but Pollock C.B., in 1858, adopted the test which has been used ever since, that damages must be calculated " in reference to *a reasonable expectation of pecuniary benefit*

---

[46] *British Columbia Electric Ry.* v. *Gentile* [1914] A.C. 1034, 1041, *per* Lord Dunedin; *Pym* v. *G.N. Ry.* (1862) 2 B. & S. 759; 4 B. & S. 396.

[47] *Haigh* v. *Royal Mail Steam Packet Co. Ltd.* (1883) 52 L.J.Q.B. 640; *The Stella* [1900] P. 161.

[48] *Nunan* v. *Southern Ry.* [1924] 1 K.B. 223; *Grein* v. *Imperial Airways* [1937] 1 K.B. 50.

[49] *Read* v. *G.E. Ry.* (1868) L.R. 3 Q.B. 555. Apparently the liability in tort is destroyed from the moment that the agreement to accept compensation is made, even before the money is actually paid; *British Russian Gazette, etc.* v. *Associated Newspapers Ltd.* [1933] 2 K.B. 616.

[50] *Williams* v. *Mersey Docks and Harbour Board* [1905] 1 K.B. 804.

[51] Fatal Accidents Act 1846, s. 3, as amended by the Law Reform (Limitation of Actions, etc.) Act 1954, s. 3.

[52] For a striking example of the independence of the dependant's claim from that of the deceased, see *Pigney* v. *Pointer's Transport Services Ltd.* [1957] 1 W.L.R. 1121, where the deceased had committed suicide in a fit of depression caused by his injury. *Cf. Farmer* v. *Rash* [1969] 1 W.L.R. 160.

[53] *Ante*, pp. 108–118.

[54] Law Reform (Contributory Negligence) Act 1945, s. 1 (4).

[55] s. 2.

as of right, or otherwise, from the continuance of the life." [56] If, therefore, the dependants have suffered only nominal damages, or none at all, they can recover nothing,[57] nor can they recover if the deceased had earned his living by crime, for then their claim arises *ex turpi causa.*[58] No award in the nature of a *solatium* for mental suffering and anguish for the loss of the deceased will be made.[59] Where a son, who worked for his father at full wages under a contract, was killed, his father was held to have no claim; for though he had lost the son's services, he could not prove that he had lost any pecuniary benefit since he had paid full wages for them.[60] An additional reason for rejecting the father's claim in that case was that the father could not show any benefit accruing to him from his relationship with his son, but only that he had lost an advantage derived from a contract with him, and this was insufficient.[61] " The benefit, to qualify under the Act, must be a benefit which arises from the relationship between the parties." [62] In *Malyon* v. *Plummer* [63] the plaintiff widow had been in receipt of a salary of about £600 per annum for somewhat nominal services' to her husband's " one-man " company. The Court of Appeal estimated the value of her services to the company at £200 per annum and held that the balance, but only the balance, was attributable to her relationship as wife to the deceased. The £200 represented payment for services rendered under her contract of employment and could not therefore be recovered. Nor is a mere speculative possibility of pecuniary benefit sufficient, as where the person killed was aged four years and his father proved nothing except that he had intended to give the child a good education.[64]

On the other hand, there may be a reasonable expectation of pecuniary benefit although the relatives had no legal claim to support by the deceased, as where a son who was killed had voluntarily assisted his father in the father's work,[65] or where he once gave him money during a period of unemployment,[66] or where a wife who was killed had gratui-

---

[56] *Franklin* v. *S.E. Ry.* (1858) 3 H. & N. 211, 213–214. It has been held that where the deceased's estate is substantial and pays estate duty, that duty is recoverable by the dependants/beneficiaries from the tortfeasor: *Davies* v. *Whiteways Cyder Co. Ltd.* [1974] 3 W.L.R. 597.

[57] *Duckworth* v. *Johnson* (1859) 29 L.J.Ex. 257.

[58] *Burns* v. *Edman* [1970] 2 Q.B. 541.

[59] *Blake* v. *Midland Ry.* (1852) 18 Q.B. 93. The reasons given for the decision are not wholly satisfactory, but the rule is undoubted law. See, *e.g. Davies* v. *Powell Duffryn Associated Collieries* [1942] A.C. 601, 716, *per* Lord Wright. No damages can be awarded to a child for the loss of its mother's care: *Pevec* v. *Brown* (1964) 108 S.J. 219.

[60] *Sykes* v. *N.E. Ry.* (1875) 44 L.J.C.P. 191.

[61] *Burgess* v. *Florence Nightingale Hospital for Gentlewomen* [1955] 1 Q.B. 349.

[62] *Ibid.* at p. 360, *per* Devlin J.

[63] [1964] 1 Q.B. 330.

[64] *Barnett* v. *Cohen* [1921] 2 K.B. 461. Formerly nothing could be recovered for funeral or mourning expenses: *Dalton* v. *S.E. Ry.* (1858) 4 C.B.(N.S.) 296; *Clark* v. *London General Omnibus Co. Ltd.* [1906] 2 K.B. 648. Now, however, the Law Reform (Miscellaneous Provisions) Act 1934, s. 2 (3), allows recovery of funeral expenses which have been incurred by the persons for whose benefit the action is brought.

[65] *Franklin* v. *S.E. Ry.* (1858) 3 H. & N. 211.

[66] *Hetherington* v. *N.E. Ry.* (1882) 9 Q.B.D. 160.

tously performed the ordinary household duties.[67] Indeed, it is not necessary that the deceased should have been actually earning anything or giving any help, provided there was a reasonable probability, as distinct from a bare possibility, that he would do so, as there was where the deceased was a girl of 16 who lived with her parents, was on the eve of completing her apprenticeship as a dressmaker, and was likely in the near future to earn a wage which might quickly have become substantial.[68]

In assessing whether there was a reasonable expectation of benefit in the above sense, the court is not concerned with a balance of probabilities in the same way as when it is ajudicating upon facts. Thus if a wife is separated from her husband at the time of his death, it is unnecessary for her to show that on a balance of probabilities she would have returned to live with her husband. The correct approach is for the court to determine whether there was a reasonable chance rather than a mere speculative possibility, of reconciliation. If there was such a chance, the award should be scaled down to take account of the probability of the reconciliation taking place.[69]

In a case under the Fatal Accidents Acts the court is concerned with assessing what would have happened if the deceased had lived. But since the loss for which damages are awarded is pecuniary loss which will be suffered by dependants in the future, it is also inevitably concerned with the prospects of the dependants: for example, if the dependant himself has a short expectation of life the damages will be small.[70] The most controversial aspect of this matter related to the dependent widow's prospects of remarriage, but there the law has undergone a fundamental alteration by statute. The common law rule was that the court had to estimate the widow's chances of remarriage and reduce the damages accordingly,[71] but some judges tended to revolt against this " guessing game " [72] and a campaign against the rule led to its reversal by the Law Reform (Miscellaneous Provisions) Act 1971.[73] Now, in assessing the damages payable to a widow in respect of the death of her husband in any action under the Fatal Accidents Acts there shall not be taken into account the remarriage of the widow nor her prospects of remarriage.[74]

---

[67] *Berry* v. *Humm* [1915] 1 K.B. 627. See also *Burgess* v. *Florence Nightingale Hospital for Gentlewomen* [1955] 1 Q.B. 349, 361–362.

[68] *Taff Vale Ry.* v. *Jenkins* [1913] A.C. 1; *Wathen* v. *Vernon* [1970] R.T.R. 471.

[69] *Davies* v. *Taylor* [1974] A.C. 207; Fleming [1973] C.L.J. 20; see also *Wathen* v. *Vernon* [1970] R.T.R. 471; *Gray* v. *Barr* [1971] 2 Q.B. 554.

[70] Thus where the deceased's widow actually died before the trial damages were awarded to her estate in respect only of the period during which she actually survived him: *Williamson* v. *John I. Thornycroft Ltd.* [1940] 2 K.B. 658; *Voller* v. *Dairy Produce Packers Ltd.* [1962] 1 W.L.R. 960.

[71] *Goodburn* v. *Thomas Cotton Ltd.* [1968] 1 Q.B. 845. Where the widow had actually remarried before the trial or before the time for appeal had expired the case was *a fortiori* for a reduction in the award: *Curwen* v. *James* [1963] 1 W.L.R. 748.

[72] See, *e.g.* Phillimore J. in *Buckley* v. *John Allen and Ford (Oxford) Ltd.* [1967] 2 Q.B. 637, 645.

[73] C. 43.

[74] Law Reform (Miscellaneous Provisions) Act 1971, s. 4 (1).

The good intentions of this provision are more evident than its logic, for it undermines the basic principle that damages for fatal accidents are awarded for future pecuniary loss. Even if it be accepted that the courts had to be relieved of the " guessing game " of estimating the chances of future remarriage, it is hard to see the justification for ignoring a re-marriage which has actually taken place.[75] Strangely enough, the Act has not succeeded in entirely abolishing the " guessing game." First, it only applies to a *widow's* claim under the Fatal Accidents Acts, and marriage prospects may be a relevant consideration in the assessment of damages for an injured but living female plaintiff.[76] Secondly, damages under the Fatal Accidents Acts are also payable to child dependants of the victim and since the 1971 Act makes no reference to their claim, the court may have to take into account their mother's prospects of remarriage.[77]

ASSESSMENT OF DAMAGES.[78] Although the action is normally brought by the executor or administrator of the deceased, and not by the dependants themselves, the remedy given by the statute is to individuals, not to a class.[79] In calculating the damages, therefore, the pecuniary loss suffered by each dependant should be separately assessed.[80] In practice, however, it will frequently be necessary first of all to determine a figure for the total liability of the defendants and then to apportion the damages between the various dependants [81] and this has been said to be the more usual method.[82]

Lord Wright in *Davies* v. *Powell Duffryn Associated Collieries Ltd.*[83] expressed the general principles to be applied in estimating the amount of damages to be awarded. " There is no question here of

---

[75] For the possible consequences of this provision see Atiyah, *Accidents, Compensation and the Law,* p. 177, n. 6. When the Act was in the Lords an amendment was put forward deleting what is now s. 4 and substituting a provision enabling the court to award " periodical payments," but this solution has problems of its own: see p. 553, *post.*

[76] See, *e.g. Harris* v. *Harris* [1973] 1 Lloyd's Rep. 445.

[77] *Thompson* v. *Price* [1973] Q.B. 838; *cf. Howitt* v. *Heads* [1973] Q.B. 64. In *Thompson* v. *Price* the widow *had* remarried, but Boreham J. clearly thought the same principle applied to prospects of remarriage. The sum involved here will in the case of minor children be small, because the cost of the child's " keep " will fall to be assessed as part of the widow's damages, which are not subject to reduction: *Thompson* v. *Price, supra* at p. 843.

The Law Commission has recommended the correction of this anomaly in relation to assessment of the child's damages. With a commendable desire for symmetry, it has also proposed that s. 4 (1) of the 1971 Act be extended to the assessment of a widower's claim for damages for the death of his wife.

Where children are looked after by relatives, no deduction is to be made on account of this benevolence: *Rawlinson* v. *Babcock and Wilcox Ltd.* [1967] 1 W.L.R. 481; *Hay & Toone* v. *Hughes* [1975] 2 W.L.R. 34.

[78] See Street, *Principles of the Law of Damages,* pp. 148–166.

[79] *Pym* v. *Great Northern Ry.* (1863) 4 B. & S. 396; *Avery* v. *London & N.E. Ry.* [1938] A.C. 613; *Jeffrey* v. *Kent County Council* [1958] 1 W.L.R. 926; *Dietz* v. *Lennig Chemicals Ltd.* [1969] 1 A.C. 170, 183, *per* Lord Morris.

[80] A good example is *Williamson* v. *Thornycroft & Co.* [1940] 2 K.B. 658.

[81] *Bishop* v. *Cunard White Star Co. Ltd.* [1950] P. 240, 248, *per* Hodson J. Once the total liability of the defendant has been determined, the apportionment of that sum is no concern of the defendant: *Eifert* v. *Holt's Transport Co. Ltd.* [1951] 2 All E.R. 655n.

[82] *Kassam* v. *Kampala Aerated Water Co. Ltd.* [1965] 1 W.L.R. 668, 672, *per* Lord Guest. See Street, *op. cit.,* pp. 149–158.

[83] [1942] A.C. 601, 617; Weir, *Casebook on Tort,* 3rd ed. p. 547; *Nance* v. *British Columbia Electric Ry.* [1951] A.C. 600, 614–617.

what may be called sentimental damage, bereavement or pain and suffering. It is a hard matter of pounds, shillings and pence, subject to the element of reasonable future probabilities. The starting point is the amount of wages which the deceased was earning, the ascertainment of which to some extent may depend on the regularity of his employment. Then there is an estimate of how much was required or expended for his own personal and living expenses. The balance will give a datum or basic figure which will generally be turned into a lump sum by taking a number of years' purchase. That sum, however, has to be taxed down by having regard to the uncertainties, for instance, that the widow might have again married and thus ceased to be dependent, and other like matters of speculation and doubt." The number of years' purchase is left fluid and will vary according to the deceased's expectation of working life as it was at his death,[84] the probable duration of the dependency of the dependants,[85] and so on.[86] Indeed each case depends upon all its own special facts[87] and no single rule can be laid down for the assessment of the damages in every case. Even the general method of assessment set out by Lord Wright, for example, is only appropriate where the deceased was the breadwinner of the family and is obviously inapplicable in a case where the claim is brought for the loss of a mere expectation of pecuniary benefit or where the deceased's contribution was in kind and not in cash.

The basic approach to assessment of damages under the Fatal Accidents Acts is the same as that for assessment of loss of earnings in claims by living plaintiffs. Proposals for fundamental reforms of the method of assessment (*e.g.* in the use of actuarial techniques) are considered later.[88]

DEDUCTIONS.[89] The action being founded upon pecuniary loss, in principle the dependants must bring into account against their loss

---

[84] See, *e.g. Gilbertson* v. *Harland and Wolff Ltd.* [1966] 2 Lloyd's Rep. 190, where the deceased aged 70 had been active, keen to continue in work and able to do so. It was held that damages should be assessed on the basis that he was likely to have worked until he was 75 or older.

[85] See, *e.g. Whittome* v. *Coates* [1965] 1 W.L.R. 1285, where the plaintiff widow's ill-health was taken into account, and *Kassam* v. *Kampala Aerated Water Co. Ltd.* [1965] 1 W.L.R. 668, where the periods of dependency of the deceased's children were all different. In *Dolbey* v. *Godwin* [1955] 1 W.L.R. 553, it was held that the damages awarded to the widowed mother of the deceased could not be assessed on the same basis as if she had been his widow, as it was likely that the deceased would have married in due course and that his contributions to his mother's upkeep would then have been reduced.

[86] Other factors to be taken into account include, at least in the case of a large award, that tax will be payable on the income from the capital sum awarded and, according to some, the prospect of future inflation: *Taylor* v. *O'Connor* [1971] A.C. 115. *Cf. Mallett* v. *McMonagle* [1970] A.C. 166.

[87] Thus, for example, the assessment may well be affected by the fact that the deceased was, or was not, a wholehearted and successful provider for his family: *Daniels* v. *Jones, supra.* For the assessment of the damages where the deceased's widow died 17 months after her husband, leaving a 16-year-old daughter, see *Rawlinson* v. *Babcock and Wilcox Ltd.* [1967] 1 W.L.R. 481.

[88] See p. 575, *post.*

[89] See Street, *op. cit.*, pp. 158–166; Ganz, " Mitigation of Damages by Benefits Received " (1962) 25 M.L.R. 559.

any pecuniary benefit accruing in consequence of the death.[90] This principle is, however, now subject to so many exceptions that in the ordinary case the only benefit that is likely to have to be brought into account will be the sums (if any) which are received by the dependants in consequence of an award of damages to the deceased's estate under the Law Reform (Miscellaneous Provisions) Act 1934.[91] The Fatal Accidents Act 1908 laid down that no account should be taken of any sum paid or payable on the death of the deceased under any contract of assurance [92] and this statutory exemption has been extended by the Fatal Accidents Act 1959 [93] to cover " any insurance money, benefit, pension or gratuity which has been or will or may be paid as a result of the death." These words, it is submitted, are apt to include any payment which is likely to be made to the deceased's family upon his death [94] except, perhaps, some purely voluntary payment such as might be made by the fellow workmen of the deceased, but such a payment would in any event be left out of account.[95]

Property left by the deceased and inherited by his dependants deserves separate mention. It might at first appear that the value of such property should be deducted in full in calculating the dependants' pecuniary loss, but in fact such a deduction would only rarely be correct. Not only will the inheriting dependant receive no more than the net value of the property after estate duty has been paid,[96] but it will also often be the case that the real value of the inheritance, especially in the case of a widow, is small. In *Heatley* v. *Steel Co. of Wales Ltd.*,[97] for example, the widow inherited from her husband the house in which she lived with her children, but it was held that no deduction should be made. As Lord Goddard C.J. said,[98] " she will simply continue to live in this house and provide a home there for the children until it is sold, and if and when it is sold she will have to get another house." Even where the dependant inherits stocks and shares or other income-producing investments, no more should be deducted than the value of the accelerated receipt of the inherit-

---

[90] *Grand Trunk Ry.* v. *Jennings* (1888) 13 App.Cas. 800; *Baker* v. *Dalgleish S.S. Co.* [1922] 1 K.B. 361.No deduction is to be made for what the widow earns by going out to work: *Howitt* v. *Heads* [1973] Q.B. 64; *Usher* v. *Williams* (1955) 60 W.A.L.R. 69.

[91] *Ante*, pp. 498–500. See *Bishop* v. *White Star Co. Ltd.* [1950] P. 240, 248 and *post*, pp. 512–515.

[92] See *Green* v. *Russell* [1959] 2 Q.B. 226.

[93] s. 2.

[94] See *Malyon* v. *Plummer* [1964] 1 Q.B. 330.

[95] *Baker* v. *Dalgleish S.S. Co. Ltd.* [1922] 1 K.B. 361, 380, *per* Younger L.J.; *Peacock* v. *Amusement Equipment Co. Ltd.* [1954] 2 Q.B. 347.

[96] See *Baker* v. *T. E. Hopkins & Sons Ltd.* [1958] 1 W.L.R. 993, 1005, affd., but no appeal on this point, [1959] 1 W.L.R. 966. Estate duty is abolished and replaced by capital transfer tax in respect of transfers of property on deaths occurring after March 13, 1975: Finance Act 1975.

[97] [1953] 1 W.L.R. 405; *Bishop* v. *Cunard White Star Co. Ltd.* [1950] P. 240, 248; *Buckley* v. *John Allen and Ford (Oxford) Ltd.*, *supra*. *Cf. Voller* v. *Dairy Produce Packers Ltd.* [1962] 1 W.L.R. 960.

[98] At 407.

ance,[99] and often less than that.[1] Where the deceased had been a generous husband, for example, Holroyd Pearce L.J. pointed out that " there was but little profit to the wife in having the capital (shorn by death duties) in her own hands instead of having a larger sum (not so shorn) in her husband's hands." [2] Cases in which some pecuniary benefit accruing upon the death must be deducted in full will probably continue to occur from time to time, but it is submitted that since the Act of 1959 they will provide the exceptions rather than the rule.[3]

Even where it is proper to make some deduction on account of accelerated receipt of the deceased's property, it does not follow that this is the end of the matter, for the court may then have to set off against that deduction the fact that by reason of the premature death the widow may be receiving a substantially smaller capital sum than she might have received at a later date.[4]

The Law Commission has recommended that *no* benefits from the estate of the deceased should be taken into account.[5]

CONTRIBUTORY NEGLIGENCE. As we have seen [6] the contributory negligence of the deceased is taken into account in actions under the Fatal Accidents Acts and the damages awarded to the dependants are reduced by the appropriate proportion. The question now arises whether the fact that one of the dependants may himself have been negligent and so have contributed to the death of the deceased, has any effect upon the damages which may be recovered. If, for example, A is being driven in a car by his wife, Mrs. A, and is killed in an accident caused by the combined negligence of Mrs. A and of B, are the damages for which B is liable affected by the negligence of Mrs. A? This a question to which neither the Fatal Accidents Acts nor the Law Reform (Contributory Negligence) Act 1945 give any direct answer, nor has it been the subject of any English decision.[7]

---

[99] *Grand Trunk Ry.* v. *Jennings* (1883) 13 App.Cas. 800; *Roughead* v. *Railway Executive* (1949) 65 T.L.R. 435; *Nance* v. *British Columbia Electric Ry.* [1951] A.C. 601, 615; *Taylor* v. *O'Connor* [1971] A.C. 115. But in the extreme case, where the whole family income is derived from the husband's investments and the widow takes his whole estate upon his death, it would seem that she has suffered no pecuniary loss: *Bishop* v. *Cunard White Star Co. Ltd.* [1950] P. 240, 248, *per* Hodson J.

[1] *Muirhead* v. *Railway Executive* (1951), unreported; Kemp & Kemp, *The Quantum of Damages*, 2nd ed., Vol. 2, pp. 226, 236, *per* Singleton L.J.; *Daniels* v. *Jones* [1961] 1 W.L.R. 1103, 1110, *per* Pearce L.J., 1114, *per* Willmer L.J., 1116, *per* Pearson L.J.; *Kassam* v. *Kampala Aerated Water Co. Ltd.* [1965] 1 W.L.R. 668, 673, *per* Lord Guest.

[2] *Daniels* v. *Jones* [1961] 1 W.L.R. 1103, 1110.

[3] *Cf. Ganz, loc. cit.*

[4] *Taylor* v. *O'Connor* [1971] A.C. 115. This may be done either by increasing the annual figure for loss of support or by making a separate assessment to represent " lost savings ": see McGregor, *Damages*, 13th ed., pp. 837–838; *Gavin* v. *Wilmot Breeden Ltd.* [1973] 1 W.L.R. 1117.

[5] Report on Personal Injury Litigation—Assessment of Damages, Law Com. No. 56 (1973), para. 256.

[6] *Ante,* p. 500.

[7] The facts of *Dawrant* v. *Nutt* [1961] 1 W.L.R. 253 raised the problem, but it was not in fact considered. See Dias [1961] C.L.J. 17, 19–20. The question is answered in the affirmative in Ontario (*Trueman* v. *Hydro-Electric Power Commission* [1924] 1 D.L.R. 405),

It is submitted that on principle the damages awarded to the negligent dependant should be reduced under the Act of 1945, s. 1 (1), in proportion to his share of responsibility, but that the other dependants should receive their damages in full.[8] The remedy under the Fatal Accidents Acts is given to individuals, not to the dependants as a group,[9] and each dependant can therefore be regarded, for present purposes at least, as if he were a separate plaintiff. Moreover, since the defendant must be provided with particulars of all persons on whose behalf the action is brought,[10] he should have no technical difficulty in pleading the contributory negligence of any one of them. The one objection to this view that has been taken is that the pecuniary loss suffered by a dependant is not " damage " within the meaning of section 1 (1) of the Act of 1945, for it has been said that the word does not. include pecuniary loss.[11] It is submitted that this objection is unsound,[12] but even if it were sustained, it would not follow that the negligent dependant should recover in full. The position would then be that the case is one of contributory negligence but that the Act of 1945 does not apply, and the result of that is that the negligent dependant should recover nothing.[13] Such a result is unlikely to commend itself to the court.[14]

Liability under the Fatal Accidents Acts does not cancel liability on other grounds, and an action may be brought both under the Acts and on one of these other grounds.[15] It is, of course, extremely common for an action on behalf of the dependants of the deceased to be joined with one on behalf of his estate under the Act of 1934.[16]

Carriage by Air Act 1961. The Carriage by Air Act 1961 [17] gives the force of law to the Warsaw Convention as amended at

---

in Victoria (*Benjamin* v. *Currie* [1958] V.R. 259) and in Northern Ireland (*Mulholland* v. *McCrea* [1961] N.I. 135). In the U.S., where few states have any equivalent to the Act of 1945 so that contributory negligence is normally a complete bar, the majority of states deny recovery to the negligent dependant but allow the others to recover in full. In some states, however, all the dependants are barred from any remedy if any one of them was negligent. And in some no dependant is barred unless all were negligent. See Prosser, *Torts*, 4th ed., p. 913; Harper and James, *Law of Torts*, p. 1282, n. 24.

[8] Glanville Williams, *Joint Torts and Contributory Negligence,* pp. 443–444.
[9] *Ante,* p. 503.
[10] *Ante,* p. 503, n. 38.
[11] *Drinkwater* v. *Kimber* [1951] 2 All E.R. 713, 715, *per* Devlin J. The decision was affirmed on other grounds [1952] 2 Q.B. 281.
[12] Glanville Williams, *op. cit.,* pp. 443–444, n. 25.
[13] *Cf. Ginty* v. *Belmont Building Supplies Ltd.* [1959] 1 All E.R. 144, 424, *per* Pearson J.
[14] There seems no reason why the defendant should not claim contribution from a negligent dependant under the Law Reform (Married Women and Tortfeasors) Act 1935, s. 6, and this would be the better course where the negligent dependant is not the only dependant. It would also be the appropriate course where the executor or administrator of the deceased, *i.e.* the nominal plaintiff, has contributed to the death but is not himself the principal dependant.
[15] *Leggott* v. *G.N. Ry.* (1876) 1 Q.B.D. 599.
[16] *Ante,* p. 501. See also *post,* pp. 512–515.
[17] And see Carriage by Air (Supplementary Provisions) Act 1962. The Act as a whole came into force on receiving the Royal Assent (June 22, 1961), but s. 1, which gives the force of law to the Convention and repeals the Carriage by Air Act 1932, did not come into force until June 1, 1967: Carriage by Air (Convention) Order 1967 (S.I. 1967 No. 479).

The Hague, 1955, and replaces the Carriage by Air Act 1932. Article 17 of the Convention provides, *inter alia*, that the carrier is liable for damage sustained in the event of the death of a passenger if the accident which caused the damage took place on board the aircraft or in the course of any of the operations of embarking or disembarking, and section 3 of the Act provides that references in the Fatal Accidents Act 1846, s. 1, to a wrongful act, neglect or default shall include references to an occurrence which gives rise to a liability under Article 17. Liability under Article 17 is not dependent upon proof of fault [18] and section 3 thus makes available an action under the Fatal Accidents Acts in which the plaintiff need not prove any actual wrongful act, neglect or default. The persons by whom and for whose benefit the action may be brought are the same as for an ordinary action under the Fatal Accidents Acts, presumably both the measure of damages and the period of limitation will also be the same,[19] and the Contributory Negligence Act 1945 applies.[20] The carrier's liability is, however, limited to 250,000 " gold " francs (approximately £7,000) for each passenger unless a special contract fixes a higher amount.[21] The Act and the Convention apply only to " international carriage," [22] but they are extended by Order to non-international carriage.[23] The substantial difference between liability under the Order and liability under the Carriage by Air Act 1961 is that the former sets a limit of liability of 875,000 gold francs (about £24,000).

Coal-Mining (Subsidence) Act 1957. The Coal-Mining (Subsidence) Act 1957, s. 12, in effect subjects the National Coal Board to liability under the Fatal Accidents Acts in respect of a death caused by coal-mining subsidence, even though the subsidence was not the result of any wrongful act, neglect or default. The damages recoverable are reduced if the deceased was guilty of contributory negligence and nothing can be recovered under the Act for the death of a trespasser or if the person killed was at the time underground in a mine of coal.

Interrelation of the Fatal Accidents Acts 1849 to 1959 and the Law Reform (Miscellaneous Provisions) Act 1934. Two important

---

[18] The carrier is not liable if he proves that he and his servants or agents have taken all necessary measures to avoid the damage or that it was impossible for him or them to take such measures: Art. 20.

[19] These two points are a little doubtful because (a) the Convention itself provides a general limitation period of two years for actions for damages (Art. 29) while the period for actions under the Fatal Accidents Acts is three years from the death, and (b) under the Carriage by Air Act 1932, which simply gave the force of law to an Article in identical language to that of Art. 17 without any equivalent to s. 3 of the Act of 1961, the damages recoverable could exceed those recoverable under the Fatal Accidents Acts: see *Preston* v. *Hunting Air Transport Ltd.* [1956] 1 Q.B. 454.

[20] s. 6.

[21] Art. 22. The carrier is not entitled to limit his liability under this Article if it is proved that the damage resulted from an act or omission of the carrier, his servants or agents, done with intent to cause damage or recklessly and with knowledge that damage would probably result: Art. 25.

[22] Art. 1. See *Grein* v. *Imperial Airways Ltd.* [1937] 1 K.B. 50; *Philippson* v. *Imperial Airways Ltd.* [1939] A.C. 332; McNair, *op. cit.*, pp. 168–171.

[23] s. 10; Carriage by Air Acts (Application of Provisions) Order 1967 (S.I. 1967 No. 480).

distinctions between actions under the Fatal Accidents Acts and under the Act of 1934 must be noticed: (i) Damages recovered under the Act of 1934 form part of the deceased's estate in which his creditors and the beneficiaries under his will may be interested, and they are subject to estate duty. Damages recovered under the Fatal Accidents Acts, on the other hand, go directly to the dependants of the deceased and form no part of his estate. Not only are they safe from the clutches of the creditors of the deceased and the officials of the Estate Duty Office, but they can be awarded even if the deceased committed suicide, provided that the death remains attributable to the wrongful act, neglect or default of the defendant.[24] (ii) The Act of 1934 provides for damages suffered between the wrong and the death, such damages as the deceased himself might have recovered if he had lived, while the Fatal Accidents Acts are concerned with damage suffered after death—" compensation to the dependants for the loss of the breadwinner." But funeral expenses may be recovered under either Act according as to whether they are paid out of the estate or by the dependants.

The rights conferred by the Act of 1934 for the benefit of the estates of deceased persons are stated to be "in addition to and not in derogation of any rights conferred on the dependants of deceased persons by the Fatal Accidents Acts," [25] but this does not mean that damages can be recovered twice over.[26] If damages recovered under the Act of 1934 devolve on the dependants under the deceased's will or intestacy, the net amount received by the dependants after deduction of administration expenses and estate duty must be taken into account in reduction of the damages recoverable under the Fatal Accidents Acts.[27] Normally an action under the Fatal Accidents Acts is joined with one under the Act of 1934 so that this rule occasions no difficulty in administration. If the actions are not so joined then, in an action under the Fatal Accidents Acts, any damages which have been or may be awarded to the estate

---

[24] *Pigney* v. *Pointer's Transport Services Ltd.* [1957] 1 W.L.R. 1121. *Cf. Farmer* v. *Rash* [1969] 1 W.L.R. 160. There is a rule of public policy that no one should be allowed to benefit himself by his own criminal act, and in a case of suicide this rule prevented the suicide's personal representatives from suing on behalf of his estate: *Beresford* v. *Royal Insurance Co. Ltd.* [1938] A.C. 586. But damages awarded under the Fatal Accident Acts do not benefit the deceased's estate and the rule of public policy did not, therefore, bar an action on behalf of the suicide's dependants. It is respectfully submitted, however, that Pilcher J. was wrong in *Pigney* v. *Pointer's Transport Services Ltd.* to make an award of damages to the estate in respect of the deceased's loss of expectation of life. By the Suicide Act 1961 (9 & 10 Eliz. 2, c. 60), s. 1, suicide is no longer a crime and presumably therefore, *Beresford's* case is no longer binding. But perhaps the decision might be upheld on other grounds. For a different application of the rule of public policy, see *Burns* v. *Edman* [1970] 2 Q.B. 541, *ante*, p. 505.

[25] Law Reform (Miscellaneous Provisions) Act 1934, s. 1 (5).

[26] *Davies* v. *Powell Duffryn Associated Collieries Ltd.* [1942] A.C. 601.

[27] This is in accordance with the general rule regarding benefits which accrue in consequence of the death: *ante*, p. 509. See *Feay* v. *Barnwell* [1938] 1 All E.R. 31; *Baker* v. *T. E. Hopkins & Son Ltd.* [1958] 1 W.L.R. 993 (affd. but no appeal on this point [1959] 1 W.L.R. 966); *Voller* v. *Dairy Produce Packers Ltd.* [1962] 1 W.L.R. 960; *Rawlinson* v. *Babcock and Wilcox Ltd.* [1967] 1 W.L.R. 481; Kemp and Kemp, *Quantum of Damages,* Vol. 2, *Fatal Injury Claims,* 2nd ed., pp. 10–11.

under the Act of 1934 must be taken into account to the extent that they benefit the dependants.[28] In an action under the Act of 1934, however, any possible award under the Fatal Accidents Acts is irrelevant. The damages are awarded to the deceased's estate, and cannot be affected by anything which the dependants may recover in respect of an entirely separate cause of action.[29]

Criticism of the existing law

The mere reading of the preceding sections of this chapter is enough to show that the law was in a deplorable condition until the Act of 1934 and that even now it is not entirely satisfactory. That causes of action should in general survive against estates of deceased tortfeasors seems obvious and the exclusion of defamation, even if not that of the other expected torts, from the provisions of the Act of 1934 is hard to justify. Not only does the victim of a libellous attack lose his right to damages if his defamer dies, but he also loses the opportunity of vindicating his character in a court of law.[30] It is with regard to the survival of causes of action for the benefit of a deceased person's estate, however, that the law is most open to criticsm. Winfield thought that it was consonant neither with abstract justice nor with the law of tort that a man's successors should profit by a wrong which in origin did *them* no harm [31] and though there may be something to be said for allowing the survival of causes of action for torts which are unconnected with the death, the value of allowing an action in respect of the very acts which caused the death is doubtful.[32] In 1934 the Law Revision Committee gave two main reasons for allowing such an action to survive, namely, that the Fatal Accidents Acts gave no remedy to adopted or illegitimate children and that under those Acts neither medical nor funeral expenses, even if actually incurred, could be recovered.[33] All that is left of these reasons today, however, is that medical expenses incurred by the deceased before his death cannot be recovered in an action under the Fatal Accidents Acts. Moreover, in the great majority of cases the existence of a claim under the Act of 1934 benefits no one,[34] for any damages awarded to the

---

[28] *Davies* v. *Powell Duffryn Associated Collieries Ltd.* [1942] A.C. 601, 608, *per* Lord Russell of Killowen.

[29] *Davies* v. *Powell Duffryn Associated Collieries Ltd., supra,* 615, *per* Lord Wright. Lord Wright here corrected his previous dictum in *Rose* v. *Ford* [1937] A.C. 826, 852. *Cf. The Aizkari Mendi* [1938] P. 263, 276, *per* Langton J.

[30] The reasons given by the Law Revision Committee for excluding these causes of action from the general rule of survival are unconvincing. " In actions which are regarded as purely personal, such as defamation or seduction, where the presence of the plaintiff may be of the greatest importance, we do not suggest any change ": Interim Report (1934) Cmd. 4540, p. 7.

[31] 5th ed., p. 204. Winfield was not, of course, referring here to wrongs affecting property. Causes of action in respect of torts to property survived the death of the tortfeasor before 1934.

[32] See the observations of Salmon L.J. in *Naylor* v. *Yorkshire Electricity Board* [1967] 1 Q.B. 244, 257–260. See also *ibid.* [1968] A.C. 529, 550, *per* Lord Devlin.

[33] Interim Report, p. 4.

[34] Except the Inland Revenue, if the deceased's estate is large enough to attract estate duty.

estate which pass to the dependants are taken into account in assessing the damages under the Fatal Accidents Acts. Only if the deceased left no dependants, or if his residuary estate passes to a stranger, does the survival of his own cause of action have any practical effect.[35] And yet the courts must go through the solemn farce of putting a value on such an incalculable thing as his lost expectation of life.[36] It would, perhaps, have been better to enlarge the rights of the dependants under the Fatal Accidents Acts as so to include general damages for the loss they have sustained, as distinct from loss of a purely financial character.

The Law Commission has recently published proposals which would effect a substantial alteration of the law in respect of some of the matters discussed above.[37] First, no deduction would be made from Fatal Accidents Acts damages in respect of benefits coming from the estate of the deceased,[38] so that the problems arising from the interrelation of those Acts and the Act of 1934 would disappear.[39] Secondly, the law would make some allowance for the non-pecuniary loss suffered by the close relatives of the deceased, a " tariff " figure of £1,000 being set as compensation for the loss of a spouse or minor child.[40]

---

[35] Unless, of course, no claim under the Fatal Accidents Acts is made at all, as in *Yorkshire Electricity Board* v. *Naylor* [1968] A.C. 529, or the claim under those Acts fails altogether as it did in *Burns* v. *Edman* [1970] 2 Q.B. 541.

[36] See Allen, " Is Life a Boon? " (1941) 57 L.Q.R. 462 and *post*, pp. 564–567.

[37] Report on Personal Injury Litigation—Assessment of Damages, Law Com. No. 56 (1973).

[38] *Ibid.*, para. 256.

[39] " Loss of expectation of life," which is often the only substantial claim under the Act of 1934 would in fact disappear as a separate head of damage: see p. 566, *post*.

[40] Law Com. No. 56, paras, 160–180.
In effect, though not in principle, English Law at present allows such a *solatium*: viz., where the deceased is a young child. In such a case the child's action for loss of expectation of life (a conventional sum of £750) survives for the benefit of the estate and passes to the parents, though they will generally have suffered no financial loss.
Other legal systems which grant a *solatium* tend either to set a conventional maximum (*e.g.* South Australia, £500 for child, £700 for spouse) or leave the matter at large for the court or jury (Scotland, though awards rarely exceed £1,500). The Law Commission proposal for a fixed tariff seems the only way to avoid judicial inquiry into the unassessable.

Chapter 25

VICARIOUS LIABILITY [1]

MASTER AND SERVANT

THE expression " vicarious liability " signifies the liability which A may incur to C for damage caused to C by the negligence or other tort of B. It is not necessary that A shall have participated in any way in the commission of the tort nor that a duty owed in law by A to C shall have been broken. What is required is that A should stand in a particular relationship to B and that B's tort should be referable in a certain manner to that relationship. The commonest instance of this in modern law is the liability of a master for the torts of his servants done in the course of their employment. The relationship required is the specific one of master and servant and the tort must be referable to that relationship in the sense that it must have been committed by the servant in the course of his employment. It is with this instance of vicarious liability that the first part of this chapter is concerned, but there are other instances which cannot be included in a work of this kind. Such are the liability of partners for each other's torts and, perhaps, the liability of a principal for the torts of his agent.[2]

Unfortunately for precision in the use of legal terms the expression " vicarious liability " is today often used also to describe cases in which A is liable for damage caused to C by the act of B even though A's liability is in truth not vicarious at all but primary. Such is the position, for example, where an employer is held liable for damage caused by the act of an independent contractor, for in that case, as we shall see, the employer is not liable unless the independent contractor's act is one which has the legal result that some duty owed directly by the employer to the plaintiff has been broken. Unlike the case of master and servant, nothing in particular turns on the precise relationship between the employer and the contractor. What matters is the duty owed by the employer to the plaintiff, and the employer's liability, if any, is for a breach of that duty.[3]

Historical outline

Historically, the idea of vicarious responsibility is common enough. A good deal of primitive law is founded on revenge, and revenge tends to be indiscriminate. In the Mosaic Code it is significant that it was found

---

[1] Weir, *Casebook on Tort*, 3rd ed., Chaps. 6 and 7; Atiyah, *Vicarious Liability in the Law of Torts*.

[2] Atiyah, *op. cit.*, pp. 99–115. See also p. 534, *post*.

[3] The contents of the above two paragraphs are, it must be admitted, somewhat controversial today, for the distinction between primary and vicarious liability has been blurred. For reasons of convenience, however, their justification is left until the law itself has been discussed. See *post*, pp. 540–543.

necessary to state expressly that each man should be put to death only for his own sin and not for that of his father or son, and Plato thought it advisable to assert a similar principle in his laws.[4]

In our own law [5] the early Anglo-Norman period is a transitional one in which the idea of complete liability for the wrongs of servants or slaves is changing to the idea of liability only where there has been command or consent on the part of the master of the servant's wrong. From 1300 onwards the change continues until by the early sixteenth century the command theory has become established. Thenceforward, during that century and the seventeenth, the master's liability was restricted to the case where he had particularly commanded the very act complained of.[6] On this basis the liability clearly is not vicarious, for a man who orders an unlawful act is a direct participant in the tort.

By the latter part of the seventeenth century so limited a form of liability had become inadequate in view of rising commercial prosperity and the increasing complexities of trade, but nothing changed until the time of Sir John Holt.[7] At last, however, Holt established the rule that the master was liable not only for acts done at his express command but also for those done by his implied command, this to be inferred from the general authority he had given his servant in his employment.[8] The new rule may appear to be but a slight extension of the old one. In truth, however, it involves a major change, for while an express command is something to be proved by direct evidence, an implied command is something which can only be inferred from the general scope of the servant's employment considered as a whole. Liability is related to the scope of the employment and the foundation of the modern law is laid.[9] Nevertheless the principle of primary liability was for the time retained and in form at least the question was still whether the master could be shown to have been a direct participant in the tort as having impliedly commanded it. The relationship of master and servant was not itself a

---

[4] Salmond, *Jurisprudence*, 12th ed., p. 105.

[5] See Wigmore's article in *Select Essays in Anglo-American Legal History* (1909), iii, pp. 520 *et seq.*; Holdsworth, H.E.L., iii, 382–387, viii, 472–482.

[6] See, *e.g. Southern* v. *How* (1617) 2 Rolle 5. As late as 1682 the following points were laid down by the court in *Kingston* v. *Booth* (1682) Skin. 288: (i) " If I command my servant to do what is lawful, and he misbehaves himself, or do more, I shall not answer for my servant but my servant for himself, for that it was his own act; otherwise it was in the power of every servant to subject his master to what actions or penalties he pleased."
(ii) " If I command my servant to do a lawful act, as in this case to pull down a little wooden house (wherein the plaintiff was and would not come out, and which was carried upon wheels into the land to trick the defendant out of possession) and bid them take care they hurt not the plaintiff; if in this doing my servants wound the plaintiff, in trespass of assault and wounding brought against me, I may plead Not Guilty, and give this in evidence, for that I was not guilty of the wounding; and the pulling down of the house was a lawful act."

[7] Chief Justice 1688–1710. Parliament itself intervened in some special cases. See, *e.g.* the Act for making Navigable the Rivers Aire and Calder, 1698 (10 Will. III, c. 25), s. 5.

[8] The new rule is stated with great clarity in *Tuberville* v. *Stamp* (1697) 1 Ld. Raym. 264.

[9] It can be said with some confidence that the modern law of vicarious liability can be traced back to Holt, but not beyond. See authorities cited by Glanville Williams, " Vicarious Liability and the Master's Indemnity " (1957) 20 M.L.R. 220, 228.

legal requirement of liability—it was merely a factual element in the case from which a command or " authority " could be implied, and other relationships might serve the same purpose equally well.[10] By the end of the eighteenth century, however, the idea began to grow up that some special importance attached to the relationship of master and servant as such,[11] and in 1849 it was finally held that the existence of that relationship was essential.[12] Thereafter, though primary liability on the part of anyone could be established on proof of direct participation in the tort, such direct participation was not even theoretically required to make a master liable for his servant's tort. The liability is derived from the relationship and is truly vicarious. At the same time the phrase " implied authority " which had been the cornerstone of the master's primary liability gives way gradually to the modern " course of employment." [13]

Who is a servant?

At one time it was generally accepted that the test of the relationship of master and servant was that of control.[14] A servant is employed under a contract of service, as distinct from a contract for services, and a contract of service was thought to be one by virtue of which the employer " can not only order or require what is to be done, but how it shall be done." [15] The control test probably retains a good deal of importance in cases to which it can be applied,[16] but in modern conditions the notion that a master has the right to control the manner of work of all his servants, save perhaps in the most attenuated form,[17] contains more of fiction than of fact. It is clearly the law that such professionally trained persons as the master of a ship, the captain of an aircraft and the house surgeon at a hospital are all servants for whose torts their masters are responsible, and it is unrealistic to suppose that a theoretical right in a

---

[10] For late examples, see *Bush* v. *Steinman* (1799) 1 Bos. & Pul. 404; *Sly* v. *Edgely* (1806) 6 Esp. 6; *Matthews* v. *West London Waterworks* (1813) 3 Camp. 403; *Randleson* v. *Murray* (1838) 8 Ad. & E. 109.

[11] See, *e.g. Stone* v. *Cartwright* (1795) 6 T.R. 411; *Brucker* v. *Fromont* (1796) 6 T.R. 659 and the cases concerning temporary servants such as *Laugher* v. *Pointer* (1826) 5 B. & C. 547; *Quarman* v. *Burnett* (1840) 6 M. & W. 499.

[12] *Reedie* v. *London and North Western Ry.* (1849) 4 Exch. 244. *Bush* v. *Steinman, supra*, was expressly overruled.

[13] Wigmore regards Lord Kenyon as chiefly responsible for the change, but the cases which he cites in support of this are tenuous, and in one of them (*Laugher* v. *Pointer* (1826) 5 B. & C. 547, 577) an opinion of Abbott C.J. is attributed to Lord Kenyon: *Essays in Anglo-American Legal History*, iii, pp. 533–534. The development of the " scope of employment " rule may be traced in the following cases: *McManus* v. *Crickett* (1800) 1 East 106; *Bowcher* v. *Noidstrom* (1809) 1 Taunt. 568; *Croft* v. *Alison* (1821) 4 B. & Ald. 590; *Laugher* v. *Pointer* (*supra, per* Abbott C.J.: note that his brethren speak in much looser terms); *Joel* v. *Morison* (1834) 6 C. & P. 502; *Sleath* v. *Wilson* (1839) ibid. 607; *Lamb* v. *Palk* (1840) 9 C. & P. 629. Chitty, *Practice of the Law*, 2nd ed. (1834), i, pp. 79–80 states the rule.

[14] For an early statement of the control test, see *Yewens* v. *Noakes* (1880) 6 Q.B.D. 530, 532–533, *per* Bramwell B. For its development see Atiyah, *op. cit.*, pp. 40–44.

[15] *Collins* v. *Hertfordshire County Council* [1947] K.B. 598, 615, *per* Hilbery J.

[16] *Argent* v. *Minister of Social Security* [1968] 1 W.L.R. 1749, 1759, *per* Roskill J.

[17] " What matters is lawful authority to command so far as there is scope for it. And there must always be some room for it, if only in incidental or collateral matters ": *Zuijs* v. *Wirth Brothers Pty. Ltd.* (1955) 93 C.L.R. 561, 571, *per* Dixon C.J.

master, who is as likely as not to be a corporate and not a natural person, to control how any skilled worker does his job, can have much substance.[18] It has, therefore, now been recognised that the absence of such control is not conclusive against the existence of a contract of service [19] and various attempts to find a more suitable test have been made.[20]

In an often cited statement [21] Lord Thankerton has said that there are four indicia of a contract of service, (a) the master's power of selection of his servant, (b) the payment of wages or other remuneration, (c) the master's right to control the method of doing the work, and (d) the master's right of suspension or dismissal. It is respectfully suggested, however, that this does not carry the matter much further; the first and last, and perhaps also the second, are indicia rather of the existence of a contract than of the particular kind of contract which is a contract of service,[22] and some judges have preferred to leave the question in very general terms. Somervell L.J. thought that one could not get beyond the question whether the contract was " a contract of service within the meaning which an ordinary person would give under those words," [23] but more helpful than this is Denning L.J.'s well-known statement that " It is often easy to recognise a contract of service when you see it, but difficult to say wherein the distinction lies. A ship's master, a chauffeur and a reporter on the staff of a newspaper are all employed under a contract of service; but a ship's pilot,[24] a taxi-man, and a newspaper contributor are employed under a contract for services. One feature which seems to run through the instances is that, under a contract of service, a man is employed as part of a business, and his work is done as an integral part of the business; whereas under a contract for services, his work, although done for the business, is not integrated into it but is only accessory to it." [25]

The most elaborate recent discussion of the matter is to be found in the judgment of MacKenna J. in *Ready Mixed Concrete (South East) Ltd.* v. *Minister of Pensions and National Insurance,*[26] where the learned

---

[18] Kahn-Freund, " Servants and Independent Contractors " (1951) 14 M.L.R. 504.

[19] *Morren* v. *Swinton and Pendelbury Borough Council* [1965] 1 W.L.R. 576; *Whittaker* v. *Minister of Pensions and National Insurance* [1967] 1 Q.B. 156; *Ready Mixed Concrete (South East) Ltd.* v. *Minister of Pensions and National Insurance* [1968] 2 Q.B. 497; *Market Investigations Ltd.* v. *Minister of Social Security* [1969] 2 Q.B. 173.

[20] Many of the more recent cases are not concerned with vicarious liabil·y but with the question whether or not a contract of service exists for the purposes of certain statutory provisions such as the National Insurance Acts. It seems to be assumed that that question should receive the same answer almost regardless of the context in which it is asked. See Atiyah, *op. cit.,* pp. 32–33.

[21] *Short* v. *J. & W. Henderson Ltd.* (1946) 62 T.L.R. 427, 429.

[22] *Ready Mixed Concrete (South East) Ltd.* v. *Minister of Pensions and National Insurance* [1968] 2 Q.B. 497, 524, *per* MacKenna J.

[23] *Cassidy* v. *Ministry of Health* [1951] 2 K.B. 343, 352–353; *Argent* v. *Minister of Social Security* [1968] 1 W.L.R. 1749, 1760, *per* Roskill J.

[24] But see Pilotage Act 1913, s. 15.

[25] *Stevenson, Jordan and Harrison Ltd.* v. *Macdonald* [1952] 1 T.L.R. 101, 111; Weir, *Casebook on Tort,* 3rd ed., p. 212; *cf. Petter* v. *Metropolitan Properties Co. Ltd.* (1973) 229 E.G. 973.

[26] [1968] 2 Q.B. 497.

judge held three conditions must be fulfilled; a contract of service exists
if (i) the servant agrees that, in consideration of a wage or other remuneration, he will provide his own work and skill in the performance
of some service for his master; (ii) he agrees, expressly or impliedly, that
in the performance of that service he will be subject to the other's control
in a sufficient degree to make that other master; (iii) the other provisions
of the contract are consistent with its being a contract of service.
Although MacKenna J. gave some examples of provisions inconsistent
with a contract of service, such as a requirement that the person employed should provide all necessary equipment and materials at his own
expense,[27] it is difficult to avoid the conclusion that much of this com-
posite test assumes what it sets out to prove. Nevertheless it is probable
that no more complete general test exists; the fact is that it is not
possible even to compile an exhaustive list of all the relevant considerations.[28] " The most that can be said is that control will no doubt always
have to be considered, although it can no longer be regarded as the sole
determining factor; and that factors which may be of importance are
such matters as whether the man performing the services provides his
own equipment, whether he hires his own helpers, what degree of
financial risk he takes, what degree of responsibility for investment and
management he has, and whether and how far he has an opportunity of
profiting from sound management in the performance of his task." [29]

Hospitals

It was to a substantial extent a consequence of developments in the
liability of hospitals for the negligence of their staffs that dissatisfaction
with the test of control developed, for while it was originally held that a
hospital authority could not be liable for negligence in matters involving
the exercise of professional skills,[30] this view has not been accepted
since 1942. Since then it has been held that radiographers,[31] house-
surgeons,[32] whole time-assistant medical officers [33] and, probably, staff
anaesthetists [34] are the servants of the authority for the purposes of
vicarious liability. It has also been suggested that even visiting consultants and surgeons under the National Health Service are servants for
this purpose.[35] However, in many of the cases there has been a tendency
to treat the question of a hospital authority's liability not as one of
vicarious liability only but also as one of the primary liability of the

---

[27] *Ibid.* at pp. 516–517.
[28] *Market Investigations Ltd.* v. *Minister of Social Security* [1969] 2 Q.B. 173, 184, *per*
Cooke J.
[29] *Ibid.* at p. 185.
[30] *Hillyer* v. *St. Bartholomew's Hospital* [1909] 2 K.B. 820. Note that the hospital in
this case was a charitable body.
[31] *Gold* v. *Essex County Council* [1942] 2 K.B. 293.
[32] *Collins* v. *Hertfordshire County Council* [1947] K.B. 598; *Cassidy* v. *Ministry of
Health* [1951] 2 K.B. 343.
[33] *Cassidy* v. *Ministry of Health, supra.*
[34] *Roe* v. *Minister of Health* [1954] 2 Q.B. 66.
[35] Street, *Torts*, 5th ed., p. 416.

authority for breach of its own duty to the patient.[36] This approach is made easier by the National Health Service Act,[37] and if a surgeon or consultant is negligent it is probable that the hospital authority concerned will itself be primarily liable for breach of its own duty under the Act. If this is so there is no need for the patient to have recourse to vicarious liability in order to obtain redress, and it is unnecessary to go to the lengths of holding such persons to be servants of the hospital authority.

Police

Until 1964 no person or body stood in the position of " master " to a police officer,[38] and accordingly anyone injured by the tortious conduct of the police could have redress only against the individual officers concerned. Now, however, it is provided by the police Act 1964, s. 48, that the chief officer of police for any police area shall be liable for torts committed by constables under his direction and control in the performance or purported performance of their functions. This statutory liability is equated with the liability of a master for the torts of his servants committed in the course of their employment, but the chief officer of police does not, of course, have to bear the damages personally. Any damages or costs awarded against him are paid out of the police fund.[39]

Lending a servant

Difficult cases arise where A is the general employer of B but C, by agreement with A (whether contractual or otherwise), is making temporary use of B's services. If B, in the course of his employment, commits a tort against X, is it A or C who is vicariously liable to X?[40] In *Mersey Docks and Harbour Board* v. *Coggins and Griffith (Liverpool) Ltd.*,[41] A employed B as the driver of a mobile crane, and let the crane together with B as driver to C. The contract between A and C provided that B should be the servant of C but B was paid by A, and A alone had power to dismiss him. In the course of loading a ship X was injured by

---

[36] See, *e.g. Gold* v. *Essex County Council, supra*, at p. 301, *per* Lord Greene M.R.; *Cassidy* v. *Ministry of Health, supra*, at pp. 362–365, *per* Denning L.J. See *post*, pp. 552–553.

[37] The Act states, in s. 3 (1), that it shall be the duty of the Minister to provide, *inter alia*, " medical, nursing and other services required at or for the purposes of hospitals " and " the services of specialists." This duty is not discharged by the appointment of competent doctors, nurses and specialists: *Razzel* v. *Snowball* [1954] 1 W.L.R. 1382. See also Salmond, *Torts*, 16th ed., pp. 468–469; Hamson, " The Liability of Hospitals for Negligence," *The Law in Action*, I, p. 19.

[38] Under the Crown Proceedings Act 1947 the Crown is only liable in respect of persons who are paid wholly out of moneys provided by Parliament (Crown Proceedings Act 1947, s. 2 (6)) and this excludes the police. Nor are the police servants of the police authority: *Fisher* v. *Oldham Corporation* [1930] 2 K.B. 364.

[39] For the " police fund " see the Police Act 1964, s. 62 and 8th Sched. If an action against a chief of police is settled the damages are payable out of the police fund only if the settlement is approved by the police authority: *ibid.* s. 48 (2) (*b*).

[40] The law *might*, of course, say that they were *both* liable; but that would require both to insure against the same risk.

[41] [1947] 1 A.C. 1; Weir, *Casebook on Tort*, 3rd ed., p. 214. See the observations of Sellers L.J. on this case in *McArdle* v. *Andmac Roofing Co.* [1967] 1 W.L.R. 356, 361.

the negligent way in which B worked the crane. At the time of the accident C had the immediate direction and control of the operations to be executed by B and his crane, e.g., to pick up and move a piece of cargo, but he had no power to direct how B should work the crane and manipulate its controls. The House of Lords held that A as the general or permanent employer of B was liable to X.

In such cases, the burden of proof, which is a heavy one and can only be discharged in exceptional circumstances [42] rests on A, the general or permanent employer, to shift the prima facie responsibility for the negligence of B, on to the hirer, C, who for the time being has the advantage of B's services. A distinction is to be drawn between cases where a complicated piece of machinery and a driver are lent, and cases where labour only, particularly where it is not of a highly skilled character,[43] is lent. In the former case, it is easier to infer that the general employer continues to control the method of perform-ance since it is his machinery and the driver remains responsible to him for its safe keeping. In the latter case it is easier to infer that the hirer has control not merely in the sense of being able to tell the workman what he wants done, but also of deciding the manner of doing it.[44]

The question whether A or C is liable depends on many factors " Who is paymaster, who can dismiss,[45] how long the alternative service lasts, what machinery is employed, have all to be kept in mind." [46] But in cases of this kind the courts have generally adhered to the view that the most satisfactory test, if it can be applied, is, who at the particular time has authority to tell B not only what he is to do, but how he is to do it. It is a question of fact involving all the circumstances of the case. C may control the particular task to be performed, but he is not liable unless he also controls the method of performing it. If C, though he has no authority to do so, expressly directs B to do the act which is negligently done and causes damage, C is generally liable with B as a joint tortfeasor,[47] but A is not liable. A term in the contract between A and C that B shall be the servant of C on the particular occasion is not conclusive, for there cannot be the transfer of the servant from one master to another without the servant's consent, either express or implied, and even then there will always

---

[42] Ibid. at p. 10, per Lord Simon; Ready Mixed Concrete (East Midlands) Ltd. v. Yorkshire Traffic Area Licensing Authority [1970] 2 Q.B. 397.
[43] Brogan v. William Allen Smith & Co. Ltd., 1965 S.L.T. 175; McGregor v. Duthie & Sons & Co. Ltd., 1966 S.L.T. 133. Cf. Savory v. Holland and Hannen and Cubitts (Southern) Ltd. [1964] 1 W.L.R. 1158; Ready Mixed Concrete (East Midlands) Ltd. v. Yorkshire Traffic Area Licensing Authority, supra.
[44] [1947] A.C. at p. 17, per Lord Porter; ibid. at p. 22, per Lord Uthwatt; Garrard v. Southey & Co. [1952] 2 Q.B. 174, 179, per Parker J.
[45] Garrard v. Southey [1952] 2 Q.B. 174, 180. Nowhere is it suggested that this is the sole or the conclusive test: per Parker J.
[46] Mersey Docks case, supra, at p. 17, per Lord Porter. " Where (does) the authority lie to direct, or delegate to the workman, the manner in which the vehicle is to be driven? " ibid. at p. 12, per Lord Simon; ibid. at p. 21, per Lord Uthwatt.
[47] Ibid. at p. 12, per Lord Simon.

remain a question as to the extent and effect of the transfer.[48] Such a contract may entitle A to claim indemnity from C for the damages he has had to pay to X,[49] but beyond determining the liability of A and C *inter se*, "it has only an indirect bearing upon the question which of them is to be regarded as master of the workman, B, on a particular occasion." [50]

By statute, owners of hackney carriages (including taxicabs) are made responsible for the torts of the driver while he is plying for hire as if the relationship of master and servant existed between them even though it does not in fact exist,[51] but the tort must be committed in the course of the driver's employment (using the word " employment " in this fictitious sense).[52]

What is the course of employment ?

Unless the wrong done falls within the course of the servant's employment, the master is not liable. It may be asked, " How can any wrong be in the course of a servant's employment? No sane or law-abiding master ever hires a man to tell lies, give blows or act carelessly." But that is not what course of employment means. A wrong falls within the scope of employment if it is expressly or impliedly authorised by the master or is an unauthorised manner of doing something which is authorised, or is necessarily incidental to something which the servant is employed to do.[53] Course of employment has supplanted scope of authority, but it contains no criteria

---

[48] *Ibid.* at p. 14, *per* Lord Macmillan; *ibid.* at pp. 21–22, *per* Lord Uthwatt; *ibid.* at p. 20, *per* Lord Simonds.

[49] *Herdman* v. *Walker* (*Tooting*) *Ltd.* [1956] 1 W.L.R. 209; *Spalding* v. *Tarmac Civil Engineering Ltd.* [1966] 1 W.L.R. 156.

[50] *Ibid.* at p. 15, *per* Lord Porter. As to requisition by the government of A's vehicle, to be driven by A's servant, see *Marney* v. *Campbell, Symonds & Co. Ltd.* (1946) 62 T.L.R. 324. See, too *Bontex Knitting Works Ltd.* v. *St. John's Garage* [1943] 2 All E.R. 690. A similar problem arises where a workman is lent by one employer to another and is then himself injured by a failure of the borrowing employer, *e.g.* to provide reasonably safe working conditions. In such cases it may be a little easier to infer an actual transfer of service, but the general principles are the same. Even if the borrowing employer has not become the temporary master of the injured workman he may still be liable for breach of his duty under the Occupiers' Liability Act 1957, or of a general duty of care. Diplock L.J. has even said that questions of transfer of service are irrelevant except for the purposes of vicarious liability: *Savory* v. *Holland and Hannen and Cubitts* (*Southern*) *Ltd.* [1964] 1 W.L.R. 1158, 1165, but this is doubtful. See *ante*, p. 152.

[51] *Keen* v. *Henry* [1894] 1 Q.B. 292; *Bygraves* v. *Dicker* [1923] 2 K.B. 585; London Hackney Carriages Act 1843 (6 & 7 Vict. c. 86) and (outside London) Town Police Clauses Act 1847 (10 & 11 Vict. c. 89).

[52] *Venables* v. *Smith* (1877) 2 Q.B.D. 279. For the position of a carrier by sea with respect to the torts of a stevedore employed by him, see Carriage of Goods by Sea Act 1924 (14 & 15 Geo. 5, c. 22), as interpreted in *Brown & Co.* v. *Harrison* (1927) 96 L.J. K.B. 1025. *Cf. Leesh River Tea Co. Ltd.* v. *British India S.N. Co. Ltd.* [1967] 2 Q.B. 250.

[53] " The expressions ' acting within his authority,' ' acting in the course of his employment,' and ' acting within the scope of his agency,' as applied to an agent, speaking broadly, mean one and the same thing. What is meant by those expressions it is not easy to define with exactitude. To the circumstances of a particular case one may be more appropriate than the other. Whichever expression is used, it must be construed liberally ": *per* Lord Macnaghten, *Lloyd* v. *Grace, Smith & Co.* [1912] A.C. 716, 736; *Dyer* v. *Munday* [1895] 1 Q.B. 742, 748, *per* Rigby L.J.; *Navarro* v. *Moregrand Ltd.* [1951] 2 T.L.R. 674, 680–681, *per* Denning L.J.; and see *Heatons Transport* (*St. Helens*) *Ltd.* v. *T.G.W.U.* [1973] A.C. 15, 100.

to decide when or why an act is within or outside the scope of employment and no single test is appropriate to cover all cases.[54] It is often an extremely difficult question to decide whether conduct is or is not within the course of employment as thus defined, and it would seem that the question is ultimately one of fact to be decided in the light of general principles.[55]

The decided cases are not very amenable to any scientific classification, and the best that can be done is to select and illustrate a few of the more conspicuous sub-rules.

Carelessness of servant

By far the commonest kind of wrong which the servant commits is one due to unlawful carelessness, whether it be negligence of the kind which is in itself a tort, or negligence which is a possible ingredient in some other tort. It should be noted also that in some torts intention or negligence is immaterial; the doer is liable either way. In cases of this sort the master may well be responsible for conduct of the servant to which no moral blame attaches.[56] But, assuming that the tort is negligence or that it is one in which inadvertence is a possible element in its commission, it may still be in the course of employment even if the servant is not acting strictly in the performance of his duty, provided he is not " on a frolic of his own." [57] Thus a first-aid attendant at a colliery is still within the course of his employment while cycling across his employer's premises to go to an office to collect his wages,[58] and so is a man sent to work at a place away from his employer's premises who drives some distance from his place of work to get a midday meal.[59] But if a driver deviates from his proper route so extensively that he can be said to have gone on an entirely new journey,[60] or if he grossly abuses the permission given to him to use his vehicle for the purpose of going for refreshment,[61] then his master will not be liable for any negligence in the course of such journeys of which he may be guilty. In cases of this kind a question of degree is necessarily involved and no hard-and-fast rule can be laid down.

---

[54] Staton v. National Coal Board [1957] 1 W.L.R. 893, 895, per Finnemore J.; Kay v I.T.W. Ltd. [1968] 1 Q.B. 140, 153, per Sellers L.J.

[55] Marsh v. Moores [1949] 2 K.B. 208, 215; " It must be a question of fact whether an unauthorised act by a servant is within the scope of his employment or outside his employment," per Lynskey J.; Whatman v. Pearson (1868) L.R. 3 C.P. 422; Mitchell v. Crassweller (1853) 13 C.B. 237; Lloyd v. Grace, Smith & Co. [1912] A.C. 716.

[56] Gregory v. Piper (1829) 9 B. & C. 591.

[57] This famous phrase was coined by Parke B. in Joel v. Morison (1834) 6 C. & P. 501, 503.

[58] Staton v. National Coal Board [1957] 1 W.L.R. 893. A servant on his way to or from work will not generally be in the course of his employment; cf. Stitt v. Woolley (1971) 115 S.J. 708 and Elleanor v. Cavendish Woodhouse (1972) 117 S.J. 14.

[59] Harvey v. R. G. O'Dell Ltd. [1958] 2 Q.B. 78; Whatman v. Pearson (1868) L.R. 3 C.P. 422. Cf. Higbid v. Hammett (1932) 49 T.L.R. 104; Crook v. Derbyshire Stone Ltd. [1956] 1 W.L.R. 432; Nottingham v. Aldridge [1971] 3 W.L.R. 1.

[60] Storey v. Ashton (1869) L.R. 4 Q.B. 476. Cf. A. & W. Hemphill Ltd. v. Williams, 1966 S.L.T. 33.   [61] Hilton v. Thomas Burton (Rhodes) Ltd. [1961] 1 W.L.R. 705.

In *Century Insurance Co. Ltd.* v. *Northern Ireland Road Transport Board*,[62] the driver of a petrol lorry, employed by the defendants, while transferring petrol from the lorry to an underground tank in the plaintiff's garage, struck a match to light a cigarette and threw it on the floor and thereby caused a conflagration and an explosion which damaged the plaintiff's property. The defendants were held liable, for the careless act of their driver was done in the course of his employment. Lord Wright pointed out that the act of the driver in lighting his cigarette was done for his own comfort and convenience; it was in itself both innocent and harmless. But the act could not be treated in abstraction from the circumstances as a separate act; the negligence was to be found by considering the time when and the circumstances in which the match was struck and thrown down, and this made it a negligent method of conducting his work.

Mistake of servant

So far we have been dealing with the incompetent *dilettante* and we now pass to the misguided enthusiast. *Bayley* v. *Manchester, Sheffield and Lincolnshire Ry.*[63] is an illustration. The defendants' porter violently pulled out of a train the plaintiff who said his destination was Macclesfield and who was in a train that was going there. The porter mistakenly thought it was going elsewhere. The defendants were held liable. The porter was doing in a blundering way something which he was authorised to do—to see that passengers were in the right trains and to do all in his power to promote their comfort.

Another application of the same principle is an act done in protection of the master's property. The servant has an implied authority to make reasonable efforts to protect and preserve it in an emergency which endangers it. For wrongful, because mistaken, acts done within the scope of that authority the master is liable, and it is a question of degree whether there has been an excess of the authority so great as to put the act outside the scope of authority. A carter, who suspected on mistaken but reasonable grounds that a boy was pilfering sugar from the wagon of the carter's employer, struck the boy on the back of the neck with his hand. The boy fell and a wheel of the wagon went over his foot. The employer was held liable because the blow given by the carter, although somewhat excessive, was not sufficiently so to make it outside the scope of employment.[64] But a servant has no implied authority to arrest a person whom he suspects of attempting

---

[62] [1942] A.C. 509, approving *Jefferson* v. *Derbyshire Farmers Ltd.* [1921] 2 K.B. 281, where the facts were very similar, and for all practical purposes overruling *Williams* v. *Jones* (1865) 3 H. & C. 602; Weir, *Casebook on Tort*, 3rd ed., p. 224, *Spencer* v. *Curtis Bros.* [1962] C.L.Y. 1136. *Cf. Kirby* v. *National Coal Board*, 1958 S.L.T. 47; *Att.-Gen.* v. *Hartley* [1964] N.Z.L.R. 785 (Sup.Ct. of N.Z.).

[63] (1873) L.R. 8 C.P. 148. The reasoning of Willes J. in (1873) L.R. 7 C.P. at p. 420 is of importance. See also *Lucas* v. *Mason* (1875) L.R. 10 Ex. 251, 253, *per* Pollock B.

[64] *Polland* v. *Parr & Sons* [1927] 1 K.B. 236.

to steal after the attempt has ceased, for the arrest is then made not for the protection of the master's property but for the vindication of justice.[65]

The existence of an emergency gives no implied authority to a servant to delegate his duty to a stranger, so as to make his employer liable for the defaults of the stranger,[66] but it may be that the servant himself was negligent in the course of his employment in allowing the stranger to do his job. In *Ilkiw* v. *Samuels*,[67] a lorry driver in the employment of the defendants permitted a stranger to drive his lorry, and an accident resulted from the stranger's negligent driving. The defendants were held liable, not for the stranger's negligence, for he was not their servant,[68] but on the ground that the driver himself had been guilty of negligence in the course of his employment in permitting the stranger to drive without even having inquired whether he was competent to do so.[69] Equally, the master may sometimes be liable even though the servant has usurped the job of another, provided that what he does is sufficiently closely connected with his master's business and is not too gross a departure from the kind of thing he is employed to do. In *Kay* v. *I.T.W. Ltd.*,[70] a storekeeper employed by the defendants needed to return a fork-lift truck to a warehouse but found his way blocked by a large lorry belonging to a third party. Although there was no urgency and without first inquiring for the driver of the lorry, he attempted to move the lorry himself, and by his negligence in doing so caused an injury to the plaintiff. The Court of Appeal considered that the case fell near the borderline, for it cannot be for every act, however excessive, that the servant may do in an attempt to serve his master's interests that the master is liable.[71] Nevertheless, taking into account the fact that it was clearly within the terms of the storekeeper's employment to move certain obstacles out of the way if they blocked the entrance to the warehouse, and since it was part of his normal employment to drive trucks and small vans,[72] the court held that his act of trying to move the lorry was not so gross and extreme as to take it outside the course of his employment.

---

[65] e.g. *Abrahams* v. *Deakin* [1891] 1 Q.B. 516; *Hanson* v. *Waller* [1901] 1 Q.B. 390; *Radley* v. *L.C.C.* (1913) 109 L.T. 162.

[66] *Houghton* v. *Pilkington* [1912] 3 K.B. 308; *Gwilliam* v. *Twist* [1895] 2 Q.B. 84. If the reasoning of Diplock L.J. in *Ilkiw* v. *Samuels* [1963] 1 W.L.R. 991, 1003–1006 is accepted it may be that these cases would be differently decided today.

[67] [1963] 1 W.L.R. 991; *Ricketts* v. *Thomas Tilling Ltd.* [1915] 1 K.B. 644.

[68] [1963] 1 W.L.R. at p. 996, *per* Willmer L.J.

[69] See, however, the different and more complex reasoning of Diplock L.J., *ibid.* at pp. 1003–1006.

[70] [1968] 1 Q.B. 140; *East* v. *Beavis Transport Ltd.* [1969] 1 Lloyd's Rep. 302. *Cf. Beard* v. *London General Omnibus Co.* [1900] 2 Q.B. 530 and see the explanation of that case by Sellers L.J.: [1968] 1 Q.B. at p. 152.

[71] [1968] 1 Q.B. at pp. 151–152, *per* Sellers L.J. It is, however, odd that the master may be vicariously liable for a fraud by the servant against the master's interests, but not liable in some cases when he is seeking to forward those interests: *Iqbal* v. *London Transport Executive* (1973) 16 K.I.R. 329, 336, *per* Megaw L.J.

[72] *Ibid.* at p. 156, *per* Sachs L.J.

Wilful wrong of servant

Next, as to the servant's wilful wrongdoing. Here two rules are well settled.

In the first place the act done may still be in the course of employment even if it was expressly forbidden by the master.[73] The prohibition by the master of an act or class of acts will only protect him from a liability which he would otherwise incur if it actually restricts what it is the servant is employed to do: the mere prohibition of a mode of performing the employment is of no avail.[74] It is a question of fact in each case whether the prohibition relates to the sphere of the employment or to the mode of performance, and " the matter must be looked at broadly, not dissecting the servant's task into its component activities . . . by asking: what was the job on which he was engaged for his employer? "[75]

In *Limpus* v. *London General Omnibus Co.*,[76] a driver of the defendants' omnibus had printed instructions not to race with, or obstruct, other omnibuses. In disobedience to this order he obstructed the plaintiff's omnibus and caused a collision which damaged it. The defendants were held liable because what he did was merely a wrongful, improper and unauthorised mode of doing an act which he was authorised to do, namely, to promote the defendants' passenger-carrying business in competition with their rivals.[77] Again, in *L.C.C.* v. *Cattermoles (Garages) Ltd.*[78] a garage-hand was not allowed to drive vehicles, but it was part of his duty to move them by hand. His employers were held liable for his negligence while driving a vehicle. On the other hand, in *Twine* v. *Bean's Express Ltd.*[79] the employers had expressly forbidden the driver of one of their vans to give a lift to any unauthorised person and affixed a notice to this effect on the dashboard of the van. Nevertheless the driver gave a lift to a person who knew of the breach of instructions and was killed owing to the driver's negligence. The Court of Appeal held that he was not acting within the scope of his employment, and his employers consequently were not liable. " He was doing something that he had no right whatsoever to do, and *qua* the deceased man he was as much

---

[73] *C.P.R.* v. *Lockhart* [1942] A.C. 591, 600, *per* Lord Thankerton; *Ilkiw* v. *Samuels* [1963] 1 W.L.R. 991, 998, *per* Willmer L.J.; *Stone* v. *Taffe* [1974] 1 W.L.R. 1575.

[74] *Plumb* v. *Cobden Flour Mills Ltd.* [1914] A.C. 62, 67, *per* Lord Dunedin; *C.P.R.* v. *Lockhart, supra*, at p. 599, *per* Lord Thankerton; *L.C.C.* v. *Cattermoles (Garages) Ltd.* [1953] 1 W.L.R. 997, 1002, *per* Evershed M.R.; *Ilkiw* v. *Samuels, supra*, *per* Diplock L.J. at p. 1004; *Kay* v. *I.T.W. Ltd.* [1968] 1 Q.B. 140, 158, *per* Sellers L.J. Compare *Ruddiman* v. *Smith* (1889) 60 L.T. 708 with *Stevens* v. *Woodward* (1881) 6 Q.B.D. 318.

[75] *Ilkiw* v. *Samuels, supra*, at p. 1004, *per* Diplock L.J.

[76] (1862) 1 H. & C. 526.

[77] " The law casts upon the master a liability for the act of his servant in the course of his employment; and the law is not so futile as to allow a master, by giving secret instructions to his servant, to discharge himself from liability ": *ibid.* at p. 539, *per* Willes J.; *C.P.R.* v. *Lockhart, supra*; *McKean* v. *Raynor Bros. Ltd.* [1942] 2 All E.R. 591.

[78] [1953] 1 W.L.R. 997; *Ilkiw* v. *Samuels, supra*; *cf. Iqbal* v. *London Transport Executive* (1973) 16 K.I.R. 329.

[79] (1946) 62 T.L.R. 155; affirmed 62 T.L.R. 458; Weir, *Casebook on Tort*, 3rd ed., p. 220.

on a frolic of his own as if he had been driving somewhere on some amusement of his own quite unauthorised by his employers." [80] Giving a lift to an unauthorised person " was not merely a wrongful mode of performing the act of the class this driver was employed to perform but was the performance of an act of a class which he was not employed to perform at all." [81]

In the second place, it does not necessarily follow that the servant is acting outside the scope of his employment because he intended to benefit himself and not his employer. It was generally thought that Willes J. in *Barwick* v. *English Joint Stock Bank* [82] had laid down the rule that the wrong must be intended to benefit the master; but in *Lloyd* v. *Grace, Smith & Co.*[83] the House of Lords surprised the profession by holding not only that this was not the law but also that *Barwick's* case had never been any authority for supposing that it was.[84] In *Lloyd's* case, the defendants, a firm of solicitors, employed a managing clerk who conducted their conveyancing business without supervision. The plaintiff, a widow, owned some cottages. She was dissatisfied with the money which they produced and went to the defendants' office where she saw the clerk, who induced her to give him instructions to sell the cottages and to execute two documents which he falsely told her were necessary for the sale but which in fact were a conveyance of the cottages to himself. He then dishonestly disposed of the property for his own benefit. The Court of Appeal by a majority held that the defendants were not liable for the clerk's fraud [85]; the House of Lords unanimously held that they were liable. It cannot be said, however, that as a result of *Lloyd's* case the question of benefit is invariably irrelevant, for it will still be found in some cases that it is the fact that the servant intended to benefit himself alone that prevents his tort from being in the course of his employment. This will be so, for example, in the case of a driver who takes his master's vehicle " on a frolic of his own." It is because the journey was made solely for the driver's benefit that the master is not liable

---

[80] *Ibid.* at p. 459, *per* Lord Greene M.R.: " In driving his van along a proper route he was acting within the scope of his employment when he ran into the omnibus. The other thing he was doing simultaneously was something totally outside the scope of his employment, namely, giving a lift to a person who had no right whatsoever to be there "; *Conway* v. *George Wimpey & Co. Ltd.* [1951] 2 K.B. 266. *Cf. Young* v. *Edward Box & Co.* [1951] 1 T.L.R. 789. Weir, *Casebook on Tort*, 3rd ed., p. 223.

[81] *Conway* v. *George Wimpey & Co. Ltd.* [1951] 2 K.B. 266, 276, *per* Asquith L.J. Nothing in ss. 143, 145 or 148 of the Road Traffic Act 1972 affects these cases. The reason for the non-liability is not any antecedent agreement between him and the unauthorised hitch-hiker, nor any voluntary assumption of risk by the latter.

[82] (1867) L.R. 2 Ex. 259, 265.

[83] [1912] A.C. 716. See, too, *Uxbridge Permanent, etc. Society* v. *Pickard* [1939] 2 K.B. 248; *British Ry., etc. Co. Ltd.* v. *Roper* (1940) 162 L.T. 217; *United Africa Co.* v. *Saka Owoade* [1955] A.C. 130; *Morris* v. *C. W. Martin & Sons Ltd.* [1966] 1 Q.B. 716. Cases such as *Century Insurance Co. Ltd.* v. *Northern Ireland Road Transport Board* [1942] A.C. 509, *ante,* p. 525, can also be regarded as involving acts done by the servant for his own benefit.

[84] But those who made this error were at any rate in the respectable company of Lord Bowen and Lord Davey, whose dicta in earlier cases were overruled in *Lloyd's* case.

[85] [1911] 2 K.B. 489.

to a person injured by the negligence of the driver. Similarly, if the servant has committed an assault upon the plaintiff, that will be in the course of his employment if his intention was to further his master's business,[86] but if the assault was a mere act of personal vengeance, it will not.[87]

Theft by servant

It was at one time the view that if a servant stole goods his master could not be vicariously liable to their owner on the ground that the act of stealing necessarily took the servant outside the course of his employment.[88] This view fails to recognise, however, that theft by a servant to whom the goods stolen have been entrusted is the dishonest performance by the servant of what he was employed to do honestly, namely, to take care of the goods; and this is sufficient for liability. In *Morris* v. *C. W. Martin & Sons Ltd.*,[89] where some of the older cases were overruled, the plaintiff had sent her fur coat to X to be cleaned, and X, with her permission, sent it on to the defendants, who were specialist cleaners. The defendants handed the coat to their servant, M, for him to clean it, and M stole the coat. It was held by the Court of Appeal that on these facts the defendants were liable.

It is submitted that *Morris* v. *C. W. Martin & Sons Ltd.* could have been decided on the short ground that the servant's tort—conversion of the coat—was a wrongful mode of performing the task entrusted to him by the defendants, namely, cleaning and taking care of the coat, and was thus committed in the course of his employment. The Court of Appeal, however, placed much reliance on the duty owed to the plaintiff by the defendants themselves as bailees of the coat and, in effect, held that the theft of the coat by the servant to whom they had delegated their own duty of reasonable care in respect of it, constituted a breach of that duty. This, no doubt, is an alternative ground for holding the defendants liable, but an essential element of their liability on any ground was that they had entrusted the coat to their servant. Had this not been the case it could not have been said that they had delegated to him their own duty as bailees, nor would the theft have been committed by him in the course of his

---

[86] *Dyer* v. *Munday* [1895] 1 Q.B. 742.

[87] *Warren* v. *Henlys Ltd.* [1948] 2 All E.R. 935. For criticism, see (1949) 65 L.Q.R. 26–28; *Petterson* v. *Royal Oak Hotel Ltd.* [1948] N.Z.L.R. 136; *Daniels* v. *Whetstone Entertainments Ltd.* [1962] 2 Lloyd's Rep. 1. *Cf. Rutherford* v. *Hawke's Bay Hospital Board* [1949] N.Z.L.R. 400; *Smith* v. *Crossley Bros. Ltd.* (1951) 95 S.J. 655.

[88] See *e.g. Cheshire* v. *Bailey* [1905] 1 K.B. 237; *Mintz* v. *Silverton* (1920) 36 T.L.R. 399. *Cf. Abraham* v. *Bullock* (1902) 86 L.T. 796, where the servant negligently facilitated a theft by a stranger and his master was held liable. The master may be primarily liable as *e.g.* where the theft can be attributed to his own negligence in employing a dishonest servant or if his own negligence led to the theft: *Williams* v. *The Curzon Syndicate Ltd.* (1919) 35 T.L.R. 475; *De Parell* v. *Walker* (1932) 49 T.L.R. 37; *Adams (Durham) Ltd.* v. *Trust Houses Ltd.* [1960] 1 Lloyd's Rep. 380.

[89] [1966] 1 Q.B. 716; *Mendelssohn* v. *Normand Ltd.* [1970] 1 Q.B. 177. See Jolowicz [1965] C.L.J. 200; Weir, *Casebook on Tort*, 3rd ed., p. 226.

employment.[90] The result is thus the same whether the case is considered in terms of the defendants' own duty as bailees or in terms of vicarious liability. It is suggested, therefore, that unless there are specific terms in the contract of bailment which displace the general rules of vicarious liability,[91] the simplest approach to the problem of the servant's theft is to inquire whether or not the goods stolen had been entrusted to his care. If this is not the case, then, unless the primary liability of the defendant can somehow be made out, the defendant is not liable: but if it is, then the theft was committed by the servant in the course of his employment and this is sufficient to make the master liable.[92]

Damage to goods bailed

The same approach serves to solve the problem of damage caused by a servant to goods which are the subject of a bailment to his master. If the goods have been entrusted by the master to the care of his servant and the servant negligently damages them, his master will be vicariously liable to their owner, for the servant has done carelessly what he was employed to do carefully, namely, to look after the goods. For this purpose it makes no difference that the servant at the time of his negligence was using the goods improperly for purposes entirely of his own, as, for example, if he uses a car, bailed to his master and entrusted to his care, for taking his friends for a ride, and then negligently damages the car in an accident.[93] He is as much guilty of negligence in looking after the car as he would have been if the accident had occurred while he was using the car for an authorised purpose. Nevertheless some difficulty has been felt to exist in such a case because the servant would, in relation to a third party injured in the same accident, be held to have been " on a frolic of his own." " How can this be? " Lord Denning M.R. has asked.[94] " How can the servant, on one and the same journey, be acting both within and without the course of his employment? " The answer, it is respectfully suggested, is not, as Lord Denning proposes,[95] to abandon the notion of vicarious liability in favour of that of the primary liability of the bailee, but to recognise that the facts relevant to the two claims—that brought by the car owner and that brought by the third party—are different. The car owner's

[90] " I base my decision in this case on the ground that the fur was stolen by the very servant whom the defendants as bailees for reward had employed to take care of it and clean it ": *Morris'* case, *supra*, at p. 737, *per* Diplock L.J.
[91] See *e.g. John Carter (Fine Worsteds) Ltd.* v. *Hanson Haulage (Leeds) Ltd.* [1965] 2 Q.B. 495, where it appears to be recognised that a carrier's liability for a theft by his servant is vicarious: *ibid.* at p. 524, *per* Davies L.J.; *ibid.* at p. 533, *per* Russell L.J.
[92] For a similar approach, see Salmond, *Torts*, 16th ed., pp. 480–481. *Cf. Leesh River Tea Co. Ltd.* v. *British India Steam Navigation Co. Ltd.* [1967] 2 Q.B. 250.
[93] *Coupe Co.* v. *Maddick* [1891] 2 Q.B. 413; *Aitchison* v. *Page Motors Ltd.* (1935) 154 L.T. 128; *Central Motors (Glasgow) Ltd.* v. *Cessnock Garage and Motor Co.*, 1925 S.C. 796. *Cf. Sanderson* v. *Collins* [1904] 1 K.B. 628.
[94] *Morris* v. *C. W. Martin & Sons Ltd.* [1966] 1 Q.B. 716, 724–725. See also Newark, " *Twine* v. *Bean's Express Ltd.*" (1954) 17 M.L.R. 102, 114.
[95] *Ibid.* at p. 725.

claim is based on the fact that the servant was negligent in looking after the car, which he was employed to do. The third party's claim is based upon the fact that the servant was guilty of negligent driving at the time and place in question. And if the servant was using the car for a joy-ride then he was not at that place at that time in the course of his employment.[96]

Fraud of servant

It has been said that there is "no difference in the liability of a master for wrongs whether for fraud or any other wrong committed by a servant in the course of his employment," [97] but this, with respect, is true only on the basis that the question whether a tort is or is not committed by a servant within the course of his employment is regarded as a pure question of fact.[98] If it is conceded that an element of principle is involved, then it must be recognised that cases of fraud raise special problems because of the special character of fraud itself. Of its very nature, fraud involves the persuasion of the victim, by deception, to part with his property or in some other way to act to his own detriment and to the profit of the person practising the fraud. Thus in *Lloyd* v. *Grace, Smith & Co.*[99] the defendants' clerk fraudulently persuaded the plaintiff to transfer her property to him, and what is significant for the purposes of vicarious liability is that it was the position in which he had been placed by the defendants that enabled him to do this. His acts were within the scope of the apparent or ostensible authority with which he had been clothed by the defendants and it is for this reason that they were liable.[1] In *Uxbridge Permanent Benefit Building Society* v. *Pickard*,[2] as in *Lloyd's* case, the clerk had full authority to conduct the business of a solicitor's office in the name and on behalf of his principal. It was not within his actual authority to commit a fraud, but it was within his ostensible authority to perform acts of the kind that come within the business conducted by a solicitor. " So long as he is acting within the scope of that class of act, his employer is bound whether or not the clerk is acting for his own purposes or for his employer's purposes." [3] In torts involving fraud, the

---

[96] See these ideas explained more fully in [1965] C.L.J. 200, 201–203. See also *Twine* v. *Bean's Express Ltd.* (1946) 62 T.L.R. 458, 459, *per* Lord Greene M.R., cited *ante*, p. 527, and note 80.

[97] *United Africa Co. Ltd.* v. *Saka Owoade* [1955] A.C. 130, 144, *per* Lord Oaksey (P.C.).

[98] As was, evidently, the opinion of Lord Oaksey in the *United Africa Co.* case, *supra*, at p. 144.

[99] [1912] A.C. 716, *ante*, pp. 528–529.

[1] " If the agent commits the fraud purporting to act in the course of business such as he was authorised, *or held out as authorised*, to transact on account of his principal, then the latter may be held liable for it ": *ibid.* at p. 725, *per* Earl Loreburn (italics added). See also *ibid.* at pp. 738–739, *per* Lord Macnaghten; *ibid.* at p. 740, *per* Lord Shaw.

[2] [1939] 2 K.B. 248.

[3] *Ibid.* at p. 254, *per* Sir Wilfrid Greene M.R. " In the case of a servant who goes off on a frolic of his own, no question arises of any actual or ostensible authority upon the faith of which some third person is going to change his position. The very essence of the present case is that the actual authority and the ostensible authority to [the clerk] were of a kind which in the ordinary course of an everyday transaction were going to lead third persons, on the faith of them, to change their position ": *ibid.* at pp. 254–255.

question of ostensible or apparent authority arises, but " it is totally different in the case of a servant driving a motor-car or cases of that kind where there is no question of the action of third parties being affected in the least degree by any apparent authority on the part of the servant." [4]

If the servant's fraudulent conduct did not fall within the scope of his authority, actual or ostensible, then the master will not be liable,[5] and in applying this rule it must be borne in mind that the mere fact that the servant's position in his master's service created the opportunity for his tort is not sufficient.[6] What is required is that the plaintiff should have *reasonably* regarded the servant as having been appointed by the defendant to perform that class of acts the dishonest performance of which caused his loss.[7] If this requirement is met, but not otherwise, the servant's fraud will be found to have been committed within the course of his employment and his master will accordingly be liable.

THE MASTER'S INDEMNITY

Vicarious liability being a form of joint liability, the provisions of the Law Reform (Married Women and Tortfeasors) Act 1935, s. 6,[8] may enable the master to recover from his servant some or all of the damages he has had to pay on account of the servant's tort.[9] Additionally, however, the master can in some cases recover damages from his servant at common law, and so, in effect, recoup himself for the damages he has had to pay. In *Lister* v. *Romford Ice and Cold Storage Co.*[10] L. was a lorry driver employed by R. Co. who by his negligent driving in the course of his employment, had caused an injury to his father, another servant of R. Co. R. Co. paid the father's damages and then sued L. It was held that L.'s negligent driving was not only a tort against his father but also a breach of an implied undertaking in

---

[4] *Ibid.* at p. 255.

[5] *Slingsby* v. *District Bank* [1932] 1 K.B. 544.

[6] See *Morris* v. *C. W. Martin & Sons Ltd.* [1966] 1 Q.B. 716, 727, *per* Lord Denning M.R., citing *Ruben* v. *Great Fingall Consolidated* [1906] A.C. 439. See also *Grant* v. *Norway* (1851) 10 C.B. 665; *Coleman* v. *Riches* (1855) 16 C.B. 104; *George Whitchurch Ltd.* v. *Cavanagh* [1902] A.C. 117, 125, *per* Lord Macnaghten. The consequences of the last-named case are reversed by the Companies Act 1948, s. 79.

[7] For full discussion of " apparent authority," see *Freeman and Lockyer* (*A Firm*) v. *Buckhurst Park Properties* (*Mangal*) *Ltd.* [1964] 2 Q.B. 480 and especially *per* Diplock L.J. at pp. 502–505. The case concerned liability in contract, but the master's liability for his servant's fraud is closely related to the principal's liability on contracts entered into by his agent.

[8] 25 & 26 Geo. 5, c. 30. See *post*, pp. 548–551.

[9] For cases in which a full indemnity was awarded to the master under the Act, see *Ryan* v. *Fildes* [1938] 3 All E.R. 517; *Semtex* v. *Gladstone* [1954] 1 W.L.R. 945; *Harvey* v. *O'Dell Ltd.* [1958] 2 Q.B. 78.

[10] [1957] A.C. 555. See also the judgment of the C.A.: [1956] 2 Q.B. 180; Jolowicz, " The Right to Indemnity between Master and Servant " [1956] C.L.J. 101; [1957] C.L.J. 21; Glanville Williams, " Vicarious Liability and the Master's Indemnity " (1957) 20 M.L.R. 220, 437. *Cf. Gregory* v. *Ford* [1951] 1 All E.R. 121. See also *Digby* v. *General Accident Fire and Life Insurance Co.* [1943] A.C. 121.

his contract of service that he would exercise reasonable care,[11] for which R. Co. were entitled to damages equivalent to the amount which they had had to pay to the father. "That an employee who is negligent and causes grave damage to his employers should be heard successfully to say that he should not make any contribution to the resulting damage, is a proposition which does not in the least commend itself to me and I do not see why it should be so. I find that justice, as we conceive justice in these courts, says that the person who caused the damage is the person who must in law be called upon to pay damages arising therefrom." [12]

However, the justice of this decision has not commended itself so strongly to others and the matter was considered by an interdepartmental committee [13] with the result that employers' liability insurers entered into a " gentleman's agreement " not to take advantage of the principle unless there was evidence of collusion or wilful misconduct. Indeed, there are strong grounds for arguing that the *Lister* principle is unjustifiable in modern conditions: the employer would rarely, if ever, wish to take advantage of it because of the disastrous effect on labour relations and the real plaintiff is likely to be an insurer acting under the doctrine of subrogation.[14] If it be objected that to deny the right of indemnity against the servant is to put him above the law, it may be replied that it is sufficient that he is liable to the victim of the tort, though admittedly judgment will rarely be enforced against him.[15]

There is, however, one important limit to the principle of *Lister's* case. The decision in that case constitutes, in effect, an exception to the common law rule of *Merryweather* v. *Nixan* [16] that there can be no contribution between joint tortfeasors, for that rule was held not to apply in the case of plaintiffs whose liability " arose solely from the fact that they were answerable for the negligence of the

---

[11] See *Harmer* v. *Cornelius* (1858) 5 C.B.(N.S.) 236.

[12] *Semtex* v. *Gladstone* [1954] 1 W.L.R. 945, 953, *per* Finnemore J., cited with approval in the *Lister* case in the C.A. at [1956] 2 Q.B. 213, *per* Romer L.J. In *Harvey* v. *O'Dell Ltd.* [1958] 2 Q.B. 78 McNair J. held that a servant's implied undertaking to exercise reasonable care extended only to those acts which he was specifically employed to do and that therefore the negligent *driving* of the servant, who was employed as a store-keeper, did not constitute a breach of his contract of service. Whatever one's views of the basic principle of *Lister's* case, it is submitted that *Harvey* v. *O'Dell* is an unsound restriction on that principle: see Jolowicz, " The Master's Indemnity—Variations on a Theme " (1959) 22 M.L.R. 71, 189, at pp. 73–76. *Cf.* Lord Denning M.R. in *Vandyke* v. *Fender* [1970] 2 Q.B. 292, 303.

[13] Report published 1959. See Gardiner (1959) 22 M.L.R. 652.

[14] See Parsons, " Individual Responsibility Versus Enterprise Liability " (1956) 29 A.L.J. 714. Despite the " gentlemen's agreement " referred to above, *Lister's* case is not dead: see *Morris* v. *Ford Motor Co. Ltd.* [1973] 2 W.L.R. 843, where the right was sought to be exercised by a third party who was bound to indemnify the employer; Weir, " Subrogation and Indemnity " (privately published case note, 1973).

[15] Weir, *loc. cit.*, comments, " the devices of subrogation and indemnity are not part of the law of tort at all, whose role is exhausted once the primary victim is paid." The employer is equally " above the law " so long as his policy is valid and his insurers are solvent.

[16] (1799) 8 T.R. 186.

defendant himself." [17] If, therefore, the master has himself, or through some other servant, been guilty of culpable fault, the principle of *Lister's* case does not apply and the master can only recover, if at all, under the Act of 1935.[18]

LIABILITY FOR AGENTS: VEHICLE DRIVERS

Thus far we have spoken of the relationship of master and servant. However, many cases on vicarious liability speak in the language of agency and numerous dicta can be found equating agency with a contract of service for this purpose.[19] It has recently been said on high authority that in principle the law governing vicarious liability for servants and agents is the same and depends upon the question, " was the servant or agent acting on behalf of, and within the scope of the authority conferred by the master or principal? " The answer will often differ simply because the authority of a servant is usually more general.[20] While this may be so in the field of economic torts or for such matters as fraud, it can hardly be true for liability for accidents, since it is clearly established that the principal is not liable (except in certain isolated instances) for accidents caused by the negligence of his independent contractors performing the tasks entrusted to them.[21]

Whatever may be the correct principle as to liability for agents, it is convenient to treat here a doctrine which fits easily into no existing legal category [22] but which has developed because of the insurance position in relation to road traffic liability. The doctrine may be stated as follows. Where A, the owner [23] of a vehicle, expressly or impliedly requests or

---

[17] [1956] 2 Q.B. at p. 210, *per* Romer L.J. This aspect of the problem was not considered by the House of Lords. See Jolowicz [1957] C.L.J. 21.

[18] *Jones* v. *Manchester Corporation* [1952] 2 Q.B. 852. " A chauffeur who, through negligence, causes damage for which his employer is held responsible, may well be liable to his master. On the other hand, if the chauffeur is young and inexperienced, and is suddenly told to drive another and bigger car or lorry, which he does not understand, and an accident follows, it is by no means certain that the employer will be entitled to an indemnity ": *ibid.* at p. 865, *per* Singleton L.J.

[19] See Atiyah, *op. cit.*, Ch. 9.

[20] *Heatons Transport (St. Helens) Ltd.* v. *T.G.W.U.* [1973] A.C. 15, 99. The judgments in the Court of Appeal in this case should also be looked at: [1973] A.C. 39. The case was not an action in tort, but for an " unfair industrial practice " under the Industrial Relations Act 1971. Lord Wilberforce disclaimed any intention to deal with tort liability: see p. 100.

[21] See pp. 536–540, *post.* An independent contractor will commonly be an " agent " in the sense in which that term is generally understood. A servant acting on my behalf is always an agent, though the reverse is not necessarily true. Sometimes, of course, a question arises of liability for a third party who is not servant, nor agent, nor independent contractor: *e.g.* the manufacturer in *Davie* v. *New Merton Board Mills Ltd.* [1959] A.C. 604, pp. 154–156, *ante.*

[22] Winfield sought to explain the doctrine in terms of " casual delegation " of the use of a chattel, but the leading case now talks in terms of agency: *Morgans* v. *Launchbury* [1973] A.C. 127. The doctrine has been applied to a boat (*The Thelma (Owners)* v. *The Endymion (Owners)* [1953] 2 Lloyd's Rep. 613) but it seems unlikely that it applies to all chattels. It *might* be possible to bring the cases within the rubric of master and servant, but only at the price of admitting that one may be a servant though rendering only a single, gratuitous service. *Cf.* Lord Denning in a review (1947) 63 L.Q.R. 517; Salmond, *Torts*, 16th ed., p. 470; *Gramak Ltd.* v. *O'Connor* (1973) 41 D.L.R. (3d) 14.

[23] Ownership as such is probably not necessary: *Nottingham* v. *Aldridge* [1971] 2 Q.B. 739. In *Morgans* v. *Launchbury, infra*, the husband was held liable for the negligence of

instructs B to drive the vehicle in performance of some task or duty carried out for A, A will be vicariously liable for B's negligence in the operation of the vehicle.[24] Thus in *Ormrod* v. *Crosville Motor Services Ltd.*[25] A, the owner of a car, asked B to drive the car from Birkenhead to Monte Carlo, where they were to start a holiday together. It was held that A was liable for B's negligent driving even though B might be said to be partly pursuing his own interests in driving A's car. On the other hand, liability was not imposed in *Morgans* v. *Launchbury* [26] where the husband, who normally used his wife's car to go to work, got a third person to drive him home after visits to several public houses. In no sense was the husband acting as his wife's agent in using the car for his work and still less was the third person her agent.[27] It is now clear that mere permission to drive without any interest or concern of the owner in the driving does not make the owner vicariously liable,[28] nor is there any doctrine of the " family car." [29] Where, however, the facts of the relationship between owner and driver are not fully known, proof of ownership may give rise to a presumption that the driver was acting as the owner's agent.[30]

The development of a separate head of vicarious liability for vehicle drivers has clearly been prompted by a desire to ensure a claim-worthy defendant, but the House of Lords has now denied that the courts may go on a voyage of discovery into the insurance position in these cases and has said that any alteration of the law must be left to the legislature with its superior capacity for making decisions of policy.[31] However, to confine our attention in this context to instances of vicarious liability risks giving a false impression. If there is in force a policy of insurance covering the liability of the driver [32] there will generally be no point in suing the owner. If, on the other hand, the owner

---

the driver and there was no appeal against that decision. If an owner bails his vehicle to A and A gets B to drive it, the owner is not liable for B's negligence: *Chowdhary* v. *Gillot* [1947] 2 All E.R. 541.

[24] *Morgans* v. *Launchbury* [1973] A.C. 127.

[25] [1953] 1 W.L.R. 1120; Weir, *Casebook on Tort*, 3rd ed., p. 248. See also *Samson* v. *Aitchison* [1912] A.C. 844; *Pratt* v. *Patrick* [1924] 1 K.B. 488; *Parker* v. *Miller* (1926) 42 T.L.R. 408; *The Trust Co. Ltd.* v. *De Silva* [1956] 1 W.L.R. 376, P.C.; *Vandyke* v. *Fender* [1970] 2 Q.B. 292. The germ of the doctrine which was originally based on a " right of control," may have appeared in *Booth* v. *Mister* (1835) 7 C. & P. 66. Brooke-Smith, " Liability for the Negligence of Another—Servant or Agent " (1954) 70 L.Q.R. 253.

[26] [1973] A.C. 127.

[27] *Cf.* the valiant attempt of Lord Denning M.R. and Edmund Davies L.J. in the C.A. to fit the facts into a traditional agency framework: [1971] 2 Q.B. 245.

[28] *Morgans* v. *Launchbury, supra*; *Hewitt* v. *Bonvin* [1940] 1 K.B. 188 (father permitting son to take girlfriends home in car); *cf. Carberry* v. *Davies* [1968] 1 W.L.R. 1103 (owner suggesting to driver that he take owner's son out in car). See also *Britt* v. *Galmoye* (1928) 44 T.L.R. 294; *Higbid* v. *Hammett* (1932) 49 T.L.R. 104; *Norton* v. *Canadian Pacific Steamships Ltd.* [1961] 1 W.L.R. 1957. A person who has " borrowed " a car, with or without the owner's permission is not acting as his agent when driving it back to him: *Klein* v. *Caluori* [1971] 1 W.L.R. 619.

[29] *Cf.* the view of Lord Denning M.R. in *Launchbury* v. *Morgans* [1971] 2 Q.B. 245.

[30] *Barnard* v. *Sully* (1931) 47 T.L.R. 557; *Rambarran* v. *Gurrucharan* [1970] 1 W.L.R. 556; *Morgans* v. *Launchbury, supra*, at p. 139, *per* Viscount Dilhorne.

[31] *Morgans* v. *Launchbury, supra. Cf.* Jolowicz [1972A] C.L.J. 209.

[32] *e.g.* under a " named driver " clause in the policy.

has permitted an uninsured driver to drive, then, whether or not he is vicariously liable, he will be liable for breach of statutory duty under *Monk* v. *Warbey* [33] if the driver is unable to satisfy the judgment. In other words, the owner will nearly always be liable in these cases, but if the liability is of the *Monk* v. *Warbey* type he will have to meet it out of his own pocket.[34]

EMPLOYER AND INDEPENDENT CONTRACTOR

In principle an employer is not responsible for the torts of his independent contractor. It is no exception to say that he is liable (a) for torts authorised or ratified by him or where the contractor is employed to do an illegal act, for here they are both liable as joint tortfeasors,[35] or (b) for his own negligence (c) Cases of strict liability are sometimes treated as exceptions, but it is doubtful if they are so in theory. (d) Nor is it an exception that he is liable if he personally interferes with the contractor or his servants and in fact directs the manner in which the work is to be done, for he is then again liable as a joint tortfeasor.[36]

It is submitted that the true question in every case in which an employer is sued for damage caused by his independent contractor is whether the employer himself was in breach of some duty which he himself owed to the plaintiff.[37] Such a breach of duty may exist if the employer has not taken care to select a competent contractor or has employed an inadequate number of men.[38] It may also exist if the contractor alone has been at fault, provided that the duty cast upon the employer is of the kind commonly described as " non-delegable." [39] Strictly speaking no duty is delegable,[40] but if my duty is merely to take reasonable care, then, if I have taken care to select a competent con-

---

[33] See p. 131, *ante*.

[34] It should be noted that at the time of the accident in *Morgans* v. *Launchbury* insurance for passengers was not còmpulsory. It now is, and in consequence a victim who cannot find an insured defendant may be able to recover his damages from the Motor Insurers' Bureau, subject to assignment of his judgment to that body. For the M.I.B. agreements, see Ivamy, *Fire and Motor Insurance*, 2nd ed., App. XI.

[35] *Ellis* v. *Sheffield Gas Consumers Co.* (1853) 2 El. & Bl. 767. The defendants, *without authority*, employed contractor to dig trench in street for gas pipes. Contractor's servants carelessly left heap of stones on footpath; plaintiff fell over them and was injured. The contract was to do an illegal act, a public nuisance, and defendants were liable.

[36] *M'Laughlin* v. *Pryor* (1842) 4 Man. & G. 48; *Hardaker* v. *Idle D.C.* [1896] 1 Q.B. 335. In *Brooke* v. *Bool* [1928] 2 K.B. 578 the defendant was held liable on the basis of participation in a joint enterprise. It is respectfully submitted that *Scarsbrook* v. *Mason* [1961] 3 All E.R. 767 takes this much too far: see Jolowicz [1962] C.L.J. 24 and *Bown* v. *Chatfield* [1963] C.L.Y. 2348 (Cty. Ct.).

[37] *Salsbury* v. *Woodland* [1970] 1 Q.B. 324, 347, *per* Sachs L.J.

[38] *Pinn* v. *Rew* (1916) 32 T.L.R. 451.

[39] For criticism of this term, and generally, see Glanville Williams, " Liability for Independent Contractors " [1956] C.L.J. 180. See also Chapman, " Liability for the Negligence of Independent Contractors " (1934) 50 L.Q.R. 71; Barak, " Mixed and Vicarious Liability—A Suggested Distinction " (1966) 29 M.L.R. 160 (where the point is made that the liability under discussion here is neither truly vicarious not yet truly personal, for the defendant is held liable for damage which he did not himself cause by his own act).

[40] *Cassidy* v. *Ministry of Health* [1951] 2 K.B. 343, 363, *per* Denning L.J.

tractor to do the work, I have done all that is required of me.[41] If, on the other hand, my duty is, *e.g.* " to provide that care is taken " [42] or is to achieve some actual result such as the secure fencing of dangerous parts of machinery,[43] then my duty is not performed unless care is taken or the machinery is fenced. It is no defence that I delegated the task to an independent contractor if he failed to fulfil his duties.

It is a question of law whether the duty in a given case is " non-delegable," but unfortunately, so far as common law duties are concerned, little by way of principle is to be gathered from the cases.[44] We must content ourselves, therefore, with a number of examples.

1. Cases of strict liability at common law

(i) *Withdrawal of support from neighbouring land*

This furnished the earliest example of a " non-delegable " duty at common law. If A, in the course of work done on his land causes subsidence on B's adjoining land and B's land is entitled to the support of A, A is liable to B, and it is no defence that the work had been entrusted to an independent contractor.[45]

(ii) *Operations on or adjoining a highway other than normal user for the purpose of passage*

In *Tarry* v. *Ashton* [46] the defendant employed an independent contractor to repair a lamp attached to his house and overhanging the footway. As it was not securely fastened the lamp fell on the plaintiff, a passer-by, and the defendant was held liable, because " it was the defendant's duty to make the lamp reasonably safe . . . the contractor has failed to do that . . . therefore the defendant has not done his duty and is liable to the plaintiff for the consequences." [47] In *Gray* v. *Pullen* [48]

---

[41] See *Phillips* v. *Britannia Hygienic Laundry Co.* [1923] 1 K.B. 539; *Stennett* v. *Hancock* [1939] 2 All E.R. 578; *Salsbury* v. *Woodland* [1970] 1 Q.B. 324.

[42] *The Pass of Ballater* [1942] P. 112, 117, *per* Langton J. See also *The Lady Gwendolen* [1965] P. 294, where Winn L.J. (at p. 350) described the duty owed by a shipowner to other ships and to persons who might be affected by the navigation of his own ships as a duty " that all concerned in any capacity with the navigation of those ships should exercise such care as a reasonable person would exercise in that capacity."

[43] Factories Act 1961, s. 14 (1).

[44] Glanville Williams, *loc. cit. Cf.* Jolowicz, " Liability for Independent Contractors in the English Common Law—A Suggestion " (1957) 9 Stanford L.Rev. 690. In *Salsbury* v. *Woodland, supra.* the Court of Appeal proceeded upon the assumption that there was simply a limited number of special exceptions to the general rule of non-liability for the negligence of independent contractors.

[45] *Bower* v. *Peate* (1876) 1 Q.B.D. 321; *Dalton* v. *Angus* (1881) 6 App.Cas. 740; *Hughes* v. *Percival* (1883) 8 App.Cas. 443.

[46] (1876) 1 Q.B.D. 314.

[47] *Ibid.* 319, *per* Blackburn J.

[48] (1864) 5 B. & S. 970; *Hole* v. *Sittingbourne Ry.* (1861) 6 H. & N. 488 (bridge obstructing navigation); *Hardaker* v. *Idle D.C.* [1896] 1 Q.B. 335 (gas main broken by failure to pack soil round it while constructing a sewer); *Penny* v. *Wimbledon U.D.C.* [1899] 2 Q.B. 72 (heap of soil left unlighted in road); *Pickard* v. *Smith* (1861) 10 C.B.(N.S.) 314 (cellar flap on railway platform left open); *Daniel* v. *Rickett, etc.* [1938] 2 K.B. 322 (cellar flap left open on pavement); *Holliday* v. *National Telephone Co.* [1899] 2 Q.B. 392 (explosion in highway caused by dipping benzoline lamp in molten solder); *Walsh* v. *Holst & Co. Ltd.* [1958] 1 W.L.R. 800 (building operations adjoining highway).

the defendant owned a house adjoining a highway and had statutory authority to cut a trench across the road to make a drain from his premises to a sewer. For this purpose he employed a contractor who negligently filled in the trench improperly and the plaintiff, a passenger on the highway, was injured. The defendant was held liable although he was not negligent. On the other hand, in *Salsbury* v. *Woodland* [49] the defendant had employed an apparently competent contractor to fell a tree in the front garden of his house near the highway. Done competently this would have involved no risk to anyone, but owing to the negligence of the contractor, the tree fouled some telephone wires, causing them to fall into the highway, and an accident resulted in which the plaintiff was injured. The Court of Appeal held that these facts did not bring the case within the special category comprising cases of work done on the highway [50] and that there was no equivalent category comprising cases in which work is done *near* the highway. Accordingly the general principle applied and the defendant was not liable for the negligence of the independent contractor.

(iii) *Other cases of strict liability*

The rule in *Rylands* v. *Fletcher*,[51] damage by fire,[52] and, in some cases, nuisance,[53] impose a liability for the default of an independent contractor. Analogous to these instances is a class of " extra hazardous acts, that is, acts which, in their very nature, involve in the eyes of the law special danger to others " [54] such as acts causing fire and explosion, where an employer cannot escape liability by delegating their performance to an independent contractor.[55] He has not merely a duty to take care, but a duty to provide that care is taken, where implements or substances dangerous in themselves, such as flame-bearing instruments or explosives are necessarily incidental to the work to be performed.[56] In *Honeywill and Stein Ltd.* v. *Larkin Bros. Ltd.*[57] it was held that the

---

[49] [1970] 1 Q.B. 324; Weir, *Casebook on Tort*, 3rd ed., p. 244.

[50] Widgery L.J. observed that the cases within this category would be found on analysis to be cases where the work done was of a character which would have been a nuisance unless authorised by statute: [1970] 1 Q.B. at p. 338. *Cf. ibid.* at p. 348, *per* Sachs L.J.

[51] (1866) L.R. 1 Ex. 265; (1868) L.R. 3 H.L. 330.

[52] *Black* v. *Christchurch Finance Co.* [1894] A.C. 48; *Spicer* v. *Smee* [1946] 1 All E.R. 489; *Balfour* v. *Barty-King* [1957] 1 Q.B. 496; *H. N. Emanuel Ltd.* v. *G.L.C., The Times*, March 10, 1971. *Cf. Eriksen* v. *Clifton* [1963] N.Z.L.R. 705 (Sup.Ct. of N.Z.).

[53] *Matania* v. *National Provincial Bank* (1936) 155 L.T. 74 (nuisance by dust and noise the inevitable consequence of extensive building operations), *ante*, p. 336. The duty of a bailee for reward is also non-delegable: *B.R.S.* v. *A. V. Crutchley & Co. Ltd.* [1968] 1 All E.R. 811. See too *Riverstone Meat Co. Pty. Ltd.* v. *Lancashire Shipping Co. Ltd.* [1961] A.C. 807. *Cf. W. Angliss & Co. (Australia) Pty. Ltd.* v. *P. & O. Steam Navigation Co.* [1927] 2 K.B. 456; *Leesh River Tea Co. Ltd.* v. *British India Steam Navigation Co. Ltd.* [1967] 2 Q.B. 250.

[54] The existence of this class of case is confirmed by *Salsbury* v. *Woodland* [1970] 1 Q.B. 324, but see Clerk and Lindsell, *Torts*, 13th ed., pp. 154–155.

[55] *Honeywill and Stein Ltd.* v. *Larkin Bros. Ltd.* [1934] 1 K.B. 191, 197, *per* Slesser L.J.

[56] *The Pass of Ballater* [1942] P. 112, 117, *per* Langton J.; *Brooke* v. *Bool* [1928] 2 K.B. 578, 587, *per* Talbot J.

[57] [1934] 1 K.B. 191; *Municipality of County of Cape Breton* v. *Chappell's Ltd.* (1963) 36 D.L.R. (2d) 58 (Nova Scotia Supreme Court); *Peters* v. *North Star Oil Ltd.* (1965) 54 D.L.R. (2d) 364 (Manitoba Q.B.). *Bluett* v. *King Core Demolition Services* (1973) 227 E.G. 503.

plaintiffs who procured the defendants as independent contractors to take photographs of X's cinema by flashlight were liable for the defendants' negligence is setting fire to X's cinema.

(iv) *The master's common law duties*

The master's common law duties in respect of his servant's safety as laid down in *Wilsons and Clyde Coal Co. v. English* [58] are probably " non delegable." This matter has already been dealt with.[59]

2. Cases of statutory duty

" Where a special duty is laid by statute on an individual or class of individuals either to take care or even to ensure safety (an absolute duty in the true sense) . . . they cannot in any way escape from or evade the full implication of and responsibility for that duty: *Smith v. Cammell Laird & Co. Ltd.*" [60] Whether the duty is absolute in this sense depends upon the true construction of the statute. Many of the duties imposed by the Factories Act 1961, *e.g.* to guard dangerous machinery, are absolute.[61] Where a statute authorises something to be done which would otherwise be illegal, the duty is generally such that there is liability if the work is done by an independent contractor.[62]

Collateral or casual negligence of independent contractor

There is a recognised exception that an employer is not liable for the collateral or casual negligence of an independent contractor, that is, negligence in some collateral respect, as distinct from negligence with regard to the very matter delegated to be done.[63] The distinction between the two kinds of negligence is difficult to draw [64] but is established by the cases. In *Padbury* v. *Holliday and Greenwood Ltd.*[65] the defendants

---

[58] [1938] A.C. 57.

[59] *Ante*, pp. 153–156.

[60] [1940] A.C. 242, *per* Langton J. in *The Pass of Ballater* [1942] P. 112, 117; *Donaghey* v. *Boulton and Paul Ltd.* [1968] A.C. 1.

[61] *Hosking* v. *De Havilland Aircraft Co. Ltd.* [1949] 1 All E.R. 540; *Galashiels Gas Co. Ltd.* v. *O'Donnell* [1940] A.C. 275; *Lochgelly Iron and Coal Co.* v. *M'Mullan* [1934] A.C. 1, 8–9, *per* Lord Atkin. ·

[62] Chapman, *loc. cit.*, at p. 78, citing *Hardaker* v. *Idle D.C.* [1896] 1 Q.B. 335, 351, *per* Rigby L.J.; *Darling* v. *Att.-Gen.* [1950] 2 All E.R. 793 (Minister of Works having statutory *power* to do work on land liable for negligence of independent contractor in leaving heap of timber on field which injured plaintiff's horse). See Baker, " Independent Contractors and the Liability of their Principals " (1954) 27 Australian L.J. 546.

[63] *Pickard* v. *Smith* (1861) 10 C.B.(N.S.) 470, 480, *per* Williams J.: " If an independent contractor is employed to do a lawful act, and in the course of the work he or his servants commit some casual act of wrong or negligence, the employer is not answerable. . . . The rule, however, is inapplicable to cases in which the act which occasions the injury is the one which the contractor was employed to do." " It is settled law that one employing another is not liable for his collateral negligence unless the relation of master and servant exists between them ": *per* Lord Blackburn, *Dalton* v. *Angus* (1881) 6 App.Cas. 740, 829; *Cassidy* v. *Ministry of Health* [1951] 2 K.B. 343, 363–364, *per* Denning L.J.

[64] See the criticism of Sachs L.J. in *Salsbury* v. *Woodland* [1970] 1 Q.B. 324, 348. Prosser, *Torts*, 4th ed., p. 475, suggests that the test of collateral negligence is not its character as a minor incident or operative detail of the work to be done, but rather its dissociation from any inherent risk created by the work itself. See also Jolowicz, *loc. cit.*, pp. 707–708.

[65] (1912) 28 T.L.R. 494.

employed a subcontractor to put metallic casements into the windows of a house which the defendants were building. While one of these casements was being put in, an iron tool was placed by a servant of the subcontractor on the window sill, and the casement having been blown in by the wind, the tool fell and injured the plaintiff in the street below. The tool was not placed on the window sill in the ordinary course of doing the work which the subcontractor was employed to do. It was held that the plaintiff's injuries were caused by an act of collateral negligence and the defendants were not liable. In *Holliday* v. *National Telephone Co.*[66] the defendants were laying telephone wires under a street and employed an independent contractor to make certain connections. A plumber employed by the contractor dipped a blowlamp into molten solder causing an explosion which injured the plaintiff. In the court below Willes J., in no uncertain terms, treated this as an act of collateral negligence, but the Court of Appeal reversed his decision and held the defendants were liable. If an employer has a lamp which overhangs the highway, he himself is under a duty to passers-by to use reasonable care to see that it is safe. He is liable if his independent contractor fails to discover a defect which a reasonable man would have discovered, and in consequence a pedestrian is injured. He is not liable if the contractor drops a hammer on a pedestrian, because that is casual or collateral negligence, not negligence in the employer's department of duty.[67]

THE BASIS OF VICARIOUS LIABILITY

The theoretical basis of the rule that a master is liable for the torts of his servants committed in the course of their employment cannot even today be regarded as finally settled.[68] As we have seen, so long as the liability was thought to depend on the fact that the master had, expressly or impliedly, authorised the servant's tort it was at least theoretically a primary one. The master was himself guilty of a tort against the plaintiff.[69] Once it was decided that the absence of the relationship of master and servant between the defendant and the wrongdoer was fatal to liability in certain cases, however, the liability of the master came to

---

[66] [1899] 2 Q.B. 392. *Cf. Reedie* v. *L. & N.W. Ry.* (1849) 4 Ex. 244 (railway company employed contractor to build a bridge. Contractor's workman negligently caused the death of a person, passing beneath along the highway, by allowing a stone to drop on him. Railway company held not liable). " I am not liable if my contractor in making a bridge happens to drop a brick . . . but I am liable if he makes a bridge which will not open . . . The liability of the employer depends on the existence of a duty . . . it only extends to the limit of that duty. I owe a duty with regard to the structure of the bridge; I owe a duty to see that my bridge will open; but I owe no duty with regard to the disposition of bricks and hammers in the course of construction ": Chapman, *loc. cit.*, 80–81.

[67] Equally, it is submitted, he is not liable if the contractor, by his negligent driving, causes an accident on the way to or from the place of work.

[68] Laski, " The Basis of Vicarious Liability " (1916) 26 Yale L.J. 105; Hughes and Hudson, " The Nature of a Master's Liability in the Law of Tort " (1953) 31 Can.Bar Rev. 18; Glanville Williams, " Vicarious Liability: Tort of the Master or the Servant " (1956) 72 L.Q.R. 522.

[69] *Ante*, pp. 517–518.

be treated as a case apart.[70] As was stated at the beginning of this chapter, the necessary and sufficient conditions for liability are that the relationship of master and servant should exist and that the servant should have committed the tort in the course of his employment. Nothing turns on any duty which the master may himself owe to the plaintiff. " To make a master liable for the conduct of his servant the first question is to see whether the servant is liable. If the answer is Yes, the second question is to see whether the employer must shoulder the servant's liability." [71]

Nevertheless, in *Twine* v. *Bean's Express Ltd.*,[72] Uthwatt J. said that the law attributes to the employer the acts of a servant done in the course of his employment, that, generally, the duty of both master and servant is the same, but that that is a coincidence and not a rule of law. " The general question in an action against an employer, . . . is technically: ' Did the employer in the circumstances which affected him owe a duty ' —for the law does not attribute to the employer the liability which attaches to the servant." [73] These observations have led to a second view as to the basis of a master's vicarious liability, expressed as follows: " It is the master who owes a duty to the plaintiff, and who breaks it as a result of the acts and mental states of his servant. In discussing the liability of the master it is not necessary to consider whether the servant owes a duty to the plaintiff or had committed a tort. A master may be under a so-called vicarious liability even though the servant has not committed any tort or any actionable tort." [74]

It is submitted that neither on principle nor on the balance of authority does this view represent the law. As to principle, it is difficult, if not impossible, to reconcile insistence on the presence of the specific master and servant relationship with the view that the master is primarily liable for breach of his own duty. If the act of B has the legal result that A's duty to C is broken, then A is liable to C whatever his relationship to B. Furthermore, if the master's liability is primary, how does the law distinguish between that liability and liability for damage caused by an independent contractor? The latter is undoubtedly a primary liability based upon a breach by the employer of a duty which he himself owes

---

[70] *Reedie* v. *London and North Western Ry.* (1849) 4 Exch. 244, *ante*, p. 518.

[71] *Young* v. *Edward Box & Co. Ltd.* [1951] 1 T.L.R. 789, 793, *per* Denning L.J.; *Launchbury* v. *Morgans* [1971] 2 W.L.R. 602, 606, *per* Lord Denning M.R. The Crown Proceedings Act 1947, s. 2 (1), and the Police Act 1964, s. 48, adopt this view. It does, however, seem to be the case that an occupier cannot be held vicariously liable for the breach of duty of his servant whereby damage is caused to an entrant upon his premises. The occupier's liability depends exclusively upon his own duty to the entrant; *Herrington* v. *B.R.B.* [1971] 2 W.L.R. 477, 486, *per* Salmon L.J. See too *Perkowski* v. *Wellington Corporation* [1959] A.C. 53 and *cf. Commissioner for Railways* v. *McDermott* [1967] 1 A.C. 169.

[72] [1946] 1 All E.R. 202, *ante*, p. 527; *Norton* v. *Canadian Pacific Steamships* [1961] 1 W.L.R. 1057, 1063, *per* Pearson L.J.

[73] *Ibid.* at p. 204. *Cf.* Newark, " *Twine* v. *Bean's Express Ltd.*" (1954) 17 M.L.R. 102.

[74] Glanville Williams, *Crown Proceedings*, p. 43. *W. B. Anderson & Sons Ltd.* v. *Rhodes (Liverpool) Ltd.* [1967] 2 All E.R. 850. But see Dias [1967] C.L.J. 155.

to the plaintiff.[75] If this is true also of liability for servants, how are we to explain, for example, that a man is liable for the negligent driving of his chauffeur (servant) but not for that of his taxi-driver (independent contractor)?[76]

So far as authority is concerned, though Uthwatt J.'s approach can find some support in decisions in the Court of Appeal and elsewhere,[77] its correctness has been denied on at least two occasions in the House of Lords. In *Staveley Iron and Chemical Co. Ltd.* v. *Jones*,[78] while recognising that a master may be liable for the breach of his own personal duty to his servants, it was held that this was something different from vicarious liability. " Cases . . . where an employer's liability is vicarious are wholly distinct from cases where an employer is under a personal liability to carry out a duty imposed upon him as an employer by common law or statute." [79] Again in *I.C.I.* v. *Shatwell* [80] it plainly stated that if the servant himself was not liable then the master could not be held liable either. " Since in this case the employer, if liable at all, is liable only by virtue of vicarious responsibility, I agree that the primary issue if the respondent . . . is to succeed here, is whether he could maintain an action for damages against (his fellow servant)." [81]

To deny that the master's liability rests upon a notional breach of his own duty brought about by the act of his servant is not, of course, to deny that a master may sometimes be liable for breach of his own duty even though the act causing the damage was done by his servant. Wherever the law imposes a duty of the kind known as " non-delegable " upon A and the act of B produces the result that that duty is broken, A is liable whatever his relationship with B. So in all the cases in which a defendant has been held liable for the acts of his independent contractor the result would have been exactly the same if the defendant had stood in the relation of master to the actual wrongdoer. A master may thus in some cases be liable on two separate grounds.[82] He may be primarily

---

[75] *Salsbury* v. *Woodland* [1970] 1 Q.B. 324, 336–337, *per* Widgery L.J.; *ibid.* at p. 345, *per* Harman L.J.; *ibid.* at p. 347, *per* Sachs L.J.

[76] See *Cassidy* v. *Ministry of Health* [1951] 2 K.B. 343, 363, *per* Denning L.J. " If I am at home while my servant is driving my car on the highway, I personally owe no duty to road users in respect of that car, but my servant does owe a duty, and if he injures someone through his negligence, I am inflicted with his liability ": Chapman, " Liability for the Negligence of Independent Contractors " (1934) 50 L.Q.R. 71, 75.

[77] In addition to cases already cited, see *Conway* v. *George Wimpey & Co. Ltd.* [1951] 2 K.B. 266; *Smith* v. *Moss* [1940] 1 K.B. 424; *Broom* v. *Morgan* [1953] 1 Q.B. 597; *Tooth & Co. Ltd.* v. *Tillyer* (1956) 95 C.L.R. 605 (H.Ct. of Aust.); *Darling Island Stevedoring Co. Ltd.* v. *Long* (1957) 97 C.L.R. 36 (H.Ct. of Aust.); *Morris* v. *C. W. Martin & Sons Ltd.* [1966] 1 Q.B. 716.

[78] [1956] A.C. 627; Weir, *Casebook on Tort*, 3rd ed., p. 216. See also *Harrison* v. *N.C.B.* [1951] A.C. 639; *N.C.B.* v. *England* [1954] A.C. 403. It is doubtful whether the decision in *Lister* v. *Romford Ice and Cold Storage Co. Ltd.* [1957] A.C. 555 could have been reached on the basis that the master is primarily liable. See *ante*, pp. 532–534.

[79] [1956] A.C. at p. 639, *per* Lord Morton.   [80] [1965] A.C. 656.

[81] *Ibid.* at p. 676, *per* Viscount Radcliffe. See also *ibid.* at p. 670, *per* Lord Reid; *ibid.* at p. 681, *per* Lord Hodson; *ibid.* at p. 686, *per* Lord Pearce; *ibid.* at p. 694, *per* Lord Donovan.

[82] See Barak, " Mixed and Vicarious Liability—A Suggested Distinction " (1966) 29 M.L.R. 160; Street, *Governmental Liability*, p. 36, citing *R.* v. *Anthony* [1946] 3 D.L.R. 577, 585, *per* Rand J.

liable for the breach, through his servant, of his own " non-delegable " duty; and he may at the same time and on the same facts also be liable vicariously for the tort of his servant committed in the course of the employment. Where this is so, though it is desirable that the two forms of liability should be kept distinct, it is natural that they should sometimes be confused. In *Morris* v. *C. W. Martin & Sons Ltd.*,[83] for example, the defendants owed the plaintiff the duty of a bailee for reward and it was to this duty that the Court of Appeal directed most of its attention. As has already been suggested, however, the same result could have been more easily achieved had the court concentrated on the defendant's vicarious liability. Conversely, in the hospital cases,[84] where there are obvious difficulties in holding that some of the persons concerned with the treatment of the plaintiff, such as visiting surgeons or consultants, are " servants " of the hospital authority, it may be easier to determine the question of liability by reference to the hospital authority's own duty to its patients. If a breach of that duty can be shown, then the precise relationship between the authority and the negligent surgeon or consultant does not matter. Nevertheless, the fact that vicarious and primary liability can co-exist on the same facts does not make them identical conceptions, and the now traditional view of the master's liability as master, namely, that it is truly vicarious, is still to be preferred. " It is a rule of law that an employer, though guilty of no fault himself, is liable for damage done by the fault or negligence of his servant acting in the course of his employment." [85]

THE REASONS FOR VICARIOUS LIABILITY

The foregoing discussion of the nature of the master's liability does nothing to explain why the master should be liable for the torts of his servants,[86] and the traditional phrases " *respondeat superior* " and " *qui facit per alium facit per se* " give no help. " The former merely states the rule baldly in two words, and the latter merely gives a fictional explanation of it." [87] Many other explanations have been put forward from time to time,[88] such as that the master must have been negligent in employing a negligent servant [89] or in failing adequately to control him, that the

---

[83] [1966] 1 Q.B. 716, *ante*, p. 529. See too *Boyle* v. *Kodak Ltd.* [1969] 1 W.L.R. 661, 672–673, *per* Lord Diplock where, it is respectfully submitted, his Lordship runs together " vicarious " performance of a duty through others, which is the only kind of performance possible to a corporation, and failure in which leads to primary liability, with vicarious liability properly so called.

[84] *Ante*, pp. 520–521.

[85] *Staveley Iron and Chemical Co. Ltd.* v. *Jones* [1956] A.C. 627, 643, *per* Lord Reid.

[86] In addition to articles already cited, see Glanville Williams, " Vicarious Liability and the Master's Indemnity " (1957) 20 M.L.R. 220, 437.

[87] *Staveley Iron and Chemical Co. Ltd.* v. *Jones* [1956] A.C. 627, 643, *per* Lord Reid.

[88] Baty, *Vicarious Liability*, p. 148, lists nine reasons, none of them, in his view, satisfactory.

[89] " The most hoary reason ": Street, *Foundations of Legal Liability*, II, p. 458.

master has " set the whole thing in motion," [90] that the master benefits from the servant's work and so should bear the responsibility for damage the servant may cause in its performance,[91] and that the master has the deeper pocket.[92] Probably the most popular today, at least with academic writers, is the last, though in a much more sophisticated form. In short, the argument is that a " master " today is normally not an individual but a substantial enterprise or undertaking, and that, by placing liability on the enterprise, what is in fact achieved is the distribution of losses caused in the conduct of its business over all the customers to whom it sells its services or products. Knowing of its potential liability for the torts of it servants, the enterprise insures against this liability and the cost of this insurance is reflected in the price it charges to its customers. In the result, therefore, losses caused by the torts of the enterprise's servants are borne in small and probably unnoticeable amounts by the body of its customers, and the injured person is compensated without the necessity of calling upon an individual, whose personal fault may be slight or even non-existent, to suffer the disastrous financial consequences that may follow liability in tort.[93]

None of these explanations, even the last,[94] is, however, sufficient to explain all the aspects of the present law, and it is difficult not to agree with Lord Pearce when he said [95] " The doctrine of vicarious liability has not grown from any very clear, logical or legal principle but from social convenience and rough justice. The master having (presumably for his own benefit) employed the servant, and being (presumably) better able to make good any damage which may occasionally result from the arrangement, is answerable to the world at large for all the torts committed by his servant within the scope of it." This may not satisfy the purist or the logician, but it probably represents the prevailing state of legal opinion on the matter and, though the future may bring further extensions of vicarious liability, it is inconceivable that a serious proposal for its abolition will be made so long as the law of tort as we know it remains alive.

---

[90] Duncan v. Findlater (1839) 6 Cl. & F. 894, 910, per Lord Brougham; Hutchinson v. York, Newcastle and Berwick Ry. (1850) 5 Exch. 343, 350, per Alderson B.; Jones v. Staveley Iron and Chemical Co. Ltd. [1955] 1 Q.B. 474, 480, per Denning L.J.

[91] Taff Vale Ry. v. Amalgamated Society of Railway Servants [1901] A.C. 426, 439, per Farwell J.; Broom v. Morgan [1953] 1 Q.B. 597, 608, per Denning L.J.

[92] Limpus v. L.G.O.C. (1862) 1 H. & C. 526, 539, per Willes J.

[93] See ante, pp. 3–4. Whatever the merits of the decision in Lister v. Romford Ice and Cold Storage Co. Ltd. [1957] A.C. 555, ante, pp. 532–534, it cannot be denied that it militates against this result.

[94] This theory proves too much. If the principle of " enterprise liability " is right then it should apply to all damage caused by the activities of the enterprise and not only to that caused by conduct which the law regards as tortious (see ante, pp. 4–6). It is also difficult to use it to explain those cases in which there is liability for the negligence of independent contractors. See Glanville Williams, " Liability for Independent Contractors " [1956] C.L.J. 180, 193–198.

[95] Imperial Chemical Industries Ltd. v. Shatwell [1965] A.C. 656, 685.

CHAPTER 26

JOINT AND SEVERAL TORTFEASORS

WHERE two or more people by their independent breaches of duty to the plaintiff cause him to suffer distinct injuries, no special rules are required, for each tortfeasor is liable for the damage which he has caused and only for that damage.[1] Where, however, two or more breaches of duty by different persons cause the plaintiff to suffer a single injury,[2] the position is different, principally because in that case the plaintiff is entitled to recover his damages in full from any or all of them,[3] and so special rules as to the possibility of successive actions in respect of that damage and as to the possibility of claims for contribution or indemnity by one tortfeasor against the others are required.

There i a well-known distinction between joint tortfeasors and several tortfeasors which was formerly of considerable importance. At common law, judgment against one of a number of joint tortfeasors, even if it remained unsatisfied, barred any subsequent action against the others for the cause of action was single and indivisible,[4] and for the same reason the release of one operated as the release of all,[5] but neither of these rules applied to several tortfeasors. Now, however, the first of them has been abolished by statute [6] while the importance of the second has been much reduced by a distinction between a release, which probably means a release from liability given under seal or by way of accord and satisfaction only,[7] and a mere covenant by the plaintiff not to sue one of the tortfeasors, which does not affect his right to claim against the others.[8] Although there was in the past a good deal of litigation on the question whether torts were joint or several, today the matter can be dealt with fairly shortly.

Joint tortfeasors

" Persons are said to be joint tortfeasors when their separate shares in the commission of the tort are done in furtherance of a common de-

---

[1] See *Performance Cars Ltd.* v. *Abraham* [1962] 1 Q.B. 33; *Baker* v. *Willoughby* [1970] A.C. 467, *ante*, pp. 87–88.

[2] See Fleming, *Torts*, 4th ed., pp. 174–176.

[3] *Clark* v. *Newsam* (1847) 1 Ex. 131; *Egger* v. *Viscount Chelmsford* [1965] 1 Q.B. 248, 264, *per* Lord Denning M.R.

[4] *Brinsmead* v. *Harrison* (1872) L.R. 7 C.P. 547.

[5] *Duck* v. *Mayeu* [1892] 2 Q.B. 511; *Cutler* v. *McPhail* [1962] 2 Q.B. 292.

[6] Law Reform (Married Women and Tortfeasors) Act 1935 (25 & 26 Geo. 5, c. 30), s. 6 (1) (*a*). See *Wah Tat Bank Ltd.* v. *Chan Cheng Kum* [1975] 2 All E.R. 257.

[7] *Gardiner* v. *Moore* [1969] 1 Q.B. 55, 92, *per* Thesiger J.

[8] *Ibid.*; *Apley Estates Ltd.* v. *De Bernales* [1947] Ch. 217. The ground for this distinction has been said to be that the rule as to releases has often worked hardship and should not be extended; [1947] Ch. at p. 221, *per* Morton L.J. There is also the point that a plaintiff who settles his claim against one of two defendants may well intend to continue his action against the other and, at least if his intention to do so is known to that other, there is no reason why he should be prevented from doing so: *Gardiner* v. *Moore, supra.*

sign." [9] So, in *Brooke* v. *Bool*,[10] where two men searching for a gas leak each applied a naked light to a gas pipe in turn and one of them caused an explosion, they were held to be joint tortfeasors; but where two ships collided because of the independent acts of negligence of each of them, and one of them then, without further negligence, collided with a third, it was held that the owner of the third ship had independent causes of action against the two negligent ships. They had no community of design but were independent tortfeasors whose acts had combined to produce a single damage.[11] It must be noted, however, that whether the case is covered by the above definition or not, where the master is liable vicariously for his servant's tort, master and servant are joint tortfeasors.[12] On the other hand, the parent or custodian of a child whose personal negligence enables the child to commit a tort, though he may be liable for the resulting damage, is not a joint tortfeasor with the child. His liability is for his own independent tort.[13] It was formerly thought that all persons concerned in the publication of defamatory matter, such as the author, publisher and printer of a book, must be joint tortfeasors,[14] but it is now known that this is not necessarily the case. If the publication is fair comment on a matter of public interest, or if it is made on an occasion of qualified privilege, then no person is liable unless he was himself malicious.[15] Accordingly the liability of each person concerned in the publication is dependent upon his own state of mind, and the mere fact of publication does not make all who join in it joint tortfeasors. It is not possible to hold " that a defendant C is a joint tortfeasor with defendants A and B unless it is proved, in a case where that is necessary to constitute a tort, that all three had, at the time of the common act, a common state of mind such as malice." [16] It should be added to the above definition, therefore, that persons are not joint tortfeasors unless they are liable upon the same cause of action, that is, speaking generally, that the same evidence would support an action against each. [17]

---

[9] *The Koursk* [1924] P. 140, 151, *per* Bankes L.J., citing Clerk and Lindsell, *Torts*, 7th ed., p. 59; *ibid.* at p. 156, *per* Scrutton L.J.; *ibid.* at pp. 159–160, *per* Sargant L.J.

[10] [1928] 2 K.B. 578. See too *Arneil* v. *Paterson* [1931] A.C. 560. *Cf. Cook* v. *Lewis* [1952] 1 D.L.R. 1, *ante*, pp. 72–73.

[11] *The Koursk, supra.* See also *Sadler* v. *G.W. Ry.* [1896] A.C. 450; *Thompson* v. *L.C.C.* [1899] 1 Q.B. 840. Street, *Torts*, 5th ed., usefully calls such defendants " several concurrent tortfeasors " to distinguish them from the " several independent tortfeasors " whose acts cause separate items of damage.

[12] " I could never see why an employer, whose only liability is the vicarious liability of being responsible for what his servant does, should be called a joint tortfeasor, which should mean a person who took some part in the tort which is the subject of the action ": *Semtex* v. *Gladstone* [1954] 1 W.L.R. 945, 949, *per* Finnemore J. In *Romford Ice and Cold Storage Co.* v. *Lister* [1956] 2 Q.B. 180, 209, Romer L.J. expressed some sympathy with this view but regarded the matter as settled by authority. See also *ibid.* 200–201, *per* Birkett L.J.

[13] See *Bebee* v. *Sales* (1916) 32 T.L.R. 413; *Newton* v. *Edgerley* [1959] 1 W.L.R. 1031. *Cf. Donaldson* v. *McNiven* [1952] 2 All E.R. 691; *Gorely* v. *Codd* [1967] 1 W.L.R. 19.

[14] Report on Defamation, Cmd. 7536, paras. 116–137; *Cutler* v. *McPhail* [1962] 2 Q.B. 292.

[15] *Egger* v. *Viscount Chelmsford* [1965] 1 Q.B. 248, *ante*, p. 296.

[16] *Gardiner* v. *Moore* [1969] 1 Q.B. 55, 91, *per* Thesiger J.

[17] See, *e.g. Brunsden* v. *Humphrey* (1884) 14 Q.B.D. 141, 147, *per* Bowen L.J. and Clerk

Successive actions

So far as several tortfeasors are concerned, it has always been the law that judgment against one does not bar proceedings against another unless the judgment is actually satisfied,[18] and, since the Law Reform (Married Women and Tortfeasors) Act 1935,[19] the same is true also in the case of joint tortfeasors. It is, however, obviously desirable that a plaintiff should, if he reasonably can, sue in the same proceedings all the tortfeasors who are liable to him for the same damage. It is therefore provided that, even though successful, the plaintiff may not recover costs in any but the first action unless the court is of opinion that there was reasonable ground for bringing a subsequent action.[20] And, to avoid the possibility of differing awards of damages, it is also provided that if successive actions are brought the sums recoverable under judgments given in those actions shall not in the aggregate exceed the amount awarded by the judgment first given.[21]

Contribution

At common law the general rule was that a joint tortfeasor, even though he had satisfied the plaintiff's claim against him in full, could recover neither an indemnity nor a contribution towards his liability from any other joint tortfeasor. This was laid down in *Merryweather* v. *Nixan* [22] and was later extended from joint tortfeasors to independent tortfeasors causing the same damage.[23] The harshness of this common law rule has, however, been modified to a limited extent, and it does not apply where the tort was not clearly illegal in itself,[24] and the person claiming contribution or indemnity acted in the belief that his conduct was lawful; nor does it apply where even though the tort was clearly illegal in itself, one of the parties has been vicariously liable for another's wrong to which he gave neither his authority nor assent and of which he

and Lindsell, *Torts*, 13th ed., pp. 112–114. It has been held in New Zealand that where one person is vicariously liable at common law for the tort of X and another person is similarly liable by statute, then the two are joint tortfeasors: *Everett's Blinds Ltd.* v. *Thomas Ballinger Ltd.* [1965] N.Z.L.R. 266.

[18] *Smith* v. *Pywell* [1959] C.L.Y. 3215.

[19] s. 6 (1) (*a*), *ante*, p. 545.

[20] s. 6 (1) (*b*).

[21] *Ibid.*; s. 6 (3) (*b*). For judgments of foreign courts, see *Kohne* v. *Karger* [1951] 2 K.B. 670. See further, Clerk and Lindsell, *Torts*, 13th ed., pp. 337–338.

[22] (1799) 8 T.R. 186: criticised in *Palmer* v. *Wick, etc. Co. Ltd.* [1894] A.C. 318, 324; (1901) 17 L.Q.R. 293–301. See also *Romford Ice and Cold Storage Co.* v. *Lister* [1956] 2 Q.B. 180; affd. [1957] A.C. 555. The rule in *Merryweather* v. *Nixan* was regarded as resting on the maxim *ex turpi causa non oritur actio*. In the extraordinary case of *Everet* v. *Williams* (1725) (1893) 9 L.Q.R. 197–199, the plaintiff and defendant were in partnership as highway robbers and " dealt with several gentlemen for divers watches, rings, swords, canes, hats, cloaks, horses, bridles, saddles and other things " at Bagshot, Salisbury, Hampstead and elsewhere. The partnership realised some £2,000. The plaintiff brought a partnership action for an account of this sum. His claim was dismissed as scandalous and impertinent, his solicitors were fined £50 each for contempt, and at later dates both plaintiff and defendant were hanged.

[23] *Horwell* v. *L.G.O. Co.* (1877) 2 Ex.D. 365, 379, *per* Kelly C.B.; *The Koursk* [1924] P. 140, 158, *per* Scrutton L.J.

[24] *Betts* v. *Gibbins* (1834) 2 Ad. & E. 57, 74, *per* Lord Denman; *Moxham* v. *Grant* [1900] 1 Q.B. 88, 93, *per* Collins L.J.

had no knowledge.[25] In *Adamson* v. *Jarvis* [26] the plaintiff, an auctioneer acting on the instructions of the defendant, who falsely told him that he (the defendant) was the owner of certain goods, sold the goods by auction and was subsequently compelled to make good their value to the true owner. It was held that the plaintiff could recoup himself against the defendant for the full amount. Best C.J. said that the rule in *Merry-weather* v. *Nixan* " is confined to cases where the person seeking redress must be presumed to have known that he was doing an unlawful act." [27]

The Law Reform (Married Women and Tortfeasors) Act 1935

The rule in *Merryweather* v. *Nixan* is for most practical purposes reversed by section 6 (1) (c) of the Act of 1935 [28] which enables a tortfeasor to recover contribution from any other tortfeasor who is or would if sued have been liable in respect of the same damage, whether as a joint tortfeasor or otherwise,[29] and the Act provides that " the amount of the contribution recoverable from any person shall be such as may be found by the court to be just and equitable having regard to the extent of that person's responsibility for the damage." [30] It might seem reasonable to regard " responsibility " as referring to the moral accountability of a person, but it has been held that the extent to which the wrongdoers respectively caused the injury should also be taken into account.[31] In any case the question of apportionment is one of proportion, not of principle; it involves an individual exercise of discretion by the trial judge, and for that reason appellate courts will rarely interfere with an apportionment as determined by the judge.[32] If it considers it appropriate on the facts of the case the

---

[25] *Romford Ice and Cold Storage Co.* v. *Lister* [1956] 2 Q.B. 180; affd. [1957] A.C. 555, *ante*, pp. 532–534.

[26] (1827) 4 Bing. 66.

[27] 4 Bing. at p. 73. This exception may hold good even where the joint enterprise proves to be criminal: *Burrows* v. *Rhodes* [1899] 1 Q.B. 816.

[28] But the common law rule may still be important in some cases. See *Lister* v. *Romford Ice and Cold Storage Co.* [1957] A.C. 555. *Cf. Jones* v. *Manchester Corporation* [1952] 2 Q.B. 852, *ante*, p. 534, n. 18. See also *post*, p. 657. There are two statutory exceptions to the rule in *Merryweather* v. *Nixan* which are older than the Act of 1935: Maritime Conventions Act 1911 (1 & 2 Geo. 5, c. 57), s. 3, and Companies Act 1908 (8 Edw. 7, c. 69), s. 84, now Companies Act 1948 (11 & 12 Geo. 6, c. 38), s. 43 (4).

[29] Contribution cannot be recovered by a tortfeasor from another tortfeasor whom he is himself liable to indemnify, *e.g.* by virtue of some contract between them.

[30] s. 6 (2).

[31] *The Miraflores and The Abadesa* [1967] 1 A.C. 826, especially at p. 845, *per* Lord Pearce (a case under the Maritime Conventions Act 1911; but in relation to this question there is no reason to distinguish between cases under that Act and cases under the Act of 1935); *Randolph* v. *Tuck* [1962] 1 Q.B. 175, 185, *per* Lawton J. See also *Smith* v. *Bray* (1939) 56 T.L.R. 200; *Collins* v. *Hertfordshire C.C.* [1947] K.B. 598; *Weaver* v. *Commercial Press Ltd.* (1947) 63 T.L.R. 466. The principles are the same as for the apportionment of the damages in a case of contributory negligence, discussed *ante*, pp. 115–118, and see Chapman, " Apportionment of Liability between Tortfeasors," 64 L.Q.R. 26; Payne, " Reduction of Damages for Contributory Negligence " (1955) 18 M.L.R. 344. In determining the apportionment the court must have regard only to the parties before it and cannot take into account the possibility that some other person may also have been to blame: *Maxfield* v. *Llewellyn* [1961] 1 W.L.R. 1119.

[32] *The Macgregor* [1943] A.C. 197, 201, *per* Lord Wright; *Ingram* v. *United Automobile Service Ltd.* [1943] K.B. 612; *The Miraflores and The Abadesa, supra*; *Brown* v. *Thompson* [1968] 1 W.L.R. 1003.

court may exempt the defendant from any liability to contribute, or may direct that the contribution recoverable shall amount to a complete indemnity.[33]

A tortfeasor may be able to recover an indemnity, or damages equivalent to an indemnity or contribution, from another person by virtue of a contract between them,[34] and it is irrelevant to this contractual claim that the extent of the tortfeasor's liability has already been determined as between himself and another tortfeasor in proceedings under the Act. In *Sims* v. *Foster Wheeler Ltd.*[35] the plaintiff's husband was killed when defective staging collapsed, and both his employers and the constructors of the staging were liable in tort. As between these two tortfeasors it was held that the employers must bear 25 per cent. of the damages. They were, however, entitled to recover this amount from their sub-contractors by way of damages for the sub-contractors' breach of an implied warranty in the contract between them that the staging should be properly constructed for safe use as scaffolding. On the other hand, nothing in the section renders enforceable any agreement for indemnity which would not have been enforceable if the section had not been passed.[36] This appears to refer to cases where the party seeking indemnity knew or may be presumed to have known that he was committing an unlawful act. In *W. H. Smith & Son* v. *Clinton*,[37] the defendants had contracted to indemnify the plaintiffs, a printing and publishing firm, against any claims made against them for libels appearing in the defendants' paper, *Vanity Fair*. This indemnity was held to be irrecoverable because the plaintiffs well knew that the matter published was libellous. If the plaintiffs had been innocent they could have recovered upon the indemnity clause.[38] Although they might still be unable to recover on the express contract of indemnity,[39] the courts would probably award contribution under the Act to the printer or publisher of a libel as against its more culpable author.[40]

---

[33] s. 6 (2); *Croston* v. *Vaughan* [1938] 1 K.B. 540; *Ryan* v. *Fildes* [1938] 3 All E.R. 517; *Whitby* v. *Burt, Boulton and Hayward Ltd.* [1947] K.B. 918; *Hosking* v. *De Havilland Aircraft Co. Ltd.* [1949] 1 All E.R. 540; *Semtex* v. *Gladstone* [1954] 1 W.L.R. 945; *Lister* v. *Romford Ice and Cold Storage Co.* [1957] A.C. 555; *Harvey* v. *O'Dell Ltd.* [1958] 2 Q.B. 78.

[34] *Spalding* v. *Tarmac Civil Engineering Ltd.* [1966] 1 W.L.R. 156; *Sims* v. *Foster Wheeler Ltd.* [1966] 1 W.L.R. 769; *Wright* v. *Tyne Improvement Commissioners* [1968] 1 W.L.R. 336. Cf. *Hadley* v. *Droitwich Construction Co. Ltd.* [1968] 1 W.L.R. 37; *AMF International Ltd.* v. *Magnet Bowling Ltd.* [1968] 1 W.L.R. 1028. See Clerk and Lindsell, *Torts*, 13th ed., pp. 117–119.

[35] *Supra.*

[36] s. 6 (4) (c).

[37] (1908) 99 L.T. 840, 841; (1933) 49 L.Q.R. 161–162.

[38] *Daily Mirror Newspapers Ltd.* v. *Exclusive News Agency* (1937) 81 S.J. 924, cited Williams, *Joint Torts*, p. 139, n. 4.

[39] The Defamation Act 1952, s. 11, provides that agreements for indemnity against civil liability shall not be unlawful unless at the time of the publication the person claiming to be indemnified knows the matter is defamatory and does not reasonably believe there is a good defence to any action brought upon it.

[40] Williams, *Joint Torts*, pp. 139–145.

The right to contribution

The Act gives the right to contribution to any " tortfeasor " who is " liable " in respect of the plaintiff's damage, and it is given to him only against another " tortfeasor who is, or would if sued have been, liable in respect of the same damage, whether as a joint tortfeasor or otherwise." [41] It follows that where a plaintiff, P, has been injured by the concurrent negligence of two defendants, D1 and D2,[42] then if D1 is not liable to P because of some defence open to him the entire loss must be borne by D2. Formerly, therefore, when actions in tort between spouses were generally prohibited, if P was the spouse of D1 he or she could recover damages in full from D2, and D2 could claim no contribution from D1.[43] Now, however, contribution can be recovered from D1 in such a case since the rule prohibiting actions in tort between spouses has been abrogated.[44]

The right of contribution between tortfeasors is not itself a right of action in tort, but is a right *sui generis* conferred by statute,[45] and it accrues only when the liability of the claimant tortfeasor, D1, has been ascertained.[46] " Liable," as used in describing D1 means " held liable," *i.e.* sued to judgment successfully [47] or has settled the action, with or without an admission of liability.[48] Where the word is used to describe D2, the tortfeasor from whom contribution may be recovered, " liable " means " held liable," and if a person has been sued to judgment and held not liable, then no contribution may be recovered from him.[49] The words " who . . . would if sued have

---

[41] s. 6 (1) (c).

[42] P may sue D1 and D2 in the same action, or P may sue either D1 or D2 and either may claim contribution from the other (a) under third-party procedure or (b) by a separate action. See *Hordern-Richmond* v.ǀ*Duncan* [1947] K.B. 545, 551–552, *per* Cassels J. for a lucid explanation of third-party procedure. See also *Croston* v. *Vaughan* [1938] 1 K.B. 540; *Bell* v. *Holmes* [1956] 1 W.L.R. 1359. *Cf. Clayson* v. *Rolls-Royce Ltd.* [1951] 1 K.B. 746; *Calvert* v. *Pick* [1954] 1 W.L.R. 456.

[43] *Chant* v. *Read* [1939] 2 K.B. 346; *Drinkwater* v. *Kimber* [1952] 2 Q.B. 281. For other examples, see Williams, *op. cit.*, pp. 99–110.

[44] Law Reform (Husband and Wife) Act 1962. If a wife is injured in an accident caused partly by her own fault and partly by the fault of X, her husband's damages for loss of consortium may be recovered by him from X in full, notwithstanding the wife's contributory negligence: *Mallett* v. *Dunn* [1949] 2 K.B. 180; *Drinkwater* v. *Kimber* [1951] 2 All E.R. 713, 715, *per* Devlin J. This is still law.

[45] *George Wimpey & Co. Ltd.* v. *B.O.A.C.* [1955] A.C. 189; *Harvey* v. *O'Dell Ltd.* [1958] 2 Q.B. 78.

[46] *Hordern-Richmond Ltd.* v. *Duncan* [1947] K.B. 545; *Wimpey's* case, *supra*; *Harvey* v. *O'Dell Ltd.*, *supra*. See the Limitation Act 1963, s. 4, *post*, p. 657.

[47] *Wimpey's* case, *supra*.

[48] *Stott* v. *West Yorkshire Road Car Co. Ltd.* [1971] 2 Q.B. 651. Notwithstanding the slight indication in s. 4 (2) of the Limitation Act 1963 that " liable " in the 1935 Act was meant to be confined to " held liable " or " admitted liability," the practical arguments in favour of the *Stott* decision are overwhelming, since it is the normal practice upon settlement not to admit liability. D1 must, of course, show that he was responsible in law: *James P. Cory & Co. Ltd.* v. *Clarke* [1967] N.I. 62.

[49] *Wimpey's* case, *supra*. There was much difference of opinion in the House of Lords in *Wimpey's* case, and it is submitted that it is authority only for the proposition stated in the text: *Harvey* v. *O'Dell Ltd.*, *supra*. In *Hart* v. *Hall and Pickles Ltd.* [1969] 1 Q.B. 405 the Court of Appeal held that contribution could be claimed from a tortfeasor notwithstanding that the action against him in respect of the tort had been dismissed for want of prosecution. See also *Walsh* v. *Curry* [1955] N.I. 112.

been liable " have, however, no reference to any particular moment of time when the hypothetical action is supposed to have been brought, and mean " who would, if sued at any time, have been liable." [50] In *Harvey* v. *O'Dell Ltd.*,[51] contribution was claimed by D1 against the estate of a deceased tortfeasor, D2, but neither the writ in the action against D1 nor the notice claiming contribution from D2's estate was issued until more than six months after the grant of letters of administration to D2's estate. If the hypothetical action against D2's estate had been brought at the date contribution was claimed, therefore, the estate would not have been liable, for actions in tort against deceased persons' estates had, when the case was decided, to be brought within six months of the date when the personal representatives took out representation.[52] This fact, however, did not prevent contribution from being recovered from the estate, for the estate would have been liable in respect of D2's tort if it had been sued in time.

---

[50] *Harvey* v. *O'Dell Ltd.* [1958] 2 Q.B. 78.

[51] *Supra.* Jolowicz, " The Master's Indemnity—Variations on a Theme " (1959) 22 M.L.R. 189.

[52] This rule concerning actions in tort against deceased persons' estates has since been repealed: *ante*, p. 501.

CHAPTER 27

REMEDIES

IN this chapter we shall consider the remedies which may be available to the victim of a tort. Of these the most important is an award of damages, and the first part of this chapter is devoted to the rules governing the action for damages and their assessment. In the second part the other remedies, namely, self-help, injunction and an order for the specific restitution of property, will be discussed.

PART I. DAMAGES [1]

DAMAGES RECOVERABLE ONCE ONLY

It is a characteristic feature of the law of damages that, subject to the special classes of case mentioned below, the damages to which a plaintiff is entitled from the defendant in respect of a wrongful act must be recovered once and for all. He cannot bring a second action upon the same facts simply because his injury proves to be more serious than was thought when judgment was given. This rule was laid down in *Fetter* v. *Beale*,[2] where some rather unconvincing reasons were given for it,[3] and Winfield considered that the rule was unsound in principle and in general operated unfairly against the plaintiff.[4] It is suggested, however, that the general rule that only one action may be brought in respect of one cause of action is a sound one. The principal difficulties arise in actions for personal injuries, because there the judge has so often to base his award of damages upon an estimate of many future uncertainties, particularly the plaintiff's future from a medical point of view.[5] But the solution is not to abolish the rule in *Fetter* v. *Beale* so as

---

[1] Weir, *Casebook on Tort*, 3rd ed., Chap. 18. The principal modern monographs are McGregor, *Damages*, 13th ed. (1972); Street, *Principles of the Law of Damages* (1962); and Ogus, *The Law of Damages* (1973).

[2] (1701) 1 Ld.Raym. 339, 692; *alias Fitter* v. *Veal* (1701) 12 Mod. 542.

[3] The main reason given was, in effect, that an award of damages must be taken to cover the whole of the damage suffered by the plaintiff, but this merely states the rule in a different form. Coke's reason was *interest reipublicae ut sit finis litium*, which seems fair enough, and others have based it on *nemo bis vexari pro eadem causa*. See also *Richardson* v. *Mellish* (1824) 2 Bing. 229, 240, *per* Best C.J.

[4] See the seventh edition of this work, pp. 97–98, where Winfield's views are retained. Winfield conceded that the rule might sometimes work to the plaintiff's advantage.

[5] Particularly striking examples are *Hawkins* v. *New Mendip Engineering Ltd.* [1966] 1 W.L.R. 1341; *Jones* v. *Griffith* [1969] 1 W.L.R. 795. The issue of damages may be postponed to that of liability: [1966] 1 W.L.R. at p. 1347, *per* Winn L.J. *Report of the Committee on Personal Injuries Litigation*, 1968. Cmnd. 3691, paras. 494–495.

The Law Commission has proposed the creation of a power to make a " provisional " award to deal with such " chance " cases: Report on Personal Injury Litigation—Assessment of Damages, Law Com. No. 56 (1973), paras. 239–244.

There is now power to make an interim award in cases of personal injury or death if the court is satisfied that liability will be established without substantial reduction: R.S.C., Ord. 29, Part II.

to allow more than one action to be brought for the same injury. It is rather to enable the court, in its discretion, to make an award of damages by way of periodical payments, the amount of such payments to be reviewable from time to time so as to take into account changes in the plaintiff's condition and also of other relevant factors, such as changes in the value of money.[6]

Cases outside the rule

(a) Where two distinct rights are violated. Where distinct wrongful acts of the defendant cause damage to distinct rights of the plaintiff, successive actions can obviously be brought; a plaintiff is not obliged to consolidate in one action all the different causes of action he may have against the defendant. And the same is true even where there has been only one wrongful act, provided two distinct rights of the plaintiff are violated. Thus in *Brunsden* v. *Humphrey* [7] the plaintiff's cab was damaged by the defendant's negligence and the plaintiff himself was injured. Having recovered damages in respect of the cab alone, the plaintiff was held entitled to bring a second action for his personal injuries. This does not mean, however, that a plaintiff who has recovered damages for, say, a broken leg, can later bring fresh proceedings against the defendant in respect of the same accident on the ground that he has now discovered that the accident also caused him to suffer from some nervous illness. There is only one cause of action for personal injuries,[8] and that is the test.[9]

(b) Continuing injury. If I wrongfully place something on your land and leave it there, that is not simply a single act of trespass, but is a continuing trespass giving rise to a fresh cause of action *de die in diem*.[10] Similarly, a continuing nuisance gives rise to a fresh cause of action each time damage occurs as a result of it, and accordingly successive actions can be brought.[11] In fact in a case of continuing nuisance prospective damages cannot be claimed, however probable the occurrence

---

[6] See *Jenkins* v. *Richard Thomas and Baldwins Ltd.* [1966] 1 W.L.R. 476, 480, *per* Salmon L.J. But there are grave practical difficulties in such a proposal and the Law Commission has rejected it after full consideration of the evidence: Law Com. No. 56.

[7] (1884) 14 Q.B.D. 141; *Goldrei, Foucard & Son* v. *Sinclair and Russian Chamber of Commerce in London* [1918] 1 K.B. 180; *Sandberg* v. *Giesbrecht* (1963) 42 D.L.R. (2d) 107 (Sup.Ct. of B.C., where the plaintiff was penalised in costs for the unnecessary multiplicity of proceedings). *Cf. Cahoon* v. *Franks* (1967) 63 D.L.R. (2d) 274 (Sup.Ct. of Canada, where *Brunsden* v. *Humphrey* was disapproved).

[8] *Watson* v. *Powles* [1968] 1 Q.B. 596, 603, *per* Lord Denning M.R.; *Fletcher* v. *Autocar and Transporters Ltd.* [1968] 2 Q.B. 322, 336, *per* Lord Denning M.R.

[9] Note, however, that the Court of Appeal may, under certain restrictive conditions, admit additional evidence relating to the assessment of damages if it transpires that the factual basis for the trial judge's assessment was incorrect. See *e.g. Jenkins* v. *Richard Thomas and Baldwins Ltd.* [1966] 1 W.L.R. 476; *Murphy* v. *Stone-Wallwork* (*Charlton*) *Ltd.* [1969] 1 W.L.R. 1023 (H.L.); *Mulholland* v. *Mitchell* [1971] 2 W.L.R. 93 (H.L.).

[10] *Hudson* v. *Nicholson* (1839) 5 M. & W. 437; *Konskier* v. *B. Goodman Ltd.* [1928] 1 K.B. 421. Distinguish the case of a single act of trespass, such as the digging of a hole on the plaintiff's land, where it is only the consequence of the trespass, not the trespass itself, which continues.

[11] *Darley Main Colliery Co.* v. *Mitchell* (1886) 11 App.Cas. 127. *Cf. Alan Maberley* v. *Peabody & Co. Ltd.* [1946] 2 All E.R. 192.

of future damage may be; the plaintiff must await the event and then bring fresh proceedings.[12] It follows, somewhat unfortunately, that if the defendant has caused a subsidence of part of the plaintiff's land, damages can be awarded only for what has already occurred, and the plaintiff cannot recover damages for the depreciation in the value of his property attributable to the risk of further subsidence.[13]

(c) **Torts actionable only on proof of damage.** It has sometimes been suggested that a particular distinction falls to be taken between torts actionable *per se* and those actionable only on proof of damage: in the former case it is impossible for more than one action to be brought while in the latter a fresh action may be brought each time fresh damage occurs as a result of the wrongful act.[14] While it is probably correct that only one action can be brought in respect of a tort which is actionable *per se*, however, it is submitted that this should be seen as no more than a reflection of the general rule that only one action may be brought in respect of one cause of action, not that cases of torts actionable only on proof of damage form a special exception to that rule. Just as I have two causes of action if your negligent act causes separate damage to my property and to my person,[15] so also I have two causes of action if on quite separate occasions your single act of negligence causes me to suffer distinct personal injuries. But this does not mean that if you negligently hit me on the head I can bring fresh proceedings each time I suffer from a headache; and the reason is that I have suffered only one injury, the blow upon the head, not that negligently hitting me on the head is trespass and that trespass is actionable *per se*. It is better to consider in each case whether the facts relied on by the plaintiff to establish his cause of action in subsequent proceedings are substantially identical with those on which he relied in the first, than to treat torts not actionable *per se* as constituting a special exception to the general rule.

KINDS OF DAMAGES

Ordinarily an award of damages is made in order to compensate the plaintiff for his injury, and the assessment of compensatory damages is considered in detail below. An award of damages may, however, be

---

[12] *Cf. Toronto General Trusts Corp.* v. *Roman* (1962) 37 D.L.R. (2d) 16 (Ontario C.A.) where, notwithstanding a judgment against him in an action of detinue for the return of shares, the defendant nevertheless failed to return them for a substantial period of time. A second action claiming damages for that detention was allowed but damages were not awarded in the second action for a period of detention prior to judgment in the first. Under certain conditions damages in respect of probable future harm may be awarded in lieu of an injunction under Lord Cairns' Act, *post*, pp. 589–590. See, however, *Redland Bricks Ltd.* v. *Morris* [1970] A.C. 652.
[13] *West Leigh Colliery Co. Ltd.* v. *Tunnicliffe and Hampson Ltd.* [1908] A.C. 27.
[14] Salmond, *Torts*, 16th ed., pp. 606–607. The matter is more fully discussed in the 7th ed., para. 37 (10). See too Gatley, *Libel and Slander*, 7th ed., pp. 356, 562–563, and *Darley Main Colliery Co. Ltd.* v. *Mitchell* (1886) 11 App.Cas. 127, 145, *per* Lord Bramwell; *ibid.* at p. 151, *per* Lord Fitzgerald. *Cf. ibid.* at pp. 142–143, *per* Lord Blackburn.
[15] *Brunsden* v. *Humphrey* (1884) 14 Q.B.D. 141, *ante*, p. 553.

avowedly non-compensatory in intention. If not compensatory, damages may be 1. contemptuous, 2. nominal or 3. exemplary or punitive.

1. Contemptuous

The amount awarded here is merely derisory—formerly one farthing, then one halfpenny and now, presumably, one new halfpenny—and indicates that the court has formed a very low opinion of the plaintiff's bare legal claim, or that his conduct was such that he deserved, at any rate morally, what the defendant did to him. Damages of this kind may imperil the plaintiff's chances of getting his costs, for although costs now usually follow the event of the action, yet their award is in the discretion of the judge, and although the insignificance of damages is not by itself enough to justify him in depriving the plaintiff of his costs, yet it is a material factor in the exercise of his discretion. Contemptuous damages are not uncommon in libel actions.[16]

2. Nominal

Nominal damages are awarded when the plaintiff's legal right has been infringed but he has suffered no actual damage, as can most readily occur in the case of torts which are actionable *per se*. In *Constantine* v. *Imperial Hotels Ltd.*[17] the defendants were guilty of a breach of their duty as common innkeepers when they unjustifiably refused accommodation in one of their hotels to the plaintiff, the well-known West Indian cricketer. Although he was given accommodation elsewhere, he was awarded nominal damages of five guineas. An award of nominal damages does not, therefore, connote any moral obliquity on the plaintiff's part, but even so the judge may in his discretion deprive the plaintiff of his costs or even make him pay the costs of both sides.[18]

3. Exemplary or punitive [19]

In any case in which damages are at large, that is, where they cannot be precisely calculated in money terms, the court may take into account the motives and conduct of the defendant, and where these aggravate the plaintiff's injury the damages will be correspondingly increased.[20]

---

[16] For a recent example, where the plaintiff got no costs, see *Dering* v. *Uris* [1964] 2 Q.B. 669.

[17] [1944] K.B. 693.

[18] *Anglo-Cyprian Trade Agencies Ltd.* v. *Paphos Wine Industries Ltd.* [1951] 1 All E.R. 873 (a case of contract); McGregor, *op. cit.*, pp. 298–299. But the plaintiff cannot be ordered to pay the costs of both sides if he has been completely successful and there has been no misconduct on his part: *Kierson* v. *Thompson & Sons Ltd.* [1913] 1 K.B. 587. If nominal damages are awarded in an action for waste, judgment may be entered for the defendant: *Harrow School* v. *Alderton* (1800) 2 B. & C. 86; *Doherty* v. *Allman* (1878) 3 App.Cas. 709, 725. But this rule is peculiar to waste; it is of considerable antiquity and was based upon the maxim *de minimis non curat lex*: Y.B.Mich. 19 Hen. 6, pl. 19, f. 8b; Br.Abr. Waste, 123; Coke, 2 Inst. 306.

[19] " Exemplary " is now more popular than " punitive ": see Lord Devlin in *Rookes* v. *Barnard* [1964] A.C. 1129 and Lord Hailsham L.C., Viscount Dilhorne and Lords Morris and Diplock in *Cassell & Co. Ltd.* v. *Broome* [1972] A.C. 1027.

[20] Street, *op. cit.*, pp. 22–23.

These " aggravated damages " are truly compensatory, being given for the injury to the plaintiff's proper feelings of dignity and pride.[21] Exemplary damages, on the other hand, are not compensatory but are awarded to punish the defendant and to deter him from similar behaviour in the future. This distinction, though clear in theory,[22] is obviously difficult to apply in practice; it was also, until recently, relatively insignificant, for it was thought that exemplary damages, like aggravated damages, could be awarded in any case of tort.[23] Now, however, in *Rookes* v. *Barnard*,[24] the House of Lords, through Lord Devlin, has restated the law regarding exemplary damages and has severely limited their scope, and this restriction has again been affirmed by the House in *Cassell & Co. Ltd.* v. *Broome*.[25] It is true that Lord Devlin thought that this would not make a great difference to the substance of the law, for aggravated damages can do most of the work of exemplary damages,[26] but, subject to what is said below, it is now clear that, except in the rare cases where exemplary damages are still allowed, any award must be strictly justifiable as compensation for the injury sustained.[27]

In Lord Devlin's view exemplary damages are in principle objectionable because they confuse the civil and the criminal functions of the law [28] and, apart from cases where they are allowed by statute,[29] exemplary damages can now be awarded in only two classes of case [30]:
(a) Oppressive, arbitrary or unconstitutional action by servants of the Government.[31] A well-known example of this, approved by Lord

---

[21] *Rookes* v. *Barnard* [1964] A.C. 1129, 1221, *per* Lord Devlin. *Cassell & Co. Ltd.* v. *Broome* [1972] A.C. 1027. The £250 awarded for the " insolent and high handed trespass " in *Jolliffe* v. *Willmett & Co.* [1971] 1 All E.R. 478 would seem to fall into this category. Although those aggravated damages are given for the offence to the plaintiff's dignity or pride, there is little evidence that the courts inquire into the question of the extent to which the plaintiff *was* affronted; *cf.* Viscount Dilhorne in *Cassell* v. *Broome* at p. 1111 and *Ansell* v. *Thomas, The Times,* May 25, 1973.

[22] See *McCarey* v. *Associated Newspapers Ltd.* (*No. 2*) [1965] 2 Q.B. 86, 104–105, *per* Pearson L.J. Perhaps the best discussion is in the judgment of McCardie J. in *Butterworth* v. *Butterworth* [1920] P. 126, a case on damages for adultery where it had long been settled that damages must be compensatory only. For a recent case on the same topic see *Pritchard* v. *Pritchard* [1967] P. 195. Claims for damages for adultery can no longer be made: Law Reform (Miscellaneous Provisions) Act 1970, *ante,* p. 439.

[23] See *e.g. Loudon* v. *Ryder* [1953] 2 Q.B. 202.

[24] *Supra. Loudon* v. *Ryder, supra,* is expressly overruled: [1964] A.C. at p. 1229.

[25] [1972] A.C. 1027.

[26] [1964] A.C. at p. 1230.

[27] *McCarey* v. *Associated Newspapers Ltd.* (*No. 2*), *supra.*

[28] [1964] A.C. at p. 1221.

[29] Lord Devlin cites the Reserve and Auxiliary Forces (Protection of Civil Interests) Act 1951, s. 13 (2): *ibid.* at p. 1225. Perhaps also the Copyright Act 1956 permits the award of exemplary damages. As to this, see *Williams* v. *Settle* [1960] 1 W.L.R. 1072 and Lord Devlin's comments: [1964] A.C. at pp. 1225 and 1229. Lord Kilbrandon in *Cassell* v. *Broome, supra,* at p. 1133, doubted whether any existing statute contemplated the award of exemplary damages in the proper sense.

[30] It is submitted, notwithstanding dicta in *Cassell* v. *Broome, supra,* at pp. 1076, 1131, that exemplary damages may be awarded in a case of deceit fulfilling the conditions of Lord Devlin's second category: *Mafo* v. *Adams* [1970] 1 Q.B. 548, 555, *per* Widgery L.J.; *cf. ibid.* at p. 555, *per* Sachs L.J.

[31] [1964] A.C. at p. 1226. It is now almost certain that " the Government " in this context includes local government and the police: *Cassell & Co. Ltd.* v. *Broome, supra,* at pp. 1077–1078, 1130, 1134, *per* Lord Hailsham L.C. and Lords Diplock and Kilbrandon. Lord Devlin's speech in *Rookes* v. *Barnard* is not to be read as if it were a

Devlin, is *Huckle* v. *Money*,[32] one of the cases deciding against the legality of the search warrants which were issued against John Wilkes and others during the latter part of the eighteenth century. The plaintiff was detained under one of these warrants for no more than six hours and the defendant " used him very civilly by treating him with beef-steaks and beer." Yet the court refused to interfere with a verdict for £300 damages, for " to enter a man's house by virtue of a nameless warrant, in order to procure evidence, is worse than the Spanish Inquisition . . . it is a most daring public attack made upon the liberty of the subject." [33] This class of case does not extend to oppressive action by private corporations or individuals and is justified in the case of servants of the Government because they " are also the servants of the people and the use of their power must always be subordinate to their duty of service." [34] (b) Cases where the defendant's conduct has been calculated by him to make a profit for himself which may well exceed the compensation payable to the plaintiff.[35] The point here is that the defendant must not be allowed to make a profit from his own deliberate wrongful act, and it is not sufficient to justify exemplary damages simply that part of the defendant's purpose in doing the act complained of was to make a profit. So the mere fact that everything published in a newspaper is published with a view to selling the newspaper and making a profit does not mean that every defamatory statement in a newspaper should be redressed with an award of exemplary damages.[36] There must be something much more calculated and deliberate, though it is unnecessary that the defendant should have indulged in any precise balancing of the chances of profit and loss. The essence of the matter is that the defendant, with knowledge that his proposed act is unlawful, directs his mind to the material advantage of committing the tort and comes to the conclusion that it is worth the risk that he may have to compensate the plaintiff if he should bring an action.[37]

---

statute. The malicious levying of excessive distress probably falls under this head: *Moore* v. *Lambeth County Court Registrar (No.* 2) [1970] 1 Q.B. 560, 572, *per* Sachs L.J.

[32] (1763) 2 Wils. 205.

[33] *Ibid.* at p. 207, *per* Pratt C.J. See also *Wilkes* v. *Wood* (1763) Lofft. 1. In *Wilkes* v. *Lord Halifax* the jury awarded John Wilkes the then phenomenal sum of £4,000 for false imprisonment: 19 State Trials 1466.

[34] [1964] A.C. at p. 1226, *per* Lord Devlin.

[35] *Ibid.* at pp. 1226–1227. It has been said that this is not really exemplary damages but is " merely preventing the defendant from obtaining a reward for his wrongdoing . . . the plaintiff is the accidental beneficiary of a rule of law based on public policy rather than on the reparation of private wrongs ": *McCarey* v. *Associated Newspapers Ltd. (No.* 2) [1965] 2 Q.B. 86, 107, *per* Diplock L.J.

[36] *McCarey* v. *Associated Newspapers Ltd. (No.* 2) [1965] 2 Q.B. 86; *Broadway Approvals Ltd.* v. *Odhams Press Ltd. (No.* 2) [1965] 1 W.L.R. 805; *Manson* v. *Associated Newspapers Ltd.* [1965] 1 W.L.R. 1038.

[37] *Cassell & Co. Ltd.* v. *Broome, supra,* a case which all the members of the House of Lords agreed fell clearly within Lord Devlin's second category. A case may fall within this category even though the defendant estimates the potential damages as very high if he calculates that the plaintiff, through poverty or intimidation, will not sue at all.

There are arguments both for and against exemplary damages,[38] though perhaps the " noes " have marginally the best of it in logic[39] and it is unlikely that anyone now sitting down to draft a civil code would include an article providing for such damages.[40] The main arguments against them are that they confuse the purposes of the civil and criminal law, import the possibility of punishment into civil litigation without the safeguards of the criminal process and provide an unmerited windfall for the plaintiff. On the other hand, exemplary damages under Lord Devlin's second category in *Rookes* v. *Barnard* may serve as a makeshift remedy to prevent the unjust enrichment of the tortfeasor.[41] Further, it is perhaps unsafe to lay too much stress on the division of function between the civil and criminal law: first, the award of exemplary damages is in practice confined to situations where the prosecuting authorities may be unwilling to act[42] (abuse of power by government) or where the criminal law is moribund (libel); secondly, one should not too readily assume that the boundaries between civil and criminal law are rigid and immutable.[43] As a high authority has recently said, " over the range of torts for which punitive damages may be given . . . there is much to be said before one can safely assert that the true or basic principle of the law of damages in tort is compensation, or, if it is, what that compensation is for, . . . or, if there is compensation, whether there is not in all cases, or at least in some, of which defamation may be an example, also a delictual element which contemplates some penalty for the defendant." [44] The verdict on the case for abolition of exemplary damages must at the moment be " not proven." [45]

Where the case is a proper one for the award of exemplary damages, the court does not have an absolute discretion.[46] In particular, awards

---

[38] See particularly the speeches in *Cassell* v. *Broome, supra,* and Street, *op. cit.,* pp. 33–34. Hodgin and Veitch, " Punitive Damages Reassessed " (1972) 21 I.C.L.Q. 119.

[39] *Cassell & Co. Ltd.* v. *Broome, supra.,* at p. 1114, *per* Lord Wilberforce.

[40] *Ibid.* at p. 1134, *per* Lord Kilbrandon. Any such article could hardly in logic confine exemplary damages to Lord Devlin's categories: see *ibid.* at p. 1088.

[41] *Ibid.* at p. 1129, *per* Lord Diplock; McGregor, *op. cit.,* pp. 228–229. But as far as the plaintiff is concerned, the damages still represent a windfall.

[42] The right of private prosecution exists for most offences, but this right has recently been criticised. The administrative law remedies referred to by Lord Diplock in *Broome* v. *Cassell* at p. 1130 are, with respect, little use to a plaintiff who has been assaulted or deprived of his liberty by the state.

[43] See *e.g.* the compensation provisions in the Criminal Justice Act 1972.

[44] *Cassell & Co. Ltd.* v. *Broome, supra.,* at p. 1114, *per* Lord Wiberforce.

[45] Exemplary damages enjoy a continuing vitality in common law jurisdictions not so far removed in social habits from our own and the courts there have rejected the restrictions of *Rookes* v. *Barnard: Uren* v. *John Fairfax & Sons Pty. Ltd.* (1966) 117 C.L.R. 118, approved by the P.C. in *Australian Consolidated Press Ltd.* v. *Uren* [1969] 1 A.C. 590 (Australia); *Fogg* v. *McKnight* [1968] N.Z.L.R. 330 (New Zealand); as to Canada, see Fridman, " Punitive Damages in Tort " (1970) 48 Can. Bar Rev. 373. For a vigorous argument for the extension of exemplary damages to contract see Weir, *Casebook on Tort,* 3rd ed., p. 273.

[46] McGregor, *op. cit.,* p. 233, argues that the considerations here set out have no relevance where the case is in Lord Devlin's second category, for that provides a " method for extracting profits tortiously obtained by the defendant," but support for all of them can be found in *Cassell* v. *Broome,* a second category case. It is submitted that the law has not finally committed itself to a restitutionary posture.

should be "moderate"[47] (though the House of Lords by a bare majority has recently upheld an award of £25,000),[48] the conduct of the plaintiff as well as the defendant should be taken into account[49] and the jury should be directed that before they make an award of exemplary damages they should consider whether the sum they have set for compensatory (including aggravated) damages is sufficient to punish the defendant.[50] Where a plaintiff sues more than one joint defendant in the same action, the sum which may be awarded by way of exemplary damages is the lowest which the conduct of any of the defendants deserves.[51]

MEASURE OF DAMAGES

Scope of subject

In theory even if not always in practice this subject is distinct from that of the chapter on Remoteness of Damage,[52] though, obviously, both topics have a direct bearing upon the amount of money the plaintiff will ultimately recover. Remoteness of damage concerns the question, "in respect of what consequences of an established breach of duty can the injured party recover?"[53] Now we must see how the law attempts to answer the different question, "how much compensation can the injured party recover for consequences of the breach of legal duty which have already been held to be not too remote?"[54]

In the case of some torts such as conversion, detinue and deceit specific rules for the assessment of damages exist, and these have been noticed in their appropriate chapters.[55] For the rest, and most notably

---

[47] *Rookes* v. *Barnard, supra*, at pp. 1227–1228, *per* Lord Devlin.

[48] *Cassell & Co. Ltd.* v. *Broome, supra.*

[49] *Lane* v. *Holloway* [1968] 1 Q.B. 379, 391, *per* Salmon L.J. (though in this case there is perhaps some confusion between aggravated and exemplary damages); *Fontin* v. *Katapodis* (1962) 108 C.L.R. 177. In *Cassell* v. *Broome* at p. 1071 Lord Hailsham L.C. speaks of this factor in the context of aggravated damages.

[50] *Cassell & Co. Ltd.* v. *Broome, supra.* The costs system in English litigation may itself be regarded as punitive: *ibid.* at pp. 1114–1115, *per* Lord Wilberforce. If the trial judge is in any doubt as to the correctness of leaving the issue of exemplary damages to the jury he should ask them, in the event of their awarding such damages, what smaller sum they would have awarded if they had confined themselves to compensation (including aggravation), but awards should not otherwise be "split": *Cassell* v. *Broome* at pp. 1082, 1094, 1116.

[51] *Cassell & Co. Ltd.* v. *Broome, supra.* As to aggravated damages, see *ibid.* at pp. 1063, 1131; but *cf.* McGregor, *op. cit.*, pp. 232–233.
This result flows from the rule that only a single award may be made against joint tortfeasors. The rule seems not to have any real justification. Where the joint tortfeasors are master and servant, it is the conduct of the servant as the actual wrongdoer that is to be taken into account: *Carrington* v. *Att.-Gen.* [1972] N.Z.L.R. 1106. *Cf.* Atiyah, *Vicarious Liability in the Law of Torts*, p. 435.

[52] *Ante*, pp. 84–106. See Wilson and Slade, "A Re-examination of Remoteness," 15 M.L.R. 458.

[53] Wilson and Slade, *ibid.*

[54] *Ibid. Cf.* Chapman (Book Review) [1964] C.L.J. 136, 138.

[55] For the measure of damages in defamation, see Gatley, *Libel and Slander*, 7th ed., pp. 1358–1374, Samuels, "Problems of Assessing Damages for Defamation" (1963) 79 L.Q.R. 63; *Lewis* v. *Daily Telegraph Ltd.* [1963] 1 Q.B. 340 (for proceedings in the H.L., where the question of damages was not fully considered, see [1964] A.C. 234); *McCarey* v. *Associated Newspapers Ltd.* (*No. 2*) [1965] 2 Q.B. 86; *Fielding* v. *Variety Incorporated* [1967] 2 Q.B. 841.

so far as damages for personal injury are concerned, the courts have in the past been content to leave the assessment of damages to the jury with only general guidance from the judges,[56] and many statements can be found to the effect that the quantum of damages in each case is a question of fact.[57]

It is no doubt true that ultimately the exact sum which the plaintiff is awarded in any case is dependent upon all the detailed circumstances of the case, but this does not mean that the topic is devoid of principle.[58] On the contrary, at least where so-called pecuniary damage is concerned, some quite firm rules have developed, and even in the case of non-pecuniary damage, such as pain and suffering and what is called " loss of amenity," where precise valuation in money terms is obviously impossible,[59] the courts are now beginning to elucidate the bases of their awards.[60] In this chapter, therefore, we shall consider some of the rules governing the assessment of damages in cases of personal injury and of loss or damage to property, acting always on the assumptions that a tort has been committed and that the damage in question is not too remote.[61]

General and special damages [62]

Before dealing in any detail with the measure of damages in tort it is necessary to say something of these expressions for their indiscriminate use in more than one sense has been the source of much confusion. Originally " special damage " was used to denote the actual damage which the plaintiff must prove in order to show a cause of action in a tort not actionable *per se* [63] and was thus contrasted with the " general damage " that is presumed in the case of other torts.[64] This usage is still extant, but it is submitted that " actual " or " particular " damage is now to be preferred, and that " special damage " is better reserved to

---

[56] For an important exception where the measure of damages was fully considered see *Phillips* v. *L.S.W. Ry.* (1879) 4 Q.B.D. 406; (1879) 5 Q.B.D. 78; (1879) 5 C.P.D. 280. The case was tried twice before a jury, twice before a Divisional Court and twice before the Court of Appeal.

[57] *e.g. Mehmet Dogan Bey* v. *Abdeni & Co. Ltd.* [1951] 2 All E.R. 162, 165, *per* McNair J., applying the statement of Lord Haldane in *British Westinghouse Electric and Manufacturing Co. Ltd.* v. *Underground Electric Rys. Co. of London Ltd.* [1912] A.C. 673, 688.

[58] See the caustic observations of Lord Sumner in *Admiralty Commissioners* v. *SS. Chekiang* [1926] A.C. 637, 643.

[59] *Cf.* Munkman, *Damages for Personal Injuries and Death*, 5th ed., pp. 14–23; and see Street, *Principles of the Law of Damages*, pp. 4–13.

[60] See in particular *Wise* v. *Kaye* [1962] 1 Q.B. 638; *H. West & Son Ltd.* v. *Shephard* [1964] A.C. 326.

[61] It is not always possible in practice to maintain the distinction between remoteness and measure of damages. A professional violinist injured by negligence can certainly recover damages for loss of earnings but it is doubtful whether he can recover the fee which he would have received for a particular recital had he not been injured. The argument could be either that loss of the fee is too remote or that reference to the fee is an inadmissible way of measuring the non-remote loss, loss of earnings. *Cf.* Street, *op. cit.*, p. 58.

[62] Street, *op. cit.*, pp. 18–22; McGregor, *Damages*, 13th ed., pp. 12–16; Jolowicz, " The Changing Use of ' Special Damage ' and its Effect on the Law " [1960] C.L.J. 214.

[63] *e.g. Iveson* v. *Moore* (1699) 1 Ld.Raym. 486, 488, *per* Gould J.

[64] *e.g. Ashby* v. *White* (1703) 2 Ld.Raym. 938, 955, *per* Holt C.J.

denote some special or material [65] item of the plaintiff's loss which is not an obvious consequence of the tort committed against him and of which, therefore, the defendant should be given notice in the pleadings. " General damage " is damage which will be presumed,[66] but " special damage " means " the particular damage (beyond the general damage), which results from the particular circumstances of the case, and of the plaintiff's claim to be compensated, for which he ought to give warning in his pleadings in order that there may be no surprise at the trial." [67] This is a sensible distinction resulting in a rule proper to the law of pleading and is one which need have no direct bearing on the substantive law of damages [68] but unfortunately it has led to another, and unjustifiable, distinction between damages which are capable of substantially exact pecuniary assessment and those which are not.[69] This has the strange result, for example, that loss of earnings which has accrued by the date of the trial is regarded as special damage while future loss of earning falls under the head of general damage [70]; and the application to " special damage " in this sense of the rule that " special damage " must be strictly pleaded and proved may have led to the under-compensation of the plaintiff in some cases.[71] The distinction between " special " and " general " damage should, it is submitted, be regarded as appertaining exclusively to the rules of pleading and as being largely irrelevant to the substantive law. Owing to its ambiguity, however, it cannot be ignored even in a textbook not directly concerned with problems of procedure.

Restitutio in integrum

The basic principle for the measure of damages in tort as well as in contract is that there should be *restitutio in integrum*. Apart from cases in which exemplary damages are awarded,[72] " where any injury is to be compensated by damages, in settling the sum of money to be given for reparation of damages you should as nearly as possible get at that sum

---

[65] *Cassell & Co. Ltd.* v. *Broome* [1972] A.C. 1027, 1073, *per* Lord Hailsham L.C.

[66] " Every libel is of itself a wrong in regard of which the law . . . implies general damage. By the very fact that he has committed such a wrong, the defendant is prepared for the proof that some general damage may have been done ": *Ratcliffe* v. *Evans* [1892] 2 Q.B. 524, 529, *per* Bowen L.J.; *Ströms Bruks Aktie Bolag* v. *John and Peter Hutchinson* [1905] A.C. 515, 525, *per* Lord Macnaghten.

[67] *Ratcliffe* v. *Evans* [1892] 2 Q.B. 524, 528, *per* Bowen L.J.; *Ströms Bruks Aktie Bolag* v. *John and Peter Hutchinson* [1905] A.C. 515, 525–526, *per* Lord Macnaghten; *Perestrello Ltda.* v. *United Paint Co. Ltd.* [1969] 1 W.L.R. 570; *Domsalla* v. *Barr* [1969] 1 W.L.R. 630.

[68] A plaintiff who claims some specific item of loss as special damages but fails to prove it may nevertheless recover general damages: *The Hebridean Coast* [1961] A.C. 545 (damage to ship; cost of chartering a substitute claimed as special damages but this loss not proved; plaintiff nevertheless allowed general damages for loss of the use of the ship). *Cf. Ilkiw* v. *Samuels* [1963] 1 W.L.R. 991.

[69] *Shearman* v. *Folland* [1950] 2 K.B. 43, 51, *per* Asquith L.J.; *British Transport Commission* v. *Gourley* [1956] A.C. 185, 206, *per* Lord Goddard.

[70] *Supra, per* Lord Goddard. For an explanation, valid for the purposes of the rules of pleading and for those purposes only, see *Perestrello Ltda.* v. *United Paint Co. Ltd.* [1969] 1 W.L.R. 570, 579, *per* Lord Donovan.

[71] It almost certainly did so in *Ilkiw* v. *Samuels, supra.*

[72] *Ante*, pp. 555–559.

of money which will put the party who has been injured, or who has suffered, in the same position as he would have been in if he had not sustained the wrong for which he is now getting his compensation or reparation."[73] So, in an action for deceit, the proper starting point for the assessment of damages is to compare the position of the plaintiff as it was before the fraudulent statement was made to him with his position as it became as a result of his reliance upon the statement.[74] In a case of personal injury, too, this criterion can and should be applied to the pecuniary elements of the plaintiff's loss such as his loss of earnings,[75] but it is difficult to see that it can be applied to the non-pecuniary elements such as pain and suffering, and there the plaintiff receives compensation not restitution.[76] Indeed compensation in the literal sense is no more possible than restitution, and what is given has been described as " notional or theoretical compensation to take the place of that which is not possible, namely, actual compensation."[77]

ACTIONS FOR PERSONAL INJURY

Heads of damage

If *restitutio in integrum* is the object of damages awarded for pecuniary loss and compensation the object of damages for non-pecuniary loss, it might have been expected that in calculating the plaintiff's total damages in a given case the court would always have drawn a clear distinction between these two aspects of his damage. The distinction has, of course, been acknowledged many times,[78] but the practice of the courts has tended until recently to cut across and obscure it by the making of global awards which did not distinguish between the different aspects of damages.[79] This practice was supported by the Court of

---

[73] *Livingstone* v. *Rawyards Coal Co.* (1880) 5 App.Cas. 25, 39, *per* Lord Blackburn; *Monarch Steamship Co. Ltd.* v. *Karlshamns Oljefabriker (A/B)* [1949] A.C. 196, 221, *per* Lord Wright; *Shearman* v. *Folland* [1950] 2 K.B. 43, 49. In *Liesbosch Dredger* v. *Edison SS.* [1933] A.C. 449, 463, Lord Wright described the principle of *restitutio in integrum* as " the dominant rule of law "; " Subsidiary rules can only be justified if they give effect to that rule." *Cf. Admiralty Commissioners* v. *SS. Valeria* [1922] 2 A.C. 242, 248, *per* Lord Dunedin.

[74] *Doyle* v. *Olby Ironmongers Ltd.* [1969] 2 Q.B. 158. See *ante*, p. 220.

[75] *British Transport Commission* v. *Gourley* [1956] A.C. 185; *Parry* v. *Cleaver* [1970] A.C. 1, 22, *per* Lord Morris.

[76] *British Transport Commission* v. *Gourley*, *supra*, at p. 208, *per* Lord Goddard.

[77] *Rushton* v. *National Coal Board* [1953] 1 Q.B. 495, 502, *per* Romer L.J.; *H. West & Son Ltd.* v. *Shephard* [1964] A.C. 326, 346, *per* Lord Morris. See too *Fletcher* v. *Autocar and Transporters Ltd.* [1968] 2 Q.B. 322, 335, *per* Lord Denning M.R.; *ibid.* at pp. 339–340, *per* Diplock L.J.; *ibid.* at p. 363, *per* Salmon L.J.; *S.* v. *Distillers Co. (Biochemicals) Ltd.* [1970] 1 W.L.R. 114 (children born deformed, having been injured *in utero* by the drug " thalidomide " used by their mothers).

[78] Street, *op. cit.*, p. 43; Kemp and Kemp, *Quantum of Damages*, 3rd ed., I, p. 9. Munkman, *Damages for Personal Injuries and Death*, 5th ed., pp. 12–13, distinguishes between " pecuniary loss " and " personal loss." This comes to the same thing.

[79] The courts have always distinguished between " special " and " general " damages in the sense of pecuniary losses accruing before trial and other losses (see p. 561, *ante*), but in the nature of things damages for the former will generally be rather low. What might be very large sums for loss of future earnings are general damages and might not be distinguished from pain and suffering, loss of amenities of life, etc. See especially *British Transport Commission* v. *Gourley* [1956] A.C. 185, 206, *per* Lord Goddard; *S.* v. *Distillers Co. (Biochemicals) Ltd.*, *supra*, at p. 125, *per* Hinchcliffe J.; Street, *op. cit.*, pp. 132–133.

Appeal, partly on the ground that separate assessment and addition of individual items might lead to " overlapping " and a consequently excessive award.[80] However, the Court of Appeal in *Jefford* v. *Gee* [81] has now acknowledged that recent changes in the law governing the award of interest on damages, whereby different treatment is given to separate items,[82] has made some degree of " itemisation " inevitable. As a result of this decision the court must at least distinguish between " special damage " in the sense of pre-trial pecuniary losses,[83] future loss of earnings and non-pecuniary loss.[84] There has so far been no acceptance of the need to divide up further any of these classes so as to show how a figure for each was reached, though the Law Commission has proposed that such a duty should be imposed on the courts.[85] However, a variety of cases, each presenting some unusual feature, has forced the courts to consider particular " heads of damage " within the broad classes recognised in *Jefford* v. *Gee* and to these we must now turn. Whatever the arguments for and against further itemisation, it is impossible to understand the *principles* of the law of damages unless the broad classes are further broken down.

1. Non-pecuniary loss

(i) *Pain and suffering* [86]

This phrase suggests a double head of damage,[87] but in fact it means no more than the suffering attributable to the injury itself and to any consequential surgical operations.[88] Compensation must be given for both past and future pain and suffering,[89] including that attributable

---

[80] *Watson* v. *Powles* [1968] 1 Q.B. 596; *Fletcher* v. *Autocar and Transporters Ltd.* [1968] 2 Q.B. 322; *cf. Ford* v. *Middlesbrough Co-operative Society Ltd.* (1969) 113 S.J. 735; *Kirby* v. *Vauxhall Motors Ltd. ibid.*, p. 736.

[81] [1970] 2 Q.B. 130.

[82] Administration of Justice Act 1969 (c. 58), s. 22. *Post*, p. 580.

[83] See n. 70, *supra*.

[84] Where damages have been agreed, it is helpful to tell the court the basis of the calculation so that it may be recorded and embodied in the judgment: *Bennett* v. *Chemical Construction (G.B.) Ltd.* [1971] 1 W.L.R. 1571.

[85] Report on Personal Injury Litigation—Assessment of Damages, Law Com. No. 56 (1973), paras. 181–214. Note the proposal for a change in the rules of pleading to require the plaintiff to " itemise " in his statement of claim. *Cf.* McGregor, *op. cit.*, p. 737, who considers that any further itemisation beyond *Jefford* v. *Gee* would be undesirable. The " overlap" problem has given the courts much difficulty. Thus in *Fletcher* v. *Autocar and Transporters, supra*, it was held to be wrong to assess damages for loss of future earnings and then assess independently the award for loss of amenities, because this took no account of the fact that the plaintiff, had he not been injured, would have had to pay for those amenities out of his earnings. See also *Smith* v. *Central Asbestos Co. Ltd.* [1972] 1 Q.B. 244. There are grave risks of over-subtlety in this approach and the Law Commission has recommended that it should not be followed: Law Com. No. 56, paras. 198–200.

[86] There is no particular conventional sum for slight injuries having no permanent effect: *Parry* v. *English Electric Co. Ltd.* [1971] 1 W.L.R. 664.

[87] See McGregor, *op. cit.*, p. 771; *Wise* v. *Kaye* [1962] 1 Q.B. 638, 650, *per* Sellers L.J.

[88] Munkman, *op. cit.*, p. 123. It is probable that the court may award damages for inconvenience under this head: McGregor, *op. cit.*, p. 771.

[89] *Heaps* v. *Perrite Ltd.* [1937] 2 All E.R. 60; *West & Son Ltd.* v. *Shephard* [1964] A.C. 326. For the assessment of damages in a case of nervous shock where a wife witnessed the death of her husband, see *Hinz* v. *Berry* [1970] 2 Q.B. 40.

to " compensation neurosis " which will cease on the determination of the plaintiff's claim for damages,[90] and both its severity and duration must be taken into account. No damages will be awarded under this head, however severe the injury, if the plaintiff suffered no pain because he remained unconscious or was otherwise incapable of experiencing pain,[91] or if the pain is not attributable to the defendant's tort,[92] but this head of damage includes both the physical pain and the mental anguish caused by the injury. A person is entitled to damages for the mental suffering caused by the knowledge that his life has been short-ened[93] or that his capacity for enjoying life has been curtailed through physical handicaps.[94] It has been suggested that the fact that the plaintiff is wealthy may be a reason for awarding a smaller sum by way of damages for personal injuries,[95] but this view is untenable.[96] It is irrelevant that the plaintiff will be unable to enjoy the benefits that an award of damages may bring,[97] and it seems equally irrelevant that he could, if he wished, provide those benefits from his own resources.

(ii) *Loss of expectation of life*

As has been mentioned in the chapter on Death in Relation to Tort, the Court of Appeal in *Flint* v. *Lovell*[98] held that where the plaintiff's expectation of life has been reduced by his injuries he may recover damages on that account, and in *Rose* v. *Ford*[99] the House of Lords held that this claim survived for the benefit of a deceased person's estate.[1] At first it was thought that the damages were based upon the subjective effect upon the mind of the injured person from his knowing that his expectation of life had been reduced,[2] but in *Rose* v. *Ford*[3] this was held to be wrong. The subject-matter of the claim is normal expec-tancy of life, and this is " a thing of temporal value, so that its impair-ment is something for which damages can be given." [4]

---

[90] *James* v. *Woodall Duckham Construction Co. Ltd.* [1969] 1 W.L.R. 903, where it was also held that the plaintiff could not recover in respect of a period of delay in determining his claim which was due to his own dilatoriness in proceeding with it. See the observations of Winn L.J. [1969] 1 W.L.R. at p. 908 on post-accident neurosis and Cretney, " Compen-sation for Neurosis " (1970) 114 S.J. 307.

[91] *Wise* v. *Kaye, supra*; *West & Son Ltd.* v. *Shephard, supra.*

[92] *Cutler* v. *Vauxhall Motors Ltd.* [1971] 1 Q.B. 418, *ante*, pp. 86–87.

[93] *Davies and Davies* v. *Smith and Smith* (1958) Kemp and Kemp, *op. cit.*, 2nd ed., pp. 353, 358, *per* Lord Goddard C.J. (omitted from 3rd ed.); *Forrest* v. *Sharp* (1963) 10 S.J. 536.

[94] *West & Son Ltd.* v. *Shephard, supra*; *Cutts* v. *Chumley* [1967] 1 W.L.R. 742. Munkman, *op. cit.*, p. 124, refers in particular to the " distress which a permanent cripple must experience because he is constantly dependent upon the care of other persons."

[95] *Phillips* v. *L.S.W. Ry.* (1879) 5 C.P.D. 280, 294, *per* Cotton L.J.

[96] *Fletcher* v. *Autocar and Transporters Ltd.* [1968] 2 Q.B. 322, 340, 361 (the dicta in fact relate to loss of amenities, but it is submitted that the same applies to pain and suffering); *West & Son Ltd.* v. *Shephard, supra*, at p. 350, *per* Lord Morris.

[97] *Oliver* v. *Ashman* [1962] 2 Q.B. 210; *Wise* v. *Kaye* [1962] 1 Q.B. 638; *H. West & Son Ltd.* v. *Shephard, supra*; *Andrews* v. *Freeborough* [1967] 1 Q.B. 1, 18, *per* Davies L.J.

[98] [1935] 1 K.B. 354, *ante*, p. 499.

[99] [1937] A.C. 826.

[1] This is so even if the death is " instantaneous ": *Morgan* v. *Scoulding* [1938] 1 K.B. 786. See Allen, " Is Life a Boon? " (1941) 57 L.Q.R. 462.

[2] *Slater* v. *Spreag* [1936] 1 K.B. 83.

[3] *Supra.*   [4] *Rose* v. *Ford, supra*, at p. 849, *per* Lord Wright.

Following *Rose* v. *Ford*, where the assessment of the damages was not in issue, considerable difficulty was experienced in measuring in money terms this normal expectancy of life,[5] but in *Benham* v. *Gambling* [6] the House of Lords laid down rules with respect to this which may be thus summarised: (a) The thing to be valued is not the prospect of length of days but of a predominantly happy life.[7] Therefore the actuarial test is not of much value, though it may be relevant, *e.g.* in cases of extreme old age. (b) The capacity of the deceased to appreciate that his further life would bring him happiness is irrelevant; the test is objective, not subjective.[8] (c) Damages are in respect of loss of life, not loss of future pecuniary prospects. (d) Assessment is so difficult that very moderate damages should be given, and even less for a very young child, because its future is so uncertain.[9] (e) Wealth and social status must be ignored, for happiness does not depend on them.

The unreality of an assessment of damages under this head is apparent and has been judicially recognised [10]; the latest decision of the House of Lords upon the matter, *Yorkshire Electricity Board* v. *Naylor*,[11] comes close to a ruling that, given the then purchasing power of the pound awards should always be of the order of £500 and in subsequent cases it has, for practical purposes, been so regarded.[12] In *Naylor's* case the deceased had been a young man of 20 with very favourable prospects of a happy life and the Court of Appeal had increased to £1,000 the trial judge's award of £500.[13] The House of Lords restored the figure to £500, this being a sum which was approximately equivalent to the £200 awarded in *Benham* v. *Gambling* in 1941. The majority of their Lordships, it is true, paid lip service to the principle that the award in each case must be determined in the light of its own particular facts, but at the same time they denied that there was any justification for differtiating sharply between the case of a very young child and that of an

---

[5] See, *e.g. The Aizkari Mendi* [1938] P. 263; *Mills* v. *Stanway Coaches Ltd.* [1940] 2 K.B. 334.

[6] [1941] A.C. 157. This case concerned a deceased victim, but it is now clear that the same principle applies to a living plaintiff: *Wise* v. *Kaye* [1962] 1 Q.B. 638, 648, *per* Sellers L.J.; *Oliver* v. *Ashman* [1962] 2 Q.B. 210, 231, *per* Holroyd Pearce L.J. But see note 93, *ante*.

[7] *Jordan* v. *Mullis* [1952] C.L.Y. 905; *Burns* v. *Edman* [1970] 2 Q.B. 541. In the latter case Crichton J. awarded lower damages to the estate of a deceased criminal because he took judicial notice " of the fact that the life of a criminal is an unhappy one."

[8] See *Wise* v. *Kaye* [1962] 1 Q.B. 638.

[9] In *Benham's* case the House reduced an award of £1,000 in respect of a child, two and a half years old and favourably situated, to £200.

[10] *H. West & Son Ltd.* v. *Shephard* [1964] A.C. 326, 342–343, *per* Lord Reid; *ibid.* at p. 361, *per* Lord Devlin; *ibid.* at p. 367, *per* Lord Pearce; *Yorkshire Electricity Board* v. *Naylor*]1968] A.C. 529, 543, *per* Lord Morris; *ibid.* at p. 546, *per* Lord Guest; *ibid.* at p. 550, *per* Lord Devlin. In *Fletcher* v. *Autocar and Transporters Ltd.* [1968] 2 Q.B. 322, 353, Diplock L.J. described this head of damage as " the modern substitute for blood-money."

[11] *Supra.*

[12] *Andrews* v. *Freeborough* [1967] 1 Q.B. 1; *Cutts* v, *Chumley* [1967] 1 W.L.R. 742; *Cain* v. *Wilcock* [1968] 1 W.L.R. 1961; *Mallett* v. *McMonagle* [1970] A.C. 166 (£500 agreed between the parties). See now *McCann* v. *Shepherd* [1973] 1 W.L.R. 540 (£750).

[13] [1967] 1 Q.B. 244.

adult.[14] Lord Devlin, more realistically, pointed out that while every assessment of damages for non-pecuniary loss must start from a more or less conventional figure, " the conventional figure for loss of a limb or a faculty is only the starting-point for a voyage of assessment which may, and generally does, end up at a different figure. . . . But while the loss of a single faculty may be more serious for one individual than for another, the loss of all the faculties is, generally speaking, the same for all. Thus for loss of expectation of life the conventional figure has become the norm, unless the case is definitely abnormal." [15] His Lordship thought that judges derive little assistance either from the artificialities in Viscount Simon's speech in *Benham* v. *Gambling* or from the " customary exhortations to use common sense." It would be a great improvement if this head of damage was abolished and replaced by a short Act of Parliament fixing a suitable sum for the wrongdoer to pay into the deceased's estate and " while the law remains as it is, I think it is less likely to fall into disrespect if judges treat *Benham* v. *Gambling* as an injunction to stick to a fixed standard than if they start revaluing happiness, each according to his own ideas." [16]

The traditional exposition of the law is, however, somewhat misleading for nearly all the cases on loss of expectation of life concern dead victims, in which event a claim on behalf of the estate will generally be combined with one on behalf of the dependants under the Fatal Accidents Acts.[17] Where, however, the victim is alive he may in fact recover substantially more than the conventional sum because the court can take account of his consciousness of his shortened life expectancy in awarding damages for pain and suffering,[18] and it is submitted that this principle should remain so long as there are *any* damages for non-pecuniary loss. The only real controversy therefore concerns the survival of the cause of action for loss of expectation of life where the victim is dead. In many, if not most, cases the assessment is irrelevant,[19] but where it is relevant (*e.g.* in the case of a child, where there will be no Fatal Accidents Acts claim from which to deduct the loss of expectation of life award) it has been argued that this highly personal loss should not survive for the benefit of the victim's relatives. On the other hand, it may be contended that it is wrong that, say, the parents of a young child should recover no damages upon the child's death by negligence: the survival of claims for loss of expectation of life provides both a legal recognition that the tortfeasor committed a wrong against the deceased and an indirect form of *solatium* for the parents. The Law Commission has recently proposed that all claims for loss of

---

[14] [1968] A.C. at p. 539, *per* Viscount Dilhorne; *ibid.* at p. 544, *per* Lord Morris; *ibid.* at p. 547, *per* Lord Guest.
[15] *Ibid.* at p. 549.
[16] *Ibid.* at p. 550.
[17] See pp. 512–515, *ante.* The result will be that the nominal award to the estate will nearly always be deducted from the Fatal Accidents Acts award.
[18] See n. 93, *ante.*
[19] See n. 17, *ante.*

expectation of life should be abolished,[20] but the practical result of this would not be so very different from the present position in view of the other proposal for a direct right of action by certain relatives for a conventional sum by way cf *solatium*.[21]

(iii) *Loss of amenity* [22]

It has for long been recognised that if the plaintiff's injuries deprive him of some enjoyment, for example, if an amateur footballer loses a leg, then he is entitled to damages on this account.[23] It has recently become clear, however, that this is to a large extent an objective element of the plaintiff's loss separate and distinguishable from pain and suffering, so that even though the plaintiff never regains consciousness after the accident and never appreciates the condition to which he has been reduced, he may nevertheless recover substantial damages under this head. In *H. West & Son Ltd.* v. *Shephard* [24] the plaintiff was a married woman aged 41 at the time of her accident and sustained severe head injuries resulting in cerebral atrophy and paralysis of all four limbs. There was no prospect of improvement in her condition and her expectation of life was reduced to about five years. There was evidence that she might appreciate to some extent the condition in which she was, but she was unable to speak. The House of Lords, by a majority, upheld an award of £17,500 [25] in addition to £500 for loss of expectation of life. As Lord Morris said, " The fact of unconsciousness does not . . . eliminate the actuality of the deprivations of the

---

[20] Law Com. No. 56, para. 99. The principle referred to in n. 93, *ante*, would receive statutory recognition.

[21] *Ibid.*, paras. 177–178. See also p. 515, *ante*.

[22] Sometimes referred to as " loss of enjoyment of life " or " loss of faculty." Perhaps this last is the most accurate description: *Andrews* v. *Freeborough* [1967] 1 Q.B. 1, 18, *per* Davies L.J.

[23] *Heaps* v. *Perrite Ltd.* [1937] 2 All E.R. 60; *Manley* v. *Rugby Portland Cement Co. Ltd.* (1951) Kemp and Kemp, *op. cit.*, 2nd ed., pp. 624, 626, *per* Birkett L.J. (omitted from 3rd ed.); *Keating* v. *Elvan Reinforced Concrete Co. Ltd.* [1967] 3 All E.R. 611 (for proceedings in the Court of Appeal, see [1968] 1 W.L.R. 722). And see the cases cited by Street, *op. cit.*, p. 63.

[24] [1964] A.C. 326; *Wise* v. *Kaye* [1962] 1 Q.B. 638; *Andrews* v. *Freeborough* [1967] 1 Q.B. 1; *Hindmarsh* v. *H. & L. Slater Ltd.* (1966) 110 S.J. 429; *Cutts* v. *Chumley* [1967] 1 W.L.R. 742; *Ward* v. *Hertfordshire C.C.* [1969] 1 W.L.R. 790. Weir, *Casebook on Tort*, 3rd ed., p. 537. While conceding the existence of this objective element, Lord Devlin, in his dissenting speech in *West's* case, considered that in the assessment of damages it should be rated low: [1964] A.C. at p. 359.

[25] An increase of £2,500 over the award in *Wise* v. *Kaye*, *supra*, where the plaintiff had no appreciation of her condition. In *Cutts* v. *Chumley* [1967] 1 W.L.R. 742, the plaintiff, though her physical injuries were perhaps less gross than those of the plaintiff in *Shephard's* case, had more awareness of her condition and her expectation of life was much greater. There was thus an extension of the period of suffering and deprivation which it was anticipated that she must endure, and, accordingly, Willis J. awarded a substantially larger sum. See too *Povey* v. *Governors of Rydal School* [1970] 1 All E.R. 841. The majority and minority in *West* v. *Shephard* did not disagree about the factors making up the award, but about the relative weight given to the factors. The majority took the view that the largest factor was the objective loss which might be increased on account of consciousness of the loss or the deprivation of an amenity peculiarly important to the victim; the minority would reverse the relative importance of these factors. For instances of pleading deprivation of special activities, see Ogus, *op. cit.*, p. 212, n. 5.

ordinary experiences and amenities of life which may be the inevitable result of some physical injury." [26]

Powerful objections have been voiced against the decision in *West* v. *Shephard*.[27] The principal objections to it are that one can no more compensate an unconscious person than a dead one and that, though a deceased person's estate is entitled to damages under the head of loss of expectation of life, awards under this head are of a comparatively small, conventional sum [28] while the award to a living, though unconscious, plaintiff is almost inevitably substantial. There may therefore be a very great difference between the total sum awarded to the estate of a deceased person and that awarded to an unconscious, living one, even though the latter will be unable to use the money for his benefit and the whole sum will probably at some future date pass to his relatives.[29] On the other hand, there is a natural reluctance to treat a living plaintiff as if he were already dead.[30] A more general argument which is not aimed at the present treatment of the unconscious plaintiff but which supports the " conceptual " or " objective " approach upon which that treatment rests is the undesirability of making compensation depend upon the individual unhappiness caused by loss of amenities. "It would be lamentable if the trial of a personal injury claim put a premium on protestations of misery and if a long face was the only safe passport to a large award. Under the present practice there is no call for a parade of personal unhappiness. A plaintiff who cheerfully admits that he is as happy as he ever was, may yet receive a large award as reasonable compensation for the grave injury and loss of amenity over which he has managed to triumph." [31] The arguments are fairly evenly balanced and the Law Commission has recommended no change in the law.[32]

---

[26] [1964] A.C. at p. 349.

[27] See the dissenting speeches of Lords Devlin and Reid in that case, the dissenting judgment of Diplock L.J. in *Wise* v. *Kay, supra,* and the decision of the High Court of Australia in *Skelton* v. *Collins* (1966) 115 C.L.R. 94, as to which see Cornish in (1966) 29 M.L.R. 570. But the *West* v. *Shephard* approach has found favour in Canada: *The Queen in right of the Province of Ontario* v. *Jennings* (1966) 57 D.L.R. (2d) 644 (Can.Sup. Ct.).

[28] See pp. 564–567, *ante.* The contrast would be even greater if, as the Law Commission propose, damages for loss of expectation of life were, as such, abolished.

[29] See *Naylor* v. *Yorkshire Electricity Board* [1967] 1 Q.B. 244, 258–259, *per* Salmon L.J. No member of the House of Lords in *Naylor's* case ([1968] A.C. 529) adverted to this aspect of the problem.

But against this argument may be set the following factors: (1) the court has never exercised any general power to control the damages awarded to the victim of an accident; (2) some victims who are conscious but unable to " use " their damages might feel compensated by being able to benefit their relatives. *Cf.* Ogus, *op. cit.,* pp. 216–217.

[30] *Wise* v. *Kaye* [1962] 1 Q.B. 638; *H. West & Son Ltd.* v. *Shephard* [1964] A.C. 326. In *Andrews* v. *Freeborough* [1967] 1 Q.B. 1, the victim of the accident, a child of eight, had died before the trial, but had survived the accident in an unconscious condition for one year. The Court of Appeal, by a majority, upheld an award of £2,000 for loss of amenities during that year, in addition to £500 for loss of expectation of life.

In these " living death " cases, the possibility of advances in medical science bringing about some amelioration of the condition may contribute to the present judicial attitude.

[31] *West* v. *Shephard, supra,* at pp. 368–369, *per* Lord Pearce.

[32] Law Com. No. 56, *op. cit.,* para. 31. A fuller discussion appears in the Law Commission's Published Working Paper No. 41 (October 18, 1971). An alternative approach, also rejected by the Law Commission, is for a legislative tariff of compensation for non-

(iv) *The injury itself*

The heads of damage so far mentioned are all consequences of the injury, and in the majority of cases the consequences are more significant to the injured person than the injury itself. It must not be forgotten, however, that the injury itself is a proper subject of compensation and that damages may be awarded for an injury, quite apart from pain and suffering, even though the injury causes no disability whatever.[33] It is not uncommon, where the injury is a very specific one such as the loss of an eye, for the courts to pay regard in the assessment of the damages as much to the injury itself as to its consequences for the plaintiff.[34]

Basis of assessment

It is the nature of non-pecuniary loss that it cannot be translated directly into money,[35] but nevertheless the only form of compensation available is an award of monetary damages, and an assessment of damages has to be made.[36] These damages have been said to be " at large " and their quantification to be a jury question for which " no rigid rules, or rules that apply to all cases, can be laid down." [37] On the other hand, it is important to retain a measure of uniformity in the amounts awarded. Justice will neither be seen to be done nor will it in fact be done if widely divergent awards are made in essentially similar cases. Recently, therefore, the courts have not only permitted the citation of previous awards as guides to the assessment of damages [38] but the Court of Appeal has declared that in general juries should not be used for the assessment of damages in actions for personal injuries.[39] This will certainly tend to encourage consistency, for judges know the

---

pecuniary loss. A sort of precedent for this already exists in the Schedule under the Industrial Injuries Benefit scheme, but that Schedule does not seek to indicate compensation in the form of an award but indicates a percentage disablement related to loss of faculty which can then be applied to the current rate of benefit. See further Law Commission's Working Paper No. 41, paras. 98–104.

[33] Munkman, *op. cit.*, pp. 121–123; *Forster* v. *Pugh* [1955] C.L.Y. 741 (damages for loss of spleen though no evidence that absence of spleen causes any disability).

[34] See, *e.g. Gardner* v. *Dyson* [1967] 1 W.L.R. 1497; *Watson* v. *Heslop* (1971) 115 S.J. 308 (loss of an eye); *Kearns* v. *Higgs and Hill* (1968) 112 S.J. 252 (loss of sense of smell).

[35] Street, *op. cit.*, p. 5. *Cf.* Munkman, *op. cit.*, pp. 14–24, where it is contended that everything, including bodily integrity, can be given a value.

[36] *The Mediana* [1900] A.C. 113, 116, *per* Earl of Halsbury L.C.

[37] *The Susquehanna* [1926] A.C. 655, 662, *per* Viscount Dunedin. His Lordship added " but in each set of circumstances certain relevant considerations will arise which . . . it would be the duty of the judge in the case to bring before the jury."

[38] *Bird* v. *Cocking & Sons Ltd.* [1951] 2 T.L.R. 1260; *Rushton* v. *N.C.B.* [1953] 1 Q.B. 495; *Waldon* v. *War Office* [1956] 1 W.L.R. 50; *Bastow* v. *Bagley & Co. Ltd.* [1961] 1 W.L.R. 1494; *Jag Singh* v. *Toong Fong Omnibus Co. Ltd.* [1964] 1 W.L.R. 1382 (P.C.). Previous awards cannot, of course, be cited as binding precedents, only as guides, and they cannot be cited at all to the jury if there is one. Indeed no specific figure may be mentioned to the jury and no maximum or minimum may be indicated: *Bates* v. *Stone Parish Council* [1954] 1 W.L.R. 1249, 1258, *per* Birkett L.J.; *Ward* v. *James* [1966] 1 Q.B. 273, 301–303, *per* Lord Denning M.R.

[39] *Ward* v. *James, supra,* a decision of the Full Court. See also *Hennell* v. *Ranabaldo* [1963] 1 W.L.R. 1391; *Sims* v. *William Howard & Son Ltd.* [1964] 2 Q.B. 409. A jury may properly be ordered in an exceptional case where no pattern of awards exists: *Hodges* v. *Harland and Wolff Ltd.* [1965] 1 W.L.R. 523.

patterns of awards which have developed for various common kinds of injury [40] while juries do not, and, moreover, juries give no details, which makes comparison of their awards extremely difficult, if not dangerous. [41] But even if all cases are tried by judge alone, as a technique the comparison of awards has one serious drawback. Comparison of one case with another is only useful if like can really be compared with like, but the circumstances of each case are so variable that it is hard to find a basis for the comparison. Even if judges regularly divided their awards between the various applicable heads of damage, which they do not, how can a realistic comparison be made between cases involving different kinds of injury? If, for example, £5,000, to take a figure at random, is appropriate for the loss of a leg, what guidance does that give to the damages appropriate for the loss of an eye?

It was considerations of this kind which led to the remarkable dissenting judgment of Diplock L.J. in *Wise* v. *Kaye*,[42] where the plaintiff had been deprived of all the attributes of life but life itself. The case was itself remarkable in isolating, as no previous case had done, the actual physical injuries from the physical pain and mental anguish which usually accompany an injury, for the plaintiff remained unconscious from the moment of the accident,[43] and this, according to Diplock L.J., necessitated an attempt to ascertain the principles for the assessment of damages for non-pecuniary loss. A basis must be found for the comparison of one case with another and, in his lordship's view, the only possible yardstick was the loss of pleasure or happiness suffered by the plaintiff. " The loss of an eye restricts the sufferer's activities from which pleasure can be derived less than the loss of a leg, and it is primarily for this reason that . . . a lesser sum is awarded in compensation." [44]

It is almost certainly true that the only factor common to all cases of

---

[40] There is no single pattern to which awards for every kind of injury can be made to conform: Clerk and Lindsell, *Torts*, 13th ed., p. 241 and n. 74.

[41] Nevertheless it is of interest to note that in two cases of quadriplegia juries made identical awards of £50,000. In the earlier, *Morey* v. *Woodfield (No. 2)* [1964] 1 W.L.R. 16n., the Court of Appeal found no fault in the summing-up and felt constrained to allow the award to stand. In the second, *Warren* v. *King* [1964] 1 W.L.R. 1, a new trial was ordered. In both cases the Court of Appeal clearly regarded the awards as very high. For a case where the jury evidently erred, see *Every* v. *Miles* (1964), unreported, cited by Lord Denning M.R. in *Ward* v. *James* [1966] 1 Q.B. 273, 297.

[42] [1962] 1 Q.B. 638. See also the dissenting speeches of Lords Reid and Devlin in *H. West & Son Ltd.* v. *Shephard* [1964] A.C. 326. Ganz, " Compensation for loss of Humanity," 25 M.L.R. 479; Hamson [1962] C.L.J. 153.

[43] She died some time after the hearing in the Court of Appeal without regaining consciousness.

[44] [1962] 1 Q.B. at p. 665. A standard for comparison does not produce by itself any actual figure in money for any injury. For that a datum figure must be found, and this can only be done empirically. For the empirical considerations which, in the view of Diplock L.J., operate to provide the datum figure, see *ibid.* pp. 669–671. *Cf.* the differing views of Lord Denning M.R. and Salmon L.J. as to the relevance of the fact that most defendants are insured: *Fletcher* v. *Autocar and Transporters Ltd.* [1968] 2 Q.B. at pp. 335–336 and 362, respectively. It is of interest that Lord Denning M.R. and Diplock L.J. (*supra*), both of whom regard the fact as relevant, seem to treat it as a reason for avoiding large awards rather than the reverse, while Salmon L.J., who regards it as irrelevant, would be more generous to plaintiffs.

personal injury is that the sufferer's happiness is reduced, but the majority of the Court of Appeal in *Wise* v. *Kaye* nevertheless rejected Diplock L.J.'s solution. Not only would it involve the court in an invidious, undesirable and well-nigh unattainable investigation of the inner feelings and outward manifestations of conduct of and affecting a claimant,[45] but its application would produced strange and unpalatable results.[46]

In *H. West & Son Ltd.* v. *Shephard*[47] the House of Lords approved the majority decision in *Wise* v. *Kaye* and Diplock L.J.'s attempt to rationalise the assessment of damages for non-pecuniary loss failed. Its rejection as impracticable by the majority was probably inevitable, for so subtle an inquiry as it requires could seldom be carried out successfully, and Diplock L.J. himself has now said that the standard of comparison which the law applies, " if it is not wholly instinctive and incommunicable, is based, apart from pain and suffering, upon the degree of deprivation—that is, the extent to which the victim is unable to do those things which, but for the injury, he would have been able to do." [48]

This is not very satisfactory as a principle, and the result is that little more can be said in general terms than that the damages awarded should be fair and reasonable compensation for the injury, bearing in mind all the relevant heads of damage, that awards should keep pace with the times,[49] and that, so far as is possible, the sums awarded should bear a reasonable relationship to one another. As a practical matter, however, it is now generally acknowledged that awards of damages for personal injuries are based upon conventional figures derived from experience [50] and the need for consistency is fully recognised.[51] So long as " conventional " is not taken to mean artificial [52] and if judges can be persuaded to apportion the total sum awarded between the various heads of damage and to set out the factors which they take into account [53] there is no reason why a reasonable degree both of consistency and of fairness between litigants should not be achieved. But it remains true that every case must ultimately be decided on its own facts and that " the choice of the right order of figure is empirical and in practice results from a

---

[45] [1962] 1 Q.B. at pp. 649, 651, *per* Sellers L.J.; *H. West & Son Ltd.* v. *Shephard* [1964] A.C. 326, 368–369, *per* Lord Pearce.

[46] See text to n. 31, *supra*.

[47] *Supra*.

[48] *Fletcher* v. *Autocar and Transporters Ltd.* [1968] 2 Q.B. at p. 340. *Cf.* Street, *op. cit.*, pp. 6–13.

[49] *Senior* v. *Barker and Allen Ltd.* [1965] 1 W.L.R. 429.

[50] *Ward* v. *James* [1966] 1 Q.B. 273, 303, *per* Lord Denning M.R. See also *e.g. Jag Singh* v. *Toong Fong Omnibus Co. Ltd.* [1964] 1 W.L.R. 1382, 1386, *per* Lord Morris; *Fletcher* v. *Autocar and Transporters Ltd.* [1968] 2 Q.B. 322, 352, *per* Diplock L.J.; *ibid.* at p. 363, *per* Salmon L.J.

[51] In *Bastow* v. *Bagley & Co. Ltd.* [1961] 1 W.L.R. 1494 the Court of Appeal actually changed its decision on learning the result of another case.

[52] *Gardner* v. *Dyson* [1967] 1 W.L.R. 1497, 1501–1502, *per* Salmon L.J.

[53] This is not a suggestion that the total award should necessarily be assessed by adding together the sums found to be appropriate. There will often be overlap between the various heads of damage and this has to be taken into account: see p. 563, *ante*.

general consensus of opinion of damage-awarding tribunals—juries, judges and appellate courts." [54]

2. Pecuniary loss

(i) *Loss of earnings or earning capacity* [55]

If the plaintiff's injuries interfere with his ability to earn his living he is entitled to damages for loss of earnings, actual and prospective. Actual loss of earnings which has already accrued at the trial is classed as " special damage " and will normally be calculated simply by reference to the period of disability and the pre-accident rate of earning.[56] Future loss cannot, however, be so easily calculated because of the many imponderables which enter into the assessment and it is therefore classed as " general damage." [57] The court must estimate the period of future disability and the plaintiff's probable future rate of earning to arrive at a lump sum, and this must then be discounted to allow for the fact that he receives a lump sum instead of payments spread over a period of time and for the normal vicissitudes of life.[58] The fact that the plaintiff is not earning at the time of the accident, *e.g.* because he is a young child, does not prevent his recovering damages under this head if his capacity for earning in the future is reduced.[59] In assessing damages under this head, however, the fact that the plaintiff would have paid tax on his earnings had he earned them must be taken into account for he will pay no tax on his damages,[60] and where the

---

[54] *Ibid.* at p. 1498, *per* Diplock L.J. For the principles on which the Court of Appeal will disturb an award of damages made in the court below, see Clerk and Lindsell, *Torts*, 13th ed., pp. 252–254. Awards are reported monthly in *Current Law*, and are collected, together with much useful commentary and extracts from the judgments in many cases, in Kemp and Kemp, *Quantum of Damages*, Vol. I, *Personal Injury Claims*, 3rd ed.

[55] Street, *op. cit.*, pp. 44–55; Munkman, *op. cit.*, pp. 59–82; McGregor, *op. cit.*, pp. 739–752; Kemp and Kemp, *op. cit.*, pp. 121–139; Jolowicz, " Damages and Income Tax " [1959] C.L.J. 86, 94–96. " Earnings " includes fees and shares of profits: *Phillips* v. *L.S.W. Ry.* (1879) 5 C.P.D. 280; *Lee* v. *Sheard* [1956] 1 Q.B. 192. In *Milvanie* v. *Joseph* (1968) 112 S.J. 927, the plaintiff, a professional golfer, was awarded damages for the loss of the opportunity of competing in a number of tournaments.

While there is a clear theoretical difference between loss of future earnings and loss of future earning capacity, the courts have proceeded pragmatically rather than conceptually. However, as a general rule it can be said that the courts have concerned themselves with what the plaintiff *would* have earned, rather than with what he *could* have earned: *Tzouvelis* v. *Victorian Railway Commissioners* [1968] V.R. 112, 136; *Burns* v. *Edman* [1970] 2 Q.B. 541; Atiyah, " Loss of Earnings or Earning Capacity " (1971) 45 A.L.J. 228.

[56] *British Transport Commission* v. *Gourley* [1958] A.C. 185, 206, *per* Lord Goddard. The validity of this calculation depends upon the assumption that but for this injury the plaintiff would have continued earning at the same rate. If the assumption is unjustified, allowance must be made accordingly: *Phillips* v. *L.S.W. Ry.* (1879) 5 C.P.D. 280, 291, *per* Brett L.J.; *Rouse* v. *P.L.A.* [1953] 2 Lloyd's Rep. 179. For the duty to mitigate by submitting to medical treatment or accepting a suitable offer of re-employment, see *McAuley* v. *London Transport Executive* [1957] 2 Lloyd's Rep. 500; *Barnes* v. *Port of London Authority* [1957] 1 Lloyd's Rep. 486; *Taplin* v.-*T. F. Maltby Ltd.* [1966] 1 Lloyd's Rep. 650; *Luker* v. *Chapman* (1970) 114 S.J. 788.

[57] See *ante*, pp. 560–561.

[58] *Phillips* v. *L.S.W. Ry.* (1879) 5 C.P.D. 280; *Roach* v. *Yates* [1938] 1 K.B. 256.

[59] *Jones* v. *Richards* [1955] 1 W.L.R. 444, 458; *Oliver* v. *Ashman* [1962] 2 Q.B. 210; *Cutts* v. *Chumley* [1967] 1 W.L.R. 742; *Jones* v. *Lawrence* [1969] 3 All E.R. 267; *S.* v. *Distillers Co. (Biochemicals) Ltd.* [1970] 1 W.L.R. 114.

[60] *British Transport Commission* v. *Gourley* [1956] A.C. 185. *Cf. Pryce* v. *Elwood* (1964) 108 S.J. 583; *Taylor* v. *O'Connor* [1971] A.C. 115 (" in a sense *British Transport Com-*

plaintiff's expectation of life is reduced by his injuries, damages for future loss may be awarded only in respect of the period of life left to the plaintiff, not by reference to his expectation of working life as it would have been if he had not suffered the injury.[61] This last principle, forbidding compensation for earnings during the " lost years," is capable of working grave injustice to the dependants of an accident victim, for if the victim dies from his injuries after having sued the tortfeasor to judgment the dependants will probably be unable to bring a claim under the Fatal Accidents Acts,[62] even though the victim's claim will have been assessed on a life expectation which may be far less than it would have been but for the accident. The Law Commission has recommended that in any case where it is established that the plaintiff's expectation of life has been reduced by his injuries, he should himself be compensated for the loss during the period he would otherwise have lived on the basis of his probable income during that period, less what he would have spent on his own maintenance.[63]

Deductions.[64] From the figure thus assessed for loss of earnings certain deductions may have to be made in order to arrive at the final award. The Law Reform (Personal Injuries) Act 1948, s. 2, requires the deduction from damages for loss of earnings of one half of the value of certain benefits under the National Insurance Acts receivable by the plaintiff in the five years following the accident,[65] but other forms of

---

mission v. *Gourley* in reverse ": *ibid.* at p. 129, *per* Lord Reid). See Law Reform Committee's Seventh Report (Effect of Tax Liability on Damages), August 1958, Cmnd. 501; Baxter, " British Transport Commission v. Gourley " (1956) 19 M.L.R. 365; (1956) 72 L.Q.R. 153; Hall, " Taxation of Compensation for Loss of Income " (1957) 73 L.Q.R. 212; Jolowicz, " Damages and Income Tax " [1959] C.L.J. 86; Tucker, " Damages and Income Tax, A Miracle of Alchemy? " [1959] C.L.J. 185; Kemp and Kemp, *op. cit.*, pp. 140–150. National Insurance contributions which would have been payable by the plaintiff but for his injury must similarly be taken into account (*Cooper* v. *Firth Brown Ltd.* [1963] 1 W.L.R. 418). Note that the principle of *Gourley's* case may apply in cases of libel: *Lewis* v. *Daily Telegraph Ltd.* [1964] A.C. 234.
[61] *Harris* v. *Brights Asphalt Contractors Ltd.* [1953] 1 Q.B. 617; *Oliver* v. *Ashman*, *supra*; *Wise* v. *Kaye* [1962] 1 Q.B. 638. But see *per* Sellers L.J. in the last-named case at p. 646; *Pope* v. *D. Murphy & Son Ltd.* [1961] 1 Q.B. 222; Street, *op. cit.*, pp. 48–53; Jolowicz [1960] C.L.J. 160; Fleming, " The Lost Years: A Problem in the Computation and Distribution of Damages " (1962) 50 California L.R. 598.
[62] The dependants' right of action under these Acts depends upon the existence of a right of action in the deceased at the time of his death (see pp. 503–504, *ante*) and his cause of action merges in judgment or settlement: *Read* v. *Great Eastern Ry.* (1868) L.R. 3 Q.B. 55; *Murray* v. *Shuter* [1972] 1 Lloyd's Rep. 6, 7; *McCann* v. *Sheppard* [1973] 1 W.L.R. 540 (Stamp L.J. expressing no opinion). The injustice of the present rule is amply illustrated by the last case, in which, by reason of the victim's death between trial and appeal the damages for loss of earnings were reduced from £15,000 to £400. Even if the dependants were not barred by merger of the victim's claim they might face limitation problems. In *Murray* v. *Shuter*, *supra*, the court sought to evade the *Oliver* v. *Ashman* problem by adjourning the case for nine months to allow the plaintiff to die.
[63] Law Com. No. 56, para. 87. This is in effect the solution adopted by the High Court of Australia in *Skelton* v. *Collins* (1966) 115 C.L.R. 94. Two other solutions were considered by the Law Commission but rejected as being too complicated: (i) to allow the dependants to bring a separate action before the victim's death; (ii) to allow the victim to join dependants in his action.
[64] Ganz, " Mitigation of Damages by Benefits Received " (1962) 25 M.L.R. 559.
[65] See *Stott* v. *Sir William Arrol & Co. Ltd.* [1953] 2 Q.B. 92; *Flowers* v. *Wimpey & Co. Ltd.* [1956] 1 Q.B. 73; *Hultquist* v. *Universal Pattern and Precision Engineering Co. Ltd.* [1960] 2 Q.B. 467; *Eley* v. *Bedford* [1972] 1 Q.B. 155; Clerk and Lindsell, *Torts*, 13th ed.,

insurance payments received by the plaintiff on account of his injuries are not set against damages.[66] Other " collateral benefits " depend upon the principles of the common law and a good deal of order has now been brought to these principles by the House of Lords. Wages or sick pay paid by an employer under contractual entitlement are certainly deductible,[67] but the position where such payments are made *ex gratia* is doubtful: the better view is that they are probably not deductible.[68] On the other hand, a disablement pension does not fall to be deducted from a plaintiff's claim for loss of earnings, for such a pension is really equivalent to a policy of insurance.[69] Charitable payments are not taken into account, for otherwise there would be a risk that the springs of charity would dry up.[70] As for welfare state benefits not mentioned in the Law Reform (Personal Injuries) Act [71] it is submitted that unemployment benefit is deductible,[72] but supplementary benefit [73] and state retirement pensions are not.[74]

---

pp. 230–231. Where the plaintiff fails to claim these benefits (whether, it seems, through ignorance or otherwise) no deduction is to be made in respect of them because s. 2 provides an exhaustive statement of the grounds upon which a reduction may be made: *Eley* v. *Bedford, supra.*

[66] *Bradburn* v. *G.W. Ry.* (1874) L.R. 10 Ex. 1; *Parry* v. *Cleaver* [1970] A.C. 1.

[67] *Parry* v. *Cleaver* [1970] A.C. 1; Weir, *Casebook on Tort*, 3rd ed., p. 540; *Receiver for Metropolitan Police District* v. *Croydon Corporation* [1957] 2 Q.B. 154; *Turner* v. *Ministry of Defence* (1969) 113 S.J. 505. The employer is not, however, entitled to recover the wages from the wrongdoer except in the few cases in which the action *per quod servitium amisit* is available: *Receiver for Metropolitan Police District* v. *Croydon Corporation, supra.* The Law Commission has recommended that this type of action be abolished, there being no particular demand from employers for any form of recovery from the tortfeasor: Law Com. No. 56, paras. 142–150, 158. See also Shalgi, " A Benefactor's Right of Action Against a Tortfeasor: A New Approach in Israel " (1966) 29 M.L.R. 42 and Tedeschi, " An Israel Law on Personal Injuries " (1966) 15 I.C.L.Q. 1195.

[68] *Dennis* v. *L.P.T.B.* [1948] 1 All E.R. 779 is some authority for this view. However, the theme running through *Parry* v. *Cleaver, supra,* is the nature of the benefit conferred rather than the conditions under which it is paid, so it may be that even a gratuitous payment of wages is deductible. If so, the difficulty is then to distinguish between gratuitously paid wages and charitable payments, the latter being clearly not deductible. In *Cunningham* v. *Harrison* [1973] Q.B. 942, where no deduction was made, Lord Denning M.R. refers to the plaintiff as being on " virtually half-pay for the rest of his days," but the contract of employment in that case had been terminated and it would seem better to regard the payment as in the nature of a voluntary pension. *Quaere* as to the correctness of the course adopted in *Dennis* v. *L.P.T.B., supra,* of requiring the plaintiff to give an undertaking that he would reimburse his employer out of the damages. See, however, the Commonwealth cases cited in Cooper, " A Collateral Benefits Principle " (1971) 39 C.B.R. 501 at 506–507.

[69] *Parry* v. *Cleaver, supra* (overruling, for practical purpo s, *Browning* v. *War Office* [1963] 1 Q.B. 750; *Hewson* v. *Downs* [1970] 1 Q.B. 73. The approach of the majority in *Parry* v. *Cleaver* is to classify the loss as " wages " and the benefit as " pension." The approach of the minority is to treat both as " money." However, the question is at bottom one of policy, and neither conceptual classification is decisive: Jolowicz [1969] C.L.J. 183; Atiyah, " Collateral Benefits Again " (1969) 32 M.L.R. 697. Cooper, *loc. cit.,* argues for a principle whereby the intended purpose of the benefit would be the crucial factor.

[70] *Redpath* v. *Belfast and County Down Ry.* [1947] N.I. 167; *Parry* v. *Cleaver, supra.* The reasons of policy behind this approach seem overwhelming.

[71] See n. 65, *supra.* An income tax rebate is deductible: *Hartley* v. *Sandholme Iron Co.* [1974] 3 W.L.R. 445.

[72] This was deducted in *Parsons* v. *B.N.M. Laboratories Ltd.* [1964] 1 Q.B. 95 (not a personal injuries case) and *Foxley* v. *Oulton* [1965] 2 Q.B. 306. The C.A. in *Cheeseman* v. *Bowaters United Kingdom Paper Mills Ltd.* [1971] 1 W.L.R. 1173 assumed that such benefits were still deductible, though it is arguable that they are more akin to the proceeds of insurance under the *Parry* v. *Cleaver* dispensation.

Footnotes 73 and 74 on p. 575

Actuarial computation. It is obvious that damages for future loss of earnings cannot be assessed by a simple arithmetical calculation, and it is not always possible for this to be done even for accrued loss, for it cannot always be certain what the plaintiff would have earned had he not been injured.[75] The courts have, therefore, not always attempted to calculate pecuniary loss to a high degree of exactness and, as we have seen, damages for future loss of earnings have often been awarded in one lump sum together with damages for non-pecuniary loss. Nevertheless, it has been urged [76] that actuarial calculation can provide a considerable measure of precision in calculating damages for loss of earnings and that " actuarial evidence in personal injury . . . litigation in England ought to become the standard procedure forthwith." [77] This is not the place for a detailed investigation of so complicated a matter, but it is of interest that the Law Commission has demonstrated how actuarial techniques could be brought into regular use for the purpose of calculating the present value of future pecuniary loss.[78] The Commission has now recommended legislation to promote the use of actuarial evidence and the introduction of a set of official actuarial tables.[79] Despite the possibility of some extra costs [80] it is to be hoped that these proposals will be adopted: it is, after all, admitted that the object of an award of damages to the plaintiff is " so far as possible, to make good to him the financial loss which he has suffered and will probably suffer as a result of the wrong done to him for which the defendant is responsible." [81]

(ii) *Medical expenses*

The plaintiff is entitled to the cost of medical and similar services which he reasonably incurs as a result of his injuries, and it has been enacted that in determining the reasonableness of any expenses the possibility of avoiding them by making use of the National Health

[73] It was held in *Foxley* v. *Oulton, supra,* that the then national assistance benefit was not deductible because of its discretionary nature. The element of formal discretion in the present supplementary benefits scheme is in fact limited, but the discretion-right distinction is less important after *Parry* v. *Cleaver.* In *Ruffley* v. *Frisby, Jarvis Ltd.,* May 18, 1972 (unreported) Willis J. held that supplementary benefit was not deductible.

[74] *Hewson* v. *Downs, supra.* See also Law Com. No. 56, paras. 132–137.

[75] *Ante,* p. 572, note 56.

[76] Street, *op. cit.,* Chap. 5; Kemp and Kemp, *op. cit.,* pp. 44–78; Prevett, " Actuarial Assessment of Damages: the Thalidomide Case " (1972) 35 M.L.R. 140, 257.

[77] Street, *op. cit.,* p. 137. See also Munkman, *op. cit.,* pp. 63–66. There is no doubt that actuarial evidence is admissible, but its use has been discouraged by the decisions in *Taylor* v. *O'Connor* [1971] A.C. 115 and *Mitchell* v. *Mulholland (No. 2)* [1972] 1 Q.B. 65, which expressed a clear preference for the " multiplicand and multiplier " method.

[78] Published Working Paper No. 27, *Personal Injury Litigation: Assessment of Damages,* 1970.

[79] Law Com. No. 56, paras. 215–230.

[80] The cost of actuarial evidence may have been exaggerated: see Law Com. No. 56, n. 194.

[81] *British Transport Commission* v. *Gourley* [1956] A.C. 185, 212, *per* Lord Reid; *ibid.* at pp. 197–198, *per* Earl Jowitt. Another grave problem in this field is that of the effect of inflation. The predominant attitude is that no allowance should be made for this because the effect could be largely off-set by investment in good growth equities: *Mallett* v. *McMonagle* [1970] A.C. 166, 175–176, *per* Lord Diplock. Recent events have falsified this, though continuing very high interest rates tend towards the same result. See further, Law Com. No. 56, paras. 217–230 and *Young* v. *Percival* [1975] 1 W.L.R. 17.

Service is to be disregarded.[82] Damages under this head may be awarded in respect of both past and prospective expenses[83] and may include not only the cost of medical treatment and attendance but all such matters as increased living expenses if, e.g. the plaintiff has to live in a special institution because of his injuries,[84] or be supplied with special equipment[85] or, presumably, has to adhere to a special and expensive diet.[86] Transport costs to and from hospital may similarly be recovered.[87] Less easy to support is the decision that if the plaintiff will be supported free of charge for the rest of his life in a National Health Service hospital no deduction is to be made from his damages for loss of earnings in respect of what would have been his general living expenses had he not been injured.[88]

It may happen that services for which the plaintiff would otherwise have had to pay are rendered by a friend to whom the plaintiff incurs no legal obligation, and the question then arises whether the plaintiff is entitled to damages under this head. It is true that he will himself have suffered no relevant loss, but the friend may have incurred actual expense or have given up his employment in order to look after the plaintiff, and the plaintiff will thus normally feel himself under a moral obligation to reimburse his friend. For many years there was doubt whether any damages were recoverable by the plaintiff[89] on this account and, if so, on what basis. The matter has now been put on a firm footing by the decision of the Court of Appeal in *Donnelly* v. *Joyce*[90] that the plaintiff is entitled to recover that proper and reasonable cost of nursing or other services which he needs as a result of the accident, and on this issue it is irrelevant whether he is under any legal[91] or " moral " obligation to pay the person who provides the services. The sum

---

[82] Law Reform (Personal Injuries) Act 1948, s. 2 (4). If the plaintiff in fact receives treatment under the National Health Service he cannot claim for what the treatment would have cost if he had contracted for it privately: *Harris* v. *Brights Asphalt Contractors Ltd.* [1963] 1 Q.B. 617, 635, *per* Slade J.; *Oliver* v. *Ashman* [1962] 2 Q.B. 210.

[83] They will, however, be divided between the " special " and the " general " damages: *ante*, pp. 560–561; *Shearman* v. *Folland* [1950] 2 K.B. 43, 51, *per* Asquith L.J.

[84] *Shearman* v. *Folland, supra*; *Oliver* v. *Ashman, supra*; *Cutts* v. *Chumley* [1967] 1 W.L.R. 742.

[85] *S.* v. *Distillers (Biochemicals) Ltd.* [1970] 1 W.L.R. 114.

[86] Munkman, *op. cit.*, pp. 90–91.

[87] *Ibid.* p. 75.

[88] *Daish* v. *Wauton* [1972] 2 Q.B. 262; see the comment on this case in Weir, *Casebook on Tort*, 3rd ed., pp. 546–547. It is submitted that since the benefit in this case was not in the form of money, *Parry* v. *Cleaver* does not provide the close analogy which the C.A. assumed. Unless the plaintiff is institutionalised the problem does not, of course, arise, since he has to continue to support himself.

[89] There is no question of any right of action in the person rendering the assistance in the absence of the special circumstances set out in the next section.

[90] [1974] Q.B. 454; Jolowicz [1974] C.L.J. 40; *Roach* v. *Yates* [1938] 1 K.B. 256; *Liffen* v. *Watson* [1940] 1 K.B. 556; *Cunningham* v. *Harrison* [1973] Q.B. 942; *Davies* v. *Tenby Corporation, The Times*, April 10, 1974.

[91] The device had sometimes been adopted of the plaintiff and the person giving him assistance making a contract: *Haggar* v. *de Placido* [1972] 1 W.L.R. 716.

recoverable under this head will not, of course, necessarily be the same as the earnings given up by the friend who renders the assistance.[92]

Domestic relations.[93] If a father incurs medical expenses on behalf of his injured child or a husband does so on behalf of his wife, the father or husband can himself recover damages from the wrongdoer in respect of those expenses, but the basis and thus the scope of this remedy is not entirely clear. Is the right of action in these cases derived from the ancient actions *per quod servitium* and *per quod consortium amisit*,[94] or does it depend upon a man's legal obligation to support and maintain his wife and children? Probably the latter solution is the more favoured today,[95] but the former cannot be entirely abandoned as it is beyond dispute that a husband whose wife has been injured may recover not only medical expenses incurred on her behalf, but also the cost of domestic help necessitated by his wife's incapacity.[96] Lord Goddard has said,[97] " As to the first, I think his claim really lies in his legal obligation to provide proper maintenance and comfort, including medical and surgical aid, for his wife, and the fact that a wrong does cause that obligation to be incurred is regarded as giving him a right to recover [98] while the latter is truly a remnant, and perhaps the last, of his right to sue for the loss of servitium." It follows that a person who incurs medical expenses on behalf of a child but who neither has a legal obligation to maintain the child nor is in position to make use of the action *per quod servitium amisit* is unable to recover those expenses in a direct action against the tortfeasor.[99] So far as prospective medical expenses are concerned, however, damages may be awarded to the plaintiff wife or child even though it is clear that contractual liability to pay them will be incurred

---

[92] The lost earnings might be far in excess of the reasonable value of the services. Conversely, the person rendering the assistance might not have given up any paid employment. *Donnelly* v. *Joyce* renders the implementation of the proposal in Law Com. No. 56, para. 155, unnecessary. Indeed, the decision is wider than that proposal: Jolowicz, *loc. cit.* at p. 42 and p. 578, *post.*

[93] Street, *op. cit.*, Chap. 9.

[94] *Ante*, pp. 441–443, 440–441.

[95] See, *e.g. Kirkham* v. *Boughey* [1958] 1 Q.B. 338, 342, *per* Diplock J.

[96] See, too, *Hare* v. *British Transport Commission* [1956] 1 W.L.R. 250; *Cutts* v. *Chumley* [1967] 1 W.L.R. 742.

[97] *Best* v. *Samuel Fox & Co. Ltd.* [1952] A.C. 716, 733.

[98] The nature of this right, whether it exists in tort or in quasi-contract, seems never to have been considered. There are difficulties in either approach, but on the whole it is thought that the quasi-contractual explanation is the better. *Receiver for Metropolitan Police District* v. *Croydon Corporation* [1957] 2 Q.B. 154 may be distinguished from the situation now under consideration on the ground that in that case the plaintiff incurred no additional expenditure as a result of the tort whereas the medical expenses incurred by the husband would not have been incurred if the wife had not been injured (*cf.* Street, *op. cit.*, p. 224). A claim based on loss of consortium or servitium is plainly founded upon tort.

[99] *Kirkham* v. *Boughey* [1958] 2 Q.B. 338, 342, *per* Diplock J.; *Donnelly* v. *Joyce* [1974] Q.B. 454, 462. In *Square* v. *Model Farm Dairies (Bournemouth) Ltd.* [1938] 2 All E.R. 740, 750 (this point not considered by the C.A. [1939] 2 K.B. 365) Lewis J. held that a mother is under no obligation to provide for her daughter while the father is alive and that therefore she could not recover in respect of medical expenses incurred on the daughter's behalf. It is respectfully submitted that the decision that the mother is under no obligation is incorrect (Street, *op. cit.*, pp. 221–223) but that otherwise the decision is correct.

by others.[1] So far as expenses already incurred are concerned, if the person incurring them cannot recover directly from the tortfeasor, it is submitted that on the principle of *Donnelly* v. *Joyce* [2] the plaintiff himself may recover and then reimburse his benefactor, since there is no distinction between the rendering of services by the benefactor and expenditure by him on the plaintiff's behalf.[3] If, for example, a child is staying with its aunt when it is injured by the defendant's negligence and the aunt incurs medical expenses on the child's behalf, she will have no direct action against the defendant, but the child could recover damages for the expenses incurred by its aunt and then reimburse her.

Closely allied to this topic is the problem of the husband whose wife is injured and who gives up his employment in order to remain with her. It appears that he can claim damages for the consequent loss of earnings, if but only if, the loss can be justified either on the ground that it formed part of the medical expenses because visits by him might well be a factor in her recovery [4] or that it was a reasonable alternative to loss of consortium for which he could otherwise have claimed.[5] Evidently cases in which a husband is justified in giving up his employment altogether in order to remain with his injured wife must be rare, but *McNeill* v. *Johnstone* [6] illustrates when a husband's claim for loss of earnings may be upheld. The husband was a U.S. Air Force officer stationed near Margate and his wife was injured in an accident caused by the defendant's negligence. She was sent to a U.S. Air Force hospital at Swindon and the husband took a month's leave without pay in order to stay near her. The cost of treatment there was very much less than it would have been at a nursing home in Margate where the husband could have visited her without cost to himself, and Devlin J. held that he could recover his loss of earnings as an alternative to damages for loss of consortium. " If he could have claimed damages of £100 for loss of consortium during a month—I take £100 as a notional figure—and can say: ' In order to preserve my consortium and therefore save the defendant paying me £100, I gave up my earnings during that month so as to be free to see my wife,' he must be entitled to the earnings as an alternative." [7] In *Kirkham* v. *Boughey*,[8] on the other hand, the husband was home on leave from his highly paid work in Africa when his wife was injured and he refused to return there, ultimately accepting employment in England at a much lower wage. Diplock J. held that although his conduct had been reasonable in the circumstances he could not

---

[1] See, *e.g. Oliver* v. *Ashman* [1962] 2 Q.B. 210 (child aged 4 at date of trial and rendered a low-grade mental defective entitled to damages in respect of prospective medical expenses).
[2] [1974] Q.B. 454, *ante*, p. 576; see also *Schneider* v. *Eisovitch* [1960] 2 Q.B. 430.
[3] *Donnelly* v. *Joyce, supra.*
[4] *Kirkham* v. *Boughey* [1958] 2 Q.B. 338, 343, *per* Diplock J.
[5] *Behrens* v. *Bertram Mills Circus Ltd.* [1957] 2 Q.B. 1; *McNeill* v. *Johnstone* [1958] 1 W.L.R. 888. *Cf. McDonnell* v. *Stevens, The Times,* April 8, 1967.
[6] *Supra.*
[7] At p. 892.
[8] [1958] 2 Q.B. 338.

recover damages under this head. The decision can be distinguished from *McNeill* v. *Johnstone* on the ground that the husband's claim was not based upon loss of consortium,[9] but it must be admitted that the distinction is a technical one. It may be permissible to suggest that the real difference between the cases is to be found in the fact that whereas an award of damages to the husband in *Kirkham* v. *Boughey* would have substantially increased the defendant's liability, the award in *McNeill* v. *Johnstone* merely brought the liability up to what it would have been if the wife had been treated in an ordinary nursing home. Both decisions appear to be correct upon their facts,[10] but the law upon which they are based seems less satisfactory.

The Law Commission has now recommended the total abolition of the action *per quod consortium et servitium amisit.*[11] If its recommendations are carried into effect, the victim himself will be able to recover from the tortfeasor the value of gratuitous services which he rendered to the family[12] but nothing is proposed to replace the *consortium* element in the present action. *McNeill* v. *Johnstone* would accordingly fall with the form of action upon which it rests.

(iii) *Other pecuniary loss*

The heads of damage so far mentioned are not exhaustive, nor can an exhaustive list be given, for the plaintiff is entitled to damages for any item of loss he may have suffered provided only that it is not too remote. The following examples provide some indication, however, of the kinds of loss that may have to be considered in any given case. If his employer provided board and lodging and he has to give up his employment, the plaintiff may recover the value of that board and lodging as well as his actual loss of earnings,[13] and if he has to give up a pensionable employment he can recover for any consequent loss of pension rights.[14] A man whose injuries leave him with a permanent disability may recover for the consequent handicap he will suffer in seeking employment in the future, even if at the time of the trial he is working at his full pre-accident wage,[15] and an unmarried woman who suffers disfigurement may recover damages for the consequent reduction of her prospects of marriage.[16]

---

[9] It may be observed also that in *Kirkham* v. *Boughey* the husband and wife did not normally live together. The husband worked in Africa and his wife and children lived in England.

[10] In *McNeill* v. *Johnstone* [1958] 1 W.L.R. at p. 892, Devlin J. expressed his concurrence with Diplock J.'s decision in *Kirkham* v. *Boughey*.

[11] Law Com. No. 56, para. 158. For earlier proposals see the Law Reform Committee's Eleventh Report (Loss of Services) 1963, Cmnd. 2017; Law Commission Published Working Papers Nos. 19 (1968) and 41 (1971) and the 9th ed. of this work. See generally Chap. 20, *ante*. [12] See Chap. 20, *ante*.

[13] *Liffen* v. *Watson* [1940] 1 K.B. 556. It is immaterial that a relative provides the plaintiff with free accommodation and food: *ibid*.

[14] *Judd* v. *Hammersmith, etc. Hospital Board* [1960] 1 W.L.R. 328; *Parry* v. *Cleaver* [1970] A.C. 1.

[15] Kemp and Kemp, *op. cit.*, pp. 97–99, and cases there cited.

[16] Similarly a married woman whose husband leaves her on account of her disfigurement may recover for her loss: *Lampert* v. *Eastern National Omnibus Co.* [1954] 1 W.L.R. 1047. Loss of marriage prospects is an item of pecuniary as well as non-pecuniary loss: Kemp and Kemp, *op. cit.*, p. 100.

Even a man's hobbies may have to be considered.[17] If he had a profitable hobby which he can no longer pursue, or if, for example, he formerly tended his own garden and now has to employ another to do it for him, he has suffered a loss for which he is entitled to compensation.[18]

(iv) *Interest on damages for personal injury* [19]

Although there is now power for the court in certain circumstances to order an interim payment on account of damages,[20] it is obvious that there will always be a lapse of time between the injury and the payment of the damages, and that frequently the plaintiff will have to wait a considerable time until his claim has been determined and the damages found due to him are paid. Until recently the court had a discretion to award interest,[21] but this is now mandatory in an action for personal injuries in which the plaintiff recovers more than £200, unless the court is satisfied that there are special reasons why interest should not be given.[22] The principles upon which interest should be awarded were laid down by the Court of Appeal in *Jefford* v. *Gee*.[23] On the damages for pain and suffering and for loss of amenity, interest should be paid from the date of service of the writ [24]; interest on the " special " damages, *i.e.* accrued pecuniary losses, should be dealt with broadly and in normal cases interest at half the current rate should be paid from the date of the accident. But, since interest is awarded to a plaintiff for being kept out of money which ought to have been paid to him, no interest is payable on the damages awarded for future pecuniary loss.

Loss of or Damage to Property [25]

As we have seen, the basic principle for the assessment of damages is that there should be *restitutio in integrum*,[26] and in cases of loss of or damage to property this principle can be more fully applied than in cases of personal injury. It is, in fact, the dominant rule to which the

---

[17] *i.e.* apart from their relevance to the claim for loss of amenities, *ante*, pp. 567–568.

[18] See Street, *op. cit.*, p. 58, where it is pointed out that there are some twelve to fifteen million practitioners of " Do-it-Yourself." Obviously, serious financial consequences may follow the incapacity of such a person.

[19] The Law Commission has proposed certain alterations of the principles discussed below: Law Com. No. 56, paras. 263–286.

[20] Administration of Justice Act 1969 (c. 58), s. 20; R.S.C., Ord. 29, Part II. The conditions for an order for an interim payment are quite stringent and it will be by no means in every case in which the plaintiff ultimately succeeds that an order will be made.

[21] Law Reform (Miscellaneous Provisions) Act 1934, s. 3.

[22] Administration of Justice Act 1969, s. 22. The section applies also to actions under the Fatal Accidents Acts. Interest on damages for personal injuries is not subject to income tax: Income and Corporation Taxes Act 1970, s. 375A, as inserted by Finance Act 1971, s. 19; *Mason* v. *Harman* [1972] R.T.R. 1.

[23] [1970] 2 Q.B. 130; *May* v. *A. G. Bassett & Sons* (1970) 114 S.J. 269; *Newall* v. *Tunstall* [1971] 1 W.L.R. 105; *Chadwick* v. *Parsons, The Times*, January 23, 1971. Walker, " Interest on damages " (1970) 120 New L.J. 308.

[24] But a third party should pay interest on general damages only from the date of issue of the third party notice: *Slater* v. *Hughes* [1971] 1 W.L.R. 1438.

[25] For the measure of damages in detinue and conversion, see *ante*, pp. 410–412, 433–436.

[26] *Ante*, pp. 561–562.

subsidiary rules which follow must conform.[27] In working out these subsidiary rules the courts have been mainly concerned with cases involving ships, but the rules are the same in Admiralty and under the common law.[28]

1. Loss

Where property is totally destroyed as a result of the defendant's tort the normal measure of damage is its value [29] at the time and place of the destruction, and this is so even if the plaintiff has only a limited interest in the property destroyed.[30] In principle the plaintiff is entitled to such a sum of money as would enable him to purchase a replacement at the prices prevailing at the date of destruction,[31] and where no market exists in which such prices can be ascertained, the tendency is to look to replacement cost.[32] Merely to enable the plaintiff to acquire a replacement, however, will often be insufficient to effect a full *restitutio in integrum*, at least if the property destroyed is used by the plaintiff in the course of his business. " The true rule seems to be that the measure of damages in such cases is the value of the ship to her owner as a going concern at the time and place of the loss. In assessing that value regard must naturally be had to her pending engagements, either profitable or the reverse." [33] In *Liesbosch Dredger* v. *SS. Edison* [34] the plaintiff's dredger, which they were using in the course of contract work at Patras Harbour, was sunk by the negligence of the defendants. It was held that they were entitled to recover the market price of a comparable dredger, the cost of adapting the new dredger and transporting it to Patras, and compensation for disturbance in the carrying out of their contract from the date of the loss until the new dredger could reasonably have been available in Patras.[35]

---

[27] *Liesbosch Dredger* v. *SS. Edison* [1933] A.C. 449, 463, per Lord Wright.

[28] *Admiralty Commissioners* v. *SS. Susquehanna* [1926] A.C. 655, 661, *per* Viscount Dunedin.

[29] For the difficulties involved in the concept of value, see Street, *op. cit.*, pp. 188–203.

[30] *The Winkfield* [1902] P. 42.

[31] *Liesbosch Dredger* v. *SS. Edison* [1933] A.C. 449; Weir, *Casebook on Tort*, 3rd ed., p. 553.

[32] Street, *op. cit.*, p. 201, citing *Clyde Navigation Trustees* v. *Bowring* (1929) 34 Ll.L.R. 319. *Cf. Ucktos* v. *Mazzetta* [1956] 1 Lloyd's Rep. 209 (destruction of boat of unusual type. Damages restricted to cost of another boat of a different type which would reasonably meet the plaintiff's needs). In cases involving the destruction of buildings the measure of damages is normally the diminution in value of the plaintiff's interest in the land, not the cost of replacement: *Moss* v. *Christchurch R.D.C.* [1925] 2 K.B. 750. *Cf. Hollebone* v. *Midhurst and Fernhurst Builders Ltd.* [1968] 1 Lloyd's Rep. 38, where the building was unique and its reinstatement reasonable. See also p. 584, *post*.

[33] *Liesbosch Dredger* v. *SS. Edison* [1933] A.C. 449, 463–464, *per* Lord Wright; *Jones* v. *Port of London Authority* [1954] 1 Lloyd's Rep. 489 (lorry).

[34] [1933] A.C. 449. See *ante*, pp. 101–102, where the case is considered from the point of view of remoteness of damage. The plaintiffs' claim for the cost of hire of a substitute dredger failed because this damage flowed from their own impecuniosity. But a plaintiff whose chattel is destroyed will normally be entitled to the reasonable cost of hire of a substitute *until a replacement can be bought*: *Moore* v. *D.E.R. Ltd.* [1971] 1 W.L.R. 1476; *cf. Watson Norrie* v. *Shaw* (1967) 111 S.J. 117.

[35] It is to be remembered that negligent interference with contract does not of itself give rise to a cause of action: *ante*, pp. 51–53.

As Lord Wright pointed out in *Liesbosch Dredger* v. *SS. Edison*,[36] in assessing the value of a ship as a going concern, care must be taken to avoid awarding damages twice over. The market value of a profit-earning chattel such as a ship will normally recognise that the chattel will be used in a profit-earning capacity and the actual loss of prospective freights or other profits cannot, therefore, simply be added to that market value.[37] What is needed, it may be suggested, is a recognition in the assessment of the damages of the difference between the profit-earning potential of a ship without any engagement but with the chance or probability of making a profit, which will be reflected in the market value, and the actual profits which would have been made by the plaintiff's ship had it not been destroyed.[38] Nevertheless, if a ship is actually under charter at the time of her loss or has charters which would have commenced shortly thereafter, the loss of those charters may be allowed in some cases [39] as damages for loss of use of the ship from the time of its destruction until the time when it could reasonably be replaced.[40] It is submitted that in deciding whether or not these damages may be added to the market value, the manner in which the market value itself has been determined is of critical importance. If it is determined on the basis that the ship was in any case virtually certain of profitable employment, then nothing may be added for the loss of actual charters,[41] but if the market value does not assume the full employment of the ship then the loss of actual charters must be taken into account.

2. Damage

Where property is damaged the normal measure of damages is the amount by which its value has been diminished, and in the case of ships and other chattels this will usually be ascertained by reference to the cost of repair.[42] It does not matter that the repairs have not been carried out at the date of the trial,[43] or even that they are never carried out at all, as where a ship is lost from other causes before the repairs are done.[44] The estimated cost of the repairs can be recovered as indicating the amount by which the chattel's value is reduced. On the other hand, if a ship is damaged while on its way to the breaker's yard it is submitted that the cost of repairing the ship could not be recovered, for that cost

---

[36] *Supra*, at p. 464.

[37] *The Llanover* [1947] P. 80.

[38] For this distinction see *The Philadelphia* [1917] P. 101, 108, *per* Swinfen Eady L.J.

[39] *The Kate* [1899] P. 165; *The Racine* [1906] P. 273; *The Philadelphia* [1917] P. 101; *The Fortunity* [1961] 1 W.L.R. 351.

[40] See the explanation of Greer L.J. in *The Arpad* [1934] P. 189, 217; *The Fortunity, supra*; Street, *op. cit.*, p. 195.

[41] *The Llanover* [1947] P. 80.

[42] *The London Corporation* [1935] P. 70, 77, *per* Greer L.J.; McGregor, *op. cit.*, pp. 638–642. It is irrelevant that the value of the chattel after repair is greater than it was before the damage was caused by reason of the incorporation of new materials in place of old: *The Gazelle* (1844) 2 W.Rob.(Adm.) 279; *The Munster* (1896) 12 T.L.R. 264; and the same is true for land and buildings: *Harbutt's " Plasticine " Ltd.* v. *Wayne Tank and Pump Co. Ltd.* [1970] 1 Q.B. 447. *Cf.* Street, *op. cit.*, p. 212.

[43] *The Kingsway* [1918] P. 344.

[44] *The York* [1929] P. 178, 184–185, *per* Scrutton L.J.; *The London Corporation, supra*.

would not represent the true reduction in the value of the ship. All that could be recovered would be the diminution, if any, in the value of the ship as scrap.[45] Similarly, if the cost of repairing the chattel exceeds its total value, then, unless the chattel is in some way unique or irreplaceable, no more than its value can be recovered.[46]

In the majority of cases the plaintiff will not only have incurred the cost of repairing his chattel, he will also have been deprived of its use for a period of time and for this loss he is entitled to damages whether he used the damaged chattel in a profit-earning capacity and whether he has suffered actual pecuniary loss or not.[47] In *The Mediana*[48] a light-ship belonging to the plaintiff harbour board was damaged and replaced by a standby vessel kept by the board for such an emergency but the board was, nevertheless, entitled to damages for loss of use. " Supposing a person took away a chair out of my room and kept it for 12 months, could anybody say you had a right to diminish the damages by showing that I did not usually sit in that chair, or that there were plenty of other chairs in the room? The proposition so nakedly stated appears to me to be absurd."[49] There is no reason, therefore, why a person whose motor-car is damaged by the negligence of the defendant should not recover damages for loss of use, even though he only uses his car for pleasure purposes and has a second car in his garage.[50] Damages for loss of use cannot, of course, be claimed if the loss is due not to the defendant's tort but to some extraneous cause.[51]

No fixed rules can be laid down for the assessment of damages for loss of use; subject to the rules concerning remoteness of damage, the amount recoverable in each case depends on the use which the owner would, but for the damage, have had of his chattel, and, in the case of a profit-earning chattel, what the owner would have earned by its use.[52]

---

[45] See *The London Corporation* [1935] P. 70, 77–78, where Greer L.J. seems to have been in two minds on this point. In any event it will be for the defendant to prove that the damage he has caused to the plaintiff's ship has not reduced its value to the plaintiff: *ibid.*

[46] *Darbishire* v. *Warran* [1963] 1 W.L.R. 1067, distinguishing *O'Grady* v. *Westminster Scaffolding Ltd.* [1962] 2 Lloyd's Rep. 238; Weir, *Casebook on Tort*, 3rd ed., p. 555.

[47] *The Greta Holme* [1897] A.C. 596 (dredger owned by trustees deriving their funds from rates and not operating for profit); *The Marpessa* [1907] A.C. 241; *Admiralty Commissioners* v. *SS. Chekiang* [1926] A.C. 637 (warship); *Admiralty Commissioners* v. *SS. Susquehanna* [1926] A.C. 655 (naval oil tanker); *The Hebridean Coast* [1961] A.C. 545; *AMF International Ltd.* v. *Magnet Bowling Ltd.* [1968] 1 W.L.R. 1028, 1049–1051, per Mocatta J. (damage to property giving rise to liability under the Occupiers' Liability Act 1957—consequential loss may be recovered); *Birmingham Corporation* v. *Sowsbery* (1969) 113 S.J. 877 (non-profit-earning bus); *Dixons (Scholar Green) Ltd.* v. *J. L. Cooper Ltd.* (1970) 114 S.J. 319 (profit-earning lorry).

[48] [1900] A.C. 113; Weir, *Casebook on Tort*, 3rd ed., p. 552.

[49] *The Mediana* [1900] A.C. 113, 117, per Earl of Halsbury L.C.

[50] See *Macrae* v. *Swindells* [1954] 1 W.L.R. 597. *Cf. Berrill* v. *Road Haulage Executive* [1952] 2 Lloyd's Rep. 490, criticised Street, *op. cit.*, p. 206; *Watson Norie* v. *Shaw* (1967) 111 S.J 117.

[51] *Carslogie Steamship Co. Ltd.* v. *Royal Norwegian Government* [1952] A.C. 292, *ante*, p. 103, *The Hassell* [1962] 2 Lloyd's Rep. 139. *Cf. Admiralty Commissioners* v. *SS. Chekiang* [1926] A.C. 637 (damages for loss of use awarded although plaintiffs took the opportunity, when the ship was in dock, of carrying out other repairs which had not yet become necessary when the damage was caused). See McGregor, *op. cit.*, pp. 649–652.

[52] *The Argentino* (1888) 13 P.D. 191, 201, per Bowen L.J.; *ibid.* (1889) 14 App.Cas. 519, 523, *per* Lord Herschell; *The Hassell, supra*; McGregor, *op. cit.*, pp. 643–649.

Thus in the case of a profit-earning ship the normal measure of damage will be the loss of profits calculated at the freight rates prevailing during the period of detention of the ship,[53] but in the actual case this measure may prove too high or too low. It will be too high if the ship was operating at a loss at the time of the damage [54] and too low if the damage prevented the ship from fulfilling an actual charter already entered into at favourable rates.[55] In the case of a non-profit-earning chattel, whether used by its owner for the purposes of his business, or, it is submitted,[56] purely for his pleasure, the owner will be entitled to the reasonable cost of hiring a substitute if one is in fact hired.[57] If no substitute is hired the owner is entitled to general damages for loss of use of his chattel and these will normally be calculated on the basis of interest on the capital value of the damaged chattel plus depreciation and expenses,[58] if any, for the period of non-use.[59]

Land and buildings [60]

The principles considered thus far have been worked out in the context of injuries to chattels; those governing injuries to land or buildings are not fundamentally different, though there is probably a greater readiness to allow the cost of repair or reinstatement than in the case of chattels.[61] Where, however, the cost of reinstatement greatly exceeds the diminution in value and it would be unreasonable for the plaintiff to insist on reinstatement, the diminution in value will be the measure.[62]

---

[53] *The Soya* [1956] 1 W.L.R. 714. *Cf. The Pacific Concord* [1961] 1 W.L.R. 873. The cost of hiring a substitute is often used as the basis of the calculation: Street, *op. cit.*, p. 207. *Cf. Admiralty Commissioners* v. *SS. Valeria* [1922] 2 A.C. 242. If a substitute is hired and the plaintiff is thereby enabled to make a greater profit than he would have done if his own chattel had never been damaged, credit for this must be given: *The World Beauty* [1969] P. 12, revd. without affecting this point: [1970] P. 144.

[54] *The Bodlewell* [1907] P. 286. See also *SS. Strathfillan* v. *SS. Ikala* [1929] A.C. 196.

[55] *The Argentino, supra.*

[56] See, too, Street, *op. cit.*, p. 206.

[57] *The Mediana* [1900] A.C. 113, 122, *per* Lord Shand; 123, *per* Lord Brampton; *Macrae* v. *Swindells* [1954] 1 W.L.R. 597 (private car used by veterinary surgeon in his practice). *Cf. The Hebridean Coast* [1961] A.C. 545, where the chartering of a substitute ship was not proved.

[58] Such as crew's wages in the case of a ship.

[59] *The Marpessa* [1907] A.C. 241; *Admiralty Commissioners* v. *SS. Chekiang* [1926] A.C. 637; *Admiralty Commissioners* v. *SS. Susquehanna* [1926] A.C. 655; *The Hebridean Coast* [1961] A.C. 545. Interest on capital value will not always prove an appropriate measure (see *Admiralty Commissioners* v. *SS. Chekiang, supra*, at pp. 647–648, *per* Lord Sumner; *Birmingham Corporation* v. *Sowsbery* (1969) 113 S.J. 319) and it must be borne in mind that these are general damages, the quantification of which is a jury-type question: *Admiralty Commissioners* v. *SS. Susquehanna, supra*, at p. 661, *per* Viscount Dunedin. A plaintiff who has suffered the loss of his " no-claim " bonus under his motor insurance policy may recover its value from a defendant liable in respect of the damage to the insured motor-car: *Ironfield* v. *Eastern Gas Board* [1964] 1 W.L.R. 1125.

[60] See McGregor, *op. cit.*, pp. 711–722.

[61] See *Harbutt's* " *Plasticine* " *Ltd.* v. *Wayne Tank and Pump Co. Ltd.* [1970] 1 Q.B. 447, 467, 472. The market in land and buildings is more limited and inflexible than in, *e.g.* secondhand cars.

[62] *Jones* v. *Gooday* (1841) 8 M. & W. 146; *Lodge Holes Colliery Co. Ltd.* v. *Wednesbury Corporation* [1908] A.C. 323; *Taylor* v. *Auto Trade Supply Ltd.* [1972] N.Z.L.R. 102.

PART II. OTHER REMEDIES

1. Self-help

Self-help is apt to be a perilous remedy, for the person exercising it is probably the worst judge of exactly how much he is entitled to do without exceeding his rights. Still, it is well recognised as a remedy for certain torts. A trespasser, or trespassing animal, may be expelled with no more force than is reasonable. A person wrongfully imprisoned may escape. A building set up by a trespasser may be pulled down, nor is it necessary to notify the trespasser of one's intention to do so, unless the building is inhabited; then reasonable notice to quit is required, for it is not permissible to assert one's rights by knocking down a house about the ears of its occupants without giving them an opportunity of evacuation. This is certainly the law with respect to removal by a commoner of a building which is unlawfully erected on land over which he has a right of common,[63] and it is probably necessary to give such notice where the trespasser has built upon any land, whether subject to right of common or not.[64]

Again, goods wrongfully taken may be peaceably retaken; and chattels of another which encumber one's land may be detained until adequate compensation is paid for the harm they have done. These forms of self-help have been considered more fully in the chapters on trespass and conversion.[65]

Abatement of nuisance

A nuisance may be abated, i.e. removed. But this is a remedy which the law does not favour, because, as Sir Matthew Hale said, " this many times occasions tumults and disorders," [66] and its exercise destroys any right of action in respect of the nuisance.[67] In the first place, before abatement is attempted, notice should be given to the offending party to remedy the nuisance, unless it be one of omission and the security of lives and property does not allow time for notice,[68] or unless the nuisance can be removed by the abator without entry on the wrongdoer's land: I may lop the branches of my neighbour's tree which project over or into my land without notice to him,[69] although I must not appropriate what I sever.[70] The law as to notice is, however, not quite certain beyond

---

[63] Perry v. Fitzhowe (1846) 8 Q.B. 757; Davies v. Williams (1851) 16 Q.B. 546; Jones v. Jones (1862) 1 H. & C. 1.

[64] Burling v. Read (1850) 11 Q.B. 904 might appear to be the other way, but the fifth plea in that case (at p. 906) seems to indicate that the trespasser had notice that the owner intended to destroy the building. See, too, Lane v. Capsey [1891] 3 Ch. 411, 415–416, per Chitty J.

[65] Ante, Chaps. 14, 19.

[66] De Portubus Maris, Pt. 2, Chap. VII.

[67] Lagan Navigation Co. v. Lambeg, etc. Bleaching Co. Ltd. [1927] A.C. 226, 244, per Lord Atkinson.

[68] Ibid.

[69] Lemmon v. Webb [1895] A.C. 1. Roots of a tree projecting into one's soil from neighbouring land may be sawn off, but it is not clear whether notice to the neighbouring land occupier must first be given. Butler v. Standard Telephones, etc. Ltd. [1940] 1 K.B. 399.

[70] Mills v. Brooker [1919] 1 K.B. 555.

this. During the last century it has veered from the view that notice need be given only exceptionally to the view that notice ought always to be given subject to the exceptions just stated.[71] The explanation is that the riper a system of law becomes the more it tends to restrict self-help. Secondly, unnecessary damage must not be done: e.g. tearing up a picture which is publicly exhibited and which is a libel on oneself is too drastic, even though it be a nuisance.[72] Thirdly, where there are two ways of abatement, the less mischievous should be followed, unless it would inflict some wrong on an innocent third party or on the public.[73]

2. Injunction

An injunction is a judgment or order of the court restraining the commission or continuance of some wrongful act, or the continuance of some wrongful omission. Originally only the Court of Chancery could issue an injunction, but now any Division of the High Court may do so in any case in which it appears to the court to be " just or convenient." [74] Like other equitable remedies, the issue of an injunction is in the discretion of the court; an injunction cannot be demanded as of right and one will not be granted where damages would be a sufficient remedy.[75]

Injunctions are generally sought against such torts as nuisance, continuing or repeated trespass, infringement of copyright and the like and libel, but there is no theoretical reason why an injunction should not be issued to restrain the repetition or continuation of a tort of any kind.[76] On the other hand, if the wrong suffered by the plaintiff is trivial [77] or of a very temporary character an injunction will normally be refused. So too will an injunction be refused if the plaintiff has acquiesced in the

---

[71] Compare *Jones* v. *Williams* (1843) 11 M. & W. 176 with *Lemmon* v. *Webb* [1895] A.C. 1, and the *Lagan Navigation Co.* case [1927] A.C. 226; and see Salmond, 16th ed., p. 627; Clerk and Lindsell, *Torts*, 13th ed., pp. 299–300.

[72] *Du Bost* v. *Beresford* (1801) 2 Camp. 511, where the point was left open, but it may probably be regarded as settled now.

[73] Blackburn J. in *Roberts* v. *Rose* (1865) L.R. 1 Ex. 82, 89; adopted by Lord Atkinson in *Lagan Navigation Co.* v. *Lambeg, etc. Bleaching Co. Ltd.* [1927] A.C. 226, 244–246, where the abators satisfied none of these three conditions.

[74] Supreme Court of Judicature (Consolidation) Act 1925 (15 & 16 Geo. 5, c. 49), s. 45. An injunction can only be granted in a county court if it is ancillary to a claim for damages: *R.* v. *Cheshire County Court Judge* [1921] 2 K.B. 694.

[75] *London and Blackwall Ry.* v. *Cross* (1886) 31 Ch.D. 354, 369, *per* Lindley L.J. But if the plaintiff proves that his proprietary rights are being wrongfully interfered with by the defendant and that the defendant intends to continue his wrong, the plaintiff is prima facie entitled to an injunction unless special circumstances exist: *Pride of Derby and Derbyshire Angling Association* v. *British Celanese Ltd.* [1953] Ch. 149, 181, *per* Evershed M.R. See too *Warder* v. *Cooper* [1970] Ch. 495, where the plaintiff had no proprietary right. Conversely, the operation of the injunction can be suspended. See *e.g. Woollerton and Wilson Ltd.* v. *Richard Costain Ltd.* [1970] 1 W.L.R. 411, *ante*, p. 305, n. 43, and *cf. Charrington* v. *Simons & Co. Ltd.* [1971] 1 W.L.R. 598.

[76] In *Bird* v. *O'Neal* [1960] A.C. 907, the Privy Council granted an injunction to restrain picketing which was being carried on with intimidation and threats. But some legal right of the plaintiff must have been infringed: *Thorne* v. *British Broadcasting Corporation* [1967] 1 W.L.R. 1104.

[77] *Llandudno U.D.C.* v. *Woods* [1899] 2 Ch. 705; *Armstrong* v. *Sheppard and Short Ltd.* [1959] 2 Q.B. 384. *Cf. Woollerton and Wilson Ltd.* v. *Richard Costain Ltd.* [1970] 1 W.L.R. 411 where, however, the operation of the injunction was postponed; criticised by Dworkin (1970) 33 M.L.R. 552.

defendant's infringement of his legal rights,[78] and, *a fortiori*, if he has actually misled the defendant into believing that he acquiesced.[79]

Interlocutory injunction

An injunction which is issued at the conclusion of a trial upon the merits is known as a perpetual injunction, but an injunction may be issued provisionally until the hearing of the case on the merits, when it is known as an interlocutory injunction. The court on an application for an interlocutory injunction does not profess to anticipate the final outcome of the action but will normally proceed upon the balance of convenience,[80] the main question being whether an injunction is necessary to preserve the *status quo* until the trial. In cases of libel, interlocutory injunctions are rare for it is almost impossible for the court to avoid anticipating the verdict of the jury,[81] but in other cases the plaintiff need do little more than establish a prima facie breach of duty and that the defendants are threatening or intending to repeat the breach of duty.[82] Since it is always possible that when the case actually comes to trial the defendant will be found to have been in the right after all, if an interlocutory injunction is issued the plaintiff may be required to give an undertaking to pay damages to the defendant for any loss suffered by him while the injunction was in force, should it prove to have been wrongly issued. On the other hand, in practice the parties often treat the application for an interlocutory injunction as the trial of the action.[83]

Mandatory injunction

Normally injunctions are prohibitory, they forbid the defendant from persisting in his wrongful conduct, but the court has power also to grant a mandatory injunction by virtue of which the defendant is actually ordered to take positive action to rectify the consequences of what he

---

[78] *Gaskin* v. *Balls* (1879) 13 Ch.D. 324.

[79] *Armstrong* v. *Sheppard and Short Ltd.*, *supra*.

[80] *Canadian Pacific Railway* v. *Gaud* [1949] 2 K.B. 239, 249–250, *per* Cohen L.J. Note that considerations of the balance of convenience do not apply to the issue of perpetual injunctions, but the loss to the defendant which the issue of an injunction would cause may be taken into account, especially where a mandatory injunction (*post*, pp. 587–588) is in question. See Clerk and Lindsell, *Torts*, 13th ed., pp. 279–280. If there is no arguable defence to the plaintiff's claim it would be a misuse of the process of the court to withhold even an interlocutory injunction, and where this is so no question of the convenience of the defendant arises: *Manchester Corporation* v. *Connolly* [1970] Ch. 420.

[81] Gatley, *Libel and Slander*, 7th ed., pp. 605–609. If there is a plea of justification an interlocutory injunction cannot be granted for it is always for the jury to decide whether the words complained of are true: *Mosley* v. *Matthews* [1962] C.L.Y. 2430; *Argyll (Duchess)* v. *Argyll (Duke)* [1967] Ch. 302, 315, *per* Ungoed-Thomas J. See too *Sim* v. *H. J. Heinz Co. Ltd.* [1959] 1 W.L.R. 313.

[82] *J. T. Stratford & Son Ltd.* v. *Lindley* [1965] A.C. 269, 338, *per* Lord Upjohn. Interlocutory injunctions are quite commonly granted in cases arising out of labour disputes. See *e.g. J. T. Stratford & Son Ltd.* v. *Lindley*, *supra*; *Daily Mirror Newspapers Ltd.* v. *Gardner* [1968] 2 Q.B. 762; *Torquay Hotel Co. Ltd.* v. *Cousins* [1969] 2 Ch. 106, *ante*, pp. 450–452.

[83] In cases of great urgency the plaintiff can obtain an " interim " injunction on an *ex parte* application (*i.e.* in the absence of the defendant) which will remain in force for a few days until there can be a hearing: *Beese* v. *Woodhouse* [1970] 1 W.L.R. 586.

has already done.[84] In *Redland Bricks Ltd.* v. *Morris* [85] the defendants' excavations on their own land had caused part of the plaintiff's land to subside and had endangered part of the remainder. In the county court the plaintiffs recovered damages in respect of the subsidence which had already occurred, and the judge also granted them a mandatory injunction requiring the defendants to restore support to their land, the estimated cost of doing which was very great, and, indeed, actually exceeded the value of the whole of the plaintiff's land. In the House of Lords the defendants' appeal against this injunction was allowed and, while emphasising that the issue of a mandatory injunction is entirely discretionary and that each case depends upon its own circumstances. Lord Upjohn laid down certain general principles.[86] These may be summarised as follows:

1. There must be a very strong probability that grave damages for which an award of damages would not be a sufficient remedy will accrue to the plaintiff in the future.[87]

2. If the defendant has acted wantonly or has tried to steal a march on the plaintiff or on the court,[88] then the expense which the issue of a mandatory injunction would cause the defendant to incur is immaterial, but where the defendant has acted reasonably though, in the event, wrongly, the cost of remedying his earlier activities is a most important consideration.

3. If a mandatory injunction is issued, the court must be careful to see that the defendant knows as a matter of fact exactly what he has to do so that he can give proper instructions to contractors for the carrying out of the work.

Quia timet injunction

Normally injunctions are issued only when a tort has already been committed, and, in the case of torts actionable only on proof of damage, it is premature for the plaintiff to seek an injunction before any damage has actually occurred. Where, however, the conduct of the defendant is such that, if it is allowed to continue, substantial damage to the plaintiff is almost bound to occur, the plaintiff may bring a " *quia timet* " action, that is, an action for an injunction to prevent an apprehended legal wrong.[89] The existence of the court's power to grant a *quia timet*

---

[84] A mandatory injunction can be granted on an interlocutory application, but only in exceptional circumstances: *Thompson* v. *Park* [1944] K.B. 408; *Canadian Pacific Railway* v. *Gaud* [1949] 2 K.B. 239. For examples, see *Kennard* v. *Cory Bros. & Co.* [1922] 2 Ch. 1; *Truckell* v. *Stock* [1957] 1 W.L.R. 161; *Kelsen* v. *Imperial Tobacco Co. Ltd.* [1957] 2 Q.B. 334; *Prudential Assurance Co. Ltd.* v. *Lorenz, The Times,* April 29, 1971.
[85] [1970] A.C. 652.
[86] *Ibid.* at pp. 665–667. The other members of the House of Lords agreed with Lord Upjohn's speech.
[87] *Taylor* v. *Auto Trade Supply Ltd.* [1972] N.Z.L R. 102.
[88] See *e.g. Daniel* v. *Ferguson* [1891] 2 Ch. 27.
[89] *Redland Bricks Ltd.* v. *Morris* [1970] A.C. 652, 664, *per* Lord Upjohn. In his Lordship's opinion, an action is still *quia timet* even though damage has already occurred, if that damage has been redressed by an award of damages: *ibid.* at p. 665.

injunction is undoubted,[90] but it is not often exercised for the plaintiff must show both a near certainty that damage will occur [91] and that it is imminent.[92] And even then an injunction will not be issued to compel the defendant to do something which he is willing to do without the intervention of the court.[93]

Damages in lieu of injunction

The Court of Chancery had no power to award damages for torts which brought no profit to the wrongdoer, but by Lord Cairns's Act 1858,[94] the court was enabled to award damages either in addition to, or in substitution for, an injunction, and later legislation has conferred this jurisdiction on the High Court.[95] Such damages are given in full satisfaction not only for all damage already done in the past, but also for all future damage which may occur if the injunction is not granted. The jurisdiction to award damages in substitution for an injunction will, therefore, be exercised only if it would be oppressive to the defendant to issue an injunction, and so long as the injury to the plaintiff's rights is small, is capable of being estimated in money, and is one which can be adequately compensated by a money payment.[96]

It has been held that damages may be awarded in substitution for an injunction even in a *quia timet* action.[97] This, in effect, is to allow the defendant to purchase the right to commit a tort in the future but, illogical though this may be, it is really no more illogical than the idea, inherent in Lord Cairns's Act itself, that damages can ever be " adequate " compensation for damage which has not yet occurred, which can be avoided, and to which the plaintiff does not consent.[98] Practical considerations must, however, be taken into account and on practical grounds there may be considerable advantage in awarding a plaintiff damages only, where his probable future damage is likely to be much

---

[90] For a recent example, see *Torquay Hotel Co. Ltd.* v. *Cousins* [1969] 2 Ch. 106, 120, *per* Stamp J.

[91] *Att.-Gen.* v. *Nottingham Corporation* [1904] 1 Ch. 673; *Redland Bricks Ltd.* v. *Morris, supra.*

[92] *Lemos* v. *Kennedy Leigh Developments* (1961) 105 S.J. 178.

[93] *Bridlington Relay Ltd.* v. *Yorkshire Electricity Board* [1965] Ch. 436.

[94] 21 & 22 Vict. c. 27, s. 2.

[95] Lord Cairns's Act was repealed by the Statute Law Revision Act 1883 (46 & 47 Vict. c. 49), s. 3, but the jurisdiction was preserved by the joint effect of the Judicature Act 1873 (36 & 37 Vict. c. 66), s. 16 (now s. 18 of the Supreme Court of Judicature (Consolidation) Act 1925 (15 & 16 Geo. 5, c. 39)) and Statute Law Revision Act 1898 (61 & 62 Vict. c. 22), s. 1. Kerr, *op. cit.,* p. 655. For the conditions on which damages will be granted in lieu of an injunction, see *Shelfer* v. *London Electric Lighting Co.* [1895] 1 Ch 287, 322–323; *per* A. L. Smith L.J.; applied in *Alan Maberley* v. *Peabody & Co. Ltd.* [1946] 2 All E.R. 192, 195. See also *Armstrong* v. *Sheppard and Short Ltd.* [1959] 2 Q.B. 384, 397, *per* Lord Evershed M.R.

[96] *Shelfer* v. *City of London Electric Lighting Co.* [1895] 1 Ch. 287, 322, *per* A. L. Smith L.J. These principles were elaborately considered by the Court of Appeal in *Morris* v. *Redland Bricks Ltd.* [1967] 1 W.L.R. 967, but in the House of Lords it was held that no question under Lord Cairns's Act arose: [1970] A.C. 652.

[97] *Leeds Industrial Co-operative Society Ltd.* v. *Slack* [1924] A.C. 851. The decision of the House of Lords was by a bare majority.

[98] *Leeds Industrial Co-operative Society Ltd.* v. *Slack, supra,* at pp. 867–868, *per* Lord Sumner, dissenting.

less than the cost to the defendant of preventing it, provided, of course, that the defendant has acted honestly and without the deliberate intention of committing or continuing to commit an unlawful act. Otherwise there is a danger that proceedings for injunctions will be used by unscrupulous plaintiffs, not to protect their rights, but to extort from defendants sums of money greater in value than any damage that is likely to occur.[99]

3. Specific restitution of property

Orders for the specific restitution of property may be for the recovery of land or for the recovery of chattels. But whether it is restitution of land or of goods that is sought, the remedies are confined to cases where one man is in possession of another's property and this limits them to torts infringing such possession. They have, therefore, been considered in their appropriate chapters.[1]

---

[99] *Colls* v. *Home and Colonial Stores Ltd.* [1904] A.C. 179, 193, *per* Lord Macnaghten. Another useful purpose of Lord Cairns's Act, it is suggested, is that its use may avoid the necessity for further proceedings where it is anticipated that the defendant's act is likely to lead to future damage unless positive steps are taken to prevent it and yet the court considers that a mandatory injunction should not be issued, as occurred in *Redland Bricks Ltd.* v. *Morris, supra.* It is respectfully submitted that Lord Upjohn's conclusion that Lord Cairns's Act had nothing to do with the principles applicable in that case ([1970] A.C. at p. 665) and that the plaintiffs should bring further proceedings if further damage occurred is capable of unfortunate consequences. See Clerk and Lindsell, *Torts,* 13th ed., Supplement, 505.

[1] *Ante,* pp. 312–315, 410–412.

CHAPTER 28

CAPACITY [1]

Capacity explained

The title of this chapter is a compendious abbreviation of " Variation in capacity to sue, or liability to be sued, in tort." The word " status " would have done equally well, but unluckily there is not much agreement in books on jurisprudence as to what exactly it comprises. Where it is used it is employed as equivalent to " capacity " in the sense stated above.

Every system of law and every branch of each system must recognise variations in favour of, or against, abnormal members of the community. Who are to be reckoned as abnormal is a question of policy which each country must settle for itself. The hangman had a status in some parts of Europe; he never had one with us. Further, it will often happen that even in the same country a person is counted as abnormal in one age and as normal in another. Heretics and Jews were once under disabilities in England which have now disappeared. In the law of tort the chief variations in capacity are to be found with the state and its officials, minors, married women, persons of unsound mind and corporations. They are all much the sort of people whom one would expect to be classed as abnormal, except the married woman, and she has now been put into virtually the same position, so far as the law of tort is concerned, as any other person.

THE STATE AND ITS SUBORDINATES

The Crown and state officials [2]

At common law no action in tort lay against the Crown [3] for wrongs expressly authorised by the Crown or for wrongs committed by its servants in the course of their employment.[4] Moreover, the head of the department or other superior official was not, and is not, personally liable for wrongs committed by his subordinates, unless he has expressly authorised them, for all the servants of the Crown are fellow servants

---

[1] For the position of trade unions, see p. 468, ante.
[2] Hogg, Liability of the Crown (1971).
[3] Or against government departments, for these enjoyed the immunity of the Crown unless a statute expressly provided otherwise. See Minister of Supply v. British Thomson-Houston Co. [1943] K.B. 478.
[4] Canterbury (Viscount) v. Att.-Gen. (1842) 1 Ph. 306. The remedy by way of petition of right was available for breach of contract, and to recover property which had been wrongfully taken and withheld. France, Fenwick & Co. Ltd. v. R. [1927] 1 K.B. 52. Proceedings by way of petition of right were abolished by the Crown Proceedings Act 1947, Sched. I, para. 2, but only with regard to liability in respect of Her Majesty's Government in the United Kingdom. A petition of right may, therefore, still lie in certain cases, but in the common law form used prior to the Petitions of Right Act 1860: Franklin v. Att.-Gen. [1974] Q.B. 185.

of the Crown and not of one another.[5] On the other hand, the actual wrongdoer could, and still can, be sued in his personal capacity.[6] In practice the Treasury Solicitor usually defended an action against the individual Crown servant and the Treasury as a matter of grace undertook to satisfy any judgment awarded against him for a tort committed in the course of his employment.[7] If the actual wrongdoer could not be identified the Treasury Solicitor would supply the name of a merely nominal defendant for the purpose of the action, *i.e.* a person who, though a government servant, had nothing to do with the alleged wrong. But in *Royster* v. *Cavey*[8] it was held that the court had no jurisdiction to try the case unless the subordinate named by the Treasury Solicitor was the person who apparently had committed the tort. Since the Crown is today one of the largest employers of labour and occupiers of property in the country, this system of providing compensation for the victims of torts committed by Crown servants in the course of their employment was plainly inadequate and, finally, some 20 years after it was mooted, the Crown Proceedings Act 1947[9] put an end to Crown immunity in tort.

Crown Proceedings Act 1947

Under the Act the old maxim that " the King can do no wrong " is retained to the extent that no proceedings can be instituted against the Sovereign in person,[10] and there are savings in respect of the Crown's prerogative and statutory powers,[11] but otherwise the general effect of the Act is to equate the Crown with a private person of full age and capacity for the purposes of tortious liability. Section 2 (1) provides that the Crown shall be liable[12] as if it were such a person: (a) in respect of torts committed by its servants or agents[13]; (b) in respect of any breach of those duties which a person owes to his servants or agents at common law by reason of being their employer; and (c) in respect of any breach of the duties attaching at common law to the

---

[5] *Raleigh* v. *Goschen* [1898] 1 Ch. 73, 83; *Bainbridge* v. *Postmaster-General* [1906] 1 K.B. 178. See also *Lane* v. *Cotton* (1701) 1 Ld.Raym. 646.

[6] He could not, and cannot now, plead the orders of the Crown or State necessity as a defence. *Entick* v. *Carrington* (1765) 19 St.Tr. 1030; *Wilkes* v. *Wood* (1763) *ibid.* 1153.

[7] Dicey, *Law of the Constitution*, 9th ed., p. 531 (omitted from 10th ed.); Crown Proceedings Report (1927) Cmd. 2842. In 1942 the Lord Chancellor appointed an independent person to certify (if the claimant should so desire) whether the subordinate was acting in the course of his employment. This was in consequence of a debate on the topic in the House of Lords, April 13, 1942. *Hansard*, Vol. 122, cols. 535–568. Previously, the decision on this point had been with the department concerned.

[8] [1947] K.B. 204, the Court of Appeal acting upon emphatic *obiter dicta* of the House of Lords in *Adams* v. *Naylor* [1946] A.C. 543.

[9] 10 & 11 Geo. 6, c. 44.   [10] s. 40 (1).

[11] s. 11 (1).

[12] The action is brought against the appropriate government department in accordance with a list published by the Treasury, otherwise the Attorney-General may be made defendant (s. 17). See Bickford Smith, *The Crown Proceedings Act*, 1947; Bell, *Crown Proceedings*; Glanville Williams, *Crown Proceedings*; Street, *Governmental Liability*, pp. 25–52.

[13] " Agent " includes an independent contractor (s. 38 (2)) but the Crown is not on this account subject to any greater liability for the tort of an independent contractor employed by it than it would be if it were a private person: s. 40 (2) (*d*).

ownership, occupation, possession or control of property.[14] Section 2 (2) makes the Crown liable for breach of statutory duty, provided that the statute in question is one which binds other persons besides the Crown and its officers. Moreover, the apportionment provisions of the Law Reform (Married Women and Tortfeasors) Act 1935 and the Law Reform (Contributory Negligence) Act 1945, as well as the analogous provisions of the Maritime Conventions Act 1911, apply to proceedings in which the Crown is a party.[15] It is an open question whether an action lies against the Crown on behalf of a deceased person's estate under the Law Reform (Miscellaneous Provisions) Act 1934 or on behalf of his dependants under the Fatal Accidents Acts 1846 to 1959, but it is submitted that on principle the Crown should be liable.[16]

There are, however, certain limitations on the Crown's general liability in tort:

1. Officers, that is, servants or Ministers of the Crown,[17] who may render the Crown liable are only those appointed directly or indirectly by the Crown and paid wholly out of moneys provided by Parliament or a fund certified by the Treasury as equivalent.[18] This excludes liability for police officers who are not paid out of such funds, even·in the case of the Metropolitan Police,[19] and also for public corporations which are, normally, liable themselves like any other corporation.[20]

2. The Crown cannot be made liable for an act or omission of its servant unless that act or omission would, apart from the Act, have given rise to a cause of action against the servant himself.[21] This preserves such defences as act of state but does not, it is submitted, extend so far as to exempt the Crown from liability in those exceptional cases where the master is vicariously liable even though his servant is immune from liability himself.[22]

---

[14] The duties owed by an occupier of premises to his invitees and licensees are now contained in the Occupiers' Liability Act 1957, which binds the Crown. The liability of the Crown under the Act thus falls under s. 2 (2), but s. 2 (1) (c) continues to apply to the other duties which attach to the ownership, occupation, possession or control of property such as those in the tort of nuisance.

[15] s. 4. So also do the provisions of the Merchant Shipping Acts 1894 to 1940 concerning limitation of liability: s. 5; *The Truculent* [1952] P. 1.

[16] Clerk and Lindsell, *Torts*, 13th ed., pp. 90–91, Glanville Williams, *op. cit.*, pp. 55–58; Treitel, " Crown Proceedings: Some Recent Developments " [1957] *Public Law* 321, 322–326.

[17] s. 38 (2). The Crown is not expressly defined, but it appears to include all government departments, officers, servants and agents of the Crown.

[18] s. 2 (6). S. 1 provides that where a petition of right was formerly available, *e.g.* for detinue, " the claim may be enforced as of right." S. 2 need not be invoked for the recovery of property, and the definition of " officer " in s. 2 (6) is inapplicable. Street, *Governmental Liability*, p. 35.

[19] See now the Police Act 1964, s. 48, *ante*, p. 521.

[20] *Tamlin* v. *Hannaford* [1950] 1 K.B. 18. *Cf. Glasgow Corporation* v. *Central Land Board*, 1956 S.L.T. 41 (H.L.). See also *Bank Voor Handel en Scheepvaart* v. *Administrator of Hungarian Property* [1954] A.C. 584. For the special position of the Post Office, see *post*, p. 595.

[21] s. 2, proviso. The Crown has the benefit of any statute regulating or limiting the liability of a government department or officer of the Crown: s. 2 (4).

[22] Clerk and Lindsell, *Torts*, 13th ed., p. 85. *Contra*, Glanville Williams, *Crown Proceedings*, pp. 44–45.

3. The Crown is not liable for anything done by any person in discharging responsibilities of a judicial nature vested in him or any responsibilities he has in connection with the execution of the judicial process.[23]

4. Section 10 exempts the Crown from liability in tort for death or personal injury caused by a member of the armed forces when on duty to another member of the armed forces,[24] provided the latter is on duty or even if not on duty, is on any land, premises, ship or vehicle being used for the purposes of the armed forces of the Crown, and the Secretary of State for Social Services certifies that his suffering is attributable to service for the purposes of pension.[25] There is a similar immunity if death or personal injuries are caused in consequence of the condition of such premises or equipment or supplies. The actual wrongdoer is also exempted from liability unless the court is satisfied that his act or omission was not connected with the execution of his duties as a member of the armed forces. As the section refers to death or personal injury and no other head of damage, it does not apply to defamation and torts involving damage to property and in such cases both the Crown and the member of the armed forces would be liable.

Act of state

It is proposed to deal with this matter very shortly since it belongs much more to the realm of constitutional and international law than to the law of tort.[26] There is no doubt that no action may be brought either against the Crown or anyone else in respect of an act of state, but there is little agreement on the meaning of this phrase. Certainly an injury inflicted upon a foreigner abroad which is either authorised or ratified by the Crown is for this purpose an " act of state " and cannot be made the subject of an action in the English courts,[27] but it is doubtful whether, as an answer to a claim for tort, act of state goes any further than that. It will probably not avail a defendant to plead act of state in respect of an act done within British territory, whether against a British subject or a friendly alien,[28] and it may well be unavailing against a British subject wherever he may be.[29] An act of the Crown

---

[23] s. 2 (5).

[24] This includes the W.R.N.S., Q.A.R.N.N.S., and any other organisation established under the control of the Admiralty, the Army Council or the Air Council: s. 38 (5).

[25] *Adams* v. *War Office* [1955] 1 W.L.R. 1117. Thus, a private person who is a joint tortfeasor with the Crown will be responsible for the whole of the damages awarded to a soldier without any right of contribution under the Law Reform (Married Women and Tortfeasors) Act 1935.

[26] For a somewhat fuller treatment see the 8th ed. of this work, pp. 712–715 and, in addition to authorities there cited, *Att.-Gen.* v. *Nissan* [1970] A.C. 179; Collier, " Act of State as a Defence against a British Subject " [1968] C.L.J. 102; [1969] C.L.J. 166.

[27] *Buron* v. *Denman* (1848) 2 Ex. 167. *Cf. Carr* v. *Fracis Times & Co.* [1902] A.C. 176.

[28] *Johnstone* v. *Pedlar* [1921] 2 A.C. 262, where the alien was " friendly " in a rather technical sense only.

[29] Collier. *loc. cit.* at p. 111 suggests that there can be no such thing as an act of state against a British subject and it seems that Lord Reid agrees with him: *Att.-Gen.* v. *Nissan, supra,* at p. 213. The other members of the House of Lords were more cautious and reserved their opinions.

may, of course, be lawful as an act of the prerogative, and section 11 of the Crown Proceedings Act preserves the Crown's rights to exercise its statutory and prerogative powers, but there is no prerogative power to seize or destroy the property of a subject without paying compensation.[30]

The Post Office

The Post Office was until 1969 a department of government, but, despite the general provisions of the Crown Proceedings Act 1947, no proceedings in tort lay against the Crown for any act or omission of a servant of the Crown in relation to a postal packet or telephonic communication.[31] Now the Post Office has become a statutory corporation,[32] but the immunity from liability in tort is preserved.[33] However, by a provision similar to that formerly contained in the Crown Proceedings Act[34] it is enacted that the Post Office shall be liable for the loss of or damage to a *registered inland* postal packet when that loss or damage is caused by the wrongful act, neglect or default of an officer, servant or agent of the Post Office.[35] Unless the contrary is shown, it is presumed that the loss or damage was so caused,[36] but the amount recoverable is limited to the market value of the packet or the maximum available under a scheme made in accordance with the provisions of the Act, whichever is the less.[37] The cause of action thus created is a statutory cause of action of a tortious character similar to an action for breach of bailment and, subject to the limits provided for, damages should be assessed on that basis.[38]

JUDICIAL ACTS [39]

The general rule is that " no action lies for acts done or words spoken by a judge in the exercise of his judicial office, although his motive is

---

[30] *Att.-Gen.* v. *De Keyser's Royal Hotel* [1920] A.C. 508; *Burmah Oil Co. Ltd.* v. *Lord Advocate* [1965] A.C. 75; *Att.-Gen.* v. *Nissan, supra*, at p. 227, *per* Lord Pearce. The common law right to compensation is considerably restricted by the War Damage Act 1965, *post*, p. 638.

[31] Crown Proceedings Act 1947, s. 9 (1).

[32] Post Office Act 1969 (c. 48). It is expressly enacted that the Post Office is not to be regarded as a servant or agent of the Crown: *ibid*. s. 6 (5).

[33] *Ibid*. s. 29. The immunity is, if anything, more extensive than that previously provided for, and the immunity of servants or agents of the Post Office, previously contained in the Crown Proceedings Act, s. 9 (2), is also preserved in a more extensive form: s. 29 (2). No contract exists between the Post Office and the sender of a postal packet and so the provisions of s. 29 cannot be avoided by basing a claim on breach of contract: *Triefus & Co. Ld.* v. *Post Office* [1957] 2 Q.B. 352.

[34] s. 9 (2).

[35] Post Office Act 1969, s. 30 (1).

[36] *Ibid*. s. 30 (2).

[37] *Ibid*. s. 30 (3). Schemes are made under s. 28 of the Act and replace the old Post Office Regulations.

[38] *Building and Civil Engineering Holidays Scheme Management Ltd.* v. *Post Office* [1966] 1 Q.B. 247, a decision on the Crown Proceedings Act, s. 9 (2). Proceedings under s. 30 must be begun within twelve months of the date of posting and, unless the court grants leave to the contrary, only the sender or addressee of the packet may claim: *ibid*. s. 30 (5).

[39] The topic is dealt with at length in Winfield, *Present Law of Abuse of Legal Procedure* (1921), Chap. 7.

malicious and the acts or words are not done or spoken in the honest exercise of his office."[40] If it were otherwise, the administration of justice would lack one of its essentials—the independence of the judges. It is better to take the chance of judicial incompetence, irritability, or irrelevance, than to run the risk of getting a Bench warped by apprehension of the consequences of judgments which ought to be given without fear or favour. Moreover, there are, as will be seen later, modes of redress of judicial misconduct even if there is no civil remedy.

This exemption from liability to civil proceedings has been rather infelicitously styled a " privilege." But that might imply that the judge has a private right to be malicious, whereas its real meaning is that in the public interest it is not desirable to inquire whether acts of this kind are malicious or not. It is rather a right of the public to have the independence of the judges preserved than a privilege of the judges themselves.[41]

Scope of exemption

The exemption has a wide scope. It includes [42] not only judges of the superior courts, but also those of inferior courts, such as quarter sessions, county courts, coroners, vice-chancellors exercising judicial authority under the charter of a university,[43] the Palatine Court of Durham, Censors of the Royal College of Physicians, ecclesiastical courts, and the official receiver, for he is under a statutory duty to make a judicial inquiry, and the Disciplinary Committee of the Law Society.[44] The position of justices of the peace has varied. Actions were maintainable against them in the older law, but the tide turned in their favour about the middle of the nineteenth century and they now appear to have judicial immunity.[45] In *Law* v. *Llewellyn*,[46] a magistrate, in allowing the prosecutor to withdraw a charge, said that the Bench regarded the charge as a gross attempt to blackmail and that if the prosecutor found himself in gaol for 12 months it would possibly do him good. The prosecutor sued the magistrate for slander, urging that whatever exemption he might have had as a judge was destroyed by the fact that what he had said was uttered after he had allowed the charge to be withdrawn and was, therefore, outside the course of his judicial duty. This

---

[40] *Anderson* v. *Gorrie* [1895] 1 Q.B. 668, 671, *per* Lord Esher M.R.; *Fray* v. *Blackburn* (1863) 3 B. & S. 576.

[41] *Bottomley* v. *Brougham* [1908] 1 K.B. 584, 586–587, *per* Channell J.; *Sirros* v. *Moore* [1974] 3 All E.R. 776.

[42] Authorities are cited in Winfield, *op. cit.*, pp. 208–211.

[43] *Kemp* v. *Neville* (1861) 10 C.B.(N.S.) 523; the famous case which led to the abolition of the old " Spinning-house " prison at Cambridge.

[44] *Addis* v. *Crocker* [1961] 1 Q.B. 11.

[45] See Winfield, *op. cit.*, pp. 216–219; Sheridan, " Protection of Justices " (1951) 14 M.L.R. 267; Thomson, " Judicial Immunity and the Protection of Justices " (1958) 21 M.L.R. 523–524. The Justices' Protection Act 1848, s. 1, assumes the existence of a remedy against justices and lays down that the action is an action on the case which shall only be maintainable if the plaintiff proves malice and want of reasonable and probable cause. But the section does not create a cause of action and it may be that it " only baptises something that never existed or has since died." Winfield, *op. cit.*, p. 217.

[46] [1906] 1 K.B. 487.

argument was not accepted by the Court of Appeal, who held that it
would be lamentable if a magistrate, when he sees that a charge ought
never to have been made, were not at liberty to say so. On the other
hand, the protection accorded to judicial acts does not extend to
ministerial acts. If a person whose usual functions are judicial refuses
to do a ministerial act which is in his province, an action may lie
against him.[47]

Tribunals of inquiry

Judicial exemption also applies on grounds of public policy wherever
there is an authorised inquiry which, though not before a court of
justice, is before a tribunal which has similar attributes.[48] Such is a military board of inquiry, and this was so even at the time when it had no
power to administer an oath [49]; much more is a court-martial, which
perhaps has always had power to do so.[50] But a meeting of the London
County Council for the purpose of granting music and dancing licences
is not a court for this purpose. " Judicial " has two meanings in this
connection. It may refer to the discharge of duties exercisable by a
judge (whether in a law court or in a private room) or to administrative
duties which need not be performed in court, but in respect of which it
is necessary to use a judicial mind—a mind to determine what is fair
and just as to the matters under consideration. Licensing meetings of a
county council fall under this second head.[51] Bodies like this, such as
the Inns of Court and the General Medical Council, do well enough
with such protection as quasi-judicial functions imply.[52]

Witnesses, etc.

Judicial exemption extends also to witnesses in a court in the sense
that they incur no liability for what they say if it has reference to the
inquiry on which they are testifying [53]; and the protection afforded to

---

[47] *Ferguson* v. *Kinnoull* (1842) 9 Cl. & Fin. 251.

[48] *Royal Aquarium Society Ltd.* v. *Parkinson* [1892] 1 Q.B. at p. 442, *per* Lord Esher,
cited by Collins M.R. in *Barratt* v. *Kearns* [1905] 1 K.B. 504, 510; and approved by the
Judicial Committee in *O'Connor* v. *Waldron* [1935] A.C. 76. As to domestic tribunals, see
Abbott v. *Sullivan* [1952] 1 K.B. 189 (committee enforcing discipline over London dockers);
Lee v. *Showmen's Guild of Great Britain* [1952] 2 Q.B. 329 (trade union); *Bonsor* v.
Musicians' Union [1956] A.C. 104 (trade union); Lloyd, " Disciplinary Powers of Pro-
fessional Bodies " (1950) 13 M.L.R. 281.

[49] *Dawkins* v. *Rokeby* (1875) L.R. 7 H.L. 744. The Army Act 1955, s. 135, enables the
board to administer an oath.

[50] This may be inferred from *Dawkins* v. *Rokeby* (1875) L.R. 7 H.L. 744. For other
examples, see Winfield, *op. cit.*, pp. 209–210.

[51] *Royal Aquarium Society Ltd.* v. *Parkinson* [1892] 1 Q.B. 431, 452. Approved in
O'Connor v. *Waldron* [1935] A.C. 76. See, too, *Smith* v. *National Meter Co. Ltd.* [1945]
2 All E.R. 35.

[52] Fry L.J. [1892] 1 Q.B. at p. 447. For quasi-judicial functions, see *ante*, pp. 489–490.

[53] *Seaman* v. *Netherclift* (1876) 2 C.P.D. 53. *Cf. Roy* v. *Prior* [1970] 3 W.L.R. 202,
ante, p. 485. The authorities were fully reviewed by Pigott C.B. in *Kennedy* v. *Hilliard*
(1859) 10 Irish C.L.R. 195. No action for damages lies at the suit of one who claims that
he has suffered damage as the result of the perjury of a witness: *Hargreaves* v. *Bretherton*
[1959] 1 Q.B. 45; *Marrinan* v. *Vibart* [1963] 1 Q.B. 234.

counsel in the discharge of their functions is at least as large.[54] Jurors are also free from liability.[55]

Excess of jurisdiction

The scope of judicial immunity formerly varied according to the status of the judge in the judicial hierarchy.[56] So, a judge of a superior court was immune from liability for any act of a judicial character even though he was acting in excess of jurisdiction, whether as a result of a mistake of fact or law.[57] But a judge of an inferior court was liable for acts done outside his jurisdiction,[58] unless he had no reason to know facts which put the case outside that jurisdiction.[59] Whatever the merits of this distinction in former times it can no longer march with our changed judicial structure [60] and a majority of the Court of Appeal has taken a recent opportunity of restating the law in simpler terms. The rule now is that *any* judge, whether of a superior or inferior court, and including a magistrate, is immune from civil liability in respect of an act done in the *bona fide* exercise of his office and in the belief that it is within his jurisdiction.[61] The fact that his erroneous belief stems from an error of law no longer subjects him to liability.[62]

We have said that even where civil remedies are not available against a judge, the criminal law nevertheless supplies some for acts done whether within jurisdiction or in excess of it.[63] The Bench in early times did not lack men with an itching palm, but the standard of judicial

[54] *Munster* v. *Lamb* (1883) 11 Q.B.D. 588. See *Rondel* v. *Worsley* [1969] 1 A.C. 191 and *ante*, pp. 63–64.
[55] *Bushell's Case* (1670) 6 St.Tr. 999.
[56] For a slightly different formulation see the 9th ed. of this work, p. 609.
[57] *Sirros* v. *Moore* [1974] 3 All E.R. 776, 784; *Hamond* v. *Howell* (1674) 1 Mod.Rep. 119, 184. An act done *with knowledge* that there was no jurisdiction to do it would not be a " judicial act "; *cf. Miller* v. *Seare* (1777) 2 Wm.Bl. 1141, 1145. On the other hand, malicious exercise of a power *ex facie* applicable to the case before him can hardly be an excess of jurisdiction, otherwise there would be nothing left of the general principle of *Anderson* v. *Gorrie, supra.*
[58] *Comyn* v. *Sabine* (1737) 1 Smith's *Leading Cases*, 13th ed., p. 651; *Houlden* v. *Smith* (1850) 14 Q.B. 841; *Willis* v. *Mclachlan* (1876) 1 Ex.D. 376; *O'Connor* v. *Isaacs* [1956] 2 Q.B. 288.
No action can be brought against justices for anything done under a conviction until that conviction has been quashed (Justices' Protection Act 1848, s. 2) but this does not apply to committal to prison under a maintenance order: *O'Connor* v. *Isaacs, supra.*
[59] *Calder* v. *Halket* (1839) 3 Moo.P.C. 28, 77; *Palmer* v. *Crone* [1927] 1 K.B. 804; *Sammy-Joe* v. *G.P.O. Mount Pleasant Post Office* [1967] 1 W.L.R. 370.
[60] For example, the Crown Court is a superior court of record (Courts Act 1971, s. 4 (1)), though for practical purposes it is an inferior court for some types of jurisdiction (*ibid.*, s. 10 (5)) and its judicial personnel cover the whole scale from puisne judges to lay justices. Furthermore, there is now a fully developed appellate structure supplemented by habeas corpus and other prerogative orders.
[61] *Sirros* v. *Moore* [1974] 3 All E.R. 776, *per* Lord Denning M.R. and Ormrod L.J.
[62] The judgment of Buckley L.J., who agreed with the decision of his brethren, holds to a more traditional classification. In his view, a judge of a superior court of record is absolutely immune from liability for any judicial act. A judge of an inferior court is immune if (1) the act was judicial and (2) the act was either within his jurisdiction or, if not within his jurisdiction, was an act done in the conscientious belief that it was within that jurisdiction and this belief was based upon a justifiable ignorance of some relevant fact. The difference between superior and inferior courts rests not so much on any point of principle but on the fact that the former is the sole arbiter of its own jurisdiction.
[63] For fuller details, see Winfield, *op. cit.* pp. 212–228.

integrity has been raised so greatly during the last two centuries that legal proceedings for corruption are unknown now.

Nor has it ever been found necessary to take advantage of the legislation now embodied in the Supreme Court of Judicature (Consolidation) Act 1925, which enables the Crown to remove judges of the High Court and the Court of Appeal on address by both Houses of Parliament.[64] And even with their humbler brethren, the justices of the peace, there is less need now to have recourse to the statutes which, as Lambard said, " do now and then correct the dulnesse of these Justices, with some strokes of the rodde, or spur." [65]

Officers of the law

An officer of the law who executes process apparently regular, without knowing in fact that the person who authorised him to do so has exceeded his powers, is protected in spite of the proceedings being ill founded.[66] Again by the Constables Protection Act 1750,[67] no action can be brought against a constable for anything done in obedience to any warrant issued by a justice of the peace until the would-be plaintiff has made a written demand for a copy of the warrant and the demand has not been complied with for six days. If it is complied with, then the constable, if he produces the warrant at the trial of the action against him, is not liable in spite of any defect of jurisdiction in the justice. But if he arrests a person not named in the warrant or seizes goods of one who is not mentioned in it, he does so at his peril. His mistake, however honest, will not excuse him. In *Hoye* v. *Bush* [68] Richard Hoye was suspected of stealing a mare. A warrant was issued for his arrest, but it described him as " John Hoye," which in fact was his father's name. Richard was arrested under this warrant and subsequently sued Bush, the constable, for false imprisonment. Bush was held liable, for although Richard was the man who actually was wanted, still the warrant described somebody else and it did not help Bush that John Hoye was not really wanted.

MINORS

After an early period of uncertainty, the common law adopted twenty-one years as the age of majority for most purposes [69] and it remained at this until 1970, when it was reduced by statute to 18.[70] So far as the law of tort is concerned, only two questions arise concerning minors, namely their capacity to sue and to be sued for tort.

---

[64] 15 & 16 Geo. 5, c. 49, s. 12.
[65] *Eirenarcha* (1614), 370.
[66] *Sirros* v. *Moore* [1974] 3 All E.R. 776; *London (Mayor of)* v. *Cox* (1867) L.R. 2 H.L. 239, 269, *per* Willes J.; Pollock, *Torts*, 15th ed., p. 85.
[67] 24 Geo. 2, c. 44, s. 6.
[68] (1840) 1 M. & G. 775; Weir, *Casebook on Tort*, 3rd ed., p. 317; *Diamond* v. *Minter* [1941] 1 K.B. 656. See too *Horsfield* v. *Brown* [1932] 1 K.B. 355.
[69] Holdsworth, H.E.L. iii, pp. 510–511.
[70] Family Law Reform Act 1969 (c. 46), s. 1.

Capacity to sue

In general no distinction falls to be taken between a minor and an adult so far as their respective capacities to sue for tort are concerned, save that a minor must sue by his " next friend." The only substantial question is whether a minor can sue for an injury done to him before he was born.[71] Certainly an action may be brought under the Fatal Accidents Act on behalf of a posthumous child of the deceased,[72] and if a tort is committed before a child's birth against property to which he becomes entitled on birth, there is no reason why he should be prevented from suing for it. It is in relation to injuries suffered by the child himself while *en ventre sa mère* that the most doubt arises for there is no English authority directly in point. In *S. v. Distillers Co. (Biochemicals) Ltd.*,[73] where the court had to assess the damages payable to children who were born deformed as a result of the use of the drug thalidomide by their mothers during pregnancy, the issue of liability was settled by agreement between the parties.[74] Nevertheless, provided that the necessary ingredients of tortious liability can be made out (and this, admittedly, will not always be easy [75]) there seems to be no reason why an action should not lie.[76] To clear up doubt, the Law Commission has proposed the enactment of a short Bill creating liability for injury to an unborn child. Considerations of space prevent full treatment of the proposals and the Report itself will repay study,[77] but the following salient features of their proposed scheme of liability may be noted: (1) No action would lie unless the child were born alive; (2) liability would rest upon a breach of duty to the mother, though she need have suffered no actionable injury; (3) the child would be " identified " with the mother's contributory negligence; (4) the mother should not be liable to the child in respect of pre-natal injury except if the injury

---

[71] See Winfield, " The Unborn Child " (1942) 8 C.L.J. 76; Barry, " The Child en ventre sa mere " (1941) 14 A.L.J. 351; Gordon, " The Unborn Plaintiff " (1965) 63 Mich.L.R. 579 and, for a wide ranging discussion, Tedeschi, " On Tort Liability for ' Wrongful Life ' " (1966) 1 Israel L.R. 513 and Lovell and Griffith-Jones, " The Sins of the Fathers—Tort Liability for Pre-Natal Injuries " (1974) 90 L.Q.R. 531.

[72] *The George and Richard* (1871) L.R. 3 Ad. & E. 466.

[73] [1970] 1 W.L.R. 114.

[74] The settlement was on the basis that the defendants would pay 40 per cent. of the damages to which the plaintiffs would be entitled if wholly successful in the action and that all allegations of negligence against the defendants were withdrawn. Clearly, questions of fact as well as of law were in doubt.

[75] Consider the differences, from the point of view of establishing reasonable foreseeability of damage to the plaintiff, between an action against the manufacturer of a drug intended for use by expectant mothers and one against a person whose negligent act has injured a woman who is, but who is not known by the defendant to be, pregnant. In the former case there is little substance in the objection that the plaintiff might not even have been conceived when the drug was manufactured: *cf.* Street, *Torts*, 5th ed., p. 109, n. 1.

[76] It is most unlikely that the old Irish case to the contrary of *Walker* v. *G.N. Ry. of Ireland* (1890) 28 L.R.Ir. 69 would now be followed. Liability has recently been imposed for injuries caused to the plaintiff while a foetus in car accidents in *Watt* v. *Rama* [1972] V.R. 353 and *Duval* v. *Seguin* (1972) 26 D.L.R. (3d) 418. The majority of writers favour this view. In addition to those cited, n. 71, *ante*, see Clerk and Lindsell, *Torts*, 13th ed., p. 101; Salmond, *Torts*, 16th ed., p. 446. Fleming, *Torts*, 4th ed., pp. 155–157 and Street, *Torts*, 5th ed., p. 109, are more doubtful.

[77] Injuries to Unborn Children, Law Com. No. 56 (1974).

is caused by her negligent driving of a motor vehicle; (5) no special exemption should be given to the father; (6) there should be no liability for " wrongful life " in the sense of failure to prevent the birth of an already conceived child, which is at risk of disability.

Capacity to be sued

In the law of tort there is no defence of infancy as such and a minor is as much liable to be sued for his torts as is an adult. In *Gorely* v. *Codd*,[78] Nield J. had no hesitation in holding that a boy of $16\frac{1}{2}$ had been negligent when he accidentally shot the plaintiff with an air-rifle in the course of " larking about," and it is obvious that a motorist of $17\frac{1}{2}$ is as responsible for negligent driving as one six months older. Where, however, the minor is very young, then, it appears, his age is relevant if he is sued for a tort involving negligence or malice. This is to be inferred from the fact that a young child may well be incapable of the necessary mental state for liability in such torts, from the English cases concerning the contributory negligence of children,[79] and from a number of decisions in other jurisdictions.[80] In an action for negligence against a young child, therefore, it is insufficient to show that he behaved in a way which would amount to negligence on the part of an adult. It must be shown that his behaviour was unreasonable for a child of his age.

Tort and contract

In general contracts entered into by minors are void and unenforceable, and the question arises, therefore, whether if the facts show both a breach of a (void) contract and a tort, the contract rule can be evaded by framing the claim against the minor in tort. The answer, unsatisfactory though it may be from a theoretical point of view,[81] seems to be that a minor cannot be sued if the cause of action against him arises substantially *ex contractu* or if to allow the action would be to enforce the contract indirectly, but if the wrong is independent of the contract, then the minor may be sued even though but for the contract he would have had no opportunity of committing the tort.[82] In *R. Leslie Ltd.* v. *Shiell*[83] a minor had fraudulently represented to the plaintiffs that he was of full age and had thereby persuaded them to lend him money. He was held not liable for deceit or on any other ground for a judgment against him would have amounted to the enforcement of the contract of

---

[78] [1967] 1 W.L.R. 19; *Buckpitt* v. *Oates* [1968] 1 All E.R. 1145, 1149, *per* John Stephenson J.

[79] *Ante*, pp. 111–112.

[80] *Walmsley* v. *Humenick* [1954] 2 D.L.R. 232 (Sup.Ct. of B.C.); *McHale* v. *Watson* (1966) 115 C.L.R. 199 (H.Ct. of Aus.); *Yokton Agriculture and Industrial Exhibition Society* v. *Morley* (1967) 66 D.L.R. (2d) 37 (Sask.C.A.).

[81] See *ante*, pp. 11–12, 17–18.

[82] Pollock, *Contract*, 13th ed., pp. 62–63, approved by Kennedy L.J. in *R. Leslie Ltd.* v. *Shiell* [1914] 3 K.B. 607, 620; Cheshire and Fifoot, *Law of Contract*, 8th ed., p. 407.

[83] *Supra*. This was first established in *Johnson* v. *Pye* (1665) 1 Sid. 258. See too *Stocks* v. *Wilson* [1913] 2 K.B. 235.

loan in a roundabout way. On the other hand, in *Burnard* v. *Haggis*,[84] the defendant, an undergraduate of Trinity College, Cambridge, and a minor, was held liable in the following circumstances. He hired from the plaintiff a mare for riding on the express stipulation that she was not to be used for " jumping or larking." He nevertheless lent the mare to a friend who, while they were galloping about fields in the neighbourhood of Cambridge, tried to jump her over a fence, on which she was staked; she died from the wound. The defendant's conduct was, as Willes J. said,[85] " as much a trespass, notwithstanding the hiring for another purpose, as if, without any hiring at all, the defendant had gone into a field and taken the mare out and hunted her and killed her. It was a bare trespass, not within the object and purpose of the hiring. It was not even an excess. It was doing an act towards the mare which was altogether forbidden by the owner." [86]

So long as it is considered necessary to protect minors against liability in contract it is difficult to see that a different rule from that represented by these cases could be found. Its most unfortunate practical consequence is that the fraudulent minor is able to enjoy the fruits of his deceit free from civil liability, but now that the age of majority has been reduced to 18, this is probably of less importance than it has been in the past.

Liability of parent

A parent or guardian [87] is not in general liable for the torts of a child; but to this there are two exceptions. First, where the child is employed by his parent and commits a tort in the course of his employment, the parent is vicariously responsible just as he would be for the tort of any other servant of his. Secondly, the parent will be liable if the child's tort were due to the parent's negligent control of the child in respect of the act that caused the injury, or if the parent expressly authorised the commission of the tort, or possibly if he ratified the child's act. Thus, where a father gave his boy, about 15 years old, an airgun and allowed him to retain it after he had smashed a neighbour's window with it, he was held liable for the boy's tort in injuring the eye of another boy with the gun.[88] Where, however, a boy aged 13 had promised his father never

---

[84] (1863) 14 C.B.(N.S.) 45. *Cf. Jennings* v. *Rundall* (1799) 8 T.R. 335; *Fawcett* v. *Smethurst* (1915) 84 L.J.K.B. 473.
[85] *Ibid.* at p. 53.
[86] See too *Ballett* v. *Mingay* [1943] K.B. 281.
[87] Note in this connection that school authorities are under no greater duty than that of a reasonably careful parent: *Ricketts* v. *Erith B.C.* [1943] 2 All E.R. 629; *Rich* v. *London County Council* [1953] 1 W.L.R. 895, C.A. (no practical alternative to keeping coke in school playground, infant plaintiff injured by coke thrown at him by another schoolboy, found as a fact there had been adequate supervision, it was not necessary to ensure coke was not accessible to the boys, reasonable care had been taken); *Nicholson* v. *Westmorland County Council* [1962] C.L.Y. 2087 (schoolteacher in charge of a class of 20 children. Test of reasonable care that of a parent with a family of 20 children). *Cf. Carmarthenshire County Council* v. *Lewis* [1955] A.C. 549.
[88] *Bebee* v. *Sales* (1916) 32 T.L.R. 413; *Newton* v. *Edgerley* [1959] 1 W.L.R. 1031. See, too, the Scottish case, *Brown* v. *Fulton* (1881) 9 R. 36.

to use his air-rifle outside the house (where there was a cellar in which the rifle could be fired) and subsequently broke that promise, the Court of Appeal refused to disturb the trial judge's finding that the father had not been negligent.[89] Nor will he be liable to one who is bitten by a dog which belongs to his daughter who is old enough (*e.g.* 17 years) to be able to exercise control over it, and this is so even if the father knows of the dog's ferocious temper.[90]

MARRIED WOMEN

Until 1935, the English law as to wives presented a rather barbarous hotch-potch of humiliating disabilities and scandalous immunities. The cause of this was the sharp difference between the harsh policy of the common law and the benignant attitude of equity towards the married woman. If she was the spoiled child of equity, she was also the Cinderella of the common law. In the law of property equity won the day, for its main doctrine was embodied in various Married Women's Property Acts. At present the Law Reform (Married Women and Tortfeasors) Act 1935 and the Law Reform (Husband and Wife) Act 1962 put married women in almost exactly the same position as their unmarried sisters.[91]

In the law of tort there was neither disability nor immunity at common law. She could sue and be sued, but her husband had to be joined with her as she had no procedural existence apart from him. The necessity for joining him was abolished by the Married Women's Property Act 1882.[92]

But this simple statement of the law was subject to several qualifications and additions.

1. Extent of liability

A married woman was not liable beyond her separate property.[93] The Law Reform (Married Women and Tortfeasors) Act 1935 [94] abolished the word " separate " in connection with her property and, subject to what is stated below, puts her in the same position as a *feme sole* with respect to property. Judgment against her is not, as it used to be, limited to her separate property.[95]

2. Actions between spouses

Actions in tort between husband and wife were not possible at com-

---

[89] *Donaldson* v. *McNiven* (1952) 96 S.J. 747; *Gorely* v. *Codd* [1967] 1 W.L.R. 19. Contrast *Newton* v. *Edgerley, supra,* where Lord Parker C.J. seems to put the father in an inescapable dilemma.

[90] *North* v. *Wood* [1914] 1 K.B. 629. *Cf.* pp. 395–396, *ante.*

[91] For the history of the law down to 1879, see C. S. Kenny, *History of the Law of Married Women's Property.*

[92] 45 & 46 Vict. c. 75, s. 1 (2).

[93] *Ibid.*

[94] 25 & 26 Geo. 5, c. 30, s. 1.

[95] *Scott* v. *Morley* (1887) 20 Q.B.D. 120; Act of 1935, s. 1 (*d*).

mon law,[96] and this rule was retained by the Married Women's Property Act 1882, s. 12, except that under the section a wife could sue her husband in tort " for the protection and security of her property." [97] In modern times, however, the prohibition of actions in tort between spouses has been productive of serious anomalies and injustices,[98] and it has been abolished by the Law Reform (Husband and Wife) Act 1962.[99] Each of the parties to a marriage now has the same right of action in tort against the other as if they were not married, but, in order to prevent them from using the court as a forum for trivial domestic disputes, the proceedings may be stayed if it appears that no substantial benefit will accrue to either party from their continuation.[1] The proceedings may also be stayed if it appears that the case can be more conveniently disposed of under section 17 of the Married Women's Property Act 1882, which provides a summary procedure for determining questions of title or possession of property between husband and wife.[2]

One anomaly does, however, remain. If a wife is injured as the result partly of her husband's negligence and partly as a result of the negligence of X she can recover her damages in full from X, and X can now recover contribution from the husband.[3] But if the wife is injured partly as a result of her own negligence and partly as the result of that of X, then, though her own damages will be reduced on account of her contributory negligence, X will be liable to the husband in full for his loss of *consortium*.[4]

3. Husband's liability for wife's torts

At common law a husband was liable for torts committed by his wife during the marriage,[5] and this rule was upheld by a bare majority of the House of Lords as late as 1925.[6] The Act of 1882 made him liable also for his wife's pre-nuptial torts to the extent of any property he acquired through her.[7] The Act of 1935 has abolished this form of

---

[96] The reason being the fiction that they were one flesh. A better and more modern reason, though not a convincing one, is that such litigation is " unseemly, distressing and embittering," *per* McCardie J. in *Gottliffe* v. *Edelston* [1930] 2 K.B. 378, 392.

[97] There was no similar exception in favour of the husband: *Baylis* v. *Blackwell* [1952] 1 K.B. 154.

[98] See Kahn-Freund, " Inconsistencies and Injustices in the Law of Husband and Wife " (1952) 15 M.L.R. 133; Glanville Williams, " Some Reforms in the Law of Tort " (1961) 24 M.L.R. 101–102; Law Reform Committee, 9th Report (Liability in Tort between Husband and Wife) (1961) Cmnd. 1268, and comment thereon, Stone (1961) 24 M.L.R. 481.

[99] s. 1 (1). For the earlier law see, 6th ed., pp. 118–125.

[1] s. 1 (2) (*a*). See *McLeod* v. *McLeod* (1963) 113 L.J. 420 (Cty.Ct.).

[2] s. 1 (2) (*b*).

[3] The Act of 1962 reverses *Chant* v. *Read* [1939] 2 K.B. 346; *Drinkwater* v. *Kimber* [1952] 2 Q.B. 281. For contribution under the Law Reform (Married Women and Tortfeasors) Act 1935, see *ante*, pp. 558–561.

[4] *Mallett* v. *Dunn* [1949] 2 K.B. 180. This decision is unaffected by the Act of 1962. *Cf. Enridge* v. *Copp* (1966) 57 D.L.R. 239 (Br.Col.Sup.Ct.). For the action for loss of *consortium*, see *ante*, pp. 439–441.

[5] So was she, to the extent of her separate property.

[6] *Edwards* v. *Porter* [1925] A.C. 1.   [7] s. 14.

vicarious liability by providing that a husband shall not, merely because he is a husband, be liable in respect of any tort committed by his wife whether before or during marriage,[8] but he may, of course, be liable as a joint tortfeasor with his wife if in fact he was one.[9]

CORPORATIONS

A corporation is an artificial person created by the law. It may come into existence either by the common law, or by royal charter, or by parliamentary authority, or by prescription or by custom. Whatever their origin may be, the characteristics common to most corporations are a distinctive name, a common seal and perpetuity of existence. This existence is quite independent of the human beings who are members of the corporation. Fellow of a college and shareholders of a brewery company may perish, but the college and brewery company still continue.

1. Capacity to sue in tort

A corporation can sue for torts committed against it,[10] but there are certain torts which, by their very nature, it is impossible to commit against a corporation, such as assault or false imprisonment. A corporation can sue for the malicious presentation of a winding-up petition[11] or for defamation, though the precise limits of the latter are unclear. It is certain that a trading corporation may sue in respect of defamation affecting its business or property,[12] but the law probably goes further and allows any corporation to sue in respect of matter defamatory of its conduct of its affairs.[13] Thus a local government authority is entitled to sue if defamed in respect of its " governing " reputation.[14]

2. Liability to be sued

Many corporations are expressly limited by the terms of their incorporation as to the acts which they may lawfully do.[15] If they observe

---

[8] s. 3.

[9] s. 4 (2) (c).

[10] *Semble,* even if engaged in an *ultra vires* undertaking at the material time: *National Telephone Co.* v. *Constable of St. Peter Port* [1900] A.C. 317, 321, *per* Lord Davey (*obiter*), a decision of the Privy Council on appeal from the Royal Court of Guernsey.

[11] *Quartz Hill Consolidated Gold Mining Co.* v. *Eyre* (1883) 11 Q.B.D. 674.

[12] *Metropolitan Saloon Omnibus Co.* v. *Hawkins* (1859) 4 H. & N. 87.

[13] *Bognor Regis U.D.C.* v. *Campion* [1972] 2 Q.B. 169; *D. & L. Caterers Ltd.* v. *D'Ajou* [1945] K.B. 364; *National Union of General and Municipal Workers* v. *Gillian* [1946] K.B. 81; *Willis* v. *Brooks* [1947] 1 All E.R. 191. *South Hetton Coal Co. Ltd.* v. *N.E. News Association Ltd.* [1894] 1 Q.B. 133, though inconclusive on the point, seems to support this view. Dicta in *Manchester Corporation* v. *Williams* (1891) 63 L.T. 805, 806 (the fuller report) and *Lewis* v. *Daily Telegraph Ltd.* [1964] A.C. 234, 262, seem to support the narrower view.

[14] *Bognor Regis U.D.C.* v. *Campion, supra.* But defamation which reflects solely upon the individual officers or workers is not actionable by the corporation.

[15] It is generally accepted that a chartered corporation has all the powers of a natural person: *The Case of Sutton's Hospital* (1613) 10 Co.Rep. 23a. See Gower, *Modern Company Law,* 3rd ed., p. 83.

those restrictions they are said to be acting *intra vires*, and this is still the case even when they commit a tort, provided it is done as an incident of some act which falls within their powers. If it is not connected in this way with what they are lawfully entitled to do, the tort is said to be *ultra vires*.

(i) *Intra vires torts*

If the tort is committed by a servant or other agent of the corporation acting in the course of his employment, then the corporation is liable on exactly the same principle that any employer is vicariously responsible in the like circumstances. In time past there were procedural difficulties in the way of suing the corporation,[16] but these have long since disappeared. In 1812, it was held that a corporation could be sued in trover,[17] in 1842 in trespass,[18] and 1858 for libel,[19] and many other decisions have made it clear that wherever it is possible for a corporation to commit a tort at all, it can be sued.[20]

In one class of torts there was a difficulty which has been dispelled in only comparatively recent times—those which require malice in the sense of actual ill will, such as malicious prosecution. It was urged that a corporation had no mind and that therefore malice could not be imputed to it. But this was a needless and fallacious metaphysical subtlety, for the reason why a corporation is liable, if at all, for tort is because it is responsible (like any other employer) for the torts of its servants committed in the course of their employment, and they have the requisite mental equipment even if the corporation has none.[21]

(ii) *Ultra vires torts*

In *Poulton* v. *L. & S.W. Ry.*[22] the defendants' stationmaster wrongfully detained the plaintiff because he refused to pay the fare of his horse. The power to detain in such circumstances was quite outside the defendants' powers. It was held that they were not liable, for the stationmaster could not be said to have been impliedly authorised to do such an act. Winfield considered that it followed that a corporation could not be vicariously liable for the torts of its servants committed in the course of an *ultra vires* undertaking, but it is submitted that this is not so. When *Poulton's* case was decided the " course of employment " test of vicarious liability was in its infancy; the need for " implied authority " was still much in the judges' minds [23] and there is obvious difficulty in holding that a corporation has impliedly authorised the doing of an act which it has itself no power to perform. Today, how-

---

[16] Pollock, *Torts*, 15th ed., p. 51, n. 19; Holdsworth, H.E.L., iii, 488–489.
[17] *Yarborough* v. *Bank of England* (1812) 16 East 6.
[18] *Maund* v. *Monmouthshire Canal Co.* (1842) 4 Man. & G. 452.
[19] *Whitfield* v. *S.E. Ry.* (1858) E.B. & E. 115.
[20] 9 Halsbury's *Laws of England*, 4th ed., §§ 1374–1378.
[21] *Cornford* v. *Carlton Bank Ltd.* [1899] 1 Q.B. 392; [1900] 1 Q.B. 22; *Citizens' Life Assurance Co. Ltd.* v. *Brown* [1904] A.C. 423, 426, *per* Lord Lindley.
[22] (1867) L.R. 2 Q.B. 534; *Ormiston* v. *G.W. Ry.* [1917] 1 K.B. 598.
[23] See *ante*, pp. 517–518.

ever, so long, at least, as the view is accepted that a master's liability for his servants' torts is truly vicarious,[24] there is no need for this technical argument to succeed. It will, no doubt, be comparatively rare for an *ultra vires* tort to be committed by a servant of a corporation in the course of his employment, but if such a case arises there is no valid reason why the corporation should not be liable.[25]

If this is correct, then the case of a tort which is expressly authorised by the corporation, whether *ultra vires* or not, will normally present no problem. If the act constituting the tort is done by a servant of the corporation and with its express authority, it is hard to see that it will not be done in the course of his employment. It may, however, sometimes be necessary, if the corporation is to be liable, to attribute to it the *act* of another, whether its servant or not, and where this is the case it may be thought that the *ultra vires* doctrine presents a stumbling block. How, it may be asked, can an act which the corporation has no power to perform nevertheless be the corporation's act? The answer, it is suggested, is that if a corporation acts in the only way in which a corporation, being an artificial person,[26] can act—that is, if the central governing body of the corporation orders or ratifies an act—then the act must be attributed to the corporation itself. This commonsense solution was regarded as obvious in *Campbell,* v. *Paddington Corporation* [27] and it is submitted that there is no valid reason why it should not be accepted.[28] Indeed, if it is not accepted, it is difficult to see how any unlawful act can ever be regarded as the corporation's act, and yet we know that a corporation can not only be primarily liable in tort, but can even be held guilty of " actual fault " within the meaning of the Merchant Shipping Acts.[29]

PARTNERS

In English law a partnership is not a legal person distinct from its members and consequently has no capacity to sue or be sued,[30] but

---

[24] See *ante*, pp. 516, 540–543.

[25] If the employment of the servant was itself *ultra vires* the corporation, then there may be some difficulty, for an *ultra vires* contract is certainly void at common law (*Ashbury Railway Carriage and Iron Co. Ltd.* v. *Riche* (1875) L.R. 7 H.L. 653; but in certain circumstances the contract may be valid under s. 9 of the European Communities Act 1972) and it can, therefore, be argued that in fact the relationship of master and servant does not exist. See Goodhart, " Corporate Liability in Tort and the Doctrine of Ultra Vires " (1926) 2 C.L.J. 350.

[26] Artificial, not fictitious. A wooden leg may be artificial: it is not a fiction.

[27] [1911] 1 K.B. 869, 875, *per* Avory J.; *ibid.* at pp. 877–878, *per* Lush J.

[28] But see Goodhart, *loc. cit.*, and *cf.* Warren, " Torts by Corporations in Ultra Vires Undertakings " (1926) 2 C.L.J. 180. See also Ashton-Cross, " Suggestions regarding the Liability of Corporations for the Torts of their Servants " (1950) 10 C.L.J. 419. Other textbooks are in general agreement with the view expressed above: Salmond, *Torts*, 16th ed., pp. 438–439; Street, *Torts* 5th ed., pp. 462–463; Clerk and Lindsell, *Torts*, 13th ed., pp. 106–107.

[29] *Lennard's Carrying Co. Ltd.* v. *Asiatic Petroleum Co. Ltd.* [1915] A.C. 705; *The Lady Gwendolen* [1965] P. 294.

[30] But the partners may sue or be sued in the name of the firm: R.S.C., Ord. 80.

each partner is liable jointly and severally with his co-partners for a tort committed by any of them against an outsider in the course of business.[31]

CLUBS [32]

In the case of proprietary and incorporated clubs, it would seem that the ordinary rules as to the liability of a master or principal for the torts of his servants or agents apply.[33] In the case of an unincorporated club which is not an entity known to the law and which cannot be sued in its own name, liability involves a question of substantive law and one of procedure. The first question is, who is liable for the wrongful act or breach of duty? This depends on the circumstances of the particular case, and it may be the members of the committee, or someone such as a steward who is in control of the club or possibly the whole body of members.[34] Membership of the club and even membership of the committee does not involve any special duty of care towards other *members* of the club [35] nor, it seems, towards a *stranger*, though in the latter case the members of the committee (at the time when the cause of action arose) will be liable personally to the exclusion of other members, if they act personally, as by employing an incompetent person to erect a stand as the result of which a stranger is injured.[36] In the case of torts involving vicarious liability, apart from the actual wrongdoer's liability, the question depends upon whose servant or agent the wrongdoer was at the material time.[37] Where liability arises out of the ownership or occupation of property, as in nuisance or under the Occupiers' Liability Act 1957, the occupiers of the premises in question will normally be the proper persons to sue.[38] If the property is vested in trustees they may be the proper persons to sue, but in the absence of trustees it is a question of fact as to who are the occupiers of the premises.[39] As to the procedural point, the need for a representative action only arises where it is desired to sue the whole body of members, and a representation

---

[31] Partnership Act 1890, ss. 10 and 12. See Lindley, *Partnership*, 13th ed., pp. 187–193. The partners may, of course, also be liable for the torts of their servants, or agents under ordinary principles: see, *e.g. Lloyd* v. *Grace, Smith & Co.* [1912] A.C. 716.

[32] For the position of trade unions, see p. 468, *ante.*

[33] Halsbury, *Laws of England*, 4th ed., Vol. 6, para. 277; for different kinds of clubs, see paras. 204–216. In a proprietary club the property and funds of the club belong to a proprietor, who may sue or be sued in his own name or in the name of the club. The members are in contractual relation with the proprietor, and have a right to use the club premises in accordance with the rules, but they are not his servants or agents. An incorporated club may sue or be sued in its corporate name. An unincorporated members' club has no legal existence apart from its members, who are jointly entitled to the property and funds, though usually the property is vested in trustees. It cannot sue or be sued in the club name, nor can the secretary or any other officer sue or be sued on behalf of the club.

[34] Lloyd (1953) 16 M.L.R. 359.

[35] *Prole* v. *Allen* [1950] 1 All E.R. 476; *Shore* v. *Ministry of Works* [1950] 2 All E.R. 228 (C.A.).

[36] Halsbury, *Laws of England*, 4th ed., Vol. 6, para. 233; *Brown* v. *Lewis* (1896) 12 T.L.R. 445. *Bradley Egg Farm Ltd.* v. *Clifford* [1943] 2 All E.R. 378 (C.A.).

[37] Lloyd, *loc. cit.*, p. 359.

[38] *Ibid.* pp. 359–360.

[39] *Ibid.* p. 360.

order may be made, provided that the members whose names appear on the writ are persons who may fairly be taken to represent the body of club members and that they and all the other club members have the same interest in the action.[40]

PERSONS OF UNSOUND MIND

There is singularly little English authority as to the liability of persons of unsound mind for torts committed by them.[41] Sir Matthew Hale thought that *dementia* was one of several other forms of incapacity which might exempt a person from criminal liability, but which ordinarily do not excuse him from civil liability, for that " is not by way of penalty, but a satisfaction for damage done to the party " [42]; and there are dicta in the older cases which regard lunacy as no defence.[43] More to the purpose is a dictum of Lord Esher M.R., in 1892,[44] that a lunatic is liable unless the disease of his mind is so great that he cannot understand the nature and consequences of his act. In *Morriss* v. *Marsden* [45] the defendant, who attacked and seriously injured the plaintiff, had been found unfit to plead in earlier criminal proceedings. He was then sued by the plaintiff for damages for assault and battery. Stable J. found that the defendant's mind was so disturbed by his disease that he did not know that what he was doing was wrong, but that the assault was a voluntary act on his part and that the defendant was therefore liable.

Unsoundness of mind is thus certainly not in itself a ground of immunity from liability in tort, and it is submitted that the true question in each case is whether the defendant was possessed of the requisite state of mind for liability in the particular tort with which he is charged. In trespass to the person it is enough that the defendant intended to strike the plaintiff and the defendant in *Morriss* v. *Marsden* was therefore rightly held liable; but had his disease been so severe that his act was not a voluntary one at all he would not have been liable.[46] In defamation it is enough that the defendant published matter defamatory of the plaintiff and it would certainly be no defence that in his disturbed mental state he believed it to be true. Again, as Stable J. said, " I cannot think that, if a person of unsound mind converts my property under a delusion that he is entitled to do it or that it was not property at all, that affords a defence." [47] The tort of negligence probably creates the greatest diffi-

---

[40] *Campbell* v. *Thompson* [1953] 1 Q.B. 445. See Lloyd, *loc. cit.*, 360–363.
[41] See Fridman, " Mental Incompetency " (1963) 79 L.Q.R. 502, (1964) 80 L.Q.R. 84.
[42] 1 Hist. of Pleas of Crown (ed. 1778), pp. 15–16. So, too, in effect Bacon (Spedding's ed. of his works, vii, 348).
[43] *e.g. Weaver* v. *Ward* (1616) Hob. 134.
[44] *Hanbury* v. *Hanbury* (1892) 8 T.L.R. 559, 569. *Cf. Mordaunt* v. *Mordaunt* (1870) L.R. 2 P. & D. 103, 142, *per* Kelly C.B.
[45] [1952] 1 All E.R. 925. See (1952) 68 L.Q.R. 300; Todd (1952) 15 M.L.R. 486. *Morriss* v. *Marsden* was followed in *Phillips* v. *Soloway* (1957) 6 D.L.R. (2d) 570 (Manitoba Queen's Bench) and in *Beals* v. *Hayward* [1960] N.Z.L.R. 131.
[46] *Ibid.* at p. 927, *per* Stable J.
[47] *Ibid.*

culty, since it is uncertain to what extent, if at all, the personal weaknesses of the defendant can be taken into account if his conduct has fallen short of what a reasonable man would have done in the circumstances. It is submitted that the better view is that the defendant's unsoundness of mind, at least if unknown to the plaintiff, is irrelevant unless it is so severe as to make him a virtual automaton. It is, for example, unthinkable that a motorist who has failed to drive with the care and skill of a reasonably competent driver should escape liability for damages because of his unsoundness of mind.[48]

ALIENS [49]

Friendly aliens have had a chequered career in the English law courts. The early common law had little application to them, for when they came here it was generally under royal charters and their business took them into boroughs created by royal charter. Thus began a conflict which veered this way and that for some centuries. The burghers did not want aliens, because they filched away their trade. The King and nobles on the whole favoured them, because they lent money, kept prices down and paid for royal favours.[50] Littleton in his *Tenures* (c. 1481–82) denies any action, real or personal, to an alien born out of allegiance to the King.[51] Coke, in his commentary upon Littleton (1628), qualifies this by saying that " an alien that is in league [with the King] shall maintain personal actions . . . but he cannot maintain either real or mixt actions." [52] Real actions were practically concerned with the recovery of land, and as an alien could hold no land, he could not sue for the loss of it, nor was this disability extinct until the Naturalisation Act 1870.[53] A friendly alien today is under no disability and has no immunity.

An alien enemy is one whose state or sovereign is at war with the sovereign of England, or one who, whatever his nationality, is voluntarily resident or carries on business in an enemy's country. But it is possible for a subject of an enemy state, who is neither residing nor carrying on business in an enemy's country, not to be an alien enemy with regard to civil rights.[54] As thus defined, an alien enemy, unless he be within the realm by the licence of the Queen, cannot sue in the

---

[48] See *White* v. *White* [1950] P. 39, 58–59, *per* Denning L.J.; *Adamson* v. *Motor Vehicle Trust* (1957) W.A.L.R. 56, cited Salmond, *Torts*, 16th ed., p. 447. In *Morriss* v. *Marsden*, *supra*, at p. 927 Stable J. said, " If a sleepwalker inadvertently, without intention or without carelessness, broke a valuable vase, that would not be actionable." His Lordship thus evidently contemplated a negligent sleepwalker as a logical possibility and would presumably have held such a person liable for the damage he caused.
[49] Foreign sovereigns and ambassadors are more appropriately dealt with in books on nternational law. The law of tort relating to them is epitomised in Salmond, *Torts*, 16th ed., pp. 436–437; Clerk and Lindsell, *Torts*, 13th ed., pp. 92–96.
[50] Pollock and Maitland, *History of English Law*, 2nd ed. (1898), i, pp. 464–466.
[51] s. 98.
[52] Co.Litt. 129*b*.
[53] 33 & 34 Vict. c. 14. For the history of the topic, see Holdsworth, H.E.L., ix, 72–99.
[54] 4 Halsbury's *Laws of England*, 4th ed., § 950.

Queen's courts. He can, however, be sued and can defend an action and, if the decision goes against him, he can appeal.[55]

PERSONS HAVING PARENTAL OR QUASI-PARENTAL AUTHORITY

Parents and other persons in similar positions are necessarily immune against liability for many acts which in other people would be assault, battery or false imprisonment. They have control, usually but not necessarily, of a disciplinary character, over those committed to their charge. The nature of the control varies according to the relationship and, provided that it is exercised reasonably and moderately, acts done in pursuance of it are not tortious.

Parental authority needs no illustration,[56] it ceases when the child attains 18 years. Quasi-parental authority is exemplified by the control of schoolmasters over pupils, husband over wife, master over apprentice and custodian over person of unsound mind.

Schoolmasters

The control of a schoolmaster over his pupil may be delegated to him by the parent.[57] The delegation seems to include implied assent of the parent to any reasonable rule or custom of the school relating to discipline, whether the parent knew of it or not [58]; unless the child was sent to the school on the understanding that some rule or custom prevalent there (a) should not apply to him, or, perhaps, (b) should not be materially altered without giving the parent an opportunity of refusing to permit the change to apply to his child.[59] It is not limited to the school premises, for " there is not much opportunity for a boy to exhibit his moral conduct while in school under the eye of the master: the opportunity is while he is at play or outside the school." [60] Hence it is no assault if the master canes him for fighting in the street or for smoking in public.[61] Supposing that the boy were to break a rule of the school which directly conflicts with his father's instructions to him, how can

---

[55] *Porter* v. *Freudenberg* [1915] 1 K.B. 857. For further details as to alien enemies, see McNair, *Legal Effects of War*, 4th ed., Chaps. 2, 3, 15; W. E. Davies, *Aliens* (1931), Chap. XI; and, as to their position during the World War, 1939–1945: Butterworth's Emergency Legislation Service. An alien enemy interned in England cannot maintain a claim for habeas corpus: *R.* v. *Bottrill* [1947] 1 K.B. 41; it is doubtful whether he can sue for false imprisonment on the ground that statutory powers have been exceeded by those who intern him: *Hirsch* v. *Somervell* [1946] 2 All E.R. 430.. *Quaere,* whether an alien enemy resident in England without the licence of the Queen can sue in tort? Winfield was inclined to agree with Rogers, *Effect of War on Contract*, pp. 127–128, that he can sue: (1947) 9 C.L.J. 129–130 (book review).

[56] It is assumed by the Children and Young Persons Act 1933, s. 1 (7). Eekelaar, " What are Parental Rights " (1973) 89 L.Q.R. 210.

[57] *Fitzgerald* v. *Northcote* (1865) 4 F. & F. 656, 689, *per* Cockburn C.J.; *Mansell* v. *Griffin* [1908] 1 K.B. 160, affd. *ibid.* 947. *Cf.* Street, *Torts*, 5th ed., pp. 87–88.

[58] *R.* v. *Newport (Salop) Justices* [1929] 2 K.B. 416; *Ryan* v. *Fildes* [1938] 3 All E.R. 517; *Ridley* v. *Little* [1960] C.L.Y. 1088.

[59] *Mansell* v. *Griffin* [1908] 1 K.B. at p. 167, *per* Phillimore J., *sed. qu.* See Street, *supra,* n. 2.

[60] *Cleary* v. *Booth* [1893] 1 Q.B. 465, 469, *per* Collins J.

[61] *R.* v. *Newport (Salop) Justices* [1929] 2 K.B. 416.

he escape a flogging? At present the law is doubtful. If both rules are foolish, perhaps his only consolation in the dilemma is the Horatian quotation, " *Quid-quid delirant reges, plectuntur Achivi.*" [62] If the school rule was reasonable, perhaps that would be a defence to the schoolmaster unless he had agreed with the parent that the boy should be exempted from it. Assistant teachers may inflict corporal punishment provided it is moderate, is such as is usual in the school and as the parent might expect that the child would receive if it did wrong, and is not dictated by any bad motive.[63] Whether an assistant teacher, even if he satisfies these requirements, is still within his rights if the school regulations forbid him to inflict corporal punishment is doubtful.[64]

Husband and wife

As to husband and wife, in the older law he had the right to beat her moderately as a method of correction.[65] " But, with us," said Blackstone in 1768, " in the politer reign of Charles the Second, this power of correction began to be doubted: and a wife may now have security of the peace against her husband; or in return a husband against his wife. Yet the lower rank of people, who are always fond of the old common law, still claim and exert their antient privilege." [66] The right is now obsolete, nor can the husband even use force to recapture his wife if she has left him in breach of his conjugal rights.[67] It is unlikely that the husband can now restrain his wife even if she is about to leave to meet her lover.[68]

Master of ship

Authority similar to quasi-parental authority may be implied by law. Thus the master of a merchant ship can use force to preserve discipline for the safety of the ship, its crew, passengers and cargo. If he has reasonable cause to believe and does in fact believe that it is necessary

---

[62] *Ibid.* at p. 429, *per* Lord Hewart C.J. The American *Restatement of Torts*, Vol. 1, § 153, solves the problem by making the schoolmaster liable unless the school is one provided by the state, for then the schoolmaster is the delegate of the state and not of the parent. See also *Craig* v. *Frost* (1936) 30 Q.J.P. 140 (Queensland), cited Street, *Law of Torts*, 5th ed., p. 88, n. 3.

[63] *Mansell* v. *Griffin* [1908] 1 K.B. 160, 947.

[64] The Divisional Court in *Mansell's* case, *supra*, seemed to think that the teacher still has such power; but the reasoning of Phillimore J. at p. 167 is not convincing, and the Court of Appeal, while otherwise affirming the decision, declined to express an opinion on this point: [1908] 1 K.B. 947.

[65] " For that is a poynt of an honest man,
For to bete his wife well nowe and than."
Johan Johan (one of Heywood's Comedies, *circa* 1533).

[66] 1 *Commentaries*, 444–445.

[67] *R.* v. *Jackson* [1891] 1 Q.B. 671; *R.* v. *Reid* [1973] Q.B. 299. If he uses force or violence for the purpose of exercising his right to intercourse he does not commit rape (unless there has been a decree of judicial separation: *R.* v. *Clarke* [1949] 2 All E.R. 448) but he does commit a criminal assault: *R.* v. *Miller* [1954] 2 Q.B. 282. Presumably, therefore, since the prohibition against actions in tort between husband and wife has been removed (*ante*, p. 604) the wife has a cause of action in tort.

[68] *Cf. R.* v. *Jackson* [1891] 1 Q.B. 671, 679–680, *per* Lord Halsbury L.C.

for these purposes he may arrest and confine anyone on board.[69] If possible, an inquiry should precede punishment, and the accused " should have the benefit of that rule of universal justice of being heard in his own defence." [70] The punishment must of course not be excessive,[71] and it must always be a question of fact whether the occasion justifies arrest.[72]

---

[69] *Hook* v. *Cunard Steamship Co.* [1953] 1 W.L.R. 682. See also *Aldworth* v. *Stewart* (1866) 4 F. & F. 957.

[70] *The Agincourt* (1824) 1 Hagg.Ecc. 271, 174, *per* Lord Stowell.

[71] It was so in *The Agincourt, supra*, where a member of the crew was cruelly kicked and beaten.

[72] If a passenger describes the captain of a ship as the " landlord of an hotel," that does not justify the captain putting him in irons in the belief that mutiny is imminent: *King* v. *Franklin* (1858) 1 F. & F. 360; *Hook* v. *Cunard Steamship Co.* [1953] 1 W.L.R. 682.

CHAPTER 29

DEFENCES

A PLAINTIFF who fails to prove the necessary ingredients of the particular tort or torts on which he relies will, of course, fail in his action.
Even if he does prove these ingredients, however, he may still fail if the
defendant shows that he is entitled to rely upon some specific defence.
Some of these defences are peculiar to particular torts, as is justification
to the tort of defamation, and these have been noticed in their appropriate chapters. We must now consider those defences which apply
more generally throughout the law of tort.[1]

1. Consent. Volenti non fit injuria

There are many occasions on which harm—sometimes grievous
harm—may be inflicted on a person for which he has no remedy in
tort, because he consented, or at least assented, to the doing of the act
which caused his harm.[2] Simple examples are the injuries received in
the course of a lawful game or sport, or in a lawful surgical operation.
The effect of such consent or assent is commonly expressed in the
maxim " Volenti non fit injuria," which is certainly of respectable antiquity. The idea underlying it has been traced as far back as Aristotle,[3]
and it was also recognised in the works of the classical Roman jurists,[4]
and in the Canon law. In English law, Bracton in his De Legibus Angliae
(c. A.D. 1250–1258) uses the maxim, though not with the technicality
that attached to it later,[5] and in a Year Book case of 1305 it appears
worded exactly as it is now.[6] So far as actual citation of the maxim goes,
most of the modern cases use it in connection with harm to the person
rather than to property. The explanation seems to be that if the assent
is to the infliction of harm on, or at any rate to the use of, the plaintiff's
property, such assent is more usually styled leave and licence of the
plaintiff. But this phrase expresses much the same idea.[7] Moreover,
there is no reason for thinking that the maxim itself was confined in
time past to injuries to the person.[8]

---

[1] Winfield described these as " conditions which in general negative liability."
[2] " One who has invited or assented to an act being done towards him cannot, when he
suffers from it, complain of it as a wrong ": Smith v. Baker [1891] A.C. 325, 360, per
Lord Herschell.
[3] T. Beven in Journal of Comparative Legislation (1907), p. 185.
[4] Dig. 47, 10. 1. 5: " nulla injuria est quae in volentem fiat." See, too, Dig. 9. 2. 7. 4:
50. 17. 203.
[5] Ed. Woodbine (1942), Vol. 4, p. 286: " cum volenti et scienti non fiat injuria."
[6] 33–5 Edw. 1 (Rolls Series), 9 Hunt arguendo, " volenti non fit injuria."
[7] e.g. Park v. Jobson & Son [1945] 1 All E.R. 222. Cf. Armstrong v. Sheppard and
Short Ltd. [1959] 2 Q.B. 384. For a case of loss of property where volenti non fit injuria was
pleaded, but unsuccessfully, see Saunders (Mayfair) Furs Ltd. v. Chas. Wm. Davies Ltd.
(1965) 109 S.J. 922.
[8] Bracton, in the passage cited in note 6, supra, uses it generally, and in the Year Book
case (note 6, supra) it was used in a property action; Manwood J. in Grendon v. Bishop of
Lincoln (1576) Plowden 493, 501 makes it of general application. In Horne v. Widlake
(1607) Yelv. 141 it was the basis of the decision in a property case.

The maxim is of general application but no question of *volens* arises until it is established that the defendant has committed a tort, at least a presumptive [9] one, against the plaintiff. It is only then that the defendant need defend himself by proving that the plaintiff was *volens*.[10] This, a point of considerable importance, is often overlooked and the maxim invoked where there is no occasion for its use. If I engage in a boxing match with you then, no doubt, the reason why I cannot sue you for trespass if you succeed in hitting me is that I have consented to this. But if I undertake, for example, to repair the roof of your house, and while doing so I fall off and am injured, the reason that I cannot sue you is not that I have consented to the risk (though I may have done so in fact) but that you have committed no tort against me.[11]

For the defence of consent to succeed it is necessary for the defendant to establish not simply that the plaintiff consented to the *physical* risk, *i.e.* the risk of actual damage, but to the *legal* risk, *i.e.* the risk of actual damage for which there will be no redress at law.[12] Such consent may be easily proved if the plaintiff has contracted to bear a particular risk himself, as where his contract with the defendant excludes the defendant's liability for damage caused by negligence or in some other way,[13] but a contractual relationship between the parties is not essential. In at least three cases [14] it was [15] held that where a person accepted a lift in a car which, to his knowledge, carried a notice that passengers travelled at their own risk, he could not sue the driver for negligence. However, in most of the cases of tort in which the maxim is usually invoked, there is neither a contract nor any express consent by the plaintiff to take the risk upon himself. What, essentially, is argued, is that the facts justify or require the inference that the plaintiff has assumed the legal risk.

There is usually little difficulty in deciding whether or not this inference should be drawn in cases of intentional torts. The very act of

---

[9] That is, conduct that is a tort apart from the issue of *volens*.

[10] *Smith* v. *Baker* [1891] A.C. 325, 366, " If there had been no breach of duty it would not have been necessary to inquire whether the maxim, *volenti non fit injuria*, afforded a defence ": *per* Lord Herschell; *Wooldridge* v. *Sumner* [1963] 2 Q.B. 43, 56, *per* Sellers L.J.; *ibid.* at pp. 68–69, *per* Diplock L.J.; Glanville Williams, *Joint Torts and Contributory Negligence*, p. 295; Gordon, " Wrong Turns in the *Volens* Cases " (1945) 62 L.Q.R. 140.

[11] Compare the judgments of Scott and Goddard L.JJ. in *Bowater* v. *Rowley Regis Corporation* [1944] K.B. 476.

[12] Glanville Williams, *Joint Torts and Contributory Negligence*, p. 308; Lord Wright (1953) 2 Univ. of Western Austr. Annual Law Rev. 546, 558.

[13] Cases involving exclusion clauses in contracts are not generally discussed in terms of *volenti non fit injuria* but in terms of the law of contract. Many such clauses do not, of course, concern the law of tort at all, for they only seek to exclude certain contractual duties which would otherwise arise. However, where a defendant relies upon a contractual clause for protection against a claim founded upon tort he does in truth raise the defence of consent. In *Chapman* v. *Ellesmere* [1932] 2 K.B. 431, Slesser L.J. held that *volenti non fit injuria* prevented a trainer from suing for the publication of a libel in the *Racing Calendar* for, in getting his licence from the Stewards of the Jockey Club, he had impliedly assented to the publication in the *Calendar* of their subsequent decision to cancel his licence.

[14] *Buckpitt* v. *Oates* [1968] 1 All E.R. 1145; *Bennett* v. *Tugwell* [1971] 2 W.L.R. 847; *Birch* v. *Thomas* [1972] 1 W.L.R. 294. *Cf. Geier* v. *Kujara* [1970] 1 Lloyd's Rep. 364.

[15] It should be noted that these cases would now be decided differently: Road Traffic Act 1972, s. 148 (3); Symmons (1973) 123 N.L.J. 373.

taking part in a boxing match, for example, clearly implies that each participant consents to the other trying to hit him, but where the tort of negligence is involved much greater difficulty has been experienced. Diplock L.J. has even gone so far as to say, " In my view, the maxim in the absence of expressed contract has no application to negligence simpliciter where the duty of care is based solely upon proximity or ' neighbourship ' in the Atkinian sense." [16] It is respectfully submitted, however, that this should not be regarded as laying down a general proposition of law. The point is that, express consent apart, a quite extraordinary situation would have to exist for the court to be justified in holding that the plaintiff had consented generally to lack of reasonable care by the defendant. So, for example, in *Slater* v. *Clay Cross Co. Ltd.*,[17] where the plaintiff was lawfully walking along a narrow tunnel on a railway track owned and occupied by the defendants when she was struck by a train owing to the negligence of the driver, Denning L.J. said,[18] " It seems to me that when this lady walked in the tunnel, although it may be said that she voluntarily took the risk of danger from the running of the railway in the ordinary and accustomed way, nevertheless she did not take the risk of negligence by the driver."

On the other hand, it may be possible to establish consent, express or implied, to particular conduct of the defendant which would, in the absence of consent, give rise to a cause of action for negligence. In *Imperial Chemical Industries Ltd.* v. *Shatwell* [19] the plaintiff and his brother, James, were working in the defendants' quarry, and they agreed to disregard the defendants' orders, and also certain statutory regulations imposed upon themselves, and to test some detonators without taking the required precautions. In the result an explosion occurred which injured the plaintiff, and he sought to hold his employers liable vicariously on the grounds of James' negligence and breach of statutory duty in the course of his employment. It was held that the defence of *volenti non fit injuria* would have been available to James had he been sued, and therefore that the defendants were not vicariously liable. The plaintiff had consented to the very conduct which had caused his injury and, moreover, had fully appreciated the risk of injury to himself by explosion which it entailed.[20]

---

[16] *Wooldridge* v. *Sumner* [1963] 2 Q.B. 43, 69; *Morrison* v. *United S.S. Co. of N.Z. Ltd.* [1964] N.Z.L.R. 468, 478, *per* Turner J., is to similar effect, but Turner J. does admit that if there is a " transaction between the parties of such a nature that assent to the risk of damage is a proper inference to be drawn " then a plaintiff may be *volens* to future negligence: *ibid.* at p. 474.
[17] [1956] 2 Q.B. 264.
[18] *Ibid.* at p. 271.
[19] [1965] A.C. 656; *Bolt* v. *William Moss & Sons Ltd.* (1966) 110 S.J. 385.
[20] [1965] A.C. at p. 673, *per* Lord Reid; 682, *per* Lord Hodson (" If they (the plaintiff and his brother) did not appreciate the risk, of course the doctrine of ' volens ' would have no application, but I cannot accept that the risk was not truly appreciated." There was no appreciation of the risk in *White* v. *Blackmore* [1972] 2 Q.B. 651. For a case where consent to particular negligent conduct was most clearly to be inferred see *Frehlick* v. *Anderson* (1961) 27 D.L.R. (2d) 46 (plaintiff rode on front of defendant's car and thereby consented to defendant driving with his vision thus obscured).

In deciding whether the necessary consent should be inferred, a number of points must be noted:

(a) Knowledge does not necessarily imply assent. The maxim is *volenti non fit injuria*; it is not *scienti non fit injuria*.

The test of consent is objective and is not an inquiry into what the plaintiff felt or inwardly consented to,[21] but it does not follow that a person assents to a risk merely because he knows of it. The most conspicuous illustrations of this have occurred in cases of harm sustained by workers in the course of their employment. Until the latter half of the nineteenth century, very little attention was paid by the law to the safety of manual labourers, and several of the decisions on *volenti non fit injuria* went near to holding that knowledge of risk in the employment invariably implied assent to it. Protective legislation began to make notable headway from about 1860 onwards. And, quite apart from legislation, the courts, beginning with the judgment of Bowen L.J. in *Thomas* v. *Quartermaine*,[22] have declined to identify, as a matter of course, knowledge of a risk with acceptance of it.

This doctrine was driven home by the House of Lords in *Smith* v. *Baker*,[23] where it was held that *volenti non fit injuria* had no application to harm sustained by a man from the negligence of his employers in not warning him of the moment of a recurring danger, although the man knew and understood that he personally ran risk of injury if and when the danger did recur. He worked in a cutting on the top of which a crane often jibbed (*i.e.* swung) heavy stones over his head while he was drilling the rock face in the cutting. Both he and his employers knew that there was a risk of the stones falling, but no warning was given to him of the moment at which any particular jibbing commenced. A stone from the crane fell upon and injured him. The House of Lords held that the defendants were liable. Lord Herschell admitted that " where a person undertakes to do work which is intrinsically dangerous, notwithstanding that reasonable care has been taken to render it as little dangerous as possible, he no doubt voluntarily subjects himself to the risks inevitably accompanying it, and cannot, if he suffers, be permitted to complain that a wrong has been done to him, even though the cause from which he suffers might give to others a right of action "; but he added, " where . . . a risk to the employed, which may or may not result in injury, has been created or enhanced by the negligence of the employer, does the mere continuance in service,

---

[21] *Bennett* v. *Tugwell* [1971] 2 W.L.R. 847, 852, *per* Ackner J., citing Gordon, " Drunken Drivers and Willing Passengers " (1966) 82 L.Q.R. 62, 71.
[22] (1887) 18 Q.B.D. 683. *Cf. Bloor* v. *Liverpool, etc. Co. Ltd.* [1936] 3 All E.R. 399. The actual decision in *Thomas* v. *Quartermaine* has not escaped criticism: *Smith* v. *Baker* [1891] A.C. 325, 366–367, *per* Lord Herschell. *Cf. ibid.* at pp. 368–369, *per* Lord Morris; also Pollock, *Torts*, 15th ed., pp. 119–120; Glanville Williams, *Joint Torts and Contributory Negligence*, pp. 298–299.
[23] [1891] A.C. 325. Of the other cases concerning employer and workman, see in particular *Bowater* v. *Rowley Regis Corporation* [1944] K.B. 476.

with knowledge of the risk, preclude the employed, if he suffer from such negligence, from recovering in respect of his employer's breach of duty? I cannot assent to the proposition that the maxim, ' Volenti non fit injuria,' applies to such a case, and that the employer can invoke its aid to protect him from liability for his wrong." [24]

The rule that *sciens* is not *volens* has given rise to great difficulty in cases between passengers in cars and drunken or inexperienced drivers. [25] In *Nettleship* v. *Weston* [26] the plaintiff agreed to give the defendant driving lessons in the defendant's car and was injured when the defendant lost control of the car because of her inexperience. All members of the Court of Appeal rejected the defence of *volenti* [27] but Lord Denning M.R. and Megaw L.J. suggested that nothing short of an agreement could found the defence, so that merely getting into a car with a driver known to be totally inexperienced could never be *volenti*. [28] Salmon L.J., by way of contrast, thought that on the facts of *Nettleship*'s case the defence would have been clearly established had it not been for a prior conversation about insurance which rebutted the inference of *volenti* arising from such facts. [29] On the basis of this case, Asquith J. was probably correct in *Dann* v. *Hamilton* [30] to reject *volenti* against a plaintiff who had taken a lift with a drunken driver, though the actual *decision* may have been wrong. [31]

(b) The consent must be freely given. The main point to notice here is that " a man cannot be said to be truly ' willing ' unless he is in a position to choose freely, and freedom of choice predicates, not only

---

[24] *Ibid.* at pp. 360, 362.

[25] The extent to which these cases remain relevant is in some doubt. The Road Traffic Act 1972, s. 148 (3) provides that where a person uses a motor vehicle in circumstances where compulsory liability insurance is required (and this now includes liability to passengers), then any antecedent agreement or understanding between the driver and passenger (whether intended to be legally binding or not) shall be of no effect so far as it purports or might be held (a) to negative or restrict any such liability as is required to be covered by a policy of insurance, or (b) to impose any conditions with respect to the enforcement of such liability; " and the fact that a person so carried has willingly accepted as his the risk of negligence on the part of the [driver] shall not be treated as negativing any such liability of the user." It is doubtful whether the subsection covers the implied " *volenti* " in the cases here dealt with: Symmons, " Volenti Non Fit Injuria and Passenger Liability " (1973) 123 N.L.J. 373.

[26] [1971] 2 Q.B. 691; (1971) 87 L.Q.R. 444; Rogers [1972A] C.L.J. 24.

[27] They also rejected another defence based on a low duty of care by an inexperienced driver to his instructor: see p. 62, *ante.*

[28] [1971] 2 Q.B. 691, 701. See also *Burnett* v. *British Waterways Board* [1973] 1 W.L.R. 700.

[29] [1971] 2 Q.B. 691, 704,705. All three judges attach some weight to this conversation, but it is submitted that Lord Denning M.R. and Megaw L.J. would have come to the same conclusion without it.

[30] [1939] 1 K.B. 509, not followed by the High Court of Australia in *Insurance Commissioner* v. *Joyce* (1948) 77 C.L.R. 39; *Loggenkamp* v. *Bennett* (1950) 80 C.L.R. 292. See also *Davis* v. *Jones* [1958] L.J. 58; *Dawrant* v. *Nutt* [1961] 1 W.L.R. 253. For a full review of the authorities, see Gordon, " Drunken Drivers and Willing Passengers " (1966) 82 L.Q.R. 62.

[31] Because contributory negligence may be applicable in such a case: *Nettleship* v. *Weston, supra,* at p. 703; *Dawrant* v. *Nutt, supra* (contributory negligence was not pleaded in *Dann* v. *Hamilton* (1953) 69 L.Q.R. 317). Megaw L.J. in *Nettleship* v. *Weston* at p. 710 suggested that the passenger of a drunken driver may be unable to sue because he may be aiding and abetting a criminal offence. *Sed quaere?*

full knowledge of the circumstances on which the exercise of choice is conditional, so that he may be able to choose wisely, but the absence of any feeling of constraint so that nothing shall interfere with the freedom of his will." [32] The plaintiff in *Imperial Chemical Industries Ltd.* v. *Shatwell* [33] was obviously under no pressure from the defendants to adopt the dangerous method of work which caused his injury, for they had, to his knowledge, specifically forbidden it; but usually there will be economic or other pressures upon a workman which will make it unjust for an employer to say that he ran the risk with his eyes open, being fully aware of the danger he incurred.[34] In the absence of some such relationship as employer and workman between the parties it will, no doubt, be easier to establish the necessary freedom of consent, but if such consent is absent the defence of *volenti non fit injuria* cannot prevail.[35]

Three further points may be briefly mentioned. In principle consent obtained by fraud should not be sufficient, but a difficulty arises from the rule of the criminal law of assault that where the fraud on the victim induces a mistake, not as to the real nature of the transaction but merely as to its consequences, no assault has been committed.[36] It has been suggested that a similar rule applies in the tort of battery.[37] In the Irish case of *Hegarty* v. *Shine* [38] the plaintiff was infected by her paramour with a venereal disease the existence of which he concealed. She sued him for assault but her action was dismissed, partly on the ground that mere concealment was not such a fraud as to vitiate consent and partly because *ex turpi causa non oritur actio.*[39] There is, however, no English authority on the point and it is submitted that while there is reason for the rule in the criminal law, there is none in the law of tort.[40] For the purposes of *volenti non fit injuria* it should be fully accepted that consent obtained by fraud is no consent.[41]

The second point concerns children of tender years and persons of

---

[32] *Bowater* v. *Rowley Regis Corporation* [1944] K.B. 476, 479, *per* Scott L.J., cited with approval by Lord Hodson in *Imperial Chemical Industries Ltd.* v. *Shatwell* [1965] A.C. 656, 681–682; *Merrington* v. *Ironbridge Metal Works Ltd.* [1952] 2 All E.R. 1101. For a case where constraint was put upon an employee by someone other than his employer, see *Burnett* v. *British Waterways Board* [1973] 1 W.L.R. 700.

[33] [1965] A.C. 656, *ante*, p. 616.

[34] *Ibid.* at p. 681, *per* Lord Hodson; *ibid.* at p. 686, *per* Lord Pearce. See also the observations of the same learned Lords on *Williams* v. *Port of Liverpool Stevedoring Co. Ltd.* [1956] 1 W.L.R. 551 ([1965] A.C. at pp. 681, 687–688) and the cases cited *supra*, note 32.

[35] *Hambley* v. *Shepley* (1967) 63 D.L.R. (2d) 94 (Ont. C.A.) is an interesting example.

[36] Compare *R.* v. *Clarence* (1888) 22 Q.B.D. 23 with *R.* v. *Williams* [1923] 1 K.B. 340.

[37] Clerk and Lindsell, *Torts*, 13th ed., pp. 343–344.

[38] (1878) 14 Cox C.C. 145.

[39] For this maxim, see *post*, pp. 626–628.

[40] If no consent is given to sexual connection and this is held to be a criminal assault it must also logically be the very serious crime of rape.

[41] There appears to be no authority on the position where consent is obtained by a false representation honestly made, but it is submitted that in principle such consent should not be sufficient. See *T.* v. *T.* [1964] P. 85, 99, *per* Donovan L.J., a divorce case where, however, the wife's consent to sodomy was made out.

unsound mind. Children frequently protest vigorously [42] against requisite medicine or surgery, but it seems to be generally accepted that the medical practitioner has sufficient legal protection in the consent of the child's parent or guardian. How such consent, given as it is by a third party, can logically provide a defence it is difficult to understand [43] and it may perhaps be better to say that the practitioner has the defence of necessity.[44] But whatever the reasoning it is certain that the child has no action provided that the treatment was reasonably necessary [45] and was given without negligence; and no doubt the same is true also in the case of persons of unsound mind.

Lastly, certain medical procedures may be justifiable without express consent even in the case of persons of full age and capacity if the patient is incapable of expressing his wishes but he is not known to object to the procedure, and it is urgently necessary.[46] The limits of this justification are not entirely clear, but it seems to rest more on " implied " consent than on necessity,[47] and it is submitted that it could never justify a procedure to which the patient was known to object.[48]

(c) **Consent to illegal act.** It is generally true that the consent of the victim affords no defence to one charged with a criminal offence. " No person can license another to commit a crime " [49] and the question may be asked, therefore, whether there are cases in which *volenti non fit injuria* is excluded in a civil case because of the illegality of the act assented to. Certainly it cannot be true that the maxim is excluded whenever the act constitutes a crime as well as a tort, for every assult is criminal, and so are some libels, and yet it is possible, by assent, to negative tortious liability for many kinds of assault and libel. Winfield took the view, however, that whenever the act is contrary to public policy, an admittedly vague conception, *volenti non fit injuria* is inapplicable, but he did not conclude from this that in such cases the plaintiff can always succeed.[50] Public policy itself may deny him a remedy,[51] and the critical question, therefore, is whether there are cases

---

[42] A minor may, of course, give a valid consent himself, certainly under s. 8 of the Family Law Reform Act 1969 and probably independently of that section at common law if he is capable of a full understanding of the consequences: see Skegg, " Consent to Medical Proceedings on Minors " (1973) 36 M.L.R. 370.

[43] See Glanville Williams, *op. cit.* p. 315; Devlin, *Samples of Lawmaking*, p. 86.

[44] *Post*, pp. 625–628.

[45] Even this probably puts the matter too high: a parent can lawfully arrange for his child's blood grouping to be tested to determine paternity (*S.* v. *McC* [1972] A.C. 24); and it would be absurd to hold that circumcision for religious reasons was tortious.

[46] See, *e.g. Marshall* v. *Curry* [1933] 3 D.L.R. 260; *cf. Murray* v. *McMurchy* [1949] 2 D.L.R. 442.

[47] *Cf.* Skegg, " A Justification for Medical Proceedings Performed Without Consent." (1974) 90 L.Q.R. 512.

[48] *Cf.* Bates, " Consenting to the Necessary " (1972) 46 A.L.J. 73.

[49] *R.* v. *Donovan* [1934] 2 K.B. 498, 507, *per* Swift J.; *R.* v. *Coney* (1882) 8 Q.B.D. 534. Consent of the prosecutrix is a defence to a charge of rape, for the offence consists of carnal knowledge of a woman without her consent.

[50] Winfield's views are fully stated in *Province*, pp. 82–91.

[51] *Post*, pp. 625–628.

in which public policy excludes consent and yet allows the plaintiff to recover. If there are not, discussion of the question when public policy excludes consent is sterile, for whatever the answer the plaintiff's action will fail.

Winfield clearly thought that there were cases in which the plaintiff might succeed despite his consent, and gave this example: in a boxing match, the plaintiff may have inadvertently committed a breach of the rules and this may have provoked the defendant to retaliate with a deliberate foul blow. To an action for this assault, the defendant cannot plead *volenti non fit injuria*, for such a blow is not a lawful incident in boxing. Nor can it be doubted that the plaintiff could recover at least nominal damages for the assault. There would be nothing contrary to public policy in allowing him to do so. On the other hand, if the whole contest be illegal, like a fight with bare fists, it would appear to be against public policy to allow either combatant to bring an action for assault against the other.[52] It is submitted, however, that the reason why the boxer can succeed in the first of these cases is not that his consent is vitiated by the foul blow, but that it never extended to such a blow in the first place. A boxer may consent to accidental fouls, but not to deliberate ones.[53]

It is true that the maxim *ex turpi causa non oritur actio* is of extremely limited application in the law of tort,[54] but it does have its place,[55] and, it is submitted, is sufficient to defeat a plaintiff whose consent to a tort is invalidated on the grounds of public policy. In *R.* v. *Coney*[56] Hawkins J. said, " It may be that consent can in all cases be given so as to operate as a bar to a civil action," and even if this is not wholly correct in theory, for all practical purposes it can be accepted.[57]

Consent and the standard of care

It has already been pointed out that *volenti non fit injuria* has no place unless a presumptive tort has been committed, but this is not to

---

[52] *R.* v. *Coney* (1882) 8 Q.B.D. 534, a criminal case. *Cf. Lane* v. *Holloway* [1968] 1 Q.B. 379 and see *post*, pp. 627–628. Winfield also thought that if one of the combatants in an illegal prize-fight were killed, his dependants could sue the other under the Fatal Accidents Act 1846; *Province*, p. 89. But this seems a very difficult question in itself, the answer to which cannot be assumed in order to support a given view of the more general problem.

[53] In *Lane* v. *Holloway, supra*, after a verbal altercation the elderly plaintiff struck the young defendant on the shoulder and the defendant replied with an extremely severe blow to the plaintiff's eye. Although each of the parties to an ordinary fight voluntarily accepts the risk of incidental injuries, the Court of Appeal held that the plaintiff had not consented to the risk of a savage blow out of all proportion to the occasion: [1968] 1 Q.B. at pp. 386–387, *per* Lord Denning M.R.; *ibid.* at p. 389, *per* Salmon L.J. *Cf.* the approach of Winn L.J., *ibid.* at pp. 393–395. See Weir's comments on this case, *Casebook on Tort,* 3rd ed., p. 324.

[54] *National Coal Board* v. *England* [1954] A.C. 403, 418–420, *per* Lord Porter; *ibid.* at pp. 424–425, *per* Lord Reid; *ibid.* at pp. 428–429, *per* Lord Asquith.

[55] It is discussed *post*, pp. 626–628.

[56] (1882) 8 Q.B.D. at p. 553.

[57] Clerk and Lindsell, *Torts,* 13th ed., p. 343; *Salmond on Torts,* 16th ed., p. 519; Street, *Law of Torts,* 5th ed., p. 76. *Contra,* Pollock, 15th ed., pp. 113–115. In *Dann* v. *Hamilton* [1939] 1 K.B. 509, 519, Asquith J. doubted whether consent to the illegal act of driving under the influence of drink would exclude the operation of the maxim; *cf. Nettleship* v. *Weston* [1971] 2 Q.B. 691, 710.

say that the element of consent is invariably irrelevant in the absence of a prima facie breach of duty by the defendant. The plaintiff may have consented to a certain disregard for his safety by the defendant with the result that conduct which would in other circumstances amount to negligence does not in the event involve the defendant in a breach of his duty of care. This is most clearly brought out in cases where a spectator is injured in the course of some game or sport which he is watching. A spectator does not consent to negligence on the part of the participants,[58] but " provided the competition or game is being performed within the rules and the requirement of the sport and by a person of adequate skill and competence the spectator does not expect his safety to be regarded by the participant." [59]

In *Wooldridge* v. *Sumner* [60] the plaintiff was a photographer at a horse show and had stationed himself at the edge of the arena when he was injured by a galloping horse. The facts were obscure, but even accepting that the accident occurred because the defendant, the horse's rider, had caused or permitted it to take a corner " too fast," it was held that there had been no negligence. Had the defendant acted in disregard of all safety of others so as to have departed from the standards which might reasonably be expected in anyone pursuing the competition, he might well have been liable [61]; but all he had in fact done was to commit an error of judgment in the course of doing his best to win, and it was everyone's intention that he should do his best to win. The result is summarised by Diplock L.J. in these words: " A person attending a game or competition takes the risk of any damage caused to him by any act of a participant done in the course of and for the purposes of the game or competition notwithstanding that such act may involve an error of judgment or a lapse of skill, unless the participant's conduct is such as to evince a reckless disregard of the spectator's safety." [62]

---

[58] See *Cleghorn* v. *Oldham* (1927) 43 T.L.R. 465 and the unreported cases referred to by Sellers L.J. in *Wooldridge* v. *Sumner* [1963] 2 Q.B. 43, 55–56. For the position of the occupier of the premises where the game or sport is taking place, see *Cox* v. *Coulson* [1916] 2 K.B. 177; *Hall* v. *Brooklands Auto Racing Club* [1933] 1 K.B. 205; *Murray* v. *Harringay Arena Ltd.* [1951] 2 K.B. 529. For the liability of occupiers generally, see Chap. 10, *ante.*

[59] *Wooldridge* v. *Sumner, supra,* at p. 56, *per* Sellers L.J.; *ibid.* at p. 67, *per* Diplock L.J.; *Hall* v. *Brooklands Auto Racing Club, supra,* at p. 214, *per* Scrutton L.J.; *Wilks* v. *Cheltenham Home Guard Motor Cycle and Light Car Club* [1971] 1 W.L.R. 668.

[60] *Supra;* Weir, *Casebook on Tort,* 3rd ed., p. 78. For criticism, see Goodhart, " The Sportsman's Charter " (1962) 78 L.Q.R. 490; *Wilks* v. *Cheltenham Home Guard Motor Cycle and Light Car Club, supra,* at pp. 670, 673–674, *per* Lord Denning M.R. and Edmund Davies L.J.

[61] [1963] 2 Q.B. at p. 57, *per* Sellers L.J.: " There would, I think, be a difference, for instance, in assessing blame which is actionable between an injury caused by a tennis ball hit or a racket accidentally thrown in the course of play into the spectators at Wimbledon and a ball hit or a racket thrown into the stands in temper or annoyance when play was not in progress." See also *ibid.* at p. 68, *per* Diplock L.J.

[62] *Ibid.* at p. 68. *Nettleship* v. *Weston* [1971] 2 Q.B. 691 is an effective obstacle against the application of this idea to drunken or incompetent drivers: see pp. 62 and 618, *ante.*

Rescue cases [63]

What are called " rescue cases " deserve a separate paragra
they straddle three branches of the law—*volenti non fit injuria*, i
ness of consequence and contributory negligence, and the two latter
may for convenience' sake be considered here as well as the former in
this connection. Rescue cases are typified by A's death or injury in
rescuing or endeavouring to rescue B from an emergency of danger to
B's life or limb created by the negligence of C.[64] Is C liable to A? Or
can C successfully plead (a) *volenti non fit injuria*; or (b) that A's conduct is a *novus actus interveniens* which makes his injury too remote a
consequence of C's initial negligence; or (c) that A's injury was due to
contributory negligence on his own part?

Until 1924, our law was almost destitute of any decision on these
questions.[65] The American law reports, on the other hand, from 1871
onwards had contained numerous cases which, subject to the limitations stated below, conferred a right of action upon the rescuer or his
representatives. In 1935, in *Haynes* v. *Harwood* [66] the Court of Appeal
adopted a similar principle.

We can best consider the three arguable defences of C to such an
action separately:

(a) Volenti non fit injuria. Dr. Goodhart, in summarising the American cases, says: " The American rule is that the doctrine of assumption
of risk does not apply where the plaintiff has, under an exigency caused
by the defendant's wrongful misconduct, consciously and deliberately
faced a risk, even of death, to rescue another from imminent danger of
personal injury or death, whether the person endangered is one to
whom he owes a duty of protection or is a mere stranger to whom he
owes no such special duty." [67] This was accepted as an accurate representation of English law by Greer L.J. in *Haynes* v. *Harwood*,[68] where
the Court of Appeal affirmed a judgment of Finlay J. in favour of a
policeman who had been injured in stopping some runaway horses
with a van in a crowded street. The defendant had left the horses and
van unattended on the highway and they had bolted. The policeman,
who was on duty, not in the street, but in a police station, darted out
and was crushed by one of the horses which fell upon him while he was
stopping it. It was also held that the rescuer's act need not be instinctive
in order to be reasonable, for the man who deliberately encounters

---

[63] Goodhart, " Rescue and Voluntary Assumption of Risk " (1934) 5 C.L.J. 192;
Allen, *Legal Duties* (1931), pp. 217–220; Tiley, " The Rescue Principle " (1967) 30 M.L.R.
25; Linden, " Rescuers and Good Samaritans " (1971) 34 M.L.R. 241.
[64] For a case in which the rescuer himself was sued, see *Horsley* v. *McLaren* [1971]
2 Lloyd's Rep. 410; (Sup.Ct. of Canada); Spencer [1970] C.L.J. 30.
[65] *Roebuck* v. *Norwegian Titanic Co.* (1884) 1 T.L.R. 117 seems to have been forgotten
soon after it was reported.
[66] [1935] 1 K.B. 146. *Baker* v. *T. E. Hopkins & Son Ltd.* [1959] 1 W.L.R. 966 (Weir,
Casebook on Tort, 3rd ed., p. 54) provides a classic example of a rescue case.
[67] *Loc. cit.* at p. 196.
[68] [1935] 1 K.B. at pp. 156–157, applied in *The Gusty* [1940] P. 159; *Morgan* v. *Aylen*
[1942] 1 All E.R. 489; *Baker* v. *T. E. Hopkins & Son Ltd.*, *supra.*

peril after reflection may often be acting more reasonably than one who acts upon impulse.[69] There are several reasons why *volenti non fit injuria* is no answer to the rescuer's claim. In the first place, it is now clear that he founds upon a duty owed directly to himself by the defendant, and not upon one derived from that owed to the person imperilled, for he may recover notwithstanding that the person imperilled is a trespasser and has no claim.[70] If the defendant ought to have foreseen an emergency and that someone would expose himself to danger in order to effect a rescue, then he owes a duty directly to the rescuer.[71] To go on to hold that the rescuer was *volens* would be flatly self-contradictory. In the second place, a rescuer acts under the impulse of duty, legal, moral or social, and does not therefore exercise that freedom of choice which is essential to the success of the defence. Thirdly, it is in the nature of a rescue case that the defendant's negligence precedes the plaintiff's act of running the risk. The plaintiff does not assent to the defendant's negligence at all, and, indeed, may be wholly ignorant of it at the time. All he knows is that someone is in a position of peril which calls for his intervention as a rescuer.[72]

(b) **Novus actus interveniens, or remoteness of consequence.** The policeman's act was that of a normally courageous man in the like circumstances, and therefore was both the direct and foreseeable consequence of the defendant's unlawful act; hence the injury which he suffered was not too remote. " The reasonable man here must be endowed with qualities of energy and courage, and he is not to be deprived of a remedy because he has in a marked degree a desire to save human life when in peril." [73] And, even if his duty to intervene were merely a moral one, still " the law does not think so meanly of mankind as to hold it otherwise than a natural and probable consequence of a helpless person being put in danger that some able-bodied person should expose himself to the same danger to effect a rescue." [74] This covers the case, not only of a policeman, who may be said to be under some kind of duty to attempt a rescue, but also that of any other person who makes such an attempt with any reasonable prospect of success. So, in *Chadwick* v. *British Railways Board* [75] the defendant railway authority was held liable where the plaintiff's husband, who lived near a railway line, had gone from his home to the scene of a

---

[69] [1935] 1 K.B. at pp. 158–159, *per* Greer L.J.; *ibid.* at p. 164, *per* Maugham L.J.; *Baker* v. *T. E. Hopkins & Son Ltd.* (*supra*); *Videan* v. *British Transport Commission* [1963] 2 Q.B. 650, 669, *per* Lord Denning M.R.; *Chadwick* v. *B.R.B.* [1967] 1 W.L.R. 912.

[70] *Videan* v. *British Transport Commission* [1963] 2 Q.B. 650.

[71] *Ibid.*

[72] *Baker* v. *T. E. Hopkins & Son Ltd.* [1959] 1 W.L.R. at p. 976, *per* Morris L.J.

[73] [1935] 1 K.B. at p. 162, *per* Maugham L.J.

[74] Pollock, *Torts*, 15th ed., p. 370, adopted by Maugham L.J. in *Haynes* v. *Harwood* [1935] 1 K.B. at p. 163.

[75] [1967] 1 W.L.R. 912; *Morgan* v. *Aylen* [1942] 1 All E.R. 489; *Baker* v. *T. E. Hopkins & Son Ltd.* [1959] 1 W.L.R. 966.

major railway disaster and, having played a major part in rescue operations there, subsequently became psychoneurotic as a result of his experiences. On the other hand, the principle does not sanction any foolhardy or unnecessary risks, such as an attempt to stop a runaway horse on a desolate country road.[76] Here, as elsewhere in innumerable legal relations, the test is, " What is reasonable? " And it is unreasonable to go to the assistance of a driver of a horse and cart merely because he shouts for help to pacify a restive horse which has bolted into a field but which is endangering nobody.[77]

(c) **Contributory negligence.** In *Haynes* v. *Harwood*, this was set up but was not much pressed. Indeed, the earlier case of *Brandon* v. *Osborne, Garrett & Co. Ltd.*[78] had made it improbable that it would have met with any success. There, X and his wife were in a shop as customers. Owing to the negligence of the defendants who were repairing the shop roof, some glass fell from a skylight and struck X. His wife, who was unharmed herself, but who reasonably believed X to be in danger, instinctively clutched his arm and tried to pull him from the spot, and thus injured her leg. Swift J. held that there was no contributory negligence on her part, provided, as was the fact, she had done no more than any reasonable person would have done. " Bearing in mind that danger invites rescue, the court should not be astute to accept criticism of the rescuer's conduct from the wrongdoer who created the danger." [79]

Do the rules just stated apply where the person who is rescued is the person who was negligent, instead of being some third party endangered by the negligent person's conduct? So far we have been considering a case in which A is injured in trying to rescue B from the effects of C's negligence. But is the position the same if A is injured in trying to rescue C himself from peril caused by C's negligence? Would it have made any difference in *Haynes* v. *Harwood* if the person by whose negligence the horses had bolted had been imperilled and had been saved by the policeman? On principle, it seems that there ought to be no difference. C ought to be just as much liable in the one case as in the other. In *Baker* v. *T. E. Hopkins & Son Ltd.*[80] a doctor was killed in an attempt to rescue two workmen from a well which was filled with the poisonous fumes of a petrol-driven pump. His widow sued the men's employers and succeeded on the ground of their negligence, but it was also argued that the employers were vicariously liable for the

---

[76] [1935] 1 K.B. at p. 163, *per* Maugham L.J.

[77] *Cutler* v. *United Dairies (London) Ltd.* [1933] 2 K.B. 297. That seems to be the interpretation of this case by the Court of Appeal in *Haynes* v. *Harwood*, who while they recognised the decision as sound, disapproved of some dicta of Scrutton L.J. in it. *Cf.* Tiley, *loc. cit.*, pp. 32–33. See, too, *Sylvester* v. *Chapman Ltd.* (1935) 79 S.J. 777; and Goodhart, *loc. cit.*, at pp. 192–203.

[78] [1924] 1 K.B. 548.

[79] *Baker* v. *T. E. Hopkins Ltd.*, *supra* at p. 984, *per* Willmer L.J.

[80] [1958] 1 W.L.R. 993, not following *Dupuis* v. *New Regina Trading Co. Ltd.* [1943] 4 D.L.R. 275. See [1959] C.L.J. 23. The Court of Appeal did not consider the point.

negligence of the men themselves. Barry J. thought that this raised a difficult question and said, " Were I called upon to decide it, I should, with some hesitation and doubt have taken this view:—Although no one owes a duty to anyone else to preserve his own safety, yet if, by his own carelessness a man put himself into a position of peril of a kind that invites rescue, he would in law be liable for any injury caused to someone whom he ought to have foreseen would attempt to come to his aid." [81]

Another question is whether a man would be justified in running risks of life or limb in order to save his own or other people's property from evil consequences threatened by the wrongful conduct of another person. In *Hyett* v. *G.W. Ry.*,[82] the plaintiff was injured in attempting such a rescue and the Court of Appeal held that, on the facts, his conduct was reasonable and that the defendants were liable; the court held that the doctrine of *Haynes* v. *Harwood* applies to rescue of property as well as to rescue of the person; and pointed out that in either case it is necessary for the court to consider the relationship of the rescuer to the property in peril, or to the person in peril, and also to consider the degree of danger.[83] In America the decisions are not uniform, but Dr. Goodhart's suggestion is that the only difference between the life and the property cases is that a rescuer would not be justified in exposing himself to as great danger in saving property as he would in saving human life.[84] In general, this seems sound in principle, though particular cases are imaginable in which the rescuer might reasonably encounter just as much danger in trying to preserve property as to preserve life; *e.g.* where documents of great national importance, and of which no copies exist, are in peril of being destroyed by a fire caused by the tortious conduct of some person other than the rescuer.[85]

Public policy

It is convenient to notice here that, independently of all questions of consent, public policy may occasionally intervene to deny the plaintiff a remedy for what would otherwise be a tort on the ground that the act complained of formed part of an unlawful joint venture of both plaintiff and defendant. As Lord Asquith said, " If two burglars, A

• [81] [1958] 1 W.L.R. at p. 1004. Barry J.'s view is, it is submitted, confirmed by the decision in *Videan* v. *British Transport Commission* [1963] 2 Q.B. 650, *ante*, p. 624, that the rescuer's right in the more usual three-party situation is an independent one and not derived from that of the person imperilled. See also Tiley, *loc. cit.*, pp. 33–35, 42–44.

[82] [1948] 1 K.B. 345. See *Hutterly* v. *Imperial Oil and Calder* (1956) 3 D.L.R. (2d) 719; *Russell* v. *McCabe* [1962] N.Z.L.R. 392. In the Scottish decision *Steel* v. *Glasgow Iron and Steel Co.*, 1944 S.C. 237, such an action was held to be maintainable subject to the conditions that (1) the rescuer's act ought reasonably to have been contemplated by the defendant, and (2) the risk undertaken must be reasonable in relation to the interests protected.

[83] [1948] 1 K.B. at p. 348, *per* Tucker L.J. Note that the National Insurance (Industrial Injuries) Act 1965, s. 9, includes in the " course of employment " steps taken by the insured person to rescue persons or property on his employer's premises.

[84] 5 C.L.J. 198.

[85] See *Russell* v. *McCabe* [1962] N.Z.L.R. 392, 404, *per* North J.

and B, agree to open a safe by means of explosives, and A so negligently handles the explosive charge as to injure B, B might find some difficulty in maintaining an action for negligence against A." [86] This, a rule of public policy, is sometimes put in terms of the maxim *ex turpi causa non oritur actio* and, although there are cogent reasons for confining that maxim to cases of contract,[87] its use in the present context is common and it does provide a convenient form of speech.

Cases of tort to which the maxim can be applied are rare, and it must be emphasised that the mere fact that the plaintiff himself is a wrongdoer is no defence. If the rule were otherwise it would lead to the absurd result that if you stole a bottle of whisky belonging to me, I could not sue you for the tort of conversion if it appeared that I had bought the bottle during hours prohibited by the Licensing Acts. The plaintiff's own unlawful conduct may give the defendant an answer to the claim on some well-recognised ground such as that it made the damage too remote a consequence of the defendant's act,[88] but no importance attaches to the mere fact that the plaintiff may himself have committed some offence. To the example already given, Lord Asquith added, " But if A and B are proceeding to the premises which they intend burglariously to enter, and before they enter them, B picks A's pocket and steals A's watch, I cannot prevail upon myself to believe that A could not sue in tort. . . . The theft is totally unconnected with the burglary." [89]

There is a dearth of English authority on the effect of this rule of public policy, but the matter was elaborately considered by the High Court of Australia in *Smith* v. *Jenkins*.[90] In that case the plaintiff was a passenger in a car driven by the defendant and was injured as a result of the defendant's negligent driving. The car had been stolen by a gang of youths of which both plaintiff and defendant were members, and both were therefore at the time of the accident parties to the same criminal offence of using the car without the consent of its owner. It was held that the plaintiff could not succeed on the broad ground that public policy led to the conclusion that the defendant owed no duty of care to the plaintiff.[91] It should not be taken from this, however, that whenever one criminal causes an injury to another there can be no liability in tort between them. In *Smith* v. *Jenkins* the negligence complained of occurred in the course of performing the criminal act itself,

---

[86] *National Coal Board* v. *England* [1954] A.C. 403, 429.
[87] *Smith* v. *Jenkins* (1970) 44 A.L.J.R. 78, 82–84, *per* Windeyer J. (H.Ct. of Aus.).
[88] See *e.g. Ginty* v. *Belmont Building Supplies Ltd.* [1959] 1 All E.R. 414; *Rushton* v. *Turner Brothers Asbestos Ltd.* [1960] 1 W.L.R. 96; *Boyle* v. *Kodak Ltd.* [1969] 1 W.L.R. 661, 672–673, *per* Lord Diplock.
[89] See too Hilbery J.'s criticism of *Johnson* v. *Croggan & Co. Ltd.* [1954] 1 W.L.R. 195 in *Charles* v. *S. Smith (England) Ltd.* [1954] 1 W.L.R. 451.
[90] (1970) 44 A.L.J.R. 78.
[91] Windeyer J. pointed out that just as a " special relationship " may give rise to a duty of care (as in *Hedley Byrne & Co. Ltd.* v. *Heller and Partners Ltd.* [1964] A.C. 465), so also a " special relationship " such as that of " companions in crime " may exclude it: (1970) 44 A.L.J.R. at pp. 86–87.

and a decision in the plaintiff's favour would have involved saying that the defendant owed him a duty to carry out their joint criminal venture with reasonable care. The matter would stand very differently if the act complained of as a tort was unconnected with the criminal venture, as in the second of Lord Asquith's examples, and it seems likely that their Honours agreed that if the criminal aspect of the parties' joint conduct was merely incidental, as would be the case where with the agreement of both a car was being driven on a lawful errand but without a licence, or, perhaps, at a speed in excess of the statutory limit, the plaintiff would not necessarily fail in an action for negligence.[92]

Being ultimately a rule of public policy, the rule that a party to a criminal offence cannot treat as a tort against himself the manner in which his companion in crime has conducted himself in the performance of their joint criminal venture, is a flexible one,[93] and a variety of considerations may become relevant when its application to a given case is under discussion. It may be suggested, however, that the most important question is whether the act complained of as a tort does or does not go beyond the performance, in whole or in part, of the criminal activity on which the parties are engaged. Even in the case of a fight which starts by being unlawful, one of the parties can probably sue the other for damages for a subsequent injury if it was inflicted by a weapon or a savage blow out of all proportion to the occasion,[94] for such a blow goes beyond their *joint* criminal activity; but if in the course of murdering C, A, by carelessly handling the knife or gun injures B, with whom he had set out to murder C, B cannot recover from A. A's carelessness was neither more nor less than carelessness while taking a " step in the execution of the common illegal purpose." [95]

2. Mistake

Usually no defence

Mistake, whether of law or of fact, is usually no ground of exemption from liability in tort. There is no need to discuss the rule, *ignorantia juris non excusat*, for that is not peculiar to the law of tort and has been analysed in books on jurisprudence. But the rule as to mistake of fact needs some investigation. It has been pushed to harsh lengths, especially in the tort of conversion where an auctioneer, who innocently sells A's goods in the honest and reasonable belief that they belong to B on whose instructions he sells them, has been held liable to A.[96] The rule

---

[92] Unless it is precisely the absence of licence or the excessive speed of which the plaintiff complains as the cause of his damage. This seems to be implicit in the language of Windeyer J. ((1970) 44 A.L.J.R. at p. 87) and of Walsh J. (*ibid.* at pp. 89–90, 92).

[93] (1970) 44 A.L.J.R. at pp. 92–93, *per* Walsh J.

[94] *Lane* v. *Holloway* [1968] 1 Q.B. 379, 386, *per* Lord Denning M.R. His Lordship demurred " entirely " to the suggestion that the maxim *ex turpi causa non oritur actio* had any application to the facts of the case. Only Winn L.J. referred to *R.* v. *Coney* (1882) 8 Q.B.D. 534, and he only to deny its relevance to the case before the court.

[95] *Smith* v. *Jenkins* (1970) 44 A.L.J.R. at p. 87, *per* Windeyer J., citing Lord Asquith's phrase in *National Coal Coard* v. *England* [1954] A.C. at p. 429.

[96] *Consolidated Co.* v. *Curtis* [1892] 1 Q.B. 495.

has been defended on the ground that, if it were otherwise, the courts would find it difficult to discover, as a matter of evidence, whether the belief were honest and reasonable.[97] But this is not convincing, for the courts actually do make this inquiry in criminal law, where mistake of fact is, subject to certain limitations, a defence. Moreover, in the law of tort itself they are repeatedly called upon to ascertain whether a man has acted " reasonably " (e.g. in negligence), whatever may be the evidential difficulties incidental to the question; and, be it noted, mistake is sometimes an element in determining reasonableness. Finally, if the burden of proving mistake were, as it always ought to be, on the defendant, it is not likely that he would undertake it without solid reasons in support of it.

But however much the rule may be open to criticism there is no doubt that it is law and it is probably due historically to the stringent liability attaching to trespass to property and to the person. This heritage still sticks in the law in many directions, though it has been removed in others. Matters have perhaps gone too far now to make mistake of fact a general defence in the law of tort, for a good deal of the law relating to trespass, conversion and wrongs of strict liability would need recasting; so, too, as to torts analogous to trespass, such as interference with easements and *profits à prendre*. The typical example of strict liability is *Rylands* v. *Fletcher*.[98] Once admit reasonable mistake as a defence to it, then almost the whole of such liability would disappear and coalesce with the ordinary tort of negligence.

Exceptions

Such exceptions as there are to the rule depend upon whether the defendant acted reasonably or not. There are several torts in which liability hangs upon whether a reasonable man would have done what the defendant did, and mistake becomes relevant here, because a man may quite well make one and yet be behaving reasonably. Thus the plaintiff in malicious prosecution must prove lack of reasonable and probable cause for the prosecution, and in false imprisonment reasonable belief on the defendant's part that he has a right to arrest the plaintiff is in certain circumstances a defence. In defamation, mistake is relevant in some instances of publication and privilege. A mistaken belief is a defence to an action for deceit. Again, vicarious responsibility of a master for the tort of his servant may be negatived by a mistake of the servant which puts his wrongdoing outside the course of his employment.[99] And a mistake induced by the plaintiff himself may be a defence, e.g. where, as a practical joke, he leads a policeman to arrest him for a crime which he has not committed.

---

[97] Salmond, *Torts*, 7th ed. (1928) § 3 (3); not included in later editions.
[98] (1868) L.R. 3 H.L. 330; *ante*, Chap. 16.
[99] *Cf. Poland* v. *Parr* [1927] 1 K.B. 236.

3. Inevitable accident

Inevitable accident is defined by Sir Frederick Pollock as an accident " *not avoidable by any such precautions as a reasonable man, doing such an act then and there, could be expected to take.*" [1] It does not mean a catastrophe which could not have been avoided by any precaution whatever, but such as could not have been avoided by a reasonable man at the moment at which it occurred, and it is common knowledge that a reasonable man is not credited by the law with perfection of judgment. " People must guard against reasonable probabilities, but they are not bound to guard against fantastic possibilities." [2]

To speak of inevitable accident as a defence, therefore, is to say that there are cases in which the defendant will escape liability if he succeeds in proving that the accident occurred despite the exercise of reasonable care on his part, but it is also to say that there are cases in which the burden of proving this is placed upon him. In an ordinary action for negligence, for example, it is for the plaintiff to prove the defendant's lack of care, not for the defendant to disprove it, and the defence of inevitable accident is accordingly irrelevant [3]; and it is equally irrelevant in any other class of case in which the burden of proving the defendant's negligence is imposed upon the plaintiff. It was for long thought that the burden of proof in trespass rested with the defendant and that trespass, therefore, offered scope to the defence of inevitable accident, but it has now been held that here too the burden is with the plaintiff.[4] In trespass as well as in negligence, therefore, inevitable accident has no place.

In these cases inevitable accident is irrelevant because the burden is on the plaintiff to establish the defendant's negligence, but it does not follow that it is any more relevant if the plaintiff has no such burden. If, as in *Rylands* v. *Fletcher*,[5] the defendant is liable notwithstanding that he has taken reasonable care, it can avail him nothing to prove inevitable accident, and the same is true in those cases where liability for nuisance is strict,[6] and, subject to the Defamation Act 1952, s. 4, in cases of defamation.

---

[1] *Torts*, 15th ed., p. 97. *Cf. The Marpesia* (1872) L.R. 4 P.C. 212, 220, *per* Sir James Colville: " An inevitable accident in point of law is this: *viz.* that which the party charged with the offence could not possibly prevent by the exercise of ordinary care, caution, and maritime skill." *The Saint Angus* [1938] P. 225; *Ryan* v. *Youngs* [1938] 1 All E.R. 522 Beven, *Negligence in Law*, 4th ed. (1928) i, pp. 697–712, gives the history of the topic.

[2] *Fardon* v. *Harcourt-Rivington* (1932) 146 L.T. 391, *per* Lord Dunedin.

[3] " I do not find myself assisted by considering the meaning of the phrase ' inevitable accident.' I prefer to put the problem in a more simple way, namely, has it been established that the driver of the car was guilty of negligence? " *Browne* v. *De Luxe Car Services* [1941] 1 K.B. 549, 552, *per* Greene M.R. This should not be understood to mean that the defendant in an action for negligence need never bring any evidence to exculpate himself. The plaintiff's evidence may raise a presumption or prima facie case which, if nothing more appears, will entitle the court to infer that the defendant was negligent. But the legal burden of proof remains with the plaintiff, and when all the evidence has been heard the court must decide whether it has been discharged: *Brown* v. *Rolls-Royce Ltd.* [1960] 1 W.L.R. 210, 215–216, *per* Lord Denning.

[4] *Ante*, pp. 81–83.   [5] (1868) L.R. 3 H.L. 330, *ante*, Chap. 16.

[6] *Rapier* v. *London Tramways* [1893] 2 Ch. 588, 599, *ante*, pp. 352–355.

There seems, in fact, to be only one class of case in which the conception of inevitable accident has any meaning, and even there it is in truth misleading. In cases to which the maxim *res ipsa loquitur* applies [7] the plaintiff can rely upon the mere happening of the accident as evidence of negligence, and then it is sometimes said that the defendant is liable unless he proves inevitable accident.[8] But this, it is submitted, is to over-simplify the position in cases of *res ipsa loquitur*, and perhaps to falsify it.[9] It therefore seems that the conception of inevitable accident has no longer any useful function and it is doubtful whether much advantage is gained by the continued use of the phrase.[10]

Act of God

This defence is limited to negation of liability under the rule in *Rylands* v. *Fletcher* [11] and has already been dealt with.[12]

4. Private defence

Reasonable defence of oneself,[13] of one's property, and of those whom one is bound to protect negatives any liability in tort. Some authorities regard it as a species of self-help, *i.e.* as one of the remedies for tort.[14] Certainly what begins as self-defence often ends as self-help, but the better view is that private defence is allowed " not for the redress of injuries, but for their prevention," [15] and much more injury may in certain circumstances be incidental to the expulsion of a trespasser than would ever be permissible in merely keeping him out.

Defence of the person

There is no doubt that the right extends to the protection of one's spouse and family, and, whatever the limits of this defence, almost cer-

---

[7] *Ante*, pp. 73–80.

[8] *The Merchant Prince* [1892] P. 179; *Southport Corporation* v. *Esso Petroleum Co. Ltd.* [1954] 2 Q.B. 182, 200, *per* Denning L.J. (the Court of Appeal's decision was reversed by the House of Lords [1956] A.C. 218).

[9] See the observations of Devlin J. on *The Merchant Prince* in *Southport Corporation* v. *Esso Petroleum Co. Ltd.* [1956] A.C. at pp. 229–232 and *ante*, pp. 77–80.

[10] See Pape, " The Burden of Proof of Inevitable Accident in Actions for Negligence " (1965) 38 A.L.J. 395. *Cf.* Clerk and Lindsell, *Torts*, 13th ed., pp. 82–83. It may be that a new use for " inevitable accident " exists under the Highways (Miscellaneous Provisions) Act 1961, s. 1 (*ante*, pp. 355–357), which abolishes the former non-liability of highway authorities for non-feasance. If a person suffers injury from a danger resulting from the authority's failure to repair the highway, the authority is liable unless it proves that it had taken reasonable care to secure that the part of the highway in question was not dangerous to traffic: s. 1 (2). " It may be that if the highway authority could show that no amount of reasonable care on its part could have prevented the danger the common law defence of inevitable accident would be available to it ": *Griffiths* v. *Liverpool Corporation* [1967] 1 Q.B. 374, 391, *per* Diplock L.J.

[11] (1868) L.R. 3 H.L. 330. *Ante*, Chap. 16.

[12] pp. 376–377.

[13] Including defence against an unlawful arrest: " If a person is purporting to arrest another without lawful warrant, the person arrested may use force to avoid being arrested, but he must not use more force than necessary ": *R.* v. *Wilson* [1955] 1 W.L.R. 493, 494, *per* Lord Goddard C.J.; *Kenlin* v. *Gardiner* [1967] 2 Q.B. 510.

[14] Salmond, *Torts*, 7th ed., § 46; but his editors impliedly preferred the other view. See now 16th ed., p. 130. *Turner* v. *M.G.M. Ltd.* [1950] 1 All E.R. 449, 470–471 (Lord Oaksey).

[15] Pollock, *Torts*, 15th ed., pp. 135–136.

tainly anyone can be protected against unlawful force for the independent reason that there is a general liberty, even as between strangers, for the use of such force as is reasonable in the circumstances in the prevention of crime.[16]

It must always be a question of fact, rather than of law, whether violence done by way of self-protection is proportionate to warding off the harm which is threatened. On the one hand, I am certainly not bound to wait until a threatened blow falls before I hit in self-defence; thus my blow may be justified when my assailant does no more than shake his stick at me, uttering taunts at the same time [17]; much less do I commit any assault by merely putting myself in a fighting attitude in order to defend myself.[18] On the other hand, not every threat will justify a blow in self-defence; still less can B be excused " if upon a little blow given by A to B, B gives him a blow that maims him." [19]

Defence of property

Actual possession (whether with a good title or not), or the right to possession of property is necessary to justify force in keeping out (or, for that matter, expelling) a trespasser. Thus, in *Holmes* v. *Bagge*,[20] the plaintiff and defendant were both members of the committee of a cricket club. During a match in which the defendant was captain and the plaintiff was a spectator, the defendant asked the plaintiff to act as substitute for one of the eleven. He did so, but being annoyed at the tone of the defendant in commanding him to take off his coat, he refused either to remove the garment or to leave the playing part of the field. He was then forcibly removed by the defendant's direction. The defendant, when sued for assault, pleaded possession of the ground, but the plea was held bad because possession was in the committee of the club. Note, however, that if the defendant had pleaded that he removed the plaintiff for disturbing persons lawfully playing a lawful game, he would probably have been justified.

The idea that a burglar may be shot at sight or that a trespasser must always take premises as he finds them goes beyond what the law allows. The broad test here, as elsewhere in private defence, is reasonableness. No one is bound to make his premises safe for trespassers, and if burglars fall into sawpits or are bitten by dogs, tossed by bulls or mauled by savage horses, they must put up with it.[21] But there is a difference between harm suffered from what may be called the ordinary condition of premises and harm suffered from means of defence deliberately adopted. These means must be reasonable, *i.e.* proportionate to the injuries which they are likely to inflict. Such would be broken glass

---

[16] Criminal Law Act 1967 (c. 58), s. 3; *R.* v. *Duffy* [1967] 1 Q.B. 63.
[17] *Dale* v. *Wood* (1822) 7 Moore C.P. 33.
[18] Lord Lyndhurst C.B. in *Moriarty* v. *Brooks* (1834) 6 C. & P. 684.
[19] *Cockcroft* v. *Smith* (1705) 2 Salk. 642; *Lane* v. *Holloway* [1968] 1 Q.B. 379.
[20] (1853) 1 E. & B. 782; see also *Dean* v. *Hogg* (1834) 10 Bing. 345 and *Roberts* v. *Taylor* (1845) 1 C.B. 117.
[21] For the liability of occupiers to trespassers generally, see *ante*, pp. 187–190.

or spikes on a wall, or a fierce dog,[22] but not deadly implements like spring-guns. The infliction of grave bodily harm is too high a price to demand for keeping one's property intact. Even at common law a trespasser wounded in this way could recover damages [23] unless he knew that the guns were somewhere on the land [24] and it is an offence against the Offences Against the Person Act 1861 [25] to set a spring-gun or similar device except, probably, in and for the protection of a dwelling-house between sunset and sunrise. Consistently with the principle of proportion in the means of defence, more latitude is permissible in protecting premises by night than in the daytime, or when the occupier is not in the presence of the trespasser than when he is. Thus an intruder who tears himself on a spiked wall has no ground of complaint, but he certainly would have one if he, being peaceable and unarmed, had a spike thrust into him by the occupier.[26] " Presence [of the occupier] in its very nature is more or less protection . . . presence may supply means [of defence] and limit what it supplies." [27]

Injury to innocent third person

Suppose that in protecting myself from an unlawful attack by A, I injure you, an innocent passer-by. On what principles ought my liability to you to be discussed? Certainly not on those of private defence, for I cannot " defend " myself against one who has done me no unlawful harm. It would seem that the true principles applicable are that I committed no tort if I did not intend the harm and was not negligent, and that I may rely on the defence of necessity [28] if I did. But this does not mean that whatever I may do is justifiable under the one head or the other. Provided I acted reasonably I am excused, and not otherwise.

In *Scott* v. *Shepherd*,[29] A threw a lighted squib into a crowded market-house. It fell upon the gingerbread stall of Yates. A bystander, Willis, to prevent injury to himself and the wares of Yates, instantly picked up the squib and threw it away. It fell upon the gingerbread stall of Ryal, who, to save his own goods from injury, threw the squib farther. It struck B in the face, exploded and blinded him in one eye. Now it was held without any difficulty, except as to the exact form of action, that A was liable to B for trespass and assault. No proceedings were taken

---

[22] *Sarch* v. *Blackburn* (1830) 4 C. & P. 297. The position is now governed by s. 5 (3) (b) of the Animals Act 1971, which is to the like effect: see p. 397, *ante*.
[23] *Bird* v. *Holbrook* (1828) 4 Bing. 628.
[24] *Ilott* v. *Wilkes* (1820) 3 B. & Ald. 304.
[25] 24 & 25 Vict. c. 100, s. 31, re-enacting 7 & 8 Geo. 4, c. 18. *Cf. Wooton* v. *Dawkins* (1857) 5 W.R. 469.
[26] In *Pickwick Papers*, Captain Boldwig's mode of ejecting Mr. Pickwick, whom he found asleep in a wheelbarrow in his grounds, was excessive. He directed his gardener first to wheel Mr. Pickwick to the devil and then, on second thoughts, to wheel him to the village pound.
[27] *Deane* v. *Clayton* (1817) 7 Taunt. 489, 521, *per* Dallas J. For the defences available to the occupier of land who kills or injures a dog, see Animals Act 1971, s. 9.
[28] *Post*, pp. 635–638.
[29] (1773) 2 W.Bl. 892.

against Willis or Ryal, but supposing that they had been sued by B, would they have been liable? Two of the judges thought not, because they acted " under a compulsive necessity for their own safety and self-preservation." [30] No exact technicality was attached by the judges to " necessity " or " self-preservation," but one difficulty is the question whether Willis and Ryal really did behave as reasonable men would have done. Willis, it will be noted, acted to prevent injury to himself as well as to the wares of Yates, and it must be recollected that a man may well act reasonably even if he shows no great presence of mind. A cooler man would have stopped the danger by putting his foot on the squib, but perhaps Willis did all that the lawyer, if not the moralist, could expect of him. Ryal, on the other hand, appears to have acted merely to preserve his goods, and we may doubt whether a man of ordinary presence of mind would throw a squib into a crowd to save his gingerbread from ruin.

Defence against " common enemy "

The doctrine now under consideration has been applied to the protection of one's land against a " common enemy " like the sea or flood water. Where the incursion of the noxious substance is not due to the fault of anyone, such protection really falls under the defence of " necessity." [31] A landowner may defend himself against the incursion by erecting barricades or heightening banks on his own land even if the foreseeable result is the flooding of his neighbour's land by the diverted water. The law allows a kind of reasonable selfishness in such matters. [32] Altruism is not demanded; ordinary skill and care are. [33] This applies not only to private landowners but also to any authority charged with protecting landowners from the incursion of water. [34] Nor is it material that the barriers were erected at some distance within the boundaries of the land instead of on the edge of it; for it would be illogical to allow a landowner to protect the whole of his land against floods and yet to hold him liable because he had set his embankment farther back and so had left part of his land undefended. [35]

But this repulsion of a temporary incursion must be distinguished from accumulating water on one's land and then getting rid of it by artificial means in such a way as to flood a neighbour's land. That is not lawful. [36] And this is so even if the accumulation of the water is due, not to the act of the landowner, but to an extraordinary rainfall. Thus, in *Whalley* v. *Lancashire and Yorkshire Ry.,* [37] an unprecedented storm

---

[30] *Ibid.* at p. 900, *per* De Grey C.J.; *ibid.* at p. 898, *per* Gould J.
[31] *Post*, pp. 635–638.
[32] *Nield* v. *L. & N.W. Ry.* (1874) L.R. 10 Ex. 4, 7, *per* Bramwell B.
[33] *Maxey Drainage Board* v. *G.N. Ry.* (1912) 106 L.T. 429.
[34] *R.* v. *Pagham* (1828) 8 B. & C. 356.
[35] *Gerrard* v. *Crowe* [1921] 1 A.C. 395, 400, *per* Viscount Cave.
[36] *Hurdman* v. *N.E. Ry.* (1878) 3 C.P.D. 168. *Maxey Drainage Board* v. *G.N. Ry.* (1912) 106 L.T. 429; *Gerrard* v. *Crowe, supra.*
[37] (1884) 13 Q.B.D. 131.

and rainfall flooded the drains bordering on the railway embankment of the defendants so that a large quantity of water was dammed up against the embankment. The water afterwards rose so as to endanger the embankment. The defendants then pierced it with gullies and the water flowed away and flooded the plaintiff's land. The defendants were held liable, although the jury found that if they had had only the preservation of their own land to consider, their act would have been reasonable. They could lawfully have turned away the flood if they had seen it coming, but " there is a difference between protecting yourself from an injury which is not yet suffered by you, and getting rid of the consequences of an injury which has occurred to you." [38]

Greyvensteyn v. *Hattingh*,[39] an appeal case from South Africa, related to a plague of locusts. They entered the plaintiff's land, and the defendants, in the reasonable belief that they were trekking towards their land, entered a strip of land belonging to third parties and turned away the locusts so that they re-entered the plaintiff's land and devoured his crops. The defendants were held not liable either because they were repelling an extraordinary misfortune or because, if locusts were to be regarded in South Africa as a normal incident of agriculture, the defendants were entitled to get rid of them just as they would be allowed to scare away crows regardless of the direction they took in leaving.[40]

5. Necessity

This negatives liability in tort, provided, of course, that the occasion of necessity does not arise from the defendant's own negligence,[41] though the authority on it is scanty.[42] It differs from private defence in that in necessity the harm inflicted on the plaintiff was not provoked by any actual or threatened illegal wrong on the plaintiff's part, and that what the defendant did may be entirely for the good of other people and not necessarily for the protection of himself or his property. Its basis is a mixture of charity, the maintenance of the public good and self-protection, and it is probably limited to cases involving an urgent situation of imminent peril. It does not, for example, furnish a defence

---

[38] *Ibid.* at p. 140, *per* Lindley L.J.

[39] [1911] A.C. 355.

[40] Scaring crows is a normal incident in the occupation of land; piercing a railway embankment is not an ordinary use of the embankment: *Whaley* v. *Lancashire and Yorkshire Ry.* (1884) 13 Q.B.D. at p. 138, *per* Brett M.R.

[41] *Southport Corporation* v. *Esso Petroleum Ltd.* [1954] 2 Q.B. 182, 194, *per* Singleton L.J.; *ibid.* at p. 198, *per* Denning L.J.; *Esso Petroleum Ltd.* v. *Southport Corporation* [1956] A.C. 218, 242, *per* Lord Radcliffe.

[42] *Esso Petroleum Ltd.* v. *Southport Corporation* [1956] A.C. 218, 228, *per* Devlin J.; *ibid.* at p. 235, *per* Earl Jowitt; *ibid.* at p. 242, *per* Lord Radcliffe; *Southwark London Borough Council* v. *Williams* [1971] 2 W.L.R. 467; Pollock, *Torts*, 15th ed., pp. 121–123; Clerk and Lindsell, *Torts*, 13th ed., p. 75; Salmond, *Torts*, 16th ed., pp. 504–506; Street, *Law of Torts*, 5th ed., pp. 81–82. Glanville Williams (1953) 6 *Current Legal Problems*, 216–235. *Contra*, Newark (1956) 19 M.L.R. 320 (book review). For " agency of necessity," see *Sachs* v. *Miklos* [1948] 2 K.B. 23; *Munro* v. *Willmott* [1949] 1 K.B. 295.

to an action for trespass brought against homeless persons who enter and " squat " in unoccupied premises.[43]

Familiar examples are pulling down a house on fire to prevent its spread to other property,[44] destroying a building made ruinous by fire to prevent its collapse into the highway,[45] throwing goods overboard to lighten a boat in a storm,[46] and perhaps assistance, medical [47] or otherwise, rendered to a person unconscious at the time. So, too, the removal of the plaintiff's barge because it is frozen hard to the defendant's barge which he is lawfully moving.[48] The measures which are taken must be reasonable, and this will depend, amongst other things, upon whether there is human life or merely property in danger.[49] In *Kirk v. Gregory*,[50] X died in a state of *delirium tremens*. His servants were feasting and drinking in the house. X's sister-in-law removed X's jewellery from the room where he lay dead to another room for safety's sake. Some unknown person stole it. The sister-in-law was held liable to X's executor for trespass to the jewellery because there was no proof that her interference was reasonably necessary. On the other hand, the justification for interference depends upon the state of things at the moment at which interference takes place. Subsequent events may show that interference was not needed at all, but that will not deprive the doer of his defence. In *Cope v. Sharpe*,[51] a fire broke out on A's land. While A's servants were trying to beat it out, the gamekeeper of C (who had shooting rights over A's land) set fire to some strips of heather between the fire and some nesting pheasants of C. Shortly afterwards, A's servants succeeded in extinguishing the fire. A sued the gamekeeper for trespass. He was held not liable, for there was real and imminent danger to the game at the moment at which he acted, and what he did was reasonably necessary.

So far we have been dealing with harm inflicted on property. There

---

[43] *Southwark London Borough Council* v. *Williams, supra*, where the Court of Appeal was concerned that the defence of necessity should not become a " mask for anarchy ": [1971] 2 W.L.R. at p. 474, *per* Edmund Davies L.J.; *ibid.* at p. 473, *per* Lord Denning M.R.

[44] Shelley *arguendo* in Y.B.Trin. 13 Hen. 8, f. 15, pl. 1, at f. 16*a*; Kingsmill J. in Y.B. Trin. 21 Hen. 7, f. 27*b*, pl. 5; *Saltpetre Case* (1606) 12 Rep. 12, 13. But officious interference with a fire brigade which is adequately coping with the fire is not justified: *Carter* v. *Thomas* [1893] 1 Q.B. 673.

[45] *Dewey* v. *White* (1827) M. & M. 56 (A, whose adjoining house was inevitably damaged, had no remedy). See, however, the observations of Lord Upjohn in *Burmah Oil Co.* (*Burma Trading*) *Ltd.* v. *Lord Advocate* [1965] A.C. 75, 164–165.

[46] *Mouse's Case* (1609) 12 Rep. 63. It should be noted that this case took place on an inland waterway. The position as to jettison at sea may be affected by the principle of general average.

[47] Bates, " Consenting to the Necessary " (1972) 46 A.L.J. 73. But see p. 620, *ante*.

[48] *Milman* v. *Dolwell* (1810) 2 Camp. 378. Defendant lost his case because he did not plead necessity. *Cf. Romney Marsh* v. *Trinity House* (1870) L.R. 5 Ex. 204.

[49] " The safety of human lives belongs to a different scale of values from the safety of property. The two are beyond comparison and the necessity for saving life has at all times been considered a proper ground for inflicting such damages as may be necessary upon another's property ": *Esso Petroleum Ltd.* v. *Southport Corporation* [1956] A.C. 218, 228, *per* Devlin J.; Weir, *Casebook on Tort*, 3rd ed., p. 330. *Cf.* Glanville Williams, *loc. cit.* at pp. 234–235.

[50] (1876) 1 Ex.D. 55.

[51] [1912] 1 K.B. 496.

is no reported decision that is of any real assistance on necessity as a defence for inflicting injuries to the person. The dicta in *Scott* v. *Shepherd* [52] were only *obiter*. In *Gregson* v. *Gilbert*,[53] where 150 negro slaves were thrown overboard owing to shortage of water, it was held in an action upon a policy of insurance for the value of the slaves that, upon the facts, no sufficient evidence of necessity had been shown for the captain's act, but the decision is obviously of little value for modern purposes. All that it is safe to hazard is that the principle of reasonableness applies here also, that more latitude would be allowed in the protection of the actor's person than of his property, and still more where he acts for the public safety and not for his own.[54]

Is compensation demandable?

Another point not free from doubt is whether, assuming that the defence of necessity has been established, the defendant must make compensation or at least restitution for the harm which he has inflicted. It is clear that no damages can be claimed in tort where the defendant's act is justified by necessity,[55] but that does not settle the question whether the defendant is liable to make restitution, *i.e.* to restore to its former condition the property of the plaintiff which has been affected by the defendant's act, or, if restoration be impossible, to pay the plaintiff equivalent compensation. Here, the basis of the plaintiff's claim would be quasi-contract, not tort, the practical difference being that compensation payable on a quasi-contractual claim may be considerably less than damages on a claim in tort. Perhaps a distinction exists between (a) an act done for the common weal, and (b) an act done simply in protection of one's person or property. As to (a), in the *Saltpetre Case*,[56] it was said that every man, as well as the King and his officials, may, for the defence of the realm, enter upon another man's land and make trenches or bulwarks there; " but after the danger is over, the trenches and bulwarks ought to be removed, so that the owner shall not have prejudice in his inheritance "; and in *Burmah Oil Co. (Burma Trading) Ltd.* v. *Lord Advocate* [57] it was held by a majority of the House of Lords that the Crown must pay compensation for pro-

---

[52] (1773) 2 W.Bl. 892, *ante*, p. 634.
[53] (1783) 3 Dougl. 232.
[54] The driver of a fire engine is in no privileged position; he must observe traffic signals: *Ward* v. *L.C.C.* [1938] 2 All E.R. 341. Road Traffic Act 1934 (24 & 25 Geo. 5, c. 50), s. 3 (now Road Traffic Regulation Act 1967, s. 79), exempts fire engines, ambulances and police cars from speed limits, but does not affect the civil liability of the driver: *Gaynor* v. *Allen* [1959] 2 Q.B. 403.
[55] *Cope* v. *Sharpe* [1912] 1 K.B. 496. Tindal C.J. in *Anthony* v. *Haney* (1823) 8 Bing. 186, 192–193 said *obiter* that an owner who peaceably retakes his goods from the land of another, who refuses to give them up, must pay for such damage as he commits. But this relates to the limits of self-help rather than to necessity. In *Southport Corporation* v. *Esso Petroleum Co. Ltd.* [1965] A.C. 218, 227, Devlin J. was not prepared to hold without further consideration that a man is entitled to damage the property of another without compensating him merely because the infliction of such damage is necessary to save his own property.
[56] (1606) 12 Rep. 12, 13, *per* the justices consulting in Serjeants Inn.
[57] [1965] A.C. 75.

perty destroyed, by an exercise of the Royal prerogative during the War, in order to prevent it from falling into enemy hands. The effect of this decision was, however, removed by the War Damage Act 1965, which provides that " No person shall be entitled *at common law* to receive from the Crown compensation in respect of damage to, or destruction of, property caused . . . by acts lawfully done by, or on the authority of, the Crown during, or in contemplation of the outbreak of, a war in which the Sovereign was, or is, engaged." [58] Notwithstanding the dictum in the *Saltpetre Case* it may be doubted whether a private person, who, of course, does not act under the prerogative and is unaffected by the Act of 1965, need ever have made any compensation for acts justifiably done in defence of the realm.[59] It is, however, exceedingly difficult to conceive that today a private citizen could justify an otherwise tortious action on the ground that it was done in defence of the realm.[60] As to (b), it is suggested that bare restitution or compensation for the use or consumption of property might be claimed on quasi-contractual grounds: *e.g.* using a neighbour's fire extinguisher to put out a fire in one's own house.[61]

Duress

Duress, or threatened injury to a person unless he commits a tort, appears to be no defence if he does commit it. In *Gilbert* v. *Stone*,[62] 12 unknown armed men threatened to kill the defendant unless he entered the plaintiff's house with them, which he did. To an action for trespass he was held to have no defence, " for one cannot justify a trespass upon another for fear, and the defendant hath remedy against those that compelled him." But actual physical compulsion, as distinct from mere threat of it, is a defence.[63]

---

[58] s. 1 (1), italics added. On this provision see *Nissan* v. *Att.-Gen.* [1968] 1 Q.B. at pp. 309–310, *per* John Stephenson J.; *ibid.* [1970] A.C. at p. 229, *per* Lord Pearce. The normal situation is, of course, that special statutory provisions for compensation will apply.

[59] The whole passage in 12 Rep. 12–13 is rather confused and the earlier authorities do not support Coke, who reported the case. See, *e.g. Maleverer* v. *Spinke* (1538) Dyer 35b, 36b, para. 40.

[60] See *Burmah Oil Co.* (*Burma Trading*) *Ltd.* v. *Lord Advocate, supra*, at pp. 164–165, *per* Lord Upjohn. Lord Reid, *ibid.* at p. 99, conceded that there might be occasions when a subject is entitled to act on his own initiative in defence of the realm, particularly if there is no one in authority there to direct him, but he thought it impossible that any subject could have been entitled to carry out the major demolitions with which the case was concerned.

[61] There is no English decision in point, but an example put by Lord Mansfield in *Hambly* v. *Trott* (1776) 1 Cowp. 371, 375 is consistent with the suggestion. For a case the facts of which would seem to call for such a remedy see *Esso Petroleum Ltd.* v. *Southport Corporation* [1956] A.C. 218. The American *Restatement of Restitution*, § 122, is to the like effect and applies the rule also where A harms B's property in order to preserve C or C's property, for " a person is not entitled to be a good Samaritan at the expense of another." § 122, however, exempts A from any obligation to make restitution to B if A's act appeared reasonably necessary to avert a *public* catastrophe.

[62] (1647) Aleyn 35. *Cf.* Fleming, *Torts*, 4th ed., p. 95.

[63] *Smith* v. *Stone* (1647) Style 65; dictum in *Weaver* v. *Ward* (1616) Hob. 134.

6. Statutory authority

When a statute authorises the commission of what would otherwise be a tort, then the party injured has no remedy apart from the compensation (if any) which the statute allows him. This principle, of course, applies to any tort, but it is most commonly illustrated in the tort of nuisance. Statutory powers are not, however, charters of immunity for any injurious act done in the exercise of them. In the first place, courts will not impute to the legislature any intention to take away the private rights of individuals without compensation, unless it be proved that there was such an intention; and the burden of proving it is said to rest with those who exercise the statutory powers.[64] Next, when the legislature confers such powers it may do so in one of two ways.[65]

1. It may, in effect, order a particular thing to be done regardless of whether it inflicts an injury upon another person. Then the authority covers not only harm which must obviously occur, but also that which is necessarily incidental to the exercise of the authority. It is impossible to build a railway without interfering with private land. But it is equally impossible to run trains on it without some noise and vibration, and there is no more a remedy for this incidental harm, provided the work has been carried out without negligence, than there is for the more obvious harm. " Where there is a mandatory obligation . . . there would be, in our opinion, no liability if what had been done was that which was expressly required by statute to be done or was reasonably incidental to that requirement and was done without negligence." [66]

2. It may merely permit a particular thing to be done. Here, too, there is no liability except for negligence, unless the statute contains a section retaining liability for nuisance.[67] In *Metropolitan Asylum District* v. *Hill* [68] it was held that a smallpox hospital was a nuisance because, although the statute enabled the managers of the district to purchase land and to erect buildings on it for the care of the sick and the infirm poor, yet it conferred this power only subject to the managers obtaining by free bargain and contract the means of doing so; much less did it condone the commission of any nuisance by them. With this case may

---

[64] *Farnworth* v. *Manchester Corporation* [1929] 1 K.B. 533, 556, *per* Lawrence L.J. For proceedings in the House of Lords, see [1930] A.C. 171. But the question would seem to be one purely of statutory construction and as such not to involve questions of the burden of proof at all. The point is that unless the clearest language is used it is to be assumed that Parliament did not intend an encroachment upon the liberties of the subject: *Att.-Gen.* v. *Nissan* [1970] A.C. 179, 229, *per* Lord Pearce.

[65] These principles are not necessarily applicable when the authority is to undertake an activity rather than specific works: see Fleming, *Torts*, 4th ed., pp. 365–367; the judgment of Jenkins L.J. in *Marriage* v. *E. Norfolk Catchment Board* [1950] 1 K.B. 284; and the speech of Lord Diplock in *Home Office* v. *Dorset Yacht Co. Ltd.* [1970] A.C. 1004.

[66] *Dunne* v. *N.W. Gas Board* [1964] 2 Q.B. 806, 835, *per curiam* (Sellers L.J.). But see the observation of Rees J. in *Pearson* v. *N.W. Gas Board* [1968] 2 All E.R. 669, 672. See also the famous statement of Lord Blackburn in *Geddis* v. *Proprietors of Bann Reservoir* (1878) 3 App.Cas. 430, 455; *Pride of Derby, etc.* v. *British Celanese Ltd.* [1953] Ch. 149; *Smeaton* v. *Ilford Corporation* [1954] Ch. 450.

[67] *Dunne* v. *N.W. Gas Board* [1964] 2 Q.B. 806. *Cf. Charing Cross Electricity Supply Co.* v. *Hydraulic Power Co.* [1914] 3 K.B. 772.

[68] (1881) 6 App.Cas. 193.

be compared *Att.-Gen.* v. *Nottingham Corporation.*[69] There the corporation proposed to use a building as a smallpox hospital, and the court declined to issue a *quia timet* injunction to prevent them from doing so, because they did not regard the theory of the aerial dissemination of smallpox as unequivocally established.

The distinction between the cases seems to be this. The argument of the managers in *Hill's* case was, " Because we have authority to erect a smallpox hospital, we can erect it *anywhere.*" The argument of the plaintiff in *Att.-Gen.* v. *Nottingham Corporation* was, in effect, " You cannot erect a smallpox hospital *anywhere* in a populous neighbourhood." In fact, both arguments were overstatements, for the first would have twisted the statute into a licence to commit any nuisance by means of the hospital, while the second assumed the hospital to be a nuisance without any proof that it was. In fact, with smallpox hospitals, as with every other kind of potential nuisance, it is a question of time, place and circumstance whether there is an actual nuisance or not.

---

[69] [1904] 1 Ch. 673. See, too, *Edgington* v. *Swindon Corporation* [1939] 1 K.B. 86; *East Suffolk, etc. Board* v. *Kent* [1941] A.C. 74.

CHAPTER 30

EXTINCTION OF LIABILITY IN TORT

EXTINCTION of liability in tort may take place in several ways, some of them by act of the parties, others by operation of law.[1]

WAIVER

An injured party may waive his remedy in tort in favour of some other remedy and, if he does so, this extinguishes the right of action in tort. He cannot change his mind after he has elected the other remedy, and sue upon the action which he has put aside; nor can he ask the court to elect for him.[2] The reason stated in various guises is that " he cannot have it both ways," " he cannot both approbate and reprobate," [3] " he cannot blow hot and blow cold." The remedy which he actually elects may be some other action in tort, e.g. he may have waived trespass for trover [4]; or it may be an action on contract [5]; or an action on quasi-contract, as where he sues for money had and received in preference to bringing trover [6]; or some other kind of proceeding, like a petition in bankruptcy.[7]

What he does must, of course, amount to waiver, and there has been some litigation on what constitutes election of a remedy. Final judgment in an action on the injured party's claim is certainly a waiver which will preclude him from exploiting an alternative action on the same claim [8]; but the mere commencement of an action for money lent (*i.e.* an action on contract) or for money had and received (*i.e.* an action on quasi-contract) is not a waiver of an action in tort on the same facts, if for one reason or another the first action is not pushed to judgment.[9] Receipt of a sum of money paid by the tortfeasor and accepted as a complete discharge of the tortfeasor's liability bars a subsequent action. So, where A was the agent of B and wrongfully converted B's goods, B had the choice of suing A in tort or of adopting his acts as agent; but, having chosen the latter course and received payment from A in that capacity, B could not subsequently sue in tort for the conversion.[10] Beyond such clear cases as these, waiver is a question of fact to be determined by the circumstances of each case. Once a

---

[1] For extinction of liability by death, now more the exception than the rule, see *ante*, pp. 498–501.
[2] *British Ry., etc. Co.* v. *Roper* (1940) 162 L.T. 217.
[3] *Lissenden* v. *C.A.V. Bosch Ltd.* [1940] A.C. 412, 416–419, *per* Lord Maugham.
[4] *Rodgers* v. *Maw* (1846) 15 M. & W. 444, 448, *per* Pollock C.B.
[5] *Verschures Creameries Ltd.* v. *Hull, etc., SS. Co. Ltd.* [1921] 2 K.B. 608.
[6] *Post*, pp. 642–645.
[7] *Smith* v. *Baker* (1873) L.R. 8 C.P. 350; *Roes* v. *Mutual Loan Fund* (1887) 19 Q.B.D. 347.
[8] *Smith* v. *Baker, supra.*
[9] *United Australia Ltd.* v. *Barclays Bank Ltd.* [1941] A.C. 1.
[10] *Brewer* v. *Sparrow* (1827) 7 B. & C. 310.

person has committed himself unequivocally to one of two inconsistent rights he cannot afterwards resort to the other,[11] but if an act is ambiguous in character, it does not amount to election [12]; much less where it is explicable on some other ground. A mere demand for payment of compensation for a tort is no waiver of an action for it [13]; nor is part payment of what is due, unless it is accepted as a full discharge [14]; nor is the commencement of an action with alternative claims in tort and for money had and received [15]; and if one and the same act constitutes two different torts, the suing of an action for both of them is no waiver of either of them.[16]

Waiver of tort in favour of quasi-contract

There is one form of waiver which is important enough to deserve special examination.[17] This is where the waiver consists in selecting an action upon quasi-contract in preference to suing upon the tort. There are several varieties of quasi-contract, but the particular one with which we are concerned here is that which, when the old forms of action were in force, was redressed by a claim upon *indebitatus assumpsit*.[18]

Why employed?

At the outset, why should a plaintiff ever wish to waive his action in tort for one in quasi-contract? His preference may seem to be the more remarkable in view of the fact that in such waiver he has got to prove in the first instance that the tort has been committed, although the court does not insist on the establishment of mere technical ingredients in the wrong.[19] The original explanation is that under the old system of pleading *indebitatus assumpsit* had many advantages over an action in tort.[20] Modern procedural reforms have obliterated many of these advantages, most recently by the abolition of the special period

---

[11] *Re United Railways of Havana and Regla Warehouses Ltd.* [1961] A.C. 1007, 1065, *per* Lord Denning.

[12] *Rice* v. *Reed* [1900] 1 Q.B. 54, 66, *per* A. L. Smith L.J.

[13] *Valpy* v. *Sanders* (1848) 5 C.B. 886; *Morris* v. *Robinson* (1824) 3 B. & C. 196.

[14] *Burn* v. *Morris* (1834) 4 Tyrw. 485; *Lythgoe* v. *Vernon* (1860) 5 H. & N. 180.

[15] *Rice* v. *Reed* [1900] 1 Q.B. 54, 65, *per* A. L. Smith L.J. Claims in the alternative are quite common; see *e.g. Chesworth* v. *Farrar* [1967] 1 Q.B. 407.

[16] *Caxton Publishing Co. Ltd.* v. *Sutherland Publishing Co. Ltd.* [1939] A.C. 178, 199.

[17] Goff and Jones, *Restitution,* Chap. 33. *Cf.* Fridman, " Waiver of Tort " (1955) 18 M.L.R. 1, where the view is expressed that waiver of tort " as a device and a doctrine is otiose and ripe for abolition." Both the history and much of the present law of waiver of a tort in favour of an action on quasi-contract have been thoroughly explored by Jackson, *History of Quasi-Contract in English Law* (1936), pp. 61–84; Winfield, *Province of the Law of Tort,* pp. 168–176, and *The Law of Quasi-Contracts,* pp. 91–100; *United Australia Ltd.* v. *Barclays Bank Ltd.* [1941] A.C. 1, 11–19, *per* Lord Simon L.C.; 26–30, *per* Lord Atkin; *ibid.* at pp. 40–43, *per* Lord Porter; Lord Wright, " United Australia Ltd. *v.* Barclays Bank Ltd." (1941) 57 L.Q.R. 184–202; and his *Legal Essays and Addresses,* pp. 53–54.

[18] " Thoughts much too deep for tears subdue the court
When I *assumpsit* bring, and god-like waive a tort."
                                              The Circuiteers, 1 L.Q.R. 233.

[19] *Heilbut* v. *Nevill* (1870) L.R. 5 C.P. 478.

[20] They are detailed in Winfield, *op. cit.,* pp. 143–146.

of limitation for actions in tort against the estates of deceased persons,[21] but even nowadays a plaintiff may still find it useful to waive a tort.[22] By doing so he can, for example, avoid the rule that a claim for unliquidated damages for tort cannot be proved in a bankruptcy,[23] since his quasi-contractual claim will be for a liquidated sum.[24] Again, if the defendant has converted his goods and sold them for more than their value the plaintiff can claim the proceeds of sale in quasi-contract.[25]

What torts can be waived ?

In 1831 Tindal C.J. thought that there was no limit except that the defendant must not be prejudiced.[26] But this is of little help at the present day, and it is inconceivable that waiver can apply to some torts. The essence of *indebitatus assumpsit* was that the plaintiff claimed that the defendant " had and received " money which belonged to the plaintiff, and that is still the essence of the particular species of quasi-contractual claim which has succeeded to the *indebitatus* counts. Now, if the tort committed by the defendant is assault or defamation, no money has been " had and received " by him and a claim in quasi-contract is obviously inapplicable. So there must be some limit to the torts that can be waived, but what it is can only be conjectured in view of some of the decided cases.[27] We can at any rate enumerate the torts which do admit of waiver, and we can then consider the doubtful cases. Conversion has long been recognised as capable of waiver [28] and waiver of trespass to land, where it results in the sale of things extracted from the land, is permissible [29] unless the trespass was committed merely as a mode of establishing a right or unless exemplary damages are claimed.[30] So, too, waiver of trespass to goods if the trespasser has subsequently, either in fact or in the eye of the law, turned the goods into money.[31] The tort of deceit in its modern sense can be waived,[32] although there

---

[21] Proceedings Against Estates Act 1970 (c. 17), *ante*, p. 501. For a case where waiver of tort successfully avoided this particular limitation period, see *Chesworth* v. *Farrar* [1967] 1 Q.B. 407.

[22] *Bavins* v. *L. & S.W. Bank* [1900] 1 Q.B. 270; *United Australia Ltd.* v. *Barclays Bank Ltd.* [1941] A.C. 1.

[23] Bankruptcy Act 1914, s. 30.

[24] Goff and Jones, *op. cit.*, p. 437.

[25] *Ibid.* For a list of the advantages in waiving the tort, see *ibid.* pp. 436–437. *Cf.* Marshall Evans, " Waiving the Tort " (1966) 82 L.Q.R. 167.

[26] *Young* v. *Marshall*, 8 Bing. at p. 44.

[27] Goff and Jones, *op. cit.*, p. 429, suggests that " in every case where the tortfeasor has gained an unjust benefit at the plaintiff's expense, whether his assets have been increased or whether he has merely been saved expense, the plaintiff should be allowed to waive the tort and recover in quasi-contract the value of that benefit." They admit that *Phillips* v. *Homfray* (1883) 24 Ch.D. 439 is something of a stumbling block but consider that that case should be overruled: *ibid.* p. 433.

[28] This was regarded as settled by Park J., giving the opinion of the judges to the House of Lords in *Marsh* v. *Keating* (1834) 1 Bing.N.C. 198, 215–216. See, too, *Thomas* v. *Whip* (1715) Buller N.P. 130.

[29] *Powell* v. *Rees* (1837) 7 A. & E. 426.

[30] Jackson, *op. cit.*, p. 75.

[31] *Oughton* v. *Seppings* (1830) 1 B. & Ad. 241; *Rodgers* v. *Maw* (1846) 15 M. & W. 444, 448, *per* Pollock C.B.; *Neate* v. *Harding* (1851) 6 Ex. 349, 351, *per* Parke B.

[32] For application of waiver to deceit in its older meaning of swindling a court of justice, see Jackson, *op. cit.*, p. 74.

are exceptions to this; deceit alone is the appropriate action and waiver is not possible if, for example, the right to rescind a contract for fraud no longer exists because restitution of the property is impossible. " If you are fraudulently induced to buy a cake, you may return it and get back the price, but you cannot both eat your cake and return your cake." [33] If you have eaten it, you can sue in tort for deceit, but not for the return of the price; and it is obvious that the damages recoverable in such circumstances for deceit may well be less than the price paid for the article. In this connection, it is better to include under waiver of deceit the action upon an obligation to compensate a person for having obtained his services by fraud. [34] Another tort which can be waived is usurpation of an office which in fact belongs to the plaintiff. Thus in *Howard* v. *Wood* [35] the defendant had wrongfully taken the fees of a stewardship which properly belonged to the plaintiff, who was allowed to recover them by *indebitatus assumpsit*. [36]

Doubtful cases of waiver

So much for torts which certainly can be waived. Outside them we are in a region of doubt. Two older cases push the doctrine to such lengths that it becomes scarcely recognisable. In *Lightly* v. *Clouston*, [37] A induced B's apprentice, in breach of his apprenticeship, to work for A. B was allowed to waive A's tort and to sue A in *indebitatus assumpsit* for work and labour done by the apprentice for A. Mansfield C.J. regarded it as long settled in cases of sale that if the plaintiff chose to sue for the produce of the sale, he might do so, and that the like principle applied here; it was not competent to the defendant to argue that he got the apprentice's labour, not by contract but by tort. A few years later this decision was followed with some hesitation by Lord Ellenborough C.J. in *Foster* v. *Stewart*. [38] It is uncertain whether either decision would be adopted at the present day. Their dates are material in the sense that many of the procedural advantages given by *indebitatus assumpsit* have been extinguished by later legislation, so that now there is not so much reason for giving a wide scope to waiver. Again it is difficult to find a complete answer to counsel's argument in *Foster* v. *Stewart* that, if waiver were allowed there, " as well might it be said, that if a man take the goods of another, the owner of the goods may have *assumpsit* against him for goods sold." [39] On the other hand, waiver is possible where the tort is extortion by threats and there is not

---

[33] *Clarke* v. *Dickson* (1858) E.B. & E. 148, 152, *per* Crompton J.
[34] *Rumsey* v. *N.E. Ry.* (1863) 14 C.B.(N.S.) 641; discussed in Winfield, *op. cit.*. p. 171.
[35] (1678) 2 Show. 21; 2 Lev. 245; Freeman K.B. 478; T. Jones 126. This appears to have been the earliest class of case to allow waiver of tort: Goff and Jones, *op. cit.*, p. 427.
[36] For other cases, see Jackson, *op. cit.*, pp. 61–64; Goff and Jones, *op. cit.*, pp. 428–430.
[37] (1808) 1 Taunt. 112.
[38] (1814) 3 M. & S. 191.
[39] 3 M. & S. 196.

much difference between that and waiving the conversion which consists in taking a man's goods without any threat.[40] Upon the whole, it may be conjectured that even if *Lightly* v. *Clouston* and *Foster* v. *Stewart* are still law, the courts would not now be disposed to add to the list of torts which can be waived.[41]

ACCORD AND SATISFACTION [42]

Tortious liability can be extinguished by agreement for valuable consideration between the injured party and the tortfeasor.[43] This is styled accord and satisfaction but is really little more than a specialised form of contract and so, to be effective, it must comply with the rules for the formation of contract.[44] " Accord " signifies the agreement, " satisfaction " the consideration which makes it operative. The satisfaction may be either executed, *e.g.* " I release you from your obligation in consideration of £100 now paid by you to me "; or it may be executory, *e.g.* " I release you from your obligation in consideration of your promise to pay me £100 in six months." [45]

Accord and satisfaction may be conditional. A person injured in an accident brought about by the negligence of the defendant may accept an offer of compensation, reserving to himself the right to renew his claim if his injuries turn out to be worse than they were at the time of the accord.[46]

Non-performance of accord and satisfaction

What is the position of the parties if the accord and satisfaction are not carried out? Are they in the same situation as if it had never been made or must the party aggrieved sue upon the broken accord and satisfaction and upon that only? The answer is that it depends upon the construction of the agreement which embodies the accord and satisfaction.[47] If the satisfaction consists of a promise on the part of the

---

[40] Jackson, *op. cit.*, pp. 76–77, regards the test of possibility of waiver of a tort as " the principle that an action for money had and received would not lie unless a specific sum of money had been received, *or could be deemed to have been received.*" But the learned author admits that the words italicised make the principle vague and difficult to apply.

[41] *Cf. United Australia Ltd.* v. *Barclays Bank Ltd.* [1941] A.C. 1 at pp. 12–13, *per* Viscount Simon L.C.; Goff and Jones, *op. cit.*, p. 429.

[42] Salmond and Williams, *Contracts*, § 178; Chitty, *Contracts*, 23rd ed., Vol. I, pp. 573–575.

[43] *Peytoe's Case* (1611) 9 Rep. 77b. It is also possible for the parties, by an agreement falling short of full accord and satisfaction, to limit the issues between them, as in *Tomlin* v. *Standard Telephones and Cables Ltd.* [1969]]1 W.L.R. 1378, an action for damages for personal injuries, where it was agreed that the defendants would pay 50 per cent. of the plaintiff's damages, leaving only the amount of those damages to be determined. See also *S.* v. *Distillers Co. (Biochemicals) Ltd.* [1970] 1 W.L.R. 114.

[44] See *D. & C. Builders Ltd.* v. *Rees* [1966] 2 Q.B. 617.

[45] *British Russian Gazette, etc. Ltd.* v. *Associated Newspapers Ltd.* [1933] 2 K.B. 616, *per* Scrutton L.J.; *ibid.* at p. 650, *per* Greer L.J.

[46] *Lee* v. *L. & Y. Ry.* (1871) L.R. 6 Ch. 527; *Ellen* v. *G.N. Ry.* (1901) 17 T.L.R. 453; *North British Ry.* v. *Wood* (1891) 18 R. 27 (H.L.).

[47] Although the agreement will usually be contained in " without prejudice " correspondence, which means that the correspondence cannot be used in evidence, this correspondence can be produced to the court if the question is whether a binding agreement

tortfeasor, the interpretation of the agreement may be, " I accept this promise as an absolute discharge of your tortious liability "; if so, all that the injured party can sue upon in the event of the tortfeasor not carrying out his promise, is the contract which has been substituted for the tortious liability. Alternatively, the interpretation of the agreement may be, " I accept this promise as a discharge of your liability provided you carry it out "; in that case, if the promise is not fulfilled, the injured party has two alternative remedies: he can either fall back upon his original claim in tort, or he can sue upon the contract which was intended to take its place. Somewhat different considerations apply to an accord and satisfaction which is expressed to be conditional in the first instance, as in the example given above of provisional acceptance of compensation in an accident. Here the injured party cannot have recourse to his action in tort unless the condition is not fulfilled. If it is fulfilled within the time specified by the agreement or, if no time is specified, within a reasonable time, then the tortious liability is extinguished. If it is not thus fulfilled, then the injured party can either rely upon his claim in tort or sue upon the conditional agreement which was substituted for it and which has been broken.[48]

Release

Closely akin to accord and satisfaction is release of tortious liability given by the injured party. In fact, there seems to be little difference between the two except that a release is usually, but not necessarily, embodied in an instrument under seal and the necessity for consideration is thus avoided.[49] Release is apparently effective whether it is given before or after an action against the tortfeasor is commenced.[50]

JUDGMENT

Final judgment by a court of competent jurisdiction extinguishes a right of action. It has a twofold effect. First, it estops any party to the litigation from disputing afterwards the correctness of the decision either in law or in fact. Secondly, it operates as a merger of the original cause of action in the rights created by the judgment; and these are either to levy execution against the defendant or to bring a new action upon the judgment (not upon the original claim, for that has perished).

The reason why judgment wipes out the plaintiff's original cause of action is put on either of two grounds. One is public policy: *interest reipublicae ut sit finis litium*; the other is private justice: *nemo debet bis*

---

has actually been reached between the parties (*Tomlin* v. *Standard Telephones and Cables Ltd.* [1969] 1 W.L.R. 1378) and, presumably, also when a question of the interpretation of the agreement has to be decided.

[48] Salmond and Williams, *Contracts*, § 178.

[49] *Phillips* v. *Clagett* (1843) 11 M. & W. 84. See *ante*, p. 545, for the position regarding release of joint tortfeasors.

[50] *Apley Estates Co. Ltd.* v. *De Bernales* [1946] 2 All E.R. 338, 340, *per* Evershed J. The C.A. affirmed his decision, but without reference to this point: [1947] Ch. 217.

vexari pro uno et eodem delicto.[51] However, as we have seen,[52] judgment is no bar to another action unless the cause of action is the same.

STATUTES OF LIMITATION [53]

Whether a person's claim is based upon tort or upon any other form of injury, he will lose his remedy if he falls asleep upon it. The reasons for this are twofold. In the first place, no one ought to be exposed to the risk of stale demands of which he may be quite ignorant and which, owing to changed circumstances, he may be unable to satisfy. Secondly, it may have become impossible or difficult, owing to the loss of documents or the death of witnesses, to establish a defence which would have negatived the claim if it had been prosecuted more promptly. The older law was contained in a rambling and slovenly piece of legislation, the Statute of Limitation 1623.[54] The principal Act today is the Limitation Act 1939,[55] and this Act, as amended, provides that actions founded on simple contract or tort shall not be brought after the expiration of six years, or in the case of actions for personal injuries, three years, from the date on which the cause of action accrued.[56] The defendant must plead the Act if he wishes to rely on it,[57] for the court will not of its own motion take notice that an action is out of time.[58]

Commencement of period

According to the Act of 1939 the period of limitation runs " from the date on which the cause of action accrued." No further explanation of " accrued " is given, so the authorities on the older law are still in point. They show that the period begins to run " from the earliest time at which an action could be brought." [59] " ' Cause of action ' means

---

[51] Bower, *Res Judicata* (1924), pp. 1–2.

[52] *Ante*, pp. 552–554. The facts of a case may be such as to enable the defendant successfully to plead *res judicata*, or to have the action dismissed as frivolous and vexatious: *Wright* v. *Bennett* [1948] 1 All E.R. 227. See, too, *Marginson* v. *Blackburn Borough Council* [1939] 2 K.B. 426; *Bell* v. *Holmes* [1956] 1 W.L.R. 1359; *Wood* v. *Luscombe* [1966] 1 Q.B. 169. *Cf. Randolph* v. *Tuck* [1962] 1 Q.B. 175. See Clerk and Lindsell, *Torts*, 13th ed., pp. 315–317.

[53] The best statement of the principles of these statutes is in the Fifth Interim Report of the Law Revision Committee (Statutes of Limitation) (1936) Cmd. 5334. It is cited in this section as " 5th Report." Modern works on the subject are Preston and Newsom, *Limitation of Actions*, 3rd ed.; Franks, *Limitation of Actions*.

[54] 21 Jac. 1, c. 16; discussed at length in the first edition of this book, pp. 679–690.

[55] 2 & 3 Geo. 6, c. 21.

[56] s. 2 (1) (*a*). This three-year period was introduced by the Law Reform (Limitation of Actions, etc.) Act 1954 (2 & 3 Eliz. 2, c. 36) which also abolished the specially favourable periods of limitation formerly applicable to actions against public authorities.

[57] R.S.C., Ord. 18, r. 8. The benefit a defendant derives from the limitation of actions is procedural and accordingly can be regulated by Rules of the Supreme Court under the Supreme Court of Judicature (Consolidation) Act 1925, s. 99: *Rodriguez* v. *R. J. Parker (Male)* [1967] 1 Q.B. 116; *Mitchell* v. *Harris Engineering Co. Ltd.* [1967] 2 Q.B. 703. See also *Chatsworth Investments Ltd.* v. *Cussins (Contractors) Ltd.* [1969] 1 W.L.R. 1. *Cf. Braniff* v. *Holland and Hannen and Cubitts (Southern) Ltd.* [1969] 1 W.L.R. 1533.

[58] *Dismore* v. *Milton* [1938] 3 All E.R. 762 (C.A.); Preston and Newsom, *op. cit.*, pp. 23–24.

[59] *Reeves* v. *Butcher* [1891] 2 Q.B. 509, 511, *per* Lindley L.J. A highly technical variant of this was laid down by Lord Esher M.R. in *Coburn* v. *Colledge* [1897] 1 Q.B. 702, 706–707. The day on which the cause of action arose is excluded: *Marren* v. *Dawson*,

that which makes action possible." [60] A cause of action arises, therefore, at the moment when a state of facts occurs which gives a potential plaintiff a right to succeed against a potential defendant. There must be a plaintiff who can succeed, and a defendant against whom he can succeed.[61] The fact that the potential plaintiff could not at that first possible moment identify the defendant does not prevent a cause of action accruing.[62]

Where the tort is actionable *per se*, as in trespass and libel,[63] time begins to run, in general, at the moment the wrongful act was committed, whether the injured party knows of it or not, provided there is no fraudulent concealment.[64] This applies though the resulting damage does not occur or is not discovered until a later date, for such damage is not a new cause of action, but is merely an incident of the other.[65] On the other hand, where the tort is actionable only on proof of actual damage, that is, when damage is the gist of the action, as in nuisance, negligence and deceit, time runs from the damage.[66] If, therefore, you are injured by my negligent manufacture of ginger beer, you will not be barred from bringing an action against me even though more than three years have passed before you actually drank the ginger beer and suffered damage.[67] It is the date at which the damage is caused, however, not the date at which it is discovered, which governs, and in such cases a man's right of action may be barred before he is aware that he has it.[68] Because of the particular hardship this may cause in certain cases of personal injury, the law for them has been altered by the Limitation Act 1963, which is described below,[69] but in all other cases this remains the rule.

Some torts, however, may be of a continuing nature, while others are done once and for all (though their consequences and the damage

---

Bentley & Co. Ltd. [1961] 2 Q.B. 135; *Kour* v. *S. Russell & Sons* [1973] 2 W.L.R. 147. See generally Preston and Newsom, *op. cit.*, Chap. 2.

[60] Preston and Newsom, *op. cit.*, p. 4, citing Lord Dunedin in *Board of Trade* v. *Cayzer, Irvine & Co. Ltd.* [1927] A.C. 610, 617. Or in terms of pleading, " Every fact which it would be necessary for the plaintiff to prove, if traversed, in order to support his right to the judgment of the court ": *Read* v. *Brown* (1888) 22 Q.B.D. 128, 131, *per* Lord Esher M.R.

[61] Preston and Newsom, *op. cit.*, p. 4, referring to dicta of Vaughan Williams L.J. in *Thomson* v. *Clanmorris* [1900] 1 Ch. 718, 728–729.

[62] *R. B. Policies at Lloyd's* v. *Butler* [1950] 1 K.B. 76. Ignorance of the identity of the defendant may therefore be a reason for the giving of leave to commence proceedings after the expiry of the three-year period of limitation in actions for damages for personal injury: *Clark* v. *Forbes Stuart (Thames Street) Ltd. (Intended Action)* [1964] 1 W.L.R. 836, decided under the Limitation Act 1963. For this Act, see *post*, pp. 654–656. See Goodman, " First Catch Your Defendant " (1966) 29 M.L.R. 366.

[63] *Brunswick (Duke)* v. *Harmer* (1849) 14 Q.B. 185.

[64] *Granger* v. *George* (1826) 5 B. & C. 149.

[65] *Howell* v. *Young* (1826) 5 B. & C. 259.

[66] *Backhouse* v. *Bonomi* (1861) 9 H.L.C. 503. *Cf.* the position in Scotland under the Law Reform (Limitation of Actions, etc.) Act 1954, s. 6 (1), and see *Watson* v. *Winget Ltd.*, 1960 S.L.T. 321.

[67] See *Watson* v. *Winget Ltd.*, 1960 S.L.T. 321. *Cf. Higgins* v. *Arfon B. C.* [1975] 2 All E.R. 589.

[68] *Cartledge* v. *Jopling & Sons Ltd.* [1963] A.C. 758; *Archer* v. *Catton & Co. Ltd.* [1954] 1 W.L.R. 775. *Cf. Clarkson* v. *Modern Foundries Ltd.* [1957] 1 W.L.R. 1210. See also *Howell* v. *Young* (1826) 5 B. & C. 259.   [69] *Post*, pp. 654–656.

arising from them may be continuous or may occur only after an interval). Nuisance is usually a continuing tort and frequently false imprisonment and occasionally trespass to land or even negligence.[70] In that event, a fresh cause of action arises *de die in diem* so long as the wrongful state of affairs continues, and the plaintiff can recover for such portions of the tort as lie within the time allotted by the statute, although the first commission of the tort occurred outside the six-year or three-year period.[71]

Parties must be in existence

The period does not begin to run until there is someone in existence capable of suing, for until then no cause of action has accrued. Thus, for example, when goods belonging to a person who has died intestate have been converted after his death, the proper party to sue is, of course, the administrator and time does not begin to run until he has taken out letters of administration.[72] So, too, there must be a defendant capable of being sued; thus, where the tortfeasor is entitled to diplomatic immunity, time does not begin to run in his favour until the termination of his period of office, for until then no action will lie against him.[73] If, however, time has once begun to run, it will continue to do so even over a period during which there is no one capable of suing or of being sued.[74]

Disabilities

A person who is under a disability on the date when his cause of action accrues [75] is in a special position so far as limitation is concerned, for his action may be brought at any time before the expiration of six years (or three years in an action for personal injuries) from the date when he either (a) ceased to be under a disability or (b) died, whichever event first occurred.[76] For these purposes the law now recognises only two forms of disability, infancy and unsoundness of mind.[77] Infancy presents no difficulty, for it means simply a person under the age of 18, but the Limitation Act contains no definition of unsoundness of mind. This question fell to be considered by the Court

---

[70] *Clarkson* v. *Modern Foundries Ltd., supra.*

[71] *Coventry* v. *Apsley* (1691) 2 Salk. 420; *Massey* v. *Johnson* (1809) 12 East 67; *Bailey* v. *Warden* (1815) 4 M. & S. 400; *Hardy* v. *Ryle* (1829) 9 B. & C. 603. *Cf. O'Connor* v. *Isaacs* [1956] 2 Q.B. 288.

[72] *Pratt* v. *Swaine* (1828) 8 B. & C. 285. The principle was laid down generally in *Murray* v. *East India Co.* (1821) 5 B. & Ald. 204, which, however, was not an action in tort.

[73] *Musurus Bey* v. *Gadban* [1894] 2 Q.B. 352.

[74] *Rhodes* v. *Smethurst* (1838) 4 M. & W. 42; 6 M. & W. 351.

[75] This includes a person whose disability is caused by an accident in respect of which the action is brought, for such a person is under a disability on the day of the accident and the law takes no account of part of a day: *Kirby* v. *Leather* [1965] 2 Q.B. 367, 382–383, *per* Lord Denning M.R. *Cf. Penrose* v. *Mansfield, The Times,* March 19, 1971.

[76] s. 22.

[77] Limitation Act 1939, s. 31 (2). The Criminal Justice Act 1948 abolished the status of " convict."

of Appeal in *Kirby* v. *Leather*,[78] where a young man of 24 was injured in an accident which was partly due to the negligence of the defendant. Before his accident the plaintiff had been perfectly normal, but as a result of his injuries he suffered continuously from mental illness due to brain trauma which rendered him paranoic and aggressive, with defective comprehension and memory. Though not totally incapable, he was incapable of instructing a solicitor or of exercising any reasonable judgment upon a possible settlement of his claim. The Court of Appeal held that for the purposes of limitation a person is of unsound mind " when he is, by reason of mental illness, incapable of managing his affairs in relation to the accident as a reasonable man would do," [79] and accordingly that the plaintiff was under a disability.

By section 2 (2) of the Law Reform (Limitation of Actions, etc.) Act 1954, in an action for *personal injuries*, where the person to whom the right of action accrued was under a disability, the period of six years is now reduced to three, but no additional time will be allowed unless the plaintiff proves that the person under disability was not, at the time when the right of action accrued to him, in the custody of a parent.[80] The meaning of " custody " here has given the courts some trouble in recent years for, while it is perfectly clear that an infant living at home and dependent on his parents is " in the custody of a parent," cases of an infant living away from home at a farm training centre [81] or in the care of a local authority [82] or living at home but independently,[83] have required the courts to investigate more clearly the meaning of that phrase. After a period of uncertainty [84] it is now clear that what is in issue is a question of fact, not of legal custody as it is known in matrimonial law.[85] The point of the provision is that there is no need to suspend the running of time against a person who is under a disability if he is being looked after by a parent who can be relied upon to protect his interests, and for this purpose what matters is not legal custody but actual and effective care and control.

Subject to this, the rule that the running of time is not suspended

---

[78] [1965] 2 Q.B. 367. In *Harnett* v. *Fisher* [1927] A.C. 573, it was held that a person who was wrongfully detained as a lunatic under the Lunacy Act 1890 was not under a disability on the ground of lunacy. The Act of 1939, s. 31 (2), conclusively presumes that, for the purposes of the Act, such a person is of unsound mind. See Preston and Newsom, *op. cit.*, p. 222.

[79] [1965] 2 Q.B. at p. 383, *per* Lord Denning M.R.; *ibid.* at p. 387, *per* Danckwerts L.J.; *ibid.* at p. 387, *per* Winn L.J.; but note Winn L.J.'s caveat, *ibid.*, and see *Penrose* v. *Mansfield, The Times,* March 19, 1971. The court considered that the definition contained in R.S.C., Ord. 80, r. 1 (which deals with the appointment of a guardian *ad litem* or a next friend and refers to " a person who, by reason of mental disorder . . . is incapable of managing and administering his property and affairs "), could be applied by analogy.

[80] In actions other than for personal injuries, custody of a parent is of no consequence, and the period applicable after disability ceases remains at six years as before.

[81] *Hewer* v. *Bryant* [1969] 1 Q.B. 415; [1970] 1 Q.B. 357.

[82] *Duncan* v. *Lambeth London Borough Council* [1968] 1 Q.B. 747.

[83] *Brook* v. *Hoar* [1967] 1 W.L.R. 1336. The infant had his own key, paid for his board and lodging, and was described by his father as a " young lodger."

[84] The decisions at first instance in the three cases cited above are irreconcilable. See Clerk and Lindsell, *Torts,* 13th ed., pp. 332–334.

[85] *Hewer* v. *Bryant, supra*; *Todd* v. *Davison* [1972] A.C. 392.

when the person under disability is in the custody of a parent is perfectly comprehensible in the case of an infant, but it makes little sense in relation to an adult person of unsound mind.[86] Probably it is restricted to a " harmless imbecile or mongol who could be expected to be actually in the custody of his parents." [87] At all events, it does not cover an adult who was of sound mind until his accident, even though once out of hospital he was looked after by his mother.[88]

No disability of the defendant prevents the running of the period. Formerly his absence beyond the seas delayed the commencement of the period until his return, but modern facilities for service of a writ on a defendant who is abroad made this concession to the plaintiff of little practical value, and it vanished under the Act of 1939.

Cumulative disabilities

What is the position of a plaintiff who was of sound mind when time began to run but later becomes of unsound mind; or of a plaintiff who was an infant when his cause of action accrued but who becomes of unsound mind after he reaches 18; or of a plaintiff who is under a disability at the moment when he succeeds to the title of a predecessor who was under no disability? The Act of 1939 in effect provides that a disability which arises after time began to run has no effect.[89] It is true that this rule may be hard on the plaintiff, but facts which give rise to its application are not likely to occur often and there might be quite as much hardship to the defendant if the rule were otherwise.[90] Where there are successive disabilities in the same person, *e.g.* unsoundness of mind supervening on infancy, time does not run until the last of the disabilities has ended, provided that there is no interval of ability between any of the disabilities,[91] but if a right of action accrues to A, who is under a disability, and A dies and B, who is also under a disability, succeeds to A's right, no further extension of time is allowed by reason of B's disability.[92]

Extinction of title by limitation

Before 1939 it was only in cases affecting title to land that the expiry of the period of limitation affected title; in all other cases it merely barred the plaintiff from pursuing his remedy before the courts. Even though a person who had been wrongfully deprived of his chattel might lose his right to sue for conversion or detinue, he retained his title to the chattel, and if he could recover possession of it otherwise than by action

---

[86] *Kirby* v. *Leather* [1965] 2 Q.B. 367, 383, *per* Lord Denning M.R.; *ibid.* at pp. 385–386, *per* Danckwerts L.J.

[87] *Ibid.* at p. 386, *per* Danckwerts L.J.

[88] *Kirby* v. *Leather, supra.*

[89] s. 22 (*a*); giving effect to *Garner* v. *Wingrove* [1905] 2 Ch. 233.

[90] Fifth Report, s. 16.

[91] *Borrows* v. *Ellison* (1871) L.R. 6 Ex. 128 (the Act of 1939 gives statutory effect to this: Preston and Newsom, *op. cit.*, pp. 220–221).

[92] s. 22 (*b*).

he was entitled to do so. Moreover any act of conversion or wrongful detention of the chattel by a third party gave rise to a fresh cause of action against the third party, and in respect of that cause of action time ran afresh from its accrual.[93]

So far as most causes of action in tort are concerned, the Act of 1939 retains the principle that the expiry of the period of limitation only bars the remedy, not the right, but this is no longer true for detinue or conversion. In the first place, it is enacted by section 3 (1) that once a cause of action in detinue or conversion has accrued in respect of a chattel, no action may be brought for any subsequent conversion or wrongful detention after the expiry of six years from the accrual of the original cause of action unless, of course, the owner has recovered possession of it in the meanwhile.[94] What is more, it is enacted by section 3 (2) that once the period of limitation in respect of the original cause of action has expired, then the owner's title to his chattel is extinguished. So, if you take my goods wrongfully and later sell them to someone else, once six years have elapsed from the taking, not only have I lost my right to sue either you or the person who bought the goods from you, but he is in a position to deal with them as absolute owner notwithstanding that at the time of the sale to him you had no title which you could pass on to him.

Fraud and concealed fraud

Two distinct points arise here. First, as would seem to be no more than fair, where the plaintiff's cause of action is based upon the fraud of the defendant (or his agent [95] or of any person through whom he claims or his agent), section 26 (a) of the Act of 1939 provides that time does not begin to run until such time as the plaintiff did discover, or could with reasonable diligence have discovered, the fraud. This part of the section is limited to cases where the plaintiff's cause of action is actually founded upon fraud, as is the position in an action for deceit,[96] but by section 26 (b) the same suspension of the running of time applies where the right of action [97] has been concealed by the fraud of the defendant (or of any other of the persons mentioned above). Here " fraud " has a much wider meaning and is treated on broad equitable principles; it extends to wrongs done furtively which have not come to the plaintiff's knowledge, such as the surreptitious abstraction of minerals from under ground, and covers any " conduct which, having regard to some special relationship between the two parties concerned,

---

[93] See *Wilkinson* v. *Verity* (1871) L.R 6 C.P. 206; *Spackman* v. *Foster* (1883) 11 Q.B.D. 99; *Miller* v. *Dell* [1891] 1 Q.B. 468.

[94] *Eddis* v. *Chichester Constable* [1969] 2 Ch. 345, 360, *per* Winn L.J.

[95] Which includes an independent contractor: *Applegate* v. *Moss* [1971] 1 Q.B. 406; *King* v. *Victor Parsons & Co.* [1973] 1 W.L.R. 658.

[96] *Beaman* v. *A.R.T.S. Ltd.* [1949] 1 K.B. 550, 558, *per* Lord Greene M.R.; *ibid.* at p. 567, *per* Somervell L.J.

[97] See Goodman, " First Catch Your Defendant " (1966) 29 M.L.R. 366, 368–371.

is an unconscionable thing for the one to do towards the other." [98] It is not necessary that active steps to prevent detection shall have been taken, and a wrongdoer who " chooses his opportunity so wisely and acts so warily that he can safely calculate on not being found out for many a long day," will not be allowed to take advantage of the Limitation Act.[99] So, in *Beaman* v. *A.R.T.S. Ltd.*[1] a bailee disposed of his bailor's goods during the war and in order to suit his own convenience; he did not try to obtain the bailor's instructions and he did not even attempt to inform her of what he had done when communication became easier than it had been. This was held to be a concealment by fraud of the bailor's right of action and time did not, therefore, begin to run against her until she learnt of what had been done.

The combined effect of sections 3 and 26 was considered in the difficult case of *Eddis* v. *Chichester Constable* [2] where the assumed facts [3] were that the tenant for life of a picture of which the plaintiff trustees were owners, had sold it in 1951 to an art consortium; that their right of action was concealed by his fraud; and that the agent of the consortium who bought the picture had reason to believe that fraud had been committed. Subsequently, the consortium sold the picture to an American art gallery, but none of this became known to the plaintiffs until the death of the life tenant in 1963. In 1966 they brought proceedings against, *inter alios*, the consortium, for conversion of the picture, and the question for the Court of Appeal was whether the defence of limitation should prevail.

Two distinct rulings in point of law seem to emerge from the judgments. In the first place the life tenant, who originally converted the picture, was a " person through whom " the consortium claimed so that his fraudulent concealment of the plaintiff's right of action prevented time from running in favour of the consortium.[4] Secondly it was also held that section 26 governs section 3 (2) as well as section 3 (1) so that in cases in which it applies it prevents the extinction of title as well as the barring of the action.[5] Notwithstanding the existence of a proviso to section 26 which, even in a case of fraud, protects the bona fide purchaser for value of property, so long as he was not a

---

[98] *Kitchen* v. *R.A.F. Association* [1958] 1 W.L.R. 563, 573, *per* Lord Evershed M.R.

[99] *Ibid.* at p. 570, *per* Somervell L.J. See also *Eddis* v. *Chichester Constable* [1969] 2 Ch. 345, 356, *per* Lord Denning.

[1] *Supra*; *Kitchen* v. *R.A.F. Association, supra,* where it was held in an action for negligence against solicitors that their failure to inform the plaintiff of her possible claim against X was not concealed fraud, but that their failure to inform her of an offer by X to pay £100 was concealed fraud and therefore that the running of time against them was suspended. Mere negligence by the defendant which leads to the plaintiff being ignorant of his rights is not " fraud " for this purpose: *semble, Applegate* v. *Moss* and *King* v. *Victor Parsons & Co., supra.*

[2] [1969] 2 Ch. 345. Jackson (1969) 32 M.L.R. 691.

[3] The case came before the Court of Appeal on a preliminary point of law.

[4] [1969] 2 Ch. at p. 357, *per* Lord Denning M.R.; *ibid.* at pp. 362–363, *per* Winn L.J. (but with hesitation); *ibid.* at p. 364, *per* Fenton Atkinson L.J.

[5] *Ibid.* at p. 356, *per* Denning L.J.; *ibid.* at pp. 361–362, *per* Winn L.J. (but with hesitation); *ibid.* at p. 364, *per* Fenton Atkinson L.J. See too *Beaman* v. *A.R.T.S. Ltd.* [1949] 1 K.B. 550, 557, *per* Lord Greene M.R.

party to the fraud and neither knew nor had reason to believe that a fraud had been committed,[6] it therefore followed that the plaintiff's action against the consortium for conversion was not statute barred.

Special periods of limitation
(i) *Personal injuries*
Section 2 (1) of the Law Reform (Limitation of Actions, etc.) Act 1954[7] amends section 2 (1) of the Limitation Act 1939 by providing a special period of three years instead of the usual six years for " actions for damages for negligence, nuisance or breach of duty (whether the duty exists by virtue of a contract or of provision made by or under a statute or independently of any contract or any such provision) where the damages claimed by the plaintiff for the negligence, nuisance or breach of duty consist of or include damages in respect of personal injuries to any person." These words are wide enough to include actions for trespass to the person,[8] and the three-year period applies generally in all actions for personal injuries, including those brought for the benefit of a deceased person's estate under the Law Reform (Miscellaneous Provisions) Act 1934.[9] The expression " personal injuries " includes any disease and any impairment of a person's physical or mental condition.[10]

It has been noticed that a cause of action accrues when the damage is caused, not when it is discovered.[11] This rule is most obviously likely to cause hardship in cases where the plaintiff contracts a lung disease such as pneumoconiosis as a result of the defendant's breach of statutory duty or negligence, for these diseases, though present to a more than negligible extent, can still remain unknown to the sufferer for a considerable period of time. This is what happened in *Cartledge* v. *E. Jopling & Sons Ltd.*,[12] where a number of miners found themselves without a remedy because their diseases had not revealed themselves in time, and following this case the law has been altered by the Limitation Act 1963.[13]

This Act,[14] which is quite remarkably complicated,[15] is intended to

---

[6] Although this proviso refers, so far as material, only to actions to *recover* any property, the court held that it must be applied so as to cover also actions for conversion, *i.e.* actions for damages, as well as to actions in detinue in those cases in which its conditions are fulfilled: *ibid.* at pp. 357–358, *per* Lord Denning M.R.; *ibid.* at p. 364, *per* Fenton Atkinson L.J. *Cf. ibid.* at p. 362, *per* Winn L.J.   [7] 2 & 3 Eliz. 2, c. 36.

[8] *Letang* v. *Cooper* [1965] 1 Q.B. 232; *Long* v. *Hepworth* [1968] 1 W.L.R. 1299.

[9] See *ante*, pp. 498–501.

[10] Law Reform (Limitation of Actions, etc.) Act 1954, s. 2 (3).

[11] *Ante*, p. 648.   [12] [1963] A.C. 758.

[13] c. 47. Following the Court of Appeal's decision in *Cartledge* v. *E. Jopling & Sons Ltd.* [1962] 1 Q.B. 189, a committee was set up by the Lord Chancellor and its report had already been published at the time of the House of Lords decision: Report of the Committee on Limitation of Actions in Cases of Personal Injury (1962) Cmnd. 1829.

[14] See Woolf, *The Time Barrier in Personal Injury Claims*; Dworkin, " Limitation Act 1963 " (1964) 27 M.L.R. 199; Jolowicz, " Limitation Act 1963 " [1964] C.L.J. 47. The Act was substantially amended by ss. 1–3 of the Law Reform (Miscellaneous Provisions) Act 1971, implementing the Law Commission's Report on the 1963 Act, Law Com. No. 35 (1970).

[15] Lord Denning M.R. has described it as " very complicated and obscure ": *Re Pickles* v. *National Coal Board (Intended Action)* [1968] 1 W.L.R. 997, 1000.

give a reasonable period within which persons who remain for a time ignorant of the existence of their claims may start proceedings, while at the same time safeguarding the position of defendants. It provides, in effect, that a plaintiff may apply for the leave of the court to bring his action notwithstanding the expiry of the normal three-year period, and, if leave is granted and if, also, the plaintiff proves that certain stringent conditions are fulfilled, then the expiry of that period shall not be a defence.[16]

The application for leave is made *ex parte* [17] and, although no decision taken on the application for leave is binding at the trial,[18] to obtain leave the plaintiff must produce evidence by affidavit so that it appears, in the absence of evidence to the contrary, that (a) he will be able to establish his cause of action apart from the defence of limitation and (b) that the conditions prescribed by the Act are fulfilled.[19] These conditions are, shortly, that the *material facts* relating to the plaintiff's cause of actions were or included *facts of a decisive character* which were at all times *outside the knowledge (actual or constructive)* of the plaintiff until a date which was not earlier than three years before the date on which the action was brought.[20]

The detailed working of the Act cannot be considered here,[21] but it has already given a good deal of trouble to the courts. One point which needs urgently to be settled is whether the plaintiff's knowledge that he has a cause of action against the defendant is a " material fact." Though the issue came before the House of Lords in *Central Asbestos Co. Ltd.* v. *Dodd* [22] there is no discernible *ratio decidendi* in that case and the Court of Appeal has accordingly continued to follow its own earlier decisions which held that time did not run against the plaintiff until he had knowledge (actual or constructive) that his condition is attributable to the negligence or other tort of the defendant.[23] There is, no doubt, considerable difficulty in working out a suitable compromise

---

[16] ss. 3, 3A and 3B of the Act (as substituted by the Law Reform (Miscellaneous Provisions) Act 1971, s. 2, Sched. 1) contain provisions designed to meet the same problem, as it arises in actions on behalf of estates of deceased persons and in actions under the Fatal Accidents Acts.

[17] Appeal against a refusal of leave lies to the Court of Appeal but not to the House of Lords: s. 2 (4). The defendant cannot apply to set the grant of leave aside (*Cozens* v. *North Devon Hospital Management Committee* [1966] 2 Q.B. 330) but, if he believes that the necessary conditions are not fulfilled, the defendant can apply for this to be tried as a preliminary issue: *Goodchild* v. *Greatness Timber Co. Ltd.* [1968] 2 Q.B. 372.

[18] *Re Clark* v. *Forbes Stuart (Thames Street) Ltd.* [1964] 1 W.L.R. 836; *Cozens* v. *North Devon Hospital Management Committee, supra.*

[19] The Court of Appeal has insisted that this evidence should be scrutinised very carefully: *Goodchild* v. *Greatness Timber Co. Ltd., supra.*

[20] s. 1 (3), as amended by the Law Reform (Miscellaneous Provisions) Act 1971, s. 1 (1). The words italicised all receive elaborate definition by the Act itself in s. 7.

[21] For a somewhat more detailed account, see Clerk and Lindsell, *Torts*, 13th ed., pp. 328–332. For proposals for further reform, see the 20th Report of the Law Reform Committee (1974), Cmnd. 5630.   [22] [1973] A.C. 518.

[23] *Harper* v. *N.C.B.* [1974] 2 All E.R. 441; see also *Pickles* v. *N.C.B.* [1968] 1 W.L.R. 997; *Skingsley* v. *Cape Asbestos Co. Ltd.* [1968] 2 Lloyd's Rep. 201; *Newton* v. *Cammell Laird & Co.* [1969] 1 W.L.R. 415; *Drinkwater* v. *Joseph Lucas Ltd.* [1970] 3 All E.R. 769; *Smith* v. *Central Asbestos Ltd.* [1972] 1 Q.B. 244; *Knipe* v. *British Railways Board* [1972] 1 Q.B. 361.

between the interest of a plaintiff who is, through no fault of his own, unaware of the existence of his cause of action or of the identity of the person whom he should sue, and the interest of the defendant that he should not be confronted by a stale claim. Certainly the latter should not be too readily discounted, but it is hard to avoid the conclusion that the Limitation Act 1963 is designed to do no more than remove the worst injustices while detracting as little as possible from the protection given to defendants.[24] But, as we have seen, in the case of torts not actionable without proof of damage, and it is with those torts that actions for personal injury are almost invariably concerned, it is not and never has been the law that the action is barred after the expiry of a certain time from the date of the wrongful act; it is only barred after the expiry of a certain time from the occurrence of the damage. As Lord Reid has said, " there seems little if any practical difference between causing damage which occurs at a later date and causing damage which can only be discovered at a later date. If a defendant has to pay in the one case, why should he not have to pay in the other case? "[25] Could not equal justice for both parties have been achieved by a provision that the cause of action should not be deemed to have accrued until the plaintiff could reasonably have known of its existence?[26]

(ii) Maritime cases

The Maritime Conventions Act 1911[27] fixes two years as the period of limitation for damage to a vessel, her cargo, freight or any property on board her, or for damages for loss of life or personal injuries suffered by any person on board caused by the fault of any other vessel. The court may, however, extend this period to such extent and upon such conditions as it thinks fit.[28] But the Act applies only to actions brought against ships other than that on which the damage actually occurred, and, accordingly, where an action was brought against shipowners in

---

[24] Note that the requirement that the plaintiff produce evidence in support of his application for leave under the Act to the effect not only that the conditions prescribed by the Act are satisfied, but also that he has a prima facie cause of action, gives the defendant the compensating advantage of advance information of the plaintiff's evidence. The equivalent provisions for Scotland (Limitation Act 1963, s. 8) do not require this. See also Woolf, op. cit., p. 60.

[25] Cartledge v. E. Jopling & Sons Ltd. [1963] A.C. 758, 773. His Lordship referred to Davie v. New Merton Board Mills Ltd. [1959] A.C. 604, where seven years elapsed between the last negligent act of the defendant and the date when the cause of action accrued.

[26] See Cartledge v. E. Jopling & Sons Ltd., supra, at p. 772, per Lord Reid. This is, in fact, the position in some other jurisdictions. See Sacks, " Statutes of Limitations and Undiscovered Malpractice " (1967) 16 Clev.-Mar.L.Rev. 65. In many continental countries two periods of limitation are provided, a long one running from the date of the wrongful act or the date of the damage, and a considerably shorter one running from the date when the injured person learnt of his injury and of the identity of the person responsible. See e.g. para. 852 BGB (Germany).

[27] 1 & 2 Geo. 5, c. 57, s. 8. The period of limitation under the Act is unaffected by the Law Reform (Limitation of Actions, etc.) Act 1954: The Alnwick [1965] P. 357.

[28] Ibid. For a recent case on the exercise of this discretion, see The Alnwick [1965] P. 357.

respect of the death of a seaman on their ship, it was held that the normal three-year period applied.[29]

(iii) *Cases of contribution*

It was formerly thought that the period of limitation for claims for contribution between tortfeasors under the Law Reform (Married Women and Tortfeasors) Act 1935 [30] was six years, for no special period had been laid down. Now, however, it is provided by the Limitation Act 1963, s. 4, that such claims must be brought within two years of the date when the right to contribution first accrued.[31] If the tortfeasor claiming contribution has himself been sued by the victim of the tort, then the right to contribution accrues when judgment is given against him [32]; if he admits his liability, then the right accrues when the amount to be paid by him to the victim has been agreed.[33] In the case of claims for contribution between shipowners in respect of their liabilities for loss of life or personal injuries on board ship, which are governed by the Maritime Conventions Act 1911,[34] however, the period of limitation is one year only.[35]

ASSIGNMENT OF RIGHT OF ACTION IN TORT [36]

This topic may be conveniently treated here, although it relates not to extinction of liability in tort, but to transfer of a right of action in tort.

It is a familiar rule in the law of assignment of choses in action that, while property can be lawfully assigned, a bare right to litigate cannot. Consistently with this, a right of action in tort is not in general assignable. The reason suggested in Elizabethan times was that the damages in such an action are at the date of the purported assignment uncertain, " and perhaps the assignee may be a man of great power, who might procure a jury to give him greater damages." [37] The first part of this reasoning is unconvincing and the latter part is obsolete. A reason better suited to modern law is that such an assignment is contrary to public policy.[38] It is obvious that if the rule were otherwise, speculation in lawsuits of an undesirable kind would be encouraged.

Exceptions

The following exceptions to the rule are recognised.

(i) *Transmission on death*

This has already been considered.[39]

---

[29] *The Niceto de Larrinaga* [1966] P. 80.

[30] *Ante*, pp. 548–551.

[31] The Act of 1963 thus gives added importance to the possibility of a common law claim between tortfeasors, *e.g.* by virtue of an express contract between them (*ante*, p. 549) or under *Lister* v. *Romford Ice and Cold Storage Co. Ltd.* [1957] A.C. 555 (*ante*, pp. 532–534) since the limitation period for such claims remains at six years.

[32] s. 4 (2) (*a*).

[33] s. 4 (2) (*b*).

[34] Maritime Conventions Act 1911, s. 3.

[35] *Ibid.* s. 8.

[36] Winfield, *Present Law of Abuse of Procedure*, pp. 67–69.

[37] Argument in *Anon.* (1600) Godbolt 81.

[38] *Defries* v. *Milne* [1913] 1 Ch. 98.

[39] *Ante*, Chap. 24.

(ii) *Bankruptcy*

One of the rules in the law of bankruptcy is that demands in the nature of unliquidated damages arising otherwise than by reason of a contract, promise, or breach of trust are not provable.[40] Hence, as actions in tort are usually for unliquidated damages, neither the liability of the tortfeasor nor the right of action of the injured party ought, in general, to pass to the trustee in bankruptcy of either. With respect to liability this is true almost without qualification. The tortfeasor, if he becomes bankrupt, remains liable and it is he and not the trustee in bankruptcy who must be sued. But where the claim has become liquidated before the bankruptcy, either by agreement, or by reference and award, or by final judgment, the injured party can prove for it in bankruptcy. Thus in *Ex p. Mumford*,[41] A seduced B's daughter. B sued A for seduction. A compromised the claim by giving B promissory notes for £223. A then became bankrupt and it was held that B could prove for the value of the notes against A's trustee.

As to the right of action for a tort, the law seems to be this. If the tort is a purely personal one, like assault or defamation, the right of action for it remains exercisable by the injured party himself, and does not pass to his trustee in bankruptcy [42]; but where the tort is to property, *e.g.* conversion of goods, then the right to sue for it passes to the trustee who can sell or assign it to any one else, as he, in his discretion, thinks fit. Now the same set of facts may give rise to injuries to both the person and the property of X. That often happens with the tort of negligence. So, too, trespass to land is occasionally accompanied by violence to the person in possession of it. It is probable, but not certain, that in such circumstances the claim for the personal injury remains with the bankrupt while that for injury to his property passes to his trustee.[43] At any rate the suggestion has in its favour, first, the general principle that it is the bankrupt's *property* with which the trustee is primarily concerned, and, secondly, the argument that if a claim for personal injuries done to the bankrupt passed to the trustee, he might find it awkward to prosecute it if the bankrupt were unwilling to engage in the action at all.

---

[40] Bankruptcy Act 1914 (4 & 5 Geo. 5, c. 59), s. 30 (1). By the Law Reform (Miscellaneous Provisions) Act 1934, s. 1 (6), if the estate against which proceedings are maintainable under this section is insolvent, any liability is a debt provable in the administration of the estate.

[41] (1808) 15 Ves.Jun. 289; *Re Newman, ex p. Brooke* (1876) 3 Ch.D. 494, C.A. (judgment signed before adjudication is sufficient, but a verdict is not). If a claim may be made either in contract or in tort, the tort may be waived and the claim made on the contract: *Re Great Orme Tramways Co.* (1934) 50 T.L.R. 450.

[42] See Halsbury's *Laws of England*, 4th ed, Vol. 3, para. 558.

[43] *Rogers* v. *Spence* (1846) 12 Cl. & F. 700, 720–721, *per* Lord Campbell. *Cf. Beckham* v. *Drake* (1849) 2 H.L.C. 579, 626, *per* Parke B.; *Wetherell* v. *Julius* (1850) 10 C.B. 267; *Wilson* v. *United Counties Bank Ltd.* [1920] A.C. 102, 120, *per* Viscount Finlay. See Clerk and Lindsell, *Torts*, 13th ed., pp. 97–98.

(iii) *Subrogation* [44]

The commonest example of subrogation in this connection is in the law of insurance. An insurance company which has compensated a policy-holder under an indemnity insurance policy stands in his shoes with regard to his claims against the person who caused the injury. Hence, if A by negligent driving of his car damages B's car, and the X company, with whom B is insured, compensates him, the X company can exploit B's action for negligence against A.[45]

(iv) *Judgment*

Where judgment has been entered for damages in an action for tort, the damages become a judgment debt and are therefore assignable.[46] Closely akin to this is the rule which permits assignment of the fruits of an action which has been commenced but has not yet proceeded to judgment. This is not an assignment of a cause of action, but of property, *i.e.* the proceeds of the action as and when they are recovered. Thus in *Glegg* v. *Bromley* [47] an assignment *pendente lite* of the fruits of an action for slander was upheld.[48]

Whether, apart from these exceptions, there is any other modification of the rule that a right of action in tort is not assignable, is doubtful. None has been traced so far as judicial decisions go, but there is some ground for thinking that the courts might take a distinction between assignment of an action for such a purely personal tort as slander (which obviously ought not to be hawked about like a marketable commodity) and assignment of an action for damage to property, *e.g.* running down a ship, where there appears to be much less objection. At any rate the distinction was thought to be not unreasonable or inconsistent with law and morals more than a century ago.[49]

---

[44] For a statement of the principle, see *Castellain* v. *Preston* (1883) 11 Q.B.D.at pp. 387 *et seq.*, *per* Brett L.J.; *Burnand* v. *Rodocanachi* (1882) 7 App.Cas. at p. 339, *per* Lord Blackburn; *Morris* v. *Ford Motor Co.* [1973] Q.B. 792.

[45] In *Lister* v. *Romford Ice and Cold Storage Co. Ltd.* [1957] A.C. 555 the action was in fact brought by the employers' insurers, and the employers themselves were not consulted about the action: [1956] 2 Q.B. at p. 185, *per* Denning L.J. Normally the action is brought in the name of the insured, but if there has been an assignment which complies with the requirements of the Law of Property Act 1925, s. 136, the insurer can bring the action in his own name: *Compania Colombiana de Seguros* v. *Pacific Steam Navigation Co.* [1965] 1 Q.B. 101, 121–122, *per* Roskill J.

[46] *Carrington* v. *Harway* (1662) 1 Keb. 803; *Goodman* v. *Robinson* (1886) 18 Q.B.D. 332.

[47] [1912] 3 K.B. 474.

[48] *Cohen* v. *Mitchell* (1890) 25 Q.B.D. 262 can also be supported on this ground, although other reasons were given for the decision.

[49] *Stanley* v. *Jones* (1831) 7 Bing. 369, 375, *per* Park J., *obiter*. *Cf.* Winfield, *Present Law of Abuse of Procedure*, pp. 68–69.

INDEX